American Constitutional Law
Volume II

Civil Rights and Li

American Constitutional Law
Volume II
Civil Rights and Liberties

SIXTH EDITION

OTIS H. STEPHENS, JR.
University of Tennessee, Knoxville

JOHN M. SCHEB II
University of Tennessee, Knoxville

COLIN GLENNON
East Tennessee State University

CENGAGE
Learning·

Australia • Brazil • Mexico • Singapore • United Kingdom • United States

CENGAGE
Learning·

American Constitutional Law, Volume II: Civil Rights and Liberties,
Sixth Edition

Otis H. Stephens, Jr., John M. Scheb II, and Colin Glennon

Product Director: Suzanne Jeans

Product Manager: Carolyn Merrill

Content Developer: Renee Eckhoff

Content Coordinator: Jessica Wang

Product Assistant: Abigail Hess

Media Developer: Laura Hildebrand

Marketing Manager: Valerie Hartman

Senior Rights Acquisitions Specialist: Jennifer Meyer Dare

Manufacturing Planner: Fola Orekoya

Art and Design Direction, Production Management, and Composition: PreMediaGlobal

Cover Image: Photography and Artwork by Joel Gendron

For product information and technology assistance, contact us at
Cengage Learning Customer & Sales Support, 1-800-354-9706

For permission to use material from this text or product,
submit all requests online at **www.cengage.com/permissions**
Further permissions questions can be e-mailed to
permissionrequest@cengage.com

Library of Congress Control Number: 2013957827

Student Edition:

ISBN-13: 978-1-285-73692-1

ISBN-10: 1-285-73692-3

Cengage Learning
200 First Stamford Place, 4th Floor
Stamford, CT 06902
USA

Cengage Learning is a leading provider of customized learning solutions with office locations around the globe, including Singapore, the United Kingdom, Australia, Mexico, Brazil, and Japan. Locate your local office at: **www.cengage.com/global**

Cengage Learning products are represented in Canada by Nelson Education, Ltd.

To learn more about Cengage Learning Solutions, visit **www.cengage.com**

Purchase any of our products at your local college store or at our preferred online store **www.cengagebrain.com**

Printed in the United States of America
1 2 3 4 5 6 7 18 17 16 15 14

About the Authors

Otis H. Stephens, Jr. is Professor Emeritus of Political Science and Law at the University of Tennessee. He received his Ph.D. in political science from Johns Hopkins University and his J.D. from the University of Tennessee. During a distinguished academic career that spanned six decades, Professor Stephens taught courses in constitutional law, judicial process, civil rights and liberties, law and public policy, and jurisprudence. He authored or coauthored five books, including this one, and many more articles, essays, and book chapters. Dr. Stephens is a member of the Tennessee Bar and has been admitted to the Bar of the United States Supreme Court.

John M. Scheb II is Professor and Head of Political Science at the University of Tennessee, where he teaches courses and conducts research in American government, constitutional law, civil rights and liberties, administrative law, criminal law and procedure, the judicial process, judicial administration, and law in American society. Professor Scheb received his Ph.D. from the University of Florida in 1982. He has authored or coauthored numerous articles in professional journals and also coauthored four other textbooks.

Colin Glennon is Assistant Professor of Political Science at East Tennessee State University, where he teaches courses in American government, constitutional law, the judicial process, law and society, and American political institutions. Professor Glennon received his Ph.D. from the University of Tennessee in 2011. He has authored or coauthored articles in a number of professional journals. His research interests include American political institutions, judicial politics, public law, federalism in the courts, public policy in the courts, the impact of public opinion on judicial outcomes, judicial public policy, and state court administration.

This edition of American Constitutional Law *is dedicated to our many students—past, present, and future. Our wish for them is that their study of constitutional law will enrich their lives as citizens of this great republic.*

Contents

Preface

We are pleased to present Volume II of *American Constitutional Law*, 6th edition. This volume focuses on civil rights and liberties, including all of the freedoms protected by the Bill of Rights and subsequent amendments to the Constitution. Particular attention is given to the Fourteenth Amendment and the obligations it imposes on the states with respect to liberty, due process, and equal protection of the laws. Our goal is to present a compressive and current compendium of constitutional law in these vital areas of American public life.

About the Edited Cases

With the exception of Chapter 1 in Volume I, each introductory essay is followed by a set of edited Supreme Court decisions focusing on salient constitutional issues. In selecting and editing these cases, we have emphasized recent trends in major areas of constitutional interpretation. At the same time, we have included many landmark decisions, some of which retain importance as precedents while others illustrate the transient nature of constitutional interpretation. Because it is not possible to include edited versions of all important Supreme Court decisions, additional edited cases can be found on the free companion website located at www.cengagebrain.com. Just log in and search for your book to access these free resources.

What's New in the Sixth Edition?

We have endeavored to update the book since the last edition, taking into account the most significant decisions of the Supreme Court as well as other major constitutional developments. In this edition we pay particular attention to the recent controversies over gun control, terrorism, same-sex marriage, voting rights and campaign finance.

Acknowledgments

At the outset we must acknowledge the editorial team at Cengage, especially Carolyn O. Merrill, executive editor for political science,for their ongoing support, assistance, and encouragement. We also want to express our gratitude to Renee Eckhoff of Ohlinger Publishing Services, for her assistance throughout the project. Finally, we wish to thank the many scholars who reviewed this edition and its predecessors. Their comments, criticisms, and suggestions havebeen extremely helpful as this book has evolved over six editions.

Although many people contributed to the development and production of this book, we, as always, assume full responsibility for any errors that may appear herein.

Otis H. Stephens, Jr.
John M. Scheb II
Colin Glennon
January 3, 2014.

List of Edited Cases Located on the Free Companion Website

www.cengagebrain.com

VOLUME ▌▌

Civil Rights and Liberties

CHAPTER 1

Constitutional Sources of Civil Rights and Liberties

"History teaches us that grave threats to liberty often come in times of urgency, when constitutional rights seem too extravagant to a endure."

—*Justice Thurgood Marshall, dissenting in* Skinner v. Railway Labor Executives *(1989)*

Historical Pictures/Stock Montage

Thurgood Marshall: Associate Justice, 1967–1991

Introduction

One of the principal objectives of the U.S. Constitution, as stated in its preamble, is "to secure the Blessings of Liberty to ourselves and our Posterity." The Framers of the Constitution thus recognized the protection of individual liberty as a fundamental goal of constitutional government. Paraphrasing John Locke, the Declaration of Independence (1776) had declared the **unalienable rights** of man to be "life, liberty and the pursuit of happiness." Other more specific rights, including trial by jury, freedom of religion, and freedom of speech, were generally embraced by Americans, legacies of the Magna Carta (1215) and the English Bill of Rights (1689). The Framers of the Constitution sought to protect these rights by creating a system of government that would be inherently restricted in power and, hence, limited in its ability to transgress the rights of the individual.

The founders were heavily influenced by the theory of **natural rights**, in which rights are seen as inherently belonging to individuals, not as created by government. According to this view, individuals have the right to do whatever they please unless (1) they interfere with the rights of others or (2) government is constitutionally empowered to restrict the exercise of that freedom. The founders thus conceived of the powers of government as mere islands in a vast sea of individual rights. This was especially true of the newly created national government, which was limited to the exercise of expressly delegated powers. The original unamended

Constitution thus contained no provision guaranteeing freedom of speech, because the Constitution gave the federal government no authority to regulate that freedom. Yet the Framers did recognize certain rights, at least indirectly, by enumerating specific limitations on the national government and the states.

During the debate over ratification of the Constitution, a consensus emerged that the Constitution should be more explicit as to the rights of individuals. Reflecting this consensus, the First Congress in 1789 adopted the Bill of Rights, ratified in 1791. This prompt response by Congress and the states underscored the strong national commitment to individual freedom and fear of an intrusive tyrannical government.

Liberty, however, is only one aspect of constitutional rights. Equally critical in a constitutional democracy is the ideal of **equality**. Although the Framers of the original Constitution were less interested in equality than in liberty, the Constitution has come to be considerably more egalitarian over the years, both through formal amendment and through judicial interpretation. In its constitutional sense, equality means that all citizens are considered to be equal before the law, equal before the state, and equal in their possession of rights. The term **civil rights**, as distinct from **civil liberties**, is generally used to denote citizens' equality claims, as distinct from their liberty claims.

The subject matter of civil rights and liberties is far ranging, touching on most contemporary social, political, and economic issues. Gun control, same-sex marriage, abortion, doctor-assisted suicide, and affirmative action are a few of the more salient policy questions the courts have addressed in recent years in disputes over the meaning of particular civil rights and liberties protections. The Supreme Court's rulings on such issues comprise a major aspect of contemporary American constitutional law and, accordingly, are the subject of Volume II of this textbook.

Judicial Protection of Civil Rights and Liberties

Although formal constitutional amendments are very important, constitutional law affecting civil rights and liberties often develops through judicial interpretation of the language of the Constitution. Both the state and federal courts interpret the Constitution in the course of deciding cases. When a court finds that a statute or some other government policy is contrary to its understanding of the Constitution, it is empowered to declare the former null and void. Ever since *Marbury v. Madison* (1803), American courts have exercised this power, known as **judicial review**. Historically, judicial review has been crucial to the protection, as well as the development, of civil rights and liberties in the United States. Courts are not the only protectors of civil rights and liberties— legislatures and executives have a role to play as well. But quite often the protection of rights involves a declaration that a legislature or an executive body has acted unconstitutionally, and this responsibility falls to the courts.

The power of judicial review, although quite formidable, is not unlimited. The most basic limitation on judicial review is that it may be exercised only as needed to resolve court cases between adverse parties. These cases begin in one of two ways: as **civil suits** or **criminal prosecutions**.

Civil Suits

A civil suit begins when one party, the plaintiff, files a suit against another party, the defendant. Often, a civil suit consists of one party making a claim against another. Sometimes, a plaintiff files a class action on behalf of all "similarly situated" persons. While a large number of civil suits are between two private parties, in some civil cases, the plaintiff accuses the defendant of violating his or her constitutional rights. Because constitutional rights are essentially limitations on the actions of government, the respondent in such a civil suit is generally a government official. Suits against government agencies per se are often, but not always, barred by the doctrine of sovereign immunity. Congress and every state legislature have passed laws waiving sovereign immunity with regard to certain types of claims.

Every civil suit seeks a remedy for an alleged wrong. The remedy may be monetary compensation for actual or punitive damages. It may be a court order requiring specific performance from or barring specified action by the defendant. It may be a simple declaratory judgment—a statement from the court declaring the rights of the litigants. Sometimes, a plaintiff will seek an injunction against a defendant to cause an ongoing injury to cease or to prevent an injury from occurring.

In a civil suit alleging the violation of a constitutional right, all of the aforementioned remedies are available to the plaintiff. However, because many government officials (judges, legislators, governors, and so forth) are immune from suits for monetary damages stemming from their official decisions or actions, suits against government officials tend to seek declaratory judgments and/or injunctions. A person who is threatened with criminal prosecution under an unconstitutional statute may seek an injunction against enforcement of the law by filing a civil suit against the prosecutor. *Roe v. Wade*, the landmark abortion decision, began when Jane Roe, an unmarried pregnant woman, brought a suit against Henry Wade, the district attorney in Dallas, Texas, seeking to permanently enjoin Wade from enforcing the state's abortion law against her and other similarly situated women (see Chapter 6).

In certain instances, individuals whose constitutional rights have been violated may recover monetary damages. The Civil Rights Act of 1866 (codified at 42 U.S.C. § 1983) permits courts to award monetary damages to plaintiffs whose constitutional rights are violated by persons acting under "color of law." A good example of this type of action is seen in the Rodney King case, in which the plaintiff recovered monetary damages in a Section 1983 lawsuit stemming from an incident of police brutality in Los Angeles that was witnessed on TV by many millions of people across the United States and beyond.

Criminal Prosecutions

Criminal prosecutions often raise constitutional issues. In criminal cases, a governmental agency has brought charges against an individual on behalf of a jurisdiction's citizens. As noted earlier, one who is threatened with criminal prosecution under an unconstitutional statute can seek an injunction to bar the prosecutor from enforcing the law. Once a prosecution is under way, however, the usual means of challenging a statute is by filing a demurrer to an indictment or through the appropriate pretrial motion. If one is convicted under an arguably unconstitutional statute, the appropriate remedy is, of course, an appeal to a higher court. Many criminal convictions are challenged in this way. As an illustration, consider the case of *Texas v. Johnson* (1989), the landmark "flag burning" case. Gregory Johnson was convicted of violating the Texas law, making it a crime to desecrate the American flag. He appealed his conviction to the Texas Court of Criminal Appeals, the state court of last resort in criminal cases, arguing that the conviction violated his constitutional rights. The Court of Criminal Appeals agreed, saying that the state flag desecration law was unconstitutional. The state of Texas obtained review in the U.S. Supreme Court on a writ of certiorari, but to no avail. The Supreme Court, in a highly publicized and controversial decision, agreed with the Texas Court of Criminal Appeals: It was held unconstitutional to punish someone for the act of burning the American flag as a form of political protest (see Chapter 3).

Very often constitutional issues arise in criminal cases owing to the actions of the police or the prosecutor, or decisions made by the trial judge on the admission of evidence or various trial procedures. The federal Constitution provides a host of protections to persons accused of crimes, including freedom from unreasonable searches and seizures, compulsory self-incrimination, double jeopardy, and cruel and unusual punishments (see Chapter 5). Frequently, these protections are invoked by persons challenging their convictions on appeal. While the overwhelming majority of these appeals are resolved by intermediate appellate courts or state courts of last resort, a small number of such cases are heard each term by the U.S. Supreme Court. Some of the Supreme Court's most famous decisions, for example, *Mapp v. Ohio* (1961), *Gideon v. Wainwright* (1963), and *Miranda v. Arizona* (1966), have involved the rights of persons accused of crimes. (These landmark cases are discussed and excerpted in Chapter 5.)

Habeas Corpus

The Constitution in Article I, Section 9, Clause 2, explicitly recognizes the writ of **habeas corpus**, an ancient common law device that persons can use to challenge the legality of arrest or imprisonment. One who believes that he or she is being illegally detained, even if he or she is in prison after being duly convicted and exhausting the ordinary appeals process, may seek a writ of habeas corpus in the appropriate court. In 2002, relatives of foreign nationals apprehended in the "war on terrorism" and incarcerated at the American naval base at Guantanamo Bay, Cuba, sought habeas corpus relief in the federal courts. Despite lower court decisions holding that federal courts did not have jurisdiction, the Supreme Court in *Rasul v. Bush* (2004) held that "[a]liens held at the base, no less than American citizens, are entitled to invoke the federal courts' authority." This controversial decision opened the door to judicial review of the confinement of hundreds of alleged enemy combatants being held in indefinite detention by the military pursuant to an order of the president.

The federal habeas corpus statute affords opportunities to persons convicted of crimes to obtain review of their convictions in federal courts, even if they received appellate review in the state courts. Some of the Supreme Court's most important decisions in the area of criminal procedure, for example, *Gideon v. Wainwright* (1963), have come in federal habeas corpus cases filed by state prisoners. A proliferation of such cases beginning in the 1960s led critics to call for the curtailment or outright abolition of federal habeas corpus review of state criminal cases. Although it has not been abolished, federal habeas corpus review has been restricted in recent years, through both congressional and judicial action (see Chapter 5).

How Civil Rights and Liberties Cases Get to the Supreme Court

As noted in the previous section, cases raising federal constitutional questions can begin in the state or federal courts. The Supreme Court has jurisdiction to review these cases and will consider doing so as long as parties have exhausted their remedies in the lower courts. There are three mechanisms by which the Supreme Court reviews lower court decisions. By far the rarest is certification, in which a federal appeals court formally asks the Supreme Court to certify or "make certain" a point of law. The second is on appeal by right in which, at least theoretically, the Court must rule on the merits of the appeal. As noted earlier, however, Congress has restricted such appeals to a few narrow categories of cases. By far the most common means by which the Court grants review is through the writ of certiorari. One who loses an appeal in a state court of last resort or a federal court of appeals may file a petition for certiorari in the Supreme Court. At least four of the Court's nine justices must vote affirmatively on a petition in order for certiorari to be granted. Of the approximately 10,000 "cert petitions" coming to it each year, the Court will normally grant review in only about a hundred, and even some of these cases will be dismissed later without a decision on the merits. A denial of certiorari, just like the dismissal of an appeal, has the effect of sustaining the lower court decision under challenge, although the denial of review has no precedential value.

Like all appellate courts, the Supreme Court decides cases collegially. Normally, all nine justices participate in each decision. Once review is granted, parties submit briefs setting forth their positions. Outside parties, typically interest groups, often file *amicus curiae* briefs supporting one side or the other. After briefs have been submitted, cases are scheduled for oral argument, during which counsel for both sides appear before the Court in a public hearing to make statements and answer questions from the bench. The justices will then confer in private to discuss and decide the case—majority rules. One justice will be assigned the responsibility of authoring the Opinion of the Court, which states the judgment of the Court and expresses a supporting rationale. If the chief justice is in the majority, he or she will write the Opinion of the Court or assign that task to another justice in the majority. If the chief justice is in the minority, opinion assignment falls to the senior justice in the majority.

The Opinion of the Court, often referred to as the majority opinion when the Court is not unanimous, has the great advantage of providing a coherent statement of the Court's position to the parties, the lower courts, and the larger legal and political communities. It must be understood, however, that even a unanimous vote in support of a particular judgment does not guarantee that there will be an Opinion of the Court. Justices can and do differ on the rationales they adopt for voting in a particular way. Every justice retains the right to produce an opinion in every case, either for or against the judgment of the Court. A concurring opinion is one written in support of the Court's decision; a dissenting opinion is one that disagrees with the decision. An opinion concurring in the judgment is one that supports the Court's decision, but disagrees with the rationale expressed in the majority opinion. Occasionally, in cases that review multiple questions of constitutional principle, a justice will author an opinion that concurs in part and dissents in part, specifically outlining the reasons for this conclusion. All the opinions produced by the Court are important and are studied carefully by lawyers, judges, scholars, and students of the law.

To Summarize:

♦ *Ever since* Marbury v. Madison *(1803), American courts have exercised judicial review, the power to strike down legislation and other government actions determined to be unconstitutional.*

♦ *The courts exercise judicial review in the context of cases—live disputes between adverse parties. These cases begin as civil suits or criminal prosecutions. A special type of proceeding, habeas corpus, enables a court to determine the lawfulness of confinement.*

♦ *The Supreme Court has jurisdiction to review lower court decisions as long as federal questions are involved and parties seeking review have exhausted their remedies in the lower courts.*

♦ *There are three mechanisms by which the Supreme Court reviews lower court decisions: certification, in which a federal appeals court formally asks the Supreme Court to certify or "make certain" a point of law; appeal by right in which, at least theoretically, the Court must rule on the merits of the appeal; and certiorari, which is granted at the discretion of the Court.*

♦ *When a case is brought before the Supreme Court, parties submit briefs and engage in oral argument. The justices make their decisions in private conferences and announce their decisions through the issuance of written opinions. These opinions provide guidance to the lower courts and are closely studied by judges, lawyers, scholars, and students.*

Briefing Cases

The study of American constitutional law involves careful consideration of important decisions of the Supreme Court and other courts. Each chapter in this textbook includes a number of excerpts from important Supreme Court decisions. These excerpts have been chosen to illustrate some of the important concepts and principles described in the chapters. "Briefing" cases is an excellent way to digest the facts, issues, holdings, and rationales of judicial decisions. A case brief is simply a summary of a court decision, usually in outline format. Whether or not the instructor requires case briefs, students may find briefing cases useful for learning material and preparing for examinations. Typically, a case brief contains the following elements:

- The name of the case and the date of the decision
- The essential facts of the case
- The key issue(s) of law involved
- The holding of the court
- A brief summary of the court's opinion, especially as it relates to the key issue(s) in the case
- Summaries of concurring and dissenting opinions, if any
- A statement commenting on the significance of the decision and/or stating the student's view as to the correctness of the decision

Here is a sample case brief:

Plessy v. Ferguson *(1896)*

Issue: Is a state law requiring "equal but separate" facilities for whites and blacks a violation of the Thirteenth or Fourteenth Amendment?

Facts: Homer Plessy, who was seven-eighths white and one-eighth black, was arrested after refusing to vacate a seat in a railroad car reserved for whites. He was convicted under a Louisiana statute mandating "equal but separate" accommodations on railroads. After unsuccessfully attacking the statute in the Louisiana state courts, Plessy appealed to the U.S. Supreme Court.

Supreme Court Decision: Judgment of state court affirmed; conviction and statute upheld. Vote: 7–1 (Justice Brewer not participating).

Opinions:

Majority (Brown): Segregation is a reasonable exercise of the state's police power in that it is conducive to the maintenance of public order and peace. Segregation is not per se a "badge of slavery" and is therefore not a violation of the Thirteenth Amendment. The compulsory segregation of the races is permissible under the Equal Protection Clause of the Fourteenth Amendment as long as equal accommodations are provided. The Fourteenth Amendment was not intended to abolish all distinctions based on color, nor was it intended to enforce social as distinct from political equality.

Dissenting (Harlan): Compulsory segregation is an infringement on the personal liberties of persons of African descent. The Constitution is color-blind; therefore, government is prohibited from treating people differently merely on account of their race. Forcible segregation is a badge of inferiority, a vestige of slavery, and therefore a violation of the Thirteenth Amendment.

Comment:

The "separate but equal" doctrine propounded in Plessy provided a justification for the entire regime of Jim Crow laws enacted in the late nineteenth century. The Supreme Court eventually repudiated this doctrine, beginning with Brown v. Board of Education (1954).

Rights Recognized in the Original Constitution

With these preliminary matters out of the way, we now begin our examination of constitutional law affecting civil rights and liberties. The original, unamended Constitution contained few explicit protections of individual rights, not because the Framers did not value rights, but because they thought it unnecessary to deal with them explicitly. Significantly, most of the state constitutions adopted during the American Revolution contained fairly detailed bills of rights placing limits on state and local governments. The Framers did not anticipate the growth of a pervasive national government and thus did not regard the extensive enumeration of individual rights in the federal Constitution as critical. They did, however, recognize a few important safeguards in the original Constitution.

Trial by Jury

Article III, Section 2, Clause 4, provides that "The Trial of all Crimes, except in Cases of Impeachment, shall be by Jury; and such Trial shall be held in the State where the said Crimes shall have been committed; but when not committed within any State, the Trial shall be at such Place or Places as the Congress may by Law have directed." The right to a jury trial in criminal cases is reaffirmed in the Sixth Amendment, and the right to trial by jury in civil cases is enumerated in the Seventh Amendment. The Sixth and Seventh Amendments are discussed more fully later in this chapter.

Circumscribing the Crime of Treason

The crime of treason involves betraying one's country, either by making war against it or giving aid and comfort to its enemies. Under the English common law, treason was in a category by itself, because it was considered far worse than any felony. English kings had used the crime of treason to punish and deter political opposition. The Framers of the U.S. Constitution, aware of these abuses, sought to prohibit the federal government from using the offense of treason to punish political dissent. The Framers of the Constitution, having recently participated in a successful revolution, were understandably sensitive to the prospect that government could employ the crime of **treason** to stifle political dissent. Thus, they provided in Article III, Section 3, that "Treason against the United States, shall consist only in levying War against them, or in adhering to their Enemies, giving them Aid and Comfort." To protect citizens against unwarranted prosecution for treason, the Framers further specified that "[n]o Person shall be convicted of Treason unless on the Testimony of two Witnesses to the same overt Act, or on Confession in open Court."

In *Ex Parte Bollman* (1807), Chief Justice John Marshall observed "that the crime of treason should not be extended by construction to doubtful cases." In presiding over the treason trial of Aaron Burr in 1807, Chief Justice Marshall so instructed the jury, which returned a verdict of not guilty. The upshot of John Marshall's opinion and the acquittal of Aaron Burr was that subsequent prosecutions for treason became infrequent and convictions became rare.

In *Cramer v. United States* (1945), the Supreme Court reversed the treason conviction of Anthony Cramer, a German immigrant accused of giving aid and comfort to two Nazi saboteurs who infiltrated the United States in 1942. Writing for the Court, Justice Robert Jackson pointed out that to be guilty of treason, a defendant must both adhere to the enemy and provide them aid and comfort:

> *A citizen intellectually or emotionally may favor the enemy and harbor sympathies or convictions disloyal to this country's policy or interest, but so long as he commits no act of aid and comfort to the enemy, there is no treason. On the other hand, a citizen may*

take actions, which do aid and comfort the enemy—making a speech critical of the government or opposing its measures, profiteering, striking in defense plants or essential work, and the hundred other things which impair our cohesion and diminish our strength—but if there is no adherence to the enemy in this, if there is no intent to betray, there is no treason.

Two years later, in *Haupt v. United States* (1947), the Court upheld the treason conviction of a German-American who sheltered one of the Nazi saboteurs. Again writing for the majority, Justice Robert Jackson observed that "[t]he law of treason makes and properly makes conviction difficult but not impossible."

No one has been convicted of treason in the United States since World War II. Many people incorrectly believe that Julius and Ethel Rosenberg, who provided the Soviet Union with top-secret information about the construction of the atomic bomb, were convicted of treason. Prosecutors considered charging the Rosenbergs with treason but concluded that they could not obtain a conviction due to the constitutional two-witness requirement. Instead, they elected to charge the Rosenbergs with espionage. The defendants were convicted in 1951 and sentenced to death. The couple was executed in 1953.

More recently, some believed that John Walker Lindh, an American citizen captured by American military forces in Afghanistan in December 2001, was guilty of treason based on his involvement with the Taliban regime and Osama Bin Laden's al-Qaeda terrorist organization. As in the Rosenberg case, federal prosecutors decided not to charge Lindh with treason. Rather, he agreed to plead guilty to two lesser offenses and was sentenced to twenty years in federal prison.

Prohibition of Religious Tests for Public Office

Article VI of the Constitution provides, among other things, that "no religious Test shall ever be required as a Qualification to any Office or public Trust under the United States." This clause means, in effect, that personal views regarding religion may not officially qualify or disqualify one for public service. The prohibition against **religious tests** reflects the Framers' commitment to the idea that government ought to be neutral with respect to matters of religion, a view that was strongly reinforced by adoption of the **Establishment Clause** of the First Amendment (see Chapter 3).

Because the Religious Test Clause referred only to *federal* offices, states remained free to require religious tests as conditions of holding public office or securing public employment. At the time the U.S. Constitution was adopted, most states did have such requirements. The Supreme Court's decision in *Cantwell v. Connecticut* (1940), applying the First Amendment's **Free Exercise Clause** to the states by way of the Fourteenth Amendment, ultimately set the stage for the Supreme Court to review religious tests for *state* offices. (The doctrine of incorporation, by which most Bill of Rights protections have been enforced against the states via the Fourteenth Amendment, is discussed extensively later in this chapter.)

In *Torcaso v. Watkins* (1961), the Court reviewed a provision of the Maryland constitution stating that "no religious test ought ever to be required as a qualification for any office of profit or trust in this State, other than a declaration of belief in the existence of God." The appellant, Torcaso, was denied a commission as a notary public because he refused to acknowledge the existence of God. Speaking for the Court, Justice Hugo L. Black concluded that the "Maryland religious test for public office unconstitutionally invades the appellant's freedom of belief and religion and therefore cannot be enforced against him." Seventeen years later, in *McDaniel v. Paty* (1978), the Court invalidated a Tennessee statute barring priests and ministers from serving as delegates to state constitutional conventions. In an opinion announcing the judgment of the Court, Chief Justice

Warren E. Burger explained that the historical origin of state bans on clergy holding public office "was primarily to assure the success of a new political experiment, the separation of church and state." Nevertheless, Burger concluded that the ban violated the First Amendment right to the free exercise of religion. *Torcaso v. Watkins* and *McDaniel v. Paty* have rendered unenforceable all similar state religious tests and restrictions on clergy holding public office.

Protecting the Writ of Habeas Corpus

As noted earlier, the writ of habeas corpus enables a court to review a custodial situation and order the release of an individual who is found to have been illegally incarcerated. Article I, Section 9, of the Constitution states that "the Privilege of the Writ of Habeas Corpus shall not be suspended, unless when in Cases of Rebellion or Invasion the public Safety may require it." Grounded in English common law, the writ of habeas corpus gives effect to the all-important right of the individual not to be held in unlawful custody.

In adopting the habeas corpus provision, the Framers wanted not only to recognize the right but also to limit its suspension to emergency situations. The Constitution is ambiguous as to which branch of government has the authority to suspend the writ of habeas corpus during emergencies. Early in the Civil War, President Lincoln authorized military commanders to suspend the writ. Congress ultimately confirmed the president's action through legislation. In *Ex Parte Milligan* (1866), the Supreme Court held that only Congress can suspend the writ of habeas corpus. During World War II, the writ of habeas corpus was suspended in the territory of Hawaii.

SIDEBAR

Habeas Corpus: The Guantanamo Cases

Access to habeas corpus became a hotly contested issue after hundreds of "enemy combatants" captured as part of the "war on terrorism" were incarcerated at the American naval base at Guantanamo Bay, Cuba. Under an executive order issued by President George W. Bush after September 11, 2001, these detainees were to be tried by military tribunals. Moreover, the government took the position that the detainees were beyond the reach of federal habeas corpus review.

In *Rasul v. Bush* (2004), the Supreme Court ruled that the federal courts had jurisdiction under the federal habeas corpus statute to review the legality of the detention of the Guantanamo inmates. This opened the door for hundreds of alleged enemy combatants to seek judicial review of their detention. One of these detainees, Salim Ahmed Hamdan, employed the writ of habeas corpus to successfully challenge President George W. Bush's authority to establish military tribunals to try the detainees (see *Hamdan v. Rumsfeld* [2006], discussed and excerpted in Chapter 4, Volume I).

In *Boumediene v. Bush* (2008), the Supreme Court reviewed the Military Commissions Act (MCA), passed in response to the *Hamdan* decision in an effort to prevent enemy combatants held outside of the United States from obtaining writs of habeas corpus to challenge their detention. Here the Court held that because procedures specified in the Detainee Treatment Act of 2005 were not adequate substitutes for the writ of habeas corpus, the MCA, in stripping the courts of jurisdiction to hear habeas petitions, operated as an unconstitutional suspension of the writ.

In closing his opinion for the Court in *Boumediene*, Justice Anthony Kennedy remarked that:

The laws and Constitution are designed to survive, and remain in force, in extraordinary times. Liberty and security can be reconciled; and in our system they are reconciled within the framework of the law. The Framers decided that habeas corpus, a right of first importance, must be a part of that framework, a part of that law.

Writing for four dissenters, Chief Justice John Roberts chided the Court for striking down "the most generous set of procedural protections ever afforded aliens detained by this country as enemy combatants."

The writ of habeas corpus is an important element in modern criminal procedure. As a result of legislation passed by Congress in 1867 and subsequent judicial interpretation of that legislation, a person convicted of a crime in a state court and sentenced to state prison may petition a federal district court for habeas corpus relief. This permits a federal court to review the constitutional correctness of the arrest, trial, and sentencing of a state prisoner.

Under Chief Justice Earl Warren, the Supreme Court broadened the scope of federal habeas corpus review of state criminal convictions by permitting prisoners to raise issues in a federal court that they did not raise in their state appeals (see, for example, *Fay v. Noia* [1963]). The more conservative Burger and Rehnquist Courts significantly restricted state prisoners' access to federal habeas corpus (see, for example, *Stone v. Powell* [1976]; *McCleskey v. Zant* [1991]; *Hererra v. Collins* [1993]). Nevertheless, the continuing controversy over federal habeas corpus review of state criminal convictions prompted Congress to place further restrictions on the availability of the writ. The Antiterrorism and Effective Death Penalty Act of 1996 curtailed habeas corpus petitions by state prisoners who have already filed such petitions in federal court. Of course, because Congress initially provided this jurisdiction to the federal courts by statute, Congress may modify or abolish this jurisdiction if it so desires. It is unlikely, though, that Congress would eliminate federal habeas review of state criminal cases altogether (for further discussion, see Chapter 5).

Ex Post Facto Laws

Article I, Section 9, of the Constitution prohibits Congress from passing **ex post facto laws**. Article I, Section 10, imposes the same prohibition on state legislatures. **Ex post facto** laws (literally, "after the fact") are laws passed after the occurrence of an act that alter the legal status or consequences of that act. In *Calder v. Bull* (1798), the Supreme Court held that the *ex post facto* clauses applied to criminal but not to civil laws. According to Justice Samuel Chase's opinion in that case, impermissible *ex post facto* laws are those that "create or aggravate … [a] crime; or increase the punishment, or change the rules of evidence, for the purpose of conviction." Retrospective laws dealing with civil matters are thus not prohibited by the *ex post facto* clauses.

In two cases decided during the late nineteenth century, *Kring v. Missouri* (1883) and *Thompson v. Utah* (1898), the Supreme Court broadened the definition of *ex post facto* laws to prohibit certain changes in criminal procedure that might prove disadvantageous to the accused. However, in *Collins v. Youngblood* (1990), the Supreme Court overruled these precedents and returned to the definition adopted in *Calder v. Bull*. For an act to be invalidated as an *ex post facto* law, two key elements must exist. First, the act must be retroactive—it must apply to events that occurred before its passage. Second, it must seriously disadvantage the accused, not merely by changes in procedure but by means that render conviction more likely or punishment more severe.

Judicial decisions relying on the *Ex Post Facto* Clause are uncommon today. But during its 1999 term, the Supreme Court handed down a ruling in this area. In *Carmell v. Texas* (2000), the Court reversed convictions on four sexual assault charges. The convictions were for assaults that occurred in 1991 and 1992, when Texas law provided that a defendant could not be convicted merely on the testimony of the victim unless he or she was under age 14. At the time of the alleged assaults, the victim was 14 or 15. The law was later amended to extend the "child victim exception" to victims under 18 years old. Carmell was convicted under the amended law, which the Supreme Court held to be an *ex post facto* law. Writing for the Court, Justice Stevens observed that "[u]nder the law in effect at the time the acts were committed, the prosecution's case was legally insufficient ... unless the State could produce both the victim's testimony *and* corroborative evidence."

Bills of Attainder

Article I, Sections 9 and 10, also prohibits Congress and the states, respectively, from adopting bills of attainder. A **bill of attainder** is a legislative act that imposes punishment on a person without benefit of a trial in a court of law. Perhaps the best known cases involving bills of attainder are the test oath cases of 1867. In *Ex parte Garland*, the Court struck down an 1865 federal statute, forbidding attorneys from practicing before federal courts unless they took an oath that they had not supported the Confederacy during the Civil War. In *Cummings v. Missouri* (1866), the Court voided a provision of the Missouri Constitution that required a similar oath of all persons who wished to be employed in a variety of occupations, including the ministry. Cummings, a Catholic priest, had been fined $500 for preaching without having taken the oath. The Court found that these laws violated both the bill of attainder and *ex post facto* provisions of Article I.

Since World War II, the Supreme Court has declared only two acts of Congress invalid as bills of attainder. The first instance was *United States v. Lovett* (1946), in which the Court struck down a rider to an appropriation measure that prohibited three named federal employees from receiving compensation from the government. The three individuals had been branded by the House Un-American Activities Committee as "subversives." The Court said that legislative acts "that apply either to named individuals or to easily ascertainable members of a group in such a way as to inflict punishment on them without a judicial trial are bills of attainder prohibited by the Constitution." In *United States v. Brown* (1965), the Court invalidated a law that prohibited members of the Communist Party from serving as officers in trade unions, saying that Congress had inflicted punishment on "easily ascertainable members of a group." Four justices dissented, however, citing a number of legislative prohibitions on members of the Communist Party that the Court had previously upheld (see, for example, *American Communications Association v. Douds* [1950]).

Additionally, the Supreme Court considered an interesting bill of attainder issue in *Nixon v. Administrator of General Services* (1977). In this case, former president Richard Nixon challenged the Presidential Recordings and Materials Preservation Act of 1974, in which Congress had placed control of Nixon's presidential papers and recordings in the hands of the General Services Administration, an agency of the federal government. Nixon argued that the law singled him out for punishment by depriving him of the traditional right of presidents to control their own presidential papers. The Court ruled 7 to 2 that the act was not a bill of attainder, concluding that Congress's purpose in passing the law was not punitive.

The Contracts Clause

After the Revolutionary War, the thirteen states comprising the newly formed Union experienced a difficult period of political and economic instability. Numerous citizens, especially farmers, defaulted on their loans. Many were imprisoned under the harsh debtor laws of the period. Some state legislatures adopted laws to alleviate the plight of debtors. Cheap paper money was made legal tender; bankruptcy laws were adopted; in some states, creditors' access to the courts was restricted; some states prohibited imprisonment for debt. These policies, while commonplace today, were at that time anathema to the wealthy. Members of the creditor class believed that serious steps had to be taken to prevent the states from abrogating debts and interfering with contracts generally.

It is fair to say that one of the motivations behind the Constitutional Convention of 1787 was the desire to secure overriding legal protection for contracts. Thus, Article I, Section 10, prohibits states from passing laws "impairing the Obligation of Contracts." The **Contracts Clause** must be included among the provisions of the original Constitution that protect individual rights—in this case, the right of individuals to be free from governmental interference with their contractual relationships.

In *Dartmouth College v. Woodward* (1819), the seminal Contracts Clause decision of the Supreme Court, Chief Justice John Marshall said that:

> [I]t must be understood as intended to guard against a power, of at least doubtful utility, the abuse of which had been extensively felt; and to restrain the legislature in future from violating the right to property. That, anterior to the formation of the constitution, a course of legislation had prevailed in many, if not in all, of the states, which weakened the confidence of man in man, and embarrassed all transactions between individuals, by dispensing with a faithful performance of engagements. To correct this mischief, by restraining the power which produced it, the state legislatures were forbidden "to pass any law impairing the obligation of contracts," that is, of contracts respecting property, under which some individual could claim a right to something beneficial to himself; and that, since the clause in the constitution must in construction receive some limitation, it may be confined, and ought to be confined, to cases of this description; to cases within the mischief it was intended to remedy.

By protecting contracts, Article I, Section 10, performed an important function in the early years of American economic development. Historically, the Contracts Clause was an important source of litigation in the federal courts. However, in modern times, it is seldom interpreted to impose significant limits on the states in the field of economic regulation. (The Contracts Clause is discussed more fully in Chapter 2.)

To Summarize:

- *A number of provisions of Article I, Sections 9 and 10, recognize individual rights by placing restrictions on the federal government and the states, respectively.*
- *The specific provisions defining and limiting the crime of treason apply only to the federal government, as does the prohibition against religious tests for holding public office.*
- *The protection of the writ of habeas corpus also applies specifically to the federal government and, in effect, may not be suspended except in cases of national emergency.*
- *Two provisions of the original Constitution protect certain individual rights against both federal and state encroachment. These are the prohibitions of* ex post facto *laws and bills of attainder.*
- *The Contracts Clause of Article I, Section 10, imposes limitations on state interference with contractual rights and obligations. In the early years of the republic, this provision served as a major basis for federal judicial protection of private property rights.*

The Bill of Rights

As previously noted, the original Constitution contained little by way of explicit protection of individual rights. In *The Federalist*, No. 84, Alexander Hamilton argued that since the Constitution provided for limited government through enumerated powers, a Bill of

Rights was unnecessary. In rebuttal, Anti-Federalists argued that the Necessary and Proper Clause of Article I, Section 8, could be used to justify expansive government power that might threaten individual liberties. As we saw in Chapter 5, Volume I, the Anti-Federalists were definitely on target.

The omission of a bill of rights from the original Constitution was regarded as a major defect by numerous critics and significantly threatened to derail ratification in some states. Thomas Jefferson, who had not participated in the Constitutional Convention due to his diplomatic duties in France, was among the most influential critics. In a letter to his close friend James Madison, Jefferson argued, "You must specify your liberties, and put them down on paper." Madison, the acknowledged father of the Constitution, thought it unwise and unnecessary to enumerate individual rights, but Jefferson's view eventually prevailed. Honoring a "gentleman's agreement" designed to secure ratification of the Constitution in several key states, the First Congress considered a proposed bill of rights drafted by Madison.

Madison's original bill of rights called for limitations on the states as well as the federal government, but this proposal was defeated by states' rights advocates in Congress. Madison originally purposed seventeen amendments, but only twelve amendments to the Constitution were adopted by Congress in September 1789. Although two of these amendments were rejected by the states, the other ten were ratified in November 1791 and added to the Constitution as the Bill of Rights.

The First Amendment

The **First Amendment** contains what many believe to be the most crucial guarantees of freedom. The Establishment Clause prohibits Congress from making laws "respecting an establishment of religion," while the Free Exercise Clause enjoins the national government from "prohibiting the free exercise thereof." These first two clauses demonstrate the fundamental character of the founders' devotion to freedom of religion. Today, the Religion Clauses remain both important and controversial, involving such emotional issues as prayer and the teaching of "creation science" in the public schools. (The Religion Clauses of the First Amendment are examined in Chapter 4.)

The First Amendment also protects **freedom of speech** and **freedom of the press**, often referred to jointly as **freedom of expression**. One can argue that freedom of expression is the most vital freedom in a democracy, in that it permits the free flow of information between the people and their government. Finally, the First Amendment protects the "right of the people peaceably to assemble and petition the Government for a redress of grievances." Freedom of assembly remains an important right, and one that is often controversial, as when an extremist group such as the Ku Klux Klan stages a public rally. The freedom to petition government tends to be less controversial but no less important. Today, it embraces "lobbying," the principal activity of interest groups, but the right of petition also extends to less organized efforts. (The freedoms of speech, press, and assembly are examined in Chapter 3.)

The Second Amendment

Most Americans believe that the Constitution protects their individual **right to keep and bear arms** and, in recent years, the Supreme Court has affirmed that belief. Yet the **Second Amendment** refers not only to the keeping and bearing of arms but also to the need for a **well-regulated militia**. It provides: "A well-regulated Militia, being necessary to the security of a free State, the right of the people to keep and bear Arms, shall not be infringed." In *United States v. Cruikshank* (1875), the Supreme Court held that the Second Amendment guaranteed states the right to maintain militias but did not guarantee to individuals the right to possess guns.

Subsequently, in *United States v. Miller* (1939), the Court upheld a federal law banning the interstate transportation of certain firearms. Miller, who had been arrested for transporting a double-barreled sawed-off shotgun from Oklahoma to Arkansas, sought the protection of the Second Amendment. The Court rejected Miller's argument, asserting that "we cannot say that the Second Amendment guarantees the right to keep and bear such an instrument." In *Lewis v. United States* (1980), the Court reaffirmed the *Miller* precedent. In upholding a federal gun control act, the Court said:

> *These legislative restrictions on the use of firearms are neither based on constitutionally suspect criteria, nor do they trench upon any constitutionally protected liberties.... [T]he Second Amendment guarantees no right to keep and bear a firearm that does not have "some reasonable relationship to the preservation or efficiency of a well regulated militia."*

The Court's statement in *Lewis* did not end the debate over the Second Amendment. In fact, the debate intensified as the National Rifle Association and various conservative groups urged that the Second Amendment should be viewed as protecting an individual's right to possess guns irrespective of any service in a militia.

As Attorney General of the United States during George W. Bush's first presidential term, John Ashcroft adopted the "individual rights" interpretation of the Second Amendment. In a May 17, 2001, letter to the National Rifle Association, Ashcroft wrote, "[L]et me state unequivocally.... the Second Amendment clearly protect(s) the right of individuals to keep and bear firearms." The Attorney General's letter reflected a widely held view among conservative Americans who opposed many of the state and federal gun control laws.

In a dramatic turnaround, a five-member majority of the Supreme Court decided in *District of Columbia v. Heller* (2008) that the Second Amendment protects *a personal* right to keep and bear arms. Speaking for the Court, Justice Antonin Scalia insisted that the Court was returning to the original understanding of the Second Amendment:

> *Undoubtedly some think that the Second Amendment is outmoded in a society where our standing army is the pride of our Nation, where well-trained police forces provide personal security, and where gun violence is a serious problem. That is perhaps debatable, but what is not debatable is that it is not the role of this Court to pronounce the Second Amendment extinct.*

In dissent, Justice John Paul Stevens took issue with the Court's interpretation of the original understanding of the Second Amendment:

> *The Court would have us believe that over 200 years ago, the Framers made a choice to limit the tools available to elected officials wishing to regulate civilian uses of weapons, and to authorize this Court to use the common-law process of case-by-case judicial lawmaking to define the contours of acceptable gun control policy. Absent compelling evidence that is nowhere to be found in the Court's opinion, I could not possibly conclude that the Framers made such a choice.*

Two years later, in *McDonald v. Chicago* (2010), a narrowly divided Court held, in an opinion by Justice Alito, that "the Second Amendment right is fully applicable to the States." Alito noted that the Court in *Heller* had recognized that "individual self-defense [was] 'the central component' of the Second Amendment right." Echoing Justice Scalia's observations in *Heller*, Justice Alito emphasized that the Court did not intend to question laws banning possession of guns by felons or mentally ill persons or restrictions on carrying guns in sensitive places such as schools and government buildings. Nor did the Court question the reasonable regulation of the commercial sale of firearms.

The four dissenters in *McDonald*, led by Justice Stevens, reiterated their view that *Heller* had been wrongly decided, adding that they would not have extended its protections to state and local jurisdictions even if it had been decided correctly. The obvious question remaining in the aftermath of *Heller* and *McDonald* is the extent to which the Supreme Court will be willing to defer to legislative and administrative restrictions on the possession and use of firearms.

It should be noted that most of the state constitutions contain language similar to the Second Amendment. As interpreted by the various state courts, these provisions vary considerably in the degree to which they restrict state legislatures and local governing bodies from enacting gun control laws. There is a general distinction, however, between the right to gun ownership, which is generally protected, and the carrying of guns, which generally is not protected. Of course, in the wake of *McDonald v. Chicago*, state and local restrictions on firearms are subject to challenge under the Second Amendment as well as under relevant provisions of state constitutions.

In 2013, the Obama administration asked Congress to enact a law requiring universal background checks on prospective gun buyers, banning military-style assault weapons, and limiting the number of rounds in gun magazines. The proposal came in the wake of a horrendous school shooting in Newtown, Connecticut, in December 2012 and a rash of similar incidents of gun violence in movie theaters, malls, and other public places throughout America. President Obama characterized his proposal as a common-sense measures that would not infringe on Second Amendment rights. His critics disagreed and mounted an intense effort to defeat the measures in Congress. The bill failed to pass, but even had it become law, litigation would have been inevitable. One of the consequences of the *Heller* decision has been to make gun rights advocates believe that they have a reasonable chance of getting any federal gun control measures declared unconstitutional.

The Third Amendment

The **Third Amendment** prohibits military authorities from quartering troops in citizens' homes without their consent. This was a matter of serious concern to the founders, because English troops had been forcibly billeted in colonists' homes during the Revolutionary War. Today, the Third Amendment is little more than a historical curiosity, since it has not been the subject of any significant litigation. Indeed, the Supreme Court has rarely mentioned the amendment. Justice Robert H. Jackson's concurring opinion in *Youngstown Sheet and Tube Company v. Sawyer* (1952) cited the Third Amendment as an example of a constitutional limitation on presidential executive power during wartime. Writing for the Court in *Griswold v. Connecticut* (1965), Justice William O. Douglas relied, in small part, on the Third Amendment in justifying a constitutional right of privacy as implicit in the Bill of Rights. But the Court has never based a decision squarely on the Third Amendment.

The Fourth Amendment

The **Fourth Amendment** protects citizens from **unreasonable searches and seizures** conducted by police and other government agents. Reflecting a serious concern of the founders, the Fourth Amendment remains extremely important today, especially in light of the pervasiveness of crime, the ongoing war on drugs, and the more recent war on terrorism. In the twentieth century, the Fourth Amendment was the source of numerous important Supreme Court decisions and generated a tremendous and complex body of legal doctrine. For example, in *Katz v. United States* (1967), the Supreme Court under Chief Justice Warren expanded the scope of Fourth Amendment protection to include

wiretapping, an important tool of modern law enforcement. With a few notable exceptions, the Burger, Rehnquist, and Roberts Courts have been decidedly more conservative in this area, facilitating police efforts to ferret out crime. (The Fourth Amendment as it relates to criminal justice is examined in some depth in Chapter 5.)

In 2013, revelations about the National Security Agency's program of monitoring telephone calls, e-mails, and other electronic communications prompted a national discussion about government surveillance and the Fourth Amendment. Defenders of the NSA program argued that it was essential to protection of the national security in an age of terrorism. Critics objected to the fact that the NSA apparently was collecting massive amounts of data on Americans without suspicion that they were involved in any improper activity. In a statement posted on the American Civil Liberties Union Web site, ACLU deputy legal director Jameel Jaffer asserted that the NSA program "is surely one of the largest surveillance efforts ever launched by a democratic government against its own citizens" and "represents a gross infringement of the freedom of association and the right to privacy." (This issue is also addressed in Chapter 4, Volume I.)

The Fifth Amendment

The **Fifth Amendment** contains a number of important provisions involving the rights of persons accused of crime. It requires the federal government to obtain an **indictment** from a **grand jury** before trying someone for a major crime. It also prohibits **double jeopardy**—that is, being tried twice for the same offense. Additionally, the Fifth Amendment protects persons against **compulsory self-incrimination**, commonly referred to as "taking the Fifth." (Fifth Amendment rights of the accused are dealt with in Chapter 5.) The Fifth Amendment also protects people against arbitrary use of **eminent domain**, the power of government to take private property for public use. The Just Compensation Clause forbids government from taking private property without paying **just compensation** to the owner (see Chapter 2). Finally, the Fifth Amendment prohibits the federal government from depriving persons of life, liberty, or property without **due process of law**. A virtually identical clause is found in the **Fourteenth Amendment**, applied specifically to the states. The Due Process Clauses have implications for both civil and criminal cases, as well as for a variety of relationships between citizen and government.

The Meaning of Due Process   Due process of law may be the broadest and most basic protection afforded by the Constitution. In its most generic sense, due process refers to the exercise of governmental power under the rule of law with due regard for the rights and interests of individuals. The roots of due process can be traced to Magna Carta (1215), which provided that "No Freeman shall be taken, or imprisoned, or be disseized of his Freehold, or Liberties, or free Customs, or be outlawed, or exiled, or any otherwise destroyed; nor will we pass upon him, nor condemn him, but by lawful Judgment of his Peers, or by the Law of the Land." The term "due process of law" first appeared in a statute adopted by Parliament in 1354. The law provided: "No man of what state or condition he be, shall be put out of his lands or tenements nor taken, nor disinherited, nor put to death, without he be brought to answer by *due process of law*." Thereafter, the term became shorthand for the protection of life, liberty, and property by appropriate legal procedures, including **fair notice** and a **fair hearing**. This is sometimes referred to as **procedural due process**.

In the infamous Dred Scott Case of 1857, the Supreme Court imparted a substantive dimension to the concept of due process. Writing for the Supreme Court, Chief Justice Roger B. Taney opined that "[a]n Act of Congress which deprives a citizen of the United States of his liberty or property, merely because he came himself or brought his property into a particular Territory of the United States, and who had committed no offense

Due Process of Law under the Federal and State Constitutions

"No person shall be ... deprived of life, liberty, or property, without due process of law."

—U.S. Constitution, Amendment V

"[N]or shall any State deprive any person of life, liberty, or property, without due process of law."

—U.S. Constitution, Amendment XIV, Sec. 1

"[N]o man shall be taken or imprisoned, or disseized of his freehold, liberties or privileges, or outlawed, or exiled, or in any manner destroyed or deprived of his life, liberty or property, but by the judgment of his peers or the law of the land."

—Tennessee Constitution, Art. I, Sec. 8

"No member of this state shall be disfranchised, or deprived of any of the rights or privileges secured to any citizen thereof, unless by the law of the land."

—New York Constitution, Art. I, Sec. 1

against the laws, could hardly be dignified with the name of due process of law." Of course, the "property" Taney referred to was the human being held in bondage. The abolition of slavery and the overturning of the Dred Scott decision by the Thirteenth and Fourteenth Amendments, respectively, would discredit the concept of substantive due process in this context. But it would re-emerge, beginning in the late nineteenth century as a basis for limiting various governmental regulations of the economy. (The concept of due process is more fully explicated later in this chapter, as part of the discussion of the Fourteenth Amendment.)

The Sixth Amendment

The **Sixth Amendment** is concerned exclusively with the rights of the accused. It requires, among other things, that people charged with crimes be provided a "**speedy and public trial**, by an impartial jury." The right of **trial by jury** is one of the most cherished rights in the Anglo-American tradition, predating Magna Carta. The Sixth Amendment also grants defendants the right to confront (examine or cross-examine) witnesses for the prosecution and the right to have "compulsory process" (the power of **subpoena**) to require favorable witnesses to appear in court. Significantly, considering the incredible complexity of the criminal law, the Sixth Amendment guarantees that accused persons have the "Assistance of Counsel" for their defense. The Supreme Court has regarded the **right to counsel** as crucial to a fair trial, holding that defendants who are unable to afford private counsel must be provided counsel at public expense (*Gideon v. Wainwright* [1963]). (Sixth Amendment rights in the context of criminal justice are examined in Chapter 5.)

The Seventh Amendment

The **Seventh Amendment** guarantees the right to a jury trial in federal civil suits "at common law" where the amount at issue exceeds $20. Originally, it was widely assumed that the Seventh Amendment required jury trials only in traditional common law cases— for example, actions for libel, wrongful death, and trespass. But over the years, the Supreme Court expanded the scope of the Seventh Amendment to encompass civil suits seeking enforcement of statutory rights. For example, in *Curtis v. Loether* (1974), an African-American woman brought suit against a number of white defendants, charging them with refusing to rent her an apartment in violation of the Fair Housing Act of 1968. The defendants requested a trial by jury, but the district court ruled that the

Seventh Amendment did not apply to lawsuits seeking to enforce the rights created by the Fair Housing Act. In reversing the district court, the Supreme Court said:

The Seventh Amendment does apply to actions enforcing statutory rights, and requires a jury trial on demand, if the statute creates legal rights and remedies, enforceable in an action for damages in the ordinary courts of law.... We recognize ... the possibility that jury prejudice may deprive a victim of discrimination of the verdict to which he or she is entitled. Of course, the trial judge's power to direct a verdict, to grant judgment notwithstanding the verdict, or to grant a new trial provides substantial protection against this risk.

Although it does apply to suits enforcing statutory rights, the Seventh Amendment does not apply to the adjudication of certain issues by administrative or regulatory agencies. In *Thomas v. Union Carbide* (1985), the Supreme Court said that the Seventh Amendment does not provide the right to a jury trial where Congress "has created a 'private' right that is so closely integrated into a public regulatory scheme as to be a matter appropriate for agency resolution with limited involvement by the Article III judiciary." Under current interpretation, the Seventh Amendment does not require the traditional common law twelve-person jury in civil trials. In *Colgrove v. Battin* (1973), the Supreme Court held that a six-person jury was sufficient to try a civil case in federal court. The defendant in the case argued that the Seventh Amendment's reference to "suits at common law" required federal courts to adopt the traditional common law jury. The Supreme Court, dividing 5 to 4, disagreed. Writing for the Court, Justice William Brennan said:

Consistently with the historical objective of the Seventh Amendment, our decisions have defined the jury right preserved in cases covered by the Amendment, as "the substance of the common-law right of trial by jury, as distinguished from mere matters of form or procedure." The Amendment, therefore, does not bind the federal courts to the exact procedural incidents or details of jury trial according to the common law in 1791.

In a lengthy dissent, Justice Thurgood Marshall stressed the need for fidelity to the traditions of the common law:

Since some definition of "jury" must be chosen, I would ... rely on the fixed bounds of history which the Framers, by drafting the Seventh Amendment, meant to "preserve...." It may well be that the number 12 is no more than a "historical accident" and is "wholly without significance." ... But surely there is nothing more significant about the number six, or three or one. The line must be drawn somewhere, and the difference between drawing it in the light of history and drawing it on an ad hoc basis is, ultimately, the difference between interpreting a constitution and making it up as one goes along.

The controversy over the appropriate size of the jury in federal civil trials parallels the issue of jury size in criminal cases, a question examined in Chapter 5.

The Eighth Amendment

The **Eighth Amendment** protects persons accused of crimes from being required to post **excessive bail** to secure **pretrial release**. In *Stack v. Boyle* (1951), the Supreme Court held that bail is excessive if it is higher than is necessary to ensure a defendant's appearance for trial. But in *United States v. Salerno* (1987), a case involving the prosecution of an organized crime figure, the Court said that the Eighth Amendment does not require that defendants be released on bail, only that, if the court grants bail, it must not be "excessive." (The issue of **pretrial detention** is discussed more thoroughly in Chapter 5.)

The Eighth Amendment also forbids the imposition of **excessive fines** and the inflic-tion of **cruel and unusual punishments** on persons convicted of crimes. Originally thought to proscribe torture, the Cruel and Unusual Punishments Clause now figures prominently in the ongoing national debate over the death penalty (see Chapter 5). Writing for the Supreme Court in *Trop v. Dulles* (1958), Chief Justice Earl Warren ob-served that the Cruel and Unusual Punishments Clause "must draw its meaning from the evolving standards of decency that mark the progress of a maturing society." In the *Trop* case, a soldier had lost his citizenship after being found guilty of desertion from the U.S. Army. The Supreme Court restored Trop's citizenship, noting that "[t]he civilized na-tions of the world are in virtual unanimity that statelessness is not to be imposed as pun-ishment for a crime."

Civil Forfeitures   Federal law provides for forfeiture of the proceeds of a variety of criminal activities. Most controversial are the federal law provisions allowing **forfeiture** of property used in illicit drug activity. Under federal law a "conveyance," which includes aircraft, motor vehicles, and vessels, is subject to forfeiture if it is used to transport con-trolled substances. Real estate may be forfeited if it is used to commit or facilitate com-mission of a drug-related felony. Many states have similar statutes. Though technically such forfeitures are civil, not criminal, sanctions, the Supreme Court has recognized that forfeiture constitutes significant punishment and is thus subject to constitutional limitations under the Eighth Amendment. In *Austin v. United States* (1993), the Court said that forfeiture "constitutes 'payment to a sovereign as punishment for some offense' ... and, as such, is subject to the limitations of the Eighth Amendment's Excessive Fines Clause." However, the Court left it to state and lower federal courts to determine the tests of "excessiveness" in the context of forfeiture.

The Ninth Amendment

The **Ninth Amendment** was included in the Bill of Rights as a solution to a problem raised by James Madison—namely, that the specification of particular liberties might suggest that individuals possessed only those specified. The Ninth Amendment makes it clear that individuals retain a reservoir of rights and liberties beyond those listed in the Constitution: "The enumeration in the Constitution, of certain rights, shall not be con-strued to deny or disparage others retained by the people." This amendment reflects the dominant thinking of late eighteenth-century America: Individual rights precede and transcend the power of government; individuals possess all rights except those that have been surrendered to government for the protection of the public good. Yet prior to 1965, the Ninth Amendment had little significance in constitutional law. In the words of Justice Potter Stewart:

> *The Ninth Amendment, like its companion the Tenth, which this Court has held "states but a truism that all is retained which has not been surrendered," was framed by James Madison and adopted by the States simply to make clear that the adoption of the Bill of Rights did not alter the plan that the Federal government was to be a government of express and limited powers, and that all rights and powers not delegated to it were retained by the people and the individual States. (Griswold v. Connecticut [1965] [dissenting opinion])*

But in *Griswold v. Connecticut* (1965), a Supreme Court majority, in recognizing a constitutional right of privacy (discussed more fully in Chapter 6), relied in part on the Ninth Amendment. Here, the Court invalidated a Connecticut statute that made it a crime to use birth control devices. In dissent, Justice Stewart expressed dismay, observing that "the idea that a federal court could ever use the Ninth Amendment to annul a law passed by the elected representatives of the people of the State of Connecticut would have caused James Madison no little wonder." Although they have seldom relied explicitly on the Ninth Amendment, federal and state courts have over the years recognized a number of rights that Americans take for granted but which are not specifically enumerated in the Constitution. The right to marry, to determine how one's children are to be reared and educated, to choose one's occupation, to start a business, to travel freely across state lines, to sue in the courts, and to be presumed innocent of a crime until proven guilty are all examples of individual rights that have been recognized as "constitutional," despite their absence from the text of the Constitution. Quite often these rights have been recognized under the broad Due Process Clauses of the Fifth and Fourteenth Amendments.

The Tenth Amendment

The Bill of Rights is generally considered to be the first ten amendments to the Constitution. But the Tenth Amendment is of a fundamentally different character from the nine amendments that precede it. The Tenth Amendment provides: "The powers not delegated to the United States by the Constitution, nor prohibited by it to the States, are reserved to the States respectively, or to the people." Unlike other provisions of the Bill of Rights, and despite its reference to "the people," the Tenth Amendment recognizes the powers of the states vis-à-vis the federal government and does not directly address individual rights. However, the Framers of the Constitution and Bill of Rights believed that the federal structure guaranteed by the Tenth Amendment was conducive to the maintenance of freedom generally.

In the wake of the Constitutional Revolution of 1937, it appeared that the Tenth Amendment had been relegated to the dustbin of constitutional interpretation. In fact, in *United States v. Darby* (1941), the Supreme Court said that the Amendment "states but a truism that all is retained [by the states] which has not been surrendered [to the national government]." Not everyone agrees with this minimalist view of the Tenth Amendment. Judges and commentators of a more conservative orientation are apt to agree with Justice Lewis Powell that the Tenth Amendment plays "an integral role … in our constitutional theory" by maintaining the balance of power between the national government and the states, "a balance designed to protect our fundamental liberties" (*San Antonio Metro Transit Authority v. Garcia* [1985], Powell, J., dissenting).

> **To Summarize:**
> - *The omission of a more detailed enumeration of rights from the original Constitution was regarded in many quarters as a major deficiency and even threatened to undermine ratification of the Constitution.*
> - *The first ten amendments to the Constitution, known today as the Bill of Rights, were adopted by Congress in 1789 and ratified by the states in 1791. Most of these amendments (the First, Fourth, Fifth, Sixth, Eighth, and Ninth) are of fundamental importance in the field of civil rights and liberties and are discussed in detail in later chapters.*
> - *The Second Amendment recognizes an individual's "right to keep and bear Arms," independent of the provision regarding a "well-regulated Militia." Nevertheless, the Court has upheld federal statutes regulating the sale, possession, and use of certain weapons.*
> - *The Third Amendment, which prohibits the nonconsensual quartering of troops in private homes, has never been the subject of significant constitutional adjudication.*

> ♦ *The Seventh Amendment, which guarantees the common law right to a jury trial in a civil suit, has been expanded to include civil suits seeking enforcement of statutory rights. Under prevailing interpretation, the Seventh Amendment permits some variation from the use of the traditional twelve-member jury in a civil trial.*
>
> ♦ *The Tenth Amendment, often referred to as the "states' rights" amendment, applies to matters of federalism and is not directly related to individual rights and liberties.*

The Civil War Amendments

Next to the Bill of Rights, the most important amendments to the Constitution are the Thirteenth, Fourteenth, and Fifteenth, ratified in 1865, 1868, and 1870, respectively. Passed during Reconstruction, the underlying motive was to protect the civil rights of the newly freed former slaves. Yet in the fullness of time, these amendments, and most especially the Fourteenth, would provide the basis for a dramatic expansion of civil rights and liberties in this country.

The Thirteenth Amendment

On January 1, 1863, in the middle of the Civil War, President Abraham Lincoln issued the Emancipation Proclamation, declaring that "all persons held as slaves within any State, or designated part of a State, the people whereof shall then be in rebellion against the United States, shall be then, thenceforward, and forever free." Because the Emancipation Proclamation did not apply to slaves residing in border states that had remained loyal to the Union, and because there were doubts as to the Proclamation's constitutional efficacy, Congress proposed the **Thirteenth Amendment** to the U.S. Constitution. The amendment was adopted by the Senate on April 8, 1864, and passed the House of Representatives on January 31, 1865. The amendment secured ratification by the necessary number of states on December 6, 1865, when Georgia became the twenty-seventh state to approve it.

Section 1 of the Thirteenth Amendment provides "Neither slavery nor involuntary servitude, except as a punishment for crime whereof the party shall have been duly convicted, shall exist within the United States, or any place subject to their jurisdiction." Moreover, Section 2 authorizes Congress to enforce the abolition of slavery through "appropriate legislation."

To effectuate the guarantee of freedom implicit in the Thirteenth Amendment, Congress enacted the Civil Rights Act of 1866, the first in a series of important federal civil rights statutes. The act guaranteed that the newly freed former slaves would not be denied basic economic freedoms and property rights or access to the courts to enforce these rights.

In 1875, Congress passed another civil rights statute, one specifically aimed at racial discrimination by privately owned hotels, taverns, and other places of public accommodation. But in *The Civil Rights Cases* (1883), the Supreme Court struck it down, holding that Congress did not have the power to prohibit private discrimination. The Court rejected the argument that racial discrimination by private establishments was a badge or incident of slavery, and thus held that it was beyond the legislative powers of Congress under the Thirteenth Amendment.

Eighty-five years later, the Supreme Court took a very different view. In *Jones v. Alfred H. Mayer Company* (1968), the Supreme Court invoked the Thirteenth

Amendment in a decision upholding a provision of the Civil Rights Act of 1866. The issue in the case was whether Congress had the constitutional power to prohibit purely private discrimination in the sale of real estate. Writing for the Court, Justice Potter Stewart reasoned that "[w]hen racial discrimination herds men into ghettos and makes their ability to buy property turn on the color of their skin, then it too is a relic of slavery." Thus, in Stewart's view, Section 2 of the Thirteenth Amendment endowed Congress with ample authority to prohibit racial discrimination in the sale of housing.

Is Military Conscription Tantamount to Slavery?   Although the Thirteenth Amendment was designed solely to eliminate slavery, during World War I some critics of the military draft claimed that conscription was tantamount to involuntary servitude. In *Arver v. United States* (1918), the Supreme Court, speaking through Chief Justice Edward D. White, gave this argument short shrift, saying:

> [W]e are unable to conceive upon what theory the exaction by government from the citizen of the performance of his supreme and noble duty of contributing to the defense of the rights and honor of the nation as the result of a war declared by the great representative body of the people can be said to be the imposition of involuntary servitude in violation of the prohibitions of the Thirteenth Amendment.

The Fourteenth Amendment

Although slavery had been formally abolished by the Thirteenth Amendment, questions remained about the legal status of the former slaves. In *Dred Scott v. Sandford* (1857), the Supreme Court not only defended the institution of slavery but indicated that blacks were not citizens of the United States and possessed "no rights or privileges but such as those who held the power and the Government might choose to grant them." Section 1 of the Fourteenth Amendment made clear that *Dred Scott* was no longer the law of the land:

> All persons born or naturalized in the United States, and subject to the jurisdiction thereof are citizens of the United States and of the State wherein they reside. No State shall make or enforce any law which shall abridge the privileges or immunities of citizens of the United States; nor shall any State deprive any person of life, liberty, or property, without due process of law; nor deny to any person within its jurisdiction the equal protection of the laws.

There had also been questions about the constitutionality of the Civil Rights Act of 1866. It was not entirely clear that Section 2 of the Thirteenth Amendment provided a firm textual basis for the enactment of civil rights legislation that went beyond the prohibition of slavery per se. Section 5 of the Fourteenth Amendment, giving Congress "power to enforce, by appropriate legislation, the provisions of this article," when combined with the broad provisions of Section 1 of the Fourteenth Amendment, provided a solid foundation for federal civil rights legislation. It is appropriate at this juncture to examine in some detail the three principal provisions of Section 1: the Privileges or Immunities Clause, the Due Process Clause, and the Equal Protection Clause.

The Privileges or Immunities Clause   The Privileges or Immunities Clause of the Fourteenth Amendment echoes a similar clause found in Article IV, Section 2, of the Constitution, which in turn stemmed from a provision in the Articles of Confederation. The Privileges and Immunities Clause of Article IV, Section 2, provides: "The Citizens of each State shall be entitled to all privileges and Immunities of Citizens in the several States." In *Corfield v. Coryell* (1823), Justice Bushrod Washington asserted that the clause protected privileges and immunities "which are, in their nature, fundamental; which belong of right to the citizens of all free governments; and which have, at all times, been enjoyed by the citizens of the several states." Among those rights were "protection by the government; the enjoyment of life and liberty, with the right to acquire and possess property of every kind, to pursue and obtain happiness and safety; subject nevertheless to such restraints as the government may justly prescribe for the general good of the whole." Justice Washington's dictum was well known to the Framers of the Fourteenth Amendment. But there is evidence that at least some of those who framed the Fourteenth Amendment, including the author of Section 1, Representative John A. Bingham of Ohio, believed that the Privileges or Immunities Clause would provide a textual basis for the application of the Bill of Rights to the states.

In *The Slaughterhouse Cases* (1873), the Supreme Court adopted a very narrow view of the Privileges or Immunities Clause. Interpreting the clause for the first time, the Court held that it required the states to respect only the privileges and immunities of *national* citizenship, which the Court defined to include the right of access to the seat of the national government, the right to demand the federal government's protection on the high seas, the right to use the navigable waters of the United States, the privilege of habeas corpus, and other rights secured by treaties to which the United States was a signatory. Later, in *Twining v. New Jersey* (1908), the Court expanded the list to include the right to travel freely between states, the right to vote in elections for federal offices, the right to have access to public lands, and the right to petition Congress for a redress of grievances. While these rights are by no means unimportant, they pale in comparison to the liberties enumerated in the Bill of Rights. By adopting such a restrictive interpretation of the Privileges or Immunities Clause, the Court restricted the power of both Congress and the federal judiciary to protect citizens from state action.

In *Bradwell v. Illinois* (1873), the Supreme Court ruled that the Privileges or Immunities Clause did not prohibit a state from denying a woman a license to practice law. Speaking for eight of the nine members of the Court, Justice Samuel F. Miller concluded that "the right to control and regulate the granting of license to practice law in the courts of a State is one of those powers which are not transferred for its protection to the Federal Government, and its exercise is in no manner governed or controlled by citizenship of the United States." Two years later, in *Minor v. Happersett* (1875), the Court ruled that denying women the right to vote was not a violation of the Privileges or Immunities Clause. Writing for the majority, Chief Justice Morrison R. Waite asserted that national citizenship does not confer a right to vote and that the Fourteenth Amendment in no way deprived states of their powers with respect to determining eligibility to vote.

Given this very restrictive interpretation of the Privileges or Immunities Clause, it is not surprising that the clause has generated very little constitutional litigation. In *Saenz v. Roe* (1999), the Supreme Court relied on the clause in striking down a California law requiring people to have lived in the state for one year in order to obtain full welfare benefits. Writing for the majority, Justice John P. Stevens invoked *The Slaughterhouse Cases*, where the Court had said that "a citizen of the United States can, of his own volition, become a citizen of any State of the Union by a *bona fide* residence therein, with the same rights as other citizens of that State." However, to date, the *Saenz* decision has not spawned a new progeny of Supreme Court decisions under the Privileges or Immunities Clause.

The Due Process Clause   As we noted earlier in our discussion of the Fifth Amendment, the Framers of the Bill of Rights provided that no person shall "be deprived of life, liberty, or property, without due process of law." However, this provision applied only to the federal government. Thus citizens had to look to their state constitutions and state courts for protection against their respective state governments. Of course, all the state constitutions had, and still have, their own versions of the due process clause. For example, the Tennessee Constitution of 1796 adopted language reminiscent of Magna Carta, and this language remains in the current state constitution, which dates from 1870. Article I, Section 8, provides that "no man shall be taken or imprisoned, or disseized of his freehold, liberties or privileges, or outlawed, or exiled, or in any manner destroyed or deprived of his life, liberty or property, but by the judgment of his peers or the law of the land." Notwithstanding state constitutional guarantees of due process, the Framers of the Fourteenth Amendment wanted to provide for federal judicial protection of life, liberty, and property from arbitrary and capricious actions of the states. Therefore, they included in Section 1 the following injunction: "nor shall any State deprive any person of life, liberty, or property, without due process of law."

Early on, the Supreme Court adopted a narrow interpretation of the Fourteenth Amendment **Due Process Clause**. In *The Slaughterhouse Cases* (1873) and *Munn v. Illinois* (1877), the Court insisted that the clause provided only minimal procedural protection against state action. In *Munn*, Chief Justice Waite observed that, "For protection against abuses by legislatures the people must resort to the polls, not to the courts." However, in *Hurtado v. California* (1884), the Court adopted a broader view of due process. Speaking for the Court, Justice Stanley Matthews opined:

> *Arbitrary power, enforcing its edicts to the injury of the persons and property of its subjects, is not law, whether manifested as the decree of a personal monarch or of an impersonal multitude. And the limitations imposed by our constitutional law upon the action of the governments, both state and national, are essential to the preservation of public and private rights, notwithstanding the representative character of our political institutions. The enforcement of these limitations by judicial process is the device of self-governing communities to protect the rights of individuals and minorities, as well against the power of numbers, as against the violence of public agents transcending the limits of lawful authority, even when acting in the name and wielding the force of the government.*

From this language, it was a short jump to the reassertion of the doctrine of **substantive due process**. In essence, this doctrine holds that government is barred from enforcing policies that are irrational, unfair, unreasonable, or unjust, even if such policies do not run counter to other specific constitutional prohibitions. For example, in *Lochner v. New York* (1905), the Court struck down a state law setting maximum working hours in bakeries. The Court held that the restriction violated both the employer's and the employee's **liberty of contract**, a right not specifically enumerated in the Constitution but held to be embraced within the substantive prohibitions of the Due Process Clause of the Fourteenth Amendment. For almost fifty years (roughly 1890–1937), the Supreme Court relied on substantive due process to invalidate a variety of state and federal laws regulating aspects of economic life. (Substantive due process as it relates to economic freedom and property rights is discussed extensively in Chapter 2.) Although the modern Supreme Court has repudiated the notion of liberty of contract, substantive due process lives on under the rubric of the constitutional **right of privacy** (see Chapter 6).

In the modern era, the Supreme Court has relied on the Due Process Clause of the Fourteenth Amendment in numerous landmark decisions expanding the rights of persons accused of crimes, prisoners, public school students, public employees, and even welfare beneficiaries. Thus, while there is no constitutional right to receive welfare assistance, government may not terminate a person's welfare benefits without observing certain procedural safeguards (see, for example, *Goldberg v. Kelly* [1970], discussed and excerpted in Chapter 5, Volume I). In 1967 the Court invoked due process to revolutionize the juvenile justice system, holding that juveniles must be afforded certain procedural protections before they can be judged delinquent and sent to a reformatory (see *In re Gault,* 1967).

The Equal Protection Clause   As with other provisions of the Civil War Amendments, the principal motivation behind the **Equal Protection Clause** of the Fourteenth Amendment was the desire to protect the rights of the former slaves. Yet the text of the clause does not limit the right to equal protection of the laws to any particular group. It says, rather, that "nor shall any State ... deny to *any person within its jurisdiction* the equal protection of the laws" (emphasis added). But, early on the Supreme Court viewed the clause as limited to the protection of former slaves, thus saying in *The Slaughterhouse Cases* (1873) that its purpose was "the protection of the newly-made freeman and citizen from the oppressions of those who had formerly exercised unlimited dominion over him." However, in *Plessy v. Ferguson* (1896), the Court seemed oblivious to such "oppressions" when it rejected an equal protection challenge to a state law requiring racial segregation on trains. Speaking for a nearly unanimous Court, Justice Henry B. Brown opined that "[t]he object of the [Fourteenth] amendment was undoubtedly to enforce the absolute equality of the two races before the law, but, in the nature of things, it could not have been intended to abolish distinctions based upon color, or to enforce social, as distinguished from political, equality, or a commingling of the two races upon terms unsatisfactory to either."

The narrow view of the Equal Protection Clause adopted in *Plessy* was repudiated by the Supreme Court in *Brown v. Board of Education* (1954), where the Court invalidated compulsory racial segregation in public schools, and in a series of subsequent decisions in which the Court struck down other types of Jim Crow laws. Since *Brown,* the federal courts have relied heavily on the Equal Protection Clause in advancing the civil rights not only of African-Americans, but also of women and various minority groups (see Chapter 7). The courts have also relied upon the Equal Protection Clause in seeking to ensure fundamental fairness in the political process (see Chapter 8).

The State Action Doctrine   Normally one thinks of the Fourteenth Amendment, as well as the provisions of the Bill of Rights, as placing constraints on government action. The Supreme Court has said on numerous occasions, the first being in *The Civil Rights Cases* (1883), that the prohibitions of the Fourteenth Amendment apply to state action but not to actions by private individuals or corporations. (This important doctrine of constitutional law is discussed at some length in Chapter 7.) An action that is ostensibly private in character, however, may be treated as "state action" within the purview of the Fourteenth Amendment if there is a "close nexus" between the state and the private actor.

Thus, for example, the Supreme Court in 1944 invalidated the Texas Democratic Party's whites-only primary election, even though the party was not, strictly speaking, an agency of the state (see *Smith v. Allwright* [1944], discussed and excerpted in Chapter 8). Similarly, in *Shelley v. Kraemer* (1948), the Court held that a state court's enforcement of a racially restrictive covenant with respect to the sale of private housing constituted state action in violation of the Fourteenth Amendment.

Congressional Enforcement Powers under the Fourteenth Amendment   Section 5 of the Fourteenth Amendment grants to Congress the power to enforce the broad provisions of Section 1 through "appropriate legislation." Congress has relied on Section 5 in passing numerous civil rights laws, although it should be noted that the enforcement provisions of the Thirteenth, Fifteenth, and Nineteenth Amendments also provide constitutional support for federal civil rights legislation.

In *The Civil Rights Cases,* the Supreme Court said that because the Fourteenth Amendment prohibits *state action* contrary to the principles of Section 1, Congress's

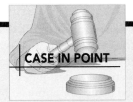

Can Governmental Inaction Be "State Action"?

DeShaney v. Winnebago Social Services (1989)

In modern times, the **state action doctrine** has been criticized as being too restrictive. Indeed, some have argued that the Fourteenth Amendment should be interpreted to impose an affirmative duty on government to protect persons against harm in some circumstances. This argument was made in dramatic form in the 1989 case of *DeShaney v. Winnebago Social Services*. There, the Supreme Court, dividing 6 to 3, held that a social services agency, regardless of its prior knowledge of the danger, did not violate the Fourteenth Amendment by failing to protect young Joshua DeShaney from his abusive father. Writing for the majority, Chief Justice Rehnquist noted that the Court had previously recognized a state's constitutional obligation to protect the safety and well-being of those within its custody, including mentally retarded persons in state institutions. But this "affirmative duty to protect" did not arise "from the state's knowledge of [Joshua's] predicament or from its expressions of its intent to help him." Since the state had no constitutional duty to protect Joshua from his father, its failure to do so, although calamitous, did not constitute a violation of the Due Process Clause. In a dissenting opinion, Justice Harry Blackmun excoriated the Court for its "sterile formalism." Blackmun asserted that the "broad and stirring clauses of the Fourteenth Amendment" were "designed, at least in part, to undo the formalistic legal reasoning that infected antebellum jurisprudence." Blackmun preferred a "sympathetic reading" of the Fourteenth Amendment that recognized that "compassion need not be exiled from the province of judging."

enforcement powers under Section 5 are limited to punishing state actions that contravene Section 1. It was for this reason that the Court struck down the Civil Rights Act of 1875. By prohibiting private discrimination, Congress had exceeded its enforcement powers under Section 5.

In the Civil Rights Acts of 1870 and 1871, respectively, Congress provided criminal and civil penalties for civil rights violations perpetrated "under color of state law." This language allowed individuals to be found liable for violating the civil rights of others, as long as there was some element of state action supporting or condoning the violation. The Civil Rights Act of 1870 (also known as the Enforcement Act) also contained a provision criminalizing conspiracies to deprive persons of their civil rights. The language of the statute did not indicate that such conspiracies had to involve unconstitutional state action, but in *United States v. Cruikshank* (1875), the Supreme Court indicated that in the absence of state action, the statute could not be constitutionally enforced against private conspiracies. Although that view still applies today, modern courts tend to be fairly liberal in finding an element of state action in such conspiracies (see, for example, *United States v. Guest* [1966]).

In *South Carolina v. Katzenbach* (1966), the Court noted that "[t]he constitutional propriety of [legislation adopted under Section 5] must be judged with reference to the historical experience … it reflects." Thus the courts have afforded broad latitude to Congress in crafting measures to eliminate or remedy racial discrimination (see, for example, *Katzenbach v. Morgan* [1966]). However, in *City of Boerne v. Flores* (1997), a more conservative Supreme Court made clear that Congress may not use Section 5 to create new constitutional rights or alter the meaning of constitutional rights that have been defined through judicial interpretation. Similarly, in *United States v. Morrison* (2000), the Supreme Court struck down a provision of the federal Violence Against Women Act that allowed victims of gender-based violence to bring suits for damages in federal courts. The Court said that the provision was unconstitutional not only as a violation of the Commerce Clause but also insofar as it permitted suits in cases where the gender-based violence was purely private in character.

The Fifteenth Amendment

Like the Thirteenth and Fourteenth Amendments, the **Fifteenth Amendment** (ratified in 1870) was an outgrowth of the Civil War. Unlike the Fourteenth Amendment, however, the Fifteenth Amendment is targeted fairly narrowly, its only concern being the denial of voting rights in state and federal elections on grounds of race. Section 1 states quite simply, "The right of citizens of the United States to vote shall not be denied or abridged by the United States or by any State on account of race, color, or previous condition of servitude." As in the Thirteenth and Fourteenth Amendments, Section 2 of the Fifteenth Amendment grants Congress the power to adopt "appropriate legislation" to enforce the prohibition contained in Section 1. Almost a century later, Congress employed its enforcement powers under Section 2 in adopting the landmark Voting Rights Act of 1965. Among other things, the act allowed the federal government to actively supervise electoral systems in states where racial discrimination had been pervasive. It also granted individuals the right to sue in federal court to challenge features of state and local elections deemed to be discriminatory. Without question, the Voting Rights Act of 1965 has had an enormous impact on ending racial discrimination in this area. (The topic of voting rights is examined in detail in Chapter 8.)

To Summarize:

- *Beyond the Bill of Rights, Civil War Amendments are the most important amendment to the U.S. Constitution. The common thread tying these amendments together was the need to protect the civil rights of the newly freed former slaves.*
- *The Thirteenth Amendment, ratified in 1865, abolished slavery and gave Congress power to enforce this abolition by appropriate legislation.*
- *The Fourteenth Amendment (1868) overturned the Dred Scott decision by conferring citizenship on all persons born or naturalized in the United States. The Fourteenth Amendment also required states to provide due process of law and equal protection of the laws to all persons within their jurisdiction and gave Congress power to enforce these requirements by appropriate legislation.*
- *The courts have distinguished between two aspects of due process: procedural and substantive. Procedural due process, which embodies the requirements of notice and hearing, requires fundamental fairness in governmental proceedings against individuals. Substantive due process prohibits government from enforcing policies that are deemed unreasonable, unfair, or unjust, even if they do not violate specific constitutional prohibitions. The right of privacy can be seen as a contemporary manifestation of substantive due process.*
- *The Fifteenth Amendment (1870) prohibits states from engaging in racial discrimination with respect to voting rights.*
- *Collectively, the Civil War Amendments have given rise to numerous federal statutes and court decisions protecting and expanding civil rights and liberties.*

The Nationalization of the Bill of Rights

One of the most important impacts of the Fourteenth Amendment has been the effective "nationalization" of the Bill of Rights. There is little doubt that, at the time of its ratification in 1791, the Bill of Rights was widely perceived as imposing limitations only on the powers and actions of the national government. Historical evidence suggests that states would not have ratified the document had the limitations been seen as proscribing state action and is further suggested by the first clause of the First Amendment, which begins,

"Congress shall make no law...." The Court held as much in 1833 in the case *of Barron v. Baltimore*, when it refused to permit a citizen to sue a local government for violating his or her property rights under the Just Compensation Clause of the Fifth Amendment. Speaking for the Court, Chief Justice John Marshall said: "We are of the opinion, that, the provision in the Fifth Amendment to the Constitution, declaring that private property shall not be taken for public use without just compensation is intended solely as a limitation on the power of the United States, and is not applicable to the legislation of the states."

The ratification of the Fourteenth Amendment in 1868 provided an opportunity for the Supreme Court to reconsider the relationship between the Bill of Rights and state and local governments. As we have seen, Section 1 of the Fourteenth Amendment imposed broad restrictions on state power, requiring the states to provide equal protection of the law to all persons, to respect the "privileges and immunities" of citizens of the United States, and, most importantly, to protect the "life, liberty, and property" of all persons. More to the point, the Fourteenth Amendment enjoined states from depriving persons of these basic rights "without due process of law." Although there was no full agreement as to whether the provisions of the Bill of Rights were "incorporated" into the Fourteenth Amendment and thus applicable to the states, plaintiffs in federal cases began to make this argument fairly soon after the amendment was ratified.

Initially, the Supreme Court was not favorably disposed toward the **doctrine of incorporation**. In *Hurtado v. California* (1884), the Court rejected the argument that the grand jury procedure required in federal criminal cases by the Fifth Amendment was an essential feature of due process and thus required in state criminal cases by the Fourteenth Amendment. Justice Stanley Matthews delivered the Opinion of the Court, saying in part:

> *Due process of law [in the Fifth Amendment] refers to that law of the land, which derives its authority from the legislative powers conferred upon Congress by the Constitution of the United States, exercised within the limits therein prescribed, and interpreted according to the principles of the common law. In the Fourteenth Amendment, by parity of reason, it refers to that law of the land in each State, which derives its authority from the inherent and reserved powers of the State, exerted within the limits of those fundamental principles of liberty and justice which lie at the base of all our civil and political institutions, and the greatest security for which resides in the right of the people to make their own laws, and alter them at their pleasure.*

Today, the *Hurtado* decision remains good law; states are not required by the federal Constitution to use grand juries to bring criminal charges, although many still do. But the Supreme Court soon repudiated the underlying philosophy of *Hurtado*, that due process for the purposes of the Fourteenth Amendment must be defined solely in terms of the law of each state.

Selective Incorporation

The fact that the *Hurtado* decision remains valid indicates that the Supreme Court, in spite of mounting historical evidence to the contrary, has never accepted the argument that the Fourteenth Amendment incorporates the Bill of Rights *en toto*. The Court has, however, endorsed a doctrine of **selective incorporation** by which most of the provisions of the Bill of Rights have been extended to limit actions of the state and local governments. The process of selective incorporation began in 1897 in the case of *Chicago, Burlington, & Quincy Railroad Company v. Chicago*. There, a conservative Court concerned about protecting private enterprise against a rising tide of government interventionism held that the Due Process Clause of the Fourteenth Amendment imposed on state and local governments the same obligation to respect private property that the Fifth Amendment imposed on the federal government. The Court said that when a state or local government takes private property under its power of eminent domain, it must provide just compensation to the owner. Thus, the Court had "incorporated" the Just Compensation Clause of the Fifth Amendment into the Due Process Clause of the Fourteenth Amendment.

The doctrine of incorporation was next applied to First Amendment freedoms, specifically the freedoms of speech and press. In *Gitlow v. New York* (1925), the Supreme Court said that "we may and do assume that freedom of speech and of the press—which are protected by the First Amendment from abridgment by Congress—are among the fundamental personal rights and 'liberties' protected by the due process clause of the Fourteenth Amendment from impairment by the states." This dictum was soon followed by decisions in which the Court relied on the doctrine of incorporation to invalidate state actions abridging the freedoms of speech and press.

In *Fiske v. Kansas* (1927), the Court invalidated a state statute that prohibited mere advocacy of violent action, finding it to be a violation of freedom of speech. Four years later, in *Near v. Minnesota* (1931), the Court struck down a state law that permitted **censorship** of "malicious, scandalous and defamatory" periodicals, finding it to be a clear violation of freedom of the press. In the wake of these and related decisions, state and local policies impinging on freedom of expression became subject to challenge in the courts under the same First Amendment standards that applied to federal legislation.

In *Palko v. Connecticut* (1937), the Supreme Court refused to incorporate the Double Jeopardy Clause of the Fifth Amendment into the Due Process Clause of the Fourteenth. To merit incorporation, said Justice Benjamin N. Cardozo, a provision of the Bill of Rights must be essential to "a scheme of ordered liberty." Cardozo's majority opinion suggested that the First Amendment freedoms that had been previously incorporated represented "the matrix, the indispensable condition, of nearly every other form of freedom." The Double Jeopardy Clause, in Cardozo's view, lay on "a different plane of social and moral values." Following *Palko v. Connecticut*, the doctrine of incorporation became the subject of an intense debate among the justices of the Supreme Court. In *Cantwell v. Connecticut* (1940), the Court incorporated the Free Exercise of Religion Clause of the First Amendment. Similarly, in *Everson v. Board of Education* (1947), the Court extended the Establishment Clause to the states under the Fourteenth Amendment (for more discussion of both cases and clauses, see Chapter 4). Yet in *Adamson v. California* (1947) and in *Rochin v. California* (1952), the Court refused to extend the Fifth Amendment privilege against compulsory self-incrimination to state criminal trials.

The Court's highly selective approach to incorporation of the Bill of Rights drew the particular ire of Justices Hugo Black and William O. Douglas. In the 1960s, the views of Justices Black and Douglas as to the applicability of the Bill of Rights to state criminal prosecutions came to be supported by a majority of justices on the Supreme Court (although Justice Black's total incorporation position was never embraced by the Court). Indeed, one of the priorities of the Court under the leadership of Chief Justice Warren was to increase the legal protections afforded to persons accused of crimes, both in state and in federal courts. In a series of landmark decisions, the Warren Court incorporated nearly all of the relevant provisions of the Bill of Rights into the Due Process Clause of the Fourteenth Amendment and thus made them applicable to state criminal cases (see Table 1.1). In one of the most significant of these decisions, *Duncan v. Louisiana* (1968), the Court made the ancient right of trial by jury applicable to defendants in state criminal cases. In a concurring opinion joined by Justice Douglas, Justice Black expressed his satisfaction with what the Court had done under the mantle of selective incorporation:

I believe as strongly as ever that the Fourteenth Amendment was intended to make the Bill of Rights applicable to the States. I have been willing to support the selective incorporation doctrine, however, as an alternative, although perhaps less historically

TABLE 1.1 CHRONOLOGY OF INCORPORATION OF THE BILL OF RIGHTS

YEAR	ISSUE AND AMENDMENT INVOLVED	CASE
1897	Just compensation (V)	*Chicago, Burlington, & Quincy RR v. Chicago*
1927	Speech (I)	*Fiske v. Kansas*
1931	Press (I)	*Near v. Minnesota*
1937	Assembly and petition (I)	*De Jonge v. Oregon*
1940	Free exercise of religion (I)	*Cantwell v. Connecticut*
1947	Separation of church and state (I)	*Everson v. Board of Education*
1948	Public trial (VI)	*In re Oliver*
1949	Unreasonable searches and seizures (IV)	*Wolf v. Colorado*
1962	Cruel and unusual punishment (VIII)	*Robinson v. California*
1963	Right to counsel (VI)	*Gideon v. Wainwright*
1964	Compulsory self-incrimination (V)	*Malloy v. Hogan*
1965	Confrontation of hostile witnesses (VI)	*Pointer v. Texas*
1966	Impartial jury (VI)	*Parker v. Gladden*
1967	Compulsory process to obtain favorable witnesses (VI)	*Washington v. Texas*
1967	Speedy trial (VI)	*Klopfer v. North Carolina*
1968	Jury trial in nonpetty criminal cases (VI)	*Duncan v. Louisiana*
1969	Double jeopardy (V)	*Benton v. Maryland*
2010	Right to keep and bear arms (II)	*McDonald v. Chicago*

supportable than complete incorporation.... [M]ost importantly for me, the selective incorporation process has the virtue of having already worked to make most of the Bill of Rights protections applicable to the States.

The Warren Court's final selective incorporation decision came in 1969. In that year, in *Benton v. Maryland*, the Supreme Court overruled its earlier decision in *Palko v. Connecticut* and decided, after all, that the Double Jeopardy Clause of the Fifth Amendment warranted incorporation into the Fourteenth Amendment. It would be almost forty years before the Court would extend the incorporation doctrine to another provision of the Bill of Rights.

As we noted earlier, the Court in *McDonald v. Chicago* (2010) incorporated the Second Amendment right to keep and bear arms in the Fourteenth Amendment. Although five members of the Court supported the judgment that the right applies to the states, only four justices adhered to the familiar due process rationale of selective incorporation. Justice Thomas, in an extensively researched "originalist" analysis covering some fifty-six pages, asserted by contrast that the Privileges or Immunities Clause of the Fourteenth Amendment incorporates the right to keep and bear arms. According to Thomas, "the ratifying-era public understood—just as the Framers of the Second Amendment did— that the right to keep and bear arms was essential to the preservation of liberty." In his view the record made it "equally plain that they deemed this right necessary to include in the minimum baseline of federal rights that the Privileges or Immunities Clause established in the wake of the War over slavery."

In flatly rejecting the Fourteenth Amendment due process rationale in favor of a Privileges or Immunities alternative, Thomas repudiated the Court's long-standing rationale in the *Slaughterhouse Cases* of 1873. Thomas explicitly identified the right to keep and bear arms with African-Americans' right to self-defense during the period of post–Civil War reconstruction. He asserted that "Militias such as the Ku Klux Klan, the Knights of the White Camellia, the White Brotherhood, the Pale Faces, and the '76 Association spread terror among blacks and white Republicans by breaking up Republican meetings, threatening political leaders, and whipping black militiamen." He concluded that "use of firearms for self-defense was often the only way black citizens could protect themselves from mob violence."

It is interesting to note that no other member of the Court made mention of this extraordinary opinion by Justice Thomas. Either his colleagues were attempting to distance themselves from a perceived outburst, or they found no basis for questioning the accuracy of his observations.

Thus, as the Court began its 2013 term, the only provisions of the Bill of Rights that had not been absorbed into the Fourteenth Amendment were the Third and Seventh Amendments, the Fifth Amendment grand jury clause, and the Eighth Amendment prohibitions against "excessive fines" and "excessive bail." The principal thrust of the process of selective incorporation is that today, with very few exceptions, policies of state and local governments are subject to judicial scrutiny under the same standards that the Bill of Rights imposes on the federal government.

Thus, for example, the prohibition of the First Amendment against establishment of religion applies with the same force to a school board in rural Arkansas as it does to the Congress of the United States. Likewise, the Eighth Amendment injunction against cruel and unusual punishments applies equally to high-profile federal prosecutions for treason and to sentences imposed by local courts for violations of city or county ordinances. Note, however, that in a few instances, such as those governed by the Sixth Amendment right to trial by jury, the Supreme Court has been willing to give the states slightly greater latitude than the federal government in complying with Bill of Rights requirements (for further discussion, see Chapter 5).

To Summarize:

◆ *In a long series of cases beginning in the late nineteenth century, the Supreme Court has held that the Due Process Clause of the Fourteenth Amendment incorporates most of the provisions of the Bill of Rights, thus making them applicable to the states.*

◆ *Today, only the Third and Seventh Amendments, the Fifth Amendment grand jury clause, and the Eighth Amendment prohibitions against "excessive fines" and "excessive bail" are not considered essential to the liberty protected against state action by the Fourteenth Amendment.*

Later Amendments Protecting Voting Rights

The original Constitution left the matter of voting rights to the states. In 1787, voting in the United States was confined for the most part to "freeholders"—that is, white male landowners above age 21. As American society became more democratic, the Constitution was amended to make the franchise more inclusive. We have already seen that the Fifteenth Amendment was adopted after the Civil War to ensure that voting rights would not be denied by states on account of race. Of course, it would be many years before the promise of the Fifteenth Amendment would be realized (see Chapter 8). The **right to vote** is essential to the very definition of democracy, and no polity that does not observe **universal suffrage** can claim to be a genuine democracy.

The Nineteenth Amendment

Like most African-Americans, women were originally excluded from participation in elections in the United States. In 1848, a delegation of women, including the famous suffragist Elizabeth Cady Stanton, met at Seneca Falls, New York, to address the "social, civil, and religious conditions and rights of woman." The Seneca Falls Convention adopted a resolution stating that "it is the duty of the women of this country to secure to themselves their sacred right to the elective franchise." Securing the franchise would not be easy. In 1872, Susan B. Anthony was prosecuted for attempting to vote in the presidential election. Three years later, the Supreme Court rebuffed a woman seeking to cast a ballot in a Missouri election, saying that "the Constitution of the United States does not confer the right of suffrage upon anyone" (*Minor v. Happersett* [1875]). In the last decades of the nineteenth century, a few states changed their statutes to permit female suffrage. By 1912, nine states had extended the franchise to include women. In 1918, President Woodrow Wilson took a stand in favor of women's suffrage.

Following Wilson's lead, Congress adopted a constitutional amendment granting women the right to vote and submitted it to the states for ratification. In 1920, the **Nineteenth Amendment** was added to the Constitution:

> *The right of the citizens of the United States to vote shall not be denied or abridged by the United States or by any State on account of sex. Congress shall have the power, by appropriate legislation, to enforce the provision of this article.*

In one fell swoop, the size of the potential electorate was doubled! Political participation by women did not, as some critics feared, radically alter the political system or its public policy outputs.

The Twenty-Fourth Amendment

Although formally granted the right to vote by the Fifteenth Amendment, many African-Americans were still effectively disenfranchised by practices such as **grandfather clauses**, **literacy tests**, the "**white primary**," and poll taxes (see Chapter 8). The **poll tax** was a fee required as a condition for voting. Typically, the unpaid fees would accumulate from election to election, posing an ever-greater economic impediment to voting. Poll taxes had been common in the United States at the time the Constitution was adopted but fell into disuse by the mid-nineteenth century. They were resurrected after the ratification of the Fifteenth Amendment as a means of preventing African-Americans, most of whom were poor, from voting. In *Breedlove v. Suttles* (1937), the Supreme Court ruled that poll taxes, in and of themselves, did not violate the Fourteenth or Fifteenth Amendment. The *Breedlove* decision gave impetus to a movement to abolish the poll tax, and by 1960, poll taxes existed in only five southern states. The **Twenty-Fourth Amendment,** ratified in 1964, outlawed poll taxes as a requirement to vote in federal elections. Two years later, the Supreme Court extended this policy when it overturned *Breedlove* and struck down poll taxes in state elections as well (*Harper v. Virginia State Board of Elections* [1966]) (see Chapter 8).

The Twenty-Sixth Amendment

During the 1960s, young people, galvanized primarily by the Vietnam War, began to assert themselves politically. Often, political participation by the young was unconventional, taking the form of demonstrations and protests. Many youth leaders argued that if 18-year-olds were old enough to be drafted into military service and placed in combat, they were also old enough to cast a ballot. This line of argument was not new; it had persuaded Georgia and Kentucky to lower the minimum voting age to 18 during World War II. In 1970, Congress passed a measure, lowering the voting age from 21 to 18 in both state and federal elections. The Supreme Court, however, declared this measure unconstitutional in *Oregon v. Mitchell* (1970). Dividing 5 to 4, the Court held that although Congress possessed the authority to lower the voting age in federal elections, it could not by simple statute lower the voting age in state elections. This decision prompted Congress to adopt the **Twenty-Sixth Amendment,** which was ratified by the states in record time—five weeks. Unlike women, however, young people have not taken full advantage of the extension of the franchise. People aged 18 to 21 are still considerably less likely to vote than their elders, although the presidential candidacy of Barack Obama in 2008 stimulated significantly higher turnout by young voters.

To Summarize:

◆ *The right to vote, one of the most essential rights in a democracy, has been protected and enlarged by several amendments to the Constitution as interpreted by the Supreme Court.*

◆ *The Fifteenth Amendment (1870) prohibits racial discrimination in defining and implementing the right to vote and empowers Congress to enact legislation to achieve this purpose.*

◆ *The Nineteenth Amendment (1920) removes gender as a qualification for voting.*

◆ *The Twenty-Fourth Amendment (1964) prohibits the imposition of a poll tax as a precondition for voting in federal elections. In 1966, the Supreme Court interpreted the Equal Protection Clause of the Fourteenth Amendment to extend this prohibition to state elections as well.*

◆ *The Twenty-Sixth Amendment (1971) lowered the minimum voting age to 18 in both state and federal elections.*

Standards of Judicial Review in Civil Rights and Liberties Cases

As we near the end of this introductory chapter, we return to the theme with which we began: judicial protection of civil rights and liberties. The Supreme Court has developed several different standards of review in determining the constitutionality of laws affecting civil rights and liberties. These standards can be categorized as **minimal scrutiny**, **heightened scrutiny**, and **strict scrutiny**.

Minimal Scrutiny: The Rational Basis Test

Minimal scrutiny, the most lenient standard of judicial review, typically involves the application of the **rational basis test**. In *Massachusetts Board of Retirement v. Murgia* (1976), the Supreme Court said that a law that touches on a constitutionally protected interest must, at a minimum, be "rationally related to furthering a legitimate government interest." For example, a state law that prohibits performing surgery without a license impinges on constitutionally protected interests by depriving laypersons of their right to make contracts freely and discriminating against those unable or unwilling to obtain a license. Yet the prohibition is obviously a rational means of advancing the state's legitimate interests in public health and safety. There is no doubt that, if it were challenged, the prohibition would withstand judicial review.

In applying the rational basis test, courts begin with a strong presumption that the challenged law or policy is valid. The burden of proof is on the party making the challenge to show that the law or policy is unconstitutional. To carry this burden, the party must demonstrate that there is no rational basis for the law or policy. Since this is a difficult showing to make, application of the rational basis test usually leads to a judgment sustaining the constitutionality of the challenged law or policy.

Strict Scrutiny: The Compelling Government Interest Test

When a law or policy impinges on a right explicitly protected by the Constitution, such as the right to vote, it is subjected to a more searching judicial scrutiny. This approach also applies in the case of unenumerated rights that the courts have identified as fundamental, such as the right of privacy (see *Roe v. Wade* [1973]) and the right of interstate travel (see *Shapiro v. Thompson* [1969]). Strict judicial scrutiny is also warranted in cases involving forms of discrimination, such as that based on race, that have been held to be "inherently suspect" (see *Korematsu v. United States* [1944]).

Under strict scrutiny, the ordinary **presumption of constitutionality** is reversed, which means, in effect, that the challenged law or policy is presumed to be unconstitutional. The burden shifts to the government (local, state, or federal) to show that the law or policy furthers a **compelling government interest**. Moreover, the government must show that the law is **narrowly tailored** to achieve this interest. This is a heavy burden for the government to carry. Consequently, most laws subjected to strict judicial scrutiny are declared unconstitutional. However, the application of strict scrutiny is not necessarily tantamount to a declaration of unconstitutionality. For example, in *New York v. Ferber* (1982), the Supreme Court upheld a child pornography law that impinged on the First Amendment freedom of expression because, in the view of the Court, the law served a compelling interest in protecting children from the abuse typically associated with the pornography industry. More recently, in *Grutter v. Bollinger* (2003), the Court upheld an affirmative action policy at a state law school in which minorities were afforded preferential status in admissions. The Court sustained the policy against an equal protection challenge on the ground that it was necessary to achieve the law school's compelling interest in fostering student diversity. Obviously, reasonable and well-intentioned people can and will disagree as to what governmental interests are so compelling that they warrant infringements of **fundamental rights**.

Intermediate Scrutiny

To further complicate matters, the Supreme Court has developed an intermediate level of review, often referred to as heightened scrutiny. This standard has been most important in reviewing claims of gender-based discrimination under the Equal Protection Clause of the Fourteenth Amendment. Intermediate scrutiny is also applied in resolving First Amendment issues in the field of commercial speech. (See *Central Hudson Gas and Electric Corporation v. Public Service Commission of New York* [1980].)

As an intermediate standard of review, heightened scrutiny is less rigorous than strict scrutiny, but more demanding than the rational basis test. To survive judicial review under this approach, a policy must "serve important governmental objectives and must be substantially related to achievement of those objectives" (*Craig v. Boren* [1976]). In perhaps the best-known gender discrimination case, *United States v. Virginia* (1996), the Supreme Court employed intermediate scrutiny in striking down the Virginia Military Institute's (VMI) policy of limiting admission to males. Looking at the cases in which the Court has employed heightened scrutiny, it is fair to say that as a standard of review, it is closer to strict scrutiny than to the rational basis test. Indeed, the Court recognized in the VMI case that in cases of intermediate scrutiny "the burden of justification is demanding and it rests entirely on the State." The challenged policy is presumed invalid unless the government can advance an "exceedingly persuasive" justification.

To Summarize:
- *The Supreme Court utilizes several distinctive standards of review in determining the constitutionality of laws affecting civil rights and liberties.*
- *The most lenient standard, minimal scrutiny, utilizes the rational basis test. Here the ordinary presumption of constitutionality applies, placing the burden of persuasion on the party challenging the law. To pass muster under this*

> *standard, a law need merely be rationally related to the furtherance of a legitimate government interest.*
> ◆ *The most stringent standard of review, strict scrutiny, applies in cases of racial discrimination and where other fundamental rights are at stake. Here the burden of persuasion rests with the government to show that the law serves a compelling interest and is narrowly tailored to that end.*
> ◆ *The Court has identified an intermediate standard of review, often termed heightened scrutiny, which has been applied primarily in the area of sex discrimination but also to such fields as commercial speech.*

The Importance of State Constitutions and the State Courts

In trying to understand constitutional law as it relates to civil rights and liberties, we must not ignore the role of state constitutions and courts in protecting individual rights. Under our federal system of government, the highest court of each state possesses the authority to interpret with finality its state constitution and statutes. Since every state constitution contains language protecting individual rights and liberties, many state court decisions implicate both state and federal constitutional provisions.

Under the relevant language of their constitutions and statutes, state courts are free to recognize greater (but not lesser) protections of individual rights than are provided by the U.S. Constitution as interpreted by the federal courts. This idea is sometimes referred to as the **new judicial federalism**. It holds that state courts are free to further protections of civil rights and liberties beyond the federally established minimums. For example, in *In re T. W.* (1989), the Florida Supreme Court struck down as a violation of the right of privacy a statute that required parental consent in cases where minors sought abortions. The constitutionality of a similar law had been upheld on federal grounds by the U.S. Supreme Court in *Planned Parenthood v. Ashcroft* (1983). In *T. W.*, the Florida Supreme Court made it clear that it was basing its decision on an amendment to the Florida Constitution that (unlike the federal Constitution) explicitly protects the right of privacy. Later, in *Goodridge v. Department of Public Health* (2003), the Massachusetts Supreme Court recognized the right to enter into same-sex marriage, a position other state courts have been emulating in recent years. These decisions, and numerous others like them, mean that a complete study of civil rights and liberties must encompass the provisions of state constitutions and the holdings of state courts. It is also important to note that state courts have the last word on state issues. Judgments made there can be appealed in federal court only if a federal issue is present. Thus, the reality is that overwhelmingly state issues, including questions of state-sanctioned civil rights and liberties, are often resolved in the state courts.

To Summarize:
◆ *Under our system of federalism, the U.S. Constitution provides a base level of protection for civil rights and liberties applicable at every level of government.*
◆ *Under their respective constitutions, as interpreted by their courts, states may provide higher levels of protection for individual rights than are recognized in the federal Constitution as interpreted by the federal courts.*

Conclusion

This chapter provides a broad survey of the constitutional sources of protection for civil rights and liberties. As manifestations of the ideals of liberty and equality, civil rights and liberties are regarded as indispensable features of American democracy. Yet individual rights exist in constant tension with majority rule, another essential feature of democracy. Individual rights must be balanced wisely against compelling societal interests, such as public order, national defense, and the general welfare. The task of achieving this balance rests primarily with the courts, most notably the U.S. Supreme Court. The remaining chapters of this book are devoted to an examination of the Supreme Court's jurisprudence in several key areas of civil rights and liberties.

Key Terms

unalienable rights
natural rights
liberty
equality
civil rights
civil liberties
judicial review
civil suits
criminal prosecutions
habeas corpus
treason
religious tests
Establishment Clause
Free Exercise Clause
ex post facto laws
bill of attainder
Contracts Clause
First Amendment
freedom of speech
freedom of the press
freedom of expression
right to keep and bear arms
Second Amendment
well-regulated militia
Third Amendment
Fourth Amendment
unreasonable searches and seizures
wiretapping

Fifth Amendment
indictment
grand jury
double jeopardy
compulsory self-incrimination
eminent domain
just compensation
due process of law
Fourteenth Amendment
fair notice
fair hearing
procedural due process
Sixth Amendment
speedy and public trial
trial by jury
subpoena
right to counsel
Seventh Amendment
Eighth Amendment
excessive bail
pretrial release
pretrial detention
excessive fines
cruel and unusual punishments
forfeiture
Ninth Amendment
Thirteenth Amendment
Due Process Clause

substantive due process
liberty of contract
right of privacy
Equal Protection Clause
state action doctrine
Fifteenth Amendment
doctrine of incorporation
selective incorporation
censorship
right to vote
universal suffrage
Nineteenth Amendment
grandfather clauses
literacy tests
white primary
poll tax
Twenty-Fourth Amendment
Twenty-sixth Amendment
minimal scrutiny
heightened scrutiny
strict scrutiny
rational basis test
presumption of constitutionality
compelling government interest
narrowly tailored
fundamental rights
new judicial federalism

For Further Reading

Abraham, Henry J., and Barbara A. Perry. *Freedom and the Court: Civil Rights and Liberties in the United States* (8th ed.). Lawrence: University Press of Kansas, 2003.

Amar, Akhil Reed. *The Bill of Rights: Creation and Reconstruction*. New Haven, Conn.: Yale University Press, 2000.

Barnett, Randy E. *Restoring the Lost Constitution: The Presumption of Liberty*. Princeton, N.J.: Princeton University Press, 2004.

Berger, Raoul. *Government by Judiciary: The Transformation of the Fourteenth Amendment*. Cambridge, Mass.: Harvard University Press, 1977.

Dworkin, Ronald. *Taking Rights Seriously*. Cambridge, Mass.: Harvard University Press, 1978.

Levy, Leonard D. *Origins of the Bill of Rights* (Contemporary Law Series). New Haven, Conn.: Yale University Press, 1999.

Nelson, William E. *The Fourteenth Amendment: From Political Principle to Judicial Doctrine*. Cambridge, Mass.: Harvard University Press, 1988.

Perry, Michael. *The Constitution, the Courts, and Human Rights*. New Haven, Conn.: Yale University Press, 1982.

Sarat, Austin, and Thomas R. Kearns. *Legal Rights: Historical and Philosophical Perspectives*. Ann Arbor: University of Michigan Press, 1996.

Schwartz, Bernard. *The Great Rights of Mankind: A History of the American Bill of Rights*. New York: Oxford University Press, 1977.

Schwartz, Bernard (ed.). *The Fourteenth Amendment*. New York: New York University Press, 1970.

Stephens, Otis H., and Richard A. Glenn. *Unreasonable Searches and Seizures: Rights and Liberties under the Law*. Santa Barbara, Calif.: ABC-CLIO, 2006.

Tarr, G. Alan, and Ellis Katz (eds.). *Federalism and Rights*. Lanham, Md.: Rowman & Littlefield, 1996.

Walker, Samuel. *In Defense of American Liberties: A History of the ACLU* (2nd ed.). Carbondale: Southern Illinois University Press, 1999.

EX PARTE MILLIGAN
4 Wall. (71 U.S.) 2; 18 L.Ed. 281 (1866)
Vote: 9-0

In 1864, Lambden P. Milligan, a civilian resident of Indiana, was arrested by the military on charges of inciting insurrection and giving aid and comfort to the Confederacy. After being tried and convicted by a military court, Milligan was sentenced to death. In 1865, he petitioned the federal circuit court for a writ of habeas corpus, arguing that the military did not have jurisdiction over him since, at the time of his arrest, he was a civilian living in a state where the civilian courts were still open and that, even if the military court had jurisdiction, it had violated his right to trial by jury. The circuit court was unable to reach a decision on these issues and thus certified the case to the Supreme Court. After the Supreme Court's decision, Milligan was released from custody. He later prevailed in a civil action against the military commander who had ordered his arrest.

Mr. Justice Davis delivered the opinion of the Court.

... The controlling question in the case is this: Upon the facts stated in Milligan's petition, and the exhibits filed, had the military commission ... jurisdiction, legally, to try and sentence him? Milligan, not a resident of one of the rebellious states, or a prisoner of war, but a citizen of Indiana for twenty years past, and never in the military or naval service, is, while at his home, arrested by the military power of the United States, imprisoned, and, on certain criminal charges preferred against him, tried, convicted, and sentenced to be hanged by a military commission, organized under the direction of the military commander of the military district of Indiana. Had this tribunal the legal power and authority to try and punish this man?

... The Constitution of the United States is a law for rulers and people, equally in war and in peace, and covers with the shield of its protection all classes of men, at all times, and under all circumstances. No doctrine involving more pernicious consequences was ever invented by the wit of man than that any of its provisions can be suspended during any of the great exigencies of government. Such a doctrine leads directly to anarchy or despotism, but the theory of necessity on which it is based is false; for the government, within the Constitution, has all the powers granted to it which are necessary to preserve its existence; as has been happily proved by the result of the great effort to throw off its just authority. ...

Every trial involves the exercise of judicial power; and from what source did the military commission that tried him derive their authority? Certainly no part of the judicial power of the country was conferred on them; because the Constitution expressly vests it "in one supreme court and such inferior courts as the Congress may from time to time ordain and establish," and it is not pretended that the commission was a court ordained and established by Congress. They cannot justify on the mandate of the President; because he is controlled by law, and has his appropriate sphere of duty, which is to execute, not to make, the laws; and there is "no unwritten criminal code to which resort can be had as a source of jurisdiction."

But it is said that the jurisdiction is complete under the "laws and usages of war."

It can serve no useful purpose to inquire what those laws and usages are, whence they originated, where found and on whom they operate; they can never be applied to citizens in states which have upheld the authority of the government, and where the courts are open and their process unobstructed. This court has judicial knowledge that in Indiana the Federal authority was always unopposed, and its courts always open to hear criminal accusations and redress grievances; and no usage of war could sanction a military trial there for any offence whatever or a citizen in civil life, in nowise connected with the military service. Congress could grant no such power; and to the honor of our national legislature be it said, it has never been provoked by the state of the country even to attempt its exercise. One of the plainest constitutional provisions was, therefore, infringed when Milligan was tried by a court not ordained and established by Congress, and not composed of judges appointed during good behavior.

Why was he not delivered to the Circuit Court of Indiana to be proceeded against according to law? No reason of necessity could be urged against it; because Congress had declared penalties against the offences charged, provided for their punishment, and directed that court to hear and determine them. And soon after this military tribunal was ended, the Circuit Court met, peacefully transacted its business, and adjourned. It needed no bayonets to protect it, and required no military aid to execute its judgments. It was held in a state, eminently distinguished for patriotism, by judges commissioned during the Rebellion, who were provided with juries, upright, intelligent, and selected by a marshal appointed by the President. The government had no right to conclude that Milligan, if guilty, would not receive in that court merited punishment; for its records disclose that it was constantly engaged in the trial of similar offences, and was never interrupted in its administration of criminal justice. If it was dangerous, in the distracted condition of affairs, to leave Milligan unrestrained of his liberty, because he "conspired against the government, afforded aid and comfort to rebels, and incited the people to insurrection," the law said arrest him, confine him closely, render him powerless to do further mischief; and then present

his case to the grand jury of the district, with proofs of his guilt, and, if indicted, try him according to the course of the common law. If this had been done, the Constitution would have been vindicated, the law of 1863 enforced, and the securities for personal liberty preserved and defended.

Another guarantee of freedom was broken when Milligan was denied a trial by jury.... The Sixth Amendment affirms that "in all criminal prosecutions the accused shall enjoy the right to a speedy and public trial by an impartial jury," language broad enough to embrace all persons and cases; but the Fifth, recognizing the necessity of an indictment, or presentment, before anyone can be held to answer for high crimes, "excepts cases arising in the land of naval forces, or in the militia, when in actual service in time of war or public danger"; and the framers of the Constitution, doubtless, meant to limit the right of trial by jury, in the Sixth Amendment, to those persons who were subject to indictment or presentment in the Fifth.

The discipline necessary to the efficiency of the army and navy required other and swifter modes of trial than are furnished by the common law courts; and, in pursuance of the power conferred by the Constitution, Congress has declared the kinds of trial, and the manner in which they shall be conducted, for offences committed while the party is in the military or naval service. Everyone connected with these branches of the public service is amenable to the jurisdiction which Congress has created for their government, and, while thus serving, surrenders his right to be tried by the civil courts. All other persons, citizens of states where the courts are open, if charged with crime, are guaranteed the inestimable privilege of trial by jury. This privilege is a vital principle, underlying the whole administration of criminal justice....

It is claimed that martial law covers with its broad mantle the proceedings of this military commission. The proposition is this: that in a time of war the commander of an armed force (if in his opinion the exigencies of the country demand it, and of which he is to judge), has the power, within the lines of his military district, to suspend all civil rights and their remedies, and subject citizens as well as soldiers to the role of his will; and in the exercise of his lawful authority cannot be restrained, except by his superior officer or the President of the United States.

If this position is sound to the extent claimed, then when war exists, foreign or domestic, and the country is subdivided into military departments for mere convenience, the commander of one of them can, if he

(Continued)

chooses, within his limits, on the plea of necessity, with the approval of the Executive, substitute military force for and to the exclusion of the laws, and punish all persons, as he thinks right and proper, without fixed or certain rules.

The statement of this proposition shows its importance; for, if true, republican government is a failure, and there is an end of liberty regulated by law. Martial law, established on such a basis, destroys every guaranty of the Constitution, and effectually renders the "military independent of and superior to the civil power"—the attempt to do which by the King of Great Britain was deemed by our fathers such an offence, that they assigned it to the world as one of the causes which impelled them to declare their independence. Civil liberty and this kind of martial law cannot endure together; the antagonism is irreconcilable; and in the conflict, one or the other must perish....

It is difficult to see how the safety of the country required martial law in Indiana. If any of her citizens were plotting treason, the power of arrest could secure them, until the government was prepared for their trial, when the courts were open and ready to try them. It was as easy to protect witnesses before a civil as a military tribunal; and as there could be no wish to convict, except on sufficient legal evidence, surely an ordained and established court was better able to judge of this than a military tribunal composed of gentlemen not trained to the profession of the law.

It follows, from what has been said on this subject, that there are occasions when martial rule can be properly applied. If, in foreign invasions or civil war, the courts are actually closed, and it is impossible to administer criminal justice according to law, then, in the theater of active military operations, where war really prevails, there is a necessity to furnish a substitute for the civil authority, thus overthrown, to preserve the safety of the army and society; and as no power is left but the military, it is allowed to govern by martial rule until the laws can have their free course. As necessity creates the rule, so it limits its duration; for, if this government is continued after the courts are reinstated, it is a gross usurpation of power. Martial rule can never exist where the courts are open, and in the proper and unobstructed exercise of their jurisdiction. It is also confined to the locality of actual war. Because, during the late Rebellion it could have been enforced in Virginia, where the national authority was overturned and the courts driven out, it does not follow that it should obtain in Indiana, where that authority was never disputed, and justice was always administered.

And so in the case of a foreign invasion martial rule may become a necessity in one state, when, in another, it would be "mere lawless violence." ...

The two remaining questions in this case must be answered in the affirmative. The suspension of the privilege of the writ of habeas corpus does not suspend the writ itself. The writ issues as a matter of course; and on the return made to it the court decides whether the party applying is denied the right of proceeding any further with it.

If the military trial of Milligan was contrary to law, then he was entitled, on the facts stated in his petition, to be discharged from custody by the terms of the act of Congress of March 3rd, 1863....

But it is insisted that Milligan was a prisoner of war, and, therefore, excluded from the privileges of the statute. It is not easy to see how he can be treated as a prisoner of war, when he lived in Indiana for the past twenty years, was arrested there, and had not been, during the late troubles, a resident of any of the states in rebellion. If in Indiana he conspired with bad men to assist the enemy, he is punishable for it in the courts of Indiana; but, when tried for the offence, he cannot plead the rights of war; for he was not engaged in legal acts of hostility against the government, and only such persons, when captured, are prisoners of war. If he cannot enjoy the immunities attached to the character of a prisoner of war, how can he be subject to their pains and penalties? ...

The Chief Justice delivered the following [concurring] opinion:

Four members of the Court ... unable to concur in some important particulars with the opinion which has just been read, think it their duty to make a separate statement of their views of the whole case....

The opinion ... as we understand it, asserts not only that the military commission held in Indiana was not authorized by Congress, but that it was not in the power of Congress to authorize it; from which it may be thought to follow that Congress has no power to indemnify the officers who composed the commission against liability in civil courts for acting as members of it. We cannot agree to this....

We think that Congress had power, though not exercised, to authorize the military commission which was held in Indiana....

Mr. Justice Wayne, Mr. Justice Swayne, and Mr. Justice Miller concur with me in these views.

BOUMEDIENE V. BUSH
553 U.S. 723; 128 S.Ct. 2229; 171 L.Ed.2d 41 (2008)
Vote: 5-4

In this case, the Court considers the constitutionality of the Detainee Treatment Act of 2005 and the Military Commissions Act of 2006, both of which Congress passed in response to earlier Supreme Court decisions regarding the rights of foreign nationals held at the United States Naval Station at Guantanamo Bay, Cuba. The instant case began as a petition for habeas corpus brought on behalf of Lakhdar Boumediene and other Guantanamo detainees.

'Justice Kennedy delivered the opinion of the Court.

... Petitioners present a question not resolved by our earlier cases relating to the detention of aliens at Guantanamo: whether they have the constitutional privilege of habeas corpus, a privilege not to be withdrawn except in conformance with the Suspension Clause, Art. I, § 9, cl. 2. We hold these petitioners do have the habeas corpus privilege. Congress has enacted a statute, the Detainee Treatment Act of 2005 (DTA) ... that provides certain procedures for review of the detainees' status. We hold that those procedures are not an adequate and effective substitute for habeas corpus. Therefore §7 of the Military Commissions Act of 2006 ... operates as an unconstitutional suspension of the writ....

Under the Authorization for Use of Military Force (AUMF) ... the President is authorized "to use all necessary and appropriate force against those nations, organizations, or persons he determines planned, authorized, committed, or aided the terrorist attacks that occurred on September 11, 2001, or harbored such organizations or persons, in order to prevent any future acts of international terrorism against the United States by such nations, organizations or persons."

In *Hamdi v. Rumsfeld* ... (2004), five Members of the Court recognized that detention of individuals who fought against the United States in Afghanistan "for the duration of the particular conflict in which they were captured, is so fundamental and accepted an incident to war as to be an exercise of the 'necessary and appropriate force' Congress has authorized the President to use." ... After *Hamdi*, the Deputy Secretary of Defense established Combatant Status Review Tribunals (CSRTs) to determine whether individuals detained at Guantanamo were "enemy combatants," as the Department defines that term.... A later

memorandum established procedures to implement the CSRTs.... The Government maintains these procedures were designed to comply with the due process requirements identified by the plurality in *Hamdi*....

Interpreting the AUMF, the Department of Defense ordered the detention of these petitioners, and they were transferred to Guantanamo. Some of these individuals were apprehended on the battlefield in Afghanistan, others in places as far away from there as Bosnia and Gambia. All are foreign nationals, but none is a citizen of a nation now at war with the United States. Each denies he is a member of the al Qaeda terrorist network that carried out the September 11 attacks or of the Taliban regime that provided sanctuary for al Qaeda. Each petitioner appeared before a separate CSRT; was determined to be an enemy combatant; and has sought a writ of habeas corpus in the United States District Court for the District of Columbia.

The first actions commenced in February 2002. The District Court ordered the cases dismissed for lack of jurisdiction because the naval station is outside the sovereign territory of the United States.... We granted certiorari and reversed, holding that 28 U. S. C. §2241 extended statutory habeas corpus jurisdiction to Guantanamo. See *Rasul v. Bush* ... (2004). The constitutional issue presented in the instant cases was not reached in *Rasul*....

After *Rasul*, petitioners' cases were consolidated and entertained in two separate proceedings. In the first set of cases, Judge Richard J. Leon granted the Government's motion to dismiss, holding that the detainees had no rights that could be vindicated in a habeas corpus action. In the second set of cases Judge Joyce Hens Green reached the opposite conclusion, holding the detainees had rights under the Due Process Clause of the Fifth Amendment....

While appeals were pending from the District Court decisions, Congress passed the DTA. Subsection (e) of §1005 of the DTA amended 28 U. S. C. §2241 to provide that "no court, justice, or judge shall have jurisdiction to hear or consider ... an application for a writ of habeas corpus filed by or on behalf of an alien detained by the Department of Defense at Guantanamo Bay, Cuba." ... Section 1005 further provides that the Court of Appeals for the District of Columbia Circuit shall

(Continued)

have "exclusive" jurisdiction to review decisions of the CSRTs....

In *Hamdan v. Rumsfeld* ... (2006), the Court held this provision did not apply to cases (like petitioners') pending when the DTA was enacted. Congress responded by passing the MCA, ... which again amended §2241. The text of the statutory amendment is discussed below.... (Four Members of the *Hamdan* majority noted that "[n]othing prevented] the President from returning to Congress to seek the authority he believes necessary." ... The authority to which the concurring opinion referred was the authority to "create military commissions of the kind at issue" in the case.... Nothing in that opinion can be construed as an invitation for Congress to suspend the writ.)

Petitioners' cases were consolidated on appeal, and the parties filed supplemental briefs in light of our decision in *Hamdan*. The Court of Appeals' ruling ... is the subject of our present review and today's decision.

The Court of Appeals concluded that MCA §7 must be read to strip from it, and all federal courts, jurisdiction to consider petitioners' habeas corpus applications, ... that petitioners are not entitled to the privilege of the writ or the protections of the Suspension Clause, ... and, as a result, that it was unnecessary to consider whether Congress provided an adequate and effective substitute for habeas corpus in the DTA.

We granted certiorari....

In deciding the constitutional questions now presented we must determine whether petitioners are barred from seeking the writ or invoking the protections of the Suspension Clause either because of their status, i.e., petitioners' designation by the Executive Branch as enemy combatants, or their physical location, i.e., their presence at Guantanamo Bay. The Government contends that noncitizens designated as enemy combatants and detained in territory located outside our Nation's borders have no constitutional rights and no privilege of habeas corpus. Petitioners contend they do have cognizable constitutional rights and that Congress, in seeking to eliminate recourse to habeas corpus as a means to assert those rights, acted in violation of the Suspension Clause....

Guantanamo Bay is not formally part of the United States.... And under the terms of the lease between the United States and Cuba, Cuba retains "ultimate sovereignty" over the territory while the United States exercises "complete jurisdiction and control." ...

The United States contends, nevertheless, that Guantanamo is not within its sovereign control. This was the Government's position well before the events of September 11, 2001.... And in other contexts the Court has held that questions of sovereignty are for the political branches to decide.... Even if this were a treaty interpretation case that did not involve a political question, the President's construction of the lease agreement would be entitled to great respect....

We therefore do not question the Government's position that Cuba, not the United States, maintains sovereignty, in the legal and technical sense of the term, over Guantanamo Bay.... As we did in *Rasul*, however, we take notice of the obvious and uncontested fact that the United States, by virtue of its complete jurisdiction and control over the base, maintains de facto sovereignty over this territory....

The Court has discussed the issue of the Constitution's extraterritorial application on many occasions. These decisions undermine the Government's argument that, at least as applied to noncitizens, the Constitution necessarily stops where de jure sovereignty ends.

Practical considerations weighed heavily as well in *Johnson v. Eisentrager* ... (1950), where the Court addressed whether habeas corpus jurisdiction extended to enemy aliens who had been convicted of violating the laws of war. The prisoners were detained at Landsberg Prison in Germany during the Allied Powers' postwar occupation. The Court stressed the difficulties of ordering the Government to produce the prisoners in a habeas corpus proceeding. It "would require allocation of shipping space, guarding personnel, billeting and rations" and would damage the prestige of military commanders at a sensitive time.... In considering these factors the Court sought to balance the constraints of military occupation with constitutional necessities....

True, the Court in *Eisentrager* denied access to the writ, and it noted the prisoners "at no relevant time were within any territory over which the United States is sovereign, and [that] the scenes of their offense, their capture, their trial and their punishment were all beyond the territorial jurisdiction of any court of the United States." ... The Government seizes upon this language as proof positive that the *Eisentrager* Court adopted a formalistic, sovereignty-based test for determining the reach of the Suspension Clause.... We reject this reading for three reasons.

First, we do not accept the idea that the above-quoted passage from *Eisentrager* is the only authoritative language in the opinion and that all the rest is dicta. The Court's further determinations, based on practical considerations, were integral to Part II of its opinion and came before the decision announced its holding....

Second, because the United States lacked both de jure sovereignty and plenary control over Landsberg Prison, ... it is far from clear that the *Eisentrager* Court used the term sovereignty only in the narrow technical sense and not to connote the degree of control the military asserted over the facility....

Third, if the Government's reading of *Eisentrager* were correct, the opinion would have marked not only a change in, but a complete repudiation of, the ... functional approach to questions of extraterritoriality. We cannot accept the Government's view....

The Government's formal sovereignty-based test raises troubling separation-of-powers concerns as well. ...

The Constitution grants Congress and the President the power to acquire, dispose of, and govern territory, not the power to decide when and where its terms apply. Even when the United States acts outside its borders, its powers are not "absolute and unlimited" but are subject "to such restrictions as are expressed in the Constitution." ...

As we recognized in *Rasul*, ... the outlines of a framework for determining the reach of the Suspension Clause are suggested by the factors the Court relied upon in *Eisentrager*. In addition to the practical concerns discussed above, the *Eisentrager* Court found relevant that each petitioner: "(a) is an enemy alien; (b) has never been or resided in the United States; (c) was captured outside of our territory and there held in military custody as a prisoner of war; (d) was tried and convicted by a Military Commission sitting outside the United States; (e) for offenses against laws of war committed outside the United States; (f) and is at all times imprisoned outside the United States." ...

Based on this language from *Eisentrager*, and the reasoning in our other extraterritoriality opinions, we conclude that at least three factors are relevant in determining the reach of the Suspension Clause: (1) the citizenship and status of the detainee and the adequacy of the process through which that status determination was made; (2) the nature of the sites where apprehension and then detention took place; and (3) the practical obstacles inherent in resolving the prisoner's entitlement to the writ.

Applying this framework, we note at the onset that the status of these detainees is a matter of dispute. The petitioners, like those in *Eisentrager*, are not American citizens. But the petitioners in *Eisentrager* did not contest, it seems, the Court's assertion that they were

"enemy alien[s]." ... In the instant cases, by contrast, the detainees deny they are enemy combatants. They have been afforded some process in CSRT proceedings to determine their status; but, unlike in *Eisentrager*, ... there has been no trial by military commission for violations of the laws of war. The difference is not trivial. The records from the *Eisentrager* trials suggest that, well before the petitioners brought their case to this Court, there had been a rigorous adversarial process to test the legality of their detention. The *Eisentrager* petitioners were charged by a bill of particulars that made detailed factual allegations against them.... To rebut the accusations, they were entitled to representation by counsel, allowed to introduce evidence on their own behalf, and permitted to cross-examine the prosecution's witnesses....

As to the second factor relevant to this analysis, the detainees here are similarly situated to the *Eisentrager* petitioners in that the sites of their apprehension and detention are technically outside the sovereign territory of the United States. As noted earlier, this is a factor that weighs against finding they have rights under the Suspension Clause. But there are critical differences between Landsberg Prison, circa 1950, and the United States Naval Station at Guantanamo Bay in 2008. Unlike its present control over the naval station, the United States' control over the prison in Germany was neither absolute nor indefinite. Like all parts of occupied Germany, the prison was under the jurisdiction of the combined Allied Forces.... The United States was therefore answerable to its Allies for all activities occurring there.... The Court's holding in *Eisentrager* was thus consistent with the Insular Cases, where it had held there was no need to extend full constitutional protections to territories the United States did not intend to govern indefinitely. Guantanamo Bay, on the other hand, is no transient possession. In every practical sense Guantanamo is not abroad; it is within the constant jurisdiction of the United States....

As to the third factor, we recognize, as the Court did in *Eisentrager*, that there are costs to holding the Suspension Clause applicable in a case of military detention abroad. Habeas corpus proceedings may require expenditure of funds by the Government and may divert the attention of military personnel from other pressing tasks. While we are sensitive to these concerns, we do not find them dispositive. Compliance with any judicial process requires some incremental expenditure of resources. Yet civilian courts and the Armed Forces have functioned alongside each other

(Continued)

at various points in our history.... The Government presents no credible arguments that the military mission at Guantanamo would be compromised if habeas corpus courts had jurisdiction to hear the detainees' claims. And in light of the plenary control the United States asserts over the base, none are apparent to us....

It is true that before today the Court has never held that noncitizens detained by our Government in territory over which another country maintains de jure sovereignty have any rights under our Constitution.

But the cases before us lack any precise historical parallel. They involve individuals detained by executive order for the duration of a conflict that, if measured from September 11, 2001, to the present, is already among the longest wars in American history.... The detainees, moreover, are held in a territory that, while technically not part of the United States, is under the complete and total control of our Government. Under these circumstances the lack of a precedent on point is no barrier to our holding.

We hold that Art. I, §9, cl. 2, of the Constitution has full effect at Guantanamo Bay. If the privilege of habeas corpus is to be denied to the detainees now before us, Congress must act in accordance with the requirements of the Suspension Clause.... This Court may not impose a de facto suspension by abstaining from these controversies.... The MCA does not purport to be a formal suspension of the writ; and the Government, in its submissions to us, has not argued that it is. Petitioners, therefore, are entitled to the privilege of habeas corpus to challenge the legality of their detention.

In light of this holding the question becomes whether the statute stripping jurisdiction to issue the writ avoids the Suspension Clause mandate because Congress has provided adequate substitute procedures for habeas corpus....

We do not endeavor to offer a comprehensive summary of the requisites for an adequate substitute for habeas corpus. We do consider it uncontroversial, however, that the privilege of habeas corpus entitles the prisoner to a meaningful opportunity to demonstrate that he is being held pursuant to "the erroneous application or interpretation" of relevant law.... And the habeas court must have the power to order the conditional release of an individual unlawfully detained—though release need not be the exclusive remedy and is not the appropriate one in every case in which the writ is granted.... These are the easily identified attributes of any constitutionally adequate habeas corpus proceeding. But, depending on the circumstances, more may be required....

Where a person is detained by executive order, rather than, say, after being tried and convicted in a court, the need for collateral review is most pressing. A criminal conviction in the usual course occurs after a judicial hearing before a tribunal disinterested in the outcome and committed to procedures designed to ensure its own independence. These dynamics are not inherent in executive detention orders or executive review procedures. In this context the need for habeas corpus is more urgent. The intended duration of the detention and the reasons for it bear upon the precise scope of the inquiry. Habeas corpus proceedings need not resemble a criminal trial, even when the detention is by executive order. But the writ must be effective. The habeas court must have sufficient authority to conduct a meaningful review of both the cause for detention and the Executive's power to detain. ...

For the writ of habeas corpus, or its substitute, to function as an effective and proper remedy in this context, the court that conducts the habeas proceeding must have the means to correct errors that occurred during the CSRT proceedings. This includes some authority to assess the sufficiency of the Government's evidence against the detainee. It also must have the authority to admit and consider relevant exculpatory evidence that was not introduced during the earlier proceeding. Federal habeas petitioners long have had the means to supplement the record on review, even in the postconviction habeas setting.... Here that opportunity is constitutionally required....

Assuming the DTA can be construed to allow the Court of Appeals to review or correct the CSRT's factual determinations, as opposed to merely certifying that the tribunal applied the correct standard of proof, we see no way to construe the statute to allow what is also constitutionally required in this context: an opportunity for the detainee to present relevant exculpatory evidence that was not made part of the record in the earlier proceedings.

On its face the statute allows the Court of Appeals to consider no evidence outside the CSRT record. In the parallel litigation, however, the Court of Appeals determined that the DTA allows it to order the production of all "reasonably available information in the possession of the U.S. Government bearing on the issue of whether the detainee meets the criteria to be designated as an enemy combatant," regardless of whether this evidence was put before the CSRT.... For present purposes, however, we can assume that the Court of Appeals was correct that the DTA allows introduction and consideration of relevant exculpatory evidence that was "reasonably available" to the Government at the time of the CSRT but not made part of the record. Even so, the DTA review proceeding falls short of being a constitutionally adequate substitute, for the detainee still would have no opportunity to present evidence discovered after the CSRT proceedings concluded.

Under the DTA the Court of Appeals has the power to review CSRT determinations by assessing the legality of standards and procedures. This implies the power to inquire into what happened at the CSRT hearing and, perhaps, to remedy certain deficiencies in that proceeding. But should the Court of Appeals determine that the CSRT followed appropriate and lawful standards and procedures, it will have reached the limits of its jurisdiction. There is no language in the DTA that can be construed to allow the Court of Appeals to admit and consider newly discovered evidence that could not have been made part of the CSRT record because it was unavailable to either the Government or the detainee when the CSRT made its findings. This evidence, however, may be critical to the detainee's argument that he is not an enemy combatant and there is no cause to detain him....

If a detainee can present reasonably available evidence demonstrating there is no basis for his continued detention, he must have the opportunity to present this evidence to a habeas corpus court....

Petitioners have met their burden of establishing that the DTA review process is, on its face, an inadequate substitute for habeas corpus....

Although we do not hold that an adequate substitute must duplicate §2241 in all respects, it suffices that the Government has not established that the detainees' access to the statutory review provisions at issue is an adequate substitute for the writ of habeas corpus. MCA §7 thus effects an unconstitutional suspension of the writ. In view of our holding we need not discuss the reach of the writ with respect to claims of unlawful conditions of treatment or confinement....

... We hold that petitioners may invoke the fundamental procedural protections of habeas corpus. The laws and Constitution are designed to survive, and remain in force, in extraordinary times. Liberty and security can be reconciled; and in our system they are reconciled within the framework of the law. The Framers decided that habeas corpus, a right of first importance, must be a part of that framework, a part of that law.

The determination by the Court of Appeals that the Suspension Clause and its protections are inapplicable to petitioners was in error. The judgment of the Court of Appeals is reversed....

Justice Souter, with whom *Justice Ginsburg* and *Justice Breyer* join, concurring....

Chief Justice Roberts, with whom *Justice Scalia*, *Justice Thomas*, and *Justice Alito* join, dissenting.

Today, the Court strikes down as inadequate the most generous set of procedural protections ever afforded aliens detained by this country as enemy combatants. The political branches crafted these procedures amidst an ongoing military conflict, after much careful investigation and thorough debate. The Court rejects them today out of hand, without bothering to say what due process rights the detainees possess, without explaining how the statute fails to vindicate those rights, and before a single petitioner has even attempted to avail himself of the law's operation. And to what effect? The majority merely replaces a review system designed by the people's representatives with a set of shapeless procedures to be defined by federal courts at some future date. One cannot help but think, after surveying the modest practical results of the majority's ambitious opinion, that this decision is not really about the detainees at all, but about control of federal policy regarding enemy combatants....

The majority is adamant that the Guantanamo detainees are entitled to the protections of habeas corpus—its opinion begins by deciding that question. I regard the issue as a difficult one, primarily because of the unique and unusual jurisdictional status of Guantanamo Bay. I nonetheless agree with Justice Scalia's analysis of our precedents and the pertinent history of the writ, and accordingly join his dissent. The important point for me, however, is that the Court should have resolved these cases on other grounds. Habeas is most fundamentally a procedural right, a mechanism for contesting the legality of executive detention. The critical threshold question in these cases, prior to any inquiry about the writ's scope, is whether the system the political branches designed protects whatever rights the detainees may possess. If so, there is no need for any additional process, whether called "habeas" or something else.

Congress entrusted that threshold question in the first instance to the Court of Appeals for the District of Columbia Circuit, as the Constitution surely allows Congress to do.... But before the D.C. Circuit has addressed the issue, the Court cashiers the statute, and without answering this critical threshold question itself. The Court does eventually get around to asking whether review under the DTA is, as the Court frames

(Continued)

it, an "adequate substitute" for habeas, ... but even then its opinion fails to determine what rights the detainees possess and whether the DTA system satisfies them. The majority instead compares the undefined DTA process to an equally undefined habeas right—one that is to be given shape only in the future by district courts on a case-by-case basis. This whole approach is misguided.

It is also fruitless. How the detainees' claims will be decided now that the DTA is gone is anybody's guess. But the habeas process the Court mandates will most likely end up looking a lot like the DTA system it replaces, as the district court judges shaping it will have to reconcile review of the prisoners' detention with the undoubted need to protect the American people from the terrorist threat—precisely the challenge Congress undertook in drafting the DTA. All that today's opinion has done is shift responsibility for those sensitive foreign policy and national security decisions from the elected branches to the Federal Judiciary.

I believe the system the political branches constructed adequately protects any constitutional rights aliens captured abroad and detained as enemy combatants may enjoy. I therefore would dismiss these cases on that ground. With all respect for the contrary views of the majority, I must dissent.

... For all its eloquence about the detainees' right to the writ, the Court makes no effort to elaborate how exactly the remedy it prescribes will differ from the procedural protections detainees enjoy under the DTA. The Court objects to the detainees' limited access to witnesses and classified material, but proposes no alternatives of its own. Indeed, it simply ignores the many difficult questions its holding presents. What, for example, will become of the CSRT process? The majority says federal courts should generally refrain from entertaining detainee challenges until after the petitioner's CSRT proceeding has finished.... But to what deference, if any, is that CSRT determination entitled?

There are other problems. Take witness availability. What makes the majority think witnesses will become magically available when the review procedure is labeled "habeas"? Will the location of most of these witnesses change—will they suddenly become easily susceptible to service of process? Or will subpoenas issued by American habeas courts run to Basra? And if they did, how would they be enforced? Speaking of witnesses, will detainees be able to call active-duty military officers as witnesses? If not, why not?

The majority has no answers for these difficulties. What it does say leaves open the distinct possibility

that its "habeas" remedy will, when all is said and done, end up looking a great deal like the DTA review it rejects.... But "[t]he role of the judiciary is limited to determining whether the procedures meet the essential standard of fairness under the Due Process Clause and does not extend to imposing procedures that merely displace congressional choices of policy." ...

The majority rests its decision on abstract and hypothetical concerns. Step back and consider what, in the real world, Congress and the Executive have actually granted aliens captured by our Armed Forces overseas and found to be enemy combatants: The right to hear the bases of the charges against them, including a summary of any classified evidence. The ability to challenge the bases of their detention before military tribunals modeled after Geneva Convention procedures. Some 38 detainees have been released as a result of this process.... The right, before the CSRT, to testify, introduce evidence, call witnesses, question those the Government calls, and secure release, if and when appropriate. The right to the aid of a personal representative in arranging and presenting their cases before a CSRT. Before the D.C. Circuit, the right to employ counsel, challenge the factual record, contest the lower tribunal's legal determinations, ensure compliance with the Constitution and laws, and secure release, if any errors below establish their entitlement to such relief.

In sum, the DTA satisfies the majority's own criteria for assessing adequacy. This statutory scheme provides the combatants held at Guantanamo greater procedural protections than have ever been afforded alleged enemy detainees—whether citizens or aliens—in our national history....

Justice Scalia, with whom *The Chief Justice*, *Justice Thomas*, and *Justice Alito* join, dissenting.

Today, for the first time in our Nation's history, the Court confers a constitutional right to habeas corpus on alien enemies detained abroad by our military forces in the course of an ongoing war. The Chief Justice's dissent, which I join, shows that the procedures prescribed by Congress in the Detainee Treatment Act provide the essential protections that habeas corpus guarantees; there has thus been no suspension of the writ, and no basis exists for judicial intervention beyond what the Act allows. My problem with today's opinion is more fundamental still: The writ of habeas corpus does not, and never has, run in favor of aliens abroad; the Suspension Clause thus has no application, and the Court's intervention in this military matter is entirely ultra vires....

A mere two Terms ago in *Hamdan v. Rumsfeld* ... (2006), when the Court held (quite amazingly) that the Detainee Treatment Act of 2005 had not stripped habeas jurisdiction over Guantanamo petitioners' claims, four members of today's five-Justice majority joined an opinion saying the following: "Nothing prevents the President from returning to Congress to seek the authority [for trial by military commission] he believes necessary." ...

Turns out they were just kidding. For in response, Congress, at the President's request, quickly enacted the Military Commissions Act, emphatically reasserting that it did not want these prisoners filing habeas petitions. It is therefore clear that Congress and the Executive—both political branches—have determined that limiting the role of civilian courts in adjudicating whether prisoners captured abroad are properly detained is important to success in the war that some 190,000 of our men and women are now fighting. As the Solicitor General argued, "the Military Commissions Act and the Detainee Treatment Act ... represent an effort by the political branches to strike an appropriate balance between the need to preserve liberty and the need to accommodate the weighty and sensitive governmental interests in ensuring that those who have in fact fought with the enemy during a war do not return to battle against the United States." ...

But it does not matter. The Court today decrees that no good reason to accept the judgment of the other two branches is "apparent." ... "The Government," it declares, "presents no credible arguments that the military mission at Guantanamo would be compromised if habeas corpus courts had jurisdiction to hear the detainees' claims." ... What competence does the Court have to second-guess the judgment of Congress and the President on such a point? None whatever. But the Court blunders in nonetheless. Henceforth, as today's opinion makes unnervingly clear, how to handle enemy prisoners in this war will ultimately lie with the branch that knows least about the national security concerns that the subject entails....

THE SLAUGHTERHOUSE CASES
16 Wall. (83 U.S.) 36; 21 L.Ed. 394 (1873)
Vote: 5-4

In 1869, the Louisiana legislature granted to a slaughterhouse company a monopoly for the city of New Orleans. A number of independent butchers sought injunctions against the monopoly. Unable to secure injunctions in the state courts, they turned to the Supreme Court, which granted review pursuant to a writ of error.

Mr. Justice Miller ... delivered the opinion of the Court.

The plaintiffs ... allege that the statute is a violation of the Constitution of the United States in these several particulars:

That it creates an involuntary servitude forbidden by the thirteenth article of amendment;

That it abridges the privileges and immunities of citizens of the United States;

That it denies to the plaintiffs the equal protection of the laws; and,

That it deprives them of their property without due process of law; contrary to the provisions of the first section of the fourteenth article of amendment.

This court is thus called upon for the first time to give construction to these articles.

... On the most casual examination of the language of [the Thirteenth, Fourteenth, and Fifteenth] amendments, no one can fail to be impressed with the one pervading purpose found in them all, lying at the foundation of each, and without which none of them would have been even suggested; we mean the freedom of the slave race, the security and firm establishment of that freedom, and the protection of the newly-made freeman and citizen from the oppressions of those who had formerly exercised unlimited dominion over him. It is true that only the Fifteenth Amendment, in terms, mentions the negro by speaking of his color and his slavery. But it is just as true that each of the other articles was addressed to the

(Continued)

grievances of that race, and designed to remedy them as the Fifteenth.

We do not say that no one else but the negro can share in this protection. Both the language and spirit of these articles are to have their fair and just weight in any question of construction. Undoubtedly while negro slavery alone was in the mind of the congress which proposed the thirteenth article, it forbids any other kind of slavery, now or hereafter. If Mexican peonage or the Chinese cooly labor system shall develop slavery of the Mexican or Chinese race within our territory, this amendment may safely be trusted to make it void. And so if other rights are assailed by the States which properly and necessarily fall within the protection of these articles, that protection will apply, though the party interested may not be of African descent. But what we do say, and what we wish to be understood is, that in any fair and just construction of any section or phrase of these amendments, it is necessary to look to the purpose which we have said was the pervading spirit of them all, the evil which they were designed to remedy, and the process of continued addition to the Constitution, until that purpose was supposed to be accomplished, as far as constitutional law can accomplish it....

The next observation is more important in view of the arguments of counsel in the present case. It is, that the distinction between citizenship of the United States and citizenship of a State is clearly recognized and established.

Not only may a man be a citizen of the United States without being a citizen of a State, but an important element is necessary to convert the former into the latter. He must reside within the State to make him a citizen of it, but it is only necessary that he should be born or naturalized in the United States to be a citizen of the Union.

It is quite clear, then, that there is a citizenship of the United States, and a citizenship of a State, which are distinct from each other, and which depend upon different characteristics of circumstance in the individual.

We think this distinction and its explicit recognition in this amendment of great weight in this argument, because the next paragraph of this same section, which is the one mainly relied on by the plaintiffs in error, speaks only of privileges and immunities of citizens of the United States, and does not speak of those of citizens of the several States. The argument, however, in favor of the plaintiffs rests wholly on the assumption that the citizenship is the same, and the privileges and immunities guaranteed by the clause are the same.

The language is, "No State shall make or enforce any law which shall abridge the privileges or immunities

of citizens of the United States." It is a little remarkable, if this clause was intended as a protection to the citizen of a State against the legislative power of his own State, that the [words] *citizen of the State* should be left out when it is so carefully used, and used in contradistinction to citizens of the United States, in the very sentence which precedes it. ...

Of the privileges and immunities of the citizen of the United States, and of the privileges and immunities of the citizen of the States, and what they respectively are, we will presently consider; but we wish to state here that it is only the former which are placed by this clause under the protection of the Federal Constitution, and that the latter, whatever they may be, are not intended to have any additional protection by this paragraph of the amendment.

If, then, there is a difference between the privileges and immunities belonging to a citizen of the United States as such, and those belonging to the citizen of the State as such the latter must rest for their security and protection where they have heretofore rested; for they are not embraced by this paragraph of the amendment....

It would be the vainest show of learning to attempt to prove by citations of authority, that up to the adoption of the recent amendments, no claim or pretense was set up that those rights depended on the Federal government for their existence or protection, beyond the very few express limitations which the Federal Constitution imposed upon the States—such, for instance, as the prohibition against *ex post facto* laws, bills of attainder, and laws impairing the obligation of contracts. But with the exception of these and a few other restrictions, the entire domain of the privileges and immunities of the citizens of the States, and without that of the Federal government. Was it the purpose of the Fourteenth Amendment, by the simple declaration that no States should make or enforce any law which abridge the privileges and immunities of citizens of the United States, to transfer the security and protection of all the civil rights which we have mentioned, from the states to the Federal government? And where it is declared that Congress shall have the power to enforce that article, was it intended to bring within the power of Congress the entire domain of civil rights heretofore belonging exclusively to the States?

All this and more must follow, if the proposition of the plaintiffs in error be sound. For not only are these rights subject to the control of Congress whenever in its discretion any of them are supposed to be abridged by State legislation, but that body may also pass laws in advance, limiting and restricting the exercise of legislative power of the States, in their most ordinary and usual functions, as in its judgment it may think proper on all such subjects. And still further, such a construction followed by the reversal of the judgments of the Supreme Court of Louisiana in these cases, would constitute this court a perpetual censor upon all legislation of the States, on the civil rights of their own citizens, with authority to nullify such as it did not approve as consistent with those rights, as they existed at the time of the adoption of this amendment. The argument we admit is not always the most conclusive which is drawn from the consequences urged against the adoption of a particular construction of an instrument. But when, as in the case before us, these consequences are so serious, so far-reaching and pervading, so great a departure from the structure and spirit of our institutions; when the effect is to fetter and degrade the State governments by subjecting them to the control of Congress, in the exercise of powers heretofore universally conceded to them of the most ordinary and fundamental character; when in fact it radically changes the whole theory of the relations of the State and Federal governments to each other and of both of these governments to the people; the argument has a force that is irresistible, in the absence of language which expresses such a purpose too clearly to admit of doubt.

We are convinced that no such results were intended by the Congress which proposed these amendments, nor by the legislatures of the States which ratified them.

Having shown that the privileges and immunities relied on in the argument are those which belong to citizens of the States as such, and that they are left to the State governments for security and protection, and not by this article placed under the special care of the Federal government, we may hold ourselves excused from defining the privileges and immunities of citizens of the United States which no State can abridge, until some case involving those privileges may make it necessary to do so.

But lest it be said that no such privileges and immunities are to be found if those we have been considering are excluded, we venture to suggest some which owe their existence to the Federal government, its National character, its Constitution, or its laws.

One of these is well described in the case of *Crandall v. Nevada* ... [1867]. It is said to be the right of the citizens of this great country, protected by implied guarantees of its Constitution, "to come to the seat of government to assert any claim he may have upon that government, to transact any business he may have with it, to seek its protection, to share its offices, to engage in administering its functions. He has the right of free access to its seaports, through which all operations of foreign commerce are conducted, to the subtreasuries, land offices, and courts of justice in the several States." And quoting from the language of Chief Justice Taney in another case, it is said "that for all the great purposes for which the Federal government was established, we are one people, with one common country, we are all citizens of the United States"; and it is, as such citizens, that their rights are supported in this court in *Crandall v. Nevada....*

The argument has not been much pressed in these cases that the defendant's charter deprives the plaintiffs of their property without due process of law, or that it denies to them the equal protection of the law. The first of these paragraphs has been in the Constitution since the adoption of the Fifth Amendment, as a restraint upon the Federal power. It is also to be found in some form of expression in the constitutions of nearly all the States, as a restraint upon the power of the States. This law, then, has practically been the same as it now is during the existence of the government, except so far as the present amendment may place the restraining power over the States in this matter in the hands of the Federal government.

We are not without judicial interpretation, therefore, both State and National, of the meaning of this clause. And it is sufficient to say that under no construction of that provision that we have ever seen, or any that we deem admissible, can the restraint imposed by the state of Louisiana upon the exercise of their trade by the butchers of New Orleans be held to be a deprivation of property within the meaning of that provision.

"Nor shall any State deny to any person within its jurisdiction the equal protection of the laws." In the light of the history of these amendments, and the pervading purpose of them, which we have already discussed, it is not difficult to give a meaning to this clause. The existence of laws in the states where the newly emancipated negroes resided, which discriminated with gross injustice and hardship against them as a class, was the evil to be remedied by this clause, and by it such laws are forbidden.

If, however, the states did not conform their laws to its requirements, then by the fifth section of the article of amendment Congress was authorized to enforce it by suitable legislation. We doubt very much whether any action of a State not directed by way of

(Continued)

discrimination against the negroes as a class, or on account of their race, will ever be held to come within the purview of this provision. It is so clearly a provision for that race and that emergency, that a strong case would be necessary for its application to any other. But as it is a State that is to be dealt with, and not alone the validity of its laws, we may safely leave that matter until congress shall have exercised its power, or some case of State oppression, by denial of equal justice in its courts, shall have claimed a decision at our hands. We find no such case in the one before us, and do not deem it necessary to go over the argument again, as it may have relation to this particular clause of the amendment....

The judgments of the Supreme Court of Louisiana in these cases are affirmed.

Mr. Justice Field, dissenting:

... The question presented is ... one of the gravest importance, not merely to the parties here, but to the whole country. It is nothing less than the question whether the recent amendments to the Federal Constitution protect the citizens of the United States against the deprivation of their common rights by State legislation. In my judgment the Fourteenth Amendment does afford such protection, and was so intended by the Congress which framed and the States which adopted it.

The amendment does not attempt to confer any new privileges or immunities upon citizens, or to enumerate or define those already existing. It assumes that there are such privileges and immunities which belong of right to citizens as such, and ordains that they shall not be abridged by State legislation. If this inhibition has no reference to privileges and immunities of this character, but only refers, as held by the majority of the court in their opinion, to such privileges and immunities as were before its adoption specially designated in the Constitution or necessarily implied as belonging to citizens of the United States, it was a vain and idle enactment, which accomplished nothing, and most unnecessarily excited Congress and the people on its passage. With privileges and immunities thus designated or implied no State could ever have interfered by its laws and no new constitutional provision was required to inhibit such interference. The supremacy of the Constitution and the laws of the United States always controlled any State legislation of that character. But if the amendment refers to the natural and inalienable rights which belong to all citizens, the inhibition has a profound significance and consequence.

What, then, are the privileges and immunities which are secured against abridgment by State legislation? ...

The terms, privileges and immunities, are not new in the Amendment; they were in the Constitution before the Amendment was adopted. They are found in the second section of the fourth article, which declares that "the citizens of each State shall be entitled to all privileges and immunities of citizens in the several States," and they have been the subject of frequent consideration in judicial decisions.... The privileges and immunities designated are those which of right belong to the citizens of all free governments. Clearly among these must be placed the right to pursue a lawful employment in a lawful manner, without other restraint than such as equally affects all persons....

This equality of right, with exemption from all disparaging and partial enactments, in the lawful pursuits of life, throughout the whole country, is the distinguishing privilege of citizens of the United States. To them, everywhere, all pursuits, all professions, all avocations are open without other restrictions than such as are imposed equally upon all others of the same age, sex, and condition. The State may prescribe such regulations for every pursuit and calling of life as will promote the public health, secure the good order and advance the general prosperity of society, but when once prescribed, the pursuit or calling must be free to be followed by every citizen who is within the conditions designated, and will conform to the regulations.

... The Fourteenth Amendment, in my judgment, makes it essential to the validity of the legislation of every State that this equality of right should be respected. How widely this equality has been departed from, how entirely rejected and trampled upon by the act of Louisiana, I have already shown.

And it is to me a matter of profound regret that its validity is recognized by a majority of this court, for by it the right of free labor, one of the most sacred and imprescriptible rights of man, is violated....

I am authorized by the **Chief Justice, Mr. Justice Swayne**, and **Mr. Justice Bradley**, to state that they concur with me in this dissenting opinion.

Mr. Justice Bradley, dissenting.

... The right of a State to regulate the conduct of its citizens is undoubtedly a very broad and extensive one, and not to be lightly restricted. But there are certain fundamental rights which this right of regulation cannot infringe. It may prescribe the manner of their exercise, but it cannot subvert the rights themselves....

The granting of monopolies, or exclusive privileges to individuals or corporations, is an invasion of the right of another to choose a lawful calling, and an infringement of personal liberty....

Can the Federal courts administer relief to citizens of the United States whose privileges and immunities have been abridged by a State? Of this I entertain no doubt. Prior to the Fourteenth Amendment this could not be done, except in a few instances, for the want of the requisite authority....

Admitting, therefore, that formerly the States were not prohibited from infringing any fundamental privileges and immunities of citizens of the United States, except in a few specified cases, that cannot be said now,

since the adoption of the Fourteenth Amendment. In my judgment, it was the intention of the people of this country in adopting that amendment to provide National security against violation by the States of the fundamental rights of the citizen....

In my view, a law which prohibits a large class of citizens from adopting a lawful employment, or from following a lawful employment previously adopted, does deprive them of liberty as well as property, without due process of law. Their right of choice is a portion of their liberty; their occupation is their property. Such a law also deprives those citizens of the equal protection of the laws, contrary to the last clause of the section....

Mr. Justice Swayne, dissenting....

THE CIVIL RIGHTS CASES
109 U.S. 3; 3 S.Ct. 18; 27 L.Ed. 835 (1883)
Vote: 8-1

In this landmark decision, the Court reviews the Civil Rights Act of 1875, which prohibited racial discrimination by places of public accommodation. The constitutionality of that legislation was challenged as surpassing Congress's legislative powers under the Thirteenth and Fourteenth Amendments.

Mr. Justice Bradley delivered the opinion of the Court:

These cases are all founded on the ... "Civil Rights Act," passed March 1, 1875.... Two of the cases ... are indictments for denying to persons of color the accommodations and privileges of an inn or hotel; two of them, ... for denying to individuals the privileges and accommodations of a theater.... The case of Robinson and wife against the Memphis & Charleston Railroad Company was an action ... to recover the penalty of $500 given by the second section of the act; and the gravamen was the refusal by the conductor of the railroad company to allow the wife to ride in the ladies' car, [because] she was a person of African descent.

The sections of the law referred to provide as follows:

Sec. 1. That all persons within ... United States shall be entitled to the full and equal enjoyment of the

accommodations, advantages, facilities, and privileges of inns, public conveyances on land or water, theaters, and other places of public amusement; subject only to the conditions and limitations established by law, and applicable alike to citizens of every race and color, regardless of any previous condition of servitude.

Sec. 2. That any person who shall violate the foregoing section ... shall, for every such offense, forfeit and pay the sum of $500 to the person aggrieved [and] be deemed guilty of a misdemeanor, and upon conviction thereof shall be fined not less than $500 nor more than $1,000, or shall be imprisoned not less than 30 days nor more than one year....

The first section of the Fourteenth Amendment ... declares that "no state shall make or enforce any law which shall abridge the privileges or immunities of citizens of the United States; nor shall any state deprive any person of life, liberty, or property without due process of law; nor deny to any person within its jurisdiction, the equal protection of the laws." It is state action of a particular character that is prohibited. Individual invasion of individual rights is not the subject-matter of the amendment.... It nullifies and makes void all state legislation, and state action of every kind, which

(Continued)

impairs the privileges and immunities of citizens of the United States, or which injures them in life, liberty, or property without due process of law, or which denies to any of them the equal protection of the laws.... [T]he last section of the amendment invests Congress with power to enforce it by appropriate legislation. To enforce what? To enforce the prohibition. To adopt appropriate legislation for correcting the effects of such prohibited state law and state acts, and thus to render them effectually null, void, and innocuous.... It does not invest Congress with power to legislate upon subjects which are within the domain of state legislation.... It does not authorize Congress to create a code of municipal law for the regulation of private rights; but to provide modes of redress against the operation of state laws, and the action of state officers, executive or judicial, when these are subversive of the fundamental rights specified in the amendment....

An inspection of the [Civil Rights Act of 1875] shows that it makes no reference whatever to any supposed or apprehended violation of the Fourteenth Amendment on the part of the states.... It proceeds *ex directo* to declare that certain acts committed by individuals shall be deemed offenses, and shall be prosecuted and punished by proceedings in the courts of the United States. It does not profess to be corrective of any constitutional wrong committed by the states.... [I]t steps into the domain of local jurisprudence, and lays down rules for the conduct of individuals in society towards each other ... without referring in any manner to any supposed action of the state or its authorities.

If this legislation is appropriate for enforcing the prohibitions of the amendment, it is difficult to see where it is to stop. Why may not Congress, with equal show of authority, enact a code of laws for the enforcement and vindication of all rights of life, liberty, and property? If it is supposable that the states may deprive persons of life, liberty, and property without due process of law (and the amendment itself does suppose this), why should not Congress proceed at once to prescribe due process of law for the protection of every one of these fundamental rights, in every possible case, as well as to prescribe equal privileges in inns, public conveyances, and theaters. The truth is that the implication of a power to legislate in this manner is based upon the assumption that if the states are forbidden to legislate or act in a particular way on a particular subject, and power is conferred upon Congress to enforce the prohibition, this gives Congress power to legislate generally upon that subject, and not merely power to provide modes of redress against such state legislation or action. The assumption is certainly unsound. It is repugnant to the Tenth Amendment....

... [C]ivil rights, such as are guaranteed by the Constitution against state aggression, cannot be impaired by the wrongful acts of individuals, unsupported by state authority in the shape of laws, customs, or judicial or executive proceedings. The wrongful act of an individual, unsupported by any such authority, is simply a private wrong, or a crime of that individual.... An individual cannot deprive a man of his right to vote, to hold property, to buy and to sell, to sue in the courts, or to be a witness or a juror; he may, by force or fraud, interfere with the enjoyment of the right in a particular case; ... but unless protected in these wrongful acts by some shield of state law or state authority, he cannot destroy or injure the right; he will only render himself amenable to satisfaction or punishment; and amenable therefore to the laws of the state where the wrongful acts are committed. Hence, in all those cases where the Constitution seeks to protect the rights of the citizen against discriminative and unjust laws of the state by prohibiting such laws, it is not individual offenses, but abrogation and denial of rights, which it denounces, and for which it clothes the Congress with power to provide a remedy. This abrogation and denial of rights, for which the states alone were or could be responsible, was the great seminal and fundamental wrong which was intended to be remedied....

Of course, these remarks do not apply to those cases in which Congress is clothed with direct and plenary powers of legislation over the whole subject, accompanied with an express or implied denial of such power to the states, as in the regulation of commerce with foreign nations, among the several states, and with the Indian tribes, the coining of money, the establishment of post-offices and post-roads, the declaring of war, etc. ...

But the power of Congress to adopt direct and primary, as distinguished from corrective, legislation on the subject in hand, is sought, in the second place, from the Thirteenth Amendment, which ... declares "that neither slavery, nor involuntary servitude, except as a punishment for crime, whereof the party shall have been duly convicted, shall exist within the United States, or any place subject to their jurisdiction;" and it gives Congress power to enforce the amendment by appropriate legislation....

... [I]t is assumed that the power vested in Congress to enforce the article by appropriate legislation, clothes Congress with power to pass all laws necessary and proper for abolishing all badges and incidents of slavery in the United States; and upon this assumption it is claimed that this is sufficient authority for declaring by law that all persons shall have equal accommodations and privileges in all inns, public conveyances, and places of public amusement; the argument being that the denial of such equal accommodations and privileges is in itself a subjection to a species of servitude within the meaning of the amendment....

... [T]he civil rights bill of 1866, passed in view of the Thirteenth Amendment, before the Fourteenth was adopted, understood to wipe out these burdens and disabilities, the necessary incidents of slavery, constituting its substance and visible form; and to secure to all citizens of every race and color, and without regard to previous servitude, those fundamental rights which are the essence of civil freedom, namely, the same right to make and enforce contracts, to sue, be parties, give evidence, and to inherit, purchase, lease, sell, and convey property, as is enjoyed by white citizens. Whether this legislation was fully authorized by the Thirteenth Amendment alone, without the support which it afterwards received from the Fourteenth Amendment, after the adoption of which it was re-enacted with some additions, it is not necessary to inquire. It is referred to for the purpose of showing that at that time (in 1866) Congress did not assume, under the authority given by the Thirteenth Amendment, to adjust what may be called the social rights of men and races in the community; but only to declare and vindicate those fundamental rights which appertain to the essence of citizenship, and the enjoyment or deprivation of which constitutes the essential distinction between freedom and slavery. ...

Can the act of a mere individual, the owner of the inn, the public conveyance, or place of amusement, refusing the accommodation, be justly regarded as imposing any badge of slavery or servitude upon the applicant, or only as inflicting an ordinary civil injury ...? [S]uch an act of refusal has nothing to do with slavery or involuntary servitude, ... if it is violative of any right of the party, his redress is to be sought under the laws of the state; or, if those laws are adverse to his rights and do not protect him, his remedy will be found in the corrective legislation which Congress has adopted, or may adopt, for counter-acting the effect of state laws, or state action, prohibited by the Fourteenth Amendment. It would be running the slavery argument into the ground to make it apply to every act of discrimination which a person may see fit to make as to the guests he will entertain, or as to the

people he will take into his coach or cab or car, or admit to his concert or theater, or deal with in other matters of intercourse or business. Innkeepers and public carriers, by the laws of all the states, so far as we are aware, are bound, to the extent of their facilities, to furnish proper accommodation to all unobjectionable persons who in good faith apply for them. If the laws themselves make any unjust discrimination, amenable to the prohibitions of the Fourteenth Amendment, Congress has full power to afford a remedy under that amendment and in accordance with it.

...There were thousands of free colored people in this country before the abolition of slavery, enjoying all the essential rights of life, liberty, and property the same as white citizens; yet no one, at that time, thought that it was any invasion of their personal status as freemen because they were not admitted to all the privileges enjoyed by white citizens, or because they were subjected to discriminations in the enjoyment of accommodations in inns, public conveyances, and places of amusement. Mere discriminations on account of race or color were not regarded as badges of slavery....

On the whole, we are of the opinion that no countenance of authority for the passage of the law in question can be found in either the Thirteenth or Fourteenth Amendment of the Constitution; and no other ground of authority for its passage being suggested, it must necessarily be declared void....

Mr. Justice Harlan, dissenting.

The opinion in these cases proceeds, as it seems to me, upon grounds entirely too narrow and artificial. The substance and spirit of the recent amendments of the Constitution have been sacrificed by a subtle and ingenious verbal criticism....

The Thirteenth Amendment, my brethren concede, did something more than to prohibit slavery as an institution, resting upon distinctions of race, and upheld by positive law. They admit that it established and decreed universal civil freedom throughout the United States. But did the freedom thus established involve nothing more ... than to forbid one man from owning another as property? ... I do not contend that the Thirteenth Amendment invests Congress with authority, by legislation, to regulate the entire body of the civil rights which citizens enjoy, or may enjoy, in the several states. But I do hold that since slavery ... was the moving or principal cause of the adoption of that amendment, and since that institution rested wholly upon the inferiority, as a race, of those held in bondage, their

(Continued)

freedom necessarily involved immunity from, and protection against, all discrimination against them, because of their race, in respect of such civil rights as belong to freemen of other races. Congress, therefore, under its express power to enforce that amendment, by appropriate legislation, may enact laws to protect that people against the deprivation, on account of their race, of any civil rights enjoyed by other freemen in the same state; and such legislation may be of a direct and primary character, operating upon states, their officers and agents, and also upon, at least, such individuals and corporations as exercise public functions and wield power and authority under the State....

I am of the opinion that ... discrimination practised by corporations and individuals in the exercise of their public or quasi-public functions is a badge of servitude, the imposition of which Congress may prevent under its power through appropriate legislation, to enforce the Thirteenth Amendment....

It remains now to consider these cases with reference to the power Congress has possessed since the adoption of the Fourteenth Amendment....

The first clause of the first section—"all persons born or naturalized in the United States, and subject to the jurisdiction thereof, are citizens of the United States, and of the state wherein they reside"—is of a distinctly affirmative character. In its application to the colored race, previously liberated, it created and granted, as well citizenship of the United States, as citizenship of the state in which they respectively resided.... Further, they were brought, by this supreme act of the nation, within the direct operation of the provision of the Constitution which declares that "the citizens of each state shall be entitled to all privileges and immunities of citizens in the several states."...

The citizenship thus acquired by that race, in virtue of an affirmative grant by the nation, may be protected, not alone by the judicial branch of the government, but by congressional legislation of a primary direct character; this, because the power of Congress is not restricted to the enforcement of prohibitions upon state laws or state action. It is, in terms distinct and positive, to enforce "the provisions of this article" of amendment; not simply those of a prohibitive character, but the provisions—all of the provisions—affirmative and prohibitive, of the amendment....

But what was secured to colored citizens of the United States—as between them and their respective states—by the grant to them of state citizenship? With what rights, privileges, or immunities did this grant from the nation invest them? There is one, if there be no others—exemption from race discrimination in respect of any civil right belonging to citizens of the white race in the same state.

... It is fundamental in American citizenship that, in respect of such rights, there shall be no discrimination by the state, or its officers, or by individuals, or corporations exercising public functions or authority, against any citizen because of his race or previous condition of servitude.

... [T]o hold that the amendment remits that right to the states for their protection, primarily, and stays the hands of the nation, until it is assailed by state laws or state proceedings, is to adjudge that the amendment, so far from enlarging the powers of Congress—as we have heretofore said it did—not only curtails them, but reverses the policy which the general government has pursued from its very organization. Such an interpretation of the amendment is a denial to Congress of the power, by appropriate legislation, to enforce one of its provisions. In view of the circumstances under which the recent amendments were incorporated into the Constitution, and especially in view of the peculiar character of the new rights they created and secured, it ought not to be presumed that the general government has abdicated its authority, by national legislation, direct and primary in its character, to guard and protect privileges and immunities secured by that instrument....

It is said that any interpretation of the Fourteenth Amendment different from that adopted by the court, would authorize Congress to enact a municipal code for all the states, covering every matter affecting the life, liberty, and property of the citizens of the several states. Not so. Prior to the adoption of that amendment the constitutions of the several states, without, perhaps, an exception, secured all persons against deprivation of life, liberty, or property, otherwise than by due process of law, and, in some form, recognized the right of all persons to the equal protection of the laws. These rights, therefore, existed before that amendment was proposed or adopted....

SHELLEY V. KRAEMER
334 U.S. 1; 68 S.Ct. 836, 92 L.Ed. 1161 (1948)
Vote: 6-0

In this landmark decision, the Supreme Court rules that the Fourteenth Amendment prohibits state courts from enforcing private agreements restricting the sale and rental of real property. The Court's opinion thus represents a significant expansion of the state action doctrine.

Mr. Chief Justice Vinson delivered the opinion of the Court.

These cases present for our consideration questions relating to the validity of court enforcement of private agreements, generally described as restrictive covenants, which have as their purpose the exclusion of persons of designated race or color from the ownership or occupancy of real property. Basic constitutional issues of obvious importance have been raised.

The first of these cases comes to this Court on certiorari to the Supreme Court of Missouri. On February 16, 1911, thirty out of a total of thirty-nine owners of property fronting both sides of Labadie Avenue between Taylor Avenue and Cora Avenue in the city of St. Louis, signed an agreement, which was subsequently recorded, providing in part:

… The said property is hereby restricted to the use and occupancy for the term of Fifty (50) years from this date, so that it shall be a condition all the time and whether recited and referred to as [sic!] not in subsequent conveyances and shall attach to the land, as a condition precedent to the sale of the same, that hereafter no part of said property or any portion thereof shall be, for said term of Fifty years, occupied by any person not of the Caucasian race, it being intended hereby to restrict the use of said property for said period of time against the occupancy as owners or tenants of any portion of said property for resident or other purpose by people of the Negro or Mongolian Race….

On August 11, 1945, pursuant to a contract of sale, petitioners Shelley, who are Negroes, for valuable consideration received from one Fitzgerald a warranty deed to the parcel in question. The trial court found that petitioners had no actual knowledge of the restrictive agreement at the time of the purchase.

On October 9, 1945, respondents, as owners of other property subject to the terms of the restrictive covenant, brought suit in the Circuit Court of the city of St. Louis praying that petitioners Shelley be restrained from taking possession of the property and that judgment be entered divesting title out of petitioners Shelley and revesting title in the immediate grantor or in such other person as the court should direct. The trial court denied the requested relief on the ground that the restrictive agreement, upon which respondents based their action, had never become final and complete because it was the intention of the parties to that agreement that it was not to become effective until signed by all property owners in the district, and signatures of all the owners had never been obtained.

The Supreme Court of Missouri sitting en banc reversed and directed the trial court to grant the relief for which respondents had prayed. That court held the agreement effective and concluded that enforcement of its provisions violated no rights guaranteed to petitioners by the Federal Constitution. At the time the court rendered its decision, petitioners were occupying the property in question….

Petitioners have placed primary reliance on their contentions, first raised in the state courts, that judicial enforcement of the restrictive agreements in these cases has violated rights guaranteed to petitioners by the Fourteenth Amendment of the Federal Constitution and Acts of Congress passed pursuant to that Amendment. Specifically, petitioners urge that they have been denied the equal protection of the laws, deprived of property without due process of law, and have been denied privileges and immunities of citizens of the United States. We pass to a consideration of those issues.

I

Whether the equal protection clause of the Fourteenth Amendment inhibits judicial enforcement by state courts of restrictive covenants based on race or color is a question which this Court has not heretofore been called upon to consider….

It is well, at the outset, to scrutinize the terms of the restrictive agreements involved in these cases. … Not only does the restriction seek to proscribe use and occupancy of the affected properties by members of the excluded class, but as construed by the Missouri courts, the agreement requires that title of any person who uses his property in violation of the restriction shall be divested….

(Continued)

It cannot be doubted that among the civil rights intended to be protected from discriminatory state action by the Fourteenth Amendment are the rights to acquire, enjoy, own and dispose of property. Equality in the enjoyment of property rights was regarded by the Framers of that Amendment as an essential precondition to the realization of other basic civil rights and liberties which the Amendment was intended to guarantee. Thus ... the Civil Rights Act of 1866 which was enacted by Congress while the Fourteenth Amendment was also under consideration provides: "All citizens of the United States shall have the same right, in every State and Territory, as is enjoyed by white citizens thereof to inherit, purchase, lease, sell, hold, and convey real and personal property." This Court has given specific recognition to the same principle....

It is likewise clear that restrictions on the right of occupancy of the sort sought to be created by the private agreements in these cases could not be squared with the requirements of the Fourteenth Amendment if imposed by state statute or local ordinance....

But the present cases, unlike those just discussed, do not involve action by state legislatures or city councils. Here the particular patterns of discrimination and the areas in which the restrictions are to operate, are determined, in the first instance, by the terms of agreements among private individuals. Participation of the State consists in the enforcement of the restrictions so defined. The crucial issue with which we are here confronted is whether this distinction removes these cases from the operation of the prohibitory provisions of the Fourteenth Amendment.

Since the decision of this Court in The Civil Rights Cases, ... the principle has become firmly embedded in our constitutional law that the action inhibited by the first section of the Fourteenth Amendment is only such action as may fairly be said to be that of the States. That Amendment erects no shield against merely private conduct, however discriminatory or wrongful.

We conclude, therefore, that the restrictive agreements standing alone cannot be regarded as violative of any rights guaranteed to petitioners by the Fourteenth Amendment. So long as the purposes of those agreements are effectuated by voluntary adherence to their terms, it would appear clear that there has been no action by the State and the provisions of the Amendment have not been violated....

But here there was more. These are cases in which the purposes of the agreements were secured only by judicial enforcement by state courts of the restrictive terms of the agreements. The respondents urge that judicial enforcement of private agreements does not amount to state action; or, in any event, the participation of the States is so attenuated in character as not to amount to state action within the meaning of the Fourteenth Amendment. Finally, it is suggested, even if the States in these cases may be deemed to have acted in the constitutional sense, their action did not deprive petitioners of rights guaranteed by the Fourteenth Amendment. We move to a consideration of these matters.

II

That the action of state courts and of judicial officers in their official capacities is to be regarded as action of the State within the meaning of the Fourteenth Amendment, is a proposition which has long been established by decisions of this Court. ...

The short of the matter is that from the time of the adoption of the Fourteenth Amendment until the present, it has been the consistent ruling of this Court that the action of the States to which the Amendment has reference, includes action of state courts and state judicial officials. Although, in construing the terms of the Fourteenth Amendment, differences have from time to time been expressed as to whether particular types of state action may be said to offend the Amendment's prohibitory provisions, it has never been suggested that state court action is immunized from the operation of those provisions simply because the act is that of the judicial branch of the state government.

III

Against this background of judicial construction, extending over a period of some three-quarters of a century, we are called upon to consider whether enforcement by state courts of the restrictive agreements in these cases may be deemed to be the acts of those States; and, if so, whether that action has denied these petitioners the equal protection of the laws which the Amendment was intended to insure.

We have no doubt that there has been state action in these cases in the full and complete sense of the phrase. The undisputed facts disclose that petitioners were willing purchasers of properties upon which they desired to establish homes. The owners of the properties were willing sellers; and contracts of sale were accordingly consummated. It is clear that but for the active intervention of the state courts, supported by the full panoply of state power, petitioners would have been free to occupy the properties in question without restraint.

These are not cases, as has been suggested, in which the States have merely abstained from action, leaving private individuals free to impose such discriminations as they see fit. Rather, these are cases in which the States have made available to such individuals the full coercive power of government to deny to petitioners, on the grounds of race or color, the enjoyment of property rights in premises which petitioners are willing and financially able to acquire and which the grantors are willing to sell. The difference between judicial enforcement and nonenforcement of the restrictive covenants is the difference to petitioners between being denied rights of property available to other members of the community and being accorded full enjoyment of those rights on an equal footing....

We hold that in granting judicial enforcement of the restrictive agreements in these cases, the States have denied petitioners the equal protection of the laws and that, therefore, the action of the state courts cannot stand. We have noted that freedom from discrimination by the States in the enjoyment of property rights was among the basic objectives sought to be effectuated by the Framers of the Fourteenth Amendment. That such discrimination has occurred in these cases is clear. Because of the race or color of these petitioners they have been denied rights of ownership or occupancy enjoyed as a matter of course by other citizens of different race or color....

But there are more fundamental considerations. The rights created by the first section of the Fourteenth Amendment are, by its terms, guaranteed to the individual. The rights established are personal rights. It is, therefore, no answer to these petitioners to say that the courts may also be induced to deny white persons rights of ownership and occupancy on grounds of race or color. Equal protection of the laws is not achieved through indiscriminate imposition of inequalities....

The historical context in which the Fourteenth Amendment became a part of the Constitution should not be forgotten. Whatever else the Framers sought to achieve, it is clear that the matter of primary concern was the establishment of equality in the enjoyment of basic civil and political rights and the preservation of those rights from discriminatory action on the part of the States based on considerations of race or color. Seventy-five years ago this Court announced that the provisions of the Amendment are to be construed with this fundamental purpose in mind. Upon full consideration, we have concluded that in these cases the States have acted to deny petitioners the equal protection of the laws guaranteed by the Fourteenth Amendment. Having so decided, we find it unnecessary to consider whether petitioners have also been deprived of property without due process of law or denied privileges and immunities of citizens of the United States....

Justices Reed, *Jackson*, and *Rutledge* took no part in the consideration or decision of these cases.

BARRON V. BALTIMORE
7 Pet. (32 U.S.) 243; 8 L.Ed. 672 (1833)
Vote: 7-0

Like the cases that follow in this chapter, Barron v. Baltimore deals with the issue of whether the protections of the Bill of Rights are applicable to actions of the states and their local subdivisions. The case stemmed from an incident in which the city of Baltimore diverted the flow of certain streams, causing silt to be deposited in front of John Barron's wharf, making it unusable. Barron brought suit in state court, claiming that since the City's action amounted to a taking of private property, he was entitled to "just compensation" under the Fifth Amendment to the U.S. Constitution. The trial court agreed and awarded Barron $4,500. After this judgment was reversed by a state appellate court, Barron appealed to the U.S. Supreme Court on a writ of error.

Mr. Chief Justice Marshall delivered the Opinion of the Court:

... The plaintiff in error [Barron] contends that [this case] comes within that clause in the Fifth Amendment to the Constitution which inhibits the taking of private property for public use without just compensation. He

(Continued)

insists that this amendment, being in favor of the liberty of the citizen, ought to be so construed as to restrain the legislative power of a State, as well as that of the United States. If this proposition be untrue, the Court can take no jurisdiction of the cause.

The question thus presented is, we think, of great importance, but not of much difficulty.

The Constitution was ordained and established by the people of the United States for themselves, for their own government, and not for the government of the individual States. Each State established a constitution for itself, and in that constitution provided such limitations and restrictions on the powers of its particular government as its judgment dictated. The people of the United States framed such a government for the United States as they supposed best adapted to their situation, and best calculated to promote their interests. The powers they conferred on this government were to be exercised by itself; and the limitations on power, if expressed in general terms, are naturally, and, we think, necessarily applicable to the government created by the instrument. They are limitations of power granted in the instrument itself; not of distinct governments, framed by different persons and for different purposes.

If this proposition be correct, the Fifth Amendment must be understood as restraining the power of the general government, not as applicable to the States. In their several constitutions they have imposed such restrictions on their respective governments as their own wisdom suggested; such as they deemed most proper for themselves.

It is a subject on which they judge exclusively, and with which others interfere no farther than they are supposed to have a common interest.

The counsel for the plaintiff in error insists that the Constitution was intended to secure the people of the several States against the undue exercise of power by their respective State governments; as well as against that which might be attempted by their general government. In support of this argument he relies on the inhibitions contained in the tenth section of the first article.

We think that section affords a strong if not a conclusive argument in support of the opinion already indicated by the Court.

The preceding section contains restrictions which are obviously intended for the exclusive purpose of restraining the exercise of power by the departments of the general government. Some of them use language applicable only to Congress, others are expressed in general terms. The third clause, for example, declares that "no bill of attainder or *ex post facto* law shall be passed." No language can be more general; yet the demonstration is complete that it applies solely to the government of the United States. In addition to the general arguments furnished by the instrument itself, some of which have been already suggested, the succeeding section, the avowed purpose of which is to restrain State legislation, contains in terms the very prohibition. It declares that "no State shall pass any bill of attainder or *ex post facto* law." This provision then, of the ninth section, however comprehensive its language, contains no restriction on State legislation.

The ninth section having enumerated, in the nature of a bill of rights, the limitations intended to be imposed on the powers of the general government, the tenth proceeds to enumerate those which were to operate on the State legislatures. These restrictions are brought together in the same section, and are by express words applied to the States....

... It would be tedious to recapitulate the several limitations on the powers of the States which are contained in this section. They will be found, generally, to restrain State legislation on subjects entrusted to the government of the Union, in which the citizens of all the States are interested. In these alone were the whole people concerned. The question of their application to States is not left to construction. It is averred in positive words.

If the original Constitution, in the ninth and tenth sections of the first article, draws this plain and marked line of discrimination between the limitations it imposes on the powers of the general government and on those of the States; if in every inhibition intended to act on State power, words are employed which directly express that intent, some strong reason must be assigned for departing from this safe and judicious course in framing the amendments, before that departure can be assumed.

We search in vain for that reason....

We are of opinion that the provision in the Fifth Amendment to the Constitution, declaring that private property shall not be taken for public use without just compensations, is intended solely as a limitation on the exercise of power by the government of the United States, and is not applicable to the legislation of the States. We are therefore of opinion that there is no repugnancy between the several acts of the General Assembly of Maryland, given in evidence by the defendants at the trial of this cause in the court of that State, and the Constitution of the United States....

CHICAGO, BURLINGTON, & QUINCY RAILROAD COMPANY V. CHICAGO
166 U.S. 226; 17 S.Ct. 581; 41 L.Ed. 979 (1897)
Vote: 7-1

This case arose when the city of Chicago sought to widen Rockwell Street between West Eighteenth and West Nineteenth Streets. To obtain the land necessary to widen the street, the city used its power of eminent domain, taking part of the right-of-way owned by the Chicago, Burlington, & Quincy Railroad. A state trial court awarded the railroad company a mere $1 as "just compensation" for the condemned parcels of land. The railroad took the case to the U.S. Supreme Court on a writ of error.

Although the Court ruled in favor of the city, its opinion made new law by extending the Just Compensation Clause of the Fifth Amendment to state action under the Fourteenth Amendment.

Mr. Justice Harlan delivered the opinion of the Court.

...[A] state may not, by any of its agencies, disregard the prohibitions of the Fourteenth Amendment. Its judicial authorities may keep within the letter of the statute prescribing forms of procedure in the courts and give the parties the fullest opportunity to be heard, and yet it might be that its final action would be inconsistent with that Amendment. In determining what is due process of law, regard must be had to substance, not to form. This court, referring to the Fourteenth Amendment, has said: "Can a state make anything due process of law which, by its own legislation, it chooses to declare such? To affirm this is to hold that the prohibition to the states is of no avail, or has no application where the invasion of private rights is effected under the forms of state legislation...." The same question could be propounded, and the same answer could be made, in reference to judicial proceedings inconsistent with the requirement of due process of law. If compensation for private property taken for public use is an essential element of due process of law as ordained by the Fourteenth Amendment, then the final judgment of a state court, under the authority of which the property is in fact taken, is to be deemed the act of the state within the meaning of that Amendment.

It is proper now to inquire whether the due process of law enjoined by the Fourteenth Amendment requires compensation to be made or adequately secured to the owner of private property taken for public use under the authority of a state.

... [A] statute declaring in terms, without more, that the full and exclusive title to a described piece of land belonging to one person should be and is hereby vested in another person, would, if effectual, deprive the former of his property without due process of law, within the meaning of the Fourteenth Amendment.... Such an enactment would not receive judicial sanction in any country having a written Constitution distributing the powers of government among three coordinate departments, and committing to the judiciary, expressly or by implication, authority to enforce the provisions of such Constitution. It would be treated, not as an exertion of legislative power, but as a sentence—an act of spoliation. Due protection of the rights of property has been regarded as a vital principle of republican institutions. The requirement that the property shall not be taken for public use without just compensation is but "an affirmance of a great doctrine established by the common law for the protection of private property. It is founded in natural equity, and is laid down as a principle of universal law. Indeed, in a free government almost all other rights would become worthless if the government possessed an uncontrollable power over the private fortune of every citizen." ...

... We have examined all the questions of law arising on the record of which this court may take cognizance, and which, in our opinion, are of sufficient importance to require notice at our hands, and finding no error, the judgment [of the state court] is affirmed.

Mr. Justice Brewer, dissenting:

I dissent from the judgment in this case. I approve that which is said in the first part of the opinion as to the potency of the Fourteenth Amendment to restrain action by a state through either its legislative, executive or judicial departments, which deprives a party of his property rights without due compensation....

It is disappointing after reading so strong a declaration of the protecting reach of the Fourteenth Amendment and the power and duty of this court in enforcing it as against action by a state by any of its officers or agencies, to find sustained a judgment, depriving a party—even though a railroad corporation—of valuable property without any, or, at least only nominal, compensation....

The Chief Justice took no part in the consideration or decision of this case.

PALKO V. CONNECTICUT
302 U.S. 319; 58 S.Ct. 149; 82 L.Ed. 288 (1937)
Vote: 8-1

Here, the Court sets forth a test for determining which provisions of the Bill of Rights are applicable to the states via the Fourteenth Amendment.

Mr. Justice Cardozo delivered the opinion of the Court.

A statute of Connecticut permitting appeals in criminal cases to be taken by the state is challenged by appellant as an infringement of the Fourteenth Amendment of the Constitution of the United States. Whether the challenge should be upheld is now to be determined....

The argument for appellant is that whatever is forbidden by the Fifth Amendment is forbidden by the Fourteenth also. The Fifth Amendment, which is not directed to the states, but solely to the federal government, creates immunity from double jeopardy. No person shall be "subject for the same offense to be twice put in jeopardy of life or limb." The Fourteenth Amendment ordains, "nor shall any state deprive any person of life, liberty, or property, without due process of law." To retry a defendant, though under one indictment and only one, subjects him, it is said, to double jeopardy in violation of the Fifth Amendment, if the prosecution is one on behalf of the United States. From this the consequence is said to follow that there is a denial of life or liberty without due process of law, if the prosecution is one on behalf of the People of a State....

We do not find it profitable to mark the precise limits of the prohibition of double jeopardy in federal prosecutions....

We have said that in appellant's view the Fourteenth Amendment is to be taken as embodying the prohibitions of the Fifth. His thesis is even broader. Whatever would be a violation of the original Bill of Rights (Amendments 1 to 8) if done by the federal government is now equally unlawful by force of the Fourteenth Amendment if done by a state. There is no such general rule.

The Fifth Amendment provides, among other things, that no person shall be held to answer for a capital or otherwise infamous crime unless on presentment or indictment of a grand jury. This court has held that, in prosecutions by a state, presentment or indictment by a grand jury may give way to informations at the instance of a public officer.... The Fifth Amendment provides also that no person shall be compelled in any criminal case to be a witness against himself. This court has said that, in prosecutions by a state, the exemption will fail if the state elects to end it.... The Sixth Amendment calls for a jury trial in criminal cases and the Seventh for a jury trial in civil cases at common law where the value in controversy shall exceed twenty dollars. This court has ruled that consistently with those amendments trial by jury may be modified by a state or abolished altogether....

On the other hand, the Due Process Clause of the Fourteenth Amendment may make it unlawful for a state to abridge by its statutes the freedom of speech which the First Amendment safeguards against encroachment by the Congress ... or the right of peaceable assembly, without which speech would be unduly trammeled or the right of one accused of crime to the benefit of counsel.... In these and other situations immunities that are valid as against the federal government by force of the specific pledges of particular amendments have been found to be implicit in the concept of ordered liberty, and thus, through the Fourteenth Amendment, become valid as against the states.

The line of division may seem to be wavering and broken if there is a hasty catalogue of the cases on the one side and the other. Reflection and analysis will induce a different view. There emerges the perception of a rationalizing principle which gives to discrete instances a proper order and coherence. The right to trial by jury and the immunity from prosecution except as the result of an indictment may have value and importance. Even so, they are not of the very essence of a scheme of ordered liberty. To abolish them is not to violate a "principle of justice so rooted in the traditions and conscience of our people as to be ranked as fundamental. ..." Few would be so narrow or provincial as to maintain that a fair and enlightened system of justice would be impossible without them. What is true of jury trials and indictments is true also, as the cases show, of the immunity from compulsory self-incrimination.... This too might be lost, and justice still be done. Indeed, today as in the past there are students of our penal system who look upon the immunity as a mischief rather than a benefit, and who would limit its scope or destroy it altogether. No doubt there would remain the need to give protection against torture, physical or mental.... Justice, however, would not perish if the accused were subject to a duty to respond to orderly inquiry....

We reach a different plane of social and moral values when we pass to the privileges and immunities that have been taken over from the earlier articles of the federal Bill of Rights and brought within the Fourteenth Amendment by a process of absorption. These in their origin were effective against the federal government alone. If the Fourteenth Amendment has absorbed them, the process of absorption has had its source in the belief that neither liberty nor justice would exist if they were sacrificed.... This is true, for illustration, of freedom of thought and speech. Of that freedom one may say that it is the matrix, the indispensable condition, of nearly every other form of freedom. With rare aberrations a pervasive recognition of that truth can be traced in our history, political and legal. So it has come about that the domain of liberty, withdrawn by the Fourteenth Amendment from encroachment by the states, has been enlarged by latter-day judgments to include liberty of the mind as well as liberty of action. The extension became, indeed, a logical imperative when once it was recognized, as long ago it was, that liberty is something more than exemption from physical restraint, and that even in the field of substantive rights and duties the legislative judgment, if oppressive and arbitrary, may be overridden by the courts.... Fundamental too in the concept of due process, and so in that of liberty, is the thought that condemnation shall be rendered only after trial.... The hearing, moreover, must be a real one, not a sham or a pretense.... For that reason, ignorant defendants in a capital case were held to have been condemned unlawfully when in truth, though not in form, they were refused the aid of counsel.... The decision did not turn upon the fact that the benefit of counsel would have been guaranteed to the defendants by the provisions of the Sixth Amendment if they had been prosecuted in a federal court. The decision turned upon the fact that in the particular situation laid before us in the evidence the benefit of counsel was essential to the substance of a hearing.

Our survey of the cases serves, we think, to justify the statement that the dividing line between them, if not unfaltering throughout its course, has been true for the most part to a unifying principle. On which side of the line the case made out by the appellant has appropriate location must be the next inquiry and the final one. Is that kind of double jeopardy to which the statute has subjected him a hardship so acute and shocking that our polity will not endure it? Does it violate those "fundamental principles of liberty and justice which lie at the base of all our civil and political institutions"? ... The answer surely must be "no." What the answer would have to be if the state were permitted after a trial free from error to try the accused over again or to bring another case against him, we have no occasion to consider. We deal with the statute before us and no other. The state is not attempting to wear the accused out by a multitude of cases with accumulated trials. It asks no more than this, that the case against him shall go on until there shall be a trial free from the corrosion of substantial legal error.... This is not cruelty at all, nor even vexation in any immoderate degree. If the trial had been infected with error adverse to the accused, there might have been review at his instance, and as often as necessary to purge the vicious taint. A reciprocal privilege, subject at all times to the discretion of the presiding judge ... has now been granted to the state. There is here no seismic innovation. The edifice of justice stands, in its symmetry, to many, greater than before.... The judgment is affirmed.

Mr. Justice Butler dissents.

ADAMSON V. CALIFORNIA
332 U.S. 46; 67 S.Ct. 1672; 91 L.Ed. 1903 (1947)
Vote: 5-4

In Twining v. New Jersey (1908), the Court held that the Fifth Amendment protection against compulsory self-incrimination did not have to be honored in state criminal trials. The Court revisits this question in the instant case. The student should pay close attention to the different theories of Fourteenth Amendment due process espoused in the various opinions in this case.

Mr. Justice Reed delivered the opinion of the Court.

(Continued)

The appellant, Adamson, a citizen of the United States, was convicted, without recommendation for mercy, by a jury in a Superior Court of the State of California of murder in the first degree. After considering the same objections to the conviction that are pressed here, the sentence of death was affirmed by the Supreme Court of the state. The provisions of California law which were challenged … as invalid under the Fourteenth Amendment … permit the failure of a defendant to explain or to deny evidence against him to be commented upon by court and by counsel and to be considered by court and jury. The defendant did not testify. As the trial court gave its instructions and the District Attorney argued the case in accordance with the constitutional and statutory provisions just referred to, we have for decision the question of their constitutionality.

The appellant was charged in the information with former convictions for burglary, larceny and robbery and pursuant to §1025, California Penal Code, answered that he had suffered the previous convictions. This answer barred allusion to these charges of convictions on the trial. Under California's interpretation of Sec. 1025 of the Penal Code and Sec. 2051 of the Code of Civil Procedure, however, if the defendant, after answering affirmative charges alleging prior convictions, takes the witness stand to deny or explain away other evidence that has been introduced "the commission of these crimes could have been revealed to the jury on cross-examination to impeach his testimony." This forces an accused who is a repeat offender to choose between the risk of having his prior offenses disclosed to the jury or having it draw harmful inferences from uncontradicted evidence that can only be denied or explained by the defendant.

In the first place, appellant urges that the provision of the Fifth Amendment that no person "shall be compelled in any criminal case to be a witness against himself" is a fundamental national privilege or immunity protected against state abridgment by the Fourteenth Amendment or a privilege or immunity secured, through the Fourteenth Amendment, against deprivation by state action because it is a personal right, enumerated in the federal Bill of Rights.

Secondly, appellant relies upon the due process of law clause of the Fourteenth Amendment to invalidate the provisions of the California law and as applied (a) because comment on failure to testify is permitted, (b) because appellant was forced to forego testimony in person because of danger of disclosure of his past convictions through cross-examination and (c) because the presumption of innocence was infringed by the shifting of the burden of proof to appellant in permitting comment on his failure to testify.

We shall assume, but without any intention thereby of ruling upon the issue, that permission by law to the court, counsel and jury to comment upon and consider the failure of defendant "to explain or to deny by his testimony any evidence or facts in the case against him" would infringe defendant's privilege against self-incrimination under the Fifth Amendment if this were a trial in a court of the United States under a similar law. Such an assumption does not determine appellant's rights under the Fourteenth Amendment. It is settled law that the clause of the Fifth Amendment, protecting a person against being compelled to be a witness against himself, is not made effective by the Fourteenth Amendment as a protection against state action on the ground that freedom from testimonial compulsion is a right of national citizenship, or because it is a personal privilege or immunity secured by the Federal Constitution as one of the rights of man that are listed in the Bill of Rights.

The reasoning that leads to those conclusions starts with the unquestioned premise that the Bill of Rights, when adopted, was for the protection of the individual against the federal government and its provisions were inapplicable to similar actions done by the states.… With the adoption of the Fourteenth Amendment, it was suggested that the dual citizenship recognized by its first sentence, secured for citizens' federal protection for their elemental privileges and immunities of state citizenship. *The Slaughter-House Cases* decided, contrary to the suggestion, that these rights, as privileges and immunities of state citizenship, remained under the sole protection of the state governments. This Court, without the expression of a contrary view upon that phase of the issues before the Court, has approved this determination. The power to free defendants in state trials from self-incrimination was specifically determined to be beyond the scope of the privileges and immunities clause of the Fourteenth Amendment in *Twining v. New Jersey*.…

We reaffirm the conclusion of the *Twining* and *Palko* cases that protection against self-incrimination is not a privilege or immunity of national citizenship.

A right to a fair trial is a right admittedly protected by the due process clause of the Fourteenth Amendment. Therefore, appellant argues, the due process clause of the Fourteenth Amendment protects his privilege against self-incrimination. The due process clause of the Fourteenth Amendment, however, does not draw all the rights of the federal Bill of Rights under its protection. That contention was made and rejected in *Palko v. Connecticut*.... It was rejected with citation of the cases excluding several of the rights, protected by the Bill of Rights, against infringement by the National Government. Nothing has been called to our attention that either the framers of the Fourteenth Amendment or the states that adopted it intended its due process clause to draw within its scope the earlier amendments to the Constitution. *Palko* held that such provisions of the Bill of Rights as were "implicit in the concept of ordered liberty," became secure from state interference by the clause. But it held nothing more.

For a state to require testimony from an accused is not necessarily a breach of a state's obligation to give a fair trial. ... The due process clause forbids compulsion to testify by fear of hurt, torture or exhaustion. So our inquiry is directed, not at the broad question of the constitutionality of compulsory testimony from the accused under the due process clause, but to the constitutionality of the provision of the California law that permits comment upon his failure to testify. It is, of course, logically possible that while an accused might be required, under appropriate penalties, to submit himself as a witness without a violation of due process, comment by judge or jury on inferences to be drawn from his failure to testify, in jurisdictions where an accused's privilege against self-incrimination is protected, might deny due process. For example, a statute might declare that a permitted refusal to testify would compel an acceptance of the truth of the prosecution's evidence.

Generally, comment on the failure of an accused to testify is forbidden in American jurisdictions. This arises from state constitutional or statutory provisions similar in character to the federal provisions.... California, however, is one of a few states that permit limited comment upon a defendant's failure to testify. That permission is narrow. The California law authorizes comment by court and counsel upon the "failure of the defendant to explain or to deny by his testimony any evidence or facts in the case against him." This does not involve any presumption, rebuttable or irrebuttable, either of guilt or of the truth of any fact, that is offered in evidence. It allows inferences to be drawn from proven facts. Because of this clause, the court can direct the jury's attention to whatever evidence there may be that a defendant could deny and the prosecution can argue as to inferences that may be drawn from the accused's failure to testify. California has prescribed a method for advising the jury in the search for truth. However sound may be the legislative conclusion that an accused should not be compelled in any criminal case to be a witness against himself, we see no reason why comment should not be made upon his silence. It seems quite natural that when a defendant has opportunity to deny or explain facts and determines not to do so, the prosecution should bring out the strength of the evidence by commenting upon defendant's failure to explain or deny it. ...

Appellant sets out the circumstances of this case, however, to show coercion and unfairness in permitting comment. The guilty person was not seen at the place and time of the crime. There was evidence, however, that entrance to the place or room where the crime was committed might have been obtained through a small door. It was freshly broken. Evidence showed that six fingerprints on the door were petitioner's. Certain diamond rings were missing from the deceased's possession. There was evidence that appellant, sometime after the crime, asked an unidentified person whether the latter would be interested in purchasing a diamond ring. As has been stated, the information charged other crimes to appellant and he admitted them. His argument here is that he could not take the stand to deny the evidence against him because he would be subjected to a cross-examination as to former crimes to impeach his veracity and the evidence so produced might well bring about his conviction. Such cross-examination is allowable in California. Therefore, appellant contends the California statute permitting comment denies him due process.

It is true that if comment were forbidden, an accused in this situation could remain silent and avoid evidence of former crimes and comment upon his failure to testify. We are of the view, however, that a state may control such a situation in accordance with its own ideas of the most efficient administration of criminal justice. The purpose of due process is not to protect an accused against a proper conviction but against an unfair conviction. When evidence is before a jury that threatens conviction, it does not seem unfair to require him to choose between leaving the adverse evidence unexplained and subjecting himself to impeachment through disclosures of former crimes. Indeed, this is a dilemma with which any defendant may be faced. If facts, adverse to the defendant, are proven by the prosecution, there may be no way to explain them favorably to the accused except by a witness who may be vulnerable to impeachment on cross-examination. The defendant must then decide whether or not to use such a witness. The fact that the witness may also be the defendant makes the choice more difficult but a denial of due process does not emerge from the circumstances....

(Continued)

Mr. Justice Frankfurter, concurring....

Mr. Justice Black [joined by *Mr. Justice Douglas]*, dissenting.

This decision reasserts a constitutional theory spelled out in *Twining v. New Jersey* ... that this Court is endowed by the Constitution with boundless power under "natural law" periodically to expand and contract constitutional standards to conform to the Court's conception of what at a particular time constitutes "civilized decency" and "fundamental liberty and justice." Invoking this *Twining* rule, the Court concludes that although comment upon testimony in a federal court would violate the Fifth Amendment, identical comment in a state court does not violate today's fashion in today's decency and fundamentals and is therefore not prohibited by the Federal Constitution as amended.

The *Twining* Case was the first, and it is the only, decision of this Court, which has squarely held that states were free, notwithstanding the Fifth and Fourteenth Amendments, to extort evidence from one accused of crime. I agree that if *Twining* be reaffirmed, the result reached might appropriately follow. But I would not reaffirm the *Twining* decision. I think that decision and the "natural law" theory of the Constitution upon which it relies degrade the constitutional safeguards of the Bill of Rights and simultaneously appropriate for this Court a broad power which we are not authorized by the Constitution to exercise.

Whether this Court ever will, or whether it now should, in the light of past decisions, give full effect to what the Amendment was intended to accomplish is not necessarily essential to a decision here. However that may be, our prior decisions, including *Twining* do not prevent our carrying out that purpose, at least to the extent of making applicable to the states, not a mere part, as the Court has, but the full protection of the Fifth Amendment's provision against compelling evidence from an accused to convict him of crime. And I further contend that the "natural law" formula which the Court uses to reach its conclusion in this case should be abandoned as an incongruous excrescence on our Constitution. I believe that formula to be itself a violation of our Constitution, in that it subtly conveys to courts, at the expense of legislatures, ultimate power over public policies in fields where no specific provision of the Constitution limits legislative power.

I cannot consider the Bill of Rights to be an outworn 18th Century "strait jacket" as the *Twining* opinion did. Its provisions may be thought outdated

abstractions by some. And it is true that they were designed to meet ancient evils. But they are the same kind of human evils that have emerged from century to century wherever excessive power is sought by the few at the expense of the many. In my judgment the people of no nation can lose their liberty so long as a Bill of Rights like ours survives and its basic purposes are conscientiously interpreted, enforced and respected so as to afford continuous protection against old, as well as new, devices and practices which might thwart those purposes. I fear to see the consequences of the Court's practice of substituting its own concepts of decency and fundamental justice for the language of the Bill of Rights as its point of departure in interpreting and enforcing that Bill of Rights. If the choice must be between the selective process of the *Palko* decision applying some of the Bill of Rights to the States, or the *Twining* rule applying none of them, I would choose the *Palko* selective process. But rather than accept either of these choices, I would follow what I believe was the original purpose of the Fourteenth Amendment—to extend to all the people of the nation the complete protection of the Bill of Rights. To hold that this Court can determine what, if any provisions of the Bill of Rights will be enforced, and if so to what degree, is to frustrate the great design of a written Constitution.

Conceding the possibility that this Court is now wise enough to improve on the Bill of Rights by substituting natural law concepts for the Bill of Rights, I think the possibility is entirely too speculative to agree to take that course. I would therefore hold in this case that the full protection of the Fifth Amendment's proscription against compelled testimony must be afforded by California. This I would do because of reliance upon the original purpose of the Fourteenth Amendment....

Mr. Justice Murphy, with whom *Mr. Justice Rutledge* concurs, dissenting.

... I agree that the specific guarantees of the Bill of Rights should be carried over intact into the first section of the Fourteenth Amendment. But I am not prepared to say that the latter is entirely and necessarily limited by the Bill of Rights. Occasions may arise where a proceeding falls so far short of conforming to fundamental standards of procedure as to warrant constitutional condemnation in terms of a lack of due process despite the absence of a specific provision in the Bill of Rights.

The point, however, need not be pursued here inasmuch as the Fifth Amendment is explicit in its provision that no person shall be compelled in any criminal case to be a witness against himself. That provision, as Mr. Justice Black demonstrates, is a constituent part of the Fourteenth Amendment....

Much can be said pro and con as to the desirability of allowing comment on the failure of the accused to testify. But policy arguments are to no avail in the face of a clear constitutional command. This guarantee of freedom from self-incrimination is grounded on a deep respect for those who might prefer to remain silent before their accusers. ...

We are obliged to give effect to the principle of freedom from self-incrimination. That principle is as applicable where the compelled testimony is in the form of silence as where it is composed of oral statements. Accordingly, I would reverse the judgment below.

ROCHIN V. CALIFORNIA
342 U.S. 165; 72 S.Ct. 205; 96 L.Ed. 183 (1952)
Vote: 8-0

Here, the Court again considers the meaning of the Due Process Clause of the Fourteenth Amendment and the relationship of the Bill of Rights to the states. Again, the specific issue is that of compulsory self-incrimination. The facts are contained in Justice Frankfurter's majority opinion.

Mr. Justice Frankfurter delivered the opinion of the Court.

Having "some information that [the petitioner] was selling narcotics," three deputy sheriffs of the County of Los Angeles, on the morning of July 1, 1949, made for the two-story dwelling house in which Rochin lived with his mother, common-law wife, brothers and sisters. Finding the outside door open, they entered and then forced open the door to Rochin's room on the second floor. Inside they found petitioner sitting partly dressed on the side of the bed, upon which his wife was lying. On a "night stand" beside the bed the deputies spied two capsules. When asked "Whose stuff is this?" Rochin seized the capsules and put them in his mouth. A struggle ensued, in the course of which the three officers "jumped upon him" and attempted to extract the capsules. The force they applied proved unavailing against Rochin's resistance. He was handcuffed and taken to a hospital. At the direction of one of the officers a doctor forced an emetic solution through a tube into Rochin's stomach against his will. This "stomach pumping" produced vomiting. In the vomited matter were found two capsules which proved to contain morphine.

Rochin was brought to trial before a California Superior Court, sitting without a jury, on the charge of possessing "a preparation of morphine" in violation of the California Health and Safety Code.... Rochin was convicted and sentenced to sixty days' imprisonment. The chief evidence against him was the two capsules. They were admitted over petitioner's objection, although the means of obtaining them was frankly set forth in the testimony by one of the deputies, substantially as here narrated.

On appeal, the District Court of Appeal affirmed the conviction, despite the finding that the officers "were guilty of unlawfully breaking into and entering defendant's room ... and "were guilty of unlawfully assaulting, battering, torturing and falsely imprisoning the defendant at the alleged hospital." ...

This Court granted certiorari, because a serious question is raised as to the limitations which the Due Process Clause of the Fourteenth Amendment imposes on the conduct of criminal proceedings by the States....

In our federal system the administration of criminal justice is predominantly committed to the care of the States. The power to define crimes belongs to Congress only as an appropriate means of carrying into execution its limited grant of legislative powers. Broadly speaking, crimes in the United States are what the laws of the individual States make them, subject to the limitations ... in the original Constitution, prohibiting bills of attainder and ex post facto laws, and of the Thirteenth and Fourteenth Amendments.

These limitations, in the main, concern not restrictions upon the powers of the States to define crime, except in the restricted area where federal authority has preempted the field, but restrictions upon the manner in which the States may enforce their penal codes. Accordingly, in reviewing a State criminal conviction under a claim of right guaranteed by the Due Process

(Continued)

Clause of the Fourteenth Amendment, ... "we must be deeply mindful of the responsibilities of the States for the enforcement of criminal laws, and exercise with due humility our merely negative function in subjecting convictions from state courts to the very narrow scrutiny which the Due Process Clause of the Fourteenth Amendment authorizes." Due process of law is not to be turned into a destructive dogma against the States in the administration of their systems of criminal justice.

However, this Court too has its responsibility. Regard for the requirements of the Due Process Clause "inescapably imposes upon this Court an exercise of judgment upon the whole course of the proceedings [resulting in a conviction] in order to ascertain whether they offend those canons of decency and fairness which express the notions of justice of English-speaking peoples even toward those charged with the most heinous offenses."... These standards of justice are not authoritatively formulated anywhere as though they were specifics. Due process of law is a summarized constitutional guarantee of respect for those personal immunities which, as Mr. Justice Cardozo twice wrote for the Court, are "so rooted in the traditions and conscience of our people as to be ranked as fundamental," ... or are "implicit in the concept of ordered liberty." ...

Due process of law thus conceived is not to be derided as resort to a revival of "natural law." To believe that this judicial exercise of judgment could be avoided by freezing "due process of law" at some fixed stage of time or thought is to suggest that the most important aspect of constitutional adjudication is a function for inanimate machines and not for judges, for whom the independence safeguarded by Article 3 of the Constitution was designed and who are presumably guided by established standards of judicial behavior. ...

Restraints on our jurisdiction are self-imposed only in the sense that there is from our decisions no immediate appeal short of impeachment or constitutional amendment. But that does not make due process of law a matter of judicial caprice. The faculties of the Due Process Clause may be indefinite and vague, but the mode of their ascertainment is not self-willed. In each case "due process of law" requires an evaluation based on a disinterested inquiry pursued in the spirit of science, on a balanced order of facts exactly and fairly stated, on the detached consideration of conflicting claims....

Applying these general considerations to the circumstances of the present case, we are compelled to conclude that the proceedings by which this conviction was obtained do more than offend some fastidious squeamishness or private sentimentalism about combating crime too energetically. This is conduct that shocks the conscience. Illegally breaking into the *privacy* of the petitioner, the struggle to open his mouth and remove what was there, the forcible extraction of his stomach's contents—this course of proceeding by agents of government to obtain evidence is bound to offend even hardened sensibilities. They are methods too close to the rack and the screw to permit of constitutional differentiation.

It has long since ceased to be true that due process of law is heedless of the means by which otherwise relevant and credible evidence is obtained. This was not true even before the series of recent cases enforced the constitutional principle that the States may not base convictions upon confessions, however much verified, obtained by coercion. These decisions are not arbitrary exceptions to the comprehensive right of States to fashion their own rules of evidence for criminal trials. They are not sports in our constitutional law but applications of a general principle. They are only instances of the general requirement that States in their prosecutions respect certain decencies of civilized conduct. Due process of law, as a historic and generative principle, precludes defining, and thereby confining, these standards of conduct more precisely than to say that convictions cannot be brought about by methods that offend "a sense of justice." It would be a stultification of the responsibility which the course of constitutional history has cast upon this Court to hold that in order to convict a man the police cannot extract by force what is in his mind but can extract what is in his stomach.

To attempt in this case to distinguish what lawyers call "real evidence" from verbal evidence is to ignore the reasons for excluding coerced confessions. Use of involuntary verbal confessions in State criminal trials is constitutionally obnoxious not only because of their unreliability. They are inadmissible under the Due Process Clause even though statements contained in them may be independently established as true. Coerced confessions offend the community's sense of fair play and decency. So here, to sanction the brutal conduct which naturally enough was condemned by the court whose judgment is before us, would be to afford brutality the cloak of law. Nothing would be more calculated to discredit law and thereby to brutalize the temper of a society.

Mr. Justice Minton took no part in the consideration or decision of this case.

Mr. Justice Black, concurring.

Adamson v. California ... sets out reasons for my belief that state as well as federal courts and law enforcement officers must obey the Fifth Amendment's command that "No person ... shall be compelled in any criminal case to be a witness against himself." I think a person is compelled to be a witness against himself not only when he is compelled to testify, but also when as here, incriminating evidence is forcibly taken from him by a contrivance of modern science....

Some constitutional provisions are stated in absolute and unqualified language such, for illustration, as the First Amendment stating that no law shall be passed prohibiting the free exercise of religion or abridging the freedom of speech or press. Other constitutional provisions do require courts to choose between competing policies, such as the Fourth Amendment which, by its terms, necessitates a judicial decision as to what is an "unreasonable" search or seizure. There is, however, no express constitutional language granting judicial power to invalidate every state law of every kind deemed "unreasonable" or contrary to the Court's notion of civilized decencies; yet the constitutional philosophy used by the majority has, in the past, been used to deny a state the right to fix the price of gasoline, and even the right to prevent bakers from palming off smaller for larger loaves of bread. These cases, and others, show the extent to which the evanescent standards of the majority's philosophy have been used to nullify state legislative programs passed to suppress evil economic practices. What paralyzing role this same philosophy will play in the future economic affairs of this country is impossible to predict. Of even graver concern, however, is the use of the philosophy to nullify the Bill of Rights. I long ago concluded that the accordion-like qualities of this philosophy must inevitably imperil all the individual liberty safeguards specifically enumerated in the Bill of Rights. Recent decisions of this Court sanctioning abridgment of the freedom of speech and press have strengthened this conclusion.

Mr. Justice Douglas, concurring....

DUNCAN V. LOUISIANA
391 U.S. 145; 88 S.Ct. 1444; 20 L.Ed. 2d 491 (1968)
Vote: 7-2

This case raises the question of whether, and under what circumstances, the Due Process Clause of the Fourteenth Amendment incorporates the Sixth Amendment guarantee of trial by jury in a criminal case. The facts are set forth in Justice White's majority opinion.

Mr. Justice White delivered the opinion of the Court.

Appellant, Gary Duncan, was convicted of simple battery in the Twenty-fifth Judicial District Court of Louisiana. Under Louisiana law simple battery is a misdemeanor, punishable by a maximum of two years' imprisonment and a $300 fine. Appellant sought trial by jury, but because the Louisiana Constitution grants jury trials only in cases in which capital punishment or imprisonment at hard labor may be imposed, the trial judge denied the request. Appellant was convicted and sentenced to serve 60 days in the parish prison and pay a fine of $150. Appellant sought review in the Supreme Court of Louisiana, asserting that the denial of jury trial violated rights guaranteed to him by the United States Constitution. The Supreme Court, finding "[n]o error of law in the ruling complained of," denied appellant a writ of certiorari.... [A]ppellant sought review in this Court, alleging that the Sixth and Fourteenth Amendments to the United States Constitution secure the right to jury trial in state criminal prosecutions where a sentence as long as two years may be imposed....

Appellant was 19 years of age when tried. While driving on Highway 23 in Plaquemines Parish on October 18, 1966, he saw two younger cousins engaged in a conversation by the side of the road with four white boys. Knowing his cousins, Negroes who had recently transferred to a formerly all-white high school, had reported the occurrence of racial incidents at the school, Duncan stopped the car, got out, and approached the six boys. At trial the white boys and white onlooker testified, as did appellant and his cousins. The testimony was in dispute on many points, but the witnesses agreed that appellant and the white boys spoke to each other, that appellant encouraged his cousins to break off the encounter and enter his car, and

(Continued)

that appellant was about to enter the car himself for the purpose of driving away with his cousins. The whites testified that just before getting in the car appellant slapped Herman Landry, one of the white boys, on the elbow. The Negroes testified that appellant had not slapped Landry, but had merely touched him. The trial judge concluded that the State had proved beyond a reasonable doubt that Duncan had committed simple battery, and found him guilty....

The Fourteenth Amendment denies the States the power to "deprive any person of life, liberty, or property, without due process of law." In resolving conflicting claims concerning the meaning of this spacious language, the Court has looked increasingly to the Bill of Rights for guidance; many of the rights guaranteed by the first eight Amendments to the Constitution have been held to be protected against state action by the Due Process Clause of the Fourteenth Amendment. That clause now protects the right to compensation for property taken by the State; the rights of speech, press, and religion covered by the First Amendment; the Fourth Amendment rights to be free from unreasonable searches and seizures and to have excluded from criminal trials any evidence illegally seized; the right guaranteed by the Fifth Amendment to be free of compelled self-incrimination; and the Sixth Amendment rights to counsel, to a speedy and public trial, to confrontation of opposing witnesses, and to compulsory process for obtaining witnesses.

The test for determining whether a right extended by the Fifth and Sixth Amendments with respect to federal criminal proceedings is also protected against state action by the Fourteenth Amendment has been phrased in a variety of ways in the opinions of this Court. The question has been asked whether a right is among those "fundamental principles of liberty and justice which lie at the base of all our civil and political institutions," ... whether it is "basic in our system of jurisprudence," ... and whether it is "a fundamental right, essential to a fair trial."... The claim before us is that the right to trial by jury guaranteed by the Sixth Amendment meets these tests. The position of Louisiana, on the other hand, is that the Constitution imposes upon the States no duty to give a jury trial in any criminal case, regardless of the seriousness of the crime or the size of the punishment which may be imposed. Because we believe that trial by jury in criminal cases is fundamental to the American scheme of justice, we hold that the Fourteenth Amendment guarantees a right of jury trial in all criminal cases which—were they to be tried in a federal court—would come within the Sixth Amendment's guarantee. Since we consider the appeal before us to be such a case, we

hold that the Constitution was violated when appellant's demand for jury trial was refused. ...

We are aware of prior cases in this Court in which the prevailing opinion contains statements contrary to our holding today that the right to jury trial in serious criminal cases is a fundamental right and hence must be recognized by the States as part of their obligation to extend due process of law to all persons within their jurisdiction.... None of these cases, however, dealt with a State which had purported to dispense entirely with a jury trial in serious criminal cases....

The guarantees of jury trial in the Federal and State Constitutions reflect a profound judgment about the way in which law should be enforced and justice administered. A right to jury trial is granted to criminal defendants in order to prevent oppression by the Government....

The State of Louisiana urges that holding that the Fourteenth Amendment assures a right to jury trial will cast doubt on the integrity of every trial conducted without a jury. Plainly, this is not the import of our holding. Our conclusion is that in the American States, as in the federal judicial system, a general grant of jury trial for serious offenses is a fundamental right, essential for preventing miscarriages of justice and for assuring that fair trials are provided for all defendants. We would not assert, however, that every criminal trial—or any particular trial—held before a judge alone is unfair or that a defendant may never be as fairly treated by a judge as he would be by a jury. Thus we hold no constitutional doubts about the practices, common in both federal and state courts, of accepting waivers of jury trial and prosecuting petty crimes without extending a right to jury trial. However, the fact is that in most places more trials for serious crimes are to juries than to a court alone; a great many defendants prefer the judgment of a jury to that of a court. Even where defendants are satisfied with bench trials, the right to a jury trial very likely serves its intended purpose of making judicial or prosecutorial unfairness less likely.

Louisiana's final contention is that even if it must grant jury trials in serious criminal cases, the conviction before us is valid and constitutional because here the petitioner was tried for simple battery and was sentenced to only 60 days in the parish prison. We are not persuaded. It is doubtless true that there is a category of petty crimes or offenses which is not subject to the Sixth Amendment jury trial provision and should not be subject to the Fourteenth Amendment jury trial requirement here applied to the States. Crimes carrying possible penalties up to six months do not require a jury trial if they otherwise qualify as petty offenses....

The question, then, is whether a crime carrying such a penalty is an offense which Louisiana may insist on trying without a jury.

We think not. So-called petty offenses were tried without juries both in England and in the Colonies and have always been held to be exempt from the otherwise comprehensive language of the Sixth Amendment's jury trial provisions. There is no substantial evidence that the Framers intended to depart from this established common-law practice, and the possible consequences to defendants from convictions for petty offenses have been thought insufficient to outweigh the benefits to efficient law enforcement and simplified judicial administration resulting from the availability of speedy and inexpensive nonjury adjudications. These same considerations compel the same result under the Fourteenth Amendment. Of course the boundaries of the petty offense category have always been ill defined, if not ambulatory....

... We need not, however, settle in this case the exact location of the line between petty offenses and serious crimes. It is sufficient for our purposes to hold that a crime punishable by two years in prison is, based on past and contemporary standards in this country, a serious crime and not a petty offense. Consequently appellant was entitled to a jury trial and it was error to deny it....

Mr. Justice Fortas, concurring....

Mr. Justice Black, with whom *Mr. Justice Douglas* joins, concurring.

... I believe as strongly as ever that the Fourteenth Amendment was intended to make the Bill of Rights applicable to the States. I have been willing to support the selective incorporation doctrine, however, as an alternative, although perhaps less historically supportable than complete incorporation. The selective incorporation process, if used properly, does limit the Supreme Court in the Fourteenth Amendment field to specific Bill of Rights' protections only and keeps judges from roaming at will in their own notions of what policies outside the Bill of Rights are desirable and what are not. And, most importantly for me, the selective incorporation process has the virtue of having already worked to make most of the Bill of Rights' protections applicable to the States.

Mr. Justice Harlan, whom *Mr. Justice Stewart* joins, dissenting.

... The question before us is not whether jury trial is an ancient institution, which it is; nor whether it plays a significant role in the administration of criminal justice, which it does; nor whether it will endure, which it shall. The question in this case is whether the State of Louisiana, which provides trial by jury for all felonies, is prohibited by the Constitution from trying charges of simple battery to the court alone. In my view, the answer to that question, mandated alike by our constitutional history and by the longer history of trial by jury, is clearly "no."

The States have always borne primary responsibility for operating the machinery of criminal justice within their borders, and adapting it to their particular circumstances. In exercising this responsibility, each State is compelled to conform its procedures to the requirements of the Federal Constitution. The Due Process Clause of the Fourteenth Amendment requires that those procedures be fundamentally fair in all respects. It does not, in my view, impose or encourage nationwide uniformity for its own sake; it does not command adherence to forms that happen to be old; and it does not impose on the State the rules that may be in force in the federal courts except where such rules are also found to be essential to basic fairness.

The Court's approach to this case is an uneasy and illogical compromise among the views of various Justices on how the Due Process Clause should be interpreted. The Court does not say that those who framed the Fourteenth Amendment intended to make the Sixth Amendment applicable to the States, and the Court concedes that it finds nothing unfair about the procedure by which the present appellant was tried. Nevertheless, the Court reverses his conviction: it holds, for some reason not apparent to me, that the Due Process Clause incorporates the particular clause of the Sixth Amendment that requires trial by jury in federal criminal cases—including, as I read its opinion, the sometimes trivial accompanying baggage of judicial interpretation in federal contexts. I have raised my voice many times before against the Court's continuing undiscriminating insistence upon fastening on the States federal notions of criminal justice, and I must do so again in this instance. With all respect, the Court's approach and its reading of history are altogether topsy-turvy....

MCDONALD V. CHICAGO
561 U.S., 130 S. Ct. 3020, 177 L.Ed.2d 894 (2010)
Vote: 5-4

In this landmark decision, the Supreme Court considers the constitutionality of ordinances adopted by Chicago and Oak Park, Illinois, effectively banning the possession of handguns in the home.

Justice Alito announced the judgment of the Court and delivered the opinion of the Court with respect to Parts I, II-A, II-B, II-D, III-A, and III-B, in which **The Chief Justice**, **Justice Scalia**, **Justice Kennedy**, and **Justice Thomas** join, and an opinion with respect to Parts II-C, IV, and V, in which **The Chief Justice**, **Justice Scalia**, and **Justice Kennedy** join.

Two years ago, in *District of Columbia v. Heller* (2008), we held that the Second Amendment protects the right to keep and bear arms for the purpose of self-defense, and we struck down a District of Columbia law that banned the possession of handguns in the home. The city of Chicago (City) and the village of Oak Park, a Chicago suburb, have laws that are similar to the District of Columbia's, but Chicago and Oak Park argue that their laws are constitutional because the Second Amendment has no application to the States. We have previously held that most of the provisions of the Bill of Rights apply with full force to both the Federal Government and the States. Applying the standard that is well established in our case law, we hold that the Second Amendment right is fully applicable to the States.

I

Otis McDonald, Adam Orlov, Colleen Lawson, and David Lawson (Chicago petitioners) are Chicago residents who would like to keep handguns in their homes for self-defense but are prohibited from doing so by Chicago's firearms laws. A City ordinance provides that "[n]o person shall ... possess ... any firearm unless such person is the holder of a valid registration certificate for such firearm." The Code then prohibits registration of most handguns, thus effectively banning handgun possession by almost all private citizens who reside in the City. Like Chicago, Oak Park makes it "unlawful for any person to possess ... any firearm," a term that includes "pistols, revolvers, guns and small arms ... commonly known as handguns."

Chicago enacted its handgun ban to protect its residents "from the loss of property and injury or death from firearms." ... The Chicago petitioners and their *amici*,

however, argue that the handgun ban has left them vulnerable to criminals. Chicago Police Department statistics, we are told, reveal that the City's handgun murder rate has actually increased since the ban was enacted and that Chicago residents now face one of the highest murder rates in the country and rates of other violent crimes that exceed the average in comparable cities.

After our decision in *Heller*, the Chicago petitioners and two groups filed suit against the City in the United States District Court for the Northern District of Illinois. They sought a declaration that the handgun ban and several related Chicago ordinances violate the Second and Fourteenth Amendments to the United States Constitution....

The District Court rejected plaintiffs' argument that the Chicago and Oak Park laws are unconstitutional....

The Seventh Circuit affirmed....

We granted certiorari....

II

Petitioners argue that the Chicago and Oak Park laws violate the right to keep and bear arms for two reasons. Petitioners' primary submission is that this right is among the "privileges or immunities of citizens of the United States" and that the narrow interpretation of the Privileges or Immunities Clause ... should now be rejected. As a secondary argument, petitioners contend that the Fourteenth Amendment's Due Process Clause "incorporates" the Second Amendment right.

Chicago and Oak Park (municipal respondents) maintain that a right set out in the Bill of Rights applies to the States only if that right is an indispensable attribute of *any* "civilized" legal system.... If it is possible to imagine a civilized country that does not recognize the right, the municipal respondents tell us, then that right is not protected by due process.... And since there are civilized countries that ban or strictly regulate the private possession of handguns, the municipal respondents maintain that due process does not preclude such measures....

III

[W]e ... turn directly to the question whether the Second Amendment right to keep and bear arms is incorporated in the concept of due process. In answering that question, as just explained, we must decide whether the right to keep and bear arms is fundamental to *our* scheme of ordered liberty ... or as we have said in a related context, whether this right is "deeply rooted in this Nation's history and tradition." ...

A

Our decision in *Heller* points unmistakably to the answer. Self-defense is a basic right, recognized by many legal systems from ancient times to the present day, and in *Heller*, we held that individual self-defense is "the *central component* " of the Second Amendment right.... Explaining that "the need for defense of self, family, and property is most acute" in the home, we found that ... citizens must be permitted "to use [handguns] for the core lawful purpose of self-defense." ...

... The right to keep and bear arms was considered no less fundamental by those who drafted and ratified the Bill of Rights. "During the 1788 ratification debates, the fear that the federal government would disarm the people in order to impose rule through a standing army or select militia was pervasive in Antifederalist rhetoric." ... Federalists responded, not by arguing that the right was insufficiently important to warrant protection but by contending that the right was adequately protected by the Constitution's assignment of only limited powers to the Federal Government.... Thus, Antifederalists and Federalists alike agreed that the right to bear arms was fundamental to the newly formed system of government.... This is surely powerful evidence that the right was regarded as fundamental in the sense relevant here....

B

1 By the 1850's, the perceived threat that had prompted the inclusion of the Second Amendment in the Bill of Rights—the fear that the National Government would disarm the universal militia—had largely faded as a popular concern, but the right to keep and bear arms was highly valued for purposes of self-defense....

Throughout the South, armed parties, often consisting of ex-Confederate soldiers serving in the state militias, forcibly took firearms from newly freed slaves....

Union Army commanders took steps to secure the right of all citizens to keep and bear arms, but the 39th Congress concluded that legislative action was necessary. Its efforts to safeguard the right to keep and bear arms demonstrate that the right was still recognized to be fundamental.

The most explicit evidence of Congress' aim appears in §14 of the Freedmen's Bureau Act of 1866, which provided that "the right ... to have full and equal benefit of all laws and proceedings concerning personal liberty, personal security, and the acquisition, enjoyment, and disposition of estate, real and personal, *including the constitutional right to bear arms*, shall be secured to and enjoyed by all the citizens ... without respect to race or color, or previous condition of slavery."

The Civil Rights Act of 1866, ... which was considered at the same time as the Freedmen's Bureau Act, similarly sought to protect the right of all citizens to keep and bear arms. ... The Civil Rights Act, like the Freedmen's Bureau Act, aimed to protect "the constitutional right to bear arms" and not simply to prohibit discrimination....

Congress, however, ultimately deemed these legislative remedies insufficient. Southern resistance, Presidential vetoes, and this Court's pre-Civil-War precedent persuaded Congress that a constitutional amendment was necessary to provide full protection for the rights of blacks. Today, it is generally accepted that the Fourteenth Amendment was understood to provide a constitutional basis for protecting the rights set out in the Civil Rights Act of 1866....

In sum, it is clear that the Framers and ratifiers of the Fourteenth Amendment counted the right to keep and bear arms among those fundamental rights necessary to our system of ordered liberty.

2 Despite all this evidence, municipal respondents contend that Congress, in the years immediately following the Civil War, merely sought to outlaw "discriminatory measures taken against freedmen, which it addressed by adopting a non-discrimination principle" and that even an outright ban on the possession of firearms was regarded as acceptable, "so long as it was not done in a discriminatory manner." ... They argue that Members of Congress overwhelmingly viewed §1 of the Fourteenth Amendment "as an antidiscrimination rule," and they cite statements to the effect that the section would outlaw discriminatory measures.... This argument is implausible.

[W]hile §1 of the Fourteenth Amendment contains "an antidiscrimination rule," namely, the Equal Protection Clause, municipal respondents can hardly mean that §1 does no more than prohibit discrimination. If that were so, then the First Amendment, as applied to the States, would not prohibit nondiscriminatory abridgments of the rights to freedom of speech or freedom of religion; the Fourth Amendment, as applied to the States, would not prohibit all unreasonable searches

(Continued)

and seizures but only discriminatory searches and seizures—and so on. We assume that this is not municipal respondents' view, so what they must mean is that the Second Amendment should be singled out for special—and specially unfavorable—treatment. We reject that suggestion....

IV

Municipal respondents' remaining arguments are at war with our central holding in *Heller*, that the Second Amendment protects a personal right to keep and bear arms for lawful purposes, most notably for self-defense within the home. Municipal respondents, in effect, ask us to treat the right recognized in *Heller* as a second-class right, subject to an entirely different body of rules than the other Bill of Rights guarantees that we have held to be incorporated into the Due Process Clause.

Municipal respondents' main argument is nothing less than a plea to disregard 50 years of incorporation precedent and return (presumably for this case only) to a bygone era. Municipal respondents submit that the Due Process Clause protects only those rights "recognized by all temperate and civilized governments, from a deep and universal sense of [their] justice." ... According to municipal respondents, if it is possible to imagine *any* civilized legal system that does not recognize a particular right, then the Due Process Clause does not make that right binding on the States.... Therefore, the municipal respondents continue, because such countries as England, Canada, Australia, Japan, Denmark, Finland, Luxembourg, and New Zealand either ban or severely limit handgun ownership, it must follow that no right to possess such weapons is protected by the Fourteenth Amendment....

This line of argument is, of course, inconsistent with the long-established standard we apply in incorporation cases.... And the present-day implications of municipal respondents' argument are stunning. For example, many of the rights that our Bill of Rights provides for persons accused of criminal offenses are virtually unique to this country. If *our* understanding of the right to a jury trial, the right against self-incrimination, and the right to counsel were necessary attributes *of any* civilized country, it would follow that the United States is the only civilized Nation in the world....

Municipal respondents maintain that the Second Amendment differs from all of the other provisions of the Bill of Rights because it concerns the right to possess a deadly implement and thus has implications for public safety.... And they note that there is intense disagreement on the question whether the private possession of guns in the home increases or decreases gun deaths and injuries....

The right to keep and bear arms, however, is not the only constitutional right that has controversial public safety implications. All of the constitutional provisions that impose restrictions on law enforcement and on the prosecution of crimes fall into the same category....

Municipal respondents assert that, although most state constitutions protect firearms rights, state courts have held that these rights are subject to "interest-balancing" and have sustained a variety of restrictions.... In *Heller*, however, we expressly rejected the argument that the scope of the Second Amendment right should be determined by judicial interest balancing, ... and this Court decades ago abandoned "the notion that the Fourteenth Amendment applies to the States only a watered-down, subjective version of the individual guarantees of the Bill of Rights," ...

... It is important to keep in mind that *Heller*, while striking down a law that prohibited the possession of handguns in the home, recognized that the right to keep and bear arms is not "a right to keep and carry any weapon whatsoever in any manner whatsoever and for whatever purpose." ... We made it clear in *Heller* that our holding did not cast doubt on such longstanding regulatory measures as "prohibitions on the possession of firearms by felons and the mentally ill," "laws forbidding the carrying of firearms in sensitive places such as schools and government buildings, or laws imposing conditions and qualifications on the commercial sale of arms." ... We repeat those assurances here. Despite municipal respondents' doomsday proclamations, incorporation does not imperil every law regulating firearms.

Municipal respondents argue, finally, that the right to keep and bear arms is unique among the rights set out in the first eight Amendments "because the reason for codifying the Second Amendment (to protect the militia) differs from the purpose (primarily, to use firearms to engage in self-defense) that is claimed to make the right implicit in the concept of ordered liberty." ... Municipal respondents suggest that the Second Amendment right differs from the rights heretofore incorporated because the latter were "valued for [their] own sake." ... But we have never previously suggested that incorporation of a right turns on whether it has intrinsic as opposed to instrumental value, and quite a few of the rights previously held to be incorporated—for example the right to counsel and the right to confront and subpoena witnesses—are clearly instrumental by any measure. Moreover, this contention repackages one of the chief arguments that we rejected in *Heller*, i.e., that the scope of the Second Amendment right is defined by the immediate threat that led to the inclusion of that right in the Bill of Rights. In *Heller*, we recognized that the codification of this right was prompted by fear that the Federal Government would disarm and thus disable the militias, but we rejected the suggestion that the right was valued only as a means of preserving the militias…. On the contrary, we stressed that the right was also valued because the possession of firearms was thought to be essential for self-defense. As we put it, self-defense was "the *central component* of the right itself." …

Justice Scalia, concurring. …

Justice Thomas, concurring in part and concurring in the judgment.

I agree with the Court that the Fourteenth Amendment makes the right to keep and bear arms set forth in the Second Amendment "fully applicable to the States." … I write separately because I believe there is a more straightforward path to this conclusion, one that is more faithful to the Fourteenth Amendment's text and history.

Applying what is now a well-settled test, the plurality opinion concludes that the right to keep and bear arms applies to the States through the Fourteenth Amendment's Due Process Clause because it is "fundamental" to the American "scheme of ordered liberty," … and "deeply rooted in this Nation's history and tradition." I agree with that description of the right. But I cannot agree that it is enforceable against the States through a clause that speaks only to "process." Instead, the right to keep and bear arms is a privilege of American citizenship that applies to the States through the Fourteenth Amendment's Privileges or Immunities Clause….

In my view, the record makes plain that the Framers of the Privileges or Immunities Clause and the ratifying-era public understood—just as the Framers of the Second Amendment did—that the right to keep and bear arms was essential to the preservation of liberty. The record makes equally plain that they deemed this right necessary to include in the minimum baseline of federal rights that the Privileges or Immunities Clause established in the wake of the War over slavery….

Justice Stevens, dissenting.

In *District of Columbia v. Heller* (2008), the Court answered the question whether a federal enclave's "prohibition on the possession of usable handguns in the home violates the Second Amendment to the Constitution." The question we should be answering in this case is whether the Constitution "guarantees individuals a fundamental right," enforceable against the States, "to possess a functional, personal firearm, including a handgun, within the home." … That is a different—and more difficult—inquiry than asking if the Fourteenth Amendment "incorporates" the Second Amendment….

… [W]hile "the 'liberty' specially protected by the Fourteenth Amendment" is "perhaps not capable of being fully clarified," … it is capable of being refined and delimited. We have insisted that only certain types of especially significant personal interests may qualify for especially heightened protection. Ever since "the deviant economic due process cases [were] repudiated," … our doctrine has steered away from "laws that touch economic problems, business affairs, or social conditions," … and has instead centered on "matters relating to marriage, procreation, contraception, family relationships, and child rearing and education." … These categories are not exclusive. Government action that shocks the conscience, pointlessly infringes settled expectations, trespasses into sensitive private realms or life choices without adequate justification, perpetrates gross injustice, or simply lacks a rational basis will always be vulnerable to judicial invalidation. Nor does the fact that an asserted right falls within one of these categories end the inquiry. More fundamental rights may receive more robust judicial protection, but the strength of the individual's liberty interests and the State's regulatory interests must always be assessed and compared. No right is absolute. …

The question in this case, then, is not whether the Second Amendment right to keep and bear arms (whatever that right's precise contours) applies to the States because the Amendment has been incorporated into the Fourteenth Amendment. It has not been. The question, rather, is whether the particular right asserted by petitioners applies to the States because of the Fourteenth Amendment itself, standing on its own bottom. And to answer that question, we need to determine, first, the nature of the right that has been asserted and, second, whether that right is an aspect of Fourteenth Amendment "liberty." …

While I agree with the Court that our substantive due process cases offer a principled basis for holding that petitioners have a constitutional right to possess a usable firearm in the home, I am ultimately persuaded

(*Continued*)

that a better reading of our case law supports the city of Chicago. I would not foreclose the possibility that a particular plaintiff—say, an elderly widow who lives in a dangerous neighborhood and does not have the strength to operate a long gun—may have a cognizable liberty interest in possessing a handgun. But I cannot accept petitioners' broader submission. A number of factors, taken together, lead me to this conclusion.

First, firearms have a fundamentally ambivalent relationship to liberty. Just as they can help homeowners defend their families and property from intruders, they can help thugs and insurrectionists murder innocent victims....

Hence, in evaluating an asserted right to be free from particular gun-control regulations, liberty is on both sides of the equation. Guns may be useful for self-defense, as well as for hunting and sport, but they also have a unique potential to facilitate death and destruction and thereby to destabilize ordered liberty. *Your* interest in keeping and bearing a certain firearm may diminish *my* interest in being and feeling safe from armed violence. And while granting you the right to own a handgun might make you safer on any given day—assuming the handgun's marginal contribution to self-defense outweighs its marginal contribution to the risk of accident, suicide, and criminal mischief—it may make you and the community you live in less safe overall, owing to the increased number of handguns in circulation. It is at least reasonable for a democratically elected legislature to take such concerns into account in considering what sorts of regulations would best serve the public welfare....

Limiting the federal constitutional right to keep and bear arms to the home complicates the analysis but does not dislodge this conclusion. Even though the Court has long afforded special solicitude for the privacy of the home, we have never understood that principle to "infring[e] upon" the authority of the States to proscribe certain inherently dangerous items, for "[i]n such cases, compelling reasons may exist for overriding the right of the individual to possess those materials." ... And, of course, guns that start out in the home may not stay in the home. Even if the government has a weaker basis for restricting domestic possession of firearms as compared to public carriage—and even if a blanket, statewide prohibition on domestic possession might therefore be unconstitutional—the line between the two is a porous one. A state or local legislature may determine that a prophylactic ban on an especially portable weapon is necessary to police that line.

Second, the right to possess a firearm of one's choosing is different in kind from the liberty interests

we have recognized under the Due Process Clause. Despite the plethora of substantive due process cases that have been decided in the *post-Lochner* century, I have found none that holds, states, or even suggests that the term "liberty" encompasses either the common-law right of self-defense or a right to keep and bear arms....

Indeed, in some respects the substantive right at issue may be better viewed as a property right. Petitioners wish to *acquire* certain types of firearms, or to *keep* certain firearms they have previously acquired. Interests in the possession of chattels have traditionally been viewed as property interests subject to definition and regulation by the States.... Under that tradition, Chicago's ordinance is unexceptional.

The liberty interest asserted by petitioners is also dissimilar from those we have recognized in its capacity to undermine the security of others. To be sure, some of the Bill of Rights' procedural guarantees may place "restrictions on law enforcement" that have "controversial public safety implications." ... But those implications are generally quite attenuated. A defendant's invocation of his right to remain silent, to confront a witness, or to exclude certain evidence cannot directly cause any threat. The defendant's liberty interest is constrained by (and is itself a constraint on) the adjudicatory process. The link between handgun ownership and public safety is much tighter. The handgun is itself a tool for crime; the handgun's bullets *are* the violence....

Third, the experience of other advanced democracies, including those that share our British heritage, undercuts the notion that an expansive right to keep and bear arms is intrinsic to ordered liberty. Many of these countries place restrictions on the possession, use, and carriage of firearms far more onerous than the restrictions found in this Nation.... That the United States is an international outlier in the permissiveness of its approach to guns does not suggest that our laws are bad laws. It does suggest that this Court may not need to assume responsibility for making our laws still more permissive.

Admittedly, these other countries differ from ours in many relevant respects, including their problems with violent crime and the traditional role that firearms have played in their societies. But they are not so different from the United States that we ought to dismiss their experience entirely....

Fourth, the Second Amendment differs in kind from the Amendments that surround it, with the consequence that its inclusion in the Bill of Rights is not merely unhelpful but positively harmful to petitioners' claim. Generally, the inclusion of a liberty interest in the

Bill of Rights points toward the conclusion that it is of fundamental significance and ought to be enforceable against the States. But the Second Amendment plays a peculiar role within the Bill, as announced by its peculiar opening clause. Even accepting the *Heller* Court's view that the Amendment protects an individual right to keep and bear arms disconnected from militia service, it remains undeniable that "the purpose for which the right was codified" was "to prevent elimination of the militia." ... It was the States, not private persons, on whose immediate behalf the Second Amendment was adopted. ...

The Second Amendment, in other words, "is a federalism provision." ... It is directed at preserving the autonomy of the sovereign States, and its logic therefore "resists" incorporation by a federal court *against* the States....

Fifth, although it may be true that Americans' interest in firearm possession and state-law recognition of that interest are "deeply rooted" in some important senses, ... it is equally true that the States have a long and unbroken history of regulating firearms. The idea that States may place substantial restrictions on the right to keep and bear arms short of complete disarmament is, in fact, far more entrenched than the notion that the Federal Constitution protects any such right. Federalism is a far "older and more deeply rooted tradition than is a right to carry," or to own, "any particular kind of weapon." ...

Justice Breyer, with whom *Justice Ginsburg* and *Justice Sotomayor* join, dissenting.

In my view, Justice Stevens has demonstrated that the Fourteenth Amendment's guarantee of "substantive due process" does not include a general right to keep and bear firearms for purposes of private self-defense. As he argues, the Framers did not write the Second Amendment with this objective in view.... Unlike other forms of substantive liberty, the carrying of arms for that purpose often puts others' lives at risk.... And the use of arms for private self-defense does not warrant federal constitutional protection from state regulation....

The Court, however, does not expressly rest its opinion upon "substantive due process" concerns. Rather, it directs its attention to this Court's "incorporation" precedents and asks whether the Second Amendment right to private self-defense is "fundamental" so that it applies to the States through the Fourteenth Amendment....

I shall therefore separately consider the question of "incorporation." I can find nothing in the Second Amendment's text, history, or underlying rationale that could warrant characterizing it as "fundamental" insofar as it seeks to protect the keeping and bearing of arms for private self-defense purposes. Nor can I find any justification for interpreting the Constitution as transferring ultimate regulatory authority over the private uses of firearms from democratically elected legislatures to courts or from the States to the Federal Government. I therefore conclude that the Fourteenth Amendment does not "incorporate" the Second Amendment's right "to keep and bear Arms." And I consequently dissent....

CHAPTER **2**

Property Rights and Economic Freedom

"The great and chief end ... of Men's uniting into Commonwealths, and putting themselves under Government, is the preservation of their property."

—*John Locke,* Second Treatise of Government

Historical Pictures/Stock Montage

John Locke: The English philosopher whose ideas exerted profound influence on the American founders

Introduction

The twin pillars of any **capitalist economy** are **private property** and **contracts**. For a capitalist system to flourish, it is imperative that there are legal protections for private property and legal enforcement of contracts. Unquestionably, the protection of private property and contractual relationships was particularly important to the Framers of the Constitution. This chapter focuses on historic Supreme Court decisions balancing individual **property rights** and claims of **economic freedom** against the **police power**, both of the states and the national government, to protect the health, safety, and general welfare of the community. The term *property rights* includes the ownership, acquisition, and use of private property, whereas *economic freedom* denotes the cluster of rights associated with private enterprise.

The Influence of John Locke

Americans of the eighteenth century, including those who wrote the Constitution and Bill of Rights, generally accepted the theory of **natural rights** as expounded by the English philosopher John Locke. According to Locke, basic rights to life, liberty, and property were grounded in natural law. Therefore, they were universal and timeless, transcending government and human law. Natural rights could not be taken from citizens by government because they were not given to citizens by government. According to Locke's theory of the **social contract**, individuals living originally in a "state of nature" (anarchy) subordinated themselves to civil government in exchange for the protection of fundamental rights to life, liberty, and property. Government was in turn limited in the means by which it could interfere with the use of property and the exercise of other individual rights. Of course, the very existence of social order presumed some loss of personal and economic freedom. To protect individual rights and advance the public good, government might restrict liberty and might even take private property for public use. But in the latter instance, it would have to provide just compensation to the previous owner, and in limiting individual liberty, it would be required to act reasonably. In short, under this social contract theory, governmental restrictions would be minimal, outweighed by the high priority afforded to individual rights.

This Lockean perspective is reflected in the Contracts Clause (Article I, Section 10) of the Constitution. It is also easily recognized in the Due Process Clauses of the Fifth and Fourteenth Amendments, as well as in the Fifth Amendment provision that private property shall not be "taken for public use without just compensation." As with other general provisions of the Constitution, the Supreme Court assumed principal responsibility for interpreting such phrases as "just compensation," "due process of law," and "impairment of the obligation of contracts." The interpretation of these broad phrases defined the central theme of American constitutional lawmaking during roughly the first 150 years of Supreme Court history.

SIDEBAR   James Madison on Property Rights

This term ["property"] in its particular application means "that dominion which one man claims and exercises over the external things of the world, in exclusion of every other individual."

In its larger and juster meaning, it embraces everything to which a man may attach a value and have a right; and which leaves to everyone else the like advantage.

In the former sense, a man's land, or merchandize, or money is called his property.

In the latter sense, a man has a property in his opinions and the free communication of them.

He has a property of peculiar value in his religious opinions, and in the profession and practice dictated by them.

He has a property very dear to him in the safety and liberty of his person.

He has an equal property in the free use of his faculties and free choice of the objects on which to employ them.

In a word, as a man is said to have a right to his property, he may be equally said to have a property in his rights.

Where an excess of power prevails, property of no sort is duly respected. No man is safe in his opinions, his person, his faculties, or his possessions.

Where there is an excess of liberty, the effect is the same, though from an opposite cause.

Government is instituted to protect property of every sort; as well that which lies in the various rights of individuals, as that which the term particularly expresses. This being the end of government, that alone is a just government, which impartially secures to every man, whatever is his own.

—James Madison, "Essay on Property Rights," March 29, 1792.

Early Judicial Perspectives

The *ex post facto* law provisions (Article I, Sections 9 and 10) of the original Constitution had the potential to protect property rights against governmental encroachment. But, as noted in Chapter 1, the Supreme Court held in *Calder v. Bull* (1798) that the *ex post facto* limitation applied only to retroactive criminal statutes and not to laws affecting property rights or contractual obligations. Two of the four opinions filed in this case contain important dicta on the sources of individual rights and limitations on government. These opinions, written by Justices Samuel Chase and James Iredell, merit additional attention at this point in our discussion. Without designating any specific constitutional limitations, Justice Chase asserted that "certain vital principles in our free republican governments ... will determine and overrule an apparent and flagrant abuse of legislative power." A legislative act "contrary to the great first principles of the social compact," he continued, "cannot be considered a rightful exercise of legislative authority." Chase's opinion in *Calder v. Bull* was grounded in natural rights theory. Although this perspective has never achieved dominance on the Supreme Court as a standard for determining the validity of governmental acts, it has occasionally influenced judicial interpretation of the nature and scope of individual rights. By contrast, Justice Iredell's opinion in *Calder* maintained that courts could not invalidate legislation "merely because it is, in their judgment, contrary to the principles of natural justice." If legislatures cross explicit constitutional boundaries, however, "they violate a fundamental law, which must be our guide, whenever we are called upon, as judges, to determine the validity of a legislative act." Iredell's emphasis on the written Constitution as the ultimate standard for determining the validity of legislation soon became the dominant view among the justices.

The Age of Conservative Activism

Throughout most of the nineteenth century the Supreme Court sought to balance competing public and private interests in its property-related jurisprudence. However, in the face of a rising tide of state and federal economic legislation, the Court of the late nineteenth and early twentieth centuries became more adamant in its defense of **laissez-faire capitalism**. In a series of decisions between the late 1880s and the late 1930s, the Court invoked the constitutional protections of private property and economic freedom to strike down numerous laws designed to regulate economic activity. This period of conservative activism came to an abrupt end with the constitutional revolution of 1937, brought about by a confrontation between the Court and the elected branches over the constitutionality of President Franklin Roosevelt's New Deal programs.

Modern Judicial Perspectives on Economic Freedom

Since 1937, the Supreme Court has largely deferred to other branches of government in the field of economic regulation. The post–New Deal Court's self-restraint in the economic area was juxtaposed with a more liberal activism on behalf of cultural, political, or human rights largely outside the field of economic activity. Until recently the Court has been much more concerned with matters of free expression, the rights of the accused, personal privacy, and racial and gender equality (areas of Supreme Court activity discussed in subsequent chapters). Beginning in the late 1990s, however, a sharply divided Court manifested greater interest in balancing the claims of private property and private enterprise against governmental regulation, especially in the fields of environmental protection and economic development.

One must recognize that private property and private enterprise are widely shared and deeply held cultural values in the United States. Especially in the wake of the decline of communism around the world, public policy in the United States is unlikely to threaten these values. Thus, the need for judicial protection of property rights may be substantially less now than in the early days of the republic or even during the Great Depression. Nevertheless, judicial protection of private property and free enterprise played an extremely important part in the development of American constitutional law and in the institutional history of the Supreme Court.

The Contracts Clause

The Contracts Clause of Article I, Section 10, forbids states from passing laws "impairing the obligation of contracts." Historically, this clause was extremely important in the protection of economic freedom and private property. Like many important constitutional provisions, the Contracts Clause was first given life during the era of Chief Justice John Marshall (1801–1835).

Key Decisions of the Marshall Court

In *Fletcher v. Peck* (1810), the Supreme Court invalidated as a violation of the Contracts Clause, an act of the Georgia legislature that rescinded the state's sale of land to private investors. To reach this result, it was necessary for Chief Justice Marshall, who wrote the Court's opinion, to conclude that a grant is a contract. In Marshall's view, Georgia's original grant of land carried with it an implied contractual obligation not to assert a right to reclaim the land. Once this land passed into the hands of "innocent third parties" who bought it from the original purchasers, the state could not repeal the original sale, even if it could be proved that the initial grant had been obtained by bribing members of the legislature. As Marshall and his colleagues saw it, "absolute rights" had been established under the contract—that is, they had become "vested" in the subsequent purchasers. But because the state itself was a party to the contract, how could its obligations be enforced? In Marshall's view, Georgia had a moral obligation accorded the status of law, but he was equivocal as to the ultimate source of legal authority. He concluded that Georgia was "restrained" from passing the rescinding act "either by general principles, which are common to our free institutions, or by the particular provisions of the Constitution of the United States." This ambivalence underscores the continuing influence of the "natural rights" approach adopted by Justice Chase in *Colder v. Bull*. Whereas Marshall at least recognized the appropriateness of applying constitutional provisions to protect contractual obligations, Justice William Johnson, in a concurring opinion, opted for the "natural justice" approach exclusively:

> *I do not hesitate to declare that a state does not possess the power of revoking its own grants. But I do it on a general principle on the reason and nature of things, a principle which will impose laws even on the deity.*

The Dartmouth College Case *Fletcher v. Peck* greatly broadened the scope and potential application of the Contracts Clause. But the Court's decision nine years later in *Dartmouth College v. Woodward* (1819) had far greater influence on economic development in the nineteenth century. The Court held in essence that a corporate charter was a contract, the terms of which could not be changed materially by the state without violating the Constitution. The charter in question had been issued in 1769 by the British crown for the creation of Dartmouth College. This corporate charter authorized a self-perpetuating twelve-member board of trustees to govern the college. With the American Revolution, the state of New Hampshire succeeded to the rights and obligations of the crown provided by the charter. The college soon became embroiled in state politics, leading to an attempt in 1816 to convert it from a private institution into a state university. This objective was to be accomplished by placing the college under a board of overseers appointed by the governor pursuant to state legislation. The ousted trustees sued to recover the charter, seal, and records of the college and in this way directly challenged the authority of New Hampshire to enact the legislation. Again speaking for the Court, Chief Justice Marshall determined that the charter was a valid contract and that the legislature's attempt to modify the governing structure of the college violated Article I, Section 10, of the Constitution. No specific language in the original charter required this rigid limitation on the state's power to amend it almost half a century after the charter was granted by King George III and at a time when none of the original parties to the contract remained on the scene. Nevertheless, Marshall found that the challenged legislation violated the spirit if not the letter of the Contracts Clause. Marshall indicated that any ambiguity in the charter should be construed in favor of "the adventurers" and against the state.

Although Dartmouth College was created as a charitable educational institution, the broad principle that Marshall enunciated in this case was soon applied to profit-seeking corporations. The *Dartmouth College* decision came at a time when business corporations in such fields as insurance, canal building, and road construction were beginning to proliferate. These companies and their financial backers were tangibly aided by an interpretation of the Contracts Clause that gave corporate charters firm constitutional protection.

The Marshall Court also interpreted the Contracts Clause as a protection of creditor interests against some forms of state regulation. In the same year that it decided the *Dartmouth College* case, the Court, in *Sturges v. Crowninshield* (1819), struck down a New York bankruptcy law under which debtors could obtain relief from financial obligations previously incurred. Speaking through Marshall once again, the Court found that this measure amounted to an impairment of the obligation of contracts.

Marshall himself went so far as to assert, eight years later, that the Contracts Clause barred state bankruptcy laws that applied to debts incurred *after* their passage. But on this occasion, the legislation was upheld by a majority of his brethren, leaving Marshall to record his only dissenting opinion in a constitutional case (*Ogden v. Saunders* [1827]).

The Contribution of the Taney Court

In spite of the expanded protection of property and business interests through early interpretation of the Contracts Clause, the demand for state economic regulation continued to grow. As noted in Chapter 5, Volume I, the Marshall Court itself began to provide limited recognition to the state police power, and Marshall's successor, Roger B. Taney, significantly extended this recognition. The *Dartmouth College* case implied that corporations chartered by the state could conduct their business free of governmental regulation. However, this laissez-faire approach would not survive for long, and the judicial pendulum began to swing in the other direction with the Taney Court's 1837 decision in the case of *Charles River Bridge Company v. Warren Bridge Company.*

In 1785, the Massachusetts legislature had granted a corporate charter to the Charles River Bridge Company that authorized it to build a privately owned bridge between Boston and Charlestown and to collect tolls from persons using the bridge. This highly profitable arrangement, granted for a period of seventy years, was threatened by the legislature's incorporation of the Warren Bridge Company in 1828 with authorization to build a competing bridge nearby. Within a short time, the bridge built by Warren Bridge was to become free to the public as a part of the Massachusetts highway system. The Charles River Bridge Company challenged the 1828 act as a violation of the 1785 charter, which allegedly implied "that the legislature would not authorize another bridge, and especially a free one," alongside the original bridge. Rejecting this contention, Chief Justice Taney construed the language of the charter literally. He concluded that no rights were "taken from the public, or given to the corporation, beyond those which the words of the charter, by their natural and proper construction, [purported] to convey." By contrast with Marshall's approach in the *Dartmouth College* case, Taney was unwilling to restrict legislative authority on the basis of implicit contractual rights. The Court's position was effectively summed up in Taney's assertion that "[w]hile the rights of private property are sacredly guarded, we must not forget that the community also have rights, and that the happiness and well-being of every citizen depends on their faithful preservation."

Later Developments

The decline of the Contracts Clause as a bulwark of **vested rights** began with the *Charles River Bridge* case. Some forty years later, in *Stone v. Mississippi* (1880), the Supreme Court refused to extend Contracts Clause protection to a chartered lottery company subsequently prohibited from selling lottery tickets in Mississippi. By the late 1880s, the Due Process Clause of the Fourteenth Amendment had supplanted the Contracts Clause as a source of constitutional restraint on state regulation of business.

The extent of the demise of the Contracts Clause in the twentieth century is well illustrated by the decision in the Minnesota mortgage moratorium case (*Home Building and Loan Association v. Blaisdell* [1934]). Here, by a 5-to-4 vote, the Court upheld a state law, passed in 1933 in the depths of the Great Depression, that authorized the postponement of mortgage foreclosures for periods not to extend beyond May 1, 1935. Chief Justice Charles Evans Hughes, writing for the majority, emphasized the qualified nature of the Contracts Clause as a limitation on state power. He concluded that "the reservation of the reasonable exercise of the protective power of the state is read into all contracts." In summary, the Contracts Clause figured prominently in the Supreme Court's protection of vested property rights during the early part of the nineteenth century.

Although its influence began to be undermined by the expanding doctrine of state police power during the Taney era, the Contracts Clause remained a significant weapon in defense of property interests until supplanted by the development of **substantive due process** in the late 1800s. The Supreme Court invoked the Contracts Clause in invalidating state legislation in some seventy-five cases prior to 1890. But the Contracts Clause has not been a major restraint on state regulatory power for more than a century. Nevertheless, it is not a dead letter and is still occasionally invoked as a constitutional limitation. For example, in 1977, the Court held that a New Jersey statute violated the Contracts Clause because it impaired the state's obligation to holders of bonds issued by the Port Authority of New York and New Jersey (*United States Trust Company v. New Jersey*). Similarly, in *Allied Structural Steel Company v. Spannaus* (1978), the Court invalidated under the Contracts Clause Minnesota's attempt to regulate a company's pension fund. Writing for a five-member majority, Justice Stewart observed: "If the Contracts Clause is to retain any meaning at all, … it must be understood to impose *some* limits on the power of a State to abridge existing contractual relationships" (emphasis in the original).

Any expectation in the wake of these cases that the Contracts Clause would reemerge as a significant limitation on state regulatory authority has thus far been unfulfilled. Since the late 1970s, the Court has shown no inclination to further reinvigorate the Contracts Clause. For example, in *Energy Reserves Group v. Kansas Power & Light* (1983), the Court, rejecting a Contracts Clause challenge to a state law regulating natural gas prices, recognized that the prohibition of laws impairing the obligation of contracts must be balanced against a state's "inherent police power to safeguard the vital interests of its people." The Court said that the first question is "whether the state law has, in fact, operated as a substantial impairment of a contractual relationship." If so, the state must advance a "significant and legitimate public purpose" to justify the impairment. In the *Kansas Power & Light* case and other recent Contracts Clause decisions, the Court has found that this requirement has been satisfied.

> **To Summarize:**
> ◆ *During the Marshall era (1801–1835), the Contracts Clause of Article I, Section 10, served as a significant limitation on state interference with private property rights. In particular, John Marshall's opinion for the Court in* Dartmouth College v. Woodward *(1819), which recognized that corporate charters were protected by the Contracts Clause, had great influence on nineteenth-century economic development.*
> ◆ *With the rise of the state police power during the Taney era (1836–1864), the Court began to narrow the scope of protection afforded by the Contracts Clause. In the pivotal case of* Charles River Bridge Company v. Warren Bridge Company *(1837), Chief Justice Taney effectively subordinated traditional contract rights to the interests of the community in a rapidly changing society.*
> ◆ *By the time of the Great Depression, as illustrated by the Court's decision in* Home Building and Loan Association v. Blaisdell *(1934), the Contracts Clause no longer stood as a significant impediment to state regulatory power in the economic realm. This remains true today despite a short-lived effort in the late 1970s to resuscitate a more restrictive interpretation of the Contracts Clause as a limitation on state power.*

The Rise and Fall of Economic Due Process

State police power continued to develop through the Civil War and Reconstruction, but the protection of property rights, especially in the context of business activity, remained a prime concern of American judges, including members of the U.S. Supreme Court. Due process as a substantive limitation on governmental authority began to emerge in the 1850s, but its potential was not fully realized until some years after adoption of the Fourteenth Amendment. With the exception of the *Dred Scott* case, in which congressional regulation of slavery in the territories was held to deprive slave owners of property without due process of law (see Chapter 1, Volume I), the Fifth Amendment Due Process Clause was not invoked, prior to the Civil War, as a substantive limitation on federal authority. This is not surprising, since the national government did not play an active role in the field of economic regulation until very late in the nineteenth century.

Origins of Substantive Due Process

It is generally agreed that substantive due process as a limitation on *state* economic regulation originated in an 1856 decision of the New York Court of Appeals (the state's highest court). In *Wynehamer v. New York*, the court held that a state criminal statute prohibiting the sale of liquor curtailed the economic liberty of a Buffalo tavern owner who had been prosecuted for violating its provisions. The court of appeals held that the state police power could not be used to deprive the tavern owner of his liberty to practice his livelihood, a liberty protected by the due process clause of the New York constitution.

Following the adoption of the Fourteenth Amendment, lawyers representing business interests in opposition to growing state regulation began to emphasize substantive due process arguments. These arguments drew heavily on an influential legal treatise entitled *Constitutional Limitations*, written by a Michigan judge, Thomas M. Cooley. First published in 1868, the year in which the Fourteenth Amendment was ratified, Cooley's treatise went through several editions in the late 1800s and had a significant impact on the constitutional jurisprudence of the laissez-faire era. As noted in Chapter 1, substantive due process focuses on the reasonableness of legislation. By contrast with the more familiar procedural aspect, which emphasizes such elements as notice and the right to a fair hearing (in other words, *how* government should operate in relation to the individual), substantive due process stresses *what* government may or may not do.

Early Supreme Court Resistance to Economic Due Process

For a number of years following the adoption of the Fourteenth Amendment, most members of the Supreme Court resisted the **economic due process** approach. Thus, in *The Slaughterhouse Cases* (1873), a narrowly divided Court upheld Louisiana's grant of a monopoly in the slaughtering business in and around New Orleans. Although officially designated as "An Act to Protect the Health of the City of New Orleans," the law was not in any meaningful sense a health measure. Its only apparent effect was to deprive more than a thousand persons of their right to engage in the slaughtering trade. A number of these individuals filed suit, maintaining that the state had conferred "odious and exclusive privileges upon a small number of persons at the expense of the great body of the community of New Orleans." In rejecting this contention, the Supreme Court, in an opinion by Justice Samuel F. Miller, narrowly interpreted Fourteenth Amendment restrictions on state authority. Miller virtually read out of the Fourteenth Amendment the provision that says: "No State shall make or enforce any law which shall abridge the privileges or immunities of citizens of the United States." This language, he said, extended only to rights held by Americans as citizens of the nation, as distinguished from their rights as state citizens.

In addition to this restrictive view of the Privileges or Immunities Clause, Justice Miller found no deprivation of rights under the Due Process and Equal Protection Clauses. He identified the central purpose of the Fourteenth Amendment as the protection of the civil rights of former slaves, although he was unwilling to say that no one else was entitled to this protection. In a strong dissenting opinion, Justice Stephen J. Field took issue with Miller's narrow interpretation of the Privileges or Immunities Clause: "The privileges and immunities designated," he maintained, "are those which of right belong to the citizens of all free governments." Over the years, many scholars have sharply criticized Justice Miller's narrow interpretation of the Privileges or Immunities Clause (see, for example, John Hart Ely, *Democracy and Distrust*, 1980, and Charles L. Black, *A New Birth of Freedom: Human Rights Named and Unnamed*, [1999]). With few exceptions, however, the Supreme Court has adhered to Justice Miller's narrow interpretation of the Privileges or Immunities Clause. A broader interpretation might have enabled the Court to develop a more plausible basis for protecting individual rights than that provided by the Due Process Clause.

Justice Joseph L. Bradley's dissenting opinion in *The Slaughterhouse Cases* anticipated the Court's later development of the Due Process Clause as the basis for protecting property rights. While agreeing with Justice Field's position regarding the broad protection that should be afforded by the Privileges or Immunities Clause, Bradley went one important step further, by expressing the view that a law which prohibits a large class of citizens from adopting a lawful employment previously adopted, does deprive them of liberty as well as property, without due process of law. Their right of choice is a portion of their liberty; their occupation is their property.

"Business Affected with a Public Interest"   Four years later, the Court again sustained a broad exercise of the state police power, in this instance an act of the Illinois legislature fixing maximum storage rates charged by grain elevators and public warehouses and requiring licenses to operate these facilities. This legislation grew out of the granger movement, in which thousands of farmers sought protection against excessive freight rates charged by railroads and other businesses involved in the distribution of agricultural commodities. Chief Justice Morrison R. Waite, writing for a seven-member majority in *Munn v. Illinois* (1877), sustained the rate regulation under the English common law doctrine of **business affected with a public interest**. Like common carriers, innkeepers, and other persons directly serving the public, Waite reasoned, the owners of grain elevators were equally subject to regulation under this standard. Sounding a note that aroused the anger of business leaders, Waite acknowledged that such regulatory power was subject to abuse but admonished that, in such instances, "the people must resort to the polls, and not to the courts." Dissenting in *Munn*, Justice Field contended that the regulation violated due process. He maintained that under our system of government, the legislature lacked power "to fix the price which anyone shall receive for his property of any kind." He also argued that "there is hardly any enterprise or business engaging the attention and labor of any considerable portion of the community in which the public has not an interest in the sense in which that term is used by the Court." This was a prescient observation in view of the Court's rejection, almost half a century later, of the distinction between private businesses and those affected with a public interest (*Nebbia v. New York* [1934]).

Ironically, once the concept of substantive due process came to be recognized by a Court majority as a basis for invalidating economic legislation, the Court began to apply Waite's rationale negatively. For example, regulations of labor-management disputes, theater ticket scalping, and the rates charged by private employment agencies were ruled unconstitutional on the ground that the businesses involved were not "affected with a public interest" (see, for example, *Charles Wolff Packing Company v. Court of Industrial Relations* [1923], *Tyson v. Banton* [1927], and *Ribnik v. McBride* [1928]).

The Court Reflects Growing Corporate Influence

Powerful corporate interests reacted sharply and decisively to the *Munn* decision. In fact, the American Bar Association was organized for the immediate purpose of leading the counterattack. In 1882, former senator Roscoe Conkling, in an argument before the Supreme Court, unveiled his "conspiracy theory" of the Fourteenth Amendment. Conkling had participated as a member of the joint congressional committee that drafted the Fourteenth Amendment in 1866. Referring selectively to a previously undisclosed journal of committee proceedings, Conkling maintained in essence that those who drafted the amendment intended for the word *person*, as used in the Equal Protection and Due Process clauses, to include corporations. Later research established that Conkling's conspiracy theory was of dubious validity, if not an outright fraud. But in the 1880s, the theory was eagerly received and widely supported by those who sought to justify the protection of economic rights under the Fourteenth Amendment. In 1886, the Supreme Court announced without discussion that the Equal Protection Clause did apply to corporations (*Santa Clara County v. Southern Pacific Railroad*). This conclusion extended logically to the Due Process Clause as well.

Changes in Supreme Court personnel also influenced the shift toward economic due process. Chief Justice Waite, who had written the majority opinion in the *Munn* case, died in 1888 and was succeeded by Melville W. Fuller. In 1890, David J. Brewer, a nephew of Justice Field, took the seat on the high bench vacated by Justice Stanley Matthews. These and other appointees, drawn largely from the ranks of corporation lawyers, were receptive to the limited government approach implicit in substantive due process. During this period, under the leadership of Chief Justice Fuller, the Court significantly curtailed national authority through a restrictive interpretation of the commerce and taxing powers (see Chapter 3, Volume I). Theories of economic individualism, especially the **social Darwinism** of Herbert Spencer and William Graham Sumner, were very much in vogue during the period and obviously had some impact on the justices.

The Court's changing mood was signaled clearly by Justice John Marshall Harlan (the elder) in 1887. Writing for the Court in upholding a Kansas law prohibiting the sale of certain alcoholic beverages, he warned that not all exercises of the state police power would be automatically approved: "The Courts are not bound by mere forms, nor are they to be misled by mere pretenses. They are at liberty—indeed, are under a solemn duty—to look at the substance of things" (*Mugler v. Kansas* [1887]).

Economic Due Process Comes of Age

The first major shift in the Court's position came in 1890 with the decision that a state legislature could not authorize a commission to set railroad rates with finality. Such rate making, the Court concluded, must be subject to judicial review (*Chicago, Milwaukee, & St. Paul Railway Company v. Minnesota*). In 1897, the Court invalidated Louisiana's effort to regulate out-of-state insurance companies transacting business in the state. Writing for the Court, Justice Rufus Peckham found this regulation to be an infringement of the **liberty of contract** protected by the Fourteenth Amendment Due Process Clause (*Allgeyer v. Louisiana* [1897]). ("Liberty of contract," as used by the Court in this and many subsequent due process cases, should not be confused with the Contracts Clause of Article I, Section 10, discussed earlier in this chapter.)

Lochner v. New York: The Apotheosis of Economic Due Process

Justice Peckham used the same rationale eight years later in what has become the best known case of the early twentieth century: *Lochner v. New York* (1905). In *Lochner*, the Court, dividing 5 to 4, struck down a state law specifying a maximum sixty-hour workweek for bakery employees. Seven years earlier, the Court had upheld, as a proper exercise of the police power, an act of the Utah legislature establishing an eight-hour workday for employees in "mines … smelters and all other institutions for the reduction or refining of ores or metals" (*Holden v. Hardy* [1898]). The Utah statute was recognized as a reasonable health measure, but the majority in *Lochner* found no such justification for limiting working hours "in the occupation of a baker." "To the common understanding," Peckham opined, "the trade of a baker has never been regarded as an unhealthy one." However, the Court's fundamental objection to the legislation was that it was a "meddlesome interference" with business. The majority gave no consideration to the relative bargaining power of employers and employees in the baking industry. They simply regarded the law as an unjustified infringement on "the right to labor, and with the right of free contract on the part of the individual, either as employer or employee." Justice Harlan and his celebrated colleague Oliver Wendell Holmes, Jr., filed powerful dissenting opinions in the *Lochner* case. While Harlan pursued a conventional line of analysis, Justice Holmes attacked the majority for reading laissez-faire theory into the Constitution:

> This case is decided upon an economic theory which a large part of the country does not entertain. If it were a question whether I agreed with that theory, I should desire to study it further and long before making up my mind. But I do not conceive that to be my duty, because I strongly believe that my agreement or disagreement has nothing to do with the right of a majority to embody their opinions in law…. The Fourteenth Amendment does not enact Mr. Herbert Spencer's Social Statics.

Constitutional scholars have widely accepted Justice Holmes's charge that the ruling in *Lochner* was little more than an expression of the economic policy preferences of the Court's conservative majority. However, certain revisionist scholars have challenged the Holmesian view. In his book *The Constitution Besieged: The Rise and Decline of Lochner Era Police Powers Jurisprudence*, Howard Gillman argues that the *Lochner* decision "represented a serious principled effort to maintain one of the central distinctions in nineteenth century constitutional law—the distinction between valid economic regulation, on the one hand, and invalid class legislation on the other—during a period of unprecedented class conflict." Thus, in Gillman's view, the Court invalidated the bakery statute in *Lochner* not because it regulated business per se, but because it took sides in an emerging class conflict.

Although the philosophical perspective underlying the *Lochner* ruling remained influential for a number of years, its practical effect was short-lived. In 1908, the Court upheld an Oregon act limiting the workday to ten hours for women in designated occupational fields (*Muller v. Oregon*). In this case, attorney (later associate justice) Louis D. Brandeis submitted a novel brief in support of the legislation, presenting extensive sociological and medical data in support of the state's contention that the limitation of working hours was directly related to the promotion of the health and welfare of women. The **Brandeis brief**, which added a new dimension to constitutional argumentation, underscored the relationship between legal principles and research in the social and biological sciences. Following the *Muller* precedent, the Court in 1917 sustained the constitutionality of a maximum hours limitation for men as well as women employed in mills and factories (*Bunting v. Oregon*). This decision amounted to the de facto overruling of *Lochner*, but the Court did not specifically refer to the latter case.

The Court's willingness to sustain maximum hours laws did not carry over into other areas of labor legislation. A federal law outlawing **yellow dog contracts** (employment contracts in which workers agree not to join unions) was invalidated in 1908 as a violation of the Due Process Clause of the Fifth Amendment (*Adair v. United States*). Seven years later, in *Coppage v. Kansas* (1915), the Court voided a similar state provision as a violation of the freedom of contract protected by the Fourteenth Amendment. In these cases, the Court seemed unconcerned with the blatant inequality in the bargaining positions of individual nonunion employees and corporate employers. Indeed, in the Court's view, it was unreasonable for the legislature to interfere with the "natural order" of inequalities, no matter how great the resulting disparities between employer and employee.

Wages proved to be as invulnerable to legislative regulation as yellow dog contracts. Thus, in 1923 a divided Court struck down a congressional measure authorizing the setting of minimum wages for women and minors employed in the District of Columbia (*Adkins v. Children's Hospital*). The stated purposes of the minimum wage were to provide women with "'the necessary cost of living,' … to maintain them in good health and to protect their morals." As in *Lochner*, the government's perceived interference with liberty of contract was held to violate due process—in this instance, the Fifth Amendment's restriction on federal authority. Writing for the majority, Justice George Sutherland noted that the law was demeaning to women, especially in light of the drive toward political equality that had resulted, shortly before this decision, in ratification of the Nineteenth Amendment, which removed sex as a qualification for voting. But the real object of Sutherland's concern is unmistakably apparent from the following excerpt from his majority opinion:

> *The law takes account of the necessities of only one party to the contract. It ignores the necessities of the employer by compelling him to pay not less than a certain sum, not only whether the employee is capable of earning it, but irrespective of the ability of his business to sustain the burden, generously leaving him, of course, the privilege of abandoning his business as an alternative of going on at a loss.*

During the 1920s, Chief Justice William Howard Taft often supported the Court's limitation of regulatory authority by way of substantive due process (see, for example, his majority opinion in *Charles Wolff Packing Company v. Court of Industrial Relations* [1923]). However, Taft dissented in the *Adkins* case. In an opinion supported by Justice Edward T. Sanford, Taft expressed his belief that because no meaningful distinction could be drawn between minimum wage and maximum hours legislation and since the latter had been upheld in the *Muller* and *Bunting* cases, the Washington, D.C., minimum wage should be sustained. This view was further supported, he maintained, by the fact that the law upheld in *Bunting* contained a time and a half provision for overtime pay. He emphasized, moreover, that "it is not the function of this Court to hold congressional acts invalid simply because they are passed to carry out economic views which the Court believes to be unwise or unsound." Justice Holmes wrote a separate dissenting opinion, asserting that the power of Congress to enact minimum wage legislation seemed "absolutely free from doubt." Holmes sharply criticized the Court's development of what he called the "dogma" of liberty of contract. The word *contract*, he pointed out, is not mentioned in the Due Process Clause. Holmes viewed contract merely as "an example of doing what you want to do, embodied in the word liberty. But pretty much all law," he added, "consists in forbidding men to do some things that they want to do, and contract is no more exempt from law than other acts." Substantive due process as a restriction on economic legislation continued to flourish through the 1920s and into the 1930s. It was an integral part of the Supreme Court's intellectual defense of business interests in general. This judicial philosophy also produced a number of rulings limiting the application of the antitrust acts as restrictions on corporate behavior while extending these restrictions to such labor practices as strikes and secondary boycotts (see, for example, *Loewe v. Lawlor* [1908], *Duplex Printing Company v. Deering* [1921], and *Bedford Cut Stone Company v. Journeymen Stone Cutters' Association* [1927]). The Court strongly resisted efforts during this period to restrict child labor and to regulate agricultural and industrial production.

Patterns of Supreme Court decision making, especially in complex areas of constitutional law, often do not follow unwavering lines of analytical precision or logical consistency. As we have noted, during the period marked by such decisions as *Lochner* and *Adkins*, the Court did not always invalidate challenged regulatory legislation. The Court still adhered (officially, at least) to the principle of the presumptive validity of legislation and, as a result, many regulatory measures were upheld during the heyday of economic due process. Nevertheless, enough state and federal measures were invalidated to retard serious efforts at economic and social reform.

The Decline of Economic Due Process

The Great Depression of the 1930s, with its crippling effect on employment, industrial production, and the economic well-being of millions of people, forced the Supreme Court to rethink its constitutional commitment to limited government in the field of economic policy. It did so in a variety of issue areas between the mid-1930s and the early 1940s. With this reappraisal came the Court's repudiation of substantive due process as a restriction on the regulation of business.

This fundamental change in the Court's posture was signaled by two key decisions in 1934. As previously indicated, in that year, the Court upheld the Minnesota Mortgage Moratorium Act, finding that its provisions did not violate the Contracts Clause (*Home Building and Loan Association v. Blaisdell*). Although this decision did not turn on the meaning of due process, its implications for the Court's interpretation of liberty of contract under the Fifth and Fourteenth Amendments were unmistakable.

The due process issue was confronted directly in *Nebbia v. New York* (1934), in which the Court upheld by a 5-to-4 margin the power of a state to regulate the retail price of milk. Concluding that this price regulation did not violate due process, Justice Owen J. Roberts emphasized the breadth of legislative power in relation to economic matters: "It is clear that there is no closed class or category of businesses affected with a public interest." Since the *Munn* case, the Court had gradually narrowed the category of businesses thus affected and had established a substantial constitutional barrier against state regulation in a number of areas. In fact, during the decade or so immediately prior to the *Nebbia* decision, very few businesses other than public utilities and places of public accommodation were subject to price control with full judicial approval. Consequently, the Court's obliteration of the category of "business affected with a public interest" represented a significant turning point in constitutional development. In effect, the Court was saying in *Nebbia* that all businesses, irrespective of their supposed relationship to the public interest, are subject to regulation.

This stern repudiation of judicial activism in the field of economic liberties drew a scathing dissent from Justice James C. McReynolds, supported by Justices Willis Van Devanter, George Sutherland, and Pierce Butler. The fixing of retail prices as a means of stabilizing production was, in McReynolds's view, "not regulation, but management, control, dictation," amounting to "deprivation of the fundamental right which one has to conduct his own affairs honestly and along customary lines." He strongly suggested that the Court's decision amounted to a declaration that "rights guaranteed by the Constitution exist only so long as supposed public interest does not require their extinction." McReynolds asserted that adoption of this view "would put an end to liberty under the Constitution." The "end to liberty" feared by Justice McReynolds was postponed in the field of economic rights for another three years. In fact, in 1936, the Court reaffirmed its controversial *Adkins* ruling by striking down a New York minimum wage law for women (*Morehead v. New York ex rel. Tipaldo*). In this decision, the majority simply reiterated the "liberty of contract" rationale, but the decision was given added significance because it coincided with the Court's invalidation of major New Deal legislation (see, for example, *United States v. Butler* [1936] and *Carter v. Carter Coal Company* [1936], both of which are discussed and excerpted in Chapter 2, Volume I). In seeking Supreme Court review of a New York Court of Appeals decision invalidating this minimum wage statute, attorneys sought to distinguish the New York minimum wage law from the congressional act invalidated in *Adkins*. Writing for a five-member majority, Justice Butler seized on this omission and considered only the question of whether the two cases were distinguishable. He found that they were not and thus struck down the New York law.

In dissenting opinions, Chief Justice Charles Evans Hughes and Justice Harlan Fiske Stone (supported by Justices Brandeis and Benjamin Cardozo) maintained that the two laws were, in fact, distinguishable. More significantly, however, they criticized the Court for its refusal to reconsider the validity of *Adkins*, especially in light of the country's experience during the Great Depression. Justice Stone chastised his colleagues in the majority for reading their own economic views into the Constitution:

> *It is not for the courts to resolve doubts about whether the remedy by wage regulation is as efficacious as many believe, or is better than some other, or is better even than the blind operation of uncontrolled economic forces. The legislature must be free to choose unless government is to be rendered impotent. The Fourteenth Amendment has no more embedded in the Constitution our preference for some particular set of economic beliefs than it has adopted, in the name of liberty, the system of theology that we may happen to approve.*

West Coast Hotel Company v. Parrish: A Sudden Turnaround   Ten months later in *West Coast Hotel Company v. Parrish* (1937), the Supreme Court, again by a 5-to-4 vote (Justice Roberts having changed sides), dramatically overruled the *Adkins* and *Tipaldo* decisions. Although the votes of the justices had occurred in conference several weeks before President Franklin Roosevelt unveiled his controversial Court packing plan on February 5, 1937, most political observers and the public in general regarded the *Parrish* decision, announced on March 29, as a clear indication that the Court had caved in to pressure from a popular presidential administration. Justice Roberts later claimed he had voted with the majority in *Tipaldo* simply because he believed that the only question presented in that case was whether the New York minimum wage law could be distinguished from the provision struck down in *Adkins*. Whatever the true motivations of Justice Roberts, his change of position in this and several other major constitutional decisions in the spring of 1937 figured prominently in the constitutional revolution that to this day marks the single most important transition in Supreme Court history.

In *West Coast Hotel Company v. Parrish*, the Court considered the constitutionality of a Washington State minimum wage law enacted in 1913. Chief Justice Hughes delivered the majority opinion. He noted that in upholding the minimum wage, the Washington state Supreme Court had "refused to regard the decision in the *Adkins* case as determinative." Such a ruling, Hughes declared, "demands on our part a reexamination" of the *Adkins* case. This reexamination began with the dismantling of the liberty of contract doctrine on which *Adkins* was based. Hughes pointed out that this freedom is not absolute. Moreover, "the liberty safeguarded is liberty in a social organization which requires the protection of law against the evils which menace the health, safety, morals, and welfare of the people." Thus, constitutional liberty is "necessarily subject to the restraints of due process, and regulation which is reasonable in relation to its subject and is adopted in the interests of the community is due process." Hughes enumerated a wide array of state laws in the field of employer–employee relations previously upheld by the Supreme Court. Then, after quoting approvingly from the dissenting opinions of Chief Justice Taft and Justice Holmes in *Adkins*, he branded that decision as "a departure from the true application of the principles governing the regulation by the state of the relation of employer and employed." In further support of the formal overruling of *Adkins* and in repudiation of the philosophy it represented, Hughes took judicial notice of "the unparalleled demands for relief arising during the Great Depression and still very much in evidence at the time of this decision. Interestingly, no Brandeis brief had been filed in the *Parrish* case, primarily because this approach had failed in the *Tipaldo* case the previous year.

Acknowledging the absence in the record of statistical data establishing the need for minimum wage legislation, Hughes nevertheless had no doubt, based on "common knowledge," that the state of Washington had "encountered the same social problem ... present elsewhere." The state, he concluded, was free to correct the abusive practices of "unconscionable employers" who selfishly disregard the public interest.

West Coast Hotel Company v. Parrish marked the end of an era in American constitutional law. Although the fact might not have been fully recognized at the time, substantive due process as a limitation on governmental power in the field of economic regulation was dead. Justice Sutherland, the author of the *Adkins* majority opinion, sounded a defensive, subdued note in a dissenting opinion. For him, the Constitution had a fixed meaning that did not change "with the ebb and flow of economic events." He attempted, with little success, to distinguish between the "judicial function" of constitutional interpretation and "the power of amendment under the guise of interpretation." "To miss the point of difference between the two," he said, "is to miss all that the phrase 'supreme law of the land' stands for and to convert what was intended as inescapable and enduring mandates into mere moral reflections." That was precisely what the critics of the *Lochner–Adkins–Tipaldo* approach charged that the Court had been doing. But Sutherland insisted that "[i]f the Constitution, intelligently and reasonably construed in the light of these principles, stands in the way of desirable legislation, the blame must rest upon that instrument, and not upon the Court for enforcing it according to its terms." Personnel changes, beginning only a few months after announcement of the *Parrish* decision, soon resulted in the replacement of all four dissenting justices in that case. The newly constituted "Roosevelt Court" continued the trend begun in *Parrish* and in other 1937 decisions upholding far-reaching economic and social legislation (see, for example, *National Labor Relations Board v. Jones & Laughlin Steel Corporation* [1937] and *Steward Machine Company v. Davis* [1937], both of which are discussed and excerpted in Chapter 2, Volume I). In 1939, the Court upheld the second Agricultural Adjustment Act (*Mulford v. Smith*), and in 1941, it sustained sweeping federal regulatory power in the areas of employer employee relations by validating the Fair Labor Standards Act (*United States v. Darby*, reprinted in Chapter 5, Volume I). The constitutional revolution begun by the *Parrish* case in 1937 thus applied directly not only to due process interpretation but also to other key provisions of the Constitution, including the Commerce Clause, the taxing and spending power, and the Tenth Amendment.

The Court Gives *Carte Blanche* to Legislatures

For more than seven decades, no significant state or federal regulation of business or labor-management relations has been struck down on due process grounds. The 1963 decision in *Ferguson v. Skrupa* is representative of the modern approach in this area. Here, the Supreme Court, in an opinion by Justice Hugo Black, upheld the validity of a Kansas statute conferring a virtual monopoly on the legal profession to engage in the business of "debt adjusting." Black noted that the doctrine prevailing in the *Lochner–Coppage–Adkins* line of cases authorizing courts to invalidate laws because of a belief that the legislature acted unwisely "has long since been discarded." The Court, he continued, had "returned to the original constitutional proposition that courts do not substitute their social and economic beliefs for the judgment of legislative bodies, who are elected to pass laws." Once again, we see how the original meaning of the Constitution can mean diametrically opposing things to various Supreme Court justices. In any event, for Justice Black, objections to the law on grounds of social utility should be addressed by the legislature, not the courts. "Whether the legislature takes for its textbook Adam Smith, Herbert Spencer, Lord Keynes, or some other," Black concluded, "is no concern of ours." He also found no violation of the Equal Protection Clause of the Fourteenth Amendment in the legislative decision to provide lawyers a monopoly in the field of debt adjusting.

For the most part, the Supreme Court during the last five decades has followed the approach taken in the *Skrupa* case. Substantive due process essentially has disappeared as a barrier to economic policy making by Congress and state legislatures. However, as a constitutional doctrine, substantive due process is anything but dead. It lives on in recent Court decisions recognizing various noneconomic rights under the Fifth and Fourteenth Amendments, especially the constitutional right of privacy (see Chapter 6).

Equal Protection and Economic Regulation

Our discussion has thus far focused on the substantive interpretation of due process in the protection of private enterprise. Note, however, that during the heyday of economic due process, the Court occasionally read similar protections into the Equal Protection Clause of the Fourteenth Amendment. For example, in *Yick Wo v. Hopkins* (1886), the Court invalidated a San Francisco ordinance, requiring owners of laundries housed in wooden buildings to obtain permission from the Board of Supervisors to continue operation of their businesses. The Court found that the ordinance was being administered to the serious detriment of Chinese immigrants. Whereas all of the affected Chinese laundry owners were denied licenses by the Board of Supervisors, nearly all non-Chinese applicants were granted licenses. Writing for the Court, Justice Stanley Matthews observed: "No reason whatever, except the will of the Supervisors, is assigned why they [the Chinese laundry owners] should not be permitted to carry on, in the accustomed manner, their harmless and useful occupation, on which they depend for a livelihood." Similarly, in 1915, the Court struck down an Arizona law requiring that a minimum of 80 percent of any company's workforce had to consist of American citizens (*Truax v. Raich*). In these cases, the Court was especially concerned with the adverse impact of discriminatory legislation on the conduct of business.

Equal protection, like due process, disappeared as an important limitation on state economic regulatory power after the mid-1930s. It was used, however, in the late 1950s to strike down a provision of an Illinois law exempting the American Express Company from the requirement that any firm selling or issuing money orders in the state obtain a license and submit to state regulation (*Morey v. Doud* [1957]). The effect of the discrimination here was not reasonably related to the underlying regulatory purpose of the statute. This ruling is an isolated exception to the modern Court's unwillingness to invalidate economic regulation on Fourteenth Amendment grounds.

To Summarize:
- *In the late nineteenth century, as the Supreme Court came under the influence of social Darwinism and the economic doctrine of laissez-faire, the Due Process Clause of the Fourteenth Amendment served as the basis for invalidating state economic regulation.*
- *The Court developed a substantive interpretation of due process in which "liberty of contract" prevailed over competing claims based on state police power. In the leading case of Lochner v. New York (1905), a sharply divided Court followed this approach in striking down a New York law limiting working hours in bakeries. Critics of this decision argued that the Court was merely reading its own economic theory into the Constitution.*

> ◆ *After three decades in which the Court used the liberty of contract doctrine to invalidate numerous state laws dealing with conditions of employment and related matters, the Court finally yielded to political pressures stemming from the Great Depression and the New Deal. In* West Coast Hotel Company v. Parrish *(1937), the Court overturned precedent in upholding a state law establishing a minimum wage for working women.*
> ◆ *Since 1937 the Supreme Court has steadfastly refused to invoke the Due Process Clause as a substantive limitation on the power of government to regulate the economy.*
> ◆ *During the age of laissez-faire activism, the Court on occasion also used the Equal Protection Clause of the Fourteenth Amendment to limit state economic regulation. In the post–New Deal era, equal protection, like due process, virtually disappeared as a restraint on state regulatory power in this area.*

Property Rights and the Takings Issue

The final provision of the Fifth Amendment states: "nor shall private property be taken for public use without just compensation." In *Barron v. Baltimore* (1833), the Supreme Court held that the Just Compensation Clause, like the other provisions of the Bill of Rights, was applicable only to the acts and policies of the national government. However, in 1897, this clause became the first provision of the Bill of Rights to be incorporated into the Fourteenth Amendment and thus made applicable to the states (*Chicago, Burlington, & Quincy Railroad v. Chicago*). (For further discussion of the **doctrine of incorporation** and these important cases, see Chapter 1). The salient legal questions raised by the Just Compensation Clause are these: (1) What constitutes a "taking" of private property? (2) What constitutes a "public use"? and (3) What constitutes "just compensation"?

Although the takings concept has sometimes been interpreted literally to refer only to a physical appropriation of private property by the government, there are circumstances in which a regulation may be so severe as to constitute a **taking**. The basic problem is to determine the point at which a regulation goes beyond the legitimate scope of the police power and becomes an exercise of the power of **eminent domain**.

The dominant view is that the distinction between a valid regulation and the taking of property is one of degree. Justice Holmes stated this rule in the 1922 case of *Pennsylvania Coal Company v. Mahon*. Under a duly executed deed, the coal company claimed rights to mine coal under the land on which Mahon's dwelling was located. Mahon claimed, however, that irrespective of the deed, these rights were superseded by a Pennsylvania statute preventing the mining of coal in such a way as to cause the subsidence of specified types of improved land, including that on which his house was located. The issue was whether this exercise of the state's police power amounted to a taking of the coal company's property without just compensation. Writing for the Court, Holmes concluded that it did, and that the company was entitled to compensation. "The general rule," he declared, "is that while property may be regulated to a certain extent, if regulation goes too far it will be recognized as a taking." Although the general concept remains valid, the value of the *Mahon* case as a precedent has been substantially diminished by the Supreme Court's decision in *Keystone Bituminous Coal Association v. DeBenedictis* (1987). Dividing 5 to 4, the Court held that a more recent Pennsylvania law designed to prevent subsidence damage from coal mining did not on its face violate either the Takings Clause or the Contracts Clause.

As the *Keystone* case suggests, the modern Court tends to give a narrow interpretation to the rights protected by the Takings Clause. Thus, in *Hawaii Housing Authority v. Midkiff* (1984), the Court ruled unanimously that the state of Hawaii had not violated the Public Use Clause by adopting a policy for the redistribution of land as a means of reducing the high concentration of ownership by a small number of individuals. After extensive hearings, the legislature had discovered in the mid-1960s that, whereas the state and federal governments owned almost 49 percent of the land in Hawaii, 47 percent of the total was in the hands of seventy-two private landowners. On the heavily populated island of Oahu, twenty-two landowners held 72.5 percent of the **fee simple** titles. The legislature concluded that such concentrated land ownership was responsible for skewing the state's real estate market in the area of home ownership, that it inflated land prices, and that it was detrimental to the public welfare.

Writing for the Supreme Court, Justice Sandra Day O'Connor found ample precedent for the exercise of such regulatory power. O'Connor acknowledged that there had to be a legitimate public purpose for taking land, even where, as here, compensation was provided. "But where the exercise of the eminent domain power is rationally related to a conceivable public purpose, the Court has never held a compensated taking to be proscribed by the Public Use Clause." O'Connor concluded that on this basis, the Hawaii land reform policy was clearly constitutional. The regulation of oligopoly and "the evils associated with it is a classic exercise of a state's police powers." The Court would inquire only as to the rationality of the act, not its wisdom or desirability as public policy. O'Connor concluded that the legislature passed this act "not to benefit a particular class of identifiable individuals, but to attack certain perceived evils of concentrated property ownership in Hawaii—a legitimate public purpose."

The Takings Issue under the Rehnquist Court

In a move generally applauded by conservatives, the Rehnquist Court showed renewed interest in the Takings Clause as a basis for protecting property rights. For example, in *First English Evangelical Lutheran Church v. County of Los Angeles* (1987), the Court reviewed an ordinance that prohibited the reconstruction of privately owned buildings destroyed by a flood. The prohibition applied to a parcel of land owned by the Evangelical Lutheran Church, which filed a lawsuit seeking compensation for the loss it would sustain in not being able to continue to use its land as a campground.

Dividing 6 to 3, the Court found that the ordinance at issue "denied appellant all use of its property for a considerable period of years" and held that "invalidation of the ordinance without payment of fair value for the use of the property during this period of time would be a constitutionally insufficient remedy." In another California case, the Supreme Court considered a state agency ruling that required owners of beachfront property to grant an **easement** to allow public beach access as a condition for obtaining a building permit. In *Nollan v. California Coastal Commission* (1987), the Court struck down this requirement by a 5-to-4 vote.

In another important decision involving eminent domain, the Court in 1994 held that state and local governments that refuse to allow land development unless an owner dedicates part of the land for public use must prove that the required conditions are related to the impact of the proposed development. In *Dolan v. City of Tigard*, the Court split 5 to 4 in holding that a city had taken private property without just compensation where the city was unwilling to grant a development permit because the owner refused to dedicate part of the land to a public use. According to Chief Justice Rehnquist's majority opinion, government must show a rough proportionality between the required set aside of land and the harm that will be caused by the new development. Rehnquist observed that the Takings Clause of the Fifth Amendment should no longer be "relegated to the status of a poor relation" among the provisions of the Bill of Rights. Dissenting from the decision were the Court's liberals: Justices Blackmun, Stevens, Souter, and Ginsburg.

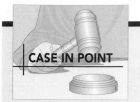

Is a Forced Easement a Taking of Property?

Nollan v. California Coastal Commission (1987)

James and Marilyn Nollan owned a beachfront lot in Ventura County, California. They wanted to tear down the small house on the lot and build a larger one. To do this they had to obtain permit from the California Coastal Commission. The commission granted the permit on the condition that the Nollans allow the public to pass across their beach, which was situated between two public beaches. The required condition was "part of a comprehensive program to provide continuous public access along Faria Beach as the lots undergo development or redevelopment." The Nollans unsuccessfully challenged this requirement in the California courts, arguing that their property was effectively being taken for public use without just compensation.

The United States Supreme Court agreed with the Nollans. Writing for the Court, Justice Antonin Scalia said that "California is free to advance its 'comprehensive program,' if it wishes, by using its power of eminent domain for this 'public purpose' ... but if it wants an easement across the Nollans' property, it must pay for it." In dissent, Justice William Brennan castigated the Court's "narrow view" of the case, saying that its "reasoning is hardly suited to the complex reality of natural resource protection in the 20th century." Brennan concluded by expressing hope "that today's decision is an aberration, and that a broader vision ultimately prevails."

The decisions in *Nollan* and *Tigard* were warmly welcomed by advocates of renewed judicial protection for property rights. On the other hand, these decisions were severely criticized by environmentalists, planners, and others who believe in regulation of private property for the general welfare. As a result of the Rehnquist Court's renewed interest in the takings issue, the volume of litigation in this area increased substantially.

The Kelo Case   The last important Takings Clause decision of the Rehnquist Court was *Kelo v. City of New London* (2005). Without question, it was also its most highly publicized and controversial ruling in this area. In *Kelo* a five-member majority held that a city could condemn over a hundred private homes to facilitate an ambitious waterfront development project. The question before the Supreme Court was whether the Constitution permits a city to take private property and ultimately transfer title to private entities with the expectation that private development will revitalize the local economy. In other words, is economic development of for-profit private entities with the expectation of benefits for society a "public use" within the meaning of the Fifth Amendment? The city claimed that the new waterfront development would create jobs, generate substantial tax revenues, and "build momentum for the revitalization of downtown New London." And even though a private developer, to whom title would be transferred, would undertake the project, there would be restaurants, stores, and other amenities that members of the public could enjoy. The Court majority agreed that this combination of benefits was sufficient to meet the requirements of the Public Use Clause. Writing for the majority, Justice Stevens noted that the Court's "public use jurisprudence has wisely eschewed rigid formulas and intrusive scrutiny in favor of affording legislatures broad latitude in determining what public needs justify the use of the takings power." Stevens concluded that New London's plan "unquestionably serves a public purpose."

In a dissenting opinion joined by Chief Justice Rehnquist and Justices Scalia and Thomas, Justice O'Connor attempted to distinguish New London's use of eminent domain from takings the Court had approved in its earlier decisions. O'Connor predicted that the beneficiaries of New London's decision "are likely to be those citizens with disproportionate influence and power in the political process, including large corporations and development firms." She bemoaned the fact that "government now has license to transfer property from those with fewer resources to those with more" and insisted that the Framers of the Constitution "cannot have intended this perverse result."

In a separate solo dissent, Justice Thomas characterized the Court's decision as "simply the latest in a string of our cases construing the Public Use Clause to be a virtual nullity, without the slightest nod to its original meaning." Thomas upbraided his colleagues for "extending the concept of public purpose to encompass any economically beneficial goal," which in his view, "guarantees that these losses will fall disproportionately on poor communities."

Because *Kelo* can be viewed as giving cities carte blanche in their exercise of eminent domain, it was roundly condemned by advocates of property rights. Modern constitutional theory calls for strict judicial scrutiny of governmental infringements of "fundamental rights" such as freedom of speech, the right of privacy, and the right to be free from racial discrimination. Although property rights were certainly perceived as fundamental by the founders, today the protection of these rights is left largely to the judgment of the people's elected representatives and, ultimately, to the sensibilities of the voters. Of course, voters can demand that their state judges, many of whom must stand for reelection, provide more protection to private property than is currently available from the federal bench. Additionally, they can demand that their state legislatures enact statutes restricting the use of eminent domain by municipalities and other state and local entities. For example, in May 2006, the Minnesota legislature enacted a law, providing that "[t]he public benefits of economic development, including an increase in [the] tax base, tax revenues, employment, or general economic health, do not by themselves constitute a public use or public purpose." Without question, the Minnesota statute and a number of similar laws passed in other states were direct responses to *Kelo*. The Supreme Court has heard fewer cases involving eminent domain cases as a result of state legislative activity prohibiting the type of action the Court appears to sanction. When the Court has had the opportunity to hear such cases recently, it has often dismissed them, as happened in the 2013 case of *Ilagan v. Ungacta*. As a result eminent domain cases remain a somewhat unsettled and controversial component of constitutional law.

Freedom of Expression versus Private Control of Property The decision in *PruneYard Shopping Center v. Robins* (1980) illustrates how property rights may be at odds with the freedom of expression and how, in such instances, the modern Court is likely to strike a balance in favor of the latter. Our discussion of this case leads logically into the examination of freedom of expression in Chapter 3. The privately owned PruneYard Shopping Center in Campbell, California, had a policy prohibiting on its premises all "expressive activity" not directly related to its commercial purposes. In accordance with this policy, the shopping center had excluded several high school students who were seeking signatures for a petition opposing a United Nations resolution against Zionism. The California Supreme Court interpreted a state constitutional provision as granting the students a right to engage in this activity on the shopping center's property.

In an opinion by Justice Rehnquist, the U.S. Supreme Court rejected the shopping center owner's allegations that his federally protected property rights and freedom of speech had been violated. The Court found no violation of the constitutional guarantee against the taking of private property without just compensation. Although Rehnquist recognized that "one of the essential sticks in the bundle of property rights is the right to exclude others," he found "nothing to suggest that preventing [the shopping center] from prohibiting this activity will unreasonably impair the value or use of [the] property as a shopping center." The students were orderly and had limited their activities to the "common area" of the shopping center. PruneYard had failed to show that its "right to exclude others" was "so essential to the use or economic value of [its] property that the state authorized limitation of it amounted to a 'taking.' " In addition, Rehnquist found that the state constitutional provision granting the right of access satisfied the test of rationality established in such cases as *Nebbia v. New York* (1934). Moreover, the state could reasonably conclude that recognizing a right of access furthered its "asserted interest in promoting more expansive rights of free speech and petition than [those] conferred by the Federal Constitution." This opinion, written by one of the most conservative justices, underscores the extent to which the modern Court has deferred to state policies limiting economic freedom.

> ### To Summarize:
>
> ♦ *The Takings Clause of the Fifth Amendment, enforceable against the states through the Fourteenth Amendment, restricts government's use of the power of eminent domain. Government can take private property only for a "public use" and only with "just compensation" to the previous owner. The "taking" of private property is not limited to its physical appropriation, but includes regulatory measures that effectively deprive the owner of the enjoyment, use, or control of the property.*
>
> ♦ *Throughout most of the twentieth century, the Takings Clause did not serve as a significant limitation on governmental power. However, in recent years the Supreme Court has found occasion to remind public policy makers, especially at the local level, that this constitutional guarantee retains some practical force.*

Conclusion

For almost a century and a half, the U.S. Supreme Court extended significant constitutional protection to property rights and economic freedom. The balance between these rights and the exercise of the police power shifted to some extent from period to period. The Marshall Court, primarily through the Contracts Clause, erected major safeguards for "vested rights." Coincident with the subsequent rise of Jacksonian democracy, these rights began to give way to the state police power. This trend continued from the beginning of the Taney era in the late 1830s into the 1880s. With significant personnel changes on the Court and the rising influence of corporate business interests, the Court began to interpret various provisions of the Constitution, particularly the Due Process Clauses of the Fifth and Fourteenth Amendments, as substantive limitations on economic legislation. This orientation, with its emphasis on "liberty of contract," became more pronounced around the turn of the twentieth century and, despite growing criticism from dissenting justices and legal commentators, continued to have a powerful influence on constitutional interpretation until the Supreme Court's confrontation with the Great Depression and the New Deal.

Because private property and free enterprise are deeply ingrained cultural values, there is little need for heightened judicial protection of these institutions. Nevertheless, it should be recognized that American judges at all levels continue to accord great weight to the protection of private property and contractual rights. Congress, the state legislatures, and local governments are unlikely to enact measures that seriously undermine economic freedom. At the same time, substantial political support exists for economic policy measures that regulate the economy "around the margins." A strong consensus exists in support of public policy designed to foster competition, reduce inequalities, stabilize the business cycle, and protect the environment, the consumer, and the worker. Facing a political consensus, the modern Supreme Court has generally acceded to these departures from laissez-faire capitalism.

During the 1980s, conservative theorists displeased with the policies of the modern regulatory state, most notably Bernard Seigan and Richard Epstein, urged the Supreme Court to resurrect its former commitment to private property and private enterprise. However, the Court did not move very far in that direction. Three decades later, battles over government regulation of the economy appear to be more in the province of the constitutional historian than the constitutional lawyer. Of course, given the vicissitudes of American constitutional politics, nothing in the law should be considered settled once and for all.

The Modern Concern for Noneconomic Rights

As the last vestiges of laissez-faire disappeared from the Court's majority opinions, the justices began to give significantly greater attention to the protection of cultural and political freedoms, especially as exercised by members of racial and religious minorities outside the mainstream of American life. Consistent with this reorientation, the Court also began to recognize broader constitutional safeguards for persons accused of crime.

To a greater or lesser degree, the Court has continued to emphasize individual rights largely outside the economic sphere. Some observers have criticized the Court for having withdrawn so completely from the defense of property interests, but even the Court's most conservative members seem disinclined to reassert the laissez-faire–oriented judicial activism of the 1920s. Of course, the Supreme Court cannot successfully pursue a course of constitutional interpretation far removed from the prevailing national political consensus. At the same time, the Court should not be expected to relinquish its position of coequality as a branch of the national government.

During the past half century, the Court has found ample opportunity to shape constitutional interpretation in many areas directly affecting the lives of the American people. The remaining chapters of this book will examine the Court's performance in the most important of these areas.

Key Terms

capitalist economy
private property
contracts
property rights
economic freedom
police power
natural rights
social contract

laissez-faire capitalism
vested rights
substantive due process
economic due process
business affected with a public
    interest
social Darwinism
liberty of contract

Brandeis brief
yellow dog contracts
doctrine of incorporation
taking
eminent domain
fee simple
easement

For Further Reading

Ackerman, Bruce. *Private Property and the Constitution.* New Haven, Conn.: Yale University Press, 1977.

Black, Charles L., Jr. *A New Birth of Freedom: Human Rights Named and Unnamed.* New Haven, Conn.: Yale University Press, 1999.

Conant, Michael. *The Constitution and Capitalism.* St. Paul, Minn.: West, 1974.

Corwin, Edward S. *Liberty against Government.* Baton Rouge: Louisiana State University Press, 1948.

Dorn, James A., and Henry G. Manne (eds.). *Economic Liberties and the Judiciary.* Fairfax, VA.: George Mason University Press, 1987.

Ely, James W., Jr. (ed.). *Property Rights in American History* (6 vols.). New York: Garland, 1997.

Ely, John Hart. *Democracy and Distrust: A Theory of Judicial Review.* Cambridge, Mass.: Harvard University Press, 1980.

Epstein, Richard A. *Takings: Private Property and the Power of Eminent Domain.* Cambridge, Mass.: Harvard University Press, 1985.

Fischel, William A. *Regulatory Takings: Law, Economics, and Politics.* Cambridge, Mass.: Harvard University Press, 1995.

Gillman, Howard. *The Constitution Besieged: The Rise and Decline of Lochner-Era Police Powers Jurisprudence.* Durham, N.C.: Duke University Press, 1993.

Horwitz, Morton J. *The Transformation of American Law, 1780–1870.* Cambridge, Mass.: Harvard University Press, 1977.

Horwitz, Morton J. *The Transformation of American Law, 1870–1960: The Crisis of Legal Orthodoxy.* New York: Oxford University Press, 1992.

Kens, Paul. *Judicial Power and Reform Politics: The Anatomy of Lochner v. New York.* Lawrence: University of Kansas Press, 1990.

Keynes, Edward. *Liberty, Property, and Privacy: Toward a Jurisprudence of Substantive Due Process.* University Park: Pennsylvania State University Press, 1996.

Mendelson, Wallace. *Capitalism, Democracy, and the Supreme Court.* New York: Appleton-Century-Crofts, 1960.

Nedelsky, Jennifer. *Private Property and the Limits of American Constitutionalism: The Madisonian Framework and Its Legacy.* Chicago, Ill.: University of Chicago Press, 1990.

Seigan, Bernard H. *Economic Liberties and the Constitution.* Chicago, Ill.: University of Chicago Press, 1980.

Wright, Benjamin F. *The Contracts Clause of the Constitution.* Cambridge, Mass.: Harvard University Press, 1938.

DARTMOUTH COLLEGE v. WOODWARD
4 Wheat. (17 U.S.) 518; 4 L.Ed. 629 (1819)
Vote: 6-1

Dartmouth College was originally chartered by King George III in 1769. Under the royal charter, the trustees of the College were "forever" granted the right to govern the institution as they saw fit. However, in 1816, the New Hampshire legislature attempted to take control of the college, believing its royal charter was no longer valid. Naturally, the trustees turned to the courts for protection. Failing in the state judiciary, they appealed to the U.S. Supreme Court on a writ of error.

The opinion of the Court was delivered by … [**Chief Justice Marshall**].

… It can require no argument to prove, that the circumstances of this case constitute a contract. An application is made to the crown for a charter to incorporate a religious and literary institution. In the application, it is stated, that large contributions have been made for the object, which will be conferred on the corporation, as soon as it shall be created. The charter is granted, and on its faith the property is conveyed. Surely, in this transaction every ingredient of a complete and legitimate contract is to be found. The points for consideration are, 1. Is this contract protected by the Constitution of the United States? 2. Is it impaired by the acts under which the defendant holds? …

… [I]t appears that Dartmouth College is an eleemosynary institution, incorporated for the purpose of perpetuating the application of the bounty of the donors to the specified objects of that bounty; that its trustees or governors were originally named by the founder, and invested with the power of perpetuating themselves; that they are not public officers, nor is it a civil institution, participating in the administration of government; but a charity school, or a seminary of education, incorporated for the preservation of its property, and the perpetual application of that property to the objects of its creation.…

This is plainly a contract to which the donors, the trustees, and the Crown (to whose rights and obligations New Hampshire succeeds) were the original parties. It is a contract made on a valuable consideration. It is a contract on the faith of which real and personal estate has been conveyed to the corporation. It is then a contract within the letter of the Constitution, and within its spirit also, unless the fact that the property is invested by the donors in trustees, for the promotion of religion and education, for the benefit of persons who are perpetually changing, though the objects remain the same, shall create a particular exception, taking this case out of the prohibition contained in the Constitution.

It is more than possible that the preservation of rights of this description was not particularly in the view of the Framers of the Constitution, when the clause under consideration was introduced into that instrument. It is probable that interferences of more frequent recurrence, to which the temptation was stronger, and of which the mischief was more extensive, constituted the great motive for imposing this restriction on the state legislatures. But although a particular and a rare case may not, in itself, be of sufficient magnitude to induce a rule, yet it must be governed by the rule, when established, unless some plain and strong reason for excluding it can be given. It is not enough to say, that this particular case was not in the mind of the Convention when the article was framed, nor of the American people when it was adopted. It is necessary to go further, and to say that, had this particular case been suggested, the language would have been so varied as to exclude it, or it would have been made a special exception. The case being within the words of the rule, must be within its operation likewise, unless there be something in the literal construction so obviously absurd or mischievous, or repugnant to the general spirit of the instrument, as to justify those who expound the Constitution in making it an exception.

On what safe and intelligible ground can this exception stand? There is no expression in the Constitution, no sentiment delivered by its contemporaneous expounders, which would justify us in making it. In the absence of all authority of this kind, is there, in the nature and reason of the case itself, that which would sustain a construction of the Constitution not warranted by its words? Are contracts of this description of a character to excite so little interest that we must exclude them from the provisions of the Constitution, as being unworthy of the attention of those who framed the instrument? Or does public policy so imperiously demand their remaining exposed to legislative alteration as to compel us, or rather permit us to say, that these words, which were introduced to give stability to contracts, and which in their plain import comprehend this contract, must yet be so construed as to exclude it? ...

If the insignificance of the object does not require that we should exclude contracts respecting it from the protection of the Constitution, neither, as we conceive, is the policy of leaving them subject to legislative alteration so apparent, as to require a forced construction of that instrument, in order to effect it. These eleemosynary institutions do not fill the place, which would otherwise be occupied by government, but that which would otherwise remain vacant. They are complete acquisitions to literature. They are donations to education; donations, which any government must be disposed rather to encourage than to discountenance. It requires no very critical examination of the human mind, to enable us to determine, that one great inducement to these gifts is the conviction felt by the giver, that the disposition he makes of them is immutable. It is probable, that no man was, and that no man ever will be, the founder of a college,

believing at the time, that an act of incorporation constitutes no security for the institution; believing, that it is immediately to be deemed a public institution, whose funds are to be governed and applied, not by the will of the donor, but by the will of the legislature. All such gifts are made in the pleasing, perhaps delusive hope, that the charity will flow forever in the channel which the givers have marked out for it. If every man finds in his own bosom strong evidence of the universality of this sentiment, there can be but little reason to imagine, that the Framers of our Constitution were strangers to it, and that, feeling the necessity and policy of giving permanence and security to contracts, of withdrawing them from the influence of legislative bodies, whose fluctuating policy, and repeated interferences, produced the most perplexing and injurious embarrassments, they still deemed it necessary to leave these contracts subject to those interferences....

We next proceed to the inquiry, whether its obligation has been impaired by those acts of the legislature of New Hampshire, to which the special verdict refers? ...

It has been already stated, that the act "to amend the charter, and enlarge and improve the corporation of Dartmouth College," increases the number of trustees to twenty one, gives the appointment of the additional members to the executive of the state, and creates a board of overseers, to consist of twenty-five persons, of whom twenty one are also appointed by the executive of New Hampshire, who have power to inspect and control the most important acts of the trustees.

On the effect of this law [of 1816], two opinions cannot be entertained. Between acting directly, and acting through the agency of trustees and overseers, no essential difference is perceived. The whole power of governing the college is transferred from trustees appointed according to the will of the founder, expressed in the charter, to the executive of New Hampshire. The management and application of the funds of this eleemosynary institution, which are placed by the donors in the hands of trustees named in the charter, and empowered to perpetuate themselves, are placed by this act under the control of the government of the state. The will of the state is substituted for the will of the donors, in every essential operation of the college. This is not an immaterial change. The founders of the college contracted, not merely for the perpetual application of the funds which they gave, to the objects for which those funds were given; they contracted, also,

(Continued)

to secure that application by the Constitution of the corporation. They contracted for a system which should, as far as human foresight can provide, retain forever the government of the literary institution they had formed, in the hands of persons approved by themselves. This system is totally changed. The charter of 1769 exists no longer. It is reorganized; and reorganized in such a manner as to convert a literary institution, moulded according to the will of its founders, and placed under the control of private literary men, into a machine entirely subservient to the will of government. This may be for the advantage of literature in general;

but it is not according to the will of the donors, and is subversive of that contract on the faith of which their property was given....

It results from this opinion, that the acts of the legislature of New Hampshire, which are stated in the special verdict found in this cause, are repugnant to the Constitution of the United States; and that the judgment on this special verdict ought to have been for the plaintiffs. The judgment of the State Court must therefore be reversed.

Mr. Justice Duvall dissented.

CHARLES RIVER BRIDGE COMPANY v. WARREN BRIDGE COMPANY
11 Pet. (36 U.S.) 420; 9 L.Ed. 773 (1837)
Vote: 5-2

This decision was one of the Taney Court's most important contributions to American constitutional development. The case grew out of a dispute involving rival companies in the business of building and operating bridges. The constitutional issue stemmed from the fact that both companies were operating under charters granted them by a state legislature. In 1785, the Massachusetts legislature incorporated the Charles River Bridge Company for forty years, for the purpose of building and operating a toll bridge over the Charles River between Boston and Cambridge. In 1792, the legislature extended the term of the charter to seventy years. In 1828, the legislature chartered another company, the Warren Bridge Company, and authorized it to build another bridge three hundred yards from the Charles River Bridge. The Charles River Bridge Company then brought suit, arguing that the legislature had implicitly granted it an exclusive right to operate a bridge in the area throughout the life of its charter. According to the Charles River Bridge Company, the grant of the charter to the Warren Bridge Company was an impairment of the obligation of contracts, forbidden by Article I, Section 10, of the Constitution. The state courts rejected this argument, and the Supreme Court took the case on a writ of error.

Mr. Chief Justice Taney delivered the opinion of the Court.

... This brings us to the act of the legislature of Massachusetts, of 1785, by which the plaintiffs were

incorporated by the name of "The Proprietors of the Charles Paver Bridge"; and it is here, and in the law of 1792, prolonging their charter, that we must look for the extent and nature of the franchise conferred upon the plaintiffs.

Much has been said in the argument of the principles of construction by which this law is to be expounded, and what undertakings, on the part of the state, may be implied. The Court think[s] there can be no serious difficulty on that head. It is the grant of certain franchises by the public to a private corporation, and in a matter where the public interest is concerned. The rule of construction in such cases is well settled, both in England and by the decisions of our own tribunals.... In the case of the *Proprietors of the Stourbridge Canal v. Wheely* and others, the Court say[s], "The canal having been made under an act of Parliament, the rights of the plaintiffs are derived entirely from that act. This, like many other cases, is a bargain between a company of adventurers and the public, the terms of which are expressed in the statute; and the rule of construction, in all such cases, is now fully established to be this; that any ambiguity in the terms of the contract must operate against the adventurers, and in favor of the public, and the plaintiffs can claim nothing that is not clearly given them by the act." And the doctrine thus laid down is abundantly sustained by the authorities referred to in this decision....

... The argument in favour of the proprietors of the Charles Paver bridge is ... that the power claimed by the state, if it exists, may be so used as to destroy the value of the franchise they have granted to the corporation.... The existence of the power does not, and cannot depend upon the circumstance of its having been exercised or not.

... [T]he object and end of all government is to promote the happiness and prosperity of the community by which it is established, and it can never be assumed, that the government intended to diminish its power of accomplishing the end for which it was created. And in a country like ours, free, active, and enterprising, continually advancing in numbers and wealth, new channels of communication are daily found necessary, both for travel and trade; and are essential to the comfort, convenience and prosperity of the people. A state ought never to be presumed to surrender this power, because, like the taxing power, the whole community have an interest in preserving it undiminished. And when a corporation alleges that a state has surrendered, for seventy years, its power of improvement and public accommodation, in a great and important line of travel, along which a vast number of its citizens must daily pass, the community have a right to insist, in the language of this court above quoted, "that its abandonment ought not to be presumed in a case in which the deliberate purpose of the state to abandon it does not appear." The continued existence of a government would be of no great value, if by implications and presumptions it was disarmed of the powers necessary to accomplish the ends of its creation, and the functions it was designed to perform, transferred to the hands of privileged corporations. The rule of construction announced by the court was not confined to the taxing power; nor is it so limited in the opinion delivered. On the contrary, it was distinctly placed on the ground that the interests of the community were concerned in preserving, undiminished, the power then in question; and whenever any power of the state is said to be surrendered and diminished, whether it be the taxing power or any other affecting the public interest, the same principle applies, and the rule of construction must be the same. No one will question that the interests of the great body of the people of the state would, in this instance, be affected by the surrender of this great line of travel to a single corporation, with the right to exact toll, and exclude competition for seventy years. While the rights of private property are sacredly guarded, we must not forget that the community also have rights, and that the happiness and well-being of every citizen depends on their faithful preservation.

Adopting the rule of construction above stated as the settled one, we proceed to apply it to the charter of 1785, to the proprietors of the Charles River bridge. This act of incorporation is in the usual form, and the privileges such as are commonly given to corporations of that kind. It confers on them the ordinary faculties of a corporation, for the purpose of building the bridge; and establishes certain rates of toll, which the company are authorized to take. This is the whole grant. There is no exclusive privilege given to them over the waters of Charles River, above or below their bridge; no right to erect another bridge themselves, nor to prevent other persons from erecting one. No engagement from the state, that another shall not be erected; and no undertaking not to sanction competition, nor to make improvements that may diminish the amount of its income. Upon all these subjects, the charter is silent, and nothing is said in it about a line of travel, so much insisted on in the argument, in which they are to have exclusive privileges....

... In short, all the franchises and rights of property, enumerated in the charter, and there mentioned to have been granted to it, remain unimpaired. But its income is destroyed by the Warren bridge; which, being free, draws off the passengers and property which would have gone over it, and renders their franchise of no value. This is the gist of the complaint. For it is not pretended, that the erection of the Warren bridge would have done them any injury, or in any degree affected their right of property, if it had not diminished the amount of their tolls. In order, then, to entitle themselves to relief, it is necessary to show, that the legislature contracted not to do the act of which they complain; and that they impaired, or in other words, violated, that contract by the erection of the Warren bridge.

The inquiry, then, is, does the charter contain such a contract on the part of the state? Is there any such stipulation to be found in that instrument? It must be admitted on all hands, that there is none; no words that even relate to another bridge, or to the [diminution] of their tolls, or to the line of travel. If a contract on that subject can be gathered from the charter, it must be by implication; and cannot be found in the words used. Can such an agreement be implied? The rule of construction before stated is an answer to the question; in charters of this description, no rights are taken from the public, or given to corporations, beyond those which the words of the charter, by their natural and proper construction, purport to convey. There are no words which import such a contract as the plaintiffs in error contend for, and none can be implied....

Indeed, the practice and usage of almost every state in the Union, old enough to have commenced the work of internal improvement, is opposed to the doctrine contended for on the part of the plaintiffs in error. Turnpike roads have been made in succession, on the same line of travel; the later ones interfering materially with the profits of the first. These corporations have, in some instances, been utterly ruined by the introduction of newer and better modes of transportation and traveling. In some cases, railroads have rendered the turnpike roads on the same line of travel so entirely useless, that the franchise of the turnpike corporation is not worth preserving. Yet in none of these cases have the corporations supposed that their privileges were invaded, or any contract violated on the part of the state. Amid the multitude of cases which have occurred, and have been daily occurring for the last forty or fifty years, this is the first instance in which such an implied contract has been contended for, and this court called upon to infer it, from an ordinary act of incorporation, containing nothing more than the usual stipulations and provisions to be found in every such law. The absence of any such controversy, when there must have been so many occasions to give rise to it, proves that neither states, nor individuals, nor corporations, ever imagined that such a contract could be implied from such charters. It shows, that the men who voted for these laws never imagined that they were forming such a contract; and if we maintain that they have made it, we must create it by a legal fiction.

And what would be the fruits of this doctrine of implied contracts, on the part of the states, and of property in a line of travel by a corporation if it should now be sanctioned by this court? To what results would it lead us? If it is to be found in the charter to this bridge, the same process of reasoning must discover it, in the various acts which have been passed, within the last forty years, for turnpike companies. And what is to be the extent of the privileges of exclusion on the different sides of the road? The counsel who have so ably argued this case, have not attempted to define it by any certain boundaries. How far must the new improvement be distant from the old one? How near may you approach, without invading its rights in the privileged line? If this court should establish the principles now contended for, what is to become of the numerous railroads established on the same line of travel with turnpike companies; and which have rendered the franchises of the turnpike

corporations of no value? Let it once be understood, that such charters carry with them these implied contracts, and give this unknown and undefined prosperity in a line of traveling; and you will soon find the old turnpike corporations awakening from their sleep and calling upon this court to put down the improvements which have taken their place. The millions of property which have been invested in railroads and canals, upon lines of travel which had been before occupied by turnpike corporations, will be put in jeopardy. We shall be thrown back to the improvements of the last century, and obliged to stand still, until the claims of the old turnpike corporations shall be satisfied; and they shall consent to permit these states to avail themselves of the lights of modern science, and to partake of the benefit of those improvements which are now adding to the wealth and prosperity, and the convenience and comfort, of every other part of the civilized word. Nor is this all. This court will find itself compelled to fix, by some kind of arbitrary rule, the width of this new kind of property in a line of travel; for if such a right of property exists, we have no lights to guide us in marking out its extent, unless, indeed, we resort to the old feudal grants, and to the exclusive rights of ferries, by prescription, between towns; and are prepared to decide that when a turnpike road from one town to another, had been made, no railroad or canal, between these two points, could afterwards be established. This court is not prepared to sanction principles which must lead to such results....

The judgment of the supreme judicial court of the commonwealth of Massachusetts, dismissing the plaintiffs' bill, must therefore, be affirmed with costs.

Mr. Justice McLean delivered an opinion [concurring in the judgment] holding that the case should be dismissed for want of jurisdiction.

Mr. Justice Story, dissenting....

... Upon the whole, my judgment is that the act of the legislature of Massachusetts granting the charter of Warren Bridge, is an act impairing the obligation of the prior contract and grant to the proprietors of Charles River bridge; and, by the Constitution of the United States, it is, therefore, utterly void. I am for reversing the decree of the state court for further proceedings....

Mr. Justice Thompson concurred in this [dissenting] opinion....

HOME BUILDING AND LOAN ASSOCIATION v. BLAISDELL
290 U.S. 398; 54 S.Ct. 231; 78 L.Ed. 413 (1934)
Vote: 5-4

In 1933, the Minnesota legislature adopted an act designed to prevent the foreclosure of mortgages on real estate during the economic emergency produced by the Great Depression. The Mortgage Moratorium Act authorized courts to extend the redemption periods of mortgages in order to prevent foreclosures. The act was to remain in effect only during the emergency period and in no case beyond May 1, 1935.

Mr. Chief Justice Hughes delivered the opinion of the Court.

... The state court upheld the statute as an emergency measure. Although conceding that the obligations of the mortgage contract were impaired, the court decided that what it thus described as an impairment was, notwithstanding the Contracts Clause of the Federal Constitution, within the police power of the state as that power was called into exercise by the public economic emergency which the legislature had found to exist....

In determining whether the provision for this temporary and conditional relief exceeds the power of the state by reason of the clause in the Federal Constitution prohibiting impairment of the obligations of contracts, we must consider the relation of emergency to constitutional power, the historical setting of the Contracts Clause, the development of the jurisprudence of this Court in the construction of that clause, and the principles of construction which we may consider to be established.

Emergency does not create power. Emergency does not increase granted power or remove or diminish the restrictions imposed upon power granted or reserved. The Constitution was adopted in a period of grave emergency. Its grants of power to the Federal Government and its limitations of the power of the states were determined in the light of emergency, and they are not altered by emergency.

What power was thus granted and what limitations were thus imposed are questions which have always been, and always will be, the subject of close examination under our constitutional system.

While emergency does not create power, emergency may furnish the occasion for the exercise of power.

"Although an emergency may not call into life a power which has never lived, nevertheless emergency may afford a reason for the exertion of a living power already enjoyed." ... The constitutional question presented in the light of an emergency is whether the power possessed embraces the particular exercise of it in response to particular conditions. Thus, the war power of the federal government is not created by the emergency of war, but it is a power to wage war successfully, and thus it permits the harnessing of the entire energies of the people in a supreme cooperative effort to preserve the nation. But even the war power does not remove constitutional limitations safeguarding essential liberties. When the provisions of the Constitution, in grant or restriction, are specific, so particularized as not to admit a state to have more than two Senators in the Congress, or permit the election of a President by a general popular vote without regard to the number of electors to which the states are respectively entitled, or permit the states to "coin money" or to "make anything but gold and silver coin a tender in payment of debts." But, where constitutional grants and limitations of power are set forth in general clauses, which afford a broad outline, the process of construction is essential to fill in the details. That is true of the Contracts Clause....

In the construction of the Contracts Clause, the debates in the Constitutional Convention are of little aid. But the reasons which led to the adoption of that clause, and of the other prohibitions of Section 10 of Article I, are not left in doubt, and have frequently been described with eloquent emphasis. The widespread distress following the revolutionary period, and the plight of debtors had called forth in the state an ignoble array of legislative schemes for the defeat of creditors and the invasion of contractual obligations. Legislative interferences had been so numerous and extreme that the confidence essential to prosperous trade had been undermined and the utter destruction of credit was threatened. "The sober people of America" were convinced that some "thorough reform" was needed which would "inspire a general prudence and industry, and give a regular course to the business of society." ...

The inescapable problems of construction have been: What is a contract? What are the obligations of

(Continued)

contracts? What constitutes impairment of these obligations? What residuum of power is there still in the states, in relation to the operation of contracts, to protect the vital interests of the community?

It is manifest … that there has been a growing appreciation of public needs and of the necessity of finding ground for a rational compromise between individual rights and public welfare…. Pressure of a constantly increasing density of population, the interrelation of the activities of our people and the complexity of our economic interests, have inevitably led to an increased use of the organization of society in order to protect the very bases of individual opportunity. Where, in earlier days, it was thought that only the concerns of individuals or of classes were involved, and that those of the state itself were touched only remotely, it has later been found that the fundamental interests of the state are directly affected; and that the question is no longer merely that of one party to a contract as against another, but of the use of reasonable means to safeguard the economic structure upon which the good of all depends.

It is no answer to say that this public need was not apprehended a century ago, or to insist that what the provision of the Constitution meant to the vision of that day it must mean to the vision of our time. If by the statement that what the Constitution meant at the time of its adoption it means today, it is intended to say that the great clauses of the Constitution must be confined to the interpretation which the Framers, with the conditions and outlook of their time, would have placed upon them, the statement carries its own refutation. It was to guard against such a narrow conception that Chief Justice Marshall uttered the memorable warning: "We must never forget, that it is a *constitution* we are expounding"; … "a constitution intended to endure for ages to come, and, consequently, to be adapted to the various *crises* of human affairs." … When we are dealing with the words of the Constitution, … "we must realize that they have called into life a being the development of which could not have been foreseen completely by the most gifted of its begetters…. The case before us must be considered in the light of our whole experience and not merely in that of what was said a hundred years ago." …

Nor is it helpful to attempt to draw a fine distinction between the intended meaning of the words of the Constitution and their intended application. When we consider the Contracts Clause and the decisions which have expounded it in harmony with the essential reserved power of the states to protect the security of their peoples, we find no warrant for the conclusion that the clause has been warped by these decisions from its proper significance or that the founders of our government would have interpreted the clause differently had they had occasion to assume that responsibility in the conditions of the later day. The vast body of law which has been developed was unknown to the fathers, but it is believed to have preserved the essential content and the spirit of the Constitution. With a growing recognition of public needs and the relation of individual right to public security, the Court has sought to prevent the perversion of the clause through its use as an instrument to throttle the capacity of the states to protect their fundamental interests….

We are of the opinion that the Minnesota statute as here applied does not violate the Contracts Clause of the Federal Constitution. Whether the legislation is wise or unwise as a matter of policy is a question with which we are not concerned….

Mr. Justice Sutherland, dissenting.

Few questions of greater moment than that just decided have been submitted for judicial inquiry during this generation. He simply closes his eyes to the necessary implications of the decision who fails to see in it the potentiality of future gradual but ever-advancing encroachments upon the sanctity of private and public contracts. The effect of the Minnesota legislation, though serious enough in itself, is of trivial significance compared with the far more serious and dangerous inroads upon the limitations of the Constitution which are almost certain to ensue as a consequence naturally following any step beyond the boundaries fixed by that instrument. And those of us who are thus apprehensive of the effect of this decision would, in a matter so important, be neglectful of our duty should we fail to spread upon the permanent records of the court the reasons which move us to the opposite view.

A provision of the Constitution, it is hardly necessary to say, does not admit of two distinctly opposite interpretations. It does not mean one thing at one time and an entirely different thing at another time. If the Contract Impairment Clause, when framed and adopted, meant that the terms of a contract for the payment of money could not be altered … by a state statute enacted for the relief of hardly pressed debtors to the end and with the effect of postponing payment or enforcement during and because of an economic or financial emergency, it is but to state the obvious to say that it means the same now. This view, at once so rational in its application to the written word, and so necessary to the stability of constitutional principles, though from time to time challenged, has never, unless recently, been put within the realm of doubt by the decisions of this Court....

The provisions of the federal Constitution, undoubtedly, are pliable in the sense that in appropriate cases they have the capacity of bringing within their grasp every new condition which falls within their meaning. But their *meaning* is changeless; it is only their *application* which is extensible.

... Constitutional grants of power and restrictions upon the exercise of power are not flexible as the doctrines of the common law are flexible. These doctrines, upon the principles of the common law itself, modify or abrogate themselves whenever they are or whenever they become plainly unsuited to different or changed conditions....

The whole aim of construction, as applied to a provision of the Constitution, is to discover the meaning, to ascertain and give effect to the intent, of its Framers and the people who adopted it.... And if the meaning be at all doubtful, the doubt should be resolved, wherever reasonably possible to do so, in a way to forward the evident purpose with which the provision was adopted....

An application of these principles to the question under review removes any doubt, if otherwise there would be any, that the Contract Impairment Clause denies to the several states the power to mitigate hard consequences resulting to debtors from financial or economic exigencies by an impairment of the obligation of contracts of indebtedness. A candid consideration of the history and circumstances which led up to and accompanied the framing and adoption of this clause will demonstrate conclusively that it was framed and adopted with the specific and studied purpose of preventing legislation designed to relieve debtors especially in time of financial distress....

The present exigency is nothing new. From the beginning of our existence as a nation, periods of depression, of industrial failure, of financial distress, of unpaid and unpayable indebtedness, have alternated with years of plenty. The vital lesson that expenditure beyond income begets poverty, that public or private extravagance, financed by promises to pay, either must end in complete or partial repudiation or the promises be fulfilled by self denial and painful effort, though constantly taught by bitter experience, seems never to be learned; and the attempt by legislative devices to shift the misfortune of debtor to the shoulders of the creditor without coming into conflict with the Contract Impairment Clause has been persistent and oft repeated.

The defense of the Minnesota law is made upon grounds which were discountenanced by the makers of the Constitution and have many times been rejected by this court. That defense should not now succeed, because it constitutes an effort to overthrow the constitutional provision by an appeal to facts and circumstances identical with those which brought it into existence. With due regard for the process of logical thinking, it legitimately cannot be urged that conditions which produced the rule may now be invoked to destroy it.

... The opinion concedes that emergency does not create power, or increase granted power, or remove or diminish restrictions upon power granted or reserved. It then proceeds to say, however, that while emergency does not create power, it may furnish the occasion for the exercise of power. I can only interpret what is said on that subject as meaning that while an emergency does not diminish a restriction upon power it furnishes an occasion for diminishing it; and this, as it seems to me, is merely to say the same thing by the use of another set of words, with the effect of affirming that which has just been denied.

It is quite true that an emergency may supply the occasion for the exercise of power, depending upon the nature of the power and the intent of the Constitution with respect thereto. The emergency of war furnishes an occasion for the exercise of certain of the war powers. This the Constitution contemplates, since they cannot be exercised upon any other occasion. The existence of another kind of emergency authorizes the United States to protect each of the states of the Union against domestic violence.

... But we are here dealing not with a power granted by the federal Constitution, but with the state policy power, which exists in its own right. Hence the question is not whether an emergency furnishes the occasion for the exercise of that state power, but whether an emergency furnishes an occasion for the relaxation of the restrictions upon the power imposed by the Contract Impairment Clause, and the difficulty is that the Contract Impairment Clause forbids state action under any circumstances, if it have the effect of impairing the obligation of contracts. That clause restricts every state power in the particular specified, no matter what may be the occasion. It does not contemplate that an emergency shall furnish an occasion for softening the restriction or making it any the less a restriction upon state action in that contingency than it is under strictly normal conditions.

The Minnesota statute either impairs the obligation of contracts or it does not. If it does not, the occasion to which it relates becomes immaterial, since then the passage of the statute is the exercise of a normal, unrestricted, state power and requires no special occasion to render it effective. If it does, the emergency no more furnishes a proper occasion for its exercise than if the emergency were nonexistent. And so, while, in form, the suggested distinction seems to put us forward in a straight line, in reality it simply carries us back in a circle, like bewildered travelers lost in a wood, to the point where we parted company with the view of the state court....

I quite agree with the opinion of the Court that whether the legislation under review is wise or unwise is a matter with which we have nothing to do. Whether it is likely to work well or work ill presents a question entirely irrelevant to the issue. The only legitimate inquiry we can make is whether it is constitutional. If it is not, its virtues, if it have any, cannot save it; if it is, its faults cannot be invoked to accomplish its destruction. If the provisions of the Constitution be not upheld when they pinch as well as when they comfort, they may as well be abandoned.

Being unable to reach any other conclusion than that the Minnesota statute infringes the constitutional restrictions under review, I have no choice but to say so.

I am authorized to say that Mr. Justice Van Devanter, Mr. Justice McReynolds, and Mr. Justice Butler concur in this opinion.

MUNN v. ILLINOIS
4 Otto (94 U.S.) 113; 24 L.Ed. 77 (1877)
Vote: 7-2

Munn, a partner in a Chicago warehouse firm, was convicted of violating an Illinois law fixing maximum storage rates charged by grain elevators and public warehouses and requiring licenses to operate these facilities. Munn appealed, arguing that the law constituted a taking of property without due process of law.

Mr. Chief Justice Waite delivered the opinion of the Court.

... [I]t is apparent that, down to the time of the adoption of the Fourteenth Amendment, it was not supposed that statutes regulating the use, or even the price of the use, of private property necessarily deprived an owner of his property without due process of law. Under some circumstances they may, but not under all. The Amendment does not change the law in this particular; it simply prevents the states from doing that which will operate as such a deprivation.

This brings us to inquire as to the principles upon which this power of regulation rests, in order that we may determine what is within and what without its operative effect. Looking, then, to the common law, from whence came the right which the Constitution protects, we find that when private property is "affected with a public interest, it ceases to be *juris privati* only." ... Property does become clothed with a public interest when used in a manner to make it of public consequence, and affect the community at large. When, therefore, one devotes his property to a use in which the public has an interest, he, in effect, grants to the public an interest in that use, and must submit to be controlled by the public for the common good, to the extent of the interest he has thus created. He may withdraw his grant by discontinuing the use; but, so long as he maintains the use, he must submit to the control....

... [W]hen private property is devoted to a public use, it is subject to public regulation. It remains only to ascertain whether the warehouses of these plaintiffs in error, and the business which is carried on there, come within the operation of this principle....

... [T]hese plaintiffs in error ... stand ... in the very "gateway of commerce," and take toll from all who pass. Their business most certainly "tends to common charge, and has become a thing of public interest and use." ... Certainly, if any business can be clothed "with a public interest, and cease to the *juris privati* only," this has been. It may not be made so by the operation of the constitution of Illinois or this statute, but it is by the facts.

We also are not permitted to overlook the fact that, for some reason, the people of Illinois, when they revised their constitution in 1870, saw fit to make it the duty of the General Assembly to pass laws "for the protection of producers, shippers and receivers of grain and produce," … to require all railroad companies receiving and transporting grain in bulk or otherwise to deliver the same at any elevator to which it might be consigned, that could be reached by any track that was or could be used by such company, and that all railroad companies should permit connections to be made with their tracks, so that any public warehouse, etc., might be reached by the cars on their railroads. This indicates very clearly that during the twenty years in which this peculiar business had been assuming its present "immense proportions," something had occurred which led the whole body of the people to suppose that remedies such as are usually employed to prevent abuses by virtual monopolies might not be inappropriate here. For our purposes we must assume that, if a state of facts could exist that would justify such legislation, it actually did exist when the statute now under consideration was passed. For us the question is one of power, not of expediency. If no state of circumstances could exist to justify such a statute, then we may declare this one void, because in excess of the legislative power of the State. But if it could, we must presume it did. Of the propriety of the legislative interference within the scope of the legislative power, the Legislature is the exclusive judge.

Neither is it a matter of any moment that no precedent can be found for a statute precisely like this. It is conceded that the business is one of recent origin, that its growth has been rapid, and that it is already of great importance. And it must also be conceded that it is a business in which the whole public has a direct and positive interest. It presents, therefore, a case for the application of a long known and well established principle in social science, and this statute simply extends the law so as to meet this new development of commercial progress. There is no attempt to compel these owners to grant the public an interest in their property, but to declare their obligations, if they use it in this particular manner.

It matters not in this case that these plaintiffs in error had built their warehouses and established their business before the regulations complained of were adopted. What they did was, from the beginning, subject to the power of the body politic to require them to conform to such regulations as might be established by the proper authorities for the common good. They entered upon their business and provided themselves with the means to carry it on subject to this condition. If they did not wish to submit themselves to such interference, they should not have clothed the public with an interest in their concerns.…

It is insisted, however, that the owner of property is entitled to a reasonable compensation for its use, even though it be clothed with a public interest, and that what is reasonable is a judicial and not a legislative question.

As has already been shown, the practice has been otherwise. In countries where the common law prevails, it has been customary from time immemorial for the Legislature to declare what shall be a reasonable compensation under such circumstances, or, perhaps more properly speaking, to fix a maximum beyond which any charge made would be unreasonable. Undoubtedly, in mere private contracts, relating to matters in which the public has no interest, what is reasonable must be ascertained judicially. But this is because the Legislature has no control over such a contract. So, too, in matters which do affect the public interest, and as to which legislative control may be exercised, if there are no statutory regulations upon the subject, the courts must determine what is reasonable. The controlling fact is the power to regulate at all. If that exists, the right to establish the maximum of charge, as one of the means of regulation, is implied. In fact, the common law rule, which requires the charge to be reasonable, is itself a regulation as to price. Without it the owner could make his rates at will, and compel the public to yield to his terms, or forego the use.

But a mere common law regulation of trade or business may be changed by statute. A person has no property, no vested interest, in any rule of the common law. That is only one of the forms of municipal law, and is no more sacred than any other. Rights of property which have been created by the common law cannot be taken away without due process; but the law itself, as a rule of conduct, may be changed at the will, or even at the whim, of the Legislature, unless prevented by constitutional limitations. Indeed, the great office of statutes is to remedy defects in the common law as they are developed, and to adapt it to the changes of time and circumstances. To limit the rate of charge for services rendered in a public employment, or for the use of property in which the public has an interest, is

(Continued)

only changing a regulation which existed before. It establishes no new principle in the law, but only gives a new effect to an old one.

We know that this is a power which may be abused; but that is no argument against its existence. For protection against abuses by Legislatures the people must resort to the polls, not to the courts....

Mr. Justice Field, dissenting:

I am compelled to dissent from the decision of the Court in this case, and from the reasons upon which that decision is founded. The principle upon which the opinion of the majority proceeds is, in my judgment, subversive of the rights of private property, heretofore believed to be protected by constitutional guarantees against legislative interference, and is in conflict with the authorities cited in its support....

The declaration of the [Illinois] Constitution of 1870, that private buildings used for private purposes shall be deemed public institutions, does not make them so. The receipt and storage of grain in a building erected by private means for that purpose does not constitute the building a public warehouse. There is no magic in the language, though used by a constitutional convention, which can change a private business into a public one, or alter the character of the building in which the business is transacted....

... The doctrine declared is that property "becomes clothed with a public interest when used in a manner to make it of public consequence, and affect the community at large;" and from such clothing the right of the Legislature is deduced to control the use of the property, and to determine the compensation which the owner may receive for it. When Sir Matthew Hale, and the sages of the law in his day, spoke of property as affected by a public interest, and ceasing from that cause to be *juris privati* solely, that is, ceasing to be held merely in private right, they referred to property dedicated by the owner to public uses, or to property the use of which was granted by the government, or in connection with which special privileges were conferred. Unless the property was thus dedicated, or some right bestowed by the government was held with the property, either by specific grant or by prescription of so long a time as to imply a grant originally, the property was not affected by any public interest so as to be taken out of the category of property held in private right. But it is not in any such sense that the terms "clothing property with a public interest" are

used in this case. From the nature of the business under consideration—the storage of grain—which, in any sense in which the words can be used, is a private business, in which the public are interested only as they are interested in the storage of other products of the soil, or in articles of manufacture, it is clear that the court intended to declare that, whenever one devotes his property to a business which is useful to the public, "affects the community at large," the Legislature can regulate the compensation which the owner may receive for its use, and for his own services in connection with it....

If this be sound law, if there be no protection, either in the principles upon which our republican government is founded, or in the prohibitions of the Constitution against such invasion of private rights, all property and all business in the state are held at the mercy of a majority of its Legislature....

No State "shall deprive any person of life, liberty or property without due process of law," says the Fourteenth Amendment to the Constitution....

By the term "liberty," as used in the provision, something more is meant than mere freedom from physical restraint or the bounds of a prison. It means freedom to go where one may choose, and to act in such manner, not inconsistent with the equal rights of others, as his judgment may dictate for the promotion of his happiness; that is, to pursue such callings and avocations as may be most suitable to develop his capacities, and give to them their highest enjoyment.

The same liberal construction which is required for the protection of life and liberty, in all particulars in which life and liberty are of any value, should be applied to the protection of private property. If the Legislature of a State, under pretense of providing for the public good, or for any other reason, can determine against the consent of the owner, the uses to which private property shall be devoted, or the prices which the owner shall receive for its uses, it can deprive him of the property as completely as by a special Act for its confiscation or destruction. If, for instance, the owner is prohibited from using his building for the purposes for which it was designed, it is of little consequence that he is permitted to retain the title and possession; or, if he is compelled to take as compensation for its use less than the expenses to which he is subject by its ownership, he is, for all practical purposes, deprived of the property, as effectually as if the Legislature had ordered his forcible dispossession. If it be admitted that the Legislature has any control over the compensation, the extent of that compensation becomes a mere matter of legislative discretion....

... I deny the power of any Legislature under our government to fix the price which one shall receive for his property of any kind. If the power can be exercised as to one article, it may as to all articles, and the prices of every thing, from a calico gown to a city mansion, may be the subject of legislative direction....

I am of opinion that the judgment of the Supreme Court of Illinois should be reversed.

Mr. Justice Strong concurred in this dissent.

LOCHNER v. NEW YORK
198 U.S. 45; 25 S.Ct. 539; 49 L.Ed. 937 (1905)
Vote: 5-4

Joseph Lochner, a bakery owner in Utica, New York, was fined $50 for violating a state law that limited employment in bakeries to ten hours a day and sixty hours a week. After the state appellate courts upheld his conviction, Lochner obtained review in the U.S. Supreme Court on a writ of error.

Mr. Justice Peckham delivered the opinion of the Court.

The indictment ... charges that the plaintiff in error violated ... the labor law of the state of New York, in that he wrongfully and unlawfully required and permitted an employee working for him to work more than sixty hours in one week.... The mandate of the statute, that "no employee shall be required or permitted to work," is the substantial equivalent of an enactment that "no employee shall contract or agree to work," more than ten hours per day; and, as there is no provision for special emergencies, the statute is mandatory in all cases. It is not an act merely fixing the number of hours which shall constitute a legal day's work, but an absolute prohibition upon the employer permitting, under any circumstances, more than ten hours work to be done in his establishment. The employee may desire to earn the extra money which would arise from his working more than the prescribed time, but this statute forbids the employer from permitting the employee to earn it.

The statute necessarily interferes with the right of contract between the employer and employees, concerning the number of hours in which the latter may labor in the bakery of the employer. The general right to make a contract in relation to his business is part of the liberty of the individual protected by the 14th Amendment of the Federal Constitution.... Under that provision no state can deprive any person of life, liberty, or property without due process of law. The right to purchase or to sell labor is part of the liberty protected by this amendment, unless there are circumstances which exclude the right. There are, however, certain powers, existing in the sovereignty of each state in the Union, somewhat vaguely termed police powers, the exact description and limitation which have not been attempted by the courts. Those powers, broadly stated, and without, at present, any attempt at a more specific limitation, relate to the safety, health, morals, and general welfare of the public. Both property and liberty are held on such reasonable conditions as may be imposed by the governing power of the state in the exercise of those powers, and with such conditions the 14th Amendment was not designed to interfere....

The state, therefore, has power to prevent the individual from making certain kinds of contracts, and in regard to them the Federal Constitution offers no protection. If the contract be one which the state, in the legitimate exercise of its police power, has the right to prohibit, it is not prevented from prohibiting it by the 14th Amendment. Contracts in violation of a statute, for immoral purposes, or to do any other unlawful act, could obtain no protection from the Federal Constitution, as coming under the liberty of person or of free contract. Therefore, when the state, by its legislature, in the assumed exercise of its police powers, has passed an act which seriously limits the right to labor or the right of contract in regard to their means of livelihood between persons who are *sui juris* (both employer and employee), it becomes of great importance to determine which shall prevail—the right of the individual to labor for such time as he may choose, or the right

(Continued)

of the state to prevent the individual from laboring, or from entering into any contract to labor, beyond a certain time prescribed by the state.

This court has recognized the existence and upheld the exercise of the police powers of the states in many cases which might fairly be considered as border ones, and it has, in the course of its determination of questions regarding the asserted invalidity of such statutes, on the ground of their violation of the rights secured by the Federal Constitution, been guided by rules of a very liberal nature, the application of which has resulted, in numerous instances, in upholding the validity of state statutes thus assailed. Among the later cases where the state law has been upheld by this court is that of *Holden v. Hardy* ... [1898]. A provision in the act of the legislature of Utah was there under consideration, the act limiting the employment of workmen in all underground mines or workings, to eight hours per day, "except in cases of emergency, where life or property is in imminent danger." It also limited the hours of labor in smelting and other institutions for the reduction or refining of ores or metals to eight hours per day, except in like cases of emergency. The act was held to be a valid exercise of the police powers of the state....

It must, of course, be conceded that there is a limit to the valid exercise of the police power by the state. There is no dispute concerning this general proposition. Otherwise the 14th Amendment would have no efficacy and the legislatures of the states would have unbounded power, and it would be enough to say that any piece of legislation was enacted to conserve the morals, the health, or the safety of the people; such legislation would be valid, no matter how absolutely without foundation the claim might be. The claim of the police power would be a mere pretext—become another and delusive name for the supreme sovereignty of the state to be exercised free from constitutional restraint. This is not contended for. In every case that comes before this court, therefore, where legislation of this character is concerned, and where the protection of the Federal Constitution is sought, the question necessarily arises. Is this a fair, reasonable, and appropriate exercise of the police power of the state, or is it an unreasonable, unnecessary, and arbitrary interference with the right of the individual to his personal liberty, or to enter into those contracts in relation to labor which may seem to him appropriate or necessary for the support of himself and his family? Of course the liberty of contract relating to labor includes both parties to it. The one has as much right to purchase as the other to sell labor.

This is not a question of substituting the judgment of the court for that of the legislature. If the act be within the power of the state it is valid, although the judgment of the court might be totally opposed to the enactment of such a law. But the question would still remain: Is it within the police power of the state? And that question must be answered by the court.

The question whether this act is valid as a labor law, pure and simple, may be dismissed in a few words. There is no reasonable ground for interfering with the liberty of person or the right of free contract, by determining the hours of labor, in the occupation of a baker. There is no contention that bakers as a class are not equal in intelligence and capacity to men in other trades or manual occupations, or that they are not able to assert their rights and care for themselves without the protecting arm of the state, interfering with their independence of judgment and of action. They are in no sense wards of the state. Viewed in the light of a purely labor law, with no reference whatever to the question of health, we think that a law like the one before us involves neither the safety, the morals, nor the welfare, of the public, and that interest of the public is not in the slightest degree affected by such an act. The law must be upheld, if at all, as a law pertaining to the health of the individual engaged in the occupation of a baker. It does not affect any other portion of the public than those who are engaged in that occupation. Clean and wholesome bread does not depend upon whether the baker works but ten hours per day or only sixty hours a week. The limitation of the hours of labor does not come within the police power on that ground.

It is a question of which of two powers or rights shall prevail—the power of the state to legislate or the right of the individual to liberty of person and freedom of contract. The mere assertion that the subject relates, though but in a remote degree, to the public health, does not necessarily render the enactment valid. The act must have a more direct relation, as a means to an end, and the end itself must be appropriate and legitimate, before an act can end, and the end itself must be appropriate and legitimate, before an act can be held to be valid which interferes with the general right of an individual to be free in his person and in his power to contract in relation to his own labor....

We think the limit of the police power has been reached and passed in this case. There is, in our judgment, no reasonable foundation for holding this to be necessary or appropriate as a health law to safeguard the public health, or the health of the individuals who are following the trade of a baker. If this statute be valid, and if, therefore, a proper case is made out in which to deny the right of an individual, *sui juris*, as employer or employee, to make contracts for the labor of the latter under the protection of the provisions of the Federal Constitution, there would seem to be no length to which legislation of this nature might not go....

We think that there can be no fair doubt that the trade of a baker, in and of itself, is not an unhealthy one to that degree which would authorize the legislature to interfere with the right to labor, and with the right of free contract on the part of the individual, either as employer or employee.

... Statutes of the nature of that under review, limiting the hours in which grown and intelligent men may labor to earn their living, are mere meddlesome interferences with the rights of the individual, and they are not saved from condemnation by the claim that they are passed in the exercise of the police power and upon the subject of the health of the individual whose rights are interfered with, unless there be some fair ground, reasonable in and of itself, to say that there is material danger to the public health or to the health of the employees if the hours of labor are not curtailed. If this be not clearly the case, the individuals whose rights are thus made the subject of legislative interference are under the protection of the Federal Constitution regarding their liberty of contract as well as of person, and the legislature of the State has no power to limit their right as proposed in this statute. All that it could properly do has been done by it with regard to the conduct of bakeries, as provided for in the other sections of the act above set forth. These several sections provide for the inspection of the premises where the bakery is carried on, with regard to furnishing proper wash rooms and water closets, apart from the bake room, also with regard to providing proper drainage, plumbing and painting; the sections, in addition, provide for the height of the ceiling, the cementing or tiling of floors, where necessary in the opinion of the factory inspector, and for other things of that nature; alterations are also provided for and are to be made where necessary in the opinion of the inspector, in order to comply with the provisions of the statute. These various sections may be wise and valid regulations, and they certainly go to the full extent of providing for the

cleanliness and the healthiness, so far as possible, of the quarters in which bakeries are to be conducted. Adding to all these requirements a prohibition to enter into any contract of labor in a bakery for more than a certain number of hours a week is, in our judgment, so wholly beside the matter of a proper, reasonable and fair provision as to run counter to that liberty of person and of free contract provided for in the Federal Constitution.

It is impossible for us to shut our eyes to the fact that many of the laws of this character, while passed under what is claimed to be the police power for the purpose of protecting the public health or welfare, are, in reality, passed from other motives. We are justified in saying so when, from the character of the law and the subject upon which it legislates, it is apparent that the public health or welfare bears but the most remote relation to the law. The purpose of a statute must be determined from the natural and legal effect of the language employed; and whether it is or is not repugnant to the Constitution of the United States must be determined from the natural effect of such statutes when put into operation, and not from their proclaimed purpose....

It is manifest to us that the limitation of the hours of labor as provided for in this section of the statute under which the indictment was found, and the plaintiff in error convicted, has no such direct relation to, and no such substantial effect upon, the health of the employee, as to justify us in regarding the section as really a health law. It seems to us that the real object and purpose were simply to regulate the hours of labor between the master and his employees ... in a private business, not dangerous in any degree to morals, or in any real and substantial degree to the health of the employees. Under such circumstances the freedom of master and employee to contract with each other in relation to their employment, and in defining the same, cannot be prohibited or interfered with, without violating the Federal Constitution.

The judgment of the Court of Appeals of New York, as well as that of the Supreme Court and of the County Court of Oneida County, must be reversed and the case remanded to County Court for further proceedings not inconsistent with this opinion.

Mr. Justice Harlan [with whom *Mr. Justice White* and *Mr. Justice Day* concurred], dissenting:

... It is plain that this statute was enacted in order to protect the physical well-being of those who work in

(Continued)

bakery and confectionery establishments. It may be that the statute had its origin, in part, in the belief that employers and employees in such establishments were not upon an equal footing, and that the necessities of the latter often compelled them to submit to such exactions as unduly taxed their strength. Be this as it may, the statute must be taken as expressing the belief of the people of New York that, as a general rule, and in the case of the average man, labor in excess of sixty hours during a week in such establishments may endanger the health of those who thus labor. Whether or not this be wise legislation it is not the province of the court to inquire. Under our system of government the courts are not concerned with the wisdom or policy of legislation. So that, in determining the question of power to interfere with liberty of contract, the court may inquire whether the means devised by the state are germane to an end which may be lawfully accomplished and have a real or substantial relation to the protection of health, as involved in the daily work of the persons, male and female, engaged in bakery and confectionery establishments. But when this inquiry is entered upon I find it impossible, in view of common experience, to say that there is here no real or substantial relation between the means employed by the state and the end sought to be accomplished by its legislation. Nor can I say that the statute has no appropriated or direct connection with that protection to health which each state owes to her citizens; or that it is not promotive of the health of the employees in question; or that the regulation prescribed by the state is utterly unreasonable and extravagant or wholly arbitrary. Still less can I say that the statute is, beyond question, a plain, palpable invasion of rights secured by the fundamental law. Therefore I submit that this court will transcend its functions if it assumes to annul the statute of New York. It must be remembered that this statute does not apply to all kinds of business. It applies only to work in bakery and confectionery establishments, in which, as all know, the air constantly breathed by workmen is not as pure and healthful as that to be found in some other establishments or out of doors....

... [T]he state is not amenable to the judiciary, in respect of its legislative enactments, unless such enactments are plainly, palpably, beyond all question, inconsistent with the Constitution of the United States. We are not to presume that the state of New York has acted in bad faith. Nor can we assume that its legislature acted without due deliberation, or that it did not determine this question upon the fullest attainable

information and for the common good. We cannot say that the state has acted without reason, nor ought we to proceed upon the theory that its action is a mere sham. Our duty, I submit, is to sustain the statute as not being in conflict with the Federal Constitution, for the reason—and such is an all sufficient reason—it is not shown to be plainly and palpably inconsistent with that instrument. Let the state alone in the management of its purely domestic affairs, so long as it does not appear beyond all question that it has violated the Federal Constitution. This view necessarily results from the principle that the health and safety of the people of a state are primarily for the state to guard and protect.

I take leave to say that the New York statute, in the particulars here involved, cannot be held to be in conflict with the 14th Amendment, without enlarging the scope of the amendment far beyond its original purpose, and without bringing under the supervision of this court matters which have been supposed to belong exclusively to the legislative departments of the several states ... to guard the health and safety of their citizens....

Mr. Justice Holmes, dissenting:

... This case is decided upon an economic theory which a large part of the country does not entertain. If it were a question whether I agreed with that theory, I should desire to study it further and long before making up my mind. But I do not conceive that to be my duty, because I strongly believe that my agreement or disagreement has nothing to do with the right of a majority to embody their opinions in law. It is settled by various decisions of this court that ... state laws may regulate life in many ways which are as legislators might think as injudicious, or if you like as tyrannical, as this, and which, equally with this, interfere with the liberty to contract. Sunday laws and usury laws are ancient examples. A more modern one is the prohibition of lotteries. The liberty of the citizen to do as he likes so long as he does not interfere with the liberty of others to do the same, which has been a shibboleth for some well known writers, is interfered with by school laws, by the post office, by every state or municipal institution which takes his money for purposes thought desirable, whether he likes it or not. The 14th Amendment does not enact Mr. Herbert Spencer's *Social Statics*.... But a Constitution is not intended to embody a particular economic theory, whether of paternalism and the organic relation of the citizen to the state or of laissez faire. It is made for people of fundamentally differing views, and the accident of finding certain opinions natural and familiar, or novel, and even shocking, ought not to conclude our judgment upon the question whether statutes embodying them conflict with the Constitution of the United States.

General propositions do not decide concrete cases. The decision will depend on a judgment or intuition more subtle than any articulate major premise. But I think that the proposition just stated, if it is accepted, will carry us far toward the end. Every opinion tends to become a law. I think that the word "liberty," in the 14th Amendment, is perverted when it is held to prevent the natural outcome of a dominant opinion, unless it can be said that a rational and fair man necessarily would admit that the statute proposed would infringe fundamental principles as they have been understood by the traditions of our people and our law. It does not end research to show that no such sweeping condemnation can be passed upon the statute before us. A reasonable man might think it a proper measure on the score of health.

Men whom I certainly could not pronounce unreasonable would uphold it as a first installment of a general regulation of the hours of work. Whether in the latter aspect it would be open to the charge of inequality I think it unnecessary to discuss.

ADKINS v. CHILDREN'S HOSPITAL
261 U.S. 525; 43 S.Ct. 394; 67 L.Ed. 785 (1923)
Vote: 5–3

In 1918, Congress created a board and empowered it to set minimum wages for women and children working in the District of Columbia. Children's Hospital obtained an injunction to prevent Adkins and other board members from enforcing the minimum wage. Adkins et al. appealed to the Supreme Court.

Mr. Justice Sutherland delivered the opinion of the Court.

… The judicial duty of passing upon the constitutionality of an act of Congress is one of great gravity and delicacy. The statute here in question has successfully borne the scrutiny of the legislative branch of the government, which, by enacting it, has affirmed its validity; and that determination must be given great weight. This Court, by an unbroken line of decisions from Chief Justice Marshall to the present day, has steadily adhered to the rule that every possible presumption is in favor of the validity of an act of Congress until overcome beyond rational doubt. But if, by clear and indubitable demonstration, a statute be opposed to the Constitution, we have no choice but to say so. The Constitution, by its own terms, is the supreme law of the land, emanating from the people, the repository of ultimate sovereignty under our form of government. A congressional statute, on the other hand, is the act of an agency of this sovereign authority, and, if it conflict with the Constitution, must fall; for that which is not supreme must yield to that which is….

The statute now under consideration is attacked upon the ground that it authorizes an unconstitutional interference with the freedom of contract included within the guarantees of the due process clause of the Fifth Amendment. That the right to contract about one's affairs is a part of the liberty of the individual protected by this clause is settled by the decisions of this Court, and is no longer open to question…. Within this liberty are contracts of employment of labor. In making such contracts, generally speaking, the parties have an equal right to obtain from each other the best terms they can as the result of private bargaining….

There is, of course, no such thing as absolute freedom of contract. It is subject to a great variety of restraints. But freedom of contract is, nevertheless, the general rule and restraint the exception; and the exercise of legislative authority to abridge it can be justified only by the existence of exceptional circumstances. Whether these circumstances exist in the present case constitutes the question to be answered….

(Continued)

In the *Muller* Case [*Muller v. Oregon* (1908)] the validity of an Oregon statute, forbidding the employment of any female in certain industries more than ten hours during any one day, was upheld. The decision proceeded upon the theory that the difference between the sexes may justify a different rule respecting hours of labor in the case of women than in the case of men. It is pointed out that these consist in differences of physical structure, especially in respect of the maternal functions, and also in the fact that historically woman has always been dependent upon man, who has established his control by superior physical strength.... But the ancient inequality of the sexes, otherwise than physical as suggested in the *Muller* Case has continued "with diminishing intensity." In view of the great—not to say revolutionary—changes which have taken place since that utterance, in the contractual, political, and civil status of women, culminating in the Nineteenth Amendment, it is not unreasonable to say that these differences have now come almost, if not quite, to the vanishing point. In this aspect of the matter, while the physical differences must be recognized in appropriate cases, and legislation fixing hours or conditions of work may properly take them into account, we cannot accept the doctrine that women of mature age, *sui juris*, require or may be subjected to restrictions upon their liberty of contract which could not lawfully be imposed in the case of men under similar circumstances. To do so would be to ignore all the implications to be drawn from the present day trend of legislation, as well as that of common thought and usage, by which woman is accorded emancipation from the old doctrine that she must be given special protection or be subjected to special restraint in her contractual and civil relationships. In passing, it may be noted that the instant statute applies in the case of a woman employer contracting with a woman employee as it does when the former is a man.

The essential characteristics of the statute now under consideration, which differentiate it from the laws fixing hours of labor, will be made to appear as we proceed. It is sufficient now to point out that the latter ... deal with incidents of the employment having no necessary effect upon the heart of the contract; that is, the amount of wages to be paid and received. A law forbidding work to continue beyond a given number of hours leaves the parties free to contract about wages and thereby equalize whatever additional burdens may be imposed upon the employer as a result of the restrictions as to hours, by an adjustment in respect of the amount of wages. Enough has been said to show that the authority to fix hours of labor cannot be exercised except in respect of those occupations where work of long-continued duration is detrimental to health. This Court has been careful in every case where the question has been raised, to place its decision upon this limited authority of the legislature to regulate hours of labor, and to disclaim any purpose to uphold the legislation as fixing wages, thus recognizing an essential difference between the two. It seems plain that these decisions afford no real support for any form of law establishing minimum wages.

If now, in the light furnished by the foregoing exceptions to the general rule forbidding legislative interference with freedom of contract, we examine and analyze the statute in question, we shall see that it differs from them in every material respect.... It is simply and exclusively a price fixing law, confined to adult women (for we are not now considering the provisions relating to minors), who are legally as capable of contracting for themselves as men. It forbids two parties having lawful capacity under penalties as to the employer to freely contract with one another in respect of the price for which one shall render service to the other in a purely private employment where both are willing, perhaps anxious, to agree, even though the consequences may be to oblige one to surrender a desirable engagement, and the other to dispense with the services of a desirable employee....

The standard furnished by the statute for the guidance of the board is so vague as to be impossible of practical application with any reasonable degree of accuracy. What is sufficient to supply the necessary cost of living for a woman worker and maintain her in good health and protect her morals is obviously not a precise or unvarying sum—not even approximately so. The amount will depend upon a variety of circumstances: The individual temperament, habits of thrift, care, ability to buy necessaries intelligently, and whether the woman lives alone or with her family. To those who practice economy, a given sum will afford comfort, while to those of contrary habit the same sum will be wholly inadequate. The cooperative economies of the family group are not taken into account, though they constitute an important consideration in estimating the cost of living, for it is obvious that the individual expense will be less in the case of a member of a family than in the case of one living alone. The relation between earnings and morals is not capable of standardization. It cannot be shown that well-paid women safeguard their morals more carefully than those who are poorly paid. Morality rests upon other considerations than wages; and there is, certainly, no such prevalent connection between the two as to justify a broad attempt to adjust the latter with reference to the former....

The law takes account of the necessities of only one party to the contract. It ignores the necessities of the employer by compelling him to pay not less than a certain sum, not only whether the employee is capable of earning it, but irrespective of the ability of his business to sustain the burden, generously leaving him, of course, the privilege of abandoning his business as an alternative for going on at a loss. Within the limits of the minimum sum, he is precluded, under penalty of fine and imprisonment, from adjusting compensation to the differing merits of his employees. It compels him to pay at least the sum fixed in any event, because the employee needs it, but requires no service of equivalent value from the employee.... To the extent that the sum fixed exceeds the fair value of the services rendered, it amounts to a compulsory exaction from the employer for the support of a partially indigent person, for whose condition there rests upon him no peculiar responsibility, and therefore, in effect, arbitrarily shifts to his shoulders a burden which, if it belongs to anybody, belongs to society as a whole.

The feature of this statute which, perhaps more than any other, puts upon it the stamp of invalidity is that it exacts from the employer an arbitrary payment for a purpose and upon a basis having no causal connection with his business, or the contract, or the work the employee engages to do.... The ethical right of every worker, man or woman, to a living wage, may be conceded. One of the declared and important purposes of trade organizations is to secure it. And with that principle and with every legitimate effort to realize it in fact, no one can quarrel; but the fallacy of the proposed method of attaining it is that it assumes that every employer is bound, at all events to furnish it. The moral requirement, implicit in every contract of employment, *viz.*, that the amount to be paid and the service to be rendered shall bear to each other some relation of just equivalence, is completely ignored.... Certainly the employer, by paying a fair equivalent for the service rendered, though not sufficient to support the employee, has neither caused nor contributed to her poverty. On the contrary, to the extent of what he pays, he has relieved it. In principle, there can be no difference between the case of selling labor and the case of selling goods. If one goes to the butcher, the baker, or grocer to buy food, he is morally entitled to obtain the worth of his money, but he is not entitled to more. If what he gets is worth what he pays, he is not justified in demanding more simply because he needs more; and the shopkeeper, having dealt fairly and honestly in that transaction, is not concerned in any peculiar sense with the question of his customer's necessities.... But a statute which prescribes payment without regard to any of these things, and solely with relation to circumstances apart from the contract of employment, the business affected by it, and the work done under it, is so clearly the product of a naked, arbitrary exercise of power, that it cannot be allowed to stand under the Constitution of the United States.

We are asked, upon the one hand, to consider the fact that several states have adopted similar statutes, and we are invited, upon the other hand, to give weight to the fact that three times as many states, presumably as well informed and as anxious to promote the health and morals of their people, have refrained from enacting such legislation. We have also been furnished with a large number of printed opinions approving the policy of the minimum wage, and our own reading has disclosed a large number to the contrary. These are all proper enough for the consideration of the lawmaking bodies, since their tendency is to establish the desirability or undesirability of the legislation; but they reflect no legitimate light upon the question of its validity, and that is what we are called upon to decide. The elucidation of that question cannot be aided by counting heads.

It is said that great benefits have resulted from the operation of such statutes, not alone in the District of Columbia, but in the several states where they have been in force. A mass of reports, opinions of special observers and students of the subject, and the like, has been brought before us in support of this statement, all of which we have found interesting but only mildly persuasive. That the earnings of women now are greater than they were formerly, and that conditions affecting women have become better in other respects, may be conceded; but convincing indications of the logical relation of these desirable changes to the law in question are significantly lacking. They may be, and quite probably are, due to other causes....

(Continued)

Baking Company v. Bryan…. This intrusion by the judiciary into the realm of legislative value judgments was strongly objected to at the time, particularly by Mr. Justice Holmes and Mr. Justice Brandeis….

The doctrine that prevailed in *Lochner, Coppage, Adkins, Burns*, and like cases—that due process authorizes courts to hold laws unconstitutional when they believe the legislature has acted unwisely—has long since been discarded. We have returned to the original constitutional proposition that courts do not substitute their social and economic beliefs for the judgment of legislative bodies, who are elected to pass laws. As this Court stated in a unanimous opinion in 1941, "We are not concerned … with the wisdom, need, or appropriateness of the legislation." Legislative bodies have broad scope to experiment with economic problems, and this Court does not sit to "subject the State to an intolerable supervision hostile to the basic principles of our Government and wholly beyond the protection which the general clause of the Fourteenth Amendment was intended to secure." It is now settled that States "have power to legislate against what are found to be injurious practices in their internal commercial and business affairs, so long as their laws do not run afoul of some specific federal constitutional prohibition or of some valid federal law." …

We conclude that the Kansas Legislature was free to decide for itself that legislation was needed to deal with the business of debt adjusting. Unquestionably, there are arguments showing that the business of debt adjusting has social utility, but such arguments are properly addressed to the legislature, not to us. We refuse to sit as a "superlegislature to weigh the wisdom of legislation," and we emphatically refuse to go back to the time when courts used the Due Process Clause "to strike down state laws, regulatory of business and industrial conditions, because they may be unwise, improvident, or out of harmony with a particular school of thought." Nor are we able or willing to draw lines by calling a law "prohibitory" or "regulatory." Whether the legislature takes for its textbook Adam Smith, Herbert Spencer, Lord Keynes, or some other is no concern of ours. The Kansas debt adjusting statute may be wise or unwise. But relief, if any be needed, lies not with us but with the body constituted to pass laws for the State of Kansas.

Nor is the statute's exception of lawyers a denial of equal protection of the laws to nonlawyers. Statutes create many classifications which do not deny equal protection; it is only "invidious discrimination" which offends the Constitution. If the State of Kansas wants to limit debt adjusting to lawyers, the Equal Protection Clause does not forbid…

Reversed.

Mr. Justice Harlan concurs in the judgment on the ground that this state measure bears a rational relation to a constitutionally permissible objective….

HAWAII HOUSING AUTHORITY v. MIDKIFF
467 U.S. 229; 104 S.Ct. 2321; 81 L.Ed.2d. 186 (1984)
Vote: 8–0

In this case, the Court considers whether the state of Hawaii may use its power of eminent domain to redistribute land previously held by a small minority of large landowners. The constitutional question is whether the state's "taking" is justified by a valid "public use."

Justice O'Connor delivered the opinion of the Court.

… The starting point for our analysis of the Act's constitutionality is the Court's decision in *Berman v. Parker* [1954]…. In *Berman*, the Court held constitutional the District of Columbia Redevelopment Act of 1945. That Act provided both for the comprehensive use of the eminent domain power to redevelop slum areas and for the possible sale or lease of the condemned lands to private interests.

In discussing whether the takings authorized by that Act were for a "public use," … the Court stated:

> We deal, in other words, with what traditionally has been known as the police power. An attempt to define its reach or trace its outer limits is fruitless, for each case must turn on its own facts. The definition is essentially the product of legislative determinations addressed to the purposes of government, purposes neither abstractly nor historically capable of complete

definition. Subject to specific constitutional limitations, when the legislature has spoken, the public interest has been declared in terms well nigh conclusive....

There is, of course, a role for courts to play in reviewing a legislature's judgment of what constitutes a public use, even when the eminent domain power is equated with the police power. But the Court in *Herman* made clear that it is "an extremely narrow" one. The Court in *Herman* cited with approval the Court's decision in *Old Dominion Company v. United States* [1925], ... which held that deference to the legislature's "public use" determination is required "until it is shown to involve an impossibility." The *Herman* Court also cited to *United States ex rel. TV A v. Welch* [1946], ... which emphasized that "[a]ny departure from this judicial restraint would result in courts deciding on what is and is not a governmental function and in their invalidating legislation on the basis of their view on that question at the moment of decision, a practice which has proved impracticable in other fields." In short, the Court has made clear that it will not substitute its judgment for a legislature's judgment as to what constitutes a public use "unless the use be palpably without reasonable foundation." ...

To be sure, the Court's cases have repeatedly stated that "one person's property may not be taken for the benefit of another private person without a justifying public purpose, even though compensation be paid." ... Thus, in *Missouri Pacific R. Company v. Nebraska* [1896], ... where the "order in question was not, and was not claimed to be, ... a taking of private property for a public use under the right of eminent domain," ... the Court invalidated a compensated taking of property for lack of a justifying public purpose. But where the exercise of the eminent domain power is rationally related to a conceivable public purpose, the Court has never held a compensated taking to be proscribed by the Public Use Clause....

On this basis, we have no trouble concluding that the Hawaii Act is constitutional. The people of Hawaii have attempted, much as the settlers of the original 13 Colonies did, to reduce the perceived social and economic evils of a land oligopoly traceable to their monarchs. The land oligopoly has, according to the Hawaii Legislature, created artificial deterrents to the normal functioning of the State's residential land market and forced thousands of individual homeowners to lease, rather than buy, the land underneath their homes. Regulating oligopoly and the evils associated with it is a classic exercise of a State's police powers.... We cannot disapprove of Hawaii's exercise of this power.

Nor can we condemn as irrational the Act's approach to correcting the land oligopoly problem. The Act presumes that when a sufficiently large number of persons declare that they are willing but unable to buy lots at fair prices the land market is malfunctioning. When such a malfunction is signaled, the Act authorizes HHA to condemn lots in the relevant tract. The Act limits the number of lots any one tenant can purchase and authorizes HHA to use public funds to ensure that the market dilution goals will be achieved. This is a comprehensive and rational approach to identifying and correcting market failure.

Of course, this Act, like any other, may not be successful in achieving its intended goals. But "whether in fact the provision will accomplish its objectives is not the question: the [constitutional requirement] is satisfied if ... the ... [state] Legislature rationally could have believed that the [Act] would promote its objective." ... When the legislature's purpose is legitimate and its means are not irrational, our cases make clear that empirical debates over the wisdom of takings—no less than debates over the wisdom of other kinds of socioeconomic legislation—are not to be carried out in the federal courts. Redistribution of fees simple to correct deficiencies in the market determined by the state legislature to be attributable to land oligopoly is a rational exercise of the eminent domain power. Therefore, the Hawaii statute must pass the scrutiny of the Public Use Clause....

The State of Hawaii has never denied that the Constitution forbids even a compensated taking of property when executed for no reason other than to confer a private benefit on a particular private party. A purely private taking could not withstand the scrutiny of the public use requirement; it would serve no legitimate purpose of government and would thus be void. But no purely private taking is involved in this case. The Hawaii Legislature enacted its Land Reform Act not to benefit a particular class of identifiable individuals but to attack certain perceived evils of concentrated property ownership in Hawaii—a legitimate public purpose. Use of the condemnation power to achieve this purpose is not irrational.

Since we assume for purposes of this appeal that the weighty demand of just compensation has been met, the requirements of the Fifth and Fourteenth Amendments have been satisfied. Accordingly, we reverse the judgment of the Court of Appeals, and remand these cases for further proceedings in conformity with this opinion....

Justice Marshall took no part in the consideration or decision of these cases.

(Continued)

DOLAN v. CITY OF TIGARD
572 U.S. 374; 114 S.Ct. 2309; 129 L.Ed.2d. 304 (1994)
Vote: 5-4

In this case, the Supreme Court addresses a city's refusal to grant a building permit unless the property owner agreed to dedicate a portion of her land for flood control and traffic improvements. In deciding the case, the Court considers a question left open in Nollan v. California Coastal Commission (1987) regarding the relationship between the impact of proposed development and the conditions imposed by government on such development.

Chief Justice Rehnquist delivered the opinion of the Court.

... The State of Oregon enacted a comprehensive land use management program in 1973.... The program required all Oregon cities and counties to adopt new comprehensive land use plans that were consistent with the statewide planning goals.... The plans are implemented by land use regulations which are part of an integrated hierarchy of legally binding goals, plans, and regulations.... Pursuant to the State's requirements, the city of Tigard a community of some 30,000 residents on the southwest edge of Portland, developed a comprehensive plan and codified it in its Community Development Code (CDC). The CDC requires property owners in the area zoned Central Business District to comply with a 15% open space and landscaping requirement, which limits total site coverage, including all structures and paving parking to 85% of the parcel.... After the completion of a transportation study that identified congestion in the Central Business District as a particular problem, the city adopted a plan for a pedestrian/bicycle pathway intended to encourage alternatives to automobile transportation for short trips. The CDC requires that new development facilitate this plan by dedicating land for pedestrian pathways where provided for in the pedestrian/bicycle pathway plan.

The city also adopted a Master Drainage Plan (Drainage Plan). The Drainage Plan noted that flooding occurred in several areas along Fanno Creek, including areas near petitioner's property.... The Drainage Plan also established that the increase in impervious surfaces associated with continued urbanization would exacerbate these flooding problems. To combat these risks, the Drainage Plan suggested a series of improvements to the Fanno Creek Basin, including channel excavation in the area next to petitioner's property.... Other recommendations included ensuring that the floodplain remains free of structures and that it be preserved as greenways to minimize flood damage to structures.... The Drainage Plan concluded that the cost of these improvements should be shared based on both direct and indirect benefits, with property owners along the waterways paying more due to the direct benefit that they would receive....

Petitioner Florence Dolan owns a plumbing and electric supply store located on Main Street in the Central Business District of the city. The store covers approximately 9,700 square feet on the eastern side of a 1.67 acre parcel, which includes a gravel parking lot. Fanno Creek flows through the southwestern corner of the lot and along its western boundary. The year-round flow of the creek renders the area within the creek's 100-year floodplain virtually unusable for commercial development. The city's comprehensive plan includes the Fanno Creek floodplain as part of the city's greenway system.

Petitioner applied to the city for a permit to redevelop the site. Her proposed plans called for nearly doubling the size of the store to 17,600 square feet, and paving a 39-space parking lot. The existing store, located on the opposite side of the parcel, would be razed in sections as construction progressed on the new building. In the second phase of the project, petitioner proposed to build an additional structure on the northeast side of the site for complementary businesses, and to provide more parking. The proposed expansion and intensified use are consistent with city's zoning scheme in the Central Business District....

The City Planning Commission granted petitioner's permit application subject to conditions imposed by the city's CDC. The CDC establishes the following standard for site development review approval: "Where landfill and/or development is allowed within and adjacent to the 100-year floodplain, the city shall require the dedication of sufficient open land area for greenway adjoining and within the floodplain. This area shall include portions at a suitable elevation for the construction of a pedestrian/bicycle pathway within the floodplain in accordance with the adopted pedestrian/bicycle plan." ...

Thus, the Commission required that petitioner dedicate the portion of her property lying within the 100-year floodplain for improvement of a storm drainage system along Fanno Creek and that she dedicate an additional 15-foot strip of land adjacent to the floodplain as a pedestrian/bicycle pathway. The dedication required by that condition encompasses approximately 7,000 square feet, or roughly 10% of the property. In accordance with city practice, petitioner could rely on the dedicated property to meet the 15% open space and landscaping requirement mandated by the city's zoning scheme.... The city would bear the cost of maintaining a landscaped buffer between the dedicated area and the new store....

Petitioner requested variances from the CDC standards. Variances are granted only where it can be shown that, owing to special circumstances related to a specific piece of the land, the literal interpretation of the applicable zoning provisions would cause "an undue or unnecessary hardship" unless the variance is granted.... Rather than posing alternative mitigating measures to offset the expected impacts of her proposed development, as allowed under the CDC, petitioner simply argued that her proposed development would not conflict with the policies of the comprehensive plan.... The Commission denied the request.

The Commission made a series of findings concerning the relationship between the dedicated conditions and the projected impacts of petitioner's project. First, the Commission noted that "[i]t is reasonable to assume that customers and employees of the future uses of this site could utilize a pedestrian/bicycle pathway adjacent to this development for their transportation and recreational needs." ... The Commission noted that the site plan has provided for bicycle parking in a rack in front of the proposed building and "[i]t is reasonable to expect that some of the users of the bicycle parking provided for by the site plan will use the pathway adjacent to Fanno Creek if it is constructed." ... In addition, the Commission found that creation of a convenient, safe pedestrian/bicycle pathway system as an alternative means of transportation "could offset some of the traffic demand on [nearby] streets and lessen the increase in traffic congestion." ... The Commission went on to note that the required floodplain dedication would be reasonably related to petitioner's request to intensify the use of the site given the increase in the impervious surface. The Commission stated that the "anticipated increased

stormwater flow from the subject property to an already strained creek and drainage basin can only add to the public need to manage the stream channel and floodplain for drainage purposes." ... Based on this anticipated increased stormwater flow, the Commission concluded that "the requirement of dedication of the floodplain area on the site is related to the applicant's plan to intensify development on the site." ... The Tigard City Council approved the Commission's final order....

Petitioner appealed to the Land Use Board of Appeals (LUBA) on the ground that the city's dedication requirements were not related to the proposed development, and, therefore, those requirements constituted an uncompensated taking of their property under the Fifth Amendment.... [This appeal was unsuccessful.]

The Oregon Court of Appeals affirmed, rejecting petitioner's contention that in *Nollan v. California Coastal Commission* ... we had abandoned the "reasonable relationship" test in favor of a stricter "essential nexus" test.... The court decided that both the pedestrian/bicycle pathway condition and the storm drainage dedication had an essential nexus to the development of the proposed site.... Therefore, the court found the conditions to be reasonably related to the impact of the expansion of petitioner's business.... We granted certiorari ... because of an alleged conflict between the Oregon Supreme Court's decision and our decision in *Nollan*.

The Takings Clause of the Fifth Amendment ... provides: "[N]or shall private property be taken for public use, without just compensation." One of the principal purposes of the Takings Clause is "to bar Government from forcing some people alone to bear public burdens which, in all fairness and justice, should be borne by the public as a whole." ... Without question, had the city simply required petitioner to dedicate a strip of land along Fanno Creek for public use, rather than conditioning the grant of her permit to redevelop her property on such a dedication, a taking would have occurred.... Such public access would deprive petitioner of the right to exclude others, "one of the most essential sticks in the bundle of rights that are commonly characterized as property." ...

... Under the well-settled doctrine of "unconstitutional conditions," the government may not require a person to give up a constitutional right—the right to receive just compensation when property is taken for a public use—in exchange for a discretionary benefit

(Continued)

conferred by the government where the property sought has little or no relationship to the benefit....

Petitioner contends that the city has forced her to choose between the building permit and her right under the Fifth Amendment to just compensation for the public easements. Petitioner does not quarrel with the city's authority to exact some forms of dedication as a condition for the grant of a building permit, but challenges the showing made by the city to justify these exactions. She argues that the city has identified "no special benefits" conferred on her, and has not identified any "special quantifiable burdens" created by her new store that would justify the particular dedications required from her which are not required from the public at large.

In evaluating petitioner's claim, we must first determine whether the "essential nexus" exists between the "legitimate state interest" and the permit condition exacted by the city.... If we find that a nexus exists, we must then decide the required degree of connection between the exactions and the projected impact of the proposed development. We were not required to reach this question in *Nollan*, because we concluded that the connection did not meet even the loosest standard.... Here, however, we must decide this question....

... Undoubtedly, the prevention of flooding along Fanno Creek and the reduction of traffic congestion in the Central Business District qualify as the type of legitimate public purposes we have upheld.... It seems equally obvious that a nexus exists between preventing flooding along Fanno Creek and limiting development within the creek's 100-year floodplain. Petitioner proposes to double the size of her retail store and to pave her now-gravel parking lot, thereby expanding the impervious surface on the property and increasing the amount of stormwater run-off into Fanno Creek.

The same may be said for the city's attempt to reduce traffic congestion by providing for alternative means of transportation. In theory, a pedestrian/bicycle pathway provides a useful alternative means of transportation for workers and shoppers....

The second part of our analysis requires us to determine whether the degree of the exactions demanded by the city's permit conditions bear the required relationship to the projected impact of petitioner's proposed development....

The city required that the petitioner dedicate "to the city as Greenway all portions of the site that fall within the existing 100-year floodplain ... and all property 15 feet above [the floodplain] boundary." In addition, the

city demanded that the retail store be designed so as not to intrude into the greenway area. The city relies on the Commission's rather tentative findings that increased stormwater flow from petitioner's property "can only add to the public need to manage the [flood-plain] for drainage purposes" to support its conclusion that the "requirement of dedication of the floodplain area on the site is related to the applicant's plan to intensify development on the site." ...

The city made the following specific findings relevant to the pedestrian/bicycle pathway: "In addition, the proposed expanded use of this site is anticipated to generate additional vehicular traffic thereby increasing congestion on nearby collector and arterial streets. Creation of a convenient, safe pedestrian/bicycle pathway system as an alternative means of transportation could offset some of the traffic demand on these nearby streets and lessen the increase in traffic congestion." ...

The question for us is whether these findings are constitutionally sufficient to justify the conditions imposed by the city on petitioner's building permit. Since state courts have been dealing with this question a good deal longer than we have, we turn to representative decisions made by them.

In some States, very generalized statements as to the necessary connection between the required dedication and the proposed development seem to suffice.... We think this standard is too lax to adequately protect petitioner's right to just compensation if her property is taken for a public purpose....

A number of state courts have taken an intermediate position, requiring the municipality to show a "reasonable relationship" between the required dedication and the impact of the proposed development....

We think the "reasonable relationship" test adopted by a majority of the state courts is closer to the federal constitutional norm than either of those previously discussed. But we do not adopt it as such, partly because the term "reasonable relationship" seems confusingly similar to the term "rational basis" which describes the minimal level of scrutiny under the Equal Protection Clause of the Fourteenth Amendment. We think a term such as "rough proportionality" best encapsulates what we hold to be the requirement of the Fifth Amendment. No precise mathematical calculation is required, but the city must make some sort of individualized determination that the required dedication is related both in nature and extent to the impact of the proposed development....

... As we have noted, [the] right to exclude others is "one of the most essential sticks in the bundle of rights that are commonly characterized as property." ... It is difficult to see why recreational visitors trampling along petitioner's floodplain easement are sufficiently related to the city's legitimate interest in reducing flooding problems along Fanno Creek, and the city has not attempted to make any individualized determination to support this part of its request....

Admittedly, petitioner wants to build a bigger store to attract members of the public to her property. She also wants, however, to be able to control the time and manner in which they enter.... [T]he city wants to impose a permanent recreational easement upon petitioner's property that borders Fanno Creek. Petitioner would lose all rights to regulate the time in which the public entered onto the Greenway, regardless of any interference it might pose with her retail store. Her right to exclude would not be regulated, it would be eviscerated.

If petitioner's proposed development had somehow encroached on existing greenway space in the city, it would have been reasonable to require petitioner to provide some alternative greenway space for the public either on her property or elsewhere.... But that is not the case here. We conclude that the findings upon which the city relies do not show the required reasonable relationship between the floodplain easement and the petitioner's proposed new building.

With respect to the pedestrian/bicycle pathway, we have no doubt that the city was correct in finding that the larger retail sales facility proposed by petitioner will increase traffic on the streets of the Central Business District. The city estimates that the proposed development would generate roughly 435 additional trips per day. Dedications for streets, sidewalks, and other public ways are generally reasonable exactions to avoid excessive congestion from a proposed property use. But on the record before us, the city has not met its burden of demonstrating that the additional number of vehicle and bicycle trips generated by the petitioner's development reasonably relate to the city's requirement for a dedication of the pedestrian/bicycle pathway easement. The city simply found that the creation of the pathway "could offset some of the traffic demand ... and lessen the increase in traffic congestion."

... No precise mathematical calculation is required, but the city must make some effort to quantify its findings in support of the dedication for the pedestrian/bicycle pathway beyond the conclusory statement that it could offset some of the traffic demand generated.

Cities have long engaged in the commendable task of land use planning, made necessary by increasing urbanization particularly in metropolitan areas such as Portland. The city's goals of reducing flooding hazards and traffic congestion, and providing for public greenways, are laudable, but there are outer limits to how this may be done....

Justice Stevens, with whom *Justice Blackmun* and *Justice Ginsburg* join, dissenting.

... If the Court proposes to have the federal judiciary micromanage state decisions of this kind, it is indeed extending its welcome mat to a significant new class of litigants. Although there is no reason to believe that state courts have failed to rise to the task, property owners have surely found a new friend today.

The Court has made a serious error by abandoning the traditional presumption of constitutionality and imposing a novel burden of proof on a city implementing an admittedly valid comprehensive land use plan. Even more consequential than its incorrect disposition of this case, however, is the Court's resurrection of a species of substantive due process analysis that it firmly rejected decades ago....

In our changing world one thing is certain: uncertainty will characterize predictions about the impact of new urban developments on the risks of floods, earthquakes, traffic congestion, or environmental harms. When there is doubt concerning the magnitude of those impacts, the public interest in averting them must outweigh the private interest of the commercial entrepreneur. If the government can demonstrate that the conditions it has imposed in a land-use permit are rational, impartial and conducive to fulfilling the aims of a valid land-use plan, a strong presumption of validity should attach to those conditions. The burden of demonstrating that those conditions have unreasonably impaired the economic value of the proposed improvement belongs squarely on the shoulders of the party challenging the state action's constitutionality. That allocation of burdens has served us well in the past. The Court has stumbled badly today by reversing it....

Justice Souter, dissenting....

KELO v. CITY OF NEW LONDON
545 U.S. 469; 125 S.Ct. 2655; 162 L.Ed.2d. 439 (2005)
Vote: 5-4

In this highly publicized and extremely controversial decision, the Supreme Court considers whether economic development constitutes a "public use" that justifies a city's exercise of eminent domain. In reviewing the opinions in the case, students should consider whether this decision represents a departure from modern Takings Clause jurisprudence as manifested in decisions like Herman v. Parker (1954) and Hawaii Housing Authority v. Midkiff (1984).

Justice Stevens delivered the opinion of the Court.

In 2000, the city of New London approved a development plan that, in the words of the Supreme Court of Connecticut, was "projected to create in excess of 1,000 jobs, to increase tax and other revenues, and to revitalize an economically distressed city, including its downtown and waterfront areas." In assembling the land needed for this project, the city's development agent has purchased property from willing sellers and proposes to use the power of eminent domain to acquire the remainder of the property from unwilling owners in exchange for just compensation. The question presented is whether the city's proposed disposition of this property qualifies as a "public use" within the meaning of the Takings Clause of the Fifth Amendment to the Constitution.

The city of New London (hereinafter City) sits at the junction of the Thames River and the Long Island Sound in southeastern Connecticut. Decades of economic decline led a state agency in 1990 to designate the City a "distressed municipality." ... In 1998, the City's unemployment rate was nearly double that of the State, and its population of just under 24,000 residents was at its lowest since 1920.

These conditions prompted state and local officials to target New London, and particularly its Fort Trumbull area, for economic revitalization. To this end, respondent New London Development Corporation (NLDC), a private nonprofit entity established some years earlier to assist the City in planning economic development, was reactivated. In January 1998, the State authorized a $5.35 million bond issue to support the NLDC's planning activities and a $10 million bond issue toward the creation of a Fort Trumbull State Park. In February, the pharmaceutical company Pfizer Inc. announced that it would build a $300 million research facility on a site immediately adjacent to Fort Trumbull; local planners hoped that Pfizer would draw new business to the area, thereby serving as a catalyst to the area's rejuvenation. After receiving initial approval from the city council, the NLDC continued its planning activities and held a series of neighborhood meetings to educate the public about the process. In May, the city council authorized the NLDC to formally submit its plans to the relevant state agencies for review. Upon obtaining state level approval, the NLDC finalized an integrated development plan focused on 90 acres of the Fort Trumbull area.

The Fort Trumbull area is situated on a peninsula that juts into the Thames River. The area comprises approximately 115 privately owned properties, as well as the 32 acres of land formerly occupied by [a] naval facility (Trumbull State Park now occupies 18 of those 32 acres). The development plan encompasses seven parcels. Parcel 1 is designated for a waterfront conference hotel at the center of a "small urban village" that will include restaurants and shopping. This parcel will also have marinas for both recreational and commercial uses. A pedestrian "riverwalk" will originate here and continue down the coast, connecting the waterfront areas of the development. Parcel 2 will be the site of approximately 80 new residences organized into an urban neighborhood and linked by public walkway to the remainder of the development, including the state park. This parcel also includes space reserved for a new U.S. Coast Guard Museum. Parcel 3, which is located immediately north of the Pfizer facility, will contain at least 90,000 square feet of research and development office space. Parcel 4A is a 2.4 acre site that will be used either to support the adjacent state park, by providing parking or retail services for visitors, or to support the nearby marina. Parcel 4B will include a renovated marina, as well as the final stretch of the riverwalk. Parcels 5, 6, and 7 will provide land for office and retail space, parking, and water dependent commercial uses.

The NLDC intended the development plan to capitalize on the arrival of the Pfizer facility and the new commerce it was expected to attract. In addition to creating jobs, generating tax revenue, and helping to "build momentum for the revitalization of downtown New London," the plan was also designed to make the

City more attractive and to create leisure and recreational opportunities on the waterfront and in the park.

The city council approved the plan in January 2000, and designated the NLDC as its development agent in charge of implementation. The city council also authorized the NLDC to purchase property or to acquire property by exercising eminent domain in the City's name. The NLDC successfully negotiated the purchase of most of the real estate in the 90-acre area, but its negotiations with petitioners failed. As a consequence, in November 2000, the NLDC initiated the condemnation proceedings that gave rise to this case.

Petitioner Susette Kelo has lived in the Fort Trumbull area since 1997. She has made extensive improvements to her house, which she prizes for its water view. Petitioner Wilhelmina Dery was born in her Fort Trumbull house in 1918 and has lived there her entire life. Her husband Charles (also a petitioner) has lived in the house since they married some 60 years ago. In all, the nine petitioners own 15 properties in Fort Trumbull. There is no allegation that any of these properties is blighted or otherwise in poor condition; rather, they were condemned only because they happen to be located in the development area.

In December 2000, petitioners brought this action in the New London Superior Court. They claimed, among other things, that the taking of their properties would violate the "public use" restriction in the Fifth Amendment. After a 7-day bench trial, the Superior Court granted a permanent restraining order prohibiting the taking of the properties located in parcel 4A (park or marina support). It, however, denied petitioners relief as to the properties located in parcel 3 (office space).

After the Superior Court ruled, both sides took appeals to the Supreme Court of Connecticut. That court held, over a dissent, that all of the City's proposed takings were valid....

Two polar propositions are perfectly clear. On the one hand, it has long been accepted that the sovereign may not take the property of *A* for the sole purpose of transferring it to another private party *B*, even though *A* is paid just compensation. On the other hand, it is equally clear that a State may transfer property from one private party to another if future "use by the public" is the purpose of the taking; the condemnation of land for a railroad with common carrier duties is a familiar example. Neither of these propositions, however, determines the disposition of this case.

As for the first proposition, the City would no doubt be forbidden from taking petitioners' land for the purpose of conferring a private benefit on a particular private party. Nor would the City be allowed to take property under the mere pretext of a public purpose, when its actual purpose was to bestow a private benefit. The takings before us, however, would be executed pursuant to a "carefully considered" development plan. The trial judge and all the members of the Supreme Court of Connecticut agreed that there was no evidence of an illegitimate purpose in this case. Therefore, ... the City's development plan was not adopted "to benefit a particular class of identifiable individuals."

On the other hand, this is not a case in which the City is planning to open the condemned land—at least not in its entirety—to use by the general public. Nor will the private lessees of the land in any sense be required to operate like common carriers, making their services available to all comers. But although such a projected use would be sufficient to satisfy the public use requirement, this "Court long ago rejected any literal requirement that condemned property be put into use for the general public." Indeed, while many state courts in the mid-19th century endorsed "use by the public" as the proper definition of public use, that narrow view steadily eroded over time. Not only was the "use by the public" test difficult to administer (e.g., what proportion of the public need have access to the property? at what price?), but it proved to be impractical given the diverse and always evolving needs of society. Accordingly, when this Court began applying the Fifth Amendment to the States at the close of the 19th century, it embraced the broader and more natural interpretation of public use as "public purpose." Thus, in a case upholding a mining company's use of an aerial bucket line to transport ore over property it did not own, Justice Holmes's opinion for the Court stressed "the inadequacy of use by the general public as a universal test." *Strickley v. Highland Boy Gold Mining Company* ... (1906). We have repeatedly and consistently rejected that narrow test ever since.

The disposition of this case therefore turns on the question whether the City's development plan serves a "public purpose." Without exception, our cases have defined that concept broadly, reflecting our longstanding policy of deference to legislative judgments in this field.

In *Herman* v. *Parker* ... (1954), this Court upheld a redevelopment plan targeting a blighted area of Washington, D.C., in which most of the housing for the area's 5,000 inhabitants was beyond repair. Under the plan, the area would be condemned and part of it utilized for the construction of streets, schools, and other public facilities. The remainder of the land would be leased or sold to private parties for the purpose of

(Continued)

redevelopment, including the construction of low-cost housing. The owner of a department store located in the area challenged the condemnation, pointing out that his store was not itself blighted and arguing that the creation of a "better balanced, more attractive community" was not a valid public use. Writing for a unanimous Court, Justice Douglas refused to evaluate this claim in isolation, deferring instead to the legislative and agency judgment that the area "must be planned as a whole" for the plan to be successful. The Court explained that "community redevelopment programs need not, by force of the Constitution, be on a piecemeal basis—lot by lot, building by building." The public use underlying the taking was unequivocally affirmed....

In *Hawaii Housing Authority v. Midkiff* ... (1984), the Court considered a Hawaii statute whereby fee title was taken from lessors and transferred to lessees (for just compensation) in order to reduce the concentration of land ownership. We unanimously upheld the statute and rejected the Ninth Circuit's view that it was "a naked attempt on the part of the state of Hawaii to take the property of A and transfer it to B solely for B's private use and benefit." Reaffirming *Berman*'s deferential approach to legislative judgments in this field, we concluded that the State's purpose of eliminating the "social and economic evils of a land oligopoly" qualified as a valid public use. Our opinion also rejected the contention that the mere fact that the State immediately transferred the properties to private individuals upon condemnation somehow diminished the public character of the taking. "[I]t is only the taking's purpose, and not its mechanics," we explained, that matters in determining public use.

In that same Term we decided another public use case that arose in a purely economic context. In *Ruckelshaus v. Monsanto, Company* ... (1984), the Court dealt with provisions of the Federal Insecticide, Fungicide, and Rodenticide Act under which the Environmental Protection Agency could consider the data (including trade secrets) submitted by a prior pesticide applicant in evaluating a subsequent application, so long as the second applicant paid just compensation for the data. We acknowledged that the "most direct beneficiaries" of these provisions were the subsequent applicants, but we nevertheless upheld the statute under *Herman* and *Midkiff*. We found sufficient Congress's belief that sparing applicants the cost of time-consuming research eliminated a significant barrier to entry in the pesticide market and thereby enhanced competition.

Viewed as a whole, our jurisprudence has recognized that the needs of society have varied between different parts of the Nation, just as they have evolved over time in response to changed circumstances. Our earliest cases in particular embodied a strong theme of federalism, emphasizing the "great respect" that we owe to state legislatures and state courts in discerning local public needs. For more than a century, our public use jurisprudence has wisely eschewed rigid formulas and intrusive scrutiny in favor of affording legislatures broad latitude in determining what public needs justify the use of the takings power....

Those who govern the City were not confronted with the need to remove blight in the Fort Trumbull area, but their determination that the area was sufficiently distressed to justify a program of economic rejuvenation is entitled to our deference. The City has carefully formulated an economic development plan that it believes will provide appreciable benefits to the community, including—but by no means limited to—new jobs and increased tax revenue. As with other exercises in urban planning and development, the City is endeavoring to coordinate a variety of commercial, residential, and recreational uses of land, with the hope that they will form a whole greater than the sum of its parts. To effectuate this plan, the City has invoked a state statute that specifically authorizes the use of eminent domain to promote economic development. Given the comprehensive character of the plan, the thorough deliberation that preceded its adoption, and the limited scope of our review, it is appropriate for us, as it was in *Berman*, to resolve the challenges of the individual owners, not on a piecemeal basis, but rather in light of the entire plan. Because that plan unquestionably serves a public purpose, the takings challenged here satisfy the public use requirement of the Fifth Amendment.

To avoid this result, petitioners urge us to adopt a new bright-line rule that economic development does not qualify as a public use. Putting aside the unpersuasive suggestion that the City's plan will provide only purely economic benefits, neither precedent nor logic supports petitioners' proposal. Promoting economic development is a traditional and long accepted function of government. There is, moreover, no principled way of distinguishing economic development from the other public purposes that we have recognized.... It would be incongruous to hold that the City's interest in the economic benefits to be derived from the development of the Fort Trumbull area has less of a public character than any of those other interests. Clearly, there is no basis for exempting economic development from our traditionally broad understanding of public purpose.

Petitioners contend that using eminent domain for economic development impermissibly blurs the boundary between public and private takings. Again, our cases foreclose this objection. Quite simply, the government's pursuit of a public purpose will often benefit individual private parties. For example, in *Midkiff*, the forced transfer of property conferred a direct and significant benefit on those lessees who were previously unable to purchase their homes. In *Monsanto*, we recognized that the "most direct beneficiaries" of the data sharing provisions were the subsequent pesticide applicants, but benefiting them in this way was necessary to promoting competition in the pesticide market. The owner of the department store in *Berman* objected to "taking from one businessman for the benefit of another businessman," referring to the fact that under the redevelopment plan land would be leased or sold to private developers for redevelopment. Our rejection of that contention has particular relevance to the instant case: "The public end may be as well or better served through an agency of private enterprise than through a department of government—or so the Congress might conclude. We cannot say that public ownership is the sole method of promoting the public purposes of community redevelopment projects."

It is further argued that without a bright line rule nothing would stop a city from transferring citizen A's property to citizen *B* for the sole reason that citizen *B* will put the property to a more productive use and thus pay more taxes. Such a one-to-one transfer of property, executed outside the confines of an integrated development plan, is not presented in this case. While such an unusual exercise of government power would certainly raise a suspicion that a private purpose was afoot, the hypothetical cases posited by petitioners can be confronted if and when they arise. They do not warrant the crafting of an artificial restriction on the concept of public use.

Alternatively, petitioners maintain that for takings of this kind we should require a "reasonable certainty" that the expected public benefits will actually accrue. Such a rule, however, would represent an even greater departure from our precedent. "When the legislature's purpose is legitimate and its means are not irrational, our cases make clear that empirical debates over the wisdom of takings—no less than debates over the wisdom of other kinds of socioeconomic legislation—are not to be carried out in the federal courts." Indeed, earlier this Term we explained why similar practical concerns (among others) undermined the use of the "substantially advances" formula in our regulatory takings doctrine. The disadvantages of a heightened form

of review are especially pronounced in this type of case. Orderly implementation of a comprehensive redevelopment plan obviously requires that the legal rights of all interested parties be established before new construction can be commenced. A constitutional rule that required postponement of the judicial approval of every condemnation until the likelihood of success of the plan had been assured would unquestionably impose a significant impediment to the successful consummation of many such plans.

Just as we decline to second-guess the City's considered judgments about the efficacy of its development plan, we also decline to second guess the City's determinations as to what lands it needs to acquire in order to effectuate the project. "It is not for the courts to oversee the choice of the boundary line nor to sit in review on the size of a particular project area. Once the question of the public purpose has been decided, the amount and character of land to be taken for the project and the need for a particular tract to complete the integrated plan rests in the discretion of the legislative branch."

In affirming the City's authority to take petitioners' properties, we do not minimize the hardship that condemnations may entail, notwithstanding the payment of just compensation. We emphasize that nothing in our opinion precludes any State from placing further restrictions on its exercise of the takings power. Indeed, many States already impose "public use" requirements that are stricter than the federal baseline. Some of these requirements have been established as a matter of state constitutional law, while others are expressed in state eminent domain statutes that carefully limit the grounds upon which takings may be exercised. As the submissions of the parties and their *amici* make clear, the necessity and wisdom of using eminent domain to promote economic development are certainly matters of legitimate public debate. This Court's authority, however, extends only to determining whether the City's proposed condemnations are for a "public use" within the meaning of the Fifth Amendment to the Federal Constitution. Because over a century of our case law interpreting that provision dictates an affirmative answer to that question, we may not grant petitioners the relief that they seek.

The judgment of the Supreme Court of Connecticut is affirmed....

Justice Kennedy, concurring.

... This Court has declared that a taking should be upheld as consistent with the Public Use Clause as long

(Continued)

as it is "rationally related to a conceivable public purpose." This deferential standard of review echoes the rational basis test used to review economic regulation under the Due Process and Equal Protection Clauses. The determination that a rational basis standard of review is appropriate does not, however, alter the fact that transfers intended to confer benefits on particular, favored private entities, and with only incidental or pretextual public benefits, are forbidden by the Public Use Clause.

A court applying rational-basis review under the Public Use Clause should strike down a taking that, by a clear showing, is intended to favor a particular private party, with only incidental or pretextual public benefits, just as a court applying rational basis review under the Equal Protection Clause must strike down a government classification that is clearly intended to injure a particular class of private parties, with only incidental or pretextual public justifications. As the trial court in this case was correct to observe, "Where the purpose [of a taking] is economic development and that development is to be carried out by private parties or private parties will be benefited, the court must decide if the stated public purpose—economic advantage to a city sorely in need of it—is only incidental to the benefits that will be confined on private parties of a development plan." ...

My agreement with the Court that a presumption of invalidity is not warranted for economic development takings in general, or for the particular takings at issue in this case, does not foreclose the possibility that a more stringent standard of review than that announced in *Herman* and *Midkiff* might be appropriate for a more narrowly drawn category of takings. There may be private transfers in which the risk of undetected impermissible favoritism of private parties is so acute that a presumption (rebuttable or otherwise) of invalidity is warranted under the Public Use Clause. This demanding level of scrutiny, however, is not required simply because the purpose of the taking is economic development.

... This taking occurred in the context of a comprehensive development plan meant to address a serious city wide depression, and the projected economic benefits of the project cannot be characterized as *de minimus*. The identity of most of the private beneficiaries were unknown at the time the city formulated its plans. The city complied with elaborate procedural requirements that facilitate review of the record and inquiry into the city's purposes. In sum, while there may be categories of cases in which the transfers are so suspicious, or the procedures employed so prone to abuse, or

the purported benefits are so trivial or implausible, that courts should presume an impermissible private purpose, no such circumstances are present in this case....

Justice O'Connor, with whom the *Chief Justice*, *Justice Scalia*, and *Justice Thomas* join, dissenting.

Over two centuries ago, just after the Bill of Rights was ratified, Justice Chase wrote:

> *An ACT of the Legislature (for I cannot call it a law) contrary to the great first principles of the social compact, cannot be considered a rightful exercise of legislative authority.... A few instances will suffice to explain what I mean.... [A] law that takes property from A and gives it to B: It is against all reason and justice, for a people to entrust a Legislature with SUCH powers; and, therefore, it cannot be presumed that they have done it. Calder v. Bull (1798).*

Today the Court abandons this long held, basic limitation on government power. Under the banner of economic development, all private property is now vulnerable to being taken and transferred to another private owner, so long as it might be upgraded—i.e., given to an owner who will use it in a way that the legislature deems more beneficial to the public—in the process. To reason, as the Court does, that the incidental public benefits resulting from the subsequent ordinary use of private property render economic development takings "for public use" is to wash out any distinction between private and public use of property—and thereby effectively to delete the words "for public use" from the Takings Clause of the Fifth Amendment. Accordingly I respectfully dissent....

When interpreting the Constitution, we begin with the unremarkable presumption that every word in the document has independent meaning, "that no word was unnecessarily used, or needlessly added." In keeping with that presumption, we have read the Fifth Amendment's language to impose two distinct conditions on the exercise of eminent domain: "the taking must be for a 'public use' and 'just compensation' must be paid to the owner."

These two limitations ... ensure stable property ownership by providing safeguards against excessive, unpredictable, or unfair use of the government's eminent domain power—particularly against those owners who, for whatever reasons, may be unable to protect themselves in the political process against the majority's will....

Where is the line between "public" and "private" property use? We give considerable deference to legislatures' determinations about what governmental activities will advantage the public. But were the political branches the sole arbiters of the public-private distinction, the Public Use Clause would amount to little more than hortatory fluff. An external, judicial check on how the public use requirement is interpreted, however limited, is necessary if this constraint on government power is to retain any meaning.

Our cases have generally identified three categories of takings that comply with the public use requirement, though it is in the nature of things that the boundaries between these categories are not always firm. Two are relatively straightforward and uncontroversial. First, the sovereign may transfer private property to public ownership—such as for a road, a hospital, or a military base. Second, the sovereign may transfer private property to private parties, often common carriers, who make the property available for the public's use—such as with a railroad, a public utility, or a stadium. But "public ownership" and "use by the public" are sometimes too constricting and impractical ways to define the scope of the Public Use Clause. Thus we have allowed that, in certain circumstances and to meet certain exigencies, takings that serve a public purpose also satisfy the Constitution even if the property is destined for subsequent private use.

This case returns us for the first time in over 20 years to the hard question of when a purportedly "public purpose" taking meets the public use requirement. It presents an issue of first impression: Are economic development takings constitutional? I would hold that they are not. We are guided by two precedents about the taking of real property by eminent domain....

In those decisions, we emphasized the importance of deferring to legislative judgments about public purpose. Because courts are ill equipped to evaluate the efficacy of proposed legislative initiatives, we rejected as unworkable the idea of courts' "'deciding on what is and is not a governmental function and ... invalidating legislation on the basis of their view on that question at the moment of decision, a practice which has proved impracticable in other fields.'" Likewise, we recognized our inability to evaluate whether, in a given case, eminent domain is a necessary means by which to pursue the legislature's ends.

Yet for all the emphasis on deference, *Herman* and *Midkiff* hewed to a bedrock principle without which our public use jurisprudence would collapse: "A purely private taking could not withstand the scrutiny of the public use requirement; it would serve no legitimate purpose of government and would thus be void." To protect that principle, those decisions reserved "a role for courts to play in reviewing a legislature's judgment of what constitutes a public use ... [though] the Court in *Herman* made clear that it is 'an extremely narrow' one."

The Court's holdings in *Herman* and *Midkiff were* true to the principle underlying the Public Use Clause. In both those cases, the extraordinary, precondemnation use of the targeted property inflicted affirmative harm on society—in *Herman* through blight resulting from extreme poverty and in *Midkiff* through oligopoly resulting from extreme wealth. And in both cases, the relevant legislative body had found that eliminating the existing property use was necessary to remedy the harm. Thus a public purpose was realized when the harmful use was eliminated. Because each taking *directly* achieved a public benefit, it did not matter that the property was turned over to private use. Here, in contrast, New London does not claim that Susette Kelo's and Wilhelmina Dery's well maintained homes are the source of any social harm. Indeed, it could not so claim without adopting the absurd argument that any single family home that might be razed to make way for an apartment building, or any church that might be replaced with a retail store, or any small business that might be more lucrative if it were instead part of a national franchise, is inherently harmful to society and thus within the government's power to condemn.

In moving away from our decisions sanctioning the condemnation of harmful property use, the Court today significantly expands the meaning of public use. It holds that the sovereign may take private property currently put to ordinary private use, and give it over for new, ordinary private use, so long as the new use is predicted to generate some secondary benefit for the public—such as increased tax revenue, more jobs, maybe even aesthetic pleasure. But nearly any lawful use of real private property can be said to generate some incidental benefit to the public. Thus, if predicted (or even guaranteed) positive side effects are enough to render transfer from one private party to another constitutional, then the words "for public use" do not realistically exclude *any* takings, and thus do not exert any constraint on the eminent domain power....

The Court protests that it does not sanction the bare transfer from A to B for B's benefit. It suggests two limitations on what can be taken after today's decision. First, it maintains a role for courts in ferreting out takings whose sole purpose is to bestow a benefit on the private transferee—without detailing how courts are to conduct that complicated inquiry. For his part,

(Continued)

Justice Kennedy suggests that courts may divine illicit purpose by a careful review of the record and the process by which a legislature arrived at the decision to take—without specifying what courts should look for in a case with different facts, how they will know if they have found it, and what to do if they do not. Whatever the details of Justice Kennedy's as yet undisclosed test, it is difficult to envision anyone but the "stupid staff[er]" failing it. The trouble with economic development takings is that private benefit and incidental public benefit are, by definition, merged and mutually reinforcing. In this case, for example, any boon for Pfizer or the plan's developer is difficult to disaggregate from the promised public gains in taxes and jobs....

Even if there were a practical way to isolate the motives behind a given taking, the gesture toward a purpose test is theoretically flawed. If it is true that incidental public benefits from new private use are enough to ensure the "public purpose" in a taking, why should it matter, as far as the Fifth Amendment is concerned, what inspired the taking in the first place? How much the government does or does not desire to benefit a favored private party has no bearing on whether an economic development taking will or will not generate secondary benefit for the public. And whatever the reason for a given condemnation, the effect is the same from the constitutional perspective—private property is forcibly relinquished to new private ownership.

A second proposed limitation is implicit in the Court's opinion. The logic of today's decision is that eminent domain may only be used to upgrade—not downgrade—property. At best this makes the Public Use Clause redundant with the Due Process Clause, which already prohibits irrational government action. The Court rightfully admits, however, that the judiciary cannot get bogged down in predictive judgments about whether the public will actually be better off after a property transfer. In any event, this constraint has no realistic import. For who among us can say she already makes the most productive or attractive possible use of her property? The specter of condemnation hangs over all property. Nothing is to prevent the State from replacing any Motel 6 with a Ritz Carlton, any home with a shopping mall, or any farm with a factory....

Finally, in a coda, the Court suggests that property owners should turn to the States, who may or may not choose to impose appropriate limits on economic development takings. This is an abdication of our responsibility. States play many important functions in our system of dual sovereignty, but compensating for our refusal to enforce properly the Federal Constitution (and a provision meant to curtail state action, no less) is not among them....

Any property may now be taken for the benefit of another private party, but the fallout from this decision will not be random. The beneficiaries are likely to be those citizens with disproportionate influence and power in the political process, including large corporations and development firms. As for the victims, the government now has license to transfer property from those with fewer resources to those with more. The Founders cannot have intended this perverse result....

Justice Thomas, dissenting.

Long ago, William Blackstone wrote that "the law of the land ... postpone[s] even public necessity to the sacred and inviolable rights of private property." The Framers embodied that principle in the Constitution, allowing the government to take property not for "public necessity," but instead for "public use." Defying this understanding, the Court replaces the Public Use Clause with a "[P]ublic [P]urpose" Clause, a restriction that is satisfied, the Court instructs, so long as the purpose is "legitimate" and the means "not irrational." This deferential shift in phraseology enables the Court to hold, against all common sense, that a costly urban-renewal project whose stated purpose is a vague promise of new jobs and increased tax revenue, but which is also suspiciously agreeable to the Pfizer Corporation, is for a "public use."

I cannot agree. If such "economic development" takings are for a "public use," any taking is, and the Court has erased the Public Use Clause from our Constitution, as Justice O'Connor powerfully argues in dissent. I do not believe that this Court can eliminate liberties expressly enumerated in the Constitution and therefore join her dissenting opinion. Regrettably, however, the Court's error runs deeper than this. Today's decision is simply the latest in a string of our cases construing the Public Use Clause to be a virtual nullity, without the slightest nod to its original meaning. In my view, the Public Use Clause, originally understood, is a meaningful limit on the government's eminent domain power. Our cases have strayed from the Clause's original meaning, and I would reconsider them....

CHAPTER 3

Expressive Freedom and the First Amendment

"If there is a bedrock principle underlying the First Amendment, it is that the government may not prohibit the expression of an idea simply because society finds the idea itself offensive or disagreeable."

—*Justice William J. Brennan, Writing for the Supreme Court in Texas v. Johnson* (1989)

William J. Brennan: Associate Justice, 1956–1990

Introduction

This chapter examines the Supreme Court's development of constitutional doctrine effectively defining **freedom of expression**, which encompasses both **freedom of speech** and **freedom of the press**. The chapter also deals with **freedom of assembly**, which is an explicit component of the First Amendment, and **freedom of association**, which the courts have recognized as an implicit First Amendment freedom as well. We deal separately with the First Amendment freedom of religion in Chapter 4. As important as freedom of religion was to the founders of the republic, one can argue that freedom of expression is *the* fundamental freedom in any democracy. To that end, writing for the Court in *Palko v. Connecticut* (1937),

Justice Benjamin Cardozo characterized freedom of speech as "the matrix, the indispensable condition, of nearly every other form of freedom."

In the wake of the constitutional revolution of 1937, the Supreme Court moved away from the protection of private property rights and toward the enhancement of personal freedoms. The First Amendment figured prominently in the Court's newfound emphasis. During the 1940s several members of the Supreme Court went so far as to suggest that the First Amendment freedoms of speech and press enjoy a "preferred position" in relation to other constitutional guarantees (see, for example, Justice William O. Douglas's majority opinion in *Murdoch v. Pennsylvania* [1943]).

Although the Court soon abandoned the **preferred freedoms** language, freedom of expression was accorded high priority during the Warren Court era (1953–1969). The Warren Court established a number of important precedents in this area, and for the most part the more conservative Burger and Rehnquist Courts adhered to these precedents. Since 2005 the Roberts Court has shown that it also recognizes the crucial importance of the First Amendment in our democratic and pluralistic society. Writing for the Court in *United States v. Stevens* (2010), Chief Justice John Roberts observed:

> *The First Amendment ... reflects a judgment by the American people that the benefits of its restrictions on the Government outweigh the costs. Our Constitution forecloses any attempt to revise that judgment simply on the basis that some speech is not worth it.*

Interpretive Foundations of Expressive Freedom

The idea of free speech is a largely modern notion that corresponds with the emergence of liberal democracy. To the ancient and medieval worlds, freedom of speech was unthinkable, especially in religious and political matters. In England the idea of freedom of speech emerged gradually, coincident with the development of parliamentary government.

The constitutional commitment to freedom of the press also has its roots in the American colonial experience, especially during the decades immediately preceding the American Revolution. The mass media of that period, consisting of small independent newspaper and pamphlet publishers, played a vital role in facilitating political debate and in disseminating information. It is worth recalling in this context that the ratification of the Constitution was vigorously debated not only in the state ratifying conventions but in the press as well. The collection of essays known as *The Federalist Papers* first appeared as a series of newspaper articles, analyzing and endorsing the new Constitution. Anti-Federalists also made wide use of newspapers to express opposition to ratification.

Despite the obvious importance of freedoms of speech and press in the establishment of American democracy, the U.S. Supreme Court did not pay major attention to these values during the early days of the republic. At times the full force of these rights was curtailed by government. For a brief period during the administration of President John Adams, the national government sought to suppress public criticism through enforcement of the Sedition Act, passed by Congress in 1798. The Sedition Act prohibited "any false, scandalous and malicious" writing against the national government. A few of Thomas Jefferson's partisans were prosecuted under this statute, and it may have had a **chilling effect** on criticism of the government. Nevertheless, the act expired on March 3, 1801, just before Jefferson and his newly victorious party took power. Jefferson pardoned those convicted under the statute, and no occasion arose for the Supreme Court to determine its constitutionality.

During the Civil War, a number of limits were imposed on freedom of expression. These included newspaper censorship and the prosecution of some of the more vociferous critics of the Lincoln administration. However, no constitutional challenges raising First Amendment issues reached the Supreme Court.

Incorporation of the Freedoms of Speech and Press

The principal reason that First Amendment controversies did not reach the Supreme Court during the nineteenth century was that, by design, the First Amendment did not apply to the state and local governments. Not until *Gitlow v. New York* (1925) did the Supreme Court recognize that the First Amendment freedoms of speech and press were applicable to the states via the Fourteenth Amendment. In addition to the **incorporation** of the First Amendment, changes in the national political environment brought questions of freedom of speech to the forefront. The national government's efforts to deal with political dissent in the early decades of the twentieth century produced a series of cases that required the Court to interpret the scope of First Amendment protection. By the 1920s, the First Amendment emerged as an important field of constitutional interpretation.

Are the Protections of the First Amendment Absolute?

Although the First Amendment begins with the seemingly absolute injunction, "Congress shall make *no* law" [emphasis added], the Supreme Court has never taken the view that First Amendment protections are absolute in character. Indeed, only a few justices who have served on the Court have argued for an absolutist interpretation.

Justice Hugo Black, the best known and most forceful of the First Amendment absolutists, believed that all speech and writing, regardless of its purpose, content, or impact, should be absolutely protected against **censorship** or sanction. Thus, Black believed that criminal laws prohibiting **obscenity**, **profanity**, and **seditious speech** were inherently unconstitutional. He also believed that laws that permitted civil suits for **libel** or **slander** could not be reconciled with the First Amendment.

In Black's view, the First Amendment gives everyone the right to say or write anything, regardless of its impact on other individuals or society in general. However, Justice Black believed that the protections of the First Amendment were limited to **pure speech** and pure writing. In his view, **picketing** and other forms of **expressive conduct** were not covered by the First Amendment.

Although Hugo Black wrote a number of important opinions for the Court on questions of freedom of speech and freedom of the press, most of his colleagues and most of the justices who came after him refused to accept Black's **First Amendment absolutism**. The Court has never taken the position that the protections of the First Amendment are absolute. Indeed, the Court has recognized that certain types of expressions, including obscenity, **fighting words** and **defamation**, are largely outside the scope of the First Amendment. It has also held that speech that is normally protected by the Constitution might not be protected depending on the circumstances in which it takes place.

On the other hand, the Court has recognized that the protections of the First Amendment are not limited to pure speech and writing. Rather, the First Amendment potentially protects communication of any kind. Protests, demonstrations, performances, advertisements, and artistic endeavors—all of these are within the ambit of expression. So too are records, films, videos, software, e-mail, broadcasts, cablecasts, and sites on the Internet. In short, the First Amendment protects communication, regardless of its nature or medium. Whether specific instances of expression merit First Amendment protection or may be censored or sanctioned by government depends on a number of factors that we will examine in this chapter.

Government can infringe on freedom of expression in two ways. It can employ censorship to prevent a specific instance of expression from reaching the public. Alternatively, it can punish someone after the fact, usually through criminal prosecution.

We begin our examination of First Amendment doctrine with the principle that limits government censorship prior to expression or publication—the rule against **prior restraint**.

> **To Summarize:**
> ♦ *Constitutional freedoms of expression came of age in the twentieth century. In the 1920s and 1930s, the Supreme Court incorporated freedoms of speech, press, and assembly into the Fourteenth Amendment, thus making them fully applicable to the states as well as the federal government.*
> ♦ *Although a majority of the Court has never regarded the First Amendment freedoms as absolute, these freedoms have come to be regarded as fundamental rights essential to the preservation of a constitutional democracy.*

The Prohibition of Prior Restraint

The authors of the Bill of Rights saw the need for the First Amendment because the common law, which the United States inherited from England, provided little protection to freedom of expression. However, one common law doctrine has been grafted onto the First Amendment through judicial interpretation. This is the rule against prior restraint. In *Commentaries on the Laws of England*, Vol. IV (1769), Sir William Blackstone stated the rule against prior restraint in the context of freedom of the press: "The liberty of the press is indeed essential to the nature of a free state; but this consists in laying no previous restraints upon publications, and not in freedom from censure for criminal matter when published." In the United States, the concept of prior restraint has been of great importance to the Supreme Court in defining both freedom of the press and freedom of speech under the First Amendment. The concept was first discussed by the Court, however, in the context of a dispute over publication of a newspaper.

The Court Adopts the Rule against Prior Restraint

In *Near v. Minnesota* (1931), the Court struck down a state law that permitted public officials to seek an injunction to stop publication of any "malicious, scandalous and defamatory newspaper, magazine or other periodical." The statute was invoked to suppress publication of a small Minneapolis newspaper, the *Saturday Press*, which had strong anti-Semitic overtones and maligned local political officials, particularly the chief of police. The state law provided that once a newspaper was enjoined, further publication was punishable as contempt of court. Writing for the Court in *Near*, Chief Justice Charles Evans Hughes characterized this mode of suppression as "the essence of censorship" and declared it unconstitutional. Note also that with its decision in *Near v. Minnesota*, the Court specifically incorporated the First Amendment freedom of the press into the Due Process Clause of the Fourteenth Amendment, thus making it fully applicable to the states.

In commenting with general approval on the rule against prior restraint, Chief Justice Hughes acknowledged, however, that this restriction is not absolute. It would not, for example, prevent the government in time of war from prohibiting publication of "the sailing dates of transports or the number and location of troops." In these and related situations, national security interests are almost certain to prevail over freedom of the press. But where is the line to be drawn? How far can the "national security" justification be extended in suppressing publication? After this decision, and likely in great part because of it, the government often would declare any type of prior restraint to be the result of a national security concern. Determining the validity of such claims is a challenge for the Supreme Court, as seen in *The Pentagon Papers Case*.

The Pentagon Papers Case   The Court revisited the question of prior restraint on the press in the much heralded Pentagon papers case decided in the summer of 1971 (*New York Times Company v. United States*). Here, the federal government attempted to prevent the *New York Times* and the *Washington Post* from publishing excerpts from a classified study titled "History of U.S. Decision-Making Process on Viet Nam Policy" (the Pentagon papers). By a 6-to-3 vote, the Supreme Court, in a brief *per curiam* opinion, held that the government's effort to block publication of this material amounted to an unconstitutional prior restraint. The majority was simply not convinced that such publication—several years after the events and decisions discussed in the Pentagon papers—constituted a significant threat to national security. The furor produced by this highly publicized case and the great pressure brought to bear on the Court for a speedy decision help explain why no detailed majority opinion was produced. The justices in fact wrote nine separate opinions, advancing a wide variety of rationales for and against application of the prior restraint concept. Excerpts from each of these opinions are reprinted at the end of this chapter, and it is important to consider the constitutional implications of the various arguments.

Does the Prior Restraint Doctrine Apply to Student Newspapers?

One notable exception to the protection of press freedom against prior restraint involves the publication of student-operated school newspapers. In *Hazelwood School District v. Kuhlmeier* (1988), the Supreme Court voted 5 to 3 to uphold a public school principal's decision to excise certain controversial material from the school newspaper. The principal objected to certain articles dealing with divorce and teenage pregnancy on the grounds that they were written in such a way as to permit students to identify classmates who had encountered such difficulties. The student newspaper staff hired a lawyer and challenged the principal's action in federal court. Writing for the majority, Justice Byron White concluded that "educators do not offend the First Amendment by exercising editorial control over the style and content of student speech in school sponsored expressive activities so long as their actions are reasonably related to legitimate pedagogical concerns." Dissenting, Justice William Brennan accused the majority of eviscerating *Tinker v. Des Moines Independent Community School District* (1969), in which the Court had accorded First Amendment protection to certain expressive activities by students in public schools. According to Brennan, the majority opinion in *Hazelwood* "denudes high school students of much of the First Amendment protection that *Tinker* itself prescribed." The controversy in *Hazelwood* centered around a student newspaper at a public high school. Would the federal courts permit officials at a state college or university to censor student-run campus newspapers? Could "legitimate pedagogical concerns" at this level ever justify such interference? Most observers doubt the Courts would permit this type of censorship on a college campus.

> **To Summarize:**
> ◆ *The prohibition of prior restraint has evolved from a technical common law rule regarding the licensing of publications into a broad First Amendment principle that restricts government censorship of expression prior to its utterance.*
> ◆ *The Supreme Court applied the rule against prior restraint most prominently in the Pentagon papers case of 1971. In this case, the Court refused to allow the federal government to bar newspapers from publishing classified documents dealing with the Vietnam War.*

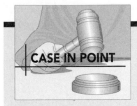

CASE IN POINT

Can the Government Prevent Publication of How to Make a Hydrogen Bomb?

United States v. The Progressive (1979)

The issue of prior restraint arose in 1979 in connection with the publication of a magazine article purporting to describe the process of making a hydrogen bomb. The federal government obtained a preliminary injunction against *The Progressive* blocking publication of the article pending a hearing. In the meantime, however, another magazine published a similar article, with no apparent damage to national security. As a result, the case against *The Progressive* was dismissed and the injunction lifted (see *United States v. The Progressive* [1979]). *The Progressive's* hydrogen bomb article was ultimately published in November 1979. In light of the Pentagon papers and *Progressive* cases, we could conclude that, although national security may justify a departure from the rule against prior restraint, in the real world of American constitutional law, such departures tend to be rare and short lived.

The Clear and Present Danger Doctrine

Even though a specific instance of expression may not be censored prior to its utterance or publication, it may still be subject to sanctions after the fact. Individuals may be subjected to criminal prosecution or civil suit for instances of expression that violate specific legal prohibitions. Whether such instances of expression are protected by the First Amendment depends on a number of factors, including the nature of the expression and context in which it takes place.

The traditional view of freedom of speech, grounded in English common law, was the bad tendency test. In essence, expression could be penalized if it had a tendency to harm the public welfare. This was the position taken by most of the state courts in interpreting their respective constitutions, and in *Patterson v. Colorado* (1907) the Supreme Court appeared to endorse this view with respect to the Federal Constitution. In *Fox v. Washington* (1915) the Court upheld a state law that explicitly adopted the bad tendency test by criminalizing publications "having a tendency to encourage or incite the commission of any crime, breach of the peace or act of violence."

In *Schenck v. United States* (1919), the first major Supreme Court decision interpreting the scope of free speech under the First Amendment, the Court moved away from the bad tendency test. Yet it made plain that there are instances in which speech that is normally subject to constitutional protection may be suppressed by the government.

Writing for the Court in *Schenck*, Justice Oliver Wendell Holmes, Jr., flatly rejected an absolutist interpretation of the First Amendment. In what has become a stock phrase in the American political lexicon, Holmes observed that "the most stringent protection of free speech would not protect a man in falsely shouting fire in a theater, and causing a panic." Holmes went on to articulate the famous **clear and present danger test**, saying that "the question in every case is whether the words used are used in such circumstances and are of such a nature as to create a clear and present danger that they will bring about the substantive evils that Congress has a right to prevent." For example, government has a right, indeed an obligation, to protect the national security. If an instance of expression creates a clear and present danger to national security, then the government has the right to prohibit the speech or punish the speaker.

In the *Schenck* case, an official of the Socialist Party was convicted for conspiring to print and circulate leaflets urging resistance to the military draft. The leaflets urged resistance to the draft on the grounds that it violated the Thirteenth Amendment. Although sharply critical of the war effort, Schenck's message was confined to the advocacy of peaceful measures, such as petition for repeal of the draft. Nevertheless, a unanimous Supreme Court believed that Schenck's activities amounted to a clear and present danger. One must remember, though, that Schenck's prosecution occurred during World War I. Many of the great Supreme Court cases have been asked to clarify constitutional provisions during times of war. As Justice Holmes observed in *Schenck*, "when a nation is at war many things that might be said in time of peace are such a hindrance to its effort that their utterance will not be endured so long as men fight, and that no court could regard them as protected by any constitutional right." It is also noteworthy that the Court's decision came down at a time when there was widespread concern about the specter of international communism. For the next four decades, as concerns grew regarding the internal spread of communism and as the United States became involved in additional military conflicts, the clear and present danger doctrine competed with other approaches to First Amendment interpretation in the area of political dissent.

A Return to the Bad Tendency Test

Although in *Schenck* the Court upheld the suppression of dissident speech, the clear and present danger test that Justice Holmes articulated meant that government could not proscribe expression simply because it disapproved of the content of that expression. However, the clear and present danger standard was ignored by a Court majority some eight months later in *Abrams v. United States* (1919). There, the Court affirmed the convictions of Jacob Abrams, a self-styled "anarchist Socialist," and several associates for distributing leaflets in New York City urging the "workers of the world" to resist, among other things, American intervention in Russia against the newly formed Bolshevik government. For Justice John H. Clarke, the Court's majority spokesman, it was enough that Abrams was advocating a general strike "in the greatest port of our land" for the purpose of "curtailing the production of ordnance and munitions necessary and essential to the prosecution of the war." Clarke accorded little importance to the free speech question, focusing instead on the possibility that Abrams's circular might in some way hinder the war effort. In this respect, his opinion amounted to an endorsement of the traditional **bad tendency test**, grounded in English common law.

In a powerful dissenting opinion, Justice Holmes, joined by Justice Louis D. Brandeis, again resorted to the clear and present danger test, but this time he used it as a basis for challenging, rather than endorsing, governmental interference with free speech:

> [T]he ultimate good desired is better reached by free trade in ideas … [t]he best test of truth is the power of the thought to get itself accepted in the competition of the market … I think that we should be eternally vigilant against attempts to check the expression of opinions that we loathe and believe to be fraught with death, unless they so imminently threaten immediate interference with the lawful and pressing purposes of the law that an immediate check is required to save the country.

Through the 1920s, a Court majority adhered to the bad tendency test, while Holmes and Brandeis further developed the clear and present danger doctrine as a rationale in support of freedom of expression and association. In *Gitlow v. New York* (1925), the Court upheld a conviction under New York's Criminal Anarchy Act that prohibited advocacy of the overthrow of government "by force or violence." Prior to this decision, the Court had addressed issues of freedom of expression arising from the states strictly on the basis of the Due Process Clause of the Fourteenth Amendment, without specific reference to the First Amendment. In fact, as late as 1922 the Court observed that "the Constitution of the United States imposes upon the States no obligation to convey upon those within their jurisdiction ... the right of free speech" (*Prudential Insurance Company v. Cheek*).

In *Meyer v. Nebraska* (1923), the Court invalidated on due process grounds a Nebraska law prohibiting the teaching of the German language in primary schools. Similarly, in *Pierce v. Society of Sisters* (1925), the Court struck down an amendment to the Oregon constitution aimed at prohibiting parents from sending their children to private schools. In the *Meyer* and *Pierce* cases, the Court focused on the deprivation of liberty and property rights protected by the Fourteenth Amendment Due Process Clause. In the *Gitlow* case, however, Justice Edward T. Sanford, writing for the majority, stated without elaboration: "For present purposes we may and do assume that freedom of speech and of the press—which are protected by the First Amendment from abridgment by Congress—are among the fundamental personal rights and 'liberties' protected by the Due Process Clause of the Fourteenth Amendment from impairment by the states." The Court would invalidate a state law on First Amendment freedom of speech grounds for the first time two years later in *Fiske v. Kansas* (1927).

The incident giving rise to the *Gitlow* case was publication of the "Left Wing Manifesto," a statement of beliefs held by what the Court characterized as the most radical section of the Socialist Party. In essence, the manifesto called for the destruction of established government and its replacement by a "revolutionary dictatorship of the proletariat." In affirming the conviction of Benjamin Gitlow, business manager of *The Revolutionary Age*, the Socialist Party paper that published the "Left Wing Manifesto," Justice Sanford stated the essence of the bad tendency test:

> *That a state, in the exercise of its police power, may punish those who abuse [freedom of speech and press] by utterances inimical to the public welfare, tending to corrupt public morals, incite to crime, or disturb the public peace, is not open to question.*

Sanford continued:

> *The state cannot reasonably be required to measure the danger from every such utterance in the nice balance of a jeweler's scale. A single revolutionary spark may kindle a fire that, smoldering for a time, may burst into a sweeping and destructive conflagration. It cannot be said that the state is acting arbitrarily or unreasonably when, in the exercise of its judgment as to the measures necessary to protect the public peace and safety, it seeks to extinguish the spark without waiting until it has enkindled the flame or blazed into the conflagration.*

Again, Justices Holmes and Brandeis dissented. They could find no clear and present danger of an effort "to overthrow the government by force on the part of the admittedly small minority who shared the defendant's views." In response to the contention that the "Left Wing Manifesto" was an incitement, Holmes asserted:

> *Every idea is an incitement. It offers itself for belief and if believed it is acted on unless some other belief outweighs it or some failure of energy stifles the movement at its birth. The only difference between the expression of an opinion and an incitement in the narrower sense is the speaker's enthusiasm for the result. Eloquence may set fire to reason. But whatever may be thought of the redundant discourse before us it had no chance of starting a present conflagration. If in the long run the beliefs expressed in proletarian dictatorship are destined to be accepted by the dominant forces of the community, the only meaning of free speech is that they should be given their chance and have their way.*

This ringing endorsement of the concept of a **free marketplace of ideas** contrasts sharply with Holmes's earlier deference, in the *Schenck* case, to governmental control of dissident expression. As we have seen in connection with judicial review of economic regulation (see Chapter 2), Holmes was inclined to give wide latitude to legislative discretion in matters of public policy. But his dissent in *Gitlow*, like his dissent in *Abrams v. United States*, reflected a decided shift in emphasis where First Amendment values were concerned. This change was probably influenced by Holmes's association on the Court with Justice Brandeis, a dedicated and an articulate defender of civil rights and liberties, and his acquaintance with Harvard University law professor Zechariah Chafee, Jr., a widely recognized authority on the First Amendment.

Brandeis himself had occasion to discuss the clear and present danger formula in a concurring opinion in *Whitney v. California* (1927). In this case, the majority, speaking again through Justice Sanford, adhered to the bad tendency test in affirming the conviction of Charlotte Anita Whitney (a niece of Justice Stephen J. Field) for violating California's Criminal Syndicalism Act. The statute defined "criminal syndicalism" as "any doctrine or precept advocating, teaching or aiding and abetting the commission of crime, sabotage … or unlawful acts of force and violence or unlawful methods of terrorism as a means of accomplishing a change in industrial ownership or control, or effecting any political change." Whitney's conviction was based on her participation in the organizing convention of the Communist Labor Party of California.

The jury rejected her contention that at this meeting she advocated lawful, nonviolent political reform. She maintained that her conviction was a deprivation of liberty without due process of law, but she did not contend specifically that her participation in organizing the Communist Labor Party constituted no clear and present danger. Sanford rejected the view that the act, as applied in this case, was "an unreasonable or arbitrary exercise of the police power of the state, unwarrantably infringing any right of free speech, assembly, or association, or that those persons are protected by the Due Process Clause who abuse such rights by joining and furthering an organization … menacing the peace and welfare of the state." Because Whitney did not raise the clear and present danger issue, Brandeis and Holmes felt compelled to concur. The jury was presented with evidence of a conspiracy and under the circumstances, they concluded, its verdict should not be disturbed.

Nevertheless, Brandeis took sharp issue with the majority's narrow view of the constitutional protection that should be afforded political dissent. The crux of the Brandeis-Holmes position is contained in the following excerpt:

It is the function of speech to free men from the bondage of irrational fears. To justify suppression of free speech there must be reasonable ground to fear that serious evil will result if free speech is practiced. There must be reasonable ground to believe that the danger apprehended is imminent. There must be reasonable ground to believe that the evil to be prevented is a serious one.

A Supreme Court majority first used the clear and present danger test in defense of free speech in the 1937 case of *Herndon v. Lowry*. This decision reversed a conviction for violation of a Georgia statute prohibiting "any attempt, by persuasion or otherwise," to incite insurrection. Following this decision, the Court began to apply the clear and present danger test not only to "seditious" speech but also to other First Amendment issues as well. For the moment, it appeared as if the Court was furthering First Amendment protections in the face of state action. This trend, however, would face great obstacle from the "Red Scare."

The Clear and Probable Danger Test

The Cold War, which had begun after World War II, deepened after the United States became embroiled in the Korean conflict—and by the early 1950s, McCarthyism, with its emphasis on the "communist menace," had achieved substantial national influence.

Against this background of Cold War paranoia, the Supreme Court reviewed and affirmed the convictions of eleven leaders of the American Communist Party in *Dennis v. United States* (1951). Eugene Dennis and his ten codefendants had been convicted after a highly publicized nine-month federal trial for violation of the Internal Security Act of 1940, more commonly known as the Smith Act.

This statute made it a crime "to knowingly or willfully advocate, abet, advise, or teach the duty, necessity, desirability, or propriety of overthrowing or destroying any government in the United States by force or violence." In essence, the defendants' convictions resulted from their activities in organizing and furthering the purposes of the Communist Party in the United States. The Court of Appeals for the Second Circuit upheld these convictions. In his opinion for that court, Chief Judge Learned Hand substituted a more limited defense of First Amendment freedoms than that of clear and present danger. This doctrine, popularly known as the **clear and probable danger test**, was adopted by Chief Justice Frederick M. Vinson in a plurality opinion, announcing the Supreme Court's judgment affirming the convictions. The new standard that Hand articulated required courts in each case to "ask whether the gravity of the 'evil,' discounted by its improbability, justifies such invasion of free speech as is necessary to avoid the danger."

Two members of the *Dennis* majority, Justices Felix Frankfurter and Robert Jackson, wrote separate concurring opinions, neither of which endorsed Hand's formula or the clear and present danger test. Frankfurter maintained that the Court should defer to the legislative balancing of competing interests in the free speech area no less than in other areas of policy making. Jackson differentiated between isolated, localized protest and what he saw as a highly organized conspiracy of international dimensions aimed at subverting American government. He regarded the clear and present danger test as an inadequate standard for assessing a conspiracy of this magnitude. Jackson found "no constitutional right to 'gang up' on the Government."

Justice Black, who dissented along with Justice Douglas, expressed the hope that "in calmer times, when present pressures, passions and fears subside, this or some later Court will restore the First Amendment liberties to the high preferred place where they belong in a free society."

Changes in public opinion and in Supreme Court personnel did in fact result in a gradual movement away from the restrictive First Amendment interpretation symbolized by the *Dennis* decision. Although, as previously indicated, the Court did not resurrect the phrase "preferred position" and did not formally overrule *Dennis*, it narrowed the scope of the Smith Act and offered greater protection to advocacy of ideas, including the forcible overthrow of government. The Court raised evidentiary standards for Smith Act prosecutions and confined its "membership clause" to "active" as distinguished from "nominal" membership in an organization advocating forcible overthrow of the government (see, for example, *Yates v. United States* [1957], *Scales v. United States* [1961], *Noto v. United States* [1961], and *Communist Party v. Subversive Activities Control Board* [1961]).

Ad Hoc Balancing

In the aftermath of *Dennis*, the Court moved away from the clear and present danger test and relied instead on **ad hoc balancing** to determine the limits of First Amendment protection in the area of internal security. This weighing of "competing private and public interests," as Justice John M. Harlan (the younger) phrased it, emphasized the particular circumstances of each case (see *Barenblatt v. United States* [1959], reprinted in Chapter 3, Volume I). Thus, ad hoc balancing in practice amounted to a process of decision making rather than a clear, interpretive doctrine. However, it is doubtful that a standard such as clear and present danger is, on close analysis, any more definite.

The Imminent Lawless Action Standard

In the early twentieth century, many states had adopted statutes prohibiting **criminal syndicalism**, which was, in essence, the crime of advocating political change through violent means. As discussed earlier, in *Whitney v. California* (1927), the Supreme Court had upheld one such law, but by the 1960s the Warren Court was ready to revisit the issue. Thus, in *Brandenburg v. Ohio* (1969), the Court invalidated a criminal syndicalism statute and explicitly overruled *Whitney v. California*. In reversing the conviction of a local Ku Klux Klan leader who had conducted a televised rally near Cincinnati, Ohio, the Court held that "the constitutional guarantees of free speech and free press do not permit a State to forbid or proscribe advocacy of the use of force or of law violation except where such advocacy is directed to inciting or producing **imminent lawless action** and is likely to incite or produce such action." The *Brandenburg* standard, with emphasis on imminent lawless action, reaffirmed and refined the clear and present danger test as articulated by Justice Holmes. The Burger Court firmly adhered to this standard in the 1970s and 1980s, as seen in *Hess v. Indiana* (1973), *Communist Party of Indiana v. Whitcomb* (1974), and *National Association for the Advancement of Colored People v. Claiborne Hardware Company* (1982). The Rehnquist Court did not extensively discuss the imminent lawless action standard, but it expressed no willingness to weaken it. To the contrary, the contemporary Court has indicated a clear willingness to protect political dissent (see, for example, *Texas v. Johnson* [1989], reprinted in this chapter).

In the aftermath of the government's response to the terrorist attacks of September 11, 2001, a number of observers expressed concern about the changing mood of the country regarding political dissent. Would the courts respond to this change in national mood by relaxing First Amendment protections? Would the imminent lawless action standard survive the war on terrorism? Yet after 9/11, constitutional law relative to free speech has remained unchanged.

To Summarize:

♦ *In Schenck v. United States (1919), the Supreme Court, speaking through Justice Holmes, first articulated the famous clear and present danger doctrine. Under this doctrine government may punish expression if it creates a clear and present danger of bringing about conditions that government has authority to prevent. Although the doctrine was first used as a rationale for upholding restrictions on radical political expression, in later years, several classic opinions by Justices Holmes and Brandeis greatly influenced the application of the doctrine as a rationale for protecting political dissent.*

♦ *In the decades following the Schenck ruling, a Court majority occasionally opted for more restrictive approaches to the First Amendment, including the bad tendency, clear and probable danger, and ad hoc balancing tests. In Brandenburg v. Ohio (1969), however, the Court eventually reaffirmed the essential concept of the clear and present danger doctrine, limiting its application to expression in situations where there is "imminent lawless action" and the expression is likely to produce such action.*

Can a Journalist Be Prosecuted for Publishing Classified Information?

Under 18 U.S.C. § 798, "whoever knowingly and willfully ... publishes ... any classified information ... concerning the communication intelligence activities of the United States or any foreign government" has committed a federal crime punishable by up to ten years in prison. If a journalist who obtained classified documents "leaked" by a government source published excerpts of these documents in the newspaper, would the courts permit the federal government to prosecute that journalist? Which should prevail in such a dispute, freedom of the press or the need for national security? The Supreme Court has not addressed the issue head-on, but in his concurrence in the Pentagon papers case, Justice White stated that "Congress appeared to have little doubt that newspapers would be subject to criminal prosecution if they insisted on publishing information of the type Congress had itself determined should not be revealed." White indicated that he "would have no difficulty in sustaining [such] convictions."

In June 2006, Congressman Peter King (R-NY) called for a criminal investigation of the *New York Times* after the newspaper published leaked information about a covert government operation to track the financing of terrorism through the international banking system. In an interview published in *Newsday* on June 26, 2006, King was quoted as saying:

This puts American lives at risk and they did it for no good reason. *The Times* thinks they are above the law. Nobody elected *The New York Times* to anything. No amendment is absolute, including the First Amendment.

In a widely publicized White House interview that same day, then president Bush also expressed outrage at the disclosure of the program, saying "We're at war with a bunch of people who want to hurt the United States of America, and for people to leak that program and for a newspaper to publish it does great harm."

In 2013 Edward Snowden, who worked for a contractor to the National Security Agency, created an international sensation when he divulged classified information about NSA's electronic surveillance programs to *The Guardian*, a London newspaper. Snowden fled the country and eventually asked for political asylum in Russia, as the American government announced its intention to prosecute Snowden under the Espionage Act. The government did not seek criminal charges against *The Guardian* or any of its employees, but presumably it could do so under 18 U.S.C. § 798.

Assuming the government did decide to prosecute such a case, and assuming a conviction resulted, how would the contemporary Supreme Court likely respond to this issue on appeal?

Fighting Words, Hate Speech, and Profanity

Does the First Amendment protect expression that is uncivil, vulgar, hateful, or profane? Prior to the 1960s, the Supreme Court took the view that offensive speech was beyond the pale of the First Amendment. In *Chaplinsky v. New Hampshire* (1942), the Court observed:

> *There are certain well defined and narrowly limited classes of speech, the prevention and punishment of which have never been thought to raise any constitutional problem. These include the lewd and obscene, the profane, the libelous, and the insulting or "fighting" words—those which by their very utterance inflict injury or tend to incite an immediate breach of the peace. It has been well observed that such utterances are no essential part of any exposition of ideas, and are of such slight social value as a step to truth that any benefit that may be derived from them is clearly outweighed by the social interest in order and morality.*

Fighting Words

The preceding excerpt from *Chaplinsky v. New Hampshire* provides the original statement of the fighting words doctrine. Under *Chaplinsky*, speech could be punished if it inflicted injury or created a danger that the person addressed would resort to violence. The Court probably underestimated the social value of what some would regard as fighting words, and no consideration was given to the question of whether police should be expected to exercise more restraint than the average person in responding to such epithets. For several decades, state courts routinely used the fighting words doctrine and the *Chaplinsky* precedent to justify prosecutions of intemperate street corner orators for incitement to riot or breach of the peace.

In 1971, the Court significantly narrowed the fighting words exception. Thus, in *Cohen v. California* the Court refused to classify as fighting words the message "Fuck the Draft" emblazoned on the back of a jacket worn by Paul Robert Cohen in the corridors of the Los Angeles County Courthouse. Reversing Cohen's conviction for breach of the peace, the Court, through Justice Harlan, reasoned as follows:

> *While the four letter word displayed by Cohen in relation to the draft is not uncommonly employed in a personally provocative fashion, in this instance it was clearly not "directed to the person of the hearer." ... No individual actually or likely to be present could reasonably have regarded the words on appellant's jacket as a direct personal insult. Nor do we have here an instance of the exercise of the State's police power to prevent a speaker from intentionally provoking a given group to hostile reaction.*

Although the Court still gives formal recognition to the fighting words exception, it has not in recent years found any specific instances of expression to qualify as fighting words.

Hate Speech

During the 1980s, a number of communities adopted laws aimed at protecting African-Americans and other minority groups from **hate crimes**, crimes motivated by racial or other group related hatred. One such ordinance was enacted by the City of St. Paul, Minnesota:

> *Whoever places on public or private property a symbol, object, appellation, characterization or graffiti, including, but not limited to, a burning cross or Nazi swastika, which one knows or has reasonable grounds to know arouses anger, alarm or resentment in others on the basis of race, color, creed, religion or gender commits disorderly conduct and shall be guilty of a misdemeanor.*

In the widely publicized case of *R.A.V. v. St. Paul* (1992), the Supreme Court declared the ordinance unconstitutional. Justice Scalia summarized the rationale of the majority as follows: "Assuming *arguendo*, that all of the expression reached by the ordinance is proscribable under the 'fighting words' doctrine, we nonetheless conclude that the ordinance is facially unconstitutional in that it prohibits otherwise permitted speech solely on the basis of the subjects the speech addresses."

The Court's decision in *R.A.V.* raised serious questions as to whether hate crimes legislation can be made to conform to constitutional standards. Nevertheless, states and communities have a number of legal means at their disposal for combating hate crimes. For example, an individual who burns a cross on someone else's front lawn may be charged with criminal trespass and possibly with malicious mischief or vandalism. Another approach to deterring hate crimes is enhancing or extending criminal penalties based on characteristics of the crime or the victim. In *Wisconsin v. Mitchell* (1993), the

Does the First Amendment Protect Web sites that Advocate Terrorism?

On April 15, 2013, the terrorist attacks on the Boston Marathon brought to the forefront of the national discussion the presence of radical Web sites that encourage violent action against United States. Two brothers, Tamerlan and Dzhokhar Tsarnaev, used homemade explosive devices placed inside of pressure cookers as their weapons to carry out the attack. During the ensuing investigation, it was reported that the Tsarnaev brothers were following directions on how to do so that they had received on a radical Jihadist Web site. One of the debates to emerge in the wake of this tragedy involved the question of allowing access to materials that advocated violence against U.S. citizens. How does this relate to the Court's treatment of "fighting words"? To date, the Supreme Court has been hesitant to support Internet censorship, see, for example, *Reno v. American Civil Liberties Union* (1997), as discussed later in this chapter. Can extremist Web sites be censored if they contain hate speech or potentially pose a threat to our national security? Would the Supreme Court uphold the constitutionality of an act of Congress that authorized the government to block Internet users from accessing Jihadist Web sites?

U.S. Supreme Court upheld a Wisconsin statute that increases the severity of punishment if a crime victim is chosen on the basis of race or other designated characteristics. Stressing the fact that the statute was aimed at conduct rather than belief, the Court held that increasing punishment because the defendant targeted the victim on the basis of his race does not infringe the defendant's freedom of conscience protected by the First Amendment. *Wisconsin v. Mitchell* was widely criticized, not so much for the merits of the majority opinion, but because many commentators thought that it could not be squared with the Court's earlier decision in *R.A.V. v. St. Paul.*

Cross Burning   Notwithstanding its earlier decision in *R.A.V.*, the Court in *Virginia v. Black* (2003) upheld a Virginia law banning cross burning with "an intent to intimidate a person or group of persons." Writing for the Court, Justice Sandra Day O'Connor concluded that the "First Amendment permits Virginia to outlaw cross burnings done with the intent to intimidate because burning a cross is a particularly virulent form of intimidation." In O'Connor's view, "Virginia may choose to regulate this subset of intimidating messages in light of cross burning's long and pernicious history as a signal of impending violence."

Profanity

Although in *Chaplinsky v. New Hampshire* (1942) the Supreme Court specifically enumerated profanity as being among those categories of speech so lacking in value as not to merit First Amendment protection, this view no longer prevails. As we discussed earlier, in *Cohen v. California* the Supreme Court overturned the conviction of a man who entered a courthouse wearing a jacket emblazoned with the slogan "Fuck the Draft." Speaking for the Court, Justice Harlan opined that

> *while the particular four letter word being litigated here is perhaps more distasteful than others of its genre, it is nevertheless often true that one man's vulgarity is another's lyric. Indeed, we think it is largely because government officials cannot make principled distinctions in this area that the Constitution leaves matters of taste and style so largely to the individual.*

Despite the Supreme Court's decision in *Cohen v. California*, most states and many cities retain laws proscribing profanity. But these laws are seldom enforced and even more rarely challenged in court. One notable exception is the case of the "cussing canoe-ist" that made national news in 1998. When Timothy Boomer fell from his canoe into Michigan's Rifle River, he unleashed a tirade of profanities in a very loud voice. He was convicted of violating a nineteenth century state law that prohibited the utterance of profanity in the presence of children. Boomer was fined $75 and ordered to perform four days of community service. With the assistance of the American Civil Liberties Union, Boomer appealed his conviction to the Michigan Court of Appeals. On April 1, 2002, the Michigan appellate court reversed Boomer's conviction and struck down the statute on which the conviction was based. Writing for the court, Judge William B. Murphy observed that the law, "as drafted, reaches constitutionally protected speech, and it operates to inhibit the exercise of First Amendment rights."

To Summarize:

◆ *In the early 1940s, the Court recognized that "fighting words," utterances that are inherently likely to produce a violent reaction, are outside the scope of First Amendment protection. In recent times, the fighting words doctrine has been honored more in the breach than in the observance.*

◆ *A more recent problem is posed by "hate speech" directed at members of targeted groups such as women and minorities. Unless a particular instance of hate speech can be identified with fighting words, defamation, or imminent lawless action, it is likely to be accorded First Amendment protection. Of course, an instance of hate speech that involves criminal conduct such as trespass or assault may be subject to criminal prosecution.*

◆ *Although profanity was once recognized as falling outside the scope of First Amendment protection, this view has eroded to the point where profanity is now considered part of ordinary speech. Thus, prosecutions for uttering profanity are very rare.*

Symbolic Speech and Expressive Conduct

As *Cohen v. California* and *R.A.V. v. St. Paul* make clear, the protection of the First Amendment is not limited to pure speech only. The term **symbolic speech** is applied to a wide range of nonverbal communication that is subject to First Amendment protection. Of course, not every symbol is entitled to constitutional protection; it depends on the circumstances in which the symbol is displayed.

The Flag Salute Controversy

An early example of the modern Court's willingness to protect symbolic speech is provided by the flag salute cases of *Minersville School District v. Gobitis* (1940) and *West Virginia State Board of Education v. Barnette* (1943). (These cases, which also implicate freedom of religion, are discussed more fully in Chapter 4.) In *Gobitis*, the Court upheld a local school board directive requiring public school students to salute the American flag as part of the daily class routine. Then, in one of the most dramatic turnabouts in its history, the Court overruled this precedent three years later in the second flag salute case. In *Barnette*, a six-member majority recognized the right of schoolchildren who were members of Jehovah's Witnesses to refrain from participation in the flag salute ritual. Writing for the Court, Justice Robert Jackson observed that "no official, high or petty, can prescribe what shall be orthodox in politics, nationalism, religion, or other matters of opinion or force citizens to confess by word or act their faith therein."

Symbolic Speech during the Vietnam Era

Protests against the Vietnam War produced a number of controversies over symbolic speech. For example, in *United States v. O'Brien* (1968), the Court rejected the First Amendment claim of a Vietnam War protester that publicly burning his draft card was a form of constitutionally protected symbolic speech. David Paul O'Brien, who had burned his Selective Service registration certificate on the steps of the South Boston Courthouse in the presence of a "sizable crowd," was convicted for violation of a federal law providing that an offense was committed by any person "who forges, alters, knowingly destroys, knowingly mutilates, or in any manner changes any such certificate." Chief Justice Earl Warren, writing for a seven-member majority, determined that Congress had ample constitutional authority to prohibit the destruction or mutilation of draft cards. After all, Warren reasoned, the card belonged to the government, not to Mr. O'Brien.

The Tinker Case   A less defiant form of symbolic speech in opposition to the Vietnam War was afforded First Amendment protection in *Tinker v. Des Moines Independent Community School District* (1969). High school students John Tinker and Christopher Eckhardt, along with Tinker's sister Mary Beth, wore black armbands to school to protest American involvement in the Vietnam War. Anticipating this protest, school officials had adopted a policy that students refusing to remove such armbands would be suspended until they agreed to return to school without them. The Tinkers and Eckhardt refused to remove their armbands when requested and were sent home under suspension. They then brought suit to recover nominal damages and to enjoin school officials from enforcing the regulation. The case eventually reached the Supreme Court, which rejected the lower court's view that the action of school officials was "reasonable" because it was based on fear that a disturbance would result from the wearing of armbands. Writing for the majority, Justice Abe Fortas concluded that the wearing of armbands in this instance "was divorced from actual or potential disruptive conduct" and as such was "closely akin to 'pure speech' which … is entitled to comprehensive protection under the First Amendment." For public school officials to justify prohibiting the "particular expression of opinion," Fortas asserted, they must be able to show that such action "was caused by something more than a mere desire to avoid the discomfort and unpleasantness that always accompany an unpopular viewpoint."

Flag Burning

During the same year in which it decided the *Tinker* case, the Court had an opportunity to address the question of whether burning the American flag is entitled to constitutional protection as symbolic speech (*Street v. New York* [1969]). The Court focused on the element of verbal expression also presented in this case, however, and effectively avoided the symbolic speech issue. After learning of the assassination attempt against civil rights leader James Meredith in Mississippi, Sidney Street burned his American flag on a Brooklyn street corner. The arresting officer testified that he heard Street say to a small crowd of onlookers: "We don't need no damn flag." Street was convicted of "malicious mischief in violation of a New York State statute making it a misdemeanor to "publicly mutilate, deface, defile, or defy, trample upon or cast contempt upon, either by words or act [any flag of the United States]." Because a general verdict was rendered by the trial court, the Supreme Court, in an opinion by Justice Harlan, observed that Street might have been punished for his speech as well as for burning the flag. The Court concluded that under the circumstances, he could not be constitutionally punished for his words alone. Harlan emphasized that the Court was not ruling on the question of whether Street could be punished for flag burning, "even though the burning was an act of protest."

The Warren Court's decision in *Street* left open the question of whether flag burning per se was a form of symbolic speech protected by the First Amendment. The Rehnquist Court, surprising many observers, answered that question in the affirmative in the highly publicized case of *Texas v. Johnson* (1989). After publicly burning the American flag outside the 1984 Republican National Convention in Dallas, Gregory Johnson was prosecuted under a Texas law prohibiting flag desecration. Johnson was convicted at trial, but his conviction was reversed by the Texas Court of Criminal Appeals, which held that Johnson's conduct was protected by the First Amendment. In an extremely controversial decision, the U.S. Supreme Court agreed, splitting 5 to 4. Perhaps most surprising to Court watchers was the fact that two Reagan appointees, Justices Antonin Scalia and Anthony Kennedy, joined the majority. On the other hand, Justice John Paul Stevens, generally considered a liberal on civil liberties issues, was among the dissenters.

Writing for the Court in *Johnson*, Justice William Brennan observed that "[t]he expressive, overtly political nature of [Johnson's] conduct was both intentional and overwhelmingly apparent." In Brennan's view:

> *Johnson was convicted for engaging in expressive conduct. The State's interest in preventing breaches of the peace does not support his conviction because Johnson's conduct did not threaten to disturb the peace. Nor does the State's interest in preserving the flag as a symbol of nationhood and national unity justify his criminal conviction for engaging in political expression.*

Dissenting, Chief Justice William Rehnquist challenged the majority's conclusion that Johnson's act of flag burning was a form of political speech, saying that "flag burning is the equivalent of an inarticulate grunt or roar that … is most likely to be indulged in not to express any particular idea, but to antagonize others." Rehnquist stressed the "unique position" of the flag "as the symbol of our Nation, a uniqueness that justifies a governmental prohibition against flag burning." But for Justice Brennan and the majority, "[t]he way to preserve the flag's special role is not to punish those who feel differently." In the wake of the *Johnson* decision, conservatives called for a constitutional amendment to place flag burning beyond the pale of First Amendment protection. In an attempt to address the issue by less drastic means, Congress passed the Federal Flag Protection Act of 1989, making flag burning a federal crime. Only one year later, in *United States v. Eichman* (1990), the Court, again dividing 5 to 4, adhered to its decision in *Texas v. Johnson* and struck down the Flag Protection Act as applied to flag burning as a means of political protest. Critics of the flag burning decisions have made several subsequent attempts to pass a constitutional amendment placing this form of protest outside the protection of the First Amendment. In June 2006, one such effort failed by only one vote to obtain the necessary two-thirds vote requisite to submitting a proposed amendment to the states. Similar measures have since been suggested, but to date have failed to gather the support necessary to move forward.

Are Nude Performances a Form of Symbolic Speech?

Every state has a prohibition against indecent exposure. Generally, these statutes are applied in situations where individuals expose themselves in public or private to unwilling viewers. But what if the exposure takes place by mutual consent, such as in a nightclub that features nude dancing? Although there is certainly no First Amendment protection for public nudity generally, the Supreme Court has consistently held that nudity may acquire constitutional protection in certain contexts. As a part of a play or performance that is not legally obscene, nudity may be considered symbolic speech protected under the First Amendment.

In *Doran v. Salem Inn* (1975), the Supreme Court said that "although the customary 'barroom' type of nude dancing may involve only the barest minimum of constitutional protection, … this form of entertainment might be entitled to First and Fourteenth Amendment protection under some circumstances." The Court faced the nude dancing issue squarely in *Barnes v. Glen Theatre, Inc.* (1991). This case involved a constitutional challenge to an Indiana statute requiring that nightclub dancers wear pasties and G-strings. The Court rejected the challenge, splitting 5 to 4. Speaking for a plurality, Chief Justice Rehnquist recognized that nude dancing was "expressive conduct within the outer perimeters of the First Amendment" but held that the state's interest in fostering order and morality justified the minimal burden on free expression associated with requiring dancers to wear pasties and G-strings. Justice Scalia's opinion concurring in the judgment was even more conservative in refusing to recognize any First Amendment protection for such activities. Justice David Souter's concurrence was more narrowly drawn. Like Rehnquist, Souter recognized the applicability of the First Amendment but concluded that the state's interest in eliminating "harmful secondary effects, including the crime associated with adult entertainment," justified the limited restriction on freedom of expression.

The four dissenting justices in *Glen Theatre* (Justices White, Marshall, Blackmun, and Stevens) found the nude dancing at issue in the case to be "communicative activity" squarely within the protection of the First Amendment, saying that "nudity is itself an expressive component of the dance, not merely incidental 'conduct.' " The dissenters quoted approvingly from the Court's previous decision in *Doran v. Salem Inn*, which observed that "while the entertainment afforded by a nude ballet at Lincoln Center to those who can pay the price may differ vastly in content (as viewed by judges) or in quality (as viewed by critics), it may not differ in substance from the dance viewed by the person who … wants some 'entertainment' with his beer or shot of rye."

In the wake of the Supreme Court's decision in *Glen Theatre*, states, cities, and counties around the country where nude dancing has been permitted began to consider laws to restrict this activity. In a 2000 decision, *Erie v. Pap's A.M.*, seven members of the Supreme Court voted to uphold an Erie, Pennsylvania, ordinance that effectively prohibited nude dancing. As in *Barnes v. Glen Theatre*, the Court was unable to produce a majority opinion. Writing for a four-member plurality, Justice O'Connor observed that "[t]he requirement that dancers wear pasties and G-strings is a minimal restriction … [and] … leaves ample capacity to convey the dancer's erotic message."

To Summarize:

- *Symbolic speech refers to nonverbal communication that is deemed entitled to First Amendment protection.*
- *The determination of whether a particular symbol is accorded constitutional protection depends on the circumstances surrounding its display.*
- *The Supreme Court has accorded First Amendment protection to the burning of the American flag as a form of nonviolent political protest.*
- *Although public nudity in general is not recognized as symbolic speech, nudity as a form of artistic expression may under some circumstances be granted this constitutionally protected status.*

Defamation

Defamation of character consists of injuring someone's reputation by making false public statements about that person. Defamation is not a crime, but rather a tort. Thus, the appropriate remedy is a civil suit for damages. Defamation may take two forms.

The verbal form is called *slander*; the written form is known as *libel*. From a legal and constitutional perspective, this distinction matters little. As a practical matter, most of the litigation in this area has involved libel, usually alleged to have been committed by newspapers.

As the Court observed in *Chaplinsky v. New Hampshire* (1942), libelous publications have traditionally been outside the scope of First Amendment protection. However, since the mid-1960s, the Supreme Court has in effect made it substantially easier for defendants in libel suits brought by "public persons" to avoid libel judgments. In so doing, the Court has substantially expanded First Amendment freedom in an area traditionally controlled by principles of tort law. This development reflects what Justice Brennan described as "a profound national commitment to the principle that debate on public issues should be uninhibited, robust, and wide open" (*New York Times Company v. Sullivan* [1964]).

New York Times v. Sullivan

Prior to the Supreme Court's decision in *New York Times Company v. Sullivan*, the primary defense in a libel action was proof that the published material was true. The *Sullivan* decision substituted a new rule that afforded far greater protection to published criticism of official conduct. As stated by Justice Brennan, this standard "prohibits a public official from recovering damages for a defamatory falsehood relating to his official conduct unless he proves that the statement was made with '**actual malice**'—that is, with knowledge that it was false or with reckless disregard of whether it was false or not." As long as there is an "absence of malice" on the part of the press, public officials are barred from recovering damages for the publication of false statements about them.

The *Sullivan* case emerged out of the civil rights struggle of the 1960s. L. B. Sullivan, a city commissioner in Montgomery, Alabama, brought suit against the *New York Times* for its publication of a paid advertisement in which civil rights leaders chastised Montgomery officials for police responses to civil rights demonstrations. The *Sullivan* decision, which broadened protection of the press against libel actions, thus reflected the Warren Court's commitment to protecting free expression by minority groups facing a politically hostile environment.

Libel Suits Brought by "Public Persons"

Although *New York Times Company v. Sullivan* applied only to cases where public officials sued for libel, the principle was soon expanded to cover a broader category designated as **public figures** (see *Curtis Publishing Company v. Butts* [1967]). This category includes prominent (and not so prominent) public figures, as well as persons who thrust themselves into the glare of publicity. The theory underlying this doctrine is that public figures have sufficient access to the media to defend themselves against false charges and thus do not require the assistance of libel suits. In *Gertz v. Robert Welch, Inc.* (1974), the Supreme Court stated that "public officials and public figures usually enjoy significantly greater access to the channels of effective communication and hence have a more realistic opportunity to counteract false statements than private individuals normally enjoy." The Court went on to discuss the concept of a "public figure":

> *In some instances an individual may achieve such pervasive fame or notoriety that he becomes a public figure for all purposes and in all contexts. More commonly, an individual voluntarily injects himself or is drawn into a particular public controversy and thereby becomes a public figure for a limited range of issues. In either case, such persons assume special prominence in the resolution of public questions.*

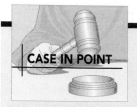

Reverend Jerry Falwell Takes on Larry Flynt

Hustler Magazine v. Falwell (1988)

In its November 1983 issue, *Hustler* ran a fictional advertisement titled "Jerry Falwell talks about his first time." The ad, which was a spoof on the popular ad campaign for Campari liqueur, portrayed Rev. Falwell as a hypocritical drunkard whose "first time" involved sex with his mother in an outhouse. At the bottom of the page, in fine print, was the disclaimer "Ad Parody—Not to be Taken Seriously." Nevertheless, Rev. Falwell took the ad very seriously, and brought a federal lawsuit alleging libel and intentional infliction of emotional distress. Given the outrageous nature of the parody, which no reasonable person could have believed to be true, the jury found for *Hustler* on the libel claim. But the jury did rule in Rev. Falwell's favor on the claim of infliction of emotional distress and awarded substantial monetary damages against *Hustler*. In a unanimous decision, the Supreme Court reversed the judgment, holding that Falwell, as a public figure, could not recover damages for infliction of emotional distress without showing that *Hustler* had published a false statement of fact with actual malice. Writing for the Court, Chief Justice Rehnquist observed that

> [I]n the world of debate about public affairs, many things done with motives that are less than admirable are protected by the First Amendment…. Thus while such a bad motive may be deemed controlling for purposes of tort liability in other areas of the law, we think the First Amendment prohibits such a result in the area of public debate about public figures.

The concept of "public figure" has been difficult to apply, but the Supreme Court has made it clear that publicity does not necessarily make a private citizen a public figure for purposes of libel law. For example, in *Time, Inc. v. Firestone* (1976), the Court rejected an attempt by a defendant in a libel suit to characterize Dorothy Firestone, a wealthy Palm Beach socialite, as a public figure merely because she was involved in a highly publicized divorce case. Speaking for the Court, Justice William Rehnquist said that for a plaintiff in a libel suit to be considered a public figure, the alleged defamation must involve a public controversy, not merely a private dispute that has been publicized in the press. While Firestone's divorce may have generated widespread public interest, it did not involve questions of vital public concern. Moreover, Firestone had not sought public attention; it was thrust upon her by an inquiring press.

Invasion of Privacy

Closely related to libel is the concept of invasion of privacy. Many jurisdictions have laws permitting private individuals to sue the press for unwarranted invasions of their privacy. Following its decision in *New York Times Company v. Sullivan*, the Supreme Court began to restrict such lawsuits. The first major decision came in *Time, Inc. v. Hill* (1967). There, the Court set aside a judgment in an **invasion of privacy** suit brought against *Life* magazine. *Life* had published a story about a family that had been held hostage by escaped prisoners. Unfortunately, not all of the statements made in the magazine story were true. Under New York law, family members could sue regardless of whether the story constituted libel. In setting aside the verdict for the plaintiffs, the Supreme Court said that the First Amendment "preclude [s] the application of the New York statute to redress false reports of matters of public interest in the absence of proof that the defendant published the report with knowledge of its falsity or in reckless disregard of the truth." In a similar vein, the Supreme Court has blocked efforts to restrict the press from reporting the identities of crime victims. In *Cox Broadcasting v. Cohn* (1975), the Court reversed a judgment for the plaintiff in a case in which a television station reported the name of a rape victim. The Court emphasized the fact that the name had been contained in the indictment and was thus a part of the public record. Similarly, in *The Florida Star v. B.J.F.* (1989), the Court overturned a verdict against a newspaper that reported the name of a rape victim. The newspaper had obtained the victim's name from a police report that had been released in violation of state law and the established policy of the police department. The *Cox Broadcasting* and *Florida Star* decisions reflect the Supreme Court's commitment to the principle that the press has the right to report any and all information that it lawfully obtains.

> **To Summarize:**
> ◆ *Defamation is outside the scope of First Amendment protection. However, since the mid-1960s the Supreme Court has extended First Amendment safeguards to defendants in libel suits brought by "public persons," thus expanding freedom of expression in a field traditionally controlled by principles of tort law.*
> ◆ *Under the rule adopted in New York Times Company v. Sullivan (1964), a public official (a term later expanded to include all "public persons") cannot recover damages for a "defamatory falsehood" relating to official conduct unless it is proved that the statement in question "was made with 'actual malice'—that is, with knowledge that it was false or with reckless disregard of whether it was false or not."*
> ◆ *In general the press is accorded freedom to publish any material lawfully obtained, even though publication may seriously invade the privacy of individuals.*

Obscenity and Pornography

In recent decades, sexually explicit magazines, books, and videos have become increasingly available in the marketplace. Soft-core pornography is readily available at most convenience stores and magazine stands. Many cable and satellite television channels also provide adult entertainment in varying degrees of explicitness. Even **hard-core pornography** is easily obtained in the back rooms of many local video rental stores or on pay-per-view from many television providers. Of course thousands of hard-core Web sites are easily accessible via the Internet as well. The commercial success of such ventures obviously indicates some degree of social acceptance, but many critics continue to regard pornography as a societal evil that should be significantly curtailed if not eliminated altogether. But what is the difference between pornographic material and obscene material? Are they always one and the same? Is there artistic value in works of pornography that are not obscene?

Anyone accused of producing or selling obscene materials will argue that the First Amendment protects his or her right to engage in such activities. One of the most difficult tasks the Supreme Court has undertaken in recent decades is that of determining the degree to which the First Amendment protects pornography.

Prior to the Supreme Court's entry into this field in 1957, most American courts adhered to a legal definition of obscenity derived from the 1868 English case of *Regina v. Hicklin*. The *Hicklin* test was "whether the tendency of the matter charged as obscenity is to deprave and corrupt those whose minds are open to such immoral influences, and into whose hands a publication of this sort may fall." By the mid-twentieth century, this standard was widely regarded as unduly restrictive of artistic and literary expression. The principal objection, among others, to the *Hicklin* test was that it sought to measure obscenity with reference to its supposed impact on the most vulnerable members of society. This was a nebulous concept and explains why the Court would seek to develop a new test for defining what was obscene.

The Prurient Interest Test

In *Roth v. United States* (1957), the Supreme Court handed down new legal guidelines for obscenity. Writing for the majority, Justice Brennan expressed the view that obscenity is "utterly without redeeming social importance" and thus entitled to no First Amendment protection. Rejecting the essence of the *Hicklin* standard, he stated the new test as "whether to the average person, applying contemporary community standards, the dominant theme of the material taken as a whole appeals to a prurient interest."

Roth v. United States, a federal case, was consolidated with the state case of *Alberts v. California* (1957), thus making the new test applicable to every level of government in the country. But in spite of its uniform applicability and apparent simplicity, the *Roth-Alberts* test drew the Court into an interpretive quagmire from which it has not yet emerged. Virtually every term contained in the new obscenity test proved elusive. The Court could never reach full agreement on what constitutes a **prurient interest**. The term **redeeming social importance** also failed to generate consensus. A majority of the Court, in the years immediately following *Roth*, could not even agree on whether "community" referred to the nation as a whole or to individual states or localities.

Although most of the justices at this time believed that hard core pornography was not entitled to First Amendment protection, they were unable to define its meaning. Justice Potter Stewart's well-known remark "I know it when I see it" (see *Jacobellis v. Ohio* [1964], concurring opinion) points up the difficulty of precise definition in this area.

The Miller Test

Partly because of the complexity of the problem and partly as a result of the refusal of Justices Hugo Black and William O. Douglas to recognize the legitimacy of *any* limitations on expression in the obscenity field, the Warren Court was unable to muster a clear majority in support of all aspects of the *Roth-Alberts* test during the 1960s. The Burger Court was also sharply divided but ultimately achieved a bare majority in restating the constitutional test of obscenity. Writing for the Court in *Miller v. California* (1973), Chief Justice Burger stated that "the basic guidelines for the trier of fact" in obscenity cases are as follows:

> *(a) whether "the average person, applying contemporary community standards" would find that the work, taken as a whole, appeals to the prurient interest, ... (b) whether the work depicts or describes, in a patently offensive way, sexual conduct specifically defined by the applicable state law, and (c) whether the work, taken as a whole, lacks serious literary, artistic, political, or scientific value.*

The *Miller* test was somewhat more restrictive of free expression than was the original *Roth-Alberts* test as embellished and applied by the Warren Court. The Burger Court explicitly rejected the "utterly without redeeming social value" standard advanced by a minority of justices in the 1960s (see *Memoirs v. Massachusetts* [1966]). Nevertheless, the new guidelines were far from clear. Exactly what is **patently offensive** material? Precisely how does a prurient interest in sex differ from a normal, healthy interest? What constitutes serious literary, artistic, political, or scientific value? And, perhaps most importantly, whose standards are to prevail in making these determinations?

In *Miller*, the Court indicated that the applicable **community standards** under the new test were local or at most statewide standards. But when authorities in Albany, Georgia, purportedly applying "community standards," attempted to ban the movie

Carnal Knowledge, the Court ruled that the test had been improperly applied. Only material showing "patently offensive hard core sexual conduct" could be proscribed under the new rules (*Jenkins v. Georgia* [1974]).

In 1987, a 5-to-4 majority of the Court modified the "contemporary community standards" yardstick. Writing for the majority in *Pope v. Illinois*, Justice Byron White declared that "the proper inquiry is not whether an ordinary member of any given community would find serious literary, artistic, political and scientific value in allegedly obscene material, but whether a reasonable person would find such value in the material, taken as a whole." Whether this "reasonable person" alternative represents a liberalization of the obscenity test or fosters "intolerable orthodoxy," as Justice John Paul Stevens predicted in a dissenting opinion, it is clear that First Amendment issues in the field of obscenity are far from resolved.

Pornography on the Internet

As a practical matter, one must recognize that pornography has become much more widely available in recent years. This is due to several factors. Most fundamentally, society's attitudes in this area have become more permissive. Second, prosecutions in this area have become increasingly rare. In the absence of a public outcry, prosecutors tend to avoid this area in favor of more "ordinary" types of crime. Finally, one must recognize the effect of the Internet, which has made pornography easily accessible to people who might not wish to enter an adult bookstore or place an order from the back of an adult magazine. With a vast number and variety of Web sites devoted to "adult entertainment," many of which feature extremely graphic, hard-core pornography, one of the principal concerns about pornography on the Internet is its availability to children.

In 1996, Congress passed the Communications Decency Act, making it a crime to display "indecent" material on the Internet in a manner that might make it available to minors. In Reno v. American Civil Liberties Union (1997), the Court declared this statute unconstitutional on First Amendment grounds. Writing for the Court, Justice Stevens concluded that, with respect to cyberspace, "the interest in encouraging freedom of expression in a democratic society outweighs any theoretical but unproven benefit of censorship." The Court's opinion in Reno left open the possibility that a more narrowly tailored statute—that is, one limited to prohibiting obscenity as distinct from indecency—might pass constitutional muster.

Child Pornography

It is now well established that government may criminalize the production and distribution of material depicting children engaged in sexual activities, irrespective of whether the material meets the legal test of obscenity. In *New York v. Ferber* (1982), the Court held that a state has a compelling interest in protecting children from sexual abuse and found a close connection between such abuse and the use of children in the production of pornographic materials. But in 2002, the Court surprised some observers by limiting government's efforts to ban child pornography. In *Ashcroft v. Free Speech Coalition*, the Court struck down as "overbroad" a provision of federal law that banned virtual child pornography as well as that employing live subjects. Dividing 6 to 3, the Court, speaking through Justice Kennedy, held that the challenged provision of the Child Pornography Prevention Act of 1996 "covers materials beyond the categories recognized in *Ferber* and *Miller*, and the reasons the Government offers in support of limiting the freedom of speech have no justification in our precedents or in the law of the First Amendment." Since then, Congress has passed legislation such as the Effective Child Pornography Act of 2007 to clarify the prohibition of such materials, meeting the Court's desire to satisfy the First Amendment while responding to societal pressures to prosecute those who engage in production and distribution of obscene depictions of children.

To Summarize:

- *The Supreme Court has said that the First Amendment does not protect expression determined to be obscene. The Court has made it clear that obscenity refers only to hard core pornography that meets a specific legal test.*
- *Under* Miller v. California *(1973), the definition of obscenity is (a) whether "the average person, applying contemporary community standards" would find that the work, taken as a whole, appeals to the prurient interest, ... (b) whether the work depicts or describes, in a patently offensive way, sexual conduct specifically defined by the applicable state law, and (c) whether the work, taken as a whole, lacks serious literary, artistic, political, or scientific value.*
- *In striking down the Communications Decency Act of 1996, the Supreme Court refused to accept the government's argument that "indecent" material on the Internet is subject to regulations similar to those upheld for the broadcast media. Thus, the Court recognized the Internet as a form of communication comparable to the printed page.*
- *It is now well established that government may criminalize the production and distribution of material depicting children engaged in sexual activities, regardless of whether the material meets the legal test of obscenity.*

The Overbreadth Doctrine

The **overbreadth doctrine** prohibits laws that are written so broadly that they potentially infringe First Amendment freedoms. The doctrine of overbreadth enables a party to contest a law imposing restrictions on First Amendment freedoms even when that person has not been charged with violating the law. This doctrine was designed to bring to the courts' attention laws that have a chilling effect on the exercise of First Amendment rights. A good illustration of this is seen in *Reno v. American Civil Liberties Union*, decided by the Supreme Court in 1997. In that case, the American Civil Liberties Union and other plaintiffs sued Attorney General Janet Reno, seeking an injunction to prevent the enforcement of the Communications Decency Act, a controversial statute aimed at protecting children from Internet pornography. Ultimately, the Supreme Court found that the statute was overbroad and declared it unconstitutional.

A similar fate befell a federal law passed in 1999 to suppress commercial trafficking in depictions of animal cruelty, in particular, so-called crush videos where small animals are crushed underfoot. As repulsive as such depictions might be to most members of society, the Supreme Court in *United States v. Stevens* (2010) found the statute, in the words of Chief Justice John Roberts, created "a criminal prohibition of alarming breadth."

To Summarize:

- *The doctrine of overbreadth was developed exclusively in the context of the First Amendment and concerns laws that are written so broadly that they potentially infringe First Amendment freedoms.*
- *Ordinarily a person can contest only a law that has been directed against him or her. However, the doctrine of overbreadth enables a person to contest a law imposing restrictions on First Amendment freedoms even when that person has not been charged with violating the law. This doctrine was designed to bring to the courts' attention laws that have a "chilling effect" on the exercise of First Amendment rights.*

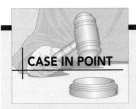

The Doctrine of Overbreadth

Coates v. City of Cincinnati (1971)

Coates was involved in a demonstration stemming from a labor dispute and as a result was arrested, charged and convicted of violating a Cincinnati ordinance making it a crime for "three or more persons to assemble ... on any of the sidewalks ... and there conduct themselves in a manner annoying to persons passing by...." On appeal, Coates argued the ordinance was unconstitutional under the First and Fourteenth Amendments of the Constitution. The Supreme Court declared the ordinance unconstitutionally overbroad, saying that while the ordinance is "broad enough to encompass many types of conduct clearly within the city's constitutional power to prohibit," the City of Cincinnati is not permitted to enact and enforce ordinances "whose violation may entirely depend upon whether or not a policeman in annoyed." Municipalities are "free to prevent people from blocking sidewalks, obstructing traffic, littering streets, committing assaults, or engaging in countless other forms of antisocial conduct," but they must "do so through the enactment and enforcement of ordinances directed with reasonable specificity toward the conduct to be prohibited."

Expressive Activities in the Public Forum

Although the Supreme Court has recognized legitimate community interests that may, under some conditions, justify limitations on speech and assembly, it has tended to favor the First Amendment right of groups to assemble and express themselves in the **public forum**, especially for the purpose of communicating a political message. Such expressive activities in the public forum are an essential part of the democratic process.

Civil Rights Demonstrations of the 1960s

Organized public protest against racial segregation in southern and border states was a critical component of the **Civil Rights Movement** of the 1950s and 1960s. In many instances these protests resulted in arrests. Several of these cases reached the Supreme Court. In *Edwards v. South Carolina* (1963), for example, the Court reversed breach of the peace convictions of 187 African-American college students who had participated in a peaceful civil rights demonstration on the grounds of the state capitol in Columbia, South Carolina. The Court held that in "arresting, convicting, and punishing" these students, South Carolina had infringed their "constitutionally protected rights of free speech, free assembly, and freedom to petition for redress of their grievances." In his opinion for the majority, Justice Stewart observed that "the Fourteenth Amendment does not permit a state to make criminal the peaceful expression of unpopular views."

In a similar case, *Cox v. Louisiana* (1965), the Court reversed convictions for breach of the peace, obstructing "public passages," and picketing near a courthouse. In this case Rev. B. Elton Cox led 2,000 African-American college students in a peaceful demonstration protesting the jailing of twenty three fellow students who had been picketing segregated lunch counters in Baton Rouge, Louisiana. When the students refused to comply with a police order to disperse, tear gas was used to break up the demonstration. In *Cox*, the Court held that the convictions for breach of the peace and for obstructing the sidewalk violated Cox's First Amendment freedoms of speech and assembly. The picketing conviction was reversed on due process grounds.

A similar factual pattern was presented in the 1966 case of *Adderley v. Florida,* but this time the Court affirmed the conviction of African-American students who were protesting local practices of racial segregation. Like the situation in *Cox,* the demonstrators were also denouncing the arrests of other students—in this instance, students from Florida A&M University who had attempted to integrate movie theaters in Tallahassee. During their demonstration, Harriet Louise Adderley and other students had allegedly blocked a jail driveway not normally used by the public. When they ignored requests to leave this area, they were arrested and charged with violating a state law that prohibited trespass "committed with a malicious and mischievous intent." In justifying defendants' convictions, Justice Black, writing for a majority of five, found that nothing in the Constitution prevented Florida from "even handed enforcement of its general trespass statute." Emphasizing the use of the driveway for vehicles providing service to the jail and playing down the symbolic significance of a civil rights protest at the place of incarceration, Black insisted: "The State, no less than a private owner of property, has power to preserve the property under its control for the use to which it is lawfully dedicated."

The *Adderley* decision may be viewed as marking the Warren Court's outer limit of tolerance for public protest. But *Adderley* is perhaps more accurately seen as a concession to public opinion. The decision was rendered at a time of great public concern over a rising tide of crime and violence in America's cities. Perhaps certain justices on the Court saw the *Adderley* case as a good opportunity to make a statement in favor of "law and order," a value that the Warren Court was seldom credited with stressing.

The Civil Rights and antiwar movements of the 1960s were characterized by frequent demonstrations, most of which stayed within constitutional parameters, others of which pressed the limits of constitutional tolerance for public protest. The relatively tranquil decades of the 1970s, 1980s, 1990s, and 2000s produced fewer cases involving large scale demonstrations.

The "Occupy" Movement　　On September 17, 2011, a different type of social protest started in New York's financial district. The Occupy Movement (or Occupy Wall Street Movement) was a protest of social and economic inequality in the United States. Protesters spoke of the perception of greed in corruption among American corporations and suggested those same corporations had undue influence on government policy makers. "We are the 99%" became the slogan of the rally, in reference to the group's feelings that the richest 1 percent of Americans had far too much wealth and power. After the original protest in New York, there were hundreds of American cities (and several international ones) that had their own Occupy protest. The groups most commonly would meet in a public space, often a park or city center, and hold demonstrations featuring speakers and music. Many vowed to camp in the public areas until their voice was heard. This presented an interesting conundrum for state and local police. Did the Occupy protestors have a right to demonstrate in the public places where they chose? Did the police need to enforce common time, place and manor restrictions to limit such events? Skirmishes with law enforcement did take place at several Occupy Movement events nationwide but predominantly the events were peaceful. Any long-term policy effects of the demonstrations are still to be determined.

Antiabortion Demonstrations

One issue that has consistently produced turmoil in the public forum in recent decades has been abortion. Pro-choice and pro-life activists have often clashed in the streets, screaming at one another and sometimes resorting to violence. Pro-life forces have been particularly aggressive in their public demonstrations, often congregating outside abortion clinics and sometimes harassing women seeking to enter these clinics. On occasion, operators of abortion clinics have gone to court to obtain injunctions limiting prolifers' protest activities.

In *Madsen v. Women's Health Center* (1994), the Court upheld a Florida court's injunction that prohibited antiabortion protesters from coming within a 36-foot buffer zone around the entrances to an abortion clinic. The state judge had found that protesters were impeding access to the clinic and harassing clients. In addition to creating a buffer zone that included a section of the public street and sidewalk, the judge banned "singing, chanting, whistling, shouting, yelling, use of bullhorns, auto horns, sound amplification equipment or other sounds or images observable to or within earshot of the patients inside the clinic" between the hours of 7:30 A.M. and noon on Mondays through Saturdays. The injunction was similar to many others that had been issued by state judges around the country to protect abortion clinics and their patrons from the activities of protesters. Judy Madsen, a member of Operation Rescue who had participated in the demonstrations, challenged the constitutionality of the injunction on First Amendment grounds. The Florida Supreme Court upheld the injunction, but in a separate case the Eleventh Circuit Court of Appeals in Atlanta struck it down.

By a 6-to-3 vote, the Supreme Court sided with Florida's highest court. Writing for the majority, Chief Justice Rehnquist concluded that the 36-foot buffer zone "burdens no more speech than necessary to accomplish the governmental interest at stake." Rehnquist noted the state's interests in ensuring public safely and order, promoting the free flow of traffic along streets and sidewalks, protecting a woman's freedom to seek abortion and other pregnancy-related services, and protecting the property rights of all citizens. The Court also upheld the noise restrictions contained in the injunction, noting that "the First Amendment does not demand that patients at a medical facility undertake Herculean efforts to escape the cacophony of political protests." But the Court invalidated other parts of the injunction, holding that the state judge had gone too far in limiting expression. In a stinging dissent, joined by Justices Thomas and Kennedy, Justice Scalia asserted that the entire injunction "departs so far from the established course of our jurisprudence that in any other context it would have been regarded as a candidate for summary reversal."

Three years later, in *Schenck v. Pro-Choice Network* (1997), the Court applied its *Madsen* rationale in upholding an injunction designed to keep demonstrators at least 15 feet away from the doorways and driveways of clinics. Consistent with *Madsen*, the Court, however, struck down a provision of the injunction creating a "floating buffer zone" around clients and staff entering and exiting abortion clinics. Particularly emotional and complex issues such as abortion highlight the Court's challenge in balancing First Amendment rights of some members of society and the legitimate government interest in maintaining peace and order.

What Constitutes a Public Forum?

A key issue for the Court in the last several decades has been defining the concept of public forum. The Supreme Court has recognized that the term *public forum* includes not only streets and parks but any property that government "has opened for use by the public as a place for expressive activity" (*Perry Educational Association v. Perry Local Educators' Association* [1983]). In *United States v. Grace* (1983), the Court recognized that the sidewalks surrounding the Court's own building in Washington, D.C., qualified as a public forum and struck down the federal law forbidding use of that space for picketing or handing out leaflets.

Not every place open to the public constitutes a public forum for purposes of the First Amendment. For example, a privately owned shopping center is not considered a public forum. In *Lloyd Corporation v. Tanner* (1972), the Supreme Court observed that a privately owned shopping center does not "lose its private character merely because the public is generally invited to use it for designated purposes." On the other hand, the Court let stand a California Supreme Court ruling that recognized shopping centers as public forums under the California Constitution (see *PruneYard Shopping Center v. Robins* [1980]). The *PruneYard* decision points up the ability of state courts and state constitutions to grant civil liberties claims transcending those recognized under the federal constitution. Justice Brennan has written on the topic many times, encouraging state courts to do so, exercising what he dubbed "new judicial federalism."

Is an Airport a Public Forum?   The Supreme Court has struggled with the problem of whether an airport is a public forum for the purposes of soliciting, proselytizing, and distributing literature. In *Board of Airport Commissioners v. Jews for Jesus* (1987) and *Lee v. International Society for Krishna Consciousness* (1992), the Court struck down policies that restricted such activities in public airport terminals. Although it relied on both decisions on First Amendment considerations, the Court was unable to reach agreement, however, as to whether an airport is a public forum. Given the prevalence of expressive activities in airports, it is unlikely that the Court will be able to avoid this question forever.

Time, Place, and Manner Regulations

It is well established that reasonable **time, place, and manner regulations** can justify the restriction of First Amendment activities in the public forum. The general rule is that such regulations must be reasonable, narrowly drawn, and **content neutral**. Applying this standard, the Supreme Court struck down, as unconstitutional on its face, a local ordinance that gave unlimited discretion to the chief of police in forbidding or permitting the use of sound amplification devices, such as loudspeakers on trucks (*Saia v. New York* [1948]). A year later, in *Kovacs v. Cooper*, the Court upheld a narrowly interpreted ordinance prohibiting vehicles on the public streets from operating amplifiers or other instruments emitting "loud and raucous noises." The requirement of content neutrality is not absolute, but government cannot depart from it without meeting a heavy burden of justification. The Court is likely to invalidate a regulation of this kind unless the government can show that it is necessary to serve a compelling interest and is narrowly drawn to achieve that purpose. The Court applied this standard in declaring unconstitutional the previously noted restriction on picketing on the sidewalks surrounding the Supreme Court building (*United States v. Grace* [1983]).

In *Boos v. Barry* (1988), the Supreme Court struck down a District of Columbia regulation that prohibited the display of signs within 500 feet of a foreign embassy if the message displayed on the signs brought the embassy's government into "disrepute." At the same time, the Court sustained the regulation permitting police to disperse assemblies within 500 feet of embassies. The former regulation was a restriction on the content of a political message; the latter, if applied evenhandedly, was regarded as a legitimate time, place, and manner regulation.

The Special Problem of Zoning Regulations

Time, place, and manner restrictions often take the form of local **zoning** requirements that have the effect of limiting freedom of expression. In the continuing process of First Amendment line drawing, the Supreme Court has had occasion to look closely at a number of these restrictions. In *Heffron v. International Society for Krishna Consciousness* (1981), a majority of five justices upheld a Minnesota "zoning" restriction limiting solicitation at the state fair, as applied to an organization wishing to distribute and sell religious literature and request donations from fair patrons. The regulation, which applied to nonprofit, charitable, and commercial enterprises alike, confined solicitation activities to booths rented on a first come, first served basis. The International Society for Krishna Consciousness (ISKCON) maintained that this restriction violated the First and Fourteenth Amendments by interfering with one of its sacred rituals, *sankirtan*, which required the faithful to distribute and sell religious literature and to solicit contributions. Writing for the majority, Justice White left no doubt that he was unimpressed by this line of argument: "None of our cases suggest that the inclusion of peripatetic solicitation as part of a church ritual entitles church members to solicitation rights in a public forum superior to those members of other religious groups who raise money but do not purport to ritualize the process." In the majority's view, the regulation at issue was content neutral and nondiscriminatory in application. Moreover, it served a significant governmental interest, that of maintaining crowd control on the congested state fairgrounds.

Five years later, the Court upheld a zoning ordinance passed by the city of Renton, Washington, prohibiting the location of "adult theaters" within 1,000 feet of residential, church, park, or school property (*Renton v. Playtime Theatres, Inc.* [1986]). Writing for a majority of seven, Justice Rehnquist found that the ordinance was "content neutral," that it served a "substantial governmental interest," and that it permitted reasonable alternative "avenues of communication." He asserted that the ordinance was a "valid governmental response to the 'admittedly serious problems' created by adult theaters." The city had not used its zoning power as a "pretext for suppressing expression" but had made areas available for adult theaters and their patrons while "preserving the quality of life in the community at large." Rehnquist concluded: "This, after all, is the essence of zoning." Justice Brennan, supported only by Justice Marshall, flatly rejected the central premise of the majority opinion when he asserted that "the circumstances here strongly suggest that the ordinance was designed to suppress expression, even that constitutionally protected, and thus was not to be analyzed as a content-neutral time, place and manner restriction." From Justice Brennan's criticism of the Court's analysis in this case, it is clear that the initial characterization of a law, for First Amendment purposes, is all important. Regulations are not automatically classified as reasonable time, place, and manner restrictions simply because the legislative body enacting them uses that rationale.

Ultimately, in matters touching freedom of expression, judges must determine whether a given law is to be viewed as primarily a content neutral time, place, and manner restriction or as a deliberate attempt, under the guise of this rationale, to limit freedom of expression. The Court may apply neat verbal formulas and strive for analytical consistency, but ultimately the question comes down to one of judgment in which intuition and ideology are often decisive factors.

To Summarize:

♦ *Because expressive activities in the public forum are an essential part of the democratic process, the Supreme Court has accorded broad First Amendment protection to groups desiring to assemble and express themselves in the public forum.*

♦ *Since the 1930s, the Supreme Court has had numerous opportunities to interpret the First Amendment in the context of political and social protests. Most notable among these are the civil rights demonstrations of the 1950s and 1960s and the public protests on both sides of the abortion issue since the 1970s.*

♦ *The Supreme Court has recognized that the term* public forum *includes not only streets and parks but any property that government "has opened for use by the public as a place for expressive activity."*

> ♦ *Although the Court strongly resists governmental efforts to control the content of expression in the public forum, the justices have repeatedly upheld reasonable "time, place, and manner" regulations on such expression.*

Electronic Media and the First Amendment

The authors of the First Amendment could not have foreseen the invention of radio and television, let alone the prevalence of **electronic media** in contemporary society. Nevertheless, because television and radio are used to express ideas in the public forum, most observers would agree that these electronic media deserve First Amendment protection, at least to some extent. Yet since their inception, radio and television have been regulated extensively by the federal government.

To operate a television or radio station, one must obtain a license from the Federal Communications Commission (FCC); to broadcast without a license from the FCC is a federal crime (as operators of "pirate" radio stations have often discovered). In granting licenses, the FCC is authorized to regulate the station's frequency, wattage, and hours of transmission. To a lesser extent, it also has the power to regulate the content of broadcasts. For example, the FCC has developed regulations to keep the airwaves free of "obscene" or "indecent" programming. Moreover, station licenses come up for renewal every three years, and the FCC is invested with tremendous discretion to determine whether a given station has been operating "in the public interest." Clearly, government regulations that apply to the electronic media would be unconstitutional if applied to books, newspapers, and magazines. The more permissive approach to government regulation of television and radio was originally predicated on the **scarcity theory**, which held that due to the limited number of available broadcast channels (there are a finite number of frequencies available to broadcast on), the government must allocate this scarce resource in the public interest. Yet, the proliferation of cable TV and radio has undermined the controlling influence of the scarcity doctrine. Moreover, changing societal norms have led to a relaxation of earlier restrictions on sexual content and profanity on radio and TV. Nevertheless, the Supreme Court continues to recognize the FCC's authority to impose restrictions on broadcast media that would not be tolerated if they were applied to the print medium.

Restrictions of "Indecent" Programming on Television and Radio

In a broad regulation that would almost certainly be declared unconstitutional if applied to a magazine or newspaper, the FCC has prohibited radio and television stations, whether public or private, from broadcasting "indecent" or "obscene" programs.

In April 1987, the FCC made national news when it threatened not to renew the licenses of certain radio stations in New York and California. These stations were engaged in so-called shock radio, which featured talk programs that were intentionally tasteless and given to heavy doses of profanity and frequent sexual references. Although the FCC's threats made headlines, there was little talk of litigation to challenge the agency's regulations. The Supreme Court had previously upheld restrictions on indecent broadcasting in *Federal Communications Commission v. Pacifica Foundation* (1978). In that case, the Court reviewed FCC regulations as applied to a radio broadcast of a monologue by comedian George Carlin that examined "seven dirty words you can't say on the radio." Attorneys for the Pacifica Foundation argued that the monologue in question did not meet the legal test of obscenity and therefore could not be banned from the radio by the FCC. Writing for the Court, Justice Stevens disagreed, observing that "when the Commission finds that a pig has entered the parlor, the exercise of its regulatory power does not depend on proof that the pig is obscene."

Under this doctrine the FCC has fined radio and television networks for particular instances of content the Commission deems to be indecent. Most memorably, the FCC fined CBS for an incident that occurred during the halftime show of the 2004 Super Bowl in which one of singer Janet Jackson's breasts was exposed to a worldwide television audience. Equally memorable were the fines imposed on Viacom/Infinity over the Howard Stern radio show. While this controversy remains a real one, in the case of radio, many of the more "shock" type programs (including Stern's) have moved to satellite radio, which lies beyond the jurisdiction of the FCC. Similarly, the FCC currently does not have statutory authority to sanction indecent content on subscription-based cable TV channels or the Internet.

Indecent Programming on Cable Television   The "Helms Amendment" to the Cable Television Consumer Protection and Competition Act of 1992 required cable systems that lease channels to commercial providers of "patently offensive" programming to scramble the signals of those channels and make them available only to subscribers who specifically request access. In *Denver Area Educational Telecommunications Consortium v. Federal Communications Commission* (1996), the Court struck down this provision. Writing for the Court, Justice Stephen Breyer observed that the provision was not carefully drafted, failed to consider less intrusive alternatives, and was not a "narrowly or reasonably tailored effort to protect children." In Breyer's view, the provision was "overly restrictive, 'sacrific[ing]' important First Amendment interests for too 'speculative a gain.' " In dissent, Justice Thomas (joined by Chief Justice Rehnquist and Justice Scalia) argued that the requirement that indecent programming be scrambled was supported by the government's compelling interest in protecting children. In Thomas's view, the provision at issue was in keeping with "precedents [which] establish that government may support parental authority to direct the moral upbringing of their children."

Some commentators were disappointed that the Court failed in the *Denver Consortium* decision to articulate a coherent general theory of the First Amendment as it relates to new technology and media. Indeed, the various opinions produced by the justices manifested uncertainty, even confusion, as to the fundamental First Amendment issues involved. This is often the case when the law is confronted by rapid technological change. By 1997, however, the Court achieved greater clarity in addressing the question of whether government could regulate "indecency" on the Internet (see previous discussion of *Reno v. American Civil Liberties Union* [1997]). While recognizing the government's legitimate role in shielding children from inappropriate expression, the Court insisted that this objective cannot justify limiting adults' access to the Internet only to material that is appropriate for children.

Editorializing by Public Television and Radio Stations

Public radio and television, as distinguished from commercial stations and networks, have long been subject to more restrictive government regulations on editorializing. Based on a 1967 act of Congress, the FCC prohibited public radio and television stations from engaging in editorializing altogether. However, in *Federal Communications Commission v. League of Women Voters* (1984), the Supreme Court declared this ban unconstitutional. Writing for a sharply divided Court, Justice Brennan concluded that the ban failed to meet a **least restrictive means test**. In Brennan's view, the ban "far exceeds what is necessary to protect against the risk of governmental interference or to prevent the public from assuming that editorials by public broadcasting stations represent the official view of government." The Court's general expansion of freedom of expression since the mid-twentieth century is reflected not only in areas of political, social, and cultural dialogue, but in the Court's growing awareness that we live in an information age.

The emergence and dynamic growth of television, radio, and the Internet have stimulated the Court's development of a First Amendment jurisprudence that elevates the overwhelming majority of communication to an almost hallowed status.

> ### To Summarize:
> ◆ *Traditionally, the Supreme Court has tolerated more extensive regulation of electronic media than of books, newspapers, and periodicals. This was originally justified by the scarcity theory, an idea that has since been undermined by the proliferation of cable TV and radio.*
> ◆ *The Court has approved the FCC's prohibition against "indecent" content on radio and TV broadcasts, but has resisted the application of such restrictions to cable TV and to the Internet.*
> ◆ *The trend of modern Court decisions is away from governmental control of the content of expression in the media. This is exemplified by the Court's invalidation of an FCC ban on editorializing by public television and radio stations.*

Commercial Speech

Prior to the mid-1970s, the Supreme Court regarded the regulation of **commercial speech** (a broad category including, but not limited to, the advertising of products and services) as simply an aspect of economic regulation, entitled to no special First Amendment protection. In an important 1976 decision, however, the Court struck down Virginia's ban on the advertisement of prescription drug prices (*Virginia State Board of Pharmacy v. Virginia Citizens Consumer Council*). Writing for the Court, Justice Harry Blackmun stated that although reasonable time, place, and manner restrictions on commercial speech are legitimate and although the state is free to proscribe "false and misleading" advertisements, consumers have a strong First Amendment interest in the free flow of information about goods and services available in the marketplace.

A Test for Judging Regulations of Commercial Speech

In his opinion for the Court in *Central Hudson Gas and Electric Corporation v. Public Service Commission of New York* (1980), Justice Lewis Powell articulated the general rationale for First Amendment protection in this area:

> *Commercial expression not only serves the economic interest of the speaker, but also assists consumers and furthers the societal interest in the fullest possible dissemination of information. In applying the First Amendment to this area, we have rejected the "highly paternalistic" view that government has complete power to suppress or regulate commercial speech.*

In the same opinion, Justice Powell outlined a four part test for evaluating regulations of commercial speech. To begin with, commercial speech must "concern lawful activity and not be misleading" if it is to be protected under the First Amendment. If this prerequisite is met, then three additional questions must be considered: (1) Is the "asserted governmental interest" in regulation substantial? (2) Does the regulation directly advance the asserted governmental interest? (3) Finally, is the regulation more extensive than is necessary to serve that purpose? This test is an attempt to balance the need for consumer protection on one hand with the value of a free marketplace of ideas on the other.

In an important decision in 1986, a narrowly divided Supreme Court opted for consumer protection over the free marketplace of ideas. In *Posadas de Puerto Rico Associates v. Tourism Company*, the Court upheld a law prohibiting advertisements inviting residents of the territory of Puerto Rico to gamble legally in local casinos. In his majority opinion, Justice Rehnquist emphasized Puerto Rico's substantial interest in reducing the demand for casino gambling among its citizens and noted that the regulation at issue directly advanced this objective. He maintained that the legislature of Puerto Rico "surely could have prohibited casino gambling by the residents of Puerto Rico altogether." He concluded that this "greater power to completely ban casino gambling necessarily includes the lesser power to ban advertising of casino gambling." In a strongly worded dissent, Justice Stevens contended that Puerto Rico had not merely banned the advertising of casino gambling, it had "blatantly" discriminated in punishing speech "depending on the publication, audience and words employed." In his view, the challenged prohibition established "a regime of prior restraint" and articulated a "hopelessly vague and unpredictable" standard.

Commercial Advertising of Alcoholic Beverages

Under the Twenty-first Amendment, states have broad authority to regulate the sale of alcoholic beverages. Does this authority extend to the ban of advertising in this area? In *44 Liquormart, Inc. v. Rhode Island* (1996), the Court struck down Rhode Island's "statutory prohibition against advertisements that provide the public with accurate information about retail prices of alcoholic beverages." Speaking for a unanimous Court, Justice Stevens concluded that "such an advertising ban is an abridgment of speech protected by the First Amendment and … is not shielded from constitutional scrutiny by the Twenty-First Amendment." In a concurring opinion, Justice Thomas wrote that "[a]ll attempts to dissuade legal choices by citizens by keeping them ignorant are impermissible."

Restrictions on Advertising of Tobacco Products

In 1965, Congress passed the Federal Cigarette Labeling and Advertising Act, which mandates warning labels on cigarette packages. In 1969, Congress adopted the Public Health Cigarette Smoking Act, which prohibits cigarette advertising on any medium of electronic communication under the jurisdiction of the Federal Communications Commission. In 1984, Congress enacted the Comprehensive Smoking Education Act, which, among other things, established a series of strong health warnings to appear in print and billboard advertisements of cigarettes. While these measures have been criticized by libertarians and various interest groups, they have come to be widely accepted—by the courts, by the society, and even by the tobacco industry. In 2001, however, the Supreme Court held that the State of Massachusetts had gone too far in its attempt to regulate advertising of tobacco products. In *Lorillard Tobacco Company v. Reilly*, the Court held that Massachusetts's regulation of cigarette advertising was preempted by federal law. It further held that regulations with respect to other tobacco products (including cigars and smokeless tobacco) violated the First Amendment. Writing for a majority of five, Justice O'Connor observed that "so long as the sale and use of tobacco is lawful for adults, the tobacco industry has a protected interest in communicating information about its products and adult customers have an interest in receiving that information."

Attorney Advertising and Solicitation

Until the late 1970s, attorneys were prohibited by their state bar associations from advertising. These prohibitions reflected a desire by the elite elements of the bar to maintain lawyering as a noble and learned profession. But critics of the prohibition, including many newly licensed attorneys, viewed it as an unwarranted restriction on the dissemination of important information in the marketplace. In *Bates v. State Bar of Arizona* (1977), the Supreme Court sided with the critics, and extended First Amendment protection to attorney advertising. As a consequence, it is now common to see ads for legal services on TV, in newspapers, online, and on buses.

Despite the relaxation of the ban on attorney advertising, many states still maintain restrictions on solicitation by lawyers. For example, the Florida Bar, a state sanctioned organization, prohibits lawyers from sending targeted direct mail solicitations to personal injury victims and their relatives for thirty days following an accident or disaster. The rule was challenged by a number of personal injury lawyers who argued that it violated the First Amendment. In *Florida Bar v. Went for It, Inc.* (1995), the Court divided 5 to 4 in upholding the challenged restriction. Justice O'Connor delivered the opinion of the Court, concluding that the Florida Bar "has substantial interest both in protecting injured Floridians from invasive conduct by lawyers and in preventing the erosion of confidence in the profession that such repeated invasions have engendered." In an unusually caustic dissent, Justice Kennedy attacked the majority opinion as "a serious departure, not only from our prior decisions involving attorney advertising, but also from the principles that govern the transmission of commercial speech." Kennedy accused the majority of unsettling precedents "at the expense of those victims most in need of legal assistance."

In spite of the somewhat restrictive (some would say paternalistic) ruling in *Florida Bar v. Went for It*, it is clear that a great many commercial messages today are entitled to First Amendment protection that was nonexistent prior to the mid-1970s. The Supreme Court has even gone so far as to protect commercial interests against "compelled speech." Thus, in *United States v. United Foods* (2001), Justice Kennedy, writing for a six member majority, concluded that a federal assessment on mushroom growers used to fund mushroom advertising violated the First Amendment.

The enlargement of freedom of expression in the commercial realm underscores the recognition that First Amendment freedoms are by no means limited to the traditional categories of political debate and social protest, important as these concerns are in a constitutional democracy. Despite the Court's recognition of commercial speech, this type of expression is still not accorded the degree of First Amendment protection extended to political and social communication. Indeed, numerous restrictions on commercial speech still abound. For example, truth-in-lending laws require creditors to disclose accurate information regarding all the terms of loans. Various state laws prohibit false advertising. In spite of enhanced legal protections of "adult-expression," the advertising of adult-oriented material is often restricted. Some scholars have urged the abandonment of any distinction between commercial speech and other forms of expression. Thus far, however, the U.S. Supreme Court has been unwilling to place commercial speech alongside political speech in the hierarchy of First Amendment values.

To Summarize:

◆ *Until the mid-1970s, the Supreme Court accorded little if any First Amendment protection to commercial speech. Since that time, however, the Court has not only recognized the First Amendment's application in this area, but has generally narrowed the gap between commercial speech and traditional areas of constitutionally protected expression.*

◆ *Under prevailing doctrine, commercial speech must "concern lawful activity and not be misleading" if it is to be protected under the First Amendment. If this prerequisite is met, then three additional questions must be considered: (1) Is the "asserted governmental interest" in regulation substantial? (2) Does the regulation directly advance the asserted governmental interest? (3) Finally, is the regulation more extensive than is necessary to serve that purpose?*

◆ *The Twenty-first Amendment, which gives states broad authority to regulate the sale of alcoholic beverages, has not been interpreted to override First Amendment protections of commercial speech as they relate to advertising in this area.*

◆ *Despite the Court's recognition of commercial speech, this type of expression is still not accorded the degree of First Amendment protection extended to political and social communication. Indeed, numerous restrictions on commercial speech still abound.*

First Amendment Rights of Public Employees and Beneficiaries

Government employment, government grants and contracts, even government programs such as Social Security are not constitutional rights but rather benefits that government may eliminate altogether or deny to particular individuals, as long as it provides due process of law. Can government make the enjoyment of such benefits contingent on the surrender of constitutional rights, in particular those rights guaranteed by the First Amendment?

Restrictions on Public Employees' Speech

Under the Federal Lobbying (Hatch) Act, federal civil servants are barred from actively participating in political campaigns. The Supreme Court upheld this prohibition in *United States v. Harris* (1954) and again in *United States Civil Service Commission v. National Association of Letter Carriers* (1973). Writing for the Court in the latter decision, Justice White asserted that it was essential that the political influence of federal government workers be limited in order to maintain the concept of a merit-based civil service.

In the 1980s and 1990s, the Court showed greater solicitude for the First Amendment rights of public employees. For example, in *Branti v. Finkel* (1980) the Court said that the First Amendment bars the firing of public prosecutors merely for expressing their political sentiments. Similarly, in *Rankin v. McPherson* (1987), the Court held that a newly hired deputy constable could not be terminated merely for making an intemperate remark about the president. Upon learning of John Hinckley's unsuccessful attempt to assassinate President Reagan in 1981, Ardith McPherson was overheard saying, "If they go for him again, I hope they get him." McPherson, who was at the time a probationary employee, was summarily discharged for making this statement. Writing for the Supreme Court, Justice Thurgood Marshall remarked that "[v]igilance is necessary to ensure that public employers do not use authority over employees to silence discourse, not because it hampers public functions but simply because superiors disagree with the content of employees' speech."

In *United States v. National Treasury Employees Union* (1995), the Court struck down a provision of the Ethics in Government Act that barred federal civil service employees from accepting honoraria for speeches and articles. Although the ban was content neutral, it applied to all honoraria, even those received for speeches and writings having nothing to do with civil servants' jobs. Writing for the Court, Justice Stevens quoted approvingly from *Pickering v. Board of Education* (1968): "Even though respondents work for the Government, they have not relinquished 'the First Amendment rights they would otherwise enjoy as citizens to comment on matters of public interest.' " The vote was 6 to 3, with Chief Justice Rehnquist and Justices Scalia and Thomas in dissent. Writing for the dissenters, Chief Justice Rehnquist complained that the majority's "application of the First Amendment understates the weight which should be accorded to the governmental justifications for the honoraria ban and overstates the amount of speech which actually will be deterred."

Is "Whistle Blowing" Protected by the First Amendment?   In 2006, the Supreme Court adopted a more conservative view of the rights of public employees. As we noted in Chapter 4, Volume I, in *Garcetti v. Ceballos* the Court held that when government employees make public statements as part of their official duties, they are not speaking as *citizens* but as *employees*, and therefore are not entitled to First Amendment protection. The *Garcetti* case involved a deputy prosecutor in Los Angeles who publicly questioned his boss's decision to proceed with a particular criminal prosecution. Richard Ceballos, who brought the lawsuit, complained that he was subsequently denied a promotion and subjected to retaliation, including reassignment and transfer. Speaking for a bare majority, Justice Kennedy rejected "the notion that the First Amendment shields from discipline the expressions employees make pursuant to their professional duties." In a strong dissent joined by Justices Stevens and Ginsburg, Justice David Souter stressed the need for constitutional protection of government whistleblowers:

> *I agree with the majority that a government employer has substantial interests in effectuating its chosen policy and objectives, and in demanding competence, honesty, and judgment from employees who speak for it in doing their work. But I would hold that private and public interests in addressing official wrongdoing and threats to health and safety can outweigh the government's stake in the efficient implementation of policy, and when they do public employees who speak on these matters in the course of their duties should be eligible to claim First Amendment protection.*

Government Employees, Facebook, and the First Amendment   One more contemporary version of this question asks if employment can be terminated as a result of social media activity. While the Supreme Court has yet to tackle this question, many labor review boards and state courts already have. Most of the employees who found themselves terminated based on social media communication have been quick to claim that the First Amendment should protect their expression. Oftentimes, employers have countered saying that the government must uphold individual free speech, but employers harbor no such responsibility. Bureaucratic review boards and state courts to date have provided a series of conflicting rulings in this burgeoning area of the law. This too seems a likely area where the Supreme Court will eventually define the limits of individual First Amendment freedoms.

First Amendment Rights of Government Contractors

In *O'Hare Trucking Service v. Northlake* (1996), the Court split 7 to 2 (Justices Scalia and Thomas dissenting) in ruling that independent contractors who do business with government agencies have the same free speech rights as government employees. Writing for the majority, Justice Kennedy stated that "government officials may indeed terminate at will [contractual] relationships … without cause; but it does not follow that this discretion can be exercised to impose conditions on expressing, or not expressing, specific political views." Given the sheer volume of federal, state, and local contracts, and the fact that political favoritism often plays a role in determining which companies obtain contracts, the decision is apt to spawn considerable litigation.

Restricting Abortion Counseling

The decision in *Rust v. Sullivan* (1991) suggests a different perspective on issues in this area. In *Rust*, the Court sustained a federal regulation barring private birth control clinics that receive federal funds from counseling their clients regarding abortion. The Department of Health and Human Services imposed this restriction in 1987 at the direction of the Reagan administration. When the Court upheld the restriction with a 5-to-4 vote in June 1991, abortion rights activists were not the only ones to protest. Civil libertarians, members of the medical profession, and even some supporters of the Bush administration expressed opposition to what they perceived as an attack on free speech. Critics of the *Rust* decision pointed out that if government could make the receipt of federal funds conditional upon the surrender of First Amendment rights, then all government benefits might be used as devices to limit constitutional rights. For example, people who live in public housing could be asked to surrender their Fourth Amendment rights or face eviction; public defenders could be limited in the defenses they provide to their indigent clients; students could have their choice of occupations dictated by conditions imposed on student loans. The most serious implication of the *Rust* ruling is that public employees, including teachers, might be prohibited from addressing controversial issues or face losing their jobs. The precedential value of *Rust* is open to question, however, given the close division among the justices and subsequent changes in Court personnel.

The NEA Funding Controversy

Since the late 1980s, controversy has surrounded National Endowment for the Arts (NEA) funding of provocative works of art that offend the religious and sexual sensibilities of many people. In 1990, Congress directed the NEA to consider "general standards of decency" in making its funding decisions. During the early stages of the 1992 presidential election campaign, President George H. W. Bush intensified the dispute by firing NEA Chairman John Frohnmeyer. Is it legitimate for the federal government to censor works of art that it subsidizes through a granting agency like the NEA? In a speech to the National Press Club on March 23, 1992, Frohnmeyer argued that "when the government does support free expression, it must do so with a level playing field—no blacklists and no ideological preconceptions." On the other hand, conservative critics of the NEA argued that the taxpayers have no obligation to support works of art that many people find offensive. In *National Endowment for the Arts v. Finley* (1998), the Supreme Court upheld the decency requirement, construing the statute as more of an exhortation than a restriction on expression.

The Military Recruitment Conflict

In the early 1990s, some law schools whose faculties were unhappy with the military's policies regarding gay and lesbian servicepersons began to restrict access of military recruiters to their students. Congress responded by enacting the Solomon Amendment in 1996. The law withholds federal funds from institutions of higher learning that restrict access of military recruiters to their students. An organization of law schools, the Forum for Academic and Institutional Rights (FAIR), brought suit to challenge the constitutionality of the Solomon Amendment on First Amendment grounds. In *Rumsfeld v. FAIR* (2006), the Supreme Court rejected the challenge. Writing for a unanimous bench, Chief Justice John Roberts concluded:

> *The Solomon Amendment neither limits what law schools may say nor requires them to say anything. Law schools remain free under the statute to express whatever views they may have on the military's congressionally mandated employment policy, all the while retaining eligibility for federal funds … As a general matter, the Solomon Amendment*

regulates conduct, not speech. It affects what law school must do—afford equal access to military recruiters—not what they may or may not say. [Emphasis in original]

> **To Summarize:**
>
> ◆ *Traditionally, public employees (especially in the federal civil service) have operated under a number of constraints on their political activities. Consistent with its expanding recognition of constitutionally protected expression, however, the Supreme Court in recent decades has shown greater solicitude for the right of public employees to express themselves on political issues.*
> ◆ *The Court has said that government contractors enjoy the same rights of free expression as those accorded to public employees.*
> ◆ *There is continuing controversy over the extent to which government can condition the provision of benefits on the surrender of First Amendment rights.*

Freedom of Association

Although the Constitution makes no explicit reference to freedom of association, the Supreme Court has long recognized association as a "penumbral" or "implicit" constitutional right. Different provisions of the Constitution have been identified as sources for the protection of various types of association, and some associational freedoms are given more protections than others. Intimate associations—for example, those between husband and wife or parent and child—are extensively protected by the constitutional right of privacy (see Chapter 6). On the other hand, economic associations, like property rights, are afforded more limited protection under the Due Process Clauses of the Fifth and Fourteenth Amendments. The right to associate with others for purposes of worship or devotion is obviously implied by the Free Exercise of Religion Clause of the First Amendment (see Chapter 4). Similarly, the First Amendment freedoms of speech, assembly, and petition implicitly protect the right of individuals to associate for political purposes.

Political Association

Political association, like political expression, occupies a high place in the Supreme Court's scheme of constitutional values. But, like political expression, freedom of political association is far from absolute. Thus, in *Scales v. United States* (1961), the Supreme Court was willing to place its stamp of approval on Section 2 of the Smith Act, which impinged on freedom of association by making it a crime merely to belong to the Communist Party. The Court majority saved the constitutionality of Section 2 by interpreting it narrowly so as to apply only to "active" members of the Communist Party who had a "specific intent" to bring about the violent overthrow of the U.S. government. Four members of the Court (Douglas, Black, Warren, and Brennan) dissented, claiming that the majority had in effect legalized guilt by association.

The constitutional controversy over communism and government efforts to rid the country of the "Red menace" greatly diminished during the 1960s. On the other hand, the Civil Rights Movement was at that time reaching its apogee. In the struggle for civil rights, the National Association for the Advancement of Colored People (NAACP) was one of the most active and significant political organizations. The NAACP had aroused tremendous hostility in the South and had occasionally been the target of state government attempts at intimidation and suppression. In *National Association for the Advancement of Colored People v. Alabama* (1958), the Supreme Court found that the state of Alabama had unconstitutionally infringed the NAACP's freedom of association by selectively enforcing a law requiring organizations based outside Alabama to register members' names and addresses with state authorities.

In ruling in favor of the NAACP, the Supreme Court had to distinguish a precedent that cut the other way. In 1928, it had upheld a New York law under which the Ku Klux Klan was forced to disclose its membership list. In that case, *Bryant v. Zimmerman*, the Court had justified the state policy by stressing the violent and unlawful tactics of the Klan. In *NAACP v. Alabama*, the Court stressed the fact that the NAACP used lawful means in seeking its political objectives.

Freedom of Association and the Problem of Discrimination

Today there is very little controversy about the rights of minorities to organize for purposes of litigation and political action. Many states use their legislative powers on behalf of minority groups and women seeking integration into the economic and cultural mainstream. Public accommodations laws have been used to force civic groups and social clubs to extend membership to women and minorities. Freedom of association has often been raised as a constitutional objection to such efforts.

In *Roberts v. United States Jaycees* (1984), a unanimous Supreme Court found that Minnesota's interest in eradicating sex discrimination was sufficiently compelling to justify a decision of its human rights commission requiring local chapters of the Jaycees to admit women. Writing for the Court, Justice Brennan recognized a political dimension to the Jaycees' activities but nevertheless held that the organization's freedom of political association must give way to the superior state interest in abolishing sex discrimination. In *Rotary International v. Rotary Club of Duarte* (1987), the Court extended its decision in the *Jaycees* case to encompass the Rotary Club as well.

In 1988, the Court upheld a city ordinance requiring large all male social clubs to admit women (*New York State Club Association v. City of New York*). The Court's decisions dealing with "private" clubs suggest that freedom of association in that context must yield to the societal interest in eradicating racial and sexual inequality.

Freedom of Association versus Gay Rights   In *Hurley v. Irish American Gay, Lesbian, and Bisexual Group of Boston* (1995), the Court held that the state of Massachusetts could not prohibit a private organization from excluding a gay rights group from its annual St. Patrick's Day parade. The Massachusetts Supreme Court had ruled against the South Boston Allied War Veterans Council, which organized the parade and refused to permit gay rights groups to participate. The state court held that gay rights groups could not be excluded under Massachusetts's long standing and broadly construed public accommodations statute. In a unanimous decision, the Supreme Court reversed, saying that the state could not compel the parade's organizers to promote a message of which they disapproved. Writing for the Court, Justice Souter insisted that the decision "rests not on any particular view about the Council's message but on the Nation's commitment to protect freedom of speech."

In *Boy Scouts of America v. Dale* (2000), the Court addressed a much more controversial question involving freedom of association and gay rights. James Dale was dismissed from his position as an assistant scoutmaster when the organization learned that Dale was gay. Dale successfully sued the Boy Scouts in the New Jersey courts, which ultimately ruled that the Boy Scouts had violated a state law prohibiting discriminating on the basis of sexual orientation by places of public accommodation.

Dividing 5 to 4, the U.S. Supreme Court reversed, holding that the Boy Scouts' freedom of association trumped the state's interest in advancing the cause of gay rights. Critics of the decision, and there were many, argued that the Court was giving its sanction to bigotry. But many in the private, not-for-profit sector applauded the Court for protecting a private organization from government control. In an official statement, the Boy Scouts of America commented that the *Dale* decision "affirms our standing as a private association with the right to set its own standards for membership and leadership ... and allows us to continue our mission of providing character building experiences for young people, which has been our chartered purpose since our founding." One of the factors that make the *Dale* case so problematic is the close relationship that the Boy Scouts have with public schools, fire departments, and other governmental entities. Critics of the *Dale* decision argue that it is unrealistic to view the Scouts as a strictly private organization. Others argue that even if the Scouts are a private group, the compelling public interest in defeating discrimination should prevail over any First Amendment claim. In 2013 the Boy Scouts of America announced that it was changing its policy and would allow gay Scouts but not gay Scout leaders in the organization. While the decision was no doubt influenced by changing attitudes in society, legally the decision was the BSA's to make.

> **To Summarize:**
> - *Although the Constitution does not explicitly provide for freedom of association, the Supreme Court has long recognized association as an implied First Amendment right.*
> - *The Court has balanced the right of individuals to associate freely against legitimate government interests such as the protection of national security and the promotion of social equality. In general, freedom of association will be protected unless the government advances a very strong justification for abridging it.*

Conclusion

The preceding discussion of major issues involving freedom of expression, assembly, and association, although necessarily selective, underscores several important First Amendment themes. The Supreme Court recognizes no absolutes in this area, but it does operate on the assumption that First Amendment freedoms are of fundamental importance in a democratic society. As a result, the Court generally imposes high standards in determining the constitutionality of legislation challenged on First Amendment grounds. In recent years, a majority of the justices have resisted easy generalizations and uncritical application of neat doctrinal tests in this particularly complex area of constitutional interpretation. In deciding difficult First Amendment cases, the Court attempts to accommodate legitimate government interests in maintaining peace, order, security, decency, and overall quality of life with an open society's vital interest in maintaining a free marketplace of ideas. In an age of an ever-expanding number of political viewpoints, increased concern about terrorism, and the ease with which social media outlets allow expression to be transmitted, this is not an easy balance to maintain. The Supreme Court continues to weigh competing concerns of public order and individual free speech, two ideals that nearly always appear to be mutually exclusive.

Key Terms

freedom of expression	preferred freedoms	profanity
freedom of speech	chilling effect	seditious speech
freedom of the press	incorporation	libel
freedom of assembly	censorship	slander
freedom of association	obscenity	pure speech

picketing
expressive conduct
First Amendment absolutism
fighting words
defamation
prior restraint
clear and present danger test
bad tendency test
free marketplace of ideas
clear and probable danger test
ad hoc balancing

criminal syndicalism
imminent lawless action
hate crimes
symbolic speech
actual malice'
public figures
invasion of privacy
hard-core pornography
prurient interest
redeeming social importance
patently offensive

community standards
overbreadth doctrine
public forum
Civil Rights Movement
time, place, and manner regulations
content neutral
zoning
electronic media
scarcity theory
least restrictive means test
commercial speech

For Further Reading

Berns, Walter. *The First Amendment and the Future of American Democracy.* New York: Basic Books, 1976.

Bollinger, Lee. *The Tolerant Society: Freedom of Speech and Extremist Speech in America.* New York: Oxford University Press, 1986.

Downs, D. A. *Nazis in Skokie: Freedom, Communication and the First Amendment.* South Bend, Ind.: Notre Dame University Press, 1985.

Fortas, Abe. *Concerning Dissent and Civil Disobedience.* New York: New American Library, 1968.

Irons, Peter. *May It Please the Court: The First Amendment.* New York: New Press, 1997.

Kalven, Harry, Jr. *A Worthy Tradition: Freedom of Speech in America.* New York: Harper and Row, 1988.

Konefsky, Samuel J. *The Legacy of Holmes and Brandeis: A Study in the Influence of Ideas.* New York: Macmillan, 1956.

Lowenthal, David. *No Liberty for License: The Forgotten Logic of the First Amendment.* Dallas: Spence Publishing, 1997.

Polenberg, Richard. *Fighting Faiths: The Abrams Case, the Supreme Court and Free Speech.* New York: Viking Press, 1987.

Shiffrin, Steven H. *Dissent, Injustice, and the Meanings of America.* Princeton, N.J.: Princeton University Press, 1999.

Tedford, Thomas L., and Dale A. *Herbeck Freedom of Speech in the United States* (5th ed.). State College, Pa.: Strata Publishing, 2005.

Walker, Sam. *Hate Speech: The History of an American Controversy.* Lincoln: University of Nebraska Press, 1994.

NEAR v. MINNESOTA
283 U.S. 697; 51 S.Ct. 625; 75 L.Ed. 1357 (1931)
Vote: 5-4

In this seminal case, the Court interprets the First Amendment as imposing a broad prohibition against prior restraints on publication. The Court also makes clear that freedom of the press is among the fundamental liberties that must be observed by state and local governments under the Fourteenth Amendment.

Mr. Chief Justice Hughes delivered the opinion of the Court.

Chapter 285 of the Sessions Laws of Minnesota for the year 1925 provides for the abatement, as a public nuisance, of a "malicious, scandalous and defamatory newspaper, magazine or other periodical." ...

Under this statute ... the county attorney of Hennepin County brought this action to enjoin the publication of what was described as a "malicious, scandalous and defamatory newspaper, magazine and periodical," known as *The Saturday Press*, published by the defendants in the city of Minneapolis. The complaint alleged that the defendants, on September 24, 1927, and on eight subsequent dates in October and November 1927, published and circulated editions of that periodical which were "largely devoted to

(Continued)

malicious, scandalous and defamatory articles" concerning [various public officials and others] …

The district court … found in general terms that the editions in question were "chiefly devoted to malicious, scandalous and defamatory articles," concerning the individuals named. The court further found that the defendants through these publications "did engage in the business of regularly and customarily producing, publishing and circulating a malicious, scandalous and defamatory newspaper," and that "the said publication … constitutes a public nuisance under the laws of the state." Judgment was thereupon entered adjudging that "the newspaper, magazine and periodical known as *The Saturday Press*, as a public nuisance, be and is hereby abated … "The defendant Near appealed from this judgment to the supreme court of the state, … asserting his right under the Federal Constitution, and the judgment was affirmed upon the authority of the former decision.…

From the judgment as thus affirmed, the defendant Near appeals to this Court.

This statute, for the suppression as a public nuisance of a newspaper or periodical, is unusual, if not unique, and raises questions of grave importance transcending the local interests involved in the particular action. It is no longer open to doubt that the liberty of the press and of speech is within the liberty safeguarded by the Due Process Clause of the Fourteenth Amendment from invasion by state action. It was found impossible to conclude that this essential personal liberty of the citizen was left unprotected by the general guaranty of fundamental rights of persons and property.… Liberty of speech and of the press is not an absolute right, and the state may punish its abuse. Liberty, in each of its phases, has its history and connotation and, in the present instance, the inquiry is as to the historic conception of the liberty of the press and whether the statute under review violates the essential attributes of that liberty.…

If we cut through mere details of procedure, the operation and effect of the statute in substance is that public authorities may bring the owner or publisher of a newspaper or periodical before a judge upon a charge of conducting a business of publishing scandalous and defamatory matter—in particular that the matter consists of charges against public officers of official dereliction—and unless the owner or publisher is able and disposed to bring competent evidence to satisfy the judge that the charges are true and are published with good motives and for justifiable ends, his newspaper or periodical is suppressed and further publication is made punishable as a contempt. This is of the essence of censorship.

The question is whether a statute authorizing such proceedings in restraint of publication is consistent with the conception of the liberty of the press as historically conceived and guaranteed. In determining the extent of the constitutional protection, it has been generally, if not universally, considered that it is the chief purpose of the guaranty to prevent previous restraints upon publication. The struggle in England, directed against the legislative power of the licenser, resulted in renunciation of the censorship of the press. The liberty deemed to be established was thus described by Blackstone:

> *The liberty of the press is indeed essential to the nature of a free state; but this consists in laying no previous restraints upon publications, and not in freedom from censure for criminal matter when published. Every freeman has an undoubted right to lay what sentiments he pleases before the public; to forbid this, is to destroy the freedom of the press; but if he publishes what is improper, mischievous or illegal, he must take the consequences of his own temerity.…*

The criticism upon Blackstone's statement has not been because immunity from previous restraint upon publication has not been regarded as deserving of special emphasis, but chiefly because that immunity cannot be deemed to exhaust the conception of the liberty guaranteed by state and Federal constitutions. The point of criticism has been "that the mere exemption from previous restraints cannot be all that is secured by the constitutional provisions"; and that "the liberty of the press might be rendered a mockery and a delusion, and the phrase itself a by word, if, while every man was at liberty to publish what he pleased, the public authorities might nevertheless punish him for harmless publications." …

The objection has also been made that the principle as to immunity from previous restraint is stated too broadly, if every such restraint is deemed to be prohibited. That is undoubtedly true; the protection even as to previous restraint is not absolutely unlimited. But the limitation has been recognized only in exceptional cases. "When a nation is at war many things that might be said in time of peace are such a hindrance to its effort that their utterance will not be endured so long as men fight and that no court could regard them as protected by any constitutional right." … No one would question but that a government might prevent actual obstruction to its recruiting service or the publication of the sailing dates of transports or the number and location of troops. On similar grounds, the primary requirements of decency may be enforced against obscene publications. The security of the community life may be protected against incitements to acts of violence and the overthrow by force of orderly government.

The exceptional nature of its limitations places in a strong light the general conception that liberty of the press, historically considered and taken up by the Federal Constitution, has meant, principally, although not exclusively, immunity from previous restraints or censorship. The conception of the liberty of the press in this country has broadened with the exigencies of the colonial period and with the efforts to secure freedom from oppressive administration. That liberty was especially cherished for the immunity it afforded from previous restraint of the publication of censure of public officers and charges of official misconduct....

The fact that for approximately one hundred and fifty years there has been almost an entire absence of attempts to impose previous restraints upon publications relating to the malfeasance of public officers is significant of the deep seated conviction that such restraints would violate constitutional rights. Public officers, whose character and conduct remain open to debate and free discussion in the press, find their remedies for false accusations in actions under libel laws providing for redress and punishment, and not in proceedings to restrain the publication of newspapers and periodicals....

The fact that the liberty of the press may be abused by miscreant purveyors of scandal does not make any the less necessary the immunity of the press from previous restraint in dealing with official misconduct. Subsequent punishment for such abuses as may exist is the appropriate remedy, consistent with constitutional privilege....

The statute in question cannot be justified by reason of the fact that the publisher is permitted to show, before injunction issues, that the matter published is true, and is published with good motives and for justifiable ends. If such a statute, authorizing suppression and injunction on such a basis, is constitutionally valid, it would be equally permissible for the legislature to provide that at any time the publisher of any newspaper could be brought before a court, or even an administrative officer (as the constitutional protection may not be regarded as resting on mere procedural details) and required to produce proof of the truth of his

publication, or of what he intended to publish, and of his motives, or stand enjoined. If this can be done, the legislature may provide machinery for determining in the complete exercise of its discretion what are justifiable ends and restrain publication accordingly. And it would be but a step to a complete system of censorship. The recognition of authority to impose previous restraint upon publication in order to protect the community against the circulation of charges of misconduct, and especially of official misconduct, necessarily would carry with it the admission of the authority of the censor against which the constitutional barrier was erected. The preliminary freedom, by virtue of the very reason for its existence, does not depend, as this court has said, on proof of truth....

For these reasons we hold the statute, so far as it authorized the proceedings in this action under clause (b) of section one, to be an infringement of the liberty of the press guaranteed by the Fourteenth Amendment. We should add that this decision rests upon the operation and effect of the statute, without regard to the question of the truth of the charges contained in the particular periodical. The fact that the public officers named in this case, and those associated with the charges of official dereliction, may be deemed to be impeccable, cannot affect the conclusion that the statute imposes an unconstitutional restraint upon publication.

Judgment reversed.

Mr. Justice Butler [joined by **Justices Van Devanter**, **McReynolds**, and **Sutherland**], dissenting:

The decision of the Court in this case declares Minnesota and every other state powerless to restrain by injunction the business of publishing and circulating among the people malicious, scandalous and defamatory periodicals that in due course of judicial procedure have been adjudged to be a public nuisance. It gives to freedom of the press a meaning and a scope not heretofore recognized and construes "liberty" in the Due Process Clause of the Fourteenth Amendment to put upon the states a Federal restriction that is without precedent....

The Minnesota statute does not operate as a previous restraint on publication within the proper meaning of that phrase. It does not authorize administrative control in advance such as was formerly exercised by the licensers and censors but prescribes a remedy to be enforced by a suit in equity. In this case there was previous publication made in the course of the business

(Continued)

of regularly producing malicious, scandalous and defamatory periodicals. The business and publications unquestionably constitute an abuse of the right of free press. The statute denounces the things done as a nuisance on the ground, as stated by the state supreme court, that they threaten morals, peace and good order. There is no question of the power of the state to denounce such transgressions. The restraint authorized is only in respect of continuing to do what has been duly adjudged to constitute a nuisance.... There is nothing in the statute purporting to prohibit publications that have not been adjudged to constitute a nuisance. ... It is well known, as found by the state supreme court, that existing libel laws are inadequate effectively to suppress evils resulting from the kind of business and publications that are shown in this case. The doctrine that measures such as the one before us are invalid because they operate as previous restraints to infringe freedom of press exposes the peace and good order of every community and the business and private affairs of every individual to the constant and protracted false and malicious assaults of any insolvent publisher who may have purpose and sufficient capacity to contrive and put into effect a scheme or program for oppression, blackmail or extortion.

The judgment should be affirmed.

NEW YORK TIMES COMPANY v. UNITED STATES (THE PENTAGON PAPERS CASE)
403 U.S. 713; 91 S.Ct. 2140; 29 L.Ed. 2d 822 (1971)
Vote: 6-3

In June 1971, Daniel Ellsberg, a disaffected Pentagon employee, turned over to the New York Times *a 7,000-page top secret study titled "History of U.S. Decision-Making Process on Viet Nam Policy." Excerpts from the study, popularly known as the Pentagon papers, appeared in the* New York Times *beginning on June 13, 1971. After the* Times *refused a request to cease publishing excerpts from the study, the Justice Department filed a motion for an injunction in federal court. On Tuesday, June 16, 1971, Judge Harold Gurfein issued the first federal court injunction against a newspaper in this nation's history. Three days later, a federal district court in Washington, D.C., refused to issue a similar injunction against the* Washington Post. *Thereupon, Judge Gurfein lifted the injunction against the* New York Times. *On appeal to the circuit courts, the injunctions were quickly reinstated. The Supreme Court granted certiorari and heard the case immediately.*

PER CURIAM:

We granted certiorari in these cases in which the United States seeks to enjoin the *New York Times* and the *Washington Post* from publishing the contents of a classified study entitled "History of U.S. Decision-Making Process on Viet Nam Policy." "Any system of prior restraints of expression comes to this Court bearing a heavy presumption against its constitutional validity." ... The Government "thus carries a heavy burden of showing justification for the imposition of such a restraint." ... The District Court for the Southern District of New York in the *New York Times* case and the District Court for the District of Columbia and the Court of Appeals for the District of Columbia Circuit in the *Washington Post* case held that the Government had not met that burden. We agree.

The judgment of the Court of Appeals for the District of Columbia Circuit is therefore affirmed. The order of the Court of Appeals for the Second Circuit is reversed and the case is remanded with directions to enter a judgment affirming the judgment of the District Court for the Southern District of New York. The stays entered June 25, 1971, by the Court are vacated. The judgments shall issue forthwith.

Mr. Justice Black, with whom **Mr. Justice Douglas** joins, concurring.

... I believe that every moment's continuance of the injunctions against these newspapers amounts to a flagrant, indefensible, and continuing violation of the First Amendment.... In my view it is unfortunate that some of my Brethren are apparently willing to hold that the publication of news may sometimes be enjoined. Such a holding would make a shambles of the First Amendment....

In seeking injunctions against these newspapers and in its presentation to the Court, the Executive Branch seems to have forgotten the essential purpose and history of the First Amendment....

In the First Amendment the Founding Fathers gave the free press the protection it must have to fulfill its essential role in our democracy. The press was to serve the governed, not the governors. The Government's power to censor the press was abolished so that the press would remain forever free to censure the Government. The press was protected so that it could bare the secrets of government and inform the people. Only a free and unrestrained press can effectively expose deception in government. And paramount among the responsibilities of a free press is the duty to prevent any part of the government from deceiving the people and sending them off to distant lands to die of foreign fevers and foreign shot and shell. In my view, far from deserving condemnation for their courageous reporting, the *New York Times*, the *Washington Post*, and other newspapers should be commended for serving the purpose that the Founding Fathers saw so clearly. In revealing the workings of government that led to the Vietnam War, the newspapers nobly did precisely that which the Founders hoped and trusted they would do....

... [W]e are asked to hold that despite the First Amendment's emphatic command, the Executive Branch, the Congress, and the Judiciary can make laws enjoining publication of current news and abridging freedom of the press in the name of "national security." The Government does not even attempt to rely on any act of Congress.

Instead it makes the bold and dangerously far reaching contention that the courts should take it upon themselves to "make" a law abridging freedom of the press in the name of equity, presidential power, and national security, even when the representatives of the people in Congress have adhered to the command of the First Amendment and refused to make such a law.

... To find that the President has "inherent power" to halt the publication of news by resort to the courts would wipe out the First Amendment and destroy the fundamental liberty and security of the very people the Government hopes to make "secure." No one can read the history of the adoption of the First Amendment without being convinced beyond any doubt that it was injunctions like those sought here that Madison and his collaborators intended to outlaw in this Nation for all time.

Mr. Justice Douglas, with whom *Mr. Justice Black* joins, concurring.

... The Government says that it has inherent powers to go into court and obtain an injunction to protect the national interest, which in this case is alleged to be national security. *Near v. Minnesota* [1931] ... repudiated that expansive doctrine in no uncertain terms.

The dominant purpose of the First Amendment was to prohibit the widespread practice of governmental suppression of embarrassing information. It is common knowledge that the First Amendment was adopted against the widespread use of the common law of seditious libel to punish the dissemination of material that is embarrassing to the powers that be ... The present cases will, I think, go down in history as the most dramatic illustration of that principle. A debate of large proportions goes on in the Nation over our posture in Vietnam. That debate antedated the disclosure of the contents of the present documents. The latter are highly relevant to the debate in progress.

Secrecy in government is fundamentally antidemocratic, perpetuating bureaucratic errors. Open debate and discussion of public issues are vital to our national health. On public questions there should be "uninhibited, robust, and wide open" debate....

Mr. Justice Brennan, concurring.

... I write separately in these cases only to emphasize what should be apparent: that our judgments in the present cases may not be taken to indicate the propriety, in the future, of issuing temporary stays and restraining orders to block the publication of material sought to be suppressed by the Government. So far as I can determine, never before has the United States sought to enjoin a newspaper from publishing information in its possession. The relative novelty of the question presented, the necessary haste with which decisions were reached, the magnitude of the interests asserted, and the fact that all the parties have concentrated their arguments upon the question whether permanent restraints were proper may have justified at least some of the restraints heretofore imposed in these cases. Certainly it is difficult to fault the several courts below for seeking to assure that the issues here involved were preserved for ultimate review by this Court. But even if it be assumed that some of the interim restraints were proper in the two cases before

(Continued)

us, that assumption has no bearing upon the propriety of similar judicial action in the future. To begin with, there has now been ample time for reflection and judgment; whatever values there may be in the preservation of novel questions for appellate review may not support any restraints in the future. More important, the First Amendment stands as an absolute bar to the imposition of judicial restraints in circumstances of the kind presented by these cases....

The error that has pervaded these cases from the outset was the granting of any injunctive relief whatsoever, interim or otherwise. The entire thrust of the Government's claim throughout these cases has been that publication of the material sought to be enjoined "could," or "might," or "may" prejudice the national interest in various ways. But the First Amendment tolerates absolutely no prior judicial restraints of the press predicated upon surmise or conjecture that untoward consequences may result....

Mr. Justice Stewart, with whom **Mr. Justice White** joins, concurring.

In the governmental structure created by our Constitution, the Executive is endowed with enormous power in the two related areas of national defense and international relations. This power, largely unchecked by the Legislative and Judicial branches, has been pressed to the very hilt since the advent of the nuclear missile age. For better or for worse, the simple fact is that a President of the United States possesses vastly greater constitutional independence in these two vital areas of power than does, say, a prime minister of a country with a parliamentary form of government.

In the absence of the governmental checks and balances present in other areas of our national life, the only effective restraint upon executive policy and power in the areas of national defense and international affairs may lie in an enlightened citizenry—in an informal and critical public opinion which alone can here protect the values of democratic government. For this reason, it is perhaps here that a press that is alert, aware, and free most vitally serves the basic purpose of the First Amendment. For without an informed and free press there cannot be an enlightened people.

Yet it is elementary that the successful conduct of international diplomacy and the maintenance of an effective national defense require both confidentiality and secrecy. Other nations can hardly deal with this Nation in an atmosphere of mutual trust unless they can be assured that their confidences will be kept. And within our own executive departments, the development of considered and intelligent international policies would be impossible if those charged with their formulation could not communicate with each other freely, frankly, and in confidence. In the area of basic national defense the frequent need for absolute secrecy is, of course, self-evident.

I think there can be but one answer to this dilemma, if dilemma it be. The responsibility must be where the power is. If the Constitution gives the Executive a large degree of unshared power in the conduct of foreign affairs and the maintenance of our national defense, then under the Constitution the Executive must have the largely unshared duty to determine and preserve the degree of internal security necessary to exercise that power successfully. It is an awesome responsibility, requiring judgment and wisdom of a high order. I should suppose that moral, political, and practical considerations would dictate that a very first principle of that wisdom would be an insistence upon avoiding secrecy for its own sake. For when everything is classified, then nothing is classified, and the system becomes one to be disregarded by the cynical or the careless, and to be manipulated by those intent on self-protection or self-promotion. I should suppose, in short, that the hallmark of a truly effective internal security system would be the maximum possible disclosure, recognizing that secrecy can best be preserved only when credibility is truly maintained. But be that as it may, it is clear to me that it is the constitutional duty of the Executive—as a matter of sovereign prerogative and not as a matter of law as the courts know law—through the promulgation and enforcement of executive regulations, to protect the confidentiality necessary to carry out its responsibilities in the fields of international relations and national defense.

This is not to say that Congress and the courts have no role to play. Undoubtedly Congress has the power to enact specific and appropriate criminal laws to protect government property and preserve government secrets. Congress has passed such laws, and several of them are of very colorable relevance to the apparent circumstances of these cases. And if a criminal prosecution is instituted, it will be the responsibility of the courts to decide the applicability of the criminal law under which the charge is brought. Moreover, if Congress should pass a specific law authorizing civil proceedings in this field, the courts would likewise have the duty to decide the constitutionality of such a law as well as its applicability to the facts proved.

But in the cases before us we are asked neither to construe specific regulations nor to apply specific laws. We are asked, instead, to perform a function that the Constitution gave to the Executive, not the Judiciary. We are asked, quite simply, to prevent the publication by two newspapers of material that the Executive Branch insists should not, in the national interest, be published. I am convinced that the Executive is correct with respect to some of the documents involved. But I cannot say that disclosure of any of them will surely result in direct, immediate, and irreparable damage to our Nation or its people. That being so, there can under the First Amendment be but one judicial resolution of the issues before us. I join the judgments of the Court.

Mr. Justice White, with whom *Mr. Justice Stewart* joins, concurring.

I concur in today's judgments, but only because of the concededly extraordinary protection against prior restraints enjoyed by the press under our constitutional system. I do not say that in no circumstances would the First Amendment permit an injunction against publishing information about government plans or operations. Nor, after examining the materials the Government characterizes as the most sensitive and destructive, can I deny that revelation of these documents will do substantial damage to public interests. Indeed, I am confident that their disclosure will have that result. But I nevertheless agree that the United States has not satisfied the very heavy burden that it must meet to warrant an injunction against publication in these cases, at least in the absence of express and appropriately limited congressional authorization for prior restraints in circumstances such as these....

Mr. Justice Marshall, concurring.

... It would ... be utterly inconsistent with the concept of separation of powers for this Court to use its power of contempt to prevent behavior that Congress has specifically declined to prohibit. There would be a similar damage to the basic concept of these coequal branches of Government if when the Executive Branch has adequate authority granted by Congress to protect "national security" it can choose instead to invoke the contempt power of a court to enjoin the threatened conduct. The Constitution provides that Congress shall make laws, the President execute laws, and courts interpret laws. It did not provide for government by injunction in which the courts and the Executive Branch can "make law" without regard to the action of Congress. It may be more convenient for the Executive Branch if it need only convince a judge to prohibit conduct rather than ask the Congress to pass a law, and it may be more convenient to enforce a contempt order than to seek a criminal conviction in a jury trial. Moreover, it may be considered politically wise to get a court to share the responsibility for arresting those who the Executive Branch has probable cause to believe are violating the law. But convenience and political considerations of the moment do not justify a basic departure from the principles of our system of government....

Mr. Chief Justice Burger, dissenting.

... I suggest ... these cases have been conducted in unseemly haste.... [T]he chronology of events demonstrat[es] the hectic pressures under which these cases have been processed and I need not restate them. The prompt setting of these cases reflects our universal abhorrence of prior restraint. But prompt judicial action does not mean unjudicial haste.

Here, moreover, the frenetic haste is due in large part to the manner in which the *Times* proceeded from the date it obtained the purloined documents. It seems reasonably clear now that the haste precluded reasonable and deliberate judicial treatment of these cases and was not warranted. The precipitate action of this Court aborting trials not yet completed is not the kind of judicial conduct that ought to attend the disposition of a great issue.

The newspapers make a derivative claim under the First Amendment; they denominate this right as the public "right to know"; by implication, the *Times* asserts a sole trusteeship of that right by virtue of its journalistic "scoop." The right is asserted as an absolute. Of course, the First Amendment right itself is not an absolute, as Justice Holmes so long ago pointed out in his aphorism concerning the right to shout "fire" in a crowded theater if there was no fire. There are other exceptions, some of which Chief Justice Hughes mentioned by way of example in *Near v. Minnesota*. There are no doubt other exceptions no one has had occasion to describe or discuss. Conceivably such exceptions may be lurking in these cases and would have been flushed had they been properly considered in the trial courts, free from unwarranted deadlines and frenetic pressures. An issue of this importance should be tried and heard in a judicial atmosphere conducive to thoughtful, reflective deliberation, especially when haste, in terms of hours, is unwarranted in light of

(Continued)

the long period the *Times,* by its own choice, deferred publication.

It is not disputed that the *Times* has had unauthorized possession of the documents for three to four months, during which it has had its expert analysts studying them, presumably digesting them and preparing the material for publication. During all of this time, the *Times* presumably in its capacity as trustee of the public's "right to know," had held up publication for purposes it considered proper and thus public knowledge was delayed. No doubt this was for a good reason; the analysis of 7,000 pages of complex material drawn from a vastly greater volume of material would inevitably take time and the writing of good news stories takes time. But why should the United States Government, from whom this information was illegally acquired by someone, along with all the counsel, trial judges, and appellate judges be placed under needless pressure? After these months of deferral, the alleged "right to know" has somehow and suddenly become a right that must be vindicated instanter.

Would it have been unreasonable since the newspaper could anticipate the Government's objections to release of secret material, to give the Government an opportunity to review the entire collection and determine whether agreement could be reached on publication? Stolen or not, if security was not in fact jeopardized, much of the material could no doubt have been declassified, since it spans a period ending in 1968. With such an approach—one that great newspapers have in the past practiced and stated editorially to be the duty of an honorable press—the newspapers and Government might well have narrowed the area of disagreement as to what was and was not publishable, leaving the remainder to be resolved in orderly litigation, if necessary. To me it is hardly believable that a newspaper long regarded as a great institution in American life would fail to perform one of the basic and simple duties of every citizen with respect to the discovery or possession of stolen property or secret government documents. That duty, I had thought—perhaps naively—was to report forthwith, to responsible public officers. This duty rests on taxi drivers, Justices and the *New York Times.* The course followed by the *Times,* whether so calculated or not, removed any possibility of orderly litigation of the issues. If the action of the judges up to now has been correct, that result is sheer happenstance....

Mr. Justice Harlan, with whom the **Chief Justice** and *Mr. Justice Blackmun* join, dissenting.

... Pending further hearings in each case conducted under the appropriate ground rules, I would continue the restraints on publication. I cannot believe that the doctrine prohibiting prior restraints reaches to the point of preventing courts from maintaining the status quo long enough to act responsibly in matters of such national importance as those involved here....

Mr. Justice Blackmun, dissenting.

... The First Amendment, after all, is only one part of an entire Constitution. Article II of the great document vests in the Executive Branch primary power over the conduct of foreign affairs and places in that branch the responsibility for the Nation's safety. Each provision of the Constitution is important, and I cannot subscribe to a doctrine of unlimited absolutism for the First Amendment at the cost of downgrading other provisions....

SCHENCK v. UNITED STATES
249 U.S. 47; 39 S.Ct. 247; 63 L.Ed. 470 (1919)
Vote: 9-0

Charles T. Schenck, general secretary of the Socialist Party, was convicted of "causing and attempting to cause insubordination in the military and naval forces of the United States," in violation of the Espionage Act of 1917. The conviction stemmed from the Socialist Party's activities in printing and distributing leaflets attacking American participation in the First World War and urging young men to oppose the military draft.

Mr. Justice Holmes delivered the opinion of the Court:

This is an indictment in three counts. The first charges a conspiracy to violate the Espionage Act of

June 15, 1917, … by causing and attempting to cause insubordination, etc., in the military and naval forces of the United States, and to obstruct the recruiting and enlistment service of the United States, when the United States was at war with the German Empire; to wit, that the defendant willfully conspired to have printed and circulated to men who had been called and accepted for military service, a document set forth and alleged to be calculated to cause such insubordination and obstruction. The court alleges overt acts in pursuance of the conspiracy, ending in the distribution of the document set forth. The second count alleges a conspiracy to commit an offense against the United States; to wit, to use the mails for the transmission of matter declared to be non mailable, … to wit, the above mentioned document, with an averment of the same overt acts. The third count charges an unlawful use of the mails for the transmission of same matter and otherwise as above. The defendants were found guilty on all the counts. They set up the First Amendment to the Constitution, forbidding Congress to make any law abridging the freedom of speech or of the press.…

According to the testimony Schenck said he was general secretary of the Socialist party and had charge of the Socialist headquarters from which the documents were sent. He identified a book found there as the minutes of the executive committee of the party. The book showed a resolution of August 13, 1917, that 15,000 leaflets should be printed … to be mailed to men who had passed exemption boards, and for distribution. Schenck personally attended to the printing. On August 20 the general secretary's report said, "Obtained new leaflets from the printer and started work addressing envelopes," etc.; and there was a resolve that Comrade Schenck be allowed $125 for sending leaflets through the mail. He said that he had about fifteen or sixteen thousand printed. There were files of the circular in question in the inner office … Copies were proved to have been sent through the mails to drafted men. Without going into confirmatory details that were proved, no reasonable man could doubt that the defendant Schenck was largely instrumental in sending the circulars about.…

The document in question, upon its first printed side, recited the 1st section of the Thirteenth Amendment, said that the idea embodied in it was violated by the Conscription Act, and that a conscript is little better than a convict. In impassioned language it intimated that conscription was despotism in its worst form and a monstrous wrong against humanity, in the interest of Wall Street's chosen few. It said: "Do not submit to intimidation"; but in form at least confined itself to peaceful measures, such as a petition for the repeal of the act. The other and later printed side of the sheet was headed, "Assert Your Rights." It stated reasons for alleging that anyone violated the Constitution when he refused to recognize "your right to assert your opposition to the draft," and went on: "If you do not assert and support your rights, you are helping to deny or disparage rights which it is the solemn duty of all citizens and residents of the United States to retain." It described the arguments on the other side as coming from cunning politicians and a mercenary capitalist press, and even silent consent to the Conscription Law as helping to support an infamous conspiracy. It denied the power to send our citizens away to foreign shores to shoot up the people of other lands, and added that words could not express the condemnation such cold blooded ruthlessness deserves, etc., etc., winding up, "You must do your share to maintain, support, and uphold the rights of the people of this country." Of course the document would not have been sent unless it had been intended to have some effect, and we do not see what effect it could be expected to have upon persons subject to the draft except to influence them to obstruct the carrying of it out. The defendants do not deny that the jury might find against them on this point.

But it is said, suppose that that was the tendency of this circular, it is protected by the First Amendment to the Constitution. Two of the strongest expressions are said to be quoted respectively from well known public men. It well may be that the prohibition of laws abridging the freedom of speech is not confined to previous restraints, although to prevent them may have been the main purpose.… We admit that in many places and in ordinary times the defendants, in saying all that was said in the circular, would have been within their constitutional rights. But the character of every act depends upon the circumstances in which it is done. … The most stringent protection of free speech would not protect a man in falsely shouting fire in a theater, and causing a panic. It does not even protect a man from an injunction against uttering words that may have all the effect of force.… The question in every case is whether the words used are used in such circumstances and are of such a nature as to create a clear and present danger that they will bring about the substantive evils that Congress has a right to prevent. It is a question of proximity and degree. When a nation is at war many things that might be said in time of peace are such a hindrance to its effort that their utterance will not be endured so long as men fight, and that no

(Continued)

court could regard them as protected by any constitutional right. It seems to be admitted that if an actual obstruction of the recruiting service were proved, liability for words that produced that effect might be enforced. The Statute of 1917 punishes conspiracies to obstruct as well as actual obstruction. If the act (speaking, or circulating a paper), its tendency and the intent with which it is done, are the same, we perceive no ground for saying that success alone warrants making the act a crime....

BRANDENBURG v. OHIO
395 U.S. 444; 89 S.Ct. 1827; 23 L.Ed. 2d 430 (1969)
Vote: 9-0

In Whitney v. California (1927), the Court upheld a state criminal syndicalism statute. Here the Court reconsiders the constitutionality of such laws. The court also reconsiders the formulation of the clear and present danger test.

PER CURIAM:

The appellant, a leader of a Ku Klux Klan group, was convicted under the Ohio Criminal Syndicalism statute for "advocat[ing] ... the duty, necessity, or propriety of crime, sabotage, violence, or unlawful methods of terrorism as a means of accomplishing industrial or political reform" and for "voluntarily assembl[ing] with any society, group, or assemblage of persons formed to teach or advocate the doctrines of criminal syndicalism." ... He was fined $1,000 and sentenced to one to 10 years' imprisonment.

The appellant challenged the constitutionality of the criminal syndicalism statute under the First and Fourteenth Amendments to the United States Constitution, but the intermediate appellate court of Ohio affirmed his conviction without opinion. The Supreme Court of Ohio dismissed his appeal.... It did not file an opinion or explain its conclusions. Appeal was taken to this Court, and we noted probable jurisdiction. We reverse.

The record shows that a man, identified at trial as the appellant, telephoned an announcer-reporter on the staff of a Cincinnati television station and invited him to come to a Ku Klux Klan "rally" to be held at a farm in Hamilton County. With the cooperation of the organizers, the reporter and a cameraman attended the meeting and filmed the events. Portions of the films were later broadcast on the local station and on a national network.

The prosecution's case rested on the films and on testimony identifying the appellant as the person who communicated with the reporter and who spoke at the rally. The State also introduced into evidence several articles appearing in the film, including a pistol, a rifle, a shotgun, ammunition, a Bible, and a red hood worn by the speaker in the films.

One film showed 12 hooded figures, some of whom carried firearms. They were gathered around a large wooden cross, which they burned. No one was present other than the participants and the newsmen who made the film. Most of the words uttered during the scene were incomprehensible when the film was projected, but scattered phrases could be understood that were derogatory of Negroes and, in one instance, of Jews. Another scene on the same film showed the appellant, in Klan regalia, making a speech. The speech, [in part], was as follows: "We're not a revengent organization, but if our President, our Congress, our Supreme Court, continues to suppress the white, Caucasian race, it's possible that there might have to be some revengeance taken."

The second film showed six hooded figures, one of whom, later identified as the appellant, repeated a speech very similar to that recorded on the first film. The reference to the possibility of "revengeance" was omitted, and one sentence was added: "Personally, I believe the nigger should be returned to Africa, the Jew returned to Israel." Though some of the figures in the films carried weapons, the speaker did not.

The Ohio Criminal Syndicalism Statute was enacted in 1919. From 1917 to 1920, identical or quite similar laws were adopted by 20 States and two territories.... In 1927, this Court sustained the constitutionality of California's Criminal Syndicalism Act, the text of which is quite similar to that of the laws of Ohio.... The Court upheld that statute on the ground that, without more, "advocating" violent means to effect political and economic change involves such danger to the security of the State that the State may outlaw it.... But [this view] has been thoroughly discredited by later decisions. ... These later decisions have fashioned the principle that the constitutional guarantees of free speech and free press do not permit a State to forbid or proscribe advocacy of the use of force or of law violation except where such advocacy is directed to inciting or producing imminent lawless action and is likely to incite or produce such action. As we said in *Noto v. United States* ... [1961], "the mere abstract teaching ... of the moral propriety or even moral necessity for a resort to force and violence, is not the same as preparing a group for violent action and steeling it to such action." ... A statute which fails to draw this distinction impermissibly intrudes upon the freedoms guaranteed by the First and Fourteenth Amendments. It sweeps within its condemnation speech which our Constitution has immunized from governmental control....

... [W]e are here confronted with a statute which, by its own words and as applied, purports to punish mere advocacy and to forbid, on pain of criminal punishment, assembly with others merely to advocate the described type of action. Such a statute falls within the condemnation of the First and Fourteenth Amendments. The contrary teaching of *Whitney v. California* ... cannot be supported and that decision is therefore overruled....

Mr. Justice Black, concurring.

Mr. Justice Douglas, concurring.

... I see no place in the regime of the First Amendment for any "clear and present danger" test, whether strict and tight as some would make it, or freewheeling....

The line between what is permissible and not subject to control and what may be made impermissible and subject to regulation is the line between ideas and overt acts.

The example usually given by those who would punish speech is the case of one who falsely shouts fire in a crowded theatre. This is, however, a classic case where speech is brigaded with action.... They are indeed inseparable and a prosecution can be launched for the overt acts actually caused. Apart from rare instances of that kind, speech is, I think, immune from prosecution. Certainly there is no constitutional line between advocacy of abstract ideas ... and advocacy of political action.... The quality of advocacy turns on the depth of the conviction; and government has no power to invade that sanctuary of belief and conscience.

COHEN v. CALIFORNIA
403 U.S. 15; 91 S.Ct. 1780; 29 L.Ed. 2d 284 (1971)
Vote: 5-4

Paul Robert Cohen was convicted in Los Angeles Municipal Court of "maliciously and willfully disturbing the peace" by "offensive conduct" and was sentenced to thirty days in jail. The constitutional question is whether Cohen's conduct constitutes speech as protected by the First Amendment.

Mr. Justice Harlan delivered the opinion of the Court.

... On April 26, 1968, the defendant was observed in the Los Angeles County Courthouse in the corridor outside the division 20 of the municipal court wearing a jacket bearing the words "Fuck the Draft" which were plainly visible. There were women and children present in the corridor. The defendant was arrested. The defendant testified that he wore the jacket knowing that the words were on the jacket as a means of informing the public of the depth of his feelings against the Vietnam War and the draft.

The defendant did not engage in, nor threaten to engage in, nor did anyone as the result of his conduct in fact commit or threaten to commit any act of violence. The defendant did not make any loud or unusual noise, nor was there any evidence that he uttered any sound prior to his arrest....

In affirming the conviction the Court of Appeal held that "offensive conduct" means "behavior which has a tendency to provoke others to acts of violence or to in turn disturb the peace," and that the State had proved this element because, on the facts of this case, "[i]t was certainly reasonably foreseeable that such conduct might cause others to rise up to commit a violent act against the person of the defendant or attempt to forcibly remove his jacket." ...

(Continued)

In order to lay hands on the precise issue which this case involves, it is useful first to canvass various matters which this record does not present.

The conviction quite clearly rests upon the asserted offensiveness of the words Cohen used to convey his message to the public. The only "conduct" which the State sought to punish is the fact of communication. Thus, we deal here with a conviction resting solely upon "speech," ... not upon any separately identifiable conduct which allegedly was intended by Cohen to be perceived by others as expressive of particular views but which, on its face, does not necessarily convey any message and hence arguably could be regulated without effectively repressing Cohen's ability to express himself.... Further, the State certainly lacks power to punish Cohen for the underlying content of the message the inscription conveyed. At least so long as there is no showing of an intent to incite disobedience to or disruption of the draft, Cohen could not, consistently with the First and Fourteenth Amendments, be punished for asserting the evident position on the inutility or immorality of the draft his jacket reflected....

Appellant's conviction, then, rests squarely upon his exercise of the "freedom of speech" protected from arbitrary governmental interference by the Constitution and can be justified, if at all, only as a valid regulation of the manner in which he exercised that freedom, not as a permissible prohibition on the substantive message it conveys. This does not end the inquiry, of course, for the First and Fourteenth Amendments have never been thought to give absolute protection to every individual to speak whenever or wherever he pleases, or to use any form of address in any circumstances that he chooses. In this vein, too, however, we think it important to note that several issues typically associated with such problems are not presented here....

In the first place, Cohen was tried under a statute applicable throughout the entire State. Any attempt to support this conviction on the ground that the statute seeks to preserve an appropriately decorous atmosphere in the courthouse where Cohen was arrested must fall in the absence of any language in the statute that would have put appellant on notice that certain kinds of otherwise permissible speech or conduct would nevertheless, under California law, not be tolerated in certain places....

In the second place, as it comes to us, this case cannot be said to fall within those relatively few categories of instances where prior decisions have established the power of government to deal more comprehensively with certain forms of individual expression simply upon a showing that such a form was employed. This is not, for example, an obscenity case. Whatever else may be necessary to give rise to the States' broader power to prohibit obscene expression, such expression must be, in some significant way, erotic ... It cannot plausibly be maintained that this vulgar allusion to the Selective Service System would conjure up such psychic stimulation in anyone likely to be confronted with Cohen's crudely defaced jacket.

This Court has also held that the States are free to ban the simple use, without a demonstration of additional justifying circumstances, of so called "fighting words," those personally abusive epithets which, when addressed to the ordinary citizen, are, as a matter of common knowledge, inherently likely to provoke violent reaction.... While the four letter word displayed by Cohen in relation to the draft is not uncommonly employed in a personally provocative fashion, in this instance it was clearly not "directed to the person of the hearer." ... No individual actually or likely to be present could reasonably have regarded the words on appellant's jacket as a direct personal insult.

Finally, in arguments before this Court much has been made of the claim that Cohen's distasteful mode of expression was thrust upon unwilling or unsuspecting viewers, and that the State might therefore legitimately act as it did in order to protect the sensitive from otherwise unavoidable exposure to appellant's crude form of protest. Of course, the mere presumed presence of unwitting listeners or viewers does not serve automatically to justify curtailing all speech capable of giving offense.... While this Court has recognized that government may properly act in many situations to prohibit intrusion into the privacy of the home of unwelcome views and ideas which cannot be totally banned from the public dialogue, ... we have at the same time consistently stressed that "we are often 'captives' outside the sanctuary of the home and subject to objectionable speech." ... The ability of government, consonant with the Constitution, to shut off discourse solely to protect others from hearing it is, in other words, dependent upon a showing that substantial privacy interests are being invaded in an essentially intolerable manner. Any broader view of this authority would effectively empower a majority to silence dissidents simply as a matter of personal predilections.

In this regard, persons confronted with Cohen's jacket were in a quite different posture than, say, those subjected to the raucous emissions of sound trucks blaring outside their residences. Those in the Los Angeles courthouse could effectively avoid further bombardment of their sensibilities simply by averting their eyes ... Given the subtlety and complexity of the factors involved, if Cohen's "speech" was otherwise entitled to constitutional protection, we do not think the fact that some unwilling "listeners" in a public building may have been briefly exposed to it can serve to justify this breach of the peace conviction where, as here, there was no evidence that persons powerless to avoid appellant's conduct did in fact object to it ...

Against this background, the issue flushed by this case stands out in bold relief. It is whether California can excise, as "offensive conduct," one particular scurrilous epithet from the public discourse, either upon the theory of the court below that its use is inherently likely to cause violent reaction or upon a more general assertion that the States, acting as guardians of public morality, may properly remove this offensive word from the public vocabulary.

The rationale of the California court is plainly untenable. At most it reflects an "undifferentiated fear or apprehension of disturbance [which] is not enough to overcome the right to freedom of expression." ... We have been shown no evidence that substantial numbers of citizens are standing ready to strike out physically at whoever may assault their sensibilities with execrations like that uttered by Cohen. There may be some persons with such lawless and violent proclivities, but that is an insufficient base upon which to erect, consistently with constitutional values, a governmental power to force persons who wish to ventilate their dissident views into avoiding particular forms of expression. The argument amounts to little more than the self-defeating proposition that to avoid physical censorship of one who has not sought to provoke such a response by a hypothetical coterie of the violent and lawless, the State may more appropriately effectuate that censorship themselves....

Admittedly, it is not so obvious that the First and Fourteenth Amendments must be taken to disable the States from punishing public utterance of this unseemly expletive in order to maintain what they regard as a suitable level of discourse within the body politic. We think, however, that examination and reflection will reveal the shortcomings of a contrary viewpoint.

... [W]e cannot overemphasize that, in our judgment, most situations where the State has a justifiable interest in regulating speech will fall within one or more of the various established exceptions, discussed above but not applicable here, to the usual rule that governmental bodies may not prescribe the form or content of individual expression. Equally important to

our conclusion is the constitutional backdrop against which our decision must be made. The constitutional right of free expression is powerful medicine in a society as diverse and populous as ours. It is designed and intended to remove governmental restraints from the arena of public discussion, putting the decision as to what views shall be voiced largely into the hands of each of us, in the hope that use of such freedom will ultimately produce a more capable citizenry and more perfect polity and in the belief that no other approach would comport with the premise of individual dignity and choice upon which our political system rests....

To many, the immediate consequence of this freedom may often appear to be only verbal tumult, discord, and even offensive utterance. These are, however, within established limits, in truth necessary side effects of the broader enduring values which the process of open debate permits us to achieve. That the air may at times seem filled with verbal cacophony is, in this sense, not a sign of weakness but of strength.

Against this perception of the constitutional policies involved, we discern certain more particularized considerations that peculiarly call for reversal of this conviction. First, the principle contended for by the State seems inherently boundless. How is one to distinguish this from any other offensive word? Surely the State has no right to cleanse public debate to the point where it is grammatically palatable to the most squeamish among us. Yet no readily ascertainable general principle exists for stopping short of that result were we to affirm the judgment below. For, while the particular four letter word being litigated here is perhaps more distasteful than most others of its genre, it is nevertheless often true that one man's vulgarity is another's lyric. Indeed, we think it is largely because governmental officials cannot make principled distinctions in this area that the Constitution leaves matter of taste and style so largely to the individual.

Additionally, we cannot overlook the fact, because it is well illustrated by the episode involved here, that much linguistic expression serves a dual communicative function: it conveys not only ideas capable of relatively precise detached explication, but otherwise inexpressible emotions as well. In fact, words are often chosen as much for their emotive as their cognitive force. We cannot sanction the view that the Constitution, while solicitous of the cognitive content of individual speech, has little or no regard for that emotive function which, practically speaking, may often be the more important element of the overall message sought to be communicated. Indeed, as Mr. Justice

(Continued)

Frankfurter has said, "[o]ne of the prerogatives of American citizenship is the right to criticize public men and measures—and that means not only informed and responsible criticism but the freedom to speak foolishly and without moderation." ...

Finally, and in the same vein, we cannot indulge the facile assumption that one can forbid particular words without also running a substantial risk of suppressing ideas in the process. Indeed, governments might soon seize upon the censorship of particular words as a convenient guise for banning the expression of unpopular views. We have been able, as noted above, to discern little social benefit that might result from running the risk of opening the door to such grave results.

It is, in sum, our judgment that, absent a more particularized and compelling reason for its actions, the State may not, consistently with the First and Fourteenth Amendments, make the simple public display here involved of this single four letter expletive a criminal offense....

Mr. Justice Blackmun, with whom the *Chief Justice* and *Mr. Justice Black* join, dissenting.

... Cohen's absurd and immature antic, in my view, was mainly conduct and little speech.... The California Court of Appeal appears so to have described it, ... and I cannot characterize it otherwise. Further, the case appears to me to be well within the sphere of *Chaplinsky v. New Hampshire* ... [1942], where Mr. Justice Murphy, a known champion of First Amendment freedoms, wrote for a unanimous bench. As a consequence, this Court's agonizing over First Amendment values seems misplaced and unnecessary....

Mr. Justice White [dissenting]....

TEXAS v. JOHNSON
491 U.S. 397; 109 S.Ct. 2533; 105 L.Ed. 2d 342 (1989)
Vote: 5-4

After burning an American flag as part of a public protest, Gregory Lee Johnson was convicted of desecrating a flag in violation of Texas law. The Texas Court of Criminal Appeals reversed the conviction, holding that the statute under which Johnson was convicted was unconstitutional as applied to his particular conduct.

Justice Brennan delivered the opinion of the Court.

... We must first determine whether Johnson's burning of the flag constituted expressive conduct, permitting him to invoke the First Amendment in challenging his conviction.... If his conduct was expressive, we next decide whether the State's regulation is related to the suppression of free expression.... If the State's regulation is not related to expression, then the less stringent standard we announced in *United States v. O'Brien* [1968] for regulations of noncommunicative conduct controls. ... If it is, then we are outside of *O'Brien*'s test, and we must ask whether this interest justifies Johnson's conviction under a more demanding standard.... A third possibility is that the State's asserted interest is simply not implicated on these facts, and in that event the interest drops out of the picture....

The First Amendment literally forbids the abridgment only of "speech," but we have long recognized that its protection does not end at the spoken or written word. While we have rejected "the view that an apparently limitless variety of conduct can be labeled 'speech' whenever the person engaging in the conduct intends thereby to express an idea," ... we have acknowledged that conduct may be "sufficiently imbued with elements of communication to fall within the scope of the First and Fourteenth Amendments." ...

In deciding whether particular conduct possesses sufficient communicative elements to bring the First Amendment into play, we have asked whether "[a]n intent to convey a particularized message was present, and [whether] the likelihood was great that the message was present, and [whether] the likelihood was great that the message would be understood by those who viewed it." Hence, we have recognized the expressive nature of students' wearing of black armbands to protest American military involvement in Vietnam, ... of the wearing of American military uniforms in a dramatic presentation criticizing American involvement in Vietnam, ... and of picketing about a wide variety of causes....

Especially pertinent to this case are our decisions recognizing the communicative nature of conduct relating to flags. Attaching a peace sign to the flag, ... saluting the flag, ... and displaying a red flag, ... we have held, all may find shelter under the First Amendment.... That we have had little difficulty identifying an expressive element in conduct relating to flags should not be surprising. The very purpose of a national flag is to serve as a symbol of our country; it is, one might say, "the one visible manifestation of two hundred years of nationhood." ... Pregnant with expressive content, the flag as readily signifies this Nation as does the combination of letters found in "America." We have not automatically concluded, however, that any action taken with respect to our flag is expressive. Instead, in characterizing such action for First Amendment purposes, we have considered the context in which it occurred.

The State of Texas conceded for purposes of its oral argument in this case that Johnson's conduct was expressive conduct ... Johnson burned an American flag as part—indeed, as the culmination—of a political demonstration that coincided with the convening of the Republican Party and its renomination of Ronald Reagan for President. The expressive, overtly political nature of this conduct was both intentional and overwhelmingly apparent....

The government generally has a freer hand in restricting expressive conduct than it has in restricting the written or spoken word.... It may not, however, proscribe particular conduct because it has expressive elements.... It is, in short, not simply the verbal or nonverbal nature of the expression, but the governmental interest at stake, that helps to determine whether a restriction on that expression is valid....

Texas claims that its interest in preventing breaches of the peace justifies Johnson's conviction for flag desecration. However, no disturbance of the peace actually occurred or threatened to occur because of Johnson's burning of the flag. Although the State stresses the disruptive behavior of the protestors during their march toward City Hall, ... it admits that no actual breach of the peace "occurred at the time of the flag burning or in response to the flag burning." The State's emphasis on the protestors' disorderly actions prior to arriving at City Hall is not only somewhat surprising given that no charges were brought on the basis of this conduct, but it also fails to show that a disturbance of the peace was a likely reaction to Johnson's conduct. The only evidence offered by the State at trial to show the reaction to Johnson's actions was the testimony of several persons who had been seriously offended by the flag burning.

The State's position, therefore, amounts to a claim that an audience that takes serious offense at particular expression is necessarily likely to disturb the peace and that the expression may be prohibited on this basis. Our precedents do not countenance such a presumption. On the contrary, they recognize that a principal "function of free speech under our system of government is to invite dispute. It may indeed best serve its high purpose when it induces a condition of unrest, creates dissatisfaction with conditions as they are, or even stirs people to anger." ...

... Johnson's expressive conduct [does not] fall within that small class of "fighting words" that are "likely to provoke the average person to retaliation, and thereby cause a breach of the peace." ... No reasonable onlooker would have regarded Johnson's generalized expression of dissatisfaction with the policies of the Federal Government as a direct personal insult or an invitation to exchange fisticuffs.

We thus conclude that the State's interest in maintaining order is not implicated on these facts. The State need not worry that our holding will disable it from preserving the peace. We do not suggest that the First Amendment forbids a State to prevent "imminent lawless action." ...

The State also asserts an interest in preserving the flag as a symbol of nationhood and national unity.... The State, apparently, is concerned that ... [flag burning] will lead people to believe either that the flag does not stand for nationhood and national unity, but instead reflects other, less positive concepts, or that the concepts reflected in the flag do not in fact exist, that is, we do not enjoy unity as a Nation. These concerns blossom only when a person's treatment of the flag communicates some message, and thus are related "to the suppression of free expression"...

It remains to consider whether the State's interest in preserving the flag as a symbol of nationhood and national unity justifies Johnson's conviction.

... Johnson was not ... prosecuted for the expression of just any idea; he was prosecuted for his expression of dissatisfaction with the policies of this country, expression situated at the core of our First Amendment values....

Moreover, Johnson was prosecuted because he knew that his politically charged expression would cause "serious offense." If he had burned the flag as a means of disposing of it because it was dirty or torn, he would not have been convicted of flag desecration under this Texas law: federal law designates burning as the preferred means of disposing of a flag "when it is in such condition that it is no longer a fitting emblem for display," ... and Texas has no quarrel

(Continued)

with this means of disposal. The Texas law is thus not aimed at protecting the physical integrity of the flag in all circumstances, but is designed instead to protect it only against impairments that would cause serious offense to others....

Whether Johnson's treatment of the flag violated Texas law thus depended on the likely communicative impact of his expressive conduct.... [T]his restriction on Johnson's expression is content based.

... Johnson's political expression was restricted because of the content of the message he conveyed. We must therefore subject the State's asserted interest in preserving the special symbolic character of the flag to "the most exacting scrutiny." ...

If there is a bedrock principle underlying the First Amendment, it is that Government may not prohibit the expression of an idea simply because society finds the idea itself offensive or disagreeable....

There is, moreover, no indication—either in the text of the Constitution or in our cases interpreting it—that a separate judicial category exists for the American flag alone. Indeed, we would not be surprised to learn that the persons who framed our Constitution and wrote the Amendment that we now construe were not known for their reverence for the Union Jack.... We decline, therefore to create for the flag an exception to the joust of principles protected by the First Amendment.

We are tempted to say ... that the flag's deservedly cherished place in our community will be strengthened, not weakened, by our holding today. Our decision is a reaffirmation of the principles of freedom and inclusiveness that the flag best reflects, and of the conviction that our toleration of criticism such as Johnson's is a sign and source of our strength.

The way to preserve the flag's special role is not to punish those who feel differently about these matters. It is to persuade them that they are wrong.

... [P]recisely because it is our flag that is involved, one's response to the flag burners may exploit the uniquely persuasive power of the flag itself. We can imagine no more appropriate response to burning a flag than waving one's own, no better way to counter a flag burner's message than by saluting the flag that burns, no surer means of preserving the dignity even of the flag that burned than by—as one witness here did—according its remains a respectful burial. We do not consecrate the flag by punishing its desecration, for in doing so we dilute the freedom that this cherished emblem represents....

The judgment of the Texas Court of Criminal Appeals is ... affirmed.

Justice Kennedy, concurring....

Chief Justice Rehnquist, with whom **Justice White** and **Justice O'Connor** join, dissenting.

In holding this Texas statute unconstitutional, the Court ignores Justice Holmes's familiar aphorism that "a page of history is worth a volume of logic." ... For more than 200 years, the American flag has occupied a unique position as the symbol of our Nation, a uniqueness that justifies a governmental prohibition against flag burning in the way respondent Johnson did here....

Here it may equally well be said that the public burning of the American flag by Johnson was no essential part of any exposition of ideas, and at the same time it had a tendency to incite a breach of the peace. Johnson was free to make any verbal denunciation of the flag that he wished; indeed, he was free to burn the flag in private. He could publicly burn other symbols of the Government or effigies of political leaders. He did lead a march through the streets of Dallas, and conducted a rally in front of the Dallas City Hall. He engaged in a "die in" to protest nuclear weapons. He shouted out various slogans during the march, including: "Reagan, Mondale which will it be? Either one means World War III"; "Ronald Reagan, killer of the hour, perfect example of US power"; and "red, white and blue, we spit on you, you stand for plunder, you will go under." ... For none of these acts was he arrested or prosecuted; it was only when he proceeded to burn publicly an American flag stolen from its rightful owner that he violated the Texas statute....

The Court concludes its opinion with a regrettably patronizing civics lecture, presumably addressed to the Members of both Houses of Congress, the members of the 48 state legislatures that enacted prohibitions against flag burning, and the troops fighting under that flag in Vietnam who objected to its being burned: "The way to preserve the flag's special role is not to punish those who feel differently about these matters. It is to persuade them that they are wrong." ... The Court's role as the final expositor of the Constitution is well established, but its role as a platonic guardian admonishing those responsible to public opinion as if they were truant school children has no similar place in our system of government. The cry of "no taxation without representation" animated those who revolted against the English Crown to found our Nation—the idea that those who submitted to government should have some say as to what kind of laws would be passed. Surely one of the high purposes of a democratic society is to legislate against conduct that is regarded as evil and profoundly offensive to the majority of people—whether it be murder, embezzlement, pollution, or flag burning.

Our Constitution wisely places limits on powers of legislative majorities to act, but the declaration of such limits by this Court "is, at all times, a question of much delicacy which ought seldom, if ever, to be decided in the affirmative, in a doubtful case." ... Uncritical extension of constitutional protection to the burning of the flag risks the frustration of the very purpose for which organized governments are instituted. The Court decides that the American flag is just another symbol, about which not only must opinions pro and con be tolerated, but for which the most minimal public respect may not be enjoined. The government may conscript men into the Armed Forces where they must fight and perhaps die for the flag, but the government may not prohibit the public burning of the banner under which they fight. I would uphold the Texas statute as applied in this case.

Justice Stevens, dissenting.

... A country's flag is a symbol of more than "nationhood and national unity." ... It also signifies the ideas that characterize the society that has chosen that emblem as well as the special history that has animated the growth and power of those ideas. The *fleur de lis* and the tricolor both symbolized "nationhood and national unity," but they had vastly different meanings. The message conveyed by some flags—the swastika, for example—may survive long after it has outlived its usefulness as a symbol of regimented unity in a particular nation.

So it is with the American flag. It is more than a proud symbol of the courage, the determination, and the gifts of nature that transformed 13 fledgling Colonies into a world power. It is a symbol of freedom, of equal opportunity, of religious tolerance, and of goodwill for other peoples who share our aspirations. The symbol carries its message to dissidents both at home and abroad who may have no interest at all in our national unity or survival.

The value of the flag as a symbol cannot be measured. Even so, I have no doubt that the interest in preserving that value for the future is both significant and legitimate. Conceivably that value will be enhanced by the Court's conclusion that our national commitment to free expression is so strong that even the United States as ultimate guarantor of that freedom is without power to prohibit the desecration of its unique symbol. But I am unpersuaded. The creation of a federal right to post bulletin boards and graffiti on the Washington Monument might enlarge the market for free expression, but at a cost I would not pay....

The Court is ... quite wrong in blandly asserting that respondent "was prosecuted for his expression of dissatisfaction with the policies of this country, expression situated at the core of our First Amendment values." ... Respondent was prosecuted because of the method he chose to express his dissatisfaction with those policies. Had he chosen to spray paint—or perhaps convey with a motion picture projector—his message of dissatisfaction on the facade of the Lincoln Memorial, there would be no question about the power of the Government to prohibit his means of expression. The prohibition would be supported by the legitimate interest in preserving the quality of an important national asset. Though the asset at stake in this case is intangible, given its unique value, the same interest supports a prohibition on the desecration of the American flag....

VIRGINIA v. BLACK
538 U.S. 343; 123 S.Ct. 1536; 155 L.Ed. 2d 535 (2003)
Vote: 6-3

In this case, the Supreme Court considers a Virginia law banning cross burning with "an intent to intimidate a person or group of persons." The statute further specified that "[a]ny such burning.... shall be prima facie evidence of an intent to intimidate a person or group." Three

defendants, Black, O'Mara, and Elliott, were convicted in separate proceedings of violating the statute. Consolidating the three cases on appeal, the Virginia Supreme Court declared the statute unconstitutional on its face. That court found the law to be indistinguishable from

(Continued)

the ordinance struck down by the U.S. Supreme Court in R.A.V v. St. Paul (1992). It also found that the "prima facie evidence" provision rendered the statute unconstitutionally overbroad. In a badly fragmented decision, the U.S. Supreme Court affirmed in part, vacated in part, and remanded the case to the Virginia Supreme Court for further proceedings. For our purposes in this textbook, the essential point is that six of the justices (O'Connor, Rehnquist, Stevens, Breyer, Scalia, and Thomas) agreed that Virginia could ban cross burnings done with the intent to intimidate. Three justices (Souter, Kennedy, and Ginsburg) took the position that the statute was inescapably flawed.

Justice O'Connor announced the judgment of the Court and delivered the opinion of the Court....

... Respondents Barry Black, Richard Elliott, and Jonathan O'Mara were convicted separately of violating Virginia's cross burning statute. That statute provides:

> *It shall be unlawful for any person or persons, with the intent of intimidating any person or group of persons, to burn, or cause to be burned, a cross on the property of another, a highway or other public place. Any person who shall violate any provision of this section shall be guilty of a Class 6 felony. Any such burning of a cross shall be prima facie evidence of an intent to intimidate a person or group of persons.*

On August 22, 1998, Barry Black led a Ku Klux Klan rally in Carroll County, Virginia. Twenty-five to thirty people attended this gathering, which occurred on private property with the permission of the owner, who was in attendance....

At the conclusion of the rally, the crowd circled around a 25- to 30-foot cross. The cross was between 300 and 350 yards away from the road. According to the sheriff [of Carroll County], the cross "then all of a sudden ... went up in a flame." As the cross burned, the Klan played Amazing Grace over the loudspeakers....

When the sheriff observed the cross burning, he ... entered the rally, and asked "who was responsible for burning the cross." Black responded, "I guess I am because I'm the head of the rally." The sheriff then told Black, "[T]here's a law in the State of Virginia that you cannot burn a cross and I'll have to place you under arrest for this."

Black was charged with burning a cross with the intent of intimidating a person or group of persons.... At his trial, the jury was instructed that "intent to intimidate means the motivation to intentionally put a person

or a group of persons in fear of bodily harm. Such fear must arise from the willful conduct of the accused rather than from some mere temperamental timidity of the victim." The trial court also instructed the jury that "the burning of a cross by itself is sufficient evidence from which you may infer the required intent." ... The jury found Black guilty, and fined him $2,500. The Court of Appeals of Virginia affirmed Black's conviction.

On May 2, 1998, respondents Richard Elliott and Jonathan O'Mara, as well as a third individual, attempted to burn a cross on the yard of James Jubilee. Jubilee, an African American, was Elliott's next door neighbor in Virginia Beach, Virginia. Four months prior to the incident, Jubilee and his family had moved from California to Virginia Beach. Before the cross burning, Jubilee spoke to Elliott's mother to inquire about shots being fired from behind the Elliott home. Elliott's mother explained to Jubilee that her son shot firearms as a hobby, and that he used the backyard as a firing range.

On the night of May 2, respondents drove a truck onto Jubilee's property, planted a cross, and set it on fire. Their apparent motive was to "get back" at Jubilee for complaining about the shooting in the backyard. Respondents were not affiliated with the Klan....

Elliott and O'Mara were charged with attempted cross burning and conspiracy to commit cross-burning. O'Mara pleaded guilty to both counts, reserving the right to challenge the constitutionality of the cross burning statute. The judge sentenced O'Mara to 90 days in jail and fined him $2,500. The judge also suspended 45 days of the sentence and $1,000 of the fine....

Each respondent appealed to the Supreme Court of Virginia, arguing that [the statute] is facially unconstitutional. The Supreme Court of Virginia consolidated all three cases, and held that the statute is unconstitutional on its face. It held that the Virginia cross-burning statute "is analytically indistinguishable from the ordinance found unconstitutional in R.A.V. [v. St. Paul (1992)]." The Virginia statute, the court held, discriminates on the basis of content since it "selectively chooses only cross burning because of its distinctive message." The court also held that the prima facie evidence provision renders the statute overbroad because "[t]he enhanced probability of prosecution under the statute chills the expression of protected speech." ...

In R.A.V., we held that a local ordinance that banned certain symbolic conduct, including cross burning, when done with the knowledge that such conduct would "arouse anger, alarm or resentment in others on the basis of race, color, creed, religion or gender" was unconstitutional. We held that the ordinance did not pass constitutional muster because it discriminated on the basis of content by targeting only those individuals who "provoke violence" on a basis specified in the law. The ordinance did not cover "[t]hose who wish to use 'fighting words' in connection with other ideas—to express hostility, for example, on the basis of political affiliation, union membership, or homosexuality." This content based discrimination was unconstitutional because it allowed the city "to impose special prohibitions on those speakers who express views on disfavored subjects." ...

We did not hold in *R.A.V.* that the First Amendment prohibits *all* forms of content based discrimination within a proscribable area of speech. Rather, we specifically stated that some types of content discrimination did not violate the First Amendment: "When the basis for the content discrimination consists entirely of the very reason the entire class of speech at issue is proscribable, no significant danger of idea or viewpoint discrimination exists."...

... Virginia's statute does not run afoul of the First Amendment insofar as it bans cross burning with intent to intimidate. Unlike the statute at issue in *R.A.V.*, the Virginia statute does not single out for opprobrium only that speech directed toward "one of the specified disfavored topics." It does not matter whether an individual burns a cross with intent to intimidate because of the victim's race, gender, or religion, or because of the victim's "political affiliation, union membership, or homosexuality." Moreover, as a factual matter it is not true that cross burners direct their intimidating conduct solely to racial or religious minorities. Indeed, in the case of Elliott and O'Mara, it is at least unclear whether the respondents burned a cross due to racial animus.

The First Amendment permits Virginia to outlaw cross burnings done with the intent to intimidate because burning a cross is a particularly virulent form of intimidation. Instead of prohibiting all intimidating messages, Virginia may choose to regulate this subset of intimidating messages in light of cross burning's long and pernicious history as a signal of impending violence. Thus, just as a State may regulate only that obscenity which is the most obscene due to its prurient content, so too may a State choose to prohibit only those forms of intimidation that are most likely to inspire fear of bodily harm. A ban on cross burning carried out with the intent to intimidate is fully consistent with our holding in *R.A.V.* and is proscribable under the First Amendment....

The Supreme Court of Virginia ruled in the alternative that Virginia's cross burning statute was unconstitutionally overbroad due to its provision stating that "[a]ny such burning of a cross shall be prima facie evidence of an intent to intimidate a person or group of persons." ...

The prima facie evidence provision, as interpreted by the jury instruction, renders the statute unconstitutional. ... The ... provision permits a jury to convict in every cross burning case in which defendants exercise their constitutional right not to put on a defense. And even where a defendant like Black presents a defense, the prima facie evidence provision makes it more likely that the jury will find an intent to intimidate regardless of the particular facts of the case. The provision permits the Commonwealth to arrest, prosecute, and convict a person based solely on the fact of cross burning itself.

It is apparent that the provision as so interpreted "would create an unacceptable risk of the suppression of ideas." ... The act of burning a cross may mean that a person is engaging in constitutionally proscribable intimidation. But that same act may mean only that the person is engaged in core political speech. The prima facie evidence provision in this statute blurs the line between these two meanings of a burning cross. As interpreted by the jury instruction, the provision chills constitutionally protected political speech because of the possibility that the Commonwealth will prosecute—and potentially convict—somebody engaging only in lawful political speech at the core of what the First Amendment is designed to protect.

The prima facie provision makes no effort to distinguish among ... different types of cross burnings. It does not distinguish between a cross burning done with the purpose of creating anger or resentment and a cross burning done with the purpose of threatening or intimidating a victim. It does not distinguish between a cross burning at a public rally or a cross burning on a neighbor's lawn. It does not treat the cross burning directed at an individual differently from the cross burning directed at a group of like-minded believers. It allows a jury to treat a cross burning on the property of another with the owner's acquiescence in the same manner as a cross burning on the property of another without the owner's permission....

It may be true that a cross burning, even at a political rally, arouses a sense of anger or hatred among the vast majority of citizens who see a burning cross. But this sense of anger or hatred is not sufficient to ban all cross burnings. As Gerald Gunther has stated, "The lesson I have drawn from my childhood in Nazi Germany and my happier adult life in this country is the need to walk the sometimes difficult path of

(Continued)

denouncing the bigot's hateful ideas with all my power, yet at the same time challenging any community's attempt to suppress hateful ideas by force of law." The prima facie evidence provision in this case ignores all of the contextual factors that are necessary to decide whether a particular cross burning is intended to intimidate. The First Amendment does not permit such a shortcut.

For these reasons, the prima facie evidence provision, as ... applied in Barry Black's case, is unconstitutional on its face. We recognize that the Supreme Court of Virginia has not authoritatively interpreted the meaning of the prima facie evidence provision.... [A] 11 we hold is that ... the provision makes the statute facially invalid at this point. We also recognize the theoretical possibility that the court, on remand, could interpret the provision in a manner different from that so far set forth in order to avoid the constitutional objections we have described. We leave open that possibility. We also leave open the possibility that the provision is severable, and if so, whether Elliott and O'Mara could be retried....

With respect to Barry Black, we agree with the Supreme Court of Virginia that his conviction cannot stand, and we affirm the judgment of the Supreme Court of Virginia. With respect to Elliott and O'Mara, we vacate the judgment of the Supreme Court of Virginia, and remand the case for further proceedings.

Justice Souter, with whom *Justice Kennedy* and *Justice Ginsburg* join, concurring in the judgment in part and dissenting in part.

... I conclude that the statute under which all three of the respondents were prosecuted violates the First Amendment, since the statute's content-based distinction was invalid at the time of the charged activities, regardless of whether the prima facie evidence provision was given any effect in any respondent's individual case. In my view, severance of the prima facie evidence provision now could not eliminate the unconstitutionality of the whole statute at the time of the respondents' conduct. I would therefore affirm the judgment of the Supreme Court of Virginia vacating the respondents' convictions and dismissing the indictments. Accordingly, I concur in the Court's judgment as to respondent Black and dissent as to respondents Elliott and O'Mara.

NEW YORK TIMES COMPANY v. SULLIVAN
376 U.S. 254; 84 S.Ct. 710; 11 L.Ed. 2d 686 (1964)
Vote: 9-0

In this case, the Court determines the extent to which the First Amendment limits a state's power to award damages in a libel suit brought by a public official against critics of his official conduct.

Mr. Justice Brennan delivered the opinion of the Court.

... Respondent L. B. Sullivan is one of the three elected Commissioners of the City of Montgomery, Alabama. He testified that he was "Commissioner of Public Affairs and the duties are supervision of the Police Department, Fire Department, Department of Cemetery and Department of Scales." He brought this civil libel action against the four individual petitioners, who are Negroes and Alabama clergymen, and against petitioner the New York Times Company, a New York corporation which publishes the *New York Times*, a daily newspaper. A jury in the Circuit Court of Montgomery County awarded him damages of $500,000, the full amount claimed, against all the petitioners and the Supreme Court of Alabama affirmed....

Respondent's complaint alleged that he had been libeled by statements in a full-page advertisement that was carried in the *New York Times* on March 29, 1960. Entitled "Heed Their Rising Voices," the advertisement began by stating that "As the whole world knows by now, thousands of Southern Negro students are engaged in widespread nonviolent demonstrations in positive affirmation of the right to live in human dignity as guaranteed by the U.S. Constitution and the Bill of Rights." It went on to charge that "in their efforts to uphold these guarantees, they are being met by an unprecedented wave of terror by those who would deny and negate that document which the whole world looks upon as setting the pattern for modern freedom...." Succeeding paragraphs purported to illustrate the "wave of terror" by describing certain alleged events. The text concluded with an appeal for funds for three purposes: support of the student movement, "the struggle for the right-to-vote," and the legal defense of Dr. Martin Luther King, Jr., leader of the movement, against a perjury indictment then pending in Montgomery.

The text appeared over the names of 64 persons, many widely known for their activities in public affairs, religion, trade unions, and the performing arts. Below these names, and under a line reading "We in the south who are struggling daily for dignity and freedom warmly endorse this appeal," appeared the names of the four individual petitioners and of 16 other persons, all but two of whom were identified as clergymen in various Southern cities. The advertisement was signed at the bottom of the page by the "Committee to Defend Martin Luther King and the Struggle for Freedom in the South," and the officers of the Committee were listed.

Of the 10 paragraphs of text in the advertisement, the third and a portion of the sixth were the basis of respondent's claim of libel. They read as follows:

Third paragraph:

In Montgomery, Alabama, after students sang "My Country, 'Tis of Thee" on the State Capitol steps, their leaders were expelled from school, and truckloads of police armed with shotguns and tear gas ringed the Alabama State College Campus. When the entire student body protested to state authorities by refusing to register, their dining hall was padlocked in an attempt to starve them into submission.

Sixth paragraph:

Again and again the Southern violators have answered Dr. King's peaceful protests with intimidation and violence. They have bombed his home almost killing his wife and child. They have assaulted his person. They have arrested him seven times—for "speeding," "loitering" and similar "offenses." And now they have charged him with "perjury"—a felony under which they could imprison him for ten years....

Although neither of these statements mentions respondent by name, he contended that the word "police" in the third paragraph referred to him as the Montgomery Commissioner who supervised the Police Department, so that he was being accused of "ringing" the campus with police. He further claimed that the paragraph would be read as imputing to the police,

and hence to him, the padlocking of the dining hall in order to starve the students into submission. As to the sixth paragraph, he contended that since arrests are ordinarily made by the police, the statement "They have arrested [Dr. King] seven times" would be read as referring to him; he further contended that the "They" who did the arresting would be equated with the "They" who committed the other described acts and with the "Southern violators." Thus, he argued, the paragraph would be read as accusing the Montgomery police, and hence him, of answering Dr. King's protests with "intimidation and violence," bombing his home, assaulting his person, and charging him with perjury. Respondent and six other Montgomery residents testified that they read some of all of the statements as referring to him in his capacity as Commissioner.

It is uncontroverted that some of the statements contained in the two paragraphs were not accurate descriptions of events which occurred in Montgomery. Although Negro students staged a demonstration on the State Capitol steps, they sang the National Anthem and not "My Country, 'Tis of Thee." Although nine students were expelled by the State Board of Education, this was not for leading the demonstration at the Capitol, but for demanding service at a lunch counter in the Montgomery County Courthouse on another day. Not the entire student body, but most of it, had protested the expulsion, not by refusing to register, but by boycotting classes on a single day; virtually all the students did register for the ensuing semester. The campus dining hall was not padlocked on any occasion, and the only students who may have been barred from eating there were the few who had neither signed a preregistration application nor requested temporary meal tickets. Although the police were deployed near the campus in large numbers on three occasions, they did not at any time "ring" the campus, and they were not called to the campus in connection with the demonstration on the State Capitol steps, as the third paragraph implied. Dr. King had not been arrested seven times, but only four; and although he claimed to have been assaulted some years earlier in connection with his arrest for loitering outside a courtroom, one of the officers who made the arrest denied that there was such an assault.

On the premise that the charges in the sixth paragraph could be read as referring to him, respondent was allowed to prove that he had not participated in the events described. Although Dr. King's home had in fact been bombed twice when his wife and child were there, both of these occasions antedated respondent's tenure as Commissioner, and the police were not only

(Continued)

not implicated in the bombings, but had made every effort to apprehend those who were. Three of Dr. King's four arrests took place before respondent became Commissioner. Although Dr. King had in fact been indicted (he was subsequently acquitted) on two counts of perjury, each of which carried a possible five year sentence, respondent had nothing to do with procuring the indictment....

Because of the importance of the constitutional issues involved, we granted the separate petitions for certiorari of the individual petitioners and of the *Times*.... We reverse the judgment. We hold that the rule of law applied by the Alabama courts is constitutionally deficient for failure to provide the safeguards for freedom of speech and of the press that are required by the First and Fourteenth Amendments in a libel action brought by a public official against critics of his official conduct. We further hold that under the proper safeguards the evidence presented in this case is constitutionally insufficient to support the judgment for respondent....

Under Alabama law as applied in this case, a publication is "libelous per se" if the words "tend to injure a person ... in his reputation" or to "bring [him] into public contempt"; the trial court stated that the standard was met if the words are such as to "injure him in his public office, or impute misconduct to him in his office, or want of official integrity, or want of fidelity to a public trust.... "The jury must find that the words were published "of and concerning" the plaintiff, but where the plaintiff is a public official his place in the governmental hierarchy is sufficient evidence to support a finding that his reputation has been affected by statements that reflect upon the agency of which he is in charge. Once "libel per se" has been established, the defendant has no defense as to stated facts unless he can persuade the jury that they were true in all their particulars.... His privilege of "fair comment" for expressions of opinion depends on the truth of the facts upon which the comment is based.... Unless he can discharge the burden of proving truth, general damages are presumed, and may be awarded without proof of pecuniary injury. A showing of actual malice is apparently a prerequisite to recovery of punitive damages, and the defendant may in any event forestall a punitive award by a retraction meeting the statutory requirements. Good motives and belief in truth do not negate an inference of malice, but are relevant only in mitigation of punitive damages if the jury chooses to accord them weight....

The question before us is whether this rule of liability, as applied to an action brought by a public official against critics of his official conduct, abridges the freedom of speech and of the press that is guaranteed by the First and Fourteenth Amendments.

[W]e consider this case against the background of a profound national commitment to the principle that debate on public issues should be uninhibited, robust, and wide open, and that it may well include vehement, caustic, and sometimes unpleasantly sharp attacks on government and public officials....

A rule compelling the critic of official conduct to guarantee the truth of all his factual assertions—and to do so on pain of libel judgments virtually unlimited in amount—leads to a comparable "self censorship." Allowance of the defense of truth, with the burden of proving it on the defendant, does not mean that only false speech will be deterred. Even courts accepting this defense as an adequate safeguard have recognized the difficulties of adducing legal proofs that the alleged libel was true in all its factual particulars ... Under such a rule, would be critics of official conduct may be deterred from voicing their criticism, even though it is believed to be true and even though it is in fact true, because of doubt whether it can be proved in court or fear of the expense of having to do so.

The constitutional guarantees require, we think, a federal rule that prohibits a public official from recovering damages for a defamatory falsehood relating to his official conduct unless he proves that the statement was made with "actual malice"—that is, with knowledge that it was false or with reckless disregard of whether it was false or not....

Such a privilege for criticism of official conduct is appropriately analogous to the protection accorded a public official when he is sued for libel by a private citizen.... The reason for the official privilege is said to be that the threat of damage suits would otherwise "inhibit the fearless, vigorous, and effective administration of policies of government" and "dampen the ardor of all but the most resolute, or the most irresponsible, in the unflinching discharge of their duties." ... Analogous considerations support the privilege for the citizen critic of government. It is as much his duty to criticize as it is the official's duty to administer.... It would give public servants an unjustified preference over the public they serve, if critics of official conduct did not have a fair equivalent of the immunity granted to the officials themselves....

We hold today that the Constitution delimits a State's power to award damages for libel in actions brought by public officials against critics of their official conduct. Since this is such an action, the rule requiring proof of actual malice is applicable. While Alabama law apparently requires proof of actual malice for an award of punitive damages, where general damages are concerned malice is "presumed." Such a presumption is inconsistent with the federal rule.... Since the trial judge did not instruct the jury to differentiate between general and punitive damages, it may be that the verdict was wholly an award of one or the other. But it is impossible to know, in view of the general verdict returned. Because of this uncertainty, the judgment must be reversed and the case remanded....

Mr. Justice Black, with whom *Mr. Justice Douglas* joins, concurring.

... I base my vote to reverse on the belief that the First and Fourteenth Amendments not merely "delimit" a State's power to award damages to "public officials against critics of their official conduct" but completely prohibit a State from exercising such a power. The Court goes on to hold that a State can subject such critics to damages if "actual malice" can be proved against them. "Malice," even as defined by the Court, is an elusive, abstract concept, hard to prove and hard to disprove. The requirement that malice be proved provides at best an evanescent protection for the right critically to discuss public affairs and certainly does not measure up to the sturdy safeguard embodied in the First Amendment. Unlike the Court, therefore, I vote to reverse exclusively on the ground that the *Times* and the individual defendants had an absolute, unconditional constitutional right to publish in the *Times* advertisement their criticisms of the Montgomery agencies and officials....

MILLER v. CALIFORNIA
473 U.S. 15; 93 S.Ct. 2607; 37 L.Ed. 2d 419 (1973)
Vote: 5-4

In this case, the Supreme Court sets forth the constitutional standards for determining obscenity. The defendant, Miller, was convicted in the Orange County Superior Court of "knowingly distributing obscene matter," a misdemeanor under California law. The appellate court affirmed his conviction without opinion.

Mr. Chief Justice Burger delivered the opinion of the Court.

... Appellant conducted a mass mailing campaign to advertise the sale of illustrated books, euphemistically called "adult" material. After a jury trial, he was convicted of violating California Penal Code § 311.2 (a), a misdemeanor, by knowingly distributing obscene matter, and the Appellate Department, Superior Court of California, County of Orange, summarily affirmed the judgment without opinion. Appellant's conviction was specifically based on his conduct in causing five unsolicited advertising brochures to be sent through the mail in an envelope addressed to a restaurant in Newport Beach, California. The envelope was opened by the manager of the restaurant and his mother. They had not requested the brochures; they complained to the police.

The brochures advertise four books entitled "Intercourse," "Man Woman," "Sex Orgies Illustrated," and "An Illustrated History of Pornography," and a film entitled "Marital Intercourse." While the brochures contain some descriptive printed material, primarily they consist of pictures and drawings very explicitly depicting men and women in groups of two or more engaging in a variety of sexual activities, with genitals often prominently displayed....

... This much has been categorically settled by the Court, that obscene material is unprotected by the First Amendment.... "The First and Fourteenth Amendments have never been treated as absolutes." ... We acknowledge, however, the inherent dangers of undertaking to regulate any form of expression. State statutes designed to regulate obscene materials must be carefully limited.... As a result, we now confine the permissible scope of such regulation to works which depict or describe sexual conduct. That conduct must be specifically defined by the applicable state law, as written or authoritatively construed. A state offense must also be limited to works which, taken as a whole, appeal to the prurient interest in sex, which portray sexual conduct in a patently offensive way, and which, taken as a

(Continued)

whole, do not have serious literary, artistic, political, or scientific value.

The basic guidelines for the trier of fact must be: (a) whether "the average person, applying contemporary community standards" would find that the work, taken as a whole, appeals to the prurient interest, ... (b) whether the work depicts or describes, in a patently offensive way, sexual conduct specifically defined by the applicable state law, and (c) whether the work, taken as a whole, lacks serious literary, artistic, political, or scientific value. We do not adopt as a constitutional standard the "*utterly* without redeeming social value" test of *Memoirs v. Massachusetts* ... [1966]; that concept has never commanded the adherence of more than three Justices at one time.... If a state law that regulates obscene material is thus limited, as written or construed, the First Amendment values applicable to the States through the Fourteenth Amendment are adequately protected by the ultimate power of appellate courts to conduct an independent review of constitutional claims when necessary....

We emphasize that it is not our function to propose regulatory schemes for the States. That must await their concrete legislative efforts. It is possible, however, to give a few plain examples of what a state statute could define for regulation ...:

> *Patently offensive representations or descriptions of ultimate sexual acts, normal or perverted, actual or simulated.*
> *(a) Patently offensive representations or descriptions of masturbation, excretory functions, and lewd exhibition of the genitals.*

Sex and nudity may not be exploited without limit by films or pictures exhibited or sold in places of public accommodation any more than live sex and nudity can be exhibited or sold without limit in such public places. At a minimum, prurient, patently offensive depiction or description of sexual conduct must have serious literary, artistic, political, or scientific value to merit First Amendment protection....

Under the holdings announced today, no one will be subject to prosecution for the sale or exposure of obscene materials unless these materials depict or describe patently offensive "hard core" sexual conduct specifically defined by the regulating state law, as written or construed. We are satisfied that these specific prerequisites will provide fair notice to a dealer in such materials that his public and commercial activities may bring prosecution....

It is certainly true that the absence, since *Roth v. United States* [1957] of a single majority view of this Court as to proper standards for testing obscenity has placed a strain on both state and federal courts. But today, for the first time since ... 1957, a majority of this Court has agreed on concrete guidelines to isolate "hard core" pornography from expression protected by the First Amendment....

This may not be an easy road, free from difficulty. But no amount of "fatigue" should lead us to adopt a convenient "institutional" rationale—an absolutist, "anything goes" view of the First Amendment—because it will lighten our burdens. "Such an abnegation of judicial supervision in this field would be inconsistent with our duty to uphold the constitutional guarantees." ... Nor should we remedy "tension between state and federal courts" by arbitrarily depriving the States of a power reserved to them under the Constitution, a power which they have enjoyed and exercised continuously from before the adoption of the First Amendment to this day....

Under a national Constitution, fundamental First Amendment limitations on the powers of the States do not vary from community to community, but this does not mean that there are, or should or can be, fixed, uniform national standards of precisely what appeals to the "prurient interest" or is "patently offensive." These are essentially questions of fact, and our nation is simply too big and too diverse for this Court to reasonably expect that such standards could be articulated for all 50 States in a single formulation, even assuming the prerequisite consensus exists. When triers of fact are asked to decide whether "the average person, applying contemporary community standards" would consider certain materials "prurient," it would be unrealistic to require that the answer be based on some abstract formulation. The adversary system, with lay jurors as the usual ultimate fact finders in criminal prosecution, has historically permitted triers of fact to draw on the standards of their community, guided always by limiting instructions on the law. To require a State to structure obscenity proceedings around evidence of a national "community standard" would be an exercise in futility....

It is neither realistic nor constitutionally sound to read the First Amendment as requiring that the people of Maine or Mississippi accept public depiction of conduct found tolerable in Las Vegas, or New York City.... People in different States vary in their tastes and attitudes, and this diversity is not to be strangled by the absolutism of imposed uniformity....

The dissenting Justices sound the alarm of repression. But, in our view, to equate the free and robust exchange of ideas and political debate with commercial exploitation of obscene material demeans the grand conception of the First Amendment and its high purposes in the historic struggle for freedom. It is a "misuse of the great guarantees of free speech and free press." ... The First Amendment protects works which, taken as a whole, have serious literary, artistic, political or scientific value, regardless of whether the government or a majority of the people approve the ideas these works represent. "The protection given speech and press was fashioned to assure unfettered interchange of *ideas* for the bringing about of political and social changes desired by the people." ... But the public portrayal of hard core sexual conduct for its own sake, and for the ensuing commercial gain, is a different matter.

One can concede that the "sexual revolution" of recent years may have had useful byproducts in striking layers of prudery from a subject long irrationally kept from needed ventilation. But it does not follow that no regulation of patently offensive "hard core" materials is needed or permissible; ...

Mr. Justice Douglas, dissenting.

... The idea that the First Amendment permits government to ban publications that are "offensive" to some people puts an ominous gloss on freedom of the press. That test would make it possible to ban any paper or any journal or magazine in some benighted place. The First Amendment was designed "to invite dispute," to induce "a condition of unrest," to "create dissatisfactions with conditions as they are," and even to stir "people to anger." ... The idea that the First Amendment permits punishment for ideas that are "offensive" to the particular judge or jury sitting in judgment is astounding. No greater leveler of speech or literature has ever been designed. To give the power to the censor, as we do today, is to make a sharp and radical break with the traditions of a free society. The use of the standard "offensive" gives authority to government that cuts the very vitals out of the First Amendment. As is intimated by the Court's opinion, the materials before us may be garbage. But so is much of what is said in political campaigns, in the daily press, on TV or over the radio. By reason of the First Amendment—and solely because of it—speakers and publishers have not been threatened or subdued because their thoughts and ideas may be "offensive" to some....

Mr. Justice Brennan, with whom *Mr. Justice Stewart* and *Mr. Justice Marshall* join, dissenting....

RENO v. AMERICAN CIVIL LIBERTIES UNION
527 U.S. 844; 117 S.Ct. 2329; 138 L.Ed. 2d 874 (1997)
Vote: 7-2

In this widely publicized case, the Court considers the constitutionality of the Communications Decency Act (CDA), federal legislation enacted to protect minors from "indecent" and "patently offensive" communications on the Internet.

Justice Stevens delivered the opinion of the Court.

... Notwithstanding the legitimacy and importance of the congressional goal of protecting children from harmful materials, we agree with the three judge District Court that the statute abridges "the freedom of speech" protected by the First Amendment....

... In its appeal, the Government argues that the District Court erred in holding that the CDA violated both the First Amendment because it is overbroad and the Fifth Amendment because it is vague. While we discuss the vagueness of the CDA because of its relevance to the First Amendment overbreadth inquiry, we conclude that the judgment should be affirmed without reaching the Fifth Amendment issue. We begin our analysis by reviewing the principal authorities on which the Government relies. Then, after describing the overbreadth of the CDA, we consider the Government's specific contentions, including its submission that we save portions of the statute either by severance or by fashioning judicial limitations on the scope of its coverage.

In arguing for reversal, the Government contends that the CDA is plainly constitutional under three of our prior decisions: (1) *Ginsberg v. New York* ... (1968); (2) *FCC v. Pacifica Foundation* ... (1978); and

(Continued)

(3) *Kenton v. Playtime Theatres, Inc.* ... (1986). A close look at these cases, however, raises—rather than relieves—doubts concerning the constitutionality of the CDA.... *[Justice Stevens proceeds to discuss these precedents.]*

These precedents ... surely do not require us to uphold the CDA and are fully consistent with the application of the most stringent review of its provisions.

In *Southeastern Promotions, Ltd. v. Conrad* ... (1975), we observed that "[e]ach medium of expression ... may present its own problems." Thus, some of our cases have recognized special justifications for regulation of the broadcast media that are not applicable to other speakers, see *Red Lion Broadcasting Company v. FCC* ... (1969); *FCC v. Pacifica Foundation* ... (1978). In these cases, the Court relied on the history of extensive government regulation of the broadcast medium; the scarcity of available frequencies at its inception; and its "invasive" nature.

Those factors are not present in cyberspace. Neither before nor after the enactment of the CDA have the vast democratic fora of the Internet been subject to the type of government supervision and regulation that has attended the broadcast industry. Moreover, the Internet is not as "invasive" as radio or television. The District Court specifically found that "[c]ommunications over the Internet do not 'invade' an individual's home or appear on one's computer screen unbidden. Users seldom encounter content 'by accident.' " It also found that "[a]lmost all sexually explicit images are preceded by warnings as to the content," and cited testimony that "'odds are slim' that a user would come across a sexually explicit sight by accident." ...

Finally, unlike the conditions that prevailed when Congress first authorized regulation of the broadcast spectrum, the Internet can hardly be considered a "scarce" expressive commodity. It provides relatively unlimited, low cost capacity for communication of all kinds. The Government estimates that "[a]s many as 40 million people use the Internet today, and that figure is expected to grow to 200 million by 1999." This dynamic, multifaceted category of communication includes not only traditional print and news services, but also audio, video, and still images, as well as interactive, real time dialogue. Through the use of chat rooms, any person with a phone line can become a town crier with a voice that resonates farther than it could from any soapbox. Through the use of Web pages, mail exploders, and newsgroups, the same individual can become a pamphleteer. As the District Court found, "the content on the Internet is as diverse as human thought." ... We agree with its conclusion that our cases provide no basis for qualifying the level of First Amendment scrutiny that should be applied to this medium.

Regardless of whether the CDA is so vague that it violates the Fifth Amendment, the many ambiguities concerning the scope of its coverage render it problematic for purposes of the First Amendment. For instance, each of the two parts of the CDA uses a different linguistic form. The first uses the word "indecent," ... while the second speaks of material that "in context, depicts or describes, in terms patently offensive as measured by contemporary community standards, sexual or excretory activities or organs." Given the absence of a definition of either term, this difference in language will provoke uncertainty among speakers about how the two standards relate to each other and just what they mean. Could a speaker confidently assume that a serious discussion about birth control practices, homosexuality, the First Amendment issues raised by the Appendix to our *Pacifica* opinion, or the consequences of prison rape would not violate the CDA? This uncertainty undermines the likelihood that the CDA has been carefully tailored to the congressional goal of protecting minors from potentially harmful materials.

The vagueness of the CDA is a matter of special concern for two reasons. First, the CDA is a content based regulation of speech. The vagueness of such a regulation raises special First Amendment concerns because of its obvious chilling effect on free speech.... Second, the CDA is a criminal statute. In addition to the opprobrium and stigma of a criminal conviction, the CDA threatens violators with penalties including up to two years in prison for each act of violation. The severity of criminal sanctions may well cause speakers to remain silent rather than communicate even arguably unlawful words, ideas, and images.... As a practical matter, this increased deterrent effect, coupled with the "risk of discriminatory enforcement" of vague regulations, poses greater First Amendment concerns....

We are persuaded that the CDA lacks the precision that the First Amendment requires when a statute regulates the content of speech. In order to deny minors access to potentially harmful speech, the CDA effectively suppresses a large amount of speech that adults have a constitutional right to receive and to address to one another. That burden on adult speech is unacceptable if less restrictive alternatives would be at least as effective in achieving the legitimate purpose that the statute was enacted to serve.

In evaluating the free speech rights of adults, we have made it perfectly clear that "[s]exual expression which is indecent but not obscene is protected by the First Amendment." ... Indeed, *Pacifica* itself admonished that "the fact that society may find speech offensive is not a sufficient reason for suppressing it." ...

It is true that we have repeatedly recognized the governmental interest in protecting children from harmful materials.... But that interest does not justify an unnecessarily broad suppression of speech addressed to adults. As we have explained, the Government may not "reduc[e] the adult population ... to ... only what is fit for children." ...

In arguing that the CDA does not so diminish adult communication, the Government relies on the incorrect factual premise that prohibiting a transmission whenever it is known that one of its recipients is a minor would not interfere with adult to adult communication. The findings of the District Court make clear that this premise is untenable.

Given the size of the potential audience for most messages, in the absence of a viable age verification process, the sender must be charged with knowing that one or more minors will likely view it. Knowledge that, for instance, one or more members of a 100 person chat group will be minor—and therefore that it would be a crime to send the group an indecent message—would surely burden communication among adults.

The breadth of the CDA's coverage is wholly unprecedented.... [T]he scope of the CDA is not limited to commercial speech or commercial entities. Its open ended prohibitions embrace all nonprofit entities and individuals posting indecent messages or displaying them on their own computers in the presence of minors. The general, undefined terms "indecent" and "patently offensive" cover large amounts of non-pornographic material with serious educational or other value. Moreover, the "community standards" criterion as applied to the Internet means that any communication available to a nationwide audience will be judged by the standards of the community most likely to be offended by the message. The regulated subject matter includes any of the seven "dirty words" used in the Pacifica monologue, the use of which the Government's expert acknowledged could constitute a felony.... It may also extend to discussions about prison rape or safe sexual practices, artistic images that include nude subjects, and arguably the card catalogue of the Carnegie Library....

The breadth of this content based restriction of speech imposes an especially heavy burden on the Government to explain why a less restrictive provision would not be as effective as the CDA. It has not done so. The arguments in this Court have referred to possible alternatives such as requiring that indecent material be "tagged" in a way that facilitates parental control of material coming into their homes, making exceptions for messages with artistic or educational value, providing some tolerance for parental choice, and regulating some portions of the Internet—such as commercial Web sites—differently than others, such as chat rooms. Particularly in the light of the absence of any detailed findings by the Congress, or even hearings addressing the special problems of the CDA, we are persuaded that the CDA is not narrowly tailored if that requirement has any meaning at all....

In this Court, though not in the District Court, the Government asserts that—in addition to its interest in protecting children—its "[e]qually significant" interest in fostering the growth of the Internet provides an independent basis for upholding the constitutionality of the CDA. ... The Government apparently assumes that the unregulated availability of "indecent" and "patently offensive" material on the Internet is driving countless citizens away from the medium because of the risk of exposing themselves or their children to harmful material.

We find this argument singularly unpersuasive. The dramatic expansion of this new marketplace of ideas contradicts the factual basis of this contention. The record demonstrates that the growth of the Internet has been and continues to be phenomenal. As a matter of constitutional tradition, in the absence of evidence to the contrary, we presume that governmental regulation of the content of speech is more likely to interfere with the free exchange of ideas than to encourage it. The interest in encouraging freedom of expression in a democratic society outweighs any theoretical but unproven benefit of censorship.

For the foregoing reasons, the judgment of the district court is affirmed.

Justice O'Connor, with whom the *Chief Justice* joins, concurring in the judgment in part and dissenting in part.

... I view the Communications Decency Act of 1996 (CDA) as little more than an attempt by Congress to create "adult zones" on the Internet. Our precedent indicates that the creation of such zones can be constitutionally sound. Despite the soundness of its purpose, however, portions of the CDA are unconstitutional because they stray from the blueprint our prior cases have developed for constructing a "zoning law" that passes constitutional muster....

(Continued)

... [T]o prevail in a facial challenge, it is not enough for a plaintiff to show "some" overbreadth. Our cases require a proof of "real" and "substantial" overbreadth, ... and appellees have not carried their burden in this case. In my view, the universe of speech constitutionally protected as to minors but banned by the CDA—i. e., the universe of material that is "patently offensive," but which nonetheless has some redeeming value for minors or does not appeal to their prurient interest—is a very small one. Appellees cite no examples of speech falling within this universe and do not attempt to explain why that universe is substantial "in relation to the statute's plainly legitimate sweep." ... That the CDA might deny minors the right to obtain material that has some "value," ... is largely beside the point. While discussions about prison rape or nude art ... may have some redeeming education value for adults, they do not necessarily have any such value for minors, and ... minors only have a First Amendment right to obtain patently offensive material that has "redeeming social importance for minors." ... There is also no evidence in the record to support the contention that "many [e]mail transmissions from an adult to a minor are conversations between family members," ... and no support for the legal proposition that such speech is absolutely immune from regulation. Accordingly, in my view, the CDA does not burden a substantial amount of minors' constitutionally protected speech.

... [T]he constitutionality of the CDA as a zoning law hinges on the extent to which it substantially interferes with the First Amendment rights of adults. Because the rights of adults are infringed only by the "display" provision and by the "indecency transmission" and "specific person" provisions as applied to communications involving more than one adult, I would invalidate the CDA only to that extent. Insofar as the "indecency transmission" and "specific person" provisions prohibit the use of indecent speech in communications between an adult and one or more minors, however, they can and should be sustained. The Court reaches a contrary conclusion, and from that holding that I respectfully dissent.

UNITED STATES v. STEVENS
559 U.S. 460; 130 S. Ct. 1577; 176 L.Ed. 2d 435 (2010)
Vote: 8-1

In this case, the Supreme Court strikes down a federal statute, 18 U.S.C. §48, which made it a felony for anyone to knowingly create, sell, or possess a depiction of animal cruelty if done for commercial gain. The law exempted depictions with serious religious, political, scientific, educational, journalistic, historical, or artistic value. The law was enacted in 1999 primarily to prohibit so called "crush videos," which depict small animals being crushed, usually by human feet and often in a sexual context. However, more recent concerns about dogfighting led to the law being applied to purveyors of dogfighting videos. Robert J. Stevens, who ran a website selling such videos, was convicted of violating the statute and was sentenced to three years in prison followed by three years of supervised release. The U.S. Court of Appeals for the Third Circuit reversed and declared the statute facially invalid under the First Amendment. The Supreme Court granted certiorari.

Chief Justice Roberts delivered the opinion of the Court.

... The First Amendment provides that "Congress shall make no law ... abridging the freedom of speech." "[A]s a general matter, the First Amendment means that government has no power to restrict expression because of its message, its ideas, its subject matter, or its content." ... Section 48 explicitly regulates expression based on content: The statute restricts "visual [and] auditory depiction[s]," such as photographs, videos, or sound recordings, depending on whether they depict conduct in which a living animal is intentionally harmed. As such, §48 is " 'presumptively invalid,' and the Government bears the burden to rebut that presumption." ... "From 1791 to the present," however, the First Amendment has "permitted restrictions upon the content of speech in a few limited areas," and has never "include[d] a freedom to disregard these traditional limitations." … These "historic and traditional categories long familiar to the bar," … including obscenity, … defamation, … fraud, … incitement, … and speech integral to criminal conduct, … are "well-defined and narrowly limited classes of speech, the prevention and punishment of which have never been thought to raise any Constitutional problem." …

The Government argues that "depictions of animal cruelty" should be added to the list. It contends that depictions of "illegal acts of animal cruelty" that are "made, sold, or possessed for commercial gain" necessarily "lack expressive value," and may accordingly "be regulated as *unprotected* speech." … The claim is not just that Congress may regulate depictions of animal cruelty subject to the First Amendment, but that these depictions are outside the reach of that Amendment altogether—that they fall into a "First Amendment Free Zone." …

As the Government notes, the prohibition of animal cruelty itself has a long history in American law, starting with the early settlement of the Colonies.… But we are unaware of any similar tradition excluding *depictions* of animal cruelty from "the freedom of speech" codified in the First Amendment, and the Government points us to none.

The Government contends that "historical evidence" about the reach of the First Amendment is not "a necessary prerequisite for regulation today," … and that categories of speech may be exempted from the First Amendment's protection without any long-settled tradition of subjecting that speech to regulation. Instead, the Government points to Congress's "legislative judgment that … depictions of animals being intentionally tortured and killed [are] of such minimal redeeming value as to render [them] unworthy of First Amendment protection," … and asks the Court to uphold the ban on the same basis. The Government thus proposes that a claim of categorical exclusion should be considered under a simple balancing test: "Whether a given category of speech enjoys First Amendment protection depends upon a categorical balancing of the value of the speech against its societal costs." …

As a free-floating test for First Amendment coverage, that sentence is startling and dangerous. The First Amendment's guarantee of free speech does not extend only to categories of speech that survive an ad hoc balancing of relative social costs and benefits. The First Amendment itself reflects a judgment by the American people that the benefits of its restrictions on the Government outweigh the costs. Our Constitution forecloses any attempt to revise that judgment

simply on the basis that some speech is not worth it. The Constitution is not a document "prescribing limits, and declaring that those limits may be passed at pleasure." …

To be fair to the Government, its view did not emerge from a vacuum. As the Government correctly notes, this Court has often *described* historically unprotected categories of speech as being ' "of such slight social value as a step to truth that any benefit that may be derived from them is clearly outweighed by the social interest in order and morality.' " … In *New York v. Ferber* … (1982), we noted that within these categories of unprotected speech, "the evil to be restricted so overwhelmingly outweighs the expressive interests, if any, at stake, that no process of case-by-case adjudication is required," because "the balance of competing interests is clearly struck." … The Government derives its proposed test from these descriptions in our precedents.…

But such descriptions are just that—descriptive. They do not set forth a test that may be applied as a general matter to permit the Government to imprison any speaker so long as his speech is deemed valueless or unnecessary, or so long as an ad hoc calculus of costs and benefits tilts in a statute's favor.

When we have identified categories of speech as fully outside the protection of the First Amendment, it has not been on the basis of a simple cost-benefit analysis. In *Ferber,* for example, we classified child pornography as such a category.… We noted that the State of New York had a compelling interest in protecting children from abuse, and that the value of using children in these works (as opposed to simulated conduct or adult actors) was *de minimis*.… But our decision did not rest on this "balance of competing interests" alone.… We made clear that *Ferber* presented a special case: The market for child pornography was "intrinsically related" to the underlying abuse, and was therefore "an integral part of the production of such materials, an activity illegal throughout the Nation." … As we noted, " '[i]t rarely has been suggested that the constitutional freedom for speech and press extends its immunity to speech or writing used as an integral part of conduct in violation of a valid criminal statute.' " … *Ferber* thus grounded its analysis in a previously recognized, long-established category of unprotected speech, and our subsequent decisions have shared this understanding.…

Our decisions in *Ferber* and other cases cannot be taken as establishing a freewheeling authority to declare new categories of speech outside the scope of the First Amendment.

Because we decline to carve out from the First Amendment any novel exception for §48, we review Stevens's First Amendment challenge under our existing doctrine. ...

Stevens challenged §48 on its face, arguing that any conviction secured under the statute would be unconstitutional. The court below decided the case on that basis, ... and we granted the Solicitor General's petition for certiorari to determine "whether 18 U.S.C. 48 is facially invalid under the Free Speech Clause of the First Amendment." ...

To succeed in a typical facial attack, Stevens would have to establish "that no set of circumstances exists under which [§48] would be valid," ... or that the statute lacks any "plainly legitimate sweep." ... Which standard applies in a typical case is a matter of dispute that we need not and do not address.... Here the Government asserts that Stevens cannot prevail because §48 is plainly legitimate as applied to crush videos and animal fighting depictions. Deciding this case through a traditional facial analysis would require us to resolve whether these applications of §48 are in fact consistent with the Constitution.

In the First Amendment context, however, this Court recognizes "a second type of facial challenge," whereby a law may be invalidated as overbroad if "a substantial number of its applications are unconstitutional, judged in relation to the statute's plainly legitimate sweep." ... Stevens argues that §48 applies to common depictions of ordinary and lawful activities, and that these depictions constitute the vast majority of materials subject to the statute.... The Government makes no effort to defend such a broad ban as constitutional. Instead, the Government's entire defense of §48 rests on interpreting the statute as narrowly limited to specific types of "extreme" material.... As the parties have presented the issue, therefore, the constitutionality of §48 hinges on how broadly it is construed. It is to that question that we now turn. ...

As we explained two Terms ago, "[t]he first step in overbreadth analysis is to construe the challenged statute; it is impossible to determine whether a statute reaches too far without first knowing what the statute covers." ...

We read §48 to create a criminal prohibition of alarming breadth. To begin with, the text of the statute's ban on a "depiction of animal cruelty" nowhere requires that the depicted conduct be cruel. That text applies to "any ... depiction" in which "a living animal is intentionally maimed, mutilated, tortured, wounded, or killed." ... "[M]aimed, mutilated, [and] tortured" convey cruelty, but "wounded" or "killed" do not suggest any such limitation....

What is more, the application of §48 to depictions of illegal conduct extends to conduct that is illegal in only a single jurisdiction.... A depiction of entirely lawful conduct runs afoul of the ban if that depiction later finds its way into another State where the same conduct is unlawful. This provision greatly expands the scope of §48, because although there may be "a broad societal consensus" against cruelty to animals, ... there is substantial disagreement on what types of conduct are properly regarded as cruel. Both views about cruelty to animals and regulations having no connection to cruelty vary widely from place to place.

In the District of Columbia, for example, all hunting is unlawful.... Other jurisdictions permit or encourage hunting, and there is an enormous national market for hunting-related depictions in which a living animal is intentionally killed. Hunting periodicals have circulations in the hundreds of thousands or millions, ... and hunting television programs, videos, and Web sites are equally popular.... The demand for hunting depictions exceeds the estimated demand for crush videos or animal fighting depictions by several orders of magnitude.... Nonetheless, because the statute allows each jurisdiction to export its laws to the rest of the country, §48(a) extends to *any* magazine or video depicting lawful hunting, so long as that depiction is sold within the Nation's Capital.

Those seeking to comply with the law thus face a bewildering maze of regulations from at least 56 separate jurisdictions....

The only thing standing between defendants who sell such depictions and five years in federal prison—other than the mercy of a prosecutor—is the statute's exceptions clause. Subsection (b) exempts from prohibition "any depiction that has serious religious, political, scientific, educational, journalistic, historical, or artistic value." The Government argues that this clause substantially narrows the statute's reach: News reports about animal cruelty have "journalistic" value; pictures of bullfights in Spain have "historical" value; and instructional hunting videos have "educational" value. ... Thus, the Government argues, §48 reaches only crush videos, depictions of animal fighting ... and perhaps other depictions of "extreme acts of animal cruelty." ... The Government's attempt to narrow the statutory ban, however, requires an unrealistically broad reading of the exceptions clause....

Not to worry, the Government says: The Executive Branch construes §48 to reach only "extreme" cruelty, ... and it "neither has brought nor will bring a prosecution for anything less." ... The Government hits this theme hard, invoking its prosecutorial discretion several times.... But the First Amendment protects against the Government; it does not leave us at the mercy of *noblesse oblige*. We would not uphold an unconstitutional statute merely because the Government promised to use it responsibly....

This prosecution is itself evidence of the danger in putting faith in government representations of prosecutorial restraint. When this legislation was enacted, the Executive Branch announced that it would interpret §48 as covering only depictions "of wanton cruelty to animals designed to appeal to a prurient interest in sex." ... No one suggests that the videos in this case fit that description. The Government's assurance that it will apply §48 far more restrictively than its language provides is pertinent only as an implicit acknowledgment of the potential constitutional problems with a more natural reading....

Our construction of §48 decides the constitutional question; the Government makes no effort to defend the constitutionality of §48 as applied beyond crush videos and depictions of animal fighting. It argues that those particular depictions are intrinsically related to criminal conduct or are analogous to obscenity (if not themselves obscene), and that the ban on such speech is narrowly tailored to reinforce restrictions on the underlying conduct, prevent additional crime arising from the depictions, or safeguard public mores. But the Government nowhere attempts to extend these arguments to depictions of any other activities—depictions that are presumptively protected by the First Amendment but that remain subject to the criminal sanctions of §48.

Nor does the Government seriously contest that the presumptively impermissible applications of §48 (properly construed) far outnumber any permissible ones. However "growing" and "lucrative" the markets for crush videos and dogfighting depictions might be, ... they are dwarfed by the market for other depictions, such as hunting magazines and videos, that we have determined to be within the scope of §48.... We therefore need not and do not decide whether a statute limited to crush videos or other depictions of extreme animal cruelty would be constitutional. We hold only that §48 is not so limited but is instead substantially overbroad, and therefore invalid under the First Amendment....

Justice Alito, dissenting.

The Court strikes down in its entirety a valuable statute, 18 U.S.C. §48, that was enacted not to suppress speech, but to prevent horrific acts of animal cruelty—in particular, the creation and commercial exploitation of "crush videos," a form of depraved entertainment that has no social value. The Court's approach, which has the practical effect of legalizing the sale of such videos and is thus likely to spur a resumption of their production, is unwarranted. Respondent was convicted under §48 for selling videos depicting dogfights. On appeal, he argued, among other things, that §48 is unconstitutional as applied to the facts of this case, and he highlighted features of those videos that might distinguish them from other dogfight videos brought to our attention. The Court of Appeals—incorrectly, in my view—declined to decide whether §48 is unconstitutional as applied to respondent's videos and instead reached out to hold that the statute is facially invalid. Today's decision does not endorse the Court of Appeals' reasoning, but it nevertheless strikes down §48 using what has been aptly termed the "strong medicine" of the overbreadth doctrine, ... a potion that generally should be administered only as "a last resort." ...

Instead of applying the doctrine of overbreadth, I would vacate the decision below and instruct the Court of Appeals on remand to decide whether the videos that respondent sold are constitutionally protected. If the question of overbreadth is to be decided, however, I do not think the present record supports the Court's conclusion that §48 bans a substantial quantity of protected speech....

... §48 may validly be applied to at least two broad real-world categories of expression covered by the statute: crush videos and dogfighting videos. Thus, the statute has a substantial core of constitutionally permissible applications. Moreover, ... the record does not show that §48, properly interpreted, bans a substantial amount of protected speech in absolute terms. *A fortiori,* respondent has not met his burden of demonstrating that any impermissible applications of the statute are "substantial" in relation to its "plainly legitimate sweep." ... Accordingly, I would reject respondent's claim that §48 is facially unconstitutional under the overbreadth doctrine....

EDWARDS v. SOUTH CAROLINA
372 U.S. 229; 83 S.Ct. 680; 9 L.Ed. 2d 697 (1963)
Vote: 8-1

In this case, the Court considers the issues of freedom of assembly and freedom of speech in the public forum in the context of a civil rights demonstration on the grounds of a State capitol.

Mr. Justice Stewart delivered the opinion of the Court.

The petitioners, 187 in number, were convicted in a magistrate's court in Columbia, South Carolina, of the common law crime of breach of the peace....

There was no substantial conflict in the trial evidence. Late in the morning of March 2, 1961, the petitioners, high school and college students of the Negro race, met at the Zion Baptist Church in Columbia. From there, at about noon, they walked in separate groups of about 15 to the South Carolina State House grounds, an area of two city blocks open to the general public. Their purpose was "to submit a protest to the citizens of South Carolina, along with the Legislative Bodies of South Carolina, our feelings and our dissatisfaction with the present condition of discriminatory actions against Negroes, in general, and to let them know that we were dissatisfied and that we would like for the laws which prohibited Negro privileges in this State to be removed."

Already on the State House grounds when the petitioners arrived were 30 or more law enforcement officers, who had advance knowledge that the petitioners were coming. Each group of petitioners entered the grounds through a driveway and parking area known in the record as the "horseshoe." As they entered, they were told by the law enforcement officials that "they had a right, as a citizen, to go through the State House grounds, as any other citizen has, as long as they were peaceful." During the next half hour or 45 minutes, the petitioners, in the same small groups, walked single file or two abreast in an orderly way through the grounds, each group carrying placards bearing such messages as "I am proud to be a Negro" and "Down with segregation."

During this time a crowd of some 200 to 300 onlookers had collected in the horseshoe area and on the adjacent sidewalks. There was no evidence to suggest that these onlookers were anything but curious, and no evidence at all of any threatening remarks, hostile gestures, or offensive language on the part of any member of the crowd. The City Manager testified that he recognized some of the onlookers, whom he did not identify, as "possible trouble makers," but his subsequent testimony made clear that nobody among the crowd actually caused or threatened any trouble. There was no obstruction of pedestrian or vehicular traffic within the State House grounds. No vehicle was prevented from entering or leaving the horseshoe area. Although vehicular traffic at a nearby street intersection was slowed down somewhat, an officer was dispatched to keep traffic moving. There were a number of bystanders on the public sidewalks adjacent to the State House grounds, but they all moved on when asked to do so, and there was no impediment of pedestrian traffic. Police protection at the scene was at all times sufficient to meet any foreseeable possibility of disorder.

In the situation and under the circumstances thus described, the police authorities advised the petitioners that they would be arrested if they did not disperse within 15 minutes. Instead of dispersing, the petitioners engaged in what the City manager described as "boisterous," "loud," and "flamboyant" conduct, which, as his later testimony made clear, consisted of listening to a "religious harangue" by one of their leaders, and loudly singing "The Star Spangled Banner" and other patriotic and religious songs, while stamping their feet and clapping their hands. After 15 minutes had passed, the police arrested the petitioners and marched them off to jail.

Upon this evidence the state trial court convicted the petitioners of breach of the peace, and imposed sentences ranging from a $10 fine or five days in jail, to a $100 fine or 30 days in jail. In affirming the judgments, the Supreme Court of South Carolina said that under the law of that State the offense of breach of the peace "is not susceptible for exact definition," but that the "general definition of the offense" is as follows:

In general terms, a breach of the peace is a violation of public order, a disturbance of the public tranquility, by any act or conduct inciting to violence ... , it includes any violation of any law enacted to preserve peace and good order. It may consist of an act of violence or an act likely to produce violence. It is not necessary that the peace be actually broken to lay the foundation for a prosecution for this offense.

If what is done is unjustifiable and unlawful, tending with sufficient directness to break the peace, no more is required. Nor is actual personal violence an essential element in the offense....

By "peace," as used in the law in this connection, is meant the tranquility enjoyed by citizens of a municipality or community where good order reigns among its members, which is the natural right of all persons in political society....

... It has long been established that these First Amendment freedoms are protected by the Fourteenth Amendment from invasion by the States.... The circumstances in this case reflect an exercise of these basic constitutional rights in their most pristine and classic form. The petitioners felt aggrieved by laws of South Carolina which allegedly "prohibited Negro privileges in this State." They peaceably assembled at the site of the State Government and there peaceably expressed their grievances "to the citizens of South Carolina, along with the Legislative Bodies of South Carolina." Not until they were told by police officials that they must disperse on pain of arrest did they do more. Even then, they but sang patriotic and religious songs after one of their leaders had delivered a "religious harangue." There was no violence or threat of violence on their part, or on the part of any member of the crowd watching them. Police protection was "ample."

This, therefore, was a far cry from the situation in *Feiner v. New York* ... [1951], where two policemen were faced with a crowd which was "pushing, shoving, and milling around," ... where at least one member of the crowd "threatened violence if the police did not act," ... where "the crowd was pressing closer around petitioner and the officer," ... and where "the speaker passes the bounds of argument or persuasion and undertakes incitement to riot." ... And the record is barren of any evidence of "fighting words." ...

We do not review in this case criminal convictions resulting from the even handed application of a precise and narrowly drawn regulatory statute evincing a legislative judgment that certain specific conduct be limited or proscribed. If, for example, the petitioners had been convicted upon evidence that they had violated a law regulating traffic, or had disobeyed a law reasonably limiting the periods during which the State House grounds were open to the public, this would be a different case.... These petitioners were convicted of an offense so generalized as to be, in the words of the South Carolina Supreme Court, "not susceptible of

exact definition." And they were convicted upon evidence which showed no more than that the opinions which they were peaceably expressing were sufficiently opposed to the views of the majority of the community to attract a crowd and necessitate police protection....

Mr. Justice Clark, dissenting.

... Beginning, as did the South Carolina courts, with the premise that the petitioners were entitled to assemble and voice their dissatisfaction with segregation, the enlargement of constitutional protection for the conduct here is as fallacious as would be the conclusion that free speech necessarily includes the right to broadcast from a sound truck in the public street. Here the petitioners were permitted without hindrance to exercise their rights of free speech and assembly. Their arrests occurred only after a situation arose in which the law enforcement officials on the scene considered that a dangerous disturbance was imminent. The County Court found that "[t]he evidence is clear that the officers were motivated solely by a proper concern for the preservation of order and prevention of further interference with traffic upon the public streets and sidewalks." ...

... Here 200 youthful Negro demonstrators were being aroused to a "fever pitch" before a crowd of some 300 people who undoubtedly were hostile. Perhaps their speech was not so animated but in this setting their actions, their placards reading "You may jail our bodies but not our souls" and their chanting of "I Shall Not Be Moved," accompanied by stamping feet and clapping hands, created a much greater danger of riot and disorder. It is my belief that anyone conversant with the almost spontaneous combustion in some Southern communities in such a situation will agree that the [city's] action may well have averted a major catastrophe.

The gravity of the danger here surely needs no further explication. The imminence of that danger has been emphasized at every stage of this proceeding, from the complaints charging that the demonstrations "tended directly to immediate violence" to the State Supreme Court's affirmance on the authority of *Feiner....* This record, then, shows no steps backward from a standard of "clear and present danger." But to say that the police may not intervene until the riot has occurred is like keeping out the doctor until the patient dies. I cannot subscribe to such a doctrine.

ADDERLEY v. FLORIDA
385 U.S. 39; 87 S.Ct. 242; 17 L.Ed. 2d 149 (1966)
Vote: 5-4

In this case, the Supreme Court reviews the convictions of thirty-two college students who marched onto the premises of the county jail in Tallahassee, Florida, to protest the arrest of other students the previous day. The key question in the case is: Are the premises of a county jail a public forum?

Mr. Justice Black delivered the opinion of the Court.

Petitioners, Harriett Louise Adderley and 31 other persons, were convicted by a jury in a joint trial in the County Judge's Court of Leon County, Florida, on a charge of "trespass with a malicious and mischievous intent" upon the premises of the county jail contrary to § 821.18 of the Florida statutes set out below. Petitioners, apparently all students of the Florida A&M University in Tallahassee, had gone from the school to the jail about a mile away, along with many other students, to "demonstrate" at the jail their protests of arrests of other protesting students the day before, and perhaps to protest more generally against state and local policies and practices of racial segregation, including segregation of the jail. The county sheriff, legal custodian of the jail and jail grounds, tried to persuade the students to leave the jail grounds. When this did not work, he notified them that they must leave, that if they did not leave he would arrest them for trespassing, and that if they resisted he would charge them with that as well. Some of the students left but others, including petitioners, remained and they were arrested. On appeal the convictions were affirmed by the Florida Circuit Court and then by the Florida District Court of Appeal.... That being the highest state court to which they could appeal, petitioners applied to us for certiorari contending that, in view of petitioners' purpose to protest against jail and other segregation policies, their conviction denied them "rights of free speech, assembly, petition, due process of law and equal protection of the laws as guaranteed by the Fourteenth Amendment to the Constitution of the United States." ...

Petitioners have insisted from the beginning of this case that it is controlled by and must be reversed because of our prior cases *of Edwards v. South Carolina* ... [1963] and *Cox v. Louisiana* ... [1965]. We cannot agree....

Petitioners argue that "petty criminal statutes may not be used to violate minorities' constitutional rights." This of course is true but this abstract proposition gets us nowhere in deciding this case....

Nothing in the Constitution of the United States prevents Florida from even handed enforcement of its general trespass statute against those refusing to obey the sheriff's order to remove themselves from what amounted to the curtilage of the jailhouse. The State, no less than a private owner of property, has power to preserve the property under its control for the use to which it is lawfully dedicated. For this reason there is no merit to the petitioners' argument that they had a constitutional right to stay on the property, over the jail custodian's objections, because this "area chosen for the peaceful civil rights demonstration was not only 'reasonable' but also particularly appropriate ..." Such an argument has as its major unarticulated premise the assumption that people who want to propagandize protests or views have a constitutional right to do so whenever and however and wherever they please. That concept of constitutional law was vigorously and forthrightly rejected in ... *Cox v. Louisiana*.... We reject it again....

Mr. Justice Douglas, with whom the **Chief Justice**, **Mr. Justice Brennan**, and **Mr. Justice Fortas** concur, dissenting.

... The jailhouse, like an executive mansion, a legislative chamber, a courthouse, or the statehouse itself ... is one of the seats of government, whether it be the Tower of London, the Bastille, or a small county jail. And when it houses political prisoners or those who many think are unjustly held, it is an obvious center for protest. ...

The Court forgets that prior to this day our decisions have drastically limited the application of state statutes inhibiting the right to go peacefully on public property to exercise First Amendment rights....

There may be some public places which are so clearly committed to other purposes that their use for the airing of grievances is anomalous. There may be some instances in which assemblies and petitions for redress of grievances are not consistent with other necessary purposes of public property.... But this is quite different from saying that all public places are off limits to people with grievances....

Today a trespass law is used to penalize people for exercising a constitutional right. Tomorrow a disorderly conduct statute, a breach of the peace statute, a vagrancy statute will be put to the same end. It is said

that the sheriff did not make the arrests because of the views which petitioners espoused ... by allowing these orderly and civilized protests against injustice to be suppressed, we only increase the forces of frustration which the conditions of second class citizenship are generating amongst us.

LORILLARD TOBACCO COMPANY v. REILLY
533 U.S. 525; 121 S.Ct. 2404; 150 L.Ed. 2d 532 (2001)
Vote: 5-4

In 1999, the attorney general of the State of Massachusetts adopted regulations governing the advertising and sale of tobacco products. The regulations prohibited outdoor advertising of cigarettes, cigars, and smokeless tobacco within 1,000 feet of any playground or school. They also required that ads inside stores be at least 5 feet off the floor, away from the usual sight of children. A group of tobacco product manufacturers and retailers brought suit to challenge the legality and constitutionality of these regulations. In the instant case, the Supreme Court holds that the Federal Cigarette Labeling and Advertising Act (FCLAA) preempts the Massachusetts regulations with respect to cigarette advertising. The Court then considers the constitutionality of the remaining regulations.

Justice O'Connor delivered the opinion of the Court.

... For over 25 years, the Court has recognized that commercial speech does not fall outside the purview of the First Amendment.... Instead, the Court has afforded commercial speech a measure of First Amendment protection commensurate with its position in relation to other constitutionally guaranteed expression.... In recognition of the distinction between speech proposing a commercial transaction, which occurs in an area traditionally subject to government regulation, and other varieties of speech, ... we developed a framework for analyzing regulations of commercial speech that is substantially similar to the test for time, place, and manner restrictions. *Central Hudson Gas & Electric Corporation v. Public Service Commission of New York* ... (1980). The analysis contains four elements:

At the outset, we must determine whether the expression is protected by the First Amendment. For

commercial speech to come within that provision, it at least must concern lawful activity and not be misleading. Next, we ask whether the asserted governmental interest is substantial. If both inquiries yield positive answers, we must determine whether the regulation directly advances the governmental interest asserted, and whether it is not more extensive than is necessary to serve that interest....

Petitioners urge us to reject the *Central Hudson* analysis and apply strict scrutiny. They are not the first litigants to do so.... Admittedly, several Members of the Court have expressed doubts about the *Central Hudson* analysis and whether it should apply in particular cases.... But ... we see no need to break new ground. *Central Hudson,* as applied in our more recent commercial speech cases, provides an adequate basis for decision....

The State's interest in preventing underage tobacco use is substantial, and even compelling, but it is no less true that the sale and use of tobacco products by adults is a legal activity. We must consider that tobacco retailers and manufacturers have an interest in conveying truthful information about their products to adults, and adults have a corresponding interest in receiving truthful information about tobacco products....

In some instances, Massachusetts outdoor advertising regulations would impose particularly onerous burdens on speech. For example, we disagree with the Court of Appeals conclusion that because cigar manufacturers and retailers conduct a limited amount of advertising in comparison to other tobacco products, the relative lack of cigar advertising also means that the burden imposed on cigar advertisers is correspondingly small.... If some retailers have relatively small advertising budgets, and use few avenues of

(Continued)

communication, then the Attorney General's outdoor advertising regulations potentially place a greater, not lesser, burden on those retailers' speech. Furthermore, to the extent that cigar products and cigar advertising differ from that of other tobacco products, that difference should inform the inquiry into what speech restrictions are necessary.

In addition, a retailer in Massachusetts may have no means of communicating to passersby on the street that it sells tobacco products because alternative forms of advertisement, like newspapers, do not allow that retailer to propose an instant transaction in the way that onsite advertising does. The ban on any indoor advertising that is visible from the outside also presents problems in establishments like convenience stores, which have unique security concerns that counsel in favor of full visibility of the store from the outside. It is these sorts of considerations that the Attorney General failed to incorporate into the regulatory scheme.

We conclude that the Attorney General has failed to show that the outdoor advertising regulations for smokeless tobacco and cigars are not more extensive than necessary to advance the State's substantial interest in preventing underage tobacco use. Justice Stevens urges that the Court remand the case for further development of the factual record.... We believe that a remand is inappropriate in this case because the State had ample opportunity to develop a record with respect to tailoring (as it had to justify its decision to regulate advertising), and additional evidence would not alter the nature of the scheme before the Court....

A careful calculation of the costs of a speech regulation does not mean that a State must demonstrate that there is no incursion on legitimate speech interests, but a speech regulation cannot unduly impinge on the speaker's ability to propose a commercial transaction and the adult listeners opportunity to obtain information about products. After reviewing the outdoor advertising regulations, we find the calculation in this case insufficient for purposes of the First Amendment....

Massachusetts may wish to target tobacco advertisements and displays that entice children, much like floor level candy displays in a convenience store, but the blanket height restriction does not constitute a reasonable fit with that goal. The Court of Appeals recognized that the efficacy of the regulation was questionable, but decided that [i]n any event, the burden on speech imposed by the provision is very limited.... There is no *de minimis* exception for a speech restriction that lacks sufficient tailoring or justification.

We conclude that the restriction on the height of indoor advertising is invalid under *Central Hudson's* third and fourth prongs....

We have observed that tobacco use, particularly among children and adolescents, poses perhaps the single most significant threat to public health in the United States.... From a policy perspective, it is understandable for the States to attempt to prevent minors from using tobacco products before they reach an age where they are capable of weighing for themselves the risks and potential benefits of tobacco use, and other adult activities. Federal law, however, places limits on policy choices available to the States.

To the extent that federal law and the First Amendment do not prohibit state action, States and localities remain free to combat the problem of underage tobacco use by appropriate means. The judgment of the United States Court of Appeals for the First Circuit is therefore affirmed in part and reversed in part, and the cases are remanded for further proceedings consistent with this opinion....

Justice Kennedy, with whom *Justice Scalia* joins, concurring in part and concurring in the judgment.

The obvious overbreadth of the outdoor advertising restrictions suffices to invalidate them under the fourth part of the test in *Central Hudson Gas* ... (1980). As a result, in my view, there is no need to consider whether the restrictions satisfy the third part of the test, a proposition about which there is considerable doubt.... Neither are we required to consider whether *Central Hudson* should be retained in the face of the substantial objections that can be made to it.... My continuing concerns that the test gives insufficient protection to truthful, nonmisleading commercial speech require me to refrain from expressing agreement with the Court's application of the third part of *Central Hudson*.... With [this] exception ... I join the opinion of the Court.

Justice Thomas, concurring in part and concurring in the judgment.

I join the opinion of the Court ... because I agree that the Massachusetts cigarette advertising regulations are preempted by the Federal Cigarette Labeling and Advertising Act.... I also agree with the Court's disposition of the First Amendment challenges to the other regulations at issue here, and I share the Court's view that the regulations fail even the intermediate scrutiny of *Central Hudson Gas* ... (1980). At the same time,

I continue to believe that when the government seeks to restrict truthful speech in order to suppress the ideas it conveys, strict scrutiny is appropriate, whether or not the speech in question may be characterized as commercial.... I would subject all of the advertising restrictions to strict scrutiny and would hold that they violate the First Amendment....

Justice Souter, concurring in part and dissenting in part....

Justice Stevens, with whom *Justice Ginsburg* and *Justice Breyer* join, and with whom *Justice Souter* joins as to Part I, concurring in part, concurring in the judgment in part, and dissenting in part.

This suit presents two separate sets of issues. The first involving preemption is straightforward. The second involving the First Amendment is more complex.

Because I strongly disagree with the Court's conclusion that the Federal Cigarette Labeling and Advertising Act of 1965 (FCLAA or Act) ... precludes States and localities from regulating the location of cigarette advertising, I dissent from Parts IIA and IIB of the Court's opinion. On the First Amendment questions, I agree with the Court both that the outdoor advertising restrictions imposed by Massachusetts serve legitimate and important state interests and that the record does not indicate that the measures were properly tailored to serve those interests. Because the present record does not enable us to adjudicate the merits of those claims on summary judgment, I would vacate the decision upholding those restrictions and remand for trial on the constitutionality of the outdoor advertising regulations. Finally, because I do not believe that either the point of sale advertising restrictions or the sales practice restrictions implicate significant First Amendment concerns, I would uphold them in their entirety.

NATIONAL ENDOWMENT FOR THE ARTS v. FINLEY
524 U.S. 569; 118 S.Ct. 2168; 141 L.Ed. 2d 500 (1998)
Vote: 8-1

Here, the Court considers a statutory requirement that the National Endowment for the Arts take into account "general standards of decency" in deciding which artistic endeavors will receive public support. In a case brought by performance artist Karen Finley, a federal district judge in California declared the provision unconstitutional under the First Amendment. The Ninth Circuit Court of Appeals affirmed.

Justice O'Connor delivered the opinion of the Court.

The National Foundation on the Arts and Humanities Act, as amended in 1990, requires the Chairperson of the National Endowment for the Arts (NEA) to ensure that "artistic excellence and artistic merit are the criteria by which [grant] applications are judged, taking into consideration general standards of decency and respect for the diverse beliefs and values of the American public." 20 U.S.C. § 954(d)(1)....

Since 1965, the NEA has distributed over three billion dollars in grants to individuals and organizations, funding that has served as a catalyst for increased state,

corporate, and foundation support for the arts. Congress has recently restricted the availability of federal funding for individual artists, confining grants primarily to qualifying organizations and state arts agencies, and constraining sub granting.... By far the largest portion of the grants distributed in fiscal year 1998 were awarded directly to state arts agencies. In the remaining categories, the most substantial grants were allocated to symphony orchestras, fine arts museums, dance theater foundations, and opera associations....

Throughout the NEA's history, only a handful of the agency's roughly 100,000 awards have generated formal complaints about misapplied funds or abuse of the public's trust. Two provocative works, however, prompted public controversy in 1989 and led to congressional reevaluation of the NEA's funding priorities and efforts to increase oversight of its grant making procedures. The Institute of Contemporary Art at the University of Pennsylvania had used $30,000 of a visual arts grant it received from the NEA to fund a 1989 retrospective of photographer Robert Mapplethorpe's work. The exhibit,

(Continued)

entitled The Perfect Moment, included homoerotic photographs that several Members of Congress condemned as pornographic ... Members also denounced artist Andres Serrano's work Piss Christ, a photograph of a crucifix immersed in urine.... Serrano had been awarded a $15,000 grant from the Southeast Center for Contemporary Art, an organization that received NEA support.

When considering the NEA's appropriations for fiscal year 1990, Congress reacted to the controversy surrounding the Mapplethorpe and Serrano photographs by eliminating $45,000 from the agency's budget, the precise amount contributed to the two exhibits by NEA grant recipients. Congress also enacted an amendment providing that no NEA funds "may be used to promote, disseminate, or produce materials which in the judgment of [the NEA] may be considered obscene, including but not limited to, depictions of sadomasochism, homoeroticism, the sexual exploitation of children, or individuals engaged in sex acts and which, when taken as a whole, do not have serious literary, artistic, political, or scientific value." ... The NEA implemented Congress's mandate by instituting a requirement that all grantees certify in writing that they would not utilize federal funding to engage in projects inconsistent with the criteria in the 1990 appropriations bill. That certification requirement was subsequently invalidated as unconstitutionally vague by a Federal District Court ... and the NEA did not appeal the decision.

In the 1990 appropriations bill, Congress also agreed to create an Independent Commission of constitutional law scholars to review the NEA's grant making procedures and assess the possibility of more focused standards for public arts funding. The Commission's report, issued in September 1990, concluded that there is no constitutional obligation to provide arts funding, but also recommended that the NEA rescind the certification requirement and cautioned against legislation setting forth any content restrictions. Instead, the Commission suggested procedural changes to enhance the role of advisory panels and a statutory reaffirmation of "the high place the nation accords to the fostering of mutual respect for the disparate beliefs and values among us." ...

Informed by the Commission's recommendations, and cognizant of pending judicial challenges to the funding limitations in the 1990 appropriations bill, Congress debated several proposals to reform the NEA's grant making process when it considered the agency's reauthorization in the fall of 1990 ... Ultimately,

Congress adopted ... a bipartisan compromise between Members opposing any funding restrictions and those favoring some guidance to the agency. In relevant part, [this compromise] became § 954(d)(1)....

... Respondents raise a facial constitutional challenge to § 954(d)(1), and consequently they confront "a heavy burden" in advancing their claim.... Facial invalidation "is, manifestly, strong medicine" that "has been employed by the Court sparingly and only as a last resort." ... To prevail, respondents must demonstrate a substantial risk that application of the provision will lead to the suppression of speech....

Respondents argue that the provision is a paradigmatic example of viewpoint discrimination because it rejects any artistic speech that either fails to respect mainstream values or offends standards of decency. The premise of respondents' claim is that § 954(d)(1) constrains the agency's ability to fund certain categories of artistic expression. The NEA, however, reads the provision as merely hortatory, and contends that it stops well short of an absolute restriction. Section 954(d)(1) adds "considerations" to the grant making process; it does not preclude awards to projects that might be deemed "indecent" or "disrespectful," nor place conditions on grants, or even specify that those factors must be given any particular weight in reviewing an application....

That § 954(d)(1) admonishes the NEA merely to take "decency and respect" into consideration, and that the legislation was aimed at reforming procedures rather than precluding speech, undercut respondents' argument that the provision inevitably will be utilized as a tool for invidious viewpoint discrimination. In cases where we have struck down legislation as facially unconstitutional, the dangers were both more evident and more substantial....

... Thus, we do not perceive a realistic danger that § 954(d)(1) will compromise First Amendment values. As respondents' own arguments demonstrate, the considerations that the provision introduces, by their nature, do not engender the kind of directed viewpoint discrimination that would prompt this Court to invalidate a statute on its face.

Respondents' claim that the provision is facially unconstitutional may be reduced to the argument that the criteria in § 954(d)(1) are sufficiently subjective that the agency could utilize them to engage in viewpoint discrimination. Given the varied interpretations of the criteria and the vague exhortation to "take them into consideration," it seems unlikely that this provision will introduce any greater element of selectivity than the determination of "artistic excellence" itself. And we are reluctant, in any event, to invalidate legislation "on the basis of its hypothetical application to situations not before the Court." ...

Finally, although the First Amendment certainly has application in the subsidy context, we note that the Government may allocate competitive funding according to criteria that would be impermissible were direct regulation of speech or a criminal penalty at stake. So long as legislation does not infringe on other constitutionally protected rights, Congress has wide latitude to set spending priorities....

Section 954(d)(1) merely adds some imprecise considerations to an already subjective selection process. It does not, on its face, impermissibly infringe on First or Fifth Amendment rights. Accordingly, the judgment of the Court of Appeals is reversed and the case is remanded for further proceedings consistent with this opinion.

Justice Scalia, with whom *Justice Thomas* joins, concurring in the judgment.

"The operation was a success, but the patient died." What such a procedure is to medicine, the Court's opinion in this case is to law. It sustains the constitutionality of § 954(d)(1) by gutting it. The most avid congressional opponents of the provision could not have asked for more. I write separately because, unlike the Court, I think that § 954(d)(1) must be evaluated as written, rather than as distorted by the agency it was meant to control. By its terms, it establishes content and viewpoint based criteria upon which grant applications are to be evaluated. And that is perfectly constitutional....

The nub of the difference between me and the Court is that I regard the distinction between "abridging" speech and funding it as a fundamental divide, on this side of which the First Amendment is inapplicable. The Court, by contrast, seems to believe that the First Amendment, despite its words, has some ineffable effect upon funding, imposing constraints of an indeterminate nature which it announces (without troubling to enunciate any particular test) are not violated by the statute here—or, more accurately, are not violated by the quite different, emasculated statute that it imagines. "[T]he Government," it says, "may allocate competitive funding according to criteria that would be impermissible were direct regulation of speech or a criminal penalty at stake." ... The government,

I think, may allocate both competitive and noncompetitive funding *ad libitum*, insofar as the First Amendment is concerned. Finally, what is true of the First Amendment is also true of the constitutional rule against vague legislation: it has no application to funding. Insofar as it bears upon First Amendment concerns, the vagueness doctrine addresses the problems that arise from government regulation of expressive conduct, ... not government grant programs. In the former context, vagueness produces an abridgment of lawful speech; in the latter it produces, at worst, a waste of money. I cannot refrain from observing, however, that if the vagueness doctrine were applicable, the agency charged with making grants under a statutory standard of "artistic excellence"—and which has itself thought that standard met by everything from the playing of Beethoven to a depiction of a crucifix immersed in urine—would be of more dubious constitutional validity than the "decency" and "respect" limitations that respondents (who demand to be judged on the same strict standard of "artistic excellence") have the humorlessness to call too vague.

In its laudatory description of the accomplishments of the NEA, ... the Court notes with satisfaction that "only a handful of the agency's roughly 100,000 awards have generated formal complaints." ... The Congress that felt it necessary to enact § 954(d)(1) evidently thought it much more noteworthy that any money exacted from American taxpayers had been used to produce a crucifix immersed in urine, or a display of homoerotic photographs. It is no secret that the provision was prompted by, and directed at, the funding of such offensive productions. Instead of banning the funding of such productions absolutely, which I think would have been entirely constitutional, Congress took the lesser step of requiring them to be disfavored in the evaluation of grant applications. The Court's opinion today renders even that lesser step a nullity. For that reason, I concur only in the judgment.

Justice Souter, dissenting.

... The decency and respect proviso mandates viewpoint based decisions in the disbursement of government subsidies, and the Government has wholly failed to explain why the statute should be afforded an exemption from the fundamental rule of the First Amendment that viewpoint discrimination in the exercise of public authority over expressive activity is unconstitutional....

(Continued)

"If there is a bedrock principle underlying the First Amendment, it is that the government may not prohibit the expression of an idea simply because society finds the idea itself offensive or disagreeable." ... Because this principle applies not only to affirmative suppression of speech, but also to disqualification for government favors, Congress is generally not permitted to pivot discrimination against otherwise protected speech on the offensiveness or unacceptability of the views it expresses....

It goes without saying that artistic expression lies within this First Amendment protection.... The constitutional protection of artistic works turns not on the political significance that may be attributable to such productions, though they may indeed comment on the political, but simply on their expressive character, which falls within a spectrum of protected "speech" extending outward from the core of overtly political declarations. Put differently, art is entitled to full protection because our "cultural life," just like our native politics, "rests upon [the] ideal" of governmental viewpoint neutrality.... When called upon to vindicate this ideal, we characteristically begin by asking "whether the government has adopted a regulation of speech

because of disagreement with the message it conveys. The government's purpose is the controlling consideration." ... The answer in this case is damning. One need do nothing more than read the text of the statute to conclude that Congress's purpose in imposing the decency and respect criteria was to prevent the funding of art that conveys an offensive message; the decency and respect provision on its face is quintessentially viewpoint based, and quotations from the Congressional Record merely confirm the obvious legislative purpose. In the words of a cosponsor of the bill that enacted the proviso, "[w]orks which deeply offend the sensibilities of significant portions of the public ought not to be supported with public funds." ... Indeed, if there were any question at all about what Congress had in mind, a definitive answer comes in the succinctly accurate remark of the proviso's author, that the bill "add[s] to the criteria of artistic excellence and artistic merit, a shell, a screen, a viewpoint that must be constantly taken into account." ...

Since the [challenged legislation] is substantially overbroad and carries with it a significant power to chill artistic production and display, it should be struck down on its face.

BOY SCOUTS OF AMERICA v. DALE
530 U.S. 640; 120 S.Ct. 2446; 147 L.Ed. 2d 554 (2000)
Vote: 5-4

James Dale, a former Eagle Scout, was dismissed from his position as an assistant scoutmaster of a New Jersey Boy Scout troop when the organization learned that Dale was openly gay. Dale sued the Boy Scouts in the New Jersey courts, asserting that the organization was in violation of a state statute barring discriminating on the basis of sexual orientation by places of public accommodation.

Chief Justice Rehnquist delivered the opinion of the Court.

... The Boy Scouts is a private, not for profit organization engaged in instilling its system of values in young people. The Boy Scouts asserts that homosexual conduct is inconsistent with the values it seeks to instill

... The New Jersey Supreme Court held that New Jersey's public accommodations law requires that the Boy Scouts admit Dale. This case presents the question whether applying New Jersey's public accommodations law in this way violates the Boy Scouts' First Amendment right of expressive association. We hold that it does.

... In *Roberts v. United States Jaycees* ... (1984), we observed that "implicit in the right to engage in activities protected by the First Amendment" is "a corresponding right to associate with others in pursuit of a wide variety of political, social, economic, educational, religious, and cultural ends." This right is crucial in preventing the majority from imposing its views on groups that would rather express other, perhaps unpopular, ideas.... Government actions that may unconstitutionally burden this freedom may take many forms, one of which is "intrusion into the internal structure or affairs of an association" like a "regulation that forces the group to accept members it does not desire." ... Forcing a group to accept certain members may impair the ability of the group to express those views, and only those views, that it intends to express. Thus, "[f]reedom of association ... plainly presupposes a freedom not to associate." ...

The forced inclusion of an unwanted person in a group infringes the group's freedom of expressive association if the presence of that person affects in a significant way the group's ability to advocate public or private viewpoints.... But the freedom of expressive association, like many freedoms, is not absolute. We have held that the freedom could be overridden "by regulations adopted to serve compelling state interests, unrelated to the suppression of ideas, that cannot be achieved through means significantly less restrictive of associational freedoms." ...

To determine whether a group is protected by the First Amendment's expressive associational right, we must determine whether the group engages in "expressive association." The First Amendment's protection of expressive association is not reserved for advocacy groups. But to come within its ambit, a group must engage in some form of expression, whether it be public or private.

... [T]he general mission of the Boy Scouts is clear: "[T]o instill values in young people." ... The Boy Scouts seeks to instill these values by having its adult leaders spend time with the youth members, instructing and engaging them in activities like camping, archery, and fishing. During the time spent with the youth members, the scoutmasters and assistant scoutmasters inculcate them with the Boy Scouts' values—both expressly and by example. It seems indisputable that an association that seeks to transmit such a system of values engages in expressive activity....

Given that the Boy Scouts engages in expressive activity, we must determine whether the forced inclusion of Dale as an assistant scoutmaster would significantly affect the Boy Scouts' ability to advocate public or private viewpoints. This inquiry necessarily requires us first to explore, to a limited extent, the nature of the Boy Scouts' view of homosexuality.

The values the Boy Scouts seeks to instill are "based on" those listed in the Scout Oath and Law.... The Boy Scouts explains that the Scout Oath and Law provide "a positive moral code for living; they are a list of 'do's'

rather than 'don'ts.' " ... The Boy Scouts asserts that homosexual conduct is inconsistent with the values embodied in the Scout Oath and Law, particularly with the values represented by the terms "morally straight" and "clean."

Obviously, the Scout Oath and Law do not expressly mention sexuality or sexual orientation.... And the terms "morally straight" and "clean" are by no means self defining. Different people would attribute to those terms very different meanings....

The New Jersey Supreme Court analyzed the Boy Scouts' beliefs and found that the "exclusion of members solely on the basis of their sexual orientation is inconsistent with Boy Scouts' commitment to a diverse and 'representative' membership ... [and] contradicts Boy Scouts' overarching objective to reach 'all eligible youth.' " ... The court concluded that the exclusion of members like Dale "appears antithetical to the organization's goals and philosophy." ... But our cases reject this sort of inquiry; it is not the role of the courts to reject a group's expressed values because they disagree with those values or find them internally inconsistent....

The Boy Scouts asserts that it "teach[es] that homosexual conduct is not morally straight," ... and that it does "not want to promote homosexual conduct as a legitimate form of behavior." ... We accept the Boy Scouts' assertion. We need not inquire further to determine the nature of the Boy Scouts' expression with respect to homosexuality. But because the record before us contains written evidence of the Boy Scouts' viewpoint, we look to it as instructive, if only on the question of the sincerity of the professed beliefs....

We must then determine whether Dale's presence as an assistant scoutmaster would significantly burden the Boy Scouts' desire to not "promote homosexual conduct as a legitimate form of behavior." ... As we give deference to an association's assertions regarding the nature of its expression, we must also give deference to an association's view of what would impair its expression ... That is not to say that an expressive association can erect a shield against antidiscrimination laws simply by asserting that mere acceptance of a member from a particular group would impair its message. But here Dale, by his own admission, is one of a group of gay Scouts who have "become leaders in their community and are open and honest about their sexual orientation." ... Dale was the copresident of a gay and lesbian organization at college and remains a gay rights activist. Dale's presence in the Boy Scouts would, at the very least, force the organization to send a message, both to the youth

(Continued)

members and the world, that the Boy Scouts accepts homosexual conduct as a legitimate form of behavior....

Having determined that the Boy Scouts is an expressive association and that the forced inclusion of Dale would significantly affect its expression, we inquire whether the application of New Jersey's public accommodations law to require that the Boy Scouts accept Dale as an assistant scoutmaster runs afoul of the Scouts' freedom of expressive association. We conclude that it does.

State public accommodations laws were originally enacted to prevent discrimination in traditional places of public accommodation—like inns and trains.... New Jersey's statutory definition of "[a] place of public accommodation" is extremely broad. The term is said to "include, but not be limited to," a list of over 50 types of places.... Many on the list are what one would expect to be places where the public is invited. For example, the statute includes as places of public accommodation taverns, restaurants, retail shops, and public libraries. But the statute also includes places that often may not carry with them open invitations to the public, like summer camps and roof gardens. In this case, the New Jersey Supreme Court went a step further and applied its public accommodations law to a private entity without even attempting to tie the term "place" to a physical location. As the definition of "public accommodation" has expanded from clearly commercial entities, such as restaurants, bars, and hotels, to membership organizations such as the Boy Scouts, the potential for conflict between state public accommodations laws and the First Amendment rights of organizations has increased.

... We have already concluded that a state requirement that the Boy Scouts retain Dale as an assistant scoutmaster would significantly burden the organization's right to oppose or disfavor homosexual conduct. The state interests embodied in New Jersey's public accommodations law do not justify such a severe intrusion on the Boy Scouts' rights to freedom of expressive association. That being the case, we hold that the First Amendment prohibits the State from imposing such a requirement through the application of its public accommodations law....

... We are not, as we must not be, guided by our views of whether the Boy Scouts' teachings with respect to homosexual conduct are right or wrong; public or judicial disapproval of a tenet of an organization's expression does not justify the State's effort to compel the organization to accept members where such acceptance would derogate from the organization's expressive message. "While the law is free to promote all sorts of conduct in place of harmful behavior, it is not free to interfere with speech for no better reason than promoting an approved message or discouraging a disfavored one, however enlightened either purpose may strike the government." ...

The judgment of the New Jersey Supreme Court is reversed, and the cause remanded for further proceedings not inconsistent with this opinion....

Justice Stevens, with whom *Justice Souter*, *Justice Ginsburg*, and *Justice Breyer* join, dissenting.

... The majority holds that New Jersey's law violates BSA's right to associate and its right to free speech. But that law does not "impos[e] any serious burdens" on BSA's "collective effort on behalf of [its] shared goals," ... nor does it force BSA to communicate any message that it does not wish to endorse. New Jersey's law, therefore, abridges no constitutional right of the Boy Scouts....

... [T]here is "no basis in the record for concluding that admission of [homosexuals] will impede the [Boy Scouts'] ability to engage in [its] protected activities or to disseminate its preferred views" and New Jersey's law "requires no change in [BSA's] creed." ...

... The State of New Jersey has decided that people who are open and frank about their sexual orientation are entitled to equal access to employment as school teachers, police officers, librarians, athletic coaches, and a host of other jobs filled by citizens who serve as role models for children and adults alike. Dozens of Scout units throughout the State are sponsored by public agencies, such as schools and fire departments, that employ such role models. BSA's affiliation with numerous public agencies that comply with New Jersey's law against discrimination cannot be understood to convey any particular message endorsing or condoning the activities of all these people....

Unfavorable opinions about homosexuals "have ancient roots." ... Like equally atavistic opinions about certain racial groups, those roots have been nourished by sectarian doctrine.... Over the years, however, interaction with real people, rather than mere adherence to traditional ways of thinking about members of unfamiliar classes, have modified those opinions....

That such prejudices are still prevalent and that they have caused serious and tangible harm to countless members of the class New Jersey seeks to protect are established matters of fact that neither the Boy Scouts nor the Court disputes. That harm can only be aggravated by the creation of a constitutional shield for a policy that is itself the product of a habitual way of thinking about strangers. As Justice Brandeis so wisely advised, "we must be ever on our guard, lest we erect our prejudices into legal principles."

If we would guide by the light of reason, we must let our minds be bold. I respectfully dissent.

Justice Souter, with whom *Justice Ginsburg* and *Justice Breyer* join, dissenting....

CHAPTER **4**

Religious Liberty and Church–State Relations

"We are a people whose institutions presuppose a Supreme Being."
—Justice William O. Douglas, Writing for the Court
in Zorach v. Clauson *(1952)*

"[O]ne of the mandates of the First Amendment is to promote a viable, pluralistic society and to keep government neutral, not only between sects, but also between believers and nonbelievers."
—Justice William O. Douglas, Dissenting in
Walz v. Tax Commission *(1970)*

Library of Congress Prints and Photographs Division

William O. Douglas: Associate Justice, 1939–1975

Introduction

Religion is one of the hallmarks of American society. Americans are more likely than people in other Western democracies to hold religious beliefs, affiliate with religious denominations, and attend religious services. Another distinguishing feature of American social life is the great diversity of religious beliefs and practices that coexist peacefully. No other society on earth has such a wide array of creeds and denominations.

Despite obvious differences in doctrine and styles of worship, most religions are united by their common belief in a Supreme Being and their commitment to standards of right and wrong. Nevertheless, history and current events teach us that human beings are given to zealotry, intolerance, persecution, and even warfare in the name of God. Peaceful coexistence among competing religious groups is one of the major accomplishments of modern democracy.

The authors of the Bill of Rights were well aware of the excesses that can result when one denomination is established as the official religion and recognized and supported by government. Indeed, a profound thirst for the freedom to worship in one's own way, without coercion or persecution by government, was one of the principal motivations in the formation of the American colonies. However, nine of the thirteen original American colonies set up official churches and provided them with financial support. In fact, at the time the Bill of Rights was ratified in 1791, Connecticut, Massachusetts, and New Hampshire continued to recognize the Congregational Church as the official, state-sponsored denomination. Nevertheless, opposition to officially established religion ultimately prevailed. The First Amendment to the Constitution provides that "Congress shall make no law respecting an establishment of religion, or prohibiting the free exercise thereof." That the protection of religious freedom was of fundamental importance is underscored by the fact that the Religion Clauses are listed first among the safeguards contained in the Bill of Rights. These clauses not only reflect the strong desire for religious freedom held by eighteenth-century Americans, but they also protect and foster the religious diversity that exists in America today.

Interpretive Foundations of the Religion Clauses

Widespread agreement exists regarding the abstract value of the **Religion Clauses of the First Amendment**. Nevertheless, there is equally broad disagreement about what these clauses specifically require, permit, and forbid. Some of the Supreme Court's least popular decisions are in the realm of government involvement with religion, specifically in the area of **school prayer**. Note, however, that these decisions are often as misunderstood as they are unpopular. This chapter attempts to clarify and explain what the Supreme Court has said in many of its decisions interpreting the Religion Clauses of the First Amendment. Sadly, too often those who are given to strong opinions on the subject of religion are unwilling or unable to understand clearly what has been decided by the courts. While informed debate over judicial decisions is to be encouraged, criticism based on ignorance is counterproductive.

The Incorporation of the Religion Clauses

In his original draft of the Bill of Rights, James Madison proposed that state as well as federal establishments of religion be prohibited. The First Congress rejected Madison's suggestion in this respect, preferring to allow states to make their own determinations in this area. Thus, the First Amendment proscribed establishments of religion by the national government only. By the late 1940s, the Supreme Court had ruled, however, that the Religion Clauses of the First Amendment were of sufficient importance in a "scheme of ordered liberty" to warrant their application to the states through the Due Process Clause of the Fourteenth Amendment (for a full discussion of the doctrine of incorporation, see Chapter 1). The **Free Exercise Clause** was definitively applied to the states in *Cantwell v. Connecticut* (1940); arguably, it had been incorporated in the 1934 case of *Hamilton v. Regents of the University of California*, yet after the ruling in *Cantwell* there was no doubt. The **Establishment Clause** was incorporated in *Everson v. Board of Education* (1947). Thus, all levels of government, from local school boards to the U.S. Congress, are now required to abide by the strictures of the Religion Clauses of the First Amendment.

What Constitutes Religion for First Amendment Purposes?

Before one can define "establishment of religion" or "the free exercise thereof," one must understand what is meant by the term *religion*. It comes from the Latin *religare*, which means "to tie down" or "to restrain." Since its appearance in the English language at the beginning of the thirteenth century, the term *religion* has had a distinctly theological connotation. In *Davis v. Beason* (1890), the Supreme Court first had occasion to define religion. In a majority opinion authored by Justice Stephen J. Field, the Court stated that "the term 'religion' has reference to one's view of his relations to his Creator, and to the obligations they impose of reverence for His being and character, and obedience to His will." This conception of religion was strictly theistic, which no doubt mirrored popular attitudes circa 1890. By the 1960s, however, American society had become much more religiously diverse, and nontheistic creeds from Asia, such as Buddhism and Taoism, were beginning to find adherents in this country.

Religion Broadly Defined   In 1965, the Supreme Court attempted to define religion in a fashion broad enough to respect the diversity of creeds that coexist in modern America. The definitional problem arose in *United States v. Seeger*, a case involving four men who claimed **conscientious objector** status in refusing to serve in the Vietnam War. In the Universal Military Training and Service Act of 1940, Congress exempted from combat duty anyone "who, by reason of religious training and belief, is conscientiously opposed to participation in war in any form." The act defined "religious training and belief" as training or belief "in a relation to a Supreme Being involving duties superior to those arising from any human relation." Although some organized religions (such as the Quakers) do not approve of participation in war, Daniel Seeger was not a member of any such group. Nevertheless, he sought conscientious objector status on religious grounds. When specifically asked about his belief in a Supreme Being, Seeger stated that "you could call [it] a belief in the Supreme Being or God. These just do not happen to be the words that I use." Forest Peter, another man whose refusal to serve in Vietnam was before the Supreme Court in *Seeger*, claimed that after considerable meditation and reflection "on values derived from the Western religious and philosophical tradition," he determined that it would be "a violation of his moral code to take human life and that he considered this belief superior to any obligation to the state." In deciding the *Seeger* case, the Court avoided a constitutional question by interpreting the statutory definition of religion broadly. Writing for the Court, Justice Tom C. Clark concluded that "Congress, in using the expression 'Supreme Being' rather than the designation 'God,' was merely clarifying the meaning of religious tradition and belief so as to embrace all religions and to exclude essentially political, sociological, or philosophical views." According to Clark's majority opinion, the test was "whether a given belief that is sincere and meaningful occupies a place in the life of its possessor parallel to the orthodox belief in God." Apparently the Court was persuaded that Seeger, Peter, and the others whose refusal to serve in Vietnam possessed such a belief and recognized them as conscientious objectors on religious grounds.

A Working Definition of Religion   Subsequent decisions in both federal and state tribunals have expanded the definition of religion adopted by the Supreme Court in the *Seeger* case. Essentially, a creed must meet four criteria to qualify as a religion as this term is used in the First Amendment. First, as noted earlier, there must be a belief in God or some parallel belief that occupies a central place in the believer's life. Second, the religion must involve a moral code that transcends individual belief—it cannot be purely subjective. Third, some associational ties must be involved. That is, there must be some community of people united by common beliefs. Fourth, there must be a demonstrable sincerity of belief. Under these criteria, even nontheistic creeds, such as Taoism or Zen Buddhism, qualify as religions. But frivolous or ridiculous beliefs, such as Stanley Oscar Brown's professed "faith" in Kozy Kitten Cat Food (see *Brown v. Pena* [1977]), fail to meet any of the four criteria. Of course, there is a long continuum between ludicrous beliefs such as Brown's and conventional religions.

> **To Summarize:**
> ◆ *The Religion Clauses of the First Amendment have been incorporated into the Due Process Clause of the Fourteenth Amendment. Thus, all levels of government, from local school boards to the U.S. Congress, are now required to abide by the strictures of the Religion Clauses.*
> ◆ *The Supreme Court has said that a creed must meet four criteria to qualify as a religion under the First Amendment: (1) There must be a belief in God or some parallel belief that occupies a central place in the believer's life; (2) it must involve a moral code that transcends individual belief; (3) some associational ties must be involved; and (4) there must be a demonstrable sincerity of belief.*

Religious Belief and the Right to Proselytize

The First Amendment provides virtually absolute protection with respect to individual religious convictions and beliefs. The government may never question a person's beliefs or impose penalties or disabilities based solely on those beliefs. Thus, in *Torcaso v. Watkins* (1961), the Court unanimously struck down a Maryland constitutional provision requiring persons seeking public office to take an oath declaring their belief in God. Likewise, in *McDaniel v. Paty* (1978), the Court was unanimous in holding that states may not bar priests and ministers from serving as delegates to state constitutional conventions.

The Free Exercise Clause obviously protects more than belief—it carries over into the realm of action. Were it otherwise, there would be no need of the Free Exercise Clause; religious belief is subsumed under the "freedom of conscience" implicitly protected by the Free Speech Clause. But the protections of religiously motivated conduct are somewhat attenuated. Whether specific actions are protected by the First Amendment depends on the character of those actions and the government's rationale for trying to regulate them. Thus, while the Court has ruled that religious beliefs are afforded the highest of legal protections, not all action or conduct in the name of religion is granted such lofty constitutional status.

Religious Solicitation

The highest degree of protection is accorded to **religious speech** and other **expressive religious conduct**. Thus, in *Cantwell v. Connecticut* (1940), the Court struck down a state law that prohibited door-to-door solicitation for any religious or charitable cause without prior approval of a state agency. The law was challenged by Newton Cantwell, a member of the Jehovah's Witnesses, a sect committed to active proselytizing.

Cantwell and his sons routinely went from door to door or stopped people on the street in order to communicate a message that was highly critical of the Roman Catholic Church and other organized religions. Eventually they were arrested and charged with failure to obtain approval for solicitation under the state law, as well as with common law breach of the peace. The Court reversed the breach-of-the-peace conviction and invalidated the state statute, saying in part:

> *In the realm of religious faith, and in that of political belief, sharp differences arise. In both fields the tenets of one man may seem the rankest error to his neighbor. To persuade others to his point of view, the pleader, as we know, resorts to exaggeration, to vilification of men who have been, or are, prominent in church or state, and even to false statement. But the people of this nation have ordained in the light of history, that, in spite of the probability of excesses and abuses, these liberties are, in the long view, essential to enlightened opinion and right conduct on the part of citizens of a democracy.*

Three years later, the Court in *Douglas v. City of Jeanette* (1943) held that police could not prohibit members of the Jehovah's Witnesses from peaceable and orderly proselytizing on Sundays merely because other citizens complained. In another 1943 case involving the Jehovah's Witnesses, *Murdoch v. Pennsylvania,* the Court held that a state law requiring the payment of a tax for the privilege of solicitation could not be constitutionally applied to religious solicitation. Writing for the Court, Justice William O. Douglas observed that "a person cannot be compelled to purchase ... a privilege freely granted by the Constitution." In still another case involving members of the Jehovah's Witnesses, *Niemotko v. Maryland* (1951), the Supreme Court held unconstitutional a city council's denial of a permit to the Jehovah's Witnesses to use the city park for a public meeting. The city council had refused to grant the permit because the Jehovah's Witnesses' answers to questions about Catholicism, military service, and other issues were "unsatisfactory." A unanimous Supreme Court regarded this denial of the public forum to an unpopular religious group as blatant censorship.

Time, Place, and Manner Regulations

As we saw in Chapter 3, the First Amendment does not guarantee the right to communicate one's views at all times and places or in any manner that may be desired. Religious expression in the **public forum** is subject to reasonable **time, place, and manner regulations**. Airports, courthouses, and other public buildings may be declared off-limits to all First Amendment activities, as long as particular groups are not singled out. Similarly, religious proselytizing in congested areas may be limited to certain areas so as to maintain the safe and orderly flow of pedestrian and vehicular traffic (see, for example, *Heffron v. International Society for Krishna Consciousness* [1981]).

To Summarize:
- ◆ *The First Amendment affords unlimited protection to freedom of belief per se.*
- ◆ *The actions of believers in proselytizing and soliciting contributions are also highly protected by the First Amendment, but any religious expression in the public forum is subject to reasonable time, place, and manner restrictions.*

Unconventional Religious Practices

Although the Supreme Court has consistently defended the right of unpopular religious groups to meet, canvass, solicit, and proselytize in the public forum, it has generally rejected arguments that the Free Exercise Clause allows religious groups to engage in activities that are proscribed as detrimental to public health, safety, or morality.

Subsequently, the Supreme Court has upheld laws that limit practices in the name of religion, such as polygamy, drug use, and other unconventional practices. For example, in 1975 the Court refused to review a lower court decision upholding Tennessee's law prohibiting the handling of poisonous snakes in religious ceremonies (see *State ex rel. Swann v. Pack*). In *Employment Division v. Smith* (1990), the Supreme Court rejected a claim made by members of the Native American Church that their ritualistic use of peyote constituted free exercise of religion.

The Mormon Polygamy Case

The first major pronouncement from the Supreme Court on the subject of **unconventional religious practices** came in *Reynolds v. United States* (1879). In this landmark case, the Court upheld application of the federal antipolygamy statute to a Mormon who claimed it was his religious duty to have several wives. The federal law in question merely adopted the long-standing common law prohibition against bigamy (the crime of having more than one spouse). Although the law applied to everyone regardless of religion, it is clear from the congressional debates surrounding this legislation that the law was aimed at the Mormons, a highly controversial sect in nineteenth-century America. Writing for a unanimous bench, Chief Justice Morrison R. Waite opined:

> *Laws are made for the government of actions, and while they cannot interfere with mere religious belief and opinions, they may with practices. ... So here, as a law of the organization of society under the exclusive dominion of the United States, it is provided that plural marriages shall not be allowed. Can a man excuse his practices to the contrary because of his religious belief? To permit this would be to make the professed doctrines of religious belief superior to the law of the land, and in effect to permit every citizen to become a law unto himself.*

The *Reynolds* decision was based on a sharp distinction between belief and conduct that would be untenable today. Although the Supreme Court has occasionally reiterated the distinction between religious belief and conduct, it has largely repudiated the position taken in *Reynolds* that religious conduct is beyond the pale of the Free Exercise Clause. After all, few if any government policies infringe on religious belief per se; rather, they are aimed at particular kinds of actions deemed socially undesirable.

The Warren Court Establishes the Compelling Interest Test

In its post–New Deal expansion of civil liberties, the Court markedly increased the degree of judicial protection of religiously motivated conduct, but this did not mean that religious activity received absolute immunity from government regulation. The Court remained willing to uphold public policies that infringed on religious practices if the government could point to an important secular justification for such infringement.

In *Sherbert v. Verner* (1963), the Court said that freedom of religion is a **fundamental right** that could be abridged only if necessary to protect a **compelling government interest**. Although the justices often disagreed over precisely which government interests should be viewed as compelling, this general standard established a strong presumption in favor of the free exercise of religion.

The *Sherbert* case arose when Adelle Sherbet, a Seventh-Day Adventist, was fired from her job in a textile mill after she refused on religious grounds to work on Saturday. The South Carolina Employment Security Commission denied her application for unemployment benefits. The Supreme Court held that the state's denial of benefits amounted to an abridgment of Sherbert's right to freely exercise her religion. In his opinion for the Court, Justice Brennan found no compelling state interest that would sustain the state's decision: "The appellees suggest no more than a possibility that the filing of fraudulent claims by unscrupulous claimants feigning religious objections to Saturday work might not only dilute the unemployment compensation fund but also hinder the scheduling by employers of necessary Saturday work." In Brennan's view, these arguments were not enough to justify the infringement of a fundamental right.

Throughout the 1970s and 1980s, the Supreme Court continued to apply the rationale established in *Sherbert v. Verner* (see, for example, *Thomas v. Review Board* [1981] and *Hobbie v. Unemployment Appeals Division* [1987]). These cases stood for the proposition that, in the absence of a compelling justification, a state could not withhold unemployment compensation from an employee who resigned or was discharged due to unwillingness to depart from religious practices or beliefs that conflicted with job requirements.

The Oregon Peyote Case

In 1990, however, a sharply divided Court departed dramatically from the approach taken in *Sherbert v. Verner* and its progeny. In *Employment Division v. Smith*, a state's interest in prohibiting the use of illicit drugs came into conflict with well-established practices of the Native American Church, a sect outside the Judeo-Christian mainstream of American religion. Two members of this church, Alfred Smith and Galen Black, worked as drug rehabilitation counselors for a private social service agency in Oregon. Along with other church members, Smith and Black ingested peyote, a hallucinogenic drug, at a sacramental ceremony practiced by Native Americans for hundreds of years. Citing their use of peyote as "job-related misconduct," the social service agency fired Smith and Black. Recognizing no exception, even for sacramental purposes, Oregon's controlled substances statute made the possession of peyote a criminal offense. Although Smith and Black were not charged with violation of this law, its existence figured prominently in the Supreme Court's ultimate resolution of the free exercise issue.

Shortly after they were fired, Smith and Black applied for unemployment compensation. The Oregon Employment Appeals Board denied their applications, accepting the employer's explanation that the employees had been discharged for job-related misconduct. Smith and Black successfully challenged this administrative ruling in the Oregon Court of Appeals, thus initiating a lengthy and complex judicial struggle that generated several state court decisions and two rulings by the U.S. Supreme Court. On remand from the first of these rulings, the Oregon Supreme Court held that the controlled substance law, as applied in this case, violated the Free Exercise Clause of the First Amendment and that Smith and Black were thus entitled to unemployment compensation.

Reviewing the case for a second time and finally reaching the basic constitutional issue, the U.S. Supreme Court reversed. Justice Antonin Scalia, writing for the majority, ruled that "if prohibiting the exercise of religion … is … merely the incidental effect of a generally applicable and otherwise valid [criminal] law, the First Amendment has not been offended." According to this reasoning, the Free Exercise Clause would be violated only if a particular religious practice were singled out for proscription.

In supporting this holding, Scalia relied heavily on *Reynolds v. United States* (1879), in effect equating Oregon's drug prohibition with the federal antipolygamy statute. He contended that "[t]o make an individual's obligation to obey such a law contingent upon the law's coincidence with his religious beliefs except where the state's interest is compelling … contradicts both constitutional tradition and common sense." The legislature, Scalia maintained, is free to make accommodations for religious practices. Such accommodations, however, are not required, no matter how "central" a particular practice might be to one's religious beliefs.

As Justice Sandra Day O'Connor's concurring opinion indicates, Scalia's rejection of the compelling governmental interest test was the most controversial aspect of this decision. Although she supported the Court's judgment that the Free Exercise Clause had not been violated, O'Connor sharply criticized the majority opinion as a dramatic departure "from well-settled First Amendment jurisprudence ... and ... [as] incompatible with our Nation's fundamental commitment to individual religious liberty." This part of O'Connor's opinion was supported by Justices Brennan, Marshall, and Blackmun, who dissented from the Court's decision. "The compelling interest test," O'Connor asserted, "effectuates the First Amendment's command that religious liberty is an independent liberty, that it occupies a preferred position, and that the Court will not permit encroachments upon this liberty, whether direct or indirect, unless required by clear and compelling governmental interests 'of the highest order.'"

In a separate dissenting opinion, Justice Harry Blackmun, joined by Justices Brennan and Marshall, charged the majority with "mischaracterizing" precedents and "overturning ... settled law concerning the Religion Clauses of our Constitution." With evident sarcasm, Blackmun expressed the hope that the Court was "aware of the consequences" and that the result was not a "product of overreaction to the serious problems the country's drug crisis [had] generated." He pointed out that the Native American Church restricted and supervised the sacramental use of peyote. The state thus had no significant health or safety justification for regulating this form of drug use. Blackmun also noted that Oregon had not attempted to prosecute Smith and Black or, for that matter, any other Native Americans for the sacramental use of peyote. He concluded that "Oregon's interest in enforcing its drug laws against religious use of peyote [was] not sufficiently compelling to outweigh respondents' right to the free exercise of their religion."

The Religious Freedom Restoration Act

Negative public reaction to the Court's decision in *Smith*, especially from the religious community, convinced a majority in Congress to pass the **Religious Freedom Restoration Act (RFRA)** of 1993. The RFRA prohibited government at all levels from substantially burdening a person's free exercise of religion, even if such burden resulted from a generally applicable rule, unless the government could demonstrate a compelling interest and that the rule constituted the least restrictive means of furthering that interest. In passing the RFRA, Congress sought to restore the status quo ante—to return the law in this area to what it was prior to the *Smith* decision. In adopting this statute, Congress relied on its broad powers under Section 5 of the Fourteenth Amendment.

In *City of Boerne v. Flores* (1997), the Supreme Court, dividing 6 to 3, declared the RFRA unconstitutional as applied to the states. While conceding that Congress has broad power to enforce the provisions of the Fourteenth Amendment, Justice Kennedy, writing for the majority, concluded that "RFRA contradicts vital principles necessary to maintain separation of powers and the federal balance." In this decision the Court stressed the primacy of its role as interpreter of the Constitution. It was firm and unequivocal in rejecting, on broad institutional grounds, a direct congressional challenge of final judicial authority on a question of constitutional interpretation (this case is excerpted in Chapter 3, Volume I).

It is noteworthy that in 1994, in the wake of *Boerne v. Flores*, Congress enacted an amendment to the American Indian Religious Freedom Act of 1978 in order to exempt the sacramental use of peyote by Native Americans from prosecution under both federal and state drug laws. Without question, Congress can create an exemption to prosecution under federal drug laws; whether it can do so with respect to state laws remains an open question. The Supreme Court has not yet found the occasion to address that issue.

It is also important to note that RFRA applied to the federal government as well as the states. The *Boerne* decision did not challenge the constitutionality of this statute with respect to the former. In the 2006 decision of *Gonzales v. O Centro Espirita*, the federal government was barred from enforcing the Controlled Substances Act because doing so would offend RFRA. In *O Centro Espirita*, a 130-member religious sect used in its practice a sacramental tea brewed from a plant called *hoasca*, which was banned under federal law because it contains a hallucinogen. The sect argued that prohibiting the use of hoasca violated RFRA because the prohibition would impose a substantial burden on the exercise of their religion. In affirming a preliminary injunction against enforcement of the Controlled Substances Act, the Court held that the federal government must demonstrate proof that the substantial burden on religious freedom actually furthered a compelling interest. It was not enough merely to show that hoasca was covered by the Controlled Substances Act.

Ritualistic Animal Sacrifice

In 1987, the city of Hialeah, a Miami suburb, passed an ordinance making it a crime to "unnecessarily kill, torment, torture, or mutilate an animal in a public or private ritual or ceremony not for the primary purpose of food consumption." The ordinance came in response to local concern over the sacrificial practices associated with Santeria, a blend of Roman Catholicism and West African religions brought to the Caribbean by East African slaves. Santeria, which literally means "worship of the saints," involves occasional sacrifices of live animals, usually goats or chickens. According to some estimates, there were as many as 70,000 devotees of Santeria in the Miami area, and perhaps as many as one million nationwide. Ernesto Pichardo, a Santeria priest, challenged the Hialeah law as a violation of the First Amendment.

In *Church of the Lukumi Babalu Aye v. City of Hialeah* (1993), the justices unanimously invalidated the Hialeah ordinance. Writing for the Supreme Court, Justice Kennedy observed that "the laws in question were enacted by officials who did not understand, failed to perceive, or chose to ignore the fact that their official actions violated the Nation's essential commitment to religious freedom." Justice Kennedy was careful to point out that the ordinance in question was not a generally applicable criminal prohibition, but rather singled out practitioners of Santeria in that it forbade animal slaughter only insofar as it took place within the context of religious rituals. Thus, the decision in *Lukumi Babalu Aye* is consistent with the Court's decision in *Employment Division v. Smith*.

The Court Refuses to Extend the **Lukumi** ***Rationale*** In a 2004 decision, *Locke v. Davey*, the Court considered the question of whether its rationale in *Lukumi* required the invalidation of a Washington State policy excluding from a general state scholarship program students who chose to pursue college majors in "devotional theology." Joshua Davey qualified for a Promise Scholarship under a program designed to assist academically gifted students to defray their college expenses. In accordance with the Washington Constitution, however, students could not use the scholarships at institutions where they chose to pursue degrees in devotional theology. Mr. Davey chose to attend a private Christian college that qualified as an eligible institution under the program. He was informed, however, that he could not use the scholarship if he pursued his chosen major in pastoral ministries. Davey challenged the constitutionality of this restriction, claiming that it violated his First Amendment freedom of religion. The Supreme Court, in an opinion by Chief Justice Rehnquist, rejected his challenge, holding that this exclusion from an otherwise inclusive financial aid program did not violate the Free Exercise

Clause. In reaching this conclusion, Rehnquist recognized that while the Establishment and Free Exercise Clauses of the First Amendment "are frequently in tension … we have long said that 'there is room for play in the joints' between them." In a sharply worded dissent, Justice Scalia, joined by Justice Thomas, asserted: "When the state makes a public benefit generally available, that benefit becomes part of the baseline against which burdens on religion are measured; and when the state withholds that benefit from some individuals solely on the basis of religion, it violates the Free Exercise Clause no less than if it had imposed a special tax."

To Summarize:

- ◆ *In contrast to proselytizing and solicitation of contributions, unconventional religious practices such as polygamy and use of illicit drugs receive far less protection under the Free Exercise Clause.*
- ◆ *Although generally applicable prohibitions that incidentally burden religion are likely to be upheld, prohibitions that single out particular religious groups are less likely to survive constitutional challenge. For example, the Court invalidated as a violation of the Free Exercise Clause a restriction designed to bar the religious practice of animal sacrifice; but upheld a state's refusal to include students of devotional theology within its otherwise inclusive scholarship program.*

Patriotic Rituals and Civic Duties

Some religious groups prefer to live largely in isolation from the mainstream of modern society, pursuing lifestyles and embracing virtues reminiscent of the early nineteenth century. For the most part, they are uninterested in things political, preferring to concentrate on their families' moral and spiritual development. Because they are opposed to war in any form, they are generally unwilling to serve in the armed forces.

They also avoid displays of nationalism or even citizenship. Sometimes, they refuse to school their children formally beyond the primary grades. To what extent does the First Amendment protect such groups from being forced to observe patriotic rituals and civic duties that are readily observed by most Americans?

The Flag Salute Cases

In *Minersville School District v. Gobitis* (1940), the Supreme Court upheld a local school board requirement that all public school students participate in a daily flag salute program. The requirement had been challenged by a member of the Jehovah's Witnesses whose children were being forced to salute the American flag in violation of their religious training, which held the flag salute to be the worship of a "graven image" (see Exodus 20:4–5). In a dramatic turnabout, the *Gobitis* decision was overruled three years later in *West Virginia State Board of Education v. Barnette* (1943). In the *Gobitis* decision, Justice Felix Frankfurter had justified the compulsory flag salute as an appropriate means for the attainment of national unity, which he viewed as "the basis of national security." Writing for the Court that overruled Frankfurter's position, Justice Robert Jackson stated that "compulsory unification of opinion leads only to the unanimity of the graveyard," obviously referring to the situation in Europe in 1943. For Justice Jackson, "to believe that patriotism will not flourish if patriotic ceremonies are voluntary and spontaneous instead of a compulsory routine is to make an unflattering estimate of the appeal of our institutions to free minds." Nothing that the Supreme Court has decided since *Barnette* indicates that government has any justification for forcing citizens to make professions of patriotism. The Court has even gone so far as to prohibit the state of New Hampshire from requiring that an automobile display a license plate inscribed with the state's motto "Live Free or Die" if such motto offends the religious sensibilities of the car's owner (see *Wooley v. Maynard* [1977]). Although the Court has not faced the question since 1931 (see *United States v. Bland*), it is interesting to speculate as to whether the current Court would require a religious pacifist who wishes to become a citizen to swear that he or she would "defend the Constitution and the laws of the United States against all enemies, foreign or domestic," which is the oath required of all naturalized citizens. The Court upheld the oath requirement in 1931. Would it do so today?

Free Exercise of Religion and Military Service

Another interesting constitutional question involves conscientious objection to military service, alluded to earlier in the discussion of the *Seeger* case. Although Congress has provided an exemption from military service for religiously motivated conscientious objectors, is such an exemption required by the Free Exercise Clause? In other words, would the Supreme Court permit religiously motivated refusal to serve in combat on constitutional grounds if there were no act of Congress providing such an exemption? On the other hand, is it not possible to argue that, in granting an exemption only to those whose refusal to serve is based on religion, Congress has run afoul of the Establishment Clause? The Court has never squarely addressed these questions.

One of the most controversial Supreme Court decisions in the area of free exercise of religion dealt with military regulations that were alleged to infringe First Amendment rights. In *Goldman v. Weinberger* (1986), the Court upheld an Air Force dress code requirement against the challenge of an Orthodox Jew who was disciplined for wearing a yarmulke while in uniform. Stressing the need for discipline and uniformity in the military, the Court rejected the challenge by a vote of 5 to 4. Writing for the sharply divided Court, Justice William Rehnquist maintained that "when evaluating whether military needs justify a particular restriction on religiously motivated conduct, courts must give great deference to the professional judgment of military authorities concerning the relative importance of a particular military interest." In *Goldman*, the Supreme Court thus reiterated the position taken five years before that "[j]udicial deference ... is at its apogee when legislative action under the congressional authority to raise and support armies and make rules and regulations for their governance is challenged" (*Rostker v. Goldberg* [1981]). In 1988 Congress passed legislation providing that "a member of the armed forces may wear an item of religious apparel while wearing the uniform of the member's armed force." However, this legislation authorized the Department of Defense to restrict the wearing of apparel that "would interfere with the performance of ... military duties" or is "not neat and conservative."

To Summarize:

- *The First Amendment prohibits government from compelling individuals to make public affirmations of belief whether religious or political.*
- *Because Congress has created a statutory basis for conscientious objection to military service, the Supreme Court has not faced the issue of whether exemptions for conscientious objectors are required by the Free Exercise Clause.*
- *The Court tends to be deferential to military regulations such as dress codes that impinge upon the free exercise of religion by persons in military service, as long as such regulations do not single out or discriminate against particular religions.*

Freedom of Religion versus *Parens Patriae*

Our legal traditions recognize government as *parens patriae*, meaning literally "parent of the country." This term refers to the role of government as guardian of persons who are not legally competent to make their own decisions, such as children, the severely retarded, and the mentally ill. Occasionally, the state uses this power to take custody of children who are the victims of neglect or abuse. The state's role as *parens patriae* has sometimes come into conflict with the Free Exercise Clause when parents refuse on religious grounds to allow their children to receive medical treatment. Some devoutly religious persons believe that medical science is blasphemous—that true faith is all that is necessary to promote healing. For example, in a 1983 Tennessee case that attracted wide attention, a fundamentalist preacher refused to allow a hospital to treat his young daughter for cancer. The state intervened as *parens patriae* and secured a court order requiring medical treatment (see *In the Matter of Hamilton* [1983]).

Although some state and federal court decisions have recognized a competent adult's **right to refuse medical treatment** on religious and/or privacy grounds, courts are generally disinclined to uphold such free exercise claims where the health of children is involved. Judges generally assume that children are not sufficiently mature to make rational choices regarding medical treatment and, in some instances, must be protected against the consequences of their parents' unusual religious convictions.

In *Prince v. Massachusetts* (1944), the Supreme Court upheld a child labor law against an attack based on the Free Exercise Clause. The law prohibited boys under age 12 and girls under 18 from selling newspapers on the streets. The law was challenged by a member of the Jehovah's Witnesses whose children normally assisted her in the sale and distribution of religious literature. Dividing 8 to 1, the Court held that the state's role as *parens patriae* in protecting the safety of children overrode Prince's free exercise claim.

Compulsory School Attendance

In *Wisconsin v. Yoder* (1972), the Supreme Court held that a state's compulsory high school attendance law could not be constitutionally applied to members of the Old Order Amish faith, which does not permit secular education beyond the eighth grade. Writing for the Court, Chief Justice Warren E. Burger placed great stress on the fact that the education of the Amish teenager continued in the home, with emphasis on practical skills as well as religious and moral values. Based on Burger's opinion in *Yoder*, it seems unlikely that the Court would grant the Amish an exemption from compulsory primary education. Nor would it grant an exemption to members of a religion that strikes the Court as silly, faddish, or insincere.

One wonders whether the Amish would prevail if their case came before the current Supreme Court. After all, compulsory school attendance laws are generally applicable rules. In *Minnesota v. Hershberger* (1990), the Court vacated a state supreme court decision exempting the Amish from compliance with state traffic laws. On the other hand, the Court has long recognized the rights of parents in matters pertaining to the education of their children (see, for example, *Meyer v. Nebraska* [1923]). One can make good arguments for the current Court deciding the compulsory school attendance issue either way.

Today, states permit parents to "home school" their children as long as certain state educational standards are met. Many parents who choose this option do so for religious reasons; they object to the secular character of the public schools but are unable or unwilling to place their children in private, sectarian schools. The home schooling option helps to defuse many potential conflicts between states and parents whose religious convictions make them unwilling to send their children to public schools.

> ### To Summarize:
>
> ◆ *Courts have recognized the right of competent adults to refuse medical treatment on religious grounds, but generally do not permit parents to refuse life-saving medical treatment for their minor children.*
> ◆ *The Supreme Court has held that the Free Exercise Clause exempts members of the Old Order Amish faith from compliance with state laws requiring children to attend school beyond the eighth grade. The Court recognized the exceptional circumstances under which this exemption was granted, making it clear that a mere claim of religious liberty is not enough to warrant such special treatment.*

Separation of Church and State

The Establishment Clause of the First Amendment was adopted in contradiction to the practice, prevalent not only in Europe but among the American colonies, of having official churches supported by taxation. Indeed, as previously noted, some states maintained their established churches well into the nineteenth century. Thus, the concept of "a wall of separation between church and state," as Thomas Jefferson referred to it, was an American invention whose application remained to be worked out in practice.

Competing Interpretations of the Establishment Clause

Since its ratification more than two centuries ago, Americans both on and off the Supreme Court have disagreed sharply over the meaning of the Establishment Clause. The debate has become especially heated in the modern era. One view is that it merely forbids the establishment of an official, state-supported religion. According to this conservative interpretation, Congress does not run afoul of the First Amendment as long as it refrains from selecting one denomination as the official or preferred religion of the United States. However, even the literal language of the First Amendment suggests a broader prohibition. It does not say that Congress shall make no law establishing an official religion; rather, it states that "Congress shall make no law *respecting an establishment of religion*" (emphasis added). This general language, as interpreted by a majority of the justices, indicates a broader restriction than mere prohibition of an established church.

In *Everson v. Board of Education* (1947), the Supreme Court explicitly adopted Thomas Jefferson's "wall of separation" metaphor as encapsulating the meaning of the Establishment Clause. Justice Hugo Black's majority opinion in *Everson* delineated the boundaries between government and religion:

> *Neither a State nor the Federal Government can set up a church. Neither can pass laws which aid one religion, aid all religions, or prefer one religion over another. Neither can force nor influence a person to go to or to remain away from church against his will or force him to profess a belief or disbelief in any religion. No person can be punished for entertaining or professing religious beliefs or disbeliefs, for church attendance or nonattendance. No tax in any amount, large or small, can be levied to support any religious activities or institutions, whatever they may be called, or whatever form they may adopt to teach or practice religion. Neither a state nor the Federal Government can, openly or secretly, participate in the affairs of any religious organizations or groups and vice versa. In the words of Jefferson, the clause against establishment of religion by law was intended to erect "a wall of separation between church and State."*

Today, there is little prospect of government at any level engaging in any of the activities enumerated by Justice Black. Yet the controversy over the establishment of religion remains very much alive. Most contemporary Americans support the abstract concept of **separation of church and state**. Yet there is no consensus on how high or how thick the wall of separation should be. Some believe that government must be strictly neutral in matters of religion and that any trace of governmental support for religious belief or practice must be expunged.

The modern Supreme Court's decisions in the Establishment Clause field have been even more controversial than its decisions under the Free Exercise Clause. Many of these controversial decisions involve education, notably prayer in public schools and state aid to private religious schools. Another area of tremendous controversy involves governmental affirmations or endorsements of religious beliefs, such as the public display of nativity scenes or the Ten Commandments.

Potential Establishment Clause questions are implicit in many traditional government practices. For example, consider the practice of Congress and every state legislature of paying a chaplain, usually of a particular Protestant denomination, to lead our representatives in public prayer (see *Marsh v. Chambers* [1983]). What about the inscription "In God We Trust" on American currency; or the Supreme Court's time-honored practice of opening oral argument with the invocation "God save the United States and this honorable Court"; or the recognition of America as "one nation under God" in the official pledge of allegiance to the flag? These and other common practices indicate the degree to which religion figures prominently in the public life of this nation. Although many Americans no doubt approve of such official endorsement and invocation of religion, what about the rights of nonbelievers?

How far does the First Amendment allow the government to go in recognizing, endorsing, or accommodating religious beliefs? As the controversial Supreme Court decisions interpreting the Establishment Clause demonstrate, the answer to this question is far from clear.

The *Lemon* Test

In 1971, the Court laid down a three-pronged test for determining the constitutionality of policies challenged under the Establishment Clause (see *Lemon v. Kurtzman*). The so-called ***Lemon* test** synthesized various elements of the Court's Establishment Clause jurisprudence as it had evolved during the 1940s, 1950s, and 1960s. Although controversial from its inception, the *Lemon* test has been applied to a broad range of issues involving separation of church and state. Under the *Lemon* test, a challenged policy must meet the following criteria in order to pass constitutional muster under the Establishment Clause: (1) It must have a "secular legislative purpose"; (2) it must not have the principal or primary effect of "inhibiting or advancing religion"; and (3) it must avoid an "excessive government entanglement with religion."

It should go without saying that the *Lemon* test does not contain hard and fast criteria for judicial decision making. Rather, like all judicial doctrines, it is subject to some degree of manipulation by those who are predisposed to a particular result. For example, how can the "purpose" of a challenged law be determined with certainty by the courts? How does one distinguish the principal or primary effects of a law from its secondary or tertiary effects? Finally, how much entanglement between religion and government is excessive? During the 1970s and 1980s, the Court was often criticized for inconsistency in its application of the *Lemon* test, leading some scholars to question the value of the test altogether. Perhaps as a result, since the 1990s the Court has moved away from a strict application of the *Lemon* test, but has stopped short of repudiating it altogether (see, for example, *Agostini v. Felton* [1997], discussed later and excerpted at the end of the chapter).

> ## To Summarize:
> ◆ *The Supreme Court has adopted Thomas Jefferson's metaphor of a "wall of separation between church and state" to capture the essential meaning of the Establishment Clause. Since its first decision in this area, however, the Court has sought to balance the idea of separation of church and state with the equally important constitutional commitment to free exercise of religion.*
> ◆ *In* Lemon v. Kurtzman *(1971), the Court fashioned a three-part test for determining whether a particular policy constitutes an establishment of religion. To survive challenge, the policy must have a secular purpose, its principal effect must not be to advance or inhibit religion, and it must avoid excessive entanglement between government and religion.*
> ◆ *The Court has moved away from a strict application of the* Lemon *test but has stopped short of repudiating it altogether.*

Religion and Public Education

In *Everson v. Board of Education* (1947), the first case in which the Supreme Court applied the Establishment Clause to the states via the Fourteenth Amendment, the issue was whether a local school board could reimburse parents for expenses they incurred in transporting their children to and from Catholic schools. The payments to parents of children in parochial schools were part of a general program under which all parents of children in public schools and nonprofit private schools, regardless of religious affiliation, were entitled to reimbursement for transportation costs.

It is worth noting that the overwhelming number of children attending nonprofit private schools in this New Jersey school district were enrolled in Catholic schools. Writing for a sharply divided Court, Justice Hugo Black justified the challenged payments on the theory that the school board was merely furthering the state's legitimate interest in getting children, "regardless of their religion, safely and expeditiously to and from accredited schools." Justice Wiley Rutledge, joined by Justices Felix Frankfurter, Robert Jackson, and Harold Burton, dissented vigorously. Professing sympathy for the economic hardships involved in sending one's children to private, religious schools, Justice Rutledge nevertheless asserted:

> *Like St. Paul's freedom, religious liberty with a great price must be bought. And for those who exercise it most fully, by insisting upon religious education for their children mixed with secular, by the terms of our Constitution the price is greater than for others.*

The **child benefit theory** articulated in *Everson* has for the most part been maintained. Thus, for example, in *Board of Education v. Allen* (1968), the Supreme Court upheld a New York statute requiring local public school districts to lend textbooks on secular subjects to students in private and parochial schools. And in *Meek v. Pittenger* (1975), the Court reaffirmed this position. The Supreme Court has consistently ruled that state policies that primarily benefit the education of children are not in violation of the Establishment Cause simply because such policies may have the side effect of enhancing religion.

Released-Time Programs and Equal Access Policies

To accommodate the religious beliefs of public school students, the Court has upheld **released-time programs**, which allow students to leave campus to attend religious exercises. Distinguishing a 1948 decision in which it struck down an on-campus released-time program (*McCollum v. Board of Education*), the Court in *Zorach v. Clauson*

(1952) upheld a New York policy under which public school students who received parental permission left campus to attend religious services while other students attended study hall. Writing for the Court, Justice Douglas stressed the need for governmental accommodation of religious practices, a position from which he would later retreat.

Released-time programs, although constitutionally permissible under *Zorach v. Clauson*, are not in widespread use in public schools today. More common today are policies under which religiously oriented student groups are permitted **equal access** to school facilities. In *Widmar v. Vincent* (1981), the Supreme Court said that public school facilities that have been designated an open forum may not be placed off limits to religious groups. In *Board of Education v. Mergens* (1990), the Court upheld the Equal Access Act of 1984, in which Congress prohibited public secondary schools that receive federal funds from disallowing meetings of student groups on the basis of "religious, political, philosophical or other content of the speech at such meetings." Three years later, in *Lamb's Chapel v. Center Moriches Union Free School District* (1993), the Court held that the limited public forum approach could not be used to bar a religious organization from showing a film after school hours dealing with family planning and child-rearing issues, while permitting discussion of these issues by nonreligious groups. According to the Court, the school district rule at issue in this case amounted to viewpoint discrimination in violation of the First Amendment's free speech guarantee. The Court rejected the argument that Lamb's Chapel's after-hours use of school property violated the *Lemon* test. In *Good News Club v. Milford Central School* (2001), the Court went one step further by holding that if a school permits after-hours activities concerning moral or character development, it cannot prohibit activities even if they involve religious instruction of elementary school students.

Government Efforts to Assist Religious Schools

In *Lemon v. Kurtzman* (1971), the Court struck down Pennsylvania and Rhode Island policies providing publicly funded salary supplements to teachers in parochial schools as fostering "excessive entanglement." Similarly, in *Committee for Public Education v. Nyquist* (1973), the Court used the three-pronged test in striking down a New York law that provided various forms of economic aid to parochial schools. Although the released-time programs approved in *Zorach* have not been recently litigated before the Supreme Court, it is highly unlikely such programs could survive a rigorous application of the *Lemon* test. The Supreme Court reinforced its holdings in *Lemon* and *Nyquist* in two significant decisions of the mid-1980s. In *Aguilar v. Felton* (1985), the Court struck down a New York City program that used federal funds to supplement the salaries of public school teachers who taught remedial courses on the premises of religious schools. Similarly, in *Grand Rapids School District v. Ball* (1985), the Court invalidated a program in which supplementary classes for students in sectarian schools were taught by public school teachers at public expense. Writing for the Court in the *Grand Rapids* case, Justice Brennan observed that "the symbolic union of church and state inherent in the provision of secular, state-provided instruction in the religious school buildings threatens to convey a message of state support for religion to students and to the general public." Justice Byron White used the occasion to dissent not only from the Court's *Grand Rapids* holding but from the entire thrust of the Court's decisions in the area of state aid to religious schools:

> *I am firmly of the belief that the Court's decisions in these cases … are not required by the First Amendment and [are] contrary to the long-range interest of the country.... I am satisfied that what the States have sought to do in these cases is well within their authority and is not forbidden by the Establishment Clause.*

In 1994 the Court reaffirmed its decisions in *Aguilar* and *Grand Rapids* by striking down a New York law that created a new special school district in a community occupied exclusively by Hassidic Jews. Virtually all of the community's children were being educated in private schools. The new district was established for the purpose of enabling the community to avail itself of public funds for the education of children with disabilities. Under *Aguilar* and *Grand Rapids*, this kind of assistance could not be provided directly to the community's private schools, thus explaining the creation of a new public school district. In *Kiryas Joel School District v. Grumet* (1994), the Court found this arrangement to be an unconstitutional establishment of religion. In this case the Court conspicuously avoided relying on the *Lemon* test, leading commentators to wonder whether this three-pronged formulation was being phased out. Recalling Justice White's dissent in *Grand Rapids*, Justice Scalia's dissenting opinion (joined by Chief Justice Rehnquist and Justice Thomas) sharply criticized the Court's decision and indeed its general approach in this area.

By 1997 a Court majority was willing to give ground in the area of aid to parochial schools. Thus, in *Agostini v. Felton*, a bare majority of justices voted to overturn *Aguilar v. Felton* and corresponding portions of *Grand Rapids School District v. Ball*. In her majority opinion, Justice O'Connor maintained that *Aguilar* was inconsistent with the Court's later Establishment Clause decisions. O'Connor stressed the neutrality of the federally funded remedial instruction and the procedural safeguards surrounding the program. She also noted that this program could not "reasonably be viewed as an endorsement of religion." With the concurrence of Chief Justice Rehnquist and Justices Scalia, Kennedy, and Thomas, Justice O'Connor therefore concluded that "*Aguilar*, as well as the portion of *Ball* addressing Grand Rapids' 'shared time' program, are no longer good law." In dissent, Justices Stevens, Souter, Ginsburg, and Breyer continued to express concern about the difficulty of limiting government assistance in this area to purely secular objectives.

In *Mitchell v. Helms* (2000), the Court, by a 6-to-3 vote, expanded the types of public aid that government may provide to parochial schools. Relying heavily on the *Agostini* precedent, the Court upheld a Louisiana statute permitting state and local governments to lend library books, projectors, televisions, computers, software, and similar equipment to parochial and other private not-for-profit elementary and secondary schools. The six members of the majority could not agree on a single opinion, however. Justice Thomas, in a plurality opinion joined by Chief Justice Rehnquist and Justices Scalia and Kennedy, indicated his willingness to venture beyond the Court's holding, suggesting that he and his three colleagues in the plurality would be willing to support even broader public assistance to religious schools. His position is summarized in the following statement: "If religious, irreligious and areligious are all eligible for governmental aid, no one would conclude that any indoctrination that any particular recipient conducts has been done at the behest of the government."

In a separate opinion concurring in the judgment only, Justice O'Connor, joined by Justice Breyer, criticized what she viewed as the "unprecedented breadth" of the rule announced by the plurality. She contended that considerations of neutrality alone are not sufficient in determining whether governmental aid to religious schools violates the Establishment Clause. Such factors as "endorsement" of religion should also be taken into account. Thomas's opinion, she maintained, foreshadowed "the approval of direct monetary subsidies to religious organizations, even when they use the money to advance their religious objectives." In dissent, Justice Souter, supported by Justices Stevens and Ginsburg, expressed alarm at the scope of the plurality opinion:

> *As a break with consistent doctrine the plurality's new criterion is unequaled in the history of Establishment Clause interpretation. Simple on its face, it appears to take evenhandedness neutrality and in practical terms promote it to a single and sufficient test for the establishment [sic] constitutionality of school aid.*

If evenhanded neutrality were the sole standard for determining the constitutionality of public aid, Souter reasoned, "religious schools could be blessed with government funding as massive as expenditures made for the benefit of their public school counterparts and religious missions would thrive on public money."

Mitchell v. Helms has had the effect of expanding parochial school students' access to the Internet. Computers, by contrast with textbooks loaned to parochial schools at public expense, can be used in an endless variety of ways, both secular and religious. Barry W. Lynn, executive director of Americans United for Separation of Church and State, observed that as a result of this decision, "religious schools can now have students surf the Internet to read the Bible in religion classes, learn theology from Jerry Falwell, or download crucifixes as screen savers." On the other hand, children in religious schools also can use the Internet to access ideas that run counter to the religious views of their teachers and parents.

The Continuing School Prayer Controversy

Few decisions of the modern Supreme Court have been criticized more intensely than the **school prayer decisions** of the early 1960s. In *Engel v. Vitale* (1962), the Court invalidated a New York Board of Regents policy that established the voluntary recitation of a brief generic prayer by children in the public schools at the start of each school day. Justice Black wrote the opinion for the majority, saying that "in this country it is no part of the business of government to compose official prayers for any group of the American people to recite as part of a religious program carried on by government." Justice Potter Stewart, the lone dissenter in *Engel v. Vitale*, compared the recitation of the regents' prayer to other official recognitions of God and religion, such as the pledge of allegiance to the flag, the president's oath of office, and the invocation said prior to oral argument in the Supreme Court:

> *I do not believe that this Court, or the Congress, or the President has by the actions and practices I have described established an "official religion" in violation of the Constitution. And I do not believe the State of New York has done so in this case. What each has done has been to recognize and to follow the deeply entrenched and highly cherished spiritual traditions of our Nation.*

In 1963, the Court reinforced the *Engel* decision in the companion cases of *Abington School District v. Schempp* and *Murray v. Curlett* by striking down the practice of Bible reading and the recitation of the Lord's Prayer in the Pennsylvania and Maryland public schools. Again, only Justice Stewart dissented.

The reaction to the Court's school prayer decisions came fast and furious and, indeed, has still not disappeared. The Court was roundly condemned by religious leaders and conservative members of Congress and through resolutions passed by several state legislatures. Polls have consistently shown that a majority of Americans oppose the Court's ban on school prayer. For example, a 2007 Gallop poll found that 76 percent of Americans favored a constitutional amendment which would allow for voluntary prayer in public schools. It is hardly surprising then that the public has lower regard for the Court's work in this area than in other policy areas.

On several occasions, constitutional amendments have been introduced in Congress aimed specifically at overturning the school prayer decisions. In November 1971, one such proposal in the House of Representatives fell only 28 votes short of the two-thirds majority required for constitutional amendments. In the election of 1980, Ronald Reagan capitalized on public sentiment about school prayer by advocating a "school prayer amendment." However, once in office, President Reagan was either unwilling or unable to push this proposal through Congress.

Negative public reaction and widespread noncompliance notwithstanding, the Supreme Court has maintained, although by a shrinking majority, the position articulated in the school prayer cases. For example, in *Stone v. Graham* (1980), the Court invalidated a Kentucky law requiring that the Ten Commandments be posted in all public school classrooms. In *Wallace v. Jaffree* (1985), the Court struck down an Alabama law that required public school students to observe a **moment of silence** "for the purpose of meditation or voluntary prayer" at the start of each school day. In *Lee v. Weisman* (1992), the Court held unconstitutional the practice of inviting a member of the clergy to deliver a nonsectarian prayer at a public school graduation ceremony. More recently, in *Santa Fe Independent School District v. Doe* (2000), the Court split 5 to 4 in striking down a public high school's policy of allowing students to elect a chaplain to deliver invocations before football games.

The reactions to the Court's decisions in this area have been predictable. Conservative organizations and religious activists have been harshly critical. In the wake of the *Santa Fe* decision, conservative activist and Republican presidential candidate Gary Bauer said the decision "proves that a majority of the court is at war with the religious tradition of America." On the other hand, civil liberties groups have applauded the Court for these decisions. Barry W. Lynn, of Americans United for Separation of Church and State, said that the *Santa Fe* decision "was a major victory for people who believe that mob rule—majority rule—is not appropriate in matters of religion." Note that in no case has the Court held that it is unconstitutional for a student to pray voluntarily in the public school classroom, although some school officials have interpreted the Court's position this way. What the Court has said is that it is unconstitutional for the state schools to require, endorse, or sanction prayer, either directly or indirectly. One might think that if this were better understood, some of the public hostility toward the Court's decisions would abate. On the other hand, given the nature and intensity of feelings on this issue, it is unlikely that an accurate public perception of the Court's holdings would diminish the public opprobrium.

The Evolution–Creationism Conflict

With the rapid expansion of public education in the early twentieth century, especially in rural areas dominated by fundamentalist Protestantism, a controversy erupted over the teaching of evolution in the public schools. The controversy achieved national prominence in 1925 when John T. Scopes, a high school biology teacher in Dayton, Tennessee, was prosecuted for teaching evolution in violation of a state law that had been passed earlier that year. Amid a carnival-like atmosphere, the **Scopes trial**—or the "Monkey Trial," as it was caricatured by the press—pitted famous politician and orator William Jennings Bryan against celebrated lawyer Clarence Darrow in a battle royal in the courtroom. Although Darrow might have outsmarted Bryan in a much-publicized debate over biblical literalism, Scopes was nevertheless convicted of violating the state statute. The Tennessee Supreme Court reversed the conviction on technical grounds, however, preventing the U.S. Supreme Court from having to consider what was potentially the most explosive constitutional question of that decade.

In the wake of the Scopes trial, two states, Arkansas and Mississippi, enacted legislation similar to the Tennessee antievolution law. Yet it was not until 1965 that one of these laws was challenged in court. In that year, Susan Epperson, a high school biology teacher in Little Rock, Arkansas, filed a lawsuit challenging the state's statute. Although the Arkansas trial court ruled in favor of Epperson and struck down the antievolution law, the state Supreme Court reversed and reinstated the statute. On certiorari, the U.S. Supreme Court reversed (*Epperson v. Arkansas* [1968]). Writing for the Court, Justice

Abe Fortas asserted that Arkansas could not "prevent its teachers from discussing the theory of evolution because it is contrary to the belief of some that the book of Genesis must be the exclusive source of doctrine as to the origins of man." The *Epperson* decision put to rest the issue of whether states could prohibit the teaching of evolution in their public schools. But two decades later, the evolution–creationism conflict resurfaced in Louisiana. This time, the question was whether the state could mandate that creationism, or **creation science**, be given equal time in the classroom along with the theory of evolution. The state law required neither in the classroom, but held that if evolution was taught then creationism also had to be taught. In *Edwards v. Aguillard* (1987), the Supreme Court struck down the statute. Writing for a majority of seven, Justice Brennan averred that "the primary purpose" of the Louisiana Creationism Act was "to endorse a particular religious doctrine," rather than further the legitimate interests of the state in fostering different points of view in the classroom.

In the wake of such decisions as *Edwards v. Aguillard* and *Epperson v. Arkansas*, as well as the school prayer decisions discussed previously, fundamentalist Christians began to argue that, in its attempt to expunge religious teaching and symbols from the public schools, the Supreme Court had fostered a religion of **secular humanism**. According to its detractors, secular humanism is a philosophy emphasizing the view that morality is a human invention and that moral choices are largely matters of personal values. In the view of some fundamentalists, the pervasiveness of secular humanism in public school curricula was highly corrosive to traditional values and institutions.

In 1987, a federal district court barred the use of certain widely used history, social studies, and home economics textbooks in the public schools of Mobile County, Alabama. In essence, the district judge held that these books advanced the religion of secular humanism. In embracing this philosophy, the textbooks allegedly ignored or understated the historical and contemporary significance of traditional religion in American life, thus abridging the Free Exercise rights of students holding theistic beliefs. The teaching of secular humanism amounted to "a sweeping fundamental belief that must not be promoted by the public schools." Such promotion, the district court concluded, was a violation of the Establishment Clause of the First Amendment. The Court of Appeals for the Eleventh Circuit promptly overruled this novel decision, finding that the purpose for using the textbooks in question was "purely secular" (see *Smith v. Board of School Commissioners of Mobile County* [1987]).

In a similar case initiated in 1986, fundamentalist parents in Hawkins County, Tennessee, sued their county school board over the reading curriculum in the local public schools, complaining of the humanist perspective embodied in the curriculum. Although plaintiffs won at trial, the judgment was overruled on appeal by the Court of Appeals for the Sixth Circuit. The U.S. Supreme Court declined to review the case (*Mozert v. Hawkins County Public Schools* [1988]), thus letting the appeals court's decision stand.

Discrimination against Religious Expression in the Public Educational Arena

If a public school or university subsidizes a variety of student newspapers, can it withhold funds from a particular paper solely because it "promotes or manifests a particular belief in or about a deity or an ultimate reality"? This was the issue before the Court in *Rosenberger v. University of Virginia* (1995). The university denied a subsidy to "Wide Awake: A Christian Perspective at the University of Virginia." The student publisher of the paper went to court. The Supreme Court found the denial of support violative of free speech, in that the university was discriminating against the paper based on its content. Moreover, the Court rejected the argument that to subsidize the paper, the university would be breaching the wall of separation between church and state. Justices O'Connor and Thomas wrote concurring opinions. Four justices (Souter, Stevens, Ginsburg, and Breyer) dissented, claiming that for the university to provide the subsidy in question would constitute a clear violation of the Establishment Clause.

In 2010 the Court confronted a similar issue in *Christian Legal Society v. Martinez.* The Hastings College of Law, which is part of the California system of higher education, refused to allow the Christian Legal Society (CLS) to become a registered student organization because of CLS's stand against homosexuality. Writing for the Supreme Court, Justice Ruth Ginsburg observed, "In requiring CLS—in common with all other student organizations—to choose between welcoming all students and forgoing the benefits of official recognition, we hold, Hastings did not transgress constitutional limitations." In a somewhat caustic dissent, Justice Samuel Alito chided the five-member majority for holding that there is "no freedom for expression that offends prevailing standards of political correctness in our country's institutions of higher learning." *Rosenberger* and *Christian Legal Society v. Martinez* highlight the fact that the Free Exercise clause and the Establishment Clause are all too often on a collision course with one another. When religious organizations seek to use public space, it appears the competing constraints cannot each be satisfied. Thus the Court faces harsh critics of any decision in such cases, regardless of its ruling.

To Summarize:

♦ *The Supreme Court has struggled with the question of whether various kinds of governmental support for education extending to private, parochial school can be justified under a general "child benefit" theory or must be barred as a violation of the Establishment Clause.*

♦ *The Court has aroused deep and protracted controversy with its persistent efforts to proscribe officially sponsored religious exercises in the public schools. From its school prayer decisions of the early 1960s through its "moment of silence" ruling in 1985 to its 1992 and 2000 holdings regarding clerical prayer at commencement exercises and student-led prayer at high school football games, the Court has steadfastly applied a principle of strict separation in this area.*

♦ *The Court has also applied the principle of separation of church and state in thwarting state efforts dating from the 1920s to forbid the teaching of evolution and later attempts to promote the teaching of "creation science" in the public schools.*

♦ *The Court has continued to struggle with the issue of discrimination against religious belief expression and belief in the sphere of public education.*

Governmental Affirmations of Religious Belief

In a religious society such as that in the United States, it is inevitable (and, many would say, desirable) for there to be numerous public affirmations of belief. The Court's decision in *Abington v. Schempp* suggests, however, that government sponsorship of such affirmations may be unconstitutional. Nevertheless, the Supreme Court has been unwilling to hold government-sponsored displays or affirmations of belief to the same standard of **strict neutrality** that underlies the school prayer decisions. For example, in *McGowan v. Maryland* (1961), the Court upheld laws that prohibited certain businesses from operating on Sunday, despite the obvious religious underpinnings of such restrictions. In the Court's view, these **Sunday closing laws** had a secular purpose in that they represented the community's desire for a day of rest and relaxation, independent of any religious significance. The fact that this day of rest happened to be the day of worship for most Christians was merely incidental. Writing for the Court in *McGowan*, Chief Justice Earl Warren noted that:

> *[It] is common knowledge that the first day of the week has come to have special signif-icance as a rest day in this country. People of all religions and people with no religion regard Sunday as a time for family activity, for visiting friends and relatives, for late sleeping, for passive and active entertainments, for dining out, and the like.*

Perhaps the best example of the Court's unwillingness to extend the holding of *Abington v. Schempp* to its logical conclusion came in *Marsh v. Chambers* (1983). Here, the Court refused to invalidate Nebraska's policy of beginning legislative sessions with prayers offered by a Protestant chaplain retained at the taxpayers' expense. Writing for the Court, Chief Justice Burger made no pretense of applying the strict three-part test laid down in his own majority opinion in *Lemon v. Kurtzman*. Instead, Burger's opinion relied heavily on history and the need for accommodation of popular religious beliefs. In a caustic dissent, Justice Brennan observed that "if any group of law students were asked to apply the principles of *Lemon* to the question of legislative prayer, they would nearly unanimously find the practice to be unconstitutional." The decision in *Marsh v. Chambers* suggested to some observers that the Supreme Court was prepared to abandon the strict tripartite *Lemon* test for determining establishment of religion. To others, *Marsh* was a mere aberration, based on the pragmatic realization that the Court would inevitably be embarrassed if it were to attempt to strike down a practice that occurs in nearly every legislature in the United States, including the U.S. Congress. This case provides a good illustration of the practical limits of judicial power.

Religious Displays on Public Property

The decision in *Lynch v. Donnelly* (1984) suggests that *Marsh* was more than a mere aberration. In *Lynch*, the Court upheld a city-sponsored nativity scene in Pawtucket, Rhode Island. Chief Justice Burger's majority opinion barely mentioned the *Lemon* test. Again Burger relied on history and the fact that the crèche had become for many a "neu-tral harbinger of the holiday season," rather than a symbol of Christianity.

Five years later, in the Pennsylvania case of *County of Allegheny v. American Civil Liberties Union* (1989), the Court reexamined the constitutional question posed by tradi-tional holiday displays on public property. Here, the justices considered two separate dis-plays: a crèche prominently situated on the grand staircase inside the county courthouse and an arrangement featuring a Christmas tree and a Hanukkah menorah placed just outside the nearby city-county building. A sign bearing the mayor's name and the slogan "Salute to Liberty" was placed at the foot of the Christmas tree. Justice Blackmun, for a majority of the Court, maintained that the display of the crèche inside the courthouse, with the accompanying words "Gloria in Excelsis Deo," clearly conveyed a religious mes-sage. By authorizing the display, the county had, in Blackmun's view, indicated its endorsement of that message. Such endorsement, he concluded, was a violation of the Establishment Clause. By contrast, the Christmas tree and menorah display, in tandem with the mayor's message, was not in the Court's view "an endorsement of religious faith, but simply a recognition of cultural diversity." The overall display conveyed a pre-dominantly secular message and thus did not violate the Establishment Clause.

The Supreme Court's decisions in *Marsh* and *Lynch* indicate that the Burger Court retreated from the strict neutrality of the Warren Court in favor of an approach that might be labeled **accommodation** or **benevolent neutrality**. The *Allegheny County* decision suggested, however, that the Rehnquist Court was seeking a middle ground in this area. That certainly appeared to be the case in 2005, when the Court ruled in two cases involving the public display of the Ten Commandments. In *McCreary County v. ACLU*, the Court struck down such displays in two Kentucky courthouses. But in *Van Orden v. Perry*, decided the same day, the Court upheld a monument bearing the inscription of the Ten Commandments on the grounds of the Texas statehouse. Of course, the majorities in these two seemingly contradictory decisions were different. Writing for the Court in the *McCreary County* case, Justice David Souter was not persuaded by the argument that the public display of the Ten Commandments in a county courthouse has a useful secular purpose:

> *This is not to deny that the Commandments have had influence on civil or secular law; a major text of a majority religion is bound to be felt. The point is simply that the original text viewed in its entirety is an unmistakably religious statement dealing with religious obligations and with morality subject to religious sanction. When the government initiates an effort to place this statement alone in public view, a religious object is unmistakable.*

Justice Breyer, who concurred in both decisions, wrote in *Van Orden* that:

> *the Establishment Clause does not compel the government to purge from the public sphere all that in any way partakes of the religious. Such absolutism is not only inconsistent with our national traditions, but would also tend to promote the kind of social conflict the Establishment Clause seeks to avoid.*

There is perhaps no greater indicator of the difficulty in pinning down Establishment Clause jurisprudence than the Court's decisions in *McCreary County* and *Van Orden*. These were two separate cases concerned with public displays of the Ten Commandments, where the ruling was made on the same day, yet the Court ruled in seemingly contradictory directions.

To Summarize:

◆ *With respect to the issue of governmental affirmation of popular religious beliefs, the Court has sought a middle ground in which considerations of tradition and established practice are balanced against the principle of church–state separation.*

Tax Exemptions, Tax Credits, Vouchers, and Subsidies

Traditionally, church properties have been exempt from local property taxes, and church incomes have been exempt from federal and state income taxes. Such exemptions generally are not limited to churches but extend to various private, nonprofit organizations that can be classified as charitable institutions. The existence of **tax exemptions** for churches and religious schools raises questions under both the Establishment and Free Exercise Clauses of the First Amendment. On the one hand, it can be argued that a tax exemption is an indirect subsidy. Arguably, for government to exempt churches and church schools from paying taxes is to subsidize them in violation of the requirement of separation of church and state. On the other hand, one can argue that failure to exempt churches from taxation amounts to an infringement of the Free Exercise Clause, since, as Chief Justice John Marshall pointed out in *McCulloch v. Maryland* (1819), "the power to tax involves the power to destroy."

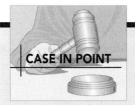

CASE IN POINT

Does a Cross in the Mojave National Preserve Violate the Establishment Clause?

Salazar v. Buono (2010)

In 1934, members of the Veterans of Foreign Wars (VFW) placed an eight-foot cross on a granite outcropping in the Mojave National Preserve. Their stated purpose was to honor Americans who died in World War I. In 2001, Frank Buono, a former National Park Service assistant superintendent at the preserve, filed a suit claiming that the display violated the Establishment Clause and seeking an injunction requiring that the cross be removed. The federal district court concluded that the display conveyed an impression of governmental endorsement of religion and granted the injunction. In 2004, while the decision was on appeal, Congress passed a law directing the Department of the Interior to transfer the land where the cross was placed to the VFW. Buono went back to court claiming that the congressional action was nothing more than an attempt to circumvent the court's order. The district court agreed and permanently enjoined the government from transferring the land. The Court of Appeals affirmed.

The case produced a fragmented decision by the Supreme Court. In a 5-to-4 vote, the Court reversed the Court of Appeals and remanded the case to the district court for reconsideration. Two justices, Thomas and Scalia, took the position that Buono lacked standing to bring the challenge to the land transfer law. Justice Kennedy, joined by Justice Alito and Chief Justice Roberts, asserted that the district court erred in

determining that the display violated the Establishment Clause. In Justice Kennedy's view, the display "evokes far more than religion. It evokes thousands of small crosses in foreign fields marking the graves of Americans who fell in battles, battles whose tragedies are compounded if the fallen are forgotten."

One of the four dissenters, Justice Breyer, did not address the constitutional question but argued that the Court had erred in accepting the case for review. The other three dissenters, Justices Stevens, Ginsburg and Sotomayor, concluded that the display was an "unambiguous endorsement of a sectarian message" and that the land transfer would only perpetuate a constitutional violation. Justice Stevens concluded by observing that "the Government's interest in honoring all those who have rendered heroic public service regardless of creed, as well as its constitutional responsibility to avoid endorsement of a particular religious view, should control wherever national memorials speak on behalf of our entire country."

Because the case was remanded for reconsideration, the Supreme Court's decision did not end the controversy over the cross in the Mojave Desert. A few days after the decision, the cross was cut down and taken away by vandals. Supporters of the display pledged to replace the cross with an even larger one. When the Mojave cross case is finally resolved, the larger issue of display of religious symbols on public lands will continue, probably for decades to come.

The Supreme Court considered the constitutionality of property tax exemptions for churches in the case of *Walz v. Tax Commission* (1970). Frederick Walz brought suit against the New York City Tax Commission, arguing that the commission's grant of property tax exemptions to churches (as allowed by state law) required him to subsidize those churches indirectly. Relying heavily on the long-standing practice of religious tax exemptions and the Court's traditional deference to legislative bodies with regard to the taxing power, the Court found no constitutional violation. Writing for a majority of eight, Chief Justice Burger noted that "[few concepts are more deeply embedded in the fabric of our national life, beginning with pre-Revolutionary colonial times, than for the government to exercise … this kind of benevolent neutrality toward churches and religious exercise generally so long as none was favored over others and none suffered interference."

Dissenting vigorously, Justice Douglas argued for strict government neutrality toward religion as distinct from the chief justice's "benevolent neutrality" approach:

If believers are entitled to public financial support, so are nonbelievers. A believer and nonbeliever under the present law are treated differently because of the articles of their faith. Believers are doubtless comforted that the cause of religion is being fostered by this legislation. Yet one of the mandates of the First Amendment is to promote a viable, pluralistic society and to keep government neutral, not only between sects, but also between believers and nonbelievers.

It is interesting to compare Justice Douglas's dissent in *Walz* with his majority opinion in *Zorach v. Clauson*. In 1952, Douglas had written, apparently in earnest, about the importance of governmental accommodation of religion. In concurring opinions in the school prayer decisions of 1962 and 1963, Douglas indicated that he was reconsidering his position on the Establishment Clause generally. By 1970, his stance had shifted from accommodation to strict neutrality. Justice Douglas's forceful dissent in *Walz* to the contrary notwithstanding, it is unlikely that the Supreme Court would go so far as to invalidate religious tax exemptions. There is simply too much public support for these long-standing policies.

To take advantage of tax exemptions for religious property, a small minority of unscrupulous individuals have established "churches" in their homes after obtaining inexpensive "doctor of divinity" degrees through the mail. For example, in the late 1970s in one small town in New York, nearly 85 percent of the residents became "ministers" and claimed tax-exempt status for their homes. This subterfuge was finally ended through state legislation that was upheld by a later court decision. The U.S. Supreme Court dismissed the appeal, thus allowing the state court decision to stand (*Hardenbaugh v. New York* [1981]). One wonders, given the ease with which online ministers licenses are earned today, what the status of this area of the law would be today had the Court ruled differently in 1981?

One of the most controversial Supreme Court decisions of the early 1980s dealt with the question of whether tax-exempt status could be withdrawn from religious schools that practice race discrimination. In *Bob Jones University v. United States* (1983), the Court held that the Internal Revenue Service (IRS) could indeed deny federal income tax exemptions to such institutions. Prior to 1975, Bob Jones University, a fundamentalist Christian college in Greenville, South Carolina, had refused to admit African-Americans. After 1975, African-Americans were admitted, but interracial dating and marriage were strictly prohibited. The IRS formally revoked the school's long-standing tax exemption in 1976. Then, in 1982, the Reagan administration announced that the IRS was restoring tax-exempt status to all segregated private schools, claiming that the IRS lacked the authority to remove tax exemptions without specific authorizing legislation from Congress. The Court's 8-to-1 decision in *Bob Jones* repudiated the Reagan administration's view that the IRS lacked authority to revoke the tax-exempt status of religious schools that practice racial discrimination.

With regard to the First Amendment issue, the Court held that:

[t]he governmental interest at stake here is compelling.... The government has a fundamental, overriding interest in eradicating racial discrimination in education.... That governmental interest substantially outweighs whatever burden denial of tax benefits places on petitioners' exercise of their religious beliefs.

The Court's decision in *Bob Jones* implies that tax exemptions for religious enterprises are not a matter of constitutional entitlement—they are granted through governmental benevolence and can be withdrawn for reasons of public policy.

Tuition Tax Credits

A number of States and communities have considered the idea of providing tax credits or **vouchers** to parents of children in private and parochial schools. Indeed, in 1982, President Reagan proposed **tuition tax credits** of $500 per child for parents whose children attend private and parochial schools. Although the proposal did not obtain congressional approval, serious questions were raised about its constitutionality. In *Committee for Public Education v. Nyquist* (1973), the Supreme Court had struck down a state tax deduction for parents of children in parochial schools. However in the 1980s, the Court began moving away from the *Nyquist* decision, at least insofar as it dealt with tax benefits. In 1983, in *Mueller v. Allen*, the Court upheld a Minnesota law that allowed parents of children in private and parochial schools to deduct as much as $700 of school expenses from their incomes subject to state income tax. More recently, in *Zelman v. Simmons-Harris* (2002), the Court upheld a voucher program established by the state of Ohio for the Cleveland school district. Chief Justice Rehnquist's opinion for the sharply divided Court concluded that the Cleveland voucher program at issue was "entirely neutral with respect to religion." He regarded the program as one of "true private choice." In keeping with an unbroken line of decisions rejecting challenges to similar programs," he continued, "we hold that the program does not offend the Establishment Clause." In a lengthy dissenting opinion, Justice Souter, joined by Justices Stevens, Ginsburg, and Breyer, condemned the majority opinion, concluding that it was a "dramatic departure from basic Establishment Clause principle," first enunciated in the *Everson* decision.

> **To Summarize:**
> ◆ *While state and local governments are not constitutionally required to provide tax exemptions for religious institutions, such exemptions have been upheld so long as they extend to all nonprofit charitable entities.*
> ◆ *The Supreme Court has permitted the Internal Revenue Service to revoke tax-exempt status from private schools that engage in racial discrimination in clear violation of fundamental public policy commitments.*
> ◆ *In spite of the Court's diverse opinions in the area of government aid to parochial school, it now appears that the Court is willing to approve tuition tax credits to parents of children attending such schools.*

Conclusion

Although the United States is a decidedly religious nation, much more so than other advanced democracies, it is also committed to secular government and religious freedom. These competing values create tensions that can never be fully resolved. Inevitably, constitutional law on the subject of religious liberty remains unsettled, reflecting the evolving views of a maturing society. With respect to the free exercise of religion, the modern Supreme Court has protected religious minorities from governmental intrusions and restrictions aimed specifically at them, but has not been willing to extend constitutional protections to unconventional religious practices that violate generally applicable rules of conduct. With respect to the Establishment Clause, the Court continues to accord some legitimacy to governmental efforts to accommodate traditional religious practices. In the field of public education, the Court continues to insist on a strict separation of church and state, but has shown its willingness to uphold policies that facilitate the existence of private religious schools.

Key Terms

Religion Clauses of the First
  Amendment
school prayer
Free Exercise Clause
Establishment Clause
conscientious objector
religious speech
expressive religious conduct
public forum
time, place, and manner regulations
unconventional religious practices
fundamental right

compelling government interest
Religious Freedom Restoration Act
  (RFRA)
parens patriae
right to refuse medical treatment
separation of church and state
Lemon test
child benefit theory
released-time programs
equal access
school prayer decisions
moment of silence

Scopes trial
creation science
secular humanism
strict neutrality
Sunday closing laws
accommodation
benevolent neutrality
tax exemptions
vouchers
tuition tax credits

For Further Reading

Bellah, Robert, Richard Madsen, William Sullivan, Ann Swidler, and Steven M. Tipton. *The Good Society.* New York: Knopf, 1991.

Carter, Lief. *An Introduction to Constitutional Interpretation: Cases in Law and Religion.* New York: Longman, 1991.

Carter, Stephen. *The Culture of Disbelief.* New York: Anchor Books, 1994.

Curry, Thomas J. *The First Freedoms.* New York: Oxford University Press, 1986.

Eisgruber, Christopher L., and Lawrence G. Sager. *Religious Freedom and the Constitution.* Cambridge, Mass.: Harvard University Press, 2007.

Howe, Mark DeWolfe. *The Garden and the Wilderness: Religion and Government in American Constitutional History.* Chicago, Ill.: University of Chicago Press, 1985.

Irons, Peter. *The Courage of Their Convictions: Sixteen Americans Who Fought Their Way to the Supreme Court.* New York: Penguin Books, 1990. See, in particular, Chapters 1, 7, 9, and 15.

Kauper, Paul. *Religion and the Constitution.* Baton Rouge: Louisiana State University Press, 1964.

Levy, Leonard. *The Establishment Clause: Religion and the First Amendment.* New York: Macmillan, 1986.

Manwaring, David. *Render unto Caesar: The Flag Salute Controversy.* Chicago, Ill.: University of Chicago Press, 1962.

Miller, William Lee. *The First Liberty: Religion and the American Republic.* Washington, D.C.: Georgetown University Press, 2003.

Oaks, Dallin (ed.). *The Wall between Church and State.* Chicago, Ill.: University of Chicago Press, 1963.

Pfeffer, Leo. *God, Caesar and the Constitution.* Boston, Mass.: Beacon Press, 1975.

Sorauf, Frank. *The Wall of Separation: The Constitutional Politics of Church and State.* Princeton, N.J.: Princeton University Press, 1976.

Stokes, Anson, and Leo Pfeffer. *Church and State in the United States.* New York: Harper and Row, 1965.

Tussman, Joseph. *The Supreme Court on Church and State.* New York: Oxford University Press, 1962.

WEST VIRGINIA STATE BOARD OF EDUCATION v. BARNETTE
319 U.S. 624; 63 S.Ct. 1178; 87 L.Ed. 1628 (1943)
Vote: 6-3

In Minersville School District v. Gobitis *(1940), the Supreme Court, in an 8-to-1 decision, upheld a local school board directive in Minersville, Pennsylvania, requiring public school students and teachers to participate in a flag salute ceremony conducted as a regular* *part of the daily classroom schedule. This requirement had been challenged by Walter Gobitis, a member of the Jehovah's Witnesses sect, whose children, Lillian and William (ages 12 and 10), were expelled from school for refusing to salute the flag. In upholding the flag salute requirement, the Court rejected Gobitis's contention that it violated First Amendment principles of religious liberty as applied to the states through the Due Process Clause of the Fourteenth Amendment.*

Three years later, in a dramatic and highly publicized reversal of its position, the Supreme Court, by a 6-to-3 margin, overruled the Gobitis case by striking down a virtually identical flag salute requirement imposed by the West Virginia Board of Education. The board was acting under authority of a statute passed by the West Virginia legislature in the immediate aftermath of the Gobitis decision. This law required all schools in the state to offer classes in civics, history, and the federal and state constitutions "for the purpose of teaching, fostering, and perpetuating the ideals, principles, and spirit of Americanism, and increasing the knowledge of the organization and machinery of the Government." Walter Barnette and two other Jehovah's Witnesses, all of whom had children in the public schools, filed suit to enjoin the compulsory flag salute on grounds that it violated a constitutionally protected religious precept contained in the Old Testament (Exodus 20:4–5) forbidding the worship of "any graven image." Under their reading of the Scriptures, the flag salute constituted such forbidden worship.

Because this decision represents such a swift and decisive overruling of constitutional precedent, it is interesting to compare the alignments of the justices in Gobitis and Barnette. Justice Frankfurter wrote the majority opinion in the Gobitis case, with only Justice Stone dissenting. Justice Jackson, who along with Justice Rutledge joined the Court after that decision was announced, wrote the majority opinion in Barnette. Justices Black, Douglas, and Murphy, all of whom had supported Frankfurter's original majority position, switched sides and supported the majority opinion in Barnette. Justices Frankfurter, Reed, and Roberts dissented in the latter case.

Mr. Justice Jackson delivered the opinion of the Court.

… National unity as an end which officials may foster by persuasion and example is not in question. The problem is whether under our Constitution compulsion as here employed is a permissible means for its achievement.

Struggles to coerce uniformity of sentiment in support of some end thought essential to their time and country have been waged by many good as well as by evil men. Nationalism is a relatively recent phenomenon but at other times and places the ends have been racial or territorial security, support of a dynasty or regime, and particular plans for saving souls. As first and moderate methods to attain unity have failed, those bent on its accomplishment must resort to an ever increasing severity. As governmental pressure toward unity becomes greater, so strife becomes more bitter as to whose unity it shall be. Probably no deeper division of our people could proceed from any provocation than from finding it necessary to choose what doctrine and whose program public educational officials shall compel youth to unite in embracing. Ultimate futility of such attempts to compel coherence is the lesson of every such effort from the Roman drive to stamp out Christianity as a disturber of its pagan unity, the Inquisition, as a means to religious and dynastic unity, the Siberian exiles as a means to Russian unity, down to the fast failing efforts of our present totalitarian enemies. Those who begin coercive elimination of dissent soon find themselves exterminating dissenters. Compulsory unification of opinion achieves only the unanimity of the graveyard.

It seems trite but necessary to say that the First Amendment to our Constitution was designed to avoid these ends by avoiding these beginnings. There is no mysticism in the American concept of the State or of the nature or origin of its authority. We set up government by consent of the governed, and the Bill of Rights denies those in power any legal opportunity to coerce that consent. Authority here is to be controlled by public opinion, not public opinion by authority.

The case is made difficult not because the principles of its decision are obscure but because the flag involved is our own. Nevertheless, we apply the limitations of the Constitution with no fear that freedom to be intellectually and spiritually diverse or even contrary will disintegrate the social organization. To believe that patriotism will not flourish if patriotic ceremonies are voluntary and spontaneous instead of a compulsory routine is to make an unflattering estimate of the appeal of our institutions to free minds. We can have intellectual individualism and the rich cultural diversities that we owe to exceptional minds only at the price of occasional eccentricity and abnormal attitudes. When they are so harmless to others or to the State as those we deal with here, the price is not too great. But freedom to differ is not limited to things that do not matter much. That would be a mere shadow of freedom. The test of its substance is the right to differ as to things that touch the heart of the existing order.

If there is any fixed star in our constitutional constellation, it is that no official, high or petty, can

(Continued)

prescribe what shall be orthodox in politics, nationalism, religion, or other matters of opinion or force citizens to confess by word or act their faith therein. If there are any circumstances which permit an exception, they do not now occur to us.

We think the action of the local authorities in compelling the flag salute and pledge transcends constitutional limitations on their power and invades the sphere of intellect and spirit which it is the purpose of the First Amendment to our Constitution to reserve from all official control.

The decision of this Court in *Minersville School Dist. v. Gobitis* and the holdings of those few *per curiam* decisions which preceded and foreshadowed it are overruled, and the judgment enjoining enforcement of the West Virginia Regulation is affirmed.

Mr. Justice Roberts and *Mr. Justice Reed* adhere to the views expressed by the Court in *Minersville School Dist. v. Gobitis* … and are of the opinion that the judgment below should be reversed.

Mr. Justice Black and *Mr. Justice Douglas*, concurring.

We are substantially in agreement with the opinion just read, but since we originally joined with the Court in the *Gobitis* case, it is appropriate that we make a brief statement of reasons for our change of view.

Reluctance to make the Federal Constitution a rigid bar against state regulation of conduct thought inimical to the public welfare was the controlling influence which moved us to consent to the *Gobitis* decision. Long reflection convinced us that although the principle is sound, its application in the particular case was wrong…. We believe that the statute before us fails to accord full scope to the freedom of religion secured to the appellees by the First and Fourteenth Amendments….

No well ordered society can leave to the individuals an absolute right to make final decisions, unassailable by the State, as to everything they will or will not do. The First Amendment does not go so far. Religious faiths, honestly held, do not free individuals from responsibility to conduct themselves obediently to laws which are either imperatively necessary to protect society as a whole from grave and pressingly imminent dangers or which, without any general prohibition, merely regulate time, place or manner of religious activity. Decisions as to the constitutionality of particular laws which strike at the substance of religious tenets and practices must be made by this Court. The duty is a solemn one, and in meeting it we cannot say

that a failure, because of religious scruples, to assume a particular physical position and to repeat the words of a patriotic formula creates a grave danger to the nation. Such a statutory exaction is a form of test oath, and the test oath has always been abhorrent in the United States.

Words uttered under coercion are proof of loyalty to nothing but self-interest. Love of country must spring from willing hearts and free minds, inspired by a fair administration of wise laws enacted by the people's elected representatives within the bounds of express constitutional prohibitions. These laws must, to be consistent with the First Amendment, permit the widest toleration of conflicting viewpoints consistent with a society of free men.

Neither our domestic tranquility in peace nor our martial effort in war depend on compelling little children to participate in a ceremony which ends in nothing for them but a fear of spiritual condemnation. If, as we think, their fears are groundless, time and reason are the proper antidotes for their errors. The ceremonial, when enforced against conscientious objectors, more likely to defeat than to serve its high purpose, is a handy implement for disguised religious persecution. As such, it is inconsistent with our Constitution's plan and purpose.

Mr. Justice Murphy, concurring….

Mr. Justice Frankfurter, dissenting.

One who belongs to the most vilified and persecuted minority in history is not likely to be insensible to the freedoms guaranteed by our Constitution. Were my purely personal attitude relevant I should wholeheartedly associate myself with the general libertarian views in the Court's opinion, representing as they do the thought and action of a lifetime. But as judges we are neither Jew nor Gentile, neither Catholic nor agnostic. We owe equal attachment to the Constitution and are equally bound by our judicial obligations whether we derive our citizenship from the earliest or the latest immigrants to these shores. As a member of this Court I am not justified in writing my private notions of policy into the Constitution, no matter how deeply I may cherish them or how mischievous I may deem their disregard. The duty of a judge who must decide which of two claims before the Court shall prevail, that of a State to enact and enforce laws within its general competence or that of an individual to refuse obedience because of the demands of his conscience, is not that of the ordinary person. It can never be emphasized too much that one's own opinion about the wisdom or evil of a law should be excluded altogether when one is doing one's duty on the bench. The only opinion of our own even looking in that direction that is material is our opinion whether legislators could in reason have enacted such a law. In the light of all the circumstances, including the history of this question in this Court, it would require more daring than I possess to deny that reasonable legislators could have taken the action which is before us for review. Most unwillingly, therefore, I must differ from my brethren with regard to legislation like this. I cannot bring my mind to believe that the "liberty" secured by the Due Process Clause gives this Court authority to deny to the State of West Virginia the attainment of that which we all recognize as a legitimate legislative end, namely, the promotion of good citizenship, by employment of the means here chosen....

Of course patriotism cannot be enforced by the flag salute. But neither can the liberal spirit be enforced by judicial invalidation of illiberal legislation. Of constant preoccupation with the constitutionality of legislation rather than with its wisdom tends to preoccupation of the American mind with a false value. The tendency of focusing attention on constitutionality is to make constitutionality synonymous with wisdom, to regard a law as all right if it is constitutional. Such an attitude is a great enemy of liberalism. Particularly in legislation affecting freedom of thought and freedom of speech much which should offend a free-spirited society is constitutional. Reliance for the most precious interests of civilization, therefore, must be found outside of their vindication in courts of law. Only a persistent positive translation of the faith of a free society into the convictions and habits and actions of a community is the ultimate reliance against unabated temptations to fetter the human spirit.

WISCONSIN v. YODER
406 U.S. 205; 92 S.Ct. 1526; 32 L.Ed.2d. 15 (1972)
Vote: 6-1

Here, the Court considers whether members of the Old Order Amish have a constitutional right to refuse to comply with a state's compulsory high school attendance law.

Mr. Chief Justice Burger delivered the opinion of the Court.

... Respondents Jonas Yoder and Wallace Miller are members of the Old Order Amish religion, and respondent Adin Yutzy is a member of the Conservative Amish Mennonite Church. They and their families are residents of Green County, Wisconsin. Wisconsin's compulsory school-attendance law required them to cause their children to attend public or private school until ... age 16 but the respondents declined to send their children, ages 14 and 15, to public school after they completed the eighth grade. The children were not enrolled in any private school, or within any recognized exception to the compulsory-attendance law, and they are conceded to be subject to the Wisconsin statute.

On complaint of the school district administrator for the public schools, respondents were charged,

tried, and convicted of violating the compulsory-attendance law in Green County Court and were fined the sum of $5 each. Respondents defended on the ground that the application of the compulsory-attendance law violated their rights under the First and Fourteenth Amendments. The trial testimony showed that respondents believed, in accordance with the tenets of Old Order Amish communities generally, that their children's attendance at high school, public or private, was contrary to the Amish religion and way of life. They believed that by sending their children to high school, they would not only expose themselves to the danger of the censure of the church community, but, as found by the county court, also endanger their own salvation and that of their children. The State stipulated that respondents' religious beliefs were sincere.

In support of their position, respondents presented as expert witnesses scholars on religion and education whose testimony is uncontradicted. They expressed their opinions on the relationship of the Amish belief concerning school attendance to the more general tenets of their religion, and described the impact that

(Continued)

compulsory high school attendance could have on the continued survival of Amish communities as they exist in the United States today. The history of the Amish sect was given in some detail, beginning with the Swiss Anabaptists of the 16th century who rejected institutionalized churches and sought to return to the early, simple, Christian life de-emphasizing material success, rejecting the competitive spirit, and seeking to insulate themselves from the modern world. As a result of their common heritage, Old Order Amish communities today are characterized by a fundamental belief that salvation requires life in a church community separate and apart from the world and worldly influence. This concept of life aloof from the world and its values is central to their faith....

Amish objection to formal education beyond the eighth grade is firmly grounded in these central religious concepts. They object to the high school, and higher education generally, because the values they teach are in marked variance with Amish values and the Amish way of life; they view secondary school education as an impermissible exposure of their children to a "worldly" influence in conflict with their beliefs. The high school tends to emphasize intellectual and scientific accomplishments, self-distinction, competitiveness, worldly success, and social life with other students. Amish society emphasizes informal learning-through-doing; a life of "goodness," rather than a life of intellect; wisdom, rather than technical knowledge, community welfare, rather than competition; and separation from, rather than integration with, contemporary worldly society....

The Amish do not object to elementary education through the first eight grades as a general proposition because they agree that their children must have basic skills in the "three R's" in order to read the Bible, to be good farmers and citizens, and to be able to deal with non-Amish people when necessary in the course of daily affairs. They view such a basic education as acceptable because it does not significantly expose their children to worldly values or interfere with their development in the Amish community during the crucial adolescent period. While Amish accept compulsory elementary education generally, wherever possible they have established their own elementary schools in many respects like the small local schools of the past. In the Amish belief higher learning tends to develop values they reject as influences that alienate man from God....

Although the trial court in its careful findings determined that the Wisconsin compulsory school-attendance law "does interfere with the freedom of the Defendants to act in accordance with their sincere religious belief it also concluded that the requirement of high school attendance until age 16 was a "reasonable and constitutional" exercise of governmental power, and therefore denied the motion to dismiss the charges. The Wisconsin Circuit Court affirmed the convictions. The Wisconsin Supreme Court, however, sustained respondents' claim under the Free Exercise Clause of the First Amendment and reversed the convictions. A majority of the court was of the opinion that the State had failed to make an adequate showing that its interest in "establishing and maintaining an educational system overrides the defendants' right to the free exercise of their religion." ...

There is no doubt as to the power of a State, having a high responsibility for education of its citizens, to impose reasonable regulations for the control and duration of basic education. See, e.g., *Pierce v. Society of Sisters* ... (1925). Providing public schools ranks at the very apex of the function of a State. Yet even this paramount responsibility was, in *Pierce,* made to yield to the right of parents to provide an equivalent education in a privately operated system. There the Court held that Oregon's statute compelling attendance in a public school from age eight to age 16 unreasonably interfered with the interest of parents in directing the rearing of their offspring, including their education in church-operated schools. As that case suggests, the values of parental direction of the religious upbringing and education of their children in their early and formative years have a high place in our society.... Thus, a State's interest in universal education, however highly we rank it, is not totally free from a balancing process when it impinges on fundamental rights and interests, such as those specifically protected by the Free Exercise Clause of the First Amendment, and the traditional interest of parents with respect to the religious upbringing of their children so long as they, in the words of *Pierce,* "prepare [them] for additional obligations." ...

It follows that in order for Wisconsin to compel school attendance beyond the eighth grade against a claim that such attendance interferes with the practice of a legitimate religious belief, it must appear either that the State does not deny the free exercise of religious belief by its requirement, or that there is a state interest of sufficient magnitude to override the interest claiming protection under the Free Exercise Clause....

... A way of life, however virtuous and admirable, may not be interposed as a barrier to reasonable state regulation of education if it is based on purely secular considerations; to have the protection of the Religion

Clauses, the claims must be rooted in religious belief. Although a determination of what is a "religious" belief or practice entitled to constitutional protection may present a most delicate question, the very concept of ordered liberty precludes allowing every person to make his own standards on matters of conduct in which society as a whole has important interests....

... [T]he record in this case abundantly supports the claim that the traditional way of life of the Amish is not merely a matter of personal preference, but one of deep religious conviction, shared by an organized group, and intimately related to daily living....

The impact of the compulsory-attendance law on respondents' practice of the Amish religion is not only severe, but inescapable, for the Wisconsin law affirmatively compels them, under threat of criminal sanction, to perform acts undeniably at odds with fundamental tenets of their religious beliefs.... Nor is the impact of the compulsory-attendance law confined to grave interference with important Amish religious tenets from a subjective point of view. It carries with it precisely the kind of objective danger to the free exercise of religion that the First Amendment was designed to prevent. As the record shows, compulsory school attendance to age 16 for Amish children carries with it a very real threat of undermining the Amish community and religious practice as they exist today; they must either abandon belief and be assimilated into society at large, or be forced to migrate to some other and more tolerant region.

In sum, the unchallenged testimony of acknowledged experts in education and religious history, almost 300 years of consistent practice, and strong evidence of a sustained faith pervading and regulating respondents' entire mode of life support the claim that enforcement of the State's requirement of compulsory formal education after the eighth grade would gravely endanger if not destroy the free exercise of respondents' religious beliefs....

Wisconsin concedes that under the Religion Clauses religious beliefs are absolutely free from the State's control, but it argues that "actions," even though religiously grounded, are outside the protection of the First Amendment. But our decisions have rejected the idea that religiously grounded conduct is always outside the protection of the Free Exercise Clause. It is true that activities of individuals, even when religiously based, are often subject to regulation by the States in the exercise of their undoubted power to promote the health, safety, and general welfare, or the Federal government in the exercise of its delegated powers.... But to agree that religiously grounded conduct must often be subject to the broad police power of the State is not to deny that there are areas of conduct protected by the Free Exercise Clause of the First Amendment and thus beyond the power of the State to control, even under regulations of general applicability.... This case, therefore, does not become easier because respondents were convicted for their "actions" in refusing to send their children to the public high school; in this context belief and action cannot be neatly confined in logic-tight compartments....

Nor can this case be disposed of on the grounds that Wisconsin's requirement for school attendance to age 16 applies uniformly to all citizens of the State and does not, on its face, discriminate against religions or a particular religion, or that it is motivated by legitimate secular concerns. A regulation neutral on its face may, in its application, nonetheless offend the constitutional requirement for governmental neutrality if it unduly burdens the free exercise of religion.... The Court must not ignore the danger that an exception from a general obligation of citizenship on religious grounds may run afoul of the Establishment Clause, but that danger cannot be allowed to prevent any exception no matter how vital it may be to the protection of values promoted by the right of free exercise....

The State advances two primary arguments in support of its system of compulsory education. It notes, as Thomas Jefferson pointed out early in our history, that some degree of education is necessary to prepare citizens to participate effectively and intelligently in our open political system if we are to preserve freedom and independence. Further, education prepares individuals to be self-reliant and self-sufficient participants in society. We accept these propositions.

However, the evidence adduced by the Amish in this case is persuasively to the effect that an additional one or two years of formal high school for Amish children in place of their long-established program of informal vocational education would do little to serve those interests. Respondents' experts testified at trial, without challenge, that the value of all education must be assessed in terms of its capacity to prepare the child for life. It is one thing to say that compulsory education for a year or two beyond the eighth grade may be necessary when its goal is the preparation of the child for life in modern society as the majority live, but is quite another if the goal of education be viewed as the preparation of the child for life in the separated

(Continued)

agrarian community that is the keystone of the Amish faith....

The State attacks respondents' position as one fostering "ignorance" from which the child must be protected by the State. No one can question the State's duty to protect children from ignorance but this argument does not square with the facts disclosed in the record. Whatever their idiosyncrasies as seen by the majority, this record strongly shows that the Amish community has been a highly successful social unit within our society, even if apart from the conventional "mainstream." Its members are productive and very law-abiding members of society; they reject public welfare in any of its usually modern forms. The Congress itself recognized their self-sufficiency by authorizing exemption of such groups as the Amish from the obligation to pay social security taxes.

It is neither fair nor correct to suggest that the Amish are opposed to education beyond the eighth grade level. What this record shows is that they are opposed to conventional formal education of the type provided by a certified high school because it comes at the child's crucial adolescent period of religious development....

... There can be no assumption that today's majority is "right" and the Amish and others like them are "wrong." A way of life that is odd or even erratic but interferes with no rights or interests of others is not to be condemned because it is different.

The State, however, supports its interest in providing an additional one or two years of compulsory high school education to Amish children because of the possibility that some such children will choose to leave the Amish community, and that if this occurs they will be ill-equipped for life. The State argues that if Amish children leave their church they should not be in the position of making their way in the world without the education available in the one or two additional years the State requires. However, on this record, that argument is highly speculative. There is no specific evidence of the loss of Amish adherents by attrition, nor is there any showing that upon leaving the Amish community Amish children, with their practical agricultural training and habits of industry and self-reliance, would become burdens on society because of educational shortcomings....

Insofar as the State's claim rests on the view that a brief additional period of formal education is imperative to enable the Amish to participate effectively and intelligently in our democratic process, it must fall. The Amish alternative to formal secondary school education has enabled them to function effectively in their day-to-day life under self-imposed limitations on relations with the world, and to survive and prosper in contemporary society as a separate, sharply identifiable and highly self-sufficient community for more than 200 years in this country. In itself this is strong evidence that they are capable of fulfilling the social and political responsibilities of citizenship without compelled attendance beyond the eighth grade at the price of jeopardizing their free exercise of religious belief....

Finally, the State ... argues that a decision exempting Amish children from the State's requirement fails to recognize the substantive right of the Amish child to a secondary education, and fails to give due regard to the power of the State as *parens patriae* to extend the benefit of secondary education to children regardless of the wishes of their parents....

The State's argument proceeds without reliance on any actual conflict between the wishes of parents and children. It appears to rest on the potential that exemption of Amish parents from the requirements of the compulsory education law might allow some parents to act contrary to the best interests of their children by foreclosing their opportunity to make an intelligent choice between the Amish way of life and that of the outside world. The same argument could, of course, be made with respect to all church schools short of college. There is nothing in the record or in the ordinary course of human experience to suggest that non-Amish parents generally consult with children of ages 14-16 if they are placed in a church school of the parents' faith.

Indeed it seems clear that if the State is empowered, as *parens patriae*, to "save" a child from himself or his Amish parents by requiring an additional two years of compulsory formal high school education, the State will in large measure influence, if not determine, the religious future of the child. [T]his case involves the fundamental interest of parents, as contrasted with that of the State, to guide the religious future and education of their children....

For the reasons stated we hold, with the Supreme Court of Wisconsin, that the First and Fourteenth Amendments prevent the State from compelling respondents to cause their children to attend formal high school to age 16....

Nothing we hold is intended to undermine the general applicability of the State's compulsory school-attendance statutes or to limit the power of the State to promulgate reasonable standards that, while not impairing the free exercise of religion, provide for continuing agricultural vocational education under parental and church guidance by the Old Order Amish or others similarly situated. The States have had a long history of amicable and effective relationships with church-sponsored schools, and there is no basis for assuming that, in this related context, reasonable standards cannot be established concerning the content of the continuing vocational education of Amish children under parental guidance, provided always that state regulations are not inconsistent with what we have said in this opinion.

Affirmed.

Mr. Justice Powell and *Mr. Justice Rehnquist* took no part in the consideration or decision of this case.

Mr. Justice Stewart, with whom *Mr. Justice Brennan* joins, concurring....

Mr. Justice Douglas, dissenting in part.

I agree with the Court that the religious scruples of the Amish are opposed to the education of their children beyond the grade schools, yet I disagree with the Court's conclusion that the matter is within the dispensation of parents alone. The Court's analysis assumes that the only interests at stake in the case are those of the Amish parents on the one hand, and those of the State on the other. The difficulty with this approach is that, despite the Court's claim, the parents are seeking to vindicate not only their own free exercise claims, but also those of their high-school-age children....

... Our opinions are full of talk about the power of the parents over the child's education.... And we have in the past analyzed similar conflicts between parent and State with little regard for the views of the child.... Recent cases, however, have clearly held that the children themselves have constitutionally protectible interests....

On this important and vital matter of education, I think the children should be entitled to be heard. While the parents, absent dissent, normally speak for the entire family, the education of the child is a matter on which the child will often have decided views. He may want to be a pianist or an astronaut or an oceanographer. To do so he will have to break from the Amish tradition.

It is the future of the student, not the future of the parents, that is imperiled by today's decision. If a parent keeps his child out of school beyond the grade school, then the child will be forever barred from entry into the new and amazing world of diversity that we have today. The child may decide that that is the preferred course, or he may rebel. It is the student's judgment, not his parents', that is essential if we are to give full meaning to what we have said about the Bill of Rights and of the right of students to be masters of their own destiny. If he is harnessed to the Amish way of life by those in authority over him and if his education is truncated, his entire life may be stunted and deformed. The child, therefore, should be given an opportunity to be heard before the State gives the exemption which we honor today.

The views of the two children in question were not canvassed by the Wisconsin courts. The matter should be explicitly reserved so that new hearings can be held on remand of the case....

EMPLOYMENT DIVISION v. SMITH
494 U.S. 872; 110 S.Ct. 1595; 108 L.Ed.2d. 876 (1990)
Vote: 6-3

Alfred Smith and Galen Black, both members of the Native American Church, were fired from their jobs as drug rehabilitation counselors on the grounds that they had used peyote during a religious ritual. They were subsequently denied unemployment benefits because they had been discharged for misconduct. The question before the U.S. Supreme Court is whether the refusal of the state to grant unemployment benefits in this situation constitutes an abridgement of rights under the Free Exercise Clause of the First Amendment.

Justice Scalia delivered the opinion of the Court.

... Respondents' claim for relief rests on our decisions in *Sherbert v. Venter* ... (1963); *Thomas v. Review Board* ... (1981); and *Hobbie v. Unemployment Appeals*

(Continued)

Comm'n of Florida ... (1987), in which we held that a State could not condition the availability of unemployment insurance on an individual's willingness to forego conduct required by his religion.... [H]owever, the conduct at issue in those cases was not prohibited by law.... [T]hat distinction [is] critical, for "if Oregon does prohibit the religious use of peyote, and if that prohibition is consistent with the Federal Constitution, there is no federal right to engage in that conduct in Oregon," and "the State is free to withhold unemployment compensation from respondents for engaging in work-related misconduct, despite its religious motivation." ... Now that the Oregon Supreme Court has confirmed that Oregon does prohibit the religious use of peyote, we proceed to consider whether that prohibition is permissible under the Free Exercise Clause....

The free exercise of religion means, first and foremost, the right to believe and profess whatever religious doctrine one desires. Thus, the First Amendment obviously excludes all "governmental regulation of religious beliefs as such." ...

But the "exercise of religion" often involves not only belief and profession but the performance of (or abstention from) physical acts: assembling with others for a worship service, participating in sacramental use of bread and wine, proselytizing, abstaining from certain foods or certain modes of transportation. It would be true, we think (though no case of ours has involved the point), that a state would be "prohibiting the free exercise [of religion]" ... if it sought to ban such acts or abstentions only when they are engaged in for religious reasons, or only because of the religious belief that they display. It would doubtless be unconstitutional, for example, to ban the casting of "statues that are to be used for worship purposes," ... or to prohibit bowing down before a golden calf.

Respondents in the present case, however, seek to carry the meaning of "prohibiting the free exercise [of religion]" one large step further. They contend that their religious motivation for using peyote places them beyond the reach of a criminal law that is not specifically directed at their religious practice, and that is concededly constitutional as applied to those who use the drug for other reasons. They assert, in other words, that "prohibiting the free exercise [of religion]" includes requiring any individual to observe a generally applicable law that requires (or forbids) the performance of an act that his religious belief forbids (or requires). As a textual matter, we do not think the words must be given that meaning. It is no more necessary to regard the collection of a general tax, for example, as "prohibiting the free exercise [of religion]" by those citizens who believe support of organized government to be sinful, than it is to regard the same tax as "abridging the freedom ... of the press" of those publishing companies that must pay the tax as a condition of staying in business. It is a permissible reading of the text, in the one case as in the other, to say that if prohibiting the exercise of religion (or burdening the activity of printing) is not the object of the tax but merely the incidental effect of a generally applicable and otherwise valid provision, the First Amendment has not been offended....

Our decisions reveal that the latter reading is the correct one. We have never held that an individual's religious beliefs excuse him from compliance with an otherwise valid law prohibiting conduct that the State is free to regulate....

The only decisions in which we have held that the First Amendment bars application of a neutral, generally applicable law to religiously motivated action have involved not the Free Exercise Clause alone, but the Free Exercise Clause in conjunction with other constitutional protections, such as freedom of speech and of the press....

The present case does not present such a hybrid situation, but a free exercise claim unconnected with any communicative activity or parental right. Respondents urge us to hold, quite simply, that when otherwise prohibitable conduct is accompanied by religious convictions, not only the convictions but the conduct itself must be free from governmental regulation....

Respondents argue that even though exemption from generally applicable criminal laws need not automatically be extended to religiously motivated actors, at least the claim for a religious exemption must be evaluated under the balancing test set forth in *Sherbert v. Verner* (1963).... Under the *Sherbert* test, governmental actions that substantially burden a religious practice must be justified by a compelling governmental interest.... Applying that test we have, on three occasions, invalidated state unemployment compensation rules that conditioned the availability of benefits upon an applicant's willingness to work under conditions forbidden by his religion.... We have never invalidated any governmental action on the basis of the *Sherbert* test except the denial of unemployment compensation....

Even if we were inclined to breathe into *Sherbert* some life beyond the unemployment compensation field, we would not apply it to require exemptions from a generally applicable criminal law....

We conclude today that the sounder approach, and the approach in accord with the vast majority of our precedents, is to hold the test inapplicable to such challenges. The government's ability to enforce generally applicable prohibitions of socially harmful conduct, like its ability to carry out other aspects of public policy, "cannot depend on measuring the effects of a governmental action on a religious objector's spiritual development." … To make an individual's obligation to obey such a law contingent upon the law's coincidence with his religious beliefs, except where the State's interest is "compelling"—permitting him, by virtue of his beliefs, "to become a law unto himself," …—contradicts both constitutional tradition and common sense.

The "compelling government interest" requirement seems benign, because it is familiar from other fields. But using it as the standard that must be met before the government may accord different treatment on the basis of race, … is not remotely comparable to using it for the purpose asserted here. What it produces in those other fields—equality of treatment, and an unrestricted flow of contending speech—are constitutional norms; what it would produce here—a private right to ignore generally applicable laws—is a constitutional anomaly.

Nor is it possible to limit the impact of respondents' proposal by requiring a "compelling state interest" only when the conduct prohibited is "central" to the individual's religion. It is no more appropriate for judges to determine the "centrality" of religious beliefs before applying a "compelling interest" test in the free exercise field, than it would be for them to determine the "importance" of ideas before applying the "compelling interest" test in the free speech field. What principle of law or logic can be brought to bear to contradict a believer's assertion that a particular act is "central" to his personal faith? …

If the "compelling interest" test is to be applied at all, then, it must be applied across the board, to all actions thought to be religiously commanded. Moreover, if "compelling interest" really means what it says (and watering it down here would subvert its rigor in the other fields where it is applied), many laws will not meet the test. Any society adopting such a system would be courting anarchy, but that danger increases in direct proportion to the society's diversity of religious beliefs, and its determination to coerce or suppress none of them.…

Values that are protected against government interference through enshrinement in the Bill of Rights are not thereby banished from the political process. Just as a society that believes in the negative protection accorded to the press by the First Amendment is likely to enact laws that affirmatively foster the dissemination of the printed word, so also a society that believes in the negative protection accorded to religious belief can be expected to be solicitous of that value in its legislation as well. It is therefore not surprising that a number of States have made an exception to their drug laws for sacramental peyote use. But to say that a nondiscriminatory religious-practice exemption is permitted, or even that it is desirable, is not to say that it is constitutionally required, and that the appropriate occasions for its creation can be discerned by the courts. It may fairly be said that leaving accommodation to the political process will place at a relative disadvantage those religious practices that are not widely engaged in; but that unavoidable consequence of democratic government must be preferred to a system in which each conscience is a law unto itself or in which judges weigh the social importance of all law against the centrality of all religious beliefs.…

Because respondent's ingestion of peyote was prohibited under Oregon law, and because that prohibition is constitutional, Oregon may, consistent with the Free Exercise Clause, deny respondents unemployment compensation when their dismissal results from use of the drug. The decision of the Oregon Supreme Court is accordingly reversed.…

Justice O'Connor … [concurring in the judgment only].

Although I agree with the result the Court reaches in this case, I cannot join its opinion. In my view, today's holding dramatically departs from well-settled First Amendment jurisprudence, appears unnecessary to resolve the question presented, and is incompatible with our Nation's fundamental commitment to individual religious liberty.…

[T]he critical question in this case is whether exempting respondents from the State's general criminal prohibition "will unduly interfere with fulfillment of the governmental interest." … Although the question is close, I would conclude that uniform application of Oregon's criminal prohibition is "essential to accomplish" its overriding interest in preventing the physical harm caused by the use of a Schedule I controlled substance. Oregon's criminal prohibition represents that State's judgment that the possession and use of controlled substances, even by only one person, is inherently harmful and dangerous. Because the health

(Continued)

effects caused by the use of controlled substances exist regardless of the motivation of the user, the use of such substances, even for religious purposes, violates the very purpose of the law that prohibits them....

For these reasons, I believe that granting a selective exemption in this case would seriously impair Oregon's compelling interest in prohibiting possession of peyote by its citizens. Under such circumstances, the Free Exercise Clause does not require the State to accommodate respondents' religiously motivated conduct....

I would therefore adhere to our established free exercise jurisprudence and hold that the State in this case has a compelling interest in regulating peyote use by its citizens and that accommodating respondents' religiously motivated conduct "will unduly interfere with fulfillment of the governmental interest." ... Accordingly, I concur in the judgment of the Court.

Justice Blackmun, with whom *Justice Brennan* and *Justice Marshall* join, dissenting.

This Court over the years painstakingly has developed a consistent and exacting standard to test the constitutionality of a state statute that burdens the free exercise of religion. Such a statute may stand only if the law in general, and the State's refusal to allow a religious exemption in particular, are justified by a compelling interest that cannot be served by less restrictive means.

Until today, I thought this was a settled and inviolate principle of this Court's First Amendment jurisprudence. The majority, however, perfunctorily dismisses it as a "constitutional anomaly." As carefully detailed in Justice O'Connor's concurring opinion ... the majority is able to arrive at this view only by mischaracterizing this Court's precedents. The Court discards leading free exercise cases such as *Cantwell v. Connecticut* ... (1940), and *Wisconsin v. Yoder* (1972), as "hybrid." ... The Court views traditional free exercise analysis as somehow inapplicable to criminal prohibitions (as opposed to conditions on the receipt of benefits), and to state laws of general applicability (as opposed, presumably, to laws that expressly single out religious practices). The Court cites cases in which, due to various exceptional circumstances, we found strict scrutiny inapposite, to hint that the Court is aware of the consequences, and that its result is not a product of overreaction to the serious problems the country's drug crisis has generated.

This distorted view of our precedents leads the majority to conclude that strict scrutiny of a state law burdening the free exercise of religion is a "luxury" that

a well ordered society cannot afford, and that the repression of minority religions is an "unavoidable consequence of democratic government." ... I do not believe the Founders thought their dearly bought freedom from religious persecution a "luxury," but an essential element of liberty—and they could not have thought religious intolerance "unavoidable," for they drafted the Religion Clauses precisely in order to avoid that intolerance.

For these reasons, I agree with Justice O'Connor's analysis of the applicable free exercise doctrine.... As she points out, "the critical question in this case is whether exempting respondents from the State's general criminal prohibition: 'will unduly interfere with fulfillment of the governmental interest.' " ... I do disagree, however, with her specific answer to that question.

The State's interest in enforcing its prohibition, in order to be sufficiently compelling to outweigh a free exercise claim, cannot be merely abstract or symbolic. The State cannot plausibly assert that unbending application of a criminal prohibition is essential to fulfill any compelling interest, if it does not, in fact, attempt to enforce that prohibition. In this case, the State actually has not evinced any concrete interest in enforcing its drug laws against religious users of peyote. Oregon has never sought to prosecute respondents, and does not claim that it has made significant enforcement efforts against other religious users of peyote. The State's asserted interest thus amounts only to the symbolic preservation of an unenforced prohibition....

The State proclaims an interest in protecting the health and safety of its citizens from the dangers of unlawful drugs. It offers, however, no evidence that the religious use of peyote has ever harmed anyone....

The fact that peyote is classified as a Schedule I controlled substance does not, by itself, show that any and all uses of peyote, in any circumstance, are inherently harmful and dangerous. The Federal Government, which created the classifications of unlawful drugs from which Oregon's drug laws are derived, apparently does not find peyote so dangerous as to preclude an exemption for religious use....

The carefully circumscribed ritual context in which respondents used peyote is far removed from the irresponsible and unrestricted recreational use of unlawful drugs. The Native American Church's internal restrictions on, and supervision of, its members' use of peyote substantially obviate the State's health and safety concerns....

Moreover, just as in *Yoder*, the values and interests of those seeking a religious exemption in this case are congruent, to a great degree, with those the State seeks to promote through its drug laws.... Not only does the Church's doctrine forbid nonreligious use of peyote; it also generally advocates self-reliance, familial responsibility, and abstinence from alcohol.... Far from promoting the lawless and irresponsible use of drugs, Native American Church members' spiritual code exemplifies values that Oregon's drug laws are presumably intended to foster....

Finally, although I agree with Justice O'Connor that courts should refrain from delving into questions of whether, as a matter of religious doctrine, a particular practice is "central" to the religion, I do not think this means that the courts must turn a blind eye to the severe impact of a State's restrictions on the adherents of a minority religion....

If Oregon can constitutionally prosecute them for this act of worship, they, like the Amish, may be "forced to migrate to some other and more tolerant region." This potentially devastating impact must be viewed in light of the federal policy—reached in reaction to many years of religious persecution and intolerance—of protecting the religious freedom of Native Americans....

The American Indian Religious Freedom Act, in itself, may not create rights enforceable against government action restricting religious freedom, but this Court must scrupulously apply its free exercise analysis to the religious claims of Native Americans, however unorthodox they may be. Otherwise, both the First Amendment and the stated policy of Congress will offer to Native Americans merely an unfulfilled and hollow promise.

For these reasons, I conclude that Oregon's interest in enforcing its drug laws against religious use of peyote is not sufficiently compelling to outweigh respondents' right to the free exercise of their religion. Since the State could not constitutionally enforce its criminal prohibition against respondents, the interests underlying the State's drug laws cannot justify its denial of unemployment benefits. Absent such justification, the State's regulatory interest in denying benefits for religiously motivated "misconduct," is indistinguishable from the state interests this Court has rejected.... The State of Oregon cannot, consistently with the Free Exercise Clause, deny respondents unemployment benefits....

CHURCH OF THE LUKUMI BABALU AYE, INC. v. CITY OF HIALEAH
508 U.S. 520; 113 S.Ct. 2217; 124 L.Ed.2d. 472 (1993)
Vote: 9-0

In this case, the Court considers a challenge to a set of Hialeah, Florida, ordinances prohibiting animal sacrifice in religious rituals. The ordinances were challenged in federal district court by the Church of the Lukumi Babalu Aye, which practiced animal sacrifice in keeping with the Santeria religion. Unsuccessful in the lower courts, the Church obtained review in the Supreme Court.

Justice Kennedy delivered the opinion of the Court.

... This case involves practices of the Santeria religion, which originated in the nineteenth century. When hundreds of thousands of members of the Yoruba people were brought as slaves from eastern Africa to Cuba, their traditional African religion absorbed significant elements of Roman Catholicism. The resulting

syncretion, or fusion, is Santeria, "the way of the saints." The Cuban Yoruba express their devotion to spirits, called orishas, through the iconography of Catholic saints....

... The basis of the Santeria religion is the nurture of a personal relation with the orishas, and one of the principal forms of devotion is an animal sacrifice....

... Sacrifices are performed at birth, marriage, and death rites, for the cure of the sick, for the initiation of new members and priests, and during an annual celebration. Animals sacrificed in Santeria rituals include chickens, pigeons, doves, ducks, guinea pigs, goats, sheep, and turtles. The animals are killed by the cutting of the carotid arteries in the neck. The sacrificed animal is cooked and eaten, except after healing and death rituals....

(Continued)

The prospect of a Santeria church in their midst was distressing to many members of the Hialeah community, and the announcement of the plans to open a Santeria church in Hialeah prompted the city council to hold an emergency public session on June 9....

In September 1987, the city council adopted three substantive ordinances addressing the issue of religious animal sacrifice. Ordinance 87-52 defined "sacrifice" as "to unnecessarily kill, torment, torture, or mutilate an animal in a public or private ritual or ceremony not for the primary purpose of food consumption," and prohibited owning or possessing an animal "intending to use such animal for food purposes." It restricted application of this prohibition, however, to any individual or group that "kills, slaughters or sacrifices animals for any type of ritual, regardless of whether or not the flesh or blood of the animal is to be consumed." The ordinance contained an exemption for slaughtering by "licensed establishments]" of animals "specifically raised for food purposes." Declaring, moreover, that the city council "has determined that the sacrificing of animals within the city limits is contrary to the public health, safety, welfare and morals of the community," the city council adopted Ordinance 87-71. That ordinance defined sacrifice as had Ordinance 87-52, and then provided that "[i]t shall be unlawful for any person, persons, corporations or associations to sacrifice any animal within the corporate limits of the City of Hialeah, Florida." The final Ordinance, 87-72, defined "slaughter" as "the killing of animals for food" and prohibited slaughter outside of areas zoned for slaughterhouse use. The ordinance provided an exemption, however, for the slaughter or processing for sale of "small numbers of hogs and/or cattle per week in accordance with an exemption provided in state law." All ordinances and resolutions passed the city council by unanimous vote. Violations of each of the four ordinances were punishable by fines not exceeding $500 or imprisonment not exceeding 60 days, or both....

... In addressing the constitutional protection for free exercise of religion, our cases establish the general proposition that a law that is neutral and of general applicability need not be justified by a compelling governmental interest even if the law has the incidental effect of burdening a particular religious practice.... Neutrality and general applicability are interrelated, and, as becomes apparent in this case, failure to satisfy one requirement is a likely indication that the other has not been satisfied. A law failing to satisfy these requirements must be justified by a compelling governmental interest and must be narrowly tailored to advance that interest....

At a minimum, the protections of the Free Exercise Clause pertain if the law at issue discriminates against some or all religious beliefs or regulates or prohibits conduct because it is undertaken for religious reasons.... Indeed, it was "historical instances of religious persecution and intolerance that gave concern to those who drafted the Free Exercise Clause." ... These principles, though not often at issue in our Free Exercise Clause cases, have played a role in some....

Although a law targeting religious beliefs as such is never permissible, ... if the object of a law is to infringe upon or restrict practices because of their religious motivation, the law is not neutral; ... and it is invalid unless it is justified by a compelling interest and is narrowly tailored to advance that interest....

The record in this case compels the conclusion that suppression of the central element of the Santeria worship service was the object of the ordinances. First, though use of the words "sacrifice" and "ritual" does not compel a finding of improper targeting of the Santeria religion, the choice of these words is support for our conclusion. There are further respects in which the text of the city council's enactments discloses the improper attempt to target Santeria.... No one suggests, and on this record it cannot be maintained, that city officials had in mind a religion other than Santeria.

It becomes evident that these ordinances target Santeria sacrifice when the ordinances' operation is considered. Apart from the text, the effect of a law in its real operation is strong evidence of its object. To be sure, adverse impact will not always lead to a finding of impermissible targeting. For example, a social harm may have been a legitimate concern of government for reasons quite apart from discrimination.... The subject at hand does implicate, of course, multiple concerns unrelated to religious animosity, for example, the suffering or mistreatment visited upon the sacrificed animals, and health hazards from improper disposal. But the ordinances when considered together disclose an object remote from these legitimate concerns. The design of these laws accomplishes instead a "religious gerrymander," ... an impermissible attempt to target petitioners and their religious practices.

It is a necessary conclusion that almost the only conduct subject to [the] Ordinances ... is the religious exercise of Santeria church members. The tests show that they were drafted in tandem to achieve this result....

The legitimate governmental interests in protecting the public health and preventing cruelty to animals could be addressed by restrictions stopping far short of a flat prohibition of all Santeria sacrificial practice. If improper disposal, not the sacrifice itself, is the harm to be prevented, the city could have imposed a general regulation on the disposal of organic garbage. It did not do so. Indeed, counsel for the city conceded at oral argument that, under the ordinances, Santeria sacrifices would be illegal even if they occurred in licensed, inspected, and zoned slaughterhouses.... Thus, these broad ordinances prohibit Santeria sacrifice even when it does not threaten the city's interest in the public health. The District Court accepted the argument that narrower regulation would be unenforceable because of the secrecy in the Santeria rituals.... It is difficult to understand, however, how a prohibition of the sacrifices themselves, which occur in private, is enforceable if a ban on improper disposal, which occurs in public, is not. The neutrality of a law is suspect if First Amendment freedoms are curtailed to prevent isolated collateral harms not themselves prohibited by direct regulation....

Under similar analysis, a narrow regulation would achieve the city's interest in preventing cruelty to animals....

Ordinance 87-72—unlike the three other ordinances—does appear to apply to substantial nonreligious conduct and not to be overbroad. For our purposes here, however, the four substantive ordinances may be treated as a group for neutrality purposes....

That the ordinances were enacted " 'because of,' not merely 'in spite of,' " their suppression of Santeria religious practice is revealed by the events preceding enactment of the ordinances. Although respondent claimed at oral argument that it had experienced significant problems resulting from the sacrifice of animals within the city before the announced opening of the Church, the city council made no attempt to address the supposed problem before its meeting in June 1987, just weeks after the Church announced plans to open. The minutes and taped excerpts of the June 9 session, both of which are in the record, evidence significant hostility exhibited by residents, members of the city council, and other city officials toward the Santeria religion and its practice of animal sacrifice. The public crowd that attended the June 9 meetings interrupted statements by council members critical of Santeria with cheers and the brief comments of Pichardo with taunts. When Councilman Martinez, a

supporter of the ordinances, stated that in prerevolutionary Cuba "people were put in jail for practicing this religion," the audience applauded....

In sum, the neutrality inquiry leads to one conclusion: The ordinances had as their object the suppression of religion. The pattern we have recited discloses animosity to Santeria adherents and their religious practices; the ordinances by their own terms target this religious exercise; the texts of the ordinances were gerrymandered with care to proscribe religious killings of animals but to exclude almost all secular killings, and the ordinances suppress much more religious conduct than is necessary in order to achieve the legitimate ends asserted in their defense....

We turn next to a second requirement of the Free Exercise Clause, the rule that laws burdening religious practice must be of general applicability.... All laws are selective to some extent, but categories of selection are of paramount concern when a law has the incidental effect of burdening religious practice. The Free Exercise Clause "protect[s] religious observers against unequal treatment," ... and inequality results when a legislature decides that the governmental interests it seeks to advance are worthy of being pursued only against conduct with a religious motivation.

The principle that government, in pursuit of legitimate interests, cannot in a selective manner impose burdens only on conduct motivated by religious belief is essential to the protection of the rights guaranteed by the Free Exercise Clause. The principle underlying the general applicability requirement has parallels in our First Amendment jurisprudence.... In this case we need not define with precision the standard used to evaluate whether a prohibition is of general application, for these ordinances fall well below the minimum standard necessary to protect First Amendment rights.

Respondents claim that Ordinances 87-40, 87-52, and 87-71 advance two interests: protecting the public health and preventing cruelty to animals. The ordinances are underinclusive for those ends. They fail to prohibit nonreligious conduct that endangers these interests in a similar or greater degree than Santeria sacrifice does. The underinclusion is substantial, not inconsequential. Despite the city's proffered interest in preventing cruelty to animals, the ordinances are drafted with care to forbid few killings but those occasioned by religious sacrifice....

We conclude ... that each of Hialeah's ordinances pursues the city's governmental interests only against

(Continued)

conduct motivated by religious belief. The ordinances "ha[ve] every appearance of a prohibition that society is prepared to impose upon [Santeria worshippers] but not upon itself." ... This precise evil is what the requirement of general applicability is designed to prevent....

A law burdening religious practice that is not neutral or not of general application must undergo the most rigorous of scrutiny. To satisfy the commands of the First Amendment, a law restrictive of religious practice must advance "interests of the highest order" and must be narrowly tailored in pursuit of those interests.... A law that targets religious conduct for distinctive treatment or advances legitimate governmental interests only against conduct with a religious motivation will survive strict scrutiny only in rare cases. It follows from what we have already said that these ordinances cannot withstand this scrutiny.

First, even were the governmental interests compelling, the ordinances are not drawn in narrow terms to accomplish those interests. As we have discussed, ... all four ordinances are overbroad or underinclusive in substantial respects. The proffered objectives are not pursued with respect to analogous non-religious conduct, and those interests could be achieved by narrower ordinances that burdened religion to a far lesser degree. The absence of narrow tailoring suffices to establish the invalidity of the ordinances....

Respondent has not demonstrated, moreover, that, in the context of these ordinances, its governmental interests are compelling. Where government restricts only conduct protected by the First Amendment and fails to enact feasible measures to restrict other conduct producing substantial harm or alleged harm of the same sort, the interest given in justification of the restriction is not compelling. It is established in our strict scrutiny jurisprudence that "a law cannot be regarded as protecting an interest 'of the highest order' ... when it leaves appreciable damage to that supposedly vital interest unprohibited." ... As we show above, ... the ordinances are underinclusive to a substantial extent with respect to each of the interests that respondent has asserted, and it is only conduct motivated by religious conviction that bears the weight of the governmental restrictions. There can be no serious claim that those interests justify the ordinances....

The Free Exercise Clause commits government itself to religious tolerance, and upon even slight suspicion that proposals for state intervention stem from animosity to religion or distrust of its practices, all officials must pause to remember their own high duty to the Constitution and to the rights it secures. Those in office must be resolute in resisting importunate demands and must ensure that the sole reasons for imposing the burdens of law and regulation are secular. Legislators may not devise mechanisms, overt or disguised, designed to persecute or oppress a religion or its practices. The laws here in question were enacted contrary to these constitutional principles, and they are void....

Justice Scalia, with whom the *Chief Justice* joins, concurring in part and concurring in the judgment....

Justice Souter, concurring in part and concurring in the judgment....

Justice Blackmun, with whom *Justice O'Connor* joins, concurring in the judgment....

The Court holds today that the city of Hialeah violated the First and Fourteenth Amendments when it passed a set of restrictive ordinances explicitly directed at petitioners' religious practice. With this holding I agree. I write separately to emphasize that the First Amendment's protection of religion extends beyond those rare occasions on which the government explicitly targets religion (or a particular religion) for disfavored treatment, as is done in this case. In my view, a statute that burdens the free exercise of religion "may stand only if the law is general, and the State's refusal to allow a religious exemption in particular, are justified by a compelling interest that cannot be served by less restrictive means." *Employment Div., Oregon Dept. of Human Resources v. Smith* ... (1990) (dissenting opinion). The Court, however, applies a different test. It applies the test announced in *Smith*, under which "a law that is neutral and of general applicability need not be justified by a compelling governmental interest even if the law has the incidental effect of burdening a particular religious practice." ... I continue to believe that *Smith* was wrongly decided, because it ignored the value of religious freedom as an affirmative individual liberty and treated the Free Exercise Clause as no more than an antidiscrimination principle.... Thus, while I agree with the result the Court reaches in this case, I arrive at that result by a different route....

EVERSON v. BOARD OF EDUCATION
330 U.S. 1; 67 S.Ct. 504; 91 L.Ed. 711 (1947)
Vote: 5-4

In this case, the seminal decision in the Court's Establishment Clause jurisprudence, the issue is whether the First Amendment prohibits a local school board from reimbursing parents for costs incurred as a result of transporting their children to and from parochial schools.

Mr. Justice Black delivered the opinion of the Court.

A New Jersey statute authorizes its local school districts to make rules and contracts for the transportation of children to and from schools. The appellee, a township board of education, acting pursuant to this statute, authorized reimbursement to parents of money expended by them for the bus transportation of their children on regular buses operated by the public transportation system. Part of this money was for the payment of transportation of some children in the community to Catholic parochial schools. These church schools give their students, in addition to secular education, regular religious instruction conforming to the religious tenets and modes of worship of the Catholic Faith. The superintendent of these schools is a Catholic priest.

The appellant, in his capacity as a district taxpayer, filed suit in a state court challenging the right of the Board to reimburse parents of parochial school students. He contended that the statute and the resolution passed pursuant to it violated both the State and the Federal Constitutions. That court held that the legislature was without power to authorize such payment under the state constitution.... The New Jersey Court of Errors and Appeals reversed, holding that neither the statute nor the resolution passed pursuant to it was in conflict with the State constitution or the provisions of the Federal Constitution in issue....

Since there has been no attack on the statute on the ground that a part of its language excludes children attending private schools operated for profit from enjoying State payment for their transportation, we need not consider this exclusionary language; it has no relevancy to any constitutional question here presented. Furthermore, if the exclusion clause had been properly challenged, we do not know whether New

Jersey's highest court would construe its statutes as precluding payment of the school transportation of any group of pupils, even those of a private school run for profit. Consequently, we put to one side the question as to the validity of the statute against the claim that it does not authorize payment for the transportation generally of school children in New Jersey....

The New Jersey statute is challenged as a "law respecting the establishment of religion." The First Amendment, as made applicable to the states by the Fourteenth, ... commands that a state "shall make no law respecting an establishment of religion, or prohibiting the free exercise thereof...." These words of the First Amendment reflected in the minds of early Americans a vivid mental picture of conditions and practices which they fervently wished to stamp out in order to preserve liberty for themselves and for their posterity. Doubtless their goal has not been entirely reached; but so far has the Nation moved toward it that the expression "law respecting the establishment of religion," probably does not so vividly remind present-day Americans of the evils, fears, and political problems that caused that expression to be written into our Bill of Rights....

The meaning and scope of the First Amendment, preventing establishment of religion or prohibiting the free exercise thereof, in the light of its history and the evils it was designed forever to suppress, have been several times elaborated by the decisions of this Court prior to the application of the First Amendment to the states by the Fourteenth. The broad meaning given the Amendment by these earlier cases has been accepted by this Court in its decisions concerning an individual's religious freedom rendered since the Fourteenth Amendment was interpreted to make the prohibitions of the First applicable to state action abridging religious freedom. There is every reason to give the same application and broad interpretation to the "establishment of religion" clause....

The "establishment of religion" clause of the First Amendment means at least this: Neither a state nor the Federal Government can set up a church. Neither can pass laws which aid one religion, aid all religions, or prefer one religion over another. Neither can force

(Continued)

nor influence a person to go to or to remain away from church against his will or force him to profess a belief or disbelief in any religion. No person can be punished for entertaining or professing religious beliefs or disbeliefs, for church attendance or nonattendance. No tax in any amount, large or small, can be levied to support any religious activities or institutions, whatever they may be called, or whatever form they may adopt to teach or practice religion. Neither a state nor the Federal Government can, openly or secretly, participate in the affairs of any religious organizations or groups and vice versa. In the words of Jefferson, the clause against establishment of religion by law was intended to erect "a wall of separation between church and State." ...

We must consider the New Jersey statute in accordance with the foregoing limitations imposed by the First Amendment. But we must not strike that state statute down if it is within the State's constitutional power even though it approaches the verge of that power.... New Jersey cannot consistently with the "establishment of religion" clause of the First Amendment contribute tax-raised funds to the support of an institution which teaches the tenets and faith of any church. On the other hand, other language of the amendment commands that New Jersey cannot hamper its citizens in the free exercise of their own religion. Consequently, it cannot exclude individual Catholics, Lutherans, Mohammedans, Baptists, Jews, Methodists, Non-believers, Presbyterians, or the members of any other faith, because of their faith, or lack of it, from receiving the benefits of public welfare legislation. While we do not mean to intimate that a state could not provide transportation only to children attending public schools, we must be careful in protecting the citizens of New Jersey against state-established churches, to be sure that we do not inadvertently prohibit New Jersey from extending its general state law benefits to all its citizens without regard to their religious belief.

Measured by these standards, we cannot say that the First Amendment prohibits New Jersey from spending tax-raised funds to pay the bus fares of parochial school pupils as a part of a general program under which it pays the fares of pupils attending public and other schools. It is undoubtedly true that children are helped to get to church schools. There is even a possibility that some of the children might not be sent to the church schools if the parents were compelled to pay their children's bus fares out of their own pockets when transportation to a public school would have been paid for by the State. The same possibility exists where the state requires a local transit company to provide reduced fares to school children including those attending parochial schools, or where a municipally owned transportation system undertakes to carry all school children free of charge. Moreover, state-paid policemen, detailed to protect children going to and from church schools from the very real hazards of traffic, would serve much the same purpose and accomplish much the same result as state provisions intended to guarantee free transportation of a kind which the state deems to be best for the school children's welfare. And parents might refuse to risk their children to the serious danger of traffic accidents going to and from parochial schools, the approaches to which were not protected by policemen. Similarly, parents might be reluctant to permit their children to attend schools which the state had cut off from such general government services as ordinary police and fire protection, connections for sewage disposal, public highways and sidewalks. Of course, cutting off church schools from these services, so separate and so indisputably marked off from the religious function, would make it far more difficult for the schools to operate. But such is obviously not the purpose of the First Amendment. That Amendment requires the state to be a neutral in its relations with groups of religious believers and non-believers; it does not require the state to be their adversary. State power is no more to be used so as to handicap religions than it is to favor them.

This Court has said that parents may, in the discharge of their duty under state compulsory education laws, send their children to a religious rather than a public school if the school meets the secular educational requirements which the state has power to impose.... It appears that these parochial schools meet New Jersey's requirements. The State contributes no money to the schools. It does not support them. Its legislation, as applied, does no more than provide a general program to help parents get their children, regardless of their religion, safely and expeditiously to and from accredited schools.

The First Amendment has erected a wall between church and state. That wall must be kept high and impregnable. We could not approve the slightest breach. New Jersey has not breached it here....

Mr. Justice Jackson, dissenting.

I find myself, contrary to first impressions, unable to join in this decision. I have a sympathy, though it is not ideological, with Catholic citizens who are compelled by law to pay taxes for public schools, and also feel constrained by conscience and discipline to support other schools for their own children. Such relief to them as this case involves is not in itself a serious burden to taxpayers and I had assumed it to be as little serious in principle. Study of this case convinces me otherwise. The Court's opinion marshals every argument in favor of state aid and puts the case in its most favorable light, but much of its reasoning confirms my conclusions that there are no good grounds upon which to support the present legislation. In fact, the undertones of the opinion, advocating complete and uncompromising separation of Church from State, seem utterly discordant with its conclusion yielding support to their commingling in educational matters. The case which irresistibly comes to mind as the most fitting precedent is that of Julia who, according to Byron's reports, "whispering 'I will ne'er consent,'—consented." …

This policy of our Federal Constitution has never been wholly pleasing to most religious groups. They all are quick to invoke its protections; they are all irked when they feel its restraints. This Court has gone a long way, if not an unreasonable way, to hold that public business of such paramount importance as maintenance of public order, protection of the privacy of the home, and taxation may not be pursued by a state in a way that even indirectly will interfere with religious proselytizing….

But we cannot have it both ways. Religious teaching cannot be a private affair when the state seeks to impose regulations which infringe on it indirectly, and a public affair when it comes to taxing citizens of one faith to aid another, or those of no faith to aid all. If these principles seem harsh in prohibiting aid to Catholic education, it must not be forgotten that it is the same Constitution that alone assures Catholics the right to maintain these schools at all when predominant local sentiment would forbid them…. Nor should I think that those who have done so well without this aid would want to see this separation between Church and State broken down. If the state may aid these religious schools, it may therefore regulate them. Many

groups have sought aid from tax funds only to find that it carried political controls with it. Indeed this Court has declared that "It is hardly lack of due process for the Government to regulate that which it subsidizes." …

But in any event, the great purposes of the Constitution do not depend on the approval or convenience of those they restrain. I cannot read the history of the struggle to separate political from ecclesiastical affairs, well summarized in the opinion of Mr. Justice Rutledge in which I generally concur, without a conviction that the Court today is unconsciously giving the clock's hands a backward turn.

Mr. Justice Frankfurter joins in this opinion.

Mr. Justice Rutledge, with whom *Mr. Justice Frankfurter*, Mr. Justice Jackson, and *Mr. Justice Burton* agree, dissenting.

… No one conscious of religious values can be unsympathetic toward the burden which our constitutional separation puts on parents who desire religious instruction mixed with secular for their children. They pay taxes for others' children's education, at the same time the added cost of instruction for their own. Nor can one happily see benefits denied to children which others receive, because in conscience they or their parents for them desire a different kind of training others do not demand.

But if those feelings should prevail, there would be an end to our historic constitutional policy and command. No more unjust or discriminatory in fact is it to deny attendants at religious schools the cost of their transportation than it is to deny them tuitions, sustenance for their teachers, or any other educational expense which others receive at public cost….

… [I]t is only by observing the prohibition rigidly that the state can maintain its neutrality and avoid partisanship in the dissensions inevitable when sect opposes sect over demands for public moneys to further religious education, teaching or training in any form or degree, directly or indirectly. Like St. Paul's freedom, religious liberty with a great price must be bought. And for those who exercise it most fully, by insisting upon religious education for their children mixed with secular, by the terms of our Constitution the price is greater than for others….

ABINGTON SCHOOL DISTRICT v. SCHEMPP
374 U.S. 203; 83 S.Ct. 1560; 10 L.Ed.2d. 844 (1963)
Vote: 8-1

This is one of the controversial "school prayer decisions" handed down by the Warren Court during the early 1960s. Edward and Sidney Schempp, members of the Unitarian religion and parents of children attending a public high school, brought suit to challenge the official practice of opening the school day with Bible reading and recitation of the Lord's Prayer. A three-judge panel of the U.S. District Court for the Eastern District of Pennsylvania held the practice unconstitutional under the Establishment Clause of the First Amendment. The school district appealed.

Mr. Justice Clark delivered the opinion of the Court.

... On each school day at the Abington Senior High School ... opening exercises are conducted pursuant to [State law]. The exercises are broadcast into each room in the school building through an intercommunications system and are conducted under the supervision of a teacher by students attending the school's radio and television workshop. Selected students from this course gather each morning in the school's workshop studio for the exercises, which include readings by one of the students of 10 verses of the Holy Bible, broadcast to each room in the building. This is followed by the recitation of the Lord's Prayer, likewise over the intercommunications system, but also by the students in the various classrooms, who are asked to stand and join in repeating the prayer in unison. The exercises are closed with the flag salute and such pertinent announcements as are of interest to the students. Participation in the opening exercises, as directed by the statute, is voluntary. The student reading the verses from the Bible may select the passages and read from any version he chooses, although the only copies furnished by the school are the King James Version, copies of which were circulated to each teacher by the school district. During the period in which the exercises have been conducted the King James, the Douay and the Revised Standard versions of the Bible have been used, as well as the Jewish Holy Scriptures. There are no prefatory statements, no questions asked or solicited, no comments or explanations made and no interpretations given at or during the exercises. The students and parents are advised that the student may absent himself from the classroom or, should he elect to remain, not participate in the exercises....

The wholesome "neutrality" of which this Court's cases speak ... stems from a recognition of the teachings of history that powerful sects or groups might bring about a fusion of governmental and religious functions or a concert or dependency of one upon the other to the end that official support of the State or Federal Government would be placed behind the tenets of one or of all orthodoxies. This the Establishment Clause prohibits. And a further reason for neutrality is found in the Free Exercise Clause, which recognizes the value of religious training, teaching and observance and, more particularly, the right of every person to freely choose his own course with reference thereto, free of any compulsion from the state. This the Free Exercise Clause guarantees. Thus, the two clauses may overlap.... [T]he Establishment Clause has been directly considered by this Court eight times in the past score of years and, with only one Justice dissenting on the point, it has consistently held that the clause withdrew all legislative power respecting religious belief or the expression thereof. The test may be stated as follows: what are the purpose and the primary effect of the enactment? If either is the advancement or inhibition of religion then the enactment exceeds the scope of legislative power as circumscribed by the Constitution. That is to say that to withstand the strictures of the Establishment Clause there must be a secular legislative purpose and a primary effect that neither advances nor inhibits religion.... The Free Exercise Clause, likewise considered many times here, withdraws from legislative power, state and federal, the exertion of any restraint on the free exercise of religion. Its purpose is to secure religious liberty in the individual by prohibiting any invasions thereof by civil authority. Hence it is necessary in a free exercise case for one to show the coercive effect of the enactment as it operates against him in the practice of his religion. The distinction between the two clauses is apparent—a violation of the Free Exercise Clause is predicated on coercion while the Establishment Clause violation need not be so attended.

Applying the Establishment Clause principles to the cases at bar we find that the States are requiring the selection and reading at the opening of the school day of verses from the Holy Bible and the recitation of the Lord's Prayer by the students in unison. These exercises are prescribed as part of the curricular activities of students who are required by law to attend school. They are held in the school buildings under the supervision and with the participation of teachers employed in those schools.... The trial court ... has found that such an opening exercise is a religious ceremony and was intended by the State to be so. We agree with the trial court's finding as to the religious character of the exercises. Given that finding, the exercises and the law requiring them are in violation of the Establishment Clause....

The conclusion follows that the laws require religious exercises and such exercises are being conducted in direct violation of the rights of the appellees and petitioners. Nor are these required exercises mitigated by the fact that individual students may absent themselves upon parental request, for that fact furnishes no defense to a claim of unconstitutionality under the Establishment Clause.... Further, it is no defense to urge that the religious practices here may be relatively minor encroachments on the First Amendment. The breach of neutrality that is today a trickling stream may all too soon become a raging torrent and, in the words of Madison, "it is proper to take alarm at the first experiment on our liberties." ...

It is insisted that unless these religious exercises are permitted a "religion of secularism" is established in the schools. We agree of course that the State may not establish a "religion of secularism" in the sense of affirmatively opposing or showing hostility to religion, thus "preferring those who believe in no religion over those who do believe." ... We do not agree, however, that this decision in any sense has that effect. In addition, it might well be said that one's education is not complete without a study of comparative religion or the history of religion and its relationship to the advancement of civilization. It certainly may be said that the Bible is worthy of study for its literary and historic qualities. Nothing we have said here indicates that such study of the Bible or of religion, when presented objectively as part of a secular program of education, may not be effected consistently with the First Amendment. But the exercises here do not fall into those categories. They are religious exercises, required by the State in violation of the command of the First Amendment that the Government maintain strict neutrality, neither aiding nor opposing religion.

Finally, we cannot accept that the concept of neutrality, which does not permit a State to require a religious exercise even with the consent of the majority of those affected, collides with the majority's right to free exercise of religion. While the Free Exercise Clause clearly prohibits the use of state action to deny the rights of free exercise to anyone, it has never meant that a majority could use the machinery of the State to practice its beliefs....

The place of religion in our society is an exalted one, achieved through a long tradition of reliance on the home, the church and the inviolable citadel of the individual heart and mind. We have come to recognize through bitter experience that it is not within the power of government to invade that citadel, whether its purpose or effect be to aid or oppose, to advance or retard. In the relationship between man and religion, the State is firmly committed to a position of neutrality. Though the application of that rule requires interpretation of a delicate sort, the rule itself is clearly and concisely stated in the words of the First Amendment. Applying that rule to the facts of these cases, we affirm....

Mr. Justice Douglas, concurring....

Mr. Justice Goldberg, with whom *Mr. Justice Harlan* joins, concurring....

Mr. Justice Stewart, dissenting.

I think the records in the two cases before us are so fundamentally deficient as to make impossible an informed or responsible determination of the constitutional issues presented. Specifically, I cannot agree that on these records we can say that the Establishment Clause has necessarily been violated. But I think there exist serious questions under both that provision and the Free Exercise Clause—insofar as each is imbedded in the Fourteenth Amendment—which require the remand of these cases for the taking of additional evidence....

What our Constitution indispensably protects is the freedom of each of us, be he Jew or Agnostic, Christian or Atheist, Buddhist or Freethinker, to believe or disbelieve, to worship or not worship, to pray or keep silent, according to his own conscience, uncoerced and unrestrained by government. It is conceivable that these school boards, or even all school boards, might eventually find it impossible to administer a system of religious exercises during school hours in such a way as to meet this constitutional standard—in such a way as completely to free from any kind of official coercion those who do not affirmatively want to participate. But I think we must not assume that school boards so lack the qualities of inventiveness and good will as to make impossible the achievement of that goal.

I would remand both cases for further hearings.

WALLACE v. JAFFREE
472 U.S. 38; 105 S.Ct. 2479; 86 L.Ed.2d. 29 (1985)
Vote: 6-3

In 1978, the Alabama legislature passed a law that provided: "At the commencement of the first class each day in the first through the sixth grades in all public schools ... a period of silence, not to exceed one minute in duration, shall be observed for meditation, and during any such period silence shall be maintained and no activities engaged in." In 1981, this law was amended to authorize the period of silence "for meditation or voluntary prayer." The amended version of the Alabama "moment of silence law" is before the Supreme Court in this case.

Justice Stevens delivered the opinion of the Court.

... [T]he narrow question for decision is whether [the challenged law], which authorizes a period of silence for "meditation or voluntary prayer," is a law respecting the establishment of religion within the meaning of the First Amendment.

Appellee Ishmael Jaffree is a resident of Mobile County, Alabama. On May 28, 1982, he filed a complaint on behalf of three of his minor children; two of them were second-grade students and the third was then in kindergarten. The complaint named members of the Mobile County School Board, various school officials, and the minor plaintiffs' three teachers as defendants. The complaint alleged that the appellees brought the action "seeking principally a declaratory judgment and an injunction restraining the Defendants and each of them from maintaining or allowing the maintenance of regular religious prayer services or other forms of religious observances in the Mobile County Public Schools in violation of the First Amendment as made applicable to states by the Fourteenth Amendment to the United States Constitution." The complaint further alleged that two of the children had been subjected to various acts of religious indoctrination "from the beginning of the school year in September, 1981"; that the defendant teachers had "on a daily basis" led their classes in saying certain prayers in unison; that the minor children were exposed to ostracism from their peer group class members if they did not participate; and that Ishmael Jaffree had repeatedly but unsuccessfully requested that the devotional services be stopped. The original complaint made no reference to any Alabama statute....

Jaffree's complaint was later amended to challenge the revised "moment of silence" statute. The U.S. district court dismissed the challenge to the statute holding that "the Establishment Clause of the First Amendment to the U.S. Constitution does not prohibit the State from establishing a religion." The U.S. court of appeals reversed, finding the challenged law to be in violation of the First Amendment.

When the court has been called upon to construe the breadth of the Establishment Clause, it has examined the criteria developed over a period of many years. Thus, in *Lemon v. Kurtzman* ... we wrote:

Every analysis in this area must begin with consideration of the cumulative criteria developed by the Court over many years. Three such tests may be gleaned from our cases. First, the statute must have a secular legislative purpose; second, its principal or primary effect must be one that neither advances nor inhibits religion, ... finally, the statute must not foster "an excessive government entanglement with religion."...

It is the first of these three criteria that is most plainly implicated by this case. As the District Court correctly recognized, no consideration of the second or third criteria is necessary if a statute does not have a clearly secular purpose. For even though a statute that is motivated in part by a religious purpose may satisfy the first criterion, ... the First Amendment requires that a statute must be invalidated if it is entirely motivated by a purpose to advance religion.

In applying the purpose test, it is appropriate to ask "whether government's actual purpose is to endorse or disapprove of religion." In this case, the answer to that question is dispositive. For the record not only provides us with an unambiguous affirmative answer, but it also reveals that the enactment of [the amended statute] was not motivated by any clearly secular purpose—indeed, the statute had *no* secular purpose.

The sponsor of the bill that became [the challenged law], Senator Donald Holmes, inserted into the legislative record—apparently without dissent—a statement indicating that the legislation was an "effort to return voluntary prayer" to the public schools. Later Senator Holmes confirmed this purpose before the District

Court. In response to the question whether he had any purpose for the legislation other than returning voluntary prayer to public schools, he stated, "No, I did not have no other purpose in mind." The State did not present evidence of *any* secular purpose....

The legislative intent to return prayer to the public schools is, of course, quite different from merely protecting every student's right to engage in voluntary prayer during an appropriate moment of silence during the school day. The 1978 statute already protected that right, containing nothing that prevented any student from engaging in voluntary prayer during a silent minute of meditation. Appellants have not identified any secular purpose that was not fully served by [the original statute] before the enactment of [the amendment]. Thus, only two conclusions are consistent with the text ... (1) the statute was enacted to convey a message of State endorsement and promotion of prayer; or (2) the statute was enacted for no purpose. No one suggests that the statute was nothing but a meaningless or irrational act.

We must, therefore, conclude that the Alabama Legislature intended to change existing law and that it was motivated by the same purpose that the Governor's Answer to the Second Amended Complaint expressly admitted; that the statement inserted in the legislative history revealed; and that Senator Holmes' testimony frankly described. The Legislature enacted [the challenged statute] for the sole purpose of expressing the State's endorsement of prayer activities for one minute at the beginning of each school day. The addition of "or voluntary prayer" indicates that the State intended to characterize prayer as a favored practice. Such an endorsement is not consistent with the established principle that the Government must pursue a course of complete neutrality toward religion.

The importance of that principle does not permit us to treat this as an inconsequential case involving nothing more than a few words of symbolic speech on behalf of the political majority. For whenever the State itself speaks on a religious subject, one of the questions that we must ask is "whether the Government intends to convey a message of endorsement or disapproval of religion." The well-supported concurrent findings of the District Court and the Court of Appeals—that [the challenged law] was intended to convey a message of State approval of prayer activities in the public schools—make it unnecessary, and indeed inappropriate, to evaluate the practical significance of the addition of the words "or voluntary prayer" to the statute. Keeping in mind, as we must, "both the fundamental place held by the Establishment Clause in our constitutional scheme and the myriad, subtle ways in which Establishment Clause values can be eroded," we conclude that [the challenged statute] violates the First Amendment.

The judgment of the Court of Appeals is affirmed.

Justice Powell, concurring....

Justice O'Connor, concurring in the judgment.

Nothing in the United States Constitution as interpreted by this Court or in the laws of the State of Alabama prohibits public school students from voluntarily praying at any time before, during, or after the school day. Alabama has facilitated voluntary silent prayers of students who are so inclined by enacting [the 1978 law] which provides a moment of silence in appellees' schools each day. The parties to these proceedings concede the validity of this enactment. At issue in these appeals is the constitutional validity of an additional and subsequent Alabama statute, ... which both the District Court and the Court of Appeals concluded was enacted solely to officially encourage prayer during the moment of silence. I agree with the judgment of the Court that, in light of the findings of the Courts below and the history of its enactment, [the challenged law] violates the Establishment Clause of the First Amendment. In my view, there can be little doubt that the purpose and likely effect of this subsequent enactment is to endorse and sponsor voluntary prayer in the public schools. I write separately to identify the peculiar features of the Alabama law that render it invalid, and to explain why moment of silence laws in other States do not necessarily manifest the same infirmity. I also write to explain why neither history nor the Free Exercise Clause of the First Amendment validate the Alabama law struck down by the Court today....

After an extensive discussion of Supreme Court decisions interpreting the religion clauses of the First Amendment, Justice O'Connor concludes:

The Court does not hold that the Establishment Clause is so hostile to religion that it precludes the States from affording schoolchildren an opportunity for voluntary silent prayer. To the contrary, the moment of silence statutes of many States should satisfy the Establishment Clause standard we have here applied. The Court holds only that Alabama has intentionally crossed the line between creating a quiet

(*Continued*)

moment during which those so inclined may pray, and affirmatively endorsing the particular religious practice of prayer. This line may be a fine one, but our precedents and the principles of religious liberty require that we draw it. In my view, the judgment of the Court of Appeals must be affirmed.

Chief Justice Burger, dissenting....

Justice White, dissenting....

Justice Rehnquist, dissenting.

... The true meaning of the Establishment Clause can only be seen in its history.... As drafters of our Bill of Rights, the framers inscribed the principles that control today. Any deviation from their intentions frustrates the permanence of that Charter and will only lead to the type of unprincipled decisionmaking that has plagued our Establishment Clause cases since *Everson.*

The Framers intended the Establishment Clause to prohibit the designation of any church as a "national" one. The Clause was also designed to stop the Federal Government from asserting a preference for one religious denomination or sect over others. Given the "incorporation" of the Establishment Clause as against the States via the Fourteenth Amendment in *Everson*, States are prohibited as well from establishing a religion or discriminating between sects. As its history abundantly shows, however, nothing in the Establishment Clause requires government to be strictly neutral between religion and irreligion, nor does that Clause prohibit Congress or the States from pursuing legitimate secular ends through nondiscriminatory sectarian means.

The Court strikes down the Alabama statute ... because the State wished to "endorse prayer as a favored practice."... It would come as much of a shock to those who drafted the Bill of Rights as it will to a large number of thoughtful Americans today to learn that the Constitution, as construed by the majority, prohibits the Alabama Legislature from "endorsing" prayer. George Washington himself, at the request of the very Congress which passed the Bill of Rights, proclaimed a day of "public thanksgiving and prayer, to be observed by acknowledging with grateful hearts the many and signal favors of Almighty God." History must judge whether it was the father of his country in 1789, or a majority of the Court today, which has strayed from the meaning of the Establishment Clause.

The State surely has a secular interest in regulating the manner in which public schools are conducted. Nothing in the Establishment Clause of the First Amendment, properly understood, prohibits any such generalized "endorsement" of prayer. I would therefore reverse the judgment of the Court of Appeals....

SANTA FE INDEPENDENT SCHOOL DISTRICT v. DOE
530 U.S. 290; 120 S.Ct. 2266; 147 L.Ed.2d. 295 (2000)
Vote: 6-3

In this case, the Supreme Court considers an Establishment Clause challenge to a practice at a public high school in Texas in which a student delivers prayers over the PA system before football games. The U.S. District Court upheld the practice on the condition that the school would permit only "nonsectarian, nonproselytizing prayer." However, the U.S. Court of Appeals held that the challenged practice was unconstitutional, even as modified by the district court.

Justice Stevens delivered the opinion of the Court.

... The Santa Fe Independent School District (District) is a political subdivision of the State of Texas, responsible for the education of more than 4,000 students in a small community in the southern part of the State. The District includes the Santa Fe High School, two primary schools, an intermediate school and the junior high school. Respondents are two sets of current or former students and their respective mothers. One family is Mormon and the other is Catholic. The District Court permitted respondents (Does) to litigate anonymously to protect them from intimidation or harassment.

Respondents commenced this action in April 1995 and moved for a temporary restraining order to prevent the District from violating the Establishment Clause at the imminent graduation exercises. In their complaint the Does alleged that the District had engaged in several proselytizing practices, such as promoting attendance at a Baptist revival meeting, encouraging membership in religious clubs, chastising children who held minority religious beliefs, and distributing Gideon Bibles on school premises. They also alleged that the District allowed students to read Christian invocations and benedictions from the stage at graduation ceremonies, and to deliver overtly Christian prayers over the public address system at home football games....

We granted the District's petition for certiorari, limited to the following question: "Whether petitioner's policy permitting student-led, student-initiated prayer at football games violates the Establishment Clause." ... We conclude, as did the Court of Appeals, that it does.

...In *Lee v. Weisman* ... (1992) we held that a prayer delivered by a rabbi at a middle school graduation ceremony violated that Clause. Although this case involves student prayer at a different type of school function, our analysis is properly guided by the principles that we endorsed in *Lee*....

These invocations are authorized by a government policy and take place on government property at government-sponsored school-related events.... The Santa Fe school officials simply do not "evince either 'by policy or by practice,' any intent to open the [pregame ceremony] to 'indiscriminate use,' ... by the student body generally." Rather, the school allows only one student, the same student for the entire season, to give the invocation. The statement or invocation, moreover, is subject to particular regulations that confine the content and topic of the student's message....

Granting only one student access to the stage at a time does not, of course, necessarily preclude a finding that a school has created a limited public forum. Here, however, Santa Fe's student election system ensures that only those messages deemed "appropriate" under the District's policy may be delivered. That is, the majoritarian process implemented by the District guarantees, by definition, that minority candidates will never prevail and that their views will be effectively silenced....

... [W]hile Santa Fe's majoritarian election might ensure that most of the students are represented, it does nothing to protect the minority; indeed, it likely serves to intensify their offense.

Moreover, the District has failed to divorce itself from the religious content in the invocations. It has not succeeded in doing so, either by claiming that its policy is "one of neutrality rather than endorsement" or by characterizing the individual student as the "circuit-breaker" in the process. Contrary to the District's repeated assertions that it has adopted a "hands-off approach to the pregame invocation, the realities of the situation plainly reveal that its policy involves both perceived and actual endorsement of religion. In this case ... the "degree of school involvement" makes it clear that the pregame prayers bear "the imprint of the State and thus put school-age children who objected in an untenable position." ...

The District has attempted to disentangle itself from the religious messages by developing the two-step student election process.... The elections take place at all only because the school "board *has chosen to permit* students to deliver a brief invocation and/or message." ... The elections thus "shall" be conducted "by the high school student council" and "[u]pon advice and direction of the high school principal." ... The decision whether to deliver a message is first made by majority vote of the entire student body, followed by a choice of the speaker in a separate, similar majority election. Even though the particular words used by the speaker are not determined by those votes, the policy mandates that the "statement or invocation" be "consistent with the goals and purposes of this policy," which are "to solemnize the event, to promote good sportsmanship and student safety, and to establish the appropriate environment for the competition." ...

In addition to involving the school in the selection of the speaker, the policy, by its terms, invites and encourages religious messages. The policy itself states that the purpose of the message is "to solemnize the event." A religious message is the most obvious method of solemnizing an event. Moreover, the requirements that the message "promote good citizenship" and "establish the appropriate environment for competition" further narrow the types of message deemed appropriate, suggesting that a solemn, yet non-religious, message, such as commentary on United States foreign policy, would be prohibited. Indeed, the only type of message that is expressly endorsed in the text is an "invocation"—a term that primarily describes an appeal for divine assistance. In fact, as used in the past at Santa Fe High School, an "invocation" has always entailed a focused religious message. Thus, the expressed purposes of the policy encourage the selection of a religious message, and that is precisely how the students understand the policy. The results of the

(Continued)

elections described in the parties' stipulation make it clear that the students understood that the central question before them was whether prayer should be a part of the pregame ceremony. We recognize the important role that public worship plays in many communities, as well as the sincere desire to include public prayer as a part of various occasions so as to mark those occasions' significance. But such religious activity in public schools, as elsewhere, must comport with the First Amendment.

The actual or perceived endorsement of the message, moreover, is established by factors beyond just the text of the policy. Once the student speaker is selected and the message composed, the invocation is then delivered to a large audience assembled as part of a regularly scheduled, school-sponsored function conducted on school property. The message is broadcast over the school's public address system, which remains subject to the control of school officials. It is fair to assume that the pregame ceremony is clothed in the traditional indicia of school sporting events, which generally include not just the team, but also cheerleaders and band members dressed in uniforms sporting the school name and mascot....

The text and history of this policy, moreover, reinforce our objective student's perception that the prayer is, in actuality, encouraged by the school. When a governmental entity professes a secular purpose for an arguably religious policy, the government's characterization is, of course, entitled to some deference. But it is nonetheless the duty of the courts to "distinguis[h] a sham secular purpose from a sincere one."...

According to the District, the secular purposes of the policy are to "foste[r] free expression of private persons ... as well [as to] solemniz[e] sporting events, promot[e] good sportsmanship and student safety, and establis[h] an appropriate environment for competition." ... We note, however, that the District's approval of only one specific kind of message, an "invocation," is not necessary to further any of these purposes. Additionally, the fact that only one student is permitted to give a content-limited message suggests that this policy does little to "foste[r] free expression." Furthermore, regardless of whether one considers a sporting event an appropriate occasion for solemnity, the use of an invocation to foster such solemnity is impermissible when, in actuality, it constitutes prayer sponsored by the school. And it is unclear what type of message would be both appropriately "solemnizing" under the District's policy and yet non-religious.

Most striking to us is the evolution of the current policy from the long-sanctioned office of "Student Chaplain" to the candidly titled "Prayer at Football Games" regulation. This history indicates that the District intended to preserve the practice of prayer before football games....

School sponsorship of a religious message is impermissible because it sends the ancillary message to members of the audience who are nonadherents "that they are outsiders, not full members of the political community, and an accompanying message to adherents that they are insiders, favored members of the political community." ... The delivery of such a message—over the school's public address system, by a speaker representing the student body, under the supervision of school faculty, and pursuant to a school policy that explicitly and implicitly encourages public prayer—is not properly characterized as "private" speech.

... Even if we regard every high school student's decision to attend a home football game as purely voluntary, we are nevertheless persuaded that the delivery of a pregame prayer has the improper effect of coercing those present to participate in an act of religious worship. For "the government may no more use social pressure to enforce orthodoxy than it may use more direct means." ... As in *Lee*, "[w]hat to most believers may seem nothing more than a reasonable request that the nonbeliever respect their religious practices, in a school context may appear to the nonbeliever or dissenter to be an attempt to employ the machinery of the State to enforce a religious orthodoxy." ... The constitutional command will not permit the District "to exact religious conformity from a student as the price" of joining her classmates at a varsity football game....

Finally, the District argues repeatedly that the Does have made a premature facial challenge ... that necessarily must fail. The District emphasizes, quite correctly, that until a student actually delivers a solemnizing message under the latest version of the policy, there can be no certainty that any of the statements or invocations will be religious....

The District ... asks us to pretend that we do not recognize what every Santa Fe High School student understands clearly—that this policy is about prayer. The District further asks us to accept what is obviously untrue: that these messages are necessary to "solemnize" a football game and that this single-student, year-long position is essential to the protection of student speech. We refuse to turn a blind eye to the context in which this policy arose, and that context quells any doubt that this policy was implemented with the purpose of endorsing school prayer.

Therefore, the simple enactment of this policy, with the purpose and perception of school endorsement of student prayer, was a constitutional violation. We need not wait for the inevitable to confirm and magnify the constitutional injury.... Therefore, even if no Santa Fe High School student were ever to offer a religious message, the ... policy fails a facial challenge because the attempt by the District to encourage prayer is also at issue. Government efforts to endorse religion cannot evade constitutional reproach based solely on the remote possibility that those attempts may fail.

This policy likewise does not survive a facial challenge because it impermissibly imposes upon the student body a majoritarian election on the issue of prayer. Through its election scheme, the District has established a governmental electoral mechanism that turns the school into a forum for religious debate. It further empowers the student body majority with the authority to subject students of minority views to constitutionally improper messages. The award of that power alone, regardless of the students' ultimate use of it, is not acceptable.... Such a system encourages divisiveness along religious lines and threatens the imposition of coercion upon those students not desiring to participate in a religious exercise....

To properly examine this policy on its face, we "must be deemed aware of the history and context of the community and forum." ... Our examination of those circumstances above leads to the conclusion that this policy does not provide the District with the constitutional safe harbor it sought. The policy is invalid on its face because it establishes an improper majoritarian election on religion, and unquestionably has the purpose and creates the perception of encouraging the delivery of prayer at a series of important school events.

The judgment of the Court of Appeals is, accordingly, affirmed.

Chief Justice Rehnquist, with whom **Justice Scalia** and **Justice Thomas** join, dissenting.

The Court distorts existing precedent to conclude that the school district's student-message program is invalid on its face under the Establishment Clause. But even more disturbing than its holding is the tone of the Court's opinion; it bristles with hostility to all things religious in public life. Neither the holding nor the tone of the opinion is faithful to the meaning of the Establishment Clause, when it is recalled that George Washington himself, at the request of the very Congress which passed the Bill of Rights, proclaimed a day of "public thanksgiving and prayer, to be observed by acknowledging with grateful hearts the many and signal favors of Almighty God." ...

The Court ... applies the most rigid version of the criticized test of *Lemon v. Kurtzman* ... (1971).... *Lemon* has had a checkered career in the decisional law of this Court.... We have even gone so far as to state that it has never been binding on us.... Indeed, in *Lee v. Weisman* ... (1992), an opinion upon which the Court relies heavily today, we mentioned but did not feel compelled to apply the *Lemon* test....

Even if it were appropriate to apply the *Lemon* test here, the district's student-message policy should not be invalidated on its face. The Court applies *Lemon* and holds that the "policy is invalid on its face because it establishes an improper majoritarian election on religion, and unquestionably has the purpose and creates the perception of encouraging the delivery of prayer at a series of important school events." ... The Court's reliance on each of these conclusions misses the mark.

First, the Court misconstrues the nature of the "majoritarian election" permitted by the policy as being an election on "prayer" and "religion." ... To the contrary, the election permitted by the policy is a two-fold process whereby students vote first on whether to have a student speaker before football games at all, and second, if the students vote to have such a speaker, on who that speaker will be.... It is conceivable that the election could become one in which student candidates campaign on platforms that focus on whether or not they will pray if elected. It is also conceivable that the election could lead to a Christian prayer before 90 percent of the football games. If, upon implementation, the policy operated in this fashion, we would have a record before us to review whether the policy, as applied, violated the Establishment Clause or unduly suppressed minority viewpoints. But it is possible that the students might vote not to have a pregame speaker, in which case there would be no threat of a constitutional violation. It is also possible that the election would not focus on prayer, but on public speaking ability or social popularity. And if student campaigning did begin to focus

(Continued)

on prayer, the school might decide to implement reasonable campaign restrictions.

... Support for the Court's holding cannot be found in any of our cases. And it essentially invalidates all student elections. A newly elected student body president, or even a newly elected prom king or queen, could use opportunities for public speaking to say prayers. Under the Court's view, the mere grant of power to the students to vote for such offices, in light of the fear that those elected might publicly pray, violates the Establishment Clause.

Second, with respect to the policy's purpose, the Court holds that "the simple enactment of this policy, with the purpose and perception of school endorsement of student prayer, was a constitutional violation." ... But the policy itself has plausible secular purposes: "[T]o solemnize the event, to promote good sportsmanship and student safety, and to establish the appropriate environment for the competition." ... Where a governmental body "expresses a plausible secular purpose" for an enactment, "courts should generally defer to that stated intent."... The Court grants no deference to—and appears openly hostile toward—the policy's stated purposes, and wastes no time in concluding that they are a sham....

The Court bases its conclusion that the true purpose of the policy is to endorse student prayer on its view of the school district's history of Establishment Clause violations and the context in which the policy was written, that is, as "the latest step in developing litigation brought as a challenge to institutional practices that unquestionably violated the Establishment Clause." ... But the context—attempted compliance with a District Court order—actually demonstrates that the school district was acting diligently to come within the governing constitutional law. The District Court ordered the school district to formulate a policy consistent with Fifth Circuit precedent, which permitted a school district to have a prayer-only policy.... But the school district went further than required by the District Court order and eventually settled on a policy that gave the student speaker a choice to deliver either an invocation or a message. In so doing, the school district exhibited a willingness to comply with, and exceed, Establishment Clause restrictions. Thus, the policy cannot be viewed as having a sectarian purpose.

The Court also relies on our decision in *Lee v. Weisman* ... to support its conclusion. In *Lee*, we concluded that the content of the speech at issue, a graduation prayer given by a rabbi, was "directed and controlled" by a school official.... In other words, at issue in *Lee* was *government* speech. Here, by contrast, the potential speech at issue, if the policy had been allowed to proceed, would be a message or invocation selected or created by a student. That is, if there were speech at issue here, it would be *private* speech. The "crucial difference between *government* speech endorsing religion, which the Establishment Clause forbids, and *private* speech endorsing religion, which the Free Speech and Free Exercise Clauses protect," applies with particular force to the question of endorsement....

Had the policy been put into practice, the students may have chosen a speaker according to wholly secular criteria—like good public speaking skills or social popularity—and the student speaker may have chosen, on her own accord, to deliver a religious message. Such an application of the policy would likely pass constitutional muster....

Finally, the Court seems to demand that a government policy be completely neutral as to content or be considered one that endorses religion.... This is undoubtedly a new requirement, as our Establishment Clause jurisprudence simply does not mandate "content neutrality." That concept is found in our First Amendment *speech* cases and is used as a guide for determining when we apply strict scrutiny. For example, we look to "content neutrality" in reviewing loudness restrictions imposed on speech in public forums, ... and regulations against picketing.... The Court seems to think that the fact that the policy is not content neutral somehow controls the Establishment Clause inquiry....

But even our speech jurisprudence would not require that all public school actions with respect to student speech be content neutral.... Schools do not violate the First Amendment every time they restrict student speech to certain categories. But under the Court's view, a school policy under which the student body president is to solemnize the graduation ceremony by giving a favorable introduction to the guest speaker would be facially unconstitutional. Solemnization "invites and encourages" prayer and the policy's content limitations prohibit the student body president from giving a solemn, yet non-religious, message like "commentary on United States foreign policy." ...

The policy at issue here may be applied in an unconstitutional manner, but it will be time enough to invalidate it if that is found to be the case. I would reverse the judgment of the Court of Appeals.

EDWARDS v. AGUILLARD
482 U.S. 578; 107 S.Ct. 2573; 96 L.Ed.2d. 510 (1987)
Vote: 7-2

The teaching of evolution in the public schools has long been controversial. Indeed, some states have attempted to ban the teaching of evolution altogether. Such a prohibition was struck down in Epperson v. Arkansas (1968). More recently, states have attempted to balance the teaching of evolution with the teaching of "creation science." Whether this is a legitimate secular requirement for public school curricula or an attempt to instruct public school students in the biblical account of creation is the issue before the Supreme Court in this case.

Justice Brennan delivered the opinion of the Court.

The question for decision is whether Louisiana's "Balanced Treatment for Creation-Science and Evolution-Science in Public School Instruction" Act (Creationism Act) … is facially invalid as violative of the Establishment Clause of the First Amendment.

The Creationism Act forbids the teaching of the theory of evolution in public schools unless accompanied by instruction in "creation science." … No school is required to teach evolution or creation science. If either is taught, however, the other must also be taught…. The theories of evolution and creation science are statutorily defined as "the scientific evidences for [creation or evolution] and inferences from those scientific evidences." …

Appellees, who include parents of children attending Louisiana public schools, Louisiana teachers, and religious leaders, challenged the constitutionality of the Act in District Court, seeking an injunction and declaratory relief. Appellants, Louisiana officials charged with implementing the Act, defended on the ground that the purpose of the Act is to protect a legitimate secular interest, namely, academic freedom. Appellees attacked the Act as facially invalid because it violated the Establishment Clause and made a motion for summary judgment. The District Court granted the motion…. The court held that there can be no valid secular reason for prohibiting the teaching of evolution, a theory historically opposed by some religious denominations. The court further concluded that "the teaching of 'creation-science' and 'creationism,' as contemplated by the statute, involves teaching

'tailored to the principles' of a particular religious sect or group of sects." … The District Court therefore held that the Creationism Act violated the Establishment Clause either because it prohibited the teaching of evolution or because it required the teaching of creation science with the purpose of advancing a particular religious doctrine.

The Court of Appeals affirmed…. The court observed that the statute's avowed purpose of protecting academic freedom was inconsistent with requiring, upon risk of sanction, the teaching of creation science whenever evolution is taught…. The court found that the Louisiana legislature's actual intent was "to discredit evolution by counterbalancing its teaching at every turn with the teaching of creationism, a religious belief." … Because the Creationism Act was thus a law furthering a particular religious belief, the Court of Appeals held that the Act violated the Establishment Clause. A suggestion for rehearing *en banc* was denied over a dissent…. We noted probable jurisdiction, … and now affirm.

The Establishment Clause forbids the enactment of any law "respecting an establishment of religion." The Court has applied a three-pronged test to determine whether legislation comports with the Establishment Clause. First, the legislature must have adopted the law with a secular purpose. Second, the statute's principal or primary effect must be one that neither advances nor inhibits religion. Third, the statute must not result in an excessive entanglement of government with religion. *Lemon v. Kurtzman* … (1971). State action violates the Establishment Clause if it fails to satisfy any of these prongs….

Lemons first prong focuses on the purpose that animated adoption of the Act. "The purpose prong of the *Lemon* test asks whether government's actual purpose is to endorse or disapprove of religion." … A governmental intention to promote religion is clear when the State enacts a law to serve a religious purpose. This intention may be evidenced by promotion of religion in general, … or by advancement of a particular religious belief…. If the law was enacted for the purpose of endorsing religion, "no consideration of the second or third criteria [of *Lemon*] is necessary." … In this case, the petitioners had identified no clear secular purpose for the Louisiana Act.

(Continued)

True, the Act's stated purpose is to protect academic freedom.... This phrase might, in common parlance, be understood as referring to enhancing the freedom of teachers to teach what they will. The Court of Appeals, however, correctly concluded that the Act was not designed to further that goal. We find no merit in the State's argument that the "legislature may not [have] use[d] the terms 'academic freedom' in the correct legal sense. They might have [had] in mind, instead, a basic concept of fairness: teaching all of the evidence." ... Even if "academic freedom" is read to mean "teaching all of the evidence" with respect to the origin of human beings, the Act does not further this purpose. The goal of providing a more comprehensive science curriculum is not furthered either by outlawing the teaching of evolution or by requiring the teaching of creation science.

While the Court is normally deferential to a State's articulation of a secular purpose, it is required that the statement of such purpose be sincere and not a sham....

It is clear from the legislative history that the purpose of the legislative sponsor, Senator Bill Keith, was to narrow the science curriculum. During the legislative hearings, Senator Keith stated: "My preference would be that neither [creationism nor evolution] be taught." ... Such a ban on teaching does not promote—indeed, it undermines—the provision of a comprehensive scientific education.

It is equally clear that requiring schools to teach creation science with evolution does not advance academic freedom. The Act does not grant teachers a flexibility that they did not already possess to supplant the present science curriculum with the presentation of theories, besides evolution, about the origin of life. Indeed, the Court of Appeals found that no law prohibited Louisiana public schoolteachers from teaching any scientific theory.... As the president of the Louisiana Science Teachers Association testified, "[a]ny scientific concept that's based on established fact can be included in our curriculum already, and no legislation allowing this is necessary." ... The Act provides Louisiana schoolteachers with no new authority. Thus the stated purpose is not furthered by it....

Furthermore, the goal of basic "fairness" is hardly furthered by the Act's discriminatory preference for the teaching of creation science and against the teaching of evolution. While requiring that curriculum guides be developed for creation science, the Act says nothing of comparable guides for evolution.... Similarly, research services are supplied for creation science but not for

evolution.... Only "creation scientists" can serve on the panel that supplies the resource services.... The Act forbids school boards to discriminate against anyone who "chooses to be a creation-scientist" or to teach "creationism," but fails to protect those who choose to teach evolution or any other noncreation science theory, or who refuse to teach creation science....

If the Louisiana legislature's purpose was solely to maximize the comprehensiveness and effectiveness of science instruction, it would have encouraged the teaching of all scientific theories about the origins of humankind. But under the Act's requirements, teachers who were once free to teach any and all facets of this subject are now unable to do so. Moreover, the Act fails even to ensure that creation science will be taught, but instead requires the teaching of this theory only when the theory of evolution is taught. Thus we agree with the Court of Appeals' conclusion that the Act does not serve to protect academic freedom, but has the distinctly different purpose of discrediting "evolution by counterbalancing its teaching at every turn with the teaching of creation science." ...

... [W]e need not be blind in this case to the legislature's preeminent religious purpose in enacting this statute. There is a historic and contemporaneous link between the teachings of certain religious denominations and the teaching of evolution. It was this link that concerned the Court in *Epperson v. Arkansas* (1968), ... which also involved a facial challenge to a statute regulating the teaching of evolution. In that case, the Court reviewed an Arkansas statute that made it unlawful for an instructor to teach evolution or to use a textbook that referred to this scientific theory. Although the Arkansas antievolution law did not explicitly state its predominate religious purpose, the Court could not ignore that "[t]he statute was a product of the upsurge of 'fundamentalist' religious fervor" that has long viewed this particular scientific theory as contradicting the literal interpretation of the Bible.... After reviewing the history of antievolution statutes, the Court determined that "there can be no doubt that the motivation for the [Arkansas] law was the same [as other antievolution statutes]: to suppress the teaching of a theory which, it was thought, 'denied' the divine creation of man." ... The Court found that there can be no legitimate state interest in protecting particular religions from scientific views "distasteful to them," ... and concluded "that the First Amendment does not permit the State to require that teaching and learning must be tailored to the principles or prohibitions of any religious sect or dogma." ...

These same historic and contemporaneous antagonisms between the teachings of certain religious denominations and the teaching of evolution are present in this case. The preeminent purpose of the Louisiana legislature was clearly to advance the religious viewpoint that a supernatural being created humankind. The term "creation science" was defined as embracing this particular religious doctrine by those responsible for the passage of the Creationism Act. Senator Keith's leading expert on creation science, Edward Boudreaux, testified at the legislative hearings that the theory of creation science included belief in the existence of a supernatural creator.... Senator Keith also cited testimony from other experts to support the creation-science view that "a creator [was] responsible for the universe and everything in it." ... The legislative history therefore reveals that the term "creation science," as contemplated by the legislature that adopted this Act, embodies the religious belief that a supernatural creator was responsible for the creation of humankind.

Furthermore, it is not happenstance that the legislature required the teaching of a theory that coincided with this religious view. The legislative history documents that the Act's primary purpose was to change the science curriculum of public schools in order to provide persuasive advantage to a particular religious doctrine that rejects the factual basis of evolution in its entirety. The sponsor of the Creationism Act, Senator Keith, explained during the legislative hearings that his disdain for the theory of evolution resulted from the support that evolution supplied to views contrary to his own religious beliefs. According to Senator Keith, the theory of evolution was consonant with the "cardinal principle[s] of religious humanism, secular humanism, theological liberalism, aetheistism [sic]." ... The state senator repeatedly stated that scientific evidence supporting his religious views should be included in the public school curriculum to redress the fact that the theory of evolution incidentally coincided with what he characterized as religious beliefs antithetical to his own. The legislation therefore sought to alter the science curriculum to reflect endorsement of a religious view that is antagonistic to the theory of evolution.

In this case, the purpose of the Creationism Act was to restructure the science curriculum to conform with a particular religious viewpoint. Out of many possible science subjects taught in the public schools, the legislature chose to affect the teaching of the one scientific theory that historically has been opposed by certain religious sects. As in *Epperson*, the legislature passed the Act to give preference to those religious groups which have as one of their tenets the creation of humankind by a divine creator. The "overriding fact" that confronted the Court in *Epperson* was "that Arkansas' law selects from the body of knowledge a particular segment which it proscribes for the sole reason that it is deemed to conflict with ... a particular interpretation of the Book of Genesis by a particular religious group." ... Similarly, the Creationism Act is designed either to promote the theory of creation science which embodies a particular religious tenet by requiring that creation science be taught whenever evolution is taught or to prohibit the teaching of a scientific theory disfavored by certain religious sects by forbidding the teaching of evolution when creation science is not also taught. The Establishment Clause, however, "forbids alike the preference of a religious doctrine or the prohibition of theory which is deemed antagonistic to a particular dogma." ... Because the primary purpose of the Creationism Act is to advance a particular religious belief, the Act endorses religion in violation of the First Amendment.

We do not imply that a legislature could never require that scientific critiques of prevailing scientific theories be taught. Indeed, the Court acknowledged in *Stone* that its decision forbidding the posting of the Ten Commandments did not mean that no use could ever be made of the Ten Commandments, or that the Ten Commandments played an exclusively religious role in the history of Western civilization.... In a similar way, teaching a variety of scientific theories about the origins of humankind to schoolchildren might be validly done with the clear secular intent of enhancing the effectiveness of science instruction. But because the primary purpose of the Creationism Act is to endorse a particular religious doctrine, the Act furthers religion in violation of the Establishment Clause....

Justice Powell, with whom *Justice O'Connor* joins, concurring....

Justice White, concurring in the judgment....

Justice Scalia, with whom the *Chief Justice* joins, dissenting.

Even if I agreed with the questionable premise that legislation can be invalidated under the Establishment

(*Continued*)

Clause on the basis of its motivation alone, without regard to its effects, I would still find no justification for today's decision. The Louisiana legislators who passed the "Balanced Treatment for Creation-Science and Evolution-Science Act" (Balanced Treatment Act), ... each of whom had sworn to support the Constitution, were well aware of the potential Establishment Clause problems and considered that aspect of the legislation with great care. After seven hearings and several months of study, resulting in substantial revision of the original proposal, they approved the Act overwhelmingly and specifically articulated the secular purpose they meant it to serve. Although the record contains abundant evidence of the sincerity of that purpose (the only issue pertinent to this case), the Court today holds, essentially on the basis of "its visceral knowledge regarding what must have motivated the legislators," ... that the members of the Louisiana Legislature knowingly violated their oaths and then lied about it. I dissent. Had requirements of the Balanced Treatment Act that are not apparent on its face been clarified by an interpretation of the Louisiana Supreme Court, or by the manner of its implementation, the Act might well be found unconstitutional; but the question of its constitutionality cannot rightly be disposed of on the gallop, by impugning the motives of its supporters....

Given the many hazards involved in assessing the subjective intent of governmental decisionmakers, the first prong of *Lemon* [*v. Kurtzman*] is defensible, I think, only if the text of the Establishment Clause demands it. That is surely not the case. The Clause states that "Congress shall make no law respecting an establishment of religion." One could argue, I suppose, that any time Congress acts with the intent of advancing religion, it has enacted a "law respecting an establishment of religion"; but far from being an unavoidable reading, it is quite an unnatural one. I doubt, for example, that the Clayton Act ... could reasonably be described as a "law respecting an establishment of religion" if bizarre new historical evidence revealed that it lacked a secular purpose, even though it has no discernible nonsecular effect. It is, in short, far from an inevitable reading of the Establishment Clause that it forbids all governmental action intended to advance religion; and if not inevitable, any reading with such untoward consequences must be wrong.

In the past we have attempted to justify our embarrassing Establishment Clause jurisprudence on the ground that it "sacrifices clarity and predictability for flexibility." ... One commentator had aptly characterized this as "a euphemism ... for ... the absence of any principled rationale." ... I think it time that we sacrifice some "flexibility" for "clarity and predictability." Abandoning *Lemons* purpose test—a test which exacerbates the tension between the Free Exercise and Establishment Clause, has no basis in the language or history of the amendment, and, as today's decision shows, has wonderfully flexible consequences—would be a good place to start.

AGOSTINI v. FELTON
527 U.S. 203; 117 S.Ct. 1997; 138 L.Ed.2d. 391 (1997)
Vote: 5-4

Here, the Court reconsiders its decision in Aguilar v. Felton (1985), which held that the Establishment Clause prohibited a city from sending public school teachers into parochial schools to provide remedial education.

Justice O'Connor delivered the opinion of the Court.

... Petitioners maintain that *Aguilar* cannot be squared with our intervening Establishment Clause jurisprudence and ask that we explicitly recognize what our more recent cases already dictate: *Aguilar* is no longer good law. We agree with petitioners that *Aguilar* is not consistent with our subsequent Establishment Clause decisions....

In order to evaluate whether *Aguilar* has been eroded by our subsequent Establishment Clause cases, it is necessary to understand the rationale upon which *Aguilar*, as well as its companion case, *School Dist. of Grand Rapids v. Ball*, ... (1985), rested....

Our more recent cases have undermined the assumptions upon which *Ball* and *Aguilar* relied. To be sure, the general principles we use to evaluate whether government aid violates the Establishment Clause have not changed since *Aguilar* was decided.

For example, we continue to ask whether the government acted with the purpose of advancing or inhibiting religion, and the nature of that inquiry has remained largely unchanged…. Likewise, we continue to explore whether the aid has the "effect" of advancing or inhibiting religion. What has changed since we decided *Ball* and *Aguilar* is our understanding of the criteria used to assess whether aid to religion has an impermissible effect….

… New York City's Title I program does not run afoul of any of three primary criteria we currently use to evaluate whether government aid has the effect of advancing religion: it does not result in governmental indoctrination; define its recipients by reference to religion; or create an excessive entanglement. We therefore hold that a federally funded program providing supplemental, remedial instruction to disadvantaged children on a neutral basis is not invalid under the Establishment Clause when such instruction is given on the premises of sectarian schools by government employees pursuant to a program containing safeguards such as those present here. The same considerations that justify this holding require us to conclude that this carefully constrained program also cannot reasonably be viewed as an endorsement of religion…. Accordingly, we must acknowledge that *Aguilar*, as well as the portion of *Ball* addressing Grand Rapids' Shared Time program, are no longer good law.

The doctrine of *stare decisis* does not preclude us from recognizing the change in our law and overruling *Aguilar* and those portions of *Ball* inconsistent with our more recent decisions…. That policy is at its weakest when we interpret the Constitution because our interpretation can be altered only by constitutional amendment or by overruling our prior decisions…. Thus, we have held in several cases that *stare decisis* does not prevent us from overruling a previous decision where there has been a significant change in or subsequent development of our constitutional law…. As discussed above, our Establishment Clause jurisprudence has changed significantly since we decided *Ball* and *Aguilar*, so our decision to over-turn those cases rests on far more than "a present doctrinal disposition to come out differently from the Court of (1985)." … We therefore overrule *Ball* and *Aguilar* to the extent those decisions are inconsistent with our current understanding of the Establishment Clause….

We … conclude that our Establishment Clause law has "significant[ly] change[d]" since we decided *Aguilar*. … We are only left to decide whether this change in law entitles petitioners to relief under Rule 60(b)(5). We conclude that it does. Our general practice is to apply the rule of law we announce in a case to the parties before us…. We adhere to this practice even when we overrule a case….

We do not acknowledge, and we do not hold, that other courts should conclude our more recent cases have, by implication, overruled an earlier precedent. We reaffirm that "if a precedent of this Court has direct application in a case, yet appears to rest on reasons rejected in some other line of decisions, the Court of Appeals should follow the case which directly controls, leaving to this Court the prerogative of overruling its own decisions." … Adherence to this teaching by the District Court and Court of Appeals in this case does not insulate a legal principle on which they relied from our review to determine its continued vitality. The trial court acted within its discretion in entertaining the motion with supporting allegations, but it was also correct to recognize that the motion had to be denied unless and until this Court reinterpreted the binding precedent….

… [O]ur decision today is intimately tied to the context in which it arose. This litigation involves a party's request under Rule 60(b)(5) to vacate a continuing injunction entered some years ago in light of a bona fide, significant change in subsequent law. The clause of Rule 60(b)(5) that petitioners invoke applies by its terms only to "judgments] hav[ing] prospective application." Intervening developments in the law by themselves rarely constitute the extraordinary circumstances required for relief under Rule 60(b)(6), the only remaining avenue for relief on this basis from judgments lacking any prospective component…. Our decision will have no effect outside the context of ordinary civil litigation where the propriety of continuing prospective relief is at issue…. Given that Rule 60(b)(5) specifically contemplates the grant of relief in the circumstances presented here, it can hardly be said that we have somehow warped the Rule into a means of "allowing an 'anytime' rehearing." …

Respondents further contend that "[p]etitioners' [p]roposed [u]se of Rule 60(b) [w]ill [e]rode the [i]nstitutional [i]ntegrity of the Court." … Respondents do not explain how a proper application of Rule 60(b)(5) undermines our legitimacy. Instead, respondents focus on the harm occasioned if we were to overrule *Aguilar*. But as discussed above, we do no violence to the doctrine of *stare decisis* when we recognize bona fide changes in our decisional law. And in those

(Continued)

circumstances, we do no violence to the legitimacy we derive from reliance on that doctrine....

As a final matter, we see no reason to wait for a "better vehicle" in which to evaluate the impact of subsequent cases on *Aguilar's* continued vitality. To evaluate the Rule 60(b)(5) motion properly before us today in no way undermines "integrity in the interpretation of procedural rules" or signals any departure from "the responsive, non-agenda setting character of this Court." ... Indeed, under these circumstances, it would be particularly inequitable for us to bide our time waiting for another case to arise while the city of New York labors under a continuing injunction forcing it to spend millions of dollars on mobile instructional units and leased sites when it could instead be spending that money to give economically disadvantaged children a better chance at success in life by means of a program that is perfectly consistent with the Establishment Clause.

For these reasons, we reverse the judgment of the Court of Appeals and remand to the District Court with instructions to vacate its September 26, 1985, order.

Justice Souter, with whom **Justice Stevens** and **Justice Ginsburg** join, and with whom **Justice Breyer** joins as to Part II, dissenting.

In this novel proceeding, petitioners seek relief from an injunction the District Court entered 12 years ago to implement our decision in *Aguilar v. Felton*.... [T]he Court's holding that petitioners are entitled to relief under Rule 60(b) is seriously mistaken. The Court's misapplication of the rule is tied to its equally erroneous reading of our more recent Establishment Clause cases, which the Court describes as having rejected the underpinnings of *Aguilar* and portions of *Aguilar's* companion case, *School Dist. of Grand Rapids v. Ball*, ... (1985). The result is to repudiate the very reasonable line drawn in *Aguilar* and *Ball*, and to authorize direct state aid to religious institutions on an unparalleled scale, in violation of the Establishment Clause's central prohibition against religious subsidies by the government....

... I believe *Aguilar* was a correct and sensible decision, and my only reservation about its opinion is that the emphasis on the excessive entanglement produced by monitoring religious instructional content obscured those facts that independently called for the application of two central tenets of Establishment Clause jurisprudence. The State is forbidden to subsidize religion directly and is just as surely forbidden to act in any way that could reasonably be viewed as religious endorsement....

These principles were violated by the programs at issue in *Aguilar* and *Ball*, as a consequence of several significant features common to both Title I, as implemented in New York City before *Aguilar*, and the Grand Rapids Shared Time program: each provided classes on the premises of the religious schools, covering a wide range of subjects including some at the core of primary and secondary education, like reading and mathematics; while their services were termed "supplemental," the programs and their instructors necessarily assumed responsibility for teaching subjects that the religious schools would otherwise have been obligated to provide; the public employees carrying out the programs had broad responsibilities involving the exercise of considerable discretion; while the programs offered aid to nonpublic school students generally (and Title I went to public school students as well), participation by religious school students in each program was extensive; and, finally, aid under Title I and Shared Time flowed directly to the schools in the form of classes and programs, as distinct from indirect aid that reaches schools only as a result of independent private choice....

What, therefore, was significant in *Aguilar* and *Ball* about the placement of state paid teachers into the physical and social settings of the religious schools was not only the consequent temptation of some of those teachers to reflect the schools' religious missions in the rhetoric of their instruction, with a resulting need for monitoring and the certainty of entanglement. ... What was so remarkable was that the schemes in issue assumed a teaching responsibility indistinguishable from the responsibility of the schools themselves. The obligation of primary and secondary schools to teach reading necessarily extends to teaching those who are having a hard time at it, and the same is true of math. Calling some classes remedial does not distinguish their subjects from the schools' basic subjects, however inadequately the schools may have been addressing them.

What was true of the Title I scheme as struck down in *Aguilar* will be just as true when New York reverts to the old practices with the Court's approval after today. There is simply no line that can be drawn between the instruction paid for at taxpayers' expense and the instruction in any subject that is not identified as formally religious. While it would be an obvious sham, say, to channel cash to religious schools to be credited only against the expense of "secular" instruction, the line between "supplemental" and general education is likewise impossible to draw. If a State may constitutionally enter the schools to teach in the manner in question, it must in constitutional principle be free to assume, or assume payment for, the entire cost of instruction provided in any ostensibly secular subject in any religious school....

... [T]he object of Title I is worthy without doubt, and the cost of compliance is high. In the short run there is much that is genuinely unfortunate about the administration of the scheme under *Aguilar*'s rule. But constitutional lines have to be drawn, and on one side of every one of them is an otherwise sympathetic case that provokes impatience with the Constitution and with the line. But constitutional lines are the price of constitutional government.

Justice Ginsburg, with whom ***Justice Stevens***, Justice Souter, and ***Justice Breyer*** join, dissenting.

The Court today finds a way to rehear a legal question decided in respondents' favor in this very case

some 12 years ago.... Subsequent decisions, the majority says, have undermined *Aguilar* and justify our immediate reconsideration. This Court's Rules do not countenance the rehearing here granted. For good reason, a proper application of those rules and the Federal Rules of Civil Procedure would lead us to defer reconsideration of *Aguilar* until we are presented with the issue in another case....

Unlike the majority, I find just cause to await the arrival of ... another case in which our review appropriately may be sought, before deciding whether *Aguilar* should remain the law of the land. That cause lies in the maintenance of integrity in the interpretation of procedural rules, preservation of the responsive, non-agenda setting character of this Court, and avoidance of invitations to reconsider old cases based on "speculat[ions] on chances from changes in [the Court's membership]." ...

MARSH v. CHAMBERS
463 U.S. 783; 103 S.Ct. 3330; 77 L.Ed.2d. 1019 (1983)
Vote: 6-3

Here, the Court considers whether a State legislature's practice of opening each legislative day with a prayer by a chaplain paid from public funds violates the Establishment Clause.

Chief Justice Burger delivered the opinion of the Court.

... The Nebraska Legislature begins each of its sessions with a prayer offered by a chaplain who is chosen biennially by the Executive Board of the Legislative Council and paid out of public funds. Robert E. Palmer, a Presbyterian minister, has served as chaplain since 1965 at a salary of $319.75 per month for each month the legislature is in session.

Ernest Chambers is a member of the Nebraska Legislature and a taxpayer of Nebraska. Claiming that the Nebraska Legislature's chaplaincy practice violates the Establishment Clause of the First Amendment, he brought this action ... seeking to enjoin enforcement of the practice. After denying a motion to dismiss on the ground of legislative immunity, the District Court

held that the Establishment Clause was not breached by the prayers, but was violated by paying the chaplain from public funds.

... It therefore enjoined the legislature from using public funds to pay the chaplain; it declined to enjoin the policy of beginning sessions with prayers....

Applying the three-part test of *Lemon v. Kurtzman*, ... the [Court of Appeals] held that the chaplaincy practice violated all three elements of the test: the purpose and primary effect of selecting the same minister for 16 years and publishing his prayers was to promote a particular religious expression; use of state money for compensation and publication led to entanglement.... Accordingly, the Court of Appeals modified the District Court's injunction and prohibited the State from engaging in any aspect of its established chaplaincy practice.

We granted certiorari limited to the challenge to the practice of opening sessions with prayers by a state-employed clergyman, ... and we reverse.

The opening of sessions of legislative and other deliberative public bodies with prayer is deeply

(Continued)

embedded in the history and tradition of this country. From colonial times through the founding of the Republic and ever since, the practice of legislative prayer has coexisted with the principles of disestablishment and religious freedom.

In the very courtrooms in which the United States District Judge and later three Circuit Judges heard and decided this case, the proceedings opened with an announcement that concluded, "God save the United States and this Honorable Court." The same invocation occurs at all sessions of this Court.

The tradition in many of the colonies was, of course, linked to an established church, but the Continental Congress, beginning in 1774, adopted the traditional procedure of opening its sessions with a prayer offered by a paid chaplain.... Although prayers were not offered during the Constitutional Convention, the First Congress, as one of its early items of business, adopted the policy of selecting a chaplain to open each session with prayer. Thus on April 7, 1789, the Senate appointed a committee "to take under consideration the manner of electing Chaplains." ... On April 9, 1789, a similar committee was appointed by the House of Representatives. On April 25, 1789, the Senate elected its first chaplain, ... the House followed suit on May 1, 1789.... A statute providing for the payment of these chaplains was enacted into law on Sept. 22, 1789....

On Sept. 25, 1789, three days after Congress authorized the appointment of paid chaplains, final agreement was reached on the language of the Bill of Rights.... Clearly the men who wrote the First Amendment Religion Clauses did not view paid legislative chaplains and opening prayers as a violation of that Amendment, for the practice of opening sessions with prayer has continued without interruption ever since that early session of Congress. It has also been followed consistently in most of the states, including Nebraska, where the institution of opening legislative sessions with prayer was adopted even before the State attained statehood....

Standing alone, historical patterns cannot justify contemporary violations of constitutional guarantees, but there is far more here than simply historical patterns. In this context, historical evidence sheds light not only on what the draftsmen intended the Establishment Clause to mean, but also on how they thought that clause applied to the practice authorized by the First Congress—their actions reveal their intent....

In *Walz v. Tax Comm'n* (1970), ... we considered the weight to be accorded to history:

It is obviously correct that no one acquires a vested or protected right in violation of the Constitution by

long use, even when that span of time covers our entire national existence and indeed predates it. Yet an unbroken practice ... is not something to be lightly cast aside.

No more is Nebraska's practice of over a century, consistent with two centuries of national practice, to be cast aside.... In applying the First Amendment to the States through the Fourteenth Amendment, ... it would be incongruous to interpret that clause as imposing more stringent First Amendment limits on the States than the draftsmen imposed on the Federal Government.

This unique history leads us to accept the interpretation of the First Amendment draftsmen who saw no real threat to the Establishment Clause arising from a practice of prayer similar to that now challenged....

In light of the unambiguous and unbroken history of more than 200 years, there can be no doubt that the practice of opening legislative sessions with prayer has become part of the fabric of our society. To invoke Divine guidance on a public body entrusted with making the laws is not, in these circumstances, an "establishment" of religion or a step toward establishment; it is simply a tolerable acknowledgement of beliefs widely held among the people of this country. As Justice Douglas observed, "[w]e are a religious people whose institutions presuppose a Supreme Being." ...

We turn then to the question of whether any features of the Nebraska practice violate the Establishment Clause. Beyond the bare fact that a prayer is offered, three points have been made: first, that a clergyman of only one denomination—Presbyterian—has been selected for 16 years; second, that the chaplain is paid at public expense; and third, that the prayers are in the Judeo-Christian tradition. Weighed against the historical background, these factors do not serve to invalidate Nebraska's practice.

The Court of Appeals was concerned that Palmer's long tenure has the effect of giving preference to his religious views. We, no more than Members of Congresses of this century, can perceive any suggestion that choosing a clergyman of one denomination advances the beliefs of a particular church. To the contrary, the evidence indicates that Palmer was reappointed because his performance and personal qualities were acceptable to the body appointing him. Palmer was not the only clergyman heard by the Legislature; guest chaplains have officiated at the request of various legislators and as substitutes during Palmer's absences.... Absent proof that the chaplain's reappointment stemmed from an impermissible motive, we conclude that his long tenure does not in itself conflict with the Establishment Clause.

Nor is the compensation of the chaplain from public funds a reason to invalidate the Nebraska Legislature's chaplaincy; remuneration is grounded in historic practice initiated ... by the same Congress that adopted the Establishment Clause of the First Amendment.... The content of the prayer is not of concern to judges where, as here, there is no indication that the prayer opportunity has been exploited to proselytize or advance any one, or to disparage any other, faith or belief. That being so, it is not for us to embark on a sensitive evaluation or to parse the content of a particular prayer.

We do not doubt the sincerity of those, who like respondent, believe that to have prayer in this context risks the beginning of the establishment the Founding Fathers feared. But this concern is not well founded.... The unbroken practice for two centuries in the National Congress, for more than a century in Nebraska and in many other states, gives abundant assurance that there is no real threat "while this Court sits." ...

The judgment of the Court of Appeals is reversed.

Justice Brennan, with whom *Justice Marshall* joins, dissenting.

... The Court makes no pretense of subjecting Nebraska's practice of legislative prayer to any of the formal "tests" that have traditionally structured our inquiry under the Establishment Clause. That it fails to do so is, in a sense, a good thing, for it simply confirms that the Court is carving out an exception to the Establishment Clause rather than reshaping Establishment Clause doctrine to accommodate legislative prayer. For my purposes, however, I must begin by demonstrating what should be obvious: that, if the Court were to judge legislative prayer through the unsentimental eye of our settled doctrine, it would have to strike it down as a clear violation of the Establishment Clause.

The most commonly cited formulation of prevailing Establishment Clause doctrine is found in *Lemon v. Kurtzman* (1971): ...

Every analysis in this area must begin with consideration of the cumulative criteria developed by the Court over many years. Three such tests may be gleaned from our cases. First, the statute [at issue] must have a secular legislative purpose; second, its principal or primary effect must be one that neither advances nor inhibits religion; finally, the statute must not foster "an excessive government entanglement with religion." ...

That the "purpose" of legislative prayer is preeminently religious rather than secular seems to me to be self-evident. "To invoke Divine guidance on a public body entrusted with making the laws," ... is nothing but a religious act. Moreover, whatever secular functions legislative prayer might play—formally opening the legislative session, getting the members of the body to quiet down, and imbuing them with a sense of seriousness and high purpose—could so plainly be performed in a purely nonreligious fashion that to claim a secular purpose for the prayer is an insult to the perfectly honorable individuals who instituted and continue the practice.

The "primary effect" of legislative prayer is also clearly religious. As we said in the context of officially sponsored prayers in the public schools, "prescribing a particular form of religious worship," even if the individuals involved have the choice not to participate, places "indirect coercive pressure upon religious minorities to conform to the prevailing officially approved religion...." ... More importantly, invocations in Nebraska's legislative halls explicitly link religious belief and the prestige of the State. "[T]he mere appearance of a joint exercise of legislative authority by Church and State provides a significant symbolic benefit to religion in the minds of some by reason of the power conferred." ...

Finally, there can be no doubt that the practice of legislative prayer leads to excessive "entanglement" between the State and religion. *Lemon* pointed out that "entanglement" can take two forms: First, a state statute or program might involve the state impermissibly in monitoring and overseeing religious affairs.... In the case of legislative prayer, the process of choosing a "suitable" chaplain, whether on a permanent or rotating basis, and insuring that the chaplain limits himself to "suitable" prayers, involves precisely the sort of supervision that agencies of government should if at all possible avoid.

Second, excessive "entanglement" might arise out of "the divisive political potential" of a state statute or program.... In this case, this second aspect of entanglement is also clear. The controversy between Senator Chambers and his colleagues, which had reached the stage of difficulty and rancor long before this lawsuit was brought, has split the Nebraska Legislature

(Continued)

precisely on issues of religion and religious conformity…. The record in this case also reports a series of instances, involving legislators other than Senator Chambers, in which invocations by Reverend Palmer and others led to controversy along religious lines. And in general, the history of legislative prayer has been far more eventful—and divisive—than a hasty reading of the Court's opinion might indicate.

In sum, I have no doubt that, if any group of law students were asked to apply the principles of *Lemon* to the question of legislative prayer, they would nearly unanimously find the practice to be unconstitutional….

The argument is made occasionally that a strict separation of religion and state robs the nation of its spiritual identity. I believe quite the contrary. It may be true that individuals cannot be "neutral" on the question of religion. But the judgment of the Establishment Clause is that neutrality by the organs of government on questions of religion is both possible and imperative….

Justice Stevens, dissenting.

In a democratically elected legislature, the religious beliefs of the chaplain tend to reflect the faith of the majority of the lawmakers' constituents. Prayers may be said by a Catholic priest in the Massachusetts Legislature and by a Presbyterian minister in the Nebraska Legislature, but I would not expect to find a Jehovah's Witness or a disciple of Mary Baker Eddy or the Reverend Moon serving as the official chaplain in any state legislature. Regardless of the motivation of the majority that exercises the power to appoint the chaplain, it seems plain to me that the designation of a member of one religious faith to serve as the sole official chaplain of a state legislature for a period of 16 years constitutes the preference of one faith over another in violation of the Establishment Clause of the First Amendment.

The Court declines to "embark on a sensitive evaluation or to parse the content of a particular prayer." … Perhaps it does so because it would be unable to explain away the clearly sectarian content of some of the prayers given by Nebraska's chaplain. Or perhaps the Court is unwilling to acknowledge that the tenure of the chaplain must inevitably be conditioned on the acceptability of that content to the silent majority.

I would affirm the judgment of the Court of Appeals.

MCCREARY COUNTY v. ACLU
545 U.S. 844; 125 S.Ct. 2722; 162 L.Ed.2d. 729 (2005)
Vote: 5-4

In this case and the companion case of Van Orden v. Perry, the Court re-enters the national debate over the constitutionality of displaying the Ten Commandments on government property. In Stone v. Graham (1980), the Court had held that such a display in public school classrooms violated the Establishment Clause of the First Amendment. Students should compare the McCreary County and Van Orden decisions. Are these decisions compatible?

Justice Souter delivered the opinion of the Court.

Executives of two counties posted a version of the Ten Commandments on the walls of their courthouses. After suits were filed charging violations of the Establishment Clause, the legislative body of each county adopted a resolution calling for a more extensive exhibit meant to show that the Commandments are Kentucky's "precedent legal code." The result in each instance was a modified display of the Commandments surrounded by texts containing religious references as their sole common element. After changing counsel, the counties revised the exhibits again by eliminating some documents, expanding the text set out in another, and adding some new ones.

The issues are whether a determination of the counties' purpose is a sound basis for ruling on the Establishment Clause complaints, and whether evaluation of the counties' claim of secular purpose for the ultimate displays may take their evolution into account. We hold that the counties' manifest objective may be dispositive of the constitutional enquiry, and that the development of the presentation should be considered when determining its purpose….

In the summer of 1999, petitioners McCreary County and Pulaski County, Kentucky, put up in their respective courthouses large, gold-framed copies of an abridged text of the ... Ten Commandments ... In McCreary County, the placement of the Commandments responded to an order of the county legislative body requiring "the display [to] be posted in 'a very high traffic area' of the courthouse." In Pulaski County, amidst reported controversy over the propriety of the display, the Commandments were hung in a ceremony presided over by the county Judge-Executive, who called them "good rules to live by." ...

In each county, the hallway display was "readily visible to ... county citizens who use the courthouse to conduct their civic business, to obtain or renew driver's licenses and permits, to register cars, to pay local taxes, and to register to vote."

In November 1999, respondents American Civil Liberties Union of Kentucky ... sued the Counties in Federal District Court under 42 U.S.C § 1983, and sought a preliminary injunction against maintaining the displays, which the ACLU charged were violations of the prohibition of religious establishment included in the First Amendment of the Constitution. Within a month, and before the District Court had responded to the request for injunction, the legislative body of each County authorized a second, expanded display, by nearly identical resolutions reciting that the Ten Commandments are "the precedent legal code upon which the civil and criminal codes of ... Kentucky are founded," and stating several grounds for taking that position....

As directed by the resolutions, the Counties expanded the displays of the Ten Commandments in their locations, presumably along with copies of the resolution, which instructed that it, too, be posted. In addition to the first display's large framed copy of the edited King James version of the Commandments, the second included eight other documents in smaller frames, each either having a religious theme or excerpted to highlight a religious element....

After argument, the District Court entered a preliminary injunction on May 5, 2000, ordering that the "display ... be removed from [each] County Courthouse IMMEDIATELY" and that no county official "erect or cause to be erected similar displays." ...

The Counties ... then installed another display in each courthouse, the third within a year. No new resolution authorized this one, nor did the Counties repeal the resolutions that preceded the second. The posting consists of nine framed documents of equal size, one of them setting out the Ten Commandments ... and quoted at greater length than before....

Assembled with the Commandments are framed copies of the Magna Carta, the Declaration of Independence, the Bill of Rights, the lyrics of the Star Spangled Banner, the Mayflower Compact, the National Motto, the Preamble to the Kentucky Constitution, and a picture of Lady Justice. The collection is entitled "The Foundations of American Law and Government Display" and each document comes with a statement about its historical and legal significance....

The ACLU moved to supplement the preliminary injunction to enjoin the Counties' third display, and the Counties responded with several explanations for the new version, including desires "to demonstrate that the Ten Commandments were part of the foundation of American Law and Government" and "to educate the citizens of the county regarding some of the documents that played a significant role in the foundation of our system of law and government." ...

As requested, the trial court supplemented the injunction, and a divided panel of the Court of Appeals for the Sixth Circuit affirmed.... We granted certiorari, and now affirm....

Twenty-five years ago in a case prompted by posting the Ten Commandments in Kentucky's public schools, this Court recognized that the Commandments "are undeniably a sacred text in the Jewish and Christian faiths" and held that their display in public classrooms violated the First Amendment's bar against establishment of religion. Stone found a predominantly religious purpose in the government's posting of the Commandments, given their prominence as " 'an instrument of religion.' " The Counties ask for a different approach here by arguing that official purpose is unknowable and the search for it inherently vain. In the alternative, the Counties would avoid the District Court's conclusion by having us limit the scope of the purpose enquiry so severely that any trivial rationalization would suffice, under a standard oblivious to the history of religious government action like the progression of exhibits in this case....

Ever since *Lemon v. Kurtzman* (1971) summarized the three familiar considerations for evaluating Establishment Clause claims, looking to whether government action has "a secular legislative purpose" has been a common, albeit seldom dispositive, element of our cases. Though we have found government action motivated by an illegitimate purpose only four times

(Continued)

since *Lemon*, and "the secular purpose requirement alone may rarely be determinative …, it nevertheless serves an important function."

The touchstone for our analysis is the principle that the "First Amendment mandates governmental neutrality between religion and religion, and between religion and nonreligion." When the government acts with the ostensible and predominant purpose of advancing religion, it violates that central Establishment Clause value of official religious neutrality, there being no neutrality when the government's ostensible object is to take sides. Manifesting a purpose to favor one faith over another, or adherence to religion generally, clashes with the "understanding, reached … after decades of religious war, that liberty and social stability demand a religious tolerance that respects the religious views of all citizens." … By showing a purpose to favor religion, the government "sends the … message to … nonadherents 'that they are outsiders, not full members of the political community, and an accompanying message to adherents that they are insiders, favored members.'" …

Despite the intuitive importance of official purpose to the realization of Establishment Clause values, the Counties ask us to abandon *Lemons* purpose test, or at least to truncate any enquiry into purpose here. Their first argument is that the very consideration of purpose is deceptive: according to them, true "purpose" is unknowable, and its search merely an excuse for courts to act selectively and unpredictably in picking out evidence of subjective intent. The assertions are as seismic as they are unconvincing.

Examination of purpose is a staple of statutory interpretation that makes up the daily fare of every appellate court in the country….

The cases with findings of a predominantly religious purpose point to the straightforward nature of the test…. In each case, the government's action was held unconstitutional only because openly available data supported a commonsense conclusion that a religious objective permeated the government's action.

Nor is there any indication that the enquiry is rigged in practice to finding a religious purpose dominant every time a case is filed. In the past, the test has not been fatal very often, presumably because government does not generally act unconstitutionally, with the predominant purpose of advancing religion. That said, one consequence of the corollary that Establishment Clause analysis does not look to the veiled psyche of government officers could be that in some of the cases in which establishment complaints failed, savvy

officials had disguised their religious intent so cleverly that the objective observer just missed it. But that is no reason for great constitutional concern. If someone in the government hides religious motive so well that the "objective observer, acquainted with the text, legislative history, and implementation of the statute," cannot see it, then without something more the government does not make a divisive announcement that in itself amounts to taking religious sides. A secret motive stirs up no strife and does nothing to make outsiders of nonadherents, and it suffices to wait and see whether such government action turns out to have (as it may even be likely to have) the illegitimate effect of advancing religion….

After declining the invitation to abandon concern with purpose wholesale, we also have to avoid the Counties' alternative tack of trivializing the enquiry into it….

Lemon said that government action must have "a secular … purpose," and after a host of cases it is fair to add that although a legislature's stated reasons will generally get deference, the secular purpose required has to be genuine, not a sham, and not merely secondary to a religious objective….

Even the Counties' own cited authority confirms that we have not made the purpose test a pushover for any secular claim…. [T]he Court often does accept governmental statements of purpose, in keeping with the respect owed in the first instance to … official claims. But in those unusual cases where the claim was an apparent sham, or the secular purpose secondary, the unsurprising results have been findings of no adequate secular object, as against a predominantly religious one….

The Counties' second proffered limitation can be dispatched quickly. They argue that purpose in a case like this one should be inferred, if at all, only from the latest news about the last in a series of governmental actions, however close they may all be in time and subject. But the world is not made brand new every morning, and the Counties are simply asking us to ignore perfectly probative evidence; they want an absent-minded objective observer, not one presumed to be familiar with the history of the government's actions and competent to learn what history has to show. The Counties' position just bucks common sense: reasonable observers have reasonable memories, and our precedents sensibly forbid an observer "to turn a blind eye to the context in which [the] policy arose." …

We take *Stone* as the initial legal benchmark, our only case dealing with the constitutionality of displaying the Commandments. *Stone* recognized that the Commandments are an "instrument of religion" and that, at least on the facts before it, the display of their text could presumptively be understood as meant to advance religion: although state law specifically required their posting in public school classrooms, their isolated exhibition did not leave room even for an argument that secular education explained their being there. But *Stone* did not purport to decide the constitutionality of every possible way the Commandments might be set out by the government, and under the Establishment Clause detail is key....

The display rejected in *Stone* had two obvious similarities to the first one in the sequence here: both set out a text of the Commandments as distinct from any traditionally symbolic representation, and each stood alone, not part of an arguably secular display. *Stone* stressed the significance of integrating the Commandments into a secular scheme to forestall the broadcast of an otherwise clearly religious message, and for good reason, the Commandments being a central point of reference in the religious and moral history of Jews and Christians.... Displaying that text is thus different from a symbolic depiction, like tablets with 10 roman numerals, which could be seen as alluding to a general notion of law, not a sectarian conception of faith. Where the text is set out, the insistence of the religious message is hard to avoid in the absence of a context plausibly suggesting a message going beyond an excuse to promote the religious point of view. The display in *Stone* had no context that might have indicated an object beyond the religious character of the text, and the Counties' solo exhibit here did nothing more to counter the sectarian implication than the postings at issue in *Stone*. Actually, the posting by the Counties lacked even the *Stone* display's implausible disclaimer that the Commandments were set out to show their effect on the civil law. What is more, at the ceremony for posting the framed Commandments in Pulaski County, the county executive was accompanied by his pastor, who testified to the certainty of the existence of God. The reasonable observer could only think that the Counties meant to emphasize and celebrate the Commandments' religious message.

This is not to deny that the Commandments have had influence on civil or secular law; a major text of a majority religion is bound to be felt. The point is simply that the original text viewed in its entirety is an unmistakably religious statement dealing with religious obligations and with morality subject to religious

sanction. When the government initiates an effort to place this statement alone in public view, a religious object is unmistakable....

Once the Counties were sued, they modified the exhibits and invited additional insight into their purpose in a display that hung for about six months. This new one was the product of forthright and nearly identical Pulaski and McCreary County resolutions listing a series of American historical documents with theistic and Christian references, which were to be posted in order to furnish a setting for displaying the Ten Commandments and any "other Kentucky and American historical document" without raising concern about "any Christian or religious references" in them....

In this second display, unlike the first, the Commandments were not hung in isolation, merely leaving the Counties' purpose to emerge from the pervasively religious text of the Commandments themselves. Instead, the second version was required to include the statement of the government's purpose expressly set out in the county resolutions, and underscored it by juxtaposing the Commandments to other documents with highlighted references to God as their sole common element. The display's unstinting focus was on religious passages, showing that the Counties were posting the Commandments precisely because of their sectarian content. That demonstration of the government's objective was enhanced by serial religious references and the accompanying resolution's claim about the embodiment of ethics in Christ. Together, the display and resolution presented an indisputable, and undisputed, showing of an impermissible purpose.

Today, the Counties make no attempt to defend their undeniable objective, but instead hopefully describe version two as "dead and buried." Their refusal to defend the second display is understandable, but the reasonable observer could not forget it....

After the Counties changed lawyers, they mounted a third display, without a new resolution or repeal of the old one. The result was the "Foundations of American Law and Government" exhibit, which placed the Commandments in the company of other documents the Counties thought especially significant in the historical foundation of American government. In trying to persuade the District Court to lift the preliminary injunction, the Counties cited several new purposes for the third version, including a desire "to educate the citizens of the county regarding some of the documents that played a significant role in the foundation of our system of law and government." The Counties' claims

(Continued)

did not, however, persuade the court, intimately familiar with the details of this litigation, or the Court of Appeals, neither of which found a legitimizing secular purpose in this third version of the display....

These new statements of purpose were presented only as a litigating position, there being no further authorizing action by the Counties' governing boards. And although repeal of the earlier county authorizations would not have erased them from the record of evidence bearing on current purpose, the extraordinary resolutions for the second display passed just months earlier were not repealed or otherwise repudiated. Indeed, the sectarian spirit of the common resolution found enhanced expression in the third display, which quoted more of the purely religious language of the Commandments than the first two displays had done. No reasonable observer could swallow the claim that the Counties had cast off the objective so unmistakable in the earlier displays....

In holding the preliminary injunction adequately supported by evidence that the Counties' purpose had not changed at the third stage, we do not decide that the Counties' past actions forever taint any effort on their part to deal with the subject matter. We hold only that purpose needs to be taken seriously under the Establishment Clause and needs to be understood in light of context; an implausible claim that governmental purpose has changed should not carry the day in a court of law any more than in a head with common sense. It is enough to say here that district courts are fully capable of adjusting preliminary relief to take account of genuine changes in constitutionally significant conditions.

Nor do we have occasion here to hold that a sacred text can never be integrated constitutionally into a governmental display on the subject of law, or American history. We do not forget, and in this litigation have frequently been reminded, that our own courtroom frieze was deliberately designed in the exercise of governmental authority so as to include the figure of Moses holding tablets exhibiting a portion of the Hebrew text of the later, secularly phrased Commandments; in the company of 17 other lawgivers, most of them secular figures, there is no risk that Moses would strike an observer as evidence that the National Government was violating neutrality in religion....

Given the ample support for the District Court's finding of a predominantly religious purpose behind the Counties' third display, we affirm the Sixth Circuit in upholding the preliminary injunction.

Justice O'Connor, concurring....

Justice Scalia, with whom *The Chief Justice* and *Justice Thomas* join, and with whom *Justice Kennedy* joins [in part], dissenting.

... Historical practices ... demonstrate that there is a distance between the acknowledgment of a single Creator and the establishment of a religion. The former is, as *Marsh v. Chambers* (1983) put it, "a tolerable acknowledgment of beliefs widely held among the people of this country." The three most popular religions in the United States, Christianity, Judaism, and Islam—which combined account for 97.7% of all believers—are monotheistic. All of them, moreover (Islam included), believe that the Ten Commandments were given by God to Moses, and are divine prescriptions for a virtuous life. Publicly honoring the Ten Commandments is thus indistinguishable, insofar as discriminating against other religions is concerned, from publicly honoring God. Both practices are recognized across such a broad and diverse range of the population—from Christians to Muslims—that they cannot be reasonably understood as a government endorsement of a particular religious viewpoint....

As bad as the *Lemon* test is, it is worse for the fact that, since its inception, its seemingly simple mandates have been manipulated to fit whatever result the Court aimed to achieve. Today's opinion is no different. In two respects it modifies *Lemon* to ratchet up the Court's hostility to religion. First, the Court justifies inquiry into legislative purpose, not as an end itself, but as a means to ascertain the appearance of the government action to an " 'objective observer.' " Because in the Court's view the true danger to be guarded against is that the objective observer would feel like an "outsider" or "not [a] full member of the political community," its inquiry focuses not on the actual purpose of government action, but the "purpose apparent from government action." Under this approach, even if a government could show that its actual purpose was not to advance religion, it would presumably violate the Constitution as long as the Court's objective observer would think otherwise....

Second, the Court replaces *Lemons* requirement that the government have "a secular ... purpose," with the heightened requirement that the secular purpose "predominate" over any purpose to advance religion. The Court treats this extension as a natural outgrowth of the longstanding requirement that the government's secular purpose not be a sham, but simple logic shows the two to be unrelated. If the government's proffered secular purpose is not genuine, then the government has no secular purpose at all. The new demand that secular purpose predominate contradicts *Lemons* more limited requirement, and finds no support in our cases. In all but one of the five cases in which this Court has invalidated a government practice on the basis of its purpose to benefit religion, it has first declared that the statute was motivated entirely by the desire to advance religion....

Even accepting the Court's *Lemon-based* premises, the displays at issue here were constitutional....

In sum: The first displays did not necessarily evidence an intent to further religious practice; nor did

the second displays, or the resolutions authorizing them; and there is in any event no basis for attributing whatever intent motivated first and second displays to the third. Given the presumption of regularity that always accompanies our review of official action, the Court has identified no evidence of a purpose to advance religion in a way that is inconsistent with our cases. The Court may well be correct in identifying the third displays as the fruit of a desire to display the Ten Commandments, but neither our cases nor our history support its assertion that such a desire renders the fruit poisonous.

For the foregoing reasons, I would reverse the judgment of the Court of Appeals.

VAN ORDEN v. PERRY
545 U.S. 677; 125 S.Ct. 2854; 162 L.Ed.2d. 607 (2005)
Vote: 5-4

As in the companion case of McCreary County v. ACLU, the Court here addresses the question of whether a public display of the Ten Commandments violates the Establishment Clause of the First Amendment. The "display" in the present case took the form of a monument, six-feet high and three-and-a-half-feet wide located on the grounds of the Texas State Capitol.

Chief Justice Rehnquist announced the judgment of the Court and delivered an opinion, in which **Justice Scalia, Justice Kennedy**, and **Justice Thomas** join.

The question here is whether the Establishment Clause of the First Amendment allows the display of a monument inscribed with the Ten Commandments on the Texas State Capitol grounds. We hold that it does.

The 22 acres surrounding the Texas State Capitol contain 17 monuments and 21 historical markers commemorating the "people, ideals, and events that compose Texan identity." The monolith challenged here stands 6-feet high and 31/2-feet wide. It is located ... between the Capitol and the Supreme Court building. Its primary content is the text of the Ten Commandments. An eagle grasping the American flag, an eye inside of a pyramid, and two small tablets with what appears to be an ancient script are carved above the text of the Ten Commandments. Below the text are

two Stars of David and the superimposed Greek letters Chi and Rho, which represent Christ. The bottom of the monument bears the inscription: "PRESENTED TO THE PEOPLE AND YOUTH OF TEXAS BY THE FRATERNAL ORDER OF EAGLES OF TEXAS 1961."

The legislative record surrounding the State's acceptance of the monument from the Eagles—a national social, civic, and patriotic organization—is limited to legislative journal entries. After the monument was accepted, the State selected a site for the monument based on the recommendation of the state organization responsible for maintaining the Capitol grounds. The Eagles paid the cost of erecting the monument, the dedication of which was presided over by two state legislators.

Petitioner Thomas Van Orden is a native Texan and a resident of Austin. At one time he was a licensed lawyer, having graduated from Southern Methodist Law School. Van Orden testified that, since 1995, he has encountered the Ten Commandments monument during his frequent visits to the Capitol grounds....

Forty years after the monument's erection and six years after Van Orden began to encounter the monument frequently, he sued numerous State officials in their official capacities under ... 42 U.S.C. § 1983, seeking both a declaration that the monument's placement violates the Establishment Clause and an injunction requiring its removal. After a bench trial, the District

(Continued)

Court held that the monument did not contravene the Establishment Clause.... We granted certiorari and now affirm.

Our cases, Janus-like, point in two directions in applying the Establishment Clause. One face looks toward the strong role played by religion and religious traditions throughout our Nation's history.... The other face looks toward the principle that governmental intervention in religious matters can itself endanger religious freedom.

This case, like all Establishment Clause challenges, presents us with the difficulty of respecting both faces. Our institutions presuppose a Supreme Being, yet these institutions must not press religious observances upon their citizens. One face looks to the past in acknowledgment of our Nation's heritage, while the other looks to the present in demanding a separation between church and state. Reconciling these two faces requires that we neither abdicate our responsibility to maintain a division between church and state nor evince a hostility to religion by disabling the government from in some ways recognizing our religious heritage ...

These two faces are evident in representative cases both upholding and invalidating laws under the Establishment Clause. Over the last 25 years, we have sometimes pointed to *Lemon v. Kurtzman* ... (1971) as providing the governing test in Establishment Clause challenges. Yet, just two years after *Lemon* was decided, we noted that the factors identified in *Lemon* serve as "no more than helpful signposts." *Hunt v. McNair* ... (1973). Many of our recent cases simply have not applied the *Lemon* test. Others have applied it only after concluding that the challenged practice was invalid under a different Establishment Clause test.

Whatever may be the fate of the *Lemon* test in the larger scheme of Establishment Clause jurisprudence, we think it not useful in dealing with the sort of passive monument that Texas has erected on its Capitol grounds. Instead, our analysis is driven both by the nature of the monument and by our Nation's history.

As we explained in *Lynch v. Donnelly* ... (1984): "There is an unbroken history of official acknowledgment by all three branches of government of the role of religion in American life from at least 1789." For example, both Houses passed resolutions in 1789 asking President George Washington to issue a Thanksgiving Day Proclamation to "recommend to the people of the United States a day of public thanksgiving and prayer, to be observed by acknowledging, with grateful hearts, the many and signal favors of Almighty God." President Washington's proclamation directly attributed to the Supreme Being the foundations and successes of our young Nation ...

Recognition of the role of God in our Nation's heritage has also been reflected in our decisions. We have acknowledged, for example, that "religion has been closely identified with our history and government" and that "[t]he history of man is inseparable from the history of religion." *Engel v. Vitale* ... (1962). This recognition has led us to hold that the Establishment Clause permits a state legislature to open its daily sessions with a prayer by a chaplain paid by the State. Such a practice, we thought, was "deeply embedded in the history and tradition of this country." As we observed there, "it would be incongruous to interpret [the Establishment Clause] as imposing more stringent First Amendment limits on the States than the draftsmen imposed on the Federal Government." With similar reasoning, we have upheld laws, which originated from one of the Ten Commandments, that prohibited the sale of merchandise on Sunday. *McGowan v. Maryland* ... (1961).

In this case we are faced with a display of the Ten Commandments on government property outside the Texas State Capitol. Such acknowledgments of the role played by the Ten Commandments in our Nation's heritage are common throughout America. We need only look within our own Courtroom. Since 1935, Moses has stood, holding two tablets that reveal portions of the Ten Commandments written in Hebrew, among other lawgivers in the south frieze. Representations of the Ten Commandments adorn the metal gates lining the north and south sides of the Courtroom as well as the doors leading into the Courtroom. Moses also sits on the exterior east facade of the building holding the Ten Commandments tablets.

Similar acknowledgments can be seen throughout a visitor's tour of our Nation's Capital. For example, a large statue of Moses holding the Ten Commandments, alongside a statue of the Apostle Paul, has overlooked the rotunda of the Library of Congress's Jefferson Building since 1897. And the Jefferson Building's Great Reading Room contains a sculpture of a woman beside the Ten Commandments with a quote above her from the Old Testament. A medallion with two tablets depicting the Ten Commandments decorates the floor of the National Archives. Inside the Department of Justice, a statue entitled "The Spirit of Law" has two tablets representing the Ten Commandments lying at its feet. In front of the Ronald Reagan

Building is another sculpture that includes a depiction of the Ten Commandments. So too a 24-foot-tall sculpture, depicting, among other things, the Ten Commandments and a cross, stands outside the federal courthouse that houses both the Court of Appeals and the District Court for the District of Columbia. Moses is also prominently featured in the Chamber of the United States House of Representatives. Our opinions, like our building, have recognized the role the Decalogue plays in America's heritage. These displays and recognitions of the Ten Commandments bespeak the rich American tradition of religious acknowledgments.

Of course, the Ten Commandments are religious— they were so viewed at their inception and so remain. The monument, therefore, has religious significance. According to Judeo-Christian belief, the Ten Commandments were given to Moses by God on Mt. Sinai. But Moses was a lawgiver as well as a religious leader. And the Ten Commandments have an undeniable historical meaning, as the foregoing examples demonstrate. Simply having religious content or promoting a message consistent with a religious doctrine does not run afoul of the Establishment Clause.

There are, of course, limits to the display of religious messages or symbols. For example, we held unconstitutional a Kentucky statute requiring the posting of the Ten Commandments in every public schoolroom. *Stone v. Graham* … (1980). In the classroom context, we found that the Kentucky statute had an improper and plainly religious purpose. As evidenced by *Stone* s almost exclusive reliance upon two of our school prayer cases, it stands as an example of the fact that we have "been particularly vigilant in monitoring compliance with the Establishment Clause in elementary and secondary schools." …

The placement of the Ten Commandments monument on the Texas State Capitol grounds is a far more passive use of those texts than was the case in *Stone*, where the text confronted elementary school students every day. Indeed, Van Orden, the petitioner here, apparently walked by the monument for a number of years before bringing this lawsuit…. Texas has treated her Capitol grounds monuments as representing the several strands in the State's political and legal history. The inclusion of the Ten Commandments monument in this group has a dual significance, partaking of both religion and government. We cannot say that Texas's display of this monument violates the Establishment Clause of the First Amendment.

The judgment of the Court of Appeals is affirmed.

Justice Scalia, concurring. …

Justice Thomas, concurring. …

Justice Breyer, concurring in the judgment.

In *School Dist. of Abington Township v. Schempp* … (1963), Justice Goldberg, joined by Justice Harlan, wrote, in respect to the First Amendment's Religion Clauses, that there is "no simple and clear measure which by precise application can readily and invariably demark the permissible from the impermissible." One must refer instead to the basic purposes of those Clauses. They seek to "assure the fullest possible scope of religious liberty and tolerance for all." They seek to avoid that divisiveness based upon religion that promotes social conflict, sapping the strength of government and religion alike. They seek to maintain that "separation of church and state" that has long been critical to the "peaceful dominion that religion exercises in [this] country," where the "spirit of religion" and the "spirit of freedom" are productively "united," "reign[ing] together" but in separate spheres "on the same soil." …

The Court has made clear, as Justices Goldberg and Harlan noted, that the realization of these goals means that government must "neither engage in nor compel religious practices," that it must "effect no favoritism among sects or between religion and nonreligion," and that it must "work deterrence of no religious belief." The government must avoid excessive interference with, or promotion of, religion. But the Establishment Clause does not compel the government to purge from the public sphere all that in any way partakes of the religious. Such absolutism is not only inconsistent with our national traditions, but would also tend to promote the kind of social conflict the Establishment Clause seeks to avoid….

Justice Stevens, with whom *Justice Ginsburg* joins, dissenting. …

Justice O'Connor, dissenting. …

Justice Souter, with whom *Justice Stevens* and *Justice Ginsburg* join, dissenting.

Although the First Amendment's Religion Clauses have not been read to mandate absolute governmental neutrality toward religion, the Establishment Clause

(Continued)

requires neutrality as a general rule and thus expresses Madison's condemnation of "employ[ing] Religion as an engine of Civil policy." A governmental display of an obviously religious text cannot be squared with neutrality, except in a setting that plausibly indicates that the statement is not placed in view with a predominant purpose on the part of government either to adopt the religious message or to urge its acceptance by others.

Until today, only one of our cases addressed the constitutionality of posting the Ten Commandments, *Stone v. Graham.* A Kentucky statute required posting the Commandments on the walls of public school classrooms, and the Court described the State's purpose (relevant under the tripartite test laid out in *Lemon* as being at odds with the obligation of religious neutrality)....

... When the Fraternal Order of Eagles ... donated identical monuments to other jurisdictions, it was seeking to impart a religious message. Accordingly, it was not just the terms of the moral code, but the proclamation that the terms of the code were enjoined by God, that the Eagles put forward in the monuments they donated....

Texas seeks to take advantage of the recognition that visual symbol and written text can manifest a secular purpose in secular company, when it argues that its monument (like Moses in the frieze) is not alone and ought to be viewed as only 1 among 17 placed on the 22 acres surrounding the state capitol. Texas, indeed, says that the Capitol grounds are like a museum for a collection of exhibits, the kind of setting that several Members of the Court have said can render the exhibition of religious artifacts permissible, even though in other circumstances their display would be seen as meant to convey a religious message forbidden to the State. So, for example, the Government of the United States does not violate the Establishment Clause by hanging Giotto's Madonna on the wall of the National Gallery.

But 17 monuments with no common appearance, history, or esthetic role scattered over 22 acres is not a museum, and anyone strolling around the lawn would surely take each memorial on its own terms without any dawning sense that some purpose held the miscellany together more coherently than fortuity and the edge of the grass. One monument expresses admiration for pioneer women. One pays respect to the fighters of World War II. And one quotes the God of Abraham whose command is the sanction for moral law. The themes are individual grit, patriotic courage, and God as the source of Jewish and Christian morality; there is no common denominator....

I would reverse the judgment of the Court of Appeals.

WALZ v. TAX COMMISSION
397 U.S. 664; 90 S.Ct. 1409; 25 L.Ed.2d. 697 (1970)
Vote: 8-1

In this case, the Court considers whether a property tax exemption for religious organizations constitutes a violation of the Establishment Clause.

Mr. Chief Justice Burger delivered the opinion of the Court.

... Appellant, owner of real estate in Richmond County, New York, sought an injunction in the New York courts to prevent the New York City Tax Commission from granting property tax exemptions to religious organizations for religious properties used solely for religious worship. The exemption from state taxes is authorized by Art. 16, Sec. 1, of the New York Constitution, which provides in relevant part:

Exemptions from taxation may be granted only by general laws. Exemptions may be altered or repealed except those exempting real or personal property used exclusively for religious, educational or charitable purposes as defined by law and owned by any corporation or association organized or conducted exclusively for one or more of such purposes and not operating for profit.

The essence of appellant's contention was that the New York City Tax Commission's grant of an exemption to church property indirectly requires the appellant to make a contribution to religious bodies and thereby violates provisions prohibiting establishment of religion under the First Amendment which under the Fourteenth Amendment is binding on the States.

Appellee's motion for summary judgment was granted and the Appellate Divisions of the New York Supreme Court, and the New York Court of Appeals affirmed. We noted probable jurisdiction … and affirm.

Prior opinions of this Court have discussed the development and historical background of the First Amendment in detail…. It would therefore serve no useful purpose to review in detail the background of the Establishment and Free Exercise Clauses of the First Amendment or to restate what the Court's opinions have reflected over the years….

The course of constitutional neutrality in this area cannot be an absolutely straight line; rigidity could well defeat the basic purpose of these provisions, which is to insure that no religion be sponsored or favored, none commanded, and none inhibited. The general principle deducible from the First Amendment and all that has been said by the Court is this: that we will not tolerate either governmentally established religion or governmental interference with religion. Short of those expressly proscribed governmental acts there is room for play in the joints productive of a benevolent neutrality which will permit religious exercise to exist without sponsorship and without interference.

Each value judgment under the Religion Clauses must therefore turn on whether particular acts in question are intended to establish or interfere with religious beliefs and practices or have the effect of doing so. Adherence to the policy of neutrality that derives from an accommodation of the Establishment and Free Exercise Clauses has prevented the kind of involvement that would tip the balance toward government control of churches or governmental restraint on religious practice. Adherents of particular faiths and individual churches frequently take strong positions on public issues including … vigorous advocacy of legal or constitutional positions. Of course, churches as much as secular bodies and private citizens have that right. No perfect or absolute separation is really possible; the very existence of the Religion Clauses is an involvement of sorts—one that seeks to mark boundaries to avoid excessive entanglement….

The legislative purpose of a property tax exemption is neither the advancement nor the inhibition of religion; it is neither sponsorship nor hostility. New York, in common with the other States, has determined that certain entities that exist in a harmonious relationship to the community at large, and that foster its "moral or mental improvement," should not be inhibited in their activities by property taxation or the hazard of loss of those properties for nonpayment of taxes. It has not singled out one particular church or religious group or even churches as such; rather, it has granted exemption to all houses of religious worship within a broad class of property owned by nonprofit, quasi-public corporations which include hospitals, libraries, playgrounds, scientific, professional, historical, and patriotic groups. The State has an affirmative policy that considers these groups as beneficial and stabilizing influences in community life and finds this classification useful, desirable, and in the public interest. Qualification for tax exemption is not perpetual or immutable; some tax-exempt groups lose that status when their activities take them outside the classification and new entities can come into being and qualify for exemption.

Governments have not always been tolerant of religious activity, and hostility toward religion has taken many shapes and forms—economic, political, and sometimes harshly oppressive. Grants of exemption historically reflect the concern of authors of constitutions and statutes as to the latent dangers inherent in the imposition of property taxes; exemption constitutes a reasonable and balanced attempt to guard against those dangers. The limits of permissible state accommodation to religion are by no means coextensive with the noninterference mandated by the Free Exercise Clause. To equate the two would be to deny a national heritage with roots in the Revolution itself…. We cannot read New York's statute as attempting to establish religion; it is simply sparing the exercise of religion from the burden of property taxation levied on private profit institutions….

Granting tax exemptions to churches necessarily operates to afford an indirect economic benefit and also gives rise to some, but yet a lesser, involvement than taxing them. In analyzing either alternative the questions are whether the involvement is excessive, and whether it is a continuing one calling for official and continuing surveillance leading to an impermissible degree of entanglement. Obviously a direct money subsidy would be a relationship pregnant with involvement and, as with most governmental grant programs, could encompass sustained and detailed administrative relationships for enforcement of statutory or administrative standards, but that is not this case. The hazards of churches supporting government are hardly less in their potential than the hazards of government supporting churches, each relationship carries some

(Continued)

involvement rather than the desired insulation and separation. We cannot ignore the instances in history when church support of government led to the kind of involvement we seek to avoid.

The grant of a tax exemption is not sponsorship since the government does not transfer part of its revenue to churches but simply abstains from demanding that the church support the state. No one has ever suggested that tax exemption has converted libraries, art galleries, or hospitals into arms of the state or put employees "on the public payroll." There is no genuine nexus between tax exemption and establishment of religion. As Mr. Justice Holmes commented in a related context "a page of history is worth a volume of logic." … The exemption creates only a minimal and remote involvement between church and state and far less than taxation of churches. It restricts the fiscal relationship between church and state, and tends to complement and reinforce the desired separation insulating each from the other.

Separation in this context cannot mean absence of all contact; the complexities of modern life inevitably produce some contact and the fire and police protection received by houses of religious worship are no more than incidental benefits accorded all persons or institutions within a State's boundaries, along with many other exempt organizations. The appellant has not established even an arguable quantitative correlation between the payment of an *ad valorem* property tax and the receipt of these municipal benefits.

All of the 50 States provide for tax exemption of places of worship, most of them doing so by constitutional guarantees. For so long as federal income taxes have had any potential impact on churches—over 75 years—religious organizations have been expressly exempt from the tax. Such treatment is an "aid" to churches no more and no less in principle than the real estate tax exemption granted by States. Few concepts are more deeply embedded in the fabric of our national life, beginning with pre-Revolutionary colonial times, than for the government to exercise at the very least this kind of benevolent neutrality toward churches and religious exercise generally so long as none was favored over others and none suffered interference….

It is obviously correct that no one acquires a vested or protected right in violation of the Constitution by long use, even when that span of time covers our entire national existence and indeed predates it. Yet an unbroken practice of according the exemption to churches, openly and by affirmative state action, not covertly or by state inaction, is not something to be lightly cast aside. Nearly 50 years ago Mr. Justice Holmes stated: "If a thing has been practiced for two hundred years by common consent, it will need a strong case for the Fourteenth Amendment to affect it…." … Nothing in this national attitude toward religious tolerance and two centuries of uninterrupted freedom from taxation has given the remotest sign of leading to an established church or religion and on the contrary it has operated affirmatively to help guarantee the free exercise of all forms of religious belief. Thus, it is hardly useful to suggest that tax exemption is but the "foot in the door" or the "nose of the camel in the tent" leading to an established church. If tax exemption can be seen as this first step toward "establishment" of religion, as Mr. Justice Douglas fears, the second step has been long in coming….

The argument that making "fine distinctions" between what is and what is not absolute under the Constitution is to render us a government of men, not laws, gives too little weight to the fact that it is an essential part of adjudication to draw distinctions, including fine ones, in the process of interpreting the Constitution. We must frequently decide, for example, what are "reasonable" searches and seizures under the Fourth Amendment. Determining what acts of government tend to establish or interfere with religion falls well within what courts have long been called upon to do in sensitive areas.

It is interesting to note that while the precise question we now decide has not been directly before the Court previously, the broad question was discussed by the Court in relation to real estate taxes assessed nearly a century ago on land owned by and adjacent to a church in Washington, D.C. At that time Congress granted real estate tax exemptions to buildings devoted to art, to institutions of public charity, libraries, cemeteries, and "church buildings, and grounds actually occupied by such buildings." In denying tax exemption as to land owned by but not used for the church, but rather to produce income, the Court concluded:

In the exercise of this [taxing] power, Congress, like any State legislature unrestricted by constitutional provisions, may at its discretion wholly exempt certain classes of property from taxation, or may tax them at a lower rate than other property….

It appears that at least up to 1885 this Court, reflecting more than a century of our history and uninterrupted practice, accepted without discussion the proposition that federal or state grants of tax exemption to churches were not a violation of the Religion

Clauses of the First Amendment. As to the New York statute, we now confirm that view.

Affirmed.

Mr. Justice Brennan, concurring....

Mr. Justice Harlan [concurring]. ...

Mr. Justice Douglas, dissenting.

... [There] is a major difference between churches on the one hand and the rest of the nonprofit organizations on the other. Government could provide or finance operas, hospitals, historical societies, and all the rest because they represent social welfare programs within the reach of the police power. In contrast, government may not provide or finance worship because of the Establishment Clause any more than it may single out "atheistic" or "agnostic" centers or groups and create or finance them.

The Brookings Institution, writing in 1933, before the application of the Establishment Clause of the First Amendment to the States, said about tax exemptions of religious groups:

Tax exemption, no matter what its form, is essentially a government grant or subsidy. Such grants would seem to be justified only if the purpose for which they are made is one for which the legislative body would be equally willing to make a direct appropriation from public funds equal to the amount of the exemption. This test would not be met except in the case where the exemption is granted to encourage certain activities of private interests, which, if not thus performed, would have to be assumed by the government at an expenditure at least as great as the value of the exemption....

If believers are entitled to public financial support, so are nonbelievers. A believer and nonbeliever under the present law are treated differently because of the articles of their faith. Believers are doubtless comforted that the cause of religion is being fostered by this legislation. Yet one of the mandates of the First Amendment is to promote a viable, pluralistic society and to keep government neutral, not only between sects, but also between believers and nonbelievers. The present involvement of government in religion may seem *de minimis*. But it is, I fear, a long step down the Establishment path. Perhaps I have been misinformed. But as I have read the Constitution and its philosophy, I gathered that independence was the price of liberty.

I conclude that this tax exemption is unconstitutional.

ZELMAN v. SIMMONS-HARRIS
536 U.S. 639; 122 S.Ct. 2460; 153 L.Ed.2d. 604 (2002)
Vote: 5-4

In this case, the Supreme Court considers the constitutionality of a "school voucher" program established by the state of Ohio for the Cleveland school district. The essential facts and procedural history of the case are set forth in the majority opinion.

Chief Justice Rehnquist delivered the opinion of the Court.

There are more than 75,000 children enrolled in the Cleveland City School District. The majority of these children are from low-income and minority families. Few of these families enjoy the means to send their children to any school other than an inner-city public school. For more than a generation, however, Cleveland's public schools have been among the worst performing public schools in the Nation. In 1995, a Federal District Court declared a "crisis of magnitude" and placed the entire Cleveland school district under State control. Shortly thereafter, the State auditor found that Cleveland's public schools were in the midst of a "crisis that is perhaps unprecedented in the history of American education." The district had failed to meet any of the 18 State standards for minimal acceptable performance. Only 1 in 10 ninth graders could pass a basic proficiency examination, and students at all levels performed at a dismal rate compared with students in other Ohio public schools. More than two-thirds of high school students either dropped or failed out before graduation. Of those students who managed to reach their senior year, one of every four still failed

(Continued)

to graduate. Of those students who did graduate, few could read, write, or compute at levels comparable to their counterparts in other cities.

It is against this backdrop that Ohio enacted, among other initiatives, its Pilot Project Scholarship Program. The program provides financial assistance to families in any Ohio school district that is or has been "under federal court order requiring supervision and operational management of the district by the State superintendent." Cleveland is the only Ohio school district to fall within that category.

The program provides two basic kinds of assistance to parents of children in a covered district. First, the program provides tuition aid for students in kindergarten through third grade, expanding each year through eighth grade, to attend a participating public or private school of their parent's choosing. Second, the program provides tutorial aid for students who choose to remain enrolled in public school.

The tuition aid portion of the program is designed to provide educational choices to parents who reside in a covered district. Any private school, whether religious or nonreligious, may participate in the program and accept program students so long as the school is located within the boundaries of a covered district and meets statewide educational standards. Participating private schools must agree not to discriminate on the basis of race, religion, or ethnic background, or to "advocate or foster unlawful behavior or teach hatred of any person or group on the basis of race, ethnicity, national origin, or religion." Any public school located in a school district adjacent to the covered district may also participate in the program. Adjacent public schools are eligible to receive a $2,250 tuition grant for each program student accepted in addition to the full amount of per-pupil State funding attributable to each additional student. All participating schools, whether public or private, are required to accept students in accordance with rules and procedures established by the State superintendent....

In 1996, respondents, a group of Ohio taxpayers, challenged the Ohio program in State court on State and federal grounds. The Ohio Supreme Court rejected respondents' federal claims, but held that the enactment of the program violated certain procedural requirements of the Ohio Constitution. The state legislature immediately cured this defect, leaving the basic provisions discussed above intact.

In July 1999, respondents filed this action in United States District Court, seeking to enjoin the reenacted program on the ground that it violated the Establishment Clause of the United States Constitution. In

August 1999, the District Court issued a preliminary injunction barring further implementation of the program, which we stayed pending review by the Court of Appeals. In December 1999, the District Court granted summary judgment for respondents. In December 2000, a divided panel of the Court of Appeals affirmed the judgment of the District Court, finding that the program had the "primary effect" of advancing religion in violation of the Establishment Clause. The Court of Appeals stayed its mandate pending disposition in this Court. We granted certiorari and now reverse the Court of Appeals.

The Establishment Clause of the First Amendment, applied to the States through the Fourteenth Amendment, prevents a State from enacting laws that have the "purpose" or "effect" of advancing or inhibiting religion. *Agostini v. Felton* ... (1997). There is no dispute that the program challenged here was enacted for the valid secular purpose of providing educational assistance to poor children in a demonstrably failing public school system. Thus, the question presented is whether the Ohio program nonetheless has the forbidden "effect" of advancing or inhibiting religion.

To answer that question, our decisions have drawn a consistent distinction between government programs that provide aid directly to religious schools and programs of true private choice, in which government aid reaches religious schools only as a result of the genuine and independent choices of private individuals. While our jurisprudence with respect to the constitutionality of direct aid programs has "changed significantly" over the past two decades, our jurisprudence with respect to true private choice programs has remained consistent and unbroken. Three times we have confronted Establishment Clause challenges to neutral government programs that provide aid directly to a broad class of individuals, who, in turn, direct the aid to religious schools or institutions of their own choosing. Three times we have rejected such challenges.

In *Mueller* [*v. Allen* (1983)], we rejected an Establishment Clause challenge to a Minnesota program authorizing tax deductions for various educational expenses, including private school tuition costs, even though the great majority of the program's beneficiaries were parents of children in religious schools. We began by focusing on the class of beneficiaries, finding that because the class included "all parents," including parents with "children [who] attend nonsectarian private schools or sectarian private schools," the program was "not readily subject to challenge under the Establishment Clause." Then, viewing the program as a whole, we emphasized the principle of private choice, noting that public funds were made available to religious schools "only as a result of numerous, private choices of individual parents of school-age children." This, we said, ensured that "no 'imprimatur of state approval' can be deemed to have been conferred on any particular religion, or on religion generally." We thus found it irrelevant to the constitutional inquiry that the vast majority of beneficiaries were parents of children in religious schools…. That the program was one of true private choice, with no evidence that the State deliberately skewed incentives toward religious schools, was sufficient for the program to survive scrutiny under the Establishment Clause.

In *Witters* [*v. Washington Dept. of Services for the Blind* (1986)], we used identical reasoning to reject an Establishment Clause challenge to a vocational scholarship program that provided tuition aid to a student studying at a religious institution to become a pastor. Looking at the program as a whole, we observed that "[a]ny aid … that ultimately flows to religious institutions does so only as a result of the genuinely independent and private choices of aid recipients." We further remarked that, as in *Mueller,* "[the] program is made available generally without regard to the sectarian-non-sectarian, or public-nonpublic nature of the institution benefited." In light of these factors, we held that the program was not inconsistent with the Establishment Clause….

Finally, in *Zobrest* [*v. Catalina Foothills School District* (1993)], we applied *Mueller* and *Witters* to reject an Establishment Clause challenge to a federal program that permitted sign-language interpreters to assist deaf children enrolled in religious schools. Reviewing our earlier decisions, we stated that "government programs that neutrally provide benefits to a broad class of citizens defined without reference to religion are not readily subject to an Establishment Clause challenge." Looking once again to the challenged program as a whole, we observed that the program "distributes benefits neutrally to any child qualifying as 'disabled.' " Its "primary beneficiaries," we said, were "disabled children, not sectarian schools."….

Mueller, Witters, and *Zobrest* thus make clear that where a government aid program is neutral with respect to religion, and provides assistance directly to a broad class of citizens who, in turn, direct government aid to religious schools wholly as a result of their own genuine and independent private choice, the program is not readily subject to challenge under the Establishment Clause. A program that shares these features permits government aid to reach religious institutions only by

way of the deliberate choices of numerous individual recipients. The incidental advancement of a religious mission, or the perceived endorsement of a religious message, is reasonably attributable to the individual recipient, not to the government, whose role ends with the disbursement of benefits….

We believe that the program challenged here is a program of true private choice, consistent with *Mueller, Witters,* and *Zobrest,* and thus constitutional. As was true in those cases, the Ohio program is neutral in all respects toward religion. It is part of a general and multifaceted undertaking by the State of Ohio to provide educational opportunities to the children of a failed school district. It confers educational assistance directly to a broad class of individuals defined without reference to religion, i.e., any parent of a school-age child who resides in the Cleveland City School District. The program permits the participation of all schools within the district, religious or nonreligious. Adjacent public schools also may participate and have a financial incentive to do so. Program benefits are available to participating families on neutral terms, with no reference to religion. The only preference stated anywhere in the program is a preference for low-income families, who receive greater assistance and are given priority for admission at participating schools.

There are no "financial incentive[s]" that "ske[w]" the program toward religious schools. Such incentives "[are] not present … where the aid is allocated on the basis of neutral, secular criteria that neither favor nor disfavor religion, and is made available to both religious and secular beneficiaries on a nondiscriminatory basis." The program here in fact creates financial disincentives for religious schools, with private schools receiving only half the government assistance given to community schools and one-third the assistance given to magnet schools. Adjacent public schools, should any choose to accept program students, are also eligible to receive two to three times the state funding of a private religious school. Families too have a financial disincentive to choose a private religious school over other schools. Parents that choose to participate in the scholarship program and then to enroll their children in a private school (religious or nonreligious) must co-pay a portion of the school's tuition. Families that choose a community school, magnet school, or traditional public school pay nothing. Although such features of the program are not necessary to its constitutionality, they clearly dispel the claim that the program "creates … financial incentive[s] for parents to choose a sectarian school."

(Continued)

Respondents suggest that even without a financial incentive for parents to choose a religious school, the program creates a "public perception that the State is endorsing religious practices and beliefs." But we have repeatedly recognized that no reasonable observer would think a neutral program of private choice, where state aid reaches religious schools solely as a result of the numerous independent decisions of private individuals, carries with it the imprimatur of government endorsement. The argument is particularly misplaced here since "the reasonable observer in the endorsement inquiry must be deemed aware" of the "history and context" underlying a challenged program. Any objective observer familiar with the full history and context of the Ohio program would reasonably view it as one aspect of a broader undertaking to assist poor children in failed schools, not as an endorsement of religious schooling in general.

There also is no evidence that the program fails to provide genuine opportunities for Cleveland parents to select secular educational options for their school-age children. Cleveland schoolchildren enjoy a range of educational choices: They may remain in public school as before, remain in public school with publicly funded tutoring aid, obtain a scholarship and choose a religious school, obtain a scholarship and choose a nonreligious private school, enroll in a community school, or enroll in a magnet school. That 46 of the 56 private schools now participating in the program are religious schools does not condemn it as a violation of the Establishment Clause. The Establishment Clause question is whether Ohio is coercing parents into sending their children to religious schools, and that question must be answered by evaluating all options Ohio provides Cleveland schoolchildren, only one of which is to obtain a program scholarship and then choose a religious school....

Respondents finally claim that we should look to *Committee for Public Ed. & Religious Liberty v. Nyquist* ... (1973), to decide these cases. We disagree for two reasons. First, the program in *Nyquist* was quite different from the program challenged here. *Nyquist* involved a New York program that gave a package of benefits exclusively to private schools and the parents of private school enrollees. Although the program was enacted for ostensibly secular purposes, we found that its "function" was "unmistakably to provide desired financial support for nonpublic, sectarian institutions." Its genesis, we said, was that private religious schools faced "increasingly grave fiscal problems." The program thus provided direct money grants to religious schools. It provided tax benefits "unrelated to the amount of money actually expended by any parent on tuition," ensuring a windfall to parents of children in religious schools. It similarly provided tuition reimbursements designed explicitly to "offe[r] ... an incentive to parents to send their children to sectarian schools." Indeed, the program flatly prohibited the participation of any public school, or parent of any public school enrollee. Ohio's program shares none of these features.

Second, were there any doubt that the program challenged in *Nyquist* is far removed from the program challenged here, we expressly reserved judgment with respect to "a case involving some form of public assistance (e.g., scholarships) made available generally without regard to the sectarian-nonsectarian, or public-nonpublic nature of the institution benefited." That, of course, is the very question now before us, and it has since been answered, first in *Mueller*, then in *Witters*, and again in *Zobrest*. To the extent the scope of *Nyquist* has remained an open question in light of these later decisions, we now hold that *Nyquist* does not govern neutral educational assistance programs that, like the program here, offer aid directly to a broad class of individual recipients defined without regard to religion.

In sum, the Ohio program is entirely neutral with respect to religion. It provides benefits directly to a wide spectrum of individuals, defined only by financial need and residence in a particular school district. It permits such individuals to exercise genuine choice among options public and private, secular and religious. The program is therefore a program of true private choice. In keeping with an unbroken line of decisions rejecting challenges to similar programs, we hold that the program does not offend the Establishment Clause.

The judgment of the Court of Appeals is reversed.

Justice O'Connor, concurring....

Justice Thomas, concurring....

Justice Stevens, dissenting. ...

Justice Breyer, with whom *Justice Stevens* and *Justice Souter* join, dissenting. ...

Justice Souter, with whom *Justice Stevens*, *Justice Ginsburg*, and *Justice Breyer* join, dissenting.

The Court's majority holds that the Establishment Clause is no bar to Ohio's payment of tuition at private religious elementary and middle schools under a scheme that systematically provides tax money to support the schools' religious missions. The occasion for the legislation thus upheld is the condition of public education in the city of Cleveland. The record indicates that the schools are failing to serve their objective, and the vouchers in issue here are said to be needed to provide adequate alternatives to them. If there were an excuse for giving short shrift to the Establishment Clause, it would probably apply here. But there is no excuse. Constitutional limitations are placed on government to preserve constitutional values in hard cases, like these. "[Constitutional lines have to be drawn, and on one side of every one of them is an otherwise sympathetic case that provokes impatience with the Constitution and with the line. But constitutional lines are the price of constitutional government." I therefore respectfully dissent.

The applicability of the Establishment Clause to public funding of benefits to religious schools was settled in *Everson v. Board of Education* ... (1947), which inaugurated the modern era of establishment doctrine. The Court stated the principle in words from which there was no dissent: "No tax in any amount, large or small, can be levied to support any religious activities or institutions, whatever they may be called, or whatever form they may adopt to teach or practice religion."

The Court has never in so many words repudiated this statement, let alone, in so many words, overruled *Everson*. Today, however, the majority holds that the Establishment Clause is not offended by Ohio's Pilot Project Scholarship Program, under which students may be eligible to receive as much as $2,250 in the form of tuition vouchers transferable to religious schools. In the city of Cleveland the overwhelming proportion of large appropriations for voucher money must be spent on religious schools if it is to be spent at all, and will be spent in amounts that cover almost all of tuition. The money will thus pay for eligible students' instruction not only in secular subjects but in religion as well, in schools that can fairly be characterized as founded to teach religious doctrine and to imbue teaching in all subjects with a religious dimension. Public tax money will pay at a systemic level for teaching the covenant with Israel and Mosaic Law in Jewish schools, the primacy of the Apostle Peter and the Papacy in Catholic schools, the truth of reformed Christianity in Protestant schools, and the revelation to the Prophet in Muslim schools, to speak only of major religious groupings in the Republic.

How can a Court consistently leave *Everson* on the books and approve the Ohio vouchers? The answer is that it cannot. It is only by ignoring *Everson* that the majority can claim to rest on traditional law in its invocation of neutral aid provisions and private choice to sanction the Ohio law. It is, moreover, only by ignoring the meaning of neutrality and private choice themselves that the majority can even pretend to rest today's decision on those criteria....

If the divisiveness permitted by today's majority is to be avoided in the short term, it will be avoided only by action of the political branches at the state and national levels. Legislatures not driven to desperation by the problems of public education may be able to see the threat in vouchers negotiable in sectarian schools. Perhaps even cities with problems like Cleveland's will perceive the danger, now that they know a federal court will not save them from it.

My own course as a judge on the Court cannot, however, simply be to hope that the political branches will save us from the consequences of the majority's decision. *Everson*'s statement is still the touchstone of sound law, even though the reality is that in the matter of educational aid the Establishment Clause has largely been read away. True, the majority has not approved vouchers for religious schools alone, or aid earmarked for religious instruction. But no scheme so clumsy will ever get before us, and in the cases that we may see, like these, the Establishment Clause is largely silenced. I do not have the option to leave it silent, and I hope that a future Court will reconsider today's dramatic departure from basic Establishment Clause principle.

CHAPTER 5

The Constitution and Criminal Justice

"We could, of course, facilitate the process of administering justice to those who violate criminal laws by ignoring ... the entire Bill of Rights—but it is the very purpose of the Bill of Rights to identify values that may not be sacrificed to expediency. In a just society those who govern, as well as those who are governed, must obey the law."

—Justice John Paul Stevens, Dissenting in
United States v. Leon (1984)

John Paul Stevens: Associate Justice, 1975–2010

Introduction

Protecting citizens against crime is one of the fundamental obligations of any government. In the United States, of course, government must perform the function of crime control while respecting the constitutional rights of individuals. Balancing the public interest in crime control against the values of individual liberty and privacy is, without question, the most common problem facing trial and appellate courts. Numerous American courts, especially in major metropolitan areas, are flooded with criminal cases, many of which raise vexing questions of constitutional law. This chapter examines the development of constitutional standards in this extremely important area of the law.

Relevant Constitutional Provisions

The most obvious source of constitutional protection for persons suspected, accused, or convicted of crimes is the Bill of Rights. Numerous provisions of the Bill of Rights bear directly on the administration of criminal justice in the United States. Several restrictions in the original Constitution, together with guarantees in the Fourth, Fifth, Sixth, and Eighth Amendments, were designed to prevent government from subjecting individuals to arbitrary arrest, prosecution, and punishment. Both the national government and the states are prohibited from enacting **ex post facto** laws and **bills of attainder** (Article I, Sections 9 and 10). By contrast, the **habeas corpus** guarantee (Article I, Section 9) applies only to the national government, leaving the preservation of this right in state jurisdictions up to the states themselves. Most provisions of the Bill of Rights, including those pertaining to criminal justice, have been incorporated into the Due Process Clause of the Fourteenth Amendment, thereby making them applicable to the states as well as the national government. (For a discussion of *ex post facto* laws, bills of attainder, habeas corpus, and "incorporation" of the Bill of Rights, see Chapter 1.)

Search and Seizure

The Fourth Amendment recognizes a right of personal privacy, entitling the American people to protection against arbitrary intrusions by law enforcement officers. The framers of the Bill of Rights were acutely sensitive to the need to insulate people from unlimited governmental powers of **search and seizure**. One of the chief complaints of the American colonists was the power of police and customs officials to conduct "general" searches under the dreaded Writs of Assistance. First issued in Massachusetts in 1761, the Writs of Assistance allowed customs officials to execute "general warrants"—warrants that did not specify the persons to be searched or arrested, the premises to be searched, the number of persons or items to be seized, the nature of the items to be seized, or even the reason for the warrant. The purpose of the Writs of Assistance was to facilitate the enforcement of trade and revenue laws in colonial America, where smuggling and avoidance of customs duties were rampant. Nevertheless, many colonists regarded the 100 Writs as gross abuses of power and infringements of rights protected by common law. In a highly publicized argument opposing the writs in February 1761, Boston attorney James Otis denounced them as "the worst instrument of arbitrary power, the most destructive of English liberty and the fundamental principles of law, that ever was found in an English law book" (quoted in *Boyd v. United States* [1886]).

When the first Congress considered the Bill of Rights, most state constitutions already contained limitations on government powers in this area. Thus, there was little objection in Congress to the search and seizure amendment contained in James Madison's proposal for a Bill of Rights. After minor changes in language, the Fourth Amendment was adopted:

> *The right of the people to be secure in their persons, houses, papers, and effects, against unreasonable searches and seizures, shall not be violated, and no Warrants shall issue, but upon probable cause, supported by Oath or affirmation, and particularly describing the place to be searched, and the persons or things to be seized.*

Like many of the broad provisions of the Constitution, the Fourth Amendment raises as many questions as it answers. It is clear that government cannot subject people to unreasonable searches and seizures, but what is meant by "unreasonable"? What exactly is a search? What is the precise meaning of "probable cause"? Does this protection apply equally to all personal property (vehicles, boats, business) or just to individual "persons, houses, papers, and effects"? In our legal system, these are questions for the Supreme Court to answer. Unfortunately for the student, the police on the street, the criminal suspect, and the ordinary, law-abiding citizen, the answers to these questions can be very complicated and confusing.

Reasonable Expectations of Privacy

One of the most difficult problems in applying the eighteenth-century language of the Fourth Amendment to modern conditions is determining the scope of the privacy to be protected. Obviously, the amendment prohibits unreasonable searches of one's dwelling. But what about the search of an individual's automobile, motor home, or boat? What about one's telephone conversations, fax transmissions, e-mails, or postings on social networking sites? Are such communications protected by the Fourth Amendment?

In *Olmstead v. United States* (1928), the Supreme Court took a very strict view of the scope of the Fourth Amendment. Roy Olmstead, a suspected bootlegger, was charged with conspiracy to violate the National Prohibition Act. The government's evidence consisted of transcripts of Olmstead's telephone conversations obtained through a wiretap placed outside his property. The agents had obtained no warrant authorizing the wiretap. Although there was no search or seizure of his person or physical property, Olmstead maintained that the Fourth Amendment had been violated. The term *effects*, as used in the Fourth Amendment, could have been interpreted to include telephone conversations, but the Court opted for a narrower construction. Writing for the majority, Chief Justice William Howard Taft stated that "one who installs in his house a telephone instrument with connecting wires intends to project his voice to those quite outside" and that "the wires beyond his house, and messages passing over them, are not within the protection of the Fourth Amendment."

Justice Louis Brandeis, along with three of his colleagues, dissented. In one of his most forward-looking opinions, he asserted the need to keep the Constitution relevant to changing technological conditions:

> The progress of science in furnishing the government with means of espionage is not likely to stop with wiretapping. Ways may someday be developed by which the government, without removing papers from secret drawers, can reproduce them in court, and by which it will be enabled to expose to a jury the most intimate occurrences of the home.... Can it be that the Constitution affords no protection against such invasions of individual security?

In 1928, the telephone was in fairly wide use; today, it is omnipresent. Perhaps it was this reality that motivated the Supreme Court in 1967 to overturn *Olmstead* in the landmark decision of *Katz v. United States*. Here, the Court reversed a conviction in which government agents, acting without a warrant, attached a "bug," or listening device, to the outside of a public telephone booth from which Charles Katz, a suspected bookie, often placed calls. Writing for the Court, Justice Potter Stewart stated that "the Fourth Amendment protects people—not places." Adhering to Justice John M. Harlan's concurrence in *Katz*, the Supreme Court has since held that the Fourth Amendment extends to any place or thing in which an individual has a **reasonable expectation of privacy**. The Court has demonstrated a willingness to consider hotel rooms, garages, offices, automobiles, sealed letters, suitcases, and other closed containers as protected by the Fourth Amendment. On the other hand, the Court has held that there is no Fourth Amendment protection for abandoned or discarded property or for the **open fields exception** that covers the "open fields" around a home, even if that area is private property (see *Oliver v. United States* [1984]).

Technology and the Fourth Amendment Generally speaking, the use of wiretaps, microphones, video recorders, and other devices that permit agencies to intercept the content of what would otherwise be private communications implicates the Fourth Amendment. However, merely using technology to augment the senses does not necessarily trigger Fourth Amendment protections. For example, the Supreme Court has approved the use of searchlights, field glasses, aerial photography, and various other means of enhancing the police's powers of observation, even in the absence of a warrant or probable cause. Lower federal courts have even approved miniaturized television camera surveillance. The question is whether the police use methods that infringe on a person's reasonable expectations of privacy. If so, they need a warrant or some other form of judicial authorization before deploying these technologies. For example, in *Kyllo v. United States* (2001), the Supreme Court invalidated the warrantless use of thermal imagers to identify houses likely to contain illegal marijuana growing facilities. More recently, in *United States v. Jones* (2012), the Court prohibited the use of GPS tracking devices placed on suspects' cars without prior judicial authorization. Writing for the majority, Justice Scalia explained that the use of the device was certainly a search under the Fourth Amendment when the information it detailed about Jones' travel locations was combined with government trespass onto private property to install the device.

CASE IN POINT

Use of Thermal Imagers by Police
Kyllo v. United States (2001)

In this case, federal agents had used a thermal imaging device without first obtaining a warrant to scan a home they suspected to be housing an indoor marijuana growing operation. Having discerned the telltale infrared radiation associated with the use of indoor growing lights, and having obtained corroborating information, the agents obtained a warrant to search the premises, where they found more than 100 cannabis plants growing under artificial light.

At the time this case came to the Supreme Court, thermal imagers were being used by law enforcement agencies around the country as part of the national war on drugs. Police and prosecutors typically took the view that the thermal scan was not a search within the meaning of the Fourth Amendment, since it merely collected data on heat that was being released into the public space.

In a 5-to-4 decision, the Supreme Court disagreed with this perspective. Writing for the Court, Justice Scalia opined that "[w]here, as here, the Government uses a device that is not in general public use, to explore details of the home that would previously have been unknowable without physical intrusion, the surveillance is a search and is presumptively unreasonable without a warrant." In dissent, Justice Stevens noted that "[a]ll that the infrared camera did ... was passively measure heat emitted from the exterior surfaces of petitioners home; all that those measurements showed were relative differences in emission levels, vaguely indicating that some areas of the roof and outside walls were warmer than others." In Stevens's view, the police did not significantly intrude on the privacy of the occupants.

The *Kyllo* case is interesting because it shows how changing technology creates new and difficult Fourth Amendment problems. As technology in this area advances, courts will continue to confront such issues.

Probable Cause

The fundamental requirement imposed by the Fourth Amendment is that searches and seizures must be "reasonable." The amendment presupposes two important constraints on law enforcement: that searches will be authorized by warrants, and that warrants will not be issued without probable cause. The Supreme Court has recognized exceptions to the **warrant requirement**, but has for the most part viewed probable cause as an indispensable precondition of a valid search. **Probable cause** is a term of art that cannot be defined precisely. The Supreme Court has observed that "probable cause is a fluid concept—turning on the assessment of probabilities in particular factual contexts—not readily, or even usefully, reduced to a neat set of legal rules" (*Illinois v. Gates* [1983]). As interpreted by the Court, probable cause means in effect that for a search to be valid, a police officer must have good reason to believe that the search will produce evidence of crime. According to the Court's decision in *Brinegar v. United States* (1949), officers have probable cause when "the facts and circumstances within their knowledge, and of which they had reasonably trustworthy information, [are] sufficient in themselves to warrant a man of reasonable caution in the belief that an offense has been or is being committed."

The Warrant Requirement

A **search warrant** is simply an order issued by a judge or magistrate that authorizes a search. To obtain a search warrant, a law enforcement officer must take an oath or sign an affidavit attesting to certain facts that, if true, constitute probable cause to support the issuance of a warrant. In *Coolidge v. New Hampshire* (1971), the Supreme Court invalidated a warrant that was issued by the state's attorney general, a law enforcement officer, rather than by a judge or magistrate. Thus, the Court places great importance on the role of the **neutral and detached judicial officer** in maintaining the integrity of the Fourth Amendment. This amendment also requires that search warrants describe with particularity "the place to be searched, and the persons or things to be seized." This provision reflects the Framers' distaste for the **general warrants** used in colonial America. In *Stanford v. Texas* (1965), the Supreme Court reaffirmed this long-standing distaste for "dragnet" searches when it invalidated a five-hour search of a Communist Party headquarters resulting in the seizure of some 5,000 items, including books by Justice Hugo Black and Pope John XXIII.

Confidential and Anonymous Informants

One of the most controversial questions concerning the issuance of search warrants involves the use of **confidential or anonymous informants**. Police often use tips provided by confidential informants to obtain search warrants that lead to the discovery of incriminating evidence. In *Aguilar v. Texas* (1963), police obtained a warrant simply by swearing that they "had received reliable information from a credible person" that illegal drugs would be found at a certain location. The Supreme Court ultimately invalidated the warrant, holding that an affidavit must inform the magistrate of the underlying circumstances from which the informant concluded that the narcotics were where he claimed they were, and some of the underlying circumstances from which the officer concluded that the informant, whose identity need not be disclosed, was "credible" or his information "reliable."

Five years later, the Court reaffirmed this two-pronged test in the case of *Spinelli v. United States* (1969). The so-called *Aguilar-Spinelli* test made it more difficult for police to obtain warrants based on tips from confidential informants. Accordingly, on this issue, as on several others, the Warren Court was much criticized for "handcuffing the police." In 1983, a more conservative Supreme Court under Chief Justice Warren E. Burger abandoned the rigorous *Aguilar-Spinelli* test in favor of a **totality of circumstances** approach that makes it easier for police to get search warrants. In *Illinois v. Gates*, Justice William Rehnquist asserted that the *Aguilar-Spinelli* test could not "avoid seriously impeding the task of law enforcement" because "anonymous tips seldom could survive a rigorous application of either of the *Spinelli* prongs." Dissenting, Justice William Brennan argued that "the Court [gave] virtually no consideration to the value of insuring that findings of probable cause are based on information that a magistrate can reasonably say has been obtained in a reliable way by an honest or credible person." He stated, "I … fear that the Court's rejection of *Aguilar* and *Spinelli* … may foretell an evisceration of the probable cause standard."

In 1984, the Court held that the totality of circumstances standard announced in the *Gates* decision was to be given a broad interpretation by lower courts (*Massachusetts v. Upton*). Subsequently, the Court moved beyond *Gates* and manifested an even greater level of permissiveness toward police reliance on anonymous tips (see, for example, *Alabama v. White* [1990]). Critics of these decisions argued that the Court's interest in facilitating law enforcement had eclipsed its traditional concern for the privacy of citizens subjected to police searches.

Execution of Search Warrants

Under federal law, an officer is required to **knock and announce** upon arrival at the place to be searched. The purpose of this requirement is to reduce the potential for violence as well as to protect the occupants' right of privacy. In *Wilson v. Arkansas* (1995), the Court decided unanimously that the Fourth Amendment requires police, absent a threat of physical violence or other exigent circumstances, to knock and announce when serving a search warrant at a home. The most striking aspect of the Court's decision was that the opinion was authored by Justice Thomas, who generally takes a pro-law enforcement position in criminal cases. In keeping with his adherence to the doctrine of original intent, Thomas examined the state of the common law at the time the Fourth Amendment was adopted. He concluded that "[a]t the time of the framing, the common law of search and seizure recognized a law enforcement officer's authority to break open the doors of a dwelling, but generally indicated that he first ought to announce his presence and authority." Thomas concluded that the authors of the Bill of Rights intended for the common law knock and announce requirement to be part and parcel of the Fourth Amendment. *Wilson* resolved a conflict among lower courts as to whether the Constitution requires officers to knock and announce—a requirement that many states already observed under their respective constitutions, statutes, or judicial decisions.

One of the reasons police officers resist compliance with the knock and announce requirement is that by announcing their presence, officers risk losing evidence that is easily destroyed or disposed of. In *Wilson*, the Court said that officers facing exigent circumstances could dispense with the knock and announce requirement. But in *Richards v. Wisconsin* (1997), the Court ruled unanimously that states may not create a blanket "drug exception" to the requirement that police officers knock and announce prior to executing a search warrant. In a 5-4 decision handed down on June 15, 2006, the Court held that evidence found by the police during their execution of a valid search warrant is admissible against the accused even though the police failed to observe the constitutional requirement to "knock and announce" before entering the premises (see *Hudson v. Michigan*, discussed more fully later in this chapter in connection with the Fourth Amendment exclusionary rule).

Warrantless Searches

Although the Fourth Amendment clearly indicates a preference for search warrants, the Supreme Court has held that, under **exigent circumstances,** a **warrantless search** may nevertheless be "reasonable." One example of a legitimate warrantless search is the **search incidental to a lawful arrest.** In *Chimel v. California* (1969), Justice Potter Stewart's majority opinion stated:

> *When an arrest is made, it is reasonable for the arresting officer to search the person arrested in order to remove any weapons that the latter might seek to use in order to resist arrest or effect his escape.... In addition, it is entirely reasonable for the arresting officer to search for and seize any evidence on the arrestee's person in order to prevent its concealment or destruction. And the area into which an arrestee might reach in order to grab a weapon or evidentiary items must, of course, be governed by a like rule.*

Consent Searches   An obvious example of a legitimate warrantless search is one based on the consent of the individual whose privacy is to be invaded. It is an elementary principle of law that individuals may waive their constitutional rights; Fourth Amendment protections are no exception. In *Schneckloth v. Bustamonte* (1973), the Supreme Court upheld a **search based on consent** even though the police failed to advise the individual that he was not obligated to consent to the police request. In *Florida v. Bostick,* a highly publicized 1991 decision, the Court upheld the controversial police practice of boarding interstate buses in big-city terminals, approaching persons matching a **drug courier profile**, and asking them for permission to search their belongings. In *Ohio v. Robinette* (1996), the Court held that police are not required to inform motorists who are stopped for other reasons that they are "free to go" before asking them to consent to a search of their automobile. To determine whether consent was given voluntarily and knowingly, the Court looks to the "totality of circumstances" surrounding the search. It should be noted that some state courts have moved to limit consent searches to those situations where police have reasonable suspicion that crime is afoot. This is based on the view that people who are stopped by the police may give consent to search based on fear or intimidation.

One of the more challenging problems in the area of consent searches involves searches of dwellings inhabited by multiple parties. In *United States v. Matlock* (1974), the Supreme Court held that any of the co-occupants of a dwelling may consent to a search of any area that is jointly occupied. However, in *Georgia v. Randolph* (2006), the Court held that police without a warrant may not search a home when the occupants disagree as to whether consent should be given. Dissenting, Chief Justice John Roberts expressed concern that the ruling could have dire consequences in cases of domestic violence.

Automobile Searches   One of the most important exceptions to the warrant requirement is the **automobile search.** This is because so many searches and seizures take place incident to automobile stops. In *Carroll v. United States* (1925), the Supreme Court upheld the warrantless search of an automobile believed to be carrying illegal liquor. The Court stressed, however, that probable cause was essential to justify a warrantless automobile search. Indiscriminately stopping and searching passing motorists in an effort to discover evidence of crime could never be constitutionally justified. The case of *Arkansas v. Sanders* (1979) presented the Court with an interesting question.

Can warrantless searches of automobiles extend to all the contents of said vehicles, or do police still need a warrant to search luggage taken from the trunk? In *Sanders*, the Court disallowed the search of the luggage, suggesting to some observers that the automobile exception was "in trouble." However, in *United States v. Ross* (1982), the Supreme Court demonstrated otherwise. In a 6-to-3 decision, the Court upheld a warrantless search of a paper bag and a leather pouch found in the locked trunk of a stopped automobile, a search that produced $3,200 in cash and a sizable quantity of heroin. Writing for the Court, Justice John Paul Stevens clarified the legitimate scope of a warrantless automobile search as that "no greater than a magistrate could have authorized by issuing a warrant based on the probable cause that justified the search." Dissenting vehemently in *Ross*, Justice Thurgood Marshall assailed the majority position as "flatly inconsistent … with established Fourth Amendment principles." In 1991, the Court went one step further and formally overruled *Arkansas v. Sanders* (see *California v. Acevedo* [1991]), removing any lingering doubts about judicial distinctions between searches of automobiles and closed containers found therein. Thus, under current interpretation of the Fourth Amendment, the legitimate scope of a warrantless search, whether of an automobile or any other place, is determined more by the nature of the object of the search than by the nature of the space being searched.

One of the more controversial practices of law enforcement has been to search vehicles thoroughly after drivers and other occupants have been arrested for DUI or other offenses. In *Arizona v. Gant* (2009), the Supreme Court placed limits on a search incident to arrest of an occupant of a vehicle. Speaking through Justice Stevens, a sharply divided Court held that:

> *Police may search a vehicle incident to a recent occupant's arrest only if the arrestee is within reaching distance of the passenger compartment at the time of the search or it is reasonable to believe the vehicle contains evidence of the offense of arrest. When these justifications are absent, a search of an arrestee's vehicle will be unreasonable unless police obtain a warrant or show that another exception to the warrant requirement applies.*

Other Justifications for Warrantless Searches   Other accepted justifications for warrantless searches include **plain view** (see *Coolidge v. New Hampshire* [1971]), **hot pursuit** (see *Warden v. Hayden* [1967]), **evanescent evidence** (see *Schmerber v. California* [1966]), and **emergency searches** (see *Michigan v. Tyler* [1978]). In each of these examples, compelling exigencies make the warrant requirement itself unreasonable, at least in the view of the nation's highest court.

Investigatory Detention

One of the most controversial forms of police search is **investigatory detention**. This type of limited search involves the **stop and frisk,** and occurs when police temporarily detain suspicious persons in an effort to prevent a crime from taking place. The seminal case in this area is *Terry v. Ohio* (1968). Here, an experienced plainclothes officer observed three men acting suspiciously. The officer concluded that they were preparing to rob a nearby store and approached them. He identified himself as a police officer and asked for their names. Unsatisfied with their mumbled responses, he then subjected one of the trio to a **pat-down search**, which produced a gun for which the individual had no permit. In this instance, the police officer had no warrant; indeed, he did not have probable cause in its traditional sense. The Court nevertheless allowed the pat-down search on the basis of **reasonable suspicion**. However, given that the "sole justification of the search … is the protection of the police officer and others nearby," the Court limited the frisk to "an intrusion reasonably designed to discover guns, knives, clubs or other hidden instruments for the assault of the police officer." Of course, if police discover contraband or other evidence of crime in the process of performing the pat-down for weapons, such evidence is admissible under a theory analogous to the plain view doctrine. For example, if a pat-down reveals an object in a jacket pocket that the officer believes to be a knife, the officer may retrieve the object. If the object turns out to be a vial of cocaine, that contraband has been lawfully seized. But may an officer retrieve an object that does not appear to be a weapon but does have the characteristics of contraband or containers used to carry contraband? In *Minnesota v. Dickerson* (1993), the Supreme Court answered this question in the affirmative, saying that "the suspect's privacy interests are not advanced by a categorical rule barring the seizure of contraband plainly detected through the sense of touch." The type of police encounter upheld in *Terry v. Ohio* and numerous subsequent court decisions has come to be known as the "*Terry* stop." Police may stop and question suspicious persons, pat them down for weapons, and even subject them to nonintrusive search procedures, such as the use of metal detectors and drug-sniffing dogs.

While a suspect is being detained, a computer search can be performed to determine whether the suspect is wanted for crimes in other jurisdictions. If so, then he or she may be arrested and a search conducted incident to that arrest.

Detention Based on "Profiling"   Because police officers have been given the power to detain, question, and investigate suspected drug couriers, investigatory detention has become extremely important in the highly publicized "war on drugs." In *United States v. Sokolow* (1989), the Supreme Court upheld a search and seizure that stemmed from a *Terry* stop conducted at an international airport. The defendant in the case aroused the suspicions of federal Drug Enforcement Administration (DEA) agents by conforming to a controversial drug courier profile developed by the DEA.

United States v. Sokolow is consistent with a host of judicial decisions affording law enforcement officers wide latitude to investigate and detain suspected drug smugglers at international airports. In one widely publicized case, such a suspect was held for sixteen hours while airport security officers obtained a court order permitting a rectal examination of the suspect. During the exam, officers retrieved a plastic balloon filled with cocaine and placed the suspect under arrest. Over the next few days, the suspect passed eighty-eight similar balloons! The Supreme Court upheld the long detention, even though security personnel lacked probable cause to make the initial stop. As in *Terry v. Ohio*, the Court found that there was reasonable suspicion to justify the original detention (*United States v. Montoya de Hernandez* [1985]).

Civil rights groups have long claimed that law enforcement officers target racial minorities in conducting investigatory detentions. They claim that police are much more likely to stop African-American motorists, especially if they are driving expensive cars. Critics further maintain that minority pedestrians are more likely to be subjected to stop and frisk procedures. They also contend that minority travelers are more likely to be searched extensively by customs agents and border patrol officers. A Gallup Poll released in July 2004 found that 50 percent of whites and 67 percent of African-Americans believed that racial profiling was "widespread." Four in ten African-Americans, and three-fourths of young African-American males, claimed to have been the victims of racial profiling.

In the wake of the terrorist attacks of September 11, 2001, airport security measures were tightened considerably. Movement of people and automobiles in and around airports was restricted. Existing procedures for searching checked baggage as well as carry-on items, widely deemed to be inadequate after 9/11, were expanded and made more rigorous. Even automobiles entering airport parking lots were subjected to inspections. Americans generally applauded such precautions, and few questioned their constitutionality. However, a more difficult problem arose in connection with the investigatory detention of passengers who fit a "terrorist profile" established by the Federal Bureau of Investigation (FBI). Arab American groups claimed that persons (including American citizens) of Middle Eastern descent were being singled out for close scrutiny, detention, and in some instances harassment by airport security personnel. Despite questions over the use of profiling broadly, a 2010 Gallup poll found that Americans supported the idea of subjecting airline passengers to additional screening that fit a terrorist profile based on age, ethnicity, and gender by a 3-1 margin. While such practices do raise constitutional concern, one must remember that during times of war courts tolerate greater infringements of civil rights and liberties, as long as such infringements are related to the prosecution of the war or the maintenance of national security. Indeed, the *Korematsu* decision of 1944 (discussed and reprinted in Chapter 3, Volume I) involved what may be the ultimate example of racial profiling—the relocation of Japanese Americans from the West Coast after the outbreak of World War II.

Detention of an Automobile Based on an Anonymous Tip

The Supreme Court has become increasingly permissive as to what constitutes reasonable suspicion for purposes of investigatory detention. For example, in *Alabama v. White* (1990), the Court upheld a *Terry* stop of an automobile based solely on an anonymous tip that described a certain car that would be at a specific location. Police went to the location, found the vehicle, and detained the driver, Vanessa White. The encounter led ultimately to the discovery of marijuana and cocaine in the automobile. Writing for the Court, Justice Byron White noted that "although it is a close case, we conclude that under the totality of the circumstances, the anonymous tip, as corroborated, exhibited sufficient indicia of reliability to justify the investigatory stop of respondent's car." In a dissenting opinion joined by Justices Brennan and Marshall, Justice Stevens observed that under *Alabama v. White*, "every citizen is subject to being seized and questioned by any officer who is prepared to testify that the warrantless stop was based on an anonymous tip predicting whatever conduct the officer had just observed." Clearly, the Court's willingness to permit the detention in *Alabama v. White* stands in sharp contrast to the Warren Court's carefully drawn stop and frisk policy delineated in *Terry v. Ohio*.

Can Police Require People to Exit Their Cars during Automobile Stops?

During automobile stops, police routinely request that drivers exit their cars. Sometimes, they also request passengers to exit. These practices are justified by the police by the need to protect officers from weapons that might be concealed inside the passenger compartment of a stopped vehicle. In *Maryland v. Wilson* (1997), the Supreme Court noted that in 1994 eleven police officers were killed and more than 5,000 officers were assaulted during traffic stops. Of course, when drivers and passengers are required to exit their automobiles, police often discover contraband or observe behavior indicative of intoxication. Such was the case in *Maryland v. Wilson*, in which a passenger who had been ordered to exit a vehicle dropped a quantity of crack cocaine onto the ground. This evidence was used to secure a conviction for possession with intent to distribute and, ultimately, the conviction was sustained by the Supreme Court.

> ### To Summarize:
>
> ◆ *The Fourth Amendment recognizes a right of personal privacy entitling the American people to protection against arbitrary intrusions by law enforcement officers.*
>
> ◆ *The Supreme Court has held that the Fourth Amendment extends to any place or thing in which an individual has a reasonable expectation of privacy.*
>
> ◆ *The fundamental requirement imposed by the Fourth Amendment is that searches and seizures must be reasonable. The amendment presupposes that searches will be authorized by warrants, and that warrants will not be issued without probable cause.*
>
> ◆ *The Supreme Court has recognized exceptions to the warrant requirement, but has for the most part viewed the probable cause requirement as indispensable.*
>
> ◆ *Examples of legitimate warrantless searches include searches incidental to a lawful arrest, searches based on consent, seizures of evidence in plain view, searches for evanescent evidence, searches conducted during hot pursuit, and emergency searches.*
>
> ◆ *Police often use tips provided by confidential or anonymous informants to obtain search warrants that lead to the discovery of incriminating evidence. Such tips may or may not constitute probable cause, depending on the "totality of circumstances."*
>
> ◆ *The Supreme Court has said that, in the absence of exigent circumstances, police officers must "knock and announce" prior to executing a search warrant at a private residence.*
>
> ◆ *The Court has permitted police officers to subject persons to a "stop and frisk" as long as there is "reasonable suspicion" (a less demanding standard than probable cause) that criminal activity is afoot. This principle also applies to automobile stops and brief investigatory detentions of drivers and passengers.*

The Exclusionary Rule

In addition to the difficult questions involving police methods of obtaining incriminating evidence, we must also consider the controversial issue of how violations of the Fourth Amendment are to be remedied and deterred. As far back as 1886, in *Boyd v. United States*, the Supreme Court suggested that evidence obtained in violation of the Fourth Amendment should be excluded from trial. In *Weeks v. United States* (1914), the Court made this dictum a formal requirement of criminal procedure in federal courts. Writing for the Court in *Weeks*, Justice William R. Day suggested that the **exclusionary rule**, as it came to be known, was implicit in the requirements of the Fourth Amendment. The exclusionary rule has generally been interpreted to dictate that evidence obtained by law enforcement in violation of the Constitution usually cannot be presented during a criminal trial. Day also argued that to allow illegally obtained evidence to be used in a criminal trial would be an affront to the integrity of the judiciary.

In *Wolf v. Colorado* (1949), the Supreme Court held that the Fourth Amendment is incorporated within the Due Process Clause of the Fourteenth Amendment and is therefore applicable to state criminal justice systems. However, the Court refused to apply the exclusionary rule to the state courts, preferring instead to view the rule as a procedural device that the Supreme Court imposed on federal criminal cases by virtue of its **supervisory power** over the lower federal courts. According to Justice Felix Frankfurter's opinion for the Court, considerations of federalism and judicial restraint prohibited the Court from imposing the exclusionary rule on the states.

The Warren Court Expands the Exclusionary Rule

Under *Wolf v. Colorado*, states were free to adopt or ignore the *Weeks* exclusionary rule. Some adopted the rule; most did not. The discrepancy between the rules applicable to state and federal courts gave rise to the **silver platter doctrine**. Federal authorities could (and did) provide illegally obtained evidence to prosecutors in states which did not have the exclusionary rule. Moreover, because the *Weeks* decision applied only to illegal seizures by *federal* authorities, federal prosecutors could use evidence obtained illegally by state and local law enforcement agencies.

In *Mapp v. Ohio* (1961), the Court overturned *Wolf v. Colorado* and extended the exclusionary rule to state criminal prosecutions by way of the Fourteenth Amendment. Writing for the Court, Justice Tom Clark made clear that the exclusionary rule was "an essential ingredient of the Fourth Amendment," which was "vouchsafed against the states by the Due Process Clause" of the Fourteenth Amendment. In dissent, Justice Harlan accused the Court of forgetting its sense of judicial restraint and failing to show due regard for *stare decisis*.

The *Mapp* decision was certainly one of the Warren Court's major contributions to the law of criminal procedure and, accordingly, it remains a very controversial holding. Those who believe the exclusionary rule is merely a judicially created rule have criticized the Supreme Court for extending its supervisory power to the state courts. On the other hand, if the exclusionary rule is implicit in the Fourth Amendment and if the Fourth Amendment is made applicable to the states through the Fourteenth Amendment (see *Wolf v. Colorado* [1949]), then it follows that the exclusionary rule must be respected in state criminal prosecutions.

The Burger Court Curtails the Exclusionary Rule

The Supreme Court under Chief Justice Burger substantially curtailed the application of the exclusionary rule. In *United States v. Calandra* (1974), the Burger Court made its philosophy quite clear: "[T]he rule is a judicially created remedy designed to safeguard Fourth Amendment Rights generally through its deterrent effect, rather than a personal constitutional right of the party aggrieved." The Burger Court's approach to cases involving the exclusionary rule was to weigh the perceived costs of its application against the potential benefits of deterring police misconduct. Using this approach, the Court refused to extend the exclusionary rule to grand jury proceedings (*United States v. Calandra* [1974]) and to federal civil proceedings where evidence was obtained unlawfully by state agents (*United States v. Janis* [1976]). A majority on the Supreme Court evidently agreed with Chief Justice Burger's assessment (dissenting in *Bivens v. Six Unknown Named Federal Narcotics Agents* [1971]) of the social costs of suppressing otherwise valid evidence:

> *Some clear demonstration of the benefits and effectiveness of the exclusionary rule is required to justify it in view of the high price it extracts from society—the release of countless guilty criminals.... But there is no empirical evidence to support the claim that the rule actually deters illegal conduct of law enforcement officials.*

The Good-Faith Exception   Without question, the most important Burger Court decisions on the exclusionary rule were the companion cases of *United States v. Leon* and *Massachusetts v. Sheppard* (1984). In these cases, the Court adopted a limited **good-faith exception** to the exclusionary rule, allowing the use of evidence seized under a search warrant later held to be defective, if the officers were acting in good faith that the warrant was valid. In *Leon*, police officers obtained a search warrant acting on a tip from a confidential informant of unproven reliability. A subsequent search of a residence turned up a substantial amount of illegal drugs. At an evidentiary hearing prior to trial, a judge ruled that the warrant had been wrongly issued and that there was insufficient information to constitute probable cause. The Supreme Court ultimately held that the evidence could nevertheless be admitted against the defendants, because to exclude such evidence would have no deterrent effect on police misconduct. The error was made by the magistrate who issued the warrant, not by the police who were deemed to be acting in good faith. In like manner, in *Massachusetts v. Sheppard*, the Court held that use of the wrong warrant form as authorization for a search in a murder investigation did not render the seized evidence inadmissible. Dissenting in the *Leon* case, Justice Brennan exploded:

> *The Court seeks to justify this result on the ground that the "costs" of adhering to the exclusionary rule … exceed the "benefits." But … it is clear that we have not been treated to an honest assessment of the merits of the exclusionary rule but have instead been drawn into a curious world where the "costs" of excluding illegally obtained evidence loom to exaggerated heights and where the "benefits" of such exclusion are made to disappear with a mere wave of the hand.*

It is clear that the intense intra-Court conflict in *Leon* and *Sheppard* stemmed from basic differences of opinion as to the constitutional foundations of the exclusionary rule. If one agrees with Justice Brennan that suppression of illegally obtained evidence is a personal right under the Fourth Amendment, then clearly the exclusionary rule cannot be sacrificed on the altar of cost-benefit analysis. On the other hand, if the rule is nothing more than a judicially created rule of evidence or procedure designed to deter future police misconduct, then the Court is free to apply or dispense with the rule depending on its perceived utility.

The Rehnquist Court reaffirmed the good-faith exception in 1995. In *Arizona v. Evans* (1995), the Arizona Supreme Court had ruled that evidence seized by a police officer who acted in reliance on a police record indicating the existence of an outstanding arrest warrant—a record that was later determined to be erroneous—had to be suppressed regardless of the source of the error. In fact, the error had been committed by the court clerk's office. The U.S. Supreme Court reversed by a 7-to-2 vote. Chief Justice Rehnquist wrote for the Court, saying that the exclusionary rule need apply only where the error is attributable to the police. The *Evans* decision was based squarely on *Leon*, and did not represent a major innovation.

In 2006, the Roberts Court further delimited the exclusionary rule. Students will recall that in *Wilson v. Arkansas* (1995), the Court held that officers executing a search warrant at a home must normally "knock and announce" before effecting entry. In *Hudson v. Michigan*, the Court ruled that violations of the "knock and announce" requirement do not require suppression of evidence seized as the result of the search. Speaking for a sharply divided bench, Justice Scalia concluded that:

> *The social costs of applying the exclusionary rule to knock-and-announce violations are considerable; the incentive to such violations is minimal to begin with, and the extant deterrences against them are substantial—incomparably greater than the factors deterring warrantless entries when* Mapp *was decided. Resort to the massive remedy of suppressing evidence of guilt is unjustified.*

In dissent, Justice Breyer (joined by Justices Ginsburg, Souter, and Stevens) complained that the decision was "a significant departure from the Court's precedents" and that "it weakens, perhaps destroys, much of the practical value of the Constitution's knock-and-announce protection."

In 2009, the Court continued down the path it had blazed a quarter century earlier in *United States v. Leon*. In *Herring v. United States*, the Court said that the exclusionary rule is not applicable to a situation in which contraband is seized from a person who was falsely arrested due to police negligence. Speaking for a bare majority, Chief Justice Roberts observed that because the improper arrest was based merely on a negligent record-keeping error and not intentional misconduct, the evidence need not be suppressed. Pointing out that the exclusionary rule serves "to deter deliberate, reckless, or grossly negligent conduct," Roberts observed, "When a probable-cause determination was based on reasonable but mistaken assumptions, the person subjected to a search or seizure has not necessarily been the victim of a constitutional violation." Speaking for four dissenters, Justice Ginsburg argued that negligent record keeping errors by law enforcement are susceptible to deterrence by the exclusionary rule and cannot effectively be remedied through other means.

The controversy over the exclusionary rule is far from over. It remains to be seen whether the Court will extend the good-faith exception to warrantless searches involving unintended violations of constitutionally protected privacy. It is important to note, however, that a number of state supreme courts have refused to follow the good-faith exception with respect to interpretation of their own state constitutional protections against unlawful search and seizure.

Civil Suits to Enforce the Fourth Amendment

One alternative to the exclusionary rule is filing a civil suit for damages against the officers who performed the illegal search. This remedy is especially appealing to persons who are the victims of illegal searches or seizures but are not prosecuted for any crime. Such persons have no real alternative to filing a civil suit to obtain redress for the wrongs perpetrated against them. In *Malley v. Briggs* (1986), the Supreme Court allowed civil suits under 42 U.S. Code Section 1983 (commonly referred to as 1983 suits) against police officers who "knowingly violate the law" or act in a fashion that "no reasonably competent officer" would consider to be legal in conducting arrests, searches, and seizures. In the *Malley* case, a Rhode Island state trooper obtained a warrant for the arrest of a prominent couple who were charged with "conspiring to possess marijuana." The warrant was based on a suggestion overheard by police wiretaps that the couple had hosted a marijuana party some three months earlier. The couple was taken into custody, but no physical evidence of any crime was discovered. Consequently, the grand jury refused to hand down an indictment. Not satisfied with this after-the-fact vindication, the couple filed a civil suit for damages against the police officer. The federal district court dismissed the case, holding that a police officer could not be held liable for actions based on a warrant issued by a magistrate. Ultimately, however, the Supreme Court disagreed, underscoring its previous recognition of civil suits as means of enforcing Fourth Amendment rights.

The civil remedy was advanced as an alternative to the exclusionary rule by Justice Felix Frankfurter in the 1949 case of *Wolf v. Colorado*. In a strongly worded dissenting opinion in *Wolf*, Justice Frank Murphy cast grave doubt on the viability of the civil remedy as a realistic alternative. The Warren Court, as reflected in its decisions on the exclusionary rule, apparently agreed with Murphy's assessment. But the civil liability approach was resurrected by Chief Justice Burger in his dissent in the *Bivens* case. Finally, in *Malley*, a majority of the Court found occasion to apply the civil remedy in the context of an outrageous Fourth Amendment violation. In its recent decision permitting the admission of evidence obtained in violation of the "knock and announce" requirement, the Court majority, speaking through Justice Scalia, endorsed the view that civil liability is at present a significant deterrent to police misconduct, and consequently an important component of the Court's Forth Amendment enforcement.

> **To Summarize:**
>
> ◆ *In* Weeks v. United States *(1914), the Court held that evidence obtained in violation of the Fourth Amendment may not be used in federal criminal trials. In* Mapp v. Ohio *(1961), the Court extended this Fourth Amendment exclusionary rule to state criminal prosecutions by way of the Fourteenth Amendment.*
>
> ◆ *The Supreme Court under Chief Justice Burger and Chief Justice Rehnquist substantially curtailed the application of the exclusionary rule. The Court's current approach is to weigh the perceived costs of the rule's application against the potential benefits of deterring police misconduct.*
>
> ◆ *The Court has adopted a limited good-faith exception to the exclusionary rule, allowing the use of evidence seized under a search warrant later held to be defective, if the officers were acting in good faith that the warrant was valid.*

Arrest

An **arrest** entails the deprivation of one's liberty by a law enforcement officer or other person with legal authority. Normally, an arrest occurs when someone suspected of having committed a crime is taken into custody by a police officer. Because an arrest is, in effect, a "seizure," it must conform to the probable cause and warrant requirements of the Fourth Amendment. In *Ker v. California* (1963), the Supreme Court held that the legality of arrests by state and local officers should be determined by the same standards applicable to federal law enforcement officials.

Arrests are often made pursuant to warrants based on preliminary investigations. An **arrest warrant**, like a search warrant, is issued by a judge or magistrate upon a showing of probable cause. Under some circumstances, however, warrantless arrests are permissible. The most common of these is where police observe someone committing a crime or have direct knowledge of criminal activity. Whether or not it is made pursuant to a warrant, an arrest must be based on probable cause.

The Probable Cause Hearing

As the warrant requirement of the Fourth Amendment implies, the legality of detention after arrest also depends on the existence of probable cause. It follows logically that a person arrested *without* a warrant must be brought *promptly* before a judicial officer for a **probable cause hearing**. This principle had in fact emerged in English common law by the late seventeenth century, long before ratification of the Fourth Amendment in 1791. It was not until 1975 that the Supreme Court, in *Gerstein v. Pugh*, explicitly recognized the probable cause hearing as a Fourth Amendment requirement in cases of **warrantless arrest**. This decision, however, did not specify the maximum time that a person could be held in custody prior to a probable cause determination.

In *County of Riverside v. McLaughlin* (1991), the Rehnquist Court adopted a permissive interpretation of the probable cause hearing requirement. In this controversial 5-to-4 decision, the majority, speaking through Justice Sandra Day O'Connor, held that an individual could be detained for as long as forty-eight hours prior to a probable cause hearing without necessarily violating the Fourth Amendment. In the *McLaughlin* case, the Court balanced Fourth Amendment rights against state interests in administrative convenience and local autonomy. In a sharply worded dissent, Justice Antonin Scalia, generally favorable to law enforcement claims, criticized the majority for going far beyond the Court's prevailing concern that criminals not go unpunished. He argued that the Court had improperly applied the *Gerstein* precedent, repudiating one of the "core applications" of the Fourth Amendment "so that the presumptively innocent may be left in jail." By definition, the failure to find probable cause points to the innocence of the arrestee. According to the many critics of the *McLaughlin* decision, the majority lost sight of this consideration in its apparent zeal to accommodate the practical demands of law enforcement.

Use of Force by Police in Making Arrests

Since suspects often resist arrest, police on occasion must use force to take a person into custody. The courts have generally recognized that the Fourth Amendment permits police to use only such force as is "reasonable" and "necessary" in effectuating an arrest. In *Tennessee v. Garner* (1985), the Supreme Court held that police officers may use *deadly* force only when necessary to apprehend a fleeing felon and only when "the officer has probable cause to believe that the suspect poses a significant threat of death or physical injury to the officer or others." This decision marked a departure from previous rulings which permitted greater leeway to law enforcement in determining the amount of force warranted in a given situation.

While most police officers take care to exercise force responsibly, police have committed acts of brutality in numerous instances. In such cases, police officers are subject not only to internal departmental sanctions but also to civil suit and even criminal prosecution under applicable state and federal statutes. Perhaps the best-known case in this area stemmed from the infamous beating of Rodney King, an African-American motorist, by Los Angeles police officers in 1991. Although a jury in a California court acquitted the police officers on state charges, two of them were eventually convicted in federal court of violating Mr. King's constitutional rights and were sentenced to thirty months in prison. Moreover, King ultimately recovered $3.8 million in a federal civil suit against the City of Los Angeles.

> **To Summarize:**
> - *Because an arrest is, in effect, a "seizure," it must conform to the probable cause and warrant requirements of the Fourth Amendment.*
> - *Arrests are often made pursuant to warrants based on preliminary investigations. An arrest warrant, like a search warrant, is issued by a judge or magistrate upon a showing of probable cause.*
> - *Warrantless arrests, like warrantless searches, are permissible assuming there is probable cause to make the arrest and exigent circumstances make it impracticable for police to obtain a warrant. A person arrested without a warrant must be brought promptly before a judicial officer for a probable cause hearing.*
> - *The courts have generally recognized that the Fourth Amendment permits police to use only such force as is "reasonable" and "necessary" in effectuating an arrest. However, the Supreme Court has held that police officers may use deadly force to apprehend a fleeing felon only when the officer has probable cause to believe that the suspect poses a significant threat of death or physical injury to the officer or others.*

Police Interrogation and Confessions of Guilt

Another of the Warren Court's controversial contributions to the criminal process was its enlargement of protection for criminal suspects subjected to **custodial interrogation**. Clearly, police must have the authority to question suspects in order to solve crimes.

But the Supreme Court held as far back as 1897 (*Bram v. United States*) that a coerced confession violates the Self-Incrimination Clause of the Fifth Amendment. Of course, the Self-Incrimination Clause was not incorporated into the Fourteenth Amendment until well into the 1960s. Prior to incorporation, the Court's scrutiny of police interrogation in the states was limited to a broad due process inquiry that examined the totality of circumstances in each case with one eye on the fairness of the defendant's trial and the other on methods of police interrogation.

The traditional test used by the Court was whether a challenged confession could reasonably be deemed to have been voluntary. Subjective voluntariness, however, is extremely difficult to discern, even through direct observation, let alone through appellate hindsight years later. Consequently, the Supreme Court's decisions in this area were often unclear and inconsistent. For example, in the 1944 case of *Ashcraft v. Tennessee*, the Court overturned a murder conviction on grounds that the defendant's alleged confession was coerced because it had been preceded by a thirty-six-hour period of continuous police interrogation. Writing for a six-member majority, Justice Black made no attempt to weigh the effect of this long and intense period of questioning on the suspect. Black simply concluded that thirty-six hours of questioning was "inherently coercive" and that use of the confession violated the Due Process Clause of the Fourteenth Amendment. Justice Robert H. Jackson dissented sharply, pointing out that coerciveness could not be measured simply by reference to the clock. Just over a month later, in *Lyons v. Oklahoma* (1944), the Court, dividing 5 to 4, held to be "voluntary" a confession repeated some twelve hours after the suspect, during incommunicado detention in the dead of night, had been forced to hold in his lap a pan containing the charred bones of his alleged murder victims.

By the 1960s, many believed that another approach to the law governing police interrogation was necessary. The Court's decision in *Malloy v. Hogan* (1964) to incorporate the Self-incrimination Clause paved the way for a stricter attitude toward interrogation by state law enforcement personnel. A sharp break with the voluntariness approach came in 1964 when the Supreme Court decided *Escobedo v. Illinois*. Here, the Court held that once a police interrogation has begun to focus on a particular suspect, the suspect has been taken into custody, the police carry out a process of interrogations that lends itself to incriminating statements, the suspect has requested and been denied an opportunity to consult with his lawyer, and the police have not effectively warned him of his absolute constitutional right to remain silent … no statement elicited by the police during the interrogation may be used against him during the criminal trial.

In effect, *Escobedo* adopted an exclusionary rule similar to that of *Mapp v. Ohio* but applied to enforce Fifth and Sixth Amendment rights. Two years later, in *Miranda v. Arizona* (1966), the Court elaborated on the need for constitutional safeguards to protect citizens from "inherently coercive" police interrogation:

> *It is obvious that such an interrogation environment is created for no purpose other than to subjugate the individual to the will of his examiner. This atmosphere carries its own badge of intimidation. To be sure this is not physical intimidation, but it is equally destructive to human dignity. The current practice of incommunicado interrogation is at odds with one of our nation's most cherished principles—that the individual may not be compelled to incriminate himself.*

The *Miranda* Warnings

To safeguard the immunity against self-incrimination, the Court developed the well-known *Miranda* **warnings**. Unless police inform suspects of their rights to remain silent and have an attorney present during questioning and unless police obtain voluntary waivers of these rights, suspects' confessions and other statements are inadmissible at trial. When the *Miranda* decision came down in 1966, the Court was harshly criticized, especially by the law enforcement community, for "coddling criminals" and "hamstringing the police." However, the practice of "Mirandizing" suspects soon became standard operating procedure in law enforcement. Today, most people in law enforcement support the *Miranda* decision as a means of professionalizing police conduct and, perhaps more importantly, protecting legitimate confessions from later challenges. As long as the police provide suspects with the warning and avoid coercion, anything said by the suspect can be used against him or her in a court of law. Whereas, prior to *Miranda*, there was something of a presumption against the admissibility of a confession, today the presumption is clearly in favor of admitting confessions as evidence as long as the requirements of *Miranda* have been observed by the police.

The *Miranda* decision is firmly established in the Supreme Court's jurisprudence, as evidenced by the Court's decision in *Dickerson v. United States* (2000). In *Dickerson*, the Rehnquist Court was handed a good opportunity to overturn *Miranda* and some Court watchers expected the Court to do just that. Given the Rehnquist Court's generally conservative disposition, and given that *Miranda* is more than any other decision a symbol of the Warren Court's liberalism in the criminal justice area, there was some basis for thinking the Court might abandon this precedent. As it turned out, only two of the most conservative justices (Scalia and Thomas) voted to overturn *Miranda*. Writing for the majority, Chief Justice Rehnquist, ironically one of the foremost early critics of Miranda, observed that "*Miranda* has become embedded in routine police practice to the point where the warnings have become part of our national culture." Although the Supreme Court has consistently reaffirmed the *Miranda* decision, it has over the years carved out a number of exceptions that have considerably softened *Miranda's* impact on law enforcement. As Chief Justice Rehnquist recognized in *Dickerson*, the Court has "reduced the impact of the *Miranda* rule on legitimate law enforcement while reaffirming the decision's core ruling." For example, in *Harris v. New York* (1971), the Court ruled that confessions excluded from trial under *Miranda* could nevertheless be used to impeach the credibility of a defendant who takes the stand to testify in his or her own behalf. Writing for the Court, Chief Justice Burger pointed out that the privilege against compulsory self-incrimination "cannot be construed to include the right to commit perjury."

The Public Safety Exception to Miranda   In 1984, the Supreme Court created the public safety exception to the requirement that *Miranda* warnings be given prior to any questioning of the suspect. In *New York v. Quarks*, the Court examined an interesting factual situation. Two New York City police officers were approached by a woman who claimed she had just been raped and that her assailant had gone into a nearby grocery store. The police were informed that the assailant was carrying a gun. The officers proceeded to the store and immediately spotted Benjamin Quarles, who matched the description given by the victim. Upon seeing the police, Quarles turned and ran. One of the police officers drew his service revolver and ordered Quarles to freeze. Quarles complied with the officer's request. The officer frisked Quarles and discovered an

---

The *Miranda* Warnings

"You have the right to remain silent. Anything you say can and will be used against you in a court of law. You have the right to speak to an attorney and to have an attorney present during any questioning. If you cannot afford an attorney, one will be provided for you at government expense."

empty shoulder holster. Before reading Quarles the *Miranda* warnings, the officer asked Quarles the location of the gun. Quarles nodded in the direction of some empty boxes and said, "The gun is over there." He was then placed under arrest and given the *Miranda* warnings. Later, Quarles moved to have his statement suppressed from evidence since it was made prior to the *Miranda* warnings. He also moved for suppression of the gun under the **fruit of the poisonous tree doctrine**, which holds that evidence derived from illegally obtained evidence is itself tainted (see *Wong Sun v. United States* [1963]). The Supreme Court allowed both pieces of evidence to be used against Quarles, notwithstanding the delay in the *Miranda* warnings. Obviously, the Court felt that the officers were justified in locating a discarded weapon prior to Mirandizing Quarles. In so holding, the Court created the **public safety exception** to *Miranda*.

In 2013, the public safety exception became a matter of national media discussion when the FBI invoked the exception to delay Mirandizing a suspect in the Boston Marathon bombing. The suspect, Dzhokhar Tsarnaev, was questioned by the FBI in a hospital room for two days before a federal magistrate arrived and read the suspect his rights. Some questioned the need to Mirandize Tsarnaev at all, given that the evidence against him was very strong and the authorities really did not need his confession. Some media accounts indicated that Tsarnaev had been cooperating with authorities and stopped doing so after being given the *Miranda* warnings.

The Inevitable Discovery Exception Another exception to the *Miranda* exclusionary rule is based on inevitable discovery of physical evidence that is challenged as the fruit of the poisonous tree. In a macabre case decided in 1984 (*Nix v. Williams*), the Court allowed evidence to be admitted even though it was obtained through the statement of a suspect who had indicated his desire to remain silent until he could meet with his attorney. After one of the police officers involved made a speech emphasizing the need for a "Christian burial" for the victim, the suspect led police to the body of a young girl he had kidnapped and murdered. In allowing the body to be used as evidence, the Court reasoned that the body was not the fruit of a poisonous tree since a search under way in the area would eventually have located the body anyway. Hence, the Court created an **inevitable discovery exception** to the fruit of the poisonous tree doctrine.

Must a Suspect Speak to Invoke the Right to Remain Silent?

In 2010 the Supreme Court handed down a major decision limiting the protection that *Miranda v. Arizona* provides to suspects held in police custody. Writing for the five-member majority in *Berghuis v. Tompkins*, Justice Kennedy insisted that the right to remain silent during a police interrogation must be invoked unambiguously by a suspect. Justice Kennedy noted, "There is good reason to require an accused who wants to invoke his or her right to remain silent to do so unambiguously. [This] results in an objective inquiry that 'avoid[s] difficulties of proof ... and provides[s] guidance to officers' on how to proceed in the face of ambiguity."

Writing her first major dissent, Justice Sotomayor found it "counterintuitive" that a suspect must speak to invoke his right to remain silent. Claiming that the decision "turns *Miranda* upside down," she disagreed with the idea she found in the majority's opinion that "suspects will be legally presumed to have waived their rights even if they have given no clear expression of their intent to do so." Justice Sotomayor's reasoning adhered more closely to the original language of *Miranda* than did Justice Kennedy's majority opinion. Kennedy, however, maintained that more recent interpretations of the *Miranda* requirements supported his conclusion in this case. In short, the majority held that a suspect must positively and unambiguously invoke his right to remain silent, while the dissenters would have held that a suspect must positively and unambiguously waive that right.

The Court continued down this path in *Salinas v. Texas* (2013). Salinas, who had not been placed in custody or received the *Miranda* warnings, voluntarily answered several police officers' questions about a murder. However, when he was asked whether ballistics testing would match his shotgun to shell casings found at the scene of the crime, Salinas fell silent. He was subsequently arrested and charged with the murder. At trial, the state used Salinas' failure to answer questions as evidence of his guilt. Salinas was convicted, sentenced to twenty years in prison, and two state appellate courts upheld the conviction. The U.S. Supreme Court also affirmed the conviction, but was unable to produce a majority opinion. Speaking for a plurality of justices on the majority side, Justice Samuel Alito opined that Salinas' "Fifth Amendment claim fails because he did not expressly invoke the privilege against self-incrimination in response to the officer's question." The absence of a majority opinion gives the Salinas decision limited precedential value, but it certainly shows the direction that the Roberts Court is moving with respect to the right to remain silent.

Police Deception in Interrogations

The Court has refused to expand the scope of custodial interrogation beyond an actual arrest or significant "deprivation of freedom." In *Oregon v. Mathiason* (1977), the Court allowed the use of a confession obtained by police during voluntary interrogation of a suspect who was not at the time under arrest. An interesting fact in the *Mathiason* case is that the police officer who obtained the confession lied to the suspect about his fingerprints being found at the scene of the crime. Only after this deception did Mathiason confess. Nevertheless, he was not under formal arrest at the time and had even come to the station house unescorted to talk to police. In the Court's view, this was a "noncustodial" situation; hence, *Miranda* did not apply.

In another controversial decision involving **police deception** (*Moran v. Burbine* [1986]), the Court further delimited the scope of the *Miranda* rule. Police arrested Burbine for burglary and later obtained information that linked him to an unsolved murder. Burbine's sister, unaware of the possible murder charge, retained an attorney to represent her brother. The attorney telephoned the police, who assured her that Burbine was not to be questioned until the next day but failed to tell her of a possible murder charge against her client. Despite their assurances to the contrary, the police then interrogated Burbine, failing to tell him that an attorney had been obtained for him and had attempted to contact him. Burbine waived his rights to counsel and to remain silent and eventually confessed to the killing. The Supreme Court found no constitutional violation, holding that Burbine had knowingly, intelligently, and voluntarily waived his rights.

Can a Coerced Confession Be a "Harmless Error"?

In one of the most significant decisions in this area, *Arizona v. Fulminante* (1991), the Supreme Court disallowed the use of a confession that was obtained by a prisoner who was also a confidential FBI informant. Oreste Fulminante, who was suspected of murdering his eleven-year-old stepdaughter, Jeneane, was incarcerated in federal prison on an unrelated charge. He was befriended by Anthony Sarivola, a former police officer serving time for extortion. Sarivola led Fulminante to believe that he had connections with organized crime organizations and could protect Fulminante from other prisoners who had heard that Fulminante was suspected of killing his stepdaughter. Sarivola insisted, however, that Fulminante tell him what really happened to his stepdaughter. Fulminante then confided in Sarivola that he had indeed taken his stepdaughter on his motorcycle into the desert where, in the words of Justice White, "he choked her, sexually assaulted her, and made her beg for her life, before shooting her twice in the head." Sarivola gave this information to the FBI, which, in turn, passed it along to Arizona authorities. After being released from prison, Fulminante was indicted for the murder of his stepdaughter. Denying his motion to suppress, the Arizona trial court allowed the confession to be introduced and subsequently found Fulminante guilty of first-degree murder.

In reviewing Fulminante's conviction, the U.S. Supreme Court found that his confession had been coerced. However, the most significant aspect of the Court's decision was its holding that a coerced confession is subject to **harmless error analysis.** Prior to this holding, a defendant was automatically entitled to reversal of his or her conviction if a coerced confession had been introduced into evidence at trial. Under the *Fulminante* decision, an appellate court is permitted to affirm a conviction if it determines that the defendant would have been convicted on other evidence even in the absence of the coerced confession. Note that the Supreme Court found that the use of Fulminante's confession was not harmless error and therefore reversed his conviction. Irrespective of this result, the *Fulminante* decision has been criticized as a further erosion of the constitutional protection against coerced confessions.

To Summarize:

♦ *The Supreme Court has long held that a coerced confession violates the Self-Incrimination Clause of the Fifth Amendment as well as the due process requirements of the Fifth and Fourteenth Amendments.*

♦ *The traditional test used by the Court was whether a challenged confession could reasonably be deemed to have been voluntary. This approach often led to seemingly inconsistent decisions with respect to police interrogation practices.*

♦ *To safeguard the immunity against self-incrimination, the Court developed the well-known* Miranda *warnings. Unless police inform suspects of their rights to remain silent and have an attorney present during questioning, and unless police obtain voluntary waivers of these rights, suspects' confessions and other statements are inadmissible at trial.*

♦ *Although the Supreme Court has reaffirmed the Miranda decision, it has substantially narrowed the scope of its application. The Court has refused to expand the scope of custodial interrogation beyond an actual arrest or significant "deprivation of freedom." The Court has also recognized a number of exceptions to Miranda, including the public safety and inevitable discovery exceptions.*

♦ *The Court has ruled that an unlawfully obtained confession does not necessarily require reversal of a conviction; it depends on whether there was sufficient evidence to convict the defendant in the absence of the confession.*

The Right to Counsel

Historically, the Sixth Amendment right to counsel in "all criminal prosecutions" had meant no more than that the government could not prevent a person accused of a crime from hiring a lawyer if he or she could afford to do so. The Supreme Court moved significantly away from this traditional view in the celebrated Scottsboro case of the 1930s. Here, the Court reversed the convictions of a group of young African-American men who had been sentenced to death in an Alabama court for allegedly raping two white women. During the rushed investigation and trial, conducted in an atmosphere of extreme racial animosity, the defendants were not represented by counsel in any meaningful sense. In some cases the defendants met their council the morning their trail was to begin. In *Powell v. Alabama* (1932), the Supreme Court found that the defendants had been denied due process of law in violation of the Fourteenth Amendment. Justice George Sutherland's majority opinion placed great importance on the failure of the trial judge to ensure effective representation and adequate time to prepare a defense.

The *Gideon* Decision

Under Chief Justice Earl Warren, the Supreme Court placed enormous stress on the need for professional representation of persons suspected or accused of crimes. In its *Escobedo* and *Miranda* decisions, for example, the Warren Court was obviously concerned about the absence of defense counsel during custodial police interrogation. In *Gideon v. Wainwright* (1963), the Court overruled precedent and held that the Sixth Amendment **right to counsel** as applied to the states via the Due Process Clause of the Fourteenth Amendment requires states to provide counsel to defendants who cannot afford to hire attorneys on their own. The *Gideon* Court recognized that "in our adversary system of criminal justice, any person hauled into court, who is too poor to hire a lawyer, cannot be assured a fair trial unless counsel is provided for him." In a related case decided the same day as *Gideon* (*Douglas v. California* [1963]), the Court held that a state must provide counsel to an indigent defendant who has a right under state law to appeal a conviction to a higher court. (However, in *Pennsylvania v. Finley* [1987], the Court made clear what had been only implicit in *Douglas v. California*—namely, that "the right to appointed counsel extends to the first appeal ... and no further.") Because *Gideon* was made retroactive, it had a tremendous impact on the criminal justice system. For example, in Florida, where the *Gideon* case originated, the state was required to retry hundreds of convicted felons who had not been represented by counsel at their first trials. In many cases, the key witnesses were no longer available, and the state was forced to drop its charges. In the wake of *Gideon*, many states decided it would be more economical in the long run to set up permanent offices to handle indigent defense rather than to have judges appoint counsel ad hoc. Most states now have public defenders to make good on the state's responsibility under the Due Process Clause of the Fourteenth Amendment. Although many state judges, legislators, governors, and law enforcement officers resented the Court's "meddling" in their affairs, the *Gideon* decision has come, like so many other Supreme Court rulings, to be accepted and even praised by state officials.

For the most part, the Burger Court maintained this commitment to providing counsel to indigent defendants. In *Argersinger v. Hamlin* (1972), the Court extended the *Gideon* ruling to cover misdemeanor trials (*Gideon* applied only to felonies). The *Argersinger* decision was ambiguous, however, on the issue of whether misdemeanor defendants were entitled to counsel if they faced possible jail terms or only if their convictions *actually resulted in* incarceration. In *Scott v. Illinois* (1979), the Supreme Court clarified the situation, holding that counsel had to be provided to indigent misdemeanants only if conviction would actually result in imprisonment. Writing for the Court, Justice Rehnquist thus opted for a narrow interpretation of *Argersinger*, arguing that "any extension would create confusion and impose unpredictable, but necessarily substantial costs on fifty quite diverse states."

Effectiveness of Appointed Counsel

One of the most elusive contemporary issues in the right to counsel area is that of **ineffective representation**. As the Court recognized in *Powell v. Alabama* (1932), the right to counsel is useless unless a defendant is competently represented. Until recently, most federal courts followed the **mockery of justice test** in determining the competency of appointed counsel. The question was whether the attorney was so ineffective as to constitute "a farce or mockery of justice" (see, for example, *Edwards v. United States* [1958]).

This permissive standard was rapidly adopted by most of the state supreme courts. However, the federal circuit courts adopted different standards of varying strictness.

In 1984, the Supreme Court finally standardized the test that courts must follow to comply with the Sixth Amendment. In *Strickland v. Washington*, the Court held that an indigent appellant must show (1) that his or her trial lawyer was less than reasonably effective and (2) that there is a reasonable probability that the outcome of the trial would have been different had counsel been more effective. Obviously, this is a difficult test to meet, allowing for reversal only in cases of egregious incompetence.

Self-Representation   Although decisions such as *Powell v. Alabama* and *Gideon v. Wainwright* stressed the importance of counsel in ensuring a fair trial, the Supreme Court has made it quite clear that a defendant has a constitutional right to refuse counsel, as long as the waiver is made "knowingly and intelligently." In *Faretta v. California* (1975), the Court decided a case in which Anthony Pasquall Faretta, accused of grand theft, requested permission from the trial court to represent himself, arguing that the public defender's office was too busy to provide him with effective representation. The trial judge refused the request and appointed an assistant public defender to represent him. Faretta's conviction was ultimately vacated by the Supreme Court by a 6-to-3 vote. The majority asserted that "[t]he language and spirit of the Sixth Amendment contemplate that counsel, like the other defense tools guaranteed by the Amendment, shall be an aid to a willing defendant—not an organ of the state interposed between an unwilling defendant and his right to defend himself personally."

Although the *Faretta* decision did not produce a rash of **pro se defenses** (those in which the defendant conducts his or her own defense), occasionally a defendant will "go it alone" in the courtroom. It is important to note that while the right to represent one's self is generally upheld, a judge must first approve of this setup based on a defendant's competence to do so. One noteworthy example of **self-representation** occurred in the trial of serial killer Ted Bundy in Florida in the early 1980s. Bundy, a former law student, insisted on representing himself, although the trial judge appointed a lawyer to serve as standby counsel. Although most observers believed that Bundy did a reasonably effective job in representing himself, he still claimed on appeal that his conviction was invalid because he had ineffective representation at trial. Not surprisingly, the appellate court was unmoved by this attempt to have it both ways!

To Summarize:

- *Historically, the Sixth Amendment right to counsel in "all criminal prosecutions" meant no more than that the government could not prevent a person accused of a crime from hiring a lawyer if he or she could afford to do so.*
- *In* Gideon v. Wainwright *(1963), the Warren Court overturned precedent and held that the Sixth Amendment right to counsel as applied to the states via the Due Process Clause of the Fourteenth Amendment requires states to provide counsel to felony defendants who cannot afford to hire attorneys on their own. For the most part, the Burger, Rehnquist, and Roberts Courts have maintained this commitment to providing counsel to indigent defendants.*
- *The Supreme Court has held that indigent defendants have the right to reasonably effective counsel. To prevail in a claim of ineffective counsel, one must show that his or her trial lawyer was less than reasonably effective and that there is a reasonable probability that the outcome of the trial would have been different had counsel been more effective.*
- *The Court has made it quite clear that a defendant has a constitutional right to refuse to be represented by appointed counsel, as long as the waiver is made "knowingly and intelligently."*

Bail and Pretrial Detention

Because persons accused of crime are presumed innocent until proven guilty, it is customary for defendants to be released from custody prior to **arraignment** and trial. Ordinarily, courts require defendants to post **bail** (a sum of money), which is forfeited if the defendant fails to appear in court or flees to escape prosecution. The Eighth Amendment prohibits "excessive bail." The Supreme Court has recognized that the purpose of bail is not to inflict punishment but to ensure that a defendant appears in court. In *Stack v. Boyle* (1951), the Court said that "[b]ail set at a figure higher than an amount reasonably calculated to fulfill this purpose is 'excessive' under the Eighth Amendment." However, the Court has never held that the Excessive Bail Clause is incorporated by the Fourteenth Amendment, leaving the issue of excessive bail in state criminal prosecutions to state constitutions, legislatures, and courts.

It has been a long-standing practice for courts to deny bail to defendants who are deemed especially dangerous or pose an unusual likelihood of fleeing to avoid prosecution. This raises the question of whether the Eighth Amendment implies a right to pretrial release. In *United States v. Salerno* (1987), the Supreme Court answered this question in the negative. Here, the Court upheld the Bail Reform Act of 1984, which permits **pretrial detention** in federal cases where a court determines that the release of a defendant would pose a serious threat to public safety. Writing for the Court, Chief Justice Rehnquist agreed that "a primary function of bail is to safeguard the courts' role in adjudicating the guilt or innocence of defendants" but rejected "the proposition that the Eighth Amendment categorically prohibits the government from pursuing other admittedly compelling interests through the regulation of pretrial release." The Court's decision in *Salerno*, while applying formally only to federal criminal cases, suggests the validity of state laws denying bail to persons accused of violent felonies, especially where such persons have a record of violent crimes. It is doubtful that the Supreme Court would approve a policy of long-term pretrial detention for defendants accused of nonviolent crimes.

To Summarize:

◆ *Because persons accused of crime are presumed innocent until proven guilty, it is customary for defendants to be released from custody prior to arraignment and trial.*

◆ *The Supreme Court has upheld the common practice for courts to deny bail to defendants who are deemed especially dangerous or pose an unusual likelihood of fleeing to avoid prosecution.*

Plea Bargaining

In a typical jurisdiction, only about 5 percent of felony arrests result in trials. Many cases are dropped by the prosecution after key evidence has been suppressed on Fourth, Fifth, or Sixth Amendment grounds. Other cases must be dropped because key witnesses cannot be located or made to testify. But the main reason that criminal cases do not often result in trials is the existence of the **plea bargain**, an agreement by the accused to plead guilty in exchange for some concession from the prosecution. This concession might be a reduction in the severity or number of the charges brought, or it might simply be a promise by the prosecutor not to seek the maximum sentence allowed by law.

Conventional wisdom holds that plea bargaining occurs because of the scarce resources allocated to the processing of criminal cases. The criminal trial can be a protracted process. There simply are not enough prosecutors, public defenders, and judges to try all the criminal cases coming into the system. Nor does the public or its elected representatives seem inclined to provide the necessary resources. But even if such resources were miraculously furnished, there is reason to believe plea bargaining would still exist; the evidence indicates that plea bargaining occurs in jurisdictions where scarce resources are really not a problem. In addition, an incentive to plea bargain may be built into the very nature of the criminal justice process.

We know that organizations generally try to minimize uncertainties associated with their activities. The defense counsel group is probably no different. Lawyers especially dislike the uncertainty inherent in a trial. The legal technicalities associated with proving guilt and the unpredictability of juries make the criminal trial a very uncertain enterprise. Many prosecutors and defense lawyers would rather settle on a plea bargain that is certain than to go into the courtroom and take their chances on losing the case. This suggests that plea bargaining is here to stay. There is a clear benefit for all to participate; prosecutors secure a conviction, the defense team receives a reduced sentence, and the judge is able to remove a case from an overloaded docket.

Nevertheless, plea bargaining has been and will continue to be an object of criticism. Some are offended by what they perceive to be insufficient penalties meted out to criminals through plea bargains. Others are concerned that our historic commitment to due process of law is being sacrificed on the altar of expediency. Still others argue that plea bargaining removes a direct connection between the unlawful actions of the accused and the sentence received, as well as increasing the discrepancy in punishment for similar offenses. Collectively these objections advocate the position that plea bargaining is not aligned with any traditional American conception of "justice."

The Supreme Court has addressed the issue of plea bargaining in several cases dating from the late 1960s (see, for example, *Jackson v. United States* [1968]; *Boykin v. Alabama* [1969]; *Brady v. United States* [1970]; and *Santobello v. New York* [1971]). Basically, the Court has manifested concern over plea bargaining but nevertheless has recognized its practicality, if not its inevitability. However, the Court has stated emphatically that a trial judge must ascertain that the defendant has made a **knowing and intelligent waiver** of the right to a trial before accepting the defendant's plea of guilty. As the Court noted in *Boykin v. Alabama*:

> [A] plea of guilty is more than an admission of conduct, it is a conviction. Ignorance, incomprehension, coercion, terror, inducements, subtle or blatant threats might be a cover-up of unconstitutionality.

One of the more difficult cases decided by the Court in the area of plea bargaining was *Bordenkircher v. Hayes* (1978). Paul Hayes was indicted by a Kentucky grand jury for writing a bad check. It was not his first offense. The prosecutor informed Hayes that if he did not plead guilty, he (the prosecutor) would return to the grand jury to seek a tougher indictment based on the state's habitual offender statute. The defendant refused to "cop a plea," and the prosecutor carried out his threat. The grand jury handed down the more serious indictment. Hayes was tried, convicted, and sentenced to life imprisonment. Was this threat by the prosecutor constitutionally permissible? Dividing 5 to 4, the Supreme Court ruled that it was, since Hayes was "properly chargeable" under the recidivist statute from the start. Dissenting, Justice Harry Blackmun refused to approve what he perceived as "prosecutorial vindictiveness." In Blackmun's view, Hayes was being punished for the exercise of constitutional rights. The sharp division in *Bordenkircher* underscores the fact that reasonable people, including those trained in the law, can disagree on what offends the "fundamental fairness" required by due process.

> **To Summarize:**
> ◆ *Plea bargaining refers to an agreement by the accused to plead guilty in exchange for some concession from the prosecution.*
> ◆ *The Supreme Court has approved the practice of plea bargaining but has stated emphatically that a trial judge must ascertain that the defendant has made a knowing and intelligent waiver of the right to a trial before accepting his or her plea of guilty.*

Trial by Jury

In spite of the pervasiveness of plea bargaining, the **jury trial** still plays a prominent role in the administration of justice. Trial by jury is recognized as a federal constitutional right in criminal and civil cases. Reference to jury trial appears once in the original Constitution and twice in the Bill of Rights. Article III provides: "The Trial of all Crimes, except in Cases of Impeachment, shall be by Jury." The Seventh Amendment requires that "the right of trial by jury shall be preserved" in civil suits. Most pertinent to our concerns is the Sixth Amendment, which states: "In all criminal prosecutions, the accused shall enjoy the right to a speedy and public trial by an impartial jury." Of course, prior to the incorporation of this provision into the Fourteenth Amendment in 1968 (see *Duncan v. Louisiana*), "all criminal prosecutions" meant all *federal* criminal prosecutions. Ever since *Duncan*, however, defendants in both state and federal criminal cases have had a constitutional right to trial by jury. The only exception to the right to jury trial involves misdemeanor trials where defendants face incarceration for less than six months.

The Problem of Pretrial Publicity

Even before the Sixth Amendment right to trial by jury was incorporated into the Fourteenth Amendment, the Supreme Court had occasion to reverse jury verdicts in state criminal cases where the fairness of the trial was prejudiced by excessive publicity. In so doing, the Court used the **fair trial doctrine** under the Fourteenth Amendment, rather than the Sixth Amendment jury trial provision. *Sheppard v. Maxwell* (1966) is an excellent case in point. There, the Court reversed a murder conviction reached in a trial conducted against a backdrop of sensationalistic publicity. The circumstances surrounding the *Sheppard* case are almost comical in retrospect. Local officials, especially the trial judge, allowed Dr. Sam Sheppard's murder trial to degenerate into a circus. The jurors in the case were constantly exposed to intense media coverage of the case right up until the time at which they began their deliberations. Under these circumstances, the guilty verdict was virtually a foregone conclusion. Resolving that fundamental fairness had been denied, the Supreme Court reversed Sheppard's conviction.

Sheppard v. Maxwell leads one to wonder just what steps can be legitimately taken to insulate a jury from prejudicial **pretrial publicity** in a sensational case. One possibility is to take extreme care in the jury selection process, possibly by increasing the number of peremptory challenges available to the defense and the prosecution (such challenges, while limited in number, do not ordinarily require an explanation by counsel or a ruling by the trial judge). Another common step is to sequester the jury during the course of the trial. Another frequent measure is to postpone the trial until the publicity dies down. A less common approach is a **change of venue**—moving the trial to a locale less affected by the pretrial publicity. Although there is no question about the propriety of these measures, considerable doubt remains as to their efficacy.

Some judges have attempted more drastic means of protecting the defendant's right to a fair trial. One of these is to impose **gag orders** on the press, prohibiting the reportage of certain facts or incidents related to a sensational crime. In *Nebraska Press Association v. Stuart* (1976), the Supreme Court invalidated a gag order imposed by a trial judge to safeguard the rights of a man accused of a brutal mass murder. The Court viewed the order as a prior restraint in violation of the First Amendment's protection of the freedom of the press. The *Nebraska Press* case vividly illustrates the head-on conflict of two cherished constitutional principles: freedom of the press and the right to a fair trial. Although the Court was unanimous in striking down the gag order, Chief Justice Burger's majority opinion left open the possibility that such orders might be permissible under extreme circumstances.

Closure of Judicial Proceedings　　Another more drastic means of protecting the defendant's right to a fair trial is **closure of pretrial proceedings**. In *Gannet v. DePasquale* (1979), the Court allowed the closure of a pretrial hearing to determine the admissibility of evidence with the consent of both the prosecution and the defense. Writing for a divided Court, Justice Stewart stated that the right to a "public trial" guaranteed by the Sixth Amendment is personal to the defendant, not a general right of public access. Stewart went on to say that any First Amendment right of access by the press was outweighed by the right of the accused to receive a fair trial. In 1980, the Court appeared to alter its position somewhat. In *Richmond Newspapers v. Virginia*, the Court voted 7 to 1 to disallow the closure of a criminal trial. Although there was no majority opinion, the justices seemed to have agreed that the First Amendment prohibits trial closure. The very next year, in *Chandler v. Florida* (1981), the Court allowed television coverage of criminal trials, suggesting that *Richmond Newspapers* was no anomaly. The Court's decision in *Waller v. Georgia* (1984) also suggests a strong commitment to the value of a public trial. In *Waller*, the Court refused to allow closure of a pretrial suppression hearing that had been granted by the trial court over the objection of the accused. Although the Court in *Waller* suggested that extreme circumstances might allow the closure of a pretrial proceeding despite the objection of the defendant, the Court adopted a test that makes it very difficult to justify closure.

Jury Size

Historically, trial juries in the United States were composed of twelve persons, all of whom had to agree in order to convict a defendant. Although this is still the case in most states, some jurisdictions allow for six-person juries in noncapital cases. In *Williams v. Florida* (1970), the Supreme Court approved Florida's use of six-person juries in noncapital cases. Justice White's Opinion of the Court discussed the relationship between jury size and the Sixth Amendment:

> [T]he fact that the jury at common law was composed of precisely twelve is a historical accident, unnecessary to effect the purposes of the jury system and wholly without significance…. To read the Sixth Amendment as forever codifying a feature so incidental to the real purpose of the Amendment is to ascribe a blind formalism to the Framers.

Serious questions exist about the factual assertions made by the Court in the *Williams* case. Is it true, as the Court asserted, that "neither currently available evidence nor theory suggests that the twelve-member jury is necessarily more advantageous to the defendant"? Some experts on jury behavior have concluded otherwise. However, in *Ballew v. Georgia* (1978), the Court drew the line on jury size when it refused to permit the use of five-person juries. The Court cited studies to show that "the purpose and functioning of the jury … is seriously impaired … by a reduction in size to below six members." Thus, state legislatures are free to specify the number of persons to serve on juries in noncapital cases as long as they observe the constitutional minimum of six.

The Unanimity Principle

In *Johnson v. Louisiana* (1972) and its companion case *Apodaca v. Oregon* (1972), the Supreme Court surprised many observers by allowing state criminal trials to depart from the historic **unanimity rule**. In *Johnson*, the state of Louisiana passed a law allowing for convictions by nine votes on twelve-person juries in noncapital cases. Writing for a sharply divided Court, Justice White tried to reconcile nonunanimity with the **reasonable doubt standard** required by due process:

> *Of course, the State's proof could be regarded as more certain if it had convinced all 12 jurors instead of only nine; it would have been even more compelling if it had … convinced 24 or 36 jurors. But the fact remains that nine jurors—a substantial majority of the jury—were convinced by the evidence. In our view disagreement of three jurors does not alone establish reasonable doubt.*

One can argue, as Justice Marshall did in his dissent, that the refusal of three presumably reasonable jurors to sanction a guilty verdict might in and of itself indicate a reasonable doubt as to the guilt of the accused:

> *The juror whose dissenting voice is unheard may be a spokesman, but simply for himself—and that, in my view, is enough. The doubts of a single juror are in my view evidence that the government has failed to carry its burden of proving guilt beyond a reasonable doubt.*

The Court's decisions in *Williams v. Florida* and *Johnson v. Louisiana* left many observers wondering whether the Court would permit **nonunanimous verdicts** by six-member juries. In *Burch v. Louisiana* (1979), the Court allayed the fears of those who thought it was going too far to facilitate criminal convictions. Justice Rehnquist wrote the opinion for a unanimous Court:

> *We agree … that the question presented is a "close" one. Nevertheless, we believe that conviction by a nonunanimous six-member jury in a state criminal trial for a nonpetty offense deprives an individual of his constitutional right to trial by jury.*

Exclusion of Minorities from Juries

Another problem that has beset the courts with respect to trial juries is the exclusion of women, African-Americans, and other minority groups from juries, especially when the defendants are members of such groups. Although the Court has quite clearly stated that there is no constitutional right of a defendant to have on the jury individuals of his or her gender or ethnic identity, it has also held that the systematic exclusion of such groups is unconstitutional under the Fourteenth Amendment (see *Strauder v. West Virginia* [1879] and *Swain v. Alabama* [1965]). The Court has recognized that a jury should, at least ideally, represent a cross section of the community in order to be completely fair and just to the accused.

One of the more difficult issues in jury selection is the use of the **peremptory challenge** to eliminate prospective jurors on the grounds of race. In *Batson v. Kentucky* (1986), the Supreme Court held that a prosecutor's use of peremptory challenges to exclude African-Americans from a jury trying an African-American defendant constituted a basis for reversal on appeal. Consequently, today in the trial of an African-American defendant, the exclusion of a single African-American juror can be the basis for the trial court to deny the use of a peremptory challenge, if the judge is persuaded that the challenge is racially motivated. In 1991, the *Batson* rule was broadened so that a defendant need not be of the same race as the excluded juror to successfully challenge that juror's exclusion (*Powers v. Ohio*). In the same year, the Supreme Court extended the *Batson* rule to encompass civil trials as well (*Edmondson v. Leesville Concrete Company*).

In *Georgia v. McCollum* (1992), the Court revisited this area of the law and extended the *Batson* rule by holding that a defendant's exercise of peremptory challenges was state action, and that the Equal Protection Clause also prohibits defendants from engaging in purposeful discrimination on the ground of race. As a result of the pronouncements in *Batson*, *Powers*, and *McCollum*, federal and state courts have reevaluated their views on the exercise of peremptory challenges. In general, trial judges are still vested with broad discretion in reviewing **racially motivated peremptory challenges**, but many trial lawyers have expressed concern that peremptory challenges may become relics in our system of jurisprudence.

Gender-Based Peremptory Challenges   The view that peremptory challenges are on the way out was reinforced by a trend in the late 1980s and early 1990s to restrict **gender-based peremptory challenges**. By 1993, federal appellate courts had issued disparate rulings on the issue. Finally, in *J.E.B. v. Alabama ex rel. T. B.* (1994), the Supreme Court resolved that conflict and held that the Equal Protection Clause of the Fourteenth Amendment prohibits gender-based peremptory challenges. Writing for the majority, Justice Blackmun emphasized the relationship between racially based and gender-based peremptory challenges when he observed that "[f]ailing to provide jurors the same protection against gender discrimination as race discrimination could frustrate the purpose of *Batson* itself." There may be reason to believe that the Court is retreating somewhat from the *Batson* decision. In *Purkett v. Elem* (1995), the Court held in effect that judges are not required to disallow a peremptory challenge, even if the lawyer making the challenge gives an implausible nonracial explanation for why the juror was excluded.

> **To Summarize:**
>
> ♦ *Defendants in both state and federal criminal cases have a constitutional right to trial by jury, except in misdemeanor cases where defendants face incarceration for less than six months.*
>
> ♦ *Trial judges have at their disposal several means of protecting a defendant's right to a fair trial against potentially prejudicial media coverage. These include a change of venue, sequestration of the jury, and postponement of the trial.*
>
> ♦ *On rare occasions the Supreme Court has invoked the "fair trial doctrine" to limit media coverage of judicial proceedings. However, the Court tends to give the widest possible latitude to freedom of the press in this regard.*
>
> ♦ *Historically, trial juries have been composed of twelve persons, all of whom had to agree in order to convict a defendant. In recent decades, however, the Supreme Court has upheld state-level variations from the traditional size and unanimity requirements in noncapital cases.*
>
> ♦ *Although a defendant has no constitutional right to have on the jury individuals of his or her gender or ethnic identity, the Supreme Court has held that the systematic exclusion of such persons is unconstitutional. Since the mid-1980s, the Court has restricted the use of peremptory challenges in accordance with this principle.*

The Protection against Double Jeopardy

The Fifth Amendment provides that no person "shall ... be subject for the same offence to be twice put in jeopardy of life or limb." This protection against **double jeopardy** has deep roots in the soil of the common law. To allow the government to continue to prosecute a defendant on the same charge, using the same evidence that had previously resulted in acquittal, would seem to violate "fundamental canons of decency and fairness." Yet, in *Palko v. Connecticut* (1937), the Supreme Court held otherwise in refusing to incorporate the Double Jeopardy Clause into the Fourteenth Amendment. This holding has since been overruled (see *Benton v. Maryland* [1969]), and the Double Jeopardy Clause has taken its place among those protections deemed "essential to a scheme of ordered liberty." However, the question of what exactly constitutes double jeopardy remains open. Essentially, the clause prevents the government from attempting to convict the accused of an illegal act after it has once failed to do so. However, there are a number of exceptions to this general rule.

Successive State and Federal Prosecutions

Given our system of federalism, it is possible for one set of actions to lead to separate criminal prosecutions in the state and federal courts. In *United States v. Lanza* (1922), the Supreme Court upheld successive state and federal prosecutions for the same offense, the Double Jeopardy Clause notwithstanding. Writing for the Court in *Lanza*, Chief Justice William Howard Taft observed:

> *We have here two sovereignties, deriving power from different sources, capable of dealing with the same subject matter within the same territory.... Each government in determining what shall be an offense against its peace and dignity is exercising its own sovereignty, not that of the other.*

It follows that an act denounced as a crime by both national and state sovereignties is an offense against the peace and dignity of both and may be punished by each. Of course, the *Lanza* decision was rendered prior to the incorporation of the Double Jeopardy Clause in *Benton v. Maryland* (1969). But the Court has held that application of the Clause to the states does not abrogate the dual sovereignty principle articulated in *Lanza*. Were it otherwise, the Court noted in *United States v. Wheeler* (1978), "[p]rosecution by one sovereign for a relatively minor offense might bar prosecution by the other for a much graver one, thus effectively depriving the latter of the right to enforce its own laws."

A good example of a successive prosecution by the federal government after an acquittal in state court is provided by the case of the Los Angeles police officers involved in the videotaped beating of African-American motorist Rodney King in 1991. The California Superior Court's verdict finding the police officers not guilty of criminal misconduct was followed by considerable outrage and large-scale destructive rioting in Los Angeles. Despite the officers' acquittal on state charges, the federal government brought new charges against them for violating King's civil rights. On appeal, the officers argued that the new federal charges were barred by the double jeopardy clause. In *United States v. Koon* (1994), the Ninth circuit rejected this claim, saying that "there is no evidence that the federal prosecution was a 'sham' or a 'cover' for the state prosecution." Ultimately, the defendants were convicted and served time in federal prison.

Mistrials

Another legitimate deviation from the double jeopardy principle occurs in the case of a **mistrial** granted on the request of the defense. Judges often declare a mistrial if some extraordinary event occurs, such as the death of a juror or attorney; if some prejudicial error cannot be corrected; or if a **hung jury** (that is, a jury unable to reach a verdict) results. The declaration of a mistrial, at least on the motion of the defendant, has the effect of "wiping the slate clean," of declaring that no trial took place. Thus, the state's renewal of its prosecution of the accused does not violate the Double Jeopardy Clause.

Confinement of Sexual Predators in Mental Institutions

In *Kansas v. Hendricks* (1997), the Court upheld the Kansas Sexually Violent Predator Act, which permits the state to continue to institutionalize certain sex offenders after they have completed their prison sentences. The Court concluded that the law, which provides for involuntary confinement in mental institutions, did not inflict "punishment" and was therefore beyond the pale of the Double Jeopardy Clause. Justice Thomas wrote the Opinion of the Court, joined by Chief Justice Rehnquist and Justices O'Connor, Kennedy, and Scalia. Dissenting, Justice Breyer (joined by Justices Stevens, Souter, and Ginsburg) argued that the confinement amounted to an unconstitutional *ex post facto* law. The Court, however, rejected this argument on the grounds that the confinement resulted from a civil commitment proceeding, not a criminal prosecution. Ever since *Calder v. Bull* (1798), the Ex Post Facto Clause has been limited to criminal punishments. Technically, civil confinement is not criminal punishment, although the result may be indistinguishable from the point of view of the person who loses his freedom. In *Kansas v. Crane* (2002), the Court held that substantive due process (see Chapter 1) prohibits civil commitment of sex offenders unless the state can show that the offender has at least some difficulty controlling his or her impulses. The Court was attempting to make states distinguish between sex offenders who pose real harm to others and those who do not pose such harm after their sentences are completed.

Federal law also allows for the civil confinement of violent sex offenders who have completed their criminal sentences. In *United States v. Comstock* (2010), this statute was challenged on the ground that Congress lacked the constitutional authority to enact it. The Supreme Court, speaking through Justice Breyer, held that the Necessary and Proper Clause grants Congress sufficient authority to enact the law. According to a *New York Times* article of June 30, 2010, this case "touched off a heated debate among the justices on a question that has lately engaged the Tea Party movement and opponents of the new health care law: what limits does the Constitution impose on Congress's power to legislate on matters not specifically delegated to it in Article I?" Justice Breyer concluded that the Necessary and Proper Clause provided Congress with the needed authority as long as the statute in question was "rationally related to implementation of a constitutionally enumerated power." Justice Thomas, joined by Justice Scalia, dissented. Adhering closely to the specific language of Article I, Thomas declared: "The Necessary and Proper Clause empowers Congress to enact only those laws that 'carry into execution' one or more of the federal powers enumerated in the Constitution.... Because Section 4248 [the federal law in question] 'executes' no enumerated power, I must respectfully dissent." The *Comstock* decision shows that, within the realm of criminal justice, the Court is often willing to accord broad power to the federal government.

Sex Offender Registration Laws

In the late 1990s, states moved rapidly to adopt laws requiring convicted sex offenders who have been released from prison to register with state agencies. These sex offender registries are then made public so that people can find out if there is a sex offender living near them. The laws are known as Megan's Laws, after Megan Kanka, a seven-year old New Jersey girl who was kidnapped, raped, and killed in 1994 by a convicted sex offender who lived in her neighborhood. Defenders of the new approach argue that it is vital to protect the public from truly dangerous individuals. Critics contend that they subject persons to unconstitutional double jeopardy inasmuch as being a registered sex offender constitutes punishment in and of itself. In 2003, the Supreme Court rejected two challenges to Megan's Law—one based on due process and one based on the prohibition of *ex post facto* laws (see, respectively, *Connecticut Department of Public Safety v. John Doe* and *Smith v. Doe)*. In neither case did the Court address the double jeopardy issue, but lower federal courts and state courts have addressed this question and have by and large rejected such challenges.

Civil Forfeitures, Double Jeopardy, and Excessive Fines

Federal law provides for the **forfeiture** of real estate and other property used in illegal drug trafficking. In *United States v. Ursery* (1996), the Court held that such forfeitures do not constitute "punishment" for purposes of the Double Jeopardy Clause. Two federal circuit courts had held that the Double Jeopardy Clause prohibits both punishing a defendant for a criminal offense and forfeiting his or her property for that same offense in a separate civil proceeding. The Supreme Court reversed, with Chief Justice Rehnquist noting that "Congress long has authorized the Government to bring parallel criminal proceedings and civil forfeiture proceedings, and this Court consistently has found civil forfeitures not to constitute punishment under the Double Jeopardy Clause." In a lone dissent, Justice Stevens relied on the Court's prior decisions in *Austin v. United States* (1993) and *Department of Revenue of Montana v. Kurth Ranch* (1994). In *Austin*, the Court decided that a property forfeiture stemming from a drug crime is subject to limitation under the Eighth Amendment. In *Kurth Ranch*, the Court invoked the Double Jeopardy Clause in striking down a state tax imposed on a quantity of marijuana when the taxpayer had already been convicted of possessing the same contraband. Dissenting in the *Usery* case, Justice Stevens took the view that these precedents dictated "a far different conclusion" from that reached by the Court.

To Summarize:

- *Essentially, the Double Jeopardy Clause prevents the government from attempting to convict the accused of an illegal act after it has once failed to do so. However, there are a number of exceptions to this general rule.*
- *Given our system of federalism, it is possible for one episode of criminal misconduct to lead to separate criminal prosecutions in the state and federal courts.*
- *The renewal of a prosecution after the declaration of a mistrial does not constitute double jeopardy.*
- *The Supreme Court has held that civil confinement of violent sexual predators after completion of their criminal sentences does not violate the double jeopardy prohibition.*

Incarceration and the Rights of Prisoners

The authors of the Bill of Rights were well aware of the sordid history of torture that characterized criminal punishment in pre-Revolutionary Europe. In *O'Neil v. Vermont* (1892), the Supreme Court said that the Eighth Amendment prohibition of **cruel and unusual punishments** was directed to "punishments which inflict torture, such as the rack, the thumb-screw, the iron boot, the stretching of limbs and the like, which are attended with acute pain and suffering." Yet the Court recognized that the Eighth Amendment also proscribed "punishments which by their excessive length or severity are greatly disproportionate to the offense charged." Torture is no longer a significant legal issue in this country. Indeed, corporal punishment has been abolished as a penalty for criminal acts. Yet the question of proportionality of punishments and crimes remains a viable problem for contemporary courts of law. In *Robinson v. California* (1962), the Supreme Court held that state courts were bound by the Cruel and Unusual Punishments Clause. Since then, there have been numerous challenges to state sentencing policies as well as the conditions of state prisons.

Habitual Offender and "Three Strikes" Laws

Does an excessive term of imprisonment constitute cruel and unusual punishment? The issue is often raised in the context of **habitual offender laws** that mandate long prison terms for felony offenders with prior felony convictions. For example, in *Rummel v. Estelle* (1980), the Court reviewed a mandatory life sentence imposed on a man who had committed three nonviolent felonies. In three separate cases over a period of years, Rummel had been convicted of the fraudulent use of a credit card, forging a check, and obtaining money under false pretenses. Under Texas law, he was considered to be a habitual offender and on that basis sentenced to life in prison. Dividing 5 to 4, the Court held that the sentence did not constitute cruel and unusual punishment. Writing for the majority, Justice Rehnquist concluded that,

> given Rummel's record, Texas was not required to treat him in the same manner as it might treat him were this his first "petty property offense." Having twice imprisoned him for felonies, Texas was entitled to place upon Rummel the onus of one who is simply unable to bring his conduct within the social norms prescribed by the criminal law of the State.

Rehnquist also noted that Texas had "a relatively liberal policy of granting 'good time' credits to its prisoners," which meant that it was likely that Rummel would not be incarcerated for the duration of his life.

In *Solem v. Helm* (1983), the Court struck down a South Dakota habitual offender statute very similar to the law upheld in *Rummel v. Estelle*. However, because the South Dakota law did not provide for release on parole, the Court distinguished this case from *Rummel*. Justice Lewis Powell wrote for a Court that was, again, sharply divided:

> Applying objective criteria, we find that Helm has received that penultimate sentence for relatively minor criminal conduct. He has been treated more harshly than other criminals in the State who have committed more serious crimes. He has been treated more harshly than he would have been in any other jurisdiction, with the possible exception of a single State. We conclude that his sentence is significantly disproportionate to his crime, and is therefore prohibited by the Eighth Amendment.

In the 1980s, Congress and many state legislatures enacted tough mandatory sentences for drug crimes. In 1991, the Supreme Court, in *Harmelin v. Michigan*, upheld a life sentence without possibility of parole imposed on an individual for possessing 772 grams of cocaine. Michigan law required the automatic imposition of this sentence on anyone convicted of possessing 650 grams or more of any mixture containing cocaine. Writing for another sharply divided bench, Justice Antonin Scalia observed that "[s]evere, mandatory penalties may be cruel, but they are not unusual in the constitutional sense, having been employed in various forms throughout our Nation's history." In dissent, Justice Byron White argued that "the fact that no other jurisdiction provides such a severe, mandatory penalty for possession of this quantity of drugs is enough to establish 'the degree of national consensus this Court has previously thought sufficient to label a particular punishment cruel and unusual.'"

During the 1990s, a number of states enacted a new round of habitual offender laws known colloquially as "three strikes and you're out," because these laws mandate a long prison sentence for an offender's third felony conviction. In *Ewing v. California* (2003), the Supreme Court reviewed California's **three strikes laws**. Ewing, who had been previously convicted of four felonies and was out on parole, was convicted of grand larceny and was sentenced to twenty-five years to life in prison. In yet another 5-4 decision in this area, the Supreme Court upheld the sentence against an Eighth Amendment challenge. Justice Sandra Day O'Connor, writing for the majority, admitted Ewing's "sentence is long, but so is his criminal history." In dissent, Justice Stephen Breyer observed, "Ewing's sentence is, at a minimum, two to three times the length of sentences that other jurisdictions would impose in similar circumstances."

Prisoners' Rights

Because they have been convicted of serious crimes, the inmates in our nation's crowded prison system have lost many of the rights we take for granted. In *Price v. Johnson* (1948), the Supreme Court held that lawful incarceration necessarily requires suspension or limitation of rights. In *Hudson v. Palmer* (1984), the Court reiterated this position, stating, "The curtailment of certain rights is necessary as a practical matter, to accommodate a myriad of 'institutional needs and objectives' of prison facilities, … chief among which is internal security." The Court further observed that "these restrictions or retractions also serve, incidentally, as reminders that, under our system of justice, deterrence and retribution are factors in addition to correction." By definition, prisoners have forfeited their right to live in civil society, to move about freely, to associate with whom they choose, and to make decisions about everyday matters such as eating, sleeping, recreation, and work. Under state and federal laws, many prisoners have also forfeited their right to vote or to hold public office. But they have not been stripped of all constitutional rights and protections. Obviously, prisoners can invoke the Cruel and Unusual Punishments Clause to challenge the conditions of their confinement. They also retain rights under the Due Process and Equal Protection Clauses (see, for example, *Baxter v. Palmigiano* [1976]). Prisoners cannot be denied access to the courts or to counsel (see *Procunier v. Martinez* [1974]). The Supreme Court has even held that a prison inmate retains those First Amendment rights "that are not inconsistent with his status as a prisoner or with the legitimate penological objectives of the corrections system" (*Pell v. Procunier* [1974]).

Prior to the 1960s, courts appeared indifferent to **prisoners' rights**. The main reason for this was that so few cases were ever filed; for the most part, prisoners were denied access to counsel and the courts. As a result of favorable Supreme Court decisions of the 1950s and early 1960s, however, prisoners began to obtain access to the federal judiciary, using petitions for writs of habeas corpus. Then, in the 1970s, their cases began to reach the level of the Supreme Court. In *Cruz v. Beto* (1972), the Court held that if prison officials allow inmates who belong to mainstream religious denominations to attend worship services, then members of other religious sects must be given a reasonable opportunity to exercise their religious beliefs. In *Wolff v. McDonnell* (1974), the Court said that prisoners were entitled to due process before being subjected to disciplinary measures.

In *Hutto v. Finney* (1978), the Supreme Court upheld a federal court order imposing a thirty-day limit on the use of **punitive isolation** by a state prison. The case, which began in 1969 under the name *Holt v. Sarver*, involved an Eighth Amendment challenge to the conditions of confinement in the Arkansas prison system, particularly the notorious Cummins Farm. The challenged conditions included corporal punishment and torture; abysmal sanitation, diet, and health care; and an overall atmosphere of violence. The conditions that prevailed at Cummins Farm were not altogether atypical of conditions in maximum security state prisons at the time the litigation began. Today, as a result of increased judicial oversight, such conditions are rare exceptions.

In 1992, the Supreme Court demonstrated continuing solicitude toward prisoners subjected to inhumane treatment. In *Hudson v. McMillian*, the Court held that a prisoner who is beaten maliciously by guards may bring a civil suit to recover damages under a claim of cruel and unusual punishment, even if the injuries sustained are not serious. In one of his first dissenting opinions on the High Court, Justice Clarence

Thomas (joined by Justice Scalia) expressed the view that nonserious injury to a prisoner does not rise to the level of cruel and unusual punishment.

Many people, especially prison officials, regard judicial oversight of prisons with disdain. Few observers—beyond prisoners themselves and groups representing their interests—are prepared to lavish praise on the federal courts for their involvement in this area. As a group, prisoners have very little political power and even less public support. Nevertheless, some argue that one of the most important functions of the judiciary is to protect **discrete and insular minorities** who have no effective means of representing themselves in the political process. Certainly prisoners, particularly those who have lost their suffrage rights, are such a minority. And although they may well deserve harsh punishment, they are nevertheless persons and, as such, are entitled to the applicable protections of the Constitution.

To Summarize:

◆ *The Supreme Court has recognized that the Eighth Amendment requires that punishments, including the length of prison terms, be proportional to the offenses for which they are imposed. However, the Court's cases challenging particular sentences as excessive have yielded mixed results.*

◆ *By definition, persons serving terms of imprisonment forfeit many of their civil and constitutional rights. The Supreme Court has made clear that the rights of prisoners must be balanced against concern for prison discipline and security.*

◆ *The Court has recognized, however, that prisoners retain a few basic substantive and procedural rights. These include access to the courts and to legal counsel, the right to due process with respect to disciplinary actions against them, and protection against inhumane conditions of confinement.*

The Death Penalty

Although already in decline, the **death penalty** was in widespread use when the Constitution was adopted—not only for murder but also for an array of lesser offenses. The Due Process Clauses of the Fifth and Fourteenth Amendments explicitly recognize, although they do not necessarily endorse, the death penalty, stating that no person shall "be deprived of *life*, liberty, or property, without due process of law" [emphasis added]. In *Trop v. Dulles* (1958), however, Chief Justice Warren indicated that the Cruel and Unusual Punishments Clause "must draw its meaning from the **evolving standards of decency** that mark the progress of a maturing society." By the 1960s, it was clear that public support for the death penalty had diminished substantially. By 1966, public opinion polls were finding that a majority of Americans opposed capital punishment. Reflecting this change in societal attitudes, only two persons were executed in the United States between 1967 and the Supreme Court's decision in *Furman v. Georgia* (1972), which struck down the Georgia death penalty law.

The *Furman* Case

In *Furman v. Georgia*, five justices voted to strike down Georgia's death penalty statute. There was, however, only a brief *per curiam* opinion announcing the judgment of the Court. For the majority's rationale, one had to look at five separate concurring opinions. Two of the five justices—Brennan and Marshall—held that the death penalty itself was cruel and unusual punishment, given the "evolving standards of decency." Throughout their subsequent tenure on the Court, Brennan and Marshall steadfastly maintained the position that the death penalty is inherently unconstitutional. (Justice Brennan retired in 1990; Justice Marshall followed suit in 1991.)

It should be pointed out that if "evolving standards of decency" have anything to do with public opinion, then the Brennan-Marshall position on the death penalty is difficult to defend. In the years after *Furman*, probably as a result of the increasing salience of the crime problem, the level of support for the death penalty rose steadily; according to the Gallup Poll, public support in favor of the death penalty was at 62 percent in March of 1978, 75 percent in November of 1985, a high of 80 percent in September of 1994, then began a slow decline to 67 percent in February 2001, and was at 63 percent in January of 2013. It is, therefore, difficult to make the "evolving standards" argument unless one is talking about one's own standards! However, it is generally considered unacceptable for judges to impose their personal standards of morality on public policy under the aegis of the Constitution. Thus, Justice Marshall, dissenting in *Gregg v. Georgia* (1976), took the position that "the American people, fully informed as to the purposes of the death penalty and its liabilities, would in my view reject it as morally unacceptable." Justice Marshall's statement was regarded by many critics as arrogant, but it should be admitted that we simply do not know whether Marshall's assertion was correct.

Of the five justices who voted to invalidate the death penalty in the *Furman* case, Justice Stewart's opinion seems to have been the most influential. For Stewart, the problem with the death penalty was not the punishment itself but the manner in which it was being administered. Trial juries were being left with virtually unfettered discretion in deciding when to impose capital punishment. The result, according to Stewart, was that the death penalty was "wantonly and … freakishly imposed." Although Stewart explicitly linked his objection to the Cruel and Unusual Punishments Clause, it seems as though he was making a due process argument: The death penalty was invalid because it was being administered in an arbitrary and capricious fashion.

The Court Reinstates the Death Penalty

In the wake of the *Furman* decision, some thirty-five state legislatures rewrote their death penalty laws. Georgia's revamped death penalty statute was before the Supreme Court in the *Gregg* case of 1976. The revised Georgia law required a bifurcated trial for capital crimes: In the first stage, guilt would be determined in the usual manner; the second stage would deal with the appropriate sentence. For the jury to impose the death penalty, it would have to find at least one of several statutorily prescribed **aggravating factors**. Automatic appeal to the state supreme court would also be provided. Appellate review would be required to consider not only the procedural regularity of the trial but also whether the evidence supports the finding of the aggravating factor and whether the death sentence is disproportionate to the penalty imposed in similar cases.

The Court had little difficulty upholding the new Georgia statute, with only Justices Brennan and Marshall dissenting. Thus, after a hiatus of four years, the death penalty was effectively reinstated. Although Justice Stewart's opinion in *Gregg* makes much of the procedural safeguards required by the Georgia law, one suspects that the marked increase in public support for the death penalty that occurred during the four years after *Furman* had at least some influence on the Court's decision to uphold Georgia's revised law. In this, as in other areas, the Court seldom strays far from a clear national consensus. Fortunately for the Court, the restraint demonstrated by several of the justices in *Furman* (by deciding the case on fairly narrow grounds) facilitated the reinstatement of the death penalty in *Gregg* four years later without the necessity of overruling a recent precedent.

Although the Burger Court effectively reinstated the death penalty, it refused to allow states to execute criminals convicted of lesser crimes than first-degree murder. In *Coker v.*

Georgia (1977), the Court invalidated an attempt to execute a man convicted of rape. Writing for a plurality, Justice White characterized the death sentence for rape as "disproportionate" and "excessive."

Other Procedural Aspects of Death Sentencing

Later decisions of the Burger Court indicated an increasingly permissive stance toward imposition of capital punishment. For the most part, the Burger Court was unsympathetic to challenges to the legal sufficiency of procedures used to impose the death penalty. For example, in *Lockhart v. McCree* (1986), the Court facilitated the use of capital punishment by ruling that potential jurors could be excluded before trial if their opposition to the death penalty was so intense that it would impair their ability to perform as impartial jurors. In *Walton v. Arizona* (1990), the Rehnquist Court continued in this vein by upholding a state law permitting the trial judge, rather than the jury, to determine the existence of aggravating and **mitigating circumstances**. The Court also concluded that Arizona's characterization of "heinous, cruel, or depraved" conduct as an aggravating factor was sufficiently specific to meet the requirements of the Eighth Amendment.

Similarly, in *Proctor v. California* (1994), the Court sustained California's death penalty statute against the challenge that it was excessively vague. The 8-to-l decision, with only Justice Blackmun in dissent, came as a major disappointment to the 383 men awaiting execution on California's death row, many of whom would have been able to challenge their sentences had the Supreme Court decided differently. The challenge was brought by William Proctor, who was sentenced to death in 1982 for the murder of a woman whom he also robbed and raped. Proctor argued that California law failed to give juries adequate guidance in considering the factors that determine whether a given crime should merit a death sentence. In rejecting Proctor's challenge, the Court, speaking through Justice Kennedy, found that the law had a "commonsense core of meaning that criminal juries should be capable of understanding" (see *Tuilaepa v. California* [1994]).

In the late 1980s, growing concern for the rights of crime victims led some states to enact laws permitting the introduction of **victim impact statements**—statements related to personal characteristics of murder victims and the impact of their murders on family members—at the penalty phase of capital trials. In *Booth v. Maryland* (1987) and *South Carolina v. Gathers* (1989), the Supreme Court declared that the introduction of such victim impact evidence violated the Eighth Amendment. In a dramatic reversal of this position, a more conservative Court in 1991 held that "the Eighth Amendment erects no *per se* bar" to "the admission of victim impact evidence and prosecutorial argument on that subject" (*Payne v. Tennessee*).

While victims' rights advocates praised this decision, civil libertarians and defense attorneys objected sharply to what they perceived as an invitation to infuse excessive emotion into the criminal process. In one of the last opinions he wrote before retiring, Justice Marshall, dissenting, delivered a broadside against the Rehnquist Court's disregard of precedent:

> *In dispatching* Booth *and* Gathers *to their graves, today's majority ominously suggests that an even more extensive upheaval of this Court's precedents may be in store.... The majority today sends a clear signal that scores of established constitutional liberties are now ripe for reconsideration.*

The Death Penalty and Racial Discrimination

Whether the evenhandedness in the administration of the death penalty has been achieved through the revised procedures upheld in *Gregg* is very much open to question.

Critics continue to claim that capital punishment is racially discriminatory, in regards to both the race of the offender and the race of the murder victim. Criminologist David Baldus collected data on more than 1,000 murder cases in Georgia during the 1970s and found significant disparities in the imposition of the death penalty, based primarily on the race of the murder victims and, to a lesser extent, on the race of the defendants. The data reveal that blacks who killed whites were more than seven times more likely to receive the death sentence than were whites who killed blacks. In *McCleskey v. Kemp* (1987), the Supreme Court refused to accept statistical evidence derived from the Baldus study as a basis for reversing the death sentence of a black man who had killed a white police officer during an armed robbery. In the Court's view, even if there is statistical evidence of systemic race discrimination, a defendant sentenced to death cannot prevail on appeal unless he or she can show that his or her death sentence was imposed because of race discrimination. Obviously, this would be difficult, although certainly not impossible, for a defendant to demonstrate.

Is the Federal Death Penalty Law Constitutional?

In May 2001, Timothy McVeigh was put to death by lethal injection for his role in the bombing of the federal office building in Oklahoma City in 1995. In his federal trial, McVeigh was convicted of twenty-eight counts of murder of federal law enforcement agents on active duty. Under federal law, executions are carried out in the state where the defendant was sentenced, unless that state has no death penalty, in which case the prisoner is transferred to another state for execution. Before the McVeigh execution, the federal government had not executed anyone since 1963.

The Federal Anti-Drug Abuse Act of 1988 allows the death penalty for the so-called drug kingpins who control "continuing criminal enterprises" whose members intentionally kill or procure others to kill in furtherance of the enterprise. Moreover, the Violent Crime Control and Law Enforcement Act of 1994, better known as the Federal Crime Bill, dramatically increased the number of federal crimes eligible for the death penalty. Capital punishment is now authorized for dozens of federal crimes, including treason, murder of a federal law enforcement official, and kidnapping, carjacking, child abuse, and bank robbery that result in death. While it remains to be seen whether the federal courts will permit the death penalty for nonhomicidal crimes, the ruling in *Coker v. Georgia* (1977) would suggest otherwise.

The Death Penalty and Mental Incompetence

It is well documented that there are significantly higher rates of mental illness and mental retardation among prisoners than among the general population. This is particularly the case on death row. Human rights advocates have long criticized the American legal system for allowing mentally ill and mentally retarded prisoners to be put to death. In *Ford v. Wainwright* (1986), the Supreme Court surprised many of its critics when it held that the Eighth Amendment prohibits the execution of a prisoner who is insane. Invoking the "evolving standards of decency" test, the Court asserted that "the intuition that such an execution … offends humanity is shared across this Nation." Writing for a Court plurality, Justice Thurgood Marshall declared, "It is no less abhorrent today than it has been for centuries to exact in penance the life of one whose mental illness prevents him from comprehending the reasons for the penalty or its implications."

Three years later, though, in *Penry v. Lynaugh* (1989), the Court held that mental retardation, in and of itself, is not a sufficient basis to bar the imposition of the death penalty. Justice O'Connor wrote the opinion of the Court, observing that "mental retardation is a factor that may well lessen a defendant's culpability for a capital offense." But O'Connor was willing to leave consideration of that issue to juries, rather than impose a judicial rule. But in *Atkins v. Virginia* (2002), the Court overturned *Penry* and held that it is impermissible for a state to execute an inmate whose IQ is below 70. Writing for the Court in a 6-3 decision, Justice Stevens observed that:

> *even among those States that regularly execute offenders and that have no prohibition with regard to the mentally retarded, only five have executed offenders possessing a known IQ less than 70 since we decided Penry. The practice, therefore, has become truly unusual, and it is fair to say that a national consensus has developed against it.*

In a caustic dissent, Justice Scalia (joined by Justice Thomas and Chief Justice Rehnquist) accused the majority of reading its own policy preferences into the Constitution. In Scalia's view, the decision has:

> *no support in the text or history of the Eighth Amendment; it does not even have support in current social attitudes regarding the conditions that render an otherwise just death penalty inappropriate. Seldom has an opinion of this Court rested so obviously upon nothing but the personal views of its members.*

Capital Punishment of Juveniles

Another much litigated question about eligibility for the death penalty involves those offenders who, at the time they committed capital crimes, were below the age of legal majority. Critics have often argued that it is wrong to execute such persons, but many Americans have taken the view that a juvenile who is convicted as an adult should be punished as an adult. In *Eddings v. Oklahoma* (1982), the Supreme Court voted 5-4 to vacate the death sentence of a 16-year-old boy. In 1988, the Court divided 6-3 in ruling that the Constitution forbids execution of juveniles who are 15 or younger at the time they committed their capital crimes (*Thompson v. Oklahoma*). One year later, in *Stanford v. Kentucky* (1989), the Court split 5-4 in deciding that juveniles aged 16 and older at the time of their crimes may be sentenced to death. According to Justice O'Connor's controlling opinion, "it is sufficiently clear that no national consensus forbids the imposition of capital punishment on 16- or 17-year-old capital murderers." But in *Roper v. Simmons* (2005), much as in *Atkins v. Virginia* (2002), the Court found that such a consensus had emerged. Splitting 5-4 yet again, the Court held that "[t]he Eighth and Fourteenth Amendments forbid imposition of the death penalty on offenders who were under the age of 18 when their crimes were committed." Writing for the majority, Justice Anthony Kennedy found that "[t]he evidence of national consensus against the death penalty for juveniles is similar, and in some respects parallel, to the evidence *Atkins* held sufficient to demonstrate a national consensus against the death penalty for the mentally retarded." In another caustic dissent, Justice Scalia chided the majority's reasoning:

> *The Court reaches this implausible result by purporting to advert, not to the original meaning of the Eighth Amendment, but to "the evolving standards of decency" ... of our national society. It then finds, on the flimsiest of grounds, that a national consensus which could not be perceived in our people's laws barely 15 years ago now solidly exists.*

Some opponents of capital punishment thought that the Court's decisions in *Atkins* and *Roper* might presage a complete judicial abolition of the death penalty. But a June 2006 decision of the Roberts Court showed that such speculations were premature.

The Roberts Court and the Death Penalty

When Samuel Alito succeeded Justice Sandra Day O'Connor in 2006, one of the areas in which commentators expected to see an impact was the death penalty. In *Kansas v. Marsh* (2006), that impact was seen in a case that might well have been decided the other way had O'Connor remained on the Court. A Kansas court sentenced Michael Lee Marsh to death for the murders of Marry Ane Pusch and her 19-month-old daughter in 1996. On appeal to the Kansas Supreme Court, Marsh challenged the constitutionality of a state law requiring juries to sentence a defendant to death, rather than life in prison, when the aggravating and mitigating circumstances are equivalent. That court agreed and awarded Marsh a new trial. Splitting 5-to-4, the U.S. Supreme Court reversed. Writing for the majority, Justice Clarence Thomas observed that "our precedents establish that a state enjoys a range of discretion in imposing the death penalty." Speaking for the four dissenters, Justice Souter said the law would lead to death sentences in doubtful cases and "is obtuse by any moral or social measure."

Kansas v. Marsh revealed the deep division over the death penalty on the Roberts Court. It also suggested that the Court was not ready to abolish capital punishment by judicial decree. That was reinforced by the Court's 2008 decision in *Baze v. Rees*, in which the Court upheld Kentucky's practice of execution by lethal injection.

In *Kennedy v. Louisiana*, also decided in 2008, the Court continued to narrow the scope of offenses for which the death penalty may be given by striking down a state law allowing child rapists to be sentenced to death. Justice Anthony Kennedy, writing for a slim five-member majority, held that the Eighth Amendment "bars [imposing] the death penalty for the rape of a child where the crime did not result, and was not intended to result, in death of the victim." Citing "a consensus against the death penalty for child rape," Kennedy observed that "[d]ifficulties in administering the penalty to ensure against its arbitrary and capricious application require adherence to a rule reserving its use, at this stage of evolving standards and in cases of crimes against individuals, for crimes that take the life of the victim."

Justice Samuel Alito dissented vigorously, arguing that:

(1) This holding is not supported by the original meaning of the Eighth Amendment; (2) neither Coker nor any other prior precedent commands this result; (3) there are no reliable "objective indicia" of a "national consensus" in support of the Court's position; (4) sustaining the constitutionality of the state law before us would not "extend" or "expand" the death penalty; (5) this Court has previously rejected the proposition that the Eighth Amendment is a one-way ratchet that prohibits legislatures from adopting new capital punishment statutes to meet new problems; (6) the worst child rapists exhibit the epitome of moral depravity; and (7) child rape inflicts grievous injury on victims and on society in general.

In 2013 Maryland became the eighteenth state to abolish the death penalty and the fifth to do so since 2007. While opponents of the death penalty argue this reflects a changing national consensus that the death penalty should be repealed nationwide, supporters of the death penalty and the thirty-two states, which still make use of capital punishment would clearly disagree. Obviously, the death penalty remains a deeply divisive issue in American society, and it is likely to remain so for some time to come. This division is also manifested on the nation's highest court.

> ### To Summarize:
>
> ◆ *The Court has said that the Cruel and Unusual Punishments Clause "must draw its meaning from the evolving standards of decency that mark the progress of a maturing society." Consistent with this perspective, the Court in* Furman v. Georgia *(1972) invalidated capital punishment as it existed throughout the United States, but left the door open for states to revise their death penalty statutes. In* Gregg v. Georgia *(1976), the Court upheld several such revised statutes, thus effectively reinstating the death penalty.*
>
> ◆ *In the years after* Gregg v. Georgia, *the Court found occasion to set aside particular death sentences, but in general showed increasing deference to the states in the implementation of capital punishment. An example of this trend was seen in the Court's willingness to allow the use of victim impact statements in the sentencing stage of capital trials.*
>
> ◆ *In the current decade, the Court has imposed significant limitations on who can be executed, holding that juvenile offenders and mentally retarded offenders are exempt from the death penalty.*

Appeal and Postconviction Relief

The federal Constitution makes no mention of a defendant's right to appeal from a criminal conviction, although one could argue that such a right is implicit in the concept of procedural due process. In *McKane v. Durston* (1894), the Supreme Court held that there is no such constitutional right. Given the expansiveness of modern notions of due process, it is likely that the Supreme Court would reconsider *McKane v. Durston* but for the fact that Congress and all fifty state legislatures have created statutory rights of appeal. Indeed, a federal defendant's right of appeal is of fairly ancient vintage, having first been granted by the Judiciary Act of 1789. The so-called **appeal by right** granted by federal and state statutes applies to defendants who are convicted over their pleas of not guilty. The only situation in which a defendant who pleads guilty retains the right of appeal is where such a provision is made pursuant to a plea bargain. The prosecution is never permitted to appeal the acquittal of a defendant but may appeal certain pretrial rulings resulting in the dismissal of the case.

The appeal by right is an important means whereby defendants assert constitutional rights alleged to have been violated in their apprehension or in the investigation, prosecution, or trial of their case. The appeal by right thus permits appellate courts to perform the important function of **error correction**. Of course, not all errors constitute the basis for reversal on appeal. Only those errors deemed prejudicial to the accused necessitate reversal; other mistakes are referred to as **harmless errors** (see *Chapman v. California* [1967]).

In 1991, the Supreme Court made news when it decided that, under certain circumstances, the use of an involuntary confession as evidence at trial constitutes a harmless error (see *Arizona v. Fulminante*, discussed earlier). Previously, the use of an illegally obtained confession was considered a sufficient basis for reversal of a conviction, regardless of the strength of the other evidence against the accused.

Beyond the right to one appeal, defendants may petition higher courts to review their convictions, but such review is granted at the discretion of the higher court. In the U.S. Supreme Court and most state supreme courts, **discretionary review** involves the issuance of a writ of certiorari. In essence, the writ of certiorari is issued to the lower court, directing it to provide the record in a given case so that the higher court may conduct its review. The use of this type of discretionary review is usually limited to new and important issues of law, especially where the lower appellate courts are in conflict.

Federal Habeas Corpus Review of State Criminal Cases

A state prisoner who has exhausted his or her appeals in the state courts may petition a federal district court for a writ of habeas corpus. The power of federal courts to issue habeas corpus in state cases can be traced to an act of Congress adopted just after the Civil War (see *Ex parte McCardle* [1869], discussed and excerpted in Chapter 1, Volume I). Rarely used prior to the 1950s, in the modern era this aspect of federal jurisdiction has played an important role in the development of constitutional law as it relates to the criminal process. In *Brown v. Allen* (1953), the Supreme Court held that state prisoners could readjudicate issues on federal habeas review that had already been addressed in state proceedings. Then, in *Fay v. Noia* (1963), the Warren Court further expanded federal habeas corpus by deciding that state prisoners could raise issues in their federal habeas corpus petitions that they failed to raise in state appeals. Moreover, unless it was found that they deliberately abused the writ, there was no limit on the number of habeas corpus petitions state prisoners could file in federal district courts (see *Sanders v. United States* [1963]).

The Warren Court's decision to expand federal habeas corpus helped fuel the "criminal justice revolution" of the 1960s. Federal district courts could look at and correct the state courts' failures to implement the pronouncements of the High Court in key areas such as search and seizure, confessions, double jeopardy, and the right to counsel. Accordingly, one of the strategies of the Burger and Rehnquist Courts' "counterrevolution" in the criminal process area was to restrict federal habeas corpus review of state criminal convictions.

Judicial Limitations on Federal Habeas Corpus Review   The first significant limitation on federal habeas corpus came in *Stone v. Powell* (1976). There, the Burger Court decided that state prisoners could not use federal habeas corpus petitions to raise Fourth Amendment issues where they had been provided "a full and fair opportunity" to litigate those issues in the state courts. Subsequently, in *Engle v. Isaac* (1982), the Court refused to allow a state prisoner to use federal habeas corpus to challenge a questionable jury instruction to which he failed to object during trial. Other decisions of the Burger Court chipped away at the Warren Court's expansive interpretations of federal habeas corpus relief (see, for example, *Kuhlmann v. Wilson* [1986] and *Straight v. Wainwright* [1986]).

The Rehnquist Court continued the trend toward limiting access to federal habeas corpus. In *McCleskey v. Zant* (1991), the Court barred Warren McCleskey—whose 1987 appeal is discussed earlier in this chapter and who was executed by the state of Georgia's in 1991—from filing a second federal habeas corpus petition, holding that he had "abused the writ." In the second *McCleskey* case, the Court held that a state need not prove that a petitioner deliberately abandoned a constitutional claim in his or her first habeas corpus petition for the petitioner to be barred from raising the claim in a subsequent petition. The Court thus moved away from the "deliberate abandonment" standard the Warren Court had articulated in *Sanders v. United States* (1963). In another bitter dissent, Justice Marshall blasted the Court for departing from precedent, saying that "whatever 'abuse of the writ' today's decision is designed to avert pales in comparison with the majority's own abuse of the norms that inform the proper judicial function." In *Keeney v. Tamayo-Reyes* (1992), the Court overturned *Townsend v. Sain* (1963), in which the Warren Court had held that state prisoners had the right to seek federal habeas corpus relief unless they had deliberately bypassed the state courts.

The Supreme Court's decisions in *McCleskey v. Zant* and *Keeney v. Tamayo-Reyes* came at a time when many in Congress were calling for legislative restrictions on federal habeas corpus. Both the Supreme Court and Congress were responding to a widespread perception that state prisoners were being afforded excessive opportunities to challenge their convictions in federal courts. Indeed, some conservative commentators questioned the need for federal postconviction review of state criminal cases altogether. While federal habeas corpus has been subject to abuse by state prisoners, eliminating this aspect of federal jurisdiction altogether would remove some of the pressure that has led to an increased awareness of and appreciation for defendants' rights in the state courts. Indeed, in the *McCleskey* case, the Supreme Court expressed a commitment to the continued efficacy of habeas corpus to prevent miscarriages of justice in the state courts.

In 1993, the Supreme Court handed down two decisions, restricting federal habeas corpus review of state criminal convictions. In *Herrera v. Collins*, the Court held that a belated claim of innocence does not entitle a state prisoner on death row to a federal district court hearing prior to his execution. In *Brecht v. Abrahamson*, the Court ruled that federal district courts may not overturn state criminal convictions unless the petitioner can show that he or she suffered "actual prejudice" from the errors cited in the habeas corpus petition. Previously, the state carried the burden of proving beyond a reasonable doubt that any constitutional error committed during or prior to trial was "harmless"—that is, not prejudicial to the defendant. *Brecht v. Abrahamson* had the effect of shifting the burden of proof from the state to the petitioner in a federal habeas corpus hearing.

Congress Modifies the Federal Habeas Corpus Procedure   On April 24, 1996, President Clinton signed into law the Antiterrorism and Effective Death Penalty Act of 1996. One of the provisions of this statute curtails second habeas corpus petitions by state prisoners who have already filed such petitions in federal court. Under the new statute, any second or subsequent habeas petition must meet a particularly high standard and must pass through a "gatekeeping" function exercised by the U.S. Courts of Appeals. A circuit court must grant a motion giving the inmate permission to file the petition in a district court; denial of this motion is not appealable to the Supreme Court. In *Felker v. Turpin* (1996), an inmate awaiting execution in Georgia challenged the constitutionality of this provision, posing two constitutional objections: (1) that the new law amounted to an unconstitutional "suspension" of the writ of habeas corpus and (2) that the prohibition against Supreme Court review of a circuit court's denial of permission to file a subsequent habeas petition is an unconstitutional interference with the Supreme Court's jurisdiction as defined in Article III of the Constitution.

In a unanimous decision rendered less than one month after the case was argued, the Supreme Court rejected these challenges and upheld the statute. In a "saving construction" of the statute, the Court interpreted the law in such a way as to preserve the right of state prisoners to file habeas petitions directly in the Supreme Court. The Court stated, however, that it would exercise this jurisdiction only in "exceptional circumstances." According to Chief Justice Rehnquist, who spoke for a unanimous bench, the fact that habeas corpus relief remains available by direct petition to the Supreme Court "obviates any claim by petitioner under the Exceptions Clause of Article III, Section 2, of the Constitution." Turning to the argument that Congress had, in effect, improperly suspended the writ of habeas corpus, Rehnquist observed that "[t]he new restrictions on successive petitions constitute a ... restraint on what is called in habeas corpus practice 'abuse of the writ.' " Noting the evolving body of judicial decisions attempting to limit abuses of habeas corpus, the Chief Justice concluded that "[t]he added restrictions ... on second habeas petitions are well within the compass of this evolutionary process." Interestingly, in *Felker v. Turpin*, the Court managed to sustain what Congress had done while at the same time reaffirming its own statutory and constitutional powers.

Note, however, that the provision at issue in *Felker* was but one of several restrictions on habeas corpus petitions embodied in the Antiterrorism Act. Indeed, other challenges to various sections of the law are currently working their way through the lower federal courts. The Supreme Court will likely address these issues in the near future. The enactment of "habeas corpus reform," fully supported by the Clinton administration, and the Court's refusal to invalidate it, indicated the existence of a consensus in the national government that "abuse of the writ" of habeas corpus had to be curtailed.

To Summarize:

◆ *Although there is no constitutional right of appeal in a criminal case, federal and state statutes provide this right to persons who are convicted after having pleaded not guilty.*

◆ *Federal law permits federal courts to grant writs of habeas corpus to review state court convictions after all state appellate remedies have been exhausted. The Warren Court expanded this form of postconviction relief, but in recent years Congress and the Court have significantly curtailed federal habeas corpus review.*

Juvenile Justice

At the time of the founding of the United States, children were treated essentially as adults for the purposes of criminal justice. It was not uncommon for teenagers to be hanged, flogged, or placed in the public pillory as punishment for their crimes.

Toward the end of the nineteenth century, public outcry against such treatment led to the establishment of a separate justice system for juveniles. Reformatories and specialized courts were created to deal with young offenders, not as hardened criminals but as misguided youth in need of special care. This special treatment was legally justified by the *parens patriae* concept that the state is responsible for caring for those incapable of caring for themselves. The newly created juvenile courts were usually separate from the regular tribunals; often the judges or referees that presided over these courts did not have formal legal training. There was little procedural regularity or even opportunity for the juvenile offender to confront his or her accusers.

The abuses that came to be associated with **juvenile courts** were addressed by the Supreme Court in the landmark case *In re Gault* (1967). Along with *Mapp v. Ohio, Gideon v. Wainwright,* and *Miranda v. Arizona, Gault* is considered to be one of the "four horsemen" of the Warren Court's revolution in the criminal justice area. In *Gault,* the Court essentially made the juvenile courts adhere to standards of due process, applying most of the basic procedural safeguards enjoyed by adults accused of crimes. Moreover, *Gault* held that juvenile courts must respect the right of counsel, the freedom from compulsory self-incrimination, and the right to confront (cross-examine) hostile witnesses.

For the most part, the Supreme Court has reaffirmed the *Gault* decision (see, for example, *Breed v. Jones* [1975]). In *McKeiver v. Pennsylvania* (1971), however, the Court refused to extend the right to trial by jury to juvenile proceedings. Writing for a plurality, Justice Blackmun concluded that juries are not indispensable "to fair and equitable juvenile proceedings." Thirteen years later, in *Schall v. Martin* (1984), the Court upheld a pretrial detention program for juveniles that might well have been found violative of due process had it applied to adults. Writing for the Court, Justice Rehnquist stressed that "the Constitution does not mandate elimination of all differences in the treatment of juveniles." At this point, it appears likely that the Supreme Court will maintain the requirements imposed in *Gault* and a few subsequent cases. But further expansion of juvenile due process seems unlikely.

> **To Summarize:**
> ◆ *Persons under the age of legal majority who engage in criminal conduct are typically within the jurisdiction of specialized juvenile courts.*
> ◆ *Although juvenile courts need not conform to all of the procedural requirements that apply to adult criminal prosecutions (for example, trial by jury), the Supreme Court has held that they must respect the right of counsel, the freedom from compulsory self-incrimination, and the right to confront hostile witnesses.*

Conclusion

This chapter has summarized the development of constitutional standards in the field of criminal justice. Here, as in much of its First Amendment jurisprudence, the Supreme Court has attempted to balance legitimate interests of public safety and public order with equally legitimate interests in individual liberty and privacy. In seeking to protect the constitutional rights of persons suspected, accused, or convicted of crimes, the Court has often challenged established law enforcement methods.

This tendency began in the 1930s and was most pronounced in the areas of search and seizure and police interrogation. Sharp criticism resulted from Supreme Court efforts to "police the police" and to upgrade standards of criminal procedure in the courts. Such criticism was particularly strong near the end of the Earl Warren era in the late 1960s.

Reflecting strong currents of change in public opinion, as well as the impact of appointments by Presidents Nixon, Reagan, and Bush (the elder), the Supreme Court since the 1970s has been decidedly more sympathetic to law enforcement than was the Warren Court. By refusing to extend or in some cases by overturning Warren Court precedents, the Burger and Rehnquist Courts opened themselves to the charge of insensitivity to the rights of individuals. This criticism was particularly strident with respect to decisions in the area of search and seizure.

The reason the authors of the Bill of Rights imposed constraints on law enforcement was not that they were opposed to law and order. Rather, they were deeply distrustful of power; they feared what well-meaning but overzealous officials might do if not constrained by the rule of law. Certainly, there was ample historical evidence to support their fears. Consequently, they gave us a Bill of Rights that makes it more difficult for government to investigate, prosecute, and punish crime. Some have suggested that the very reason for such a lengthy list of criminal protections in the Constitution is that the founders felt that individuals never needed rights as much as they needed them when the government believed they had committed a criminal offense. Hence, major portions of the Fourth, Fifth, Sixth, and Eighth Amendments all aim to safeguard individual freedoms from aggressive law enforcement actors seeking to punish suspected law violators. But what we as a society lose in our ability to control crime, we gain in increased liberty and privacy. It is hard to have it both ways, but, of course, most of us would like to! The great challenge to courts, especially the Supreme Court, is to strike a delicate balance between society's need for crime control and our equally strong desires for individual privacy and freedom.

Key Terms

ex post facto laws	neutral and detached judicial officer	search incidental to a lawful arrest
bills of attainder	general warrants	search based on consent
habeas corpus	confidential or anonymous informants	drug courier profile
search and seizure		automobile search
reasonable expectation of privacy	totality of circumstances	plain view
open fields exception	knock and announce	hot pursuit
warrant requirement	exigent circumstances	evanescent evidence
probable cause	warrantless search	emergency searches
search warrant		investigatory detention

stop and frisk

pat-down search

reasonable suspicion

exclusionary rule

supervisory power

silver platter doctrine

good-faith exception

arrest

arrest warrant

probable cause hearing

warrantless arrest

custodial interrogation

Miranda warnings

fruit of the poisonous tree doctrine

public safety exception

inevitable discovery exception

police deception

harmless error analysis

right to counsel

ineffective representation

mockery of justice test

pro se defenses

self-representation

arraignment

bail

pretrial detention

plea bargain

knowing and intelligent waiver

jury trial

fair trial doctrine

pretrial publicity

change of venue

gag orders

closure of pretrial proceedings

unanimity rule

reasonable doubt standard

nonunanimous verdicts

peremptory challenge

racially motivated peremptory
challenges

gender-based peremptory
challenges

double jeopardy

mistrial

hung jury

forfeiture

cruel and unusual punishments

habitual offender laws

three strikes laws

prisoners' rights

punitive isolation

discrete and insular minorities

death penalty

evolving standards of decency

aggravating factors

mitigating circumstances

victim impact statements

appeal by right

error correction

harmless errors

discretionary review

parens patriae

juvenile courts

For Further Reading

Amar, Akhil Reed. *The Constitution and Criminal Procedure: First Principles.* New Haven, Conn.: Yale University Press, 1997.

Bedau, Hugo Adam (ed.). *The Death Penalty in America: Current Controversies.* New York: Oxford University Press, 1997.

Berns, Walter. *For Capital Punishment.* New York: Basic Books, 1979.

Black, Charles, Jr. *Capital Punishment: The Inevitability of Caprice and Mistake.* New York: Norton, 1974.

Dershowitz, Alan M. *The Best Defense.* New York: Random House, 1982.

Eisenstein, James, Roy B. Fleming, and Peter F. Nardulli. *The Contours of Justice: Communities and Their Courts.* Boston, Mass.: Little, Brown, 1988.

Heumann, Milton. *Plea Bargaining: The Experiences of Prosecutors, Judges, and Defense Attorneys.* Chicago, Ill.: University of Chicago Press, 1978.

Jacob, Herbert. *Law and Politics in the United States.* Boston, Mass.: Little, Brown, 1986.

Kalven, Harry, and Hans Zeisel. *The American Jury.* Chicago, Ill.: University of Chicago Press, 1966.

Landynski, Jacob W. *Search and Seizure and the Supreme Court.* Baltimore: Johns Hopkins University Press, 1966.

Levy, Leonard W. *Against the Law: The Nixon Court and Criminal Justice.* New York: Harper and Row, 1974.

Lewis, Anthony. *Gideons Trumpet.* New York: Vintage Books, 1964.

Miller, Leonard G. *Double Jeopardy and the Federal System.* Chicago, Ill.: University of Chicago Press, 1968.

Packer, Herbert L. *The Limits of the Criminal Sanction.* Stanford, Calif: Stanford University Press, 1968.

Scheb II, John M. *Criminal Law and Procedure* (8th ed.). Belmont, Calif.: Cengage, 2013.

Scheingold, Stuart A. *The Politics of Law and Order: Street Crime and Public Policy.* New York: Longman, 1984.

Schlesinger, Stephen. *Exclusionary Injustice.* New York: Dekker, 1977.

Sigler, Jay. *Double Jeopardy: The Development of a Legal and Social Policy.* Ithaca, NY.: Cornell University Press, 1969.

Stephens, Otis H., Jr. *The Supreme Court and Confessions of Guilt.* Knoxville: University of Tennessee Press, 1973.

Stephens, Otis H., Jr., and Richard A. Glenn. *Unreasonable Searches and Seizures: Rights and Liberties under the Law.* Santa Barbara, Calif.: ABC-Clio, 2006.

White, Welsh. *The Death Penalty in the Eighties.* Ann Arbor: University of Michigan Press, 1988.

OLMSTEAD v. UNITED STATES
277 U.S. 438; 48 S.Ct. 564; 72 L.Ed. 944 (1928)
Vote: 5-4

In this decision, which has long since been overturned, the Court considers the admissibility of evidence obtained through wiretapping conducted without prior judicial authorization.

Mr. Chief Justice Taft delivered the opinion of the Court.

These cases are here by certiorari from the Circuit Court of Appeals for the Ninth Circuit. They were granted with the distinct limitation that the hearing should be confined to the single question whether the use of evidence of private telephone conversations between the defendants and others, intercepted by means of wiretapping, amounted to a violation of the 4th and 5th Amendments.

The petitioners were convicted in the District Court for the Western District of Washington of a conspiracy to violate the National Prohibition Act by unlawfully possessing, transporting and importing intoxicating liquors and maintaining nuisances, and by selling intoxicating liquors. Seventy-two others in addition to the petitioners were indicted. Some were not apprehended, some were acquitted, and others pleaded guilty.

The evidence in the records discloses a conspiracy of amazing magnitude to import, possess and sell liquor unlawfully. It involved the employment of not less than fifty persons, of two seagoing vessels for the transportation of liquor to British Columbia, of smaller vessels for coastwise transportation to the state of Washington, the purchase and use of a ranch beyond the suburban limits of Seattle, with a large underground cache for storage and a number of smaller caches in that city, the maintenance of a central office manned with operators, the employment of executives, salesmen, deliverymen, dispatchers, scouts, bookkeepers, collectors and an attorney. In a bad month sales amounted to $176,000; the aggregate for a year must have exceeded two millions of dollars.

Olmstead was the leading conspirator and the general manager of the business. He made a contribution of $10,000 to the capital; eleven others contributed $1,000 each. The profits were divided one-half to Olmstead and the remainder to the other eleven. Of the several offices in Seattle the chief one was in a large office building. In this there were three telephones on three different lines. There were telephones in an office of the manager in his own home, at the homes of his associates, and at other places in the city. Communication was had frequently with Vancouver, British Columbia. Times were fixed for the deliveries of the "stuff," to places along Puget Sound near Seattle, and from there the liquor was removed and deposited in the caches already referred to. One of the chief men was always on duty at the main office to receive orders by the telephones and to direct their filing by a corps of men stationed in another room—the "bull pen." The call numbers of the telephones were given to those known to be likely customers. At times the sales amounted to 200 cases of liquor per day.

The information which led to the discovery of the conspiracy and its nature and extent was largely obtained by intercepting messages on the telephones of the conspirators by four Federal prohibition officers. Small wires were inserted along the ordinary telephone wires from the residences of four of the petitioners and those leading from the chief office. The insertions were made without trespass upon any property of the defendants. They were made in the basement of the large office building. The taps from house lines were made in the streets near the houses.

The gathering of evidence continued for many months. Conversations of the conspirators, of which refreshing stenographic notes were currently made, were testified to by the government witnesses. They revealed the large business transactions of the partners and their subordinates. Men at the wires heard the orders given for liquor by customers, and the acceptances; they became auditors of the conversations between the partners. All this disclosed the conspiracy charged in the indictment. Many of the intercepted conversations were not merely reports but parts of the criminal acts. The evidence also disclosed the difficulties to which the conspirators were subjected, the reported news of the capture of vessels, the arrest of their men and the seizure of cases of liquor in garages and other places. It showed the dealing by Olmstead, the chief conspirator, with members of the Seattle police, the messages to them which secured the release of arrested members of the conspiracy, and also direct promises to officers of payments as soon as opportunity offered....

The well-known historical purpose of the 4th Amendment, directed against general warrants and writs of assistance, was to prevent the use of governmental force to search a man's house, his person, his papers, and his effects, and to prevent their seizure against his will....

The Amendment itself shows that the search is to be of material things—the person, the house, his papers or his effects. The description of the warrant necessary to make the proceeding lawful is that it must specify the place to be searched and the person or things to be seized....

... The 4th Amendment may have proper application to a sealed letter in the mail because of the constitutional provision for the Post Office Department and the relations between the government and those who pay to secure protection of their sealed letters.... It is plainly within the words of the Amendment to say that the unlawful rifling by a government agent of a sealed letter is a search and seizure of the sender's papers or effects. The letter is a paper, an effect, and in the custody of a government that forbids carriage except under its protection.

The United States takes no such care of telegraph or telephone messages as of mailed sealed letters. The Amendment does not forbid what was done here. There was no searching. There was no seizure. The evidence was secured by the use of the sense of hearing and that only. There was no entry of the house or offices of the defendants.

By the invention of the telephone fifty years ago, and its application for the purpose of extending communications, one can talk with another at a far distant place.

The language of the Amendment can not be extended and expanded to include telephone wires reaching to the whole world from the defendant's house or office. The intervening wires are not part of his house or office, any more than are the highways along which they are stretched....

"The 4th Amendment is to be construed in the light of what was deemed an unreasonable search and seizure when it was adopted and in a manner which will conserve public interests as well as the interests and rights of individual citizens." ...

Congress may, of course, protect the secrecy of telephone messages by making them, when intercepted, inadmissible in evidence in Federal criminal trials, by direct legislation, and thus depart from the common law of evidence. But the courts may not adopt such a policy by attributing an enlarged and unusual meaning to the 4th Amendment. The reasonable view is that one who installs in his house a telephone instrument with connecting wires intends to project his voice to those quite outside, and that the wires beyond his house and messages while passing over them are not within the protection of the 4th Amendment. Here those who intercepted the projected voices were not in the house of either party to the conversation....

We think, therefore, that the wiretapping here disclosed did not amount to a search or seizure within the meaning of the 4th Amendment....

Mr. Justice Holmes [dissenting]....

Mr. Justice Brandeis, dissenting:

... The government makes no attempt to defend the methods employed by its officers. Indeed, it concedes that if wire-tapping can be deemed a search and seizure within the 4th Amendment, such wire-tapping as was practiced in the case at bar was an unreasonable search and seizure, and that the evidence thus obtained was inadmissible. But it relies on the language of the Amendment; and it claims that the protection given thereby cannot properly be held to include a telephone conversation....

Time and again, this court, in giving effect to the principle underlying the 4th Amendment, has refused to place an unduly literal construction upon it....

The protection guaranteed by the Amendments is much broader in scope. The makers of our Constitution undertook to secure conditions favorable to the pursuit of happiness. They recognized the significance of man's spiritual nature, of his feelings and of his intellect. They knew that only a part of the pain, pleasure and satisfactions of life are to be found in material things. They sought to protect Americans in their beliefs, their thoughts, their emotions and their sensations. They conferred, as against the government, the right to be let alone—the most comprehensive of rights and the right most valued by civilized men. To protect that right, every unjustifiable intrusion by the government upon the privacy of the individual, whatever the means employed, must be deemed a violation of the 4th Amendment...

... [T]he defendants' objections to the evidence obtained by a wiretapping must, in my opinion, be sustained. It is, of course, immaterial where the physical connection with the telephone wires leading into

(Continued)

the defendants' premises was made. And, it is also immaterial that the intrusion was in aid of law enforcement. Experience should teach us to be most on our guard to protect liberty when the government's purposes are beneficent. Men born to freedom are naturally alert to repel invasion of their liberty by evil-minded rulers. The greatest dangers to liberty lurk in insidious encroachment by men of zeal, well-meaning, but without understanding....

Decency, security, and liberty alike demand that government officials shall be subjected to the same rules of conduct that are commands to the citizen. In a government of laws, existence of the government will be imperiled if it fails to observe the law scrupulously. Our government is the potent, the omnipresent, teacher. For good or for ill, it teaches the whole people by its example. Crime is contagious. If the government becomes a law-breaker, it breeds contempt for law; it invites every man to become a law unto himself; it invites anarchy. To declare that in the administration of the criminal law the end justifies the means—to declare that the government may commit crimes in order to secure the conviction of a private criminal—would bring terrible retribution. Against that pernicious doctrine this court should resolutely set its face.

Mr. Justice Butler, dissenting....

Mr. Justice Stone, dissenting....

KATZ v. UNITED STATES
389 U.S. 347; 88 S.Ct. 507; 19 L.Ed. 2d 576 (1967)
Vote: 7-1

In this case, the Court overturns its earlier ruling in Olmstead v. United States and adopts a broad view of the scope of Fourth Amendment protection.

Mr. Justice Stewart delivered the opinion of the Court.

The petitioner was convicted in the District Court for the Southern District of California under an eight-count indictment charging him with transmitting wagering information by telephone from Los Angeles to Miami and Boston in violation of a federal statute. At trial the Government was permitted, over the petitioner's objection, to introduce evidence of the petitioner's end of telephone conversations, overheard by FBI agents who had attached an electronic listening and recording device to the outside of the public telephone booth from which he had placed his calls. In affirming his conviction, the Court of Appeals rejected the contention that the recordings had been obtained in violation of the Fourth Amendment, because "[t]here was no physical entrance into the area occupied by [the petitioner]." We granted certiorari in order to consider the constitutional questions thus presented....

... [T]he parties have attached great significance to the characterization of the telephone booth from which the petitioner placed his calls. The petitioner has strenuously argued that the booth was a "constitutionally protected area." The Government has maintained with equal vigor that it was not. But this effort to decide whether or not a given "area," viewed in the abstract, is "constitutionally protected" deflects attention from the problem presented by this case. For the Fourth Amendment protects people, not places. What a person knowingly exposes to the public, even in his own home or office, is not a subject of Fourth Amendment protection. But what he seeks to preserve as private, even in an area accessible to the public, may be constitutionally protected.

The Government stresses the fact that the telephone booth from which the petitioner made his calls was constructed partly of glass, so that he was as visible after he entered it as he would have been if he had remained outside. But what he sought to exclude when he entered the booth was not the intruding eye—it was the uninvited ear. He did not shed his right to do so simply because he made his calls from a place where he might be seen. No less than an individual in a business office, in a friend's apartment, or in a taxicab, a person in a telephone booth may rely upon the protection of the Fourth Amendment. One who occupies it, shuts the door behind him, and pays the toll that permits him to place a call is surely entitled to assume that the words he utters into the mouthpiece will not be broadcast to the world. To read the Constitution more narrowly is to ignore the vital role that the public telephone has come to play in private communication.

The Government contends, however, that the activities of its agents in this case should not be tested by Fourth Amendment requirements, for the surveillance technique they employed involved no physical penetration of the telephone booth from which the petitioner placed his calls. It is true that the absence of such penetration was at one time thought to foreclose further Fourth Amendment inquiry, ... for that Amendment was thought to limit only searches and seizures of tangible property. But "[t]he premise that property interests control the right of the Government to search and seize has been discredited." Thus, although a closely divided Court supposed in *Olmstead* that surveillance without any trespass and without the seizure of any material object fell outside the ambit of the Constitution, we have since departed from the narrow view on which that decision rested. Indeed, we have expressly held that the Fourth Amendment governs not only the seizure of tangible items, but extends as well to the recording of oral statements overheard without any "technical trespass under ... local property law." Once this much is acknowledged, and once it is recognized that the Fourth Amendment protects people—and not simply "areas"—against unreasonable searches and seizures it becomes clear that the reach of the Amendment cannot turn upon the presence or absence of a physical intrusion into any given enclosure.

We conclude that the underpinnings of ... [*Olmstead v. United States*] ... have been so eroded by our subsequent decisions that the "trespass" doctrine there enunciated can no longer be regarded as controlling. The Government's activities in electronically listening to and recording the petitioner's words violated the privacy upon which he justifiably relied while using the telephone booth and thus constituted a "search and seizure" within the meaning of the Fourth Amendment. The fact that the electronic device employed to achieve that end did not happen to penetrate the wall of the booth can have no constitutional significance.

The question remaining for decision, then, is whether the search and seizure conducted in this case complied with constitutional standards. In that regard, the Government's position is that its agents acted in an entirely defensible manner. They did not begin their electronic surveillance until investigation of the petitioner's activities had established a strong probability that he was using the telephone in question to transmit gambling information to persons in other States, in violation of federal law. Moreover, the surveillance was limited,

both in scope and in duration, to the specific purpose of establishing the contents of the petitioner's unlawful telephone communications. The agents confined their surveillance to the brief periods during which he used the telephone booth, and they took great care to overhear only the conversations of the petitioner himself.

Accepting this account of the Government's actions as accurate, it is clear that this surveillance was so narrowly circumscribed that a duly authorized magistrate, properly notified of the need for such investigation, specifically informed of the basis on which it was to proceed, and clearly apprised of the precise intrusion it would entail, could constitutionally have authorized, with appropriate safeguards, the very limited search and seizure that the Government asserts in fact took place....

... The government agents here ignored "the procedure of antecedent justification ... that is central to the Fourth Amendment," ... a procedure that we hold to be a constitutional precondition of the kind of electronic surveillance involved in this case. Because the surveillance here failed to meet that condition, and because it led to the petitioner's conviction, the judgment must be reversed....

Mr. Justice Marshall took no part in the consideration or decision of this case.

Mr. Justice Douglas, with whom *Mr. Justice Brennan* joins, concurring....

Mr. Justice Harlan, concurring.

... As the Court's opinion states, "the Fourth Amendment protects people, not places." The question, however, is what protection it affords to those people. Generally, as here, the answer to that question requires reference to a "place." My understanding of the rule that has emerged from prior decisions is that there is a twofold requirement, first that a person has exhibited an actual (subjective) expectation of privacy and, second, that the expectation be one that society is prepared to recognize as "reasonable." Thus a man's home is, for most purposes, a place where he expects privacy, but objects, activities, or statements that he exposes to the "plain view" of outsiders are not "protected" because no intention to keep them to himself has been exhibited. On the other hand, conversations in the open would not be protected against being overheard, for the expectation of privacy under the circumstances would be unreasonable.

(Continued)

The critical fact in this case is that "[o]ne who occupies it [a telephone booth], shuts the door behind him, and pays the toll that permits him to place a call is surely entitled to assume" that his conversation is not being intercepted. The point is not that the booth is "accessible to the public" at other times, but that it is a temporarily private place whose momentary occupants' expectations of freedom from intrusion are recognized as reasonable....

Mr. Justice White, concurring....

Mr. Justice Black, dissenting.

My basic objection is twofold: (1) I do not believe that the words of the Amendment will bear the meaning given them by today's decision, and (2) I do not believe that it is the proper role of this Court to rewrite the Amendment in order "to bring it into harmony with the times" and thus reach a result that many people believe to be desirable.

While I realize that an argument based on the meaning of words lacks the scope, and no doubt the appeal, of broad policy discussions and philosophical discourses on such nebulous subjects as privacy, for me the language of the Amendment is the crucial place to look in construing a written document such as our Constitution....

The first clause [of the Fourth Amendment] protects "persons, houses, papers, and effects, against un-reasonable searches and seizures...." These words connote the idea of tangible things with size, form, and weight, things capable of being searched, seized, or both. The second clause of the Amendment still further established its Framers' purpose to limit its protection to tangible things by providing that no warrants shall issue but those

"particularly describing the place to be searched, and the persons or things to be seized." A conversation overheard by eavesdropping, whether by plain snooping or wire-tapping, is not tangible and, under the normally accepted meanings of the words, can neither be searched nor seized. In addition the language of the second clause indicates that the Amendment refers not only to something tangible so it can be seized but to something already in existence so it can be described. Yet the Court's interpretation would have the Amendment apply to overhearing future conversations which by their very nature are nonexistent until they take place. How can one "describe" a future conversation, and, if one cannot, how can a magistrate issue a warrant to eavesdrop one in the future? It is argued that information showing what is expected to be said is sufficient to limit the boundaries of what later can be admitted into evidence; but does such general information really meet the specific language of the Amendment which says "particularly describing"? Rather than using language in a completely artificial way, I must conclude that the Fourth Amendment simply does not apply to eavesdropping....

Since I see no way in which the words of the Fourth Amendment can be construed to apply to eavesdropping, that closes the matter for me. In interpreting the Bill of Rights, I willingly go as far as a liberal construction of the language takes me, but I simply cannot in good conscience give a meaning to words which they have never before been thought to have and which they certainly do not have in common ordinary usage. I will not distort the words of the Amendment in order to "keep the Constitution up to date" or "to bring it into harmony with the time." It was never meant that this Court have such power, which in effect would make us a continuously functioning constitutional convention.

WEEKS v. UNITED STATES
232 U.S. 383; 34 S.Ct. 341; 58 L.Ed. 652 (1914)
Vote: 9-0

In this case, the Court first establishes the Fourth Amendment exclusionary rule, although the ruling applies only to criminal trials in federal courts.

Mr. Justice Day delivered the opinion of the Court.

An indictment was returned against the plaintiff in error, defendant below, and herein so designated, in the

District Court of the United States for the Western District of Missouri, containing nine counts. The seventh count, upon which a conviction was had, charged the use of the mails for the purpose of transporting certain coupons or tickets representing chances or shares in a lottery ... in violation of the Criminal Code. Sentence of fine and imprisonment was imposed. This writ of error is to review that judgment.

The defendant was arrested by a police officer, so far as the record shows, without warrant, at the Union Station in Kansas City, Missouri, where he was employed by an express company. Other police officers had gone to the house of the defendant, and being told by a neighbor where the key was kept, found it and entered the house. They searched the defendant's room and took possession of various papers and articles found there, which were afterwards turned over to the United States marshal. Later in the same day police officers returned with the marshal, who thought he might find additional evidence, and, being admitted by someone in the house, probably a boarder, in response to a rap, the marshal searched the defendant's room and carried away certain letters and envelopes found in the drawer of a chiffonier. Neither the marshal nor the police officers had a search warrant. ...

Upon the introduction of such papers during the trial, the defendant objected on the ground that the papers had been obtained without a search warrant, and by breaking into his home, in violation of the 4th and 5th Amendments to the Constitution of the United States, which objection was overruled by the court. Among the papers retained and put in evidence were a number of lottery tickets and statements with reference to the lottery, taken at the first visit of the police to the defendant's room, and a number of letters written to the defendant in respect to the lottery, taken by the marshal upon his search of defendant's room. ...

The effect of the 4th Amendment is to put the courts of the United States and Federal officials, in the exercise of their power and authority, under limitations and restraints as to the exercise of such power and authority, and to forever secure the people, their persons, houses, papers, and effects, against all unreasonable searches and seizures under the guise of law. This protection reaches all alike, whether accused of crime or not, and the duty of giving to it force and effect is obligatory upon all intrusted under our Federal system with the enforcement of the laws. The tendency of those who execute the criminal laws of the country to obtain conviction by means of unlawful seizures and enforced confessions, the latter often obtained after subjecting accused persons to unwarranted practices destructive of rights secured by the Federal Constitution, should find no sanction in the judgments of the courts, which are charged at all times with the support of the Constitution, and to which people of all conditions have a right to appeal for the maintenance of such fundamental rights.

What, then, is the present case? Before answering that inquiry specifically, it may be well by a process of exclusion to state what it is not. It is not an assertion of the right on the part of the government, always recognized under English and American law, to search the person of the accused when legally arrested, to discover and seize the fruits or evidences of crime. Nor is it the case of testimony offered at a trial where the court is asked to stop and consider the illegal means by which proofs, otherwise competent, were obtained—of which we shall have occasion to treat later in this opinion. Nor is it the case of burglar's tools or other proofs of guilt found upon his arrest within the control of the accused.

The case in the aspect in which we are dealing with it involves the right of the court in a criminal prosecution to retain for the purposes of evidence the letters and correspondence of the accused, seized in his house in his absence and without his authority, by a United States marshal holding no warrant for his arrest and none for the search of his premises. If letters and private documents can thus be seized and held and used in evidence against a citizen accused of an offense, the protection of the 4th Amendment, declaring his right to be secure against such searches and seizures, is of no value, and, so far as those thus placed are concerned, might as well be stricken from the Constitution. The efforts of the courts and their officials to bring the guilty to punishment, praise-worthy as they are, are not to be aided by the sacrifice of those great principles established by years of endeavor and suffering which have resulted in their embodiment in the fundamental law of the land. The United States marshal could only have invaded the house of the accused when armed with a warrant issued as required by the Constitution, upon sworn information, and describing with reasonable particularity the thing for which the search was to be made. Instead, he acted without sanction of law, doubtless prompted by the desire to bring further proof to the aid of the government, and under color of his office undertook to make a seizure of private papers in direct violation of the constitutional prohibition against such action. Under such circumstances, without sworn information and particular description, not even an order of court would have justified such procedure; much less was it within the authority of the United States marshal to thus invade the house and privacy of the accused.

We therefore reach the conclusion that the letters in question were taken from the house of the accused by an official of the United States, acting under color of his office, in direct violation of the constitutional rights of the defendant; that having made a seasonable

(Continued)

application for their return, which was heard and passed upon by the court, there was involved in the order refusing the application of denial of the constitutional rights of the accused, and that the court should have restored these letters to the accused. In holding them and permitting their use upon the trial, we think prejudicial error was committed....

It results that the judgment of the court below must be reversed, and the case remanded for further proceedings in accordance with this opinion....

MAPP v. OHIO
367 U.S. 643; 81 S.Ct. 1684; 6 L.Ed. 2d 1081 (1961)
Vote: 6-3

In this landmark case, the Supreme Court extends the Fourth Amendment exclusionary rule to state criminal prosecutions via the Due Process Clause of the Fourteenth Amendment.

Mr. Justice Clark delivered the opinion of the Court.

Appellant stands convicted of knowingly having had in her possession and under her control certain lewd and lascivious books, pictures, and photographs in violation of … Ohio's Revised Code.... [T]he Supreme Court of Ohio found that her conviction was valid though "based primarily upon the introduction in evidence of lewd and lascivious books and pictures unlawfully seized during an unlawful search of defendant's home...."

On May 23, 1957, three Cleveland police officers arrived at appellant's residence in that city pursuant to information that "a person [was] hiding out in the home, who was wanted for questioning in connection with a recent bombing, and that there was a large amount of policy [gambling] paraphernalia being hidden in the home." Miss Mapp and her daughter by a former marriage lived on the top floor of the two-family dwelling. Upon their arrival at that house, the officers knocked on the door and demanded entrance but appellant, after telephoning her attorney, refused to admit them without a search warrant. They advised their headquarters of the situation and undertook a surveillance of the house.

The officers again sought entrance some three hours later when four or more additional officers arrived on the scene. When Miss Mapp did not come to the door immediately at least one of the several doors to the house was forcibly opened and the policemen gained admittance. Meanwhile Miss Mapp's attorney arrived, but the officers, having secured their own entry, and continuing in their defiance of the law, would permit him neither to see Miss Mapp nor to enter the house. It appears that Miss Mapp was halfway down the stairs from the upper floor to the front door when the officers, in this highhanded manner, broke into the hall. She demanded to see the search warrant. A paper, claimed to be a warrant, was held up by one of the officers. She grabbed the "warrant" and placed it in her bosom. A struggle ensued in which the officers recovered the piece of paper and as a result of which they handcuffed appellant because she had been "belligerent" in resisting their official rescue of the "warrant" from her person. Running roughshod over appellant, a policeman "grabbed" her, "twisted [her] hand," and she "yelled [and] pleaded with him" because "it was hurting." Appellant, in handcuffs, was then forcibly taken upstairs to her bedroom where the officers searched a dresser, a chest of drawers, a closet and some suitcases. They also looked into a photo album and through personal papers belonging to the appellant. The search spread to the rest of the second floor including the child's bedroom, the living room, the kitchen and a dinette. The basement of the building and a trunk found therein were also searched. The obscene materials for possession of which she was ultimately convicted were discovered in the course of that widespread search.

At the trial no search warrant was produced by the prosecution, nor was the failure to produce one explained or accounted for. At best, "There is, in the record, considerable doubt as to whether there ever was any warrant for the search of defendant's home." …

The State says that even if the search were made without authority, or otherwise unreasonably, it is not prevented from using the unconstitutionally seized evidence at trial, citing *Wolf v. Colorado* (1949), in which this Court did indeed hold "that in a prosecution in a State court for a State crime the Fourteenth Amendment does not forbid the admission of evidence obtained by an unreasonable search and seizure." ... On this appeal, of which we have noted probable jurisdiction, ... it is urged once again that we review that holding....

[I]n the year 1914, in the *Weeks* Case, this Court "for the first time" held that, "in a federal prosecution the Fourth Amendment barred the use of evidence secured through an illegal search and seizure." ... This Court has ever since required of federal law officers a strict adherence to that command which this Court has held to be a clear, specific, and constitutionally required—even if judicially implied—deterrent safeguard without insistence upon which the Fourth Amendment would have been reduced to "a form of words." ... It meant, quite simply, that "conviction by means of unlawful seizures and enforced confessions ... should find no sanction in the judgments of the courts." ...

There are in the cases of this Court some passing references to the *Weeks* rule as being one of evidence. But the plain and unequivocal language of *Weeks*—and its later paraphrase in *Wolf*—to the effect that the *Weeks* rule is of constitutional origin, remains entirely undisturbed. In *Byars v. United States* ... (1927), a unanimous Court declared that "the doctrine [cannot] ... be tolerated under our constitutional system, that evidences of crime discovered by a federal officer in making a search without lawful warrant may be used against the victim of the unlawful search where a timely challenge has been interposed." ...

In 1949, 35 years after *Weeks* was announced, this Court, in *Wolf v. Colorado* for the first time discussed the effect of the Fourth Amendment upon the States through the operation of the Due Process Clause of the Fourteenth Amendment. It said: "[W]e have no hesitation in saying that were a State affirmatively to sanction such police incursion into privacy it would run counter to the guaranty of the Fourteenth Amendment." ... Nevertheless, after declaring that the "security of one's privacy against arbitrary intrusion by the police" is "implicit in 'the concept of ordered liberty' and as such enforceable against the States through the Due Process Clause," and announcing that it "stoutly adhere[d]" to the *Weeks* decision, the Court decided that the *Weeks* exclusionary rule would not then be imposed upon the States as "an essential ingredient of the right." ... The Court's reasons for not considering essential to the right to privacy, as a curb imposed upon the States by the Due Process Clause, that which decades before had been posited as part and parcel of the Fourth Amendment's limitation upon federal encroachment of individual privacy, were bottomed on factual considerations.

While they are not basically relevant to a decision that the exclusionary rule is an essential ingredient of the Fourth Amendment as the right it embodies is vouchsafed against the States by the Due Process Clause, we will consider the current validity of the factual grounds upon which *Wolf* was based.

The Court in *Wolf* first stated that "[t]he contrariety of views of the States" on the adoption of the exclusionary rule of *Weeks* was "particularly impressive"; ... and, in this connection that it could not "brush aside the experience of States which deem the incidence of such conduct by the police too slight to call for a deterrent remedy ... by overriding the [States'] relevant rules of evidence." ... While in 1949, prior to the *Wolf* Case, almost two-thirds of the States were opposed to the use of the exclusionary rule, now, despite the *Wolf* Case, more than half of those since passing upon it, by their own legislative or judicial decision, have wholly or partly adopted or adhered to the *Weeks* rule.... Significantly, among those now following the rule is California, which, according to its highest court, was "compelled to reach that conclusion because other remedies have completely failed to secure compliance with the constitutional provisions." ... The experience of California that such other remedies have been worthless and futile is buttressed by the experience of other States. The obvious futility of relegating the Fourth Amendment to the protection of other remedies has, moreover, been recognized by this Court since *Wolf*...

It, therefore, plainly appears that the factual considerations supporting the failure of the *Wolf* Court to include the *Weeks* exclusionary rule when it recognized the enforceability of the right to privacy against the States in 1949, while not basically relevant to the constitutional consideration, could not, in any analysis, now be deemed controlling....

Since the Fourth Amendment's right of privacy has been declared enforceable against the States through the Due Process Clause of the Fourteenth, it is enforceable

(Continued)

against them by the same sanction of exclusion as is used against the Federal Government. Were it otherwise, then just as without the *Weeks* rule the assurance against unreasonable federal searches and seizures would be "a form of words," valueless and undeserving of mention in a perpetual charter of inestimable human liberties, so too, without that rule the freedom from state invasions of privacy would be so ephemeral and so neatly severed from its conceptual nexus with the freedom from all brutish means of coercing evidence as not to merit this Court's high regard as a freedom "implicit in the concept of ordered liberty." At the time that the Court held in *Wolf* that the Amendment was applicable to the States through the Due Process Clause, the cases of this Court, as we have seen, had steadfastly held that as to federal officers the Fourth Amendment included the exclusion of the evidence seized in violation of its provisions. Even *Wolf* "stoutly adhered" to that proposition. The right to privacy, when conceded operatively enforceable against the States, was not susceptible of destruction by avulsion of the sanction upon which its protection and enjoyment had always been deemed dependent under the *Boyd*, *Weeks* and *Silverthorne* cases. Therefore, in extending the substantive protections of due process to all constitutionally unreasonable searches—state or federal—it was logically and constitutionally necessary that the exclusion doctrine—an essential part of the right to privacy—be also insisted upon as an essential ingredient of the right newly recognized by the *Wolf* case. In short, the admission of the new constitutional right by *Wolf* could not consistently tolerate denial of its most important constitutional privilege, namely, the exclusion of the evidence which an accused had been forced to give by reason of the unlawful seizure. To hold otherwise is to grant the right but in reality to withhold its privilege and enjoyment. Only last year the Court itself recognized that the purpose of the exclusionary rule "is to deter—to compel respect for the constitutional guaranty in the only effectively available way—by removing the incentive to disregard it." ...

Moreover, our holding that the exclusionary rule is an essential part of both the Fourth and Fourteenth Amendments is not only the logical dictate of prior cases, but it also makes very good sense. There is no war between the Constitution and common sense. Presently, a federal prosecutor may make no use of evidence illegally seized, but a State's attorney across the street may, although he supposedly is operating

under the enforceable prohibitions of the same Amendment. Thus the State, by admitting evidence unlawfully seized, serves to encourage disobedience to the Federal Constitution which it is bound to uphold. Moreover, ... "[t]he very essence of a healthy federalism depends upon the avoidance of needless conflict between state and federal courts." ...

Federal-state cooperation in the solution of crime under constitutional standards will be promoted, if only by recognition of their now mutual obligation to respect the same fundamental criteria in their approaches. "However much in a particular case insistence upon such rules may appear as a technicality that inures to the benefit of a guilty person, the history of the criminal law proves that tolerance of shortcut methods in law enforcement impairs its enduring effectiveness." ... Denying shortcuts to only one of two cooperating law enforcement agencies tends naturally to breed legitimate suspicion of "working arrangements" whose results are equally tainted....

There are those who say, as did Justice (then Judge) Cardozo, that under our constitutional exclusionary doctrine "[t]he criminal is to go free because the constable has blundered." ... In some cases this will undoubtedly be the result. But,... "there is another consideration—the imperative of judicial integrity." ... The criminal goes free, if he must, but it is the law that sets him free. Nothing can destroy a government more quickly than its failure to observe its own laws, or worse, its disregard of the charter of its own existence. As Mr. Justice Brandeis, dissenting, said in *Olmstead v. United States* (1928): "Our Government is the potent, the omnipresent teacher. For good or for ill, it teaches the whole people by its example.... If the Government becomes a lawbreaker, it breeds contempt for law; it invites every man to become a law unto himself; it invites anarchy."

The ignoble shortcut to conviction left open to the State tends to destroy the entire system of constitutional restraints on which the liberties of the people rest. Having once recognized that the right to privacy embodied in the Fourth Amendment is enforceable against the States, and that the right to be secure against rude invasions of privacy by state officers is, therefore, constitutional in origin, we can no longer permit that right to remain an empty promise. Because it is enforceable in the same manner and to like effect as other basic rights secured by the Due Process

Clause, we can no longer permit it to be revocable at the whim of any police officer who, in the name of law enforcement itself, chooses to suspend its enjoyment. Our decision, founded on reason and truth, gives to the individual no more than that which the Constitution guarantees him, to the police officer no less than that to which honest law enforcement is entitled, and, to the courts, that judicial integrity so necessary in the true administration of justice.

The judgment of the Supreme Court of Ohio is reversed and the case remanded for further proceedings not inconsistent with this opinion.

Mr. Justice Black, concurring....

Mr. Justice Douglas, concurring....

Mr. Justice Harlan, with whom *Mr. Justice Frankfurter* and *Mr. Justice Whittaker* join, dissenting.

In overruling the *Wolf* case the Court, in my opinion, has forgotten the sense of judicial restraint which, with due regard for *stare decisis*, is one element that should enter into deciding whether a past decision of this Court should be overruled. Apart from that I also believe that the *Wolf* rule represents sounder Constitutional doctrine than the new rule which now replaces it.

From the Court's statement of the case one would gather that the central, if not controlling, issue on this appeal is whether illegally state-seized evidence is constitutionally admissible in a state prosecution, an issue which would of course face us with the need for reexamining *Wolf.* However, such is not the situation. For, although that question was indeed raised here and below among appellant's subordinate points, the new and pivotal issue brought to the Court by this appeal is whether section 2905.34 of the Ohio Revised Code making criminal the mere knowing possession or control of obscene material, and under which appellant has been convicted, is consistent with the rights of free thought and expression assured against state action by the Fourteenth Amendment. That was the principal issue which was decided by the Ohio Supreme Court, which was tendered by appellant's Jurisdictional Statement, and which was briefed and argued in this Court.

In this posture of things, I think it fair to say that five members of this Court have simply "reached out"

to overrule *Wolf.* With all respect for the views of the majority, and recognizing that *stare decisis* carries different weight in Constitutional adjudication than it does in nonconstitutional decision, I can perceive no justification for regarding this case as an appropriate occasion for re-examining *Wolf* ...

I would not impose upon the States this federal exclusionary remedy. The reasons given by the majority for now suddenly turning its back on *Wolf* seem to me notably unconvincing.

First, it is said that "the factual grounds upon which *Wolf* was based" have since changed, in that more States now follow the *Weeks* exclusionary rule than was so at the time *Wolf* was decided. While that is true, a recent survey indicates that at present one-half of the States still adhere to the common-law nonexclusionary rule, and one, Maryland, retains the rule as to felonies.... But in any case surely all this is beside the point, as the majority itself indeed seems to recognize. Our concern here, as it was in *Wolf,* is not with the desirability of that rule but only with the question whether the States are constitutionally free to follow it or not as they may themselves determine, and the relevance of the disparity of views among the States on this point lies simply in the fact that the judgment involved is a debatable one. Moreover, the very fact on which the majority relies, instead of lending support to what is now being done, points away from the need of replacing voluntary state action with federal compulsion.

The preservation of a proper balance between state and federal responsibility in the administration of criminal justice demands patience on the part of those who might like to see things move faster among the States in this respect....

Memorandum of *Mr. Justice Stewart.*

Agreeing fully with Part I of Mr. Justice Harlan's dissenting opinion, I express no view as to the merits of the constitutional issue which the Court today decides. I would, however, reverse the judgment in this case, because I am persuaded that the provision ... upon which the petitioner's conviction was based is, in the words of Mr. Justice Harlan, not "consistent with the rights of free thought and expression assured against state action by the Fourteenth Amendment."

UNITED STATES v. LEON
468 U.S. 897; 104 S.Ct. 3405; 82 L.Ed. 2d 677 (1984)
Vote: 6-3

In this case, the Court recognizes a limited good-faith exception to the Fourth Amendment exclusionary rule.

Justice White delivered the opinion of the Court.

This case presents the question whether the Fourth Amendment exclusionary rule should be modified so as not to bar the use in the prosecution's case-in-chief of evidence obtained by officers acting in reasonable reliance on a search warrant issued by a detached and neutral magistrate but ultimately found to be unsupported by probable cause. To resolve this question, we must consider once again the tension between the sometimes competing goals of, on the one hand, deterring official misconduct and removing inducements to unreasonable invasions of privacy and, on the other, establishing procedures under which criminal defendants are "acquitted or convicted on the basis of all the evidence which exposes the truth." ...

In August 1981, a confidential informant of unproven reliability informed an officer of the Burbank Police Department that two persons known to him as "Armando" and "Patsy" were selling large quantities of cocaine and methaqualone from their residence at 620 Price Drive in Burbank, Cal. The informant also indicated that he had witnessed a sale of methaqualone by "Patsy" at the residence approximately five months earlier and had observed at that time a shoebox containing a large amount of cash that belonged to "Patsy." He further declared that "Armando" and "Patsy" generally kept only small quantities of drugs at their residence and stored the remainder at another location in Burbank.

On the basis of this information, the Burbank police initiated an extensive investigation focusing first on the Price Drive residence and later on two other residences as well. Cars parked at the Price Drive residence were determined to belong to respondents Armando Sanchez, who had previously been arrested for possession of marijuana, and Patsy Stewart, who had no criminal record. During the course of the investigation, officers observed an automobile belonging to respondent Ricardo Del Castillo, who had previously been arrested for possession of 50 pounds of marijuana, arrive at the Price residence. The driver of that car entered the house, exited shortly thereafter carrying a small paper sack, and drove away. A check of Del Castillo's probation records led the

officers to respondent Alberto Leon, whose telephone number Del Castillo had listed as his employer's. Leon had been arrested in 1980 on drug charges, and a companion had informed the police at that time that Leon was heavily involved in the importation of drugs into this country. Before the current investigation began, the Burbank officers had learned that an informant had told a Glendale police officer that Leon stored a large quantity of methaqualone at his residence in Glendale. During the course of this investigation, the Burbank officers learned that Leon was living at 716 South Sunset Canyon in Burbank.

Subsequently, the officers observed several persons, at least one of whom had prior drug involvement, arriving at the Price Drive residence and leaving with small packages; observed a variety of other material activity at the two residences as well as at a condominium at 7902 Via Magdalena; and witnessed a variety of relevant activity involving respondents' automobiles. The officers also observed respondents Sanchez and Stewart board separate flights for Miami. The pair later returned to Los Angeles together, consented to a search of their luggage that revealed only a small amount of marijuana, and left the airport. Based on these and other observations summarized in the affidavit, Officer Cyril Rombach of the Burbank Police Department, an experienced and well-trained narcotics investigator, prepared an application for a warrant to search 620 Price Drive, 716 South Sunset Canyon, 7902 Via Magdalena, and automobiles registered to each of the respondents for an extensive list of items believed to be related to respondent's drug-trafficking activities. Officer Rombach's extensive application was reviewed by several Deputy District Attorneys.

A facially valid search warrant was issued in September 1981 by a State Superior Court Judge. The ensuing searches produced large quantities of drugs at the Via Magdalena and Sunset Canyon addresses and a small quantity at the Price Drive residence. Other evidence was discovered at each of the residences and in Stewart's and Del Castillo's automobiles....

The respondents then filed motions to suppress the evidence seized pursuant to the warrant. The District Court ... concluded that the affidavit was insufficient to establish probable cause, but did not suppress all of the evidence as to all of the respondents because none of the respondents had standing to challenge all of the searches. In response to a request from the Government, the court made clear that Officer Rombach had acted in good faith, but it rejected the Government's suggestion that the Fourth Amendment exclusionary rule should not apply where evidence is seized in reasonable, good-faith reliance on a search warrant....

The Fourth Amendment contains no provision expressly precluding the use of evidence obtained in violation of its commands, and an examination of its origin and purposes makes clear that the use of fruits of a past unlawful search or seizure "work[s] no new Fourth Amendment wrong." ... The wrong condemned by the Amendment is "fully accomplished" by the unlawful search or seizure itself, ... and the exclusionary rule is neither intended nor able to "cure the invasion of the defendant's rights which he has already suffered." ... The rule thus operates as "a judicially created remedy designed to safeguard Fourth Amendment rights generally through its deterrent effect, rather than a personal constitutional right of the person aggrieved." ...

Whether the exclusionary sanction is appropriately imposed in a particular case, our decisions make clear, is "an issue separate from the question whether the Fourth Amendment rights of the party seeking to invoke the rule were violated by police conduct." ... Only the former question is currently before us, and it must be resolved by weighing the costs and benefits of preventing the use in the prosecution's case-in-chief of inherently trustworthy tangible evidence obtained in reliance on a search warrant issued by a detached and neutral magistrate that ultimately is found to be defective.

The substantial social costs exacted by the exclusionary rule for the vindication of Fourth Amendment rights have long been a source of concern. "Our cases have consistently recognized that unbending application of the exclusionary sanction to enforce ideals of government rectitude would impede unacceptably the truth-finding functions of judge and jury." ... An objectionable collateral consequence of this interference with the criminal justice system's truth-finding function is that some guilty defendants may go free or receive reduced sentences as a result of favorable plea bargains. Particularly when law enforcement officers have acted in objective good faith or their transgressions have been minor, the magnitude of the benefit conferred on such guilty defendants offends basic concepts of the criminal justice system.... Indiscriminate application of the exclusionary rule, therefore, may well "generat[e] disrespect for the law and the administration of justice." ... Accordingly, "[a]s with any remedial device, the application of the rule has been restricted to those areas where its remedial objectives are thought most efficaciously served." ...

... The Court has, to be sure, not seriously questioned, "in the absence of a more efficacious sanction, the continued application of the rule to suppress evidence from the [prosecution's] case where a Fourth Amendment violation has been substantial and deliberate. "... Nevertheless, the balancing approach that has evolved in various contexts—including criminal trial—"forcefully suggest[s] that the exclusionary rule be more generally modified to permit the introduction of evidence obtained in the reasonable good-faith belief that a search or a seizure was in accord with the Fourth Amendment." ...

As cases considering the use of unlawfully obtained evidence in criminal trials themselves make clear, it does not follow from the emphasis on the exclusionary rule's deterrent value that "anything which deters illegal searches is thereby commanded by the Fourth Amendment." ... In determining whether persons aggrieved solely by the introduction of damaging evidence unlawfully obtained from their co-conspirators or co-defendants could seek suppression, for example, we found that the additional benefits of such an extension of the exclusionary rule would not outweigh its costs.... Standing to invoke the rule has thus been limited to cases in which the prosecution seeks to use the fruits of an illegal search or seizure against the victim of police misconduct ...

Because a search warrant "provides the detached scrutiny of a neutral magistrate, which is a more reliable safeguard against improper searches than the hurried judgment of a law enforcement officer 'engaged in the often competitive enterprise of ferreting out crime,'" ... we have expressed a strong preference for warrants and declared that "in a doubtful or marginal case a search under a warrant may be sustainable where without one it would fall." ... Reasonable minds frequently may differ on the question whether a particular affidavit establishes probable cause, and we have thus concluded that the preference for warrants is most appropriately effectuated by according "great deference" to a magistrate's determination....

Deference to the magistrate, however, is not boundless. It is clear, first, that the deference accorded to a magistrate's finding of probable cause does not preclude inquiry into the knowing or reckless falsity of the affidavit on which that determination was based. ... Second, the courts must also insist that the magistrate purport to "perform his 'neutral and detached'

(Continued)

function and not serve merely as a rubber stamp for the police." ...

Third, reviewing courts will not defer to a warrant based on an affidavit that does not "provide the magistrate with a substantial basis for determining the existence of probable cause." ... Even if the warrant application was supported by more than a "bare bones" affidavit, a reviewing court may properly conclude that, notwithstanding the deference that magistrates deserve, the warrant was invalid because the magistrate's probable cause determination reflected an improper analysis of the totality of the circumstances, ...

Only in the first of these three situations, however, has the Court set forth a rationale for suppressing evidence obtained pursuant to a search warrant; in the other areas, it has simply excluded such evidence without considering whether Fourth Amendment interests will be advanced. To the extent that proponents of exclusion rely on its behavioral effects on judges and magistrates in these areas, their reliance is misplaced. First, the exclusionary rule is designed to deter police misconduct rather than to punish the errors of judges and magistrates. Second, there exists no evidence suggesting that judges and magistrates are inclined to ignore or subvert the Fourth Amendment or that lawlessness among those actors requires application of the extreme sanction of exclusion.

Third, and most important, we discern no basis, and are offered none, for believing that exclusion of evidence seized pursuant to a warrant will have a significant deterrent effect on the issuing judge or magistrate.... Judges and magistrates are not adjuncts to the law enforcement team; as neutral judicial officers, they have no stake in the outcome of particular criminal prosecutions. The threat of exclusion thus cannot be expected significantly to deter them. Imposition of the exclusionary sanction is not necessary meaningfully to inform judicial officers of their errors, and we cannot conclude that admitting evidence obtained pursuant to a warrant while at the same time declaring that the warrant was somehow defective will in any way reduce judicial officers' professional incentives to comply with the Fourth Amendment, encourage them to repeat their mistakes, or lead to the granting of all colorable warrant requests.

If exclusion of evidence obtained pursuant to a subsequently invalidated warrant is to have any deterrent effect, therefore, it must alter the behavior of individual law enforcement officers or the policies of their departments....

We have frequently questioned whether the exclusionary rule can have any deterrent effect when the offending officers acted in the objectively reasonable belief that their conduct did not violate the Fourth Amendment. "No empirical researcher, proponent or opponent of the rule, has yet been able to establish with any assurance whether the rule has a deterrent effect." ... But even assuming that the rule effectively deters some police misconduct and provides incentives for the law enforcement profession as a whole to conduct itself in accord with the Fourth Amendment, it cannot be expected, and should not be applied, to deter objectively reasonable law enforcement activity....

We conclude that the marginal or nonexistent benefits produced by suppressing evidence obtained in objectively reasonable reliance on a subsequently invalidated search warrant cannot justify the substantial costs of exclusion....

When the principles we have enunciated today are applied to the facts of this case, it is apparent that the judgment of the Court of Appeals cannot stand. The Court of Appeals applied the prevailing legal standards to Officer Rombach's warrant application and concluded that the application could not support the magistrate's probable cause determination. In so doing, the court clearly informed the magistrate that he had erred in issuing the challenged warrant. This aspect of the court's judgment is not under attack in this proceeding.

Having determined that the warrant should not have issued, the Court of Appeals understandably declined to adopt a modification of the Fourth Amendment exclusionary rule that this court had not previously sanctioned. Although the modification finds strong support in our previous cases, the Court of Appeals' commendable self-restraint is not to be criticized. We have now re-examined the purposes of the exclusionary rule and the propriety of its application in cases where officers have relied on a subsequently invalidated search warrant. Our conclusion is that the rule's purposes will only rarely be served by applying it in such circumstances....

Accordingly, the judgment of the Court of Appeals is reversed.

Justice Blackmun, concurring....

Justice Brennan, with whom *Justice Marshall* joins, dissenting.

Ten years ago in *United States v. Calandra* ... (1974), I expressed the fear that the Court's decision "may signal that a majority of my colleagues have positioned themselves to reopen the door [to evidence secured by official lawlessness] still further and abandon altogether the exclusionary rule in search-and-seizure cases." ... Since then, in case after case, I have witnessed the Court's gradual but determined strangulation of the rule. It now appears that the Court's victory over the Fourth Amendment is complete....

The Court seeks to justify this result on the ground that the "costs" of adhering to the exclusionary rule in cases like those before us exceed the "benefits." But the language of deterrence and of cost/benefit analysis, if used indiscriminately, can have a narcotic effect. It creates an illusion of technical precision and ineluctability. It suggests that not only constitutional principle but also empirical data supports the majority's result. When the Court's analysis is examined carefully, however, it is clear that we have not been treated to an honest assessment of the merits of the exclusionary rule, but have instead been drawn into a curious world where the "costs" of excluding illegally obtained evidence loom to exaggerated heights and where the "benefits" of such exclusion are made to disappear with a mere wave of the hand.

The majority ignores the fundamental constitutional importance of what is at stake here. While the machinery of law enforcement and indeed the nature of crime itself have changed dramatically since the Fourth Amendment became part of the Nation's fundamental law in 1791, what the Framers understood then remains true today—that the task of combating crime and convicting the guilty will in every era seem of such critical and pressing concern that we may be lured by the temptations of expediency into forsaking our commitment to protecting individual liberty and privacy. It was for that very reason that the Framers of the Bill of Rights insisted that law enforcement efforts be permanently and unambiguously restricted in order to preserve personal freedoms. In the constitutional scheme they ordained, the sometimes unpopular task of ensuring that the government's enforcement efforts remain within the strict boundaries fixed by the Fourth Amendment was entrusted to the courts.... If those independent tribunals lose their resolve, however, as the Court has done today, and give way to the seductive call of expediency, the vital guarantees of the Fourth Amendment are reduced to nothing more than a "form of words." ....

A proper understanding of the broad purposes sought to be served by the Fourth Amendment demonstrates that the principles embodied in the exclusionary rule rest upon a far firmer constitutional foundation than the shifting sands of the Court's deterrence rationale. But even if I were to accept the Court's chosen method of analyzing the question posed by these cases, I would still conclude that the Court's decision cannot be justified....

At bottom, the Court's decision turns on the proposition that the exclusionary rule is merely a "judicially created remedy designed to safeguard Fourth Amendment rights generally through its deterrent effect, rather than a personal constitutional right." ... The germ of that idea is found in *Wolf v. Colorado*, ... and although I had thought that such a narrow conception of the rule had been forever put to rest by our decision in *Mapp v. Ohio*, ... it has been revived by the present Court and reaches full flower with today's decision. The essence of this view, as expressed initially in the *Calandra* opinion and as reiterated today, is that the sole "purpose of the Fourth Amendment is to prevent unreasonable governmental intrusions into the privacy of one's person, house, papers, or effects. The wrong condemned is the unjustified governmental invasion of these areas of an individual's life. That wrong ... is *fully* accomplished by the original search without probable cause." ... This reading of the Amendment implies that its proscriptions are directed solely at those government agents, who may actually invade an individual's constitutionally protected privacy. The courts are not subject to any direct constitutional duty to exclude illegally obtained evidence, because the question of the admissibility of such evidence is not addressed by the Amendment. This view of the scope of the Amendment relegates the judiciary to the periphery. Because the only constitutionally cognizable injury has already been "fully accomplished" by the police by the time a case comes before the courts, the Constitution is not itself violated if the judge decides to admit the tainted evidence. Indeed, the most the judge *can* do is wring his hands and hope that perhaps by excluding such evidence he can deter future transgressions by the police.

Such a reading appears plausible, because, as critics of the exclusionary rule never tire of repeating, the Fourth Amendment makes no express provision of the exclusion of evidence secured in violation of its commands. A short answer to this claim, of course, is that many of the Constitution's most vital imperatives are stated in general terms and the task of giving meaning to these precepts is therefore left to subsequent judicial decision making in the context of concrete cases....

(Continued)

A more direct answer may be supplied by recognizing that the Amendment, like other provisions of the Bill of Rights, restrains the power of the government as a whole; it does not specify only a particular agency and exempt all others. The judiciary is responsible, no less than the executive, for ensuring that constitutional rights are respected....

It is difficult to give any meaning at all to the limitations imposed by the Amendment if they are read to proscribe only certain conduct by the police but to allow other agents of the same government to take advantage of evidence secured by the police in violation of its requirements. The Amendment therefore must be read to condemn not only the initial unconstitutional invasion of privacy—which is done, after all, for the purpose of securing evidence—but also the subsequent use of any evidence so obtained.

The Court evades this principle by drawing an artificial line between the constitutional rights and responsibilities that are engaged by actions of the police and those that are engaged when a defendant appears before the courts. According to the Court, the substantive protections of the Fourth Amendment are wholly exhausted at the moment when police unlawfully invade an individual's privacy and thus no substantive force remains to those protections at the time of trial when the government seeks to use evidence obtained by the police.

I submit that such a crabbed reading of the Fourth Amendment casts aside the teaching of those Justices who first formulated the exclusionary rule, and rests ultimately on an impoverished understanding of judicial responsibility in our constitutional scheme. For my part, "[t]he right of the people to be secure in their persons, houses, papers and effects, against unreasonable searches and seizures" comprises a personal right to exclude all evidence secured by means of unreasonable searches and seizures. The right to be free from the initial invasion of privacy and the right of exclusion are coordinate components of the central embracing right to be free from unreasonable searches and seizures....

Justice Stevens, dissenting....

MIRANDA v. ARIZONA
384 U.S. 436; 86 S.Ct. 1602; 16 L.Ed. 2d 694 (1966)
Vote: 5-4

In one of the most important criminal justice decisions of the Warren era, the Court imposes procedural safeguards on custodial police interrogations.

Mr. Chief Justice Warren delivered the opinion of the Court.

The cases before us raise questions which go to the roots of our concepts of American criminal jurisprudence: the restraints society must observe consistent with the Federal Constitution in prosecuting individuals for crime. More specifically, we deal with the admissibility of statements obtained from an individual who is subjected to custodial police interrogation and the necessity for procedures which assure that the individual is accorded his privilege under the Fifth Amendment to the Constitution not to be compelled to incriminate himself.

We dealt with certain phases of this problem recently in *Escobedo v. Illinois* ... (1964). We start here, as we did in *Escobedo*, with the premise that our holding is not an innovation in our jurisprudence, but is an application of principles long recognized and applied in other settings. We have undertaken a thorough re-examination of the *Escobedo* decision and the principles it announced, and we reaffirm it. That case was but an explication of basic rights that are enshrined in our Constitution—that "No person ... shall be compelled in any criminal case to be a witness against himself," and that "the accused shall ... have the Assistance of Counsel"—rights which were put in jeopardy in that case through official overbearing. These precious rights were fixed in our Constitution only after centuries of persecution and struggle. And in the words of Chief Justice Marshall, they were secured "for ages to come, and ... designed to approach immortality as nearly as human institutions can approach it." ...

Our holding will be spelled out with some specificity in the pages which follow but briefly stated it is this: the prosecution may not use statements, whether exculpatory or inculpatory, stemming from custodial interrogation of the defendant unless it demonstrates the use of procedural safeguards effective to secure the privilege against self-incrimination. By custodial interrogation, we mean questioning initiated by law enforcement officers after a person has been taken into custody or otherwise deprived of his freedom of action in any significant way. As for the procedural safeguards to be employed, unless other fully effective means are devised to inform accused persons of their right of silence and to assure a continuous opportunity to exercise it, the following measures are required. Prior to any questioning, the person must be warned that he has a right to remain silent, that any statement he does make may be used as evidence against him, and that he has a right to the presence of an attorney, either retained or appointed. The defendant may waive effectuation of these rights, provided the waiver is made voluntarily, knowingly and intelligently. If, however, he indicates in any manner and at any stage of the process that he wishes to consult with an attorney before speaking there can be no questioning. Likewise, if the individual is alone and indicates in any manner that he does not wish to be interrogated, the police may not question him. The mere fact that he may have answered some questions or volunteered some statements on his own does not deprive him of the right to refrain from answering any further inquiries until he has consulted with an attorney and thereafter consents to be questioned.

The constitutional issue we decide … is the admissibility of statements obtained from a defendant questioned while in custody or otherwise deprived of his freedom of action in any significant way. In each, the defendant was questioned by police officers, detectives, or a prosecuting attorney in a room in which he was cut off from the outside world. In none of these cases was the defendant given a full and effective warning of his rights at the outset of the interrogation process. In all the cases, the questioning elicited oral admissions, and in three of them, signed statements as well which were admitted at their trials. They all thus share salient features—*incommunicado* interrogation of individuals in a police-dominated atmosphere, resulting in self-incriminating statements without full warnings of constitutional rights.

An understanding of the nature and setting of this in-custody interrogation is essential to our decisions today. The difficulty in depicting what transpires at such interrogations stems from the fact that in this country they have largely taken place *incommunicado*. From extensive factual studies undertaken in the early 1930s, including the famous Wickersham Report to Congress by a Presidential Commission, it is clear that police violence and the "third degree" flourished at that time. In a series of cases decided by this Court long after these studies, the police resorted to physical brutality—beating, hanging, whipping—and to sustained and protracted questioning *incommunicado* in order to extort confessions. The Commission on Civil Rights in 1961 found much evidence to indicate that "some policemen still resort to physical force to obtain confessions." The use of physical brutality and violence is not, unfortunately, relegated to the past or to any part of the country. Only recently in Kings County, New York, the police brutally beat, kicked and placed lighted cigarette butts on the back of a potential witness under interrogation for the purpose of securing a statement incriminating a third party.…

The examples given above are undoubtedly the exception now, but they are sufficiently widespread to be the object of concern. Unless a proper limitation upon custodial interrogation is achieved—such as these decisions will advance—there can be no assurance that practices of this nature will be eradicated in the foreseeable future.

Again we stress that the modern practice of in-custody interrogation is psychologically rather than physically oriented. Interrogation still takes place in privacy. Privacy results in secrecy and this in turn results in a gap in our knowledge as to what in fact goes on in the interrogation rooms. A valuable source of information about present police practices, however, may be found in various police manuals and texts which document procedures employed with success in the past, and which recommended various other effective tactics. These texts are used by law enforcement agencies themselves as guides. It should be noted that these texts professedly present the most enlightened and effective means presently used to obtain statements through custodial interrogation. By considering these texts and other data, it is possible to describe procedures observed and noted around the country.

Even without employing brutality, the "third degree" or the specific strategems described above, the very fact of custodial interrogation exacts a heavy toll on individual liberty and trades on the weakness of individuals.

In the cases before us today, given this background, we concern ourselves primarily with this interrogation atmosphere and the evils it can bring.

(Continued)

In these cases, we might not find the defendants' statements to have been involuntary in traditional terms. Our concern for adequate safeguards to protect precious Fifth Amendment rights is, of course, not lessened in the slightest. In each of the cases, the defendant was thrust into an unfamiliar atmosphere and run through menacing police interrogation procedures. The potentiality for compulsion is forcefully apparent, for example, in *Miranda*, where the indigent Mexican defendant was a seriously disturbed individual with pronounced sexual fantasies....

It is obvious that such an interrogation environment is created for no purpose other than to subjugate the individual to the will of his examiner. This atmosphere carries its own badge of intimidation.... The current practice of *incommunicado* interrogation is at odds with one of our Nation's most cherished principles—that the individual may not be compelled to incriminate himself. Unless adequate protective devices are employed to dispel the compulsion inherent in custodial surroundings, no statement obtained from the defendant can truly be the product of his free choice.

From the foregoing, we can readily perceive an intimate connection between the privilege against self-incrimination and police custodial questioning. It is fitting to turn to history and precedent underlying the Self-incrimination Clause to determine its applicability in this situation.

We sometimes forget how long it has taken to establish the privilege against self-incrimination, the sources from which it came and the fervor with which it was defended. Its roots go back into ancient times.

As a "noble principle often transcends its origins," the privilege has come rightfully to be recognized in part as an individual's substantive right, a "right to a private enclave where he may lead a private life. That right is the hallmark of our democracy."... We have recently noted that the privilege against self-incrimination—the essential mainstay of our adversary system—is founded on a complex of values.... All these policies point to one overriding thought: the constitutional foundation underlying the privilege is the respect a government—state or federal—must accord to the dignity and integrity of its citizens.

We are satisfied that all the principles embodied in the privilege apply to informal compulsion exerted by law enforcement officers during in-custody questioning. An individual swept from familiar surroundings into police custody, surrounded by antagonistic forces, and subjected to the techniques of persuasion described above cannot be otherwise than under compulsion to speak. As a practical matter, the compulsion to speak in the isolated setting of the police station may well be greater than in courts or other official investigations, where there are often impartial observers to guard against intimidation or trickery.

The presence of counsel, in all the cases before us today, would be the adequate protective device necessary to make the process of police interrogation conform to the dictates of the privilege. His presence would insure that statements made in the government-established atmosphere are not the product of compulsion.

It is impossible for us to foresee the potential alternatives for protecting the privilege which might be devised by Congress or the States in the exercise of their creative rulemaking capacities. Therefore we cannot say that the Constitution necessarily requires adherence to any particular solution for the inherent compulsions of the interrogation process as it is presently conducted. Our decision in no way creates a constitutional strait-jacket which will handicap sound efforts at reform, nor is it intended to have this effect. We encourage Congress and the States to continue their laudable search for increasingly effective ways of protecting the rights of the individual while promoting efficient enforcement of our criminal laws.

A recurrent argument made in these cases is that society's need for interrogation outweighs the privilege. This argument is not unfamiliar to this Court....

In announcing these principles, we are not unmindful of the burdens which law enforcement officials must bear, often under trying circumstances. We also fully recognize the obligation of all citizens to aid in enforcing the criminal laws. This Court, while protecting individual rights, has always given ample latitude to law enforcement agencies in the legitimate exercise of their duties. The limit we have placed on the interrogation process should not constitute an undue interference with a proper system of law enforcement. As we have noted, our decision does not in any way preclude police from carrying out their traditional investigatory functions. Although confessions may play an important role in some convictions, the cases before us present graphic examples of the overstatement of the "need" for confessions.

Therefore, in accordance with the foregoing, the judgment of the Supreme Court of Arizona ... [is] reversed....

Mr. Justice Harlan, with whom ***Mr. Justice Stewart*** and ***Mr. Justice White*** join, dissenting....

Mr. Justice White, with whom ***Mr. Justice Harlan*** and ***Mr. Justice Stewart*** join, dissenting.

... The obvious underpinning of the Court's decision is a deep-seated distrust of all confessions. As the Court declares that the accused may not be interrogated without counsel present, absent a waiver of the right to counsel, and as the Court all but admonishes the lawyer to advise the accused to remain silent, the result adds up to a judicial judgment that evidence from the accused should not be used against him in any way, whether compelled or not. This is the not so subtle overtone of the opinion—that it is inherently wrong for the police to gather evidence from the accused himself. And this is precisely the nub of this dissent. I see nothing wrong or immoral, and certainly nothing unconstitutional, in the police's asking a suspect whom they have reasonable cause to arrest whether or not he killed his wife or in confronting him with the evidence on which the arrest was based, at least where he has been plainly advised that he may remain completely silent...

The rule announced today will measurably weaken the ability of the criminal law to perform these tasks. It is a deliberate calculus to prevent interrogations, to reduce the incidence of confessions and pleas of guilty and to increase the number of trials....

In some unknown number of cases the Court's rule will return a killer, a rapist or other criminal to the streets and to the environment which produced him, to repeat his crime whenever it pleases him. As a consequence, there will not be a gain, but a loss, in human dignity. The real concern is not the unfortunate consequences of this new decision on the criminal law as an abstract, disembodied series of authoritative proscriptions, but the impact on those who rely on the public authority for protection and who without it can only engage in violent self-help with guns, knives and the help of their neighbors similarly inclined. There is, of course, a saving factor: the next victims are uncertain, unnamed and unrepresented in this case.

Nor can this decision do other than have a corrosive effect on the criminal law as an effective device to prevent crime. A major component in its effectiveness in this regard is its swift and sure enforcement. The easier it is to get away with rape and murder, the less the deterrent effect on those who are inclined to attempt it. This is still good common sense. If it were not, we should posthaste liquidate the whole law enforcement establishment as a useless, misguided effort to control human conduct.

Much of the trouble with the Court's new rule is that it will operate indiscriminately in all criminal cases, regardless of the severity of the crime or the circumstances involved. It applies to every defendant, whether the professional criminal or one committing a crime of momentary passion who is not part and parcel of organized crime. It will slow down the investigation and the apprehension of confederates in those cases where time is of the essence, such as kidnapping, those involving the national security, and some of those involving organized crime. In the latter context the lawyer who arrives may also be the lawyer for the defendant's colleagues and can be relied upon to insure that no breach of the organization's security takes place even though the accused may feel that the best thing he can do is to cooperate.

At the same time, the Court's *per se* approach may not be justified on the ground that it provides a "bright line" permitting the authorities to judge in advance whether interrogation may safely be pursued without jeopardizing the admissibility of any information obtained as a consequence. Nor can it be claimed that judicial time and effort, assuming that is a relevant consideration, will be conserved because of the ease of application of the new rule. Today's decision leaves open such questions as whether the accused was in custody, whether his statements were spontaneous or the product of interrogation, whether the accused has effectively waived his rights, and whether nontestimonial evidence introduced at trial is the fruit of statements made during a prohibited interrogation, all of which are certain to prove productive of uncertainty during investigation and litigation during prosecution. For all these reasons, if further restrictions on police interrogation are desirable at this time, a more flexible approach makes much more sense than the Court's constitutional straitjacket which forecloses more discriminating treatment by legislative or rule-making pronouncements....

Mr. Justice Clark, dissenting....

DICKERSON v. UNITED STATES
530 U.S. 428, 120 S.Ct. 2326, 147 L.Ed.2d 405 (2000)
Vote: 7-2

In this case, the Supreme Court reconsiders its 1966 decision in Miranda v. Arizona. The Court also reviews a statute Congress enacted following Miranda that provided that the admissibility of incriminating statements by suspects should depend only on whether or not they were made voluntarily.

Chief Justice Rehnquist delivered the opinion of the Court.

In *Miranda v. Arizona* … (1966), we held that certain warnings must be given before a suspect's statement made during custodial interrogation could be admitted in evidence. In the wake of that decision, Congress enacted 18 U.S.C. § 3501, which in essence laid down a rule that the admissibility of such statements should turn only on whether or not they were voluntarily made. We hold that *Miranda*, being a constitutional decision of this Court, may not be in effect overruled by an Act of Congress, and we decline to overrule *Miranda* ourselves. We therefore hold that *Miranda* and its progeny in this Court govern the admissibility of statements made during custodial interrogation in both state and federal courts.

Petitioner Dickerson was indicted for bank robbery, conspiracy to commit bank robbery, and using a firearm in the course of committing a crime of violence, all in violation of the applicable provisions of Title 18 of the United States Code. Before trial, Dickerson moved to suppress a statement he had made at a Federal Bureau of Investigation field office, on the grounds that he had not received "*Miranda* warnings" before being interrogated. The District Court granted his motion to suppress, and the Government took an interlocutory appeal to the United States Court of Appeals for the Fourth Circuit. That court, by a divided vote, reversed the District Court's suppression order. It agreed with the District Court's conclusion that petitioner had not received *Miranda* warnings before making his statement. But it went on to hold that § 3501, which in effect makes the admissibility of statements such as Dickerson's turn solely on whether they were made voluntarily, was satisfied in this case. It then concluded that our decision in *Miranda* was not a constitutional holding, and that

therefore Congress could by statute have the final say on the question of admissibility….

Because of the importance of the questions raised by the Court of Appeals' decision, we granted certiorari … and now reverse….

Two years after *Miranda* was decided, Congress enacted § 3501. That section provides, in relevant part:

(a) In any criminal prosecution brought by the United States or by the District of Columbia, a confession … shall be admissible in evidence if it is voluntarily given. Before such confession is received in evidence, the trial judge shall, out of the presence of the jury, determine any issue as to voluntariness. If the trial judge determines that the confession was voluntarily made it shall be admitted in evidence and the trial judge shall permit the jury to hear relevant evidence on the issue of voluntariness and shall instruct the jury to give such weight to the confession as the jury feels it deserves under all the circumstances.

(b) The trial judge in determining the issue of voluntariness shall take into consideration all the circumstances surrounding the giving of the confession, including (1) the time elapsing between arrest and arraignment of the defendant making the confession, if it was made after arrest and before arraignment, (2) whether such defendant knew the nature of the offense with which he was charged or of which he was suspected at the time of making the confession, (3) whether or not such defendant was advised or knew that he was not required to make any statement and that any such statement could be used against him, (4) whether or not such defendant had been advised prior to questioning of his right to the assistance of counsel, and (5) whether or not such defendant was without the assistance of counsel when questioned and when giving such confession….

Given § 3501's express designation of voluntariness as the touchstone of admissibility, its omission of any warning requirement, and the instruction for trial courts to consider a nonexclusive list of factors relevant to the circumstances of a confession, we agree with the Court of Appeals that Congress intended by its enactment to overrule *Miranda*…. Because of the obvious conflict between our decision in *Miranda* and § 3501, we must address whether Congress has constitutional authority to thus supersede *Miranda*. If Congress has such authority, § 3501's totality-of-the-circumstances approach must prevail over *Miranda's* requirement of warnings; if not, that section must yield to *Mirandas* more specific requirements.

The law in this area is clear. This Court has supervisory authority over the federal courts, and we may use that authority to prescribe rules of evidence and procedure that are binding in those tribunals.... However, the power to judicially create and enforce nonconstitutional "rules of procedure and evidence for the federal courts exists only in the absence of a relevant Act of Congress." ... Congress retains the ultimate authority to modify or set aside any judicially created rules of evidence and procedure that are not required by the Constitution....

But Congress may not legislatively supersede our decisions interpreting and applying the Constitution. ... This case therefore turns on whether the *Miranda* Court announced a constitutional rule or merely exercised its supervisory authority to regulate evidence in the absence of congressional direction. Recognizing this point, the Court of Appeals surveyed *Miranda* and its progeny to determine the constitutional status of the *Miranda* decision.... Relying on the fact that we have created several exceptions to *Miranda's* warnings requirement and that we have repeatedly referred to the *Miranda* warnings as "prophylactic," ... the Court of Appeals concluded that the protections announced in *Miranda are* not constitutionally required....

We disagree with the Court of Appeals' conclusion, although we concede that there is language in some of our opinions that supports the view taken by that court. But first and foremost of the factors on the other side—that *Miranda* is a constitutional decision—is that both *Miranda* and two of its companion cases applied the rule to proceedings in state courts—to wit, Arizona, California, and New York.... Since that time, we have consistently applied *Miranda's* rule to prosecutions arising in state courts.... It is beyond dispute that we do not hold a supervisory power over the courts of the several States.... With respect to proceedings in state courts, our "authority is limited to enforcing the commands of the United States Constitution." ...

The *Miranda* opinion itself begins by stating that the Court granted certiorari "to explore some facets of the problems ... of applying the privilege against self-incrimination to in-custody interrogation, *and to give concrete constitutional guidelines for law enforcement agencies and courts to follow*" (emphasis added).

In fact, the majority opinion is replete with statements indicating that the majority thought it was announcing a constitutional rule. Indeed, the Court's ultimate conclusion was that the unwarned confessions obtained in the four cases before the Court in *Miranda* "were obtained from the defendant under circumstances that did not meet constitutional standards for protection of the privilege." ...

The Court of Appeals also relied on the fact that we have, after our *Miranda* decision, made exceptions from its rule in cases such as *New York v. Quarles* (1984), and *Harris v. New York* (1971).... But we have also broadened the application of the *Miranda* doctrine in cases such as *Doyle v. Ohio* (1976), and *Arizona v. Roberson* (1988). These decisions illustrate the principle—not that *Miranda* is not a constitutional rule—but that no constitutional rule is immutable. No court laying down a general rule can possibly foresee the various circumstances in which counsel will seek to apply it, and the sort of modifications represented by these cases are as much a normal part of constitutional law as the original decision....

As an alternative argument for sustaining the Court of Appeals' decision, the court-invited *amicus curiae* contends that the section complies with the requirement that a legislative alternative to *Miranda* be equally as effective in preventing coerced confessions. ... We agree with the *amicus'* contention that there are more remedies available for abusive police conduct than there were at the time *Miranda* was decided, ... to hold that a suspect may bring a federal cause of action under the Due Process Clause for police misconduct during custodial interrogation. But we do not agree that these additional measures supplement § 3501's protections sufficiently to meet the constitutional minimum. *Miranda* requires procedures that will warn a suspect in custody of his right to remain silent and which will assure the suspect that the exercise of that right will be honored.... As discussed above, § 3501 explicitly eschews a requirement of pre-interrogation warnings in favor of an approach that looks to the administration of such warnings as only one factor in determining the voluntariness of a suspect's confession. The additional remedies cited by *amicus* do not, in our view, render them, together with § 3501 an adequate substitute for the warnings required by *Miranda*.

The dissent argues that it is judicial overreaching for this Court to hold § 3501 unconstitutional unless we hold that the *Miranda* warnings are required by the

(Continued)

Constitution, in the sense that nothing else will suffice to satisfy constitutional requirements.... But we need not go farther than *Miranda* to decide this case. In *Miranda*, the Court noted that reliance on the traditional totality-of-the-circumstances test raised a risk of overlooking an involuntary custodial confession, ... a risk that the Court found unacceptably great when the confession is offered in the case in chief to prove guilt. The Court therefore concluded that something more than the totality test was necessary.... As discussed above, § 3501 reinstates the totality test as sufficient. Section 3501 therefore cannot be sustained *if Miranda* is to remain the law.

Whether or not we would agree with *Miranda's* reasoning and its resulting rule, were we addressing the issue in the first instance, the principles of *stare decisis* weigh heavily against overruling it now....

... *Miranda* has become embedded in routine police practice to the point where the warnings have become part of our national culture.... While we have overruled our precedents when subsequent cases have undermined their doctrinal underpinnings, ... we do not believe that this has happened to the *Miranda* decision...

The disadvantage of the *Miranda* rule is that statements which may be by no means involuntary, made by a defendant who is aware of his "rights," may nonetheless be excluded and a guilty defendant go free as a result. But experience suggests that the totality-of-the-circumstances test which § 3501 seeks to revive is more difficult than *Miranda* for law enforcement officers to conform to, and for courts to apply in a consistent manner....

In sum, we conclude that *Miranda* announced a constitutional rule that Congress may not supersede legislatively. Following the rule of *stare decisis*, we decline to overrule *Miranda* ourselves. The judgment of the Court of Appeals is therefore *Reversed*.

Mr. Justice Scalia, with whom **Mr. Justice Thomas** joins, dissenting.

Those to whom judicial decisions are an unconnected series of judgments that produce either favored or disfavored results will doubtless greet today's decision as a paragon of moderation, since it declines to overrule *Miranda v. Arizona* (1966). Those who understand the judicial process will appreciate that today's decision is not a reaffirmation of *Miranda*, but a radical revision of the most significant element of *Miranda* (as of all cases): the rationale that gives it a permanent place in our jurisprudence.

Marbury v. Madison ... held that an Act of Congress will not be enforced by the courts if what it prescribes violates the Constitution of the United States. That was the basis on which *Miranda* was decided. One will search today's opinion in vain, however, for a statement (surely simple enough to make) that what 18 U.S.C. § 3501 prescribes—the use at trial of a voluntary confession, even when a *Miranda* warning or its equivalent has failed to be given—violates the Constitution. The reason the statement does not appear is not only (and perhaps not so much) that it would be absurd, inasmuch as § 3501 excludes from trial precisely what the Constitution excludes from trial, viz., compelled confessions; but also that Justices whose votes are needed to compose today's majority are on record as believing that a violation of *Miranda* is *not* a violation of the Constitution.... And so, to justify today's agreed-upon result, the Court must adopt a significant *new*, if not entirely comprehensible, principle of constitutional law.

As the Court chooses to describe that principle, statutes of Congress can be disregarded, not only when what they prescribe violates the Constitution, but when what they prescribe contradicts a decision of this Court that "announced a constitutional rule." ... As I shall discuss in some detail, the only thing that can possibly mean in the context of this case is that this Court has the power, not merely to apply the Constitution but to expand it, imposing what it regards as useful "prophylactic" restrictions upon Congress and the States. That is an immense and frightening antidemocratic power, and it does not exist.

It takes only a small step to bring today's opinion out of the realm of power-judging and into the mainstream of legal reasoning: The Court need only go beyond its carefully couched iterations that "*Miranda* is a constitutional decision," ... that "*Miranda* is constitutionally based," ... that *Miranda* has "constitutional underpinnings," ... and come out and say quite clearly: "We reaffirm today that custodial interrogation that is not preceded by *Miranda* warnings or their equivalent violates the Constitution of the United States." It cannot say that, because a majority of the Court does not believe it. The Court therefore acts in plain violation of the Constitution when it denies effect to this Act of Congress....

... [W]hile I agree with the Court that § 3501 cannot be upheld without also concluding that *Miranda* represents an illegitimate exercise of our authority to review state-court judgments, I do not share the Court's hesitation in reaching that conclusion. For while the Court is also correct that the doctrine of *stare decisis* demands some "special justification" for a departure from longstanding precedent—even precedent of the constitutional variety—that criterion is more than met here.

Neither am I persuaded by the argument for retaining *Miranda* that touts its supposed workability as compared with the totality-of-the-circumstances test it purported to replace. *Miranda's* proponents cite *ad nauseam* the fact that the Court was called upon to make difficult and subtle distinctions in applying the "voluntariness" test in some 30-odd due process "coerced confessions" cases in the 30 years between *Brown v. Mississippi* (1936), and *Miranda*. It is not immediately apparent, however, that the judicial burden has been eased by the "bright-line" rules adopted in *Miranda*. In fact, in the 34 years since *Miranda* was decided, this Court has been called upon to decide nearly 60 cases involving a host of *Miranda* issues, most of them predicted with remarkable prescience by Justice White in his *Miranda* dissent....

Moreover, it is not clear why the Court thinks that the "totality-of-the-circumstances test ... is more difficult than *Miranda* for law enforcement officers to conform to, and for courts to apply in a consistent manner." ...

Finally, I am not convinced by petitioner's argument that *Miranda* should be preserved because the decision occupies a special place in the "public's consciousness." ... As far as I am aware, the public is not under the illusion that we are infallible. I see little harm in admitting that we made a mistake in taking away from the people the ability to decide for themselves what protections (beyond those required by the Constitution) are reasonably affordable in the criminal investigatory process. And I see much to be gained by reaffirming for the people the wonderful reality that they govern themselves—which means that "[t]he powers not delegated to the United States by the Constitution" that the people adopted, "nor prohibited ... to the States" by that Constitution, "are reserved to the States respectively, or to the people." ...

Today's judgment converts *Miranda* from a milestone of judicial overreaching into the very Cheops' Pyramid (or perhaps the Sphinx would be a better analogue) of judicial arrogance. In imposing its Court-made code upon the States, the original opinion at least *asserted* that it was demanded by the Constitution. Today's decision does not pretend that it is—and yet *still* asserts the right to impose it against the will of the people's representatives in Congress. Far from believing that *stare decisis* compels this result, I believe we cannot allow to remain on the books even a celebrated decision—*especially* a celebrated decision—that has come to stand for the proposition that the Supreme Court has power to impose extra-constitutional constraints upon Congress and the States. This is not the system that was established by the Framers, or that would be established by any sane supporter of government by the people.

I dissent from today's decision, and, until § 3501 is repealed, will continue to apply it in all cases where there has been a sustainable finding that the defendant's confession was voluntary.

POWELL v. ALABAMA
287 U.S. 45; 53 S.Ct. 55; 77 L.Ed. 158 (1932)
Vote: 7-2

In this now-classic case, the Court reviews the convictions of eight young African-American men who had been sentenced to death by an Alabama court for allegedly raping two white women.

Mr. Justice Sutherland delivered the opinion of the Court.

... The record shows that on the day when the offense is said to have been committed, these defendants, together with a number of other negroes, were upon a freight train on its way through Alabama. On the same train were seven white boys and two white girls. A fight took place between the negroes and the white boys, in the course of which the white boys, with the exception of one named Gilley, were thrown off the train. A message was sent ahead, reporting the fight and asking that every negro be gotten off the train. The participants in the fight, and the two girls, were in an open gondola car. The two girls

(Continued)

testified that each of them was assaulted by six different negroes in turn, and they identified the seven defendants as having been among the number. None of the white boys was called to testify, with the exception of Gilley, who was called in rebuttal.

Before the train reached Scottsboro, Alabama, a sheriff's posse seized the defendants and two other negroes. Both girls and the negroes then were taken to Scottsboro, the county seat. Word of their coming and of the alleged assault had preceded them, and they were met at Scottsboro by a large crowd. It does not sufficiently appear that the defendants were seriously threatened with, or that they were actually in danger of, mob violence; but it does appear that the attitude of the community was one of great hostility. The sheriff thought it necessary to call for the militia to assist in safeguarding the prisoners. Chief Justice Anderson pointed out in his opinion that every step taken from the arrest and arraignment to the sentence was accompanied by the military. Soldiers took the defendants to Gadsden for safekeeping, brought them back to Scottsboro for arraignment, returned them to Gadsden for safekeeping while awaiting trial, escorted them to Scottsboro for trial a few days later, and guarded the courthouse and grounds at every stage of the proceedings. It is perfectly apparent that the proceedings, from beginning to end, took place in an atmosphere of tense, hostile and excited public sentiment. During the entire time, the defendants were closely confined or were under military guard. The record does not disclose their ages, except that one of them was nineteen; but the record clearly indicates that most, if not all, of them were youthful, and they are constantly referred to as "the boys." They were ignorant and illiterate. All of them were residents of other states, where alone members of their families or friends resided.

However guilty defendants, upon due inquiry might prove to have been, they were, until convicted, presumed to be innocent. It was the duty of the court having their cases in charge to see that they were denied no necessary incident of a fair trial. With any error of the state court involving alleged contravention of the state statutes or constitution we, of course, have nothing to do. The sole inquiry which we are permitted to make is whether the federal Constitution was contravened ... and as to that, we confine ourselves, as already suggested, to the inquiry whether the defendants were in substance denied the right to counsel, and if so, whether such denial infringes the Due Process Clause of the Fourteenth Amendment.

First. The record shows that immediately upon the return of the indictment defendants were arraigned and pleaded not guilty. Apparently they were not asked whether they had, or were able to employ, counsel, or wished to have counsel appointed; or whether they had friends or relatives who might assist in that regard if communicated with....

It is hardly necessary to say that the right to counsel being conceded, a defendant should be afforded a fair opportunity to secure counsel of his own choice. Not only was that not done here, but such designation of counsel as was attempted was either so indefinite or so close upon the trial as to amount to a denial of effective and substantial aid in that regard. This will be amply demonstrated by a brief review of the record.

April 6, six days after indictment, the trial began. When the first case was called, the court inquired whether the parties were ready for trial. The state's attorney replied that he was ready to proceed. No one answered for the defendants or appeared to represent or defend them. Mr. Roddy, a Tennessee lawyer, not a member of the local bar, addressed the court, saying that he had not been employed, but that people who were interested had spoken to him about the case. He was asked by the court whether he intended to appear for the defendants, and answered that he would like to appear along with counsel that the court might appoint. The record then proceeds:

The Court: If you appear for these defendants, then I will not appoint counsel: if local counsel are willing to appear and assist you under the circumstances all right, but I will not appoint them.

Mr. Roddy: Your Honor has appointed counsel, is that correct?

The Court: I appointed all the members of the bar for the purpose of arraigning the defendants and then of course I anticipated them to continue to help them if no counsel appears.

Mr. Roddy: Then I don't appear then as counsel but I do want to stay in and not be ruled out in this case.

The Court: Of course I would not do that—

Mr. Roddy: I just appear here through the courtesy of Your Honor.

The Court: Of course I give you that right; ...

...[T]his action of the trial judge in respect of appointment of counsel was little more than an expansive gesture, imposing no substantial or definite obligation upon any one ... during perhaps the most critical period of the proceedings against these defendants, that is to say, from the time of their arraignment until the beginning of their trial, when consultation, thoroughgoing investigation and preparation were vitally important, the defendants did not have the aid of counsel in any real sense, although they were as much entitled to such aid during that period as at the trial itself.…

Nor do we think the situation was helped by what occurred on the morning of the trial. At that time, Mr. Roddy stated to the court that he did not appear as counsel, but that he would like to appear along with counsel that the court might appoint; that he had not been given an opportunity to prepare the case; that he was not familiar with the procedure in Alabama, but merely came down as a friend of the people who were interested; that he thought the boys would be better off if he should step entirely out of the case. Mr. Moody, a member of the local bar, expressed a willingness to help Mr. Roddy in anything he would do under the circumstances. To this the court responded, "All right, all the lawyers that will; of course I would not require a lawyer to appear if—." And Mr. Moody continued, "I am willing to do that for him as a member of the bar; I will go ahead and help do anything I can do." With this dubious understanding, the trials immediately proceeded. The defendants, young, ignorant, illiterate, surrounded by hostile sentiment, haled back and forth under guard of soldiers, charged with an atrocious crime regarded with especial horror in the community where they were to be tried, were thus put in peril of their lives within a few moments after counsel for the first time charged with any degree of responsibility began to represent them.

It is not enough to assume that counsel thus precipitated into the case thought there was no defense, and exercised their best judgment in proceeding to trial without preparation. Neither they nor the court could say what a prompt and thorough-going investigation might disclose as to the facts. No attempt was made to investigate. No opportunity to do so was given. Defendants were immediately hurried to trial. Chief Justice Anderson, after disclaiming any intention to criticize harshly counsel who attempted to represent defendants at the trials, said: "…The record indicates that the appearance was rather *pro forma* than zealous and active.…" Under the circumstances disclosed, we hold that defendants were not accorded the right of counsel in any substantial sense. To decide otherwise, would simply be to ignore actualities.…

The prompt disposition of criminal cases is to be commended and encouraged. But in reaching that result a defendant, charged with a serious crime, must not be stripped of his right to have sufficient time to advise with counsel and prepare his defense. To do that is not to proceed promptly in the calm spirit of regulated justice but to go forward with the haste of the mob.…

Second. The Constitution of Alabama provides that in all criminal prosecutions the accused shall enjoy the right to have the assistance of counsel; and a state statute requires the court in a capital case, where the defendant is unable to employ counsel, to appoint counsel for him. The state supreme court held that these provisions had not been infringed.… The question, however, which it is our duty, and within our power to decide, is whether the denial of the assistance of counsel contravenes the Due Process Clause of the Fourteenth Amendment to the federal Constitution.

An affirmation of the right to the aid of counsel in petty offenses, and its denial in the case of crimes of the gravest character, where such aid is most needed, is so outrageous and so obviously a perversion of all sense of proportion that the rule was constantly, vigorously and sometimes passionately assailed by English statesmen and lawyers. As early as 1758, Blackstone, although recognizing that the rule was settled at common law, denounced it as not in keeping with the rest of the humane treatment of prisoners by the English law. "For upon what face of reason," he says, "can that assistance be denied to save the life of a man, which yet is allowed him in prosecutions for every petty trespass?"

…In light of the facts outlined in the forepart of this opinion—the ignorance and illiteracy of the defendants, their youth, the circumstances of public hostility, the imprisonment and the close surveillance of the defendants by the military forces, the fact that their friends and families were all in other states and communication with them necessarily difficult, and above all that they stood in deadly peril of their lives—we think the failure of the trial court to give them reasonable time and opportunity to secure counsel was a clear denial of due process.

But passing that, and assuming their inability, even if opportunity had been given, to employ counsel, as the trial court evidently did assume, we are of opinion that, under the circumstances just stated, the necessity of counsel was so vital and imperative that the failure of the trial court to make an effective appointment of counsel was likewise a denial of due process within the meaning of the Fourteenth Amendment. Whether this would be so in other criminal prosecutions, or under other circumstances, we need not determine. All that it is necessary now to decide, as we do decide, is that in a capital case, where the defendant is unable to employ

(*Continued*)

counsel, and is incapable adequately of making his own defense because of ignorance, feeble-mindedness, illiteracy, or the like, it is the duty of the court, whether requested or not, to assign counsel for him as a necessary requisite of due process of law; and that duty is not discharged by an assignment at such a time or under such circumstances as to preclude the giving of effective aid in the preparation and trial of the case. To hold otherwise would be to ignore the fundamental postulate, already adverted to, "that there are certain immutable principles of justice which inhere in the very idea of free government which no member of the Union may disregard." ... In a case such as this, whatever may be the rule in other cases, the right to have counsel appointed, when necessary, is a logical corollary from the constitutional right to be heard by counsel....

The judgments must be reversed and the causes remanded for further proceedings not inconsistent with this opinion.

Mr. Justice Butler, dissenting.

If correct, the ruling that the failure of the trial court to give petitioners time and opportunity to secure counsel was denial of due process is enough, and with this the opinion should end. But the Court goes on to declare that "the failure of the trial court to make an effective appointment of counsel was likewise a denial of due process within the meaning of the Fourteenth Amendment." This is an extension of federal authority into a field hitherto occupied exclusively by the several States. Nothing before the Court calls for a consideration of the point. It was not suggested below and petitioners do not ask for its decision here. The Court, without being called upon to consider it, adjudges without a hearing an important constitutional question concerning criminal procedure in state courts.

It is a wise rule firmly established by a long course of decisions here that constitutional questions—even when properly raised and argued—are to be decided only when necessary for a determination of the rights of the parties in controversy before it....

The record wholly fails to reveal that petitioners have been deprived of any right guaranteed by the Federal Constitution, and I am of opinion that the judgment should be affirmed.

Mr. Justice McReynolds concurs in this opinion.

GIDEON v. WAINWRIGHT
372 U.S. 335; 83 S.Ct. 792; 9 L.Ed. 2d 799 (1963)
Vote: 9-0

Here, the Court considers whether state courts must as a matter of course appoint counsel to represent indigent defendants accused of felonies.

Mr. Justice Black delivered the opinion of the Court.

Petitioner was charged in a Florida State court with having broken and entered a poolroom with intent to commit a misdemeanor. This offense is a felony under Florida law. Appearing in court without funds and without a lawyer, petitioner asked the court to appoint counsel for him, whereupon the following colloquy took place:

THE COURT: *Mr. Gideon, I am sorry, but I cannot appoint Counsel to represent you in this case. Under the laws of the State of Florida, the only time the Court can appoint Counsel to represent a Defendant is when that person is charged with a capital offense. I am sorry, but I will have to deny your request to appoint Counsel to defend you in this case.*

THE DEFENDANT: *The United States Supreme Court says I am entitled to be represented by Counsel.*

Put to trial before a jury, *Gideon* conducted his defense about as well as could be expected from a layman. He made an opening statement to the jury, cross-examined the State's witnesses, presented witnesses in his own defense, declined to testify himself, and made a short argument "emphasizing his innocence to the charge contained in the Information filed in this case." The jury returned a verdict of guilty, the petitioner was sentenced to serve five years in the state prison. Later, petitioner filed in the Florida Supreme Court this habeas corpus petition attacking his conviction and sentence on the ground that the trial court's refusal to appoint counsel for him denied him rights "guaranteed by the Constitution and the Bill of Rights by the United States Government." Treating the petition for habeas corpus as properly before it, the State Supreme Court, "upon consideration thereof but without an opinion, denied all relief. Since 1942, when *Betts v. Brady* … was decided by a divided Court, the problem of a defendant's federal constitutional right to counsel in a state court has been a continuing source of controversy and litigation in both state and federal courts. To give this problem another review here, we granted certiorari. Since *Gideon* was proceeding *in forma pauperis*, we appointed counsel to represent him and requested both sides to discuss in their briefs and oral arguments the following: "Should this Court's holding in *Betts v. Brady* be reconsidered?" Since the facts and circumstances of the two cases are so nearly indistinguishable, we think the *Betts v. Brady* holding if left standing would require us to reject Gideon's claim that the Constitution guarantees him the assistance of counsel. Upon full reconsideration we conclude that *Betts v. Brady* should be overruled.

The facts upon which Betts claimed that he had been unconstitutionally denied the right to have counsel appointed to assist him are strikingly like the facts upon which *Gideon* here bases his federal constitutional claim.

The Sixth Amendment provides, "In all criminal prosecutions, the accused shall enjoy the right … to have the Assistance of Counsel for his defense." We have construed this to mean that in federal courts counsel must be provided for defendants unable to employ counsel unless the right is competently and intelligently waived. Betts argued that this right is extended to indigent defendants in state courts by the Fourteenth Amendment. In response the Court stated that, while the Sixth Amendment laid down "no rule for the conduct of the states, the question recurs whether the constraint laid by Amendment upon the national courts expresses a rule so fundamental and essential to a fair trial, and so, to due process of law, that it is made obligatory upon the States by the Fourteenth Amendment." In order to decide whether the Sixth Amendment's guarantee of counsel is of this fundamental nature, the Court in *Betts* set out and considered "[r]elevant data on the subject … afforded by constitutional and statutory provisions subsisting in the colonies and the States prior to the inclusion of the Bill of Rights in the national Constitution, and in the constitutional, legislative, and judicial history of the States to the present date." … On the basis

of this historical data the Court concluded that "appointment of counsel is not a fundamental right, essential to a fair trial." … It was for this reason the *Betts* Court refused to accept the contention that the Sixth Amendment's guarantee of counsel for indigent federal defendants was extended to or, in the words of that Court, "made obligatory upon the States by the Fourteenth Amendment." … Plainly, had the Court concluded that appointment of counsel for an indigent criminal defendant was "a fundamental right, essential to a fair trial," … it would have held that the Fourteenth Amendment requires appointment of counsel in a state court, just as the Sixth Amendment requires in a federal court.

We think the Court in *Betts* had ample precedent for acknowledging that those guarantees of the Bill of Rights which are fundamental safeguards of liberty immune from federal abridgment are equally protected against state invasion by the Due Process Clause of the Fourteenth Amendment. This same principle was recognized, explained, and applied in *Powell v. Alabama*, … a case upholding the right of counsel, where the Court held that despite sweeping language to the contrary in *Hurtado v. California*, … the Fourteenth Amendment "embraced" those "fundamental principles of liberty and justice which lie at the base of all our civil and political institutions," even though they had been "specifically dealt with in another part of the federal Constitution." … In many cases other than *Powell* and *Betts*, this Court has looked to the fundamental nature of original Bill of Rights guarantees to decide whether the Fourteenth Amendment makes them obligatory on the States.

In light of these and many other prior decisions of this Court, it is not surprising that the *Betts* Court, when faced with the contention that "one charged with crime, who is unable to obtain counsel, must be furnished counsel by the State," … conceded that "[e]xpressions in the opinions of this court lend color to the argument." … The fact is that in deciding as it did—that "appointment of counsel is not a fundamental right, essential to a fair trial" … —the Court in *Betts v. Brady* made an abrupt break with its own well-considered precedents. In returning to these old precedents, sounder we believe than the new, we but restore constitutional principles established to achieve a fair system of justice. Not only these precedents but also reason and reflection require us to recognize that in our adversary system of criminal justice, any person haled into court, who is too poor to hire a lawyer, cannot be assured a fair trial unless counsel is provided for him. This seems

(Continued)

to us to be an obvious truth. Governments, both state and federal, quite properly spend vast sums of money to establish machinery to try defendants accused of crime. Lawyers to prosecute are everywhere deemed essential to protect the public's interest in an orderly society. Similarly, there are few defendants charged with crime, few indeed, who fail to hire the best lawyers they can get to prepare and present their defenses. That government hires lawyers to prosecute and defendants who have the money hire lawyers to defend are the strongest indications of the widespread belief that lawyers in criminal courts are necessities, not luxuries. The right of one charged with crime to counsel may not be deemed fundamental and essential to fair trials in some countries, but it is in ours. From the very beginning, our state and national constitutions and laws have laid great emphasis on procedural and substantive safeguards designed to assure fair trials before impartial tribunals in which every defendant stands equal before the law.

This noble ideal cannot be realized if the poor man charged with crime has to face his accusers without a lawyer to assist him.

The Court in *Betts v. Brady* departed from the sound wisdom upon which the Court's holding in *Powell v. Alabama* rested. Florida, supported by two other States, has asked that *Betts v. Brady* be left intact. Twenty-two States, as friends of the Court, argue that *Betts* was "an anachronism when handed down" … and that it should now be overruled. We agree.

The judgment is reversed and the cause is remanded to the Supreme Court of Florida for further action not inconsistent with this opinion.

Mr. Justice Douglas, concurring.…

Mr. Justice Clark, concurring in the result.…

Mr. Justice Harlan, concurring.…

FURMAN v. GEORGIA
408 U.S. 238; 92 S.Ct. 2726; 33 L.Ed. 2d 346 (1972)
Vote: 5-4

In this landmark decision, the U.S. Supreme Court invalidates Georgia's death penalty statute. This decision represents three death penalty cases that were consolidated on appeal. All three defendants were African-American. One of them was convicted for murder; two were found guilty of rape. All three were sentenced to death by juries.

PER CURIAM

The Court holds that the imposition and carrying out of the death penalty in these cases constitutes cruel and unusual punishment in violation of the Eighth and Fourteenth Amendments. The judgment in each case is therefore reversed insofar as it leaves undisturbed the death sentence imposed, and the cases are remanded for further proceedings.

Mr. Justice Douglas, Mr. Justice Brennan, Mr. Justice Stewart, Mr. Justice White, and Mr. Justice Marshall have filed separate opinions in support of the judgments. The Chief Justice, Mr. Justice Blackmun, Mr. Justice Powell, and Mr. Justice Rehnquist have filed separate dissenting opinions.

Mr. Justice Douglas concurring.

… In each [of these cases] the determination of whether the penalty should be death or a lighter punishment was left by the State to the discretion of the judge or of the jury.… I vote to vacate each judgment, believing that the exaction of the death penalty does violate the Eighth and Fourteenth Amendments.…

The words "cruel and unusual" certainly include penalties that are barbaric. But the words, at least when read in light of the English proscription against selective and irregular use of penalties, suggest that it is "cruel and unusual" to apply the death penalty—or any other penalty—selectively to minorities whose numbers are few, who are outcasts of society, and who are unpopular, but whom society is willing to see suffer though it would not countenance general application of the same penalty across the board.…

… [W]e deal with a system of law and of justice that leaves to the uncontrolled discretion of judges or juries the determination whether defendants committing these crimes should die or be imprisoned. Under these laws no standards govern the selection of the penalty. People live or die, dependent on the whim of one man or of 12. In a Nation committed to equal protection of the laws there is no permissible "caste" aspect of law enforcement. Yet we know that the discretion of judges and juries in imposing the death penalty enables the penalty to be selectively applied, feeding prejudices against the accused if he is poor and despised, lacking political clout, or if he is a member of a suspect or unpopular minority, and saving those who by social position may be in a more protected position.…

The high service rendered by the "cruel and unusual" punishment clause of the Eighth Amendment is to require legislatures to write penal laws that are even-handed, nonselective, and nonarbitrary, and to require judges to see to it that general laws are not applied sparsely, selectively, and spottily to unpopular groups.

… [T]hese discretionary statutes are unconstitutional in their operation. They are pregnant with discrimination and discrimination is an ingredient not compatible with the idea of equal protection of the laws that is implicit in the ban on "cruel and unusual" punishments.

Mr. Justice Brennan, concurring.

Ours would indeed be a simple task were we required merely to measure a challenged punishment against those that history has long condemned. That narrow and unwarranted view of the Clause, however, was left behind with the 19th century. Our task today is more complex. We know "that the words of the [Clause] are not precise and that their scope is not static." We know, therefore, that the Clause "must draw its meaning from the evolving standards of decency that mark the progress of a maturing society." That knowledge, of course, is but the beginning of the inquiry.

… [T]he question is whether [a] penalty subjects the individual to a fate forbidden by the principle of civilized treatment guaranteed by the [Clause]." It was also said that a challenged punishment must be examined "in light of the basic prohibition against inhuman treatment" embodied in the Clause.

… "The basic concept underlying the [Clause] is nothing less than the dignity of man. While the State has the power to punish, the [Clause] stands to assure that this power be exercised within the limits of civilized standards." At bottom, then, the Cruel and Unusual Punishment Clause prohibits the infliction of uncivilized and inhuman punishments. The State, even as it punishes, must treat its members with respect for their intrinsic worth as human beings. A punishment is "cruel and unusual," therefore, if it does not comport with human dignity.…

… [T]he punishment of death is inconsistent with … four principles: Death is an unusually severe and degrading punishment; there is a strong probability that it is inflicted arbitrarily; its rejection by contemporary society is virtually total; and there is no reason to believe that it serves any penal purpose more effectively than the less severe punishment of imprisonment. The function of these principles is to enable a court to determine whether a punishment comports with human dignity. Death, quite simply, does not.…

Mr. Justice Stewart, concurring.

… Legislatures—state and federal—have sometimes specified that the penalty of death shall be the mandatory punishment for every person convicted of engaging in certain designated criminal conduct.

If we were reviewing death sentences imposed under these or similar laws, we would be faced with the need to decide whether capital punishment is unconstitutional for all crimes and under all circumstances. We would need to decide whether a legislature—state or federal—could constitutionally determine that certain criminal conduct is so atrocious that society's interest in deterrence and retribution wholly outweighs any considerations of reform or rehabilitation of the perpetrator, and that, despite the inconclusive empirical evidence, only the automatic penalty of death will provide maximum deterrence.

On that score I would say only that I cannot agree that retribution is a constitutionally impermissible ingredient in the imposition of punishment. The instinct for retribution is part of the nature of man, and channeling that instinct in the administration of criminal justice serves an important purpose in promoting the stability of a society governed by law. When people begin to believe that organized society is unwilling or unable to impose upon criminal offenders the punishment they "deserve," then there are sown the seeds of anarchy—of self-help, vigilante justice and lynch law.

The constitutionality of capital punishment in the abstract is not, however, before us in these cases. For the Georgia and Texas Legislatures have not provided that the death penalty shall be imposed upon all those who are found guilty of forcible rape. And the Georgia Legislature has not ordained that death shall be the automatic punishment for murder.

(Continued)

Instead, the death sentences now before us are the product of a legal system that brings them, I believe, within the very core of the Eighth Amendment's guarantee against cruel and unusual punishments, a guarantee applicable against the States through the Fourteenth Amendment. In the first place, it is clear that these sentences are "cruel" in the sense that they excessively go beyond, not in degree but in kind, the punishments that the state legislatures have determined to be necessary. In the second place, it is equally clear that these sentences are "unusual" in the sense that the penalty of death is infrequently imposed for murder, and that its imposition for rape is extraordinarily rare. But I do not rest my conclusion upon these two propositions alone.

These death sentences are cruel and unusual in the same way that being struck by lightning is cruel and unusual. For, of all the people convicted of rapes and murders in 1967 and 1968, many just as reprehensible as these, the petitioners are among a capriciously selected random handful upon whom the sentence of death has in fact been imposed. My concurring Brothers have demonstrated that, if any basis can be discerned for the selection of these few to be sentenced to die, it is the constitutionally impermissible basis of race. But racial discrimination has not been proved, and I put it to one side. I simply conclude that the Eighth and Fourteenth Amendments cannot tolerate the infliction of a sentence of death under legal systems that permit this unique penalty to be so wantonly and so freakishly imposed.

Mr. Justice White, concurring.

… The narrow question to which I address myself concerns the constitutionality of capital punishment statutes under which (1) the legislature authorizes the imposition of the death penalty for murder or rape; (2) the legislature does not itself mandate the penalty in any particular class or kind of case (that is, legislative will is not frustrated if the penalty is never imposed), but delegates to judges or juries the decisions as to those cases, if any, in which the penalty will be utilized; and (3) judges and juries have ordered the death penalty with such infrequency that the odds are now very much against imposition and execution of the penalty with respect to any convicted murderer or rapist. It is in this context that we must consider whether the execution of these petitioners would violate the Eighth Amendment.

… [L]ike my Brethren, I must arrive at judgment; and I can do no more than state a conclusion based on 10 years of almost daily exposure to the facts and circumstances of hundreds and hundreds of federal and state criminal cases involving crimes for which death is the authorized penalty. That conclusion, as I have said, is that the death penalty is exacted with great infrequency even for the most atrocious crimes and that there is no meaningful basis for distinguishing the few cases in which it is imposed from the many cases in which it is not. The short of it is that the policy of vesting sentencing authority primarily in juries—a decision largely motivated by the desire to mitigate the harshness of the law and to bring community judgment to bear on the sentence as well as guilt or innocence—has so effectively achieved its aims that capital punishment within the confines of the statutes now before us has for all practical purposes run its course.…

Mr. Justice Marshall, concurring.

… Perhaps the most important principle in analyzing "cruel and unusual" punishment questions is one that is reiterated again and again in the prior opinions of the Court: i.e., the cruel and unusual language "must draw its meaning from the evolving standards of decency that mark the progress of a maturing society." Thus, a penalty that was permissible at one time in our Nation's history is not necessarily permissible today.…

In judging whether or not a given penalty is morally acceptable, most courts have said that the punishment is valid unless "it shocks the conscience and sense of justice of the people."

While a public opinion poll obviously is of some assistance in indicating public acceptance or rejection of a specific penalty, its utility cannot be very great. This is because whether or not a punishment is cruel and unusual depends, not on whether its mere mention "shocks the conscience and sense of justice of the people," but on whether people who were fully informed as to the purposes of the penalty and its liabilities would find the penalty shocking, unjust, and unacceptable.

In other words, the question with which we must deal is not whether a substantial proportion of American citizens would today, if polled, opine that capital punishment is barbarously cruel, but whether they would find it to be so in the light of all information presently available.

This information would almost surely convince the average citizen that the penalty was unwise, but a problem arises as to whether it would convince him that the penalty was morally reprehensible. This problem arises from the fact that the public's desire for retribution, even though this is a goal that the legislature cannot constitutionally pursue as its sole justification for capital punishment, might influence the citizenry's view of the morality of capital punishment. The solution to the problem lies in the fact that no one has ever seriously advanced retribution as a legitimate goal of our society. Defenses of capital punishment are always mounted on deterrent or other similar theories. This should not be surprising. It is the people of this country who have urged in the past that prisons rehabilitate as well as isolate offenders, and it is the people who have injected a sense of purpose into our penology. I cannot believe that at this stage in our history, the American people would ever knowingly support purposeless vengeance. Thus, I believe that the great mass of citizens would conclude on the basis of the material already considered that the death penalty is immoral therefore unconstitutional.

In striking down capital punishment, this Court does not malign our system of government. On the contrary, it pays homage to it. Only in a free society could right triumph in difficult times, and could civilization record its magnificent advancement. In recognizing the humanity of our fellow beings, we pay ourselves the highest tribute. We achieve "a major milestone in the long road up from barbarism" and join the approximately 70 other jurisdictions in the world which celebrate their regard for civilization and humanity by shunning capital punishment.

Mr. Chief Justice Burger, with whom ***Mr. Justice Blackmun***, and ***Mr. Justice Rehnquist*** join, dissenting.

... If we were possessed of legislative power, I would either join with Mr. Justice Brennan and Mr. Justice Marshall or, at the very least, restrict the use of capital punishment to a small category of the most heinous crimes. Our constitutional inquiry, however, must be divorced from personal feelings as to the morality and efficacy of the death penalty, and be confined to the meaning and applicability of the uncertain language of the Eighth Amendment. There is no novelty in being called upon to interpret a constitutional provision that is less than self-defining, but, of all our fundamental guarantees, the ban on "cruel and unusual punishments" is one of the most difficult to translate into judicially manageable terms. The widely divergent views of the Amendment expressed in today's opinions reveals the haze that surrounds this constitutional command. Yet it is essential to our role as a court that we not seize upon the enigmatic character of the guarantee as an invitation to enact our personal predilections into law.

Although the Eighth Amendment literally reads as prohibiting only those punishments that are both "cruel" and "unusual," history compels the conclusion that the Constitution prohibits all punishments of extreme and barbarous cruelty, regardless of how frequently or infrequently imposed.

But where, as here, we consider a punishment well known to history, and clearly authorized by legislative enactment, it disregards the history of the Eighth Amendment and all the judicial comment that has followed to rely on the term "unusual" as affecting the outcome of these cases. Instead, I view these cases as turning on the single question whether capital punishment is "cruel" in the constitutional sense. The term "unusual" cannot be read as limiting the ban on "cruel" punishments or as somehow expanding the meaning of the term "cruel." For this reason I am unpersuaded by the facile argument that since capital punishment has always been cruel in the everyday sense of the word, and has become unusual due to decreased use, it is, therefore, now "cruel and unusual." ...

Mr. Justice Blackmun, dissenting.

... Cases such as these provide for me an excruciating agony of the spirit. I yield to no one in the depth of my distaste, antipathy, and, indeed, abhorrence, for the death penalty, with all its aspects of physical distress and fear and of moral judgment exercised by finite minds. That distaste is buttressed by a belief that capital punishment serves no useful purpose that can be demonstrated. For me, it violates childhood's training and life's experiences, and is not compatible with the philosophical convictions I have been able to develop. It is antagonistic to any sense of "reverence for life." Were I a legislator, I would vote against the death penalty for the policy reasons argued by counsel for the respective petitioners and expressed and adopted in the several opinions filed by the Justices who vote to reverse these convictions.

Although personally I may rejoice at the Court's result, I find it difficult to accept or to justify as a matter of history, of law, or of constitutional pronouncement. I fear the Court has overstepped. It has sought and has achieved an end.

Mr. Justice Powell, with **whom** the ***Chief Justice***, ***Mr. Justice Blackmun***, and ***Mr. Justice Rehnquist*** **join**, dissenting.

... The Court granted certiorari in these cases to consider whether the death penalty is any longer a

(Continued)

cases. The death penalty, I concluded, is a cruel and unusual punishment prohibited by the Eighth and Fourteenth Amendments. That continues to be my view.

In *Furman* I concluded that the death penalty is constitutionally invalid for two reasons. First, the death penalty is excessive. And second, the American people, fully informed as to the purposes of the death penalty and its liabilities, would in my view reject it as morally unacceptable....

The mere fact that the community demands the murderer's life in return for the evil he has done cannot sustain the death penalty, for as the plurality reminds us, "the Eighth Amendment demands more than that a challenged punishment be acceptable to contemporary society." To be sustained under the Eighth Amendment,

the death penalty must "[comport] with the basic concept of human dignity at the core of the Amendment." ... Under these standards, the taking of life "because the wrongdoer deserves it" surely must fall, for such a punishment has as its very basis the total denial of the wrongdoer's dignity and worth.

The death penalty, unnecessary to promote the goal of deterrence or to further any legitimate notion of retribution, is an excessive penalty forbidden by the Eighth and Fourteenth Amendments. I respectfully dissent from the Court's judgment upholding the sentences of death imposed upon the petitioners in these cases.

Mr. Justice Brennan, dissenting....

ROPER v. SIMMONS
543 U.S. 551; 125 S.Ct. 1183; 161 L.Ed. 2d 1 (2005)
Vote: 5-4

In this case, the Supreme Court reconsiders the constitutionality of the "juvenile death penalty." In Stanford v. Kentucky (1989) the Court had upheld the constitutionality of the death penalty as applied to defendants who were "older than 15 but younger than 18" at the time of their offenses.

Justice Kennedy delivered the opinion of the Court.

This case requires us to address, for the second time in a decade and a half, whether it is permissible under the Eighth and Fourteenth Amendments to the Constitution of the United States to execute a juvenile offender who was older than 15 but younger than 18 when he committed a capital crime. In *Stanford v. Kentucky* ... (1989), a divided Court rejected the proposition that the Constitution bars capital punishment for juvenile offenders in this age group. We reconsider the question....

At the age of 17, when he was still a junior in high school, Christopher Simmons, the respondent here, committed murder. About nine months later, after he had turned 18, he was tried and sentenced to death. There is little doubt that Simmons was the instigator of the crime. Before its commission Simmons said he wanted to murder someone. In chilling, callous terms he talked about his plan, discussing it for the most part

with two friends.... Simmons proposed to commit burglary and murder by breaking and entering, tying up a victim, and throwing the victim off a bridge. Simmons assured his friends they could "get away with it" because they were minors.

The three met at about 2 A.M. on the night of the murder, but [one friend] left before the other two set out.... Simmons and [the other friend] entered the home of the victim, Shirley Crook, after reaching through an open window and unlocking the back door.... Simmons entered Mrs. Crook's bedroom, where he recognized her from a previous car accident involving them both. Simmons later admitted this confirmed his resolve to murder her.

Using duct tape to cover her eyes and mouth and bind her hands, the two perpetrators put Mrs. Crook in her minivan and drove to a state park.... There they tied her hands and feet together with electrical wire, wrapped her whole face in duct tape and threw her from the bridge, drowning her in the waters below....

The next day, after receiving information of Simmons's involvement, police arrested him at his high school and took him to the police station in Fenton, Missouri.... Simmons confessed to the murder and agreed to perform a videotaped reenactment at the crime scene.

The State charged Simmons with burglary, kidnapping, stealing, and murder in the first degree. As

Simmons was 17 at the time of the crime, he was outside the criminal jurisdiction of Missouri's juvenile court system. He was tried as an adult. At trial the State introduced Simmons's confession and the videotaped reenactment of the crime, along with testimony that Simmons discussed the crime in advance and bragged about it later. The defense called no witnesses in the guilt phase. The jury having returned a verdict of murder, the trial proceeded to the penalty phase.

The State sought the death penalty. As aggravating factors, the State submitted that the murder was committed for the purpose of receiving money; was committed for the purpose of avoiding, interfering with, or preventing lawful arrest of the defendant; and involved depravity of mind and was outrageously and wantonly vile, horrible, and inhuman....

In mitigation Simmons' attorneys first called an officer of the Missouri juvenile justice system, who testified that Simmons had no prior convictions and that no previous charges had been filed against him. Simmons's mother, father, two younger half brothers, a neighbor, and a friend took the stand to tell the jurors of the close relationships they had formed with Simmons and to plead for mercy on his behalf....

During closing arguments, both the prosecutor and defense counsel addressed Simmons's age, which the trial judge had instructed the jurors they could consider as a mitigating factor. Defense counsel reminded the jurors that juveniles of Simmons's age cannot drink, serve on juries, or even see certain movies, because "the legislatures have wisely decided that individuals of a certain age aren't responsible enough." Defense counsel argued that Simmons' age should make "a huge difference to [the jurors] in deciding just exactly what sort of punishment to make." ...

The jury recommended the death penalty after finding the State had proved each of the three aggravating factors submitted to it. Accepting the jury's recommendation, the trial judge imposed the death penalty.

Simmons obtained new counsel, who moved in the trial court to set aside the conviction and sentence. One argument was that Simmons had received ineffective assistance at trial. To support this contention, the new counsel called as witnesses Simmons' trial attorney, Simmons' friends and neighbors, and clinical psychologists who had evaluated him.

Part of the submission was that Simmons was "very immature," "very impulsive," and "very susceptible to being manipulated or influenced." The experts testified about Simmons' background including a difficult home environment and dramatic changes in behavior, accompanied by poor school performance in adolescence. Simmons was absent from home for long periods, spending time using alcohol and drugs with other teenagers or young adults. The contention by Simmons' postconviction counsel was that these matters should have been established in the sentencing proceeding.

The trial court found no constitutional violation by reason of ineffective assistance of counsel and denied the motion for postconviction relief. In a consolidated appeal from Simmons's conviction and sentence, and from the denial of postconviction relief, the Missouri Supreme Court affirmed. The federal courts denied Simmons' petition for a writ of habeas corpus.

After these proceedings in Simmons' case had run their course, this Court held that the Eighth and Fourteenth Amendments prohibit the execution of a mentally retarded person. *Atkins v. Virginia* ... (2002). Simmons filed a new petition for state postconviction relief, arguing that the reasoning of *Atkins* established that the Constitution prohibits the execution of a juvenile who was under 18 when the crime was committed.

The Missouri Supreme Court agreed. It held that since *Stanford*, "a national consensus has developed against the execution of juvenile offenders, as demonstrated by the fact that eighteen states now bar such executions for juveniles, that twelve other states bar executions altogether, that no state has lowered its age of execution below 18 since *Stanford*, that five states have legislatively or by case law raised or established the minimum age at 18, and that the imposition of the juvenile death penalty has become truly unusual over the last decade." ... On this reasoning it set aside Simmons' death sentence and resentenced him to "life imprisonment without eligibility for probation, parole, or release except by act of the Governor." We granted certiorari, and now affirm....

The Eighth Amendment provides: "Excessive bail shall not be required, nor excessive fines imposed, nor cruel and unusual punishments inflicted." The provision is applicable to the States through the Fourteenth Amendment. As the Court explained in *Atkins*, the Eighth Amendment guarantees individuals the right not to be subjected to excessive sanctions. The right flows from the basic "precept of justice that punishment for crime should be graduated and proportioned to [the] offense." ... By protecting even those convicted of heinous crimes, the Eighth Amendment reaffirms the duty of the government to respect the dignity of all persons.

The prohibition against "cruel and unusual punishments," like other expansive language in the Constitution, must be interpreted according to its text, by considering history, tradition, and precedent, and

(Continued)

with due regard for its purpose and function in the constitutional design. To implement this framework we have established the propriety and affirmed the necessity of referring to "the evolving standards of decency that mark the progress of a maturing society" to determine which punishments are so disproportionate as to be cruel and unusual....

In *Thompson v. Oklahoma* ... (1988), a plurality of the Court determined that our standards of decency do not permit the execution of any offender under the age of 16 at the time of the crime. The plurality opinion explained that no death penalty State that had given express consideration to a minimum age for the death penalty had set the age lower than 16. The plurality also observed that "[t]he conclusion that it would offend civilized standards of decency to execute a person who was less than 16 years old at the time of his or her offense is consistent with the views that have been expressed by respected professional organizations, by other nations that share our Anglo-American heritage, and by the leading members of the Western European community." The opinion further noted that juries imposed the death penalty on offenders under 16 with exceeding rarity; the last execution of an offender for a crime committed under the age of 16 had been carried out in 1948, 40 years prior.

Bringing its independent judgment to bear on the permissibility of the death penalty for a 15-year-old offender, the *Thompson* plurality stressed that "[t]he reasons why juveniles are not trusted with the privileges and responsibilities of an adult also explain why their irresponsible conduct is not as morally reprehensible as that of an adult." ... According to the plurality, the lesser culpability of offenders under 16 made the death penalty inappropriate as a form of retribution, while the low likelihood that offenders under 16 engaged in "the kind of cost-benefit analysis that attaches any weight to the possibility of execution" made the death penalty ineffective as a means of deterrence.

The next year, in *Stanford v. Kentucky*, the Court, over a dissenting opinion joined by four Justices, referred to contemporary standards of decency in this country and concluded the Eighth and Fourteenth Amendments did not proscribe the execution of juvenile offenders over 15 but under 18. The Court noted that 22 of the 37 death penalty States permitted the death penalty for 16-year-old offenders, and, among these 37 States, 25 permitted it for 17-year-old offenders. These numbers, in the Court's view, indicated there was no national consensus "sufficient to label a particular punishment cruel and unusual." ...

The same day the Court decided *Stanford*, it held that the Eighth Amendment did not mandate a categorical exemption from the death penalty for the mentally retarded. *Penry v. Lynaugh* ... (1989). In reaching this conclusion it stressed that only two States had enacted laws banning the imposition of the death penalty on a mentally retarded person convicted of a capital offense. According to the Court, "the two state statutes prohibiting execution of the mentally retarded, even when added to the 14 States that have rejected capital punishment completely, [did] not provide sufficient evidence at present of a national consensus." ...

Three Terms ago the subject was reconsidered in *Atkins*. We held that standards of decency have evolved since *Penry* and now demonstrate that the execution of the mentally retarded is cruel and unusual punishment... the Court determined that executing mentally retarded offenders "has become truly unusual, and it is fair to say that a national consensus has developed against it." ...

Just as the *Atkins* Court reconsidered the issue decided in *Penry*, we now reconsider the issue decided in *Stanford*. The beginning point is a review of objective indicia of consensus, as expressed in particular by the enactments of legislatures that have addressed the question. This data gives us essential instruction. We then must determine, in the exercise of our own independent judgment, whether the death penalty is a disproportionate punishment for juveniles....

The evidence of national consensus against the death penalty for juveniles is similar, and in some respects parallel, to the evidence *Atkins* held sufficient to demonstrate a national consensus against the death penalty for the mentally retarded. When *Atkins* was decided, 30 States prohibited the death penalty for the mentally retarded.... By a similar calculation in this case, 30 States prohibit the juvenile death penalty.... *Atkins* emphasized that even in the 20 States without formal prohibition, the practice of executing the mentally retarded was infrequent.... In the present case, too, even in the 20 States without a formal prohibition on executing juveniles, the practice is infrequent. Since *Stanford*, six States have executed prisoners for crimes committed as juveniles.... In December 2003 the Governor of Kentucky decided to spare the life of Kevin Stanford, and commuted his sentence to one of life imprisonment without parole, with the declaration that "[w]e ought not be executing people who, legally, were children." ...

There is, to be sure, at least one difference between the evidence of consensus in *Atkins* and in this case.

Impressive in *Atkins* was the rate of abolition of the death penalty for the mentally retarded. Sixteen States that permitted the execution of the mentally retarded at the time of *Penry* had prohibited the practice by the time we heard *Atkins*. By contrast, the rate of change in reducing the incidence of the juvenile death penalty, or in taking specific steps to abolish it, has been slower. Five States that allowed the juvenile death penalty at the time of *Stanford* have abandoned it in the intervening 15 years....

Though less dramatic than the change from *Penry* to *Atkins*,... we still consider the change from *Stanford* to this case to be significant. As noted in *Atkins*, with respect to the States that had abandoned the death penalty for the mentally retarded since *Penry*, "[i]t is not so much the number of these States that is significant, but the consistency of the direction of change." ... Since *Stanford*, no State that previously prohibited capital punishment for juveniles has reinstated it. This fact, coupled with the trend toward abolition of the juvenile death penalty, carries special force in light of the general popularity of anticrime legislation, and in light of the particular trend in recent years toward cracking down on juvenile crime in other respects. Any difference between this case and *Atkins* with respect to the pace of abolition is thus counterbalanced by the consistent direction of the change.

As in *Atkins*, the objective indicia of consensus in this case—the rejection of the juvenile death penalty in the majority of States; the infrequency of its use even where it remains on the books; and the consistency in the trend toward abolition of the practice—provide sufficient evidence that today our society views juveniles, in the words *Atkins* used respecting the mentally retarded, as "categorically less culpable than the average criminal." ...

A majority of States have rejected the imposition of the death penalty on juvenile offenders under 18, and we now hold this is required by the Eighth Amendment.

Because the death penalty is the most severe punishment, the Eighth Amendment applies to it with special force. Capital punishment must be limited to those offenders who commit "a narrow category of the most serious crimes" and whose extreme culpability makes them "the most deserving of execution." This principle is implemented throughout the capital sentencing process. States must give narrow and precise definition to the aggravating factors that can result in a capital sentence.... In any capital case a defendant has wide latitude to raise as a mitigating factor "any aspect of [his

or her] character or record and any of the circumstances of the offense that the defendant proffers as a basis for a sentence less than death." There are a number of crimes that beyond question are severe in absolute terms, yet the death penalty may not be imposed for their commission. The death penalty may not be imposed on certain classes of offenders, such as juveniles under 16, the insane, and the mentally retarded, no matter how heinous the crime. These rules vindicate the underlying principle that the death penalty is reserved for a narrow category of crimes and offenders.

Three general differences between juveniles under 18 and adults demonstrate that juvenile offenders cannot with reliability be classified among the worst offenders. First, ... "[a] lack of maturity and an underdeveloped sense of responsibility are found in youth more often than in adults and are more understandable among the young. These qualities often result in impetuous and ill-considered actions and decisions." It has been noted that "adolescents are over-represented statistically in virtually every category of reckless behavior." In recognition of the comparative immaturity and irresponsibility of juveniles, almost every State prohibits those under 18 years of age from voting, serving on juries, or marrying without parental consent.

The second area of difference is that juveniles are more vulnerable or susceptible to negative influences and outside pressures, including peer pressure. This is explained in part by the prevailing circumstance that juveniles have less control, or less experience with control, over their own environment.

The third broad difference is that the character of a juvenile is not as well formed as that of an adult. The personality traits of juveniles are more transitory, less fixed.

These differences render suspect any conclusion that a juvenile falls among the worst offenders. The susceptibility of juveniles to immature and irresponsible behavior means "their irresponsible conduct is not as morally reprehensible as that of an adult." Their own vulnerability and comparative lack of control over their immediate surroundings mean juveniles have a greater claim than adults to be forgiven for failing to escape negative influences in their whole environment. The reality that juveniles still struggle to define their identity means it is less supportable to conclude that even a heinous crime committed by a juvenile is evidence of irretrievably depraved character.

In *Thompson*, a plurality of the Court recognized the import of these characteristics with respect to juveniles

(Continued)

under 16, and relied on them to hold that the Eighth Amendment prohibited the imposition of the death penalty on juveniles below that age. We conclude the same reasoning applies to all juvenile offenders under 18.

Once the diminished culpability of juveniles is recognized, it is evident that the penological justifications for the death penalty apply to them with lesser force than to adults. We have held there are two distinct social purposes served by the death penalty: "retribution and deterrence of capital crimes by prospective offenders." As for retribution, we remarked in *Atkins* that "[i]f the culpability of the average murderer is insufficient to justify the most extreme sanction available to the State, the lesser culpability of the mentally retarded offender surely does not merit that form of retribution." ... The same conclusions follow from the lesser culpability of the juvenile offender. Whether viewed as an attempt to express the community's moral outrage or as an attempt to right the balance for the wrong to the victim, the case for retribution is not as strong with a minor as with an adult. Retribution is not proportional if the law's most severe penalty is imposed on one whose culpability or blameworthiness is diminished, to a substantial degree, by reason of youth and immaturity.

As for deterrence, it is unclear whether the death penalty has a significant or even measurable deterrent effect on juveniles, as counsel for the petitioner acknowledged at oral argument. In general we leave to legislatures the assessment of the efficacy of various criminal penalty schemes. Here, however, the absence of evidence of deterrent effect is of special concern because the same characteristics that render juveniles less culpable than adults suggest as well that juveniles will be less susceptible to deterrence.

In particular, as the plurality observed in *Thompson*, "[t]he likelihood that the teenage offender has made the kind of cost-benefit analysis that attaches any weight to the possibility of execution is so remote as to be virtually nonexistent." ... To the extent the juvenile death penalty might have residual deterrent effect, it is worth noting that the punishment of life imprisonment without the possibility of parole is itself a severe sanction, in particular for a young person....

Drawing the line at 18 years of age is subject, of course, to the objections always raised against categorical rules. The qualities that distinguish juveniles from adults do not disappear when an individual turns 18. By the same token, some under 18 have already attained a level of maturity some adults will never reach. For the reasons we have discussed, however, a line must be drawn. The plurality opinion in

Thompson drew the line at 16. In the intervening years the *Thompson* plurality's conclusion that offenders under 16 may not be executed has not been challenged. The logic of *Thompson* extends to those who are under 18. The age of 18 is the point where society draws the line for many purposes between childhood and adulthood. It is, we conclude, the age at which the line for death eligibility ought to rest.

These considerations mean *Stanford v. Kentucky* should be deemed no longer controlling on this issue....

Our determination that the death penalty is disproportionate punishment for offenders under 18 finds confirmation in the stark reality that the United States is the only country in the world that continues to give official sanction to the juvenile death penalty. This reality does not become controlling, for the task of interpreting the Eighth Amendment remains our responsibility. Yet at least from the time of the Court's decision in *Trop [v. Dulles*, 1958], the Court has referred to the laws of other countries and to international authorities as instructive for its interpretation of the Eighth Amendment's prohibition of "cruel and unusual punishments."

As respondent and a number of *amici* emphasize, Article 37 of the United Nations Convention on the Rights of the Child, which every country in the world has ratified save for the United States and Somalia, contains an express prohibition on capital punishment for crimes committed by juveniles under 18. No ratifying country has entered a reservation to the provision prohibiting the execution of juvenile offenders. Parallel prohibitions are contained in other significant international covenants....

It is proper that we acknowledge the overwhelming weight of international opinion against the juvenile death penalty, resting in large part on the understanding that the instability and emotional imbalance of young people may often be a factor in the crime. The opinion of the world community, while not controlling our outcome, does provide respected and significant confirmation for our own conclusions.

... It does not lessen our fidelity to the Constitution or our pride in its origins to acknowledge that the express affirmation of certain fundamental rights by other nations and peoples simply underscores the centrality of those same rights within our own heritage of freedom.

The Eighth and Fourteenth Amendments forbid imposition of the death penalty on offenders who were under the age of 18 when their crimes were committed. The judgment of the Missouri Supreme Court setting aside the sentence of death imposed upon Christopher Simmons is affirmed.

Justice Stevens, with whom *Justice Ginsburg* joins, concurring....

Justice O'Connor, dissenting.

The Court's decision today establishes a categorical rule forbidding the execution of any offender for any crime committed before his 18th birthday, no matter how deliberate, wanton, or cruel the offense. Neither the objective evidence of contemporary societal values, nor the Court's moral proportionality analysis, nor the two in tandem suffice to justify this ruling. Although the Court finds support for its decision in the fact that a majority of the States now disallow capital punishment of 17-year-old offenders, it refrains from asserting that its holding is compelled by a genuine national consensus. Indeed, the evidence before us fails to demonstrate conclusively that any such consensus has emerged in the brief period since we upheld the constitutionality of this practice in *Stanford v. Kentucky....*

Justice Scalia, with whom the **Chief Justice** and *Justice Thomas* join, dissenting.

In urging approval of a constitution that gave life-tenured judges the power to nullify laws enacted by the people's representatives, Alexander Hamilton assured the citizens of New York that there was little risk in this, since "[t]he judiciary ... ha[s] neither FORCE nor WILL but merely judgment." ... But Hamilton had in mind a traditional judiciary, "bound down by strict rules and precedents which serve to define and point out their duty in every particular case that comes before them." ... Bound down, indeed. What a mockery today's opinion makes of Hamilton's expectation, announcing the Court's conclusion that the meaning of our Constitution has changed over the past 15 years—not, mind you, that this Court's decision 15 years ago was *wrong*, but that the Constitution *has changed*. The Court reaches this implausible result by purporting to advert, not to the original meaning of the Eighth Amendment, but to "the evolving standards of decency" ... of our national society. It then finds, on the flimsiest of grounds, that a national consensus which could not be perceived in our people's laws barely 15 years ago now solidly exists. Worse still, the Court says in so many words that what our people's laws say about the issue does not, in the last analysis, matter: "[I]n the end our own judgment will be brought to bear on the question of the acceptability of the death penalty under the Eighth Amendment." ... The Court thus proclaims itself sole arbiter of our Nation's moral standards—and in the course of discharging that awesome responsibility purports to take guidance from the views of foreign courts and legislatures. Because I do not believe that the meaning of our Eighth Amendment, any more than the meaning of other provisions of our Constitution, should be determined by the subjective views of five Members of this Court and like-minded foreigners, I dissent.

BAZE v. REES
553 U.S. 35; 128 S.Ct. 1520; 170 L.Ed. 2d 420 (2008)
Vote: 7-2

Here, the Court reviews Kentucky's practice of executing condemned prisoners by lethal injection. The specific question before the Court is whether the protocol adopted by the state carries an intolerable risk that persons to be executed will be subjected to unnecessary pain during the procedure.

Chief Justice Roberts announced the judgment of the Court and delivered an opinion, in which *Justice Kennedy* and *Justice Alito* join.

Like 35 other States and the Federal Government, Kentucky has chosen to impose capital punishment for certain crimes. As is true with respect to each of these States and the Federal Government, Kentucky has altered its method of execution over time to more humane means of carrying out the sentence. That progress has led to the use of lethal injection by every jurisdiction that imposes the death penalty....

Kentucky has adopted a method of execution believed to be the most humane available, one it shares

(Continued)

with 35 other States. Petitioners agree that, if administered as intended, that procedure will result in a painless death. The risks of maladministration they have suggested—such as improper mixing of chemicals and improper setting of IVs by trained and experienced personnel—cannot remotely be characterized as "objectively intolerable." Kentucky's decision to adhere to its protocol despite these asserted risks, while adopting safeguards to protect against them, cannot be viewed as probative of the wanton infliction of pain under the Eighth Amendment....

Throughout our history, whenever a method of execution has been challenged in this Court as cruel and unusual, the Court has rejected the challenge. Our society has nonetheless steadily moved to more humane methods of carrying out capital punishment. The firing squad, hanging, the electric chair, and the gas chamber have each in turn given way to more humane methods, culminating in today's consensus on lethal injection.... The broad framework of the Eighth Amendment has accommodated this progress toward more humane methods of execution, and our approval of a particular method in the past has not precluded legislatures from taking the steps they deem appropriate, in light of new developments, to ensure humane capital punishment. There is no reason to suppose that today's decision will be any different.

The judgment below concluding that Kentucky's procedure is consistent with the Eighth Amendment is, accordingly, affirmed.

Justice Alito, concurring....

Justice Stevens, concurring in the judgment.

... The conclusion that I have reached with regard to the constitutionality of the death penalty itself makes my decision in this case particularly difficult. It does not, however, justify a refusal to respect precedents that remain a part of our law. This Court has held that the death penalty is constitutional, and has established a framework for evaluating the constitutionality of particular methods of execution. Under those precedents, whether as interpreted by *The Chief Justice* or *Justice Ginsburg*, I am persuaded that the evidence adduced by petitioners fails to prove that Kentucky's lethal injection protocol violates the Eighth Amendment. Accordingly, I join the Court's judgment.

Justice Scalia, with whom *Justice Thomas* joins, concurring in the judgment.

... I take no position on the desirability of the death penalty, except to say that its value is eminently debatable and the subject of deeply, indeed passionately, held views—which means, to me, that it is preeminently not a matter to be resolved here. And especially not when it is explicitly permitted by the Constitution.

Justice Thomas, with whom *Justice Scalia* joins, concurring in the judgment.

... Judged under the proper standard, this is an easy case. It is undisputed that Kentucky adopted its lethal injection protocol in an effort to make capital punishment more humane, not to add elements of terror, pain, or disgrace to the death penalty. And it is undisputed that, if administered properly, Kentucky's lethal injection protocol will result in a swift and painless death. As the Sixth Circuit observed in rejecting a similar challenge to Tennessee's lethal injection protocol, we "do not have a situation where the State has any intent (or anything approaching intent) to inflict unnecessary pain; the complaint is that the State's pain-avoidance procedure may fail because the executioners may make a mistake in implementing it." ... But "[t]he risk of negligence in implementing a death-penalty procedure ... does not establish a cognizable Eighth Amendment claim." ... Because Kentucky's lethal injection protocol is designed to eliminate pain rather than to inflict it, petitioners' challenge must fail. I accordingly concur in the Court's judgment affirming the decision below.

Justice Breyer, concurring in the judgment.

... I cannot find, either in the record or in the readily available literature that I have seen, sufficient grounds to believe that Kentucky's method of lethal injection creates a significant risk of unnecessary suffering. The death penalty itself, of course, brings with it serious risks.... These risks in part explain why that penalty is so controversial. But the lawfulness of the death penalty is not before us. And petitioners' proof and evidence, while giving rise to legitimate concern, do not show that Kentucky's method of applying the death penalty amounts to "cruel and unusual punishmen[t]." ...

Justice Ginsburg, with whom *Justice Souter* joins, dissenting.

It is undisputed that the second and third drugs used in Kentucky's three-drug lethal injection protocol, pancuronium bromide and potassium chloride, would cause a conscious inmate to suffer excruciating pain. Pancuronium bromide paralyzes the lung muscles and results in slow asphyxiation.... Potassium chloride causes burning and intense pain as it circulates throughout the body.... Use of pancuronium bromide and potassium chloride on a conscious inmate, the plurality recognizes, would be "constitutionally unacceptable." ...

The constitutionality of Kentucky's protocol therefore turns on whether inmates are adequately anesthetized by the first drug in the protocol, sodium thiopental. Kentucky's system is constitutional, the plurality states, because "petitioners have not shown that the risk of an inadequate dose of the first drug is substantial." ... I would not dispose of the case so swiftly given the character of the risk at stake. Kentucky's protocol lacks basic safeguards used by other States to confirm that an inmate is unconscious before injection of the second and third drugs. I would vacate and remand with instructions to consider whether Kentucky's omission of those safeguards poses an untoward, readily avoidable risk of inflicting severe and unnecessary pain....

CHAPTER 6

Personal Autonomy and the Constitutional Right of Privacy

"The makers of the Constitution ... conferred, as against the Government, the right to be let alone—the most comprehensive of rights and the right most valued by civilized men."

—*Justice Louis D. Brandeis, Dissenting in* Olmstead v. United States *(1928)*

Historical Pictures/Stock Montage

Louis D. Brandeis: Associate Justice, 1916–1939

Introduction

The **constitutional right of privacy** protects the individual from unwarranted government interference in intimate personal relationships or activities. As it has taken shape since the mid-1960s, the right of privacy includes the freedom of the individual to make fundamental choices involving sex, reproduction, family life, and other intimate personal relationships. Of the various constitutional rights addressed in this book, the right of privacy remains perhaps the most intensely disputed. The controversy stems in part from the absence of any specific reference to privacy in the Constitution. Some scholars and judges still adhere to Justice Hugo Black's view that a right of privacy cannot reasonably be inferred from the language of the original Constitution or any of its amendments. However, it is clear that this is a minority position today. Among recent Supreme Court nominees, only Judge Robert Bork has rejected the interpretive foundation of the right of privacy. For most Americans, the debate over privacy has less to do with competing theories of constitutional interpretation than with the profound implications of the privacy principle for divisive social issues such as **abortion, gay rights,** and **euthanasia**.

In *Roe v. Wade* (1973), the Supreme Court held that the right of privacy "is broad enough to encompass a woman's decision whether or not to terminate her pregnancy." As the ongoing protest against legal abortion makes clear, abortion is hardly an ordinary issue of public policy. Nor was *Roe v. Wade* a run-of-the-mill Supreme Court decision. Unlike most constitutional decisions, *Roe* aroused deep philosophical conflict and even deeper political and emotional turmoil. *Roe v. Wade* drew the Supreme Court into a firestorm of political controversy that continues unabated four decades later. This controversy has dominated public discussion of the Court, often eclipsing other important issues and likewise influencing the debate surrounding nominations to the Supreme Court.

Although abortion is the focal point of the debate over the right of privacy, the viability of the right of privacy is not based solely on the continued vitality of *Roe v. Wade*. Even if *Roe* were to be overturned, the right of privacy would still exist as an independent constitutional right, albeit substantially circumscribed. The right of privacy is now well established in both federal and state constitutional law and has application to numerous questions of public policy beyond abortion. This chapter examines some of the more salient ones that have been addressed by the U.S. Supreme Court.

Philosophical Foundations of the Right of Privacy

When the Supreme Court invoked the right of privacy to effectively legalize abortion within stated limits, it was giving expression to a sense of **moral individualism** that is deeply rooted in American culture. However, countervailing notions of traditional morality are also deeply ingrained in American society, as the relentless and widespread attacks on *Roe v. Wade* demonstrate. In no other area of constitutional law are individualism and traditional morality so sharply antagonistic as in the area of privacy rights.

The moral individualism underlying the constitutional right of privacy was conceived in the political liberalism of the Age of Enlightenment. In his influential essay *On Liberty* (1859), the English thinker John Stuart Mill argued that "there is a sphere of action in which society, as distinguished from the individual, has, if any, only an indirect interest; comprehending all that portion of a person's life and conduct which affects only himself, or if it also affects others, only with their free, voluntary and undeceived consent and participation." In the modern era, this idea that each individual should be considered an autonomous actor with respect to personal matters is associated with the philosophy of **libertarianism**, which holds that individual freedom is the highest good and that law should be interpreted to maximize the scope of liberty. During and after the 1960s, the libertarian perspective became increasingly widespread among Americans, especially younger people. At this time, a large number of people began to question the authority of government to regulate the private lives of individuals in the name of traditional morality.

In the libertarian view, the legitimate role of government is protection of individuals from one another, not from their own vices. Thus, libertarians often object to laws which range from regulating sexual conduct, living arrangements, and private drug use to laws mandating motorcycle riders to wear helmets. Perhaps the telltale libertarian position is opposition to the criminal law against suicide. In the libertarian view, the individual has the right to make basic decisions regarding his or her own life—or death.

The countervailing position, which might be dubbed **classical conservatism**, holds that individuals must often be protected against their own vices. Classical conservatives defend not only traditional morality but the embodiment of that morality in the law.

An Excerpt from John Stuart Mill, *On Liberty* (1859)

The object of this Essay is to assert one very simple principle, as entitled to govern absolutely the dealings of society with the individual in the way of compulsion and control, whether the means used be physical force in the form of legal penalties, or the moral coercion of public opinion. That principle is, that the sole end for which mankind are warranted, individually or collectively, in interfering with the liberty of action of any of their number, is self-protection. That the only purpose for which power can be rightfully exercised over any member of a civilized community, against his will, is to prevent harm to others. His own good, either physical or moral, is not a sufficient warrant. He cannot rightfully be compelled to do or forbear because it will be better for him to do so, because it will make him happier, because, in the opinions of others, to do so would be wise, or even right. These are good reasons for remonstrating with him, or reasoning with him, or persuading him, or entreating him, but not for compelling him, or visiting him with any evil in case he do otherwise. To justify that, the conduct from which it is desired to deter him, must be calculated to produce evil to someone else. The only part of the conduct of any one, for which he is amenable to society, is that which concerns others. In the part which merely concerns himself, his independence is, of right, absolute. Over himself, over his own body and mind, the individual is sovereign.

On the contemporary Supreme Court, Justice Antonin Scalia has endorsed the classical conservative view of law and morality. Concurring in *Barnes v. Glen Theatre, Inc.* (1991) (the "nude dancing" decision discussed in Chapter 3), Scalia wrote:

> *Our society prohibits, and all human societies have prohibited, certain activities not because they harm others but because they are considered ... immoral. In American society, such prohibitions have included, for example, sadomasochism, cockfighting, bestiality, suicide, drug use, prostitution and sodomy. While there might be a great diversity of views on whether various of these prohibitions should exist, ... there is no doubt that absent specific constitutional protection for the conduct involved, the Constitution does not prohibit them simply because they regulate "morality."*

The debate over the constitutional right of privacy is ultimately a debate between two sharply divergent views of the law. In the libertarian view, the law exists to protect individuals from one another. In this view, morality is not in and of itself a legitimate basis for law. The classical conservative view, on the other hand, sees law and morality as inseparable and holds that the maintenance of societal morality is one of the essential functions of the legal system.

Constitutional Foundations of the Right of Privacy

Although libertarianism has roots in the liberalism of the Enlightenment, it is doubtful that any of the Framers of the Constitution were libertarians in the modern sense of the term. Certainly the Framers believed in individual freedom, but most did not conceive of freedom as including the right to flout traditional principles of conduct embodied in the common law. Yet the right of privacy, in essence the constitutional expression of libertarianism, has been "found" by the Supreme Court to emanate from various provisions of the Bill of Rights (see *Griswold v. Connecticut* [1965]).

Several provisions of the Bill of Rights were adopted to protect individuals from unreasonable invasions of privacy. For example, the Third Amendment explicitly protects the privacy of the home in peacetime from soldiers seeking quarters. The Fourth Amendment protects individuals from unreasonable searches and seizures where they have a "reasonable expectation of privacy" (*Katz v. United States* [1967], Harlan, J., concurring).

The Fifth Amendment prohibits compulsory self-incrimination, thus protecting the privacy of an accused individual's thoughts. The First Amendment ensures freedom of conscience in both political and religious matters, again recognizing the autonomy of the individual. Finally, the First Amendment's implicit guarantee of freedom of association protects one's right to choose one's friends, one's spouse, one's business partners, and so on. In *Griswold v. Connecticut* (1965), the Supreme Court interpreted these protections as embodying a right to be free of those government intrusions into the realm of intimate personal decisions.

Proponents of a constitutional right of privacy often cite the Ninth Amendment, which guarantees rights "retained by the people" even though they are not enumerated in the Constitution. Indeed, historically, the courts have recognized a variety of unenumerated constitutional rights. The right to marry, to choose one's spouse, to select an occupation, to travel freely within the country, and to enter into contracts are all examples of long-standing rights retained by the people although they are not explicitly provided for in the Constitution. They have achieved constitutional status by virtue of the fact that they are elements of the "liberty" protected by the Due Process Clauses of the Fifth and Fourteenth Amendments. Dissenting in *Olmstead v. United States* (1928), Justice Louis Brandeis wrote:

> *The makers of our Constitution undertook to secure conditions favorable to the pursuit of happiness. They recognized the significance of man's spiritual nature, of his feelings and his intellect. They knew that only a part of his pain, pleasure, and satisfactions of life are to be found in material things. They sought to protect Americans in their beliefs, their thoughts, their emotions and their sensations. They conferred, as against the Government, the right to be let alone—the most comprehensive of rights and the right most valued by civilized men.*

These words were written by way of dissent in a case dealing with the scope of the Fourth Amendment's protection against wiretapping (see Chapter 5). Yet they may be interpreted as foreshadowing the modern right of privacy, which is, in essence, the **right to be let alone.**

SIDEBAR

James Madison and the Ninth Amendment

Recall that during the battle for ratification of the Constitution, the Anti-Federalists' main objection to the document was its lack of an enumerated Bill of Rights. The Federalists thought that the document was sufficient without such specific guarantees, because the new national government they were creating would be so limited in power. It's unlikely that the Constitution's supporters doubted that individuals retained basic freedoms of speech, religion, association, and so forth. Rather, there were other compelling reasons that the document lacked a Bill of Rights. Some Federalists feared that the enumeration of certain rights would be perceived as insinuating that individuals lacked any additional rights. In other words, while Madison and others understood that they could not possibly list all the individual freedoms that must be protected from government intrusion, they feared that by listing any, it would be assumed later that those not listed did not exist. The specific language of the Ninth Amendment reflects precisely this concern: "The enumeration in the Constitution, of certain rights, shall not be construed to deny or disparage others retained by the people."

Substantive Due Process

To understand the emergence of the constitutional right of privacy, one must recall the discussion of substantive due process (see Chapters 1 and 2). In a landmark decision in 1905, the Supreme Court broadly interpreted the Due Process Clause of the Fourteenth Amendment to impose a restriction on the power of state legislatures to engage in economic regulation. In *Lochner v. New York*, the Court held that the "liberty of contract" protected by the Fourteenth Amendment had been infringed when the state of New York adopted a law restricting the working hours of bakery employees. Although *Lochner* and related decisions were concerned exclusively with the protection of individual property rights (see Chapter 2), they paved the way for the creation of the right of privacy by giving a substantive (as distinct from a strictly procedural) interpretation to the Due Process Clause of the Fourteenth Amendment. Under the **substantive due process** formula, courts can discover in the Fourteenth Amendment rights that are "fundamental" or "implicit in a scheme of ordered liberty." Again, the Ninth Amendment's recognition of rights "retained by the people" provides additional justification for the substantive interpretation of the Fourteenth Amendment.

In the first two decades of the twentieth century, substantive due process was by and large confined to the protection of economic liberties from government regulation. Just two months before the Court handed down its controversial decision in *Lochner*, it refused to find in the Due Process Clause a prohibition against compulsory vaccination laws (*Jacobson v. Massachusetts* [1905]). Nevertheless, Justice John M. Harlan's majority opinion did recognize that "[t]here is, of course, a sphere within which the individual may assert the supremacy of his own will and rightfully dispute the authority of any human government, especially of any free government existing under a written constitution, to interfere with the exercise of that will."

For Justice Harlan and most of his brethren, the state's interest in promoting the public health through compulsory vaccination was superior to the individual "exercise of will." Nevertheless, in *Jacobson*, the Court suggested that the Fourteenth Amendment might protect certain noneconomic aspects of individual autonomy.

The expansion of substantive due process to include noneconomic rights took a quantum leap in 1923. In that year, the Court recognized that citizens have the right to study foreign languages in private schools, state statutes to the contrary notwithstanding (*Meyer v. Nebraska*). Two years later, the Court emphasized the right to a private education by striking down an Oregon law that required parents to send their children to public schools (*Pierce v. Society of Sisters* [1925]).

> **To Summarize:**
> - *The right of privacy, aptly defined by Justice Brandeis as "the right to be let alone," can be viewed as a constitutional expression of libertarianism, the doctrine that elevates individual freedom above all other values.*
> - *Although nowhere mentioned explicitly in the Constitution, the right of privacy is generally viewed as implicit in the protections of the Bill of Rights or the broad guarantee of "liberty" found in the Due Process Clauses of the Fifth and Fourteenth Amendments.*
> - *Proponents of the right of privacy often invoke the Ninth Amendment, which guarantees rights "retained by the people" even though they are not enumerated in the Constitution.*
> - *To the extent that judicial recognition of the right of privacy relies on the Due Process Clauses of the Fifth and Fourteenth Amendments, it may be viewed as a modern application of the doctrine of substantive due process.*

Procreation and Birth Control

The slowly emerging right of privacy experienced a temporary setback in *Buck v. Bell* (1927). There, the Court refused to find in the Fourteenth Amendment a protection against **compulsory sterilization** for mentally retarded persons. Carrie Buck, an 18-year-old mentally retarded woman, was committed to the Virginia State Colony for Epileptics and Feeble Minded, where her mother was also confined. Before being committed, Carrie had been raped by a guest at the home where she had been in foster care. Officials at the Virginia institution concluded that Carrie and her mother shared hereditary traits of "feeble-mindedness and sexual promiscuity" and sought to have Carrie sterilized. After conducting an evidentiary hearing required by state law, a Virginia court ordered the director to proceed with the sterilization. The Virginia Supreme Court upheld this decision, as did the U.S. Supreme Court. Writing for a nearly unanimous Court, Justice Oliver Wendell Holmes, Jr., declared that the principle announced in *Jacobson v. Massachusetts* was "broad enough to cover cutting the Fallopian tubes." In one of his more memorable (and most gratuitous) lines, Holmes went on to write that "[t]hree generations of imbeciles are enough."

Although *Buck v. Bell* has never been formally overruled, it is unlikely that it would command a majority today. In 1942, the Court struck down a state law providing for the compulsory sterilization of criminals (*Skinner v. Oklahoma*). Although the decision was based on the Equal Protection Clause of the Fourteenth Amendment, rather than on substantive due process, *Skinner* in effect recognized a constitutional right of procreation. The Court characterized the right to procreate as "one of the basic civil rights of man." The Court's decisions in *Meyer v. Nebraska, Pierce v. Society of Sisters,* and *Skinner v. Oklahoma* paved the way for the landmark 1965 decision in *Griswold v. Connecticut* recognizing an independent constitutional right of privacy.

The Connecticut Birth Control Controversy

The *Griswold* case involved a challenge to an 1879 Connecticut law that made the sale and possession of birth-control devices a misdemeanor. The law also forbade anyone from assisting, abetting, or counseling another in the use of birth-control devices.

In *Poe v. Ullman* (1961), the Supreme Court voted 5 to 4 to dismiss a challenge to the Connecticut law. The challenge stemmed not from a criminal prosecution but from a lawsuit brought by a married couple and their physician who complained of state interference in the doctor–patient relationship. Writing for a four-member plurality, Justice Felix Frankfurter said that there was no real "case or controversy" and that the issue was unripe for judicial review. Frankfurter alluded to a "tacit agreement" whereby the birth-control law would no longer be enforced. In a forceful dissent, Justice William O. Douglas pointed out that an earlier criminal prosecution had effectively prevented birth-control clinics from operating in the state. Douglas not only asserted that the case was properly before the Court but characterized the statute as "an invasion of the privacy implicit in a free society." Douglas's sharp dissent in *Poe v. Ullman* anticipated the Court's decision in *Griswold* four years later.

Estelle Griswold was the director of Planned Parenthood in Connecticut. Just three days after Planned Parenthood opened a clinic in New Haven, Griswold was arrested. Reportedly, she had given detectives a tour of the clinic, pointing out contraceptives that the clinic was dispensing. After a short trial, Griswold was convicted and fined $100. As expected, the Connecticut courts upheld her conviction, rejecting the contention that the state law was unconstitutional. Also as expected, Griswold's attorneys filed a petition for certiorari in the U.S. Supreme Court. When the Court agreed to take the case, it was clear that the justices were going to rule on the constitutionality of the Connecticut law.

Griswold's attorneys argued that the birth-control law infringed a right of privacy implicit in the Bill of Rights, as embodied in the concept of personal liberty protected by the Fourteenth Amendment. Moreover, they maintained that the Connecticut statute lacked a reasonable relationship to a legitimate legislative purpose. The state of Connecticut responded by emphasizing its broad police powers, arguing that the birth-control law was a rational means of promoting the welfare of Connecticut's people. Interestingly, however, Connecticut's brief failed to state the particular legislative purpose behind the birth-control law. Rather, the brief was designed chiefly to persuade the justices that they should not second-guess the wisdom or desirability of social legislation.

On June 7, 1965, the Supreme Court announced its decision striking down the Connecticut birth-control law. The vote was 7 to 2. Justice Douglas was given the task of writing the majority opinion. After a disclaimer that "[w]e do not sit as a superlegislature to determine the wisdom, need and propriety of laws," Douglas proceeded to explain why, in his view, the Connecticut law ran afoul of the Constitution. As an advocate of "total incorporation" (see Chapter 1), Justice Douglas sought to identify an implicit right of privacy in the Bill of Rights, rather than in the vague notions of liberty that the Court had in the past attached to the Due Process Clause of the Fourteenth Amendment.

In what has become frequently quoted language, Douglas asserted that "specific guarantees in the Bill of Rights have penumbras, formed by emanations from those guarantees that help give them life and substance." Douglas reasoned that the explicit language of the Bill of Rights, specifically the First, Third, Fourth, Fifth, and Ninth Amendments, when considered along with their "emanations" and "penumbras" as defined by previous decisions of the Court, adds up to a general, independent right of privacy. In Douglas's view, this general right was infringed by the state of Connecticut when it outlawed birth control. In the sharpest language of the majority opinion, Douglas asked:

> Would we allow the police to search the sacred precincts of marital bedrooms for telltale signs of the use of contraceptives? The very idea is repulsive to the notions of privacy surrounding the marriage relationship.

While the prospect of the police searching one's bedroom for evidence of contraception is no doubt repulsive to many, the question is whether the law allowing such a search is constitutional. Obviously, Justices John Harlan (the younger) and Byron White, who voted to strike down the Connecticut law, were not altogether persuaded by Justice Douglas's discovery of a general right of privacy in the Bill of Rights. In their separate opinions concurring in the judgment, Harlan and White maintained that the Connecticut law infringed the liberty protected by the Fourteenth Amendment, a liberty that, in their view, transcends the particular protections of the Bill of Rights. In taking this course, Justices Harlan and White were not embarking on uncharted jurisprudential waters; they were merely using the substantive due process approach that had been employed in *Meyer v. Nebraska, Pierce v. Society of Sisters,* and the numerous cases in which the Court had used liberty of contract to invalidate economic legislation.

Dissenting sharply, Justice Black criticized what he perceived as a blatant attempt to amend the Constitution through loose interpretation. Justice Black never hesitated to urge invalidation of a legislative act if he believed it ran afoul of a specific provision of the Constitution. Consequently, he and Justice Douglas often found themselves voting together in civil liberties cases, thus earning the label "judicial activists." But, as one who preferred to adhere strictly to the text of the Constitution, Black refused in *Griswold* to go along with what he regarded as a discredited approach to constitutional interpretation:

> *I cannot rely on the Due Process Clause or the Ninth Amendment or any mysterious and uncertain natural law concept as a reason for striking down this state law.... I had thought that we had laid that formula, as a means of striking down state legislation, to rest once and for all.*

The debate over modes of constitutional interpretation is certainly a legitimate one. Cogent jurisprudential arguments can be made for and against the Court's decision in *Griswold*. However, it must be recognized that the Court's decision was not based on a radical departure from traditional jurisprudence, as a few extreme critics have claimed. Rather, there is ample precedent for the broad interpretation of the Constitution in general (for example, *Marbury v. Madison*), and the substantive due process formula in particular, in the rich history of the Court's constitutional decision making.

Although *Griswold* was sharply criticized by commentators who shared Justice Black's view of constitutional interpretation and by a few staunch social conservatives, the Court's decision was not subjected to the kind of public outcry occasioned by the desegregation decisions of the 1950s or the school prayer decisions of the early 1960s. Obviously, the average person is not particularly concerned with the legal aspects of a Supreme Court decision; he or she is much more likely to focus on the Court's substantive policy output. As a matter of public policy, *Griswold* was quite well received. A Gallup Poll conducted in 1965 found that 81 percent of the American public agreed with the statement that "birth control information should be available to anyone who wants it." There can be little doubt that changing societal attitudes about sex, procreation, and contraception had more to do with the Court's decision in *Griswold* than did "emanations" from the Bill of Rights!

Beyond the Marital Bedroom

In the *Griswold* case, the Court was careful to invalidate the Connecticut law only insofar as it invaded marital privacy, thus leaving open the question of whether states could prohibit the use of birth-control devices by unmarried persons. In *Eisenstadt v. Baird* (1972), the Court faced a challenge to a Massachusetts law that prohibited unmarried persons from obtaining and using contraceptives. William Baird, a former medical student, was arrested after he delivered a lecture on birth control at Boston University during which he provided some contraceptive foam to a female student.

In reversing Baird's conviction and striking down the Massachusetts law, the Court established the right of privacy as an individual right, not a right enjoyed solely by married couples. As Justice William Brennan's opinion for the Court stated:

> [T]he marital couple is not an independent entity with a mind and heart of its own, but an association of two individuals each with separate intellectual and emotional makeup. If the right of privacy means anything, it is the right of the individual, married or single, to be free from unwarranted governmental intrusion into matters so fundamentally affecting a person as the decision whether or not to beget a child.

Having thus articulated an independent right of privacy protecting individual decisions in the area of sex and procreation, *Eisenstadt v. Baird* paved the way for the most controversial decision the Supreme Court was to make during the chief justiceship of Warren Burger: *Roe v. Wade.*

> **To Summarize:**
> ◆ *The right of privacy was first invoked in the area of procreation and birth control. In* Griswold v. Connecticut *(1965), the Court struck down a state statute prohibiting the use of birth-control devices insofar as the statute applied to married couples. Later, the Court made clear that because the right of privacy is an individual right, laws forbidding the use of contraceptives by unmarried adults are likewise invalid.*
> ◆ *Justice William O. Douglas's opinion for the Court in* Griswold *attempted to justify the right of privacy in terms of "emanations" from the Bill of Rights. Dissenting justices criticized the majority for loosely interpreting the Constitution.*
> ◆ *The* Griswold *case set the stage for the most controversial decision of the Court's modern era:* Roe v. Wade *(1973).*

The Abortion Controversy

Abortion has been practiced in nearly all societies since ancient times. Under English common law, abortion was a misdemeanor, but only after "quickening" (that point during a pregnancy where the mother can feel the fetus moving inside her womb). This was based on the ancient Aristotelian theory of "mediate animation," a position later adopted by St. Thomas Aquinas and, until the nineteenth century, the official doctrine of the Roman Catholic Church. The idea was that the soul did not enter the body until the middle of pregnancy; quickening was the physical manifestation of "ensoulment." Before that point, the fetus was not thought to be alive. Therefore, there was no moral wrong in performing an abortion before quickening. Students need to understand that English common law was much influenced by ecclesiastical notions of morality.

As the science of medicine advanced, people came to understand that the fetus moves about in the womb throughout pregnancy. Quickening, a term not much used these days, occurs because the fetus has grown large enough that the mother can feel its movement. This realization, along with growing concern about the health risks of abortion to women, led to changes in the law, in both England and the United States. In the early nineteenth century, legislatures in the American states began to enact statutes containing stricter prohibitions of abortion. By the late 1860s, nearly all states made abortion a felony except where it was deemed medically necessary to save the life of the mother. During the 1960s, a number of states liberalized their abortion laws to make exceptions for rape and incest.

The sexual revolution and the rise of modern feminism in the 1960s resulted in widespread changes in attitudes toward abortion. In 1970, New York became the first state to legalize abortion-on-demand, as long as a licensed physician performed the procedure during the first six months of pregnancy. This movement set the stage for what is likely the most controversial social policy debate the Supreme Court ever considered.

Roe v. Wade

Norma McCorvey, also known as Jane Roe, was a 25-year-old unmarried Texas woman who was faced with an unwanted pregnancy resulting from an alleged gang rape that she later admitted never occurred. After her doctor informed her that abortion was illegal in

Texas, she went to see an attorney. The attorney, Linda Coffee, introduced McCorvey to Sarah Weddington, a young woman just out of law school, who would ultimately argue the case before the U.S. Supreme Court. Weddington expressed her view that the Constitution allows a woman to control her own body, including the decision to terminate an unwanted pregnancy. Shortly thereafter, Coffee and Weddington filed suit in federal district court against Dallas District Attorney Henry Wade, seeking to enjoin him from enforcing what was claimed to be an unconstitutional law. The suit was filed as a class action—that is, not only on behalf of Jane Roe but on behalf of all women similarly situated. The district court declared the Texas law unconstitutional but refused to issue the injunction, invoking the doctrine of abstention whereby federal courts refrain from interfering with state judicial processes (see Chapter 2, Volume I). As permitted in cases of this kind, Jane Roe appealed directly to the U.S. Supreme Court.

On January 22, 1973, the Supreme Court handed down a 7-to-2 decision striking down the Texas law. Justice Harry A. Blackmun wrote the majority opinion. After determining that the case was properly before the Court, Blackmun reviewed prior decisions on the right of privacy. In what is perhaps the best-known statement from his opinion in *Roe*, Blackmun concluded that the right of privacy "is broad enough to encompass a woman's decision whether or not to terminate her pregnancy." Yet Blackmun's analysis did not end with this pronouncement, because the right of privacy, like all constitutional rights, may be limited if there is a sufficiently strong justification to do so by the state. Specifically, because the Court identified privacy as a **fundamental right**, the state of Texas had to demonstrate a **compelling interest** to justify regulating or prohibiting abortion. The Court recognized a compelling interest in protecting maternal health that justifies reasonable state regulations of abortions performed after the first trimester of pregnancy. However, the state of Texas sought not only to regulate but also to proscribe abortion altogether and claimed a compelling state interest in protecting unborn human life. The Court recognized this interest as legitimate but held that it did not become compelling until that point in pregnancy when the fetus became viable—that is, capable of "meaningful life outside the mother's womb." Beyond the point of **viability**, according to the Court, the state may prohibit abortion, except in cases where it is necessary to preserve the life or health of the mother.

The Court summarily rejected the argument that a fetus is a "person" as that term is used in the Constitution and thus possessed of a right to life, holding that the term "has application only postnatally." If a fetus is regarded as a person from the point of conception, then any abortion is certainly homicide. If that were the case, then states could not allow abortions even in cases of rape or where the pregnancy endangers the life of the mother (as the Texas law challenged in *Roe* allowed). Nor would intrauterine devices or "morning-after" pills, both of which prevent implantation after conception, be permissible. Like abortion, these forms of birth control, which are regarded by most as morally acceptable, would be tantamount to murder. Clearly, the Court was not inclined to make such a pronouncement. Nor was it prepared to assert that the woman's right to obtain an abortion is absolute—"that she is entitled to terminate at whatever time, in whatever way and for whatever reason she alone chooses." The Court tried to steer a middle course, to accommodate what it regarded as legitimate interests on both sides of the issue.

Roe v. Wade was the product of sharp conflict, bargaining, and compromise within the Supreme Court. Although the Court's decision attempted to strike a reasonable balance between the state's interest in protecting unborn life and a woman's interest in controlling her own body, the abortion decision was not viewed by the pro-life forces as an acceptable compromise. The hostile reaction to *Roe v. Wade* was immediate and intense. Justices of the Supreme Court, especially Harry Blackmun, received hate mail and even death threats. The 1980s saw frequent public demonstrations, harassment of women entering abortion clinics, and even the occasional bombing of such facilities.

Since the *Roe* decision came down in 1973, public opinion has remained sharply divided on the abortion question. This sharp division was reflected in the U.S. Senate, which, in 1983, defeated by one vote a proposed constitutional amendment that would have provided that "[t]he right to an abortion is not secured by this Constitution." Although it is difficult to say with certainty which side of the issue is favored by public opinion, it was clear until recently that the antiabortion forces manifest greater intensity in their opposition to abortion than the pro-choice forces do in their support. In politics, intensity may count for as much as numbers. In constitutional law, neither is supposed to matter, but there is considerable evidence that both do!

Regulation of Abortion in the Wake of *Roe v. Wade*

In the wake of *Roe v. Wade*, many state and local governments enacted regulations governing the performance of abortions. As previously noted, the Court in *Roe* allowed for "reasonable" regulation of abortions to effectuate the state's legitimate interest in protecting maternal health. However, many state statutes and local ordinances affecting abortion were not intended to promote maternal health at all but rather to deter women from obtaining abortions.

In *Planned Parenthood of Central Missouri v. Danforth* (1976), the Court struck down a Missouri law that required minors to obtain the consent of their husbands or parents before obtaining an abortion. Three years later, in *Bellotti v. Baird* (1979), the Court struck down a similar law passed by the state of Massachusetts. This law required an unmarried pregnant minor to obtain parental consent for an abortion or, if parental consent was not given, to obtain authorization from a judge who was to determine whether the abortion was in the minor's best interest. Taken together, the decisions in *Bellotti* and *Danforth* emphasized the personal nature of the abortion decision: other parties, whether one's spouse, parents, or the state, could not be given a veto over the exercise of one's constitutional rights. Needless to say, these decisions produced enormous controversy. In particular, advocates of traditional family values objected to a policy under which parents would not be able to control their daughters' reproductive decisions. They questioned how it could be that parents must consent to every medical procedure performed on their children except for abortion.

In 1983, the Court appeared to back away from the strong position taken in *Bellotti* and *Danforth*. In *Planned Parenthood v. Ashcroft*, the Court upheld a Missouri law that required parental consent for unemancipated minors but apparently only because the law provided a mechanism whereby exceptionally mature minors could obtain abortions by seeking judicial intervention.

The same day *Ashcroft* came down, the Court announced its decision in *Akron v. Akron Center for Reproductive Health* (1983). In this case, the Court struck down a city ordinance that, in addition to requiring parental consent for minors' abortions, required (1) that all abortions be performed in hospitals; (2) that there be a twenty-four-hour waiting period before abortions could be performed; (3) that physicians make certain specified statements to the woman seeking abortion to ensure that her decision is truly an informed one; and (4) that all fetal remains be disposed of in a manner that is both humane and sanitary. The Court found that these requirements imposed significant burdens on a woman's exercise of her constitutional rights without substantially furthering the state's legitimate interests. The "humane and sanitary" disposal requirement was invalidated as "impermissibly vague" in obliquely suggesting an intention on the part of the city to "mandate some sort of 'decent burial' of the embryo at the earliest stages of formation."

Restrictions on Public Funding of Abortions

One of the more successful legislative assaults on abortion involves the exemption of abortions not deemed to be medically necessary from medical welfare programs. In *Maher v. Roe* (1977), the Court voted 6 to 3 to uphold a Connecticut welfare regulation that denied Medicaid benefits to indigent women seeking to have abortions, unless their attending physicians certified their abortions as medically necessary. The Court's decision was based on the new due process/equal protection analysis developed by the Court during the modern era (see Chapter 7). In a nutshell, the Court held that the denial of Medicaid benefits to poor women seeking elective abortions neither discriminated against a suspect class of persons nor unduly burdened the exercise of fundamental rights. Therefore, the Court judged the Connecticut regulation to be permissible under both the Equal Protection and Due Process Clauses of the Fourteenth Amendment.

Three years later, in *Harris v. McRae* (1980), the Court upheld a provision of federal law, commonly known as the **Hyde amendment**, forbidding the use of federal funds to support nontherapeutic abortions. Writing for a sharply divided Court, Justice Potter Stewart concluded that:

> [I]t simply does not follow that a woman's freedom of choice carries with it a constitutional entitlement to the financial resources to avail herself of the full range of protected choices.... Although government may not place obstacles in the path of a woman's exercise of her freedom of choice, it need not remove those not of its own creation. Indigency falls in the latter category.

The Hyde Amendment restricted federal funding of abortions, leaving states to decide whether to impose similar restrictions on the use of state funds. As noted, the U.S. Supreme Court upheld Connecticut's restriction on abortion funding in *Maher v. Roe* (1977). Yet several state supreme courts have invalidated similar restrictions under their state constitutions (see, for example, *Committee to Defend Reproductive Rights v. Myers* [Cal. S.Ct. 1981], *Moe v. Secretary of Administration* [Mass. S.Jud.Ct. 1981], and *Right to Choose v. Byrne* [N.J. S.Ct. 1982]).

Eroding Support for *Roe v. Wade* on the Supreme Court in the 1980s

By the early 1980s, the bloc of justices supportive of *Roe v. Wade* had begun to erode. In the *Akron Center* decision of 1983, the Court had explicitly reaffirmed *Roe* but by one less vote than the *Roe* majority of 1973. While Potter Stewart had voted with the majority in *Roe*, his successor on the Court, Sandra Day O'Connor, dissented in the *Akron* case. In one of her most significant early opinions, Justice O'Connor expressed considerable dissatisfaction with the **trimester framework** adopted by the Court in *Roe v. Wade*. O'Connor's *Akron* dissent went well beyond a critique of the particular formulation adopted by the Court in *Roe*, however. Her opinion suggested that a state has a sufficiently compelling interest in protecting potential life to allow it to ban abortion at any stage of pregnancy. O'Connor's apparent dissent from the *Roe* decision did not necessarily indicate that she opposed legalized abortion. It did suggest that O'Connor believed that the state legislature (not a court of law) is the proper forum for resolving the abortion issue. Again, quoting from her dissent in *Akron v. Akron Center:* "It is ... difficult to believe that this Court, without the resources available to those bodies entrusted with making legislative choices, believes itself competent to make these inquiries." Substantial support exists, even among those who favor some form of legalized abortion, for the position adopted by Justice O'Connor. Some would argue that the question of abortion is simply not one that courts should decide. These critics would call for judicial restraint, for deference to the legislative judgment. While many state legislators have criticized the Supreme Court for usurping the role of the legislature in deciding *Roe v. Wade*, others have expressed relief that the judiciary has taken the heat on the abortion issue. Few legislators relish the prospect of voting on the abortion question. On both sides of the issue are powerful interest groups, and a middle ground on abortion is difficult to locate, much less defend.

The Supreme Court reaffirmed *Roe v. Wade* again in *Thornburgh v. American College of Obstetricians and Gynecologists* (1986). However, in *Thornburgh*, the vote in favor of a constitutional right to abortion was 5 to 4, because Chief Justice Burger switched sides and joined the dissenters. Although Burger retired after the 1985 term, his departure did not strengthen the position of *Roe v. Wade*. President Ronald Reagan elevated Associate Justice William Rehnquist to the position of chief justice and appointed Antonin Scalia, a conservative, to fill the vacancy.

In 1987, it appeared that the opponents of legalized abortion were only one vote away from overturning *Roe v. Wade*. In that year, Justice Lewis Powell, a member of the *Roe* majority, retired from the Court. It looked as if the Court would be divided 4 to 4 on the abortion issue, possibly making the next appointee to the Court the swing vote on whether to overrule *Roe v. Wade*. To a great extent, this fact explains the furor surrounding President Reagan's nomination of conservative federal judge Robert Bork to fill the vacancy left by Justice Powell. A well-known critic of *Roe* and of the right of privacy generally, Bork entered a firestorm of political controversy when he appeared before the Senate Judiciary Committee. The Senate, controlled by the Democrats, ultimately rejected Bork, in no small measure due to his stand on the right of privacy.

Eventually, the Senate confirmed Reagan's nomination of another federal judge, Anthony Kennedy. In his confirmation hearing, Kennedy was asked repeatedly about his views on abortion. He replied, "If I had a … fixed view … I might be obliged to disclose that to you. I don't have such a view." The nation would have to wait two years for Kennedy to register his opinion in the abortion debate.

The Webster Decision

The Webster Decision   Without question, the most significant abortion case of the 1980s was *Webster v. Reproductive Health Services* (1989). Many thought the *Webster* case would be the one in which the Supreme Court would overturn *Roe v. Wade*. Those who favored such an outcome were disappointed by the decision. Yet those who supported legalized abortion found cause for alarm in what they perceived as a significant departure from the philosophy of *Roe*.

The *Webster* case involved a challenge to a Missouri statute containing a number of restrictions on abortions. Most worrisome from the pro-choice perspective was the statement in the preamble of the law that "the life of each human being begins at conception." In its various provisions, the law forbade state employees from performing, assisting in, or counseling women to have abortions. It also prohibited the use of any state facilities for these purposes. Finally, it required all doctors who would perform abortions to conduct viability tests on fetuses at or beyond twenty weeks' gestation.

The Supreme Court, splitting 5 to 4, sustained the constitutionality of the Missouri statute. Yet in deciding the issues in *Webster*, the Supreme Court could not agree on a majority opinion. A plurality (Chief Justice Rehnquist and Associate Justices White, Kennedy, and O'Connor) expressed the view that the legislation could be sustained without overruling *Roe v. Wade*. In her separate concurrence, Justice O'Connor stressed the "fundamental rule of judicial restraint," which dictates that courts not decide major issues unless absolutely necessary. Only Justice Scalia, in a separate concurrence, called for the explicit overruling of *Roe* and chided his colleagues in the majority for not facing the issue squarely: "Of the four courses we might have chosen today—to reaffirm *Roe*, to overrule it explicitly, to overrule it *sub silentio*, or to avoid the question—the last is the least responsible." Justice Blackmun, the author of the Court's opinion in *Roe v. Wade*, accused the plurality of undermining *Roe*:

> With feigned restraint, the plurality announces that its analysis leaves Roe "undis-turbed," albeit "modified and narrow[ed]." ... But this disclaimer is totally meaning-less. The plurality opinion is filled with winks, and nods, and knowing glances to those who would do away with Roe explicitly, but turns a stone face to anyone in search of what the plurality conceives as the scope of a woman's right under the Due Process Clause to terminate a pregnancy free from the coercive and brooding influence of the State.

Rust v. Sullivan: *Restricting Information about Abortion*   Supporters of legalized abortion were dealt another setback during the spring of 1991. In *Rust v. Sullivan*, the Supreme Court upheld a federal regulation that barred birth-control clinics that received federal funds from providing information about abortion services to their clients. The regulation had been imposed in 1987 by the Department of Health and Human Services (HHS) at the direction of the Reagan administration, which opposed legalized abortion. The Supreme Court found the regulation to be a legitimate condition imposed on the receipt of financial assistance from the government.

In the Court's view, the regulation was an invasion neither of privacy rights nor free-dom of speech, as plaintiffs in the lawsuit alleged. Congress, with broad public support, passed a measure designed to overturn the HHS regulation. However, this act was vetoed by President George H. W. Bush, and Congress was unable to muster the two-thirds vote necessary to override the veto.

The Court Reaffirms *Roe v. Wade*

In *Rust v. Sullivan*, as in the *Webster* decision two years earlier, the Court did not face squarely the question of whether *Roe v. Wade* should be maintained as the law of the land. Yet these decisions did send a strong signal that the Court was prepared to toler-ate greater restrictions on legalized abortion. On January 21, 1992, on the eve of the nineteenth anniversary of its landmark decision in *Roe v. Wade*, the Supreme Court announced that it would hear a case challenging a Pennsylvania law that contained a series of restrictions on abortion (*Planned Parenthood of Southeastern Pennsylvania v. Casey* [1992]). Among other things, the law required spousal notification, parental con-sent in cases of minors, and a twenty-four-hour waiting period before an abortion could be performed. Identical requirements had been declared invalid by the Supreme Court in previous decisions, but the Third Circuit Court of Appeals in Philadelphia upheld most of the provisions of the Pennsylvania statute. The appellate court based its ruling largely on the Supreme Court's 1989 *Webster* decision, which it interpreted as a significant retreat from the "strict scrutiny" to which abortion regulations had been subjected.

On April 22, 1992, the Supreme Court heard oral arguments in *Planned Parenthood v. Casey*. Ernest Preate, Jr., attorney general of Pennsylvania, defended the constitution-ality of the statute, contending, among other things, that "*Roe* did not establish an abso-lute right to abortion on demand, but rather a limited right subject to reasonable state regulations." Attacking the statute, Kathryn Kolbert, counsel for the American Civil Liberties Union, characterized Pennsylvania's regulations not only as unreasonable but as "cruel and oppressive." U.S. Solicitor General Kenneth W. Starr, speaking on behalf of the Bush administration, urged the Court to abandon the "compelling state interest" test and adopt a more lenient "rational basis test" for determining the constitutionality of statutes in this area. When asked by Justice White whether the adoption of such a test would lead to a conclusion that the Pennsylvania law should be upheld, Starr replied, "Exactly." The Supreme Court handed down its much anticipated decision in *Planned Parenthood v. Casey* on June 29, 1992, the last day of the Court's 1991 term. To the surprise of many observers, the Court reaffirmed by a 5-to-4 vote the essential holding in *Roe v. Wade* that the constitutional right of privacy is broad enough to include a woman's decision to terminate her pregnancy. The Court was highly fragmented, however, producing five opinions. Two justices, Blackmun and Stevens, took the position that *Roe v. Wade* should be reaffirmed and that all of the challenged provisions of the Pennsylvania statute should be declared invalid. Four justices—Rehnquist, Scalia, White, and Thomas—took the view that *Roe* should be overruled and all of the Pennsylvania restrictions upheld. Adopting an extremely unusual method of presentation underscoring the gravity of the case, Justices O'Connor, Kennedy, and Souter jointly authored the controlling opinion of the Court. This lengthy joint opinion thoroughly reexamined *Roe v. Wade*, its underlying rationale and formulation, and the line of cases it spawned. While joining Justices Blackmun and Stevens in explicitly reaffirming *Roe*, the joint opinion abandoned the trimester framework and declared a new "undue burden" test for judging regulations of abortion. Applying this test, the joint opinion upheld the parental consent, waiting period, and record-keeping and reporting provisions but invalidated the spousal notification requirement.

The *Casey* decision was greeted with dismay and derision from both pro-life and pro-choice groups. Pro-choice groups expressed alarm that the Court was willing to overturn recent precedent (*Akron v. Akron Center for Reproductive Health* [1983] and *Thornburgh v. American College of Obstetricians and Gynecologists* [1986]) and uphold Pennsylvania's restrictions on abortion. Pro-life advocates were disappointed that two Reagan appointees (Kennedy and O'Connor) and one Bush appointee (Souter) voted to reaffirm *Roe v. Wade.*

In their separate opinions in *Casey*, Chief Justice Rehnquist and Justice Scalia, supported by Justices White and Thomas, made it clear that four members of the Court were fully prepared to overrule *Roe v. Wade.* However, with the replacement of Justice White by Justice Ruth Bader Ginsburg in 1993, the anti-*Roe* bloc on the Court was diminished. In 1994, Justice Blackmun, the author of the *Roe* opinion, resigned from the Court. His replacement by Justice Stephen G. Breyer, the second Clinton appointee to the Court, did not weaken support of the *Roe* precedent. Since then, there have been two Republican appointments to the Court (Chief Justice Roberts and Justice Alito) and two Democratic appointments (Justices Sotomayor and Kagan). None of these appointments dramatically shifted the ideological balance of the Court, and the Court's position on the basic constitutional question of abortion remains stable. However, recent years have seen the Court shift in a more conservative direction on the volatile issue of "partial-birth abortion."

"Partial-Birth Abortion"

During the 1990s, more than thirty states adopted statutes banning so-called partial-birth abortions. Congress passed similar legislation but it was successfully vetoed by President Bill Clinton. Nebraska's statute defined partial-birth abortion as "an abortion procedure in which the person performing the abortion partially delivers vaginally a living unborn child before killing the unborn child and completing the delivery." The law provided an exception for procedures deemed necessary to protect a woman's life, but no exception for the purpose of protecting a woman's health. LeRoy Carhart, a Nebraska physician, brought suit to challenge the constitutionality of the statute. In a sharply divided decision, the Supreme Court invalidated the Nebraska law. Writing for the Court in *Stenberg v. Carhart* (2000), Justice Stephen Breyer found that the law went well beyond the prohibition of late-term abortions and could be invoked to prohibit certain early-term abortions as well. In Breyer's view, the law, if allowed to stand, could be interpreted to prohibit the "dilation and evacuation" procedure, "the most commonly used method for performing previability second trimester abortions." Breyer concluded:

> *All those who perform abortion procedures using that method must fear prosecution, conviction, and imprisonment. The result is an undue burden upon a woman's right to make an abortion decision.*

In dissent, Justice Anthony Kennedy, one of the architects of the compromise in *Planned Parenthood v. Casey*, objected that the Court had repudiated *Casey* "by invalidating a statute advancing critical state interests, even though the law denies no woman the right to choose an abortion and places no undue burden upon the right." Kennedy characterized partial-birth abortion as "a procedure many decent and civilized people find so abhorrent as to be among the most serious of crimes against human life." In his dissenting opinion, Justice Antonin Scalia stated, "Today's decision, that the Constitution of the United States prevents the prohibition of a horrible mode of abortion, will be greeted by a firestorm of criticism—as well it should."

In *Gonzales v. Carhart* (2007), the Court revisited the issue of partial-birth abortion. At issue was a federal statute passed in the wake of the *Stenberg* decision. This time, Justice Kennedy's position prevailed, albeit by the narrowest majority. Interestingly, the Court did not overturn *Stenberg*, but distinguished the new federal law from the Nebraska law it had invalidated previously. Writing for the majority, Justice Kennedy observed that "[c]ompared to the state statute at issue in *Stenberg*, the [federal] Act is more specific concerning the instances to which it applies and in this respect more precise in its coverage." In dissent, Justice Ruth Bader Ginsburg chided the majority for offering "flimsy and transparent justifications" for upholding the federal statute. It is instructive to compare and contrast the two decisions and the laws reviewed by the Court in both cases.

Abortion Rights under State Constitutions

Even if the Supreme Court were to overrule *Roe v. Wade*, this would by no means result in the immediate recriminalization of abortion. If *Roe* were overruled, state legislatures would be permitted to determine their own policies in this area, subject to limits imposed by state courts under state constitutional provisions. Thus, state courts would have to determine the scope of abortion rights under their respective state constitutions.

Indeed, some state supreme courts have moved in this direction. For example, according to the National Conference of State Legislatures, as of 2013 Florida is one of ten states whose constitutions contain explicit recognition of the right of privacy (the others are Alaska, Arizona, California, Hawaii, Illinois, Louisiana, Montana, South Carolina, and Washington). The Florida Supreme Court has said that "[s]ince the people of this state exercised their prerogative and enacted an amendment to the Florida Constitution which expressly and succinctly provides for a strong right of privacy …, it can only be concluded that the right is much broader in scope than that of the federal constitution" (*Winfield v. Division of PariMutuel Wagering* [Fla. S.Ct. 1985]). The court has also indicated quite clearly that a woman's right to choose abortion is protected by the privacy amendment to the state constitution (see *In re T.W.* [Fla. S.Ct. 1989]).

Even where state constitutions do not contain explicit rights of privacy, some state courts have recognized privacy as an implicit right and have even accorded it broader scope than the federal right as interpreted by the U.S. Supreme Court. For example, in *Planned Parenthood v. Sundquist* (2000), the Tennessee Supreme Court struck down several statutes restricting access to abortion in Tennessee. Speaking through Chief Justice Riley Anderson, the court asserted that:

> [A] woman's right to terminate her pregnancy is a vital part of the right to privacy guaranteed by the Tennessee Constitution. As this right is inherent in the concept of ordered liberty embodied in the Tennessee Constitution, we conclude that the right to terminate one's pregnancy is fundamental. The standard we have traditionally applied to fundamental rights requires that statutes regulating fundamental rights be subjected to strict scrutiny analysis. Moreover, when reviewed under the strict scrutiny standard, we conclude that none of the statutory provisions at issue withstand such scrutiny.

In *Planned Parenthood v. Sundquist*, the Tennessee Supreme Court rejected the "undue burden" test of *Planned Parenthood v. Casey* and reaffirmed the fundamental rights/ strict scrutiny approach of *Roe v. Wade*. Thus, even if the U.S. Supreme Court were to overturn *Roe*, it would not ipso facto return the abortion issue to the exclusive domain of the state legislatures. The right of privacy, including the right to abortion, is becoming well established as a matter of state constitutional law.

The abortion issue is *the* constitutional question of our time. But it is far more complex than most observers of American law and politics realize, going well beyond the domain of the U.S. Supreme Court and the fate of *Roe v. Wade*. It will be many years before this question is finally resolved.

To Summarize:

- *In* Roe v. Wade *(1973), the Court relied on the right of privacy in striking down a Texas statute criminalizing most abortions. In* Roe, *the Court held that the state's interest in protecting the fetus becomes compelling only at the point of fetal viability outside the womb. States may thus prohibit only those abortions that are performed after the point of viability.*

- *In the decades following* Roe, *the Court reviewed a number of cases in which state and local governments imposed various restrictions on abortion. During the 1970s, most of these restrictions were declared unconstitutional. In the 1980s, however, an increasingly conservative Supreme Court began to view such restrictions more favorably.*

- *By the late 1980s, it appeared that* Roe v. Wade *might be overturned. In* Planned Parenthood v. Casey *(1992), however, the Court reaffirmed its basic holding in* Roe—*but in so doing, gave states broader latitude in regulating access to abortion.*

- *In* Stenberg v. Carhart *(2000), the Court again reaffirmed* Roe *and manifested a renewed willingness to closely scrutinize state regulations on abortion. In* Stenberg, *the Court struck down a state law restricting "partial-birth abortion." However, in* Gonzales v. Carhart *(2007), the Court upheld a federal law very similar to the one it has voided in* Stenberg, *which led pro-choice advocates to worry that support for* Roe v. Wade *on the nation's highest court was waning again.*

- *Even if the Court were to overturn* Roe v. Wade, *state courts would be free to determine whether their own states' restrictions on abortion violate relevant provisions of their state constitutions.*

Privacy and Living Arrangements

While Supreme Court decisions in the area of reproductive freedom receive most of the public attention, the Court's decisions applying the constitutional right of privacy are by no means confined to contraception and abortion. The right of privacy has also been applied in reviewing city ordinances governing residential occupancy. In *Belle Terre v. Boraas* (1974), the Supreme Court upheld a village ordinance that limited residential land use to one-family dwellings. A couple who had leased a house to six unrelated college students challenged the law on the ground that it "trenche[d] on the newcomers' rights of privacy." The Court, adopting the traditional rational-basis test, found the ordinance to be a valid exercise of the police power. Justice Thurgood Marshall dissented, maintaining that fundamental rights of privacy and association were infringed and that the village failed to demonstrate a compelling justification for this infringement.

In *Moore v. City of East Cleveland* (1977), the Court struck down an ordinance that limited the occupancy of residences to members of single families. However, the East Cleveland ordinance defined family in such a way as to prohibit a grandmother from cohabiting with her two grandsons. Distinguishing the ordinance from the one upheld in *Belle Terre*, which primarily affected unrelated individuals, the Court stressed freedom of choice in matters of marriage and family life:

> *Our decisions teach that the Constitution protects the sanctity of the family precisely because the institution of the family is deeply rooted in our history and tradition. [Ours] is by no means a tradition limited to respect for [the] nuclear family. The tradition of uncles, aunts, cousins, and especially grandparents sharing a household along with parents and children has roots equally venerable and equally deserving of constitutional recognition.*

In a rather caustic concurrence, Justice Brennan noted that "in today's America, the nuclear family is the pattern so often found in much of white suburbia" but that "the Constitution cannot tolerate the imposition by government upon the rest of us of white suburbia's preference in patterns of family living."

To Summarize:

♦ *While Supreme Court decisions in the area of reproductive freedom receive most of the public attention, the Court's decisions applying the constitutional right of privacy are by no means confined to contraception and abortion.*

♦ *Stressing freedom of choice in matters of marriage and family life, the Court has used the right of privacy to scrutinize ordinances limiting residential living arrangements.*

The Demise of Sodomy Laws

In *Eisenstadt v. Baird* (1972), the Supreme Court tacitly acknowledged the right of an unmarried adult to engage in heterosexual activity. If this right is based on the premise that one may decide what to do with his or her own body without interference by the state, how can laws that prohibit private, consensual homosexual conduct be justified? What is the compelling interest on the part of the state that could be advanced to justify such prohibitions? The question has been raised in federal court. In *Doe v. Commonwealth's Attorney* (1976), the Supreme Court summarily affirmed a federal district court decision that upheld Virginia's **sodomy** law. The district court, dividing 2 to 1, cited Justice Harlan's dissent in the 1961 case of *Poe v. Ullman*, which, although supportive of sexual privacy within marriage, suggested that homosexual conduct could be prosecuted even if practiced privately. The Supreme Court, in refusing to hear the appeal in *Doe v. Commonwealth's Attorney*, in effect endorsed Justice Harlan's position.

In *Bowers v. Hardwick* (1986), the Supreme Court reached the merits of a case challenging the application of Georgia's sodomy law to homosexual activity. Michael Hardwick, an admitted homosexual, was charged with committing sodomy with a consenting male adult in the privacy of his home. Although the state prosecutor decided not to take the case to the grand jury, Hardwick brought suit in federal court, seeking a declaration that the statute was unconstitutional. The district court dismissed the case, claiming that facing no punishment under the law, Hardwick lacked standing. But the appeals court reversed, accepting Hardwick's argument that because of his lifestyle he would continually run afoul of the state law and was bound to face prosecution eventually. Yet the U.S. Supreme Court granted the state's petition for certiorari and reversed the court of appeals.

In arguing his case before the Supreme Court, Hardwick relied on *Griswold v. Connecticut* and *Roe v. Wade*, as well as on the Court's 1969 decision in *Stanley v. Georgia*. In *Stanley*, the Court held that the First Amendment prohibits a state from punishing a person merely for the private possession of obscene materials. Although ostensibly a First Amendment case, the *Stanley* decision suggested that the home was a sanctuary from prosecution for acts that might well be criminal outside the home. Dividing 5 to 4 in *Hardwick*, the Court upheld the Georgia law, refusing to recognize "a fundamental right to engage in homosexual sodomy." Writing for the Court, Justice White stressed the traditional, legal, and moral prohibitions against sodomy.

Responding to the libertarian argument that the state has no right to legislate solely on the basis of morality, White wrote that "law … is constantly based on notions of morality, and if all laws representing essentially moral choices are to be invalidated …, the Courts will be very busy indeed." Dissenting, Justice Blackmun disputed the Court's characterization of the issue. For Blackmun and three of his colleagues, the case was not about a "fundamental right to engage in homosexual sodomy" but the more general right of an adult, homosexual or heterosexual, to engage in consensual sexual acts with another adult. Striking a libertarian chord, Justice John Paul Stevens wrote that "the fact that the governing majority in a State has traditionally viewed a practice as immoral is not a sufficient reason for upholding a law prohibiting the practice."

The Court's decision in *Bowers v. Hardwick* produced a firestorm of protest and helped galvanize the gay rights movement in America. Many commentators suspected that, given the cultural trends in postmodern America, the decision would not survive the test of time. Interestingly, after his retirement Supreme Court Justice Lewis Powell, one of the members of the *Hardwick* majority, expressed reservations about his vote in that case. In talking to a group of law students at New York University in 1990, Justice Powell said, "I think I probably made a mistake in that one." In a subsequent interview, Powell said that the case was a "close call" and that his decision to support the majority was based in part on the fact that the sodomy law had been largely unenforced. Interestingly Powell also minimized the importance of the case, referring to it as frivolous and suggesting that it had been filed "just to see what the court would do" (*Washington Post*, October 26, 1990, p. A-3).

Romer v. Evans: A Pivotal Decision

The Court's decision in *Romer v. Evans* (1996) called into question the precedential value of *Bowers v. Hardwick*. In what the American Civil Liberties Union hailed as a "transforming moment in the fight for equality for lesbians and gay men," the Court struck down a Colorado constitutional amendment that barred state and local government from providing various legal protections for gays and lesbians. (For more discussion of this decision, see Chapter 7.) In dissent, Justice Scalia argued that "if it is constitutionally permissible for a State to make homosexual conduct criminal, surely it is constitutionally permissible for a State to enact other laws merely disfavoring homosexual conduct." The *Romer* decision signaled that the Supreme Court was becoming more sensitive to the cause of gay rights. But it would still be several years before the Court would be ready to cast aside *Bowers v. Hardwick*.

State Courts Invalidate Sodomy Laws

As we have noted throughout this book, a state constitution may afford more protection to its citizens than does the federal constitution. By the mid-1990s a number of state courts, including appellate courts in Tennessee, New York, and Kentucky, had invalidated their states' sodomy laws on state constitutional grounds. Perhaps the most dramatic example of judicial federalism in this context came in 1998 when the Georgia Supreme Court struck down the same sodomy law upheld by the U.S. Supreme Court in *Bowers v. Hardwick*. Writing for the Georgia Supreme Court in *Powell v. State*, Chief Justice Robert Benham found that the sodomy statute, "insofar as it criminalizes the performance of private, non-commercial acts of sexual intimacy between persons legally able to consent, 'manifestly infringes upon a constitutional provision' ... which guarantees to the citizens of Georgia the right of privacy."

The Supreme Court Overturns *Bowers v. Hardwick*

By the beginning of the twenty-first century, only a few states retained laws making sodomy an offense. In Texas, two men were convicted of having anal sex with a member of the same sex in violation of a state law that made it an offense "to engage in deviate sexual intercourse with another individual of the same sex." A Texas appellate court, in a divided opinion, rejected the defendants' federal constitutional arguments under both the Equal Protection and Due Process Clauses of the Fourteenth Amendment and affirmed the defendants' convictions. When the Supreme Court granted certiorari in *Lawrence v. Texas*, the stage was set for the continuing campaign to obtain a reversal of the 1986 decision in *Bowers v. Hardwick*.

In *Lawrence v. Texas* (2003), Justice Kennedy, writing for the Court in a 6-to-3 decision, opined that the Texas statute "furthers no legitimate state interest which can justify its intrusion into the personal and private life of the individual." The Court expressly overruled its decision in *Bowers v. Hardwick* on the ground that the Due Process Clause of the Fourteenth Amendment prohibits states from making private consensual sexual conduct of adults a crime. After referencing the English experience and decisions of the European Court of Human Rights, Justice Kennedy pointed out that the deficiencies in *Bowers* had become apparent in the years following its announcement. Observing that the twenty-five states with laws prohibiting the conduct referred to in *Bowers* were now reduced to thirteen, of which four enforce their laws only against homosexual conduct, Kennedy stated, "In those States, including Texas, that still proscribe sodomy (whether for same-sex or heterosexual conduct), there is a pattern of nonenforcement with respect to consenting adults acting in private."

Concurring in the Court's judgment, Justice O'Connor wrote separately to note that while she agreed that the Texas law was unconstitutional, she would have invalidated it on the ground that it violated the Equal Protection Clause because it was directed only against homosexual and not heterosexual conduct.

The Court was careful to note that its decision did not involve minors, persons who might be injured or coerced or who were situated in relationships where consent might not easily be refused, or public conduct or prostitution. Finally, displaying some foresight as to where the issue would next be debated, the Court emphasized that its decision did not bear on the issue of whether the government must give formal recognition to any relationship that homosexual persons seek to enter.

Chief Justice Rehnquist and Justice Thomas joined with Justice Scalia in dissenting. Scalia argued, "What Texas has chosen to do is well within the range of traditional democratic action, and its hand should not be stayed through the invention of a brand-new 'constitutional right' by a Court that is impatient of democratic change." Finally, in a separate dissent, Justice Thomas observed, "I join Justice Scalia's dissenting opinion. I write separately to note that the law before the Court today "is ... uncommonly silly." ... "If I were a member of the Texas Legislature, I would vote to repeal it. Punishing someone for expressing his sexual preference through noncommercial consensual conduct with another adult does not appear to be a worthy way to expend valuable law enforcement resources."

> ### To Summarize:
>
> ◆ *Libertarians have long argued that laws prohibiting homosexual conduct violate the right of privacy, and that traditional morality is an insufficient basis for upholding such legislation. In recent years, the courts have adopted this perspective.*
>
> ◆ *In* Bowers v. Hardwick *(1986), the Supreme Court narrowly upheld a Georgia antisodomy law as applied to homosexual conduct. In the wake of* Bowers, *a number of state courts struck down their state sodomy statutes on the basis of protections found in their respective state constitutions, thus illustrating the importance of judicial federalism in the area of civil liberties.*
>
> ◆ *In* Lawrence v. Texas *(2003), the Supreme Court overturned* Bowers v. Hardwick *by striking down a Texas law forbidding private, consensual homosexual conduct.*

The Right to Die

Since the mid-1970s, the right of privacy has been successfully asserted as a basis for refusing medical treatment. For example, in *Superintendent of Belchertown State School v. Saikewicz* (Mass. 1977), the Massachusetts Supreme Judicial Court permitted the guardian of an elderly, retarded man to assert his ward's right of privacy and refuse chemotherapy treatment for the elderly man's leukemia. Under the right of privacy, courts have also authorized the discontinuation of artificial means of life support, even if it results in the immediate death of the patient. For example, in the case of *Guardianship of Andrew Barry* (1984), a Florida appellate court allowed the removal of a respirator that was maintaining the life of a comatose infant. Andrew Barry was one of twins, the other of whom died at birth. Andrew had a serious brain defect that kept him comatose and unable to breathe without mechanical assistance. After it became clear that Andrew would never achieve a "sapient existence" and would spend his life on the ventilator, his parents asked the hospital to remove the machine. Not surprisingly, the hospital refused to do so without a court order.

The Karen Quinlan Case

In both *Saikewicz* and *Barry*, courts relied on the doctrine of "substituted judgment" whereby legal guardians are permitted to exercise the rights of persons under their authority. The best-known case involving the doctrine of substituted judgment in relation to the so-called right to die is *In re Quinlan* (N.J. 1976). Karen Quinlan was a healthy young woman who became permanently comatose after she ingested large quantities of drugs and alcohol. In this condition, she was unable to maintain normal breathing without a ventilator. After it became clear that Karen Quinlan would not regain consciousness, her parents asked her physicians to remove the respirator. The physicians refused, no doubt concerned about possible criminal prosecution or civil liability. The Quinlans went to court and obtained an order allowing removal of the life-support machine. According to the New Jersey Supreme Court, the right of privacy was "broad enough to encompass [Karen Quinlan's] decision to decline medical treatment under certain circumstances, in much the same way as it is broad enough to encompass a woman's decision to terminate pregnancy." Of course, Karen Quinlan, lying comatose in the hospital, was unable to communicate her intentions to exercise this aspect of the right of privacy. According to the Court's opinion, the "only practical way to prevent destruction of [Karen Quinlan's] right is to permit the guardian and family … to render their best judgment as to whether she would exercise [the right to decline treatment] in these circumstances." After Karen Quinlan was taken off the breathing machine, she lived for nine years in a coma, taking food and water through a nasogastric tube. Her parents never asked that this feeding be discontinued, but therein lies another troubling question. Does the right of privacy empower a terminally ill patient to refuse food and water provided through a nasogastric tube? In *Bouvia v. Superior Court* (Cal. 1986), the California Supreme Court answered this question in the affirmative in a case involving a young woman who, although competent, was suffering the terrible effects of an advanced degenerative illness.

A Right to Commit Suicide?

Court decisions such as *Quinlan* and *Bouvia* have led to a national debate over the **right to die**. In what circumstances and by what means does a person have a right to bring about his or her own demise? Critics of the right to die argue that it is a "slippery slope" leading inexorably to the legal recognition of mercy killing and suicide. If the right of privacy allows an individual to make fundamental life choices and to decide what happens to his or her body, then how can laws that forbid suicide (or aiding and abetting suicide) be constitutional? During the 1990s, the public debate over the right to die took an eerie turn when it was revealed that a doctor named Jack Kevorkian was assisting terminally ill people in committing suicide. After several unsuccessful attempts to prosecute Kevorkian, in 1999 a Michigan jury found him guilty of second-degree murder in the death of a man suffering from Lou Gehrig's disease. The court sentenced him to serve ten to twenty-five years in prison. He was paroled in 2007 after serving eight years, on the condition he no longer engage in assisting others commit suicide. The case of Dr. Kevorkian raised a troubling question: If suicide is a constitutional right, as the California Supreme Court suggested in the *Bouvia* case, how can it be a crime to assist someone in committing suicide?

The Nancy Cruzan Case

The U.S. Supreme Court's only significant decision to date involving the right to die is the 1990 case of *Cruzan v. Missouri Health Department*. When the case reached the Supreme Court, Nancy Cruzan had for six years been confined to a hospital bed in a state of unconsciousness. Her condition was the result of extreme brain damage that occurred in an automobile accident. When it became apparent that Cruzan's condition was irreversible, her parents asked the hospital to remove the nasogastric tube that was keeping her alive. The hospital refused absent a court order. The trial court issued the order, but the Missouri Supreme Court reversed, citing the state's "policy strongly favoring the preservation of life." The Missouri Supreme Court said that since Nancy Cruzan was unable to communicate, there would have to be clear and convincing evidence of her desire to have the feeding tube removed. Dividing 5 to 4, the U.S. Supreme Court upheld the Missouri Supreme Court's decision. Writing for the Court, Chief Justice Rehnquist held that, although Nancy Cruzan had a right to terminate life-prolonging treatment, it was reasonable for the state to impose the clear and convincing evidence standard as a means of guarding against potential abuse of the "substituted judgment" doctrine.

Critics of the right to die, many of whom also oppose legalized abortion, hailed the *Cruzan* decision as a victory for the pro-life movement. It remains to be seen, however, whether the *Cruzan* decision represented a turnaround in the development of the right to die or merely the fine-tuning of a right that is now well established in American jurisprudence. It is likely that state, rather than federal, courts will continue to take the lead in developing this important new area of the law.

Doctor-Assisted Suicide

The courts have recognized a sharp distinction between termination of life-support systems and the active administration of means designed to end a person's life. But recently this distinction between passive and active euthanasia has been called into question. There are those in the medical community who believe that physicians should be able to provide active assistance to terminally ill patients who wish to hasten their own

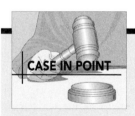

CASE IN POINT

The Terri Schiavo Case

Perhaps the best-known and most controversial case involving the right to die is the tragic Terri Schiavo case, which came to the nation's attention in 2004. Fifteen years earlier, Ms. Schiavo, at that time only 26 years old, had suffered a major heart attack and was rendered comatose. When she did not regain consciousness after several weeks, doctors diagnosed her condition as a persistent vegetative state. Because Terri had no "living will" (a legal document expressing one's wishes should one be in a persistent vegetative state and therefore unable to communicate), her husband petitioned a Florida court to remove the feeding tube that was keeping her alive. Over the strong objections of her parents, the court found that Ms. Schiavo did not wish to be kept alive and ordered her feeding tube removed. The court's decision engendered numerous unsuccessful appeals in state courts. The Florida legislature became involved in the controversy and even the U.S. Congress passed a law granting federal courts jurisdiction over this particular case, an action that raised interesting constitutional issues. The U.S. Supreme Court denied review of lower federal-court decisions denying the parents relief. Even Florida Governor Jeb Bush then unsuccessfully attempted to prohibit the removal of the feeding tube. Finally, Ms. Schiavo's feeding tube was removed, and she died on March 31, 2005, at the age of 41. The Schiavo case did not develop any new legal principles or procedures. It did, however, reaffirm the right to die in a highly public and highly politicized context. Moreover, it focused national attention on the need for individuals to execute living wills clearly defining the extent of extraordinary medical procedures to be employed in the event a person is in a persistent vegetative state.

deaths. There are those who argue that **doctor-assisted suicide** is well within the scope of privacy protected by the Constitution. But such views have yet to be accepted by the mainstream of the medical and legal communities.

To prevent assisted suicide in the state of Washington, the legislature enacted a law providing that "[a] person is guilty of promoting a suicide attempt when he knowingly causes or aids another person to attempt suicide." Promoting a suicide attempt is a felony punishable by up to five years' imprisonment and up to a $10,000 fine. In 1994, a federal judge ruled that Washington's statute banning assisted suicide was unconstitutional. Hearing the case en banc, the Ninth Circuit concluded that the state's assisted suicide ban was unconstitutional as applied to "terminally ill competent adults who wish to hasten their deaths with medication prescribed by their physicians." In *Washington v. Glucksberg* (1997), the Supreme Court reversed the Ninth Circuit's decision. Writing for a unanimous Court, Chief Justice Rehnquist discussed the historical and cultural background of laws prohibiting assisted suicide. He pointed out that in almost every state it is a crime to assist in a suicide, and that the statutes banning assisted suicide are longstanding expressions of the states' commitment to the protection and preservation of all human life. Rehnquist analyzed the interests that come into play in determining whether a statute banning assisted suicide passes constitutional muster. He rejected any parallel between a person's right to terminate medical treatment and the right to have assistance in committing suicide. The Court's decision in *Glucksberg* recognized that a serious debate was taking place throughout the nation about the morality and legality of assisted suicide—a debate that the Court's decision permitted to continue. Currently the states of Oregon and Washington are the only ones that recognize an implicit right to physician-assisted suicide. But the state of Montana, based on state court rulings, has also recognized the legitimacy of the practice. In 2012 a ballot measure to legalize assisted suicide in Massachusetts was narrowly defeated, and in 2013 the Vermont legislature passed a law similar to the model in Oregon. Though this hardly represents a national consensus on the issue, the debate over defining an individual's right to die continues. It is likely that the U.S. Supreme Court will revisit this issue in the not-too-distant future.

To Summarize:

◆ *Since the mid-1970s, the right of privacy has been successfully asserted in state courts as a basis for competent adults to refuse medical treatment. It has been extended to allow the termination of artificial life-support systems in cases where patients are found to be in a persistent vegetative state resulting from injury or illness.*

◆ *The courts have generally rejected a thoroughgoing right to die that would allow any competent adult to commit suicide under any conditions.*

◆ *In 1990, the Supreme Court recognized that terminally ill patients have the right to order removal of life-support systems, but permitted states to impose a requirement that there be clear and convincing evidence of patients' desire that such systems be removed.*

◆ *In 1997, the Court entered the debate over physician-assisted suicide, holding that there is no constitutional right to engage in such conduct. This decision effectively permits states to regulate in this area, although state courts can play a significant role under the relevant provisions of state constitutions.*

◆ *The highly politicized Terry Schiavo case, which reached its conclusion in 2005, reaffirmed the right to die and focused national attention on the need for individuals to execute living wills.*

Conclusion

The modern Supreme Court has fashioned a general, independent constitutional right of privacy by drawing on the Fourteenth Amendment and on various provisions of the Bill of Rights. While the legal logic underlying the right of privacy is debatable, the right is now firmly established in American constitutional law. The right of privacy has been recognized by the courts of most states, and several state constitutions now even contain explicit protections of the right of privacy. It is unclear whether, and how far, the courts will further extend the right of privacy.

In 1965, when the Supreme Court decided *Griswold v. Connecticut*, public sentiment had become decidedly more liberal in the area of sex and reproduction. The 1973 abortion decision did not meet with the same extent of popular approbation, and the opposition to abortion has been much more intense than the opposition to the use of devices that prevent conception. The so-called right to die, if it is limited to the withholding of extraordinary means of life prolongation, seems to be socially acceptable. But there would be considerable opposition to the legalization of active euthanasia or suicide. At this time, prevailing social norms do not condone homosexual conduct or the private use of recreational drugs. For courts to assert constitutional protections for such activities would be a bold move indeed, possibly leading to political retaliation. One certainly would not expect the U.S. Supreme Court, which has become steadily more conservative in recent years, to adopt such libertarian positions in the near future. The evolution of the right of privacy thus illustrates the give and take of American constitutional law. It also dramatizes the fact that constitutional rights do not exist in a social, political, or moral vacuum.

Key Terms

constitutional right of privacy
abortion
gay rights
euthanasia
moral individualism
libertarianism

classical conservatism
right to be let alone
substantive due process
compulsory sterilization
fundamental right
compelling interest

viability
Hyde amendment
trimester framework
sodomy
right to die
doctor-assisted suicide

For Further Reading

Barnett, Randy (ed.). *The Rights Retained by the People: The History and Meaning of the Ninth Amendment.* Fairfax, Va.: George Mason University Press, 1989.

DeRosa, Marshall. *The Ninth Amendment and the Politics of Creative Jurisprudence: Disparaging the Fundamental Right of Popular Control.* Somerset, N.J.: Transaction Publishers, 1996.

Glick, Henry R. *The Right to Die.* New York: Columbia University Press, 1994.

Greenhouse, Linda, and Reva Siegel. *Before* Roe v. Wade: *Voices That Shaped the Abortion Debate before the Supreme Court's Ruling.* Kaplan Publishing, 2010.

Hull, N. E. H., and Peter Charles Hoffer. *Roe v. Wade: The Abortion Rights Controversy in American History.* Lawrence: University Press of Kansas, 2001.

Luker, Kristin. *Abortion and the Politics of Motherhood.* Berkeley: University of California Press, 1980.

McClellan, Grant S. (ed.). *The Right to Privacy.* New York: H. W. Wilson, 1976.

Miller, Arthur R. *The Assault on Privacy.* Ann Arbor: University of Michigan Press, 1971.

Murphy, Paul L. *The Right to Privacy and the Ninth Amendment.* New York: Garland, 1990.

Neeley, G. Steven. *The Constitutional Right to Suicide: A Legal and Philosophical Examination.* New York: Peter Lang Publishing, 1994.

O'Brien, David M. *Privacy, Law, and Public Policy.* New York: Praeger, 1979.

O'Connor, Karen. *No Neutral Ground? Abortion Politics in an Age of Absolutes.* Boulder, Colo.: Westview Press, 1996.

Rubin, Eva R. *Abortion, Politics, and the Courts: Roe v. Wade and Its Aftermath.* New York: Greenwood Press, 1987.

Steiner, Gilbert Y. (ed.). *The Abortion Dispute and the American System.* Washington, D.C.: Brookings Institution, 1983.

Tribe, Laurence. *Abortion: The Clash of Absolutes.* New York: Norton, 1990.

Westin, Alan F. *Privacy and Freedom.* New York: Atheneum Press, 1970.

JACOBSON v. MASSACHUSETTS
737 U.S. 11; 25 S.Ct. 358; 49 L.Ed. 643 (1905)
Vote: 7-2

Acting under authority of state law, the board of health of Cambridge, Massachusetts, adopted a regulation requiring that, with certain exceptions, inhabitants of the city be vaccinated against smallpox. State law imposed a $5 fine for violation of the vaccination requirement. Henning Jacobson, a resident of Cambridge, refused to comply with the regulation. As a result, charges were filed against him: He was convicted, and the fine was imposed. Jacobson appealed his conviction, contending that the compulsory vaccination law and implementing regulation violated his rights under the Fourteenth Amendment. The state, in response, argued that the statute was a legitimate exercise of its police power. The Massachusetts Supreme Judicial Court sustained the constitutionality of the law, and Jacobson obtained review by the U.S. Supreme Court.

Mr. Justice Harlan delivered the opinion of the Court.

This case involves the validity, under the Constitution of the United States, of certain provisions in the statutes of Massachusetts relating to vaccination....

Is the statute ... inconsistent with the liberty which the Constitution of the United States secures to every person against deprivation by the state?

The authority of the state to enact this statute is to be referred to what is commonly called the police power—a power which the state did not surrender when becoming a member of the Union under the Constitution. Although this court has refrained from any attempt to define the limits of that power, yet it has "health laws of every description"; indeed, all laws that relate to matters completely within its territory and which do not by their necessary operation affect the people of other states. According to settled principles, the police power of a state must be held to embrace, at least, such reasonable regulations established directly by legislative enactment as will protect the public health and the public safety....

We come, then, to inquire whether any right given or secured by the Constitution is invaded by the statute as interpreted by the state court. The defendant insists that his liberty is invaded when the state subjects him to fine or imprisonment for neglecting or refusing to submit to vaccination; that a compulsory vaccination law is unreasonable, arbitrary, and oppressive, and, therefore, hostile to the inherent right of every freeman to care for his own body and health in such a way as to him seems best; and that the execution of such a law against one who objects to vaccination, no matter for what reason, is nothing short of an assault upon his person. But the liberty secured by the Constitution of the United States to every person within its jurisdiction does not import an absolute right in each person to be, at all times and in all circumstances, wholly freed from restraint. There are manifold restraints to which every person is necessarily subject for the common good. On any other basis organized society could not exist with safety to its members. Society based on the rule that each one is a law unto himself would soon be confronted with disorder and anarchy. Real liberty for all could not exist under the operation of a principle which recognizes the right of each individual person to use his own, whether in respect of his person or his property, regardless of the injury that may be done to others....

Applying these principles to the present case, it is to be observed that the legislature of Massachusetts required the inhabitants of a city or town to be vaccinated only when, in the opinion of the board of health, that was necessary for the public health or the public safety. The authority to determine for all what ought to be done in such an emergency must have been lodged somewhere or in some body; and surely it was appropriate for the legislature to refer that question, in the first instance, to a board of health composed of persons residing in the locality affected, and appointed, presumably, because of their fitness to determine such questions. To invest such a body with authority over such matters was not an unusual, nor an unreasonable or arbitrary, requirement. Upon the principle of self-defense, of paramount necessity, a community has the right to protect itself against an epidemic of disease which threatens the safety of its members....

There is, of course, a sphere within which the individual may assert the supremacy of his own will, and rightfully dispute the authority of any human government, especially of any free government existing under a written constitution, to interfere with the exercise of

(Continued)

that will. But it is equally true that in every well-ordered society charged with the duty of conserving the safety of its members the rights of the individual in respect of his liberty may at times, under the pressure of great dangers, be subjected to such restraint, to be enforced by reasonable regulations, as the safety of the general public may demand....

Whatever may be thought of the expediency of this statute, it cannot be affirmed to be, beyond question, in palpable conflict with the Constitution. Nor, in view of the methods employed to stamp out the disease of smallpox, can anyone confidently assert that the means prescribed by the state to that end has no real or substantial relation to the protection of the public health and the public safety? Such an assertion would not be consistent with the experience of this and other countries whose authorities have dealt with the disease of smallpox. And the principle of vaccination as a means to prevent the spread of smallpox has been enforced in many states by statutes making the vaccination of children a condition of their right to enter or remain in public school....

We are not prepared to hold that a minority, residing or remaining in any city or town where smallpox is prevalent, and enjoying the general protection afforded by an organized local government, may thus defy the will of its constituted authorities, acting in good faith for all, under the legislative sanction of the state. If such be the privilege of a minority, then a like privilege would belong to each individual of the community, and the spectacle would be presented of the welfare and safety of an entire population being subordinated to the notions of a single individual who chooses to remain a part of that population. We are unwilling to hold it to be an element in the liberty secured by the Constitution of the United States that one person, or a minority of persons, residing in any community and enjoying the benefits of its local government, should have the power thus to dominate the majority when supported in their action by the authority of the state. While this court should guard with firmness every right appertaining to life, liberty, or property as secured to the individual by the supreme law of the land, it is of the last importance that it should not invade the domain of local authority except when it is plainly necessary to do so in order to enforce that law...

The judgment of the court below must be affirmed.

Mr. Justice Brewer and *Mr. Justice Peckham* dissent.

MEYER v. NEBRASKA
262 U.S. 390; 43 S.Ct. 625; 67 L.Ed. 1042 (1923)
Vote: 7-2

Robert T. Meyer was fined $25 for violating a Nebraska law prohibiting the teaching of foreign languages to students who had not completed the eighth grade. His crime: teaching German to a ten-year-old boy attending a private school. The Nebraska Supreme Court affirmed the conviction and Meyer appealed to the Supreme Court. Before the U.S. Supreme Court, Meyer's counsel characterized the statute as an expression of "hatred, national bigotry and racial prejudice engendered by the World War." The state of Nebraska averred that it was "the ambition of the State to have its entire population 100% American."

Mr. Justice McReynolds delivered the opinion of the Court.

... While this Court has not attempted to define with exactness the liberty [guaranteed by the Fourteenth Amendment], the term has received much consideration and some of the included things have been definitely stated. Without doubt, it denotes not merely freedom from bodily restraint but also the right of the individual to contract, to engage in any of the common occupations of life, to acquire useful knowledge, to marry, establish a home and bring up children, to worship God according to the dictates of his own conscience, and generally to enjoy those privileges long recognized at common law as essential to the orderly pursuit of happiness by free men.... The established doctrine is that this liberty may not be interfered with, under the guise of protecting the public interest, by legislative action which is arbitrary or without reasonable relation to some purpose within the competency of the State to effect. Determination by the legislature of what constitutes proper exercise of police power is not final or conclusive but is subject to supervision by the courts....

Corresponding to the right of control, it is the natural duty of the parent to give his children education suitable to their station in life; and nearly all the States, including Nebraska, enforce this obligation by compulsory laws.

Practically, education of the young is only possible in schools conducted by especially qualified persons who devote themselves thereto. The calling always has been regarded as useful and honorable, essential, indeed, to the public welfare. Mere knowledge of the German language cannot reasonably be regarded as harmful. Heretofore it has been commonly looked upon as helpful and desirable. Plaintiff in error taught this language in school as part of his occupation. His right thus to teach and the right of parents to engage him so to instruct their children, we think, are within the liberty of the Amendment.

The challenged statute forbids the teaching in school of any subject except in English; also the teaching of any other language until the pupil has attained and successfully passed the eighth grade, which is not usually accomplished before the age of twelve. The Supreme Court of the State has held that "the so-called ancient or dead languages" are not "within the spirit or the purpose of the act." ... Latin, Greek, Hebrew are not proscribed; but German, French, Spanish, Italian and every other alien speech are within the ban. Evidently the legislature has attempted materially to interfere with the calling of modern language teachers, with the opportunities of pupils to acquire knowledge, and with the power of parents to control the education of their own....

That the State may do much, go very far, indeed, in order to improve the quality of its citizens, physically, mentally and morally, is clear; but the individual has certain fundamental rights which must be respected. The protection of the Constitution extends to all, to those who speak other languages as well as to those born with English on the tongue. Perhaps it would be highly advantageous if all had ready understanding of our ordinary speech, but this cannot be coerced by methods which conflict with the Constitution—a desirable end cannot be promoted by prohibited means....

It hardly will be affirmed that any legislature could impose such restrictions upon the people of a State without doing violence to both letter and spirit of the Constitution.

The desire of the legislature to foster a homogeneous people with American ideals prepared readily to understand current discussions of civic matters is easy to appreciate. Unfortunate experiences during the late war and aversion toward every characteristic of truculent adversaries were certainly enough to quicken that aspiration. But the means adopted, we think, exceed the limitations upon the power of the State and conflict with rights assured to plaintiff in error. The interference is plain enough, and no adequate reason therefore in time of peace and domestic tranquility has been shown.

The power of the State to compel attendance at some school and to make reasonable regulations for all schools, including a requirement that they shall give instructions in English, is not questioned. Nor has challenge been made of the State's power to prescribe a curriculum for institutions which it supports. Those matters are not within the present controversy.... No emergency has arisen which renders knowledge by a child of some language other than English so clearly harmful as to justify its inhibition with the consequent infringement of rights long freely enjoyed. We are constrained to conclude that the statute as applied is arbitrary and without reasonable relation to any end within the competency of the State.

The judgment of the court below must be reversed, and the cause remanded for further proceedings not inconsistent with this opinion.

Mr. Justice Holmes [with whom *Justice Sutherland* concurred], dissenting.

We all agree, I take it, that it is desirable that all the citizens of the United States should speak a common tongue, and therefore that the end aimed at by the statute is a lawful and proper one. The only question is whether the means adopted deprive teachers of the liberty secured to them by the Fourteenth Amendment. It is with hesitation and unwillingness that I differ from my brethren with regard to a law like this but I cannot bring my mind to believe that in some circumstances, and circumstances existing it is said in Nebraska, the statute might not be regarded as a reasonable or even necessary method of reaching the desired result. The part of the act with which we

(Continued)

are concerned deals with the teaching of young children. Youth is the time when familiarity with a language is established and if there are sections in the State where a child would hear only Polish or French or German spoken at home I am not prepared to say that it is unreasonable to provide that in his early years he shall hear and speak only English at school. But if it is reasonable it is not an undue restriction of the liberty either of teacher or scholar. No one would doubt that a teacher might be forbidden to teach many things, and the only criterion of his liberty under the Constitution that I can think of is "whether, considering the end in view, the statute passes the bounds of reason and assumes the character of a merely arbitrary fiat." ... I think I appreciate the objection to the law but it appears to me to present a question upon which men reasonably might differ and therefore I am unable to say that the Constitution of the United States prevents the experiment being tried....

BUCK v. BELL
274 U.S. 200; 47 S.Ct. 584; 71 L.Ed. 1000 (1927)
Vote: 8-1

In this notorious case, the Court considers whether the Constitution permits a state to order the sterilization of a "mentally defective" person who is in state custody.

Mr. Justice Holmes delivered the opinion of the Court.

This is a writ of error to review a judgment of the Supreme Court of Appeals of the State of Virginia, affirming a judgment of the Circuit Court of Amherst County, by which the defendant in error [Dr. J. H. Bell], the superintendent of the State Colony for Epileptics and Feeble Minded, was ordered to perform the operation of salpingectomy upon Carrie Buck, the plaintiff in error, for the purpose of making her sterile.... The case comes here upon the contention that the statute authorizing the judgment is void under the Fourteenth Amendment as denying to the plaintiff in error due process of law and the equal protection of the laws.

Carrie Buck is a feeble-minded white woman who was committed to the State Colony above mentioned in due form. She is the daughter of a feeble-minded mother in the same institution, and the mother of an illegitimate feeble-minded child. She was eighteen years old at the time of the trial of her case in the Circuit Court, in the latter part of 1924. An Act of Virginia, approved March 20, 1924, recites that the health of the patient and the welfare of society may be promoted in certain cases by the sterilization of mental defectives, under careful safeguard....

The attack is not upon the procedure but upon the substantive law.... In view of the general declarations of the legislature and the specific findings of the Court, obviously we cannot say as matter of law that the grounds do not exist, and if they exist they justify the result.... It is better for all the world, if instead of waiting to execute degenerate offspring for crime, or to let them starve for their imbecility, society can prevent those who are manifestly unfit from continuing their kind. The principle that sustains compulsory vaccination is broad enough to cover cutting the Fallopian tubes. Three generations of imbeciles are enough.

But, it is said, however it might be if this reasoning were applied generally, it fails when it is confined to the small number who are in the institutions named and is not applied to the multitudes outside. It is the usual last resort of constitutional arguments to point out shortcomings of this sort. But the answer is that the law does all that is needed when it does all that it can, indicates a policy, applies it to all within the lines, and seeks to bring within the lines all similarly situated so far and so fast as its means allow. Of course so far as the operations enable those who otherwise must be kept confined to be returned to the world, and thus open the asylum to others, the equality aimed at will be more nearly reached.

Judgment affirmed.

Mr. Justice Butler dissents.

POE v. ULLMAN
367 U.S. 497; 81 S.Ct. 1752; 6 L.Ed. 2d. 989 (1961)
Vote: 5-4

A married couple and their doctor brought suit to challenge a Connecticut law forbidding the use of artificial means of birth control. The Supreme Court dismisses the case as unripe for judicial review. However, Justice Harlan's dissenting opinion is noteworthy as an important milestone in the development of the right of privacy.

Mr. Justice Frankfurter announced the judgment of the Court and an opinion in which the **Chief Justice** [Warren], **Mr. Justice Clark**, and **Mr. Justice Whittaker** join.

... These appeals challenge the constitutionality, under the Fourteenth Amendment, of Connecticut statutes which, as authoritatively construed by the Connecticut Supreme Court of Errors, prohibit the use of contraceptive devices and the giving of medical advice in the use of such devices. In proceedings seeking declarations of law, not on review of convictions for violation of the statutes, that court has ruled that these statutes would be applicable in the case of married couples and even under claim that conception would constitute a serious threat to the health or life of the female spouse....

The Connecticut law prohibiting the use of contraceptives has been on the State's books since 1879.... During the more than three-quarters of a century since its enactment, a prosecution for its violation seems never to have been initiated, save in *State v. Nelson*.... The circumstances of that case, decided in 1940, only prove the abstract character of what is before us. There, a test case was brought to determine the constitutionality of the Act as applied against two doctors and a nurse who had allegedly disseminated contraceptive information. After the Supreme Court of Errors sustained the legislation on appeal from a demurrer to the information, the State moved to dismiss the information. Neither counsel nor our own researchers have discovered any other attempt to enforce the prohibition of distribution or use of contraceptive devices by criminal process....

... The fact that Connecticut has not chosen to press to enforcement of this statute deprives these controversies of the immediacy which is an indispensable condition of constitutional adjudication. This Court cannot be umpire to debates concerning harmless, empty shadows. To find it necessary to pass on these statutes now, in order to protect appellants from the hazards of prosecution, would be to close our eyes to reality....

Dismissed.

Mr. Justice Black dissents because he believes that the constitutional questions should be reached and decided.

Mr. Justice Brennan, concurring in the judgment....

Mr. Justice Stewart, dissenting....

Mr. Justice Douglas, dissenting....

Mr. Justice Harlan, dissenting.

... I consider that this Connecticut legislation, as construed to apply to these appellants, violates the Fourteenth Amendment. I believe that a statute making it a criminal offense for married couples to use contraceptives is an intolerable and unjustifiable invasion of privacy and in the conduct of the most intimate concerns of an individual's personal life. ...

Adultery, homosexuality and the like are sexual intimacies which the State forbids altogether, but the intimacy of husband and wife is necessarily an essential and accepted feature of the institution of marriage, an institution which the State not only must allow, but which always and in every age it has fostered and protected. It is one thing when the State exerts its power either to forbid extramarital sexuality altogether, or to say who may marry, but it is quite another when, having acknowledged a marriage and the intimacies inherent in it, it undertakes to regulate by means of the criminal law the details of that intimacy.

In sum, even though the State has determined that the use of contraceptives is as iniquitous as any act of extramarital sexual immorality, the intrusion of the whole machinery of the criminal law into the very heart of marital privacy, requiring husband and wife to render account before a criminal tribunal of their

(Continued)

uses of that intimacy, is surely a very different thing indeed from punishing those who establish intimacies which the law has always forbidden and which can have no claim to social protection.

In my view the appellants have presented a very pressing claim for Constitutional protection. Such difficulty as the claim presents lies only in evaluating it against the State's countervailing contention that it be allowed to enforce, by whatever means it deems appropriate, its judgment of the immorality of the practice this law condemns. In resolving this conflict a number of factors compel me to conclude that the decision here must most emphatically be for the appellants. Since, as it appears to me, the statute marks an abridgment of important fundamental liberties protected by the Fourteenth Amendment, it will not do to urge in justification of that abridgement simply that the statute is rationally related to the effectuation of a proper state purpose. A closer scrutiny and stronger justification than that are required....

Though the State has argued the Constitutional permissibility of the moral judgment underlying this statute, neither its brief, not its argument, nor anything in any of the opinions of its highest court in these or other cases even remotely suggests a justification for the obnoxiously intrusive means it has chosen to effectuate that policy. To me the very circumstance that Connecticut has not chosen to press the enforcement of this statute against individual users, while it nevertheless persists in asserting its right to do so at any time—in effect a right to hold this statute as an imminent threat to the privacy of the households of the State—conduces to the inference either that it does not consider the policy of the statute a very important one, or that it does not regard the means it has chosen for its effectuation as appropriate or necessary.

But conclusive, in my view, is the utter novelty of this enactment. Although the Federal Government and many States have at one time or other had on their books statutes forbidding or regulating the distribution of contraceptives, none, so far as I can find, has made the use of contraceptives a crime. Indeed, a diligent search has revealed that no nation, including several which quite evidently share Connecticut's moral policy, has seen fit to effectuate that policy by the means presented here.

Though undoubtedly the States are and should be left free to reflect a wide variety of policies and should be allowed broad scope in experimenting with various means of promoting those policies, I must agree with Mr. Justice Jackson that "[t]here are limits to the extent to which a legislatively represented majority may conduct ... experiments at the expense of the dignity and personality" of the individual.... In this instance these limits are, in my view, reached and passed....

GRISWOLD v. CONNECTICUT
381 U.S. 479; 85 S.Ct. 1678; 14 L.Ed. 2d. 510 (1965)
Vote: 7-2

In this landmark case, the Court considers the constitutionality of a state statute criminalizing the use of birth-control devices.

Mr. Justice Douglas delivered the opinion of the Court.

Appellant Griswold is Executive Director of the Planned Parenthood League of Connecticut. Appellant Buxton is a licensed physician and a professor at the Yale Medical School who served as Medical Director for the League at its Center in New Haven—a center open and operating from November 1 to November 10, 1961, when appellants were arrested.

They gave information, instruction and medical advice to *married* persons as to the means of preventing conception. They examined the wife and prescribed the best contraceptive device or material for her use. Fees were usually charged, although some couples were serviced free.

The statutes whose constitutionality is involved in this appeal [provide]:

Any person who uses any drug, medicinal article or instrument for the purpose of preventing conception shall be fined not less than fifty dollars or imprisoned not less than sixty days nor more than one year or be both fined and imprisoned.

Any person who assists, abets, counsels, causes, hires or commands another to commit any offense may be prosecuted and punished as if he were the principal offender.

The appellants were found guilty as accessories and fined $100 each, against the claim that the accessory statute as so applied violated the Fourteenth Amendment. The Appellate Division of the Circuit Court affirmed. The Supreme Court of Errors affirmed that judgment....

We think that appellants have standing to raise the constitutional rights of the married people with whom they had a professional relationship.... Certainly the accessory should have standing to assert that the offense which he is charged with assisting is not, or cannot constitutionally be, a crime....

Coming to the merits, we are met with a wide range of questions that implicate the Due Process Clause of the Fourteenth Amendment. Overtones of some arguments suggest that *Lochner v. New York* (1905) should be our guide. But we decline that invitation.... We do not sit as a superlegislature to determine the wisdom, need, and propriety of laws that touch economic problems, business affairs, or social conditions. This law, however, operates directly on an intimate relation of husband and wife and their physician's role in one aspect of that relation.

The association of people is not mentioned in the Constitution nor in the Bill of Rights. The right to educate a child in a school of the parents' choice—whether public or private or parochial—is also not mentioned. Nor is the right to study any particular subject or any foreign language. Yet the First Amendment has been construed to include certain of those rights.

By *Pierce v. Society of Sisters* (1925) the right to educate one's children as one chooses is made applicable to the States by the force of the First and Fourteenth Amendments. By *Meyer v. Nebraska* (1923) the same dignity is given the right to study the German language in a private school. In other words, the State may not, consistently with the spirit of the First Amendment, contract the spectrum of available knowledge. The right of freedom of speech and press includes not only the right to utter or to print, but the right to distribute, the right to receive, the right to read ... and freedom of inquiry, freedom of thought, and freedom to teach ... indeed the freedom of the entire university community.... Without those peripheral rights the specific rights would be less secure.

And so we reaffirm the principle of the *Pierce* and the *Meyer* cases.

In *NAACP v. Alabama* (1958) we protected the "freedom to associate and privacy in one's associations," noting that freedom of association was a peripheral First Amendment right. Disclosure of membership lists of a constitutionally valid association, we held, was invalid "as entailing the likelihood of a substantial restraint upon the exercise by petitioner's members of their right to freedom of association." In other words, the First Amendment has a penumbra where privacy is protected from governmental intrusion. In like context, we have protected forms of "association" that are not political in the customary sense but pertain to the social, legal, and economic benefit of the members....

[Previous] ... cases suggest that specific guarantees in the Bill of Rights have penumbras, formed by emanations from those guarantees that help give them life and substance. Various guarantees create zones of privacy. The right of association contained in the penumbra of the First Amendment is one, as we have seen. The Third Amendment in its prohibition against the quartering of soldiers "in any house" in time of peace without the consent of the owner is another facet of that privacy. The Fourth Amendment explicitly affirms the "right of the people to be secure in their persons, houses, papers, and effects, against unreasonable searches and seizures." The Fifth Amendment in its Self-incrimination Clause enables the citizen to create a zone of privacy which government may not force him to surrender to his detriment. The Ninth Amendment provides: "The enumeration in the Constitution, of certain rights, shall not be construed to deny or disparage others retained by the people." The Fourth and Fifth Amendments were described in *Boyd v. United States* (1886) as protection against all governmental invasions "of the sanctity of a man's home and the privacies of life." We recently referred in *Mapp v. Ohio* (1961) to the Fourth Amendment as creating a "right to privacy, no less important than any other right carefully and particularly reserved to the people." ...

We have had many controversies over these penumbral rights of "privacy and repose." ... These cases bear witness that the right of privacy which presses for recognition here is a legitimate one.

The present case, then, concerns a relationship lying within the zone of privacy created by several fundamental constitutional guarantees. And it concerns a

(Continued)

law which, in forbidding the *use* of contraceptives rather than regulating their manufacture or sale, seeks to achieve its goals by means having a maximum destructive impact upon that relationship. Such a law cannot stand in light of the familiar principle, so often applied by this Court, that a "governmental purpose to control or prevent activities constitutionally subject to state regulation may not be achieved by means which sweep unnecessarily broadly and thereby invade the area of protected freedoms." ... Would we allow the police to search the sacred precincts of marital bedrooms for telltale signs of the use of contraceptives? The very idea is repulsive to the notions of privacy surrounding the marriage relationship....

Mr. Justice Goldberg, with whom the *Chief Justice* [Warren] and *Mr. Justice Brennan* join, concurring.

... Although the Constitution does not speak in so many words of the right of privacy in marriage, I cannot believe that it offers these fundamental rights no protection. The fact that no particular provision of the Constitution explicitly forbids the State from disrupting the traditional relation of the family—a relation as old and as fundamental as our entire civilization—surely does not show that the Government was meant to have the power to do so. Rather, as the Ninth Amendment expressly recognizes, there are fundamental personal rights such as this one, which are protected from abridgment by the Government though not specifically mentioned in the Constitution....

The logic of the dissents would sanction federal or state legislation that seems to me even more plainly unconstitutional than the statute before us. Surely the Government, absent a showing of a compelling subordinating state interest, could not decree that all husbands and wives must be sterilized after two children have been born to them. Yet by their reasoning such an invasion of marital privacy would not be subject to constitutional challenge because, while it might be "silly," no provision of the Constitution specifically prevents the Government from curtailing the marital right to bear children and raise a family. While it may shock some of my Brethren that the Court today holds that the Constitution protects the right of marital privacy, in my view it is far more shocking to believe that the personal liberty guaranteed by the Constitution does not include protection against such totalitarian limitation of family size, which is at complete variance with our constitutional concepts. Yet, if

upon a showing of a slender basis of rationality, a law outlawing voluntary birth control by married persons is valid, then, by the same reasoning, a law requiring compulsory birth control also would seem to be valid. In my view, however, both types of law would unjustifiably intrude upon rights of marital privacy which are constitutionally protected.

In a long series of cases this Court has held that where fundamental personal liberties are involved, they may not be abridged by the States simply on a showing that a regulatory statute has some rational relationship to the effectuation of a proper state purpose....

Although the Connecticut birth-control law obviously encroaches upon a fundamental personal liberty, the State does not show that the law serves any "subordinating [state] interest which is compelling" or that it is "necessary ... to the accomplishment of a permissible state policy." The State, at most, argues that there is some rational relation between this statute and what is admittedly a legitimate subject of state concern—the discouraging of extra-marital relations. It says that preventing the use of birth-control devices by married persons helps prevent the indulgence by some in such extramarital relations. The rationality of this justification is dubious, particularly in light of the admitted widespread availability to all persons in the State of Connecticut, unmarried as well as married, of birth-control devices for the prevention of disease, as distinguished from the prevention of conception.... But, in any event, it is clear that the state interest in safeguarding marital fidelity can be served by a more discriminately tailored statute, which does not, like the present one, sweep unnecessarily broadly, reaching far beyond the evil sought to be dealt with and intruding upon the privacy of all married couples....

Finally, it should be said of the Court's holding today that it in no way interferes with a State's proper regulation of sexual promiscuity or misconduct....

In sum, I believe that the right of privacy in the marital relation is fundamental and basic—a personal right "retained by the people" within the meaning of the Ninth Amendment. Connecticut cannot constitutionally abridge this fundamental right, which is protected by the Fourteenth Amendment from infringement by the States. I agree with the Court that petitioners' convictions must therefore be reversed.

Mr. Justice Harlan, concurring in the judgment.

... In my view, the proper constitutional inquiry in this case is whether this Connecticut statute infringes the Due Process Clause of the Fourteenth Amendment because the enactment violates basic values "implicit in the concept of ordered liberty." ... For reasons stated at length in my dissenting opinion in *Poe v. Ullman*, I believe that it does.

While the relevant inquiry may be aided by resort to one or more of the provisions of the Bill of Rights, it is not dependent on them or any of their radiations. The Due Process Clause of the Fourteenth Amendment stands, in my opinion, on its own bottom....

Mr. Justice White, concurring in the judgment.

In my view this Connecticut law as applied to married couples deprives them of "liberty" without due process of law, as that concept is used in the Fourteenth Amendment. I therefore concur in the judgment of the Court reversing these convictions under the Connecticut aiding and abetting statute....

Mr. Justice Black, with whom *Mr. Justice Stewart* joins, dissenting.

... I get nowhere in this case by talk about a constitutional "right of privacy" as an emanation from one or more constitutional provisions. I like my privacy as well as the next one, but I am nevertheless compelled to admit that government has a right to invade it unless prohibited by some specific constitutional provision. For these reasons I cannot agree with the Court's judgment and the reasons it gives for holding this Connecticut law unconstitutional....

I realize that many good and able men have eloquently spoken and written, sometimes in rhapsodical strains, about the duty of this Court to keep the Constitution in tune with the times. The idea is that the Constitution must be changed from time to time and that this Court is charged with a duty to make those changes. For myself, I must with all deference reject that philosophy. The Constitution makers knew the need for change and provided for it. Amendments suggested by the people's elected representatives can be submitted to the people or their selected agents for ratification. That method of change was good enough for our Fathers, and being somewhat old-fashioned I must add it is good enough for me. And so, I cannot rely on the Due Process Clause or the Ninth Amendment or any mysterious and uncertain natural law

concept as a reason for striking down this state law. The Due Process Clause with an "arbitrary and capricious" or "shocking to the conscience" formula was liberally used by this Court to strike down economic legislation in the early decades of this century, threatening, many people thought, the tranquility and stability of the Nation....

That formula, based on subjective considerations of "natural justice," is no less dangerous when used to enforce this Court's views about personal rights than those about economic rights. I had thought that we had laid that formula, as a means for striking down state legislation, to rest once and for all....

Mr. Justice Stewart, with whom *Mr. Justice Black* joins, dissenting.

Since 1879 Connecticut has had on its books a law which forbids the use of contraceptives by anyone. I think this is an uncommonly silly law. As a practical matter, the law is obviously unenforceable, except in the oblique context of the present case. As a philosophical matter, I believe the use of contraceptives in the relationship of marriage should be left to personal and private choice, based upon the individual's moral, ethical, and religious beliefs. As a matter of social policy, I think professional counsel about methods of birth control should be available to all, so that each individual's choice can be meaningfully made. But we are not asked in this case to say whether we think this law is unwise, or even asinine. We are asked to hold that it violates the United States Constitution. And that I cannot do.

In the course of its opinion the Court refers to no less than six Amendments to the Constitution: the First, the Third, the Fourth, the Fifth, the Ninth, and the Fourteenth. But the Court does not say which of these Amendments, if any, it thinks is infringed by this Connecticut law.

We are told that the Due Process Clause of the Fourteenth Amendment is not, as such, the "guide" in this case. With that much I agree. There is no claim that this law, duly enacted by the Connecticut Legislature, is unconstitutionally vague. There is no claim that the appellants were denied any of the elements of procedural due process at their trial, so as to make their convictions constitutionally invalid. And, as the Court says, the day has long passed since the Due Process Clause was regarded as a proper instrument for determining "the wisdom, need, and propriety" of state

(Continued)

laws.... My Brothers Harlan and White to the contrary, "[w]e have returned to the original constitutional proposition that courts do not substitute their social and economic beliefs for the judgment of legislative bodies, who are elected to pass laws." ...

But to say that the Ninth Amendment has anything to do with this case is to turn somersaults with history. The Ninth Amendment, like its companion the Tenth, which this Court held "states but a truism that all is retained which has not been surrendered," ... was framed by James Madison and adopted by the States simply to make clear that the adoption of the Bill of Rights did not alter the plan that the Federal Government was to be a government of express and limited powers, and that all rights and powers not delegated to it were retained by the people and the individual States. Until today no member of this Court has ever suggested that the Ninth Amendment meant anything else, and the idea that a federal court could ever use the Ninth Amendment to annul a law passed by the elected representatives of the people of the State of Connecticut would have caused James Madison no little wonder.

What provision of the Constitution, then, does make this state law invalid? The Court says it is the right of privacy "created by several fundamental constitutional guarantees." With all deference, I can find no such general right of privacy in the Bill of Rights, in any other part of the Constitution, or in any case ever before decided by this Court.

At the oral argument in this case we were told that the Connecticut law does not "conform to current community standards." But it is not the function of this Court to decide cases on the basis of community standards. We are here to decide cases "agreeably to the Constitution and laws of the United States." It is the essence of judicial duty to subordinate our own personal views, our own ideas of what legislation is wise and what is not. If, as I should surely hope, the law before us does not reflect the standards of the people of Connecticut, the people of Connecticut can freely exercise their true Ninth and Tenth Amendment rights to persuade their elected representative to repeal it. That is the constitutional way to take this law off the books.

ROE v. WADE
470 U.S. 113; 93 S.Ct. 705; 35 L.Ed. 2d. 147 (1973)
Vote: 7-2

In what is perhaps the most controversial judicial decision of the modern era, the Supreme Court reviews a Texas law criminalizing abortion.

Mr. Justice Blackmun delivered the opinion of the Court.

... The Texas statutes that concern us here ... make it a crime to "procure an abortion," as therein defined, or to attempt one, except with respect to "an abortion procured or attempted by medical advice for the purpose of saving the life of the mother." Similar statutes are in existence in a majority of the States.

Texas first enacted a criminal abortion statute in 1854.... This was soon modified into language that has remained substantially unchanged to the present time....

Jane Roe, a single woman who was residing in Dallas County, Texas, instituted this federal action in March 1970 against the District Attorney of the county. She sought a declaratory judgment that the Texas criminal abortion statutes were unconstitutional on their face, and an injunction restraining the defendant from enforcing the statutes.

Roe alleged that she was unmarried and pregnant; that she wished to terminate her pregnancy by an abortion "performed by a competent, licensed physician, under safe, clinical conditions"; that she was unable to get a "legal" abortion in Texas because her life did not appear to be threatened by the continuation of her pregnancy; and that she could not afford to travel to another jurisdiction in order to secure a legal abortion under safe conditions. She claimed that the Texas statutes were unconstitutionally vague and that they abridged her right of personal privacy, protected by the First, Fourth, Fifth, Ninth, and Fourteenth Amendments. By an amendment to her complaint Roe purported to sue "on behalf of herself and all other women" similarly situated....

The principal thrust of appellant's attack on the Texas statutes is that they improperly invade a right, said to be possessed by the pregnant woman, to choose to terminate her pregnancy. Appellant would discover this right in the concept of personal "liberty" embodied in the Fourteenth Amendment's Due Process Clause; or in personal, marital, familial, and sexual privacy said to be protected by the Bill of Rights or its penumbras, … or among those rights reserved to the people by the Ninth Amendment.…

Before addressing this claim, we feel it desirable briefly to survey, in several aspects, the history of abortion, for such insight as that history may afford us, and then to examine the state purposes and interests behind the criminal abortion laws.…

Three reasons have been advanced to explain historically the enactment of criminal abortion laws in the nineteenth century and to justify their continued existence.

It has been argued occasionally that these laws were the product of a Victorian social concern to discourage illicit sexual conduct. Texas, however, does not advance this justification in the present case, and it appears that no court or commentator has taken the argument seriously.…

A second reason is concerned with abortion as a medical procedure. When most criminal abortion laws were first enacted, the procedure was a hazardous one for the woman. This was particularly true prior to the development of antisepsis. Antiseptic techniques, of course, were based on discoveries by Lister, Pasteur, and others first announced in 1867, but were not generally accepted and employed until about the turn of the century. Abortion mortality was high. Even after 1900, and perhaps until as late as the development of antibiotics in the 1940s, standard modern techniques such as dilation and curettage were not nearly so safe as they are today. Thus, it has been argued that a State's real concern in enacting a criminal abortion law was to protect the pregnant woman, that is, to restrain her from submitting to a procedure that placed her life in serious jeopardy.

Modern medical techniques have altered this situation. Mortality rates for women undergoing early abortions, where the procedure is legal, appear to be as low as or lower than the rates for normal childbirth. Consequently, any interest of the State in protecting the woman from an inherently hazardous procedure, except when it would be equally dangerous for her to forgo it, has largely disappeared. Of course, important state interests in the area of health and medical standards do remain.…

The third reason is the State's interest—some phrase it in terms of duty—in protecting prenatal life. Some of the argument for this justification rests on the theory that a new human life is present from the moment of conception. The State's interest and general obligation to protect life then extends, it is argued, to prenatal life. Only when the life of the pregnant mother herself is at stake, balanced against the life she carries within her, should the interest of the embryo or fetus not prevail. Logically, of course, a legitimate state interest in this area need not stand or fall on acceptance of the belief that life begins at conception or at some other point prior to live birth. In assessing the State's interest, recognition may be given to the less rigid claim that as long as at least potential life is involved, the State may assert interests beyond the protection of the pregnant woman alone.…

The Constitution does not explicitly mention any right of privacy. In a line of decisions … the Court has recognized that a right of personal privacy or a guarantee of certain areas or zones of privacy, does exist under the Constitution.…

This right of privacy, whether it be founded in the Fourteenth Amendment's concept of personal liberty and restrictions upon state action, as we feel it is, or, as the District Court determined, in the Ninth Amendment's reservation of rights to the people, is broad enough to encompass a woman's decision whether or not to terminate her pregnancy. The detriment that the State would impose upon the pregnant woman by denying this choice altogether is apparent. Specific and direct harm medically diagnosable even in early pregnancy may be involved. Maternity, or additional offspring, may force upon the woman a distressful life and future. Psychological harm may be imminent. Mental and physical health may be taxed by child care. There is also the distress, for all concerned, associated with the unwanted child, and there is the problem of bringing a child into a family already unable, psychologically and otherwise, to care for it. In other cases, as in this one, the additional difficulties and continuing stigma of unwed motherhood may be involved. All these are factors the woman and her responsible physician necessarily will consider in consultation.

On the basis of elements such as these, appellant and some *amid* argue that the woman's right is absolute and that she is entitled to terminate her pregnancy at whatever time, in whatever way, and for whatever

(Continued)

reason she alone chooses. With this we do not agree. Appellant's arguments that Texas either has no valid interest at all in regulating the abortion decision, or no interest strong enough to support any limitation upon the woman's sole determination, is unpersuasive. The Court's decisions recognizing a right of privacy also acknowledge that some state regulation in areas protected by the right is appropriate. As noted above, a State may properly assert important interests in safeguarding health, in maintaining medical standards, and in protecting potential life. At some point in pregnancy, these respective interests become sufficiently compelling to sustain regulation of the factors that govern the abortion decision. The privacy right involved, therefore, cannot be said to be absolute....

We, therefore, conclude that the right of personal privacy includes the abortion decision, but that this right is not unqualified and must be considered against important state interests in regulation.

We note that those federal and state courts that have recently considered abortion law challenges have reached the same conclusion. A majority, in addition to the District Court in the present case, have held state laws unconstitutional, at least in part, because of vagueness or because of overbreadth and abridgment of rights....

Although the results are divided, most of these courts have agreed that the right of privacy, however based, is broad enough to cover the abortion decision; that the right, nonetheless, is not absolute and is subject to some limitations; and that at some point the state interests as to protection of health, medical standards, and prenatal life, become dominant. We agree with this approach.

Where certain "fundamental rights" are involved, the Court has held that regulation limiting these rights may be justified only by a "compelling state interest," ... and that legislative enactments must be narrowly drawn to express only the legitimate state interests at stake....

The District Court held that the appellee failed to meet his burden of demonstrating that the Texas statute's infringement upon Roe's rights was necessary to support a compelling state interest, and that, although the appellee presented "several compelling justifications for state presence in the area of abortions," the statutes outstripped these justifications and swept "far beyond any areas of compelling state interest." Appellant and appellee both contest that holding. Appellant, as has been indicated, claims an absolute right that bars any state imposition of criminal penalties in the area.

Appellee argues that the State's determination to recognize and protect prenatal life from and after conception constitutes a compelling state interest. As noted above, we do not agree fully with either formulation.

The appellee and certain *amid* argue that the fetus is a "person" within the language and meaning of the Fourteenth Amendment. In support of this, they outline at length and in detail the well-known facts of fetal development. If this suggestion of personhood is established, the appellant's case, of course, collapses, for the fetus' right to life is then guaranteed specifically by the Amendment. The appellant conceded as much on reargument. On the other hand, the appellee conceded on reargument that no case could be cited that holds that a fetus is a person within the meaning of the Fourteenth Amendment.

The Constitution does not define "person" in so many words. Section 1 of the Fourteenth Amendment contains three references to "person." The first, in defining "citizens," speaks of "persons born or naturalized in the United States." The word also appears both in the Due Process Clause and in the Equal Protection Clause. "Person" is used in other places in the Constitution.... But in nearly all these instances, the use of the word is such that it has application only postnatally. None indicates, with any assurance, that it has any possible prenatal application.

All this, together with our observation, that throughout the major portion of the 19th century prevailing legal abortion practices were far freer than they are today, persuades us that the word "person," as used in the Fourteenth Amendment, does not include the unborn.

This conclusion, however, does not of itself fully answer the contentions raised by Texas, and we pass on to other considerations.

The pregnant woman cannot be isolated in her privacy. She carries an embryo and, later, a fetus, if one accepts the medical definitions of the developing young in the human uterus. The situation there is inherently different from marital intimacy, or bedroom possession of obscene material, or marriage, or procreation, or education.... As we have intimated above, it is reasonable and appropriate for a State to decide that at some point in time another interest, that of the health of the mother or that of potential human life, becomes significantly involved. The woman's privacy is no longer sole and any right of privacy she possesses must be measured accordingly.

Texas urges that, apart from the Fourteenth Amendment, life begins at conception and is present throughout pregnancy, and that, therefore, the State has a compelling interest in protecting that life from and after conception. We need not resolve the difficult question of when life begins. When those trained in the respective disciplines of medicine, philosophy, and theology are unable to arrive at any consensus, the judiciary, at this point in the development of man's knowledge, is not in a position to speculate as to the answer.

It should be sufficient to note briefly the wide divergence of thinking on this most sensitive and difficult question. There has always been strong support for the view that life does not begin until live birth.... Physicians and their scientific colleagues have regarded that event with less interest and have tended to focus either upon conception, upon live birth, or upon the interim point at which the fetus becomes "viable," that is, potentially able to live outside the mother's womb, albeit with artificial aid. Viability is usually placed at about seven months (28 weeks) but may occur earlier, even at 24 weeks.... Substantial problems for precise definition of this view are posed, however, by new embryological data that purport to indicate that conception is a "process" over time, rather than an event, and by new medical techniques such as menstrual extraction, the "morning-after" pill, implantation of embryos, artificial insemination, even artificial wombs.

In areas other than criminal abortion, the law has been reluctant to endorse any theory that life, as we recognize it, begins before live birth or to accord legal rights to the unborn except in narrowly defined situations and except when the rights are contingent upon live birth. For example, the traditional rule of tort law denied recovery for prenatal injuries even though the child was born alive. That rule has been changed in almost every jurisdiction. In most States, recovery is said to be permitted only if the fetus was viable, or at least quick, when the injuries were sustained, though few courts have squarely so held. In a recent development, generally opposed by the commentators, some States permit the parents of a stillborn child to maintain an action for wrongful death because of prenatal injuries. Such an action, however, would appear to be one to vindicate the parents' interest and is thus consistent with the view that the fetus, at most, represents only the potentiality of life. Similarly, unborn children have been recognized as acquiring rights or interests by way of inheritance or other devolution of property, and have been represented by guardians *ad litem*. Perfection of the interests involved, again, has generally been

contingent upon live birth. In short, the unborn have never been recognized in the law as persons in the whole sense.

In view of all this, we do not agree that, by adopting one theory of life, Texas may override the rights of the pregnant woman that are at stake. We repeat, however, that the State does have an important and legitimate interest in preserving and protecting the health of the pregnant woman, whether she be a resident of the State or a nonresident who seeks medical consultation and treatment there, and that it has still another important and legitimate interest in protecting the potentiality of human life. These interests are separate and distinct. Each grows in substantiality as the woman approaches term and, at a point during pregnancy, each becomes "compelling."

With respect to the State's important and legitimate interest in the health of the mother, the "compelling" point, in the light of present medical knowledge, is at approximately the end of the first trimester. This is so because of the now-established medical fact that until the end of the first trimester mortality in abortion may be less than mortality in normal childbirth. It follows that, from and after this point, a State may regulate the abortion procedure to the extent that the regulation reasonably relates to the preservation and protection of maternal health. Examples of permissible state regulation in this area are requirements as to the qualifications of the person who is to perform the abortion; as to the licensure of that person; as to the facility in which the procedure is to be performed, that is, whether it must be a hospital or may be a clinic or some other place of less-than-hospital status; as to the licensing of the facility; and the like.

This means, on the other hand, that for the period of pregnancy prior to this "compelling" point, the attending physician, in consultation with his patient, is free to determine, without regulation by the State that, in his medical judgment, the patient's pregnancy should be terminated. If that decision is reached, the judgment may be effectuated by an abortion free of interference by the State.

With respect to the State's important and legitimate interest in potential life, the "compelling" point is at viability. This is so because the fetus then presumably has the capability of meaningful life outside the mother's womb. State regulation protective of fetal life after viability thus has both logical and biological justifications. If the State is interested in protecting fetal life after viability, it may go so far as to proscribe

(Continued)

In my opinion, the principles established in [the] long line of cases [since *Roe v. Wade*] ... should govern our decision today. Under these principles, [the informed consent provisions] of the Pennsylvania statute are unconstitutional. Those sections require a physician or counselor to provide the woman with a range of materials clearly designed to persuade her to choose not to undergo the abortion....

The 24-hour waiting period raises even more serious concerns.... Part of the constitutional liberty to choose is the equal dignity to which each of us is entitled. A woman who decides to terminate her pregnancy is entitled to the same respect as a woman who decides to carry the fetus to term. The mandatory waiting period denies women that equal respect....

Justice Blackmun, concurring in part and dissenting in part.

Three years ago, in *Webster v. Reproductive Health Services*, ... four members of this Court appeared poised to "cas(t) into darkness the hopes and visions of every woman in this country" who had come to believe that the Constitution guaranteed her the right to reproductive choice.... All that remained between the promise of *Roe* and the darkness of the plurality was a single, flickering flame. Decisions since *Webster* gave little reason to hope that this flame would cast much light. But now, just when so many expected the darkness to fall, the flame has grown bright.

I do not underestimate the significance of today's joint opinion. Yet I remain steadfast in my belief that the right to reproductive choice is entitled to the full protection afforded by the Court before *Webster*. And I fear for the darkness as four Justices anxiously await the single vote necessary to extinguish the light....

Make no mistake, the joint opinion of Justices O'Connor, Kennedy, and Souter is an act of personal courage and constitutional principle. In contrast to previous decisions in which Justices O'Connor and Kennedy postponed reconsideration of *Roe v. Wade*, ... the authors of the joint opinion today join Justice Stevens and me in concluding that "the essential holding of *Roe* should be retained and once again reaffirmed." ... In brief, five members of this Court today recognize that "the Constitution protects a woman's right to terminate her pregnancy in its early stages." ...

A fervent view of individual liberty and the force of *stare decisis* have led the Court to this conclusion....

In one sense, the Court's approach is worlds apart from that of the Chief Justice and Justice Scalia. And

yet, in another sense, the distance between the two approaches is short—the distance is but a single vote. I am 83 years old. I cannot remain on this Court forever, and when I do step down, the confirmation process for my successor well may focus on the issue before us today. That, I regret, may be exactly where the choice between the two worlds will be made.

Chief Justice Rehnquist, with whom *Justice White*, *Justice Scalia*, and *Justice Thomas* join, concurring in part and dissenting in part. ...

Justice Scalia, with whom the *Chief Justice*, *Justice White*, and *Justice Thomas* join, concurring in part and dissenting in part.

My views on this matter are unchanged.... The states may, if they wish, permit abortion-on-demand, but the Constitution does not require them to do so.

The permissibility of abortion, and the limitations upon it, are to be resolved like most important questions in our democracy: by citizens trying to persuade one another and then voting. As the Court acknowledges, "where reasonable people disagree the government can adopt one position or the other." ...

The Court is correct in adding the qualification that this "assumes a state of affairs in which the choice does not intrude upon a protected liberty," ... but the crucial part of that qualification is the penultimate word. A State's choice between two positions on which reasonable people can disagree is constitutional even when (as is often the case) it intrudes upon a "liberty" in the absolute sense.

Laws against bigamy, for example—which entire societies of reasonable people disagree with—intrude upon men and women's liberty to marry and live with one another. But bigamy happens not to be a liberty specially "protected" by the Constitution.

That is, quite simply, the issue in this case: not whether the power of a woman to abort her unborn child is a "liberty" in the absolute sense; or even whether it is a liberty of great importance to many women. Of course it is both. The issue is whether it is a liberty protected by the Constitution of the United States. I am sure it is not.

I reach that conclusion not because of anything so exalted as my views concerning the "concept of existence, of meaning, of the universe, and of the mystery of life." ... Rather, I reach it for the same reason that bigamy is not constitutionally protected—because of two simple facts: (1) the Constitution says absolutely nothing about it, and (2) the long-standing traditions of American society have permitted it to be legally proscribed....

The Court's description of the place of *Roe* in the social history of the United States is unrecognizable. Not only did *Roe* not, as the Court suggests, resolve the deeply divisive issue of abortion; it did more than anything else to nourish it, by elevating it to the national level where it is infinitely more difficult to resolve.

National politics were not plagued by abortion protests, national abortion lobbying, or abortion marches on Congress, before *Roe v. Wade* was decided. Profound disagreement existed among our citizens over the issue—as it does over other issues, such as the death penalty—but that disagreement was being worked out at the state level. As with many other issues, the division of sentiment within each State was not as closely balanced as it was among the population of the Nation as a whole, meaning not only that more people would be satisfied with the results of state-by-state resolution, but also that those results would be more stable. Pre-*Roe*, moreover, political compromise was possible.

Roe's mandate for abortion-on-demand destroyed the compromises of the past, rendered compromises impossible for the future, and required the entire issue to be resolved, uniformly, at the national level.... Many favor all of those developments, and it is not for me to say that they are wrong. But to portray *Roe* as the statesmanlike "settlement" of a divisive issue, a jurisprudential Peace of Westphalia that is worth preserving, is nothing less than Orwellian....

STENBERG v. CARHART
530 U.S. 914; 120 S.Ct. 2597; 147 L.Ed. 2d. 743 (2000)
Vote: 5-4

In this case, the Supreme Court considers a constitutional challenge to a Nebraska law that prohibits any partial-birth abortion unless that procedure is necessary to save the life of the mother. The statute defines partial-birth abortion as a procedure in which the doctor "partially delivers vaginally a living unborn child before killing the ... child." In a suit brought by Leroy Carhart, a Nebraska doctor who performs abortions, a federal district court held the statute unconstitutional. The Court of Appeals affirmed.

Justice Breyer delivered the opinion of the Court.

... Three established principles determine the issue before us. We shall set them forth in the language of the joint opinion in [*Planned Parenthood* v.] *Casey* (1992).

First, before "viability ... the woman has a right to choose to terminate her pregnancy." ... Second, "a law designed to further the State's interest in fetal life which imposes an undue burden on the woman's decision before fetal viability" is unconstitutional.... An "undue burden is ... shorthand for the conclusion that a state regulation has the purpose or effect of placing a substantial obstacle in the path of a woman seeking an abortion of a nonviable fetus." ... Third, "subsequent to viability, the State in promoting its interest in the potentiality of human life may, if it chooses, regulate, and even proscribe, abortion except where it is necessary, in appropriate medical judgment, for the preservation of the life or health of the mother." ...

Because Nebraska law seeks to ban one method of aborting a pregnancy, we must describe and then discuss several different abortion procedures. Considering the fact that those procedures seek to terminate a potential human life, our discussion may seem clinically cold or callous to some, perhaps horrifying to others. There is no alternative way, however, to acquaint the reader with the technical distinctions among different abortion methods and related factual matters, upon which the outcome of this case depends. For that reason, drawing upon the findings of the trial court, underlying testimony, and related medical texts, we shall

(Continued)

describe the relevant methods of performing abortions in technical detail.

The evidence before the trial court, as supported or supplemented in the literature, indicates the following:

1. About 90% of all abortions performed in the United States take place during the first trimester of pregnancy, before 12 weeks of gestational age.... During the first trimester, the predominant abortion method is "vacuum aspiration," which involves insertion of a vacuum tube (cannula) into the uterus to evacuate the contents. Such an abortion is typically performed on an outpatient basis under local anesthesia.... Vacuum aspiration is considered particularly safe. The procedure's mortality rates for first trimester abortion are, for example, 5 to 10 times lower than those associated with carrying the fetus to term. Complication rates are also low.... As the fetus grows in size, however, the vacuum aspiration method becomes increasingly difficult to use....

2. Approximately 10% of all abortions are performed during the second trimester of pregnancy (12 to 24 weeks).... In the early 1970s, inducing labor through the injection of saline into the uterus was the predominant method of second-trimester abortion.... Today, however, the medical profession has switched from medical induction of labor to surgical procedures for most second-trimester abortions. The most commonly used procedure is called "dilation and evacuation" (D&E). That procedure (together with a modified form of vacuum aspiration used in the early second trimester) accounts for about 95% of all abortions performed from 12 to 20 weeks of gestational age....

3. D&E "refers generically to transcervical procedures performed at 13 weeks gestation or later." ... "D&E is similar to vacuum aspiration except that the cervix must be dilated more widely because surgical instruments are used to remove larger pieces of tissue. Osmotic dilators are usually used. Intravenous fluids and an analgesic or sedative may be administered. A local anesthetic such as a paracervical block may be administered, dilating agents, if used, are removed and instruments are inserted through the cervix into the uterus to removal fetal and placental tissue.... There are variations in D&E operative strategy. However, the common points are that D&E involves (1) dilation of the cervix; (2) removal of at least some fetal tissue using nonvacuum instruments; and (3) (after the 15th week) the potential need for instrumental disarticulation or dismemberment of the fetus or the collapse of fetal parts to facilitate evacuation from the uterus.

4. When instrumental disarticulation incident to D&E is necessary, it typically occurs as the doctor pulls a portion of the fetus through the cervix into the birth canal....

5. The D&E procedure carries certain risks. The use of instruments within the uterus creates a danger of accidental perforation and damage to neighboring organs. Sharp fetal bone fragments create similar dangers. And fetal tissue accidentally left behind can cause infection and various other complications.... Nonetheless studies show that the risks of mortality and complication that accompany the D&E procedure between the 12th and 20th weeks of gestation are significantly lower than those accompanying induced labor procedures (the next safest midsecond trimester procedures)....

6. At trial, Dr. Carhart and Dr. Stubblefield described a variation of the D&E procedure, which they referred to as an "intact D&E." ... Like other versions of the D technique, it begins with induced dilation of the cervix. The procedure then involves removing the fetus from the uterus through the cervix "intact," i.e., in one pass, rather than in several passes.... It is used after 16 weeks at the earliest, as vacuum aspiration becomes ineffective and the fetal skull becomes too large to pass through the cervix.... The intact D proceeds in one of two ways, depending on the presentation of the fetus. If the fetus presents head first (a vertex presentation), the doctor collapses the skull; and the doctor then extracts the entire fetus through the cervix. If the fetus presents feet first (a breech presentation), the doctor pulls the fetal body through the cervix, collapses the skull, and extracts the fetus through the

cervix.... The breech extraction version of the intact D is also known commonly as "dilation and extraction," or D&X.... In the late second trimester, vertex, breech, and traverse/compound (sideways) presentations occur in roughly similar proportions....

7. The intact D&E procedure can also be found described in certain obstetric and abortion clinical textbooks, where two variations are recognized. The first, as just described, calls for the physician to adapt his method for extracting the intact fetus depending on fetal presentation.... This is the method used by Dr. Carhart.... A slightly different version of the intact D procedure ... calls for conversion to a breech presentation in all cases....

8. The American College of Obstetricians and Gynecologists describes the D&X procedure in a manner corresponding to a breech-conversion intact D&E, including the following steps:
    1. deliberate dilatation of the cervix, usually over a sequence of days; 2. instrumental conversion of the fetus to a footling breech; 3. breech extraction of the body excepting the head; and 4. partial evacuation of the intracranial contents of a living fetus to effect vaginal delivery of a dead but otherwise intact fetus....

9. Despite the technical differences we have just described, intact D&E and D&X are sufficiently similar for us to use the terms interchangeably. Dr. Carhart testified he attempts to use the intact D&E procedure during weeks 16 to 20 because (1) it reduces the dangers from sharp bone fragments passing through the cervix, (2) minimizes the number of instrument passes needed for extraction and lessens the likelihood of uterine perforations caused by those instruments, (3) reduces the likelihood of leaving infection-causing fetal and placental tissue in the uterus, and (4) could help to prevent potentially fatal absorption of fetal tissue into the maternal circulation.... The District Court made no findings about the D&X procedure's overall safety.... The District Court concluded, however, that "the evidence is both clear and convincing that Carhart's D&X procedure is superior to, and safer than, the ... other abortion procedures

used during the relevant gestational period in the 10 to 20 cases a year that present to Dr. Carhart." ...

10. The materials presented at trial referred to the potential benefits of the D&X procedure in circumstances involving nonviable fetuses, such as fetuses with abnormal fluid accumulation in the brain (hydrocephaly).... Others have emphasized its potential for women with prior uterine scars, or for women for whom induction of labor would be particularly dangerous....

11. There are no reliable data on the number of D&X abortions performed annually. Estimates have ranged between 640 and 5,000 per year....

The question before us is whether Nebraska's statute, making criminal the performance of a "partial-birth abortion," violates the Federal Constitution, as interpreted in *Planned Parenthood of Southeastern Pa. v. Casey* (1992) and *Roe v. Wade* (1973). We conclude that it does for at least two independent reasons. First, the law lacks any exception "for the preservation of the ... health of the mother." ... Second, it "imposes an undue burden on a woman's ability" to choose a D&E abortion, thereby unduly burdening the right to choose abortion itself....

The fact that Nebraska's law applies both pre- and postviability aggravates the constitutional problem presented. The State's interest in regulating abortion previability is considerably weaker than postviability.... Since the law requires a health exception in order to validate even a postviability abortion regulation, it at a minimum requires the same in respect to previability regulation....

The quoted standard also depends on the state regulations "promoting [the State's] interest in the potentiality of human life." The Nebraska law, of course, does not directly further an interest "in the potentiality of human life" by saving the fetus in question from destruction, as it regulates only a *method* of performing abortion. Nebraska describes its interests differently. It says the law "show[s] concern for the life of the unborn," "prevent [s] cruelty to partially born children," and "preserve [s] the integrity of the medical profession." ... But we cannot see how the interest-related differences could make any difference to the question at hand, namely, the application of the "health" requirement.

(Continued)

the law away. The Court's holding stems from misunderstanding the record, misinterpretation of *Casey*, outright refusal to respect the law of a State, and statutory construction in conflict with settled rules. The decision nullifies a law expressing the will of the people of Nebraska that medical procedures must be governed by moral principles having their foundation in the intrinsic value of human life, including life of the unborn. Through their law the people of Nebraska were forthright in confronting an issue of immense moral consequence. The State chose to forbid a procedure many decent and civilized people find so abhorrent as to be among the most serious of crimes against human life, while the State still protected the woman's autonomous right of choice as reaffirmed in *Casey*. The Court closes its eyes to these profound concerns....

Justice Thomas, with whom the **Chief Justice** and **Justice Scalia** join, dissenting.

... In the years following *Roe*, this Court applied, and, worse, extended, that decision to strike down numerous state statutes that purportedly threatened a woman's ability to obtain an abortion....

It appeared that this era of Court-mandated abortion-on-demand had come to an end ... in our decision in *Planned Parenthood v. Casey* (1992). Although in *Casey* the separate opinions of The Chief Justice and Justice Scalia urging the Court to overrule *Roe* did not command a majority, seven Members of that Court, including six Members sitting today, acknowledged that States have a legitimate role in regulating abortion and recognized the States' interest in respecting fetal life at all stages of development.... The joint opinion authored by Justices O'Connor, Kennedy, and Souter concluded that prior case law "went too far" in "undervalu[ing] the State's interest in potential life" and in "striking down ... some abortion regulations which in no real sense deprived women of the ultimate decision." ...

My views on the merits of the *Casey* joint opinion have been fully articulated by others.... I will not restate those views here, except to note that the *Casey* joint opinion was constructed by its authors out of whole cloth. The standard set forth in the *Casey* joint opinion has no historical or doctrinal pedigree. The standard is a product of its authors' own philosophical views about abortion, and it should go without saying that it has no origins in or relationship to the Constitution and is, consequently, as illegitimate as the standard

it purported to replace. Even assuming, however, as I will for the remainder of this dissent, that *Casey's* fabricated undue-burden standard merits adherence (which it does not), today's decision is extraordinary.

Today, the Court inexplicably holds that the States cannot constitutionally prohibit a method of abortion that millions find hard to distinguish from infanticide and that the Court hesitates even to describe.... This holding cannot be reconciled with *Casey's* undue-burden standard, as that standard was explained to us by the authors of the joint opinion, and the majority hardly pretends otherwise. In striking down this statute—which expresses a profound and legitimate respect for fetal life and which leaves unimpeded several other safe forms of abortion—the majority opinion gives the lie to the promise of *Casey* that regulations that do no more than "express profound respect for the life of the unborn are permitted, if they are not a substantial obstacle to the woman's exercise of the right to choose" whether or not to have an abortion.... Today's decision is so obviously irreconcilable with *Casey's* explication of what its undue-burden standard requires, let alone the Constitution, that it should be seen for what it is, a reinstitution of the *pre-Webster* abortion-on-demand era in which the mere invocation of "abortion rights" trumps any contrary societal interest. If this statute is unconstitutional under *Casey*, then *Casey* meant nothing at all, and the Court should candidly admit it.

To reach its decision, the majority must take a series of indefensible steps. The majority must first disregard the principles that this Court follows in every context but abortion: We interpret statutes according to their plain meaning and we do not strike down statutes susceptible of a narrowing construction. The majority also must disregard the very constitutional standard it purports to employ, and then displace the considered judgment of the people of Nebraska and 29 other States. The majority's decision is lamentable, because of the result the majority reaches, the illogical steps the majority takes to reach it, and because it portends a return to an era I had thought we had at last abandoned....

In the almost 30 years since *Roe*, this Court has never described the various methods of aborting a second-or third-trimester fetus. From reading the majority's sanitized description, one would think that this case involves state regulation of a widely accepted routine medical procedure. Nothing could be further from the truth. The most widely used method of abortion during this stage of pregnancy is so gruesome that its use can be traumatic even for the physicians and medical staff who perform it.... And the particular procedure at issue in this case, "partial-birth abortion," so closely borders on infanticide that 30 States have attempted to ban it....

"Partial-birth abortion" is a term that has been used by a majority of state legislatures, the United States Congress, medical journals, physicians, reporters, even judges, and has never, as far as I am aware, been used to refer to the D&E procedure. The number of instances in which "partial-birth abortion" has been equated with the breech extraction form of intact D&E (otherwise known as "D&X") and explicitly contrasted with D&E, are numerous....

Were there any doubt remaining whether the statute could apply to a D&E procedure, that doubt is no ground for invalidating the statute. Rather, we are bound to first consider whether a construction of the statute is fairly possible that would avoid the constitutional question....

The next question, therefore, is whether the Nebraska statute is unconstitutional because it does not contain an exception that would allow use of the procedure whenever "necessary in appropriate medical judgment, for the preservation of the ... health of the mother." ... It is clear that the Court's understanding of when a health exception is required is not mandated by our prior cases. In fact, we have, *post-Casey*, approved regulations of methods of conducting abortion despite the lack of a health exception....

As if this state of affairs were not bad enough, the majority expands the health exception rule articulated in *Casey* in one additional and equally pernicious way. Although *Roe* and *Casey* mandated a health exception for cases in which abortion is "necessary" for a woman's health, the majority concludes that a procedure is "necessary" if it has any comparative health benefits.... In other words, according to the majority, so long as a doctor can point to support in the profession for his (or the woman's) preferred procedure, it is "necessary" and the physician is entitled to perform it.... But such a health exception requirement eviscerates *Casey's* undue burden standard and imposes unfettered abortion-on-demand. The exception entirely swallows the rule. In effect, no regulation of abortion procedures is permitted because there will always be *some* support for a procedure and there will always be some doctors who conclude that the procedure is preferable. If Nebraska reenacts its partial-birth abortion ban with a health exception, the State will not be able to prevent physicians like Dr. Carhart from using partial-birth abortion as a routine abortion procedure. This Court has now expressed its own conclusion that there is "highly plausible" support for the view that partial-birth abortion is safer, which, in the majority's view, means that the procedure is therefore "necessary." ... Any doctor who wishes to perform such a procedure under the new statute will be able to do so with impunity.... The majority's insistence on a health exception is a fig leaf barely covering its hostility to any abortion regulation by the States—a hostility that *Casey* purported to reject....

GONZALES v. CARHART
550 U.S. 124; 127 S.Ct. 1610; 167 L.Ed.2d. 480 (2007)
Vote: 5-4

LeRoy Carhart and other doctors who performed second-trimester abortions filed suit against the U.S. attorney general to challenge the constitutionality of the federal Partial-Birth Abortion Ban Act of 2003. The Act prohibited doctors from performing a particular form of abortion, known medically as "intact dilation and extraction," during the second trimester of pregnancy. The Act described the banned procedure as follows: "An abortion in which the person performing the abortion, deliberately and intentionally vaginally *delivers a living fetus until, in the case of a head-first presentation, the entire fetal head is outside the body of the mother, or, in the case of breech presentation, any part of the fetal trunk past the navel is outside the body of the mother, for the purpose of performing an overt act that the person knows will kill the partially delivered living fetus; and performs the overt act, other than completion of delivery, that kills the partially delivered living fetus." Although the Act contained a language permitting the intact D&E procedure if necessary to save the*

(Continued)

life of the mother, it carried no such exception for preserving the woman's health. Citing the Supreme Court's decision in Stenberg v. Carhart *(2000), the District Court declared the federal law unconstitutional and granted a permanent injunction against its enforcement. The Court of Appeals for the Eighth Circuit affirmed.*

Justice Kennedy delivered the opinion of the Court.

... In recitations preceding its operative provisions the Act refers to the Court's opinion in *Stenberg v. Carhart* ... (2000), which also addressed the subject of abortion procedures used in the later stages of pregnancy. Compared to the state statute at issue in *Stenberg*, the Act is more specific concerning the instances to which it applies and in this respect more precise in its coverage. We conclude the Act should be sustained against the objections lodged by the broad, facial attack brought against it.

... The Act's purposes are set forth in recitals preceding its operative provisions. A description of the prohibited abortion procedure demonstrates the rationale for the congressional enactment. The Act proscribes a method of abortion in which a fetus is killed just inches before completion of the birth process. Congress stated as follows: "Implicitly approving such a brutal and inhumane procedure by choosing not to prohibit it will further coarsen society to the humanity of not only newborns, but all vulnerable and innocent human life, making it increasingly difficult to protect such life." ... The Act expresses respect for the dignity of human life.

Congress was concerned, furthermore, with the effects on the medical community and on its reputation caused by the practice of partial-birth abortion. The findings in the Act explain: "Partial-birth abortion ... confuses the medical, legal, and ethical duties of physicians to preserve and promote life, as the physician acts directly against the physical life of a child, whom he or she had just delivered, all but the head, out of the womb, in order to end that life."

There can be no doubt the government "has an interest in protecting the integrity and ethics of the medical profession." ... Under our precedents it is clear the State has a significant role to play in regulating the medical profession.

[Planned Parenthood v.] Casey reaffirmed these governmental objectives. The government may use its voice and its regulatory authority to show its profound respect for the life within the woman. A central premise of the opinion was that the Court's precedents after

Roe [v. Wade] had "undervalue[d] the State's interest in potential life." ... The plurality opinion indicated "[t]he fact that a law which serves a valid purpose, one not designed to strike at the right itself, has the incidental effect of making it more difficult or more expensive to procure an abortion cannot be enough to invalidate it." ... This was not an idle assertion. The three premises of *Casey* must coexist.... The third premise, that the State, from the inception of the pregnancy, maintains its own regulatory interest in protecting the life of the fetus that may become a child, cannot be set at naught by interpreting *Casey's* requirement of a health exception so it becomes tantamount to allowing a doctor to choose the abortion method he or she might prefer. Where it has a rational basis to act, and it does not impose an undue burden, the State may use its regulatory power to bar certain procedures and substitute others, all in furtherance of its legitimate interests in regulating the medical profession in order to promote respect for life, including life of the unborn.

The Act's ban on abortions that involve partial delivery of a living fetus furthers the Government's objectives. No one would dispute that, for many, D&E is a procedure itself laden with the power to devalue human life. Congress could nonetheless conclude that the type of abortion proscribed by the Act requires specific regulation because it implicates additional ethical and moral concerns that justify a special prohibition. Congress determined that the abortion methods it proscribed had a "disturbing similarity to the killing of a newborn infant," ... and thus it was concerned with "draw[ing] a bright line that clearly distinguishes abortion and infanticide." ... The Court has in the past confirmed the validity of drawing boundaries to prevent certain practices that extinguish life and are close to actions that are condemned. ...

The Act's furtherance of legitimate government interests bears upon, but does not resolve, the next question: whether the Act has the effect of imposing an unconstitutional burden on the abortion right because it does not allow use of the barred procedure where "necessary, in appropriate medical judgment, for [the] preservation of the ... health of the mother." ... The prohibition in the Act would be unconstitutional, under precedents we here assume to be controlling, if it "subject[ed] [women] to significant health risks." ... [W]hether the Act creates significant health risks for women has been a contested factual question. The evidence presented in the trial courts and before Congress demonstrates both sides have medical support for their position.

Respondents presented evidence that intact D&E may be the safest method of abortion, for reasons similar to those adduced in *Stenberg*.... Abortion doctors testified, for example, that intact D&E decreases the risk of cervical laceration or uterine perforation because it requires fewer passes into the uterus with surgical instruments and does not require the removal of bony fragments of the dismembered fetus, fragments that may be sharp. Respondents also presented evidence that intact D&E was safer both because it reduces the risks that fetal parts will remain in the uterus and because it takes less time to complete. Respondents, in addition, proffered evidence that intact D&E was safer for women with certain medical conditions or women with fetuses that had certain anomalies....

These contentions were contradicted by other doctors who testified in the District Courts and before Congress. They concluded that the alleged health advantages were based on speculation without scientific studies to support them. They considered D&E always to be a safe alternative....

There is documented medical disagreement whether the Act's prohibition would ever impose significant health risks on women....

The question becomes whether the Act can stand when this medical uncertainty persists. The Court's precedents instruct that the Act can survive this facial attack. The Court has given state and federal legislatures wide discretion to pass legislation in areas where there is medical and scientific uncertainty....

This traditional rule is consistent with *Casey*, which confirms the State's interest in promoting respect for human life at all stages in the pregnancy. Physicians are not entitled to ignore regulations that direct them to use reasonable alternative procedures. The law need not give abortion doctors unfettered choice in the course of their medical practice, nor should it elevate their status above other physicians in the medical community....

Medical uncertainty does not foreclose the exercise of legislative power in the abortion context any more than it does in other contexts.... The medical uncertainty over whether the Act's prohibition creates significant health risks provides a sufficient basis to conclude in this facial attack that the Act does not impose an undue burden.

Justice Thomas, with whom ***Justice Scalia*** joins, concurring.

I join the Court's opinion because it accurately applies current jurisprudence, including *Planned Parenthood of Southeastern Pa. v. Casey* ... (1992). I write separately to reiterate my view that the Court's abortion jurisprudence, including *Casey* and *Roe v. Wade* ... (1973), has no basis in the Constitution.

Justice Ginsburg, with whom ***Justice Stevens***, ***Justice Souter***, and ***Justice Breyer*** join, dissenting.

I dissent from the Court's disposition. Retreating from prior rulings that abortion restrictions cannot be imposed absent an exception safeguarding a woman's health, the Court upholds an Act that surely would not survive under the close scrutiny that previously attended state-decreed limitations on a woman's reproductive choices....

The Court offers flimsy and transparent justifications for upholding a nationwide ban on intact D&E *sans* any exception to safeguard a women's health. Today's ruling, the Court declares, advances "a premise central to *[Casey's]* conclusion"—*i.e.*, the Government's "legitimate and substantial interest in preserving and promoting fetal life." ... But the Act scarcely furthers that interest: The law saves not a single fetus from destruction, for it targets only a *method* of performing abortion.... And surely the statute was not designed to protect the lives or health of pregnant women. ... In short, the Court upholds a law that, while doing nothing to "preserv[e] ... fetal life," ... bars a woman from choosing intact D&E although her doctor "reasonably believes [that procedure] will best protect [her]."...

Delivery of an intact, albeit nonviable, fetus warrants special condemnation, the Court maintains, because a fetus that is not dismembered resembles an infant. ... But so, too, does a fetus delivered intact after it is terminated by injection a day or two before the surgical evacuation, ... or a fetus delivered through medical induction or cesarean.... Yet, the availability of those procedures—along with D&E by dismemberment—the Court says, saves the ban on intact D&E from a declaration of unconstitutionality.... Never mind that the procedures deemed acceptable might put a woman's health at greater risk....

Revealing in this regard, the Court invokes an antiabortion shibboleth for which it concededly has no reliable evidence: Women who have abortions come to regret their choices, and consequently suffer from "[s]evere depression and loss of esteem." ... Because

(Continued)

of women's fragile emotional state and because of the "bond of love the mother has for her child," the Court worries, doctors may withhold information about the nature of the intact D&E procedure.... The solution the Court approves, then, is *not* to require doctors to inform women, accurately and adequately, of the different procedures and their attendant risks.... Instead, the Court deprives women of the right to make an autonomous choice, even at the expense of their safety.

This way of thinking reflects ancient notions about women's place in the family and under the Constitution—ideas that have long since been discredited.... Though today's majority may regard women's feelings on the matter as "self-evident," ... this Court has repeatedly confirmed that "[t]he destiny of the woman must be shaped ... on her own conception of her spiritual imperatives and her place in society." ...

Though today's opinion does not go so far as to discard *Roe* or *Casey*, the Court, differently composed

than it was when we last considered a restrictive abortion regulation, is hardly faithful to our earlier invocations of "the rule of law" and the "principles of *stare decisis*." Congress imposed a ban despite our clear prior holdings that the State cannot proscribe an abortion procedure when its use is necessary to protect a woman's health.... Although Congress' findings could not withstand the crucible of trial, the Court defers to the legislative override of our Constitution-based rulings.... A decision so at odds with our jurisprudence should not have staying power.

In sum, the notion that the Partial-Birth Abortion Ban Act furthers any legitimate governmental interest is, quite simply, irrational. The Court's defense of the statute provides no saving explanation. In candor, the Act, and the Court's defense of it, cannot be understood as anything other than an effort to chip away at a right declared again and again by this Court— and with increasing comprehension of its centrality to women's lives....

BOWERS v. HARDWICK
478 U.S. 186; 106 S.Ct. 2841; 92 L.Ed. 2d. 140 (1986)
Vote: 5-4

In this case, the Court considers the constitutionality of a state sodomy statute as applied to private, consensual homosexual conduct.

Justice White delivered the opinion of the Court.

In August 1982, respondent was charged with violating the Georgia statute criminalizing sodomy by committing that act with another adult male in the bedroom of respondent's home. After a preliminary hearing, the District Attorney decided not to present the matter to the grand jury unless further evidence developed.

Respondent then brought suit in the Federal District Court, challenging the constitutionality of the statute insofar as it criminalized consensual sodomy. He asserted that he was a practicing homosexual, that the Georgia sodomy statute, as administered by the defendants, placed him in imminent danger of arrest, and that the statute for several reasons violates the Federal Constitution. The District Court granted the

defendants' motion to dismiss [relying on *Doe v. Commonwealth's Attorney* (1976)]....

A divided panel of the Court of Appeals for the Eleventh Circuit reversed.... Relying on our decisions in *Griswold v. Connecticut*, ... *Eisenstadt v. Baird*, ... *Stanley v. Georgia*, ... and *Roe v. Wade*, ... the court went on to hold that the Georgia statute violated respondent's fundamental rights because his homosexual activity is a private and intimate association that is beyond the reach of the state regulation by reason of the Ninth Amendment and the Due Process Clause of the Fourteenth Amendment. The case was remanded for trial, at which, to prevail, the State would have to prove that the statute is supported by a compelling interest and is the most narrowly drawn means of achieving that end.

Because other Courts of Appeals have arrived at judgments contrary to that of the Eleventh Circuit in this case, we granted the State's petition for certiorari....

This case does not require a judgment on whether laws against sodomy between consenting adults in general, or between homosexuals in particular, are wise or desirable. It raises no question about the right or propriety of state legislative decisions to repeal their laws that criminalize homosexual sodomy, or of state court decisions invalidating those laws on state constitutional grounds. The issue presented is whether the Federal Constitution confers a fundamental right upon homosexuals to engage in sodomy and hence invalidates the laws of the many States that still make such conduct illegal and have done so for a very long time. The case also calls for some judgment about the limits of the Court's role in carrying out its constitutional mandate.

We first register our disagreement with the Court of Appeals and with respondent that the Court's prior cases have construed the Constitution to confer a right of privacy that contends to homosexual sodomy and for all intents and purposes have decided this case....

Accepting the decisions in these cases and the above description of them, we think it evident that none of the rights announced in those cases bears any resemblance to the claimed constitutional right of homosexuals to engage in acts of sodomy that is asserted in this case. No connection between family, marriage, or procreation on the one hand and homosexual activity on the other has been demonstrated, either by the Court of Appeals or by respondent. Moreover, any claim that these cases nevertheless stand for the proposition that any kind of private sexual conduct between consenting adults is constitutionally insulated from state proscription is unsupportable. Indeed, the Court's opinion in *Carey [v. Population Services]* twice asserted that the privacy right, which the *Griswold* line of cases found to be one of the protections provided by the Due Process Clause, did not reach so far....

Precedent aside, however, respondent would have us announce, as the Court of Appeals did, a fundamental right to engage in homosexual sodomy. This we are quite unwilling to do. It is true that despite the language of the Due Process Clauses of the Fifth and Fourteenth Amendments, which appears to focus only on the processes by which life, liberty, or property is taken, the cases are legion in which Clauses have been interpreted to have substantive content, subsuming rights that to a great extent are immune from federal or state regulation or proscription. Among such cases are those recognizing rights that have little or no textual support in the constitutional language....

Striving to assure itself and the public, that announcing rights not readily identifiable in the constitution's text involves much more than the imposition of the Justices' own choice of values on the States and the Federal Government, the Court has sought to identify the nature of the rights qualifying for heightened judicial protection. In *Palko v. Connecticut* ... (1937), it was said that this category includes those fundamental liberties that are "implicit in the concept of the record liberty," such that "neither liberty nor justice would exist if [they] were sacrificed." A different description of fundamental liberties appeared in *Moore v. East Cleveland* ... where they are characterized [by Justice Powell] as those liberties that are "deeply rooted in this Nation's history and tradition."

It is obvious to us that neither of these formulations would extend a fundamental right to homosexuals to engage in acts of consensual sodomy. Proscriptions against that conduct have ancient roots.... Sodomy was a criminal offense at common law and was forbidden by the laws of the original thirteen States when they ratified the Bill of Rights. In 1868, when the Fourteenth Amendment was ratified, all but 5 of the 37 States in the Union had criminal sodomy laws. In fact, until 1961, all States outlawed sodomy, and today, 24 States and the District of Columbia continue to provide criminal penalties for sodomy performed in private and between consenting adults.... Against this background, to claim that a right to engage in such conduct is "deeply rooted in this Nation's history and tradition" or "implicit in the concept of ordered liberty" is, at best, facetious....

Nor are we inclined to take a more expansive view of our authority to discover new fundamental rights imbedded in the Due Process Clause. The Court is most vulnerable and comes nearest to illegitimacy when it deals with judge-made constitutional law having little or no cognizable roots in the language or design of the Constitution.

Respondent, however, asserts that the result should be different where the homosexual conduct occurs in the privacy of the home. He relies on *Stanley v. Georgia* ... (1969), where the Court held that the First Amendment prevents conviction for possessing and reading obscene material in the privacy of his home: "If the First Amendment means anything, it means that a State has no business telling a man, sitting alone in his house, what books he may read or what films he may watch." ...

(Continued)

Stanley did protect conduct that would not have been protected outside the home, and it partially prevented the enforcement of state obscenity laws; but the decision was firmly grounded in the First Amendment. The right pressed upon us here has no similar support in the text of the Constitution, and it does not qualify for recognition under the prevailing principles for construing the Fourteenth Amendment. Its limits are also difficult to discern. Plainly enough, otherwise illegal conduct is not always immunized whenever it occurs in the home. Victimless crimes, such as the possession and use of illegal drugs, do not escape the law where they are committed at home.

Even if the conduct at issue here is not a fundamental right, respondent asserts that there must be a rational basis for the law and that there is none in this case other than the presumed belief of a majority of the electorate in Georgia that homosexual sodomy is immoral and unacceptable. This is said to be an inadequate rationale to support the law. The law, however, is constantly based on notions of morality, and if all laws representing essentially moral choices are to be invalidated under the Due Process Clause, the courts will be very busy indeed. Even respondent makes no such claim, but insists that majority sentiments about the morality of homosexuality should be declared inadequate. We do not agree, and are unpersuaded that the sodomy laws of some 25 States should be invalidated on this basis....

Accordingly, the judgment of the Court of Appeals is reversed.

Chief Justice Burger, concurring.

I join the Court's opinion, but I write separately to underscore my view that in constitutional terms there is no such thing as a fundamental right to commit homosexual sodomy.

As the Court notes, ... the proscriptions against sodomy have very "ancient roots." Decisions of individuals relating to homosexual conduct have been subject to state intervention throughout the history of Western Civilization.... The common law of England, including its prohibition of sodomy, became the received law of Georgia and the other Colonies. In 1816 the Georgia Legislature passed the statute at issue here, and that statute has been continuously in force in one form or another since that time. To hold that the act of homosexual sodomy is somehow protected as a fundamental right would be to cast aside millennia of moral teaching.

This is essentially not a question of personal "preferences" but rather that of the legislative authority of the State. I find nothing in the Constitution depriving a State of the power to enact the statute challenged here.

Justice Powell, concurring....

Justice Blackmun, with whom Justice Brennan, Justice Marshall, and Justice Stevens join, dissenting.

This case ... is about "the most comprehensive of rights and the right most valued by civilized men," namely, "the right to be let alone." ...

The statute at issue denies individuals the right to decide for themselves whether to engage in particular forms of private, consensual sexual activity. The Court concludes that [it] is valid essentially because "the laws of ... many States ... still make such conduct illegal and have done so for a very long time." ... But the fact that the moral judgments expressed by statutes like [such] may be "natural and familiar ... ought not to conclude our judgment upon the question whether statutes embodying them conflict with the Constitution of the United States." ...

I believe that "[i]t is revolting to have no better reason for a rule of law than that so it was laid down in the time of Henry IV. It is still more revolting if the grounds upon which it was laid down have vanished long since, and the rule simply persists from blind imitation of the past." ... I believe we must analyze respondent's claim in the light of the values that underlie the constitutional right to privacy. If that right means anything, it means that, before Georgia can prosecute its citizens for making choices about the most intimate aspects of their lives, it must do more than assert that the choice they have made is an "abominable crime not fit to be named among Christians." ...

In its haste to reverse the Court of Appeals and hold that the Constitution does not "confe[r] a fundamental right upon homosexuals to engage in sodomy," the Court relegates the actual statute being challenged to a footnote and ignores the procedural posture of the case before it. A fair reading of the statute and of the complaint clearly reveals that the majority has distorted the question this case presents.

First, the Court's almost obsessive focus on homosexual activity is particularly hard to justify in light of the broad language Georgia has used. Unlike the Court, the Georgia Legislature has not proceeded on the assumption that homosexuals are so different from other citizens that their lives may be controlled in a way that would not be tolerated if it limited the choices of those other citizens.... Rather, Georgia has provided that "[a] person commits the offense of sodomy when he performs or submits to any sexual act involving the sex organs of one person and the mouth or anus of another." ... The sex or status of the persons who engage in the act is irrelevant as a matter of state law. In fact, to the extent I can discern a legislative purpose for Georgia's 1968 enactment ... that purpose seems to have been to broaden the coverage of the law to reach heterosexual as well as homosexual activity. I therefore see no basis for the Court's decision to treat this case as an "as applied" challenge ... or for Georgia's attempt, both in its brief and at oral argument, to defend [the law] solely on the grounds that it prohibits homosexual activity. Michael Hardwick's standing may rest in significant part on Georgia's apparent willingness to enforce against homosexuals a law it seems not to have any desire to enforce against heterosexuals.... But his claim that [the law] involves an unconstitutional intrusion into his privacy and his right of intimate association does not depend ... on his sexual orientation.

Second, I disagree with the Court's refusal to consider whether [the sodomy law] runs afoul of the Eighth or Ninth Amendments or the Equal Protection Clause of the Fourteenth Amendment.... Respondent's complaint expressly invoked the Ninth Amendment, ... and he relied heavily before this Court on *Griswold v. Connecticut* ... (1965), which identifies that Amendment as one of the specific constitutional provisions giving "life and substance" to our understanding of privacy.... More importantly, the procedural posture of the case requires that we affirm the Court of Appeals' judgment if there is any ground on which respondent may be entitled to relief....

Despite historical views of homosexuality, it is no longer viewed by mental health professionals as a "disease" or disorder.... But, obviously, neither is it simply a matter of deliberate personal election. Homosexual orientation may well form part of the very fiber of an individual's personality. Consequently, ... the Eighth Amendment may pose a constitutional barrier to sending an individual to prison for acting on that attraction regardless of the circumstances. An individual's ability to make constitutionally protected "decisions concerning sexual relations," ... is rendered empty indeed if he or she is given no real choice but a life without any physical intimacy.

With respect to the Equal Protection Clause's applicability to [the challenged law], I note that Georgia's exclusive stress before this Court on its interest in prosecuting homosexual activity despite the gender-neutral terms of the statute may arise serious questions of discriminatory enforcement, questions that cannot be disposed of before the Court on a motion to dismiss.... The legislature having decided that the sex of the participants is irrelevant to the legality of the acts, I do not see why the State can defend [the law] on the ground that individuals singled out for prosecution are of the same sex as their partners. Thus, under the circumstances of this case, a claim under the Equal Protection Clause may well be available without having to reach the more controversial question whether homosexuals are a suspect class....

The Court concludes today that none of our prior cases dealing with various decisions that individuals are entitled to make free of governmental interference "bears any resemblance to the claimed constitutional right of homosexuals to engage in acts of sodomy that is asserted in this case." ... While it is true that these cases may be characterized by their connection to protection of the family, ... the Court's conclusion that they extend no further than this boundary ignores the warning in *Moore v. East Cleveland,*... against "clos[ing] our eyes to the basic reasons why certain rights associated with the family have been accorded shelter under the Fourteenth Amendment's Due Process Clause." We protect those rights not because they contribute, in some direct and material way, to the general public welfare, but because they form so central a part of an individual's life. "[T]he concept of privacy embodies the 'moral fact that a person belongs to himself and not others nor to society as a whole.'" ...

... The Court claims that its decision today merely refuses to recognize a fundamental right to engage in homosexual sodomy; what the Court really has refused to recognize is the fundamental interest all individuals have in controlling the nature of their intimate associations with others.

The behavior for which Hardwick faces prosecution occurred in his own home, a place to which the Fourth Amendment attaches special significance. The Court's treatment of this aspect of the case is symptomatic of its overall refusal to consider the broad principles that have informed our treatment of privacy in specific cases. Just as the right to privacy is more than the mere aggregation of a number of entitlements to engage in specific behavior, so too, protecting the

(Continued)

physical integrity of the home is more than merely a means of protecting specific activities that often take place there....

Indeed, the right of an individual to conduct intimate relationships in the intimacy of his or her own home seems to me to be the heart of the Constitution's protection of privacy....

Justice Stevens, with whom *Justice Brennan* and *Justice Marshall* join, dissenting....

LAWRENCE v. TEXAS
537 U.S. 1102; 123 S.Ct. 953; 154 L.Ed. 2d. 770 (2003)
Vote: 6-3

In this case, the Supreme Court reconsiders its decision in Bowers v. Hardwick *(1986) in the context of a Texas statute criminalizing private, consensual homosexual conduct.*

Justice Kennedy delivered the opinion of the Court.

Liberty protects the person from unwarranted government intrusions into a dwelling or other private places. In our tradition the State is not omnipresent in the home. And there are other spheres of our lives and existence, outside the home, where the State should not be a dominant presence. Freedom extends beyond spatial bounds. Liberty presumes an autonomy of self that includes freedom of thought, belief, expression, and certain intimate conduct. The instant case involves liberty of the person both in its spatial and more transcendent dimensions.

The question before the Court is the validity of a Texas statute making it a crime for two persons of the same sex to engage in certain intimate sexual conduct.

In Houston, Texas, officers of the Harris County Police Department were dispatched to a private residence in response to a reported weapons disturbance. They entered an apartment where one of the petitioners, John Geddes Lawrence, resided. The right of the police to enter does not seem to have been questioned. The officers observed Lawrence and another man, Tyron Garner, engaging in a sexual act. The two petitioners were arrested, held in custody overnight, and charged and convicted before a Justice of the Peace.

The complaints described their crime as "deviate sexual intercourse, namely anal sex, with a member of the same sex (man)." ... The applicable state law is Tex. Penal Code Ann. § 21.06(a) (2003). It provides: "A person commits an offense if he engages in deviate sexual intercourse with another individual of the same sex." The statute defines "[d]eviate sexual intercourse" as follows: "(A) any contact between any part of the genitals of one person and the mouth or anus of another person"; or "(B) the penetration of the genitals or the anus of another person with an object." § 21.01(1).

The Court of Appeals for the Texas Fourteenth District considered the petitioners' federal constitutional arguments under both the Equal Protection and Due Process Clauses of the Fourteenth Amendment. After hearing the case en banc the court, in a divided opinion, rejected the constitutional arguments and affirmed the convictions.... The majority opinion indicates that the Court of Appeals considered our decision in *Bowers v. Hardwick* ... (1986), to be controlling on the federal due process aspect of the case. *Bowers* then being authoritative, this was proper.

We granted certiorari ... to consider three questions:

"1. Whether Petitioners' criminal convictions under the Texas "Homosexual Conduct" law—which criminalizes sexual intimacy by same-sex couples, but not identical behavior by different-sex couples—violate the Fourteenth Amendment guarantee of equal protection of laws?

"2. Whether Petitioners' criminal convictions for adult consensual sexual intimacy in the home violate their vital interests in liberty and privacy protected by the Due Process Clause of the Fourteenth Amendment?

"3. Whether *Bowers v. Hardwick* ... should be overruled?" ...

The petitioners were adults at the time of the alleged offense. Their conduct was in private and consensual....

We conclude the case should be resolved by determining whether the petitioners were free as adults to engage in the private conduct in the exercise of their liberty under the Due Process Clause of the Fourteenth Amendment to the Constitution. For this inquiry we deem it necessary to reconsider the Court's holding in *Bowers* ....

There are broad statements of the substantive reach of liberty under the Due Process Clause in earlier cases, including *Pierce v. Society of Sisters* (1925), and *Meyer v. Nebraska* (1923); but the most pertinent beginning point is our decision in *Griswold v. Connecticut* (1965).

After *Griswold* it was established that the right to make certain decisions regarding sexual conduct extends beyond the marital relationship. In *Eisenstadt v. Baird* (1972), the Court invalidated a law prohibiting the distribution of contraceptives to unmarried persons. The case was decided under the Equal Protection Clause, ... but with respect to unmarried persons, the Court went on to state the fundamental proposition that the law impaired the exercise of their personal rights....

The opinions in *Griswold* and *Eisenstadt* were part of the background for the decision in *Roe v. Wade* (1973). As is well known, the case involved a challenge to the Texas law prohibiting abortions, but the laws of other States were affected as well. Although the Court held the woman's rights were not absolute, her right to elect an abortion did have real and substantial protection as an exercise of her liberty under the Due Process Clause. The Court cited cases that protect spatial freedom and cases that go well beyond it. *Roe* recognized the right of a woman to make certain fundamental decisions affecting her destiny and confirmed once more that the protection of liberty under the Due Process Clause has a substantive dimension of fundamental significance in defining the rights of the person....

The facts in *Bowers* had some similarities to the instant case.... One difference between the two cases is that the Georgia statute prohibited the conduct whether or not the participants were of the same sex, while the Texas statute, as we have seen, applies only to participants of the same sex. Hardwick was not prosecuted, but he brought an action in federal court to declare the state statute invalid. He alleged he was a practicing homosexual and that the criminal prohibition violated rights guaranteed to him by the Constitution. The Court, in an opinion by Justice White, sustained the Georgia law. Chief Justice Burger and Justice Powell joined the opinion of the Court and filed separate, concurring opinions. Four Justices dissented....

The Court began its substantive discussion in *Bowers* as follows: "The issue presented is whether the Federal Constitution confers a fundamental right upon homosexuals to engage in sodomy and hence invalidates the laws of the many States that still make such conduct illegal and have done so for a very long time." ... That statement, we now conclude, discloses the Court's own failure to appreciate the extent of the liberty at stake. To say that the issue in *Bowers* was simply the right to engage in certain sexual conduct demeans the claim the individual put forward, just as it would demean a married couple were it to be said marriage is simply about the right to have sexual intercourse. The laws involved in *Bowers* and here are, to be sure, statutes that purport to do no more than prohibit a particular sexual act. Their penalties and purposes, though, have more far-reaching consequences, touching upon the most private human conduct, sexual behavior, and in the most private of places, the home. The statutes do seek to control a personal relationship that, whether or not entitled to formal recognition in the law, is within the liberty of persons to choose without being punished as criminals....

The policy of punishing consenting adults for private acts was not much discussed in the early legal literature. We can infer that one reason for this was the very private nature of the conduct. Despite the absence of prosecutions, there may have been periods in which there was public criticism of homosexuals as such and an insistence that the criminal laws be enforced to discourage their practices. But far from possessing "ancient roots," ... American laws targeting same-sex couples did not develop until the last third of the 20th century. The reported decisions concerning the prosecution of consensual, homosexual sodomy between adults for the years 1880–1995 are not always clear in the details, but a significant number involved conduct in a public place....

It was not until the 1970s that any State singled out same-sex relations for criminal prosecution, and only nine States have done so.... *Post-Bowers* even some of these States did not adhere to the policy of suppressing homosexual conduct. Over the course of the last decades, States with same-sex prohibitions have moved toward abolishing them....

In summary, the historical grounds relied upon in *Bowers are* more complex than the majority opinion and the concurring opinion by Chief Justice Burger indicate. Their historical premises are not without doubt and, at the very least, are overstated....

(Continued)

In *Bowers* the Court referred to the fact that before 1961 all 50 States had outlawed sodomy, and that at the time of the Court's decision 24 States and the District of Columbia had sodomy laws.... Justice Powell pointed out that these prohibitions often were being ignored, however. Georgia, for instance, had not sought to enforce its law for decades....

In our own constitutional system the deficiencies in *Bowers* became even more apparent in the years following its announcement. The 25 States with laws prohibiting the relevant conduct referenced in the *Bowers* decision are reduced now to 13, of which 4 enforce their laws only against homosexual conduct. In those States where sodomy is still proscribed, whether for same-sex or heterosexual conduct, there is a pattern of nonenforcement with respect to consenting adults acting in private. The State of Texas admitted in 1994 that as of that date it had not prosecuted anyone under those circumstances....

Two principal cases decided after *Bowers* cast its holding into even more doubt. In *Planned Parenthood of Southeastern Pa. v. Casey* (1992), the Court reaffirmed the substantive force of the liberty protected by the Due Process Clause. The *Casey* decision again confirmed that our laws and tradition afford constitutional protection to personal decisions relating to marriage, procreation, contraception, family relationships, child rearing, and education.... In explaining the respect the Constitution demands for the autonomy of the person in making these choices, we stated as follows:

"These matters, involving the most intimate and personal choices a person may make in a lifetime, choices central to personal dignity and autonomy, are central to the liberty protected by the Fourteenth Amendment. At the heart of liberty is the right to define one's own concept of existence, of meaning, of the universe, and of the mystery of human life. Beliefs about these matters could not define the attributes of personhood were they formed under compulsion of the State." ...

Persons in a homosexual relationship may seek autonomy for these purposes, just as heterosexual persons do. The decision in *Bowers* would deny them this right.

The second *post-Bowers* case of principal relevance is *Romer v. Evans* (1996). There the Court struck down class-based legislation directed at homosexuals as a violation of the Equal Protection Clause. *Romer* invalidated an amendment to Colorado's constitution which named as a solitary class persons who were homosexuals, lesbians, or bisexual either by "orientation, conduct, practices or relationships," ... and deprived them of protection under state antidiscrimination laws. We concluded that the provision was "born of animosity toward the class of persons affected" and further that it had no rational relation to a legitimate governmental purpose....

Equality of treatment and the due process right to demand respect for conduct protected by the substantive guarantee of liberty are linked in important respects, and a decision on the latter point advances both interests. If protected conduct is made criminal and the law which does so remains unexamined for its substantive validity, its stigma might remain even if it were not enforceable as drawn for equal protection reasons. When homosexual conduct is made criminal by the law of the State, that declaration in and of itself is an invitation to subject homosexual persons to discrimination both in the public and in the private spheres. The central holding of *Bowers* has been brought in question by this case, and it should be addressed. Its continuance as precedent demeans the lives of homosexual persons.

The stigma this criminal statute imposes, moreover, is not trivial. The offense, to be sure, is but a class C misdemeanor, a minor offense in the Texas legal system. Still, it remains a criminal offense with all that imports for the dignity of the persons charged.

Bowers was not correct when it was decided, and it is not correct today. It ought not to remain binding precedent. *Bowers v. Hardwick* should be and now is overruled.

The present case does not involve minors. It does not involve persons who might be injured or coerced or who are situated in relationships where consent might not easily be refused. It does not involve public conduct or prostitution. It does not involve whether the government must give formal recognition to any relationship that homosexual persons seek to enter. The case does involve two adults who, with full and mutual consent from each other, engaged in sexual practices common to a homosexual lifestyle. The petitioners are entitled to respect for their private lives. The State cannot demean their existence or control their destiny by making their private sexual conduct a crime. Their right to liberty under the Due Process Clause gives them the full right to engage in their conduct without intervention of the government. "It is a promise of the Constitution that there is a realm of personal liberty which the government may not enter." ... The Texas statute furthers no legitimate state interest which can justify its intrusion into the personal and private life of the individual.

Had those who drew and ratified the Due Process Clauses of the Fifth Amendment or the Fourteenth Amendment known the components of liberty in its manifold possibilities, they might have been more specific. They did not presume to have this insight. They knew times can blind us to certain truths and later generations can see that laws once thought necessary and proper in fact serve only to oppress. As the Constitution endures, persons in every generation can invoke its principles in their own search for greater freedom.

The judgment of the Court of Appeals for the Texas Fourteenth District is reversed, and the case is remanded for further proceedings not inconsistent with this opinion.

It is so ordered.

Justice O'Connor, concurring in the judgment.

The Court today overrules *Bowers v. Hardwick* (1986). I joined *Bowers*, and do not join the Court in overruling it. Nevertheless, I agree with the Court that Texas's statute banning same-sex sodomy is unconstitutional…. Rather than relying on the substantive component of the Fourteenth Amendment's Due Process Clause, as the Court does, I base my conclusion on the Fourteenth Amendment's Equal Protection Clause.

The Equal Protection Clause of the Fourteenth Amendment "is essentially a direction that all persons similarly situated should be treated alike." … Under our rational-basis standard of review, "legislation is presumed to be valid and will be sustained if the classification drawn by the statute is rationally related to a legitimate state interest." …

The statute at issue here [Tex. Penal Code Ann. § 21.06] makes sodomy a crime only if a person "engages in deviate sexual intercourse with another individual of the same sex." … Sodomy between opposite-sex partners, however, is not a crime in Texas. That is, Texas treats the same conduct differently based solely on the participants. Those harmed by this law are people who have a same-sex sexual orientation and thus are more likely to engage in behavior prohibited by § 21.06.

The Texas statute makes homosexuals unequal in the eyes of the law by making particular conduct—and only that conduct—subject to criminal sanction. It appears that prosecutions under Texas' sodomy law

are rare…. This case shows, however, that prosecutions under § 21.06 do occur. And while the penalty imposed on petitioners in this case was relatively minor, the consequences of conviction are not. As the Court notes, see ante, at *15*, petitioners' convictions, if upheld, would disqualify them from or restrict their ability to engage in a variety of professions, including medicine, athletic training, and interior design….

Texas argues, however, that the sodomy law does not discriminate against homosexual persons. Instead, the State maintains that the law discriminates only against homosexual conduct. While it is true that the law applies only to conduct, the conduct targeted by this law is conduct that is closely correlated with being homosexual. Under such circumstances, Texas's sodomy law is targeted at more than conduct. It is instead directed toward gay persons as a class. "After all, there can hardly be more palpable discrimination against a class than making the conduct that defines the class criminal." … When a State makes homosexual conduct criminal, and not "deviate sexual intercourse" committed by persons of different sexes, "that declaration in and of itself is an invitation to subject homosexual persons to discrimination both in the public and in the private spheres." …

That this law as applied to private, consensual conduct is unconstitutional under the Equal Protection Clause does not mean that other laws distinguishing between heterosexuals and homosexuals would similarly fail under rational-basis review. Texas cannot assert any legitimate state interest here, such as national security or preserving the traditional institution of marriage. Unlike the moral disapproval of same-sex relations—the asserted state interest in this case—other reasons exist to promote the institution of marriage beyond mere moral disapproval of an excluded group.

A law branding one class of persons as criminal solely based on the State's moral disapproval of that class and the conduct associated with that class runs contrary to the values of the Constitution and the Equal Protection Clause, under any standard of review. I therefore concur in the Court's judgment that Texas's sodomy law banning "deviate sexual intercourse" between consenting adults of the same sex, but not between consenting adults of different sexes, is unconstitutional.

Justice Scalia, with whom the **Chief Justice** and **Justice Thomas** join, dissenting.

... Texas Penal Code Ann. § 21.06(a) (2003) undoubtedly imposes constraints on liberty. So do laws prohibiting prostitution, recreational use of heroin, and, for that matter, working more than 60 hours per week in a bakery. But there is no right to "liberty" under the Due Process Clause, though today's opinion repeatedly makes that claim.... The Fourteenth Amendment expressly allows States to deprive their citizens of "liberty," so long as "due process of law" is provided....

Our opinions applying the doctrine known as "substantive due process" hold that the Due Process Clause prohibits States from infringing fundamental liberty interests, unless the infringement is narrowly tailored to serve a compelling state interest.... We have held repeatedly, in cases the Court today does not overrule, that only fundamental rights qualify for this so-called "heightened scrutiny" protection—that is, rights which are "deeply rooted in this Nation's history and tradition."

Bowers held, first, that criminal prohibitions of homosexual sodomy are not subject to heightened scrutiny because they do not implicate a "fundamental right" under the Due Process Clause.... Noting that "proscriptions against that conduct have ancient roots," ... that "[s]odomy was a criminal offense at common law and was forbidden by the laws of the original 13 States when they ratified the Bill of Rights," ... and that many States had retained their bans on sodomy, ... *Bowers* concluded that a right to engage in homosexual sodomy was not "deeply rooted in this Nation's history and tradition."

The Court today does not overrule this holding. Not once does it describe homosexual sodomy as a "fundamental right" or a "fundamental liberty interest," nor does it subject the Texas statute to strict scrutiny. Instead, having failed to establish that the right to homosexual sodomy is "deeply rooted in this Nation's history and tradition," the Court concludes that the application of Texas's statute to petitioners' conduct fails the rational-basis test, and overrules *Bowers'* holding to the contrary.... "The Texas statute furthers no legitimate state interest which can justify its intrusion into the personal and private life of the individual." ...

I shall address that rational-basis holding presently. First, however, I address some aspersions that the Court casts upon *Bowers'* conclusion that homosexual sodomy is not a "fundamental right"—even though, as I have said, the Court does not have the boldness to reverse that conclusion....

The Court's description of "the state of the law" at the time of *Bowers* only confirms that *Bowers* was right.... The Court points to *Griswold v. Connecticut* (1965). But that case expressly disclaimed any reliance on the doctrine of "substantive due process," and grounded the so-called "right to privacy" in penumbras of constitutional provisions other than the Due Process Clause. *Eisenstadt v. Baird* (1972), likewise had nothing to do with "substantive due process"; it invalidated a Massachusetts law prohibiting the distribution of contraceptives to unmarried persons solely on the basis of the Equal Protection Clause. Of course *Eisenstadt* contains well-known dictum relating to the "right to privacy," but this referred to the right recognized in *Griswold*—a right penumbral to the specific guarantees in the Bill of Rights, and not a "substantive due process" right.

It is (as *Bowers* recognized) entirely irrelevant whether the laws in our long national tradition criminalizing homosexual sodomy were "directed at homosexual conduct as a distinct matter." ... Whether homosexual sodomy was prohibited by a law targeted at same-sex sexual relations or by a more general law prohibiting both homosexual and heterosexual sodomy, the only relevant point is that it was criminalized—which suffices to establish that homosexual sodomy is not a right "deeply rooted in our Nation's history and tradition." The Court today agrees that homosexual sodomy was criminalized and thus does not dispute the facts on which *Bowers* actually relied.

Next the Court makes the claim, again unsupported by any citations, that "[l]aws prohibiting sodomy do not seem to have been enforced against consenting adults acting in private." ... I do not know what "acting in private" means; surely consensual sodomy, like heterosexual intercourse, is rarely performed on stage. If all the Court means by "acting in private" is "on private premises, with the doors closed and windows covered," it is entirely unsurprising that evidence of enforcement would be hard to come by....

I turn now to the ground on which the Court squarely rests its holding: the contention that there is no rational basis for the law here under attack. This proposition is so out of accord with our jurisprudence—indeed, with the jurisprudence of any society we know—that it requires little discussion.

The Texas statute undeniably seeks to further the belief of its citizens that certain forms of sexual behavior are "immoral and unacceptable," ... [which is] the same interest furthered by criminal laws against fornication, bigamy, adultery, adult incest, bestiality, and obscenity. *Bowers* held that this was a legitimate state interest. The Court today reaches the opposite conclusion. The Texas statute, it says, "furthers no legitimate state interest which can justify its intrusion into the personal and private life of the individual." ... The Court embraces instead Justice Stevens's declaration in his *Bowers* dissent that "the fact that the governing majority in a State has traditionally viewed a particular practice as immoral is not a sufficient reason for upholding a law prohibiting the practice." ... This effectively decrees the end of all morals legislation. If, as the Court asserts, the promotion of majoritarian sexual morality is not even a legitimate state interest, none of the above-mentioned laws can survive rational-basis review....

Finally, I turn to petitioners' equal-protection challenge, which no Member of the Court ... save Justice O'Connor, embraces: On its face § 21.06(a) applies equally to all persons. Men and women, heterosexuals and homosexuals, are all subject to its prohibition of deviate sexual intercourse with someone of the same sex. To be sure, § 21.06 does distinguish between the sexes insofar as concerns the partner with whom the sexual acts are performed: men can violate the law only with other men, and women only with other women. But this cannot itself be a denial of equal protection, since it is precisely the same distinction regarding partner that is drawn in state laws prohibiting marriage with someone of the same sex while permitting marriage with someone of the opposite sex....

Justice O'Connor simply decrees application of "a more searching form of rational basis review" to the Texas statute.... The cases she cites do not recognize such a standard, and reach their conclusions only after finding, as required by conventional rational-basis analysis, that no conceivable legitimate state interest supports the classification at issue.... Nor does Justice O'Connor explain precisely what her "more searching form" of rational-basis review consists of. It must at least mean, however, that laws exhibiting "a ... desire to harm a politically unpopular group" ... are invalid even though there may be a conceivable rational basis to support them.

This reasoning leaves on pretty shaky grounds state laws limiting marriage to opposite-sex couples. Justice O'Connor seeks to preserve them by the conclusory statement that "preserving the traditional institution of marriage" is a legitimate state interest.... But "preserving the traditional institution of marriage" is just a kinder way of describing the State's moral disapproval of same-sex couples. Texas's interest in § 21.06 could be recast in similarly euphemistic terms: "preserving the traditional sexual mores of our society." In the jurisprudence Justice O'Connor has seemingly created, judges can validate laws by characterizing them as "preserving the traditions of society" (good); or invalidate them by characterizing them as "expressing moral disapproval" (bad)....

Today's opinion is the product of a Court, which is the product of a law-profession culture, that has largely signed on to the so-called homosexual agenda, by which I mean the agenda promoted by some homosexual activists directed at eliminating the moral opprobrium that has traditionally attached to homosexual conduct. I noted in an earlier opinion the fact that the American Association of Law Schools (to which any reputable law school must seek to belong) excludes from membership any school that refuses to ban from its job-interview facilities a law firm (no matter how small) that does not wish to hire as a prospective partner a person who openly engages in homosexual conduct....

One of the most revealing statements in today's opinion is the Court's grim warning that the criminalization of homosexual conduct is "an invitation to subject homosexual persons to discrimination both in the public and in the private spheres." ... It is clear from this that the Court has taken sides in the culture war, departing from its role of assuring, as neutral observer, that the democratic rules of engagement are observed. Many Americans do not want persons who openly engage in homosexual conduct as partners in their business, as scoutmasters for their children, as teachers in their children's schools, or as boarders in their home. They view this as protecting themselves and their families from a lifestyle that they believe to be immoral and destructive. The Court views it as "discrimination" which it is the function of our judgments to deter. So imbued is the Court with the law profession's anti-antihomosexual culture, that it is seemingly unaware that the attitudes of that culture are not obviously "mainstream"; that in most States what the Court calls "discrimination" against those who engage in homosexual acts is perfectly legal; that proposals to ban such "discrimination" under Title VII have repeatedly been rejected by Congress, ... that in some cases such "discrimination" is mandated by federal statute, ... and that in some cases such "discrimination" is a constitutional right....

Let me be clear that I have nothing against homosexuals, or any other group, promoting their agenda

(Continued)

through normal democratic means. Social perceptions of sexual and other morality change over time, and every group has the right to persuade its fellow citizens that its view of such matters is the best. That homosexuals have achieved some success in that enterprise is attested to by the fact that Texas is one of the few remaining States that criminalize private, consensual homosexual acts. But persuading one's fellow citizens is one thing, and imposing one's views in absence of democratic majority will is something else. I would no more require a State to criminalize homosexual acts—or, for that matter, display any moral disapprobation of them—than I would forbid it to do so. What Texas has chosen to do is well within the range of traditional democratic action, and its hand should not be stayed through the invention of a brand-new "constitutional right" by a Court that is impatient of democratic change. It is indeed true that "later generations can see that laws once thought necessary and proper in fact serve only to oppress," ... and when that happens, later generations can repeal those laws. But it is the premise of our system that those judgments are to be made by the people, and not imposed by a governing caste that knows best.

One of the benefits of leaving regulation of this matter to the people rather than to the courts is that the people, unlike judges, need not carry things to their logical conclusion. The people may feel that their disapprobation of homosexual conduct is strong enough to disallow homosexual marriage, but not strong enough to criminalize private homosexual acts—and may legislate accordingly. The Court today pretends that it possesses a similar freedom of action, so that that we need not fear judicial imposition of homosexual marriage, as has recently occurred in Canada (in a decision that the Canadian Government has chosen not to appeal).... At the end of its opinion—after having laid waste the foundations of our rational-basis jurisprudence—the Court says that the present case "does not involve whether the government must give formal recognition to any relationship that homosexual persons seek to enter." ... Do not believe it. More illuminating than this bald, unreasoned disclaimer is the progression of thought displayed by an earlier passage in the Court's opinion, which notes the constitutional protections afforded to "personal decisions relating to marriage, procreation, contraception, family relationships, child rearing, and education," and then declares that "[p]ersons in a homosexual relationship

may seek autonomy for these purposes, just as heterosexual persons do." ... Today's opinion dismantles the structure of constitutional law that has permitted a distinction to be made between heterosexual and homosexual unions, insofar as formal recognition in marriage is concerned. If moral disapprobation of homosexual conduct is "no legitimate state interest" for purposes of proscribing that conduct, ... and if, as the Court coos (casting aside all pretense of neutrality), "[w]hen sexuality finds overt expression in intimate conduct with another person, the conduct can be but one element in a personal bond that is more enduring," ... what justification could there possibly be for denying the benefits of marriage to homosexual couples exercising "[t]he liberty protected by the Constitution"? ... Surely not the encouragement of procreation, since the sterile and the elderly are allowed to marry. This case "does not involve" the issue of homosexual marriage only if one entertains the belief that principle and logic have nothing to do with the decisions of this Court. Many will hope that, as the Court comfortingly assures us, this is so.

The matters appropriate for this Court's resolution are only three: Texas's prohibition of sodomy neither infringes a "fundamental right" (which the Court does not dispute), nor is unsupported by a rational relation to what the Constitution considers a legitimate state interest, nor denies the equal protection of the laws. I dissent.

Justice Thomas, dissenting.

I join Justice Scalia's dissenting opinion. I write separately to note that the law before the Court today "is ... uncommonly silly." ... If I were a member of the Texas Legislature, I would vote to repeal it. Punishing someone for expressing his sexual preference through noncommercial consensual conduct with another adult does not appear to be a worthy way to expend valuable law enforcement resources.

Notwithstanding this, I recognize that as a member of this Court I am not empowered to help petitioners and others similarly situated. My duty, rather, is to "decide cases 'agreeably to the Constitution and laws of the United States.' " ... I "can find [neither in the Bill of Rights nor any other part of the Constitution a] general right of privacy," ... or as the Court terms it today, the "liberty of the person both in its spatial and more transcendent dimensions." ...

WASHINGTON v. GLUCKSBERG
527 U.S. 702; 117 S.Ct. 2258; 138 L.Ed. 2d. 772 (1997)
Vote: 9-0

In this case, the Court reviews a state statute prohibiting doctor-assisted suicide.

Chief Justice Rehnquist delivered the opinion of the Court.

The question presented in this case is whether Washington's prohibition against "caus[ing]" or "aid[ing]" a suicide offends the Fourteenth Amendment to the United States Constitution. We hold that it does not.

It has always been a crime to assist a suicide in the State of Washington. In 1854, Washington's first Territorial Legislature outlawed "assisting another in the commission of self-murder." Today, Washington law provides: "A person is guilty of promoting a suicide attempt when he knowingly causes or aids another person to attempt suicide." ... "Promoting a suicide attempt" is a felony, punishable by up to five years' imprisonment and up to a $10,000 fine.... At the same time, Washington's Natural Death Act, enacted in 1979, states that the "withholding or withdrawal of life sustaining treatment" at a patient's direction "shall not, for any purpose, constitute a suicide." ...

Petitioners in this case are the State of Washington and its Attorney General. Respondents Harold Glucksberg, M.D., Abigail Halperin, M.D., Thomas A. Preston, M.D., and Peter Shalit, M.D., are physicians who practice in Washington. These doctors occasionally treat terminally ill, suffering patients and declare that they would assist these patients in ending their lives if not for Washington's assisted-suicide ban. In January 1994, respondents, along with three gravely ill, pseudonymous plaintiffs who have since died and Compassion in Dying, a nonprofit organization that counsels people considering physician-assisted suicide, sued in the United States District Court, seeking a declaration that [the statute] is, on its face, unconstitutional....

The plaintiffs asserted "the existence of a liberty interest protected by the Fourteenth Amendment which extends to a personal choice by a mentally competent, terminally ill adult to commit physician assisted suicide." ... Relying primarily on *Planned Parenthood v. Casey* ... (1992), and *Cruzan v. Director, Missouri Dept. of Health* ... (1990), the District Court agreed,

... and concluded that Washington's assisted suicide ban is unconstitutional because it "places an undue burden on the exercise of [that] constitutionally protected liberty interest." ... The District Court also decided that the Washington statute violated the Equal Protection Clause's requirement that "all persons similarly situated ... be treated alike." ...

A panel of the Court of Appeals for the Ninth Circuit reversed, emphasizing that "[i]n the two hundred and five years of our existence no constitutional right to aid in killing oneself has ever been asserted and upheld by a court of final jurisdiction." ... The Ninth Circuit reheard the case en banc, reversed the panel's decision, and affirmed the District Court.... Like the District Court, the en banc Court of Appeals emphasized our *Casey* and *Cruzan* decisions.... The court also discussed what it described as "historical" and "current societal attitudes" toward suicide and assisted suicide, ... and concluded that "the Constitution encompasses a due process liberty interest in controlling the time and manner of one's death—that there is, in short, a constitutionally recognized 'right to die.'" ... After "[w]eighing and then balancing" this interest against Washington's various interests, the court held that the State's assisted suicide ban was unconstitutional "as applied to terminally ill competent adults who wish to hasten their deaths with medication prescribed by their physicians." ... The court did not reach the District Court's equal protection holding.... We granted certiorari ... and now reverse.

We begin, as we do in all due process cases, by examining our Nation's history, legal traditions, and practices.... In almost every State—indeed, in almost every western democracy—it is a crime to assist a suicide. The States' assisted suicide bans are not innovations. Rather, they are long-standing expressions of the States' commitment to the protection and preservation of all human life.... Indeed, opposition to and condemnation of suicide—and, therefore, of assisting suicide—are consistent and enduring themes of our philosophical, legal, and cultural heritages.... More specifically, for over 700 years, the Anglo American common law tradition has punished or otherwise disapproved of both suicide and assisting suicide....

(Continued)

... [C]olonial and early state legislatures and courts did not retreat from prohibiting assisting suicide.... And the prohibitions against assisting suicide never contained exceptions for those who were near death....

The earliest American statute explicitly to outlaw assisting suicide was enacted in New York in 1828 ... and many of the new States and Territories followed New York's example.... In this century, the Model Penal Code also prohibited "aiding" suicide, prompting many States to enact or revise their assisted suicide bans. The Code's drafters observed that "the interests in the sanctity of life that are represented by the criminal homicide laws are threatened by one who expresses a willingness to participate in taking the life of another, even though the act may be accomplished with the consent, or at the request, of the suicide victim." ...

Though deeply rooted, the States' assisted suicide bans have in recent years been reexamined and, generally, reaffirmed. Because of advances in medicine and technology, Americans today are increasingly likely to die in institutions, from chronic illnesses.... Public concern and democratic action are therefore sharply focused on how best to protect dignity and independence at the end of life, with the result that there have been many significant changes in state laws and in the attitudes these laws reflect. Many States, for example, now permit "living wills," surrogate health care decision making, and the withdrawal or refusal of life sustaining medical treatment.... At the same time, however, voters and legislators continue for the most part to reaffirm their States' prohibitions on assisting suicide.

The Washington statute at issue in this case ... was enacted in 1975 as part of a revision of that State's criminal code. Four years later, Washington passed its Natural Death Act, which specifically stated that the "withholding or withdrawal of life sustaining treatment ... shall not, for any purpose, constitute a suicide" and that "[n]othing in this chapter shall be construed to condone, authorize, or approve mercy killing...." ... In 1991, Washington voters rejected a ballot initiative which, had it passed, would have permitted a form of physician-assisted suicide. Washington then added a provision to the Natural Death Act expressly excluding physician-assisted suicide....

California voters rejected an assisted suicide initiative similar to Washington's in 1993. On the other hand, in 1994, voters in Oregon enacted, also through ballot initiative, that State's "Death With Dignity Act," which legalized physician-assisted suicide for competent, terminally ill adults. Since the Oregon vote, many proposals to legalize assisted suicide have been and continue to be introduced in the States' legislatures, but none has been enacted. And just last year, Iowa and Rhode Island joined the overwhelming majority of States explicitly prohibiting assisted suicide....

Thus, the States are currently engaged in serious, thoughtful examinations of physician-assisted suicide and other similar issues. For example, New York State's Task Force on Life and the Law—an ongoing, blue ribbon commission composed of doctors, ethicists, lawyers, religious leaders, and interested laymen—was convened in 1984 and commissioned with "a broad mandate to recommend public policy on issues raised by medical advances." ... Over the past decade, the Task Force has recommended laws relating to end of life decisions, surrogate pregnancy, and organ donation.... After studying physician-assisted suicide, however, the Task Force unanimously concluded that "[l]egalizing assisted suicide and euthanasia would pose profound risks to many individuals who are ill and vulnerable.... [T]he potential dangers of this dramatic change in public policy would outweigh any benefit that might be achieved." ...

... The Due Process Clause guarantees more than fair process, and the "liberty" it protects includes more than the absence of physical restraint.... The Clause also provides heightened protection against government interference with certain fundamental rights and liberty interests.... In a long line of cases, we have held that, in addition to the specific freedoms protected by the Bill of Rights, the "liberty" specially protected by the Due Process Clause includes the rights to marry, ... to have children, ... to direct the education and upbringing of one's children, ... to marital privacy, ... to use contraception, ... to bodily integrity, ... and to abortion.... We have also assumed, and strongly suggested, that the Due Process Clause protects the traditional right to refuse unwanted lifesaving medical treatment....

But we "ha[ve] always been reluctant to expand the concept of substantive due process because guideposts for responsible decision making in this uncharted area are scarce and open ended." ... By extending constitutional protection to an asserted right or liberty interest, we, to a great extent, place the matter outside the arena of public debate and legislative action. We must therefore "exercise the utmost care whenever we are asked to break new ground in this field," ... lest the liberty protected by the Due Process Clause be subtly transformed into the policy preferences of the members of this Court....

Our established method of substantive due process analysis has two primary features: First, we have regularly observed that the Due Process Clause specially protects those fundamental rights and liberties which are, objectively, "deeply rooted in this Nation's history and tradition," ... and "implicit in the concept of ordered liberty," such that "neither liberty nor justice would exist if they were sacrificed." ... Second, we have required in substantive due process cases a "careful description" of the asserted fundamental liberty interest.... Our Nation's history, legal traditions, and practices thus provide the crucial "guideposts for responsible decision making," ... that direct and restrain our exposition of the Due Process Clause. As we stated recently ..., the Fourteenth Amendment "forbids the government to infringe ... 'fundamental' liberty interests at all, no matter what process is provided, unless the infringement is narrowly tailored to serve a compelling state interest." ...

... The Washington statute at issue in this case prohibits "aid[ing] another person to attempt suicide," ... and, thus, the question before us is whether the "liberty" specially protected by the Due Process Clause includes a right to commit suicide which itself includes a right to assistance in doing so.

... [W]e are confronted with a consistent and almost universal tradition that has long rejected the asserted right, and continues explicitly to reject it today, even for terminally ill, mentally competent adults. To hold for respondents, we would have to reverse centuries of legal doctrine and practice, and strike down the considered policy choice of almost every State....

Respondents contend, however, that the liberty interest they assert is consistent with this Court's substantive due process line of cases, if not with this Nation's history and practice. Pointing to *Casey* and *Cruzan*, respondents read our jurisprudence in this area as reflecting a general tradition of "self-sovereignty," ... and as teaching that the "liberty" protected by the Due Process Clause includes "basic and intimate exercises of personal autonomy." ... According to respondents, our liberty jurisprudence, and the broad, individualistic principles it reflects, protects the "liberty of competent, terminally ill adults to make end of life decisions free of undue government interference." ... The question presented in this case, however, is whether the protections of the Due Process Clause

include a right to commit suicide with another's assistance....

The history of the law's treatment of assisted suicide in this country has been and continues to be one of the rejections of nearly all efforts to permit it. That being the case, our decisions lead us to conclude that the asserted "right" to assistance in committing suicide is not a fundamental liberty interest protected by the Due Process Clause. The Constitution also requires, however, that Washington's assisted suicide ban be rationally related to legitimate government interests.... This requirement is unquestionably met here.

As the court below recognized, ... Washington's assisted suicide ban implicates a number of state interests....

First, Washington has an "unqualified interest in the preservation of human life." ... The State's prohibition on assisted suicide, like all homicide laws, both reflects and advances its commitment to this interest....

Respondents admit that "[t]he State has a real interest in preserving the lives of those who can still contribute to society and enjoy life." ...

Relatedly, all admit that suicide is a serious public health problem, especially among persons in otherwise vulnerable groups....

Those who attempt suicide—terminally ill or not—often suffer from depression or other mental disorders. ... Research indicates, however, that many people who request physician-assisted suicide withdraw that request if their depression and pain are treated.... [B]ecause depression is difficult to diagnose, physicians and medical professionals often fail to respond adequately to seriously ill patients' needs.... Thus, legal physician-assisted suicide could make it more difficult for the State to protect depressed or mentally ill persons, or those who are suffering from untreated pain, from suicidal impulses.

The State also has an interest in protecting the integrity and ethics of the medical profession.... [T]he American Medical Association, like many other medical and physicians' groups, has concluded that "[p]hysician assisted suicide is fundamentally incompatible with the physician's role as healer." ...

Next, the State has an interest in protecting vulnerable groups—including the poor, the elderly, and disabled persons—from abuse, neglect, and mistakes.... If physician-assisted suicide were permitted, many might resort to it to spare their families the substantial financial burden of end of life health care costs.

(Continued)

... The State's assisted suicide ban reflects and reinforces its policy that the lives of terminally ill, disabled, and elderly people must be no less valued than the lives of the young and healthy, and that a seriously disabled person's suicidal impulses should be interpreted and treated the same way as anyone else's....

Finally, the State may fear that permitting assisted suicide will start it down the path to voluntary and perhaps even involuntary euthanasia.... [W]hat is couched as a limited right to "physician assisted suicide" is likely, in effect, a much broader license, which could prove extremely difficult to police and contain. Washington's ban on assisting suicide prevents such erosion.

This concern is further supported by evidence about the practice of euthanasia in the Netherlands. The Dutch government's own study revealed that in 1990, there were 2,300 cases of voluntary euthanasia (defined as "the deliberate termination of another's life at his request"), 400 cases of assisted suicide, and more than 1,000 cases of euthanasia without an explicit request. In addition to these latter 1,000 cases, the study found an additional 4,941 cases where physicians administered lethal morphine overdoses without the patients' explicit consent.... This study suggests that, despite the existence of various reporting procedures, euthanasia in the Netherlands has not been limited to competent, terminally ill adults who are enduring physical suffering, and that regulation of the practice may not have prevented abuses in cases involving vulnerable persons, including severely disabled neonates and elderly persons suffering from dementia....

We need not weigh exactly the relative strengths of these various interests. They are unquestionably important and legitimate, and Washington's ban on assisted suicide is at least reasonably related to their promotion and protection. We therefore hold that [the challenged statute] does not violate the Fourteenth Amendment, either on its face or "as applied to competent, terminally ill adults who wish to hasten their deaths by obtaining medication prescribed by their doctors." ...

Throughout the Nation, Americans are engaged in an earnest and profound debate about the morality, legality, and practicality of physician-assisted suicide. Our holding permits this debate to continue, as it should in a democratic society. The decision of the en banc Court of Appeals is reversed, and the case is remanded for further proceedings consistent with this opinion.

Justice O'Connor, concurring....

Justice Stevens, concurring in the judgments.

The Court ends its opinion with the important observation that our holding today is fully consistent with a continuation of the vigorous debate about the "morality, legality, and practicality of physician assisted suicide" in a democratic society.... I write separately to make it clear that there is also room for further debate about the limits that the Constitution places on the power of the States to punish the practice.

The morality, legality, and practicality of capital punishment have been the subject of debate for many years. In *[Gregg v. Georgia]* 1976, this Court upheld the constitutionality of the practice in cases coming to us from Georgia, Florida, and Texas. In those cases we concluded that a State does have the power to place a lesser value on some lives than on others; there is no absolute requirement that a State treat all human life as having an equal right to preservation. Because the state legislatures had sufficiently narrowed the category of lives that the State could terminate, and had enacted special procedures to ensure that the defendant belonged in that limited category, we concluded that the statutes were not unconstitutional on their face. In later cases coming to us from each of those States, however, we found that some applications of the statutes were unconstitutional.

Today, the Court decides that Washington's statute prohibiting assisted suicide is not invalid "on its face," that is to say, in all or most cases in which it might be applied. That holding, however, does not foreclose the possibility that some applications of the statute might well be invalid....

... [J]ust as our conclusion that capital punishment is not always unconstitutional did not preclude later decisions holding that it is sometimes impermissibly cruel, so is it equally clear that a decision upholding a general statutory prohibition of assisted suicide does not mean that every possible application of the statute would be valid. A State, like Washington, that has authorized the death penalty and thereby has concluded that the sanctity of human life does not require that it always be preserved, must acknowledge that there are situations in which an interest in hastening death is legitimate. Indeed, not only is that interest sometimes legitimate, I am also convinced that there are times when it is entitled to constitutional protection....

There remains room for vigorous debate about the outcome of particular cases that are not necessarily resolved by the opinions announced today. How such cases may be decided will depend on their specific facts. In my judgment, however, it is clear that the so-called "unqualified interest in the preservation of human life," … is not itself sufficient to outweigh the interest in liberty that may justify the only possible means of preserving a dying patient's dignity and alleviating her intolerable suffering.

Justice Souter, concurring in the judgment.

… Legislatures [in contrast to courts] have superior opportunities to obtain the facts necessary for a judgment about the present controversy. Not only do they have more flexible mechanisms for fact finding than the Judiciary, but their mechanisms include the power to experiment, moving forward and pulling back as facts emerge within their own jurisdictions. There is, indeed, good reason to suppose that in the absence of a judgment for respondents here, just such experimentation will be attempted in some of the States….

… Sometimes a court may be bound to act regardless of the institutional preferability of the political branches as forums for addressing constitutional claims…. Now, it is enough to say that our examination of legislative reasonableness should consider the fact that the Legislature of the State of Washington is no more obviously at fault than this Court is in being uncertain about what would happen if respondents prevailed today. We therefore have a clear question about which institution, a legislature or a court, is relatively more competent to deal with an emerging issue as to which facts currently unknown could be dispositive. The answer has to be, for the reasons already stated, that the legislative process is to be preferred. There is a closely related further reason as well.

One must bear in mind that the nature of the right claimed, if recognized as one constitutionally required, would differ in no essential way from other constitutional rights guaranteed by enumeration or derived from some more definite textual source than "due process." An unenumerated right should not therefore be recognized, with the effect of displacing the legislative ordering of things, without the assurance that its recognition would prove as durable as the recognition of those other rights differently derived. To recognize a right of lesser promise would simply create a constitutional regime too uncertain to bring with it the expectation of finality that is one of this Court's central obligations in making constitutional decisions….

Legislatures, however, are not so constrained. The experimentation that should be out of the question in constitutional adjudication displacing legislative judgments is entirely proper, as well as highly desirable, when the legislative power addresses an emerging issue like assisted suicide. The Court should accordingly stay its hand to allow reasonable legislative consideration. While I do not decide for all time that respondents' claim should not be recognized, I acknowledge the legislative institutional competence as the better one to deal with that claim at this time.

Justice Ginsburg, concurring in the judgments….

Justice Breyer, concurring in the judgments.

… I agree with the Court … that the articulated state interests justify the distinction drawn between physician-assisted suicide and withdrawal of life support. I also agree with the Court that the critical question in both of the cases before us is whether "the 'liberty' specially protected by the Due Process Clause includes a right" of the sort that the respondents assert…. I do not agree, however, with the Court's formulation of that claimed "liberty" interest. The Court describes it as a "right to commit suicide with another's assistance." … But I would not reject the respondents' claim without considering a different formulation, for which our legal tradition may provide greater support. That formulation would use words roughly like a "right to die with dignity." But irrespective of the exact words used, at its core would lie personal control over the manner of death, professional medical assistance, and the avoidance of unnecessary and severe physical suffering …

I do not believe … that this Court need or now should decide whether or a not such a right is "fundamental." That is because, in my view, the avoidance of severe physical pain (connected with death) would have to comprise an essential part of any successful claim and because, as Justice O'Connor points out, the laws before us do not force a dying person to undergo that kind of pain…. Rather, the laws of New York and of Washington do not prohibit doctors from providing patients with drugs sufficient to control pain despite the risk that those drugs themselves will kill…. And under these circumstances the laws of New York and Washington would overcome any remaining significant interests and would be justified, regardless.

(Continued)

Medical technology, we are repeatedly told, makes the administration of pain relieving drugs sufficient, except for a very few individuals for whom the ineffectiveness of pain control medicines can mean, not pain, but the need for sedation which can end in a coma.... We are also told that there are many instances in which patients do not receive the palliative care that, in principle, is available, ... but that is so for institutional reasons or inadequacies or obstacles, which would seem possible to overcome, and which do not include a prohibitive set of laws....

This legal circumstance means that the state laws before us do not infringe directly upon the (assumed) central interest (what I have called the core of the interest in dying with dignity) as, by way of contrast, the state anticontraceptive laws ... did interfere with the central interest there at stake—by bringing the State's police powers to bear upon the marital bedroom.

Were the legal circumstances different—for example, were state law to prevent the provision of palliative care, including the administration of drugs as needed to avoid pain at the end of life—then the law's impact upon serious and otherwise unavoidable physical pain (accompanying death) would be more directly at issue. And as Justice O'Connor suggests, the Court might have to revisit its conclusions in these cases.

CHAPTER **7**

CHAPTER OUTLINE

Equal Protection and the Antidiscrimination Principle

"Our constitution is color-blind, and neither knows nor tolerates classes among citizens. In respect of civil rights all are equal before the law."

—*Justice John M. Harlan, Dissenting in*

Plessy v. Ferguson *(1896)*

John M. Harlan (the elder): Associate Justice, 1877–1911

Introduction

One of the philosophical foundations of American democracy is the idea that all individuals are equal before the law. This ideal is expressed both in the Declaration of Independence and in the **Equal Protection Clause** of the Fourteenth Amendment, which provides that no state shall "deny to any person within its jurisdiction the equal protection of the laws." The Equal Protection Clause prohibits states from denying any person or class of persons the same protection and rights that the law extends to other similarly situated persons or classes of persons.

Like other rights guaranteed by the post–Civil War amendments, the Equal Protection Clause was motivated in large part by a desire to protect the civil rights of African-Americans recently freed from slavery. However, the text of the clause makes no mention of race; rather, it refers to "any person" within the jurisdiction of a state. Although the Supreme Court attempted initially to limit the scope of the Equal Protection Clause to discrimination claims brought by African-Americans (see *The Slaughter-House Cases* [1873] and *Strauder v. West Virginia* [1880]), it has developed into a broad prohibition against unreasonable governmental discrimination directed at any identifiable group.

As noted in previous chapters, during the late nineteenth century the Supreme Court emphasized the protection of private enterprise against government regulation. The Equal Protection Clause played a limited role in this protection, as the Court relied more heavily on the Due Process Clauses of the Fifth and Fourteenth Amendments. Occasionally, the Equal Protection Clause was employed as a basis for invalidating discriminatory business regulation (see *Yick Wo v. Hopkins* [1886]). In *Santa Clara County v. Southern Pacific Railroad Company* (1886), the Court declared that the word "person" in the Equal Protection Clause included corporations. The notion of corporate "personhood" is today an axiom of corporation law.

In the modern era, the Equal Protection Clause has been invoked successfully to challenge discrimination against racial and ethnic minorities, as well as discrimination against women, the poor, illegitimate children, the mentally retarded, illegal aliens, and, most recently, gay men and lesbians. Under the **New Equal Protection**, the Supreme Court has used the Equal Protection Clause to scrutinize closely any state law or practice that discriminates among groups in their enjoyment of **fundamental rights**. Without question, the scope of the Equal Protection Clause has been expanded far beyond the expectations of its authors. Along with the Due Process Clause of the Fourteenth Amendment, the Equal Protection Clause has become the principal basis for challenging the constitutionality of a broad range of state laws, actions, and policies.

The "Equal Protection Component" of the Fifth Amendment

Because the Fourteenth Amendment applies only to the states, and because the Bill of Rights contains no explicit equal protection provision, does it follow that the national government is under no constitutional obligation to provide equal protection of the laws? The Supreme Court has answered this question emphatically in the negative, "finding" an "equal protection component" in the Due Process Clause of the Fifth Amendment. The Court has concluded that the values underlying the equal protection guarantee are embraced within the broad definition of due process of law (see *Boling v. Sharpe* [1954]). Very recently, in *United States v. Windsor* (2013), a landmark decision on same-sex marriage discussed and excerpted later in this chapter, the Court observed, "The liberty protected by the Fifth Amendment's Due Process Clause contains within it the prohibition against denying to any person the equal protection of the laws." Thus the federal government, territorial governments, the fifty states, and all political subdivisions (local governments and special districts) are under the same obligation to provide equal protection of the laws to persons within their respective jurisdictions.

Because the Fourteenth Amendment contains a Due Process Clause virtually identical to that found in the Fifth Amendment, one might conclude that the Equal Protection Clause of the Fourteenth Amendment is superfluous. Although this may be true in a formal, logical sense, the Equal Protection Clause was the historic basis for judicial scrutiny of governmental policies challenged as discriminatory. In the absence of the Equal Protection Clause, such scrutiny would have been more difficult to justify.

Levels of Judicial Scrutiny in Equal Protection Cases

Although the adoption and early development of the Equal Protection Clause must be understood in the context of the historic struggle for racial equality in this country, courts have over the years entertained a variety of equal protection claims going well beyond issues of racial discrimination. The Supreme Court has developed a set of standards for judging the constitutionality of policies that are challenged on equal protection grounds.

Minimal Scrutiny: The Rational Basis Test

State and federal laws are replete with discriminations, or "classifications," of various kinds. Yet very few of these classifications are considered constitutionally offensive. For example, a state law that requires a person to possess a license to practice medicine discriminates against those persons who are unable to meet the qualifications necessary to obtain a license. Similarly, when the state limits the driving privilege to persons aged 16 and older, it is by definition engaging in age discrimination. But few would challenge the reasonableness of such discrimination. Obviously, there are good reasons for restricting the driving privilege to persons 16 and above, just as there are good reasons to limit the practice of medicine to those who are qualified.

The traditional test employed by courts in judging challenged legislative classifications is the **rational basis test** (first articulated by the Supreme Court in *Gulf, Colorado, & Santa Fe Railway Company v. Ellis* [1897]). Under this deferential approach, the Court indicates a strong presumption of the constitutionality of the action in question, and the burden is on the party challenging the statute to show that (1) the purpose of the challenged discrimination is an illegitimate state objective and (2) the means employed by the state are not rationally related to the achievement of its objective. Thus, for example, the state law requiring doctors to be licensed reflects a legitimate state interest in protecting the public health and safety and is rationally related to that end. The rational basis test remains the primary test for determining the constitutionality of classifications that impinge on economic interests.

Because the rational basis test is easily satisfied, few policies that are reviewed on this basis are declared unconstitutional. Notable exceptions include *Plyler v. Doe* (1982), where the Supreme Court struck down a Texas law that denied access to public education to the children of illegal aliens, *Cleburne v. Cleburne Living Center* (1985), in which the Court invalidated a local zoning board's denial of a permit to construct a home for the mentally retarded, and *Romer v. Evans* (1996), where the Court struck down an amendment to the Colorado constitution that prohibited the extension of civil rights protections to gays and lesbians. (All three of these decisions are discussed later in this chapter.)

The Suspect Classification Doctrine

In the wake of the constitutional revolution of 1937, the focus of Supreme Court activism moved away from the protection of economic individualism. Instead, the post–New Deal Court focused its attention on civil rights and liberties, especially the rights of traditionally disadvantaged minorities. The Equal Protection Clause figured prominently in this process. In expanding the scope of the Equal Protection Clause, the Court developed a style of analysis that to a great extent superseded the traditional rational basis test.

Footnote 4 In a famous footnote to his opinion in *United States v. Carolene Products Company* (1938), Justice Harlan Fiske Stone stated that "prejudice against discrete and insular minorities may be a special condition, which tends seriously to curtail the operation of those political processes ordinarily to be relied upon to protect minorities and … may call for a more searching judicial scrutiny." The Court's desire to protect **discrete and insular minorities** who lack political clout in Congress and/or the state legislatures resulted in numerous decisions involving the rights of the accused, prisoners, aliens (legal and illegal), persons with disabilities, unorthodox religious sects, and, of course, racial and ethnic minorities.

The Japanese Relocation Case   *Korematsu v. United States* (1944) provided the first real indication that the Court was embarking on a new approach to the Equal Protection Clause. In *Korematsu*, the Court upheld the constitutionality of the "relocation" of Japanese Americans living on the West Coast during the World War II (for further discussion and excerpts from the opinions, see Chapter 3, Volume I). In his majority opinion, Justice Hugo Black stated that:

> *all legal restrictions that curtail the civil rights of a single group are immediately suspect. That is not to say that all such restrictions are unconstitutional. It is to say that courts must subject them to the most rigid scrutiny. Pressing public necessity may sometimes justify the existence of such restrictions; racial antagonism never can.*

It is now widely recognized that no compelling justification supported the relocation order at issue in *Korematsu*. However, the Supreme Court apparently did not have full access to information, later made public, clearly indicating that the relocation order stemmed more from racial prejudice than from military necessity.

Although on its face the *Korematsu* decision was hardly a victory for civil rights, it marked the inception of the **suspect classification doctrine**, which holds that certain kinds of discrimination are inherently suspect and therefore must be subjected to **strict judicial scrutiny**. Included among those laws that are inherently suspect are those that classify persons based on race, religion, or ethnicity, as well as those that impinge on fundamental rights.

Strict Scrutiny   Operationally speaking, strict judicial scrutiny means that the ordinary **presumption of constitutionality** is reversed; the government carries the burden of proof that its challenged policy is constitutional. To carry that burden, government must show that its policy is necessary to the achievement of a **compelling interest** and that it is "narrowly tailored" to further that interest. Although judicial tests are far from precise, in that courts seldom define the terms that comprise these tests, the compelling interest test is generally understood to be far more stringent than the traditional rational basis test. Using the suspect classification doctrine, the Court has invalidated, explicitly or implicitly, virtually all public policies that overtly discriminate among persons on the basis of their race (see, for example, *Loving v. Virginia* [1967]). In the Court's view, it is virtually impossible for government to have a compelling interest that would require or justify racial or ethnic discrimination.

Intermediate or Heightened Scrutiny

To complicate matters further, the Supreme Court has developed still another level of equal protection review, falling somewhere between the rational basis test and the suspect classification doctrine. This approach, often described as **heightened scrutiny**, has been applied most prominently, but not exclusively, to gender discrimination claims. Under this approach, government must show that a challenged policy bears a "substantial" relationship to an "important" government interest. Because discriminatory policies are presumed invalid under heightened scrutiny, this level of review is closer to strict scrutiny than to the rational basis test. In fact, it is difficult to differentiate clearly between the two levels of review.

Shortly before his retirement in 1991, Justice Thurgood Marshall suggested that the Court adopt a "sliding scale" that would embrace a "spectrum of standards" of review. Others on the Court have been put off by what they regard as needless doctrinal complexity. Justice John Paul Stevens, for example, argued for a return to the rational basis standard, which he believed to be adequate to invalidate all invidious forms of discrimination. Others, most notably Chief Justice Rehnquist, expressed dissatisfaction with the Court's special solicitude for the claims of discrete and insular minorities. To date the Roberts Court has wrestled less with the wisdom of the levels of review and more in defining the appropriate occasion to make use of each of them.

To Summarize:

♦ *The Supreme Court has developed three tiers of review for determining whether challenged policies violate the Equal Protection Clause.*

♦ *The most lenient approach is the rational basis test. Under this test, the burden is on the party challenging the policy to show that its purpose is illegitimate and/or that the means employed are not rationally related to the achievement of the government's objective.*

♦ *The Court employs strict scrutiny in judging policies that discriminate on the basis of race, religion, or national origin, classifications that are deemed to be "inherently suspect." In such cases, the burden is on the government to show that its challenged policy is narrowly tailored to the achievement of a compelling governmental interest.*

♦ *In cases involving claims of gender discrimination and in certain other areas, the Court employs* heightened scrutiny *in which government must show that a challenged policy bears a "substantial" relationship to an "important" government interest.*

The Struggle for Racial Equality

Although the Equal Protection Clause is now recognized as a broad shield against arbitrary government action, little doubt exists that the Fourteenth Amendment was adopted primarily to protect the rights of the newly freed former slaves. Specifically, the Fourteenth Amendment was designed to provide constitutional authority for newly enacted federal civil rights legislation aimed at ending discrimination against African-Americans. Section 5 of the Fourteenth Amendment gives Congress the power to enforce, "by appropriate legislation," the abstract promises of the Equal Protection Clause and other provisions of the amendment.

Early Interpretations of the Equal Protection Clause

Shortly before the Fourteenth Amendment was ratified, Congress passed the **Civil Rights Act of 1866**, which, among other things, protected the right of African-Americans to inherit, own, and convey property. In the wake of the Civil War, many of the southern states had adopted the **Black Codes**, which denied such basic economic rights to former slaves. Under the new Civil Rights Act, violation of these rights was made a federal offense where it could be shown that the violator was acting "under color of state law." Apparently having some reservations about the constitutionality of this law, Congress rushed to adopt the Fourteenth Amendment, believing that the Equal Protection Clause of Section 1 together with the enforcement provision of Section 5 would provide an adequate constitutional basis for far-ranging civil rights legislation.

Judging the Disparate Impact of Facially Neutral Policies

The suspect classification doctrine applies only to policies that overtly discriminate on the basis of race, religion, or ethnicity. What standard should be applied to judge public policies that are neutral on their face but have disparate impacts on people of different races? In *Washington v. Davis* (1976), the Supreme Court considered a challenge to the practice of requiring applicants to the District of Columbia police department to pass a verbal skills test that was used widely in the federal civil service. African-American applicants were approximately four times as likely to fail this test as were white applicants. The Court rejected the argument that the testing requirement should be subjected to strict scrutiny under the suspect classification doctrine. Writing for the Court, Justice Byron White said:

> A rule that a statute designed to serve neutral ends is nevertheless invalid, absent compelling justification, if in practice it benefits or burdens one race more than another would be far-reaching and would raise serious questions about, and

perhaps invalidate, a whole range of tax, welfare, public service, regulatory and licensing statutes.

Under *Washington v. Davis* and similar decisions, a policy that is racially neutral on its face, is rationally related to a legitimate governmental objective, but has a **disparate impact** on people of different races will be upheld unless plaintiffs can show that it was adopted to serve a racially discriminatory purpose. However, it is important to note that the statutory probation against employment discrimination does not require plaintiffs to prove discriminatory intent. Under Title VII of the 1964 Civil Rights Act, an employer is barred from using a facially neutral employment practice that has an unjustified adverse impact on members of a minority group. In *Griggs v. Duke Power Co.* (1971), the Supreme Court said that "good intent or absence of discriminatory intent does not redeem employment procedures or testing mechanisms that operate as 'built-in headwinds' for minority groups and are unrelated to measuring job capability."

Federal Civil Rights Statutes Passed during Reconstruction

The Civil Rights Act of 1866 provided that citizens of all races have the same rights to make and enforce contracts, to sue and give evidence in the courts, and to own, purchase, sell, rent, and inherit real and personal property. For modern counterparts, see 42 U.S.C. §§ 1981, 1982.

The Civil Rights Act of 1870 made it a federal crime to conspire to "injure, oppress, threaten or intimidate any citizen in the free exercise of any right or privilege secured to him by the Constitution or laws of the United States." See 18 U.S.C. § 241. The statute also criminalized any act under color of state law that subjects persons to deprivations of constitutional rights. See 18 U.S.C. § 242.

The Civil Rights Act of 1871 made individuals acting under color of state law personally liable for acts violating constitutional rights of others. Civil actions under this statute are commonly referred to as "Section 1983 actions" because the Act is codified at 42 U.S.C. § 1983. The Act of 1871 also permitted civil suits against those conspiring to violate civil rights of others. See 42 U.S.C. § 1985.

The Civil Rights Act of 1875 forbade denial of equal rights and privileges by places of public accommodation. This statute was declared invalid as applied to privately owned public accommodations by the Supreme Court in *The Civil Rights Cases* (1883).

The Civil Rights Cases   While the modern Supreme Court recognizes broad congressional power under the Fourteenth Amendment, the Supreme Court's early view of congressional authority in the field of civil rights was much more restrictive. In adopting the **Civil Rights Act of 1875**, Congress made a serious attempt to eradicate racial discrimination in **places of public accommodation**, including hotels, taverns, restaurants, theaters, and "public conveyances." In *The Civil Rights Cases* (1883), however, the Supreme Court struck down the key provisions of this act, ruling that the Fourteenth Amendment limited congressional action to the prohibition of official state-sponsored discrimination as distinct from discrimination practiced by privately owned places of public accommodation. The Supreme Court's decision in *The Civil Rights Cases* may have been motivated by a desire to promote reconciliation between North and South and between the federal and state governments. Unfortunately, any such reconciliation was achieved at the expense of African-Americans.

The **state action doctrine** announced in *The Civil Rights Cases* remains authoritative to this day—and in fact not until the 1960s was Congress willing or able to prohibit discrimination in places of public accommodation. When Congress did finally act in passing the **Civil Rights Act of 1964**, it chose to rely primarily on its broad powers under the Commerce Clause, rather than on Section 5 of the Fourteenth Amendment (see Chapter 3, Volume I).

The Separate but Equal Doctrine

Not only did the Court's decision in *The Civil Rights Cases* preserve widespread practices of racial discrimination in restaurants, hotels, and the like, but it was also regarded as a green light for the passage of legislation mandating strict racial segregation. The **Jim Crow laws** adopted in the aftermath of *The Civil Rights Cases* required segregation in virtually every area of public life. They required blacks and whites to attend separate schools, to use separate parks, to ride in separate railroad cars, and even to be buried in separate cemeteries. Perhaps the most ludicrous of the many Jim Crow laws required white and black witnesses in court to take their oaths on separate Bibles!

In *Plessy v. Ferguson* (1896), the Supreme Court upheld racial segregation in the context of public transportation. The Court's ruling provided a rationale for government-mandated segregation on a broad scale. At issue in *Plessy* was an 1890 Louisiana law requiring passenger trains operating within the state to provide "equal but separate" accommodations for the "white and colored races." Homer Plessy, who was considered "colored" under Louisiana law because one of his great-grandparents was black, was ordered to leave a railroad car reserved for whites. Plessy, who intended to challenge the constitutionality of the law, refused to vacate his seat and was arrested. Dividing 7 to 1 (Justice David Brewer not participating), the Court sustained the Louisiana statute. Writing for the majority, Justice Henry Billings Brown asserted that "in the nature of things, [the Fourteenth Amendment] could not have been intended to abolish distinctions based upon color, or to enforce social, as distinguished from political, equality, or a commingling of the two races upon terms unsatisfactory to either." In one of the most widely quoted opinions in American constitutional law, Justice John M. Harlan (the elder) dissented vehemently. For Justice Harlan, ironically a former Kentucky slave owner, the "arbitrary separation of citizens on the basis of race" was tantamount to imposing a "badge of servitude" on the Negro race. He asserted that "our Constitution is color-blind, and neither knows nor tolerates classes among citizens." The **separate but equal doctrine** approved in *Plessy* remained the authoritative interpretation of the Equal Protection Clause for fifty-eight years. Ultimately, of course, it was repudiated by the Supreme Court in *Brown v. Board of Education of Topeka* (1954).

The net effect of *The Civil Rights Cases* and *Plessy v. Ferguson* was to defer the dream of legal and political equality for African-Americans for nearly a century after ratification of the Fourteenth Amendment. During this period, racial discrimination was simply a way of life for many Americans, both black and white. Even today, although considerable progress toward racial equality has been achieved, racial discrimination has by no means disappeared from American society.

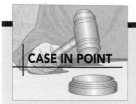

An Early Victory for Civil Rights
Buchanan v. Warley (1917)

In 1914, the city of Louisville, Kentucky, enacted "[a]n ordinance to prevent conflict and ill-feeling between the white and colored races in the city of Louisville, and to preserve the public peace and promote the general welfare, by making reasonable provisions requiring, as far as practicable, the use of separate blocks, for residences, places of abode, and places of assembly by white and colored people respectively." Ironically, the ordinance was challenged by a white man (Buchanan) who sold a house to an African-American (Warley). After losing in the Kentucky courts, Buchanan brought the case to the U.S. Supreme Court on a writ of error. Speaking for a unanimous bench, Justice William R. Day averred that Louisville's "attempt to prevent the alienation of the property in question to a person of color was not a legitimate exercise of the police power of the state, and is in direct violation of the fundamental law enacted in the Fourteenth Amendment of the Constitution preventing state interference with property rights except by due process of law." Day observed that "there exists a serious and difficult problem arising from a feeling of race hostility which the law is powerless to control, and to which it must give a measure of consideration ..." But, said Day, "its solution cannot be promoted by depriving citizens of their constitutional rights and privileges." While Day and his colleagues may have been thinking first and foremost about the property rights of the white plaintiff in the case, their decision nevertheless represented an important early victory in the struggle against racial segregation.

The Decline of de Jure Racial Segregation

The Court's decision in *Plessy v. Ferguson* rested on two obvious fictions: (1) that racial segregation conveyed no negative statement about the status of African-Americans and (2) that separate accommodations and facilities for blacks were in fact equal to those reserved for whites. Blacks, and no doubt whites as well, knew better. As time went by, it became increasingly obvious to the Supreme Court that the separate but equal doctrine was a mere rationalization for relegating African-Americans to second-class citizenship.

In a series of cases decided between 1938 and 1950, the Supreme Court chipped away at the separate but equal doctrine, as applied to higher education, without repudiating the doctrine altogether. In *Missouri ex rel. Gaines v. Canada* (1938), the Court mandated the admission of a qualified African-American resident of Missouri to the state university law school. The Court held that a state could not escape its obligation by making provisions for its African-American students to attend out-of-state law schools. The Supreme Court reaffirmed its holding in *Gaines* a decade later in *Sipuel v. Oklahoma Board of Regents* (1948). Two years later, in *McLaurin v. Oklahoma State Regents* (1950), the Court disallowed an attempt by the University of Oklahoma to segregate a black graduate student from his white colleagues after he was admitted pursuant to a court order. In class, the student, McLaurin, was required to sit in a row of desks restricted to blacks. In the cafeteria, he was required to eat alone at a particular table. He was restricted to a designated table in the library. He was even prohibited from visiting his professors during their regular office hours in order to minimize his interactions with white students. In the Court's view, this isolation significantly detracted from McLaurin's educational experience and thus could not be justified under the separate but equal doctrine.

In *Sweatt v. Painter* (1950), the Court considered an attempt by the state of Texas to provide a separate law school for African-Americans. The Court found that the newly created law school at the Texas College for Negroes was substantially inferior, in terms of both measurable and intangible factors, to the whites-only law school at the University of Texas. Chief Justice Vinson described inequities in the number of professors, students, facilities, and even library books, which amounted to a violation of the Equal Protection Clause of the Fourteenth Amendment. This set the stage for the Supreme Court's landmark ruling in 1954.

The Landmark Decision in *Brown v. Board of Education*

By the early 1950s, it was clear that the Supreme Court would no longer tolerate the provision of demonstrably inferior educational services or facilities to African-Americans under the aegis of the separate but equal doctrine. But considerable uncertainty remained, both within and outside the Court, as to whether the justices would, or should, abandon the *Plessy* doctrine altogether. The NAACP mounted a major challenge to segregated public schools, instituting lawsuits in four states and the District of Columbia. These cases were first argued before the Supreme Court in 1952, but because of the political magnitude of the issue presented, the Court directed that the cases be reargued in 1953. Before the second round of oral argument, Chief Justice Fred M. Vinson died and was succeeded by Earl Warren.

Finally, on May 17, 1954, the uncertainly regarding segregated public schools came to an end when the Court handed down its landmark decision in *Brown v. Board of Education*. In one of the most important decisions in its history, the Court unanimously struck down racial segregation in the public schools of Kansas, South Carolina, Delaware, and Virginia. Speaking for the Court in *Brown*, Chief Justice Warren declared that "in the field of public education, the doctrine of 'separate but equal' has no place. Separate educational facilities are inherently unequal." Thus, in a concise and forceful opinion, the Warren Court abandoned a long-standing constitutional precedent and precipitated a revolution in public education. In a companion case, *Boiling v. Sharpe*, the Court held that the operation of segregated schools by the District of Columbia violated the Due Process Clause of the Fifth Amendment. Here, as noted at the beginning of this chapter, the Court recognized an "equal protection component" in the Fifth Amendment due process requirement, indicating that uniform antidiscrimination mandates were to be applied to the federal government as well as the states.

Implementation of Brown   The *Brown* decision of 1954 left open the question of how and when desegregation would have to be achieved. In a follow-up decision in 1955 (referred to as *Brown II*), the Court blunted the revolutionary potential of the original decision by adopting a formula calling for implementation of **desegregation** with "all deliberate speed." Recognizing that compliance would be more difficult to achieve in the South than in other sections of the country, the Court left it up to federal district judges to apply this formula, taking into account the particular circumstances characterizing race relations within their respective jurisdictions. This approach ensured great diversity in the implementation of *Brown I* and invited the use of delaying tactics by state and local officials. Despite its concern for the difficulties public officials would face in bringing about desegregation, the Court was reviled in many quarters for "meddling" in state and local affairs. Some of the Court's harsher critics went so far as to call for the impeachment of Chief Justice Warren.

Violent Resistance to Brown   Some of the more extreme critics of school desegregation called for militant noncompliance with the Court's directive. John Kasper, a well-known white supremacist and self-styled protégé of the fascist poet Ezra Pound, went around the country preaching the use of violence and intimidation to prevent black students from entering formerly all-white public schools. In the late summer of 1956, Kasper went to Clinton, Tennessee, where he succeeded in fomenting violent resistance to court-ordered integration of Clinton High School. In late August, Kasper was ordered by federal judge Robert Taylor "to cease hindering, obstructing, or in any wise interfering" with court-ordered integration. Kasper persisted in his efforts, and Clinton experienced a turbulent fall replete with riots, beatings, death threats directed at various school officials, and harassment of African-American students. After the National Guard was called in to restore order, Kasper was arrested and convicted for violating the federal court injunction. Ultimately, peace returned to Clinton, and desegregation proceeded apace.

The Little Rock Crisis   In one of the best known and most dramatic efforts to resist the Supreme Court's desegregation decisions, Arkansas Governor Orval Faubus called out the National Guard in 1957 to prevent nine African-American students from entering Little Rock Central High School. The Guard was soon withdrawn, but an angry mob of whites continued to harass the black students. President Dwight D. Eisenhower, who had expressed serious reservations about the *Brown* decision, nevertheless intervened with federal troops to quell the violence and enforce the court-ordered integration. A year later, in *Cooper v. Aaron* (1958), the Court delivered a sharp rebuke to Arkansas officials who had attempted to frustrate the Court's mandate (see Chapter 1, Volume I). One wonders, however, if the Court's language in *Cooper v. Aaron* would have been so strong in the absence of Eisenhower's intervention in Little Rock.

The Court Repudiates "All Deliberate Speed"   In efforts less dramatic than what transpired in Little Rock, state and local governments intent on avoiding desegregation adopted a strategy of "legislate and litigate" that delayed universal compliance with *Brown* for well over a decade. But in *Alexander v. Holmes County* (1969), after many years of delay, the Supreme Court finally abandoned the permissive "all deliberate speed" policy and ordered desegregation "at once." This set the stage for the busing controversy of the 1970s.

The Busing Controversy

As previously noted, the Supreme Court's *Brown II* decision left the implementation of school desegregation largely to the discretion of federal district judges. Of the various measures that these judges employed in dismantling dual school systems, "forced busing" was by far the most controversial. In *Swann v. Charlotte-Mecklenburg Board of Education* (1971), the Supreme Court unanimously approved the use of **court-ordered busing** to achieve the goal of desegregation. In 1973, the Court turned its attention to school desegregation outside the South. In *Keyes v. Denver School District*, the Court, with only Justice Rehnquist dissenting, found **de jure discrimination** where a series of administrative decisions in the 1960s had helped to maintain racially segregated public schools in the city of Denver. Thus, in *Keyes*, as in *Swann*, the Supreme Court upheld a busing plan imposed by a federal district court.

As court-ordered busing became more pervasive, it erupted into a major political issue. In the 1972 presidential campaign, candidate George Wallace exploited the busing issue quite successfully, goading incumbent Richard Nixon into taking a stronger anti-busing posture than he had previously maintained. Perhaps as a reaction to widespread criticism of *Swann* and *Keyes*, as well as anti-busing rumblings in Congress, the Supreme Court backed away from busing in the case of *Milliken v. Bradley* (1974). *Milliken* involved a challenge to a court-ordered desegregation plan for greater Detroit that involved busing students across school district lines within the metropolitan area. Although *Milliken* by no means overturned *Swann* and *Keyes*, a 5-to-4 majority of the justices held that court-ordered busing of students across school district lines is permissible only if all affected districts had been guilty of past discriminatory practices. By thus limiting interdistrict busing plans, the Supreme Court placed substantial limits on this approach to school desegregation in metropolitan areas.

To the proponents of racial busing, the decision in *Milliken* was an unfortunate retreat from the Court's long-standing commitment to integration. For others, *Milliken* was a welcome concession to public opinion, which was generally negative toward busing. Clearly, the effect of the *Milliken* decision was to defuse much of the harsh criticism that had previously been directed at the Court over the busing issue. Nevertheless, interdistrict busing schemes continued to be ordered by federal judges where interdistrict violations were uncovered. In Boston, interdistrict busing in 1974 produced intense hostility and violence.

The use of busing to achieve desegregation continues to this day, although it is far less pervasive than it was in the early 1970s. Indeed, African-American intellectuals and educators no longer uniformly support busing. Some reject what they regard as a racist implication that black children cannot improve themselves without exposure to white children. Clearly, the political and intellectual impetus behind racial busing has diminished dramatically. Consequently, busing is no longer a salient political issue. The Supreme Court continues to hear cases in this area, but the major thrust of current litigation is toward the termination, rather than the continued implementation, of busing and related desegregation plans. In a significant 1991 decision, *Board of Education v. Dowell*, the Court granted federal district courts clear authority to terminate desegregation orders provided that two conditions are met: (1) that the local school board in question has complied in good faith with the desegregation decree, and (2) that all vestiges of prior discrimination have been effectively removed. The *Dowell* decision left many questions unanswered, but the Court made it clear that judicial supervision of school desegregation is, after all, temporary in nature.

In *Freeman v. Pitts* (1992), the Supreme Court amplified its decision in *Dowell* by permitting a federal district court that for many years had supervised desegregation of the DeKalb County, Georgia, schools to relinquish supervision over certain aspects of school administration. The Court held that district judges have discretion to relinquish supervision of school systems where racial imbalances stemming from de jure segregation have disappeared, even if schools remain "racially identifiable" due to demographic factors. Under the approach taken in *Dowell* and *Freeman*, local school districts that show good-faith efforts to comply with court-mandated desegregation plans will eventually regain full control of their school systems.

The Kansas City Desegregation Case   In *Missouri v. Jenkins* (1995), the Supreme Court reviewed a federal district judge's efforts to desegregate the Kansas City school system. The plan would redistribute the students within the system, and also included magnet schools to attract nonminority students from outside the Kansas City Metropolitan School District. Splitting 5 to 4, the Supreme Court invalidated the judge's order, finding interdistrict reassignment to be excessive and abusive of the district court's remedial powers. The Court also instructed the lower court to review the rest of its remedial orders under the stricter level of scrutiny articulated in *Freeman v. Pitts* (1992). Writing for the Court, Chief Justice Rehnquist reminded the district court "that its end purpose is not only 'to remedy the violation' to the extent practicable, but also 'to restore state and local authorities to the control of a school system that is operating in compliance with the Constitution.'" In her concurring opinion in *Jenkins*, Justice O'Connor emphasized the narrowness of the Court's holding. In contrast, Justice Thomas's twenty-seven-page concurring opinion launched a broadside against desegregation jurisprudence: "Given that desegregation has not produced the predicted leaps forward in black educational achievement, there is no reason to think that black students cannot learn as well when surrounded by members of their own race as when they are in an integrated environment." Thomas also attacked the "virtually unlimited" power of federal district judges to craft desegregation remedies: "Federal courts simply cannot gather sufficient information to render an effective decree, have limited resources to induce compliance, and cannot seek political and public support for their remedies. When we presume to have the institutional ability to set effective educational, budgetary, or administrative policy, we transform the least dangerous branch into the most dangerous one." Dissenting in *Jenkins*, Justice Souter noted that state and local officials "intentionally created this segregated system of education, and subsequently failed to correct it." Clearly, in Souter's view, officials "defaulted in their obligation to uphold the Constitution." In remedying the violation, the district court must be accorded broad latitude. It must be "authorized to remedy all conditions flowing directly from the constitutional violations committed by state or local officials, including the educational deficits that result from a segregated school system." Justice Souter was joined in this view by Justices Ginsburg, Breyer, and Stevens. In her separate dissent, Justice Ginsburg sounded a cautionary note: "Given the deep, inglorious history of segregation in Missouri, to curtail desegregation at this time and in this manner is an action at once too swift and too soon."

A Key Roberts Court Decision   In *Parents Involved in Community Schools v. Seattle School District No. 1* (2007), the Court addressed the plans of public school districts in Seattle, Washington, and Louisville, Kentucky, to create a degree of racial balance between whites and nonwhites in their public high schools by basing student admissions in part on racial criteria. The Court applied a strict scrutiny framework and struck down the racially conscious policies adopted by both local school systems. The decision distinguished between secondary and post-secondary education, and thus did not overrule *Grutter*. Chief Justice John Roberts unequivocally announced his position for a four-member plurality, rejecting the view that racial diversity advanced a compelling governmental interest and declaring that: "The way to stop discrimination on the basis of race is to stop discriminating on the basis of race." In a separate opinion concurring in the judgment, Justice Kennedy disagreed with the Chief Justice, maintaining that "diversity, depending on its meaning and definition, is a compelling educational goal a school district may pursue."

> **To Summarize:**
> ♦ *Although the Equal Protection Clause is now recognized as a broad shield against arbitrary governmental action, it is well known that the Fourteenth Amendment was adopted primarily to protect the rights of the newly freed former slaves.*
> ♦ *Section 5 of the Fourteenth Amendment gives Congress the power to enforce, "by appropriate legislation," the abstract promises of the Equal Protection Clause and other provisions of the amendment. In the wake of the Civil War, Congress adopted a number of important civil rights statutes. In the modern era, Congress has continued to rely on Section 5 of the Fourteenth Amendment in legislating in the civil rights field.*
> ♦ *The Supreme Court was slow to take up the cause of civil rights, and in early cases refused to use the Fourteenth Amendment to invalidate racial discrimination and segregation. The Warren Court, most notably in* Brown v. Board of Education *(1954), made civil rights a major priority and in so doing wrought major changes in American politics and society.*
> ♦ Brown v. Board of Education *was the beginning of a process of desegregating public schools, a process that involved considerable resistance from supporters of segregation and numerous legal controversies over busing of students and federal judicial supervision of many public school systems. Since the early 1990s the court has gradually disengaged itself from the process of implementing* Brown.

The Affirmative Action Controversy

The furor over court-ordered busing that occurred during the 1970s had largely subsided by the late 1980s. But as usually happens in American politics, a new ongoing controversy emerged to take its place. The controversy involved **affirmative action**, a broad term referring to a variety of efforts designed to assist members of traditionally disfavored minority groups. The affirmative action concept is manifested in three major areas of distributive policy: employment, government contracts, and higher education. Affirmative action actually emerged through executive orders handed down during the Kennedy, Johnson, and Nixon administrations of the 1960s and early 1970s. Initially, it was limited to the requirement that federal government contractors make increased efforts to recruit minority employees. Thereafter, state higher education programs were required to adopt affirmative action guidelines as a condition of accepting federal subsidies. Soon federal and state courts were adopting **race-conscious remedies** (for example, racial busing) in resolving desegregation lawsuits.

Eventually, what began as little more than a public exhortation became a series of goals, quotas, and timetables designed to integrate African-Americans, Hispanics, Native Americans, and other traditionally disfavored minorities into the economic and educational mainstream.

Although the ultimate objective of affirmative action was, and is, universally applauded, the means of achieving it—preferential treatment based on immutable racial characteristics—are distasteful to many and appear downright unjust to others. To many critics, affirmative action represents an unfortunate degeneration of the noble ideal of equality of opportunity into "statistical parity." For some legal critics, affirmative action is a violation of the color-blind Constitution idealized by Justice Harlan's dissent in *Plessy v. Ferguson*. Still others, some of them members of nonpreferred ethnic minorities, object to affirmative action not on principle but because they have not been given preferred status. Yet, the many defenders of affirmative action characterize it as the only practicable means of realizing the American dream for those who have been traditionally locked out.

Competing Models of Justice

Affirmative action is problematic legally because it involves two competing models of racial justice. One theory views race discrimination and its appropriate remedies in terms of identifiable groups. Under this theory, all individuals properly belonging to a traditionally disfavored minority are entitled to partake of a remedy. The competing individualistic theory holds that remedies are to be provided only to those individuals who can show that they have been the targets of invidious discrimination. The conflict can also be viewed as one between contemporary politics and traditional principles of law. In the contemporary pluralistic political process, we are accustomed to thinking in terms of group interests. However, our system of law rests on a foundation of individualism and does not easily accommodate the concept of **group rights**.

The *Bakke* and *Fullilove* Cases

Naturally, people on all sides of the affirmative action controversy looked to the Supreme Court for a settlement of the issue. The Supreme Court initially avoided the constitutionality of affirmative action when it decided *DeFunis v. Odegaard* (1974), holding that the question presented in this case was moot. Eventually, however, the Supreme Court did hand down a ruling on affirmative action, but *Regents of the University of California v. Bakke* (1978) could hardly be regarded as a definitive resolution of the issue. Alan Bakke, a thirty-seven-year-old white male engineer, brought suit to challenge the affirmative action policy of the medical school at the University of California-Davis (Cal-Davis). Bakke had been denied admission to the medical school, although his objective indicators (that is, Medical College Admission Test score and grade point average) were better than those of several of the sixteen minority students admitted under a **set-aside** policy. The California Supreme Court found this to be a violation of equal protection and ordered Bakke to be admitted to the medical school. Seeking a more authoritative resolution of the issue, the university appealed. Bakke ultimately won the appeal, completed his medical school program, and became a practicing anesthesiologist.

In a fragmented decision, the Court voted 5 to 4 to invalidate the Cal-Davis quota system and admit Alan Bakke to medical school. However, also by a 5-to-4 margin, the Court endorsed affirmative action in the abstract, by recognizing race as a legitimate criterion of admission to medical school. According to Justice Lewis Powell's controlling opinion in *Bakke*, the state has a compelling interest in achieving diversity in its medical school, and this interest justifies the use of race as one of several criteria of admission. However, the use of a rigid quota system:

> *tells applicants who are not Negro, Asian or Chicano that they are totally excluded from a specific percentage of the seats in an entering class. No matter how strong their qualifications, quantitative and extracurricular, including their own potential for contribution to educational diversity, they are never afforded the chance to compete with applicants from the preferred groups for the special admissions seats.*

For Justice Powell, this was the fatal flaw in the Cal-Davis affirmative action plan. In Powell's view, the University could consider race as one of several factors, but it could not employ quotas.

Powell's brethren were less equivocal. Four members of the Court—Burger, Stewart, Rehnquist, and Stevens—would have declared the entire policy to be in violation of the Civil Rights Act of 1964, which, in their view, required government to observe a standard of color-blindness. On the other hand, Justices Brennan, Marshall, White, and Blackmun found no statutory or constitutional violation in the minority "set-aside" policy. According to Justice William Brennan, "government may take race into account when it acts not to demean or insult any racial group, but to remedy disadvantages cast on minorities by past racial prejudice." Justice Thurgood Marshall, the first African-American justice on the Court, used his dissenting opinion to make a strong case for affirmative action:

> *It is because of a legacy of unequal treatment that we now must permit the institutions of this society to give consideration to race in making decisions about who will hold the positions of influence, affluence, and prestige in America. For far too long, the doors to those positions have been shut to Negroes. If we are ever to become a fully integrated society, one in which the color of a person's skin will not determine the opportunities available to him or her, we must be willing to take steps to open those doors. I do not believe that anyone can truly look into America's past and still find that a remedy for the effects of that past is impermissible.*

The *Bakke* decision, and in particular Justice Powell's controlling opinion, seemed to many to be an equivocation. An equally equivocal endorsement of affirmative action was provided by the Supreme Court in *Fullilove v. Klutznick* (1980). In *Fullilove*, the Court upheld a federal public works program that provided a 10 percent "set-aside" of federal funds for "minority business enterprises." Because this case involved an act of Congress, rather than state action, the "set-aside" policy was challenged as a violation of the equal protection component of the Fifth Amendment Due Process Clause. The Supreme Court upheld the minority "set-aside" by a vote of 6 to 3. Unfortunately, as in *Bakke*, the Court was unable to produce a majority opinion. Chief Justice Warren Burger's plurality opinion stressed Congress's broad powers under Section 5 of the Fourteenth Amendment but stopped far short of providing a wholesale endorsement of affirmative action. In a concurring opinion, Justice Brennan echoed the strong pro-affirmative action position he had taken in *Bakke:*

> *[The] principles outlawing the irrelevant or pernicious use of race [are] inapposite to racial classifications that provide benefits to minorities for the purpose of remedying the present effects of past racial discrimination. Such classifications may disadvantage some whites, but whites as a class lack the "traditional indicia of suspectness: the class is not saddled with such disabilities, or subjected to such a history of purposeful unequal treatment, or relegated to such a position of political powerlessness as to command extraordinary protection from the majoritarian political process."*

Justice Stewart, joined by Justice Rehnquist, cited Justice Harlan's *Plessy* dissent as a barrier to any sort of race preferences, while Justice Stevens's dissenting opinion focused on Congress's failure to demonstrate that remedial preferences were being bestowed on a truly disadvantaged class. The Court's failure to produce majority opinions in *Bakke* and *Fullilove* compounded the uncertainties surrounding the myriad affirmative action policies in effect by the early 1980s.

The Rehnquist Court Limits Affirmative Action Programs

In the wake of *Bakke* and *Fullilove*, the Supreme Court continued to grapple with the affirmative action issue, most notably through a series of decisions interpreting the federal civil rights statutes. In general, the Court continued to support various affirmative action programs (see, for example, *Steelworkers v. Weber* [1979], *Sheet Metal Workers v. Equal Employment Opportunity Commission* [1986], *Firefighters v. Cleveland* [1986], and *Johnson v. Transportation Agency of Santa Clara* [1987]). Despite its apparent acceptance of affirmative action, the Court placed limits on the scope of affirmative action policies—for example, by refusing to allow affirmative action objectives to override seniority in determining layoffs (see *Memphis Firefighters v. Stotts* [1984]). The Court also held that, if their interests are adversely affected, white employees may challenge the legality of affirmative action plans that are established under **consent decrees**, even if they were not parties to the original litigation (*Martin v. Wilks* [1989]).

The biggest change in the perspective of the Court in this area came in *City of Richmond v. J. A. Croson Company* (1989), when the Rehnquist Court dealt a serious blow to affirmative action. In 1983, the Richmond City Council passed an ordinance requiring that construction companies awarded city contracts in turn award at least 30 percent of their subcontracts to minority-owned business enterprises. A plumbing contractor, the J. A. Croson Company, sued the city in federal court, arguing that the set-aside was unconstitutional. The federal district court upheld the ordinance, relying heavily on the Supreme Court's earlier decision in *Fullilove v. Klutznick*. The Court of Appeals reversed, however, and the city of Richmond asked the Supreme Court to review the case.

The personnel on the High Court in 1989 had changed significantly since *Fullilove*, of course. Justice Stewart had been replaced by Justice Sandra Day O'Connor in 1981. Justice Antonin Scalia had joined the Court after Chief Justice Burger retired, and Justice Rehnquist became chief justice in 1986. Justice Anthony Kennedy joined the Court in 1988 after the retirement of Justice Powell. These personnel changes produced a shift in the ideological character of the Court, moving it substantially to the right. It was no surprise, therefore, that the Court, voting 6 to 3, struck down the Richmond set-aside plan. Writing for the Court, Justice O'Connor noted that "[t]he Richmond Plan denies certain citizens the opportunity to compete for a fixed percentage of public contracts based solely upon their race." After reviewing the relevant history and facts, Justice O'Connor concluded that:

> *the city has failed to demonstrate a compelling interest in apportioning public contract-*
> *ing opportunities on the basis of race. To accept Richmond's claim that past societal*
> *discrimination alone can serve as the basis for rigid racial preferences would be to*
> *open the door to competing claims for "remedial relief" for every disadvantaged group.*
> *The dream of a Nation of equal citizens in a society where race is irrelevant to personal*
> *opportunity and achievement would be lost in a mosaic of shifting preferences based on*
> *inherently unmeasurable claims of past wrongs.*

In a bitter dissent, Justice Marshall (joined by Justices Brennan and Blackmun) characterized the decision as a "deliberate and giant step backward" and "a full-scale retreat from the Court's long-standing solicitude to race-conscious remedial efforts." Marshall predicted that the decision would "inevitably discourage or prevent governmental entities, particularly States and localities, from acting to rectify the scourge of past discrimination." In her *Croson* opinion, Justice O'Connor attempted to distinguish the Richmond set-aside plan from the congressional program that the Court had approved in *Fullilove v. Klutznick*. O'Connor emphasized the broad powers of Congress under Section 5 of the Fourteenth Amendment, indicating that municipalities lack equally broad powers. Many critics of the *Croson* decision found this distinction unpersuasive.

Those who believed that affirmative action was on the way out were surprised when the Supreme Court decided *Metro Broadcasting v. Federal Communications Commission* (FCC) in 1990. In *Metro Broadcasting*, the Court upheld an FCC affirmative action policy designed to foster increased minority participation in the broadcasting industry. From a jurisprudential point of view, the significance of *Metro Broadcasting* was the distinction the Court drew between state and local affirmative action programs on the one hand and federal affirmative action programs on the other. Relying on *Fullilove v. Klutznick*, a five-member majority of the Court, in an opinion by Justice Brennan, held in effect that federal affirmative action programs were entitled to a greater presumption of validity. The Court said that federal affirmative action programs are "constitutionally permissible to the extent that they serve important governmental objectives within the power of Congress and are substantially related to achievement of those objectives." Obviously, this was a more lenient approach than the Court took in the *Croson* case, and it did not long command the support of a changing majority of the justices.

Five years later the Court repudiated *Metro Broadcasting* and the approach it embodied. In *Adarand Constructors, Inc. v. Pena* (1995), the Court held that one standard of review should govern all affirmative action programs, whether local, state, or federal. The *Adarand* case dealt with federal highway contracts. Under a policy of the U.S. Department of Transportation, general contractors were given a financial incentive to hire subcontractors controlled by "socially and economically disadvantaged individuals." Even though it submitted a lower bid, Adarand Constructors was passed over as a subcontractor on a federal highway project in favor of a company that received preferred status under the affirmative action policy. Adarand unsuccessfully argued in the lower courts that federal affirmative action programs should be subjected to the same standard as that applied to state and local programs.

In a 5-to-4 decision, the Supreme Court sent the case back to the trial court for reconsideration. Writing for the Court, Justice O'Connor held that "all racial classifications, imposed by whatever federal, state, or local governmental actor, must be analyzed by a reviewing court under strict scrutiny. In other words, such classifications are constitutional only if they are narrowly tailored measures that further compelling governmental interests." But O'Connor also recognized that, given sufficient justification, a racial preference might be sustained: "The unhappy persistence of both the practice and the lingering effects of racial discrimination against minority groups in this country is an unfortunate reality, and government is not disqualified from acting in response to it." Dissenting, Justice Stevens argued that "[i]nvidious discrimination is an engine of oppression, subjugating a disfavored group to enhance or maintain the power of the majority. Remedial race-based preferences reflect the opposite impulse: a desire to foster equality in society. No sensible conception of the Government's constitutional obligation to 'govern impartially,' should ignore this distinction." In their separate concurring opinions, Justices Scalia and Thomas stated their unequivocal opposition to affirmative action. Justice Thomas has remained vehemently opposed to affirmative action policies to date. This is a hard-line stance for any justice to take, but one that receives particular scrutiny by supporters of affirmative action given Thomas's presence as the only African-American on the Court.

The Hopwood Case   In *Hopwood v. Texas* (1995), the Fifth U.S. Circuit Court of Appeals struck down an affirmative action program at the University of Texas law school. In an effort to obtain an entering class consisting of at least 10 percent Mexican Americans and 5 percent blacks, the law school established lower test-score standards and created a separate admissions process for black and Mexican American applicants. The court of appeals ruled that this system violated the rights of four unsuccessful white applicants. In a move that startled many observers, the court went further and held that the Supreme Court's landmark 1978 *Bakke* decision was no longer good law. In *Hopwood*, the Fifth Circuit court flatly stated that "the law school may not use race as a factor in law school admissions." This decision created a firestorm of controversy among civil rights groups and within higher education. Many commentators hoped and expected that the Supreme Court would grant certiorari. The Clinton administration, the District of Columbia, and nine states filed *amicus curiae* briefs in support of Texas's cert petition. But the Supreme Court was unmoved, denying cert on the closing day of the 1995 term. Two of the Court's more liberal members, Justices Ginsburg and Souter, produced a brief opinion stating that although affirmative action "is an issue of great national importance," the case presented no live controversy because the program that motivated the lawsuit to begin with had been discontinued. The denial of cert left the *Hopwood* decision intact, but *Hopwood* applied only within the three states (Texas, Louisiana, and Mississippi) that make up the Fifth Circuit. This created an unusual legal situation in that while institutions of higher education in the Fifth Circuit were barred from using race as a criterion in their admissions, other colleges and universities across the country were under court order to do exactly that!

Proposition 209   Buoyed by favorable federal judicial decisions, opponents of affirmative action in California in 1996 succeeded in passing an amendment to the state constitution banning race and gender preferences in hiring and educational admissions. Proposition 209 provides that state and local government agencies in California may not discriminate against or grant preferential treatment to any individual or group on the basis of race, sex, color, ethnicity, or national origin. Within days after Proposition 209 was adopted by popular referendum, opponents went to federal court and obtained an injunction against its enforcement. But the federal district court eventually upheld the measure, as did the Ninth Circuit Court of Appeals. The Coalition for Economic Equity, which brought the suit, backed by civil rights groups across the country, asked the Supreme Court to grant review. But, as in the *Hopwood* case, the Court denied cert, at least in part because the controversy remained abstract (see *Coalition for Economic Equity v. Wilson* [1997]).

The Piscataway Case   In 1989, Sharon Taxman, a white teacher in Piscataway, New Jersey, was laid off so that the school board could retain a black teacher in the same department. The two teachers had been hired on the same date and were judged by supervisors to be equally qualified. Thus race was the only factor accounting for the school board's decision to lay off Taxman while retaining her black colleague. Taxman sued in federal court, claiming "reverse discrimination." The board defended its action by asserting that race-based personnel decisions could be justified in order to promote faculty diversity. In ruling in Taxman's favor, the Third Circuit Court of Appeals held that the only justification for race-based affirmative action was to remedy documented past discrimination. The school board petitioned the Supreme Court for certiorari and the Court granted review. At this point civil rights groups became concerned that the Court would use the case to review and possibly reverse its 1978 *Bakke* decision. After civil rights groups agreed to contribute more than two-thirds of the $433,500 needed to pay Taxman's back salary and legal bills, the school board voted to settle the case and Taxman agreed. The Supreme Court then dismissed the case.

The* Michigan *Cases The Court's failure to review the *Hopwood*, Prop 209, and Piscataway cases frustrated those who wished to see a definitive resolution of the affirmative action question. In 2003, the Court handed down two important affirmative action decisions that in combination helped determine the extent to which considerations of race and ethnicity might be included in higher education admissions decisions. At issue in *Gratz v. Bollinger* was the constitutionality of an undergraduate admissions policy adopted by the University of Michigan's College of Literature, Science and the Arts. Under this policy each applicant for admission was awarded a number of points based on educational and personal criteria, including, but not limited to, high school grades, strength of high school curriculum, a personal essay, standardized test scores, personal achievement or leadership, and membership in an "underrepresented" racial or ethnic minority group. Out of a maximum total of 150 points, twenty points were automatically awarded to any applicant who was a member of one of the underrepresented minority groups. Admission was virtually assured for applicants who received at least hundred points. The Court held this policy to be violative of the Equal Protection Clause of the Fourteenth Amendment. Writing for the majority, Chief Justice Rehnquist concluded that: "The University's policy, which automatically distributes 20 points, or one-fifth of the points needed to guarantee admission, to every single 'underrepresented minority' applicant solely because of race, is not narrowly tailored to achieve the interest in educational diversity that respondents claim justifies their program."

Yet, in the companion case of *Grutter v. Bollinger*, the Court, reaffirming Justice Powell's opinion in *Bakke*, upheld a more individualized admissions policy administered by the University of Michigan Law School. This policy was designed to attain the educational benefits of having a diverse student body by enrolling a "critical mass" of students drawn from underrepresented minority groups, including African-Americans, Hispanics, and Native Americans. As described in Justice O'Connor's opinion for the Court, the law school's admissions policy sought "to achieve that diversity which has the potential to enrich everyone's education and thus make a law school class stronger than the sum of its parts." The policy required admissions officials to evaluate each applicant by reviewing all information in his or her file, including a personal statement, undergraduate GPA, LSAT score, letters of recommendation, and an essay describing how the applicant would contribute to law school life and diversity. Consideration was also given to such "soft variables" as the enthusiasm of recommenders, quality of the applicant's undergraduate school, and the area and difficulty of undergraduate course selection. Applying strict scrutiny analysis, Justice O'Connor asserted that the law school had "a compelling interest in attaining a diverse student body." She distinguished this program from those that fell short of constitutional requirements by relying on racial balancing or quotas.

"When using race as a plus factor," Justice O'Connor explained, "a university's admissions program must remain flexible enough to ensure that each applicant is evaluated as an individual and not in a way that makes an applicant's race or ethnicity the defining feature of his or her application." O'Connor concluded that "the Equal Protection Clause does not prohibit the Law School's narrowly tailored use of race in admissions decisions to further a compelling interest in obtaining the educational benefits that flow from a diverse student body."

Dissenting from the judgment in *Grutter*, Justice Scalia offered the following critique of both Michigan decisions: "Unlike a clear constitutional holding that racial preferences in state educational institutions are impermissible, or even a clear anticonstitutional holding that racial preferences in state educational institutions are OK, today's *Grutter-Gratz* split double header seems perversely designed to prolong the controversy and the litigation."

Near the end of her opinion in *Grutter*, Justice O'Connor attempted to place this decision in historical perspective:

> *It has been 25 years since Justice Powell first approved the use of race to further an interest in student body diversity in the context of public higher education. Since that time, the number of minority applicants with high grades and test scores has indeed increased. We expect that 25 years from now, the use of racial preferences will no longer be necessary to further the interest approved today.*

Fisher v. University of Texas at Austin   Ten years later the Court had the opportunity to revisit affirmative action in higher education. In a sense, Justice Scalia's dissent in *Grutter* had proven correct. While it was clear that strict rigid quotas were looked upon unfavorably by the Court, the exact parameters of affirmative action policy remained nebulous. In *Fisher v. University of Texas at Austin* (2013), the Court was presented with an excellent opportunity to clarify the law in this area. Many Court-watchers were disappointed when the Court merely vacated and remanded a lower federal court decision upholding an affirmative action program at the University of Texas. In the Court's view, the district court had not applied the correct legal standard in granting summary judgment for the University. Thus, a pronouncement from the High Court on the future of affirmative action in higher education would be put off for the time being.

To Summarize:

- *Affirmative action is a broad term referring to a variety of efforts designed to assist members of traditionally disfavored minority groups. It is manifested in three major areas of distributive policy: employment, government contracts, and higher education.*
- *The affirmative action concept emerged in the 1960s, and by the 1970s it was a major topic of litigation chiefly initiated by those who challenged it as "reverse discrimination."*
- *The Burger Court sought middle ground in the affirmative action area, approving the basic concept but rejecting its more rigid applications.*
- *The Rehnquist Court initially took a more negative view of affirmative action but in 2003 approved a highly individualized law school admissions program that permitted the consideration of race as one of many criteria in creating a diverse student body.*
- *The Roberts Court has yet to render a major substantive pronouncement on affirmative action.*

Gender-Based Discrimination

Women are hardly a "discrete and insular minority." In fact, they comprise a majority of the adult population. Nevertheless, women have been historically subjected to considerable legal discrimination. Some of this discrimination was ostensibly benign, reflecting the paternalism of a patriarchal society. Not only were women once thought unfit to vote or hold public office, they were also regarded as in need of special protection from a cruel world. Thus, some **gender-based classifications** actually benefited females and burdened males. For example, a number of states, and the federal government for a time, maintained minimum-wage requirements for women but not for men. Most graphically, women have traditionally been exempted from compulsory military service.

Until very recently, the Supreme Court refused to recognize even the most blatant forms of sex discrimination as constitutionally offensive. In *Bradwell v. Illinois* (1873), the Court upheld an Illinois law that prohibited women from practicing law. Similarly, in *Minor v. Happersett* (1875), the Court held that women had no constitutional right to vote. Even as late as 1948, the Court upheld a Michigan law that prohibited women from serving as bartenders (see *Goesaert v. Cleary*). These decisions reflected broader societal attitudes that relegated women, much like African-Americans, to a position of social inferiority and second-class citizenship.

World War II did much to change the social status of women. Women in great numbers left the home and entered the industrial workplace, often assuming jobs many thought they were incapable of handling. By the 1970s, women had begun to compete with men for managerial and professional positions. Although women are still on average paid less than men, even for equal work, society has come to accept women in the workplace. This change also extended to acceptance of women in political roles. Today there are ever increasing numbers of women in Congress, in state legislatures, as mayors, governors, presidential candidates, and as justices of the Supreme Court. Naturally, the changing role of women is accompanied by demands for legal equality.

Congressional Responses to Demands for Gender Equality

Congress responded to growing demands for legal equality between the sexes by passing the Equal Pay Act of 1963, the 1972 Amendments to Title VII of the Civil Rights Act of 1964, and Title IX of the Federal Education Act of 1972. The first and second of these statutes were aimed at eliminating sex discrimination in the workplace. The third authorized the withholding of federal funds from educational institutions that engaged in sex discrimination. These statutes have been an important source of civil rights for women and have given rise to a number of significant Supreme Court decisions.

For example, in *Meritor Savings Bank v. Vinson* (1986), the Court held that Title VII of the Civil Rights Act of 1964 bars **sexual harassment** on the job. In *Faragher v. City of Boca Raton* (1998), the Court held that employers can be held liable for sexual harassment by supervisors toward their subordinates. However, in *Vance v. Ball State University* (2013), the Court narrowed the impact of this decision by ruling that victims of sexual harassment in the workplace can sue their employers for the misconduct of supervisors only if those supervisors were empowered to take "tangible employment actions" against them.

Beyond the interpretation of Title VII to prohibit sexual harassment on the job, state legislatures have passed laws aimed at eradicating sexual harassment. Yet critics contend that general norms of nonenforcement of most or all of such provisions have hindered their effect. Removing harassment from the workplace remains a work in progress in the United States today.

The Equal Rights Amendment

In 1972, Congress attempted to broaden legal protection of women's rights by adopting a constitutional amendment that read as follows:

Section 1. Equality of rights under the law shall not be denied or abridged by the United States or by any State on account of sex.

Section 2. The Congress shall have the power to enforce, by appropriate legislation, the provisions of this article.

Section 3. This amendment shall take effect two years after the date of ratification.

Like all proposed constitutional amendments, the **Equal Rights Amendment** (ERA) had to be ratified by at least three-fourths of the states to become a part of the Constitution. Initially, the ERA was met with much enthusiasm and little controversy in the state legislatures. By 1976, it had been ratified by thirty-five of the necessary thirty-eight states. However, in the late 1970s, opposition to the ERA crystallized in those states that had yet to ratify. Although Congress extended the period for ratification until 1982, the amendment ultimately failed to win approval by the requisite number of states. Women's advocacy groups still push for passage of the ERA and it is one of several amendments that are proposed in Congress nearly every year. Although no ratifying action appears imminent, supporters hope one day to see the Equal Rights Amendment added to the Constitution.

Judicial Scrutiny of Gender-Based Discrimination

The demise of the Equal Rights Amendment left constitutional interpretation in the field of sex discrimination largely in the domain of the Fourteenth Amendment. In the early 1970s, it appeared that the Supreme Court was going to add sex to the list of "suspect classifications" under the Fourteenth Amendment. In *Reed v. Reed* (1971), the Court struck down a provision of the Idaho Probate Code that required probate judges to prefer males to females in appointing administrators of estates. Writing for the majority in *Reed*, Chief Justice Burger noted that "to give a mandatory preference to members of either sex over members of the other … is to make the very kind of arbitrary legislative choice forbidden by the Equal Protection Clause." In *Frontiero v. Richardson* (1973), the Supreme Court divided 8 to 1 (Justice Rehnquist dissenting) in upholding Lt. Sharron Frontiero's claim that the Air Force violated the equal protection component of the Fifth Amendment in requiring women, but not men, to demonstrate that their spouses were in fact dependents for the purpose of receiving medical and dental benefits. While the Court was receptive to the equal protection claim, it was unable to achieve majority support for the proposition that sex is a suspect classification. Expressing the views of four members of the Court, Justice Brennan's plurality opinion was unequivocal in declaring gender-based discrimination to be inherently suspect and thus presumptively unconstitutional:

[S]ince sex, like race and national origin, is an immutable characteristic determined solely by the accident of birth, the imposition of special disabilities upon the members of a particular sex because of their sex would seem to violate "the basic concept of our system that legal burdens should bear some relationship to individual responsibility."

The remaining four members of the majority were not prepared to go so far. In an opinion concurring in the judgment only, Justice Powell wrote that "[i]t is unnecessary for the Court in this case to characterize sex as a suspect classification, with all of the far-reaching implications of such a holding."

Heightened Scrutiny   As yet, the Supreme Court has not recognized sex discrimination as being inherently suspect. It should be noted, however, that some state courts have applied strict scrutiny analysis to gender-based classifications (see, for example, the California Supreme Court's decision in *Hardy v. Stumpf* [1978]). While it has not adopted strict scrutiny for gender discrimination cases, the U.S. Supreme Court has invalidated a number of gender-based policies under a "heightened scrutiny" or "intermediate scrutiny" approach. For example, in *Weinberger v. Wiesenfeld* (1975), the Court unanimously voided a provision of the Social Security Act that authorized survivors' benefits for the widows of deceased workers but withheld them for men in the same situation. Similarly, in *Califano v. Goldfarb* (1977), a sharply divided Court struck down another Social Security requirement that widowers, but not widows, had to demonstrate their financial dependence on their deceased spouses as a condition for obtaining survivors' benefits.

In *Craig v. Boren* (1976), the Court articulated a test for judging gender-based policies under the intermediate standard of review. According to this test, a gender-based policy must be substantially related to an important government objective. Presumably, this test is stricter than the rational basis test but less strict than the compelling state interest test.

In *Craig v. Boren*, the Court struck down an Oklahoma law that forbade the sale of "3.2" beer to females under the age of eighteen and males under twenty-one. Oklahoma attempted to justify the statute as a means of promoting its interest in traffic safety, citing data that were purported to show that men in the eighteen-to-twenty-one age bracket were more likely to be arrested for drunk driving than were women in the same age bracket. Unpersuaded by the statistical evidence, the Court held that the state had failed to demonstrate a substantial relationship between its sexually discriminatory policy and its admittedly important interest in traffic safety. In a sharp dissent, Justice Rehnquist challenged the new intermediate standard of equal protection review. In Rehnquist's view, the terms "important objective" and "substantial relation" were so "elastic as to invite subjective judicial preferences or prejudices." Despite this criticism, the Court has maintained the intermediate standard of review for gender-based policies.

In *Orr v. Orr* (1979), the Court considered the question of differential alimony requirements for men and women. The Alabama law in question required divorced men, under certain circumstances, to make alimony payments to their ex-wives but exempted women in the same circumstances from paying alimony to their ex-husbands. Somewhat disingenuously, the state argued that its gender-based alimony policy was designed to compensate women for economic discrimination produced by the institution of marriage.

The Court accepted the state's asserted interest as both legitimate and important but rejected the argument that its alimony policy was substantially related to the achievement of this objective. Writing for the Court, Justice Brennan asserted that Alabama's alleged compensatory purpose may be effectuated without placing burdens solely on husbands. Progress toward fulfillment of such a purpose would not be hampered, and it would cost the state nothing more, if it were to treat men and women equally by making alimony burdens independent of sex…. Thus, "[t]he [wives] who benefit from the disparate treatment are those who were … nondependent on their husbands…." They are precisely those who are not "needy spouses" and who are the "least likely to have been victims of discrimination" by the institution of marriage.

The preceding sample of cases is not meant to suggest that the Supreme Court's sex-discrimination decisions have uniformly cut in one direction. On the contrary, the flexible approach to sex discrimination employed by the Court has resulted in a number of decisions upholding challenged gender-based policies. For example, in *Kahn v. Shevin* (1974), the Court let stand a Florida statute that gave proper tax exemptions to widows but not widowers. According to Justice William O. Douglas's majority opinion, the distinction was reasonably designed to further the state policy of "cushioning the financial impact of spousal loss upon the sex for which that loss imposes a disproportionately heavy burden.... The financial difficulties confronting the lone woman in Florida or any other state exceed those facing the man."

The same year, in *Geduldig v. Aiello* (1974), the Court upheld a state health insurance policy that excluded pregnancy from the list of disabilities for which a state employee could be compensated. In approving the policy, the Court concluded that it did not discriminate against any definable group or class in terms of the aggregate risk protection derived by the group or class from the program. There is no risk from which men are protected and women are not. Likewise, there is no risk from which women are protected and men are not. Not surprisingly, a number of observers took issue with the Court's assumption that a state's refusal to extend its disability policy to include pregnancy was **gender-neutral**.

One of the most controversial issues in the area of sex discrimination is the role that women should play in military service. Opponents of the Equal Rights Amendment argued that adoption of the amendment would result in women being drafted into combat, a prospect that many people still find unacceptable. In *Rostker v. Goldberg* (1981), the Supreme Court considered the constitutionality of the male-only draft registration law. Emphasizing its traditional deference to Congress in the area of military affairs, the Court upheld the challenged policy by a vote of 6 to 3. Writing for the majority, Justice Rehnquist asserted that exclusion of women from the draft "was not an 'accidental byproduct of a traditional way of thinking about women.'" According to Justice Rehnquist, men and women "are simply not similarly situated for purposes of a draft or registration for a draft." Would Rehnquist's assumption command wide public support today, given the current role of women as full participants in military service?

It is difficult to say with any precision what principles have guided the Court's treatment of sex discrimination cases under the intermediate scrutiny approach. Perhaps each decision rests on each justice's intuitive sense of whether the challenged discrimination is "benign" or "invidious." As Justice Oliver Wendell Holmes, Jr., pointed out in his famous dissent in *Lochner v. New York* (1905), judicial decisions often "depend on a judgment or intuition more subtle than any articulate major premise." What Holmes was suggesting was that judicial decision making is preeminently political behavior: that any exercise in legal methodology is subordinate to the assertion of judicial values. While this position can be overstated, one cannot examine the history of American constitutional decision making and deny the essential validity of Holmes's observation.

Sex Discrimination by Educational Institutions

In perhaps the most significant of its sex discrimination decisions, the Burger Court voted 5 to 4 to require the Mississippi University for Women (MUW) to admit a male student to its nursing school (*Mississippi University for Women v. Hogan* [1982]). Joe Hogan was a registered nurse working in Columbus, the city where MUW is located. Lacking a bachelor's degree, he applied for admission to the MUW nursing program and was denied solely on account of sex, although the school did inform him that he could register on a noncredit basis. Rather than quit his job to enroll in another state institution, Hogan filed suit. The state of Mississippi argued that operating a school solely for women compensated for sex discrimination in the past. Additionally, the state argued that the presence of men would detract from the performance of female students. Writing for the Supreme Court, Justice O'Connor gave both of the state's arguments short shrift. Justice O'Connor rejected the "compensation" argument as contrived since the state had made no showing that women had historically lacked opportunities in the field of nursing. O'Connor then pointed out that the state's argument that male students would adversely affect the performance of females was undermined by the university's willingness to accept male students as auditors. In O'Connor's view, the principal effect of the female-only nursing program was to "perpetuate the stereotyped view of nursing as an exclusively women's job." In a strongly worded dissent, Justice Powell asserted that the Court's decision adversely affected the opportunities of women by forbidding the "States from providing women with an opportunity to choose the type of university they prefer." Powell further suggested that the Court's decision "bows deeply to conformity."

The *Hogan* decision addressed the question of whether state-operated professional schools could limit enrollment to one sex. It did not address the broader question of whether publicly operated or supported educational institutions generally may constitutionally impose such restrictions. Of course, the only two state-supported institutions of higher education that limited enrollment to members of one sex were military schools: the Citadel in Charleston, South Carolina, and Virginia Military Institute (VMI) in Lexington. In the wake of the *Hogan* decision, young women seeking admission to these institutions brought suit in federal court. Ultimately, they prevailed.

The VMI Case In one of the most widely anticipated decisions of the 1990s, *United States v. Virginia* (1996), the Supreme Court struck down VMI's male-only admissions policy. In so doing, the Court closed the book on a case that had been in litigation for nearly six years. The suit had been brought by the Justice Department, after a complaint was filed by a female high school student who wanted to go to VMI but was barred from doing so by the Institute's prohibition against admitting women.

In a 7-to-1 decision, the Supreme Court, speaking through Justice Ginsburg, ruled that the state of Virginia had "fallen far short of establishing the 'exceedingly persuasive justification,' that must be the solid base for any gender-defined classification." Although the Court rejected the argument advanced by the Clinton administration that sex discrimination should be subjected to the same "strict scrutiny" the courts apply to race discrimination, Justice Ginsburg's opinion suggested that the current Court has raised the level of scrutiny applied to policies that treat men and women differently. According to Ginsburg, the Court should apply a "skeptical scrutiny" under which government must demonstrate an "exceedingly persuasive justification" for any gender discrimination. "The justification must be genuine, not hypothesized or invented *post hoc* in response to litigation," said Ginsburg. Moreover, it must not rely on "overbroad generalizations about the different talents, capacities, or preferences of males and females." Although technically applicable only to the VMI case, the decision in *United States v. Virginia* affected the resolution of a similar widely publicized case involving the Citadel in South Carolina. In fact, within days after the VMI decision was announced, the Citadel's governing board voted unanimously to eliminate sex as a criterion for admission, ending a 154-year tradition of admitting only men.

The sweeping character of the Court's opinion seemed to imply that it would be extremely difficult for any state to defend any single-sex educational institution. Chief Justice Rehnquist, who concurred in the judgment only, adopted a more restrained position. For Rehnquist, the state had failed in its obligation to provide equal protection because it had not demonstrated any serious effort to provide comparable opportunities to women who were interested in the kind of "citizen-soldier" training that men receive at VMI. According to Rehnquist, it was "not the 'exclusion of women' that violate [d] the Equal Protection Clause, but the maintenance of an all-men school without providing any—much less a comparable—institution for women." Rehnquist's opinion left open the possibility that single-sex public higher education might, under certain circumstances, pass constitutional muster. Of course, Rehnquist's concurrence was just one person's opinion. Six justices representing the Court's liberal and moderate blocs clearly wanted to make a stronger and a more definitive statement.

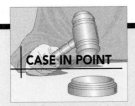

CASE IN POINT

Congress Reacts to a Court Decision Limiting Employment Discrimination Claims
Ledbetter v. Goodyear Tire and Rubber Co. (2007)

A common concern of women in the workplace is receiving pay equal to their male counterparts. In 2012 *Newsweek* reported that according to their research women made 82.2 cents for every dollar made by men in similar careers. This workplace discrimination and payment inequality is a source of much consternation for women's groups. The 82 cents figure actually represents an improvement over many measures of the same phenomenon, which certainly underscores the problem. In 1998 an anonymous tip informed Lilly Ledbetter that she was a victim of such discrimination. She was a manager at a Goodyear tire and rubber manufacturing plant in Alabama with 19 years of experience and steady work evaluations. When she learned that men in similar positions as she were making up to 40 percent more in salary, Ledbetter filed a claim with the Equal Employment Opportunity Commission and argued that the company's actions violated Article VII of the Civil Rights Act of 1964. In *Ledbetter v. Goodyear Tire and Rubber Co.* (2007) the Supreme Court ultimately ruled that she was without legal recourse because the statue required that individuals must report discriminatory pay such as she had received within 180 days of the company's salary decision. Writing for a slim 5-to-4 majority, Justice Alito stipulated that the 180 timeline does not begin anew with each paycheck as Ledbetter had argued in Court. Critics of the decision, including Justice Ginsburg, were passionate in their opposition to the Court's ruling. Many took their concerns directly to Congress in hopes of a legislative solution. In 2009 President Obama signed into law the Lilly Ledbetter Fair Pay Act, which Congress had passed in response to the ruling. The Act stipulated that the 180-day window to claim discrimination did in fact begin again with each paycheck an employee received.

In another of his scathing dissents, Justice Scalia asserted that the majority's "amorphous 'exceedingly persuasive justification' phrase" was an unwarranted departure from the "heightened scrutiny" test used by the Court in gender-discrimination cases.

Scalia concluded by lamenting the fact that, in his view, "single-sex public education is functionally dead." Scalia expressed his regret that the Court had, in his view, "shut down an institution that has served the people of the commonwealth of Virginia with pride and distinction for over a century and a half." He ended by observing that "I do not think any of us, women included, will be better off for its destruction." Not surprisingly, Justice Scalia's sentiments were shared by many students, faculty, and administrators at VMI. Major General Josiah Bunting III, the superintendent of VMI, described the Court's decision as a "savage disappointment." Of course, women's rights groups hailed the decision as a major victory.

Gender Equity in Collegiate Athletics

Title IX of the Education Amendments of 1972 applies to many facets of collegiate activity. Discrimination based on gender is prohibited in the school band, most university sponsored clubs, math, and science. Yet overwhelmingly the controversy surrounding Title IX has stemmed from questions of funding directed to athletics. Intercollegiate athletics, once the sole province of men, has witnessed considerable change in recent years. Under the rubric of **gender equity**, state colleges and universities have been putting more resources into women's athletic programs. In short, the law requires that providers of higher education that receive federal funding must provide generally equal numbers of athletic scholarships to males and females. Unquestionably Title IX has produced greater access to athletic opportunities for female students in the United States, yet critics have argued that an unintended consequence of the law has resulted in cancelation of nonrevenue men's sports which allowed institutions to balance out their numbers without increasing their costs. Still, others believe that forbidding women to participate in male-only athletic programs at state institutions constitutes invidious discrimination. Is the separate but equal doctrine appropriate when considering collegiate athletics? Suppose a female student wants to play football at a state university. Since the university does not have a women's football program, does the Equal Protection Clause require the university to let the woman try out for the men's team? While some may feel that such issues trivialize the Constitution, these matters tend to be far from trivial in the minds of plaintiffs.

To Summarize:

◆ *Since the 1970s, the Supreme Court has recognized that the Equal Protection Clause imposes significant restrictions on official discrimination on the basis of gender.*

◆ *The failure to ratify the Equal Rights Amendment left the issue of gender discrimination solely within the province of the Equal Protection Clause as interpreted by the courts.*

◆ *The Court has applied an intermediate standard of review in judging classifications based on gender, often finding that such classifications merely perpetuate sex-based stereotypes.*

◆ *The Court's most important decisions in this area have focused on discrimination against women in the military and in public institutions of higher education.*

Discrimination Based on Sexual Orientation

The 1970s saw the emergence of a movement aimed at ending discrimination against gay men and lesbians. The movement began to make progress as cities with large gay communities enacted ordinances prohibiting discrimination based on sexual orientation in employment, housing, and the enjoyment of public accommodations. Eventually a number of the more progressive state legislatures followed suit. However, Congress resisted calls to add this kind of discrimination to the federal civil rights laws. And prior to the 1990s, the federal courts had little to say about this sort of discrimination as an equal protection issue. That, of course, has changed and today the civil rights of LGBT persons are salient concerns of the federal courts.

Gay Men and Lesbians in the Military

One question of gay rights that came to the fore during the 1980s was the military's policy of discharging persons who admitted to being homosexual. In *Watkins v. U.S. Army* (1988), the U.S. Court of Appeals for the Ninth Circuit invalidated this policy. Writing for the court, Judge Norris concluded that "the Army's regulations violate the constitutional guarantee of equal protection of the laws because they discriminate against persons of homosexual orientation, a suspect class, and because the regulations are not necessary to promote a legitimate compelling governmental interest." On en banc rehearing the Court of Appeals affirmed the judgment but did so on nonconstitutional grounds, finding it "unnecessary to reach the constitutional issues." The Supreme Court denied certiorari, thus leaving open the constitutional question as to whether the military's ban on homosexuals violated constitutional equal protection standards. Shortly after his election to the presidency in November 1992, Bill Clinton announced that he intended to issue an executive order abolishing the military's ban on homosexuals. But a firestorm of controversy caused Clinton to back down. Instead, Clinton issued an order instituting a "don't ask, don't tell" policy in the military. Although this approach alleviated some of the conflict over gays in the military, gay rights activists continued to press the issue in the courts. Seventeen years after "don't ask, don't tell" went into effect, the Supreme Court still had not addressed the matter. The constitutional issue remained lively, though, as lower federal courts rendered varying decisions in lawsuits challenging the policy. By 2010 public attitudes toward gay and lesbian people had changed markedly, and most observers expected "don't ask, don't tell" to be overturned by Congress if not the Supreme Court. Indeed, Congress did repeal the policy in December of 2010. By the fall of 2011 the United States military policy of "don't ask, don't tell" officially came to an end.

Romer v. Evans: A Turning Point

In 1996, the Court took up the issue of gay rights in a case involving an unusual legal measure. In what has turned out to be a pivotal decision in this area, the Court in *Romer v. Evans* struck down Colorado's controversial Amendment 2, which barred state and local government from providing various legal protections for gays and lesbians. Writing for a majority of six, Justice Kennedy concluded that "Amendment 2 … in making a general announcement that gays and lesbians shall not have any particular protections from the law, inflicts on them immediate, continuing, and real injuries that outrun and belie any legitimate justifications that may be claimed for it." In dissent, Justice Scalia argued that Amendment 2 "is not the manifestation of a 'bare … desire to harm' homosexuals, but is rather a modest attempt by seemingly tolerant Coloradans to preserve traditional sexual mores against the efforts of a politically powerful minority to revise those mores through use of the laws." Scalia attacked the reasoning of the majority, saying that the Court's opinion "has no foundation in American constitutional law, and barely pretends to." But the Court concluded that "it is not within our constitutional tradition to enact laws of this sort." Justice Kennedy opined that "a law declaring that in general it shall be more difficult for one group of citizens than for all others to seek aid from the government is itself a denial of equal protection of the laws in the most literal sense."

The *Romer* decision halted a movement in which communities around the country sought to copy the Colorado amendment. Law professor Susan Bloch of Georgetown University observed that the Colorado amendment was "the most vulnerable to constitutional challenge" because it represented "the essence of what it is to deny people equal protection of the law." Justice Kennedy seemed to make the same point in the majority opinion, asserting that Amendment 2 was unconstitutional because "it identifies persons by a single trait and then denies them equal protection across the board." This suggests that Kennedy, as well as the other moderate members of the Court, might have been more sympathetic to a measure that merely outlawed preferential treatment for gays and lesbians. *Romer* came down at a time when the attitudes of Americans toward gay men and lesbians were shifting noticeably in the direction of tolerance. However, at the same time a reaction was developing, especially in the legislatures of the more conservative states.

Same-Sex Marriage

In 1996, the Hawaii Supreme Court ruled that the state law restricting marriage licenses to heterosexual couples violated the equal protection requirements of the Hawaii constitution. The decision produced a tremendous backlash and in 1999 Hawaii voters amended the state constitution to authorize the legislature to limit marriage to heterosexual couples, thus effectively nullifying the state supreme court's decision. In Vermont, however, a similar court decision led to a very different outcome. In *Baker v. State* (1999), the Vermont Supreme Court ruled that same-sex couples are entitled to "the same benefits and protections afforded by Vermont law to married opposite-sex couples." The decision was based on the Common Benefits Clause of the Vermont Constitution, which is that state's counterpart to the Equal Protection Clause of the Fourteenth Amendment. Although there was some negative reaction from the public, the state legislature complied with the court's mandate and adopted a law permitting same-sex couples to enter into "civil unions" having all of the legal rights and duties of marriage.

In *Goodridge v. Department of Public Health* (2003), the Massachusetts Supreme Court split 4 to 3 in striking down the state law limiting marriage licenses to heterosexual couples. The court's decision touched off a furious debate in the Massachusetts legislature. In the end, the state became the first in the United States to legalize same-sex marriage (as distinct from "civil union"). Subsequent efforts to repeal legalization were unsuccessful.

In 2008, Connecticut followed Massachusetts's lead and legalized same-sex marriage. In 2009, the state of Vermont legalized same-sex marriage, not merely civil unions. Iowa likewise legalized same-sex marriage in 2009 and New Hampshire followed suit in 2010. As of June 2013, same-sex marriage had been legalized in twelve states and the District of Columbia.

The Batle Over Proposition 8   The most interesting legal battle over same-sex marriage took place in California. In 2008 California voters approved Proposition 8, an amendment to their state's constitution overturning a decision by the California Supreme Court legalizing same-sex marriage. That amendment was successfully challenged in federal district court. Interestingly, state officials chose not to defend the amendment. The U.S. Court of Appeals for the Ninth Circuit permitted citizens who supported the amendment to appeal the district court's decision. But the Ninth Circuit also struck down the amendment, finding that it was motivated by animus toward gay men and lesbians.

In *Hollingsworth v. Perry* (2013), the Supreme Court held that defenders of Proposition 8 lacked standing to appeal the district court's decision, thus leaving intact a decision striking down Proposition 8. In response, the state of California began to issue marriage licenses to same-sex couples. Despite last-minute attempts by supporters of Proposition 8 to block the state's action, it was clear that the long battle over same-sex marriage in California had come to an end.

U.S. v. Windsor—A Milestone Decision

In *Hollingsworth v. Perry*, the Supreme Court rendered a decision that advanced the cause of marriage equality, but did so without making a pronouncement on the essential constitutional question. But in *United States v. Windsor* (2013), which came down the same day, the Court took a significant jurisprudential step in the same direction. *Windsor* involved a challenge to a key provision of the Defense of Marriage Act (DOMA), which Congress had enacted in 1996. DOMA prohibited the federal government from recognizing same-sex marriages and relieved states of the obligation of recognizing same-sex marriages entered into in other states. In *Windsor*, the Court addressed the first prong—that which prohibited the federal government from recognizing same-sex marriages. In a five-to-four decision, the Court held this prong of DOMA to be unconstitutional. Justice Anthony Kennedy's opinion for the sharply divided Court did not follow a conventional equal protection analysis. The gist of Kennedy's opinion was that the statute degraded and demeaned persons who entered into same-sex unions and disrespected the states that had sanctioned them. While one can read Kennedy's opinion as leaving the matter of same-sex marriage to the states to decide, Justice Scalia's caustic dissent predicted that *Windsor* was merely an incremental step toward an inevitable Supreme Court decision striking down all state laws forbidding same-sex marriage.

> **To Summarize:**
> ◆ *One of the most controversial issues in the equal protection area involves discrimination against gays and lesbians. In the mid-1990s the Supreme Court indicated its willingness to scrutinize policies in this area.*
> ◆ *In 2013 the Court took major steps toward the legalization of same-sex marriage when it let stand a lower court decision striking down California's ban on same-sex marriage and struck down a provision of the Defense of Marriage Act that prohibited the federal government from recognizing same-sex marriages granted by states.*

Discrimination against the Poor

A continuing controversy in the United States has been discrimination based on the economic status of individuals. Consistent with other movements of the era, the 1960s saw government begin to take a greater role in attempting to eradicate economic inequalities. For the Supreme Court this has meant determining whether policies that burden individuals unequally based on their financial status violate the Constitution. While the Court has never ruled that discrimination based on wealth is inherently suspect, some justices on the Supreme Court have indicated a desire to do so. However, the Court has often invalidated forms of economic discrimination that prevent individuals from exercising their constitutional rights. Wealth-based discriminations that burden fundamental rights have been subjected to strict judicial scrutiny; those that do not involve fundamental rights have been judged by the traditional rational basis test. For example, in the case of *Shapiro v. Thompson* (1969), described below, the Court found that the state residency requirement infringed the fundamental right of interstate travel. Similarly, in *Harper v. Virginia State Board of Elections* (1966), the Supreme Court invalidated a state's poll tax as a denial of equal protection. Certainly the imposition of a tax on voting can be seen as a burden on the exercise of a fundamental right (see Chapter 8).

In *Gideon v. Wainwright* (1963), the Court, relying on the Sixth Amendment right to counsel, required states to appoint counsel for indigent defendants accused of felonies. On the same day, in *Douglas v. California*, the Court required states to provide counsel to indigent defendants seeking appellate review in state courts. These wealth discrimination rulings of the Warren Court were closely related to the maintenance of procedural due process in the context of criminal prosecutions (see Chapter 5).

To what extent does the Equal Protection Clause require the equalization of services or benefits provided by state and local governments? Can a city's provision of public goods, such as roads, sewage systems, parks, and recreational facilities, vary according to neighborhood property tax revenues? The Supreme Court has ruled that the answer depends on whether such discriminations involve fundamental rights or "interests." But which interests are "fundamental"? Is education a fundamental right?

Inequality in Public School Funding

In *San Antonio Independent School District v. Rodriguez* (1973), the Court considered a challenge to the Texas system of financing public schools primarily through local property taxes. The Texas system, which is similar to that employed in most states, resulted in dramatically different amounts of money being spent among the state's school districts. In reviewing the Texas system of school funding, a sharply divided Court employed the traditional rational basis test, refusing to recognize wealth as a suspect classification. Using this approach, the Court found no constitutional violation. According to Justice Powell's majority opinion, the school finance system:

> *allegedly discriminates against a large, diverse, and amorphous class, unified only by the common factor of residence in districts which happen to have less taxable wealth than other districts. The system of alleged discrimination and the class it defines have none of the traditional indicia of suspectness; the class is not saddled with such disabilities, or subjected to such history of purposeful unequal treatment, or relegated to such a position of political powerlessness as to command extraordinary protection from the majoritarian political process.*

Justice Marshall protested vehemently in *Rodriguez*, arguing that education was a "fundamental interest" and that "poverty" was indeed a "suspect classification." According to Justice Marshall:

> *[The] Court has never suggested that because some "adequate" level of benefits is provided to all, discrimination in the provision of services is therefore constitutionally excusable. The Equal Protection Clause is not addressed to the minimal sufficiency but to the unjustifiable inequalities of state action.*

The Supreme Court's interpretation of the Fourteenth Amendment in *Rodriguez* in no way prevents state courts from adopting a contrary view of the relevant provisions of their state constitutions. Indeed, the California Supreme Court did so in *Serrano v. Priest* (1971). Since then, numerous state supreme courts have followed suit in holding that disparities in funding among school districts violate state constitutional equal protection requirements or state constitutional provisions guaranteeing a right to public education. A dramatic example is *Rose v. Council for Better Education, Inc.* (1989), where the Kentucky Supreme Court declared unconstitutional the entire system of public schools in that state. This forced the state legislature to overhaul the system. School funding was increased significantly and the discrepancies between wealthy and poor districts were reduced. The decision of the Kentucky Supreme Court is yet another illustration of the principle of **judicial federalism**, under which state courts are free to interpret their state laws in a way that provides additional rights beyond those secured by federal law. At a time in which the U.S. Supreme Court is dominated by conservatives, advocates of civil rights and liberties may find state tribunals receptive to claims that would be rejected by the federal courts.

Restriction of Abortion Funding for Indigent Women

Another controversial issue reaching the Burger Court under the aegis of the New Equal Protection was the dispute over legislative efforts to cut off government funds to support abortions. In *Maher v. Roe* (1977), the Court upheld the constitutionality of a Connecticut policy withholding Medicaid payments for nonessential abortions. Writing for a majority of six justices, Justice Powell opined that

> *[a]n indigent woman desiring an abortion does not come within the limited category of disadvantaged classes so recognized by our cases. Nor does the fact that the impact of the regulation falls upon those who cannot pay lead to a different conclusion. In a sense, every denial of welfare to an indigent creates a wealth classification as compared to nonindigents who are able to pay for the desired goods or services. But this Court has never held that financial need alone identifies a suspect class for purposes of Equal Protection analysis.*

Subsequently, in *Harris v. McRae* (1980), the Court upheld the **Hyde amendment**, a federal law that severely limited the use of federal funds to support abortions for indigent women. Writing for the sharply divided bench, Justice Stewart observed that:

> [t]he Hyde Amendment, like the Connecticut welfare regulation at issue in Maher, places no governmental obstacle in the path of a woman who chooses to terminate her pregnancy, but rather, by means of unequal subsidization of abortion and other medical services, encourages alternative activity deemed in the public interest. The present case does differ factually from Maher insofar as that case involved a failure to fund non-therapeutic abortions, whereas the Hyde Amendment withholds funding of certain medically necessary abortions.

Nevertheless, Justice Stewart concluded that:

> [h]ere as in Maher, the principal impact of the Hyde Amendment falls on the indigent. But that fact does not itself render the funding restriction constitutionally invalid, for this Court has held repeatedly that poverty, standing alone, is not a suspect classification.

Dissenting, Justice Marshall chastised the majority for its insensitivity to the plight of the poor, saying that "[t]here is another world 'out there,' the existence of which the Court ... either chooses to ignore or refuses to recognize." In Marshall's view, "it is only by blinding itself to that other world" that the Court could uphold the Hyde amendment. (This issue is also addressed in Chapter 6.)

Possible Interpretations of Economic Equal Protection

Although most commentators have associated an expansion of the Equal Protection Clause to protect economic interests with liberal, redistributive policy objectives, such a broadening of equal protection might well turn out to be a double-edged sword. If a more conservative Supreme Court were to make "wealth," as distinct from "poverty," a suspect classification, then government presumably would have to show a compelling interest to justify progressive taxation, subsidies, and a host of redistributive policies. Just as the Due Process Clause was once used to frustrate progressivism, populism, and the New Deal, so the Equal Protection Clause could conceivably be employed by a more conservative Supreme Court to attack the welfare state.

As we have pointed out repeatedly in this book, constitutional language, such as "due process" and "equal protection," is sufficiently broad to embrace various potential applications. Indeed, socialists could "find" in the Equal Protection Clause a requirement that government equalize material conditions in society. Similarly, the Takings Clause of the Fifth Amendment could be cited to provide a constitutional justification for the nationalization of private industries. This is not to say that the Constitution has no plain or obvious meanings, which it surely does. It is only to say that certain language in the Constitution, such as the Equal Protection Clause, is written broadly enough to allow for various, even opposing, interpretations. The constitutional values that are actualized through decision making depend greatly on the political ideologies of the justices who happen to be on the Court and on the broader political culture within which the Court functions.

To Summarize:
- *The Court has taken a decidedly conservative approach in dealing with the issue of discrimination against the poor. The Court has, for example, refused to invalidate local systems of public school finance alleged to disadvantage poor students and has upheld restrictions on public funding of nontherapeutic abortions for indigent women.*

Other Forms of Discrimination

Today, the only suspect classifications that have been identified by the Supreme Court are those based on race, national origin, and religious affiliation. As previously noted, gender-based classifications, which are the subject of much current controversy, have not been added to the inventory of suspect classifications. Rather, sex discrimination, along with illegitimacy and alienage, occupies a middle tier in what has become a complex, multi-tiered approach to judging challenged classifications. The Court has addressed other bases of discrimination, notably age and disability, using the traditional rational basis test. The Court's decisions in the areas of age and disability have focused largely on the power of Congress under Section 5 of the Fourteenth Amendment to combat discrimination.

Age Discrimination

The Supreme Court first dealt with age discrimination as a constitutional matter in the 1976 case of *Massachusetts Board of Retirement v. Murgia*. The case involved a state law requiring uniformed police officers to retire at age 50. In upholding the statute, the Court explicitly recognized the rational basis test as the appropriate one for judging claims of age discrimination. The Court reasoned that physical fitness requirements for police officers could reasonably be linked to a mandatory retirement age. The Court held 8 to 0 (Justice Stevens not participating) that mandatory retirement was rationally related to the state's legitimate objective of protecting the public by assuring that police officers are physically fit. Mandatory retirement age policies for state judges have also been upheld by the Supreme Court (see *Gregory v. Ashcroft* [1990]).

In 2000, the Court returned to the age discrimination problem in the context of its recent emphasis on issues of federalism. *Kimel v. Board of Regents* involved the application of the Age Discrimination in Employment Act of 1967 (ADEA) to state employers. The specific question was whether Congress could abrogate states' sovereign immunity by authorizing state employees to sue their state employers for damages stemming from allegations of age discrimination. In a sharply divided 5-to-4 decision, the Court answered this question in the negative. In her majority opinion, Justice O'Connor concluded:

> *A review of the ADEA's legislative record as a whole, then, reveals that Congress had virtually no reason to believe that state and local governments were unconstitutionally discriminating against their employees on the basis of age. Although that lack of support is not determinative of the § 5 inquiry, ... Congress's failure to uncover any significant pattern of unconstitutional discrimination here confirms that Congress had no reason to believe that broad prophylactic legislation was necessary in this field. In light of the indiscriminate scope of the Act's substantive requirements, and the lack of evidence of widespread and unconstitutional age discrimination by the States, we hold that the ADEA is not a valid exercise of Congress's power under § 5 of the Fourteenth Amendment. The ADEA's purported abrogation of the States' sovereign immunity is accordingly invalid.*

In dissent, Justice Stevens (joined by Justices Souter, Ginsburg, and Breyer) objected to the Court's narrow view of Congress's enforcement powers under Section 5 of the Fourteenth Amendment:

> *Congress's power to regulate the American economy includes the power to regulate both the public and the private sectors of the labor market. Federal rules outlawing discrimination in the workplace, like the regulation of wages and hours or health and safety standards, may be enforced against public as well as private employers. In my opinion, Congress's power to authorize federal remedies against state agencies that violate*

federal statutory obligations is coextensive with its power to impose those obligations on the States in the first place.

Persons with Disabilities

Although persons with disabilities can be viewed as constituting a "discrete and insular minority," policies and practices that discriminate against such persons have not been recognized as "inherently suspect" under the Fourteenth Amendment. Arguably, a government's failure to provide a wheelchair ramp at a place where votes are cast could be viewed as an unreasonable burden on the exercise of a "fundamental right." Congress has attempted to increase access to the polls for persons with disabilities through passage of the Voting Accessibility Act of 1984. For the most part Congress, not the Supreme Court, has taken the lead in recognizing the rights of persons with disabilities. With the passage of Title V of the Rehabilitation Act of 1973, the Education for All Handicapped Children Act of 1975, and especially the **Americans with Disabilities Act (ADA)** of 1990, Congress has attempted to remove barriers confronting persons with disabilities in such areas as employment, education, and public transportation.

In an important 2004 decision that surprised many disability rights observers, the Supreme Court followed the lead of Congress by holding in *Tennessee v. Lane* that an individual has a fundamental right of access to the courts. By failing to provide such access to wheelchair users, Tennessee had violated not only Title II of the ADA but, more significantly, the Due Process Clause of the Fourteenth Amendment (the *Lane* case is discussed and excerpted in Chapter 5, Volume I).

Overall it is fair to say that the Court has given mixed signals in the disability rights field. With respect to employment discrimination it has effectively insulated the states from suits brought under Title I of the ADA. On the other hand, the Court has permitted individuals to sue the state under Title II of the ADA to gain full access to the courts. This seemingly nebulous area of jurisprudence seems primed to be one of continuing controversy going forward.

Residency and Alienage

The Fifth and Fourteenth Amendments do not protect citizens alone from arbitrary or unjust government actions. Rather, the amendments use the broader term "persons." The Supreme Court has stressed the text of the Fourteenth Amendment in striking down a number of state laws that differentiate between residents and nonresidents or between citizens and aliens. For example, in *Shapiro v. Thompson* (1969), the Supreme Court struck down a series of laws that imposed one-year waiting periods on new state residents seeking welfare benefits. Then, in *Sugarman v. McDougall* (1973), the Court struck down a New York law that denied civil service jobs to aliens. In 1976, the Court extended this ruling to invalidate similar federal civil service restrictions *(Hampton v. Mow Sun Wong)*.

In a controversial 1982 decision, the Supreme Court went so far as to invalidate discrimination against the children of illegal aliens. In *Plyler v. Doe*, the Court voted 5 to 4 to strike down a Texas law that denied free public education to the children of illegal immigrants. Using elements of both rational basis and heightened scrutiny analysis, Justice Brennan found no "substantial interest" of the state to justify the denial of educational benefits to the children of illegal aliens. Dissenting sharply, Chief Justice Burger complained that "if ever a court was guilty of an unabashedly result-oriented approach, this case is a prime example." The Court's decisions in *Shapiro v. Thompson* and *Plyler v. Doe* involved not merely the distinction between residents and nonresidents or between legal residents and illegal immigrants, they also implicated the underlying issue of poverty.

> **To Summarize:**
>
> ◆ *The Supreme Court has recognized constitutional issues of discrimination in a number of areas, including classifications based on age, disability, residency, and alienage. To the extent that discriminatory practices in these areas impinge on fundamental rights, the Court has subjected them to strict scrutiny. Otherwise, the court has employed the rational basis test or, in some instances, heightened scrutiny.*

The Ongoing Problem of Private Discrimination

The repudiation of the separate but equal doctrine in *Brown* and subsequent decisions led to the virtual disappearance of de jure racial segregation—that is, segregation required or created by law or public policy. Yet, **de facto segregation** in housing, employment, and education still exists to a great extent, as a function of both social norms and economic disparities. As the Supreme Court held as far back as 1883 (see *The Civil Rights Cases*), segregation that is purely de facto is beyond the purview of the Equal Protection Clause per se. Many forms of de facto segregation, however, may be within the remedial power of both state and federal statutes. For example, under the Fair Housing Act of 1968, Congress prohibited racial discrimination in the rental or sale of homes where the transaction is handled by a licensed agent. The questions surrounding such attempts at eradicating de facto discrimination are by no means closed.

As we previously noted, the Supreme Court in 1883 drew a sharp distinction between racial discrimination that is purely private in character and that which is supported by state action. Without formally overruling *The Civil Rights Cases*, the Court has blurred this distinction as applied to racial discrimination. Nevertheless, the Court has shown no inclination to abandon the state action doctrine. For example, in the case of a racially restrictive private club's refusal to serve the African-American guest of a white member, the Court determined that the mere grant of a liquor license did not convert the club's discriminatory policy into state action under the Fourteenth Amendment (*Moose Lodge v. Irvis* [1972]). A decade earlier, in *Burton v. Wilmington Parking Authority* (1961), the Court had found state action when a state agency leased property to a restaurant that refused to serve African-Americans.

Legalistically, whether there is state action in support of discrimination depends on whether there is a "close nexus" between the functions of the state and the private discrimination. More realistically, it probably depends on whether circumstances foster a perception that the state approves of the discrimination at issue.

Restrictive Covenants

A classic form of private discrimination was the **restrictive covenant** in which a group of homeowners agreed not to sell or rent their homes to African-Americans, Jews, and other disfavored minorities. Under the decision in *The Civil Rights Cases*, this purely private form of racial discrimination was deemed to be beyond the purview of the Equal Protection Clause. However, in *Shelley v. Kraemer* (1948), the Supreme Court held such covenants to be unenforceable in state courts, because any such enforcement would amount to state action in contravention of the Fourteenth Amendment. Arguably, for a state court to enforce such an agreement would foster a public perception that the state approves of racially restrictive covenants. On the other hand, it would be a mistake to conclude that the mere judicial enforcement of every private agreement necessarily constitutes state action for purposes of the Fourteenth Amendment. In fact, ordinary contracts and other private transactions are generally not brought within the limitations of the Fourteenth Amendment merely because they are enforced in court. *Shelley v. Kraemer* seems to stand for the proposition that questions of private racial discrimination constitute a unique category.

Although restrictive covenants are no longer judicially enforceable, racial restrictions are still written into many deeds, a fact that aroused considerable public attention during the 1986 Senate confirmation hearings on the elevation of William Rehnquist to be chief justice. In the course of these hearings, it was revealed that the deed to a piece of property owned by Rehnquist himself contained a restrictive covenant.

Finally, it should be noted that although the decision in *The Civil Rights Cases* has not been overruled, Congress has employed its broad powers, chiefly under the Commerce Clause (Article I, Section 8), to prohibit racial discrimination by places of public accommodation whose operations affect interstate commerce (see Chapter 2, Volume I). In *Heart of Atlanta Motel v. United States* (1964), the Supreme Court upheld Title II of the 1964 Civil Rights Act, thus allowing Congress to accomplish under its commerce power what the Court in 1883 prevented it from doing under the Fourteenth Amendment.

State Powers to Prohibit Private Discrimination

Historically, the state governments were anything but leaders in the struggle for civil rights. Yet today, many states have civil rights or **human rights statutes**. An emerging constitutional issue is the extent to which states can act affirmatively to foster integration. Can a state adopt legislation that outlaws racial discrimination in the places of public accommodation perceived as not currently subject to federal civil rights laws? Can the states require quasi-public organizations, such as the Rotary Club, the Kiwanis, or the Jaycees, to admit women? What about private social clubs?

Can the states require racially or religiously exclusive country clubs to admit those whom their membership policies currently exclude? Here, we have a classic confrontation between the state's legitimate interest in eradicating invidious discrimination and the freedom of association protected by the First and Fourteenth Amendments. In the landmark decision *Roberts v. United States Jaycees* (1984) (see Chapter 3, Volume II), the Court upheld a Minnesota human rights law requiring a civic organization to accept women as full members, despite the organization's reliance on the First Amendment. For Justice Brennan, the state's interest in eradicating discrimination was more compelling than the Jaycees' claim to free association.

However, Justice O'Connor was careful to point out that the Jaycees behaved more like a commercial enterprise than a political organization or a private club. Justice O'Connor's concurrence left open the question of whether "less public" entities are subject to state intervention.

The principle articulated in the *Jaycees* decision has been followed fairly consistently by the Supreme Court. For example, in 1987, the Court unanimously extended this principle to encompass the Rotary Club as well *(Rotary International v. Rotary Club of Duarte)*. Likewise, in 1988, a unanimous Court relied on *Roberts v. Jaycees* in upholding a New York City ordinance that required certain all-male social clubs to admit women *(New York Club Association v. City of New York)*.

On the other hand, the Court has shown that it is not willing to eviscerate the First Amendment right of free association to achieve the goal of ending discrimination. In *Hurley v. Irish-American Gay, Lesbian, and Bisexual Group of Boston* (1995), the Court held that the state of Massachusetts could not prohibit a private organization from excluding a gay rights group from its annual St. Patrick's Day parade (see Chapter 3, Volume II). A state court had ruled that gay groups could not be excluded under

Massachusetts's **public accommodations statute**. The Supreme Court reversed, holding that the state could not compel the parade's organizers to promote a message of which they disapproved. Some commentators suggested that the Court's decision might reflect animus toward gays and lesbians and wondered whether the decision would have been the same had the parade's organizers sought to exclude women or African-Americans. Others argued that the Court had struck a blow for freedom from state coercion.

In 2000, the Court considered a more difficult case of private discrimination on the basis of sexual orientation. In *Boy Scouts of America v. Dale* (discussed and reprinted in Chapter 3, Volume II), the Court held that the Boy Scouts could not be required by state courts to accept gay Scout leaders under a state public accommodations law. In the Court's view, this requirement would be a "severe intrusion on the Boy Scouts' rights to freedom of expressive association." In a stinging dissent, Justice Stevens quoted Justice Louis Brandeis, who once wrote that "we must be ever on our guard, lest we erect our prejudices into legal principles."

To Summarize:

- *The Supreme Court held long ago that the prohibitions of the Fourteenth Amendment extend only to discrimination fostered by government. Thus, to challenge a particular discriminatory practice under the Equal Protection Clause, a plaintiff must demonstrate that there is "state action" in support of the challenged practice.*
- *The existence of state action in support of discrimination depends on whether there is a "close nexus" between the functions of the state and the challenged discriminatory practice.*
- *Discrimination that is purely de facto or private in nature is beyond the reach of the Fourteenth Amendment. However, such discrimination may violate federal, state, and local laws, such as the laws prohibiting discrimination by places of public accommodation.*
- *In some instances, courts may find that the application of civil rights laws to private organizations violates the First Amendment's implicit freedom of association.*

Conclusion

In a brief introductory essay such as this, it is impossible to discuss all the important issues of equal protection, both actual and potential. After more than four decades of the New Equal Protection, it is clear that any government policy that differentiates among identifiable groups poses a potential equal protection problem. For example, as longevity of the American population increases and more people stay on the job beyond the traditional age of retirement, discrimination against the elderly is becoming a more prominent equal protection issue. Perhaps the most polarizing question of this nature recently asked at the Supreme Court is whether laws forbidding same-sex marriage unreasonably discriminate against gay men and lesbians.

In spite of recent changes in the ideological makeup of the Supreme Court, there exists an elaborate framework of statutes and judicial decisions reflecting a strong national commitment to the antidiscrimination principle. Some observers may view recent limitations on affirmative action programs and disengagement of the federal courts from supervision of public school desegregation as departures from this commitment. The antidiscrimination principle, however, is far broader than specific remedial measures adopted to address immediate problems. The fundamental commitment to this principle is likely to outlast ephemeral changes in the political landscape.

Politically, one of the most important applications of the Equal Protection Clause has been to the historic problem of legislative malapportionment. This problem, along with other issues related to the themes of representation and political participation, is examined in Chapter 8.

Key Terms

Equal Protection Clause
New Equal Protection
fundamental rights
rational basis test
discrete and insular minorities
suspect classification doctrine
strict judicial scrutiny
presumption of constitutionality
compelling interest
heightened scrutiny
Civil Rights Act of 1866
Black Codes
disparate impact
Civil Rights Act of 1875

places of public accommodation
state action doctrine
Civil Rights Act of 1964
Jim Crow laws
separate but equal doctrine
desegregation
court-ordered busing
de jure discrimination
affirmative action
race-conscious remedies
group rights
set-aside
consent decrees
gender-based classifications

sexual harassment
Equal Rights Amendment
gender-neutral
gender equity
judicial federalism
Hyde amendment
Americans with Disabilities Act (ADA)
de facto segregation
restrictive covenant
human rights statutes
public accommodations statute

For Further Reading

Baer, Judith. *Equality under the Constitution: Reclaiming the Fourteenth Amendment.* Ithaca, NY: Cornell University Press, 1983.

Balkin, J. M., and Bruce Ackerman (eds.). *What Brown v. Board of Education Should Have Said: The Nation's Top Legal Experts Rewrite America's Landmark Civil Rights Decision.* New York: New York University Press, 2001.

Berger, Raoul. *Government by Judiciary: The Transformation of the Fourteenth Amendment.* Cambridge, MA: Harvard University Press, 1977.

Finch, Minnie. *The NAACP: Its Fight for Justice.* Metuchen, NJ: Scarecrow Press, 1981.

Franklin, John Hope. *From Slavery to Freedom: A History of Negro Americans.* New York: Knopf, 1980.

Gerstmann, Evan. *The Constitutional Underclass: Gays, Lesbians, and the Failure of Class-Based Equal Protection.* Chicago: University of Chicago Press, 1999.

Ginsberg, Ruth. *Constitutional Aspects of Sex-Based Discrimination.* St. Paul, MN: West, 1974.

Glazer, Nathan. *Affirmative Discrimination: Ethnic Inequality and Public Policy.* New York: Basic Books, 1975.

Graham, Hugh Davis. *The Civil Rights Era: Origins and Development of a National Policy.* New York: Oxford University Press, 1990.

Kennedy, Randall. *Race, Crime, and the Law.* New York: Pantheon Books, 1997.

Kluger, Richard. *Simple Justice.* New York: Vintage Books, 1975, Revised Edition 2004.

O'Connor, Karen. *Women's Organizations' Use of the Courts.* Lexington, MA: Lexington Books, 1980.

Peltason, Jack W. *Fifty-Eight Lonely Men: Southern Federal Judges and School Desegregation.* Urbana: University of Illinois Press, 1961.

Rhode, Deborah. *Justice and Gender.* Cambridge, MA: Harvard University Press, 1989.

Rossum, Ralph. *Reverse Discrimination: The Constitutional Debate.* New York: Dekker, 1980.

Schwartz, Bernard (ed.). *The Fourteenth Amendment.* New York: New York University Press, 1970.

Sindler, Allan P. *Bakke, DeFunis, and Minority Admissions.* New York: Longman, 1978.

Wasby, Stephen L., Anthony A. D'Amato, and Rosemary Metrailer. *Desegregation from Brown to Alexander: An Exploration of Supreme Court Strategies.* Carbondale: Southern Illinois University Press, 1977.

Wilkinson, J. Harvie III. *From Brown to Bakke: The Supreme Court and School Integration: 1954–1978.* New York: Oxford University Press, 1981.

Wolters, Raymond. *The Burden of Brown: Thirty Years of School Desegregation.* Knoxville: University of Tennessee Press, 1984.

Woodward, C. Vann. *The Strange Career of Jim Crow.* New York: Oxford University Press, 1968.

PLESSY v. FERGUSON
163 U.S. 537; 16 S.Ct. 1138; 41 L.Ed. 256 (1896)
Vote: 7-1

A Louisiana law passed in 1890 required all passenger trains in the state to have "equal but separate accommodations for the white, and colored races." Homer Plessy, claiming that he "was seven-eighths Caucasian and one-eighth African blood; that the mixture of colored blood was not discernible in him; and that he was entitled to every right... of the white race," was arrested after refusing to vacate a seat in a car that was reserved for white passengers. Plessy's attack on the statute's constitutionality was unsuccessful in the Louisiana courts. He appealed.

Mr. Justice Brown ... delivered the opinion of the Court.

... That [the statute] does not conflict with the Thirteenth Amendment, which abolished slavery and involuntary servitude, except as a punishment for crime, is too clear for argument. Slavery implies involuntary servitude—a state of bondage; the ownership of mankind as a chattel, or, at least, the control of the labor and services of one man for the benefit of another, and the absence of a legal right to the disposal of his own person, property, and services. This amendment ... was regarded by the statesmen of that day as insufficient to protect the colored race from certain laws which had been enacted in the Southern states, imposing upon the colored race onerous disabilities and burdens, and curtailing their rights in the pursuit of life, liberty, and property to such an extent that their freedom was of little value; and ... the Fourteenth Amendment was devised to meet this exigency....

The object of the amendment was undoubtedly to enforce the absolute equality of the two races before the law, but, in the nature of things, it could not have been intended to abolish distinctions based upon color, or to enforce social, as distinguished from political, equality, or a commingling of the two races upon terms unsatisfactory to either. Laws permitting, and even requiring, their separation, in places where they are liable to be brought into contact ... have been generally, if not universally, recognized as within the competency of the state legislatures in the exercise of their police power. The most common instance of this is connected with the establishment of separate schools for white and colored children, which have been [upheld] even by courts of states where the political rights of the colored race have been longest and most earnestly enforced.

One of the earliest of these cases is that *of Roberts v. City of Boston* ... (1849). "The great principle," said Chief Justice Shaw, "advanced by the learned and eloquent advocate for the plaintiff (Mr. Charles Sumner), is that, by the constitution and laws of Massachusetts, all persons, without distinction of age or sex, birth, or color, origin or condition, are equal before the law.... But, when this great principle comes to be applied to the actual and various conditions of persons in society, it will not warrant the assertion that men and women are legally clothed with the same civil and political powers, and that children and adults are legally to have the same functions and be subject to the same treatment; but only that the rights of all, as they are settled and regulated by law, are equally entitled to the paternal consideration and protection of the law for their maintenance and security." Similar laws have been enacted by Congress under its general power of legislation over the District of Columbia, as well as by the legislatures of many of the states, and have been generally, if not uniformly, sustained by the courts....

Laws forbidding the intermarriage of the two races may be said in a technical sense to interfere with the freedom of contract, and yet have been universally recognized as within the police power of the state....

The distinction between laws interfering with the political equality of the negro and those requiring the separation of the two races in schools, theaters, and railway carriages has been frequently drawn by this court.

[It is suggested] that the same argument that will justify the state legislature in requiring railways to provide separate accommodations for the two races will also authorize them to require separate cars to be provided for people whose hair is of a certain color, or who are aliens, or who belong to certain nationalities, or to enact laws requiring colored people to walk upon one side of the street, and white people upon the other, or requiring white men's houses to be painted white, and colored men's black, or their vehicles or business signs to be of different colors, upon the theory that one side of the street is as good as the other, or that a house or vehicle of one color is as good as one of another color. The reply to all this is that every exercise of the police power must be reasonable, and extend only to such laws as are enacted in good faith for the promotion of the public good, and not for the annoyance or oppression of a particular class....

So far, then, as a conflict with the Fourteenth Amendment is concerned, the case reduces itself to the question whether the statute of Louisiana is a reasonable regulation, and with respect to this there must necessarily be a large discretion on the part of the legislature. In determining the question of reasonableness, it is at liberty to act with reference to the established usages, customs, and traditions of the people, and with a view to the promotion of their comfort, and the preservation of the public peace and good order. Gauged by this standard, we cannot say [that this law] is unreasonable, or more obnoxious to the Fourteenth Amendment than the acts of Congress requiring separate schools for colored children in the District of Columbia, the constitutionality of which does not seem to have been questioned, or the corresponding acts of state legislatures.

We consider the underlying fallacy of the plaintiff's argument to consist in the assumption that the enforced separation of the two races stamps the colored race with a badge of inferiority. If this be so, it is not by reason of anything found in the act, but solely because the colored race chooses to put that construction upon it. The argument necessarily assumes that if, as has been more than once the case, and is not unlikely to be so again, the colored race should become the dominant power in the state legislature, and should enact a law in precisely similar terms, it would thereby relegate the white race to an inferior position. We imagine that the white race, at least, would not acquiesce in this assumption. The argument also assumes that social prejudices may be overcome by legislation, and that equal rights cannot be secured to the negro except by an enforced commingling of the two races. We cannot accept this proposition. If the two races are to meet upon terms of social equality, it must be the result of natural affinities, a mutual appreciation of each other's merits, and a voluntary consent of individuals.... Legislation is powerless to eradicate racial instincts, or to abolish distinctions based upon physical differences, and the attempt to do so can only result in accentuating the difficulties of the present situation. If the civil and political rights of both races be equal, one cannot be inferior to the other civilly or politically. If one race be inferior to the other socially, the Constitution of the United States cannot put them upon the same plane....

Mr. Justice Brewer did not ... participate in the decision of this case.

Mr. Justice Harlan dissenting.

... In respect of civil rights, common to all citizens, the Constitution of the United States does not, I think, permit any public authority to know the race of those entitled to be protected in the enjoyment of such rights. Every true man has pride of race, and under appropriate circumstances, when the rights of others, his equals before the law, are not to be affected, it is his privilege to express such pride and to take such action based upon it as to him seems proper. But I deny that any legislative body or judicial tribunal may have regard to the race of citizens when the civil rights of those citizens are involved. Indeed, such legislation as that here in question is inconsistent not only with that equality of rights which pertains to citizenship, national and state, but with the personal liberty enjoyed by everyone within the United States.

The Thirteenth Amendment does not permit the withholding or the deprivation of any right necessarily inhering in freedom. It not only struck down the institution of slavery as previously existing in the United States, but it prevents the imposition of any burdens or disabilities that constitute badges of slavery or servitude.... It was followed by the Fourteenth [and Fifteenth] amendments, which added greatly to the dignity and glory of American citizenship, and to the security of personal liberty....

It was said in argument that the statute of Louisiana does not discriminate against either race, but prescribes a rule applicable alike to white and colored citizens. But this argument does not meet the difficulty. Everyone knows that the statute in question had its origin in the purpose, not so much to exclude white persons from railroad cars occupied by blacks, as to exclude colored people from coaches occupied by or assigned to white persons.... No one would be so wanting in candor as to assert the contrary.

(Continued)

The fundamental objection, therefore, to the statute, is that it interferes with the personal freedom of citizens. "Personal liberty," it has been well said, "consists in the power of locomotion, of changing situation, or removing one's person to whatsoever places one's own inclination may direct, without imprisonment or restraint, unless by due course of law." ... If a white man and a black man choose to occupy the same public conveyance on a public highway, it is their right to do so; and no government, proceeding alone on grounds of race, can prevent it without infringing the personal liberty of each.

... If a state can prescribe, as a rule of civil conduct, that whites and blacks shall not travel as passengers in the same railroad coach, why ... may it not require sheriffs to assign whites to one side of a court room, and blacks to the other? And why may it not also prohibit the commingling of the two races in the galleries of legislative halls or in public assemblages convened for the consideration of the political questions of the day? [W]hy may not the state require the separation in railroad coaches of native and naturalized citizens of the United States, or of Protestants and Roman Catholics? ...

The white race deems itself to be the dominant race in this country. And so it is, in prestige, in achievements, in education, in wealth, and in power. So, I doubt not, it will continue to be for all time, if it remains true to its great heritage, and holds fast to the principles of constitutional liberty. But in view of the Constitution, in the eye of the law, there is in this country no superior, dominant, ruling class of citizens. There is no caste here. Our Constitution is color-blind, and neither knows nor tolerates classes among citizens....

In my opinion, the judgment this day rendered will, in time, prove to be quite as pernicious as the decision made by this tribunal in the *Dred Scott* Case ... that the descendants of Africans who were imported into this country, and sold as slaves, were not included nor intended to be included under the word "citizens" in the Constitution; ... that, at the time of the adoption of the Constitution, they were "considered as a subordinate and inferior class of beings, who had been subjugated by the dominant race, and, whether emancipated or not, yet remained subject to their authority, and had not rights or privileges but such as those who held the power and the government might choose to grant them." ... The recent amendments of the Constitution, it was supposed, has eradicated these principles from our institutions. But it seems that we have yet, in some of the states, a dominant race—a superior class of citizens—which assumes to regulate the enjoyment of civil rights, common to all citizens, upon the basis of race. The present decision ... will encourage the belief that it is possible by means of state enactments, to defeat the beneficent purposes which the people of the United States had in view when they adopted the recent amendments of the Constitution.... What can more certainly arouse race hate, what more certainly create and perpetuate a feeling of distrust between these races, than state enactments which, in fact, proceed on the ground that colored citizens are so inferior and degraded that they cannot be allowed to sit in public coaches occupied by white citizens? ... This question is not met by the suggestion that social equality cannot exist between the white and black races in this country ... for social equality no more exists between two races when traveling in a passenger coach or a public highway than when members of the same races sit by each other in a street car or in the jury box, or stand or sit with each other in a political assembly....

If evils will result from the comminglings of the two races upon public highways established for the benefit of all, they will be infinitely less than those that will surely come from state legislation regulating the enjoyment of civil rights upon the basis of race. We boast of the freedom enjoyed by our people above all other peoples. But it is difficult to reconcile that boast with a state of the law which, practically, puts the brand of servitude and degradation upon a large class of our fellow citizens—our equals before the law. The thin disguise of "equal" accommodations for passengers in railroad coaches will not mislead anyone, nor atone for the wrong this day done....

I do not deem it necessary to review the decisions of state courts to which reference was made in argument. Some, and the most important, of them, are wholly inapplicable, because rendered prior to the adoption of the last amendments of the Constitution.... Others were made at a time when public opinion, in many localities, was dominated by the institution of slavery; when it would not have been safe to do justice to the black man; and when, so far as the rights of blacks were concerned, race prejudice was, practically, the supreme law of the land. Those decisions cannot be guides in the era introduced by the recent amendments of the supreme law, which established universal civil freedom....

SWEATT v. PAINTER
339 U.S. 629; 70 S.Ct. 848; 94 L. Ed. 1114 (1950)
Vote: 9-0

In this case, the Court examines an attempt by the state of Texas to provide a separate law school for African Americans. In 1946, Heman Marion Sweatt was denied admission to law school at the University of Texas solely on account of his race. Backed by the NAACP, Sweatt filed suit in the Texas courts, arguing that because Texas refused to provide African Americans access to any state law school, it was in violation of the separate but equal doctrine established in Plessy v. Ferguson. *While the suit was pending, the state opened a law school at the Texas State University for Negroes (which was renamed Texas Southern University in 1951). Refusing to accept this accommodation, Sweatt persisted in his legal challenge and eventually the case made its way to the Supreme Court. The case was argued by Thurgood Marshall, after whom the current law school at Texas Southern University is named.*

Mr. Chief Justice Vinson delivered the opinion of the Court:

This case and *McLaurin v. Oklahoma State Regents* ... present different aspects of this general question: To what extent does the Equal Protection Clause of the Fourteenth Amendment limit the power of a state to distinguish between students of different races in professional and graduate education in a state university? Broader issues have been urged for our consideration, but we adhere to the principle of deciding constitutional questions only in the context of the particular case before the Court. We have frequently reiterated that this Court will decide constitutional questions only when necessary to the disposition of the case at hand, and that such decisions will be drawn as narrowly as possible.... Because of this traditional reluctance to extend constitutional interpretations to situations or facts which are not before the Court, much of the excellent research and detailed argument presented in these cases is unnecessary to their disposition.

In the instant case, petitioner filed an application for admission to the University of Texas Law School for the February 1946 term. His application was rejected solely because he is a Negro. Petitioner thereupon brought this suit for mandamus against the appropriate school officials, respondents here, to compel his admission. At that time, there was no law school in Texas which admitted Negroes.

The state trial court recognized that the action of the State in denying petitioner the opportunity to gain a legal education while granting it to others deprived him of the equal protection of the laws guaranteed by the Fourteenth Amendment. The court did not grant the relief requested, however, but continued the case for six months to allow the State to supply substantially equal facilities. At the expiration of the six months, in December 1946 the court denied the writ on the showing that the authorized university officials had adopted an order calling for the opening of a law school for Negroes the following February. While petitioner's appeal was pending, such a school was made available, but petitioner refused to register therein. The Texas Court of Civil Appeals set aside the trial court's judgment and ordered the case "remanded generally to the trial court for further proceedings without prejudice to the rights of any party to this suit."

On remand, a hearing was held on the issue of the equality of the educational facilities at the newly established school as compared with the University of Texas Law School. Finding that the new school offered petitioner "privileges, advantages, and opportunities for the study of law substantially equivalent to those offered by the State to white students at the University of Texas," the trial court denied mandamus. The Court of Civil Appeals affirmed.... Petitioner's application for a writ of error was denied by the Texas Supreme Court. We granted certiorari ... because of the manifest importance of the constitutional issues involved.

The University of Texas Law School, from which petitioner was excluded, was staffed by a faculty of sixteen full-time and three part-time professors, some of whom are nationally recognized authorities in their field. Its student body numbered 850. The

(Continued)

library contained over 65,000 volumes. Among the other facilities available to the students were a law review, moot court facilities, scholarship funds, and Order of the Coif affiliation. The school's alumni occupy the most distinguished positions in the private practice of the law and in the public life of the State. It may properly be considered one of the nation's ranking law schools.

The law school for Negroes which was to have opened in February 1947, would have had no independent faculty or library. The teaching was to be carried on by four members of the University of Texas Law School faculty, who were to maintain their offices at the University of Texas while teaching at both institutions. Few of the 10,000 volumes ordered for the library had arrived; nor was there any full-time librarian. The school lacked accreditation.

Since the trial of this case, respondents report the opening of a law school at the Texas State University for Negroes. It is apparently on the road to full accreditation. It has a faculty of five full-time professors; a student body of 23; a library of some 16,500 volumes serviced by a full-time staff; a practice court and legal aid association; and one alumnus who has become a member of the Texas Bar.

Whether the University of Texas Law School is compared with the original or the new law school for Negroes, we cannot find substantial equality in the educational opportunities offered white and Negro law students by the State. In terms of number of the faculty, variety of courses and opportunity for specialization, size of the student body, scope of the library, availability of law review and similar activities, the University of Texas Law School is superior. What is more important, the University of Texas Law School possesses to a far greater degree those qualities which are incapable of objective measurement but which make for greatness in a law school. Such qualities, to name but a few, include reputation of the faculty, experience of the administration, position and influence of the alumni, standing in the community, traditions and prestige. It is difficult to believe that one who had a free choice between these law schools would consider the question close.

Moreover, although the law is a highly learned profession, we are well aware that it is an intensely practical one. The law school, the proving ground for legal learning and practice, cannot be effective in isolation from the individuals and institutions with which the law interacts. Few students and no one who has practiced law would choose to study in an academic vacuum, removed from the interplay of ideas and the exchange of views with which the law is concerned. The law school to which Texas is willing to admit petitioner excludes from its student body members of the racial groups which number 85% of the population of the State and include most of the lawyers, witnesses, jurors, judges and other officials with whom petitioner will inevitably be dealing when he becomes a member of the Texas Bar. With such a substantial and significant segment of society excluded, we cannot conclude that the education offered petitioner is substantially equal to that which he would receive if admitted to the University of Texas Law School.

It may be argued that excluding petitioner from that school is no different from excluding white students from the new law school. This contention overlooks realities. It is unlikely that a member of a group so decisively in the majority, attending a school with rich traditions and prestige which only a history of consistently maintained excellence could command, would claim that the opportunities afforded him for legal education were unequal to those held open to petitioner. That such a claim, if made, would be dishonored by the State, is no answer. "Equal protection of the laws is not achieved through indiscriminate imposition of inequalities." ...

In accordance with these cases, petitioner may claim his full constitutional right: legal education equivalent to that afforded by the State to students of other races. Such education is not available to him in a separate law school as offered by the State. We cannot, therefore, agree with respondents that the doctrine of *Plessy v. Ferguson* ... requires affirmance of the judgment below. Nor need we reach petitioner's contention that *Plessy v. Ferguson* should be reexamined in the light of contemporary knowledge respecting the purposes of the Fourteenth Amendment and the effects of racial segregation.

We hold that the Equal Protection Clause of the Fourteenth Amendment requires that petitioner be admitted to the University of Texas Law School. The judgment is reversed and the cause is remanded for proceedings not inconsistent with this opinion.

BROWN v. BOARD OF EDUCATION OF TOPEKA I
347 U.S. 483; 74 S.Ct. 686; 98 L.Ed. 873 (1954)
Vote: 9-0

In what was dubbed "the case of the century," the Supreme Court invalidated compulsory racial segregation in the public schools as a denial of equal protection of the laws.

Mr. Chief Justice Warren delivered the opinion of the Court:

These cases come to us from the States of Kansas, South Carolina, Virginia, and Delaware. They are premised on different facts and different local conditions, but a common legal question justifies their consideration in this consolidated opinion.

In each of the cases, minors of the Negro race, through their legal representatives, seek the aid of the courts in obtaining admission to the public schools of their community on a nonsegregated basis. In each instance, they had been denied admission to schools attended by white children under laws requiring or permitting segregation according to race. This segregation was alleged to deprive the plaintiffs of the equal protection of the laws under the Fourteenth Amendment. In each of the cases other than the Delaware case, a three-judge federal district court denied relief to the plaintiffs on the so-called "separate but equal" doctrine announced by this Court in *Plessy v. Ferguson*.... Under that doctrine, equality of treatment is accorded when the races are provided substantially equal facilities, even though these facilities be separate. In the Delaware case, the Supreme Court of Delaware adhered to that doctrine, but ordered that the plaintiffs be admitted to the white schools because of their superiority to the Negro schools....

Because of the obvious importance of the question presented, the Court took jurisdiction. Argument was heard in the 1952 Term, and reargument was heard this Term on certain questions propounded by the Court.

Reargument was largely devoted to the circumstances surrounding the adoption of the Fourteenth Amendment in 1868. It covered exhaustively consideration of the Amendment in Congress, ratification by the states, then existing practices in racial segregation, and the views of proponents and opponents of the Amendment. This discussion and our own investigation convince us that, although these sources cast some light, it is not enough to resolve the problem with which we are faced. At best, they are inconclusive. The most avid proponents of the post-War Amendments undoubtedly intended them to remove all legal distinctions among "all persons born or naturalized in the United States." Their opponents, just as certainly, were antagonistic to both the letter and the spirit of the Amendments and wished them to have the most limited effect. What others in Congress and the state legislatures had in mind cannot be determined with any degree of certainty.

An additional reason for the inconclusive nature of the Amendment's history, with respect to segregated schools, is the status of public education at that time. In the South, the movement toward free common schools, supported by general taxation, had not yet taken hold. Education of white children was largely in the hands of private groups. Education of Negroes was almost nonexistent, and practically all of the race were illiterate. In fact, any education of Negroes was forbidden by law in some states. Today, in contrast, many Negroes have achieved outstanding success in the arts and sciences as well as in the business and professional world. It is true that public education had already advanced further in the North, but the effect of the Amendment on Northern States was generally ignored in the congressional debates. Even in the North, the conditions of public education did not approximate those existing today. The curriculum was rudimentary; ungraded schools were common in rural areas; the school term was but three months a year in many states; and compulsory school attendance was virtually unknown. As a consequence, it is not surprising that there should be so little in the history of the Fourteenth Amendment relating to its intended effect on public education.

In the first cases in this Court construing the Fourteenth Amendment, decided shortly after its adoption, the Court interpreted it as proscribing all state-imposed discriminations against the Negro race. The doctrine of "separate but equal" did not make its appearance in this Court until 1896 in the case of *Plessy v. Ferguson*, ... involving not education but transportation. American courts have since labored

(Continued)

with the doctrine for over half a century. In this Court, there have been six cases involving the "separate but equal" doctrine in the field of public education. In *Cumming v. County Board of Education* ... [1899] and *Gong hum v. Rice* ... [1927], the validity of the doctrine itself was not challenged. In more recent cases, all on the graduate school level, inequality was found in that specific benefits enjoyed by white students were denied to Negro students of the same educational qualifications.... In none of these cases was it necessary to reexamine the doctrine to grant relief to the Negro plaintiff. And in *Sweatt v. Painter* ... [1950], the Court expressly reserved decision on the question whether *Plessy v. Ferguson* should be held inapplicable to public education.

In the instant cases, that question is directly presented. Here, unlike *Sweatt v. Painter,* there are findings below that the Negro and white schools involved have been equalized, or are being equalized, with respect to buildings, curricula, qualifications and salaries of teachers, and other "tangible" factors. Our decision, therefore, cannot turn on merely a comparison of these tangible factors in the Negro and white schools involved in each of the cases. We must look instead to the effect of segregation itself on public education.

In approaching this problem, we cannot turn the clock back to 1868 when the Amendment was adopted, or even to 1896 when *Plessy v. Ferguson* was written. We must consider public education in the light of its full development and its present place in American life throughout the Nation. Only in this way can it be determined if segregation in public schools deprives these plaintiffs of the equal protection of the laws.

Today, education is perhaps the most important function of state and local governments. Compulsory school attendance laws and the great expenditures for education both demonstrate our recognition of the importance of education to our democratic society. It is required in the performance of our most basic public responsibilities, even service in the armed forces. It is the very foundation of good citizenship. Today it is a principal instrument in awakening the child to cultural values, in preparing him for later professional training, and in helping him to adjust normally to his environment. In these days, it is doubtful that any child may reasonably be expected to succeed in life if he is denied the opportunity of an education. Such an opportunity, where the state has undertaken to provide it, is a right which must be made available to all on equal terms.

We come then to the question presented: Does segregation of children in public schools solely on the basis of race, even though the physical facilities and other "tangible" factors may be equal, deprive the children of the minority group of equal educational opportunities? We believe that it does.

....To separate them from others of similar age and qualifications solely because of their race generates a feeling of inferiority as to their status in the community that may affect their hearts and minds in a way unlikely ever to be undone. The effect of this separation on their educational opportunities was well stated by a finding in the Kansas case by a court which nevertheless felt compelled to rule against the Negro plaintiffs.

Segregation of white and colored children in public schools has a detrimental effect upon the colored children. The impact is greater when it has the sanction of the law; for the policy of separating the races is usually interpreted as denoting the inferiority of the Negro group. A sense of inferiority affects the motivation of a child to learn. Segregation with the sanction of law, therefore, has a tendency to retard the educational and mental development of Negro children and to deprive them of some of the benefits they would receive in a racially integrated school system.

Whatever may have been the extent of psychological knowledge at the time of *Plessy v. Ferguson,* this finding is amply supported by modern authority. Any language in *Plessy v. Ferguson* contrary to this finding is rejected.

We conclude that in the field of public education the doctrine of "separate but equal" has no place. Separate educational facilities are inherently unequal. Therefore, we hold that the plaintiffs and others similarly situated for whom the actions have been brought are, by reason of the segregation complained of, deprived of the equal protection of the laws guaranteed by the Fourteenth Amendment. This disposition makes unnecessary any discussion whether such segregation also violates the Due Process Clause of the Fourteenth Amendment.

Because these are class actions, because of the wide applicability of this decision, and because of the great variety of local conditions, the formulation of decrees in these cases presents problems of considerable complexity. On reargument, the consideration of appropriate relief was necessarily subordinated to the primary question—the constitutionality of segregation in public education. We have now announced that such segregation is a denial of the equal protection of the laws. In order that we may have the full assistance of the parties in formulating decrees, the cases will be restored to the docket, and the parties are requested to present further argument....

BROWN v. BOARD OF EDUCATION OF TOPEKA II
349 U.S. 294; 75 S.Ct. 753; 99 L.Ed. 1083 (1955)
Vote: 9-0

Here, the Court considers how its holding in Brown I should be implemented by the lower federal courts.

Mr. Chief Justice Warren delivered the opinion of the Court.

These cases were decided on May 17, 1954. The opinions of that date, declaring the fundamental principle that racial discrimination in public education is unconstitutional, are incorporated herein by reference. All provisions of federal, state, or local law requiring or permitting such discrimination must yield to this principle. There remains for consideration the manner in which relief is to be accorded.

Because these cases arose under different local conditions and their disposition will involve a variety of local problems, we requested further argument on the question of relief. In view of the nationwide importance of the decision, we invited the Attorney General of the United States and the Attorneys General of all states requiring or permitting racial discrimination in public education to present their views on that question. The parties, the United States, and the States of Florida, North Carolina, Arkansas, Oklahoma, Maryland, and Texas filed briefs and participated in the oral argument.

These presentations were informative and helpful to the Court in its consideration of the complexities arising from the transition to a system of public education free of racial discrimination. The presentations also demonstrated that substantial steps to eliminate racial discrimination in public schools have already been taken, not only in some of the communities in which these cases arose, but in some of the states appearing as *amid curiae,* and in other states as well. Substantial progress has been made in the District of Columbia and in the communities in Kansas and Delaware involved in this litigation. The defendants in the cases coming to us from South Carolina and Virginia are awaiting the decision of this Court concerning relief.

Full implementation of these constitutional principles may require solution of varied local school problems. School authorities have the primary responsibility for elucidating, assessing, and solving these problems; courts will have to consider whether the action of school authorities constitutes good faith implementation of the governing constitutional principles. Because of their proximity to local conditions and the possible need for further hearings, the courts which originally heard these cases can best perform this judicial appraisal. Accordingly, we believe it appropriate to remand the cases to those courts.

In fashioning and effectuating the decrees, the courts will be guided by equitable principles. Traditionally, equity has been characterized by a practical flexibility in shaping its remedies and by a facility for adjusting and reconciling public and private needs. These cases call for the exercise of these traditional attributes of equity power. At stake is the personal interest of the plaintiffs in admission to public schools as soon as practicable on a nondiscriminatory basis. To effectuate this interest may call for elimination of a variety of obstacles in making the transition to school systems operated in accordance with the constitutional principles set forth in our May 17, 1954, decision. Courts of equity may properly take into account the public interest in the elimination of such obstacles in a systematic and effective manner. But it should go without saying that the vitality of these constitutional principles cannot be allowed to yield simply because of disagreement with them.

While giving weight to these public and private considerations, the courts will require that the defendants make a prompt and reasonable start toward full compliance with our May 17, 1954, ruling. Once such a start has been made, the courts may find that additional time is necessary to carry out the ruling in an effective manner. The burden rests upon the defendants to establish that such time is necessary in the public interest and is consistent with good faith compliance at the earliest practicable date. To that end, the courts may consider problems related to administration, arising from the physical condition of the school plant, the school transportation system, personnel, revision of school districts and attendance areas into compact units to achieve a system of determining admission to the public schools on a nonracial basis, and revision of local laws and regulations which may be necessary in solving the foregoing problems. They will also consider the adequacy of any plans the

(Continued)

defendants may propose to meet these problems and to effectuate a transition to a racially nondiscriminatory school system. During this period of transition, the courts will retain jurisdiction of these cases.

The judgments below, except that in the Delaware case, are accordingly reversed and remanded to the district courts to take such proceedings and enter such orders and decrees consistent with this opinion as are necessary and proper to admit to public schools on a racially nondiscriminatory basis with all deliberate speed the parties to these cases. The judgment in the Delaware case—ordering the immediate admission of the plaintiffs to schools previously attended only by white children—is affirmed on the basis of the principles stated in our May 17, 1954, opinion, but the case is remanded to the Supreme Court of Delaware for such further proceedings as that court may deem necessary in light of this opinion....

LOVING v. VIRGINIA
388 U.S. 1; 87 S.Ct. 1817; 18 L.Ed. 2d. 1010 (1967)
Vote: 9-0

Here, the Court reviews a Virginia law prohibiting interracial marriage.

Mr. Chief Justice Warren delivered the opinion of the Court.

This case presents a constitutional question never addressed by this Court: whether a statutory scheme adopted by the State of Virginia to prevent marriages between persons solely on the basis of racial classifications violates the ... Fourteenth Amendment. For reasons which seem to us to reflect the central meaning of those constitutional commands, we conclude that these statutes cannot stand consistently with the Fourteenth Amendment.

In June 1958, two residents of Virginia, Mildred Jeter, a Negro woman, and Richard Loving, a white man, were married in the District of Columbia pursuant to its laws. Shortly after their marriage, the Lovings returned to Virginia and established their marital abode in Caroline County. At the October Term, 1958, of the Circuit Court of Caroline County, a grand jury issued an indictment charging the Lovings with violating Virginia's ban on interracial marriages. On January 6, 1959, the Lovings pleaded guilty to the charge and were sentenced to one year in jail; however the trial judge suspended the sentence for a period of 25 years on the condition that the Lovings leave the State and not return to Virginia together for 25 years, stating that:

> Almighty God created the races white, black, yellow, malay, and red, and he placed them on separate continents. And but for the interference with his arrangements there would be no cause for such marriages. The fact that he separated the races shows that he did not intend for the races to mix.

After their convictions the Lovings took up residence in the District of Columbia. On November 6, 1963, they filed a motion in the state trial court to vacate the judgment and set aside the sentence on the ground that the statutes which they had violated were repugnant to the Fourteenth Amendment. The motion not having been decided by October 28, 1964, the Lovings instituted a class action in the United States District Court for the Eastern District of Virginia requesting that a three-judge court be convened to declare the Virginia antimiscegenation statutes unconstitutional and to enjoin state officials from enforcing their convictions. On January 22, 1965, the state trial judge denied the motion to vacate the sentences, and the Lovings perfected an appeal to the Supreme Court of Appeals of Virginia. On February 11, 1965, the three-judge District Court continued the case to allow the Lovings to present their constitutional claims to the highest state court.

The [Virginia] Supreme Court of Appeals upheld the constitutionality of the antimiscegenation statutes and, after modifying the sentence, affirmed the convictions. The Lovings appealed this decision, and we noted probable jurisdiction on December 12, 1966. ...

Virginia is now one of 16 States which prohibit and punish marriages on the basis of racial classifications. Penalties for miscegenation arose as an incident to slavery and have been common in Virginia since the colonial period. The present statutory scheme dates from the adoption of the Racial Integrity Act of 1924, passed during the period of extreme nativism which followed the end of the First World War. The central features of this Act, and current Virginia law, are the absolute prohibition of a "white person" marrying other than another "white person," a prohibition against issuing marriage licenses until the issuing official is satisfied that the applicants' statements as to their race are correct, certificates of "racial composition" to be kept by both local and state registrars, and the carrying forward of earlier prohibitions against racial intermarriage....

In upholding the constitutionality of these provisions in the decision below, the Supreme Court of Appeals of Virginia referred to its 1955 decision in *Nairn v. Nairn* ... as stating the reasons supporting the validity of these laws. In *Nairn,* the state court concluded that the State's legitimate purposes were "to preserve the racial integrity of its citizens," and to prevent "the corruption of blood," "a mongrel breed of citizens," and "the obliteration of racial pride," obviously an endorsement of the doctrine of White Supremacy.

The court also reasoned that marriage has traditionally been subject to state regulation without federal intervention, and, consequently, the regulation of marriage should be left to exclusive state control by the Tenth Amendment.

While the state court is no doubt correct in asserting that marriage is a social relation subject to the State's police power, ... the State does not contend in its argument before this Court that its powers to regulate marriage are unlimited notwithstanding the commands of the Fourteenth Amendment. Nor could it do so in light of *Meyer v. State of Nebraska* ... (1923) and *Skinner v. State of Oklahoma* ... (1942). Instead, the State argues that the meaning of the Equal Protection Clause, as illuminated by the statements of the Framers, is only that state penal laws containing an interracial element as part of the definition of the offense must apply equally to whites and Negroes in the sense that members of each race are punished to the same degree. Thus, the State contends that, because its miscegenation statutes punish equally both the white and the Negro participants in an interracial marriage, these statutes, despite their reliance on racial classifications do not constitute an invidious discrimination based upon race. The second argument advanced by the State assumes the validity of its equal application theory. The argument is that, if the Equal Protection Clause does not outlaw miscegenation statutes because of their reliance on racial

classifications, the question of constitutionality would thus become whether there was any rational basis for a State to treat interracial marriages differently from other marriages. On this question, the State argues, the scientific evidence is substantially in doubt and, consequently, this Court should defer to the wisdom of the state legislature in adopting its policy of discouraging interracial marriages.

Because we reject the notion that the mere "equal application" of a statute containing racial classification is enough to remove the classifications from the Fourteenth Amendment's proscription of all invidious racial discriminations, we do not accept the State's contention that these statutes should be upheld if there is any possible basis for concluding that they serve a rational purpose. The mere fact of equal application does not mean that our analysis of this statute should follow the approach we have taken in cases involving no racial discrimination where the Equal Protection Clause has been arrayed against a statute discriminating between the kinds of advertising which may be displayed on trucks in New York City, ... or an exemption in Ohio's *ad valorem* tax for merchandise owned by a non-resident in a storage warehouse.... In these cases, involving distinctions not drawn according to race, the Court has merely asked whether there is any rational foundation for the discriminations, and has deferred to the wisdom of the state legislatures. In the case at bar, however, we deal with statutes containing racial classifications, and the fact of equal application does not immunize the statute from the very heavy burden of justification which the Fourteenth Amendment has traditionally required of state statutes drawn according to race.

The State argues that statements in the Thirty-ninth Congress about the time of the passage of the Fourteenth Amendment indicate that the Framers did not intend the Amendment to make unconstitutional state miscegenation laws. Many of the statements alluded to by the State concern the debates over the Freemen's Bureau Bill, which President Johnson vetoed, and the Civil Rights Act of 1966 enacted over his veto. While these statements have some relevance to the intention of Congress in submitting the Fourteenth Amendment, it must be understood that they pertained to the passage of specific statutes and not to the broader, organic purpose of a constitutional amendment. As for the various statements directly concerning the Fourteenth Amendment, we have said in connection with a related problem, that although these historical sources "cast some light" they are not sufficient to resolve the

(Continued)

problem; "[a]t best, they are inconclusive. The most avid proponents of the post-War Amendments undoubtedly intended them to remove all legal distinctions among 'all persons born or naturalized in the United States.' Their opponents, just as certainly, were antagonistic to both the letter and the spirit of the Amendments and wished them to have the most limited effect." ... We have rejected the proposition that the debates in the Thirty-ninth Congress or in the state legislatures which ratified the Fourteenth Amendment supported the theory advanced by the State, that the requirement of equal protection of the laws is satisfied by penal laws defining offenses based on racial classifications so long as white and Negro participants in the offense were similarly punished....

There can be no question but that Virginia's miscegenation statutes rest solely upon distinctions drawn according to race. The statutes proscribe generally accepted conduct if engaged in by members of different races. Over the years, this Court has consistently repudiated "distinctions between citizens solely because of their ancestry" as being "odious to a free people whose institutions are founded upon the doctrine of equality." ... At the very least, the Equal Protection Clause demands that racial classifications, especially suspect in criminal statutes, be subjected to the "most rigid scrutiny," ... and, if they are ever to be upheld, they must be shown to be necessary to the accomplishment of some permissible state objective, independent of the racial discrimination which it was the object of the Fourteenth Amendment to eliminate. Indeed, two members of this Court have already stated that they "cannot conceive of a valid legislative purpose ... which makes the color of a person's skin the test of whether his conduct is a criminal offense."...

There is patently no legitimate overriding purpose independent of invidious racial discrimination which justifies this classification. The fact that Virginia only prohibits interracial marriages involving white persons demonstrates that the racial classifications must stand on their own justification, as measures designed to maintain White Supremacy. We have consistently denied the constitutionality of measures which restrict the rights of citizens on account of race. There can be no doubt that restricting the freedom to marry solely because of racial classification violates the central meaning of the Equal Protection Clause....

These convictions must be reversed. It is so ordered.

Mr. Justice Stewart, concurring....

SWANN v. CHARLOTTE-MECKLENBURG BOARD OF EDUCATION
402 U.S. 1; 91 S.Ct. 1267; 28 L.Ed. 2d. 554 (1971)
Vote: 9-0

In Charlotte-Mecklenburg, North Carolina, the nation's forty-third largest school district, the board of education devised a desegregation plan in order to comply with the Supreme Court's ruling in the Brown case. The U.S. district court, however, rejected the board's plan as not producing sufficient racial integration at the elementary level. Instead, the district court accepted a plan prepared by an outside expert that called for, among other things, racial quotas, alteration of attendance zones, and busing of students. In this case, the Supreme Court considers the permissibility of such measures.

Mr. Chief Justice Burger delivered the opinion of the Court.

... The central issue in this case is that of student assignment, and there are essentially four problem areas: (1) to what extent racial balance or racial quotas may be used as an implement in a remedial order to correct a previously segregated system; (2) whether every all-Negro and all-white school must be eliminated as an indispensable part of a remedial process of desegregation; (3) what are the limits, if any, on the rearrangement of school districts and attendance zones, as a remedial measure; and (4) what are the limits, if any, on the use of transportation facilities to correct state-enforced racial school segregation.

(1) Racial Balance or Racial Quotas.

The constant theme and thrust of every holding from *Brown I* (1954) to date is that state-enforced separation of races in public schools is discrimination that violates the Equal Protection clause. The remedy commanded was to dismantle dual school systems.

We are concerned in these cases with the elimination of the discrimination inherent in the dual school systems, not with myriad factors of human existence which can cause discrimination in a multitude of ways on racial, religious, or ethnic grounds. The target of the cases from *Brown I* to the present was the dual school system. The elimination of racial discrimination in public schools is a large task and one that should not be retarded by efforts to achieve broader purposes lying beyond the jurisdiction of school authorities. One vehicle can carry only a limited amount of baggage....

Our objective in dealing with the issues presented by these cases is to see that school authorities exclude no pupil or a racial minority from any school, directly or indirectly, on account of race; it does not and cannot embrace all the problems of racial prejudice, even when those problems contribute to disproportionate racial concentrations in some schools.

In this case it is urged that the District Court has imposed a racial balance requirement of 71%-29% on individual schools.... If we were to read the holding of the District Court to require, as a matter of substantive constitutional right, any particular degree of racial balance or mixing, that approach would be disapproved and we would be obliged to reverse. The constitutional command to desegregate schools does not mean that every school in every community must always reflect the racial composition of the school system as a whole....

... The use made of mathematical ratios was no more than a starting point in the process of shaping a remedy, rather than an inflexible requirement. From that starting point the District Court proceeded to frame a decree that was within its discretionary powers, an equitable remedy for the particular circumstances. As we said in *Green [v. County School Board* (1968)]*, a school authority's remedial plan or a district court's remedial decree is to be judged by its effectiveness. Awareness of the racial composition of the whole school system is likely to be a useful starting point in shaping a remedy to correct past constitutional violations. In sum, the very limited use made of mathematical ratios was within the equitable remedial discretion of the District Court.

(2) One-Race Schools.

The record in this case reveals the familiar phenomenon that in metropolitan areas minority groups are often found concentrated in one part of the city. In some circumstances certain schools may remain all or largely of one race until new schools can be provided or neighborhood patterns change. Schools all or predominately of

one race in a district of mixed population will require close scrutiny to determine that school assignments are not part of state-enforced segregation.

In light of the above, it should be clear that the existence of some small number of one-race, or virtually one-race, schools within a district is not in and of itself the mark of a system which still practices segregation by law.... Where the school authority's proposed plan for conversion from a dual to a unitary system contemplates the continued existence of some schools that are all or predominately of one race, they have the burden of showing that such school assignments are genuinely nondiscriminatory. The court should scrutinize such schools, and the burden upon the school authorities will be to satisfy the court that their racial composition is not the result of present or past discriminatory action on their part.

An optional minority-to-minority transfer provision has long been recognized as a useful part of every desegregation plan. Provision for optional transfer of those in the majority racial group of a particular school to other schools where they will be in the minority is an indispensable remedy for those students willing to transfer to other schools in order to lessen the impact on them of the state-imposed stigma of segregation. In order to be effective, such a transfer arrangement must grant the transferring student free transportation and space must be made available in the school to which he desires to move....

(3) Remedial Altering of Attendance Zones.

The maps submitted in these cases graphically demonstrate that one of the principal tools employed by school planners and by courts to break up the dual school system has been a frank—and sometimes drastic—gerrymandering of school districts and attendance zones. An additional step was "pairing," "clustering," or "grouping" of schools with attendance assignments made deliberately to accomplish the transfer of Negro students out of formerly segregated Negro schools and transfer of white students to formerly all-Negro schools. More often than not, these zones are neither compact nor contiguous; indeed they may be on opposite ends of the city. As an interim corrective measure, this cannot be said to be beyond the broad remedial powers of a court.

Absent a constitutional violation there would be no basis for judicially ordering assignment of students on a racial basis. All things being equal, with no history of discrimination, it might well be desirable to assign pupils to schools nearest their homes. But all things

(Continued)

are not equal in a system that has been deliberately constructed and maintained to enforce racial segregation....

No fixed or even substantially fixed guidelines can be established as to how far a court can go, but it must be recognized that there are limits. The objective is to dismantle the dual school system. "Racially neutral" assignment plans proposed by school authorities to a district court may be inadequate; such plans may fail to counteract the continuing effects of past school segregation resulting from discriminatory location of school sites or distortion of school size in order to achieve or maintain an artificial racial separation. When school authorities present a district court with a "loaded game board," affirmative action in the form of remedial altering of attendance zones is proper to achieve truly nondiscriminatory assignments. In short, an assignment plan is not acceptable simply because it appears to be neutral....

We hold that the pairing and grouping of noncontiguous school zones is a permissible tool and such action is to be considered in light of the objectives sought....

(4) Transportation of Students.

The scope of permissible transportation of students as an implement of a remedial decree has never been defined by this Court and by the very nature of the problem it cannot be defined with precision....

The importance of bus transportation as a normal and accepted tool of educational policy is readily discernible in this and the companion case. The Charlotte school authorities did not purport to assign students on the basis of geographically drawn zones until 1965 and then they allowed almost unlimited transfer privileges. The District Court's conclusion that assignment of children to the school nearest their home serving their grade would not produce an effective dismantling of the dual system is supported by the record.

Thus the remedial techniques used in the District Court's order were within that court's power to provide equitable relief; implementation of the decree is well within the capacity of the school authority.

The decree provided that the buses used to implement the plan would operate on direct routes. Students would be picked up at schools near their homes and transported to the schools they were to attend. The trips for elementary school pupils average about seven miles and the District Court found that they would take "not over 35 minutes at the most." This system compares favorably with the transportation plan previously operated in Charlotte under which each day 23,600 students on all grade levels were transported an average of 15 miles one way for an average trip requiring over an hour. In these circumstances, we find no basis for holding that the local school authorities may not be required to employ bus transportation as one tool of school desegregation. Desegregation plans cannot be limited to the walk-in school....

... At some point, these school authorities and others like them should have achieved full compliance with this Court's decision in *Brown I*. The systems will then be "unitary" in the sense required by our decisions in *Green [v. County School Board]* and *Alexander [v. Holmes County Board of Education]*.

It does not follow that the communities served by such systems will remain demographically stable, for in a growing, mobile society, few will do so. Neither school authorities nor district courts are constitutionally required to make year-by-year adjustments of the racial composition of student bodies once the affirmative duty to desegregate has been accomplished and racial discrimination through official action is eliminated from the system. This does not mean that federal courts are without power to deal with future problems; but in the absence of a showing that either the school authorities or some other agency of the State has deliberately attempted to fix or alter demographic patterns to affect the racial composition of the schools, further intervention by a district court should not be necessary....

PARENTS INVOLVED IN COMMUNITY SCHOOLS v. SEATTLE SCHOOL DISTRICT NO. 1
557 U.S. 701; 123 S.Ct. 2325,156 I.Ed.2d. 304 (2007)
Vote: 5-4

Here the Court considers whether school districts in Seattle, Washington, and Louisville, Kentucky, may, on their own volition, use race as a basis for assigning students to public schools. In dissent, Justice Breyer *refers to Chief Justice Roberts's opinion as a plurality opinion. That is because Justice Kennedy did not join all of Roberts's opinion. In our excerpt of this extremely long decision, we have excerpted only the portions of*

Roberts's opinion that can be characterized as the majority opinion.

Chief Justice Roberts ... delivered the opinion of the Court ...

The school districts in these cases voluntarily adopted student assignment plans that rely upon race to determine which public schools certain children may attend. The Seattle school district classifies children as white or nonwhite; the Jefferson County school district as black or "other." In Seattle, this racial classification is used to allocate slots in oversubscribed high schools. In Jefferson County, it is used to make certain elementary school assignments and to rule on transfer requests. In each case, the school district relies upon an individual student's race in assigning that student to a particular school, so that the racial balance at the school falls within a predetermined range based on the racial composition of the school district as a whole. Parents of students denied assignment to particular schools under these plans solely because of their race brought suit, contending that allocating children to different public schools on the basis of race violated the Fourteenth Amendment guarantee of equal protection. The Courts of Appeals below upheld the plans. We granted certiorari, and now reverse.

Both cases present the same underlying legal question—whether a public school that had not operated legally segregated schools or has been found to be unitary may choose to classify students by race and rely upon that classification in making school assignments....

It is well established that when the government distributes burdens or benefits on the basis of individual racial classifications, that action is reviewed under strict scrutiny.... In order to satisfy this searching standard of review, the school districts must demonstrate that the use of individual racial classifications in the assignment plans here under review is "narrowly tailored" to achieve a "compelling" government interest....

Without attempting in these cases to set forth all the interests a school district might assert, it suffices to note that our prior cases, in evaluating the use of racial classifications in the school context, have recognized two interests that qualify as compelling. The first is the compelling interest of remedying the effects of past intentional discrimination.... Yet the Seattle public schools have not shown that they were ever segregated by law, and were not subject to court-ordered desegregation decrees. The Jefferson County public schools were previously segregated by law and were subject to a desegregation decree entered in 1975. In 2000, the District Court that entered that decree dissolved it, finding that Jefferson County had "eliminated the vestiges associated with the former policy of segregation and its pernicious effects," and thus had achieved "unitary" status.... Jefferson County accordingly does not rely upon an interest in remedying the effects of past intentional discrimination in defending its present use of race in assigning students....

Nor could it. We have emphasized that the harm being remedied by mandatory desegregation plans is the harm that is traceable to segregation, and that "the Constitution is not violated by racial imbalance in the schools, without more." ... Once Jefferson County achieved unitary status, it had remedied the constitutional wrong that allowed race-based assignments. Any continued use of race must be justified on some other basis.

The second government interest we have recognized as compelling for purposes of strict scrutiny is the interest in diversity in higher education upheld in *Grutter [v. Bollinger* (2003)]. The specific interest found compelling in *Grutter* was student body diversity "in the context of higher education." ... The diversity interest was not focused on race alone but encompassed "all factors that may contribute to student body diversity." ...

... [T]he plans here employ only a limited notion of diversity, viewing race exclusively in white/nonwhite terms in Seattle and black/"other" terms in Jefferson County.... The Seattle "Board Statement Reaffirming Diversity Rationale" speaks of the "inherent educational value" in "providing students the opportunity to attend schools with diverse student enrollment."... But under the Seattle plan, a school with 50 percent Asian-American students and 50 percent white students but no African-American, Native-American, or Latino students would qualify as balanced, while a school with 30 percent Asian-American, 25 percent African-American, 25 percent Latino, and 20 percent white students would not. It is hard to understand how a plan that could allow these results can be viewed as being concerned with achieving enrollment that is "broadly diverse." ...

... In *Brown v. Board of Education* ... (1954) we held that segregation deprived black children of equal educational opportunities regardless of whether school facilities and other tangible factors were equal, because government classification and separation on grounds

(Continued)

of race themselves denoted inferiority.... It was not the inequality of the facilities but the fact of legally separating children on the basis of race on which the Court relied to find a constitutional violation in 1954.... The next Term, we accordingly stated that "full compliance" with *Brown I* required school districts "to achieve a system of determining admission to the public schools *on a nonracial basis.*" ...

The parties and their *amid* debate which side is more faithful to the heritage of *Brown,* but the position of the plaintiffs in *Brown* was spelled out in their brief and could not have been clearer: "[T]he Fourteenth Amendment prevents states from according differential treatment to American children on the basis of their color or race." ... What do the racial classifications at issue here do, if not accord differential treatment on the basis of race? As counsel who appeared before this Court for the plaintiffs in *Brown* put it: "We have one fundamental contention which we will seek to develop in the course of this argument, and that contention is that no State has any authority under the equal-protection clause of the Fourteenth Amendment to use race as a factor in affording educational opportunities among its citizens." ... What do the racial classifications do in these cases, if not determine admission to a public school on a racial basis? Before *Brown,* schoolchildren were told where they could and could not go to school based on the color of their skin. The school districts in these cases have not carried the heavy burden of demonstrating that we should allow this once again—even for very different reasons. For schools that never segregated on the basis of race, such as Seattle, or that have removed the vestiges of past segregation, such as Jefferson County, the way "to achieve a system of determining admission to the public schools on a non-racial basis," ... is to stop assigning students on a racial basis. The way to stop discrimination on the basis of race is to stop discriminating on the basis of race.

The judgments of the Courts of Appeals for the Sixth and Ninth Circuits are reversed, and the cases are remanded for further proceedings.

Justice Thomas, concurring.

Today, the Court holds that state entities may not experiment with race-based means to achieve ends they deem socially desirable. I wholly concur in The Chief Justice's opinion.... Contrary to the dissent's arguments, resegregation is not occurring in Seattle or Louisville; these school boards have no present interest in remedying past segregation; and these race-based student-assignment programs do not serve any compelling state interest. Accordingly, the plans are unconstitutional. Disfavoring a color-blind interpretation of the Constitution, the dissent would give school boards a free hand to make decisions on the basis of race—an approach reminiscent of that advocated by the segregationists in *Brown v. Board of Education* ... (1954). This approach is just as wrong today as it was a half-century ago. The Constitution and our cases require us to be much more demanding before permitting local school boards to make decisions based on race.

Justice Kennedy, concurring in part and concurring in the judgment....

Justice Breyer, with whom   Justice Stevens, Justice Souter, and Justice Ginsburg join, dissenting.

These cases consider the longstanding efforts of two local school boards to integrate their public schools. The school board plans before us resemble many others adopted in the last 50 years by primary and secondary schools throughout the Nation. All of those plans represent local efforts to bring about the kind of racially integrated education that *Brown v. Board of Education* ... (1954), long ago promised—efforts that this Court has repeatedly required, permitted, and encouraged local authorities to undertake. This Court has recognized that the public interests at stake in such cases are "compelling." We have approved of "narrowly tailored" plans that are no less race-conscious than the plans before us. And we have understood that the Constitution *permits* local communities to adopt desegregation plans even where it does not *require* them to do so.

The plurality pays inadequate attention to this law, to past opinions' rationales, their language, and the contexts in which they arise. As a result, it reverses course and reaches the wrong conclusion. In doing so, it distorts precedent, it misapplies the relevant constitutional principles, it announces legal rules that will obstruct efforts by state and local governments to deal effectively with the growing resegregation of public schools, it threatens to substitute for present calm a disruptive round of race-related litigation, and it undermines *Browns* promise of integrated primary and secondary education that local communities have sought to make a reality. This cannot be justified in the name of the Equal Protection Clause....

Justice Stevens, dissenting....

GRUTTER v. BOLLINGER
539 U.S. 306; 123 S.Ct. 2325; 156 L.Ed. 2d. 304 (2003)
Vote: 5-4

In this case, the Court considers the constitutionality of an affirmative action program designed to enhance the diversity of the student body at the University of Michigan law school. The program was challenged by Barbara Grutter, a white female who was denied admission to the law school.

Justice O'Connor delivered the opinion of the Court.

... The [University of Michigan] Law School ranks among the Nation's top law schools. It receives more than 3,500 applications each year for a class of around 350 students. Seeking to "admit a group of students who individually and collectively are among the most capable," the Law School looks for individuals with "substantial promise for success in law school" and "a strong likelihood of succeeding in the practice of law and contributing in diverse ways to the well-being of others." More broadly, the Law School seeks "a mix of students with varying backgrounds and experiences who will respect and learn from each other." In 1992, the dean of the Law School charged a faculty committee with crafting a written admissions policy to implement these goals. In particular, the Law School sought to ensure that its efforts to achieve student body diversity complied with this Court's most recent ruling on the use of race in university admissions. See *Regents of Univ. of Cal. v. Bakke* ... (1978). Upon the unanimous adoption of the committee's report by the Law School faculty, it became the Law School's official admissions policy....

The policy aspires to "achieve that diversity which has the potential to enrich everyone's education and thus make a law school class stronger than the sum of its parts." The policy does not restrict the types of diversity contributions eligible for "substantial weight" in the admissions process, but instead recognizes "many possible bases for diversity admissions." The policy does, however, reaffirm the Law School's long-standing commitment to "one particular type of diversity," that is, "racial and ethnic diversity with special reference to the inclusion of students from groups which have been historically discriminated against, like African-Americans, Hispanics and Native Americans, who without this commitment might not be represented in our student body in meaningful numbers." By enrolling a "'critical mass' of [underrepresented] minority students," the Law School seeks to "ensur[e] their ability to make unique contributions to the character of the Law School."

The policy does not define diversity "solely in terms of racial and ethnic status." Nor is the policy "insensitive to the competition among all students for admission to the [L]aw [S]chool." Rather, the policy seeks to guide admissions officers in "producing classes both diverse and academically outstanding, classes made up of students who promise to continue the tradition of outstanding contribution by Michigan Graduates to the legal profession." ...

Petitioner Barbara Grutter is a white Michigan resident who applied to the Law School in 1996 with a 3.8 GPA and 161 LSAT score. The Law School initially placed petitioner on a waiting list, but subsequently rejected her application. In December 1997, petitioner filed suit in the United States District Court for the Eastern District of Michigan ... alleging that respondents discriminated against her on the basis of race in violation of the Fourteenth Amendment; Title VI of the Civil Rights Act of 1964.

Petitioner further alleged that her application was rejected because the Law School uses race as a "predominant" factor, giving applicants who belong to certain minority groups "a significantly greater chance of admission than students with similar credentials from disfavored racial groups." ... Petitioner also alleged that respondents "had no compelling interest to justify their use of race in the admissions process." Petitioner requested compensatory and punitive damages, an order requiring the Law School to offer her admission, and an injunction prohibiting the Law School from continuing to discriminate on the basis of race. Petitioner clearly has standing to bring this lawsuit....

During the 15-day bench trial, the parties introduced extensive evidence concerning the Law School's use of race in the admissions process. Dennis Shields, Director of Admissions when petitioner applied to the Law School, testified that he did not direct his staff to admit a particular percentage or number of minority students, but rather to consider an applicant's race along with all other factors....

(Continued)

[T]he District Court concluded that the Law School's use of race as a factor in admissions decisions was unlawful. Applying strict scrutiny, the District Court determined that the Law School's asserted interest in assembling a diverse student body was not compelling because "the attainment of a racially diverse class ... was not recognized as such by *Bakke* and it is not a remedy for past discrimination." The District Court went on to hold that even if diversity were compelling, the Law School had not narrowly tailored its use of race to further that interest....

Sitting en banc, the Court of Appeals reversed the District Court's judgment and vacated the injunction....

We granted certiorari to resolve the disagreement among the Courts of Appeals on a question of national importance: Whether diversity is a compelling interest that can justify the narrowly tailored use of race in selecting applicants for admission to public universities....

We last addressed the use of race in public higher education over 25 years ago. In the landmark *Bakke* case, we reviewed a racial set-aside program that reserved 16 out of 100 seats in a medical school class for members of certain minority groups. The decision produced six separate opinions, none of which commanded a majority of the Court.... The only holding for the Court in *Bakke* was that a "State has a substantial interest that legitimately may be served by a properly devised admissions program involving the competitive consideration of race and ethnic origin." ...

Since this Court's splintered decision in *Bakke*, Justice Powell's opinion announcing the judgment of the Court has served as the touchstone for constitutional analysis of race-conscious admissions policies. Public and private universities across the Nation have modeled their own admissions programs on Justice Powell's views on permissible race-conscious policies....

We have held that all racial classifications imposed by government "must be analyzed by a reviewing court under strict scrutiny." This means that such classifications are constitutional only if they are narrowly tailored to further compelling governmental interests. "Absent searching judicial inquiry into the justification for such race-based measures," we have no way to determine what "classifications are 'benign' or 'remedial' and what classifications are in fact motivated by illegitimate notions of racial inferiority or simple racial politics." We apply strict scrutiny to all racial classifications to "'smoke out' illegitimate uses of race by assuring that [government] is pursuing a goal important enough to warrant use of a highly suspect tool." ...

Not every decision influenced by race is equally objectionable, and strict scrutiny is designed to provide a framework for carefully examining the importance and the sincerity of the reasons advanced by the governmental decisionmaker for the use of race in that particular context....

With these principles in mind, we turn to the question whether the Law School's use of race is justified by a compelling state interest. Before this Court, as they have throughout this litigation, respondents assert only one justification for their use of race in the admissions process: obtaining "the educational benefits that flow from a diverse student body." In other words, the Law School asks us to recognize, in the context of higher education, a compelling state interest in student body diversity....

As part of its goal of "assembling a class that is both exceptionally academically qualified and broadly diverse," the Law School seeks to "enroll a 'critical mass' of minority students." The Law School's interest is not simply "to assure within its student body some specified percentage of a particular group merely because of its race or ethnic origin." That would amount to outright racial balancing, which is patently unconstitutional. Rather, the Law School's concept of critical mass is defined by reference to the educational benefits that diversity is designed to produce.

These benefits are substantial. As the District Court emphasized, the Law School's admissions policy promotes "cross-racial understanding," helps to break down racial stereotypes, and "enables [students] to better understand persons of different races." These benefits are "important and laudable," because "classroom discussion is livelier, more spirited, and simply more enlightening and interesting" when the students have "the greatest possible variety of backgrounds." ...

In order to cultivate a set of leaders with legitimacy in the eyes of the citizenry, it is necessary that the path to leadership be visibly open to talented and qualified individuals of every race and ethnicity. All members of our heterogeneous society must have confidence in the openness and integrity of the educational institutions that provide this training. As we have recognized, law schools "cannot be effective in isolation from the individuals and institutions with which the law interacts." Access to legal education (and thus the legal profession) must be inclusive of talented and qualified individuals of every race and ethnicity, so that all members of our heterogeneous society may participate in the educational institutions that provide the training and education necessary to succeed in America.

The Law School does not premise its need for critical mass on "any belief that minority students always (or even consistently) express some characteristic minority viewpoint on any issue." To the contrary, diminishing the force of such stereotypes is both a crucial part of the Law School's mission, and one that it cannot accomplish with only token numbers of minority students. Just as growing up in a particular region or having particular professional experiences is likely to affect an individual's views, so too is one's own, unique experience of being a racial minority in a society, like our own, in which race unfortunately still matters. The Law School has determined, based on its experience and expertise, that a "critical mass" of underrepresented minorities is necessary to further its compelling interest in securing the educational benefits of a diverse student body.

Even in the limited circumstance when drawing racial distinctions is permissible to further a compelling state interest, government is still "constrained in how it may pursue that end: [T]he means chosen to accomplish the [government's] asserted purpose must be specifically and narrowly framed to accomplish that purpose." The purpose of the narrow tailoring requirement is to ensure that "the means chosen 'fit' th[e] compelling goal so closely that there is little or no possibility that the motive for the classification was illegitimate racial prejudice or stereotype." ...

To be narrowly tailored, a race-conscious admissions program cannot use a quota system—it cannot "insulat[e] each category of applicants with certain desired qualifications from competition with all other applicants." Instead, a university may consider race or ethnicity only as a "'plus' in a particular applicant's file," without "insulat[ing] the individual from comparison with all other candidates for the available seats." In other words, an admissions program must be "flexible enough to consider all pertinent elements of diversity in light of the particular qualifications of each applicant, and to place them on the same footing for consideration, although not necessarily according them the same weight."

We find that the Law School's admissions program bears the hallmarks of a narrowly tailored plan....

We are satisfied that the Law School's admissions program ... does not operate as a quota. Properly understood, a "quota" is a program in which a certain fixed number or proportion of opportunities are "reserved exclusively for certain minority groups." Quotas "impose a fixed number or percentage which

must be attained, or which cannot be exceeded," and "insulate the individual from comparison with all other candidates for the available seats." In contrast, "a permissible goal ... require[s] only a good-faith effort ... to come within a range demarcated by the goal itself," and permits consideration of race as a "plus" factor in any given case while still ensuring that each candidate "compete[s] with all other qualified applicants." ...

The Law School's goal of attaining a critical mass of underrepresented minority students does not transform its program into a quota. As ... Justice Powell recognized, there is of course "some relationship between numbers and achieving the benefits to be derived from a diverse student body, and between numbers and providing a reasonable environment for those students admitted." "[S]ome attention to numbers," without more, does not transform a flexible admissions system into a rigid quota....

That a race-conscious admissions program does not operate as a quota does not, by itself, satisfy the requirement of individualized consideration. When using race as a "plus" factor in university admissions, a university's admissions program must remain flexible enough to ensure that each applicant is evaluated as an individual and not in a way that makes an applicant's race or ethnicity the defining feature of his or her application. The importance of this individualized consideration in the context of a race-conscious admissions program is paramount.

Here, the Law School engages in a highly individualized, holistic review of each applicant's file, giving serious consideration to all the ways an applicant might contribute to a diverse educational environment. The Law School affords this individualized consideration to applicants of all races. There is no policy, either de jure or de facto, of automatic acceptance or rejection based on any single "soft" variable. Unlike the program at issue in *Gratz v. Bollinger*, the Law School awards no mechanical, predetermined diversity "bonuses" based on race or ethnicity.... [T]he Law School's admissions policy "is flexible enough to consider all pertinent elements of diversity in light of the particular qualifications of each applicant, and to place them on the same footing for consideration, although not necessarily according them the same weight."

We also find that ... the Law School's race-conscious admissions program adequately ensures that all factors that may contribute to student body diversity are meaningfully considered alongside race in admissions decisions. With respect to the use of race itself, all

(Continued)

underrepresented minority students admitted by the Law School have been deemed qualified. By virtue of our Nation's struggle with racial inequality, such students are both likely to have experiences of particular importance to the Law School's mission, and less likely to be admitted in meaningful numbers on criteria that ignore those experiences.

The Law School does not, however, limit in any way the broad range of qualities and experiences that may be considered valuable contributions to student body diversity. To the contrary, the 1992 policy makes clear "[t]here are many possible bases for diversity admissions," and provides examples of admittees who have lived or traveled widely abroad, are fluent in several languages, have overcome personal adversity and family hardship, have exceptional records of extensive community service, and have had successful careers in other fields. The Law School seriously considers each "applicant's promise of making a notable contribution to the class by way of a particular strength, attainment, or characteristic—e.g., an unusual intellectual achievement, employment experience, nonacademic performance, or personal background." All applicants have the opportunity to highlight their own potential diversity contributions through the submission of a personal statement, letters of recommendation, and an essay describing the ways in which the applicant will contribute to the life and diversity of the Law School.

What is more, the Law School actually gives substantial weight to diversity factors besides race. The Law School frequently accepts nonminority applicants with grades and test scores lower than underrepresented minority applicants (and other nonminority applicants) who are rejected. This shows that the Law School seriously weighs many other diversity factors besides race that can make a real and dispositive difference for nonminority applicants as well. By this flexible approach, the Law School sufficiently takes into account, in practice as well as in theory, a wide variety of characteristics besides race and ethnicity that contribute to a diverse student body. ...

... Because the Law School considers "all pertinent elements of diversity," it can (and does) select nonminority applicants who have greater potential to enhance student body diversity over underrepresented minority applicants. As Justice Powell recognized in *Bakke*, so long as a race-conscious admissions program uses race as a "plus" factor in the context of individualized consideration, a rejected applicant "will not have been foreclosed from all consideration for that seat simply because he was not the right color or had the wrong surname.... His qualifications would have been weighed fairly and competitively, and he would have no basis to complain of unequal treatment under the Fourteenth Amendment." ...

We are mindful, however, that "[a] core purpose of the Fourteenth Amendment was to do away with all governmentally imposed discrimination based on race." Accordingly, race-conscious admissions policies must be limited in time. This requirement reflects that racial classifications, however compelling their goals, are potentially so dangerous that they may be employed no more broadly than the interest demands. Enshrining a permanent justification for racial preferences would offend this fundamental equal protection principle. We see no reason to exempt race-conscious admissions programs from the requirement that all governmental use of race must have a logical end point. The Law School, too, concedes that all "race-conscious programs must have reasonable durational limits." ...

We take the Law School at its word that it would "like nothing better than to find a race-neutral admissions formula" and will terminate its race-conscious admissions program as soon as practicable. It has been 25 years since Justice Powell first approved the use of race to further an interest in student body diversity in the context of public higher education. Since that time, the number of minority applicants with high grades and test scores has indeed increased. We expect that 25 years from now, the use of racial preferences will no longer be necessary to further the interest approved today....

Justice Ginsburg, with whom *Justice Breyer* joins, concurring. ...

Justice Scalia, with whom *Justice Thomas* joins, concurring in part and dissenting in part. ...

Justice Thomas, with whom *Justice Scalia* joins, concurring in part and dissenting in part.

Frederick Douglass, speaking to a group of abolitionists almost 140 years ago, delivered a message lost on today's majority:

> ... *[I]n regard to the colored people, there is always more that is benevolent, I perceive, than just, manifested towards us. What I ask for the negro is not benevolence, not pity, not sympathy, but simply*

justice. The American people have always been anxious to know what they shall do with us.... I have had but one answer from the beginning. Do nothing with us! Your doing with us has already played the mischief with us. Do nothing with us! If the apples will not remain on the tree of their own strength, if they are worm-eaten at the core, if they are early ripe and disposed to fall, let them fall! ... And if the negro cannot stand on his own legs, let him fall also. All I ask is, give him a chance to stand on his own legs! Let him alone! ... [Y]our interference is doing him positive injury.

Like Douglass, I believe blacks can achieve in every avenue of American life without the meddling of university administrators. Because I wish to see all students succeed whatever their color, I share, in some respect, the sympathies of those who sponsor the type of discrimination advanced by the University of Michigan Law School (Law School). The Constitution does not, however, tolerate institutional devotion to the status quo in admissions policies when such devotion ripens into racial discrimination. Nor does the Constitution countenance the unprecedented deference the Court gives to the Law School, an approach inconsistent with the very concept of "strict scrutiny." ...

The majority upholds the Law School's racial discrimination not by interpreting the people's Constitution, but by responding to a faddish slogan of the cognoscenti. Nevertheless, I concur in part in the Court's opinion. First, I agree with the Court insofar as its decision, which approves of only one racial classification, confirms that further use of race in admissions remains unlawful. Second, I agree with the Court's holding that racial discrimination in higher education admissions will be illegal in 25 years. I respectfully dissent from the remainder of the Court's opinion and the judgment, however, because I believe that the Law School's current use of race violates the Equal Protection Clause and that the Constitution means the same thing today as it will in 300 months....

The Constitution abhors classifications based on race, not only because those classifications can harm favored races or are based on illegitimate motives, but also because every time the government places citizens on racial registers and makes race relevant to the provision of burdens or benefits, it demeans us all. "Purchased at the price of immeasurable human suffering, the equal protection principle reflects our Nation's understanding that such classifications ultimately have a destructive impact on the individual and our society."...

Justice Powell's opinion in *Bakke* and the Court's decision today rest on the fundamentally flawed proposition that racial discrimination can be contextualized so that a goal, such as classroom aesthetics, can be compelling in one context but not in another. This "we know it when we see it" approach to evaluating state interests is not capable of judicial application. Today, the Court insists on radically expanding the range of permissible uses of race to something as trivial (by comparison) as the assembling of a law school class. I can only presume that the majority's failure to justify its decision by reference to any principle arises from the absence of any such principle....

The interest in remaining elite and exclusive that the majority thinks so obviously critical requires the use of admissions "standards" that, in turn, create the Law School's "need" to discriminate on the basis of race. The Court validates these admissions standards by concluding that alternatives that would require "a dramatic sacrifice of ... the academic quality of all admitted students" need not be considered before racial discrimination can be employed. In the majority's view, such methods are not required by the "narrow tailoring" prong of strict scrutiny because that inquiry demands, in this context, that any race-neutral alternative work "about as well." The majority errs, however, because race-neutral alternatives must only be "workable" and do "about as well" in vindicating the compelling state interest. The Court never explicitly holds that the Law School's desire to retain the status quo in "academic selectivity" is itself a compelling state interest.... Therefore, the Law School should be forced to choose between its classroom aesthetic and its exclusionary admissions system—it cannot have it both ways....

Finally, the Court's disturbing reference to the importance of the country's law schools as training grounds meant to cultivate "a set of leaders with legitimacy in the eyes of the citizenry," through the use of racial discrimination deserves discussion. As noted earlier, the Court has soundly rejected the remedying of societal discrimination as a justification for governmental use of race. For those who believe that every racial disproportionality in our society is caused by some kind of racial discrimination, there can be no distinction between remedying societal discrimination and erasing racial disproportionalities in the country's leadership caste. And if the lack of proportional racial

(Continued)

representation among our leaders is not caused by societal discrimination, then "fixing" it is even less of a pressing public necessity.

The Court's civics lesson presents yet another example of judicial selection of a theory of political representation based on skin color—an endeavor I have previously rejected. The majority appears to believe that broader Utopian goals justify the Law School's use of race, but "[t]he Equal Protection Clause commands the elimination of racial barriers, not their creation in order to satisfy our theory as to how society ought to be organized."

As the foregoing makes clear, I believe the Court's opinion to be, in most respects, erroneous....

Chief Justice Rehnquist, with whom *Justice Scalia, Justice Kennedy,* and *Justice Thomas* join, dissenting.

I agree with the Court that, "in the limited circumstance when drawing racial distinctions is permissible," the government must ensure that its means are narrowly tailored to achieve a compelling state interest. I do not believe, however, that the University of Michigan Law School's means are narrowly tailored to the interest it asserts....

Respondents have never offered any race-specific arguments explaining why significantly more individuals from one underrepresented minority group are needed in order to achieve "critical mass" or further student body diversity. They certainly have not explained why Hispanics, who they have said are among "the groups most isolated by racial barriers in our country," should have their admission capped out in this manner. True, petitioner is neither Hispanic nor Native American. But the Law School's disparate admissions practices with respect to these minority groups demonstrate that its alleged goal of "critical mass" is simply a sham. Petitioner may use these statistics to expose this sham, which is the basis for the Law School's admission of less-qualified underrepresented minorities in preference to her. Surely strict scrutiny cannot permit these sorts of disparities without at least some explanation....

Finally, I believe that the Law School's program fails strict scrutiny because it is devoid of any reasonably precise time limit on the Law School's use of race in admissions....

Justice Kennedy, dissenting....

FRONTIERO v. RICHARDSON
411 U.S. 677; 93 S.Ct. 1764; 36 L.Ed. 2d. 583 (1973)
Vote: 8-1

In this landmark case, the Court considers the appropriate standard of equal protection review in cases alleging gender discrimination by the government.

Mr. Justice Brennan announced the judgment of the Court and an opinion in which *Mr. Justice Douglas, Mr. Justice White,* and *Mr. Justice Marshall* join.

The question before us concerns the right of a female member of the uniformed services to claim her spouse as a "dependent" for the purposes of obtaining increased quarters allowances and medical and dental benefits ... on an equal footing with male members. Under [the statutes at issue], a serviceman may claim his wife as a "dependent" without regard to whether she is in fact dependent upon him for any part of her support.

A servicewoman, on the other hand, may not claim her husband as a "dependent" under these programs unless he is in fact dependent upon her for over one-half of his support.... Thus, the question for decision is whether this difference in treatment constitutes an unconstitutional discrimination against service-women in violation of the [equal protection component] of the Fifth Amendment. A three-judge District Court for the Middle District of Alabama, one judge dissenting, rejected this contention and sustained the constitutionality of the provisions of the statutes making this distinction.... We noted probable jurisdiction .... We reverse....

In an effort to attract career personnel through reenlistment, Congress established ... a scheme for the provision of fringe benefits to members of the uniformed services on a competitive basis with business and industry.... [A] member of the uniformed services with dependents is entitled to an increased "basic allowance for quarters" and ... a member's dependents are provided comprehensive medical and dental care.

Appellant Sharron Frontiero, a lieutenant in the United States Air Force, sought increased quarters allowance, and housing and medical benefits for her husband, appellant Joseph Frontiero, on the ground that he was her "dependent." Although such benefits would automatically have been granted with respect to the wife of a male member of the uniformed services, appellant's application was denied because she failed to demonstrate that her husband was dependent on her for more than one-half of his support.

Appellants then commenced this suit, contending that, by making this distinction, the statutes unreasonably discriminate on the basis of sex in violation of the Due Process Clause of the Fifth Amendment. In essence, appellants asserted that the discriminatory impact of the statutes is two-fold: first, as a procedural matter, a female member is required to demonstrate her spouse's dependency, while no such burden is imposed upon male members; and second, as a substantive matter, a male member who does not provide more than one-half of his wife's support receives benefits, while a similarly situated female member is denied such benefits. Appellants therefore sought a permanent injunction against the continued enforcement of these statutes and an order directing the appellees to provide Lieutenant Frontiero with the same housing and medical benefits that a similarly situated male member would receive.

Although the legislative history of these statutes sheds virtually no light on the purposes underlying the differential treatment accorded male and female members, a majority of the three-judge District Court surmised that Congress might reasonably have concluded that, since the husband in our society is generally the "breadwinner" in the family—and the wife typically the "dependent" partner—"it would be more economical to require married female members claiming husbands to prove actual dependency than to extend the presumption of dependency to such members." ... Indeed, given the fact that approximately 99% of all members of the uniformed services are male, the District Court speculated that such differential treatment might conceivably lead to a "considerable saving of administrative expense and manpower." ...

At the outset, appellants contend that classifications based upon sex, like classifications based upon race, alienage, and national origin, are inherently suspect and must therefore be subjected to close judicial scrutiny. We agree and, indeed, find at least implicit support for such an approach in our unanimous decision only last Term in *Reed v. Reed....*

In *Reed,* the Court considered the constitutionality of an Idaho statute providing that, when two individuals are otherwise equally entitled to appointment as administrator of an estate, the male applicant must be preferred to the female. Appellant, the mother of the deceased, and appellee, the father, filed competing petitions for appointment as administrator of their son's estate. Since the parties, as parents of the deceased, were members of the same entitlement class, the statutory preference was invoked and the father's petition was therefore granted. Appellant claimed that this statute, by giving a mandatory preference to males over females without regard to their individual qualifications, violated the Equal Protection Clause of the Fourteenth Amendment.

The Court noted that the Idaho statute "provides that different treatment be accorded to the applicants on the basis of their sex; it thus establishes a classification subject to scrutiny under the Equal Protection Clause." ... Under "traditional" equal protection analysis, a legislative classification must be sustained unless it is "patently arbitrary" and bears no rational relationship to a legitimate governmental interest....

In an effort to meet this standard, appellee contended that the statutory scheme was a reasonable measure designed to reduce the workload on probate courts by eliminating one class of contests. Moreover, appellee argued that the mandatory preference for male applicants was in itself reasonable since "men [are] as a rule more conversant with business affairs than ... women." Indeed, appellee maintained that "it is a matter of common knowledge, that women still are not engaged in politics, the professions, business or industry to the extent that men are." And the Idaho Supreme Court, in upholding the constitutionality of this statute, suggested that the Idaho Legislature might reasonably have "concluded that in general men are better qualified to act as an administrator than are women."

Despite these contentions, however, the Court held the statutory preference for male applicants unconstitutional. In reaching this result, the Court implicitly rejected appellee's apparently rational explanation

(Continued)

of the statutory scheme, and concluded that, by ignoring the individual qualifications of particular applicants, the challenged statute provided "dissimilar treatment for men and women who are ... similarly situated." ... The Court therefore held that, even though the State's interest in achieving administrative efficiency "is not without some legitimacy," ... "[t]o give a mandatory preference to members of either sex over members of the other, merely to accomplish the elimination of hearings on the merits, is to make the very kind of arbitrary legislative choice forbidden by the [Constitution]...."... This departure from "traditional" rational basis analysis with respect to sex-based classifications is clearly justified.

There can be no doubt that our Nation has had a long and unfortunate history of sex discrimination. Traditionally, such discrimination was rationalized by an attitude of "romantic paternalism" which, in practical effect, put women not on a pedestal, but in a cage. Indeed, this paternalistic attitude became so firmly rooted in our national consciousness that, exactly 100 years ago, a distinguished member of this Court was about to proclaim:

> Man is, or should be, woman's protector and defender. The natural and proper timidity and delicacy which belongs to the female sex evidently unfits it for many of the occupations of civil life. The constitution of the family organizations, which is founded in the divine ordinance, as well as in the nature of things, indicates the domestic sphere as that which properly belongs to the domain and functions of womanhood. The harmony, not to say identity, of interests and views which belong or should belong, to the family institution is repugnant to the ideas of a woman adopting a distinct and independent career from that of her husband.... The paramount destiny and mission of woman are to fulfill the noble and benign offices of wife and mother. This is the law of the Creator....

As a result of notions such as these, our statute books gradually became laden with gross, stereotypical distinctions between the sexes and, indeed, throughout much of the 19th century the position of women in our society was, in many respects, comparable to that of blacks under the pre–Civil War slave codes. Neither slaves nor women could hold office, serve on juries, or bring suit in their own names, and married women traditionally were denied the legal capacity to hold or convey property or to serve as legal guardians of their own children.... And although blacks were

guaranteed the right to vote in 1870, women were denied even that right—which is itself "preservative of other basic civil and political rights"—until adoption of the Nineteenth Amendment half a century later.

It is true, of course, that the position of women in America has improved markedly in recent decades. Nevertheless, it can hardly be doubted that, in part because of the high visibility of the sex characteristic, women still face pervasive, although at times more subtle, discrimination in our educational institutions, on the job market and, perhaps most conspicuously, in the political arena....

Moreover, since sex, like race and national origin, is an immutable characteristic determined solely by the accident of birth, the imposition of special disabilities upon the members of a particular sex because of their sex would seem to violate "the basic concept of our system that legal burdens should bear some relationship to individual responsibility...." ... And what differentiates sex from such nonsuspect statuses as intelligence or physical disability, and aligns it with the recognized suspect criteria, is that the sex characteristic frequently bears no relation to ability to perform or contribute to society. As a result, statutory distinctions between the sexes often have the effect of invidiously relegating the entire class of females to inferior legal status without regard to the actual capabilities of its individual members.

We might also note that, over the past decade, Congress has itself manifested an increasing sensitivity to sex-based classifications. In Title VII of the Civil Rights Act of 1964, for example, Congress expressly declared that no employer, labor union, or other organization subject to the provisions of the Act shall discriminate against any individual on the basis of "race, color, religion, sex, or national origin." Similarly, the Equal Pay Act of 1963 provides that no employer covered by the Act "shall discriminate ... between employees on the basis of sex." And Section 1 of the Equal Rights Amendment, passed by Congress on March 22, 1972, and submitted to the legislatures of the States for ratification, declares that "[e] quality of rights under the law shall not be denied or abridged by the United States or by any State on account of sex." Thus, Congress has itself concluded that classifications based upon sex are inherently invidious, and this conclusion of a coequal branch of government is not without significance to the question presently under consideration....

With these considerations in mind, we can only conclude that classifications based upon sex, like classifications based upon race, alienage, or national origin, are inherently suspect, and must therefore be subjected to strict judicial scrutiny. Applying the analysis mandated by that stricter standard of review, it is clear that the statutory scheme now before us is constitutionally invalid.

The sole basis of the classification established in the challenged statutes is the sex of the individuals involved. Thus ... a female member of the uniformed services seeking to obtain housing and medical benefits for her spouse must prove his dependency in fact, whereas no such burden is imposed upon male members. In addition, the statutes operate so as to deny benefits to a female member, such as appellant Sharron Frontiero, who provides less than one-half of her spouse's support, while at the same time granting such benefits to a male member who likewise provides less than one-half of his spouse's support. Thus to this extent at least, it may fairly be said that these statutes command "dissimilar treatment for men and women who are ... similarly situated." ...

Moreover, the Government concedes that the differential treatment accorded men and women under these statutes serves no purpose other than mere "administrative convenience." In essence, the Government maintains that, as an empirical matter, wives in our society frequently are dependent upon their husbands, while husbands rarely are dependent upon their wives. Thus, the Government argues that Congress might reasonably have concluded that it would be both cheaper and easier simply conclusively to presume that wives of male members are financially dependent upon their husbands, while burdening female members with the task of establishing dependency in fact.

The Government offers no concrete evidence, however, tending to support its view that such differential treatment in fact saves the Government any money. In order to satisfy the demands of strict judicial scrutiny, the Government must demonstrate, for example, that it is actually cheaper to grant increased benefits with respect to all male members, than it is to determine which male members are in fact entitled to such benefits and to grant increased benefits only to those members whose wives actually meet the dependency requirement. Here, however, there is substantial evidence that, if put to the test, many of the wives of male members would fail to qualify for benefits. And in light of the fact that the dependency determination with respect to the husbands of female members is presently made solely on the basis of affidavits, rather than through the more costly hearing process, the Government's explanation of the statutory scheme is, to say the least, questionable.

In any case, our prior decisions make clear that, although efficacious administration of governmental programs is not without some importance, "the Constitution recognizes higher values than speed and efficiency." ... And when we enter the realm of "strict judicial scrutiny," there can be no doubt that "administrative convenience" is not a shibboleth, the mere recitation of which dictates constitutionality.... On the contrary, any statutory scheme which draws a sharp line between the sexes, solely for the purpose of achieving administrative convenience, necessarily commands "dissimilar treatment for men and women who are ... similarly situated," and therefore involves the "very kind of arbitrary legislative choice forbidden by the [Constitution]." ... We therefore conclude that, by according differential treatment to male and female members of the uniformed services for the sole purpose of achieving administrative convenience, the challenged statutes violate the Due Process Clause of the Fifth Amendment insofar as they require a female member to prove the dependency of her husband....

Mr. Justice Powell, with whom the *Chief Justice* and *Mr. Justice Blackmun* join, concurring in the judgment.

I agree that the challenged statutes constitute an unconstitutional discrimination against service women in violation of the Due Process Clause of the Fifth Amendment, but I cannot join the opinion of Mr. Justice Brennan, which would hold that all classifications based upon sex, "like classifications based upon race, alienage, and national origin," are "inherently suspect and must therefore be subjected to close judicial scrutiny." ... It is unnecessary for the Court in this case to characterize sex as a suspect classification, with all of the far-reaching implications of such a holding.... In my view, we can and should decide this case on the authority of *Reed* and reserve for the future any expansion of its rationale.

There is another, and I find compelling, reason for deferring a general categorizing of sex classifications as invoking the strictest test of judicial scrutiny. The Equal Rights Amendment, which if adopted will resolve the substance of this precise question, has been approved by the Congress and submitted for ratification by the States. If this Amendment is duly adopted, it will represent the will of the people accomplished in the manner prescribed by the Constitution.

(Continued)

By acting prematurely and unnecessarily, as I view it, the Court has assumed a decisional responsibility at the very time when state legislatures, functioning within the traditional democratic process, are debating the proposed Amendment. It seems to me that this reaching out to pre-empt by judicial action a major political decision which is currently in process of resolution does not reflect appropriate respect for duly prescribed legislative processes.

There are times when this Court, under our system, cannot avoid a constitutional decision on issues which normally should be resolved by the elected representatives of the people. But democratic institutions are weakened, and confidence in the restraint of the Court is impaired, when we appear unnecessarily to decide sensitive issues of broad social and political importance at the very time they are under consideration within the prescribed constitutional processes.

Mr. Justice Stewart concurs in the judgment, agreeing that the statutes before us work an invidious discrimination in violation of the Constitution....

Mr. Justice Rehnquist dissents.

UNITED STATES v. VIRGINIA
518 U.S. 515; 116 S.Ct. 2264; 135 L.Ed. 2d. 735 (1996)
Vote: 7-1

In this case, the Court considers the male-only admissions policy of Virginia Military Institute. Justice Ruth Ginsburg, who as an attorney argued a number of important gender discrimination cases before the High Court, authors the majority opinion.

Justice Ginsburg delivered the opinion of the Court.

Virginia's public institutions of higher learning include an incomparable military college, Virginia Military Institute (VMI). The United States maintains that the Constitution's equal protection guarantee precludes Virginia from reserving exclusively to men the unique educational opportunities VMI affords. We agree.

Founded in 1839, VMI is today the sole single-sex school among Virginia's 15 public institutions of higher learning. VMI's distinctive mission is to produce "citizen-soldiers," men prepared for leadership in civilian life and in military service. VMI pursues this mission through pervasive training of a kind not available anywhere else in Virginia. Assigning prime place to character development, VMI uses an "adversative method" modeled on English public schools and once characteristic of military instruction.

VMI constantly endeavors to instill physical and mental discipline in its cadets and impart to them a strong moral code. The school's graduates leave VMI with heightened comprehension of their capacity to deal with duress and stress, and a large sense of accomplishment for completing the hazardous course.

VMI has notably succeeded in its mission to produce leaders; among its alumni are military generals, Members of Congress, and business executives. The school's alumni overwhelmingly perceive that their VMI training helped them to realize their personal goals. VMI's endowment reflects the loyalty of its graduates; VMI has the largest per-student endowment of all undergraduate institutions in the Nation.

Neither the goal of producing citizen-soldiers nor VMI's implementing methodology is inherently unsuitable to women. And the school's impressive record in producing leaders has made admission desirable to some women. Nevertheless, Virginia has elected to preserve exclusively for men the advantages and opportunities a VMI education affords.

From its establishment in 1839 as one of the Nation's first state military colleges, ... VMI has remained financially supported by Virginia and "subject to the control of the [Virginia] General Assembly." ...

VMI today enrolls about 1,300 men as cadets. Its academic offerings in the liberal arts, sciences, and engineering are also available at other public colleges and universities in Virginia. But VMI's mission is special. It is the mission of the school "to produce educated and honorable men, prepared for the varied work of civil life, imbued with love of learning, confident in the functions and attitudes of leadership, possessing a high sense of public service, advocates of the American democracy and free enterprise system, and ready as citizen-soldiers to defend their country in time of national peril." ...

VMI produces its "citizen-soldiers" through "an adversative, or doubting, model of education" which features "[p]hysical rigor, mental stress, absolute equality of treatment, absence of privacy, minute regulation of behavior, and indoctrination in desirable values." ...

VMI cadets live in spartan barracks where surveillance is constant and privacy nonexistent; they wear uniforms, eat together in the mess hall, and regularly participate in drills.... Entering students are incessantly exposed to the rat line, "an extreme form of the adversative model," comparable in intensity to Marine Corps boot camp.... Tormenting and punishing, the rat line bonds new cadets to their fellow sufferers and, when they have completed the 7-month experience, to their former tormentors....

VMI's "adversative model" is further characterized by a hierarchical "class system" of privileges and responsibilities, a "dyke system" for assigning a senior class mentor to each entering class "rat," and a stringently enforced "honor code," which prescribes that a cadet "does not lie, cheat, steal nor tolerate those who do." ...

VMI attracts some applicants because of its reputation as an extraordinarily challenging military school, and "because its alumni are exceptionally close to the school." ... "[W]omen have no opportunity anywhere to gain the benefits of [the system of education at VMI]." ...

In 1990, prompted by a complaint filed with the Attorney General by a female high-school student seeking admission to VMI, the United States sued the Commonwealth of Virginia and VMI, alleging that VMI's exclusively male admission policy violated the Equal Protection Clause of the Fourteenth Amendment....

... Parties who seek to defend gender-based government action must demonstrate an "exceedingly persuasive justification" for that action....

Measuring the record in this case against the review standard just described, we conclude that Virginia has shown no "exceedingly persuasive justification" for excluding all women from the citizen-soldier training afforded by VMI....

Single-sex education affords pedagogical benefits to at least some students, Virginia emphasizes, and that reality is uncontested in this litigation. Similarly, it is not disputed that diversity among public educational institutions can serve the public good. But Virginia has not shown that VMI was established, or has been maintained, with a view to diversifying, by its categorical exclusion of women, educational opportunities

within the State. In cases of this genre, our precedent instructs that "benign" justifications proffered in defense of categorical exclusions will not be accepted automatically; a tenable justification must describe actual state purposes, not rationalizations for actions in fact differently grounded....

Neither recent nor distant history bears out Virginia's alleged pursuit of diversity through single-sex educational options. In 1839, when the State established VMI, a range of educational opportunities for men and women was scarcely contemplated. Higher education at the time was considered dangerous for women; reflecting widely held views about women's proper place, the Nation's first universities and colleges—for example, Harvard in Massachusetts, William and Mary in Virginia—admitted only men.... VMI was not at all novel in this respect: In admitting no women, VMI followed the lead of the State's flagship school, the University of Virginia, founded in 1819.

"[N]o struggle for the admission of women to a state university," a historian has recounted, "was longer drawn out, or developed more bitterness, than that at the University of Virginia." ...

Debate concerning women's admission as undergraduates at the main university continued well past the century's midpoint. Familiar arguments were rehearsed. If women were admitted, it was feared, they "would encroach on the rights of men; there would be new problems of government, perhaps scandals; the old honor system would have to be changed; standards would be lowered to those of other coeducational schools; and the glorious reputation of the university, as a school for men, would be trailed in the dust." ...

Ultimately, in 1970, "the most prestigious institution of higher education in Virginia," the University of Virginia, introduced coeducation and, in 1972, began to admit women on an equal basis with men.... A three-judge Federal District Court confirmed: "Virginia may not now deny to women, on the basis of sex, educational opportunities at the Charlottesville campus that are not afforded in other institutions operated by the [S]tate." ...

Virginia describes the current absence of public single-sex higher education for women as "an historical anomaly." ... But the historical record indicates action more deliberate than anomalous: First, protection of women against higher education; next, schools for women far from equal in resources and stature to schools for men; finally, conversion of the separate schools to coeducation. The state legislature, prior to

(Continued)

the advent of this controversy, had repealed "[a] 11 Virginia statutes requiring individual institutions to admit only men or women." ... And in 1990, an official commission, "legislatively established to chart the future goals of higher education in Virginia," reaffirmed the policy "of affording broad access" while maintaining "autonomy and diversity." ... Significantly, the Commission reported: "Because colleges and universities provide opportunities for students to develop values and learn from role models, it is extremely important that they deal with faculty, staff, and students without regard to sex, race, or ethnic origin." ...

This statement, the Court of Appeals observed, "is the only explicit one that we have found in the record in which the Commonwealth has expressed itself with respect to gender distinctions." ...

In sum, we find no persuasive evidence in this record that VMI's male-only admission policy "is in furtherance of a state policy of 'diversity.'" ... No such policy, the Fourth Circuit observed, can be discerned from the movement of all other public colleges and universities in Virginia away from single-sex education.... That court also questioned "how one institution with autonomy, but with no authority over any other state institution, can give effect to a state policy of diversity among institutions." ... A purpose genuinely to advance an array of educational options, as the Court of Appeals recognized, is not served by VMI's historic and constant plan—a plan to "affor[d] a unique educational benefit only to males." ... However "liberally" this plan serves the State's sons, it makes no provision whatever for her daughters. That is not equal protection....

VMI ... offers an educational opportunity no other Virginia institution provides, and the school's "prestige"—associated with its success in developing "citizen-soldiers"—is unequaled.... Women seeking and fit for a VMI-quality education cannot be offered anything less, under the State's obligation to afford them genuinely equal protection....

Justice Thomas took no part in the consideration or decision of this case.

Chief Justice Rehnquist, concurring in the judgment....

Justice Scalia, dissenting.

Today the Court shuts down an institution that has served the people of the Commonwealth of Virginia with pride and distinction for over a century and a half. To achieve that desired result, it rejects (contrary to our established practice) the factual findings of two courts below, sweeps aside the precedents of this Court, and ignores the history of our people. As to facts: it explicitly rejects the finding that there exist "gender-based developmental differences" supporting Virginia's restriction of the "adversative" method to only a men's institution, and the finding that the all-male composition of the Virginia Military Institute (VMI) is essential to that institution's character. As to precedent: it drastically revises our established standards for reviewing sex-based classifications. And as to history: it counts for nothing the long tradition, enduring down to the present, of men's military colleges supported by both States and the Federal Government....

Much of the Court's opinion is devoted to deprecating the closed-mindedness of our forebears with regard to women's education, and even with regard to the treatment of women in areas that have nothing to do with education. Closed-minded they were—as every age is, including our own, with regard to matters it cannot guess, because it simply does not consider them debatable. The virtue of a democratic system with a First Amendment is that it readily enables the people, over time, to be persuaded that what they took for granted is not so, and to change their laws accordingly. That system is destroyed if the smug assurances of each age are removed from the democratic process and written into the Constitution. So to counterbalance the Court's criticism of our ancestors, let me say a word in their praise: they left us free to change. The same cannot be said of this most illiberal Court, which has embarked on a course of inscribing one after another of the current preferences of the society (and in some cases only the counter-majoritarian preferences of the society's law-trained elite) into our Basic Law. Today it enshrines the notion that no substantial educational value is to be served by an all-men's military academy—so that the decision by the people of Virginia to maintain such an institution denies equal protection to women who cannot attend that institution but can attend others.

Since it is entirely clear that the Constitution of the United States—the old one—takes no sides in this educational debate, I dissent....

ROMER v. EVANS
577 U.S. 620; 116 S.Ct. 1620; 134 L.Ed. 2d. 855 (1996)
Vote: 6-3

Here, the Court addresses the issue of gay rights in the context of a state constitutional amendment disallowing minority status, preferred treatment, or claims of discrimination on the basis of sexual orientation.

Justice Kennedy delivered the opinion of the Court.

... The enactment challenged in this case is an amendment to the Constitution of the State of Colorado, adopted in a 1992 statewide referendum. The parties and the state courts refer to it as "Amendment 2," its designation when submitted to the voters. The impetus for the amendment and the contentious campaign that preceded its adoption came in large part from ordinances that had been passed in various Colorado municipalities.

... What gave rise to the statewide controversy was the protection the ordinances afforded to persons discriminated against by reason of their sexual orientation.... Amendment 2 repeals these ordinances to the extent they prohibit discrimination on the basis of "homosexual, lesbian or bisexual orientation, conduct, practices or relationships." ...

Yet Amendment 2, in explicit terms, does more than repeal or rescind these provisions. It prohibits all legislative, executive or judicial action at any level of state or local government designed to protect the named class, a class we shall refer to as homosexual persons or gays and lesbians. The amendment reads:

No Protected Status Based on Homosexual, Lesbian, or Bisexual Orientation. Neither the State of Colorado, through any of its branches or departments, nor any of its agencies, political subdivisions, municipalities or school districts, shall enact, adopt or enforce any statute, regulation, ordinance or policy whereby homosexual, lesbian or bisexual orientation, conduct, practices or relationships shall constitute or otherwise be the basis of or entitle any person or class of persons to have or claim any minority status, quota preferences, protected status or claim of discrimination. This Section of the Constitution shall be in all respects self-executing....

Soon after Amendment 2 was adopted, this litigation to declare its invalidity and enjoin its enforcement was commenced in the District Court for the City and County of Denver....

The trial court granted a preliminary injunction to stay enforcement of Amendment 2, and an appeal was taken to the Supreme Court of Colorado. Sustaining the interim injunction and remanding the case for further proceedings, the State Supreme Court held that Amendment 2 was subject to strict scrutiny under the Fourteenth Amendment because it infringed the fundamental right of gays and lesbians to participate in the political process.... To reach this conclusion, the state court relied on our voting rights cases ... and on our precedents involving discriminatory restructuring of governmental decision making.... On remand, the State advanced various arguments in an effort to show that Amendment 2 was narrowly tailored to serve compelling interests, but the trial court found none sufficient. It enjoined enforcement of Amendment 2, and the Supreme Court of Colorado, in a second opinion, affirmed the ruling.... We granted certiorari and now affirm the judgment, but on a rationale different from that adopted by the State Supreme Court.

The State's principal argument in defense of Amendment 2 is that it puts gays and lesbians in the same position as all other persons. So, the State says, the measure does no more than deny homosexuals special rights. This reading of the amendment's language is implausible. We rely not upon our own interpretation of the amendment but upon the authoritative construction of Colorado's Supreme Court. The state court, deeming it unnecessary to determine the full extent of the amendment's reach, found it invalid even on a modest reading of its implications....

Sweeping and comprehensive is the change in legal status effected by this law. So much is evident from the ordinances that the Colorado Supreme Court declared would be void by operation of Amendment 2. Homosexuals, by state decree, are put in a solitary class with respect to transactions and relations in both the private and governmental spheres. The amendment withdraws from homosexuals, but no others, specific legal protection from the injuries caused by discrimination, and it forbids reinstatement of these laws and policies.

(Continued)

The change that Amendment 2 works in the legal status of gays and lesbians in the private sphere is far-reaching, both on its own terms and when considered in light of the structure and operation of modern anti-discrimination laws. That structure is well illustrated by contemporary statutes and ordinances prohibiting discrimination by providers of public accommodations. "At common law, innkeepers, smiths, and others who 'made profession of a public employment,' were prohibited from refusing, without good reason, to serve a customer." … The duty was a general one and did not specify protection for particular groups. The common law rules, however, proved insufficient in many instances, and it was settled early that the Fourteenth Amendment did not give Congress a general power to prohibit discrimination in public accommodations…. In consequence, most States have chosen to counter discrimination by enacting detailed statutory schemes….

Colorado's state and municipal laws typify this emerging tradition of statutory protection and follow a consistent pattern. The laws first enumerate the persons or entities subject to a duty not to discriminate. The list goes well beyond the entities covered by the common law. The Boulder ordinance, for example, has a comprehensive definition of entities deemed places of "public accommodation." They include "any place of business engaged in any sales to the general public and any place that offers services, facilities, privileges, or advantages to the general public or that receives financial support through solicitation of the general public or through governmental subsidy of any kind." … The Denver ordinance is of similar breadth, applying, for example, to hotels, restaurants, hospitals, dental clinics, theaters, banks, common carriers, travel and insurance agencies, and "shops and stores dealing with goods or services of any kind." …

These statutes and ordinances also depart from the common law by enumerating the groups or persons within their ambit of protection. Enumeration is the essential device used to make the duty not to discriminate concrete and to provide guidance for those who must comply. In following this approach, Colorado's state and local governments have not limited antidiscrimination laws to groups that have so far been given the protection of heightened equal protection scrutiny under our cases…. Rather, they set forth an extensive catalogue of traits which cannot be the basis for discrimination, including age, military status, marital status, pregnancy, parenthood, custody of a minor child, political affiliation, physical or mental disability of an individual or of his or her associates—and, in recent times, sexual orientation….

Amendment 2 bars homosexuals from securing protection against the injuries that these public-accommodations laws address. That in itself is a severe consequence, but there is more. Amendment 2, in addition, nullifies specific legal protections for this targeted class in all transactions in housing, sale of real estate, insurance, health and welfare services, private education, and employment….

Not confined to the private sphere, Amendment 2 also operates to repeal and forbid all laws or policies providing specific protection for gays or lesbians from discrimination by every level of Colorado government. The State Supreme Court cited two examples of protections in the governmental sphere that are now rescinded and may not be reintroduced. The first is Colorado Executive Order D0035 (1990), which forbids employment discrimination against "'all state employees, classified and exempt' on the basis of sexual orientation." … Also repealed, and now forbidden, are "various provisions prohibiting discrimination based on sexual orientation at state colleges." … The repeal of these measures and the prohibition against their future reenactment demonstrates that Amendment 2 has the same force and effect in Colorado's governmental sector as it does elsewhere and that it applies to policies as well as ordinary legislation.

Amendment 2's reach may not be limited to specific laws passed for the benefit of gays and lesbians. It is a fair, if not necessary, inference from the broad language of the amendment that it deprives gays and lesbians even of the protection of general laws and policies that prohibit arbitrary discrimination in governmental and private settings…. At some point in the systematic administration of these laws, an official must determine whether homosexuality is an arbitrary and thus forbidden basis for decision. Yet a decision to that effect would itself amount to a policy prohibiting discrimination on the basis of homosexuality, and so would appear to be no more valid under Amendment 2 than the specific prohibitions against discrimination the state court held invalid.

If this consequence follows from Amendment 2, as its broad language suggests, it would compound the constitutional difficulties the law creates. The state court did not decide whether the amendment has this effect, however, and neither need we. In the course of rejecting the argument that Amendment 2 is intended to conserve resources to fight discrimination against suspect classes, the Colorado Supreme Court made the limited observation that the amendment is not intended to affect many antidiscrimination laws protecting non-suspect classes.... In our view that does not resolve the issue. In any event, even if, as we doubt, homosexuals could find some safe harbor in laws of general application, we cannot accept the view that Amendment 2's prohibition on specific legal protections does no more than deprive homosexuals of special rights. To the contrary, the amendment imposes a special disability upon those persons alone. Homosexuals are forbidden the safeguards that others enjoy or may seek without constraint. They can obtain specific protection against discrimination only by enlisting the citizenry of Colorado to amend the state constitution or perhaps, on the State's view, by trying to pass helpful laws of general applicability. This is so no matter how local or discrete the harm, no matter how public and widespread the injury. We find nothing special in the protections Amendment 2 withholds. These are protections taken for granted by most people either because they already have them or do not need them; these are protections against exclusion from an almost limitless number of transactions and endeavors that constitute ordinary civic life in a free society.

The Fourteenth Amendment's promise that no person shall be denied the equal protection of the laws must coexist with the practical necessity that most legislation classifies for one purpose or another, with resulting disadvantage to various groups or persons.... We have attempted to reconcile the principle with the reality by stating that, if a law neither burdens a fundamental right nor targets a suspect class, we will uphold the legislative classification so long as it bears a rational relation to some legitimate end....

Amendment 2 fails, indeed defies, even this conventional inquiry. First, the amendment has the peculiar property of imposing a broad and undifferentiated disability on a single named group, an exceptional and, as we shall explain, invalid form of legislation. Second, its sheer breadth is so discontinuous with the reasons offered for it that the amendment seems inexplicable by anything but animus toward the class that it affects; it lacks a rational relationship to legitimate state interests.

Taking the first point, even in the ordinary equal protection case calling for the most deferential of standards, we insist on knowing the relation between the classification adopted and the object to be attained. The search for the link between classification and objective gives substance to the Equal Protection Clause; it provides guidance and discipline for the legislature, which is entitled to know what sorts of laws it can pass; and it marks the limits of our own authority. In the ordinary case, a law will be sustained if it can be said to advance a legitimate government interest, even if the law seems unwise or works to the disadvantage of a particular group, or if the rationale for it seems tenuous.... The laws challenged in the cases just cited were narrow enough in scope and grounded in a sufficient factual context for us to ascertain that there existed some relation between the classification and the purpose it served. By requiring that the classification bear a rational relationship to an independent and legitimate legislative end, we ensure that classifications are not drawn for the purpose of disadvantaging the group burdened by the law....

Amendment 2 confounds this normal process of judicial review. It is at once too narrow and too broad. It identifies persons by a single trait and then denies them protection across the board. The resulting disqualification of a class of persons from the right to seek specific protection from the law is unprecedented in our jurisprudence. The absence of precedent for Amendment 2 is itself instructive; "[d]iscriminations of an unusual character especially suggest careful consideration to determine whether they are obnoxious to the constitutional provision." ...

It is not within our constitutional tradition to enact laws of this sort. Central both to the idea of the rule of law and to our own Constitution's guarantee of equal protection is the principle that government and each of its parts remain open on impartial terms to all who seek its assistance. "Equal protection of the laws is not achieved through indiscriminate imposition of inequalities." ... Respect for this principle explains why laws singling out a certain class of citizens for disfavored legal status or general hardships are rare. A law declaring that in general it shall be more difficult for one group of citizens than for all others to seek aid from the government is itself a denial of equal protection of the laws in the most literal sense. "The guaranty of 'equal protection of the laws is a pledge of the protection of equal laws.'" ...

... A second and related point is that laws of the kind now before us raise the inevitable inference that the disadvantage imposed is born of animosity toward the class of persons affected. "[I]f the constitutional conception of 'equal protection of the laws' means anything, it must at the very least mean that a bare ... desire to harm a politically unpopular group cannot

(Continued)

constitute a legitimate governmental interest." ... Even laws enacted for broad and ambitious purposes often can be explained by reference to legitimate public policies which justify the incidental disadvantages they impose on certain persons. Amendment 2, however, in making a general announcement that gays and lesbians shall not have any particular protections from the law, inflicts on them immediate, continuing, and real injuries that outrun and belie any legitimate justifications that may be claimed for it. We conclude that, in addition to the far-reaching deficiencies of Amendment 2 that we have noted, the principles it offends, in another sense, are conventional and venerable; a law must bear a rational relationship to a legitimate governmental purpose, ... and Amendment 2 does not.

The primary rationale the State offers for Amendment 2 is respect for other citizens' freedom of association, and in particular the liberties of landlords or employers who have personal or religious objections to homosexuality. Colorado also cites its interest in conserving resources to fight discrimination against other groups. The breadth of the Amendment is so far removed from these particular justifications that we find it impossible to credit them. We cannot say that Amendment 2 is directed to any identifiable legitimate purpose or discrete objective. It is a status-based enactment divorced from any factual context from which we could discern a relationship to legitimate state interests; it is a classification of persons undertaken for its own sake, something the Equal Protection Clause does not permit. "[C]lass legislation ... [is] obnoxious to the prohibitions of the Fourteenth Amendment...."

We must conclude that Amendment 2 classifies homosexuals not to further a proper legislative end but to make them unequal to everyone else. This Colorado cannot do. A State cannot so deem a class of persons a stranger to its laws. Amendment 2 violates the Equal Protection Clause, and the judgment of the Supreme Court of Colorado is affirmed....

Justice Scalia, with whom the ***Chief Justice*** and ***Justice Thomas*** join, dissenting.

The Court has mistaken a Kulturkampf for a fit of spite. The constitutional amendment before us here is not the manifestation of a "bare ... desire to harm" homosexuals, ... but is rather a modest attempt by seemingly tolerant Coloradans to preserve traditional sexual mores against the efforts of a politically powerful minority to revise those mores through use of the laws. That objective, and the means chosen to achieve it, are not only unimpeachable under any constitutional doctrine hitherto pronounced (hence the opinion's heavy reliance upon principles of righteousness rather than judicial holdings); they have been specifically approved by the Congress of the United States and by this Court.

In holding that homosexuality cannot be singled out for disfavorable treatment, the Court contradicts a decision, unchallenged here, pronounced only 10 years ago, see *Bowers v. Hardwick* ... (1986), and places the prestige of this institution behind the proposition that opposition to homosexuality is as reprehensible as racial or religious bias. Whether it is or not is precisely the cultural debate that gave rise to the Colorado constitutional amendment (and to the preferential laws against which the amendment was directed). Since the Constitution of the United States says nothing about this subject, it is left to be resolved by normal democratic means, including the democratic adoption of provisions in state constitutions. This Court has no business imposing upon all Americans the resolution favored by the elite class from which the Members of this institution are selected, pronouncing that "animosity" toward homosexuality ... is evil. I vigorously dissent....

... The Court's opinion contains grim, disapproving hints that Coloradans have been guilty of "animus" or "animosity" toward homosexuality, as though that has been established as Unamerican. Of course it is our moral heritage that one should not hate any human being or class of human beings. But I had thought that one could consider certain conduct reprehensible—murder, for example, or polygamy, or cruelty to animals—and could exhibit even "animus" toward such conduct. Surely that is the only sort of "animus" at issue here: moral disapproval of homosexual conduct, the same sort of moral disapproval that produced the centuries-old criminal laws that we held constitutional in *Bowers.* The Colorado amendment does not, to speak entirely precisely, prohibit giving favored status to people who are homosexuals; they can be favored for many reasons—for example, because they are senior citizens or members of racial minorities. But it prohibits giving them favored status because of their homosexual conduct—that is, it prohibits favored status for homosexuality.

But though Coloradans are, as I say, entitled to be hostile toward homosexual conduct, the fact is that the degree of hostility reflected by Amendment 2 is the smallest conceivable. The Court's portrayal of Coloradans as a society fallen victim to pointless, hate-filled "gaybashing" is so false as to be comical. Colorado not only is one of the 25 States that have repealed their antisodomy laws, but was among the first to do so.... But the society that eliminates criminal punishment for homosexual acts does not necessarily abandon the view that homosexuality is morally wrong and socially harmful; often, abolition simply reflects the view that enforcement of such criminal laws involves unseemly intrusion into the intimate lives of citizens....

There is a problem, however, which arises when criminal sanction of homosexuality is eliminated but moral and social disapprobation of homosexuality is meant to be retained. The Court cannot be unaware of that problem; it is evident in many cities of the country, and occasionally bubbles to the surface of the news, in heated political disputes over such matters as the introduction into local schools of books teaching that homosexuality is an optional and fully acceptable "alternate life style." The problem (a problem, that is, for those who wish to retain social disapprobation of homosexuality) is that, because those who engage in homosexual conduct tend to reside in disproportionate numbers in certain communities, ... and of course care about homosexual-rights issues much more ardently than the public at large, they possess political power much greater than their numbers, both locally and statewide. Quite understandably, they devote this political power to achieving not merely a grudging social toleration, but full social acceptance, of homosexuality....

By the time Coloradans were asked to vote on Amendment 2, their exposure to homosexuals' quest for social endorsement was not limited to newspaper accounts of happenings in places such as New York, Los Angeles, San Francisco, and Key West. Three Colorado cities—Aspen, Boulder, and Denver—had enacted ordinances that listed "sexual orientation" as an impermissible ground for discrimination, equating the moral disapproval of homosexual conduct with racial and religious bigotry.... The phenomenon had even appeared statewide: the Governor of Colorado had signed an executive order pronouncing that "in the State of Colorado we recognize the diversity in our pluralistic society and strive to bring an end to discrimination in any form," and directing state agency-heads to "ensure non-discrimination" in hiring and promotion based on, among other things, "sexual orientation." ... I do not mean to be critical of these legislative successes; homosexuals are as entitled to use the legal system for reinforcement of their moral sentiments as are the rest of society. But they are subject to being countered by lawful, democratic countermeasures as well.

That is where Amendment 2 came in. It sought to counter both the geographic concentration and the disproportionate political power of homosexuals by (1) resolving the controversy at the statewide level, and (2) making the election a single-issue contest for both sides. It put directly, to all the citizens of the State, the question: Should homosexuality be given special protection? They answered no. The Court today asserts that this most democratic of procedures is unconstitutional. Lacking any cases to establish that facially absurd proposition, it simply asserts that it must be unconstitutional, because it has never happened before....

I would not myself indulge in ... official praise for heterosexual monogamy, because I think it no business of the courts (as opposed to the political branches) to take sides in this culture war. But the Court today has done so, not only by inventing a novel and extravagant constitutional doctrine to take the victory away from traditional forces, but even by verbally disparaging as bigotry adherence to traditional attitudes. To suggest, for example, that this constitutional amendment springs from nothing more than "a bare ... desire to harm a politically unpopular group," ... is nothing short of insulting. (It is also nothing short of preposterous to call "politically unpopular" a group which enjoys enormous influence in American media and politics, and which, as the trial court here noted, though composing no more than 4% of the population had the support of 46% of the voters on Amendment 2....)

When the Court takes sides in the culture wars, it tends to be with the knights rather than the villains— and more specifically with the Templars, reflecting the views and values of the lawyer class from which the Court's Members are drawn... This law-school view of what "prejudices" must be stamped out may be contrasted with the more plebeian attitudes that apparently still prevail in the United States Congress, which has been unresponsive to repeated attempts to extend to homosexuals the protections of federal civil rights laws ... and which took the pains to exclude them specifically from the Americans With Disabilities Act of 1990....

Today's opinion has no foundation in American constitutional law, and barely pretends to. The people of Colorado have adopted an entirely reasonable provision which does not even disfavor homosexuals in any substantive sense, but merely denies them preferential treatment. Amendment 2 is designed to prevent piecemeal deterioration of the sexual morality favored by a majority of Coloradans, and is not only an appropriate means to that legitimate end, but a means that Americans have employed before. Striking it down is an act, not of judicial judgment, but of political will. I dissent.

UNITED STATES v. WINDSOR
570 U.S. ___; 133 S. Ct. 2675; 186 L. Ed. 2d 808 (2013)
Vote: 5-4

[In this case the Court considers the constitutionality of a provision of the Defense of Marriage Act that forbids the federal government from recognizing same-sex marriages.]

Justice Kennedy delivered the opinion of the Court.

Two women then resident in New York were married in a lawful ceremony in Ontario, Canada, in 2007. Edith Windsor and Thea Spyer returned to their home in New York City. When Spyer died in 2009, she left her entire estate to Windsor. Windsor sought to claim the estate tax exemption for surviving spouses. She was barred from doing so, however, by a federal law, the Defense of Marriage Act, which excludes a same-sex partner from the definition of "spouse" as that term is used in federal statutes. Windsor paid the taxes but filed suit to challenge the constitutionality of this provision. The United States District Court and the Court of Appeals ruled that this portion of the statute is unconstitutional and ordered the United States to pay Windsor a refund. This Court granted certiorari and now affirms the judgment in Windsor's favor.

In 1996, as some States were beginning to consider the concept of same-sex marriage ... and before any State had acted to permit it, Congress enacted the Defense of Marriage Act (DOMA). ... DOMA contains two operative sections: Section 2, which has not been challenged here, allows States to refuse to recognize same-sex marriages performed under the laws of other States. ...

Section 3 is at issue here. It amends the ... United States Code to provide a federal definition of "marriage" and "spouse." Section 3 of DOMA provides as follows:

> *"In determining the meaning of any Act of Congress, or of any ruling, regulation, or interpretation of the various administrative bureaus and agencies of the United States, the word 'marriage' means only a legal union between one man and one woman as husband and wife, and the word 'spouse' refers only to a person of the opposite sex who is a husband or a wife." ...*

The definitional provision does not by its terms forbid States from enacting laws permitting same-sex marriages or civil unions or providing state benefits to residents in that status. The enactment's comprehensive definition of marriage for purposes of all federal statutes and other regulations or directives covered by its terms, however, does control over 1,000 federal laws in which marital or spousal status is addressed as a matter of federal law....

When at first Windsor and Spyer longed to marry, neither New York nor any other State granted them that right. After waiting some years, in 2007 they traveled to Ontario to be married there. It seems fair to conclude that, until recent years, many citizens had not even considered the possibility that two persons of the same sex might aspire to occupy the same status and dignity as that of a man and woman in lawful marriage. For marriage between a man and a woman no doubt had been thought of by most people as essential to the very definition of that term and to its role and function throughout the history of civilization. That belief, for many who long have held it, became even more urgent, more cherished when challenged. For others, however, came the beginnings of a new perspective, a new insight. Accordingly some States concluded that same-sex marriage ought to be given recognition and validity in the law for those same-sex couples who wish to define themselves by their commitment to each other. The limitation of lawful marriage to heterosexual couples, which for centuries had been deemed both necessary and fundamental, came to be seen in New York and certain other States as an unjust exclusion.

Slowly at first and then in rapid course, the laws of New York came to acknowledge the urgency of this issue for same-sex couples who wanted to affirm their commitment to one another before their children, their family, their friends, and their community. And so New York recognized same-sex marriages performed elsewhere; and then it later amended its own marriage laws to permit same-sex marriage. New York, in common with, as of this writing, 11 other States and the District of Columbia, decided that same-sex couples should have the right to marry and so live with pride in themselves and their union and in a status of equality with all other married persons. After a statewide deliberative process that enabled its citizens to discuss and weigh arguments for and against same-sex marriage, New York acted to enlarge the definition of marriage to correct what its citizens and elected representatives perceived to be an injustice that they had not earlier known or understood....

Against this background of lawful same-sex marriage in some States, the design, purpose, and effect of DOMA should be considered as the beginning point in deciding whether it is valid under the Constitution. By history and tradition the definition and regulation of marriage, as will be discussed in more detail, has been treated as being within the authority and realm of the separate States....

The Federal Government, through our history, has deferred to state law policy decisions with respect to domestic relations....

The significance of state responsibilities for the definition and regulation of marriage dates to the Nation's beginning; for "when the Constitution was adopted the common understanding was that the domestic relations of husband and wife and parent and child were matters reserved to the States."... Marriage laws vary in some respects from State to State.... But these rules are in every event consistent within each State.

Against this background DOMA rejects the long established precept that the incidents, benefits, and obligations of marriage are uniform for all married couples within each State, though they may vary, subject to constitutional guarantees, from one State to the next. Despite these considerations, it is unnecessary to decide whether this federal intrusion on state power is a violation of the Constitution because it disrupts the federal balance. The State's power in defining the marital relation is of central relevance in this case quite apart from principles of federalism. Here the State's decision to give this class of persons the right to marry conferred upon them a dignity and status of immense import. When the State used its historic and essential authority to define the marital relation in this way, its role and its power in making the decision enhanced the recognition, dignity, and protection of the class in their own community. DOMA, because of its reach and extent, departs from this history and tradition of reliance on state law to define marriage....

The Federal Government uses this state-defined class for the opposite purpose—to impose restrictions and disabilities. That result requires this Court now to address whether the resulting injury and indignity is a deprivation of an essential part of the liberty protected by the Fifth Amendment. What the State of New York treats as alike the federal law deems unlike by a law designed to injure the same class the State seeks to protect.

In acting first to recognize and then to allow same-sex marriages, New York was responding "to the initiative of those who [sought] a voice in shaping the destiny of their own times." ...These actions were without doubt a proper exercise of its sovereign authority within our federal system, all in the way that the Framers of the Constitution intended. The dynamics of state government in the federal system are to allow the formation of consensus respecting the way the members of a discrete community treat each other in their daily contact and constant interaction with each other.

The States' interest in defining and regulating the marital relation, subject to constitutional guarantees, stems from the understanding that marriage is more than a routine classification for purposes of certain statutory benefits. Private, consensual sexual intimacy between two adult persons of the same sex may not be punished by the State, and it can form "but one element in a personal bond that is more enduring." ... By its recognition of the validity of same-sex marriages performed in other jurisdictions and then by authorizing same-sex unions and same-sex marriages, New York sought to give further protection and dignity to that bond. For same-sex couples who wished to be married, the State acted to give their lawful conduct a lawful status. This status is a far-reaching legal acknowledgment of the intimate relationship between two people, a relationship deemed by the State worthy of dignity in the community equal with all other marriages. It reflects both the community's considered perspective on the historical roots of the institution of marriage and its evolving understanding of the meaning of equality.

DOMA seeks to injure the very class New York seeks to protect. By doing so it violates basic due process and equal protection principles applicable to the Federal Government. ... The Constitution's guarantee of equality "must at the very least mean that a bare congressional desire to harm a politically unpopular group cannot" justify disparate treatment of that group. ... In determining whether a law is motived by an improper animus or purpose, "[d]iscriminations of an un- usual character" especially require careful consideration. ... DOMA cannot survive under these principles. The responsibility of the States for the regulation of domestic relations is an important indicator of the substantial societal impact the State's classifications have in the daily lives and customs of its people. DOMA's unusual deviation from the usual tradition of recognizing and accepting state definitions of marriage here operates to deprive same-sex couples of the

(Continued)

benefits and responsibilities that come with the federal recognition of their marriages. This is strong evidence of a law having the purpose and effect of disapproval of that class. The avowed purpose and practical effect of the law here in question are to impose a disadvantage, a separate status, and so a stigma upon all who enter into same-sex marriages made lawful by the unquestioned authority of the States.

The history of DOMA's enactment and its own text demonstrate that interference with the equal dignity of same-sex marriages, a dignity conferred by the States in the exercise of their sovereign power, was more than an incidental effect of the federal statute. It was its essence....

DOMA's principal effect is to identify a subset of state sanctioned marriages and make them unequal. The principal purpose is to impose inequality, not for other reasons like governmental efficiency. Responsibilities, as well as rights, enhance the dignity and integrity of the person. And DOMA contrives to deprive some couples married under the laws of their State, but not other couples, of both rights and responsibilities. By creating two contradictory marriage regimes within the same State, DOMA forces same-sex couples to live as married for the purpose of state law but unmarried for the purpose of federal law, thus diminishing the stability and predictability of basic personal relations the State has found it proper to acknowledge and protect. By this dynamic DOMA undermines both the public and private significance of state sanctioned same-sex marriages; for it tells those couples, and all the world, that their otherwise valid marriages are unworthy of federal recognition. This places same-sex couples in an unstable position of being in a second-tier marriage. The differentiation demeans the couple, whose moral and sexual choices the Constitution protects, ... and whose relationship the State has sought to dignify. And it humiliates tens of thousands of children now being raised by same-sex couples. The law in question makes it even more difficult for the children to understand the integrity and closeness of their own family and its concord with other families in their community and in their daily lives.

Under DOMA, same-sex married couples have their lives burdened, by reason of government decree, in visible and public ways. By its great reach, DOMA touches many aspects of married and family life, from the mundane to the profound. It prevents same-sex married couples from obtaining government healthcare benefits they would otherwise receive....

DOMA also brings financial harm to children of same-sex couples. It raises the cost of health care for families by taxing health benefits provided by employers to their workers' same-sex spouses.... And it denies or reduces benefits allowed to families upon the loss of a spouse and parent, benefits that are an integral part of family security....

DOMA divests married same-sex couples of the duties and responsibilities that are an essential part of married life and that they in most cases would be honored to accept were DOMA not in force. For instance, because it is expected that spouses will support each other as they pursue educational opportunities, federal law takes into consideration a spouse's income in calculating a student's federal financial aid eligibility.... Same-sex married couples are exempt from this requirement. The same is true with respect to federal ethics rules. Federal executive and agency officials are prohibited from "participat[ing] personally and substantially" in matters as to which they or their spouses have a financial interest.... A similar statute prohibits Senators, Senate employees, and their spouses from accepting high-value gifts from certain sources, and another mandates detailed financial disclosures by numerous high-ranking officials and their spouses.... Under DOMA, however, these Government-integrity rules do not apply to same-sex spouses....

The power the Constitution grants it also restrains. And though Congress has great authority to design laws to fit its own conception of sound national policy, it cannot deny the liberty protected by the Due Process Clause of the Fifth Amendment.

What has been explained to this point should more than suffice to establish that the principal purpose and the necessary effect of this law are to demean those persons who are in a lawful same-sex marriage. This requires the Court to hold, as it now does, that DOMA is unconstitutional as a deprivation of the liberty of the person protected by the Fifth Amendment of the Constitution.

The liberty protected by the Fifth Amendment's Due Process Clause contains within it the prohibition against denying to any person the equal protection of the laws.... While the Fifth Amendment itself withdraws from Government the power to degrade or demean in the way this law does, the equal protection guarantee of the Fourteenth Amendment makes that Fifth Amendment right all the more specific and all the better understood and preserved.

The class to which DOMA directs its restrictions and restraints are those persons who are joined in same-sex marriages made lawful by the State. DOMA singles out a class of persons deemed by a State entitled to recognition and protection to enhance their own liberty. It imposes a disability on the class by refusing to acknowledge a status the State finds to be dignified and proper. DOMA instructs all federal officials, and indeed all persons with whom same-sex couples interact, including their own children, that their marriage is less worthy than the marriages of others. The federal statute is invalid, for no legitimate purpose overcomes the purpose and effect to disparage and to injure those whom the State, by its marriage laws, sought to protect in personhood and dignity. By seeking to displace this protection and treating those persons as living in marriages less respected than others, the federal statute is in violation of the Fifth Amendment. This opinion and its holding are confined to those lawful marriages.

The judgment of the Court of Appeals for the Second Circuit is affirmed.

Chief Justice Roberts, dissenting.

… On the merits of the constitutional dispute, … Congress acted constitutionally in passing the Defense of Marriage Act (DOMA). Interests in uniformity and stability amply justified Congress's decision to retain the definition of marriage that, at that point, had been adopted by every State in our Nation, and every nation in the world.…

The majority sees a more sinister motive, pointing out that the Federal Government has generally (though not uniformly) deferred to state definitions of marriage in the past. That is true, of course, but none of those prior state-by-state variations had involved differences over something—as the majority puts it—"thought of by most people as essential to the very definition of [marriage] and to its role and function throughout the history of civilization." … That the Federal Government treated this fundamental question differently than it treated variations over consanguinity or minimum age is hardly surprising—and hardly enough to support a conclusion that the "principal purpose" …was a bare desire to harm. Nor do the snippets of legislative history and the banal title of the Act to which the majority points suffice to make such a showing. At least without some more convincing evidence that the Act's principal purpose was to codify malice, and that it furthered *no*

legitimate government interests, I would not tar the political branches with the brush of bigotry.

But while I disagree with the result to which the majority's analysis leads it in this case, I think it more important to point out that its analysis leads no further. The Court does not have before it, and the logic of its opinion does not decide, the distinct question whether the States, in the exercise of their "historic and essential authority to define the marital relation," … may continue to utilize the traditional definition of marriage.…

Justice Scalia, … dissenting.

… There are many remarkable things about the majority's merits holding. The first is how rootless and shifting its justifications are. For example, the opinion starts with seven full pages about the traditional power of States to define domestic relations—initially fooling many readers, I am sure, into thinking that this is a federalism opinion. But we are eventually told that "it is unnecessary to decide whether this federal intrusion on state power is a violation of the Constitution," and that "[t]he State's power in defining the marital relation is of central relevance in this case quite apart from principles of federalism" because "the State's decision to give this class of persons the right to marry conferred upon them a dignity and status of immense import." … But no one questions the power of the States to define marriage (with the concomitant conferral of dignity and status), so what is the point of devoting seven pages to describing how long and well established that power is? Even after the opinion has formally disclaimed reliance upon principles of federalism, mentions of "the usual tradition of recognizing and accepting state definitions of marriage" continue.… What to make of this? The opinion never explains. My guess is that the majority, while reluctant to suggest that defining the meaning of "marriage" in federal statutes is unsupported by any of the Federal Government's enumerated powers, nonetheless needs some rhetorical basis to support its pretense that today's prohibition of laws excluding same-sex marriage is confined to the Federal Government (leaving the second, state-law shoe to be dropped later, maybe next Term). But I am only guessing.

Equally perplexing are the opinion's references to "the Constitution's guarantee of equality."… …[I]f this

(Continued)

is meant to be an equal-protection opinion, it is a confusing one. The opinion does not resolve and indeed does not even mention what had been the central question in this litigation: whether, under the Equal Protection Clause, laws restricting marriage to a man and a woman are reviewed for more than mere rationality. That is the issue that divided the parties and the court below… In accord with my previously expressed skepticism about the Court's "tiers of scrutiny" approach, I would review this classification only for its rationality…. As nearly as I can tell, the Court agrees with that; its opinion does not apply strict scrutiny, and its central propositions are taken from rational-basis cases… But the Court certainly does not *apply* anything that resembles that deferential framework….

The majority opinion need not get into the strict-vs.-rational-basis scrutiny question, and need not justify its holding under either, because it says that DOMA is unconstitutional as "a deprivation of the liberty of the person protected by the Fifth Amendment of the Constitution," … that it violates "basic due process" principles, … and that it inflicts an "injury and indignity" of a kind that denies "an essential part of the liberty protected by the Fifth Amendment." … The majority never utters the dread words "substantive due process," perhaps sensing the disrepute into which that doctrine has fallen, but that is what those statements mean. Yet the opinion does not argue that same-sex marriage is "deeply rooted in this Nation's history and tradition,"… a claim that would of course be quite absurd. So would the further suggestion (also necessary, under our substantive-due-process precedents) that a world in which DOMA exists is one bereft of "ordered liberty." …

Some might conclude that this loaf could have used awhile longer in the oven. But that would be wrong; it is already overcooked. The most expert care in preparation cannot redeem a bad recipe. The sum of all the Court's nonspecific hand-waving is that this law is invalid (maybe on equal-protection grounds, maybe on substantive due process grounds, and perhaps with some amorphous federalism component playing a role) because it is motivated by a "'bare … desire to harm'" couples in same-sex marriages…. It is this proposition with which I will therefore engage.

As I have observed before, the Constitution does not forbid the government to enforce traditional moral and sexual norms…. I will not swell the U.S. Reports with restatements of that point. It is enough to say that the Constitution neither requires nor forbids our society to approve of same-sex marriage, much as it neither requires nor forbids us to approve of no-fault divorce, polygamy, or the consumption of alcohol. However, even setting aside traditional moral disapproval of same-sex marriage (or indeed same-sex sex), there are many perfectly valid—indeed, downright boring—justifying rationales for this legislation. Their existence ought to be the end of this case. For they give the lie to the Court's conclusion that only those with hateful hearts could have voted "aye" on this Act. And more importantly, they serve to make the contents of the legislators' hearts quite irrelevant: "It is a familiar principle of constitutional law that this Court will not strike down an otherwise constitutional statute on the basis of an alleged illicit legislative motive." … Or at least it *was* a familiar principle. By holding to the contrary, the majority has declared open season on any law that (in the opinion of the law's opponents and any panel of like-minded federal judges) can be characterized as mean-spirited….

… [To] defend traditional marriage is not to condemn, demean, or humiliate those who would prefer other arrangements, any more than to defend the Constitution of the United States is to condemn, demean, or humiliate other constitutions…. In the majority's judgment, any resistance to its holding is beyond the pale of reasoned disagreement…. It is one thing for a society to elect change; it is another for a court of law to impose change by adjudging those who oppose it *hostes humani generis*, enemies of the human race.

The penultimate sentence of the majority's opinion is a naked declaration that "[t]his opinion and its holding are confined" to those couples "joined in same-sex marriages made lawful by the State." … It takes real cheek for today's majority to assure us … that a constitutional requirement to give formal recognition to same-sex marriage is not at issue here—when what has preceded that assurance is a lecture on how superior the majority's moral judgment in favor of same-sex marriage is to the Congress's hateful moral judgment against it….

In my opinion, … the view that *this* Court will take of state prohibition of same-sex marriage is indicated beyond mistaking by today's opinion. As I have said, the real rationale of today's opinion … is that DOMA is motivated by "'bare … desire to harm'" couples in same-sex marriages…. How easy it is, indeed how inevitable, to reach the same conclusion with regard to state laws denying same-sex couples marital status.…

By formally declaring anyone opposed to same-sex marriage an enemy of human decency, the majority arms well every challenger to a state law restricting marriage to its traditional definition. Henceforth those challengers will lead with this Court's declaration that there is "no legitimate purpose" served by such a law, and will claim that the traditional definition has "the purpose and effect to disparage and to injure" the "personhood and dignity" of same-sex couples.… The majority's limiting assurance will be meaningless in the face of language like that, as the majority well knows. That is why the language is there. The result will be a judicial distortion of our society's debate over marriage—a debate that can seem in need of our clumsy "help" only to a member of this institution.

As to that debate: Few public controversies touch an institution so central to the lives of so many, and few inspire such attendant passion by good people on all sides. Few public controversies will ever demonstrate so vividly the beauty of what our Framers gave us, a gift the Court pawns today to buy its stolen moment in the spotlight: a system of government that permits us to rule *ourselves*. Since DOMA's passage, citizens on all sides of the question have seen victories and they have seen defeats. There have been plebiscites, legislation, persuasion and loud voices—in other words, democracy.…

In the majority's telling, this story is black-and-white: Hate your neighbor or come along with us. The truth is more complicated. It is hard to admit that one's political opponents are not monsters, especially in a struggle like this one, and the challenge in the end proves more than today's Court can handle. Too bad. A reminder that disagreement over something so fundamental as marriage can still be politically legitimate would have been a fit task for what in earlier times was called the judicial temperament. We might have covered ourselves with honor today, by promising all sides of this debate that it was theirs to settle and that we would respect their resolution. We might have let the People decide.

But that the majority will not do. Some will rejoice in today's decision, and some will despair at it; that is the nature of a controversy that matters so much to so many. But the Court has cheated both sides, robbing the winners of an honest victory, and the losers of the peace that comes from a fair defeat. We owed both of them better. I dissent.

Justice Alito, … dissenting.

Our Nation is engaged in a heated debate about same-sex marriage. That debate is, at bottom, about the nature of the institution of marriage. Respondent Edith Windsor, supported by the United States, asks this Court to intervene in that debate, and although she couches her argument in different terms, what she seeks is a holding that enshrines in the Constitution a particular understanding of marriage under which the sex of the partners makes no difference. The Constitution, however, does not dictate that choice. It leaves the choice to the people, acting through their elected representatives at both the federal and state levels. I would therefore hold that Congress did not violate Windsor's constitutional rights by enacting §3 of the Defense of Marriage Act (DOMA), … which defines the meaning of marriage under federal statutes that either confer upon married persons certain federal benefits or impose upon them certain federal obligations.

To the extent that the Court takes the position that the question of same-sex marriage should be resolved primarily at the state level, I wholeheartedly agree. I hope that the Court will ultimately permit the people of each State to decide this question for themselves. Unless the Court is willing to allow this to occur, the whiffs of federalism in the today's opinion of the Court will soon be scattered to the wind.

In any event, §3 of DOMA, in my view, does not encroach on the prerogatives of the States, assuming of course that the many federal statutes affected by DOMA have not already done so. Section 3 does not prevent any State from recognizing same-sex marriage or from extending to same-sex couples any right, privilege, benefit, or obligation stemming from state law. All that §3 does is to define a class of persons to whom federal law extends certain special benefits and upon whom federal law imposes certain special burdens. In these provisions, Congress used marital status as a way of defining this class—in part, I assume, because it viewed marriage as a valuable institution to be fostered and in part because it viewed married couples as comprising a unique type of economic unit that merits special regulatory treatment. Assuming that Congress has the power under the Constitution to enact the laws affected by §3, Congress has the power to define the category of persons to whom those laws apply.…

SAN ANTONIO INDEPENDENT SCHOOL DISTRICT v. RODRIGUEZ
411 U.S. 1; 93 S.Ct. 1278; 36 L.Ed.2d. 16 (1973)
Vote: 5-4

When this litigation began, the public school system in San Antonio, Texas, was financed by a combination of state funds and local property tax revenues. In 1971, the state markedly increased the amount of state aid to poorer school districts. Nevertheless, substantial disparities in spending still existed across districts, attributable to disparities in property tax revenues. This case raises the question of whether such spending disparities violate the Equal Protection Clause of the Fourteenth Amendment.

Mr. Justice Powell delivered the opinion of the Court.

Despite ... recent increases [in state aid], substantial interdistrict disparities in school expenditures found by the District Court to prevail in San Antonio and in varying degrees throughout the State still exist. And it was these disparities, largely attributable to differences in the amounts of money collected through local property taxation, that led the District Court to conclude that Texas's dual system of public school finance violated the Equal Protection Clause. The District Court held that the Texas system discriminates on the basis of wealth in the manner in which education is provided for its people. Finding that wealth is a "suspect" classification and that education is a "fundamental" interest, the District Court held that the Texas system could be sustained only if the State could show that it was premised upon some compelling state interest. On this issue the court concluded that "[n]ot only are defendants unable to demonstrate compelling state interests ... they fail even to establish a reasonable basis for these classifications." ...

... We must decide, first, whether the Texas system of financing public education operates to the disadvantage of some suspect class or impinges upon a fundamental right explicitly or implicitly protected by the Constitution, thereby requiring strict judicial scrutiny. If so, the judgment of the District Court should be affirmed. If not, the Texas scheme must still be examined to determine whether it rationally furthers some legitimate, articulated state purpose and therefore does not constitute an invidious discrimination in violation of the Equal Protection Clause of the Fourteenth Amendment....

The wealth discrimination discovered by the District Court in this case, and by several other courts that have recently struck down school financial laws in other States, is quite unlike any of the forms of wealth discrimination heretofore reviewed by this Court. Rather than focusing on the unique features of the alleged discrimination, the courts in these cases have virtually assumed their findings of a suspect classification through a simplistic process of analysis: since, under the traditional systems of financing public schools, some poorer people receive less expensive educations than other more affluent people, these systems discriminate on the basis of wealth. This approach largely ignores the hard threshold questions, including whether it makes a difference for purposes of consideration under the Constitution that the class of disadvantaged "poor" cannot be identified or defined in customary equal protection terms, and whether the relative—rather than absolute—nature of the asserted deprivation is of significant consequence. Before a State's laws and the justifications for the classifications they create are subjected to strict judicial scrutiny, we think these threshold considerations must be analyzed more closely than they were in the court below.

The case comes to us with no definitive description of the classifying facts or delineation of the disfavored class. Examination of the District Court's opinion and of appellees' complaint, briefs, and contentions at oral argument suggests, however, at least three ways in which the discrimination claimed here might be described. The Texas system of school finance might be regarded as discriminating (1) against "poor" persons whose incomes fall below some identifiable level of poverty or who might be characterized as functionally "indigent," or (2) against those who are relatively poorer than others, or (3) against all those who, irrespective of their personal incomes, happen to reside in relatively poorer school districts. Our task must be to ascertain whether, in fact, the Texas system has been shown to discriminate on any of these possible bases and, if so, whether the resulting classification may be regarded as suspect....

... Even a cursory examination ... demonstrates that neither of the two distinguishing characteristics of wealth classifications can be found here. First, in support of their charge that the system discriminates against the "poor," appellees have made no effort to demonstrate that it operates to the peculiar disadvantage of any class fairly definable as indigent, or as composed of persons whose incomes are beneath any designated poverty level. Indeed, there is no reason to believe that the poorest families are not necessarily clustered in the poorest property districts. A recent and exhaustive study of school districts in Connecticut concluded that "[i]t is clearly incorrect ... to contend that the 'poor' live in 'poor' districts.... Thus, the major factual assumption ... —that the educational finance system discriminates against the 'poor'—is simply false in Connecticut." ... Defining "poor" families as those below the Bureau of the Census "poverty level," the Connecticut study found, not surprisingly, that the poor were clustered around commercial and industrial areas—those same areas that provide the most attractive sources of property tax income for school districts. Whether a similar pattern would be discovered in Texas is not known, but there is no basis on the record in this case for assuming that the poorest people—defined by reference to any level of absolute impecunity—are concentrated in the poorest districts.

[N]either appellees nor the District Court addressed the fact that ... lack of personal resources has not occasioned an absolute deprivation of the desired benefit. The argument here is not that the children in districts having relatively low assessable property values are receiving no public education; rather, it is that they are receiving a poorer quality education than that available to children in districts having more assessable wealth. Apart from the unsettled and disputed question whether the quality of education may be determined by the amount of money expended for it, a sufficient answer to appellees' argument is that at least where wealth is involved the Equal Protection Clause does not require absolute equality of precisely equal advantages.... The State repeatedly asserted in its briefs in this Court that ... it now assures "every child in every school district an adequate education." No proof was offered at trial persuasively discrediting or refuting the State's assertion.

For these two reasons—the absence of any evidence that the financing system discriminates against any definable category of "poor" people or that it results in the absolute deprivation of education—the disadvantaged class is not susceptible to identification in traditional terms....

The Court here considers and repudiates the argument that there is a correlation between family income in a district and the amount spent by government on education.

This brings us, then, to the third way in which the classification scheme might be defined—district wealth discrimination. Since the only correlation indicated by the evidence is between district property wealth and expenditures, it may be argued that discrimination might be found without regard to the individual income characteristics of district residents. Assuming a perfect correlation between district property wealth and expenditures from top to bottom, the disadvantaged class might be viewed as encompassing every child in every district except the district that has the most assessable wealth and spends the most on education....

However described, it is clear that appellees ask this Court to extend its most exacting scrutiny to review a system that allegedly discriminates against a large, diverse, and amorphous class, unified only by the common factor of residence in districts that happen to have less taxable wealth than other districts. The system of alleged discrimination and the class it defines have none of the traditional indicia of suspectness: the class is not saddled with such disabilities, or subjected to such history of purposeful unequal treatment, or relegated to such a position of political powerlessness as to command extraordinary protection from the majoritarian political process.

We thus conclude that the Texas system does not operate to the peculiar disadvantage of any suspect class. But in recognition of the fact that this Court has never heretofore held that wealth discrimination alone provides an adequate basis for invoking strict scrutiny, appellees have not relied solely on this contention. They also assert that the State's system impermissibly interferes with the exercise of a "fundamental" right and that accordingly the prior decisions of this Court require the application of the strict standard of judicial review. It is this question—whether education is a fundamental right, in the sense that it is among the rights and liberties protected by the Constitution—which has so consumed the attention of courts and commentators in recent years....

Education, of course, is not among the rights afforded explicit protection under our Federal Constitution. Nor do we find any basis for saying it is implicitly so protected. It is appellees' contention, however, that education ... is itself a fundamental personal right because it is essential to the effective exercise of First Amendment freedoms and to intelligent utilization of the right to vote....

We need not dispute any of these propositions. The Court has long afforded zealous protection against

(Continued)

unjustifiable governmental interference with the individual's rights to speak and to vote. Yet we have never presumed to possess either the ability or the authority to guarantee to the citizenry the most effective speech or the most informed electoral choice....

Even if it were conceded that some identifiable quantum of education is a constitutionally protected prerequisite to the meaningful exercise of either right, we have no indication that the present levels of education expenditure in Texas provide an education that falls short....

... In one further respect we find this a particularly inappropriate case in which to subject state action to strict judicial scrutiny. The present case, in another basic sense, is significantly different from any of the cases in which the Court has applied strict scrutiny to state or federal legislation touching upon constitutionally protected rights. Each of our prior cases involved legislation which "deprived," "infringed," or "interfered" with the free exercise of some such fundamental personal right or liberty.... A critical distinction between those cases and the one now before us lies in what Texas is endeavoring to do with respect to education. Every step leading to the establishment of the system Texas utilizes today—including the decisions permitting localities to tax and expand locally, and creating and continuously expanding state aid—was implemented in an effort to extend public education and to improve its quality. Of course, every reform that benefits some more than others may be criticized for what it fails to accomplish. But we think it plain that, in substance, the thrust of the Texas system is affirmative and reformatory and, therefore, should be scrutinized under judicial principles sensitive to the nature of the State's efforts and to the rights reserved to the States under the Constitution....

We need not rest our decision, however, solely on the inappropriateness of the strict scrutiny test. A century of Supreme Court adjudication under the Equal Protection Clause affirmatively supports the application of the traditional standard of review, which requires only that the State's system be shown to bear some rational relationship to legitimate state purposes. This case represents far more than a challenge to the manner in which Texas provides for the education of its children. We have here nothing less than a direct attack on the way in which Texas has chosen to raise and disburse state and local tax revenues....

Justice Powell here defends the correctness of the more lenient standards of judicial review in the field of taxation.

... The Texas system of school finance ... permits and encourages a large measure of participation in and control of each district's schools at the local level. In an era that has witnessed a consistent trend toward centralization of the functions of government, local sharing of responsibility for public education has survived....

The persistence of attachment to government at the lowest level where education is concerned reflects the depth of commitment of its supporters. In part, local control means ... the freedom to devote more money to the education of one's children. Equally important, however, is the opportunity it offers for participation in the decision-making process that determines how those local tax dollars will be spent. Each locality is free to tailor local programs to local needs. Pluralism also affords some opportunity for experimentation, innovation, and a healthy competition for educational excellence....

... Appellees suggest that local control could be preserved and promoted under other financing systems that resulted in more equality in educational expenditures. While it is no doubt true that reliance on local property taxation for school revenues provides less freedom of choice with respect to expenditures for some districts than for others, the existence of "some inequality" in the manner in which the State's rationale is achieved is not alone a sufficient basis for striking down the entire system.... Only where state action impinges on the exercise of fundamental constitutional rights or liberties must it be found to have chosen the least restrictive alternative.... It is also well to remember that even those districts that have reduced ability to make free decisions with respect to how much they spend on education still retain under the present system a large measure of authority as to how available funds will be allocated. They further enjoy the power to make numerous other decisions with respect to the operation of the schools. The people of Texas may be justified in believing that other systems of school finance, which place more of the financial responsibility in the hands of the State, will result in a comparable lessening of desired local autonomy. That is, they may believe that along with increased control of the purse strings at the state level will go increased control over local policies....

... One also must remember that the system here challenged is not peculiar to Texas or to any other State. In its essential characteristics the Texas plan for financing public education reflects what many educators for a half century have thought was an enlightened approach to a problem for which there is no perfect solution. We are unwilling to assume for ourselves a level of wisdom superior to that of legislators, scholars, and educational authorities in 49 States, especially where the alternatives proposed are only recently conceived and nowhere yet tested. The constitutional standard under the Equal Protection Clause is whether the challenged state action rationally furthers a legitimate state purpose or interest.... We hold that the Texas plan abundantly satisfies this standard.

Mr. Justice Stewart, concurring....

Mr. Justice Brennan, dissenting.

... Here, there can be no doubt that education is inextricably linked to the right to participate in the electoral process and to the rights of free speech and association guaranteed by the First Amendment. This being so, any classification affecting education must be subjected to strict judicial scrutiny, and since even the State concedes that the statutory scheme now before us cannot pass constitutional muster under this stricter standard of review, I can only conclude that the Texas school financing scheme is constitutionally invalid....

Mr. Justice White, with whom *Mr. Justice Douglas* and *Mr. Justice Brennan* join, dissenting.

The Texas public schools are financed through a combination of state funding, local property tax revenue, and some federal funds. Concededly, the system yields wide disparity in per-pupil revenue among the various districts. In a typical year, for example, the Alamo Heights district had total revenues of $594 per pupil, while the Edgewood district had only $356 per student. The majority and the State concede, as they must, the existence of major disparities in spendable funds. But the State contends that the disparities do not invidiously discriminate against children and families in districts such as Edgewood, because the Texas scheme is designed "to provide an adequate education for all, with local autonomy to go beyond that as individual school districts desire and are able.... It leaves to the people of each district the choice whether to go beyond the minimum and, if so, by how much.... "

The difficulty with the Texas system ... is that it provides a meaningful option to Alamo Heights and

like school districts but almost none to Edgewood and those other districts with a low per-pupil real estate tax base. In these latter districts, no matter how desirous parents are of supporting their schools with greater revenues, it is impossible to do so through the use of the real estate property tax. In these districts the Texas system utterly fails to extend a realistic choice to parents, because the property tax, which is the only revenue-raising mechanism extended to school districts, is practically and legally unavailable....

In order to equal the highest yield in any other Bexar County district, Alamo Heights would be required to tax at the rate of $0.68 per $100 of assessed valuation. Edgewood would be required to tax at the prohibitive rate of $5.76 per $100. But state law places a $1.50 per $100 ceiling on the maintenance tax rate, a limit that would surely be reached long before Edgewood attained an equal yield. Edgewood is thus precluded in law, as well as in fact, from achieving a yield even close to that of some other districts.

The Equal Protection Clause permits discriminations between classes but requires that the classification bear some rational relationship to a permissible object sought to be attained by the statute. It is not enough that the Texas system before us seeks to achieve the valid, rational purpose of maximizing local initiative; the means chosen by the State must also be rationally related to the end sought to be achieved....

... Requiring the State to establish only that unequal treatment is in furtherance of a permissible goal, without also requiring the State to show that the means chosen to effectuate that goal are rationally related to its achievement, makes equal protection analysis no more than an empty gesture. In my view, the parents and children in Edgewood, and in like districts, suffer from an invidious discrimination violative of the Equal Protection Clause....

There is no difficulty in identifying the class that is subject to the alleged discrimination and that is entitled to the benefits of the Equal Protection Clause. I need go no farther than the parents and children in the Edgewood district, who are plaintiffs here and who assert that they are entitled to the same choice as Alamo Heights to augment local expenditures for schools but are denied that choice by state law. This group constitutes a class sufficiently definite to invoke the protection of the Constitution. They are as entitled to the protection of the Equal Protection Clause as were the voters in allegedly unrepresented counties in the reapportionment cases....

(Continued)

Mr. Justice Marshall, with whom *Mr. Justice Douglas* concurs, dissenting.

... We sit ... not to resolve disputes over educational theory but to enforce our Constitution. It is an inescapable fact that if one district has more funds available per pupil than another district, the former will have greater choice in educational planning than will the latter. In this regard, I believe the question of discrimination in educational quality must be deemed to be an objective one that looks to what the State provides its children, not to what the children are able to do with what they receive. That a child is forced to attend an underfunded school with poorer physical facilities, less experienced teachers, larger classes, and a narrower range of courses than a school with substantially more funds—and thus with greater choice in educational planning—may nevertheless excel is to the credit of the child, not the State.... Indeed, who can ever measure for such a child the opportunities lost and the talents wasted for want of a broader, more enriched education? Discrimination in the opportunity to learn that is afforded a child must be our standard....

... I must once more voice my disagreement with the Court's rigidified approach to equal protection analysis.... The court apparently seeks to establish today that equal protection cases fall into one of two neat categories which dictate the appropriate standard of review—strict scrutiny or mere rationality. But this Court's decisions in the field of equal protection defy such easy categorization. A principled reading of what this Court has done reveals that it has applied a spectrum of standards in reviewing discrimination allegedly violative of the Equal Protection Clause. This spectrum clearly comprehends variations in the degree of care with which the Court will scrutinize particular classifications, depending, I believe, on the constitutional and societal importance of the interest adversely affected and the recognized invidiousness of the basis upon which the particular classification is drawn....

... [It] seems to me inescapably clear that this Court has consistently adjusted the care with which it will review state discrimination in light of the constitutional significance of the interests affected and the invidiousness of the particular classification. In the context of economic interests, we find that discriminatory state action is almost always sustained, for such interests are generally far removed from constitutional guarantees. Moreover, "[t]he extremes to which the Court has gone in dreaming up rational bases for state regulation in that area may in many instances be ascribed to a healthy revulsion from the Court's earlier excesses in using the Constitution to protect interests that have more than enough power to protect themselves in the legislative halls." ... But the situation differs markedly when discrimination against important individual interests with constitutional implications and against particularly disadvantaged or powerless classes is involved. The majority suggests, however, that a variable standard of review would give this Court the appearance of a "super-legislature." Such an approach seems to me a part of the guarantees of our Constitution and of the historic experiences with oppression of and discrimination against discrete, powerless minorities which underlie that document. In truth, the Court itself will be open to the criticism raised by the majority so long as it continues on its present course of effectively selecting in private which cases will be afforded special consideration without acknowledging the true basis of its action....

The nature of our inquiry into the justifications for state discrimination is essentially the same in all equal protection cases: We must consider the substantiality of the state interests sought to be served, and we must scrutinize the reasonableness of the means by which the State has sought to advance its interests.... Differences in the application of this test are, in my view, a function of the constitutional importance of the interests at stake and the invidiousness of the particular classification. In terms of the asserted state interests, the Court has indicated that it will require, for instance, a "compelling," ... or a "substantial" or "important," ... state interest to justify discrimination affecting individual interests of constitutional significance. Whatever the differences, if any, in these descriptions of the character of the state interest necessary to sustain such discrimination, basic to each is, I believe, a concern with the legitimacy and the reality of the asserted state interests. Thus, when interests of constitutional importance are at stake, the Court does not stand ready to credit the State's classification with any conceivable legitimate purpose, but demands a clear showing that there are legitimate state interests which the classification was in fact intended to serve. Beyond the question of the adequacy of the State's purpose for the classification, the Court traditionally has become increasingly sensitive to the means by which a State chooses to act as its action affects more directly interests of constitutional significance.... Thus, by now, "less restrictive alternatives" analysis is firmly established in equal protection jurisprudence.... Here both the nature of the interest and the classification dictate close judicial scrutiny of the purposes which Texas seeks to serve with its present educational financing scheme and of the means it has selected to serve that purpose....

CHAPTER **8**

Elections, Representation, and Voting Rights

"Undoubtedly, the right of suffrage is a fundamental matter in a free and democratic society. Especially since the right to exercise the franchise in a free and unimpaired manner is preservative of other basic civil and political rights, any alleged infringement of the right of citizens to vote must be carefully and meticulously scrutinized."

—Chief Justice Earl Warren, Writing for the Court in
Reynolds v. Sims *(1964)*

Earl Warren: Chief Justice, 1953–1969

Introduction

The right to vote is essential to **representative democracy**, that form of government in which policy decisions are made by representatives of the citizenry chosen in periodic competitive elections. Because democracy is based on the principle of political equality, a genuine democracy entails **universal suffrage**, the right of all law-abiding adult citizens to vote. Of course, the right to vote is meaningless if elections are rigged or susceptible to fraud. Nor is the right to vote as meaningful if one is compelled to vote, as is the case in some countries. Ideally, then, the right to vote involves voluntary participation in free and fair elections.

From a constitutional standpoint, voting is among the most important rights that citizens possess. As the Supreme Court recognized in *Yick Wo v. Hopkins* (1886), voting is "a fundamental political right, because [it is] preservative of all rights." Like free speech, voting has important instrumental value as a means of ensuring the continuing viability of constitutional democracy in this country. Of course, voting is by no means a sufficient guarantee of liberty. Indeed, it may foster the **tyranny of the majority**, which is precisely what the Framers of the Constitution wanted to prevent.

Although the United States today is a democratic country, the term "democracy" was anathema to many of the Framers. They accepted the notion of **popular sovereignty** in the abstract, but they certainly did not believe that every question of policy was to be subjected to majority rule. Many of the delegates to the Constitutional Convention of 1787 shared Alexander Hamilton's view that democracy was little more than legitimized mob rule, an ever-present danger to personal security, liberty, and property. The Framers thus sought to establish a **constitutional republic**, in which public policy would be made by elected representatives within limits delineated in the Constitution. As we have noted in previous chapters, the Constitution was adopted to place certain values above the political fray in order to protect individual rights from the tyranny of transient majorities. With its several elitist elements and many limitations on majority rule, the Framers' Constitution can be seen as rather undemocratic. But two centuries of history have witnessed the democratization of the U.S. Constitution. What was conceived as a constitutional *republic* has become a constitutional *democracy*.

The Democratization of America

It should be remembered that property qualifications for voting still existed in 1787 and that the franchise was granted originally only to white males. With the advent of Jacksonian democracy in the 1830s, property qualifications rapidly diminished and were virtually nonexistent by the time of the Civil War. The Fifteenth Amendment, adopted in 1870, theoretically extended the franchise to African-Americans, although another century of struggle was necessary to realize the promise of the amendment.

The Nineteenth Amendment, ratified in 1920, removed sex as a qualification for voting. In addition to women's suffrage, another accomplishment of the progressive movement was passage of the Seventeenth Amendment in 1913, providing for the direct election of U.S. senators. The Twenty-fourth Amendment, ratified in 1964, abolished **poll taxes** as prerequisites for voting in federal elections. Finally, the minimum voting age was lowered to 18 with the adoption of the Twenty-sixth Amendment in 1971. Thus, through two centuries of political change highlighted by historic amendments, the U.S. Constitution has undergone a democratic transformation.

Through mass media, political parties, interest groups and public demonstrations, the American people have numerous opportunities to make their demands and preferences known to their political leaders. And, of course, many of these leaders are accountable to the public through regular, competitive elections. Comparatively, the United States elects a greater number of its officials and holds more elections than any other nation on earth. The American people elect an astonishing array of public officials from the president all the way down to local school board members. Unfortunately, however, election practices, and even the laws governing elections, have not always reflected a serious commitment to the ideal of political equality.

Policing the Democratic Process

What happens when the majority decides to strip the minority of certain rights, even to exclude it from political participation? In a political system based solely on majority rule, there would be no remedy for the minority group. The problem is far from hypothetical. History resounds with instances of majorities oppressing minorities.

Even in the United States, the "people's representatives" have passed laws isolating minority groups, diluting their right to vote, and even excluding them from the political process altogether. Such sordid conduct underscores the need for limitations on legislative power, especially in the area of voting rights. Those constitutional amendments safeguarding the right to vote and to organize politically are essential to a minority group's ability to protect itself from a hostile majority. Equally important, however, is the role that courts have played in ensuring that minorities are not locked out of the political process. Indeed, one of the paradoxes of American democracy is that the U.S. Supreme Court, an unelected, fundamentally elitist institution, has played a major part in the progressive democratization of the country. Through its exercise of judicial review, the Court, especially during the first half of the twentieth century, struck down a number of laws restricting the right to vote. In the latter half of the twentieth century it upheld and thus reinforced the constitutional legitimacy of statutes, such as the Voting Rights Act of 1965, designed to safeguard and expand the franchise.

Footnote 4 Justice Harlan Fiske Stone's famous footnote in *United States v. Carotene Products* (1938) recognized potential problems that could result from efforts to limit political participation, including "restrictions upon the right to vote," "restraints upon the dissemination of information," "interferences with political organizations," and "prohibition[s] of peaceable assembly." Stone asserted that "prejudice against discrete and insular minorities may be a special condition, which tends seriously to curtail the operation of those political processes ordinarily to be relied upon to protect minorities...." Accordingly, claims brought by groups that have been locked out of the political process call for a "more searching judicial inquiry."

SIDEBAR

Justice Samuel F. Miller on Threats to Free Elections

"It is as essential to the successful working of this government that the great organisms of its executive and legislative branches should be the free choice of the people, as that the original form of it should be so. In absolute governments, where the monarch is the source of all power, it is still held to be important that the exercise of that power shall be free from the influence of extraneous violence and internal corruption. In a republican government, like ours, where political power is reposed in representatives of the entire body of the people, chosen at short intervals by popular elections, the temptations to control these elections by violence and by corruption is a constant source of danger. Such has been the history of all republics, and, though ours has been comparatively free from both these evils in the past, no lover of his country can shut his eyes to the fear of future danger from both sources.... If the government of the United States has within its constitutional domain no authority to provide against these evils—if the very sources of power may be poisoned by corruption or controlled by violence and outrage, without legal restraint—then, indeed, is the country in danger, and its best powers, its highest purposes, the hopes which it inspires, and the love which enshrines it, are at the mercy of the combinations of those who respect no right but brute force on the one hand, and unprincipled corruptionists on the other."

—Justice Samuel F. Miller, writing for the Supreme Court in *Ex Parte Yarbrough* (1884)

Racial Discrimination in Voting Rights

As previously noted, the ratification of the Fifteenth Amendment in 1870 did not result in the immediate enfranchisement of most African-Americans. In some areas, public officials blatantly refused to honor the mandates of the Fifteenth Amendment.

In other areas, groups such as the Ku Klux Klan resorted to terrorism to prevent African-Americans from exercising their newly won right to vote. The Supreme Court initially aided such resistance by limiting congressional power to enforce the Fifteenth Amendment. In *United States v. Reese* (1876), the Court struck down the Enforcement Act of 1870, by which Congress attempted to protect the right of African-Americans to vote in state elections. By 1884, the Court changed course and recognized Congress's power to enforce the Fifteenth Amendment (see *Ex Parte Yarbrough*). By this time, however, Congress was not particularly concerned with the rights of African-Americans. Nevertheless, once it became clear that the Court would permit the federal government to secure African-Americans voting rights, states bent on maintaining African-Americans in a position of second-class citizenship resorted to disingenuous methods designed to exclude them from the political process.

Grandfather Clauses

Perhaps the most blatant official means of preventing black Americans from exercising their newly granted constitutional right to vote was the **grandfather clause**. First enacted by Mississippi in 1890, this device soon spread throughout southern and border states. Oklahoma's version, adopted as an amendment to the state constitution in 1910, was typical in that it required literacy tests for all voters whose ancestors had not been entitled to vote prior to 1866. The overall effect of grandfather clauses was to subject almost all potential African-American voters to literacy tests arbitrarily administered by white officials, while exempting numerous illiterate whites from this requirement.

Largely in response to invidious discrimination of this kind, the National Association for the Advancement of Colored People (NAACP) was formed in the early twentieth century. The first of many legal victories won by the NAACP came in 1915 when the Supreme Court struck down the Oklahoma grandfather clause *(Guinn v. United States)*. Undaunted, the Oklahoma legislature in 1916 adopted a new law aimed at keeping African-Americans from the polls. This statute granted permanent voting registration to all persons who had voted in 1914, when the grandfather clause was still in effect. All other persons were required to register to vote during a twelve-day period or be permanently disqualified from voting. Although it took more than two decades, the Supreme Court ultimately invalidated this blatant subterfuge as well (see *Lane v. Wilson* [1939]).

The White Primary

After the demise of the grandfather clause, southern states resorted to the equally infamous **white primary**. This device was an extremely effective means of keeping African-Americans from exercising their right to vote in any meaningful sense. Until the 1960s, the "solid South" maintained a virtual one-party political system. Thus, in all but a few areas, nomination by the Democratic Party was tantamount to election.

In fact, Republicans seldom bothered to run in the general elections. In order to keep African-Americans out of the political process, the Democratic Party in many states adopted a rule excluding them from party membership. Concomitantly, state legislatures closed the primaries to everyone except party members. The Supreme Court had previously ruled that political parties were private organizations, not part of the government election apparatus (see *Newberry v. United States* [1921]). Consequently, through the white primary device, African-Americans were effectively disenfranchised but, arguably, not by official state action.

In a series of cases from the late 1920s through the early 1950s, the Supreme Court grappled with the white primary issue. In two early decisions, it effectively barred formal state endorsement of the white primary (see *Nixon v. Herndon* [1927] and *Nixon v. Condon* [1932]). However, in *Grovey v. Townsend* (1935), the Supreme Court upheld a Texas white primary based not on legislative enactment but exclusively on a resolution adopted by the state Democratic Party. The Court's decision in *Grovey* thus reinforced the prevailing legal view that political parties were merely private organizations beyond the purview of the Constitution. In *United States v. Classic* (1941), however, the Court moved away from this highly artificial view of party primaries.

The *Classic* case involved the question of whether the federal government could regulate party primaries in order to prevent election fraud. In upholding this exercise of congressional power, the Court overruled *Newberry* and undercut the logic of *Grovey v. Townsend*. In *Smith v. Allwright* (1944), the Court struck down the white primary as violative of the Fifteenth Amendment, thus overruling the *Grovey* decision. Writing for the Court, Justice Stanley Reed expressed a pragmatic view of the concept of state action:

> *This grant to the people of the opportunity for choice is not to be nullified by a State through casting its electoral process in a form which permits a private organization to practice racial discrimination in the election. Constitutional rights would be of little value if they could be thus indirectly denied.*

In an attempt to circumvent the Supreme Court's ruling in *Smith v. Allwright*, Texas Democrats established the "Jaybird Democratic Association," from which African-Americans were excluded. The Jaybirds held "preprimary" elections in which candidates for the Democratic primaries were selected. This blatant attempt at further evasion of constitutional requirements was invalidated by the Supreme Court (*Terry v. Adams* [1953]). In *Terry*, the Court observed that under the preprimary scheme, both the primary and the general elections were little more than "perfunctory ratifiers" of the Jaybirds' choices for elected officials.

Literacy Tests

The eradication of grandfather clauses and white primaries was insufficient to integrate African-Americans into the political process because die-hard racism manifested itself in alternative exclusionary tactics. For example, many states relied on **literacy tests** that, despite superficial neutrality, were administered in a highly discriminatory manner. Quite frequently, white people were not required to take the tests, even if their literacy was questionable. However, since the Constitution had left the determination of voting qualifications to the states and since these tests were on their face racially neutral, the Supreme Court refused to strike them down. In *Lassiter v. Northampton County Board of Education* (1959), the Court explicitly upheld the use of literacy tests. Writing for the Court, Justice William O. Douglas reasoned that "in our society where newspapers, periodicals, books and other printed matter canvass and debate campaign issues, a State might conclude that only those who are literate should exercise the franchise." Ultimately, literacy tests as devices of racial discrimination were done away with, not by the Supreme Court but by Congress through the landmark Voting Rights Act of 1965.

Poll Taxes

Another less common but equally effective means of keeping African-Americans from voting was the poll tax. At the time the Constitution was adopted, poll taxes were widely used as a legitimate means of raising revenue. During the 1780s, however, poll taxes did not significantly hamper voting because only white property owners were entitled to vote anyway! By the mid-nineteenth century, poll taxes had virtually disappeared.

Around 1900, a number of states resurrected the poll tax for the obvious purpose of preventing African-Americans from voting. The tax generally amounted to $2 per election—quite sufficient to deter many African-Americans, as well as poor whites, from exercising the franchise. On its face, however, the poll tax was racially neutral, and the Supreme Court initially refused to strike it down (see *Breedlove v. Suttles* [1937]). Eventually, however, the poll tax was thoroughly repudiated. In 1964, the poll tax was abolished in federal elections through adoption of the Twenty-fourth Amendment. Two years later, in *Harper v. Virginia Board of Elections* (1966), the Supreme Court held that poll taxes in state elections violated the Fourteenth Amendment. Writing for the Court, Justice Douglas emphasized the arbitrariness of the tax:

> To introduce wealth, or payment of a fee as a measure of a voter's qualifications is to introduce a capricious or irrelevant factor.... Wealth, like race, creed, or color, is not germane to one's ability to participate intelligently in the electoral process.

Racial Gerrymandering

Perhaps the most outrageous attempt to disenfranchise African-American voters occurred in Tuskegee, Alabama, in 1957. At the city's behest, the all-white Alabama legislature dramatically altered the boundaries of Tuskegee from a square to a twenty-eight-sided figure. The purpose of the **gerrymander** was obvious in that all but five of the city's 400 black voters were placed outside the city limits, while no white voters were displaced. A number of the "former residents" of Tuskegee brought suit in federal court, seeking a declaratory judgment that the **racial gerrymandering** measure was unconstitutional and an injunction to prohibit its enforcement. The U.S. District Court for the Middle District of Alabama dismissed the case for lack of jurisdiction, stating that it had "no control over, no supervision over, and no power to change any boundaries of a municipal corporation fixed by a duly convened legislative body." The Court of Appeals for the Fifth Circuit agreed. But the Supreme Court reversed the decision of the lower courts and reinstated the complaint, saying that the "petitioners are entitled to prove their allegations at trial." Speaking for a unanimous bench, Justice Felix Frankfurter stated that if the plaintiffs' allegations were proven, it would be "difficult to appreciate what stands in the way of adjudging [the redistricting measure] invalid" (*Gomillion v. Lightfoot* [1960]). Indeed, plaintiffs prevailed at trial, and the gerrymander was invalidated.

The Voting Rights Act of 1965

A 1961 report of the U.S. Commission on Civil Rights documented the pervasiveness of voting discrimination in the South. According to the report, fewer than 10 percent of eligible African-Americans were registered to vote in at least 129 counties in ten southern states. In counties where African-Americans comprised a majority of the population, the average level of African-American registration was only 3 percent. As the Civil Rights movement of the early 1960s galvanized the nation's conscience, the demand for federal action grew. The federal government responded with the Civil Rights Act of 1964 and the **Voting Rights Act of 1965**, both of which were pushed through Congress under the skillful leadership of President Lyndon B. Johnson.

The Voting Rights Act employed a rough index of discrimination to apply the scrutiny of the federal government to those states that had historically been most recalcitrant in refusing to allow African-Americans to vote: Alabama, Georgia, Louisiana, Mississippi, South Carolina, and Virginia. Specifically, the Act waived accumulated poll taxes and abolished literacy tests and similar devices in those areas to which the statute applied. The Act also required the aforementioned States to obtain **preclearance** from the U.S.

Department of Justice before making changes in their electoral systems. Not surprisingly, this historic and far-reaching Act was challenged on the ground that Congress had exceeded its power to enforce the Fifteenth Amendment.

The Supreme Court, although recognizing the Voting Rights Act as "inventive," upheld the law (see *South Carolina v. Katzenbach* [1966]). Writing for a nearly unanimous Court (only Justice Hugo Black partially dissented), Chief Justice Earl Warren expressed optimism about the Voting Rights Act:

> *Hopefully, millions of non-white Americans will now be able to participate for the first time on an equal basis in the government under which they live. We may finally look forward to the day when truly "the right of citizens of the United States to vote shall not be denied or abridged by the United States or by any State on account of race, color or previous condition of servitude."*

Enforcement of the Voting Rights Act resulted in substantially higher levels of voter registration among African-Americans, particularly in the Deep South. For example, in Alabama, less than 20 percent of African-American adults were registered to vote in 1964; by 1968 more than half were registered. In Mississippi, African-American registration soared from less than 7 percent in 1964 to nearly 60 percent in 1968. The same thing happened throughout the South. Accordingly, many politicians who formerly made overt appeals to white supremacy tempered their racist rhetoric in order to draw support from new black American voters. Perhaps the best example of this metamorphosis was Alabama Governor George Wallace who, in the face of the Civil Rights movement of the 1960s, maintained a strong segregationist stance. In the late 1970s and early 1980s, Wallace dropped the racist rhetoric in order to appeal to newly enfranchised African-Americans who might be tempted to vote Republican.

The Voting Rights Act has also brought minorities into the realm of government. In a report entitled "Black Elected Officials: A Statistical Summary, 2000," the Joint Center for Political and Economic Studies reported that the number of African-American elected officials nationwide had increased 600 percent between 1970 and 2000. The report noted that African-American women made up roughly 35 percent of the 9,040 African-American elected officials in 2000. It also noted an increasing number of African-American mayors being elected in large but predominantly white cities. And, of course, the election of President Barack Obama in 2008 (as well as his reelection in 2012) would not have been possible were it not for the tremendous political gains that African-Americans made in the four decades since the Voting Rights Act was enacted.

Without question, the Voting Rights Act is a tremendous success story in the development of American constitutional democracy. However, many conservatives and "states' rights" advocates opposed renewal of the Voting Rights Act when it was due to expire in 1982. Of particular concern to many was the preclearance requirement of Section 5, under which designated states are required to submit proposed changes in election laws to the Justice Department for approval. The Reagan administration, more conservative than its Democratic and Republican predecessors in the field of civil rights, initially opposed the extension of the Act without major changes in these controversial provisions. However, bipartisan support in Congress for extending the Act forced the administration to back down. The Act was renewed and strengthened in 1982. Indeed, the Voting Rights Act has been extended and strengthened by Congress five times (1970, 1975, 1982, 1992, and 2006) and is not scheduled to expire until 2031.

The Roberts Court Hands Down a Major Decision on the Voting Rights Act

In 2013 the Roberts Court considered a major challenge to Section 5 of the Voting Rights Act. Shelby County, Alabama, which brought the case, claimed that Section 5's preclearance requirement exceeded Congress' powers to enforce the Fourteenth and Fifteenth Amendments in that preclearance was no longer necessary given the progress toward racial equality in voting and representation. Four years earlier, the Roberts Court said in *Northwest Austin Municipal Utility District No. One v. Holder* (2009) that that the burdens imposed by Section 5 had to be "justified by current needs," suggesting some sympathy with the position advocated by Shelby County. In *Shelby County v. Holder* (2013), the Supreme Court refrained from invalidating Section 5, but it did strike down the coverage formula contained in Section 4(b) of the statute, which had not been updated in forty years. Writing for a closely divided bench, Chief Justice Roberts observed that "Congress—if it is to divide the States—must identify those jurisdictions to be singled out on a basis that makes sense in light of current conditions. It cannot rely simply on the past." In dissent, Justice Ruth Ginsburg averred that "the Court errs egregiously by overriding Congress' decision." For Ginsburg and her colleagues in the minority, the Court's decision intruded on the role of Congress in deciding whether the existing coverage formula needed to be changed....

At-Large Elections

In the 1960s and 1970s, as African-Americans registered and voted in greater numbers, black politicians made substantial gains, especially at the local level. To thwart the growing influence of African-American voters, a number of white-dominated cities and counties adopted basic structural changes in their systems of representation. Because the overt racial gerrymander had been declared unconstitutional in *Gomillion v. Lightfoot* (1960), these communities converted to **at-large elections** in which local candidates ran for office on a citywide or countywide basis. This election method was by no means novel in the United States, but its use as a deliberate means of limiting the political clout of African-American voters raised new constitutional issues. At-large systems of voting were often coupled with the annexation of predominantly white suburban areas, thereby further diluting black American voting power. Since the 1970s, many of these at-large and annexation schemes have been challenged in court as unlawful attempts to undermine the voting strength of minority groups.

The Supreme Court Rules on At-Large Elections   In 1980, the Supreme Court handed down an impotent ruling on the constitutionality of at-large elections in *Mobile v. Bolden*. Since 1911, the city of Mobile, Alabama, had used at-large elections to choose its three-member city commission. At the time the lawsuit was filed, more than 35 percent of the residents of Mobile were African-American. Despite several attempts, however, no African-American had ever been elected to the city commission. Plaintiffs argued that the at-large system was unconstitutional because it had the effect of unfairly diluting the voting strength of racial minorities. The U.S. District Court for the Southern District of Alabama agreed, as did the Fifth Circuit Court of Appeals. The Supreme Court reversed, holding that there must be a showing of a discriminatory intent on the part of public officials in order to warrant a finding that the Constitution has been violated. Dissenting vehemently, Justice Thurgood Marshall asserted that "[s]uch judicial deference to official decision making has no place under the Fifteenth Amendment." Marshall went on to accuse the Court of being "an accessory to the perpetuation of racial discrimination." In spite of, or perhaps in response to, Justice Marshall's accusatory rhetoric in *Mobile v. Bolden*, the Supreme Court in 1982 demonstrated that the "intentional discrimination" standard can in fact be met. In *Rogers v. Lodge*, the Court, voting 6 to 3, struck down an at-large election scheme in Burke County, Georgia, on the basis of the standard handed down in the *Mobile* case. In this case, the Court reasserted a commitment to the Fifteenth Amendment that some critics found lacking in *Mobile v. Bolden*.

The 1982 Voting Rights Act Amendments   In its 1982 extension of the Voting Rights Act, Congress amended Section 2 to allow plaintiffs to prevail in Voting Rights Act litigation on the basis of an effects test, rather than on the intent standard of *Mobile v. Bolden*. In other words, Congress accomplished through statute what the Supreme Court refused to do under the Fifteenth Amendment. Thus, *Mobile v. Bolden* is essentially irrelevant to a group of minority plaintiffs seeking to challenge an election scheme. It matters not to plaintiffs whether they prevail under a provision of the federal Constitution or under Section 2 of the Voting Rights Act. Here is an important lesson for students of the American legal system: Civil rights law is by no means the exclusive province of courts and constitutions. Legislatures may act to enhance civil rights through their power to adopt ordinary legislation.

As amended in 1982, Section 2 of the Voting Rights Act provides that election processes must be equally open to participation by members of a minority group and that it is a violation if members of that group "have less opportunity than other members of the electorate to participate in the political process and to elect representatives of their choice." That last clause, to elect representatives of their choice, is crucial. Through judicial interpretation, this clause has given rise to a new species of legal action—the **vote dilution** claim.

In *Thornburgh v. Gingles* (1985) and subsequent cases, the Supreme Court held that splitting (or "cracking") a minority group between districts is legally suspect if, among other things, the minority group is sufficiently large and geographically compact to constitute a majority in a single-member district. In the 1980s and early 1990s, the prevailing view of the federal courts was that the Voting Rights Act requires states to maximize the number of majority-minority districts (districts in which members of a racial minority constitute a majority of voters). But as Justice Sandra Day O'Connor recognized in *Voinovich v. Quitter* (1993) "creating majority-black districts necessarily leaves fewer black voters, and therefore diminishes black voter influence in predominantly white districts." Because African-Americans tend overwhelmingly to identify themselves as Democrats, maximizing majority-minority districts causes remaining districts to be more "white" and therefore more Republican and more conservative. This may have contributed to the partisan and ideological polarization in Congress and the state legislatures.

The Rehnquist Court Restricts Race-Conscious Redistricting

In *Shaw v. Reno* (1993), the Court under Chief Justice Rehnquist ruled that strangely shaped legislative districts designed to produce African-American electoral majorities are subject to challenge under the Equal Protection Clause of the Fourteenth Amendment. White voters had sued to challenge the "racial gerrymandering" that led to the creation of the unusually shaped Twelfth Congressional District of North Carolina. A three-judge panel in the federal district court dismissed the suit for failure to state a cause of action for which relief is available under the Fourteenth Amendment. On appeal, the Supreme Court reversed by a vote of 5 to 4.

Writing for the Court, Justice O'Connor observed that "[w]hen a district is created solely to effectuate the perceived common interests of one racial group, elected officials are more likely to believe that their primary obligation is to represent only the members of that group, rather than their constituency as a whole." In O'Connor's view, such an effect would be "altogether antithetical to our system of representative democracy." In dissent, Justice White argued that "the notion that North Carolina's plan, under which whites remain a voting majority in a disproportionate number of congressional districts, and pursuant to which the State has sent its first black representatives since Reconstruction to the United States Congress, might have violated appellants' constitutional rights is both a fiction and a departure from settled equal protection principles." In *Shaw v. Reno*, the Supreme Court stopped short of invalidating the North Carolina plan, leaving that determination to the lower federal courts. On remand, the district court in North Carolina upheld the redistricting plan on the ground that the plan was narrowly tailored to further the state's compelling interests in complying with the Voting Rights Act of 1965. Not surprisingly, the Supreme Court granted certiorari and the case returned to the High Bench.

In *Shaw v. Hunt* (1996), the Supreme Court struck down the North Carolina plan. Writing for the majority of five, Chief Justice Rehnquist took issue with the district court's conclusion that the plan was justified as a means of meeting the state's responsibilities under the Voting Rights Act. Among other things, this statute protects minorities from vote dilution. In Rehnquist's view, vote dilution suffered by African-American voting in congressional elections throughout North Carolina is "not remedied by creating a safe majority-black district somewhere else in the State." The real thrust of the Court's opinion appears to have been a repudiation of the Justice Department's policy of maximizing the number of majority-black districts.

Rehnquist asserted that "this maximization policy is not properly grounded in Section 5 [of the Voting Rights Act] and the Department's authority thereunder." In a stinging dissent, Justice Stevens observed that "[t]here is no small irony in the fact that the Court's decision to intrude into the State's districting process comes in response to a lawsuit brought on behalf of white voters who have suffered no history of exclusion from North Carolina's political process, and whose only claims of harm are at best rooted in speculative and stereotypical assumptions about the kind of representation they are likely to receive from the candidates that their neighbors have chosen." In a similar case, *Bush v. Vera* (1996), the Court invalidated a Texas redistricting plan that created three minority-majority districts. Writing for a plurality, Justice O'Connor observed that the "districts' shapes are bizarre, and their utter disregard of city limits, local election precincts, and voter tabulation district lines has caused a severe disruption of traditional forms of political activity and created administrative headaches for local election officials." O'Connor noted that the "appellants adduced evidence that incumbency protection played a role in determining the bizarre district lines" but concluded, as had the district court, that "the districts' shapes are unexplainable on grounds other than race and, as such, are the product of presumptively unconstitutional racial gerrymandering is inescapably corroborated by the evidence." Justices Stevens, Souter, Ginsburg, and Breyer dissented, as they did in *Shaw v. Hunt*.

The Supreme Court Revisits the North Carolina Redistricting Plan

After the Supreme Court's decision in *Shaw v. Hunt*, the North Carolina legislature redrew the boundaries of the disputed congressional district. Again, litigation ensued. A three-judge panel of the federal district court invalidated the plan, finding that race had again been the dominant consideration. In *Hunt v. Cromartie* (2001), the Supreme Court reversed the district court and upheld the revised plan. Noting the high correlation between race and party identification, the Court concluded that the plaintiffs had failed to show that race was the predominant consideration in the legislature's redistricting plan and that the district court's contrary conclusion was "clearly erroneous."

In dissent, Justice Clarence Thomas (joined by Chief Justice Rehnquist and Justices Scalia and Kennedy) observed that "racial gerrymandering offends the Constitution whether the motivation is malicious or benign." Thomas argued that it "is not a defense that the legislature merely may have drawn the district based on the stereotype that blacks are reliable Democratic voters." *Hunt v. Cromartie* did not overturn *Shaw v. Hunt*, but it arguably makes it more difficult for plaintiffs to challenge race-conscious redistricting plans. The litigation over the use of race in redrawing the North Carolina congressional districts lasted nearly ten years and went before the Supreme Court four times. When, in 2001, the Court terminated the litigation, the 2000 census had been completed and it was time for the state legislature to begin redistricting anew. This series of cases led some to wonder if litigation in this field is simply inevitable and interminable.

Challenges to Judicial Election Systems

When Congress extended the Voting Rights Act in 1982, it changed the statutory language in a way that eventually proved to be highly significant. Instead of applying only to elections of "legislators," the act now refers to "representatives." This suggests the applicability of Voting Rights Act challenges to nonlegislative elections, but which elections? In a controversial 6-to-3 decision, the Supreme Court held in 1991 that plaintiffs may challenge judicial election systems under Section 2 of the Voting Rights Act. In *Chisom v. Roemer*, the Court decided that the statutory term "representatives" includes elected judges. The *Chisom* case is one of myriad examples of important civil rights policies being determined through statutory, as opposed to constitutional, interpretation.

Chisom v. Roemer involved a challenge to Louisiana's system for electing judges to the state supreme court. Under that system, five of the seven state supreme court judges were elected from single-member districts; the remaining two jurists were elected at large from a sixth district that included the predominantly black American Orleans Parish and several other parishes where African-Americans were in the minority. Plaintiffs in the case argued that this scheme had the effect of diluting the voting strength of black Americans in New Orleans. Had Orleans Parish been set up as a separate single-member district, an African-American candidate would have had a greater chance of being elected to the state supreme court. Under the existing system, no black American had ever been elected to Louisiana's highest tribunal, despite a number of attempts. After a bench trial, the U.S. district court concluded that there had been no violation of the Voting Rights Act under the standard set forth in the landmark case of *Thornburgh v. Gingles* (1986). On appeal, the Fifth Circuit Court of Appeals concluded that the Voting Rights Act did not apply to judicial elections, holding that the district court should have dismissed the complaint altogether. On certiorari, the U.S. Supreme Court reversed, declaring that "[w]hen each of several members of a court must be a resident of a different district, and must be elected by the voters of that district, it seems both reasonable and realistic to characterize the winners as representatives of that district." The Supreme Court expressed no opinion on the merits of the plaintiffs' case. It merely remanded the case to the Fifth Circuit Court of Appeals for further consideration.

In a related case, the Supreme Court decided that Section 2 of the Voting Rights Act applies also to the election of state trial judges. In *Houston Lawyers' Association v. Attorney General of Texas* (1991), the Court said that "[i]f a State decides to elect its trial judges, … those elections must be conducted in compliance with the Voting Rights Act." By 2012, thirty-eight states made use of some form of election (partisan, nonpartisan, or merit retention) to select or retain their judges. Thus the Court's decisions in *Chisom v. Roemer* and *Houston Lawyers' Association* have plowed a fertile field for litigation. It remains to be seen whether plaintiffs will be successful in mounting challenges to judicial elections. However, one can be sure that the Supreme Court will be revisiting this area of voting rights law.

Voter Identification Laws

Many states now have laws requiring voters to produce some sort of identification when they show up at the polling place. These laws vary in terms of what sort of identification is valid and whether an alternative measure, such as answering questions about one's residency, are available to voters who do not have the required ID. Supporters of voter ID laws argue that they are necessary to prevent voter fraud. According to public opinion polls, the public is generally favorable to this argument. But civil rights advocates sound the alarm of discrimination, fearing that these measures have the effect of suppressing the minority vote. They point out that voter fraud is not a major problem in this country and that the real danger is that states will use concern over voter fraud as a pretext for enacting measures that suppress participation by minority voters. Not surprisingly, voter ID laws have become a major partisan issue, with Republicans typically supporting them and Democrats usually in opposition.

In *Crawford v. Marion County Election Board* (2008), the Supreme Court upheld an Indiana law requiring voters to provide photo IDs. Writing for a majority of six justices, John Paul Stevens concluded that the burdens placed on voters were limited to a small percentage of the population and were offset by the state's interest in reducing voter fraud. That decision prompted other states to enact their own voter ID laws.

The National Voter Registration Act of 1993 (better known as the Motor Voter Act) was an attempt by Congress to facilitate voter registration. One of the requirements of the Act is that states allow citizens to use a uniform federal form to register to vote. In *Arizona v. Inter Tribal Council* (2013), the Supreme Court held that voters who use the federal form cannot be required to produce additional identification when they register or appear at the polls to cast their votes. However, the decision was based on statutory grounds, not constitutional interpretation. Writing for the Court, Justice Scalia concluded that the "fairest reading" of the National Voter Registration Act "is that a state-imposed requirement of evidence of citizenship not required by the Federal Form is 'inconsistent with' the NVRA's mandate that States 'accept and use' the Federal Form." In dissent, Justice Thomas said that he "would construe the law as only requiring Arizona to accept and use the form as part of its voter registration process, leaving the State free to request whatever additional information it determines is necessary to ensure that voters meet the qualifications it has the constitutional authority to establish." Although the legal effect of *Arizona v. Inter Tribal Council* is limited, symbolically the decision was an important victory for those concerned about voter suppression by the states.

On the other hand, the Court's decision in *Shelby County v. Holder* (2013) was a major victory for those on the other side of this issue. Prior to that decision, states subject to preclearance under the Voting Rights Act had to obtain prior approval of the Attorney General before implementing voter ID laws. After the Court invalidated the coverage formula and effectively imposed a moratorium on preclearance, states like Texas and North Carolina became free to move forward with implementing their voter ID laws. Of course, there are other provisions under the Voting Rights Act under which the Justice Department, or citizens who are adversely affected by voter ID laws, can go into federal court after the fact to challenge the legality of voter identification laws. As we pointed out earlier in the chapter, Section 2 of the Voting Rights Act has been interpreted to prohibit state laws that give minority voters "less opportunity than other members of the electorate to participate in the political process and to elect representatives of their choice." And, of course, the Fourteenth and Fifteenth Amendments prohibit intentional racial discrimination with respect to voting and elections. It remains to be seen whether federal courts will approve the implementation of voter ID laws in states with histories of racial discrimination in voting rights.

To Summarize:

♦ *In spite of the ratification of the Fifteenth Amendment in 1870, African-Americans did not achieve full voting rights until implementation of the Voting Rights Act of 1965.*

♦ *States intent on inhibiting electoral participation by black Americans developed a variety of mechanisms, including grandfather clauses, white primaries, literacy tests, racial gerrymanders, and poll taxes. All of these efforts to frustrate political participation by African-Americans were eventually invalidated either by Supreme Court decisions, federal statutes, or amendments to the U.S. Constitution.*

♦ *Federal courts have continued to scrutinize changes in state and local electoral systems, using both the Voting Rights Act of 1965, as amended, and the Fourteenth and Fifteenth Amendments to the U.S. Constitution. Many such changes have been challenged by minority groups on the ground that they impermissibly dilute minority influence.*

♦ *During the 1990s, the Rehnquist Court shifted the focus of judicial scrutiny away from efforts to dilute the voting power of minorities and toward efforts to increase the political influence of African-Americans through the race-conscious redrawing of district lines.*

♦ *In the recent controversy over voter ID laws, the Supreme Court has upheld such laws in principle, but it remains to be seen whether the federal courts will allow implementation of such laws in states with histories of racial discrimination with respect to voting rights.*

Reapportionment: One Person, One Vote

Questions of inequality with respect to voting rights are by no means limited to the issue of racial discrimination. For many years, one of the most intractable and pervasive forms of inequality was that of legislative **malapportionment**.

Representation in the U.S. House of Representatives, in all fifty state legislatures, and in most local governments is apportioned on the basis of population. Representatives in state legislatures and in the U.S. House are elected from single-member districts (although a few states are allotted only one representative who of course is elected state-wide). Malapportionment exists to the extent that the number of voters comprising such districts is unequal. Malapportionment can come about in two ways.

It has generally occurred as a function of natural population shifts due to urbanization and interstate migration. It has also come about through gerrymandering, where district lines are intentionally drawn to create inequalities for political purposes.

Historically, malapportionment of the state legislatures and the U.S. House favored rural over urban interests. In many states, it was not uncommon for urban districts to be ten times as populous as rural districts, thus diluting the value of urban votes by a factor of ten. A particularly egregious example of malapportionment was provided by Georgia's "county unit system" (declared unconstitutional by the Supreme Court in *Gray v. Sanders* [1963]). Under that scheme, Fulton County (comprising much of metropolitan Atlanta) with a 1960 population of more than half a million was entitled to three seats in the state House of Representatives. Echols County in rural south Georgia, with a 1960 population of only 1,876, nearly half of whom were unregistered African-Americans, was entitled to one representative. Thus, the discrepancy in representation was more than 100 to 1 in favor of Echols County!

Even though apportionment discrepancies throughout the United States were great and growing, it was unrealistic to expect elected officials (many of whom benefited from the status quo) to address the problem. Yet most Americans seemed to assume that this problem, like so many others, had a legal solution. Accordingly, voters from grossly underrepresented urban areas turned for relief to the federal courts, citing, among other things, the Equal Protection Clause of the Fourteenth Amendment.

In *Colegrove v. Green* (1946), the Supreme Court invoked the political questions doctrine to foreclose judicial relief, at least from the federal bench. Writing for a plurality of the Court, Justice Frankfurter warned of the dangers of entering the "political thicket" of malapportionment:

> It is hostile to a democratic system to involve the judiciary in the politics of the people.... The remedy for unfairness in districting is to secure state legislatures that will apportion properly, or to invoke the ample powers of Congress.

The Reapportionment Revolution

Between 1946 and 1962, groups representing urban interests tried, without much success, to secure **reapportionment** through the state legislatures and through the ballot box. Beginning in 1962, however, the Supreme Court produced a series of decisions on reapportionment that would permanently alter the American political landscape and draw the Court into a firestorm of criticism.

In *Baker v. Carr* (1962), the Supreme Court opened the doors of the federal courthouse to plaintiffs pressing reapportionment claims. The Court reversed its previous position and declared malapportionment to be justiciable (see Chapter 1, Volume I). Shortly thereafter, the Court declared malapportionment in its various contexts unconstitutional (see Table 8.1). Reapportionment, wrote Chief Justice Warren in *Reynolds v. Sims* (1964), would have to follow the principle of "one person, one vote." In *Reynolds* the Court held that "the Equal Protection Clause requires that a State make an honest and good faith effort to construct districts, in both houses of its legislature, as nearly of equal population as is practicable." Not surprisingly, many observers soon began to wonder just how strict the Court would be in requiring population equality among legislative districts. In *Reynolds*, Chief Justice Warren had observed that "it is a practical impossibility to arrange legislative districts so that each one has an identical number of residents, or citizens, or voters. Mathematical exactness is hardly a workable constitutional requirement."

TABLE 8.1 MAJOR SUPREME COURT DECISIONS EXTENDING REAPPORTIONMENT

CASE	YEAR	TARGET OF REAPPORTIONMENT
Gray v. Sanders	1963	Georgia "county unit" system of apportioning state legislature
Wesberry v. Sanders	1964	Congressional districts
Reynolds v. Sims	1964	All state legislatures
Lucas v. Colorado 44th General Assembly	1964	State legislative apportionment based on constitutional provisions
Avery v. Midland County	1968	Local governing bodies
Hadley v. Junior College District	1970	School boards

In 1969, the Court provided an indication of just how strict it intended to be when it struck down an apportionment scheme for congressional districts in Missouri. The plan invalidated by the Court in *Kirkpatrick v. Preisler* involved a 6 percent population deviation between the smallest and the largest districts and only a 1.8 percent average deviation from the ideal district population. Many praised the Court for its rigorous application of the one-person, one-vote principle. Others decried the Court's meddling in the technicalities of legislative apportionment. Regardless of the position one takes on this issue, the importance of the Court's reapportionment decisions can hardly be overstated. Indeed, on a number of occasions, Chief Justice Warren himself pointed without hesitation to the reapportionment decisions as his principal contribution to constitutional law.

Reapportionment under the Burger Court

For the most part, the Supreme Court under Chief Justice Warren Burger maintained the Warren Court's strong commitment to the one-person, one-vote principle. The counter-revolution many critics feared from a more conservative Court did not materialize, at least not in the realm of apportionment cases. The Burger Court, however, did allow state legislatures more leeway in determining state legislative boundaries than in drawing congressional district lines. The Court made it clear that, in scrutinizing state districts, it was willing to entertain "legitimate considerations incident to the effectuation of a rational state policy." Thus, in *Brown v. Thomson* (1983), the Court upheld an apportionment scheme for the Wyoming legislature based on county lines, even though the scheme had a population deviation of nearly 90 percent between the largest and the smallest districts. On the very same day, in *Karcher v. Daggett*, the Court invalidated a New Jersey scheme for congressional districts where the maximum deviation was less than 1 percent! The majority agreed with the federal district court that the plan was "not a good-faith effort to achieve population equality using the best available census data."

The Methodology of Reapportionment

Although state legislatures are responsible for drawing the boundaries of congressional districts, the Constitution empowers Congress to determine the number of representatives that each state shall have. Every ten years, after completion of the census, Congress reallocates congressional seats among the states. Article I, Section 2, of the Constitution imposes three restrictions on the exercise of Congress's discretion in this area: (1) every state is guaranteed at least one congressional seat; (2) district lines may not cross state borders; and (3) no district shall include fewer than 30,000 persons.

In 1941, Congress enacted a law specifying that "the method of equal proportions" would be used to ascertain the number of congressional seats to which each state would be entitled. Applying this method to the results of the 1990 census, Congress determined that Montana would lose one of its two congressional seats. After reapportionment, the average population of congressional districts was 572,466, while Montana's population was 803,655. Montana's single district was thus 231,189 persons larger than the average district. Had Montana retained two districts, each would have been 170,638 persons smaller than the average district. Because the loss of a congressional seat means the decline of influence in Congress and the Electoral College, Montana promptly filed suit to challenge the allocation. Relying on *Wesberry v. Sanders* (1964) and *Kirkpatrick v. Preisler* (1969), the state argued that the greater discrepancy between actual and ideal district size by its loss of a seat violated the principle of one person, one vote. A three-judge district court issued a summary judgment upholding Montana's claim and declaring the 1941 statute unconstitutional. On direct appeal, the Supreme Court unanimously reversed (see *Department of Commerce v. Montana* [1992]). Writing for the Court,

Justice John Paul Stevens concluded that Congress had ample power to adopt the method of least proportions or any other reasonable method as long as it is applied consistently after each census. The *Montana* decision signaled that the Supreme Court was willing to accord far more latitude to Congress than to state legislatures in the field of reapportionment.

Reapportionment after the 2010 Census The most recent undertaking of the national census produced several changes in the distribution of House seats across the states. Due to changes in population, New York and Ohio each lost two of their congressional seats, while Illinois, Iowa, Louisiana, Massachusetts, Missouri, New Jersey, and Pennsylvania all lost one seat. Meanwhile eight states gained seats. Arizona, Georgia, Nevada, South Carolina, Utah, and Washington each picked up a seat, while Florida gained two and Texas added four seats in the House of Representatives. Examining the list in more detail, population trends appear to be continuing as experts have generally suggested they would, with people moving away from the Northeast and Midwest and relocating in southern and western states. It is easy to understand why Republicans and conservatives are pleased with these results; they consider population decline in the liberal Northeast and simultaneous growth in the conservative South and West to be a positive development.

Assessing the Reapportionment Decisions

The Supreme Court's reapportionment decisions have been sharply criticized by conservative scholars and by some politicians. In the mid-1960s, a widely publicized effort to overrule the reapportionment decisions through constitutional amendment was spearheaded by Senate Minority Leader Everett Dirksen (R-IL). Despite auspicious beginnings, the Dirksen amendment proved to be a flash in the pan. It soon became clear that the American people fundamentally approved of the reapportionment decisions, irrespective of the strident attacks by many elected officials. A Gallup Poll conducted shortly after *Reynolds v. Sims* was decided found that 47 percent approved of the decision, 30 percent disapproved, and 23 percent expressed no opinion. Apparently the one-person, one-vote principle appealed to the American people's sense of fair play.

While many observers believe that the Supreme Court's school prayer and desegregation decisions were somewhat damaging to its prestige and credibility, the reapportionment decisions seem to have had the opposite effect. Thus, while the continuing debate over the proper role of the Court is important, the Court's legitimacy does not depend so much on fastidious adherence to legal principles, procedures, and traditions as it does on public support for the substance of the Court's decisions. One of the great ironies of American democracy (and perhaps its greatest strength) is that the judicial elite must from time to time interfere with the people's elected representatives for the purpose of maintaining the norm of political equality.

For some jurisprudential thinkers, such as the late John Hart Ely, the primary utility of and justification for judicial review is to maintain the integrity of the democratic process. Certainly the reapportionment decisions make sense from this perspective. It is noteworthy that the reapportionment decisions, although much reviled by incumbent politicians, were met with a far greater degree of compliance than, for example, the school prayer decisions. The strong public support for reapportionment as a policy was undoubtedly a critical factor promoting legislative compliance. The clarity of the Supreme Court's one-person, one-vote mandate likewise facilitated implementation of reapportionment. Finally, the obvious nature of noncompliance probably had a substantial effect on legislative willingness to abide by the Court's decisions.

> **To Summarize:**
>
> ◆ *By the mid-twentieth century, malapportionment of legislative bodies at all levels of government had become a serious problem, one that state legislatures were unwilling to address. After refusing an invitation to enter this political thicket in the mid-1940s, the Supreme Court in* Baker v. Carr *(1962) precipitated a revolution in American politics by determining that malapportionment was a justiciable issue under the Equal Protection Clause of the Fourteenth Amendment.*
>
> ◆ *In* Reynolds v. Sims *(1964) and related cases, the Court applied the principle of "one person, one vote" to legislative districts at all levels of government. As a result, reapportionment today is a regularly recurring feature of American politics.*

Political Parties and Electoral Fairness

Although the Framers of the Constitution neither desired nor anticipated the development of political parties, by 1800 a two-party system had taken root in the young republic. While particular political parties have come and gone since then, the two-party system remains an established feature of the political order. Many regard the two-party system as a source of desirable political stability, while others question the level of representation that only two dominant parties offer for the electorate. Today many Americans bemoan what they perceive as a hyperpartisan political environment in which both parties seem more interested in scoring political points at their opponent's expense than in effective governance.

The merits of the two-party system aside, there is surely a constitutional right for disaffected voters to form new parties or support independent candidates who challenge the established order. Despite ideological disagreements, the two established parties tend to collaborate in suppressing competition by rival third parties and independent candidates. State legislatures frequently adopt laws making it difficult, if not impossible, for third parties to get candidates on the ballot. Unrealistic filing deadlines and petition requirements are often employed to frustrate the electoral ambitions of third-party and independent candidates.

In 1980, independent presidential candidate John Anderson filed suit in federal court to challenge Ohio's March filing deadline for the November general elections.

In *Anderson v. Celebrezze* (1983), Anderson received a favorable ruling from the Supreme Court, which declared the Ohio regulation to be excessively burdensome on the efforts of independent candidates. Anderson's belated legal victory, however, did not altogether eliminate problems that third-party and independent candidates encounter when attempting to get their names on the ballot, as Ralph Nader and Pat Buchanan discovered in their 2000 presidential campaigns. Underscoring the challenge third parties face, by the 2012 presidential election the Libertarian Party, the largest third party in the United States, was still kept off the ballot in Michigan and Oklahoma.

Partisan Gerrymandering

Historically, one of the weapons of inter-party competition has been the gerrymander, the intentional manipulation of district lines for political purposes. Although legislative apportionment must proceed on the principle of one person, one vote and must not be based on race discrimination, there remains the prospect that the party in power in the state legislature will redraw district lines so as to minimize the likelihood that the opposing party will gain seats in the next election. The process of reapportionment, which occurs after each decennial census, thus provides an opportunity for the party holding the majority of seats in the legislature to further strengthen its position. Prior to the 1980s, this **partisan gerrymandering** was thought to be constitutionally unassailable.

In 1986, however, the Supreme Court upheld the justiciability of constitutional challenges to partisan gerrymandering. In *Davis v. Bandemer*, the Court ruled that Indiana Democrats could challenge a 1981 reapportionment plan adopted by the Republican-controlled state legislature. A plurality of four justices maintained, however, that to prevail in such cases, plaintiffs would have to make "a threshold showing of discriminatory vote dilution." In a concurring opinion reminiscent of Justice Frankfurter's plea for judicial restraint in *Colegrove v. Green*, Justice Sandra Day O'Connor lamented the Court's "far-reaching step into the 'political thicket' " and predicted dire consequences. According to Justice O'Connor, a former state legislator:

> *To turn these matters over to the federal judiciary is to inject the courts into the most heated partisan issues. It is predictable that the courts will respond by moving away from the nebulous standard a plurality of the Court fashions today and toward some form of proportional representation.*

The Supreme Court appears to have heeded Justice O'Connor's warning. Despite a number of opportunities to invalidate reapportionment schemes involving blatant political manipulation, the Court has yet to do so. In *Vieth v. Jubelirer* (2004), four justices were prepared to overturn *Davis v. Bandemer* altogether and a fifth, Justice Kennedy, expressed deep reservations about judicial review of partisan gerrymandering. In an opinion concurring in the judgment, Kennedy observed that:

> *When presented with a claim of injury from partisan gerrymandering, courts confront two obstacles. First is the lack of comprehensive and neutral principles for drawing electoral boundaries. No substantive definition of fairness in districting seems to command general assent. Second is the absence of rules to limit and confine judicial intervention. With uncertain limits, intervening courts—even when proceeding with best intentions— would risk assuming political, not legal, responsibility for a process that often produces ill will and distrust.*

Most recently, in *League of United Latin American Voters v. Perry* (2006), the Court upheld a controversial Texas congressional reapportionment plan that strongly advantaged Republican incumbents. Speaking for a plurality of a badly fragmented Court, Justice Kennedy concluded that the plaintiffs had not presented "a reliable standard for identifying unconstitutional political gerrymanders." The Court ruled in the same case, however, that the dismantling of a southwestern Texas district containing a Latino majority—a legislative action designed to improve the declining prospects of the Republican incumbent—violated the Voting Rights Act. Because a reliable standard for evaluating political gerrymanders would be very difficult to develop and apply, it is likely that the Court's brief foray into this field has come to an end.

The Supreme Court and the 2000 Presidential Election

Without question, the most salient and controversial decision of the Supreme Court since *Roe v. Wade* (1973) was *Bush v. Gore* (2000), in which the Court effectively decided the outcome of the 2000 presidential election. The case arose from a dispute over the procedures to be used and timetable to be followed in a recount of the popular vote in the state of Florida, where the margin separating candidates George W. Bush and Al Gore was razor thin. Due to the closeness of the election nationally, Florida's electoral votes would be decisive in determining the next president, but deciding who should receive Florida's electoral votes proved to be anything but simple. Although Bush ostensibly won the popular vote in Florida as recorded by the voting machines, Democrats claimed that a manual recount would prove Gore to be the winner. Litigation in the Florida courts led to decisions by that state's supreme court extending the period for a manual recount and limiting the recount to selected counties that used different procedures for conducting their recounts.

At the request of candidate Bush, the U.S. Supreme Court became involved in the dispute. In *Bush v. Gore*, the Court ruled 7 to 2 that the selective manual recount was unconstitutional, a violation of the Equal Protection Clause. According to the *per curiam* opinion issued by the Court, "[t]he recount mechanisms implemented in response to the decisions of the Florida Supreme Court do not satisfy the minimum requirement for non-arbitrary treatment of voters necessary to secure the fundamental right [to vote]." Justice David Souter, who concurred in this aspect of the decision, could "conceive of no legitimate state interest served by these differing treatments of the expressions of voters' fundamental rights." In Souter's view, the different procedures for conducting the manual recount appeared "wholly arbitrary." Under normal circumstances, the remedy for this constitutional violation would be to order a statewide manual recount under judicial supervision using standardized procedures.

Of course, the circumstances surrounding this case were anything but normal. By a bare majority, the Court decided to halt the recount and effectively declare Bush the winner. Exacerbating the controversy was the fact that the five justices who voted to halt the recount were the court's five conservatives: Rehnquist, Scalia, Thomas, Kennedy, and O'Connor. All five had been appointed by Republican presidents, making the decision appear to many observers, including the four dissenters, to be a case of partisan loyalty trumping judicial self-restraint.

In his dissenting opinion, Justice Stevens expressed worry that the decision would undermine "the Nation's confidence in the judge as an impartial guardian of the rule of law." Needless to say, Democrats around the country were outraged and looked for ways to circumvent the Court's decision. Some even called for impeachment of the five Republican appointees who constituted the Court's majority. Few scholars came to the Court's defense. Alan M. Dershowitz went so far as to accuse the Court of "hijacking" the election. Bruce Ackerman characterized *Bush v. Gore* as a "constitutional coup" and suggested that "when sitting justices retire or die, the Senate should refuse to confirm any nominations offered up by President Bush." Laurence Tribe, who took part in the oral argument of the case in support of candidate Gore, suggested that the Court had displayed its "disdain for the messy processes of democracy."

Looking at the impact of the decision more than a decade later, it is clear that *Bush v. Gore* did not result in a dramatic loss of public confidence in the Supreme Court. The dire predictions concerning the Court's loss of legitimacy in the eyes of the public have not come true. Certainly, *Bush v. Gore* was not a self-inflicted wound of the magnitude of the *Dred Scott* case, as some observers had suggested in the immediate aftermath of the decision. On September 9, 2009, the Gallup Organization reported that public approval of the Court was at the highest point in a decade—61 percent.

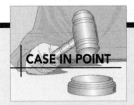

CASE IN POINT

May a State Prohibit the Election-Day Publication of a Newspaper Editorial Urging People to Vote in a Particular Way?

Mills v. Alabama (1966)

The Alabama Corrupt Practices Act made it a crime "to do any electioneering or to solicit any votes ... in support of or in opposition to any proposition that is being voted on the day on which the election affecting such candidates or propositions is being held." James E. Mills, editor of the *Birmingham Post-Herald*, was arrested for publishing an editorial on Election Day urging voters to adopt a measure to create a mayor-council form of government. The trial court sustained Mill's demurrer on constitutional grounds, but the Alabama Supreme Court reversed and remanded the case for trial. In reviewing that decision, the U.S. Supreme Court reversed and declared the law unconstitutional. Writing for a nearly unanimous bench, Justice Hugo Black noted that the Act "silences the press at a time when it can be most effective." Black found it "difficult to conceive of a more obvious and flagrant abridgment of the constitutionally guaranteed freedom of the press."

To Summarize:

◆ *Although the Supreme Court has on occasion invalidated restrictions on candidates' access to the ballot, such restrictions still pose a formidable obstacle to independent or third-party candidates.*

◆ *The Court has held that partisan gerrymandering is a justiciable issue, but has provided little guidance to lower federal courts in this area. Recent decisions indicate that the Court is reluctant to involve the judiciary in a problem that does not lend itself to principled legal resolution.*

◆ *Bush v. Gore (2000) shows the potential impact of judicial involvement in the electoral process. It remains to be seen what impact this decision will ultimately have on constitutional law in the equal protection and voting rights areas.*

The Problem of Campaign Finance

Reformers have long advocated measures designed to remove what they see as the corrupting influence of money in the political process. In particular, reformers have proposed limitations on campaign spending, restrictions on campaign contributions, and various degrees of public financing of campaigns. The most extreme proposals call for eliminating private funding altogether and providing all candidates equal amounts of public money with which to conduct their campaigns.

The Federal Election Campaign Act Amendments of 1974

In the midst of the Watergate scandal, Congress attempted to tackle the thorny problem of campaign finance. Among other things, the Federal Election Campaign Act Amendments of 1974 limited campaign spending by candidates in federal elections and limited individual contributions to such candidates. In *Buckley v. Valeo* (1976), both of these limitations were challenged as infringements of political expression as protected by the First Amendment. In a convoluted and fragmented set of opinions, the Supreme Court struck down the spending limits but upheld the limits on individual contributions. The Court also upheld provisions providing for public funding of campaigns and the limits on expenditures that accompanied the acceptance of public funds. Subsequently, in *Federal Election Commission v. National Conservative Political Action Committee* (1985), the Court said that such limits cannot be applied to persons or parties who spend money in support of a candidate who accepts public funds.

The Court reinforced this position in *Colorado Republican Federal Campaign Committee v. Federal Election Commission* (1996), where it struck down spending limits set by the Federal Election Campaign Act as applied to the Colorado Republican Party's "independent expenditures." Writing for a plurality in that decision, Justice Breyer concluded that: "We do not see how a Constitution that grants to individuals, candidates, and ordinary political committees the right to make unlimited independent expenditures could deny the same right to political parties." However, upon later review of the case, the Court held, per Justice Souter, that "a party's coordinated expenditures, unlike expenditures truly independent, may be restricted to minimize circumvention of contribution limits" (*Federal Election Commission v. Colorado Republican Federal Campaign Committee* [2001]).

While federal campaign finance reform brought a new level of scrutiny and control to political contributions, it had a number of unintended consequences. First, it prompted dramatic growth in the number and influence of political action committees (PACs), which are created by businesses, labor unions, and other interest groups in order to pool contributions which are targeted to support particular candidates. Second, campaign finance reform stimulated the growth of "soft money" contributions made to political parties ostensibly for party-building activities but in reality used to promote the parties' candidates.

The McCain–Feingold Law

In March 2002, Congress enacted the Bipartisan Campaign Reform Act, better known as the McCain–Feingold Law. The most controversial provision of the legislation prohibited the use of soft money to purchase "electioneering ads" within sixty days of a general election or thirty days of a primary. Critics of the bill—and there were many—questioned the constitutionality of these limitations on political activity. Some vowed to challenge the new law in court. Anticipating a legal challenge, the bill contained a provision calling for judicial review by a three-judge panel of the federal district court followed by expedited direct appeal to the Supreme Court.

Many observers expected the High Court to strike down at least some of the more extreme provisions of the bill on First Amendment grounds. But in *McConnell v. Federal Election Commission* (2003), the Court upheld the Act in its entirety. However, the Court was sharply divided on the most controversial aspects of the legislation: the control of soft money and the regulation of electioneering communications. In a rare joint opinion, Justices Stevens and O'Connor (joined by Justices Souter, Ginsburg, and Breyer) made the following observations about the challenged provisions:

> *Many years ago we observed that "[t]o say that Congress is without power to pass appropriate legislation to safeguard ... an election from the improper use of money to influence the result is to deny to the nation in a vital particular the power of self-protection." We abide by that conviction in considering Congress' most recent effort to confine the ill effects of aggregated wealth on our political system. We are under no illusion that [the McCain–Feingold Act] will be the last congressional statement on the*

matter. Money, like water, will always find an outlet. What problems will arise, and how Congress will respond, are concerns for another day. In the main we uphold [the Act's] two principal, complementary features: the control of soft money and the regulation of electioneering communications.

In 2006, the Court reached an opposite result in reviewing a 1997 Vermont law, Act 64, which placed strict fundraising and spending limits on campaigns for state office. Dividing 6 to 3 in *Randall v. Sorrell*, the Supreme Court found that both the fundraising and spending limits contravened the First Amendment. Writing for the majority, Justice Breyer concluded that:

Act 64's expenditure limits violate the First Amendment as interpreted in Buckley v. Valeo. We also conclude that the specific details of Act 64's contribution limits require us to hold that those limits violate the First Amendment, for they burden First Amendment interests in a manner that is disproportionate to the public purposes they were enacted to advance.

In *Federal Election Commission v. Wisconsin Right to Life, Inc.* (2007) the Court reviewed provisions of McCain–Feingold that restricted corporations and unions from funding broadcast ads mentioning candidates within close proximity to federal elections. The Court held that such restrictions were unconstitutional as applied to ads that reasonably can be interpreted as something other than an appeal to vote for or against a particular candidate.

In *Davis v. Federal Election Commission* (2008), the Court continued to chip away at McCain–Feingold by invalidating a section of the act known as the "millionaire's amendment." The provision at issue attempted to equalize campaigns by increasing limits on contributions to candidates who were greatly outspent by opposing candidates using their own funds.

Citizens United In *Citizens United v. Federal Election Commission* (2010), the Supreme Court divided 5 to 4 in striking down a provision of the McCain–Feingold Act that prohibited corporations and unions from engaging in "electioneering communications" thirty days before a presidential primary and in the sixty days before the general election. Citizens United, a conservative organization funded by corporate interests, had been prohibited from advertising a film critical of Hillary Clinton prior to the 2008 Democratic National Convention. In the Supreme Court's view, this restriction amounted to a violation of the First Amendment.

The ruling did not, as commonly thought, change the amount of money corporations and unions can contribute to campaigns, but it did allow corporations and labor unions to contribute unlimited sums of money to "independent" groups that engage in campaigning on behalf of (and often against) particular candidates.

The dissenters said the court was making a mistake treating the voices of corporations as similar to those of people. President Barack Obama expressed his concern over the Supreme Court's decision during his State of the Union speech, delivered January 27, 2011, saying,

With all due deference to separation of powers, last week the Supreme Court reversed a century of law that I believe will open the floodgates for special interests—including foreign corporations—to spend without limit in our elections. I don't think American elections should be bankrolled by America's most powerful interests, or worse, by foreign entities. They should be decided by the American people. And I'd urge Democrats and Republicans to pass a bill that helps to correct some of these problems.

President Obama also called the decision "a major victory for big oil, Wall Street banks, health insurance companies and the other powerful interests that marshal their power every day in Washington to drown out the voices of everyday Americans." This speech led to a particularly rare public spat between the president and one of the Court's justices. As President Obama was explaining who he felt would gain undue political influence from the *Citizens United* ruling, live television cameras captured Justice Samuel Alito, who was in the audience, clearly saying "not true."

In the 2012 presidential election, the effects of the *Citizens United* decision were on display as numerous "independent" groups funded by corporate and union contributions saturated the airwaves with political ads. Whether any of this affected the outcome of the election is difficult to say, as President Obama won reelection by a significant margin.

To Summarize:

♦ *Congress has attempted to regulate campaign finance, most notably through the Federal Election Campaign Act Amendments of 1974. In* Buckley v. Valeo *(1976), the Supreme Court struck down spending limits imposed on candidates but upheld the limits imposed on individual contributions. The Court recognized that campaign spending is a form of political expression protected by the First Amendment.*

♦ *Despite the decision in* Buckley v. Valeo, *the Court did uphold the most sweeping piece of federal campaign finance reform legislation since the 1970s— the McCain–Feingold Act of 2002. More recently, however, a narrowly divided Court has struck down on congressional efforts to limit electioneering communications by groups funded by corporations and unions.*

Conclusion

The fundamental question of whether courts of law ought to have the power to invalidate legislative and executive acts has long since been put to rest. Yet there remains substantial controversy over the appropriate role of courts in applying the tenets of the Constitution to challenged legislation. Many are troubled by substantive due process decisions in which the Supreme Court has invalidated legislative policies on the basis of arguably dubious principles, such as liberty of contract and the right of privacy, nowhere mentioned in the Constitution. While the appropriate role of the Supreme Court in addressing substantive issues of policy is debatable, there is little disagreement about the legitimacy of the Court's role in maintaining the integrity of the democratic process.

Applying a standard of strict scrutiny, the Supreme Court since *Baker v. Can* (1962) and *Reynolds v. Sims* (1964) has had a significant impact with respect to representation and voting rights. The Court's major decisions in this area reflect three fundamental principles: First, suffrage must be universally available; second, all votes must count equally; and third, elections must offer the voter a choice among candidates and parties.

Although politicians may resent the Court's "meddling" with the political process, the principles underlying the Court's decisions are essential to the realization of constitutional democracy. Attempts by legislative majorities to close the channels of political participation to disfavored groups of citizens, whether they are city dwellers, ethnic minorities, or rival political parties, are antithetical to the ideals underlying our system of representative government. Guarding the ideal of political equality is thus without question one of the most important obligations of the Supreme Court. Like its concern for separation of powers, checks and balances, and freedom of expression, the Court's protection of voting rights is critical to the preservation of constitutional democracy in the United States.

Key Terms

representative democracy
universal suffrage
tyranny of the majority
popular sovereignty
constitutional republic
poll taxes

grandfather clause
white primary
literacy tests
gerrymander
racial gerrymandering
Voting Rights Act of 1965

preclearance
at-large elections
vote dilution
malapportionment
reapportionment
partisan gerrymandering

For Further Reading

Ackerman, Bruce A. (ed.). *Bush v. Gore: The Question of Legitimacy.* New Haven, CT: Yale University Press, 2002.

Ackerman, Bruce A. (ed.). *Voting with Dollars: A New Paradigm for Campaign Finance.* New Haven, CT: Yale University Press, 2002.

Baker, Gordon E. *The Reapportionment Revolution.* New York: Random House, 1966.

Ball, Howard. *The Warren Court's Conceptions of Democracy: An Evaluation of the Supreme Court's Apportionment Cases.* Rutherford, NJ: Fairleigh Dickinson University Press, 1971.

Berger, Raoul. *Government by Judiciary: The Transformation of the Fourteenth Amendment.* Cambridge, MA: Harvard University Press, 1977.

Bullock, Charles S., and Kathryn S. Butler. "Voting Rights." In Tinsley E. Yarbrough (ed.), *The Reagan Administration and Human Rights.* New York: Praeger, 1985.

Cortner, Richard C. *The Reapportionment Cases.* Knoxville, TN: University of Tennessee Press, 1970.

Davidson, Chandler, and Bernard Grofman (eds.). *Quiet Revolution in the South: The Impact of the Voting Rights Act 1965–1990.* Princeton, NJ: Princeton University Press, 1994.

Dershowitz, Alan M. *Supreme Injustice: How the High Court Hijacked Election 2000.* New York: Oxford University Press, 2001.

Dixon, Robert G., Jr. *Democratic Representation: Reapportionment in Law and Politics.* New York: Oxford University Press, 1968.

Ely, John Hart. *Democracy and Distrust.* Cambridge, MA: Harvard University Press, 1980.

Grofman, Bernard. *Political Gerrymandering and the Courts.* New York: Agathon Press, 1990.

Hamilton, Howard D. (ed.). *Legislative Reapportionment: Key to Power.* New York: Harper and Row, 1964.

Hanson, Royce. *The Political Thicket: Reapportionment and Constitutional Democracy.* Englewood Cliffs, NJ: Prentice-Hall, 1966.

Issacharoff, Samuel, Pamela Karlin, and Richard Pildes. *When Elections Go Bad: The Law of Democracy and the Presidential Election of 2000.* New York: Foundation Press, 2001.

Kotz, Nick. *Judgment Days: Lyndon Baines Johnson, Martin Luther King, Jr., and the Laws That Changed America.* Boston: Houghton Mifflin, 2005.

Mendelson, Wallace. *Discrimination.* Englewood Cliffs, NJ: Prentice-Hall, 1962.

Norrell, Robert J. *Reaping the Whirlwind: The Civil Rights Movement in Tuskegee* (rev. ed). Chapel Hill: University of North Carolina Press, 1998.

Polsby, Nelson W. (ed). *Reapportionment in the 1970s.* Berkeley: University of California Press, 1971.

Taper, Bernard. *Gomillion v. Lightfoot: Apartheid in Alabama.* New York: McGraw-Hill, 1967.

United States Commission on Civil Rights. *1961 Report.* Washington, DC: U.S. Government Printing Office, 1961.

SMITH v. ALLWRIGHT
327 U.S. 649; 64 S.Ct. 757; 88 L.Ed. 987 (1944)
Vote: 8-1

*In 1927, the Texas legislature passed a law that autho-
rized political parties to set qualifications for party
membership. Pursuant to this law, the state Democratic
Party, at its convention in May 1932, adopted the following resolution: "Be it resolved that all white citizens
of the State of Texas who are qualified to vote under the
Constitution and laws of the State shall be eligible to
membership in the Democratic Party and, as such, entitled to participate in its deliberations." Lonnie Smith, a
black resident of Texas, sued S. E. Allwright, an election
judge, for refusing to allow him to vote in a Democratic
primary at which candidates for state and national
office were to be nominated. Through the efforts of the
National Association for the Advancement of Colored
People, this case ultimately reached the U.S. Supreme
Court. Thurgood Marshall, as counsel for the NAACP,
participated in the argument of the case on behalf of
Smith.*

Mr. Justice Reed delivered the opinion of the Court.

... Texas is free to conduct her elections and limit
her electorate as she may deem wise, save only as her
action may be affected by the prohibitions of the
United States Constitution or in conflict with powers
delegated to and exercised by the National Government. The Fourteenth Amendment forbids a State
from making or enforcing any law which abridges the
privileges or immunities of citizens of the United States
and the Fifteenth Amendment specifically interdicts
any denial or abridgement by a State of the right of
citizens to vote on account of color. Respondents
appeared in the District Court and the Circuit Court
of Appeals and defended on the ground that the Democratic Party of Texas is a voluntary organization with
members banded together for the purpose of selecting
individuals of the group representing the common
political beliefs as candidates in the general election.
As such a voluntary organization, it was claimed, the
Democratic Party is free to select its own membership
and limit to whites participation in the party primary.
Such action, the answer asserted, does not violate the
Fourteenth, Fifteenth or Seventeenth Amendments as
officers of government cannot be chosen at primaries
and the Amendments are applicable only to general

elections where governmental officers are actually
elected....

Since *Grovey v. Townsend* [1935] and prior to the
present suit, no case from Texas involving primary
elections has been before this Court. We did decide,
however, *United States v. Classic* ... [1941]. We there
held that Section 4 of Article I of the Constitution
authorized Congress to regulate primary as well as general elections, "where the primary is by law made an
integral part of the election machinery." ... Consequently, in the *Classic* case, we upheld the applicability
to frauds in a Louisiana primary of Sections 19 and 20
of the Criminal Code.... *Classic* bears upon *Grovey v.
Townsend* not because exclusion of Negroes from primaries is any more or less state action by reason of the
unitary character of the electoral process but because
the recognition of the place of the primary in the electoral scheme makes clear that state delegation to a
party of the power to fix the qualifications of primary
elections is delegation of a state function that may
make the party's action the action of the State. When
Grovey v. Townsend was written, the Court looked
upon the denial of a vote in a primary as a mere refusal
by a party of party membership.... As the Louisiana
statutes for holding primaries are similar to those of
Texas, our ruling in *Classic* as to the unitary character
of the electoral process calls for a reexamination as to
whether or not the exclusion of Negroes from a Texas
party primary was state action....

It may now be taken as a postulate that the right to
vote in such a primary for the nomination of candidates without discrimination by the State, like the right
to vote in a general election, is a right secured by the
Constitution.

... By the terms of the Fifteenth Amendment that
right may not be abridged by any State on account of
race. Under our Constitution the great privilege of the
ballot may not be denied a man by the State because of
his color.

We are thus brought to an examination of the qualifications for Democratic primary electors in Texas, to
determine whether state action or private action has
excluded Negroes from participation. Despite Texas'
decision that the exclusion is produced by private or
party action ... federal courts must for themselves

appraise the facts leading to that conclusion. It is only by the performance of this obligation that a final and uniform interpretation can be given to the Constitution, the "supreme Law of the Land." ...

Primary elections are conducted by the party under state statutory authority. The county executive committee selects precinct election officials and the county, district or state executive committees, respectively, canvass the returns. These party committees or the state convention certify the party's candidates to the appropriate officers for inclusion on the official ballot for the general election. No name which has not been so certified may appear upon the ballot for the general election as a candidate of a political party. No other name may be printed on the ballot which has not been placed in nomination by qualified voters who must take oath that they did not participate in a primary for the selection of a candidate for the office for which the nomination is made.

The state courts are given exclusive original jurisdiction of contested elections and of *mandamus* proceedings to compel party officers to perform their statutory duties.

We think that this statutory system for the selection of party nominees for inclusion on the general election ballot makes the party which is required to follow these legislative directions an agency of the State in so far as it determines the participants in a primary election. The party takes its character as a state agency from the duties imposed upon it by state statutes; the duties do not become matters of private law because they are performed by a political party. The plan of the Texas primary follows substantially that of Louisiana, with the exception that in Louisiana the State pays the cost of the primary while Texas assesses the cost against candidates. In numerous instances, the Texas statutes fix or limit the fees to be charged. Whether paid directly by the State or through state requirements, it is state action which compels. When primaries become a part of the machinery for choosing officials, state and national, as they have here, the same tests to determine the character of discrimination or abridgement should be applied to the primary as are applied to the general election. If the State requires a certain electoral procedure, prescribes a general election ballot made up of party nominees so chosen and limits the choice of the electorate in general elections for state offices, practically speaking, to those whose names appear on such a ballot, it endorses, adopts and enforces the discrimination against Negroes, practiced by a party entrusted

by Texas law with the determination of the qualifications of participants in the primary. This is state action within the meaning of the Fifteenth Amendment....

The United States is a constitutional democracy. Its organic law grants to all citizens a right to participate in the choice of elected officials without restriction by any State because of race. This grant to the people of the opportunity for choice is not to be nullified by a State through casting its electoral process in a form which permits a private organization to practice racial discrimination in the election. Constitutional rights would be of little value if they could be thus indirectly denied....

... In reaching this conclusion we are not unmindful of the desirability of continuity of decision in constitutional questions. However, when convinced of former error, this Court has never felt constrained to follow precedent. In constitutional questions, where correction depends upon amendment and not upon legislative action, this Court throughout its history has freely exercised its power to reexamine the basis of its constitutional decisions. This has long been accepted practice, and this practice has continued to this day. This is particularly true when the decision believed erroneous is the application of a constitutional principle rather than an interpretation of the Constitution to extract the principle itself. Here we are applying, contrary to the recent decision in *Grovey v. Townsend*, the well-established principle of the Fifteenth Amendment, forbidding the abridgement by a State of a citizen's right to vote. *Grovey v. Townsend* is overruled.

Mr. Justice Frankfurter concurs in the result.

Mr. Justice Roberts [dissenting]:

... I have expressed my views with respect to the present policy of the court freely to disregard and to overrule considered decisions and the rules of law announced in them. This tendency, it seems to me, indicates an intolerance for what those who have composed this court in the past have conscientiously and deliberately concluded, and involves an assumption that knowledge and wisdom reside in us which was denied to our predecessors. I shall not repeat what I there said for I consider it fully applicable to the instant decision, which but points the moral anew....

The reason for my concern is that the instant decision, overruling that announced about nine years ago,

(Continued)

tends to bring adjudications of this tribunal into the same class as a restricted railroad ticket, good for this day and train only. I have no assurance, in view of current decisions, that the opinion announced today may not shortly be repudiated and overruled by justices who deem they have new light on the subject. In the present term the court has overruled three cases.

In the present case, ... the court below relied, as it was bound to, upon our previous decision. As that court points out, the statutes of Texas have not been altered since *Grovey v. Townsend* was decided. The same resolution is involved as was drawn in question in *Grovey v. Townsend*. Not a fact differentiates that case from this except the names of the parties.

It is suggested that *Grovey v. Townsend* was overruled *sub silentio* in *United States v. Classic*.... If so, the situation is even worse than that exhibited by the outright repudiation of an earlier decision, for it is the fact that, in the *Classic* case, *Grovey v. Townsend* was distinguished in brief and argument by the Government without suggestion that it was wrongly decided, and was relied on by the appellee, not as a controlling decision, but by way of analogy. The case is not mentioned in either of the opinions in the *Classic* case. Again and again it is said in the opinion of the court in that case that the voter who was denied the right to vote was a fully qualified voter. In other words, there was no question of his being a person entitled under state law to vote in the primary. The offense charged was the fraudulent denial of his conceded right by an election officer because of his race. Here the question is altogether different. It is whether, in a Democratic primary, he who tendered his vote was a member of the Democratic Party....

It is regrettable that in an era marked by doubt and confusion, an era whose greater need is steadfastness of thought and purpose, this court, which has been looked to as exhibiting consistency in adjudication, and a steadiness which would hold the balance even in the face of temporary ebbs and flows of opinion, should now itself become the breeder of fresh doubt and confusion in the public mind as to the stability of our institutions.

GOMILLION v. LIGHTFOOT
364 U.S. 339; 81 S.Ct. 125; 5 L.Ed. 2d 110 (1960)
Vote: 9-0

Here, the Court confronts a blatant attempt to disenfranchise minority voters by gerrymandering the boundaries of a city.

Mr. Justice Frankfurter delivered the opinion of the Court.

This litigation challenges the validity, under the United States Constitution, of Local Act No. 140, passed by the Legislature of Alabama in 1957, redefining the boundaries of the City of Tuskegee. Petitioners, Negro citizens of Alabama who were, at the time of this redistricting measure, residents of the City of Tuskegee, brought an action in the United States District Court for the Middle District of Alabama for a declaratory judgment that Act 140 is unconstitutional, and for an injunction to restrain the Mayor and officers of Tuskegee and the officials of Macon County, Alabama, from enforcing the Act against them and other Negroes similarly situated. Petitioners' claim is that enforcement of the statute, which alters the shape of Tuskegee from a square to an uncouth twenty-eight-sided figure, will constitute a discrimination against them in violation of the Due Process and Equal Protection Clauses of the Fourteenth Amendment to the Constitution and will deny them the right to vote in defiance of the Fifteenth Amendment.

The respondents moved for dismissal of the action for failure to state a claim upon which relief could be granted and for lack of jurisdiction of the District Court. The court granted the motion, stating, "This court has no control over, no supervision over, and no power to change any boundaries of municipal corporations fixed by a duly convened and elected legislative body, acting for the people for the State of Alabama." ... On appeal, the Court of Appeals for the Fifth Circuit affirmed the judgment, one judge dissenting.... We brought the case here since serious questions were raised concerning the power of a State over its municipalities in relation to the Fourteenth and Fifteenth Amendments.... The essential inevitable effect of this redefinition of Tuskegee's boundaries is to remove from the city all save only four or five of its 400 Negro voters while not removing a single white voter or resident. The result of the Act is to deprive the Negro petitioners discriminatorily of the benefits of residence in Tuskegee, including, *inter alia,* the right to vote in municipal elections.

These allegations, if proven, would abundantly establish that Act 140 was not an ordinary geographic redistricting measure even within familiar abuses of gerrymandering. If these allegations upon a trial remained uncontradicted or unqualified, the conclusion would be irresistible, tantamount for all practical purposes to a mathematical demonstration, that the legislation is solely concerned with segregating white and colored voters by fencing Negro citizens out of town so as to deprive them of their preexisting municipal vote.

It is difficult to appreciate what stands in the way of adjudging a statute having this inevitable effect invalid in light of the principles by which this Court must judge, and uniformly has judged, statutes that, howsoever speciously defined, obviously discriminate against colored citizens. "The [Fifteenth] Amendment nullified sophisticated as well as simple-minded modes of discrimination." ...

The complaint amply alleges a claim of racial discrimination. Against this claim the respondents have never suggested, either in their brief or in oral argument, any countervailing municipal function which Act 140 is designed to serve. The respondents invoke generalities expressing the State's unrestricted power—unlimited, that is, by the United States Constitution—to establish, destroy, or reorganize by contraction or expansion its political subdivisions, to wit, cities, counties, and other local units. We freely recognize the breadth and importance of this aspect of the State's political power. To exalt this power into an absolute is to misconceive the reach and rule of this Court's decisions....

... The Court has never acknowledged that the States have power to do as they will with municipal corporations regardless of consequences. Legislative control of municipalities, no less than other state power, lies within the scope of relevant limitations imposed by the United States Constitution....

... Such power, extensive though it is, is met and overcome by the Fifteenth Amendment to the Constitution of the United States, which forbids a State from passing any law which deprives a citizen of his vote because of his race. The opposite conclusion, urged upon us by respondents, would sanction the achievement by a State of any impairment of voting rights whatever so long as it was cloaked in the garb of the realignment of political subdivisions. "It is inconceivable that guaranties embedded in the Constitution of the United States may thus be manipulated out of existence." ...

When a State exercises power wholly within the domain of state interest, it is insulated from federal judicial review. But such insulation is not carried over when state power is used as an instrument for circumventing a federally protected right. This principle has had many applications. It has long been recognized in cases which have prohibited a State from exploiting a power acknowledged to be absolute in an isolated context to justify the imposition of an "unconstitutional condition." What the Court has said in those cases is equally applicable here, viz., that "Act generally lawful may become unlawful when done to accomplish an unlawful end, ... and a constitutional power cannot be used by way of condition to attain an unconstitutional result." The petitioners are entitled to prove their allegations at trial.

For these reasons, the principal conclusions of the District Court and the Court of Appeals are clearly erroneous....

Mr. Justice Douglas, [concurring]....

Mr. Justice Whittaker, concurring.

I concur in the Court's judgment, but not in the whole of its opinion. It seems to me that the decision should be rested not on the Fifteenth Amendment, but rather on the equal Protection Clause of the Fourteenth Amendment to the Constitution. I am doubtful that the averments of the complaint, taken for present purposes to be true, show a purpose by Act No. 140 to abridge petitioners' "right ... to vote," in the Fifteenth Amendment sense. It seems to me that the "right ... to vote" that is guaranteed by the Fifteenth Amendment is but the same right to vote as is enjoyed by all others within the same election precinct, ward or other political division. And, inasmuch as no one has the right to vote in a political division, or in a local election concerning only an area in which he does not reside, it would seem to follow that one's right to vote in Division A is not abridged by a redistricting that places his residence in Division B if he there enjoys the same voting privileges as all others in that Division, even though the redistricting was done by the State for the purposes of placing a racial group of citizens in Division B rather than A. But it does seem clear to me that accomplishment of a State's purpose—to use the

Court's phrase—of "fencing Negro citizens out of Division A and into Division B is an unlawful segregation of races of citizens, in violation of the Equal Protection Clause of the Fourteenth Amendment, ... and, as stated, I would think the decision should be rested on that ground....

SHELBY COUNTY v. HOLDER
570 U.S. ___; 133 S.Ct. 2612; 186 L. Ed. 2d 651 (2013)
Vote: 5-4

Shelby County, Alabama, sued Attorney General Eric Holder to challenge the constitutionality of Section 4(b) (the coverage formula) and Section 5 (the preclearance requirement) of the Voting Rights Act, as reauthorized by Congress in 2006. The district court in Washington, D.C. rejected the challenge, holding that Congress was justified in reauthorizing §5 and continuing §4(b)'s coverage formula. The U.S. Court of Appeals for the D.C. Circuit affirmed.]

Chief Justice Roberts delivered the opinion of the Court.

The Voting Rights Act of 1965 employed extraordinary measures to address an extraordinary problem. Section 5 of the Act required States to obtain federal permission before enacting any law related to voting—a drastic departure from basic principles of federalism. And §4 of the Act applied that requirement only to some States—an equally dramatic departure from the principle that all States enjoy equal sovereignty. This was strong medicine, but Congress determined it was needed to address entrenched racial discrimination in voting, "an insidious and pervasive evil which had been perpetuated in certain parts of our country through unremitting and ingenious defiance of the Constitution." *South Carolina v. Katzenbach* (1966). As we explained in upholding the law, "exceptional conditions can justify legislative measures not otherwise appropriate." ... Reflecting the unprecedented nature of these measures, they were scheduled to expire after five years....

Nearly 50 years later, they are still in effect; indeed, they have been made more stringent, and are now scheduled to last until 2031. There is no denying,

however, that the conditions that originally justified these measures no longer characterize voting in the covered jurisdictions. By 2009, "the racial gap in voter registration and turnout [was] lower in the States originally covered by §5 than it [was] nationwide." ... Since that time, Census Bureau data indicate that African-American voter turnout has come to exceed white voter turnout in five of the six States originally covered by §5, with a gap in the sixth State of less than one half of one percent....

At the same time, voting discrimination still exists; no one doubts that. The question is whether the Act's extraordinary measures, including its disparate treatment of the States, continue to satisfy constitutional requirements. As we put it a short time ago, "the Act imposes current burdens and must be justified by current needs." ...

When upholding the constitutionality of the coverage formula in 1966, we concluded that it was "rational in both practice and theory." ... The formula looked to cause (discriminatory tests) and effect (low voter registration and turnout), and tailored the remedy (preclearance) to those jurisdictions exhibiting both. By 2009, however, we concluded that the "coverage formula raise[d] serious constitutional questions." ... As we explained, a statute's "current burdens" must be justified by "current needs," and any "disparate geographic coverage" must be "sufficiently related to the problem that it targets." The coverage formula met that test in 1965, but no longer does so.

Coverage today is based on decades-old data and eradicated practices. The formula captures States by reference to literacy tests and low voter registration and turnout in the 1960s and early 1970s. But such tests have been banned nationwide for over 40 years.

... And voter registration and turnout numbers in the covered States have risen dramatically in the years since.... Racial disparity in those numbers was compelling evidence justifying the preclearance remedy and the coverage formula.

In 1965, the States could be divided into two groups: those with a recent history of voting tests and low voter registration and turnout, and those without those characteristics. Congress based its coverage formula on that distinction. Today the Nation is no longer divided along those lines, yet the Voting Rights Act continues to treat it as if it were.

The Government falls back to the argument that because the formula was relevant in 1965, its continued use is permissible so long as any discrimination remains in the States Congress identified back then—regardless of how that discrimination compares to discrimination in States unburdened by coverage.... This argument does not look to "current political conditions," ... but instead relies on a comparison between the States in 1965. That comparison reflected the different histories of the North and South. It was in the South that slavery was upheld by law until uprooted by the Civil War, that the reign of Jim Crow denied African-Americans the most basic freedoms, and that state and local governments worked tirelessly to disenfranchise citizens on the basis of race. The Court invoked that history—rightly so—in sustaining the disparate coverage of the Voting Rights Act in 1966....

But history did not end in 1965. By the time the Act was reauthorized in 2006, there had been 40 more years of it. In assessing the "current need" for a preclearance system that treats States differently from one another today, that history cannot be ignored. During that time, largely because of the Voting Rights Act, voting tests were abolished, disparities in voter registration and turnout due to race were erased, and African-Americans attained political office in record numbers. And yet the coverage formula that Congress reauthorized in 2006 ignores these developments, keeping the focus on decades-old data relevant to decades-old problems, rather than current data reflecting current needs.

The Fifteenth Amendment commands that the right to vote shall not be denied or abridged on account of race or color, and it gives Congress the power to enforce that command. The Amendment is not designed to punish for the past; its purpose is to ensure a better future.... To serve that purpose, Congress—if it is to divide the States—must identify those

jurisdictions to be singled out on a basis that makes sense in light of current conditions. It cannot rely simply on the past....

Striking down an Act of Congress "is the gravest and most delicate duty that this Court is called on to perform." ... We do not do so lightly.... Congress could have updated the coverage formula at that time, but did not do so. Its failure to act leaves us today with no choice but to declare [the coverage formula] unconstitutional. The formula ... can no longer be used as a basis for subjecting jurisdictions to preclearance.

...We issue no holding on §5 itself, only on the coverage formula. Congress may draft another formula based on current conditions. Such a formula is an initial prerequisite to a determination that exceptional conditions still exist justifying such an "extraordinary departure from the traditional course of relations between the States and the Federal Government." ... Our country has changed, and while any racial discrimination in voting is too much, Congress must ensure that the legislation it passes to remedy that problem speaks to current conditions.

The judgment of the Court of Appeals is reversed.

Justice Thomas, concurring.

I join the Court's opinion in full but write separately to explain that I would find §5 of the Voting Rights Act unconstitutional as well. The Court's opinion sets forth the reasons.

While the Court claims to "issue no holding on §5 itself," ... its own opinion compellingly demonstrates that Congress has failed to justify "'current burdens'" with a record demonstrating "'current needs.'" ... By leaving the inevitable conclusion unstated, the Court needlessly prolongs the demise of that provision. For the reasons stated in the Court's opinion, I would find §5 unconstitutional.

Justice Ginsburg, with whom *Justice Breyer, Justice Sotomayor*, and *Justice Kagan* join, dissenting.

In the Court's view, the very success of §5 of the Voting Rights Act demands its dormancy. Congress was of another mind. Recognizing that large progress has been made, Congress determined, based on a voluminous record, that the scourge of discrimination was not yet extirpated. The question this case presents is who decides whether, as currently operative, §5 remains justifiable, this Court, or a Congress charged

(Continued)

with the obligation to enforce the post-Civil War Amendments "by appropriate legislation." With overwhelming support in both Houses, Congress concluded that, for two prime reasons, §5 should continue in force, unabated. First, continuance would facilitate completion of the impressive gains thus far made; and second, continuance would guard against backsliding. Those assessments were well within Congress' province to make and should elicit this Court's unstinting approbation....

After exhaustive evidence-gathering and deliberative process, Congress reauthorized the VRA, including

the coverage provision, with overwhelming bipartisan support. It was the judgment of Congress that "40 years has not been a sufficient amount of time to eliminate the vestiges of discrimination following nearly 100 years of disregard for the dictates of the 15th amendment and to ensure that the right of all citizens to vote is protected as guaranteed by the Constitution." ... That determination of the body empowered to enforce the Civil War Amendments "by appropriate legislation" merits this Court's utmost respect. In my judgment, the Court errs egregiously by overriding Congress' decision....

REYNOLDS v. SIMS
377 U.S. 533; 84 S.Ct. 1362; 12 L.Ed. 2d 506 (1964)
Vote: 8-1

Prior to this lawsuit, the apportionment scheme for the Alabama legislature created a thirty-five-member Senate elected from districts whose population varied from 15,417 to 634,864 and a House of Representatives with 106 members elected from districts whose populations varied from 6,731 to 104,767. Registered voters from two urban counties brought this lawsuit challenging the constitutionality of the existing apportionment.

The U.S. district court ruled for the plaintiffs and ordered a temporary reapportionment plan. On appeal, the Supreme Court affirmed the lower court's decision.

Mr. Chief Justice Warren delivered the opinion of the Court.

... A predominant consideration in determining whether a State's legislative apportionment scheme constitutes an invidious discrimination violative of rights asserted under the Equal Protection Clause is that the rights allegedly impaired are individual and personal in nature.... [T]he judicial focus must be concentrated upon ascertaining whether there has been any discrimination against certain of the State's citizens which constitutes an impermissible impairment of their constitutionally protected right to vote.... Undoubtedly, the right of suffrage is a fundamental matter in a free and democratic society. Especially since the right to exercise the franchise in a free and unimpaired manner is preservative of other basic civil

and political rights, any alleged infringement of the right of citizens to vote must be carefully and meticulously scrutinized....

Legislators represent people, not trees or acres. Legislators are elected by voters, not farms or cities or economic interests. As long as ours is a representative form of government, and our legislatures are those instruments of government elected directly by and directly representative of the people, the right to elect legislators in a free and unimpaired fashion is a bedrock of our political system. It could hardly be gainsaid that a constitutional claim had been asserted by an allegation that certain otherwise qualified voters had been entirely prohibited from voting for members of their state legislature. And, if a State should provide that the votes of citizens in one part of the State should be given two times, or five times, or 10 times the weight of votes of citizens in another part of the State, it could hardly be contended that the right to vote of those residing in the disfavored area had not been effectively diluted. It would appear extraordinary to suggest that a State could be constitutionally permitted to enact a law providing that certain of the State's voters could vote two, five, or 10 times for their legislative representatives, while voters living elsewhere could vote only once. And it is inconceivable that a state law to the effect that, in counting votes for legislators, the votes of citizens in one part of the State would be multiplied by two, five, or 10, while the votes of persons in another area would be counted only at face value, could be constitutionally sustainable. Of course, the effect of state legislative districting schemes which give the same number of representatives to unequal numbers of constituents is identical. Overweighting and overvaluation of the votes of those living here has the certain effect of dilution and undervaluation of the votes of those living there. The resulting discrimination against those individual voters living in disfavored areas is easily demonstrable mathematically. Their right to vote is simply not the same right to vote as that of those living in a favored part of the State. Two, five, or 10 of them must vote before the effect of their voting is equivalent to that of their favored neighbor. Weighting the votes of citizens differently, by any method or means, merely because of where they happen to reside, hardly seems justifiable....

State legislatures are, historically, the fountainhead of representative government in this country..., Most citizens can achieve [full and effective] participation only as qualified voters through the election of legislators to represent them. Full and effective participation by all citizens in state government requires, therefore, that each citizen have an equally effective voice in the election of members of his state legislature. Modern and viable state government needs, and the Constitution demands, no less.

Logically, in a society ostensibly grounded on representative government, it would seem reasonable that a majority of the people of a State could elect a majority of that State's legislators. To conclude differently, and to sanction minority control of state legislature bodies, would appear to deny majority rights in a way that far surpasses any possible denial of minority rights that might otherwise be thought to result. Since legislatures are responsible for enacting laws by which all citizens are to be governed, they should be bodies which are collectively responsive to the popular will. And the concept of equal protection has been traditionally viewed as requiring the uniform treatment of persons standing in the same relation to the governmental action questioned or challenged. With respect to the allocation of legislative representation, all voters, as citizens of a State, stand in the same relation regardless of where they live. Any suggested criteria for the differentiation of citizens are insufficient to justify any discrimination, as to the weight of their votes, unless relevant to the permissible purposes of legislative apportionment. Since the achieving of fair and effective

representation for all citizens is concededly the basic aim of legislative apportionment, we conclude that the Equal Protection Clause guarantees the opportunity for equal participation by all voters in the election of state legislators. Diluting the weight of votes because of place of residence impairs basic constitutional rights under the Fourteenth Amendment just as much as invidious discriminations based upon factors such as race ... or economic status.... Our constitutional system amply provides for the protection of minorities by means other than giving them majority control of state legislatures. And the democratic ideals of equality and majority rule, which have served this Nation so well in the past, are hardly of any less significance for the present and the future.

We are told that the matter of apportioning representation in a state legislature is a complex and many-faceted one. We are advised that States can rationally consider factors other than population in apportioning legislative representation. We are admonished not to restrict the power of the States to impose differing views as to political philosophy on their citizens. We are cautioned about the dangers of entering into political thickets and mathematical quagmires. Our answer is this: a denial of constitutionally protected rights demands judicial protection; our oath and our office require no less of us.

To the extent that a citizen's right to vote is debased, he is that much less a citizen. The fact that an individual lives here or there is not a legitimate reason for overweighting or diluting the efficacy of his vote. The complexions of societies and civilizations change, often with amazing rapidity. A nation once primarily rural in character becomes predominantly urban. Representation schemes once fair and equitable become archaic and outdated. But the basic principle of representative government remains, and must remain, unchanged—the weight of a citizen's vote cannot be made to depend on where he lives. Population is, of necessity, the starting point for consideration and the controlling criterion for judgment in legislative apportionment controversies. A citizen, a qualified voter, is no more nor no less so because he lives in the city or on the farm. This is the clear and strong command of our Constitution's Equal Protection Clause. This is an essential part of the concept of a government of laws and not men. This is at the heart of Lincoln's vision of "government of the people, by the people, [and] for the people." The Equal Protection Clause demands no less than substantially equal state

(Continued)

legislative representation for all citizens, of all places as well as of all races....

By holding that as a federal constitutional requisite both houses of a state legislature must be apportioned on a population basis, we mean that the Equal Protection Clause requires that a State make an honest and good faith effort to construct districts, in both houses of its legislature, as nearly of equal population as is practicable. We realize that it is a practical impossibility to arrange legislative districts so that each one has an identical number of residents, or citizens, or voters. Mathematical exactness or precision is hardly a workable constitutional requirement....

... So long as the divergences from a strict population standard are based on legitimate considerations incident to the effectuation of a rational state policy, some deviations from the equal-population principle are constitutionally permissible with respect to the apportionment of seats in either or both of the two houses of a bicameral state legislature. But neither history alone, nor economic or other sorts of group interests, are permissible factors in attempting to justify disparities from population-based representation. Citizens, not history or economic interests, cast votes. Considerations of area alone provide an insufficient justification for deviations from the equal population principle. Again, people, not land or trees or pastures, vote. Modern developments and improvements in transportation and communications make rather hollow, in the mid-1960s, most claims that deviations from population-based representation can validly be based solely on geographical considerations. Arguments for allowing such deviations in order to insure effective representation for sparsely settled areas and to prevent legislative districts from becoming so large that the availability of access of citizens to their representatives is impaired are today, for the most part, unconvincing.

A consideration that appears to be of more substance in justifying some deviations from population-based representation in state legislatures is that of insuring some voice to political subdivisions, as political subdivisions.... In many States much of the legislature's activity involves the enactment of so-called local legislation, directed only to the concerns of particular political subdivisions. And a State may legitimately desire to construct districts along political subdivision lines to deter the possibilities of gerrymandering. But if, even as a result of a clearly rational state policy of according some legislative representation to political subdivisions, population is submerged as the controlling consideration in the apportionment of seats in the particular

legislative body, then the right of all of the State's citizens to cast an effective and adequately weighted vote would be unconstitutionally impaired....

Mr. Justice Clark, concurring....

Mr. Justice Stewart, concurring....

Mr. Justice Harlan, dissenting:

... The Court's constitutional discussion ... is remarkable ... for its failure to address itself at all to the Fourteenth Amendment as a whole or to the legislative history of the Amendment pertinent to the matter at hand. Stripped of aphorisms, the Court's argument boils down to the assertion that appellee's right to vote has been invidiously "debased" or "diluted" by systems of apportionment which entitle them to vote for fewer legislators than other voters, an assertion which is tied to the Equal Protection Clause only by the constitutionally frail tautology that "equal" means "equal."

Had the Court paused to probe more deeply into the matter, it would have found that the Equal Protection Clause was never intended to inhibit the States in choosing any democratic method they pleased for the apportionment of their legislatures....

The history of the adoption of the Fourteenth Amendment provides conclusive evidence that neither those who proposed nor those who ratified the Amendment believed that the Equal Protection Clause limited the power of the States to apportion their legislatures as they saw fit. Moreover, the history demonstrates that the intention to leave this power undisturbed was deliberate and was widely believed to be essential to the adoption of the Amendment....

Although the Court—necessarily, as I believe—provides only generalities in elaboration of its main thesis, its opinion nevertheless fully demonstrates how far removed these problems are from fields of judicial competence. Recognizing that "indiscriminate districting" is an invitation to "partisan gerrymandering," ... the Court nevertheless excludes virtually every basis for the formation of electoral districts other than "indiscriminate districting." In one or another of today's opinions, the Court declares it unconstitutional for a State to give effective consideration to any of the following in establishing legislative districts: 1. history; 2. "economic or other sorts of group interests"; 3. area; 4. geographical considerations; 5. a desire "to insure effective representation for sparsely settled areas"; 6.

"availability of access of citizens to their representatives"; 7. theories of bicameralism (except those approved by the Court); 8. occupation; 9. "an attempt to balance urban and rural power"; 10. the preference of a majority of voters in the State.

So far as presently appears, the only factor which a State may consider, apart from numbers, is political subdivisions. But even "a clearly rational state policy" recognizing this factor is unconstitutional if "population is submerged as the controlling consideration...."

I know of no principle of logic or practical or theoretical politics, still less any constitutional principle, which establishes all or any of these exclusions. Certain it is that the Court's opinion does not establish them. So

far as the Court says anything at all on this score, it says only that "legislators represent people, not trees or acres," ... that "citizens, not history or economic interests, cast votes," ... that "people, not land or trees or pastures, vote." ... All this may be conceded. But it is surely equally obvious, and, in the context of elections, more meaningful to note that people are not ciphers and that legislators can represent their electors only by speaking for their interests—economic, social, political—many of which do reflect the place where the electors live. The Court does not establish, or indeed even attempt to make a case for the proposition that conflicting interests within a State can only be adjusted by disregarding them when voters are grouped for purposes of representation....

KARCHER v. DAGGETT
462 U.S. 725; 103 S.Ct. 2653; 77 L.Ed. 2d 133 (1983)
Vote: 5-4

The guiding principle is "one person, one vote," but as a practical matter, it is impossible to make legislative districts exactly equal in population. How much deviation from absolute equality is permissible? Here, the Court addresses this question in the context of a 1982 reapportionment plan for New Jersey's congressional districts.

Justice Brennan delivered the opinion of the Court.

... A three-judge District Court declared New Jersey's 1982 reapportionment plan unconstitutional on the authority of *Kirkpatrick v. Preisler* ... (1969) and *White v. Weiser* (1973), ... because the population deviations among districts, although small, were not the result of a good-faith effort to achieve population equality....

After the results of the 1980 decennial census had been tabulated, the Clerk of the United States House of Representatives notified the governor of New Jersey that the number of Representatives to which the State was entitled had decreased from 15 to 14. Accordingly, the New Jersey Legislature was required to reapportion the State's congressional districts. The State's 199th Legislature passed two reapportionment bills. One was vetoed by the Governor, and the second, although signed into law, occasioned significant dissatisfaction

among those who felt it diluted minority voting strength in the city of Newark.

... In response, the 200th Legislature returned to the problem of apportioning congressional districts when it convened in January 1982, and it swiftly passed a bill (S-711) introduced by Senator Feldman, President pro tern of the State Senate, which created the apportionment plan at issue in this case. The bill was signed by the Governor on January 19, 1982....

Like every plan considered by the legislature, the Feldman Plan contained 14 districts, with an average population per district (as determined by the 1980 census) of 526,059. Each district did not have the same population. On the average, each district differed from the "ideal" figure by 0.1384%, or about 726 people. The largest district, the Fourth District, which includes Trenton, had a population of 527,472, and the smallest, the Sixth District, embracing most of Middlesex County, a population of 523,798. The difference between them was 3,674 people, or 0.6984% of the average district. The populations of the other districts also varied. The Ninth District, including most of Bergen County, in the northeastern corner of the State, had a population of 527,349, while the population of the Third District, along the Atlantic shore, was only 524,825....

(Continued)

The legislature had before it other plans with appreciably smaller population deviations between the largest and smallest districts. The one receiving the most attention in the District Court was designed by Dr. Ernest Reock, a political science professor at Rutgers University and Director of the Bureau of Government Research. A version of the Reock Plan introduced in the 200th Legislature by Assemblyman Hardwick had a maximum population difference of 2,375, or 0.4514% of the average figure....

Almost immediately after the Feldman Plan became law, a group of individuals with varying interests, including all incumbent Republican Members of Congress from New Jersey, sought a declaration that the apportionment plan violated Article I, Section 2, of the Constitution and an injunction against proceeding with the primary election for United States Representatives under the plan....

Shortly thereafter, the District Court issued an opinion and order declaring the Feldman Plan unconstitutional. Denying the motions for summary judgment and resolving the case on the record as a whole, the District Court held that the population variances in the Feldman Plan were not "unavoidable despite a good-faith effort to achieve absolute equality." ... The court rejected appellants' argument that a deviation lower than the statistical imprecision of the decennial census was "the functional equivalent of mathematical equality." ... It also held that appellants had failed to show that the population variances were justified by the legislature's purported goals of preserving minority voting strength and anticipating shifts in population.... The District Court enjoined appellants from conducting primary or general elections under the Feldman Plan, but that order was stayed pending appeal to this Court...

Article I, Section 2, establishes a "high standard of justice and common sense" for the apportionment of congressional districts: "equal representation for equal numbers of people." ... Precise mathematical equality, however, may be impossible to achieve in an imperfect world; therefore the "equal representation" standard is enforced only to the extent of requiring that districts be apportioned to achieve population equality "as nearly as is practicable." ... As we explained further in *Kirkpatrick v. Preisler*:

[T]he "as nearly as practicable" standard requires that the State make a good-faith effort to achieve precise mathematical equality.... Unless population variances among congressional districts are shown to have resulted despite such effort, the State must justify each variance, no matter how small...

Article I, Section 2, therefore, "permits only the limited population variances which are unavoidable despite a good-faith effort to achieve absolute equality, or for which justification is shown." ...

Thus two basic questions shape litigation over population deviations in state legislation apportioning congressional districts. First, the court must consider whether the population differences among districts could have been reduced or eliminated altogether by a good-faith effort to draw districts of equal population. Parties challenging apportionment legislation must bear the burden of proof on this issue, and if they fail to show that the differences could have been avoided the apportionment scheme must be upheld. If, however, the plaintiffs can establish that the population differences were not the result of a good-faith effort to achieve equality, the State must bear the burden of proving that each significant variance between districts was necessary to achieve some legitimate goal....

Appellants' principal argument in this case is addressed to the first question described above. They contend that the Feldman Plan should be regarded per se as the product of a good-faith effort to achieve population equality because the maximum population deviation among districts is smaller than the predictable undercount in available census data....

Kirkpatrick squarely rejected a nearly identical argument. "The whole thrust of the 'as nearly as practicable' approach is inconsistent with adoption of fixed numerical standards which excuse population variances without regard to the circumstances of each particular case." ... Adopting any standard other than population equality, using the best census data available, ... would subtly erode the Constitution's ideal of equal representation. If state legislators knew that a certain *de minimis* level of population differences was acceptable, they would doubtless strive to achieve that level rather than equality....

Furthermore, choosing a different standard would import a high degree of arbitrariness into the process of reviewing apportionment plans.... In this case, appellants argue that a maximum deviation of approximately 0.7% should be considered *de minimis*. If we accept that argument, how are we to regard deviations of 0.8%, 0.9%, 1%, or 1.1%?

Any standard, including absolute equality, involves a certain artificiality. As appellants point out, even the census data are not perfect, and the well-known restlessness of the American people means that population counts for particular localities are outdated long before they are completed. Yet problems with the data at hand apply equally to any population-based standard we could choose. As between two standards—equality or something less than equality—only the former reflects the aspirations of Article I, Section 2. [Accepting the] population deviations in this case would mean to reject the basic premise *of Kirkpatrick* and *Wesberry [v. Sanders]*. We decline appellants' invitation to go that far. The unusual rigor of their standard has been noted several times. Because of that rigor, we have required that absolute population equality be the paramount objective of apportionment only in the case of congressional districts, for which the command of Article I, Section 2 as regards the National Legislature outweighs the local interests that a State may deem relevant in apportioning districts for representatives to state and local legislatures…. The principle of population equality for congressional districts has not proved unjust or socially or economically harmful in experience…. If anything, this standard should cause less difficulty now for state legislatures than it did when we adopted it in *Wesberry*. The rapid advances in computer technology and education during the last two decades make it relatively simple to draw contiguous districts of equal population and at the same time to further whatever secondary goals the State has. Finally, to abandon unnecessarily a clear and oft-confirmed constitutional interpretation would impair our authority in other cases, … would implicitly open the door to a plethora of requests that we reexamine other rules that some may consider burdensome, and would prejudice those who have relied upon the rule of law in seeking an equipopulous congressional apportionment in New Jersey…. We thus reaffirm that there are no *de minimis* population variations, which could practicably be avoided, but which nonetheless meet the standard of Article I, Section 2, without justification.

The sole difference between appellants' theory and the argument we rejected in *Kirkpatrick* is that appellants have proposed a *de minimis* line that gives the illusion of rationality and predictability: the "inevitable statistical imprecision of the census." They argue: "Where, as here, the deviation from ideal district size is less than the known imprecision of the census figures, that variation is the functional equivalent of zero." … There are two problems with this approach. First, appellants concentrate on the extent to which the census systematically undercounts actual population—a figure which is not known precisely and which, even if it were known, would not be relevant to this case. Second, the mere existence of statistical imprecisions

does not make small deviations among districts the functional equivalent of equality….

The census may systematically undercount population, and the rate of undercounting may vary from place to place. Those facts, however, do not render meaningless the differences in population between congressional districts, as determined by uncorrected census counts. To the contrary, the census data provide the only reliable—albeit less than perfect—indication of the districts' "real" relative population levels. Even if one cannot say with certainty that one district is larger than another merely because it has a higher census count, one can say with certainty that the district with a larger census count is more likely to be larger than the other district than it is to be smaller or the same size. That certainty is sufficient for decisionmaking…. Furthermore, because the census count represents the "best population data available," … it is the only basis for good-faith attempts to achieve population equality. Attempts to explain population deviations on the basis of flaws in census data must be supported with a precision not achieved here….

Given that the census-based population deviations in the Feldman Plan reflect real differences among the districts, it is clear that they could have been avoided or significantly reduced with a good-faith effort to achieve population equality. For that reason alone, it would be inappropriate to accept the Feldman Plan as "functionally equivalent" to a plan with districts of equal population.

The District Court found that several other plans introduced in the 200th Legislature had smaller maximum deviations than the Feldman Plan…. Appellants object that the alternative plans considered by the District Court were not comparable to the Feldman Plan because their political characters differed profoundly…. We have never denied that apportionment is a political process, or that state legislatures could pursue legitimate secondary objectives as long as those objectives were consistent with a good-faith effort to achieve population equality at the same time. Nevertheless, the claim that political considerations require population differences among congressional districts belongs more properly to the second level of judicial inquiry in these cases, … in which the State bears the burden of justifying the differences with particularity.

In any event, it was unnecessary for the District Court to rest its finding on the existence of alternative plans with radically different political effects. As in

(Continued)

Kirkpatrick, "resort to the simple device of transferring entire political subdivisions of known population between contiguous districts would have produced districts much closer to numerical equality." … Starting with the Feldman Plan itself and the census data available to the legislature at the time it was enacted, … one can reduce the maximum population deviation of the plan merely by shifting a handful of municipalities from one district to another.…

Thus the District Court did not err in finding that the plaintiffs had met their burden of showing that the Feldman Plan did not come as nearly as practicable to population equality.…

By itself, the foregoing discussion does not establish that the Feldman Plan is unconstitutional. Rather, appellees' success in proving that the Feldman Plan was not the product of a good-faith effort to achieve population equality means only that the burden shifted to the State to prove that the population deviations in its plan were necessary to achieve some legitimate state objective. *White v. Weiser* demonstrates that we are willing to defer to state legislative policies, so long as they are consistent with constitutional norms, even if they require small differences in the population of congressional districts.… Any number of consistently applied legislative policies might justify some variance, including, for instance, making districts compact, respecting municipal boundaries, preserving the cores of prior districts, and avoiding contests between incumbent Representatives. As long as the criteria are nondiscriminatory, … these are all legitimate objectives that on a proper showing could justify minor population deviations.…

The State must, however, show with some specificity that a particular objective required the specific deviations in its plan, rather than simply relying on general assertions. The showing required to justify population deviations is flexible, depending on the size of the deviations, the importance of the State's interests, the consistency with which the plan as a whole reflects those interests, and the availability of alternatives that might substantially vindicate those interests yet approximate population equality more closely. By necessity, whether deviations are justified requires case-by-case attention to these factors.…

The District Court properly applied the two-part test of *Kirkpatrick v. Preisler* to New Jersey's 1982 apportionment of districts for the United States House of Representatives. It correctly held that the population deviations in the plan were not functionally equal as a matter of law, and it found that the plan was not a good-faith effort to achieve population equality using the best available census data. It also correctly rejected appellants' attempt to justify the population deviations as not supported by the evidence.

The judgment of the District Court, therefore, is affirmed.

Justice Stevens, concurring.…

Justice White, with whom the **Chief Justice, Justice Powell,** and **Justice Rehnquist** join, dissenting.

… "[T]he achieving of fair and effective representation for all citizens is concededly the basic aim of legislative apportionment." … One must suspend credulity to believe that the Court's draconian response to a trifling 0.6984% maximum deviation promotes "fair and effective representation" for the people of New Jersey.…

There can be little question but that the variances in the New Jersey plan are "statistically insignificant." Although the Government strives to make the decennial census as accurate as humanly possible, the Census Bureau has never intimated that the results are a perfect count of the American population. The Bureau itself estimates the inexactitude in the taking of the 1970 census at 2.3%, a figure which is considerably larger than the 0.6984% maximum variance in the New Jersey plan, and which dwarfs the 0.2470% difference between the maximum deviations of the selected plan and the leading alternative plan.… Because the amount of undercounting differs from district to district, there is no point for a court of law to act under an unproved assumption that such tiny differences between redistricting plans reflect actual differences in population.…

Even if the 0.6984% deviation here is not encompassed within the scope of the statistical imprecision of the census, it is minuscule when compared with the variations among the districts inherent in translating census numbers into citizens' votes. First, the census "is more of an event than a process." … "It measures population at only a single instant in time. District populations are constantly changing, often at different rates in either direction, up or down." As the Court admits, "the well-known restlessness of the American people means that population counts for particular localities are outdated long before they are completed." … Second, far larger differences among districts are introduced because a substantial percentage of the total population is too young to register or is disqualified by alienage. Third, census figures cannot account for the proportion of all those otherwise eligible individuals who fail to register. The differences in the number of eligible voters per district for these reasons overwhelm the minimal variations attributable to the districting plan itself.

Accepting that the census, and the districting plans which are based upon it, cannot be perfect represents no backsliding in our commitment to assuring fair and equal representation in the election of Congress. I agree with the views of Judge Gibbons, who dissented in the District Court, that *Kirkpatrick* should not be read as a "prohibition against toleration of *de minimis* population variances which have no statistically relevant effect on relative representation." A plus-minus deviation of 0.6984% surely falls within this category.

If today's decision simply produced an unjustified standard with little practical import, it would be bad enough. Unfortunately, I fear that the Court's insistence that "there are no *de minimis* population variations, which could practically be avoided, but which nonetheless meet the standard of Article I, Section 2, without justification," ... invites further litigation of virtually every congressional redistricting plan in the Nation. At least 12 States which have completed redistricting on the basis of the 1980 census have adopted plans with a higher deviation than that presented here, and 4 others have deviations quite similar to New Jersey's. Of course, under the Court's rationale, even

Rhode Island's plan—whose two districts have a deviation of 0.02% or about 95 people—would be subject to constitutional attack.

In all such cases, state legislatures will be hard pressed to justify their preference for the selected plan. A good-faith effort to achieve population equality is not enough if the population variances are not "unavoidable." The court must consider whether the population differences could have been further "reduced or eliminated altogether."...

With the assistance of computers, there will generally be a plan with an even more minimal deviation from the mathematical ideal. Then, "the State must bear the burden of proving that each significant variance between districts was necessary to achieve some legitimate goal." ... As this case illustrates, literally any variance between districts will be considered "significant." ...

Yet no one can seriously contend that such an inflexible insistence upon mathematical exactness will serve to promote "fair and effective representation." The more likely result of today's extension of *Kirkpatrick* is to move closer to fulfilling Justice Fortas' prophecy that "a legislature might have to ignore the boundaries of common sense, running the congressional district line down the middle of the corridor of an apartment house or even dividing the residents of a single-family house between two districts." ... Such sterile and mechanistic application only brings the principle of "one man, one vote" into disrepute....

Justice Powell, dissenting....

BUSH v. GORE
537 U.S. 98; 121 S.Ct. 525; 148 L.Ed. 2d 388 (2000)
Vote: 5-4

In what may be the most controversial use of judicial power since Roe v. Wade (1973), the Supreme Court here involves itself in the 2000 presidential election process. In this highly unusual case, in which the opposing parties are rival presidential candidates, the Court reviews the Florida Supreme Court's decision upholding manual recounts of ballots cast in three counties.

Per Curiam.

I

On December 8, 2000, the Supreme Court of Florida ordered that the Circuit Court of Leon County tabulate by hand 9,000 ballots in Miami-Dade County. It also ordered the inclusion in the certified vote totals of 215 votes identified in Palm Beach County and 168 votes identified in Miami-Dade County for Vice President Albert Gore, Jr., and Senator Joseph Lieberman,

(Continued)

Democratic Candidates for President and Vice President. The Supreme Court noted that petitioner, Governor George W. Bush asserted that the net gain for Vice President Gore in Palm Beach County was 176 votes, and directed the Circuit Court to resolve that dispute on remand.... The court further held that relief would require manual recounts in all Florida counties where so-called "undervotes" had not been subject to manual tabulation. The court ordered all manual recounts to begin at once. Governor Bush and Richard Cheney, Republican Candidates for the Presidency and Vice Presidency, filed an emergency application for a stay of this mandate. On December 9, we granted the application, treated the application as a petition for a writ of certiorari, and granted certiorari....

The proceedings leading to the present controversy are discussed in some detail in our opinion in *Bush v. Palm Beach County Canvassing Bd....* (per curiam) *(Bush I)*. On November 8, 2000, the day following the Presidential election, the Florida Division of Elections reported that petitioner, Governor Bush, had received 2,909,135 votes, and respondent, Vice President Gore, had received 2,907,351 votes, a margin of 1,784 for Governor Bush. Because Governor Bush's margin of victory was less than "one-half of a percent ... of the votes cast," an automatic machine recount was conducted under § 102.141(4) of the election code, the results of which showed Governor Bush still winning the race but by a diminished margin. Vice President Gore then sought manual recounts in Volusia, Palm Beach, Broward, and Miami-Dade Counties, pursuant to Florida's election protest provisions. Fla. Stat. § 102.166 (2000). A dispute arose concerning the deadline for local county canvassing boards to submit their returns to the Secretary of State (Secretary). The Secretary declined to waive the November 14 deadline imposed by statute. §§ 102.111, 102.112. The Florida Supreme Court, however, set the deadline at November 26. We granted certiorari and vacated the Florida Supreme Court's decision, finding considerable uncertainty as to the grounds on which it was based.... On December 11, the Florida Supreme Court issued a decision on remand reinstating that date....

On November 26, the Florida Elections Canvassing Commission certified the results of the election and declared Governor Bush the winner of Florida's 25 electoral votes. On November 27, Vice President Gore, pursuant to Florida's contest provisions, filed a complaint in Leon County Circuit Court contesting the certification. Fla. Stat. § 102.168 (2000). He sought relief pursuant to § 102.168(3)(c), which provides that "[r]eceipt of a number of illegal votes or rejection of a number of legal votes sufficient to change or place in doubt the result of the election" shall be grounds for a contest. The Circuit Court denied relief, stating that Vice President Gore failed to meet his burden of proof. He appealed to the First District Court of Appeal, which certified the matter to the Florida Supreme Court.

Accepting jurisdiction, the Florida Supreme Court affirmed in part and reversed in part.... The court held that the Circuit Court had been correct to reject Vice President Gore's challenge to the results certified in Nassau County and his challenge to the Palm Beach County Canvassing Board's determination that 3,300 ballots cast in that county were not, in the statutory phrase, "legal votes." The Supreme Court held that Vice President Gore had satisfied his burden of proof under § 102.168(3)(c) with respect to his challenge to Miami-Dade County's failure to tabulate, by manual count, 9,000 ballots on which the machines had failed to detect a vote for President ("undervotes").

... Noting the closeness of the election, the Court explained that "[o]n this record, there can be no question that there are legal votes within the 9,000 uncounted votes sufficient to place the results of this election in doubt." ... A "legal vote," as determined by the Supreme Court, is "one in which there is a 'clear indication of the intent of the voter.' " ... The court therefore ordered a hand recount of the 9,000 ballots in Miami-Dade County. Observing that the contest provisions vest broad discretion in the circuit judge to "provide any relief appropriate under such circumstances," ... the Supreme Court further held that the Circuit Court could order "the Supervisor of Elections and the Canvassing Boards, as well as the necessary public officials, in all counties that have not conducted a manual recount or tabulation of the undervotes ... to do so forthwith, said tabulation to take place in the individual counties where the ballots are located." ...

The Supreme Court also determined that both Palm Beach County and Miami-Dade County, in their earlier manual recounts, had identified a net gain of 215 and 168 legal votes for Vice President Gore.... Rejecting the Circuit Court's conclusion that Palm Beach County lacked the authority to include the 215 net votes submitted past the November 26 deadline, the Supreme Court explained that the deadline was not intended to exclude votes identified after that date through ongoing manual recounts. As to Miami-Dade County, the Court concluded that although the 168 votes identified were the result of a partial recount, they were "legal votes [that] could change the outcome of the election." ... The Supreme Court therefore directed the Circuit Court to include those totals in the certified results, subject to resolution of the actual vote total from the Miami-Dade partial recount.

The petition presents the following questions: whether the Florida Supreme Court established new standards for resolving Presidential election contests, thereby violating Art. II, § 1, cl. 2, of the United States Constitution and failing to comply with 3 U.S.C. § 5, and whether the use of standardless manual recounts violates the Equal Protection and Due Process Clauses. With respect to the equal protection question, we find a violation of the Equal Protection Clause.

II

A

The closeness of this election, and the multitude of legal challenges which have followed in its wake, have brought into sharp focus a common, if heretofore unnoticed, phenomenon. Nationwide statistics reveal that an estimated 2% of ballots cast do not register a vote for President for whatever reason, including deliberately choosing no candidate at all or some voter error, such as voting for two candidates or insufficiently marking a ballot.... In certifying election results, the votes eligible for inclusion in the certification are the votes meeting the properly established legal requirements.

This case has shown that punch card balloting machines can produce an unfortunate number of ballots which are not punched in a clean, complete way by the voter. After the current counting, it is likely legislative bodies nationwide will examine ways to improve the mechanisms and machinery for voting.

B

The individual citizen has no federal constitutional right to vote for electors for the President of the United States unless and until the state legislature chooses a statewide election as the means to implement its power to appoint members of the Electoral College. U.S. Const., Art. II, § 1. This is the source for the statement in *McPherson v. Blacker* (1892), that the State legislature's power to select the manner for appointing electors is plenary; it may, if it so chooses, select the electors itself, which indeed was the manner used by State legislatures in several States for many years after the Framing of our Constitution.... History has now

favored the voter, and in each of the several States the citizens themselves vote for Presidential electors. When the state legislature vests the right to vote for President in its people, the right to vote as the legislature has prescribed is fundamental; and one source of its fundamental nature lies in the equal weight accorded to each vote and the equal dignity owed to each voter. The State, of course, after granting the franchise in the special context of Article II, can take back the power to appoint electors....

The right to vote is protected in more than the initial allocation of the franchise. Equal protection applies as well to the manner of its exercise. Having once granted the right to vote on equal terms, the State may not, by later arbitrary and disparate treatment, value one person's vote over that of another.... It must be remembered that "the right of suffrage can be denied by a debasement or dilution of the weight of a citizen's vote just as effectively as by wholly prohibiting the free exercise of the franchise." ...

There is no difference between the two sides of the present controversy on these basic propositions. Respondents say that the very purpose of vindicating the right to vote justifies the recount procedures now at issue. The question before us, however, is whether the recount procedures the Florida Supreme Court has adopted are consistent with its obligation to avoid arbitrary and disparate treatment of the members of its electorate.

Much of the controversy seems to revolve around ballot cards designed to be perforated by a stylus but which, either through error or deliberate omission, have not been perforated with sufficient precision for a machine to count them. In some cases a piece of the card—a chad—is hanging, say by two corners. In other cases there is no separation at all, just an indentation. The Florida Supreme Court has ordered that the intent of the voter be discerned from such ballots. For purposes of resolving the equal protection challenge, it is not necessary to decide whether the Florida Supreme Court had the authority under the legislative scheme for resolving election disputes to define what a legal vote is and to mandate a manual recount implementing that definition. The recount mechanisms implemented in response to the decisions of the Florida Supreme Court do not satisfy the minimum requirement for non-arbitrary treatment of voters necessary to secure the fundamental right. Florida's basic command for the count of legally cast votes is to consider the "intent of the voter." ... This is unobjectionable as

(Continued)

an abstract proposition and a starting principle. The problem inheres in the absence of specific standards to ensure its equal application. The formulation of uniform rules to determine intent based on these recurring circumstances is practicable and, we conclude, necessary.

The law does not refrain from searching for the intent of the actor in a multitude of circumstances; and in some cases the general command to ascertain intent is not susceptible to much further refinement. In this instance, however, the question is not whether to believe a witness but how to interpret the marks or holes or scratches on an inanimate object, a piece of cardboard or paper which, it is said, might not have registered as a vote during the machine count. The factfinder confronts a thing, not a person. The search for intent can be confined by specific rules designed to ensure uniform treatment.

The want of those rules here has led to unequal evaluation of ballots in various respects.... As seems to have been acknowledged at oral argument, the standards for accepting or rejecting contested ballots might vary not only from county to county but indeed within a single county from one recount team to another.

The record provides some examples. A monitor in Miami-Dade County testified at trial that he observed that three members of the county canvassing board applied different standards in defining a legal vote.... And testimony at trial also revealed that at least one county changed its evaluative standards during the counting process. Palm Beach County, for example, began the process with a 1990 guideline which precluded counting completely attached chads, switched to a rule that considered a vote to be legal if any light could be seen through a chad, changed back to the 1990 rule, and then abandoned any pretense of a per se rule, only to have a court order that the county consider dimpled chads legal. This is not a process with sufficient guarantees of equal treatment...

The State Supreme Court ratified this uneven treatment. It mandated that the recount totals from two counties, Miami-Dade and Palm Beach, be included in the certified total. The court also appeared to hold *sub silentio* that the recount totals from Broward County, which were not completed until after the original November 14 certification by the Secretary of State, were to be considered part of the new certified vote totals even though the county certification was not contested by Vice President Gore. Yet each of the counties used varying standards to determine what was a legal vote. Broward County used a more

forgiving standard than Palm Beach County, and uncovered almost three times as many new votes, a result markedly disproportionate to the difference in population between the counties.

In addition, the recounts in these three counties were not limited to so-called undervotes but extended to all of the ballots. The distinction has real consequences. A manual recount of all ballots identifies not only those ballots which show no vote but also those which contain more than one, the so-called overvotes. Neither category will be counted by the machine. This is not a trivial concern. At oral argument, respondents estimated there are as many as 110,000 overvotes statewide. As a result, the citizen whose ballot was not read by a machine because he failed to vote for a candidate in a way readable by a machine may still have his vote counted in a manual recount; on the other hand, the citizen who marks two candidates in a way discernible by the machine will not have the same opportunity to have his vote count, even if a manual examination of the ballot would reveal the requisite indicia of intent. Furthermore, the citizen who marks two candidates, only one of which is discernible by the machine, will have his vote counted even though it should have been read as an invalid ballot. The State Supreme Court's inclusion of vote counts based on these variant standards exemplifies concerns with the remedial processes that were under way.

That brings the analysis to yet a further equal protection problem. The votes certified by the court included a partial total from one county, Miami-Dade. The Florida Supreme Court's decision thus gives no assurance that the recounts included in a final certification must be complete.

Indeed, it is respondent's submission that it would be consistent with the rules of the recount procedures to include whatever partial counts are done by the time of final certification, and we interpret the Florida Supreme Court's decision to permit this.... This accommodation no doubt results from the truncated contest period established by the Florida Supreme Court in *Bush I,* at respondents' own urging. The press of time does not diminish the constitutional concern. A desire for speed is not a general excuse for ignoring equal protection guarantees.

In addition to these difficulties the actual process by which the votes were to be counted under the Florida Supreme Court's decision raises further concerns. That order did not specify who would recount the ballots. The county canvassing boards were forced to pull together ad hoc teams comprised of judges from various Circuits who had no previous training in handling and interpreting ballots. Furthermore, while others were permitted to observe, they were prohibited from objecting during the recount.

The recount process, in its features here described, is inconsistent with the minimum procedures necessary to protect the fundamental right of each voter in the special instance of a statewide recount under the authority of a single state judicial officer. Our consideration is limited to the present circumstances, for the problem of equal protection in election processes generally presents many complexities.

The question before the Court is not whether local entities, in the exercise of their expertise, may develop different systems for implementing elections. Instead, we are presented with a situation where a state court with the power to assure uniformity has ordered a statewide recount with minimal procedural safeguards. When a court orders a statewide remedy, there must be at least some assurance that the rudimentary requirements of equal treatment and fundamental fairness are satisfied.

Given the Court's assessment that the recount process under way was probably being conducted in an unconstitutional manner, the Court stayed the order directing the recount so it could hear this case and render an expedited decision. The contest provision, as it was mandated by the State Supreme Court, is not well calculated to sustain the confidence that all citizens must have in the outcome of elections. The State has not shown that its procedures include the necessary safeguards. The problem, for instance, of the estimated 110,000 overvotes has not been addressed, although Chief Justice Wells called attention to the concern in his dissenting opinion....

Upon due consideration of the difficulties identified to this point, it is obvious that the recount cannot be conducted in compliance with the requirements of equal protection and due process without substantial additional work. It would require not only the adoption (after opportunity for argument) of adequate statewide standards for determining what is a legal vote, and practicable procedures to implement them, but also orderly judicial review of any disputed matters that might arise. In addition, the Secretary of State has advised that the recount of only a portion of the ballots requires that the vote tabulation equipment be used to screen out undervotes, a function for which the machines were not designed. If a recount of overvotes were also required, perhaps even a second screening would be necessary. Use of the equipment for this purpose, and any new software developed for it, would have to be evaluated for accuracy by the Secretary of State....

The Supreme Court of Florida has said that the legislature intended the State's electors to "participate fully in the federal electoral process," as provided in 3 U.S.C. § 5.... That statute, in turn, requires that any controversy or contest that is designed to lead to a conclusive selection of electors be completed by December 12. That date is upon us, and there is no recount procedure in place under the State Supreme Court's order that comports with minimal constitutional standards. Because it is evident that any recount seeking to meet the December 12 date will be unconstitutional for the reasons we have discussed, we reverse the judgment of the Supreme Court of Florida ordering a recount to proceed.

Seven Justices of the Court agree that there are constitutional problems with the recount ordered by the Florida Supreme Court that demand a remedy.... The only disagreement is as to the remedy. Because the Florida Supreme Court has said that the Florida Legislature intended to obtain the safe-harbor benefits of 3 U.S.C. § 5, ... remanding to the Florida Supreme Court for its ordering of a constitutionally proper contest until December 18 ... contemplates action in violation of the Florida election code, and hence could not be part of an "appropriate" order....

None are more conscious of the vital limits on judicial authority than are the members of this Court, and none stand more in admiration of the Constitution's design to leave the selection of the President to the people, through their legislatures, and to the political sphere. When contending parties invoke the process of the courts, however, it becomes our unsought responsibility to resolve the federal and constitutional issues the judicial system has been forced to confront. The judgment of the Supreme Court of Florida is reversed, and the case is remanded for further proceedings not inconsistent with this opinion....

Chief Justice Rehnquist, with whom **Justice Scalia** and **Justice Thomas** join, concurring.

We join the per curiam opinion. We write separately because we believe there are additional grounds that require us to reverse the Florida Supreme Court's decision.

... In most cases, comity and respect for federalism compel us to defer to the decisions of state courts on

(Continued)

issues of state law. That practice reflects our understanding that the decisions of state courts are definitive pronouncements of the will of the States as sovereigns.... Of course, in ordinary cases, the distribution of powers among the branches of a State's government raises no questions of federal constitutional law, subject to the requirement that the government be republican in character.... But there are a few exceptional cases in which the Constitution imposes a duty or confers a power on a particular branch of a State's government. This is one of them. Article II, § 1, cl. 2, provides that "[e]ach State shall appoint, in such Manner as the Legislature thereof may direct," electors for President and Vice President.... Thus, the text of the election law itself, and not just its interpretation by the courts of the States, takes on independent significance.

In *McPherson v. Blacker* (1892), we explained that Art. II, § 1, cl. 2, "convey[s] the broadest power of determination" and "leaves it to the legislature exclusively to define the method" of appointment.... A significant departure from the legislative scheme for appointing Presidential electors presents a federal constitutional question.

3 U.S.C. § 5 informs our application of Art. II, § 1, cl. 2, to the Florida statutory scheme, which, as the Florida Supreme Court acknowledged, took that statute into account. Section 5 provides that the State's selection of electors "shall be conclusive, and shall govern in the counting of the electoral votes" if the electors are chosen under laws enacted prior to election day, and if the selection process is completed six days prior to the meeting of the electoral college....

If we are to respect the legislature's Article II powers, therefore, we must ensure that postelection state-court actions do not frustrate the legislative desire to attain the "safe harbor" provided by § 5.

In Florida, the legislature has chosen to hold statewide elections to appoint the State's 25 electors. Importantly, the legislature has delegated the authority to run the elections and to oversee election disputes to the Secretary of State (Secretary) ... Isolated sections of the code may well admit of more than one interpretation, but the general coherence of the legislative scheme may not be altered by judicial interpretation so as to wholly change the statutorily provided apportionment of responsibility among these various bodies. In any election but a Presidential election, the Florida Supreme Court can give as little or as much deference to Florida's executives as it chooses, so far as Article II is concerned, and this Court will have no cause to question the court's actions. But, with respect to a

Presidential election, the court must be both mindful of the legislature's role under Article II in choosing the manner of appointing electors and deferential to those bodies expressly empowered by the legislature to carry out its constitutional mandate.

In order to determine whether a state court has infringed upon the legislature's authority, we necessarily must examine the law of the State as it existed prior to the action of the court. Though we generally defer to state courts on the interpretation of state law ... there are of course areas in which the Constitution requires this Court to undertake an independent, if still deferential, analysis of state law....

This inquiry does not imply a disrespect for state courts but rather a respect for the constitutionally prescribed role of state legislatures. To attach definitive weight to the pronouncement of a state court, when the very question at issue is whether the court has actually departed from the statutory meaning, would be to abdicate our responsibility to enforce the explicit requirements of Article II....

II

Acting pursuant to its constitutional grant of authority, the Florida Legislature has created a detailed, if not perfectly crafted, statutory scheme that provides for appointment of Presidential electors by direct election.... Under the statute, "[v]otes cast for the actual candidates for President and Vice President shall be counted as votes cast for the presidential electors supporting such candidates." ... The legislature has designated the Secretary of State as the "chief election officer," with the responsibility to "[o]btain and maintain uniformity in the application, operation, and interpretation of the election laws." ... The state legislature has delegated to county canvassing boards the duties of administering elections.... Those boards are responsible for providing results to the state Elections Canvassing Commission, comprising the Governor, the Secretary of State, and the Director of the Division of Elections.... After the election has taken place, the canvassing boards receive returns from precincts, count the votes, and in the event that a candidate was defeated by .5% or less, conduct a mandatory recount.... The county canvassing boards must file certified election returns with the Department of State by 5 P.M. on the seventh day following the election.... The Elections Canvassing Commission must then certify the results of the election....

The state legislature has also provided mechanisms both for protesting election returns and for contesting certified election results. Section 102.166 governs protests. Any protest must be filed prior to the certification of election results by the county canvassing board. ... Once a protest has been filed, "the county canvassing board may authorize a manual recount." ... If a sample recount conducted pursuant to § 102.166(5) "indicates an error in the vote tabulation which could affect the outcome of the election," the county canvassing board is instructed to: "(a) Correct the error and recount the remaining precincts with the vote tabulation system; (b) Request the Department of State to verify the tabulation software; or (c) Manually recount all ballots," ... In the event a canvassing board chooses to conduct a manual recount of all ballots, [Florida law] prescribes procedures for such a recount.

[Under Florida law] ... [t]he grounds for contesting an election include "[r]eceipt of a number of illegal votes or rejection of a number of legal votes sufficient to change or place in doubt the result of the election." ... Any contest must be filed in the appropriate Florida circuit court, ... and the canvassing board or election board is the proper party defendant.... Section 102.168(8) provides that "[t]he circuit judge to whom the contest is presented may fashion such orders as he or she deems necessary to ensure that each allegation in the complaint is investigated, examined, or checked, to prevent or correct any alleged wrong, and to provide any relief appropriate under such circumstances." In Presidential elections, the contest period necessarily terminates on the date set by 3 U.S.C. § 5 for concluding the State's "final determination" of election controversies."

In its first decision, *Palm Beach Canvassing Bd. v. Harris* ... (*Harris 7*), the Florida Supreme Court extended the 7-day statutory certification deadline established by the legislature. This modification of the code, by lengthening the protest period, necessarily shortened the contest period for Presidential elections. Underlying the extension of the certification deadline and the shortchanging of the contest period was, presumably, the clear implication that certification was a matter of significance: The certified winner would enjoy presumptive validity, making a contest proceeding by the losing candidate an uphill battle. In its latest opinion, however, the court empties certification of virtually all legal consequence during the contest, and in doing so departs from the provisions enacted by the Florida Legislature.

The court determined that canvassing boards' decisions regarding whether to recount ballots past the certification deadline (even the certification deadline established by *Harris 7*) are to be reviewed de novo, although the election code clearly vests discretion whether to recount in the boards, and sets strict deadlines subject to the Secretary's rejection of late tallies and monetary fines for tardiness.... Moreover, the Florida court held that all late vote tallies arriving during the contest period should be automatically included in the certification regardless of the certification deadline (even the certification deadline established by *Harris 7*), thus virtually eliminating both the deadline and the Secretary's discretion to disregard recounts that violate it.

Moreover, the court's interpretation of "legal vote," and hence its decision to order a contest-period recount, plainly departed from the legislative scheme. Florida statutory law cannot reasonably be thought to require the counting of improperly marked ballots. Each Florida precinct before election day provides instructions on how properly to cast a vote; each polling place on election day contains a working model of the voting machine it uses; and each voting booth contains a sample ballot. In precincts using punch-card ballots, voters are instructed to punch out the ballot cleanly.

After voting, check your ballot card to be sure your voting selections are clearly and cleanly punched and there are no chips left hanging on the back of the card.

... No reasonable person would call it "an error in the vote tabulation," ... when electronic or electromechanical equipment performs precisely in the manner designed, and fails to count those ballots that are not marked in the manner that these voting instructions explicitly and prominently specify. The scheme that the Florida Supreme Court's opinion attributes to the legislature is one in which machines are required to be "capable of correctly counting votes," ... but which nonetheless regularly produces elections in which legal votes are predictably not tabulated, so that in close elections manual recounts are regularly required. This is of course absurd. The Secretary of State, who is authorized by law to issue binding interpretations of the election code, ... rejected this peculiar reading of the statutes.... The Florida Supreme Court, although it must defer to the Secretary's interpretations, ... rejected her reasonable interpretation and embraced the peculiar one....

But as we indicated in our remand of the earlier case, in a Presidential election the clearly expressed intent of the legislature must prevail. And there is no

(Continued)

basis for reading the Florida statutes as requiring the counting of improperly marked ballots, as an examination of the Florida Supreme Court's textual analysis shows. We will not parse that analysis here, except to note that the principal provision of the election code on which it relied ... was entirely irrelevant.... The State's Attorney General (who was supporting the Gore challenge) confirmed in oral argument here that never before the present election had a manual recount been conducted on the basis of the contention that "under-votes" should have been examined to determine voter intent.... For the court to step away from this established practice, prescribed by the Secretary of State, the state official charged by the legislature with "responsibility to ... [o]btain and maintain uniformity in the application, operation, and interpretation of the election laws," ... was to depart from the legislative scheme....

III

The scope and nature of the remedy ordered by the Florida Supreme Court jeopardizes the "legislative wish" to take advantage of the safe harbor provided by 3 U.S.C. § 5.... December 12, 2000, is the last date for a final determination of the Florida electors that will satisfy § 5. Yet in the late afternoon of December 8th—four days before this deadline—the Supreme Court of Florida ordered recounts of tens of thousands of so-called "undervotes" spread through 64 of the State's 67 counties. This was done in a search for elusive—perhaps delusive—certainty as to the exact count of 6 million votes. But no one claims that these ballots have not previously been tabulated; they were initially read by voting machines at the time of the election, and thereafter reread by virtue of Florida's automatic recount provision. No one claims there was any fraud in the election. The Supreme Court of Florida ordered this additional recount under the provision of the election code giving the circuit judge the authority to provide relief that is "appropriate under such circumstances." ...

Surely when the Florida Legislature empowered the courts of the State to grant "appropriate" relief, it must have meant relief that would have become final by the cutoff date of 3 U.S.C. § 5. In light of the inevitable legal challenges and ensuing appeals to the Supreme Court of Florida and petitions for certiorari to this Court, the entire recounting process could not possibly be completed by that date. Whereas the majority in the Supreme Court of Florida stated its confidence that "the remaining undervotes in these counties can be [counted] within the required time frame," ... it made no assertion that the seemingly inevitable appeals could be disposed of in

that time. Although the Florida Supreme Court has on occasion taken over a year to resolve disputes over local elections, ... it has heard and decided the appeals in the present case with great promptness. But the federal deadlines for the Presidential election simply do not permit even such a shortened process....

Given all these factors, and in light of the legislative intent identified by the Florida Supreme Court to bring Florida within the "safe harbor" provision of 3 U.S.C. § 5, the remedy prescribed by the Supreme Court of Florida cannot be deemed an "appropriate" one as of December 8. It significantly departed from the statutory framework in place on November 7, and authorized open-ended further proceedings which could not be completed by December 12, thereby preventing a final determination by that date.

For these reasons, in addition to those given in the *per curiam,* we would reverse.

Justice Stevens, with whom **Justice Ginsburg** and **Justice Breyer** join, dissenting.

... What must underlie petitioners' entire federal assault on the Florida election procedures is an unstated lack of confidence in the impartiality and capacity of the state judges who would make the critical decisions if the vote count were to proceed. Otherwise, their position is wholly without merit. The endorsement of that position by the majority of this Court can only lend credence to the most cynical appraisal of the work of judges throughout the land. It is confidence in the men and women who administer the judicial system that is the true backbone of the rule of law. Time will one day heal the wound to that confidence that will be inflicted by today's decision. One thing, however, is certain. Although we may never know with complete certainty the identity of the winner of this year's Presidential election, the identity of the loser is perfectly clear. It is the Nation's confidence in the judge as an impartial guardian of the rule of law....

Justice Souter, with whom **Justice Breyer** joins and with whom **Justice Stevens** and **Justice Ginsburg** join ..., dissenting.

The Court should not have reviewed either *Bush v. Palm Beach County Canvassing Bd.* or this case, and should not have stopped Florida's attempt to recount all undervote ballots, ... by issuing a stay of the Florida Supreme Court's orders during the period of this review.... If this Court had allowed the State to follow the course indicated by the opinions of its own Supreme Court, it is entirely possible that there would ultimately have been no issue requiring our review, and political tension could have worked itself out in the Congress following the procedure provided in 3 U.S.C. § 15. The case being before us, however, its resolution by the majority is another erroneous decision....

There are three issues: whether the State Supreme Court's interpretation of the statute providing for a contest of the state election results somehow violates 3 U.S. C. § 5; whether that court's construction of the state statutory provisions governing contests impermissibly changes a state law from what the State's legislature has provided, in violation of Article II, § 1, cl. 2, of the national Constitution; and whether the manner of interpreting markings on disputed ballots failing to cause machines to register votes for President (the undervote ballots) violates the equal protection or due process guaranteed by the Fourteenth Amendment. None of these issues is difficult to describe or to resolve....

The 3 U.S.C. § 5 issue is not serious. That provision sets certain conditions for treating a State's certification of Presidential electors as conclusive in the event that a dispute over recognizing those electors must be resolved in the Congress under 3 U.S.C. § 15. Conclusiveness requires selection under a legal scheme in place before the election, with results determined at least six days before the date set for casting electoral votes. But no State is required to conform to § 5 if it cannot do that (for whatever reason); the sanction for failing to satisfy the conditions of § 5 is simply loss of what has been called its "safe harbor." And even that determination is to be made, if made anywhere, in the Congress....

The second matter here goes to the State Supreme Court's interpretation of certain terms in the state statute governing election "contests," Fla. Stat. § 102.168 (2000); there is no question here about the state court's interpretation of the related provisions dealing with the antecedent process of "protesting" particular vote counts, § 102.166, which was involved in the previous case, *Bush v. Palm Beach County Canvassing Board.* The issue is whether the judgment of the state supreme court has displaced the state legislature's provisions for election contests: is the law as declared by the court different from the provisions made by the legislature, to which the national Constitution commits responsibility for determining how each State's Presidential electors are chosen? ... Bush does not, of course, claim that any judicial act interpreting a statute of

uncertain meaning is enough to displace the legislative provision and violate Article II; statutes require interpretation, which does not without more affect the legislative character of a statute within the meaning of the Constitution.... What Bush does argue, as I understand the contention, is that the interpretation of § 102.168 was so unreasonable as to transcend the accepted bounds of statutory interpretation, to the point of being a nonjudicial act and producing new law untethered to the legislative act in question.

The starting point for evaluating the claim that the Florida Supreme Court's interpretation effectively rewrote § 102.168 must be the language of the provision on which Gore relies to show his right to raise this contest: that the previously certified result in Bush's favor was produced by "rejection of a number of legal votes sufficient to change or place in doubt the result of the election." ... None of the state court's interpretations is unreasonable to the point of displacing the legislative enactment quoted....

In sum, the interpretations by the Florida court raise no substantial question under Article II. That court engaged in permissible construction in determining that Gore had instituted a contest authorized by the state statute, and it proceeded to direct the trial judge to deal with that contest in the exercise of the discretionary powers generously conferred by Fla. Stat. § 102.168(8) (2000), to "fashion such orders as he or she deems necessary to ensure that each allegation in the complaint is investigated, examined, or checked, to prevent or correct any alleged wrong, and to provide any relief appropriate under such circumstances." ...

It is only on the third issue before us that there is a meritorious argument for relief, as this Court's Per Curiam opinion recognizes. It is an issue that might well have been dealt with adequately by the Florida courts if the state proceedings had not been interrupted, and if not disposed of at the state level it could have been considered by the Congress in any electoral vote dispute. But because the course of state proceedings has been interrupted, time is short, and the issue is before us, I think it sensible for the Court to address it.

Petitioners have raised an equal protection claim ... in the charge that unjustifiably disparate standards are applied in different electoral jurisdictions to otherwise identical facts. It is true that the Equal Protection Clause does not forbid the use of a variety of voting mechanisms within a jurisdiction, even though different mechanisms will have different levels of effectiveness in recording voters' intentions; local variety can be

(Continued)

justified by concerns about cost, the potential value of innovation, and so on. But evidence in the record here suggests that a different order of disparity obtains under rules for determining a voter's intent that have been applied (and could continue to be applied) to identical types of ballots used in identical brands of machines and exhibiting identical physical characteristics (such as "hanging" or "dimpled" chads).... I can conceive of no legitimate state interest served by these differing treatments of the expressions of voters' fundamental rights. The differences appear wholly arbitrary.

In deciding what to do about this, we should take account of the fact that electoral votes are due to be cast in six days. I would therefore remand the case to the courts of Florida with instructions to establish uniform standards for evaluating the several types of ballots that have prompted differing treatments, to be applied within and among counties when passing on such identical ballots in any further recounting (or successive recounting) that the courts might order.

Unlike the majority, I see no warrant for this Court to assume that Florida could not possibly comply with this requirement before the date set for the meeting of electors, December 18. Although one of the dissenting justices of the State Supreme Court estimated that disparate standards potentially affected 170,000 votes, ... the number at issue is significantly smaller. The 170,000 figure apparently represents all uncounted votes, both undervotes (those for which no Presidential choice was recorded by a machine) and overvotes (those rejected because of votes for more than one candidate).... But ... no showing has been made of legal overvotes uncounted, and counsel for Gore made an uncontradicted representation to the Court that the statewide total of undervotes is about 60,000.... To recount these manually would be a tall order, but before this Court stayed the effort to do that the courts of Florida were ready to do their best to get that job done. There is no justification for denying the State the opportunity to try to count all disputed ballots now....

Justice Ginsburg, with whom **Justice Stevens** joins, and with whom **Justice Souter** and **Justice Breyer** join [in part], dissenting.

... The extraordinary setting of this case has obscured the ordinary principle that dictates its proper resolution: Federal courts defer to state high courts' interpretations of their state's own law. This principle reflects the core of federalism, on which all agree. "The

Framers split the atom of sovereignty. It was the genius of their idea that our citizens would have two political capacities, one state and one federal, each protected from incursion by the other." ... Were the other members of this Court as mindful as they generally are of our system of dual sovereignty, they would affirm the judgment of the Florida Supreme Court...

... The Court assumes that time will not permit "orderly judicial review of any disputed matters that might arise." ... But no one has doubted the good faith and diligence with which Florida election officials, attorneys for all sides of this controversy, and the courts of law have performed their duties. Notably, the Florida Supreme Court has produced two substantial opinions within 29 hours of oral argument. In sum, the Court's conclusion that a constitutionally adequate recount is impractical is a prophecy the Court's own judgment will not allow to be tested. Such an untested prophecy should not decide the Presidency of the United States....

Justice Breyer, with whom **Justice Stevens** and **Justice Ginsburg** join [in part] and with whom **Justice Souter** joins [in part], dissenting.

The Court was wrong to take this case. It was wrong to grant a stay. It should now vacate that stay and permit the Florida Supreme Court to decide whether the recount should resume....

The political implications of this case for the country are momentous. But the federal legal questions presented, with one exception, are insubstantial....

... The majority concludes that the Equal Protection Clause requires that a manual recount be governed not only by the uniform general standard of the "clear intent of the voter," but also by uniform subsidiary standards (for example, a uniform determination whether indented, but not perforated, "under-votes" should count). The opinion points out that the Florida Supreme Court ordered the inclusion of Broward County's undercounted "legal votes" even though those votes included ballots that were not perforated but simply "dimpled," while newly recounted ballots from other counties will likely include only votes determined to be "legal" on the basis of a stricter standard. In light of our previous remand, the Florida Supreme Court may have been reluctant to adopt a more specific standard than that provided for by the legislature for fear of exceeding its authority under Article II. However, since the use of different standards could favor one or the other of the candidates, since time was, and is, too short to permit the lower courts to iron out significant differences through ordinary judicial review, and since the relevant distinction was embodied in the order of the State's highest court, I agree that, in these very special circumstances, basic principles of fairness may well have counseled the adoption of a uniform standard to address the problem....

Nonetheless, there is no justification for the majority's remedy, which is simply to reverse the lower court and halt the recount entirely. An appropriate remedy would be, instead, to remand this case with instructions that, even at this late date, would permit the Florida Supreme Court to require recounting all undercounted votes in Florida, including those from Broward, Volusia, Palm Beach, and Miami-Dade Counties, whether or not previously recounted prior to the end of the protest period, and to do so in accordance with a single-uniform substandard....

By halting the manual recount, and thus ensuring that the uncounted legal votes will not be counted under any standard, this Court crafts a remedy out of proportion to the asserted harm. And that remedy harms the very fairness interests the Court is attempting to protect.

... [I]n a system that allows counties to use different types of voting systems, voters already arrive at the polls with an unequal chance that their votes will be counted. I do not see how the fact that this results from counties' selection of different voting machines rather than a court order makes the outcome any more fair. Nor do I understand why the Florida Supreme Court's recount order, which helps to redress this inequity, must be entirely prohibited based on a deficiency that could easily be remedied....

Despite the reminder that this case involves "an election for the President of the United States," ... no preeminent legal concern, or practical concern related to legal questions, required this Court to hear this case, let alone to issue a stay that stopped Florida's recount process in its tracks. With one exception, petitioners' claims do not ask us to vindicate a constitutional provision designed to protect a basic human right.... Petitioners invoke fundamental fairness, namely, the need for procedural fairness, including finality. But with the one "equal protection" exception, they rely upon law that focuses, not upon that basic need, but upon the constitutional allocation of power. Respondents invoke a competing fundamental consideration—the need to determine the voter's true intent. But they look to state law, not to federal constitutional law, to protect that interest. Neither side claims electoral fraud, dishonesty, or the like. And the more fundamental equal protection claim might have been left to the state court to resolve if and when it was discovered to have mattered. It could still be resolved through a remand conditioned upon issuance of a uniform standard; it does not require reversing the Florida Supreme Court.

Of course, the selection of the President is of fundamental national importance. But that importance is political, not legal. And this Court should resist the temptation unnecessarily to resolve tangential legal disputes, where doing so threatens to determine the outcome of the election.

The Constitution and federal statutes themselves make clear that restraint is appropriate. They set forth a road map of how to resolve disputes about electors, even after an election as close as this one. That road map foresees resolution of electoral disputes by state courts.... But it nowhere provides for involvement by the United States Supreme Court....

CITIZENS UNITED v. FEDERAL ELECTION COMMISSION
558 U.S. 310; 130 S.Ct. 876; 175 L.Ed.2d 753 (2010)
Vote: 5-4

In this highly controversial decision, the Court strikes down a federal statute, 2 U.S.C § 441b, that limited corporations and unions from making independent expenditures to engage in "electioneering communications" within thirty days of a primary or sixty days of a general election for federal office.

Justice Kennedy delivered the opinion of the Court.

... Limits on electioneering communications were upheld in *McConnell v. Federal Election Commission* (2003). The holding of *McConnell* rested to a large extent on an earlier case, *Austin v. Michigan Chamber*

(Continued)

of Commerce ... (1990). *Austin* had held that political speech may be banned based on the speaker's corporate identity.

In this case we are asked to reconsider *Austin* and, in effect, *McConnell*. It has been noted that "*Austin* was a significant departure from ancient First Amendment principles." ... We agree with that conclusion and hold that *stare decisis* does not compel the continued acceptance of *Austin*. The Government may regulate corporate political speech through disclaimer and disclosure requirements, but it may not suppress that speech altogether....

Citizens United is a nonprofit corporation.... [with] an annual budget of about $12 million. Most of its funds are from donations by individuals; but, in addition, it accepts a small portion of its funds from for-profit corporations.

In January 2008, Citizens United released a film entitled *Hillary: The Movie*. We refer to the film as *Hillary*. It is a 90-minute documentary about then-Senator Hillary Clinton, who was a candidate in the Democratic Party's 2008 Presidential primary elections. *Hillary* mentions Senator Clinton by name and depicts interviews with political commentators and other persons, most of them quite critical of Senator Clinton. *Hillary* was released in theaters and on DVD, but Citizens United wanted to increase distribution by making it available through video-on-demand....

Before the Bipartisan Campaign Reform Act of 2002 (BCRA), federal law prohibited—and still does prohibit—corporations and unions from using general treasury funds to make direct contributions to candidates or independent expenditures that expressly advocate the election or defeat of a candidate, through any form of media, in connection with certain qualified federal elections (2 U.S.C. § 441b [2000 ed.]). BCRA § 203 amended § 441b to prohibit any "electioneering communication" as well. An electioneering communication is defined as "any broadcast, cable, or satellite communication" that "refers to a clearly identified candidate for Federal office" and is made within 30 days of a primary or 60 days of a general election. § 434(f)(3)(A). The Federal Election Commission's (FEC) regulations further define an electioneering communication as a communication that is "publicly distributed." ...

Citizens United wanted to make *Hillary* available through video-on-demand within 30 days of the 2008 primary elections. It feared, however, that both the film and the ads would be covered by § 441b's ban on corporate-funded independent expenditures, thus subjecting the corporation to civil and criminal penalties

under § 437g. In December 2007, Citizens United sought declaratory and injunctive relief against the FEC. It argued that (1) § 441b is unconstitutional as applied to *Hillary;* and (2) BCRA's disclaimer and disclosure requirements, BCRA §§ 201 and 311, are unconstitutional as applied to *Hillary* and to the three ads for the movie....

The law before us is an outright ban, backed by criminal sanctions. Section 441b makes it a felony for all corporations—including nonprofit advocacy corporations—either to expressly advocate the election or defeat of candidates or to broadcast electioneering communications within 30 days of a primary election and 60 days of a general election. Thus, the following acts would all be felonies under § 441b: The Sierra Club runs an ad, within the crucial phase of 60 days before the general election, that exhorts the public to disapprove of a Congressman who favors logging in national forests; the National Rifle Association publishes a book urging the public to vote for the challenger because the incumbent U. S. Senator supports a handgun ban; and the American Civil Liberties Union creates a Web site telling the public to vote for a Presidential candidate in light of that candidate's defense of free speech. These prohibitions are classic examples of censorship....

Section 441b's prohibition on corporate independent expenditures is thus a ban on speech. As a "restriction on the amount of money a person or group can spend on political communication during a campaign," that statute "necessarily reduces the quantity of expression by restricting the number of issues discussed, the depth of their exploration, and the size of the audience reached." *Buckley v. Valeo*, (1976) *(per curiam)*. Were the Court to uphold these restrictions, the Government could repress speech by silencing certain voices at any of the various points in the speech process.... If § 441b applied to individuals, no one would believe that it is merely a time, place, or manner restriction on speech. Its purpose and effect are to silence entities whose voices the Government deems to be suspect.

Speech is an essential mechanism of democracy, for it is the means to hold officials accountable to the people.... The right of citizens to inquire, to hear, to speak, and to use information to reach consensus is a precondition to enlightened self-government and a necessary means to protect it. The First Amendment " 'has its fullest and most urgent application' to speech uttered during a campaign for political office." ...

For these reasons, political speech must prevail against laws that would suppress it, whether by design or inadvertence. Laws that burden political speech are "subject to strict scrutiny," which requires the Government to prove that the restriction "furthers a compelling interest and is narrowly tailored to achieve that interest" (*Federal Election Commission v. Wisconsin Right to Life, Inc.[WRTL]*). While it might be maintained that political speech simply cannot be banned or restricted as a categorical matter, the quoted language from *WRTL* provides a sufficient framework for protecting the relevant First Amendment interests in this case. We shall employ it here.

Premised on mistrust of governmental power, the First Amendment stands against attempts to disfavor certain subjects or viewpoints.... Prohibited, too, are restrictions distinguishing among different speakers, allowing speech by some but not others.... As instruments to censor, these categories are interrelated: Speech restrictions based on the identity of the speaker are all too often simply a means to control content.

Quite apart from the purpose or effect of regulating content, moreover, the Government may commit a constitutional wrong when by law it identifies certain preferred speakers. By taking the right to speak from some and giving it to others, the Government deprives the disadvantaged person or class of the right to use speech to strive to establish worth, standing, and respect for the speaker's voice. The Government may not by these means deprive the public of the right and privilege to determine for itself what speech and speakers are worthy of consideration. The First Amendment protects speech and speaker, and the ideas that flow from each....

We find no basis for the proposition that, in the context of political speech, the Government may impose restrictions on certain disfavored speakers....

The Court has recognized that First Amendment protection extends to corporations [*First Nat. Bank of Boston v. Bellotti* (1978)]....

This protection has been extended by explicit holdings to the context of political speech.... Under the rationale of these precedents, political speech does not lose First Amendment protection "simply because its source is a corporation." ... The Court has thus rejected the argument that political speech of corporations or other associations should be treated differently under the First Amendment simply because such associations are not "natural persons." ...

In *Buckley*, the Court addressed various challenges to the Federal Election Campaign Act of 1971 (FECA) as amended in 1974....

Before addressing the constitutionality of § 608(e)'s independent expenditure ban, *Buckley* first upheld § 608 (b), FECA's limits on direct contributions to candidates. The *Buckley* Court recognized a "sufficiently important" governmental interest in "the prevention of corruption and the appearance of corruption." ... This followed from the Court's concern that large contributions could be given "to secure a political *quid pro quo.*" ...

The *Buckley* Court explained that the potential for *quid pro quo* corruption distinguished direct contributions to candidates from independent expenditures. The Court emphasized that "the independent expenditure ceiling ... fails to serve any substantial governmental interest in stemming the reality or appearance of corruption in the electoral process," because "[t]he absence of prearrangement and coordination ... alleviates the danger that expenditures will be given as a *quid pro quo* for improper commitments from the candidate,"... *Buckley* invalidated § 608(e)'s restrictions on independent expenditures, with only one Justice dissenting....

Less than two years after *Buckley, Bellotti* reaffirmed the First Amendment principle that the Government cannot restrict political speech based on the speaker's corporate identity. *Bellotti* could not have been clearer when it struck down a state-law prohibition on corporate independent expenditures related to referenda issues....

Thus the law stood until *Austin v. Austin* "uph[eld] a direct restriction on the independent expenditure of funds for political speech for the first time in [this Court's] history." There, the Michigan Chamber of Commerce sought to use general treasury funds to run a newspaper ad supporting a specific candidate. Michigan law, however, prohibited corporate independent expenditures that supported or opposed any candidate for state office. A violation of the law was punishable as a felony. The Court sustained the speech prohibition.

To bypass *Buckley* and *Bellotti*, the *Austin* Court identified a new governmental interest in limiting political speech: an antidistortion interest. *Austin* found a compelling governmental interest in preventing "the corrosive and distorting effects of immense aggregations of wealth that are accumulated with the help of the corporate form and that have little or no correlation to the public's support for the corporation's political ideas." ...

If the First Amendment has any force, it prohibits Congress from fining or jailing citizens, or associations of citizens, for simply engaging in political speech. If the antidistortion rationale were to be accepted,

(Continued)

however, it would permit Government to ban political speech simply because the speaker is an association that has taken on the corporate form. The Government contends that *Austin* permits it to ban corporate expenditures for almost all forms of communication stemming from a corporation.... *If Austin* were correct, the Government could prohibit a corporation from expressing political views in media beyond those presented here, such as by printing books. The Government responds "that the FEC has never applied this statute to a book," and if it did, "there would be quite [a] good as-applied challenge." ... This troubling assertion of brooding governmental power cannot be reconciled with the confidence and stability in civic discourse that the First Amendment must secure....

Austin interferes with the "open marketplace" of ideas protected by the First Amendment... It permits the Government to ban the political speech of millions of associations of citizens.... Most of these are small corporations without large amounts of wealth.... This fact belies the Government's argument that the statute is justified on the ground that it prevents the "distorting effects of immense aggregations of wealth." ... It is not even aimed at amassed wealth....

We need not reach the question whether the Government has a compelling interest in preventing foreign individuals or associations from influencing our Nation's political process.... Section 441b is not limited to corporations or associations that were created in foreign countries or funded predominately by foreign shareholders. Section 441b therefore would be overbroad even if we assumed, *arguendo*, that the Government has a compelling interest in limiting foreign influence over our political process....

... Due consideration leads to this conclusion: *Austin*, should be and now is overruled. We return to the principle established in *Buckley* and *Bellotti* that the Government may not suppress political speech on the basis of the speaker's corporate identity. No sufficient governmental interest justifies limits on the political speech of nonprofit or for-profit corporations.

... As the Government appears to concede, overruling *Austin* "effectively invalidate[s] not only BCRA Section 203, but also 2 U. S. C. 441b's prohibition on the use of corporate treasury funds for express advocacy." ... Section 441b's restrictions on corporate independent expenditures are therefore invalid and cannot be applied to *Hillary*.

Given our conclusion we are further required to overrule the part of *McConnell* that upheld BCRA § 203's extension of § 441b's restrictions on corporate independent expenditures.... The *McConnell* Court relied on the antidistortion interest recognized in *Austin* to uphold a greater restriction on speech than the restriction upheld in *Austin*, and we have found this interest unconvincing and insufficient. This part of *McConnell* is now overruled....

Some members of the public might consider *Hillary* to be insightful and instructive; some might find it to be neither high art nor a fair discussion on how to set the Nation's course; still others simply might suspend judgment on these points but decide to think more about issues and candidates. Those choices and assessments, however, are not for the Government to make. "The First Amendment underwrites the freedom to experiment and to create in the realm of thought and speech. Citizens must be free to use new forms, and new forums, for the expression of ideas. The civic discourse belongs to the people, and the Government may not prescribe the means used to conduct it." ...

Chief Justice Roberts, with whom **Justice Alito** joins, concurring....

Justice Scalia, with whom Justice Alito joins, and with whom Justice Thomas joins in part, concurring....

Justice Stevens, with whom **Justice Ginsburg, Justice Breyer,** and **Justice Sotomayor** join, concurring in part and dissenting in part.

The real issue in this case concerns how, not if, the appellant may finance its electioneering. Citizens United is a wealthy nonprofit corporation that runs a political action committee (PAC) with millions of dollars in assets. Under the Bipartisan Campaign Reform Act of 2002 (BCRA), it could have used those assets to televise and promote *Hillary: The Movie* wherever and whenever it wanted to. It also could have spent unrestricted sums to broadcast *Hillary* at any time other than the 30 days before the last primary election. Neither Citizens United's nor any other corporation's speech has been "banned," ... All that the parties dispute is whether Citizens United had a right to use the funds in its general treasury to pay for broadcasts during the 30-day period. The notion that the First Amendment dictates an affirmative answer to that question is, in my judgment, profoundly misguided. Even more misguided is the notion that the Court must rewrite the law relating to campaign expenditures by *for-profit* corporations and unions to decide this case.

The basic premise underlying the Court's ruling is its iteration, and constant reiteration, of the proposition that the First Amendment bars regulatory distinctions based on a speaker's identity, including its "identity" as a corporation. While that glittering generality has rhetorical appeal, it is not a correct statement of the law. Nor does it tell us when a corporation may engage in electioneering that some of its shareholders oppose. It does not even resolve the specific question whether Citizens United may be required to finance some of its messages with the money in its PAC. The conceit that corporations must be treated identically to natural persons in the political sphere is not only inaccurate but also inadequate to justify the Court's disposition of this case.

In the context of election to public office, the distinction between corporate and human speakers is significant. Although they make enormous contributions to our society, corporations are not actually members of it. They cannot vote or run for office. Because they may be managed and controlled by nonresidents, their interests may conflict in fundamental respects with the interests of eligible voters. The financial resources, legal structure, and instrumental orientation of corporations raise legitimate concerns about their role in the electoral process. Our lawmakers have a compelling constitutional basis, if not also a democratic duty, to take measures designed to guard against the potentially deleterious effects of corporate spending in local and national races....

The novelty of the Court's procedural dereliction and its approach to *stare decisis* is matched by the novelty of its ruling on the merits. The ruling rests on several premises. First, the Court claims that *Austin* and *McConnell* have "banned" corporate speech. Second, it claims that the First Amendment precludes regulatory distinctions based on speaker identity, including the speaker's identity as a corporation. Third, it claims that *Austin* and *McConnell* were radical outliers in our First Amendment tradition and our campaign finance jurisprudence. Each of these claims is wrong....

Pervading the Court's analysis is the ominous image of a "categorical ba[n]" on corporate speech.... Indeed, the majority invokes the specter of a "ban" on nearly every page of its opinion.... This characterization is highly misleading, and needs to be corrected....

... Consider the statutory provision we are ostensibly evaluating in this case, BCRA § 203. It has no application to genuine issue advertising—a category of corporate speech Congress found to be far more substantial than election-related advertising ... —or to Internet, telephone, and print advocacy. Like numerous statutes, it exempts media companies' news stories, commentaries, and editorials from its electioneering restrictions, in recognition of the unique role played by the institutional press in sustaining public debate.... It also allows corporations to spend unlimited sums on political communications with their executives and shareholders, ... to fund additional PAC activity through trade associations, ... to distribute voting guides and voting records, ... to underwrite voter registration and voter turnout activities, ... to host fund-raising events for candidates within certain limits, ... and to publicly endorse candidates through a press release and press conference....

... Neither *Austin* nor *McConnell* held or implied that corporations may be silenced; the FEC is not a "censor"; and in the years since these cases were decided, corporations have continued to play a major role in the national dialogue. Laws such as § 203 target a class of communications that is especially likely to corrupt the political process, that is at least one degree removed from the views of individual citizens, and that may not even reflect the views of those who pay for it. Such laws burden political speech, and that is always a serious matter, demanding careful scrutiny. But the majority's incessant talk of a "ban" aims at a straw man....

The second pillar of the Court's opinion is its assertion that "the Government cannot restrict political speech based on the speaker's ... identity." ... The case on which it relies for this proposition is *First Nat. Bank of Boston v. Bellotti* ... (1978).... [T]he holding in that case was far narrower than the Court implies. Like its paeans to unfettered discourse, the Court's denunciation of identity-based distinctions may have rhetorical appeal but it obscures reality.

... [I]n a variety of contexts, we have held that speech can be regulated differentially on account of the speaker's identity, when identity is understood in categorical or institutional terms. The Government routinely places special restrictions on the speech rights of students, prisoners, members of the Armed Forces, foreigners, and its own employees. When such restrictions are justified by a legitimate governmental interest, they do not necessarily raise constitutional problems....

The free speech guarantee thus does not render every other public interest an illegitimate basis for qualifying a speaker's autonomy; society could scarcely function if it did. It is fair to say that our First Amendment doctrine

(Continued)

has "frowned on" certain identity-based distinctions, … particularly those that may reflect invidious discrimination or preferential treatment of a politically powerful group. But it is simply incorrect to suggest that we have prohibited all legislative distinctions based on identity or content. Not even close.…

… As we have unanimously observed, legislatures are entitled to decide "that the special characteristics of the corporate structure require particularly careful regulation" in an electoral context.… Not only has the distinctive potential of corporations to corrupt the electoral process long been recognized, but within the area of campaign finance, corporate spending is also "furthest from the core of political expression, since corporations' First Amendment speech and association interests are derived largely from those of their members and of the public in receiving information"…. Campaign finance distinctions based on corporate identity tend to be less worrisome, in other words, because the "speakers" are not natural persons, much less members of our political community, and the governmental interests are of the highest order. Furthermore, when corporations, as a class, are distinguished from noncorporations, as a class, there is a lesser risk that regulatory distinctions will reflect invidious discrimination or political favoritism.…

A third fulcrum of the Court's opinion is the idea that *Austin* and *McConnell are* radical outliers, "aberration[s]," in our First Amendment tradition.… The Court has it exactly backwards. It is today's holding that is the radical departure from what had been settled First Amendment law.…

… Corporate "domination" of electioneering … can generate the impression that corporations dominate our democracy. When citizens turn on their televisions and radios before an election and hear only corporate electioneering, they may lose faith in their capacity, as citizens, to influence public policy. A Government captured by corporate interests, they may come to believe, will be neither responsive to their needs nor willing to give their views a fair hearing. The predictable result is cynicism and disenchantment: an increased perception that large spenders "call the tune" and a reduced "willingness of voters to take part in democratic governance." … To the extent that corporations are allowed to exert undue influence in electoral races, the speech of the eventual winners of those races may also be chilled. Politicians who fear that a certain corporation can make or break their reelection chances may be cowed into silence about that corporation. On a variety of levels, unregulated corporate electioneering might diminish the ability of citizens to "hold officials accountable to the people," … and disserve the goal of a public debate that is "uninhibited, robust, and wide-open." … At the least, I stress again, a legislature is entitled to credit these concerns and to take tailored measures in response.…

… At bottom, the Court's opinion is … a rejection of the common sense of the American people, who have recognized a need to prevent corporations from undermining self-government since the founding, and who have fought against the distinctive corrupting potential of corporate electioneering since the days of Theodore Roosevelt. It is a strange time to repudiate that common sense. While American democracy is imperfect, few outside the majority of this Court would have thought its flaws included a dearth of corporate money in politics.…

The Constitution of the United States of America

We the People of the United States, in Order to form a more perfect Union, establish Justice, insure domestic Tranquility, provide for the common defence, promote the general Welfare, and secure the Blessings of Liberty to ourselves and our Posterity, do ordain and establish this Constitution for the United States of America.

Article I

Section 1

All legislative Powers herein granted shall be vested in a Congress of the United States, which shall consist of a Senate and House of Representatives.

Section 2

(1) The House of Representatives shall be composed of Members chosen every second Year by the People of the several States, and the Electors in each State shall have the Qualifications requisite for Electors of the most numerous Branch of the State Legislature.

(2) No Person shall be a Representative who shall not have attained to the age of twenty-five Years, and been seven Years a Citizen of the United States, and who shall not, when elected, be an Inhabitant of that State in which he shall be chosen.

(3) Representatives and direct Taxes shall be apportioned among the several States which may be included within this Union, according to their respective Numbers, which shall be determined by adding to the whole Number of free Persons, including those bound to Service for a Term of Years, and excluding Indians not taxed, three fifths of all other Persons. The actual Enumeration shall be made within three Years after the first Meeting of the Congress of the United States, and within every subsequent Term of ten Years, in such Manner as they shall by Law direct. The Number of Representatives shall not exceed one for every thirty Thousand, but each State shall have at Least one Representative; and until such enumeration shall be made, the State of New Hampshire shall be entitled to chuse three, Massachusetts eight, Rhode Island and Providence Plantations one, Connecticut five, New York six, New Jersey four, Pennsylvania eight, Delaware one, Maryland six, Virginia ten, North Carolina five, South Carolina five, and Georgia three.

(4) When vacancies happen in the Representation from any State, the Executive Authority thereof shall issue Writs of Election to fill such Vacancies.

(5) The House of Representatives shall chuse their Speaker and other Officers; and shall have the sole Power of Impeachment.

Section 3

(1) The Senate of the United States shall be composed of two Senators from each State, chosen by the Legislature thereof, for six Years; and each Senator shall have one Vote.

(2) Immediately after they shall be assembled in Consequence of the first Election, they shall be divided as equally as may be into three Classes. The Seats of the Senators of the first Class shall be vacated at the Expiration of the second Year, of the second Class at the Expiration of the fourth Year, and of the third Class at the Expiration of the sixth Year, so that one third may be chosen every second Year; and if Vacancies happen by Resignation, or otherwise, during the Recess of the Legislature of any State, the Executive thereof may make temporary Appointments until the next Meeting of the Legislature, which shall then fill such Vacancies.

(3) No Person shall be a Senator who shall not have attained, to the Age of thirty Years, and been nine Years a Citizen of the United States, and who shall not, when elected, be an Inhabitant of that State for which he shall be chosen.

(4) The Vice President of the United States shall be President of the Senate, but shall have no Vote, unless they be equally divided.

(5) The Senate shall chuse their other Officers, and also a President pro tempore, in the Absence of the Vice President, or when he shall exercise the Office of the President of the United States.

(6) The Senate shall have the sole Power to try all Impeachments. When sitting for that Purpose, they shall be on Oath or Affirmation. When the President of the United States is tried, the Chief Justice shall preside: And no Person shall be convicted without the Concurrence of two thirds of the Members present.

(7) Judgment in Cases of Impeachment shall not extend further than to removal from Office, and disqualification to hold and enjoy any Office of honor, Trust or Profit under the United States: but the Party convicted shall nevertheless be liable and subject to Indictment, Trial, Judgment and Punishment, according to Law.

Section 4

(1) The Times, Places and Manner of holding Elections for Senators and Representatives, shall be prescribed in each State by the Legislature thereof; but the Congress may at any time by Law make or alter such Regulations, except as to the Places of chusing Senators.

(2) The Congress shall assemble at least once in every Year, and such Meeting shall be on the first Monday in December, unless they shall by Law appoint a different Day.

Section 5

(1) Each House shall be the Judge of the Elections, Returns and Qualifications of its own Members, and a Majority of each shall constitute a Quorum to do Business; but a smaller Number may adjourn from day to day, and may be authorized to compel the Attendance of absent Members, in such Manner, and under such Penalties as each House may provide.

(2) Each House may determine the Rules of its Proceedings, punish its Members for disorderly Behaviour, and, with the Concurrence of two thirds, expel a Member.

(3) Each House shall keep a Journal of its Proceedings, and from time to time publish the same, excepting such Parts as may in their Judgment require Secrecy; and the Yeas and Nays of the Members of either House on any question shall, at the Desire of one fifth of those Present, be entered on the Journal.

(4) Neither House, during the Session of Congress, shall, without the Consent of the other, adjourn for more than three days, nor to any other Place than that in which the two Houses shall be sitting.

Section 6

(1) The Senators and Representatives shall receive a Compensation for their Services, to be ascertained by Law, and paid out of the Treasury of the United States. They shall in all Cases, except Treason, Felony and Breach of the Peace, be privileged from Arrest during their Attendance at the Session of their respective Houses, and in going to and returning from the same; and for any Speech or Debate in either House, they shall not be questioned in any other Place.

(2) No Senator or Representative shall, during the Time for which he was elected, be appointed to any civil Office under the Authority of the United States, which shall have been created, or the Emoluments whereof shall have been increased during such time; and no Person holding any Office under the United States, shall be a Member of either House during his Continuance in Office.

Section 7

(1) All Bills for raising Revenue shall originate in the House of Representatives; but the Senate may propose or concur with Amendments as on other Bills.

(2) Every Bill which shall have passed the House of Representatives and the Senate, shall, before it become a Law, be presented to the President of the United States; If he approve he shall sign it, but if not he shall return it, with his Objections to that House in which it shall have originated, who shall enter the Objections at large on their Journal, and proceed to reconsider it. If after such Reconsideration two thirds of that House shall agree to pass the Bill, it shall be sent, together with the Objections, to the other House, by which it shall likewise be reconsidered, and if approved by two thirds of that House, it shall become a Law. But in all such Cases the Votes of both Houses shall be determined by Yeas and Nays, and the Names of the Persons voting for and against the Bill shall be entered on the Journal of each House respectively. If any Bill shall not be returned by the President within ten Days (Sunday excepted) after it shall have been presented to him, the Same shall be a Law, in like Manner as if he had signed it, unless the Congress by their Adjournment prevent its Return, in which Case it shall not be a Law.

(3) Every Order, Resolution, or Vote to which the Concurrence of the Senate and House of Representatives may be necessary (except on a question of Adjournment) shall be presented to the President of

the United States; and before the Same shall take Effect, shall be approved by him, or being disapproved by him, shall be repassed by two thirds of the Senate and House of Representatives, according to the Rules and Limitations prescribed in the Case of a Bill.

Section 8

(1) The Congress shall have Power To lay and collect Taxes, Duties, Imposts and Excises, to pay the Debts and provide for the common Defence and general Welfare of the United States; but all Duties, Imposts and Excises shall be uniform throughout the United States;

(2) To borrow Money on the credit of the United States;

(3) To regulate Commerce with foreign Nations, and among the several States, and with the Indian Tribes;

(4) To establish an uniform Rule of Naturalization, and uniform Laws on the subject of Bankruptcies throughout the United States;

(5) To coin Money, regulate the Value thereof, and of foreign Coin, and to fix the Standard of Weights and Measures;

(6) To provide for the Punishment of counterfeiting the Securities and current Coin of the United States;

(7) To establish Post Offices and post Roads;

(8) To promote the Progress of Science and useful Arts, by securing for limited Times to Authors and Inventors the exclusive Right to their respective Writings and Discoveries;

(9) To constitute Tribunals inferior to the Supreme Court;

(10) To define and punish Piracies and Felonies committed on the high Seas, and Offenses against the Law of Nations;

(11) To declare War, grant Letters of Marque and Reprisal, and make Rules concerning Captures on Land and Water;

(12) To raise and support Armies, but no Appropriation of Money to that Use shall be for a longer Term than two Years;

(13) To provide and maintain a Navy;

(14) To make Rules for the Government and Regulation of the land and naval Forces;

(15) To provide for calling forth the Militia to execute the Laws of the Union, suppress Insurrections and repel Invasions;

(16) To provide for organizing, arming, and disciplining, the Militia, and for governing such Part of them as may be employed in the Service of the United States, reserving to the States respectively, the Appointment of the Officers, and the Authority of training the Militia according to the discipline prescribed by Congress;

(17) To exercise exclusive Legislation in all Cases whatsoever, over such District (not exceeding ten Miles square) as may, by Cession of particular States, and the Acceptance of Congress, become the Seat of the Government of the United States, and to exercise like Authority over all Places purchased by the Consent of the Legislature of the State in which the Same shall be, for the Erection of Forts, Magazines, Arsenals, dock-Yards, and other needful Buildings;—And

(18) To make all Laws which shall be necessary and proper for carrying into Execution the foregoing Powers, and all other Powers vested by this Constitution in the Government of the United States, or in any Department or Officer thereof.

Section 9

(1) The Migration or Importation of such Persons as any of the States now existing shall think proper to admit, shall not be prohibited by the Congress prior to the Year one thousand eight hundred and eight, but a Tax or Duty may be imposed on such Importation, not exceeding ten dollars for each Person.

(2) The Privilege of the Writ of Habeas Corpus shall not be suspended unless when in Cases of Rebellion or Invasion the public Safety may require it.

(3) No Bill of Attainder or ex post facto Law shall be passed.

(4) No Capitation, or other direct, Tax shall be laid, unless in Proportion to the Census or Enumeration herein before directed to be taken.

(5) No Tax or Duty shall be laid on Articles exported from any State.

(6) No Preference shall be given by any Regulation of Commerce or Revenue to the Ports of one State over those of another; nor shall Vessels bound to, or from, one State, be obliged to enter, clear or pay Duties in another.

(7) No Money shall be drawn from the Treasury, but in Consequence of Appropriations made by Law; and a regular Statement and Account of the Receipts and Expenditures of all public Money shall be published from time to time.

(8) No Title of Nobility shall be granted by the United States: And no Person holding any Office of Profit or Trust under them, shall, without the Consent

of the Congress, accept of any present, Emolument, Office, or Title, of any kind whatever, from any King, Prince or foreign State.

Section 10

(1) No State shall enter into any Treaty, Alliance, or Confederation; grant Letters of Marque and Reprisal; coin Money; emit Bills of Credit; make any Thing but gold and silver Coin a Tender in Payment of Debts; pass any Bill of Attainder, ex post facto Law, or Law impairing the Obligation of Contracts, or grant any Title of Nobility.

(2) No State shall, without the Consent of Congress, lay any Imposts or Duties on Imports or Exports, except what may be absolutely necessary for executing its inspection Laws: and the net Produce of all Duties and Imposts, laid by any State on Imports or Exports, shall be for the Use of the Treasury of the United States; and all such Laws shall be subject to the Revision and Control of the Congress.

(3) No State shall, without the Consent of Congress, lay any Duty of Tonnage, keep Troops, or Ships of War in time of Peace, enter into any Agreement or Compact with another State, or with a foreign Power, or engage in War, unless actually invaded, or in such imminent Danger as will not admit of Delay.

Article II

Section 1

(1) The executive Power shall be vested in a President of the United States of America. He shall hold his Office during the Term of four Years, and, together with the Vice President, chosen for the same Term, be elected, as follows:

(2) Each State shall appoint, in such Manner as the Legislature thereof may direct, a Number of Electors, equal to the whole Number of Senators and Representatives to which the State may be entitled in the Congress: but no Senator or Representative, or Person holding an Office of Trust or Profit under the United States, shall be appointed an Elector.

The Electors shall meet in their respective States, and vote by Ballot for two Persons, of whom one at least shall not be an Inhabitant of the same State with themselves. And they shall make a List of all the Persons voted for, and of the Number of Votes for each; which List they shall sign and certify, and transmit sealed to the Seat of the Government of the United States, directed to the President of the Senate. The President of the Senate shall, in the presence of the Senate and House of Representatives, open all the Certificates, and the Votes shall then be counted. The Person having the greatest Number of Votes shall be the President, if such Number be a Majority of the whole Number of Electors appointed; and if there be more than one who have such Majority, and have an equal Number of Votes, then the House of Representatives shall immediately chuse by Ballot one of them for President; and if no Person have a Majority, then from the five highest on the List the said House shall in like Manner chuse the President. But in chusing the President, the Votes shall be taken by States, the Representation from each State having one Vote; a quorum for this Purpose shall consist of a Member or Members from two thirds of the States, and a Majority of all the States shall be necessary to a Choice. In every Case, after the Choice of the President, the Person having the greatest Number of Votes of the Electors shall be the Vice President. But if there should remain two or more who have equal Votes, the Senate shall chuse from them by Ballot the Vice President.

(3) The Congress may determine the Time of chusing the Electors, and the Day on which they shall give their Votes; which Day shall be the same throughout the United States.

(4) No Person except a natural born Citizen, or a Citizen of the United States, at the time of the Adoption of this Constitution, shall be eligible to the Office of President; neither shall any Person be eligible to that Office who shall not have attained to the Age of thirty five Years, and been fourteen Years a Resident within the United States.

(5) In Case of the Removal of the President from Office, or of his Death, Resignation, or Inability to discharge the Powers and Duties of the said Office, the Same shall devolve on the Vice President, and the Congress may by Law provide for the Case of Removal, Death, Resignation or Inability, both of the President and Vice President, declaring what Officer shall then act as President, and such Officer shall act accordingly, until the Disability be removed, or a President shall be elected.

(6) The President shall, at stated Times, receive for his Services, a Compensation, which shall neither be increased nor diminished during the Period for which he shall have been elected, and he shall not receive within that Period any other Emolument from the United States, or any of them.

(7) Before he enter on the Execution of his Office, he shall take the following Oath or Affirmation:—"I do solemnly swear (or affirm) that I will faithfully execute

the Office of President of the United States, and will to the best of my Ability, preserve, protect and defend the Constitution of the United States."

Section 2

(1) The President shall be Commander in Chief of the Army and Navy of the United States, and of the Militia of the several States, when called into the actual Service of the United States; he may require the Opinion, in writing, of the principal Officer in each of the executive Departments, upon any Subject relating to the Duties of their respective Offices, and he shall have Power to grant Reprieves and Pardons for Offenses against the United States, except in Cases of Impeachment.

(2) He shall have Power, by and with the Advice and Consent of the Senate, to make Treaties, provided two thirds of the Senators present concur; and he shall nominate, and by and with the Advice and Consent of the Senate, shall appoint Ambassadors, other public Ministers and Consuls, Judges of the supreme Court, and all other Officers of the United States, whose Appointments are not herein otherwise provided for, and which shall be established by Law: but the Congress may by Law vest the Appointment of such inferior Officers, as they think proper, in the President alone, in the Courts of Law, or in the Heads of Departments.

(3) The President shall have Power to fill up all Vacancies that may happen during the Recess of the Senate, by granting Commissions which shall expire at the End of their next Session.

Section 3

He shall from time to time give to the Congress Information of the State of the Union, and recommend to their Consideration such Measures as he shall judge necessary and expedient; he may, on extraordinary Occasions, convene both Houses, or either of them, and in Case of Disagreement between them, with Respect to the Time of Adjournment, he may adjourn them to such Time as he shall think proper; he shall receive Ambassadors and other public Ministers; he shall take Care that the Laws be faithfully executed, and shall Commission all the Officers of the United States.

Section 4

The President, Vice President and all Civil Officers of the United States, shall be removed from Office on Impeachment for, and Conviction of, Treason, Bribery, or other high Crimes and Misdemeanors.

Article III

Section 1

The judicial Power of the United States, shall be vested in one supreme Court, and in such inferior Courts as the Congress may from time to time ordain and establish. The Judges, both of the supreme and inferior Courts, shall hold their Offices during good Behaviour, and shall, at stated Times, receive for their Services, a Compensation, which shall not be diminished during their Continuance in Office.

Section 2

(1) The judicial Power shall extend to all Cases, in Law and Equity, arising under this Constitution, the Laws of the United States, and Treaties made, or which shall be made, under their Authority;—to all Cases affecting Ambassadors, other public Ministers and Consuls;—to all Cases of admiralty and maritime Jurisdiction;—to Controversies to which the United States shall be a party;—to Controversies between two or more States;—between a State and Citizens of another State;—between Citizens of different States;—between Citizens of the same State claiming Lands under Grants of different States, and between a State, or the Citizens thereof, and foreign States, Citizens or Subjects.

(2) In all Cases affecting Ambassadors, other public Ministers and Consuls, and those in which a State shall be Party, the Supreme Court shall have original Jurisdiction. In all the other Cases before mentioned, the Supreme Court shall have appellate Jurisdiction, both as to Law and Fact, with such Exceptions, and under such Regulations as the Congress shall make.

(3) The Trial of all Crimes, except in Cases of Impeachment, shall be by Jury; and such Trial shall be held in the State where the said Crimes shall have been committed; but when not committed within any State, the Trial shall be at such Place or Places as the Congress may by Law have directed.

Section 3

(1) Treason against the United States, shall consist only in levying War against them, or in adhering to their Enemies, giving them Aid and Comfort. No Person shall be convicted of Treason unless on the Testimony of two Witnesses to the same overt Act, or on Confession in open Court.

(2) The Congress shall have Power to declare the Punishment of Treason, but no Attainder of Treason

shall work Corruption of Blood, or Forfeiture except during the Life of the Person attainted.

Article IV

Section 1

Full Faith and Credit shall be given in each State to the public Acts, Records, and judicial Proceedings of every other State. And the Congress may by general Laws prescribe the Manner in which such Acts, Records and Proceedings shall be proved, and the Effect thereof.

Section 2

(1) The Citizens of each State shall be entitled to all privileges and Immunities of Citizens in the several States.

(2) A Person charged in any State with Treason, Felony, or other Crime, who shall flee from Justice, and be found in another State, shall on Demand of the executive Authority of the State from which he fled, be delivered up, to be removed to the State having Jurisdiction of the Crime.

(3) No Person held to Service of Labour in one State, under the Laws thereof, escaping into another, shall, in Consequence of any Law or Regulation therein, be discharged from such Service or Labour, but shall be delivered up on Claim of the Party to whom such Service or Labour may be due.

Section 3

(1) New States may be admitted by the Congress into this Union; but no new State shall be formed or erected within the Jurisdiction of any other State; nor any State be formed by the Junction of two or more States, or Parts of States, without the Consent of the Legislatures of the States concerned as well as of the Congress.

(2) The Congress shall have power to dispose of and make all needful Rules and Regulations respecting the Territory or other Property belonging to the United States; and nothing in this Constitution shall be so construed as to Prejudice any Claims of the United States, or of any particular State.

Section 4

The United States shall guarantee to every State in this Union a Republican Form of Government, and shall protect each of them against Invasion; and on Application of the Legislature, or of the Executive (when the Legislature cannot be convened) against domestic Violence.

Article V

The Congress, whenever two thirds of both Houses shall deem it necessary, shall propose Amendments to this Constitution, or, on the Application of the Legislatures of two thirds of the several States, shall call a Convention for proposing Amendments, which, in either Case, shall be valid to all Intents and Purposes, as Part of this Constitution, when ratified by the Legislatures of three fourths of the several States, or by Conventions in three fourths thereof, as the one or the other Mode of Ratification may be proposed by the Congress; Provided that no Amendment which may be made prior to the Year One thousand eight hundred and eight shall in any Manner affect the first and fourth Clauses in the Ninth Section of the first Article; and that no State, without its Consent, shall be deprived of its equal Suffrage in the Senate.

Article VI

(1) All Debts contracted and Engagements entered into, before the Adoption of this Constitution, shall be as valid against the United States under this Constitution, as under the Confederation.

(2) This Constitution, and the Laws of the United States which shall be made in Pursuance thereof; and all Treaties made, or which shall be made, under the Authority of the United States, shall be the supreme Law of the Land; and the Judges in every State shall be bound thereby, any Thing in the Constitution or Laws of any State to the Contrary notwithstanding.

(3) The Senators and Representatives before mentioned, and the Members of the several State Legislatures, and all executive and judicial Officers, both of the United States and of the several States, shall be bound by Oath or Affirmation, to support this Constitution; but no religious Test shall ever be required as a Qualification to any Office or public Trust under the United States.

Article VII

The Ratification of the Conventions of nine States, shall be sufficient for the Establishment of this Constitution between the States so ratifying the Same.

Articles in Addition to, and Amendment of, the Constitution of the United States of America, Proposed by Congress, and Ratified by the Several States, Pursuant to the Fifth Article of the Original Constitution

Amendment I (1791)

Congress shall make no law respecting an establishment of religion, or prohibiting the free exercise thereof; or abridging the freedom of speech, or of the press; or the right of the people peaceably to assemble, and to petition the Government for a redress of grievances.

Amendment II (1791)

A well regulated Militia, being necessary to the security of a free state, the right of the people to keep and bear Arms, shall not be infringed.

Amendment III (1791)

No Soldier shall, in time of peace be quartered in any house, without the consent of the Owner, nor in time of war, but in a manner to be prescribed by law.

Amendment IV (1791)

The right of the people to be secure in their persons, houses, papers, and effects, against unreasonable searches and seizures, shall not be violated, and no Warrants shall issue, but upon probable cause, supported by Oath or affirmation, and particularly describing the place to be searched, and the persons or things to be seized.

Amendment V (1791)

No person shall be held to answer for a capital, or otherwise infamous crime, unless on a presentment or indictment of a Grand Jury, except in cases arising in the land or naval forces, or in the Militia, when in actual service in time of War or public danger; nor shall any person be subject for the same offence to be twice put in jeopardy of life or limb; nor shall be compelled in any criminal case to be a witness against himself, nor be deprived of life, liberty, or property, without due process of law; nor shall private property be taken for public use, without just compensation.

Amendment VI (1791)

In all criminal prosecutions, the accused shall enjoy the right to a speedy and public trial, by an impartial jury of the State and district wherein the crime shall have been committed, which district shall have been previously ascertained by law, and to be informed of the nature and cause of the accusation; to be confronted with the witnesses against him; to have compulsory process for obtaining witnesses in his favor, and to have the Assistance of Counsel for his defence.

Amendment VII (1791)

In Suits at common law, where the value in controversy shall exceed twenty dollars, the right of trial by jury shall be preserved, and no fact tried by a jury, shall be otherwise re-examined in any Court of the United States, than according to the rules of the common law.

Amendment VIII (1791)

Excessive bail shall not be required, nor excessive fines imposed, nor cruel and unusual punishments inflicted.

Amendment IX (1791)

The enumeration in the Constitution, of certain rights, shall not be construed to deny or disparage others retained by the people.

Amendment X (1791)

The powers not delegated to the United States by the Constitution, nor prohibited by it to the States, are reserved to the States respectively, or to the people.

Amendment XI (1798)

The Judicial power of the United States shall not be construed to extend to any suit in law or equity, commenced or prosecuted against one of the United States by Citizens of another State, or by Citizens or Subjects of any Foreign State.

Amendment XII (1804)

The Electors shall meet in their respective states and vote by ballot for President and Vice-President, one of whom, at least, shall not be an inhabitant of the same state with themselves; they shall name in their ballots the person voted for as President, and in distinct ballots the person voted for as Vice-President, and they shall make distinct lists of all persons voted for as President, and of all persons voted for as Vice-President, and of the number of votes for each, which lists they shall sign and certify, and transmit sealed to the seat of the government of the United States, directed to the President of the Senate;—The President of the Senate shall, in the presence of the Senate and House of Representatives, open all the certificates and the votes shall then be counted;—The person having the greatest number of votes for President, shall be the President, if such number be a majority of the whole number of Electors appointed; and if no person have such majority, then from the persons having the highest numbers not exceeding three on the list of those voted for as President, the House of Representatives shall choose immediately, by ballot, the President. But in choosing the President, the votes shall be taken by states, the representation from each state having one vote; a quorum for this purpose shall consist of a member or members from two-thirds of the states, and a majority of all the states shall be necessary to a choice. And if the House of Representatives shall not choose a President whenever the right of choice shall devolve upon them, before the fourth day of March next following, then the Vice-President shall act as President, as in the case of the death or other constitutional disability of the President—The person having the greatest number of votes as Vice-President, shall be the Vice-President, if such number be a majority of the whole number of Electors appointed, and if no person have a majority, then from the two highest numbers on the list, the Senate shall choose the Vice-President; A quorum for the purpose shall consist of two-thirds of the whole number of Senators, and a majority of the whole number shall be necessary to a choice. But no person constitutionally ineligible to the office of President shall be eligible to that of Vice-President of the United States.

Amendment XIII (1865)

Section 1

Neither slavery nor involuntary servitude, except as a punishment for crime whereof the party shall have been duly convicted, shall exist within the United States, or any place subject to their jurisdiction.

Section 2

Congress shall have power to enforce this article by appropriate legislation.

Amendment XIV (1868)

Section 1

All persons born or naturalized in the United States and subject to the jurisdiction thereof, are citizens of the United States and of the State wherein they reside. No State shall make or enforce any law which shall abridge the privileges or immunities of citizens of the United States; nor shall any State deprive any person of life, liberty, or property, without due process of law; nor deny to any person within its jurisdiction the equal protection of the laws.

Section 2

Representatives shall be apportioned among the several States according to their respective numbers, counting the whole number of persons in each State, excluding Indians not taxed. But when the right to vote at any election for the choice of electors for President and Vice-President of the United States, Representatives in Congress, the Executive and Judicial officers of a State, or the members of the Legislature thereof, is denied to any of the male inhabitants of such State, being twenty-one years of age, and citizens of the United States, or in any way abridged, except for participation in rebellion, or other crime, the basis of representation therein shall be reduced in the proportion which the number of such male citizens shall bear to the whole number of male citizens twenty-one years of age in such State.

Section 3

No person shall be a Senator or Representative in Congress, or elector of President and Vice-President, or hold any office, civil or military, under the United States, or under any State, who, having previously taken an oath, as a member of Congress, or as an officer of the United States, or as a member of any State legislature, or as an executive or judicial officer of any State, to support the Constitution of the United States, shall have engaged in insurrection or rebellion against the same, or given aid or comfort to the enemies thereof. But Congress may by a vote of two-thirds of each House, remove such disability.

Section 4

The validity of the public debt of the United States, authorized by law, including debts incurred for payment of pensions and bounties for services in suppressing insurrection or rebellion, shall not be questioned. But neither the United States nor any State shall assume or pay any debt or obligation incurred in aid of insurrection or rebellion against the United States, or any claim for the loss or emancipation of any slave; but all such debts, obligations and claims shall be held illegal and void.

Section 5

The Congress shall have power to enforce, by appropriate legislation, the provisions of this article.

Amendment XV (1870)

Section 1

The right of citizens of the United States to vote shall not be denied or abridged by the United States or by any State on account of race, color, or previous condition of servitude.

Section 2

The Congress shall have power to enforce this article by appropriate legislation.

Amendment XVI (1913)

The Congress shall have power to lay and collect taxes on incomes, from whatever source derived, without apportionment among the several States, and without regard to any census or enumeration.

Amendment XVII (1913)

The Senate of the United States shall be composed of two Senators from each State, elected by the people thereof, for six years; and each Senator shall have one vote. The electors in each State shall have the qualifications requisite for electors of the most numerous branch of the State legislatures.

When vacancies happen in the representation of any State in the Senate, the executive authority of such State shall issue writs of election to fill such vacancies: Provided, that the legislature of any State may empower the executive thereof to make temporary appointments until the people fill the vacancies by election as the legislature may direct.

This amendment shall not be so construed as to affect the election or term of any Senator chosen before it becomes valid as part of the Constitution.

Amendment XVIII (1919)

Section 1

After one year from the ratification of this article the manufacture, sale, or transportation of intoxicating liquors within, the importation thereof into, or the exportation thereof from the United States and all territory subject to the jurisdiction thereof for beverage purposes is hereby prohibited.

Section 2

The Congress and the several States shall have concurrent power to enforce this article by appropriate legislation.

Section 3

This article shall be inoperative unless it shall have been ratified as an amendment to the Constitution by the legislatures of the several States, as provided in the Constitution, within seven years from the date of the submission hereof to the States by the Congress.

Amendment XIX (1920)

The right of citizens of the United States to vote shall not be denied or abridged by the United States or by any State on account of sex.

Congress shall have power to enforce this article by appropriate legislation.

Amendment XX (1933)

Section 1

The terms of the President and Vice President shall end at noon on the 20th day of January, and the terms of Senators and Representatives at noon on the 3d day of January, of the years in which such terms would have ended if this article had not been ratified; and the terms of their successors shall then begin.

Section 2

The Congress shall assemble at least once in every year, and such meeting shall begin at noon on the 3d day of January, unless they shall by law appoint a different day.

Section 3

If, at the time fixed for the beginning of the term of the President, the President elect shall have died, the Vice President elect shall become President. If a President shall not have been chosen before the time fixed for the beginning of his term, or if the President elect shall have failed to qualify, then the Vice President elect shall act as President until a President shall have qualified; and the Congress may by law provide for the case wherein neither a President elect nor a Vice President elect shall have qualified, declaring who shall then act as President, or the manner in which one who is to act shall be selected, and such person shall act accordingly until a President or Vice President shall have qualified.

Section 4

The Congress may by law provide for the case of the death of any of the persons from whom the House of Representatives may choose a President whenever the right of choice shall have devolved upon them, and for the case of the death of any of the persons from whom the Senate may choose a Vice President whenever the right of choice shall have devolved upon them.

Section 5

Sections 1 and 2 shall take effect on the 15th day of October following the ratification of this article.

Section 6

This article shall be inoperative unless it shall have been ratified as an amendment to the Constitution by the legislatures of three-fourths of the several States within seven years from the date of its submission.

Amendment XXI (1933)
Section 1

The eighteenth article of amendment to the Constitution of the United States is hereby repealed.

Section 2

The transportation or importation into any State, Territory or possession of the United States for delivery or use therein of intoxicating liquors, in violation of the laws thereof, is hereby prohibited.

Section 3

This article shall be inoperative unless it shall have been ratified as an amendment to the Constitution by conventions in the several States, as provided in the Constitution, within seven years from the date of the submission hereof to the States by the Congress.

Amendment XXII (1951)
Section 1

No person shall be elected to the office of the President more than twice, and no person who has held the office of President, or acted as President, for more than two years of a term to which some other person was elected President shall be elected to the office of the President more than once. But this Article shall not apply to any person holding the office of President when this Article was proposed by the Congress, and shall not prevent any person who may be holding the office of President, or acting as President, during the term within which this Article becomes operative from holding the office of President or acting as President during the remainder of such term.

Section 2

This Article shall be inoperative unless it shall have been ratified as an amendment to the Constitution by the legislatures of three-fourths of the several States within seven years from the date of its submission to the States by the Congress.

Amendment XXIII (1961)
Section 1

The District constituting the seat of Government of the United States shall appoint in such manner as the Congress may direct:

A number of electors of President and Vice President equal to the whole number of Senators and Representatives in Congress to which the District would be entitled if it were a State, but in no event more than the least populous State; they shall be in addition to those appointed by the States, but they shall be considered, for the purposes of the election of President and Vice President, to be electors appointed by a State; and they shall meet in the District and perform such duties as provided by the twelfth article of amendment.

Section 2

The Congress shall have power to enforce this article by appropriate legislation.

Amendment XXIV (1964)
Section 1

The right of citizens of the United States to vote in any primary or other election for President or Vice President, for electors for President or Vice President, or for Senator or Representative in Congress, shall not be denied or abridged by the United States or any State by reason of failure to pay any poll tax or other tax.

Section 2

The Congress shall have power to enforce this article by appropriate legislation.

Amendment XXV (1967)
Section 1

In case of the removal of the President from office or of his death or resignation, the Vice President shall become President.

Section 2

Whenever there is a vacancy in the office of the Vice President, the President shall nominate a Vice President who shall take office upon confirmation by a majority vote of both Houses of Congress.

Section 3

Whenever the President transmits to the President pro tempore of the Senate and the Speaker of the House of Representatives his written declaration that he is unable to discharge the powers and duties of his office, and until he transmits to them a written declaration to the contrary, such powers and duties shall be discharged by the Vice President as Acting President.

Section 4

Whenever the Vice President and a majority of either the principal officers of the executive departments or of such other body as Congress may by law provide, transmit to the President pro tempore of the Senate and the Speaker of the House of Representatives their written declaration that the President is unable to discharge the powers and duties of his office, the Vice President shall immediately assume the powers and duties of the office as Acting President.

Thereafter, when the President transmits to the President pro tempore of the Senate and the Speaker of the House of Representatives his written declaration that no inability exists, he shall resume the powers and duties of his office unless the Vice President and a majority of either the principal officers of the executive department or of such other body as Congress may by law provide, transmit within four days to the President pro tempore of the Senate and the Speaker of the House of Representatives their written declaration that the President is unable to discharge the powers and duties of his office. Thereupon Congress shall decide the issue, assembling within forty-eight hours for that purpose if not in session. If the Congress, within twenty-one days after receipt of the latter written declaration, or, if Congress is not in session, within twenty-one days after Congress is required to assemble, determines by two-thirds vote of both Houses that the President is unable to discharge the powers and duties of his office, the Vice President shall continue to discharge the same as Acting President; otherwise, the President shall resume the powers and duties of his office.

Amendment XXVI (1971)

Section 1

The right of citizens of the United States, who are eighteen years of age or older, to vote shall not be denied or abridged by the United States or by any State on account of age.

Section 2

The Congress shall have power to enforce this article by appropriate legislation.

Amendment XXVII (1992)

No law, varying the compensation for the services of the Senators and Representatives, shall take effect, until an election of Representatives shall have intervened.

Chronology of Justices of the United States Supreme Court

YEAR OF COURT AS CONSTITUTED	CHIEF JUSTICE	ASSOCIATE JUSTICES								
1789	Jay	Rutledge, J.	Cushing	Wilson	Blair					
1790–91	Jay	Rutledge, J.	Cushing	Wilson	Blair	Iredell				
1792	Jay	Johnson, T.	Cushing	Wilson	Blair	Iredell				
1793–94	Jay	Paterson	Cushing	Wilson	Blair	Iredell				
1795	Rutledge, J.	Paterson	Cushing	Wilson	Blair	Iredell				
1796–97	Ellsworth	Paterson	Cushing	Wilson	Chase, S.	Iredell				
1798–99	Ellsworth	Paterson	Cushing	Washington	Chase, S.	Iredell				
1800	Ellsworth	Paterson	Cushing	Washington	Chase, S.	Moore				
1801–03	Marshall, J.	Paterson	Cushing	Washington	Chase, S.	Moore				
1804–05	Marshall, J.	Paterson	Cushing	Washington	Chase, S.	Johnson, W.				
1806	Marshall, J.	Livingston	Cushing	Washington	Chase, S.	Johnson, W.				
1807–10	Marshall, J.	Livingston	Cushing	Washington	Chase, S.	Johnson, W.	Todd			
1811–12	Marshall, J.	Livingston	Story	Washington	Duvall	Johnson, W.	Todd			
1813–25	Marshall, J.	Thompson	Story	Washington	Duvall	Johnson, W.	Todd			
1826–28	Marshall, J.	Thompson	Story	Washington	Duvall	Johnson, W.	Trimble			
1829	Marshall, J.	Thompson	Story	Washington	Duvall	Johnson, W.	McLean			
1830–34	Marshall, J.	Thompson	Story	Baldwin	Duvall	Johnson, W.	McLean			
1835	Marshall, J.	Thompson	Story	Baldwin	Duvall	Wayne	McLean			
1836	Taney	Thompson	Story	Baldwin	Barbour	Wayne	McLean			
1837–40	Taney	Thompson	Story	Baldwin	Barbour	Wayne	McLean	Catron	McKinley	
1841–44	Taney	Thompson	Story	Baldwin	Daniel	Wayne	McLean	Catron	McKinley	
1845	Taney	Nelson	Woodbury	(vacant)	Daniel	Wayne	McLean	Catron	McKinley	
1846–50	Taney	Nelson	Woodbury	Grier	Daniel	Wayne	McLean	Catron	McKinley	
1851–52	Taney	Nelson	Curtis	Grier	Daniel	Wayne	McLean	Catron	McKinley	
1853–57	Taney	Nelson	Curtis	Grier	Daniel	Wayne	McLean	Catron	Campbell	
1858–60	Taney	Nelson	Clifford	Grier	Daniel	Wayne	McLean	Catron	Campbell	
1861	Taney	Nelson	Clifford	Grier	(vacant)	Wayne	McLean	Catron	Campbell	
1862	Taney	Nelson	Clifford	Grier	Miller	Wayne	Swayne	Catron	Davis	
1863	Taney	Nelson	Clifford	Grier	Miller	Wayne	Swayne	Catron	Davis	Field
1864–65	Chase, S. P.	Nelson	Clifford	Grier	Miller	Wayne	Swayne	Catron	Davis	Field
1866–67	Chase, S. P.	Nelson	Clifford	Grier	Miller	Wayne	Swayne	(ended)*	Davis	Field
1868–69	Chase, S. P.	Nelson	Clifford	Grier	Miller	(vacant)	Swayne		Davis	Field
1870–71	Chase, S. P.	Nelson	Clifford	Strong	Miller	Bradley	Swayne		Davis	Field

*Congress ended the use of a ten-person Court in this year.

YEAR OF COURT AS CONSTITUTED	CHIEF JUSTICE	ASSOCIATE JUSTICES							
1872–73	Chase, S. P.	Hunt	Clifford	Strong	Miller	Bradley	Swayne	Davis	Field
1874–76	Waite	Hunt	Clifford	Strong	Miller	Bradley	Swayne	Davis	Field
1877–79	Waite	Hunt	Clifford	Strong	Miller	Bradley	Swayne	Harlan	Field
1880	Waite	Hunt	Clifford	Woods	Miller	Bradley	Swayne	Harlan	Field
1881	Waite	Hunt	Gray	Woods	Miller	Bradley	Matthews	Harlan	Field
1882–87	Waite	Blatchford	Gray	Woods	Miller	Bradley	Matthews	Harlan	Field
1888	Fuller	Blatchford	Gray	Lamar, L.	Miller	Bradley	Matthews	Harlan	Field
1889	Fuller	Blatchford	Gray	Lamar, L.	Miller	Bradley	Brewer	Harlan	Field
1890–91	Fuller	Blatchford	Gray	Lamar, L.	Brown	Bradley	Brewer	Harlan	Field
1892	Fuller	Blatchford	Gray	Lamar, L.	Brown	Shiras	Brewer	Harlan	Field
1893	Fuller	Blatchford	Gray	Jackson, H.	Brown	Shiras	Brewer	Harlan	Field
1894	Fuller	White	Gray	Jackson, H.	Brown	Shiras	Brewer	Harlan	Field
1895–97	Fuller	White	Gray	Peckham	Brown	Shiras	Brewer	Harlan	Field
1898–1901	Fuller	White	Gray	Peckham	Brown	Shiras	Brewer	Harlan	McKenna
1902	Fuller	White	Holmes	Peckham	Brown	Shiras	Brewer	Harlan	McKenna
1903–05	Fuller	White	Holmes	Peckham	Brown	Day	Brewer	Harlan	McKenna
1906–08	Fuller	White	Holmes	Peckham	Moody	Day	Brewer	Harlan	McKenna
1909	Fuller	White	Holmes	Lurton	Moody	Day	Brewer	Harlan	McKenna
1910–11	White, E.	Van Devanter	Holmes	Lurton	Lamar, J.	Day	Hughes	Harlan	McKenna
1912–13	White, E.	Van Devanter	Holmes	Lurton	Lamar, J.	Day	Hughes	Pitney	McKenna
1914–15	White, E.	Van Devanter	Holmes	McReynolds	Lamar, J.	Day	Hughes	Pitney	McKenna
1916–20	White, E.	Van Devanter	Holmes	McReynolds	Brandeis	Day	Clarke	Pitney	McKenna
1921	Taft	Van Devanter	Holmes	McReynolds	Brandeis	Day	Clarke	Pitney	McKenna
1922	Taft	Van Devanter	Holmes	McReynolds	Brandeis	Butler	Sutherland	Pitney	McKenna
1923–24	Taft	Van Devanter	Holmes	McReynolds	Brandeis	Butler	Sutherland	Sanford	McKenna
1925–29	Taft	Van Devanter	Holmes	McReynolds	Brandeis	Butler	Sutherland	Sanford	Stone
1930–31	Hughes	Van Devanter	Holmes	McReynolds	Brandeis	Butler	Sutherland	Roberts	Stone
1932–36	Hughes	Van Devanter	Cardozo	McReynolds	Brandeis	Butler	Sutherland	Roberts	Stone
1937	Hughes	Black	Cardozo	McReynolds	Brandeis	Butler	Sutherland	Roberts	Stone
1938	Hughes	Black	Cardozo	McReynolds	Brandeis	Butler	Reed	Roberts	Stone
1939	Hughes	Black	Frankfurter	McReynolds	Douglas	Butler	Reed	Roberts	Stone
1940	Hughes	Black	Frankfurter	McReynolds	Douglas	Murphy	Reed	Roberts	Stone
1941–42	Stone	Black	Frankfurter	Byrnes	Douglas	Murphy	Reed	Roberts	Jackson, R.
1943–44	Stone	Black	Frankfurter	Rutledge, W.	Douglas	Murphy	Reed	Roberts	Jackson, R.
1945	Stone	Black	Frankfurter	Rutledge, W.	Douglas	Murphy	Reed	Burton	Jackson, R.
1946–48	Vinson	Black	Frankfurter	Rutledge, W.	Douglas	Murphy	Reed	Burton	Jackson, R.
1949–52	Vinson	Black	Frankfurter	Minton	Douglas	Clark	Reed	Burton	Jackson, R.
1953–54	Warren	Black	Frankfurter	Minton	Douglas	Clark	Reed	Burton	Jackson, R.
1955	Warren	Black	Frankfurter	Minton	Douglas	Clark	Reed	Burton	Harlan
1956	Warren	Black	Frankfurter	Brennan	Douglas	Clark	Reed	Burton	Harlan
1957	Warren	Black	Frankfurter	Brennan	Douglas	Clark	Whittaker	Burton	Harlan
1958–61	Warren	Black	Frankfurter	Brennan	Douglas	Clark	Whittaker	Stewart	Harlan

YEAR OF COURT AS CONSTITUTED	CHIEF JUSTICE	ASSOCIATE JUSTICES						
1962–65	Warren	Black	Goldberg	Brennan	Douglas	Clark	White, B.	Stewart	Harlan
1965–67	Warren	Black	Fortas	Brennan	Douglas	Clark	White, B.	Stewart	Harlan
1967–69	Warren	Black	Fortas	Brennan	Douglas	Marshall, T.	White, B.	Stewart	Harlan
1969	Burger	Black	Fortas	Brennan	Douglas	Marshall, T.	White, B.	Stewart	Harlan
1969–70	Burger	Black	(vacant)	Brennan	Douglas	Marshall, T.	White, B.	Stewart	Harlan
1970–71	Burger	Black	Blackmun	Brennan	Douglas	Marshall, T.	White, B.	Stewart	Harlan
1972–75	Burger	Powell	Blackmun	Brennan	Douglas	Marshall, T.	White, B.	Stewart	Rehnquist
1975–81	Burger	Powell	Blackmun	Brennan	Stevens	Marshall, T.	White, B.	Stewart	Rehnquist
1981–86	Burger	Powell	Blackmun	Brennan	Stevens	Marshall, T.	White, B.	O'Connor	Rehnquist
1986–87	Rehnquist	Powell	Blackmun	Brennan	Stevens	Marshall, T.	White, B.	O'Connor	Scalia
1987–90	Rehnquist	Kennedy	Blackmun	Brennan	Stevens	Marshall, T.	White, B.	O'Connor	Scalia
1990–91	Rehnquist	Kennedy	Blackmun	Souter	Stevens	Marshall, T.	White, B	O'Connor	Scalia
1991–93	Rehnquist	Kennedy	Blackmun	Souter	Stevens	Thomas	White, B.	O'Connor	Scalia
1993–94	Rehnquist	Kennedy	Blackmun	Souter	Stevens	Thomas	Ginsburg	O'Connor	Scalia
1994–2005	Rehnquist	Kennedy	Breyer	Souter	Stevens	Thomas	Ginsburg	O'Connor	Scalia
2005–09	Roberts	Kennedy	Breyer	Souter	Stevens	Thomas	Ginsburg	Alito	Scalia
2009–10	Roberts	Kennedy	Breyer	Sotomayor	Stevens	Thomas	Ginsburg	Alito	Scalia
2010–	Roberts	Kennedy	Breyer	Sotomayor	Kagan	Thomas	Ginsburg	Alito	Scalia

Supreme Court Justices

by Appointing President, State Appointed from, and Political Party

PRESIDENT/JUSTICES APPOINTED	STATE APPOINTED FROM	POLITICAL PARTY
Washington		
John Jay (1745–1829)*	N.Y.	Federalist
John Rutledge (1739–1800)	S.C.	Federalist
William Cushing (1732–1810)	Mass.	Federalist
James Wilson (1724–1798)	Pa.	Federalist
John Blair (1732–1800)	Va.	Federalist
James Iredell (1751–1799)	N.C.	Federalist
Thomas Johnson (1732–1819)	Md.	Federalist
William Paterson (1745–1806)	N.J.	Federalist
Samuel Chase (1741–1811)	Md.	Federalist
Oliver Ellsworth (1745–1807)	Conn.	Federalist
Adams, J.		
Bushrod Washington (1762–1829)	Va.	Federalist
Alfred Moore (1755–1810)	N.C.	Federalist
John Marshall (1755–1835)	Va.	Federalist
Jefferson		
William Johnson (1771–1834)	S.C.	Dem.-Rep.
Henry Livingston (1757–1823)	N.Y.	Dem.-Rep.
Thomas Todd (1765–1826)	Va.	Dem.-Rep.
Madison		
Gabriel Duvall (1752–1844)	Md.	Dem.-Rep.
Joseph Story (1779–1845)	Mass.	Dem.-Rep.
Monroe		
Smith Thompson (1768–1843)	N.Y.	Dem.-Rep.
Adams, J. Q.		
Robert Trimble (1776–1828)	Ky.	Dem.-Rep.
Jackson		
John McLean (1785–1861)	Ohio	Dem. (later Rep.)
Henry Baldwin (1780–1844)	Penn.	Democrat
James M. Wayne (1790–1867)	Ga.	Democrat
Roger B. Taney (1777–1864)	Va.	Democrat
Philip P. Barbour (1783–1841)	Va.	Democrat

PRESIDENT/JUSTICES APPOINTED	STATE APPOINTED FROM	POLITICAL PARTY
Van Buren		
John Catron (1778–1865)	Tenn.	Democrat
John McKinley (1780–1852)	Ala.	Democrat
Peter V. Daniel (1784–1860)	Va.	Democrat
Tyler		
Samuel Nelson (1792–1873)	N.Y.	Democrat
Polk		
Levi Woodbury (1789–1851)	N.H.	Democrat
Robert C. Grier (1794–1870)	Pa.	Democrat
Fillmore		
Benjamin R. Curtis (1809–1874)	Mass.	Whig
Pierce		
John A. Campbell (1811–1889)	Ala.	Democrat
Buchanan		
Nathan Clifford (1803–1881)	Maine	Democrat
Lincoln		
Noah H. Swayne (1804–1884)	Ohio	Republican
Samuel F. Miller (1816–1890)	Iowa	Republican
David Davis (1815–1886)	Ill.	Dem. (later Rep.)
Stephen J. Field (1816–1899)	Calif.	Democrat
Salmon P. Chase (1808–1873)	Ohio	Republican
Grant		
William Strong (1808–1895)	Pa.	Republican
Joseph P. Bradley (1813–1892)	N.J.	Republican
Ward Hunt (1810–1886)	N.Y.	Republican
Morrison Waite (1816–1888)	Ohio	Republican
Hayes		
John M. Harlan (1833–1911)	Ky.	Republican
William B. Woods (1824–1887)	Ga.	Republican
Garfield		
Stanley Matthews (1824–1889)	Ohio	Republican
Arthur		
Horace Gray (1828–1902)	Mass.	Republican
Samuel Blatchford (1820–1893)	N.Y.	Republican

*Dates in parentheses indicate birth and death dates.

PRESIDENT/JUSTICES APPOINTED	STATE APPOINTED FROM	POLITICAL PARTY
Cleveland		
Lucius Q. C. Lamar (1825–1893)	Miss.	Democrat
Melville W. Fuller (1833–1910)	Ill.	Democrat
Harrison		
David J. Brewer (1837–1910)	Kans.	Republican
Henry B. Brown (1836–1913)	Mich.	Republican
George Shiras, Jr. (1832–1924)	Pa.	Republican
Howell E. Jackson (1832–1895)	Tenn.	Democrat
Cleveland		
Edward D. White (1845–1921)	La.	Democrat
Rufus W. Peckham (1838–1909)	N.Y.	Democrat
McKinley		
Joseph McKenna (1843–1926)	Calif.	Republican
Roosevelt, T.		
Oliver W. Holmes (1841–1935)	Mass.	Republican
William R. Day (1849–1923)	Ohio	Republican
William H. Moody (1853–1917)	Mass.	Republican
Taft		
Horace H. Lurton (1844–1914)	Tenn.	Democrat
Charles E. Hughes (1862–1948)	N.Y.	Republican
Willis Van Devanter (1859–1941)	Wyo.	Republican
Joseph R. Lamar (1857–1916)	Ga.	Democrat
Mahlon Pitney (1858–1924)	N.J.	Republican
Wilson		
James C. McReynolds (1862–1946)	Tenn.	Democrat
Louis D. Brandeis (1856–1941)	Mass.	Independent
John H. Clarke (1857–1945)	Ohio	Democrat
Harding		
William H. Taft (1857–1930)	Conn.	Republican
George Sutherland (1862–1942)	Utah	Republican
Pierce Butler (1866–1939)	Minn.	Democrat
Edward T. Sanford (1865–1930)	Tenn.	Republican
Coolidge		
Harlan F. Stone (1872–1946)	N.Y.	Republican
Hoover		
Owen J. Roberts (1875–1955)	Pa.	Republican
Benjamin N. Cardozo (1870–1938)	N.Y.	Democrat
Roosevelt, F. D.		
Hugo L. Black (1886–1971)	Ala.	Democrat
Stanley F. Reed (1884–1980)	Ky.	Democrat
Felix Frankfurter (1882–1965)	Mass.	Independent
William O. Douglas (1898–1980)	Conn.	Democrat
Frank Murphy (1890–1949)	Mich.	Democrat

PRESIDENT/JUSTICES APPOINTED	STATE APPOINTED FROM	POLITICAL PARTY
James F. Byrnes (1879–1972)	S.C.	Democrat
Robert H. Jackson (1892–1954)	N.Y.	Democrat
Wiley B. Rutledge (1894–1949)	Iowa	Democrat
Truman		
Harold H. Burton (1888–1964)	Ohio	Republican
Fred M. Vinson (1890–1953)	Ky.	Democrat
Tom C. Clark (1899–1977)	Texas	Democrat
Sherman Minton (1890–1965)	Ind.	Democrat
Eisenhower		
Earl Warren (1891–1974)	Calif.	Republican
John M. Harlan (1899–1971)	N.Y.	Republican
William J. Brennan (b. 1906)	N.J.	Democrat
Charles E. Whittaker (1901–1973)	Mo.	Republican
Potter Stewart (1915–1986)	Ohio	Republican
Kennedy		
Byron R. White (1917–2002)	Colo.	Democrat
Arthur J. Goldberg (1908–1990)	Ill.	Democrat
Johnson, L.B.		
Abe Fortas (1910–1982)	Tenn.	Democrat
Thurgood Marshall (1908–1993)	N.Y.	Democrat
Nixon		
Warren E. Burger (1907–1995)	Minn.	Republican
Harry R. Blackmun (1908–1999)	Minn.	Republican
Lewis F. Powell, Jr. (1907–1998)	Va.	Democrat
William H. Rehnquist (1924–2005)	Ariz.	Republican
Ford		
John Paul Stevens (b. 1920)	Ill.	Republican
Reagan		
Sandra Day O'Connor (b. 1930)	Ariz.	Republican
Antonin Scalia (b. 1936)	N.J.	Republican
Anthony M. Kennedy (b. 1936)	Calif.	Republican
Bush, George H. W.		
David Souter (b. 1939)	N.H.	Republican
Clarence Thomas (b. 1948)	Va.	Republican
Clinton		
Ruth Bader Ginsburg (b. 1933)	Wa., D.C.	Democrat
Stephen G. Breyer (b. 1938)	Mass.	Democrat
Bush, George H. W.		
John G. Roberts (b. 1955)	Md.	Republican
Samuel Alito (b. 1950)	N.J.	Republican
Obama		
Sonia Sotomayor (b. 1954)	N.Y.	Democrat
Elena Kagan (b. 1960)	Mass.	Democrat

Glossary

abate To do away with or lessen the impact of, as in abatement of a nuisance.

abortion The intentional termination of a pregnancy through destruction of the fetus.

abrogate To annul, destroy, or cancel.

abstention The doctrine under which the U.S. Supreme Court and other federal courts do not decide on, or interfere with, state cases even when empowered to do so. This doctrine is typically invoked when a case can be decided on the basis of state law.

accessory A person who aids in the commission of a crime.

accessory after the fact A person who with knowledge that a crime has been committed conceals or protects the offender.

accessory before the fact A person who aids or assists another in commission of an offense.

accommodation An approach to interpreting the Establishment Clause of the First Amendment that holds that government can and should accommodate religion whenever possible, while at the same time being officially neutral.

accomplice A person who voluntarily unites with another in commission of an offense.

accusatorial system A system of criminal justice in which the prosecution bears the burden of proving the defendant's guilt.

acquittal A judicial finding that a defendant is not guilty of a crime with which he or she has been charged.

act of omission The failure to perform an act required by law.

actual damages Money awarded to a plaintiff in a civil suit to compensate for injuries to that party's rights.

actual imprisonment standard The standard governing the applicability of the federal constitutional right of an indigent person to have counsel appointed in a misdemeanor case. In order for the right to be violated, the indigent defendant must actually be sentenced to jail time after having been tried without appointed counsel.

actual malice The degree of culpability required to establish defamation of public officials or public figures. It was defined by the Supreme Court in *New York Times v. Sullivan* (1964) as "knowledge that the information was false" or that it was published "with reckless disregard of whether it was false or not."

actual possession Possession of something with the possessor having immediate control.

actus reus A "wrongful act" that, combined with other necessary elements of crime, constitutes criminal liability.

ad hoc "For this." For a special purpose.

ad hoc balancing An effort by a court to balance competing interests in the context of the unique facts of a given case. In constitutional law, this term is used most frequently in connection with the adjudication of First Amendment issues.

adjudication The formal process by which courts decide cases.

adjudicatory hearing A proceeding in juvenile court to determine whether a juvenile has committed an act of delinquency.

ad litem "For the lawsuit"; pending the lawsuit, as in "guardian ad litem."

administrative law The body of law dealing with the structure, authority, policies, and procedures of administrative and regulatory agencies.

Administrative Procedure Act The 1946 act of Congress specifying rule making and adjudicatory procedures for federal agencies.

administrative searches Searches of premises by a government official to determine compliance with health and safety regulations.

adultery Voluntary sexual intercourse where at least one of the parties is married to someone other than the sexual partner.

ad valorem "According to the value." Referring to a tax or duty guaranteed according to the assessed value of the matter taxed.

adversary proceeding A legal action involving parties with adverse or opposing interests. A basic aspect of the American legal system, the adversary proceeding provides the framework within which most constitutional cases are decided. For an exception to this generalization, *See*: ex parte.

adversary system A system of justice involving conflicting parties where the role of the judge is to remain neutral.

advisory opinion A judicial opinion, not involving adverse parties in a "case or controversy," that is given at the request of the legislature or the executive. It has been a long-standing policy of the U.S. Supreme Court not to render advisory opinions.

affiant A person who makes an affidavit.

affidavit A person's voluntary sworn declaration attesting to a set of facts.

affirm To uphold, ratify, or approve.

affirmative action A program under which women and/or persons of particular minority groups are granted special consideration in employment, government contracts, and/or admission to programs of higher education.

a fortiori "With greater force of reason."

aggravating circumstances Factors attending the commission of a crime that make the crime or its consequences worse.

aggravating factors *See*: aggravating circumstances.

aiding and abetting Assisting in or otherwise facilitating the commission of a crime.

alibi Defense to a criminal charge that places the defendant at some place other than the scene of the crime at the time the crime occurred.

allegation Assertion or claim made by a party to a legal action.

amendment   A modification, addition, or deletion.

Americans with Disabilities Act   The 1990 federal statute forbidding discrimination on grounds of disability and guaranteeing access for the handicapped to public buildings.

amici   "Friends," usually in reference to "friends of the Court." *See: amicus curiae.*

amicus curiae   "Friend of the court." An individual or organization allowed to take part in a judicial proceeding, not as one of the adversaries, but as a party interested in the outcome. Usually an *amicus curiae* files a brief in support of one side or the other but occasionally takes a more active part in the argument of the case.

amnesty   A blanket pardon issued to a large group of lawbreakers.

anonymous informant   An informant whose identity is unknown to the police. *See also:* confidential informant.

anonymous tip   Information from an unknown source concerning alleged criminal activity.

answer brief   The appellee's written response to the appellant's law brief filed in an appellate court.

anticipatory search warrant   A search warrant issued based on an affidavit that at a future time evidence of a crime will be at a specific place.

appeal   Review by a higher court of a lower court decision.

appeal by right   An appeal brought to a higher court as a matter of right under federal or state law.

appellant   A person who takes an appeal to a higher court.

appellate courts   Judicial tribunals that review decisions from lower tribunals.

appellate jurisdiction   The legal authority of a court of law to hear an appeal from or otherwise review a decision by a lower court.

appellee   The party against whom a case is appealed to a higher court.

appointment power   The power of the president to appoint, with the consent of the Senate, judges, ambassadors, and high-level executive officials.

apportionment   The allocation of representatives among a set of legislative districts.

arguendo   "For the sake of argument."

arraignment   An appearance before a court of law for the purpose of pleading to a criminal charge.

arrest   To take someone into custody or otherwise deprive that person of freedom of movement.

arrestee   A person who is arrested.

arrest warrant   A document issued by a magistrate or judge directing that a named person be taken into custody for allegedly having committed an offense.

Article I, Section 8   Key section of the Constitution outlining the powers of Congress.

Articles of Confederation   The constitution under which the United States was governed between 1781 and 1789.

assault   The attempt or threat to inflict bodily injury upon another person.

assign   To transfer or grant a legal right.

assignee   One to whom a legal right is transferred.

assignments of error   A written presentation to an appellate court identifying the points the appellant claims constitute errors made by the lower tribunal.

asylum   Sanctuary; a place of refuge.

at bar   Before the court, as in "the case at bar."

at-large election   An election in which a number of officials are chosen to represent the entire district, as opposed to an arrangement under which each of the officials would represent one smaller district or ward.

attempt   An intent to commit a crime coupled with an act taken toward committing the offense.

attorney-client privilege   The right of a person (client) not to testify about matters discussed in confidence with an attorney in the course of the attorney's representation.

attorney general   The highest legal officer of a state or of the United States.

automobile exception   An exception to the Fourth Amendment search warrant requirement that allows the warrantless search of a vehicle by police who have probable cause to search, but for which it is impracticable to secure a warrant because of exigent circumstances.

automobile search   The search of an automobile by police, usually performed without a warrant.

bad tendency test   A restrictive interpretation of the First Amendment under which government may prohibit expression having a tendency to cause people to break the law.

bail   The conditional release from custody of a person charged with a crime pending adjudication of the case.

battery   The unlawful use of force against another person, entailing some injury or offensive touching.

bench trial   A trial before a judge rather than a jury.

bench warrant   An arrest warrant issued by a judge.

benevolent neutrality   An approach to interpreting the Establishment Clause of the First Amendment that holds that government can and should take a benevolent posture toward religion while at the same time being officially neutral on such matters.

beyond a reasonable doubt   The standard of proof that is constitutionally required to be introduced before a defendant can be found guilty of a crime or before a juvenile can be adjudicated a delinquent.

bicameralism   The characteristic of having two houses or chambers. The U.S. Congress is a bicameral body in that it has a Senate and a House of Representatives.

bifurcated trial   A capital trial with separate phases for determining guilt and punishment.

bigamy   The crime of being married to more than one person at the same time.

bill of attainder   A legislative act imposing punishment on a party without the benefit of a judicial proceeding.

Bill of Rights   The first ten amendments to the Constitution, ratified in 1791, concerned primarily with individual rights and liberties.

Black Codes Statutes enacted in southern states after the Civil War denying African-Americans a number of basic rights.

bloc A group of decision makers in a collegial body who usually vote the same way. In judicial politics, the term refers to groups of judges or justices on appellate courts who usually vote together.

bona fide "In good faith"; without the attempt to defraud or deceive.

border search A search of persons entering the borders of the United States.

bounty hunter A person paid a fee or commission to capture a defendant who had fled a jurisdiction to escape punishment.

Brady Bill Legislation passed by Congress in 1993 requiring a five-day waiting period before the purchase of a handgun during which time a background check is conducted on the buyer.

Brandeis brief Pioneered by attorney Louis D. Brandeis in 1908, a type of appellate brief that emphasizes empirical evidence of the social or economic impact of law, as distinguished from a conventional brief that focuses solely on legal analysis.

breach of contract The violation of a provision in a legally enforceable agreement that gives the damaged party the right to recourse in a court of law.

breach of the peace The crime of disturbing the public tranquility and order. A generic term encompassing disorderly conduct, riot, and similar behaviors.

brief (1) In the judicial process, a document submitted by counsel setting forth legal arguments germane to a particular case. (2) In the study of constitutional law, a summary of a given case, reviewing the essential facts, issues, holdings, and reasoning of the court.

burden of persuasion The legal responsibility of a party to convince a court of the correctness of a position asserted.

burden of production of evidence The obligation of a party to produce some evidence in support of a proposition asserted.

burden of proof The requirement to introduce evidence to prove an alleged fact or set of facts.

bureaucracy Any large, complex, hierarchical organization staffed by appointed officials.

business affected with a public interest A nineteenth century doctrine holding that certain businesses are more closely associated with the public interest and are therefore more subject to government regulation.

cabinet The collective term for the heads of the executive departments of the federal government, such as the secretary of state, the attorney general, and the secretary of defense.

capias "That you take." A general term for various court orders requiring that some named person be taken into custody.

capitalist economy An economy based on private ownership and free enterprise.

capital offense A crime punishable by death.

capital punishment The death penalty.

carnal knowledge Sexual intercourse.

case A legal dispute between adverse parties to be resolved by a court of law.

case law Law derived from judicial decisions, also known as the decisional law.

case or controversy requirement The requirement, under Article III of the Constitution, that the federal judicial power shall be extended to actual cases or controversies, not to hypothetical or abstract questions of law.

case reporters A series of books reprinting the decisions of a given court or set of courts. For example, the decisions of the U.S. Courts of Appeals are reported in the *Federal Reporter*, published by West Publishing Company.

castle doctrine The doctrine that "a man's home is his castle." At common law, the right to use whatever force is necessary to protect one's dwelling and its inhabitants from an unlawful entry or attack.

causation An act that produces an event or an effect.

cause A synonym for case; a reason or justification. *See also*: probable cause; show cause.

caveat emptor "Let the buyer beware." Common law maxim requiring the consumer to judge the quality of a product before making a purchase.

censorship Broadly defined, any restriction imposed by the government on speech, publication, or other form of expression.

certification A procedure under which a lower court requests a decision by a higher court on specified questions in a case, pending a final decision by the lower court.

certiorari "To be informed." A petition similar to an appeal, but it may be granted or refused at the discretion of the appellate court.

***certiorari*, writ of** An order from a higher court to a lower court directing that the record of a particular case be sent up for review. *See also*: certiorari.

challenge for cause Objection to a prospective juror on some specified ground (for example, a close relationship to a party to the case).

change of venue The removal of a legal proceeding, usually a trial, to a new location.

checks and balances The constitutional powers granted each branch of government to prevent one branch from dominating the others.

child benefit theory The doctrine that government assistance to religious schools can be justified if the effect is to benefit the child rather than to promote religion.

chilling effect The effect of discouraging persons from exercising their rights.

circumstantial evidence Indirect evidence from which the existence of certain facts may be inferred.

citation (1) A summons to appear in court, often used in traffic violations. (2) A reference to a statute or court decision, often designating a publication where the law or decision appears.

civil action A lawsuit brought to enforce private rights and to remedy violations thereof.

civil case *See*: civil action.

civil infractions Noncriminal violation of a law, often referring to minor traffic violations.

civil law (1) The law relating to rights and obligations of parties. (2) The body of law, based essentially on Roman law, that exists in most non-English-speaking nations.

civil liberties The freedoms protected by the Constitution and statutes—for example, freedom of speech, religion, and assembly.

civil rights Legal protection against invidious discrimination in citizens' exercise of the rights of life, liberty, and property. The right to equality before the law and equal treatment by government.

Civil Rights Act of 1866 Federal civil rights law passed after the Civil War, aimed at eliminating the discriminatory Black Codes enacted by southern states.

Civil Rights Act of 1875 Federal civil rights law aimed at ending racial discrimination by places of public accommodation. Declared unconstitutional in 1883.

Civil Rights Act of 1964 Landmark civil rights statute aimed at ending racial discrimination in employment and by places of public accommodation.

Civil Rights movement The social movement beginning in the 1950s aimed at securing civil rights for African-Americans.

civil service The system under which government employees are selected and retained based on merit, rather than political patronage.

civil suit *See*: civil action.

Civil War Amendments Reference to the Thirteenth, Fourteenth, and Fifteenth Amendments to the Constitution, designed primarily to protect the civil rights of former slaves.

claim of right A contention that an item was taken in a good-faith belief that it belonged to the taker; sometimes asserted as a defense to a charge of larceny or theft.

class action A lawsuit brought by one or more parties on behalf of themselves and others similarly situated.

classical conservatism Traditional conservatism stressing preservation of order and maintenance of traditional values.

clear and convincing evidence standard An evidentiary standard that is higher than the standard of "preponderance of the evidence" applied in civil cases, but lower than the standard of "beyond a reasonable doubt" applied in criminal cases. For example, under the new federal standard for the affirmative defense of insanity, the defendant must establish the defense of insanity by "clear and convincing evidence."

clear and present danger test The First Amendment test that protects expression up to the point that it poses a clear and present danger of bringing about some substantive evil that government has a right to prevent.

clear and probable danger test A somewhat more restrictive First Amendment test than clear and present danger. The test is "whether the gravity of the 'evil,' discounted by its improbability, justifies such invasion of speech as is necessary to avoid the danger."

clemency A grant of mercy by an executive official commuting a sentence or pardoning a criminal.

closing arguments Arguments presented at trial by counsel at the conclusion of the presentation of evidence.

closure of pretrial proceedings Decision by a judge to close proceedings prior to trial of a criminal case in order to protect the defendant's right to a fair trial.

code A systematic collection of laws.

coercive federalism Term used to describe the fact that the federal government often uses federal grants to coerce states into adopting policies that it cannot directly mandate.

collateral attack The attempt to defeat the outcome of a judicial proceeding by challenging it in another court.

collateral estoppel A rule barring the making of a claim in one judicial proceeding that has been adjudicated in another, earlier proceeding.

comity Courtesy, respect, civility. A matter of goodwill and tradition, rather than of right; particularly important in a federal system where one jurisdiction is bound to respect the judgments of another.

commander in chief Term describing the president's authority to command the armed forces of the country.

commercial speech Commercial advertising, now viewed as entitled to some protection under the First Amendment.

common law A body of law that develops primarily through judicial decisions, rather than legislative enactments. The common law is not a fixed system but an ever-changing body of rules and principles articulated by judges and applied to changing needs and circumstances. *See also*: English Common law.

community control A sentence imposed on a person found guilty of a crime that requires the offender to be placed in an individualized program of noninstitutional confinement.

community service A sentence requiring that the criminal perform some specific service to the community for some specified period of time.

community standards Standards of decency, which may vary from community to community.

commutation A form of clemency that lessens the punishment for a person convicted of a crime.

comparative proportionality review A judicial examination to determine whether the sentence imposed in a given criminal case is proportionate to sentences imposed in similar cases.

compelling government interest A government interest sufficiently strong that it overrides the fundamental rights of persons adversely affected by government action or policy.

compelling interest An interest or justification of the highest order.

competency The state of being legally fit to give testimony or stand trial.

complicity A person's voluntary participation with another person in commission of a crime or wrongful act.

comprehensive planning A guide for the orderly development of a community, usually implemented by enactment of zoning ordinances.

compulsory process The requirement that witnesses appear and testify in court or before a legislative committee. *See also*: subpoena.

compulsory self-incrimination The requirement that an individual give testimony leading to his or her own criminal conviction; forbidden by the Fifth Amendment.

compulsory sterilization The requirement that an individual undergo procedures that render him or her unable to conceive children.

concurrent jurisdiction   Jurisdiction that is shared by different courts of law.

concurrent powers   Powers exercised jointly by the state and federal governments.

concurrent resolution   An act expressing the will of both houses of the legislature but lacking a mechanism through which to enforce that will on parties outside the legislature.

concurrent sentencing   The practice in which a trial court imposes separate sentences that may be served at the same time.

concurring in the judgment   An agreement by a judge or justice in the judgment of an appellate court without necessarily agreeing to the court's reasoning processes.

concurring opinion   An opinion by a judge or justice agreeing with the decision of the court. A concurring opinion may or may not agree with the rationale adopted by the court in reaching its decision. *See also*: Opinion of the Court.

conditions of probation   A set of rules that must be observed by a person placed on probation.

conference   As applied to the appellate courts, a private meeting of judges to decide a case or to determine whether to grant review in a case.

confidential informant   An informant known to the police but whose identity is held in confidence. *See also*: anonymous informant.

conscientious objector   One who opposes military service on religious or moral grounds.

consecutive sentencing   The practice in which a trial court imposes a sentence or sentences to be served following completion of a prior sentence or sentences.

consent   Voluntarily yielding to the will or desire of another person.

consent decree   A court-enforced agreement reached by mutual consent of parties in a civil case or administrative proceeding.

conspiracy   The crime of two or more persons planning to commit a specific criminal act.

constitutional case   A judicial proceeding involving an issue of constitutional law.

Constitutional Convention of 1787   Convention of state delegates held in Philadelphia during the summer of 1787, ostensibly for the purpose of revising the Articles of Confederation. The convention resulted in a new Constitution, which was ratified in 1788.

constitutional democracy   A democratic system of government in which majority rule is limited by constitutional principles such as limited government and individual rights.

constitutional law   The fundamental and supreme law of the land defining the structure and powers of government and the rights of individuals vis-à-vis government.

constitutional republic   A republican form of government based on a written constitution. The Framers of the U.S. Constitution avoided the term *democracy*, which they equated with unrestrained majoritarianism. They preferred the term *republican form of government*, which connoted representative institutions constrained by the rule of law.

constitutional right of privacy   The right to make choices in matters of intimate personal concern without interference by government.

constitutional supremacy   The doctrine that the Constitution is the supreme law of the land and that all actions and policies of government must be consistent with it.

constitutional theory   (1) Broad term referring to theories about the Constitution generally, or particular theories about particular provisions of the Constitution. (2) In the area of the presidency, the theory that the president can exercise only those powers specifically granted by Article II.

construction   Interpretation.

contemnor   A person found to be in contempt of court.

contempt   An action that embarrasses, hinders, obstructs, or is calculated to lessen the dignity of a judicial or legislative body.

contempt of Congress   Any action that embarrasses, hinders, obstructs, or is calculated to lessen the dignity of Congress.

contempt of court   Any action that embarrasses, hinders, obstructs, or is calculated to lessen the dignity of a court of law.

content-neutral   Term referring to a time, place, or manner regulation that is enforced without regard to the content of expression.

continuance   Delay of a judicial proceeding on the motion of one of the parties.

contraband   Any property that is inherently illegal to produce or possess.

contracts   Legally binding agreements between or among specific parties.

Contracts Clause   Provision of Article I, Section 10, forbidding states from impairing the obligations of contracts.

contractual immunity   A grant by a prosecutor with approval of the court that makes a witness immune from prosecution for the witness's testimony.

controlled substance   A drug designated by law as contraband.

convening authorities   The military authorities with jurisdiction to convene a court-martial for trial of persons subject to the Uniform Code of Military Justice.

conversion   The unlawful assumption of the rights of ownership to someone else's property.

cooperative federalism   A modern approach to American federalism in which powers and functions are shared among national, state, and local authorities.

corporal punishment   Punishment that inflicts pain or injury on a person's body.

corpus delicti   "The body of the crime." The material thing upon which a crime has been committed (for example, a burned-out building in a case of arson).

corrections system   The system of prisons, jails, and other penal and correctional institutions.

corroboration   Evidence that strengthens or validates evidence already given.

counsel   A lawyer who represents a party.

court-martial   A military tribunal convened by a commander of a military unit to try a person subject to the Uniform Code of Military Justice who is accused of violating a provision of that code.

Court of Appeals for the Armed Forces   A court consisting of five civilian judges that reviews sentences affecting a general or flag officer or imposing the death penalty as well as cases certified for review by the judge advocate general of a branch of service. May grant review of convictions and sentences on petitions by service members.

court of general jurisdiction A court that conducts trials in felony and major misdemeanor cases. Also refers to a trial court with broad authority to hear and decide a wide range of civil and criminal cases.

court of last resort The highest court in a judicial system; the last resort for deciding appeals.

court of limited jurisdiction A trial court with narrow authority to hear and decide cases, typically pretrial matters, misdemeanors, and/or small claims.

court-ordered busing The transportation of public school students to schools outside their area, under court orders to alleviate racial segregation.

court system A set of trial and appellate courts established to resolve legal disputes in a particular jurisdiction.

creation science The idea that there are scientific reasons to believe in creationism as opposed to evolution.

criminal Pertaining to crime; a person convicted of a crime.

criminal action A judicial proceeding initiated by government against a person charged with the commission of a crime.

criminal case A judicial proceeding in which a person is accused of a crime.

criminal conspiracy *See*: conspiracy.

criminal contempt Punishment imposed by a judge against a person who violates a court order or otherwise intentionally interferes with the administration of the court.

criminal intent A necessary element of a crime; the evil intent associated with the criminal act.

criminal law The law defining crimes and punishments.

criminal negligence A failure to exercise the degree of caution or care necessary to avoid being charged with a crime.

criminal procedure The rules of law governing the procedures by which crimes are investigated, prosecuted, adjudicated, and punished.

criminal prosecution Legal action brought against a person accused of a crime.

criminal responsibility Term referring to the set of doctrines under which individuals are held accountable for criminal conduct.

criminal syndicalism The crime of advocating violence as a means to accomplish political change (archaic).

criminology The study of the nature of, causes of, and means of dealing with crime.

critical pretrial stages Significant procedural steps that occur preliminary to a criminal trial. A defendant has the right to counsel at these critical stages.

cross-examination The process of interrogating a witness who has testified on direct examination by asking the witness questions concerning testimony given. Cross-examination is designed to bring out any bias or inconsistencies in the witness's testimony.

cruel and unusual punishments Degrading punishments that shock the moral standards of the community, such as torturing or physically beating a prisoner.

culpability Guilt.

curtilage At common law, the enclosed space surrounding a dwelling house; in modern codes this space has been extended to encompass other buildings.

custodial interrogation Questioning by the police of a suspect in custody.

damages Monetary compensation awarded by a court to a person who has suffered injuries or losses to person or property as a result of someone else's conduct.

deadlocked jury A jury where the jurors cannot agree on a verdict. *See also*: hung jury.

deadly force The degree of force that may result in the death of the person against whom the force is applied.

death penalty Capital punishment; a sentence to death for the commission of a crime.

death-qualified jury A trial jury composed of persons who do not entertain scruples against imposing a death sentence.

decisional law Law declared by appellate courts in their written decisions and opinions.

decision on the merits A judicial decision that reaches the subject matter of a case.

declaratory judgment A judicial ruling conclusively declaring the rights, duties, or status of the parties but imposing no additional order, restriction, or requirement on them.

de facto "In fact"; as a matter of fact.

de facto **segregation** Racial segregation that exists in fact, even though it is not required by law.

defamation A tort involving the injury to one's reputation by the malicious or reckless dissemination of a falsehood.

defendant A person charged with a crime or against whom a civil action is brought.

defense A defendant's stated reasons of law or fact as to why the prosecution or plaintiff should not prevail.

defense attorneys Lawyers who represent defendants in criminal cases.

definite sentencing Legislatively determined sentencing with no discretion given to judges or corrections officials to individualize punishment.

de jure "In law"; as a matter of law.

de jure **discrimination** Discrimination that results from law, whether on its face or as applied.

delegation of legislative power A legislative act authorizing an administrative or regulatory agency to promulgate rules and regulations having the force of law.

delinquency petition A written document alleging that a juvenile has committed an offense and asking the court to hold an adjudicatory hearing to determine the merits of the petition.

de minimis Minimal, trifling, trivial.

demurrer An action of a defendant admitting to a set of alleged facts but nevertheless challenging the legal sufficiency of a complaint or criminal charge.

de novo   Anew; for a second time.

Department of Justice   The department of the federal government that is headed by the attorney general and staffed by U.S. attorneys.

deposition   The recorded sworn testimony of a witness; not given in open court.

derivative evidence   Evidence that is derived from or obtained only as a result of other evidence.

desegregation   Efforts to eliminate de jure or de facto racial segregation.

detention   Holding someone in custody.

detention hearing   A proceeding held to determine whether a juvenile charged with an offense should be detained pending an adjudicatory hearing.

determinate sentence   Variation on definite sentencing whereby a judge fixes the term of incarceration within statutory limits.

deterrence   Prevention of criminal activity by punishing criminals so that others will not engage in such activity.

dicta   See: obiter dicta.

diplomatic immunity   A privilege to be free from arrest and prosecution, granted under international law to diplomats, their staffs, and household members.

direct contempt   An obstructive or insulting act committed by a person in the immediate presence of the court.

directed verdict   A verdict rendered by a jury upon direction of the presiding judge.

direct evidence   Evidence that applies directly to proof of a fact or proposition. For example, a witness who testifies to having seen an act performed or having heard a statement made is giving direct evidence.

direct filing   The filing of information by a prosecutor charging a juvenile with an offense, rather than filing a petition in juvenile court to declare the juvenile delinquent for having committed the offense.

direct–indirect test   A test once used by the Supreme Court in its Commerce Clause jurisprudence. Under this test, a statute was valid only if the targeted activity had a direct impact on interstate commerce.

discrete and insular minorities   Minority groups that are locked out of the political process.

discretion   The power of public officials to act in certain situations according to their own judgment rather than relying on set rules or procedures.

discretionary review   Form of appellate court review of lower court decisions that is not mandatory but occurs at the discretion of the appellate court. *See also*: certiorari.

discuss list   The list of petitions for certiorari that are deemed worthy of discussion in conference.

dismissal   A judicial order terminating a case.

disorderly conduct   Illegal behavior that disturbs the public peace or order.

disparate impact   Differential, often discriminatory effect of a facially neutral law or policy on members of different races or genders.

disposition   The final settlement of a case.

dissent   An appellate judge's formal vote against the judgment of the court in a given case.

dissenting opinion   A written opinion by a judge or justice setting forth reasons for disagreeing with a particular decision of the court.

distinction between manufacturing and commerce   An important element of the Supreme Court's Commerce Clause jurisprudence in the late nineteenth and early twentieth centuries. The distinction between manufacturing, or production, on the one hand, and commerce, or distribution, on the other hand, served to limit the reach of Congress's power under the Commerce Clause.

distributive articles   Articles I, II, and III of the U.S. Constitution, delineating the powers and functions of the legislative, executive, and judicial branches, respectively, of the national government.

diversity jurisdiction   The authority of a federal court to entertain a civil suit in which the parties are citizens of different states and the amount in controversy exceeds $50,000.

diversity of citizenship action   A federal civil suit in which the parties are citizens of different states and the amount in controversy exceeds $75,000.

diversity of citizenship jurisdiction   The authority of federal courts to hear lawsuits in which the parties are citizens of different states and the amount in controversy exceeds $75,000.

docket   The set of cases pending before a court of law.

doctor-assisted suicide   Administration by a physician of lethal drugs or gas to a terminally ill patient in order to produce death.

doctrine   A legal principle or rule developed through judicial decisions.

doctrine of abstention   The doctrine that federal courts should refrain from interfering with state judicial processes.

doctrine of incorporation   The doctrine under which provisions of the Bill of Rights are held to be incorporated within the Due Process Clause of the Fourteenth Amendment and are thereby made applicable to actions of the state and local governments.

doctrine of original intent   The doctrine that the Constitution is to be understood in terms of the intentions of the Framers.

doctrine of overbreadth   The doctrine under which a person makes a facial challenge to a law on the ground that the law might be applied in the future against activities protected by the First Amendment.

doctrine of saving construction   The doctrine under which courts adopt an interpretation of a statute that saves the statute from being declared unconstitutional.

doctrine of strict necessity   The doctrine under which courts engage in judicial review only when strictly necessary to the settlement of a case.

double jeopardy   The condition of being prosecuted a second time for the same offense.

drug courier profile   A controversial law enforcement practice of identifying possible drug smugglers by relying on a set of characteristics and patterns of behavior believed to typify persons who smuggle drugs.

drug paraphernalia   Items closely associated with the use of illegal drugs.

drug testing The practice of subjecting employees to urine tests to determine whether they are using illegal substances.

dual federalism A concept of federalism in which the national and state governments exercise authority within separate, self-contained areas of public policy and public administration.

Due Process Clause The clause found in both the Fifth and Fourteenth Amendments that prohibits government from taking a person's life, liberty, or property without due process of law.

Due Process Clause of the Fourteenth Amendment The provision of the Fourteenth Amendment that prohibits states from taking a person's life, liberty, or property without due process of law.

due process of law Procedural and substantive rights of citizens against government actions that threaten the denial of life, liberty, or property.

duress The use of illegal confinement or threats of harm to coerce someone to do something he or she would not do otherwise.

duty An obligation that a person has by law or contract.

easement A right of use over the property of another; frequently refers to a right-of-way across privately owned land.

ecclesiastical Pertaining to religious laws or institutions.

economic due process The doctrine under which the Supreme Court in the late nineteenth and early twentieth centuries used the Due Process Clauses of the Fifth and Fourteenth Amendments to protect free enterprise from government intervention.

economic freedom Another term for free enterprise—that is, the ability to conduct one's business without interference by government.

economic protectionism An attempt by one state to protect its domestic economy from outside competition.

Eighth Amendment Amendment included in the Bill of Rights prohibiting excessive bail, excessive fines, and cruel and unusual punishments.

Electoral College The body of electors chosen by the voters of each state and the District of Columbia for the purpose of formally electing the president and vice president of the United States. The number of electors (538) is equivalent to the total number of representatives and senators to which each state is entitled, plus three electors from the District of Columbia.

electronic eavesdropping Covert listening to or recording of a person's conversations by electronic means.

electronic media Electronic means of mass communication, including television, radio, and the Internet.

Eleventh Amendment Amendment to the Constitution prohibiting federal courts from hearing suits brought by a citizen of one state against the government of another state.

emergency search A warrantless search performed during an emergency, such as a fire or potential explosion.

eminent domain The power of government, or of individuals and corporations authorized to perform public functions, to take private property for public use.

enabling legislation As applied to public law, a statute authorizing the creation of a government program or agency and defining the functions and powers thereof.

en banc "In the bench."

en banc **rehearing** A rehearing in an appellate court in which all or a majority of the judges participate.

enforcement power under the Fourteenth Amendment Congress's authority, recognized by Section 5 of the Fourteenth Amendment, to legislate in furtherance of the substantive provisions of the amendment.

English common law A system of legal rules and principles recognized and developed by English judges prior to the colonization of America and accepted as a basic aspect of the American legal system.

entrapment The act of government agents in inducing someone to commit a crime that the person otherwise would not be disposed to commit.

enumerated powers Powers specified in the text of the federal and state constitutions.

equal access Policies that permit religious and secular groups the same access to public buildings for purposes of meetings.

equality A condition in which persons hold the same status with respect to a particular criterion such as wealth, standing, or power.

Equal Protection Clause Clause in Section 1 of the Fourteenth Amendment that prohibits states from denying equal protection of the laws to persons within their jurisdictions.

equal protection of the laws Constitutional requirement that the government not engage in prohibited forms of discrimination against persons under its jurisdiction.

Equal Rights Amendment Failed attempt to amend the Constitution to guarantee equal rights for women.

equity Historically, a system of rules, remedies, customs, and principles developed in England to supplement the harsh common law by emphasizing the concept of fairness. In addition, because the common law served only to recompense after injury, equity was devised to prevent injuries that could not be repaired or recompensed after the fact. While American judges continue to distinguish between law and equity, these systems of rights and remedies are, for the most part, administered by the same courts.

error correction The function of appellate courts in correcting more or less routine errors committed by lower courts.

error, writ of An order issued by an appellate court for the purpose of correcting an error revealed in the record of a lower court proceeding.

escape Unlawfully fleeing to avoid arrest or confinement.

Establishment Clause Clause in the First Amendment prohibiting Congress from enacting laws "respecting an establishment of religion."

establishment of religion Official government support of religion or religious institutions. Prohibited by the First Amendment. *See also*: separation of church and state.

et al. "And others."

euthanasia Mercy killing.

evanescent evidence Evidence that will likely disappear if not immediately seized.

evidence Testimony, writings, or material objects offered in proof of an alleged fact or proposition.

evidentiary Pertaining to the rules of evidence or the evidence in a particular case.

evidentiary hearing A hearing on the admissibility of evidence into a civil or criminal trial.

evidentiary presumption A situation in which the establishment of one fact allows inference of another fact or circumstance.

evolving standards of decency Doctrine that holds that what constitutes cruel and unusual punishment must be determined in light of changing social standards of acceptable government conduct.

excessive bail An unreasonably large dollar amount or unreasonable conditions imposed by a court as a prerequisite for a defendant to be released before trial; prohibited by the Eighth Amendment.

excessive fines Fines that are deemed to be greater than is appropriate for the punishment of a particular crime.

exclusionary rule Judicial doctrine forbidding the use of evidence in a criminal trial where the evidence was obtained in violation of the defendant's constitutional rights.

exculpatory That which tends to exonerate a person of allegations of wrongdoing.

excusable homicide A death caused by accident or misfortune.

executive agreement An agreement between the United States and one or more foreign countries entered into by the president without ratification by the Senate.

executive order An order by a president or governor directing some particular action to be taken.

executive privilege The right of the president to withhold certain information from Congress or a court of law.

exhaustion of remedies The requirement that a party seeking review by a court first exhaust all legal options for resolution of the issue by nonjudicial authorities or lower courts.

exigent circumstances Situations that demand unusual or immediate action.

ex officio "By virtue of the office."

ex parte Term for a proceeding in which only one party is involved or represented.

expert witness A witness with specialized knowledge or training called to testify in his or her field of expertise.

ex post facto "After the fact."

ex post facto **law** A retroactive law that criminalizes actions that were innocent at the time they were taken or that increases punishment for a criminal act after it was committed.

expressive conduct Conduct undertaken to express a message.

expressive religious conduct Conduct undertaken to express a religious message.

ex proprio vigore "By its own force."

ex rel. "On the relation or information of." A term usually designating the name of a person on whose behalf the government is bringing legal action against another party.

extradition The surrender of a person by one jurisdiction to another for the purpose of criminal prosecution.

ex vi termini "By definition"; from the very meaning of the term or expression used.

facial attack A legal attack on the constitutionality of a law as it is written, as opposed to how it is applied in practice.

facial neutrality Condition existing when a law, on its face, does not discriminate between or among classes of persons.

facial validity The quality of being legitimate or permissible on its face. A law may nevertheless be invalid as applied in a given case.

fair hearing A hearing in a court of law that conforms to standards of procedural justice.

fair notice The requirement stemming from due process that government provide adequate notice to a person before it deprives that person of life, liberty, or property.

fair trial doctrine The doctrine whereby, under the Fourteenth Amendment, states are required to provide fair trials to persons accused of crimes.

federal bureaucracy The collective term for the myriad departments, agencies, and bureaus of the federal government.

Federal Bureau of Investigation The primary agency charged with investigating violations of federal criminal laws.

federal courts The courts operated by the U.S. government.

federal habeas corpus review Review of a state criminal trial by a federal district court on a writ of habeas corpus after the defendant has been convicted, incarcerated, and has exhausted appellate remedies in the state courts.

federalism The constitutional distribution of government power and responsibility between the national government and the states.

The Federalist Papers The collection of essays written in 1788 by James Madison, Alexander Hamilton, and John Jay in support of ratification of the Constitution.

federal preemption The doctrine that federal law preempts states from enforcing regulations in areas necessarily occupied solely by the federal government.

federal question An issue arising under the U.S. Constitution or a federal statute, executive order, regulation, or treaty.

federal question jurisdiction The authority of federal courts to decide issues of national law.

Federal Register The publication containing all regulations proposed and promulgated by federal agencies.

Federal Rules of Appellate Procedure Rules governing the practice of law in the U.S. Courts of Appeals.

federal system A political system in which sovereignty is shared by national and regional governments.

fee simple Ownership of real property; the highest interest in real estate the law will permit.

felony A serious crime for which a person may be incarcerated for more than one year.

felony murder A homicide committed during the course of committing another felony other than murder (for example, armed robbery). The felonious act substitutes for malice aforethought ordinarily required in murder.

field sobriety test A test administered by police to persons suspected of driving while intoxicated. Usually consists of requiring the suspect to demonstrate the ability to perform such physical acts as touching one's finger to nose or walking backward.

Fifteenth Amendment Amendment to the Constitution, ratified in 1870, that prohibits states from denying the right to vote on account of race.

Fifth Amendment Amendment included in the Bill of Rights providing for due process of law and prohibiting compulsory self-incrimination.

Fifth Amendment Due Process Clause The clause of the Fifth Amendment that forbids the federal government from depriving persons of life, liberty, or property without due process of law.

fighting words Utterances that are inherently likely to provoke a violent response from the audience.

fighting words doctrine The First Amendment doctrine that holds that certain utterances are not constitutionally protected as free speech if they are inherently likely to provoke a violent response from the audience.

First Amendment Amendment included in the Bill of Rights that protects freedom of religion and freedom of expression.

First Amendment absolutism The idea that the First Amendment prohibits any and all attempts by government to regulate the content of expression.

first appearance An initial judicial proceeding at which the defendant is informed of the charges, and the right to counsel, and a determination is made as to bail.

first degree murder The highest degree of unlawful homicide usually defined as "an unlawful act committed with the premeditated intent to take the life of a human being."

force The element of compulsion in such crimes against persons as rape and robbery.

forcible rape Rape, as defined by common law; that is, sexual intercourse with a female, other than the offender's wife, by force and against the will of the victim.

forensic experts Persons qualified in the application of scientific knowledge to legal principles, usually applied to those who participate in discourse or who testify in court.

forensic methods Investigatory procedures that apply scientific knowledge to legal principles.

foreperson The person selected by fellow jurors to chair deliberations and report the jury's verdict.

forfeiture Sacrifice of ownership or some right (usually property) as a penalty.

forgery The crime of making a false written instrument or materially altering a written instrument (such as a check, promissory note, or college transcript) with the intent to defraud.

fornication Sexual intercourse between unmarried persons; an offense in some jurisdictions.

Fourteenth Amendment Amendment to the Constitution, ratified in 1868, prohibiting states from depriving persons in their jurisdiction of due process of law.

Fourth Amendment Amendment within the Bill of Rights prohibiting unreasonable searches and seizures.

fraud Intentional deception or distortion in order to gain something of value.

freedom of assembly The right of people to peaceably assemble in a public place.

freedom of association The right of people to associate freely without unwarranted interference by government; implicitly protected by the First Amendment.

freedom of expression A summary term embracing freedom of speech and freedom of the press as well as symbolic speech and expressive conduct.

Freedom of Information Act Federal statute providing citizens a broad right of access to government information.

freedom of religion The First Amendment right to free exercise of one's religion.

freedom of speech The right to speak or express oneself freely without unreasonable interference by government.

freedom of the press The right to publish newspapers, magazines, and other print media free from prior restraint or sanctions by the government.

Free Exercise Clause Clause in the First Amendment prohibiting Congress from abridging the free exercise of religion.

free exercise of religion The constitutional right to be free from government coercion or restraint with respect to religious beliefs and practices; guaranteed by the First Amendment.

free marketplace of ideas The notion that expression should be unrestricted so that ideas can be traded freely in society, much as goods are freely exchanged in the marketplace.

frivolous appeals An appeal wholly lacking in legal merit.

fruit of the poisonous tree doctrine The doctrine that evidence derived from illegally obtained and thus inadmissible evidence is itself tainted and therefore likewise inadmissible.

Full Faith and Credit Clause The constitutional requirement (Article IV, Section 1) that states recognize and give effect to the records and legal proceedings of other states.

full opinion decision An appellate judicial decision rendered with one or more written opinions expressing the views of the judges in the case.

fundamental constitutional rights Those constitutional rights that have been declared to be fundamental by the courts. Includes First Amendment freedoms, the right to vote, and the right to privacy.

fundamental error An error in a judicial proceeding that adversely affects the substantial rights of the accused.

fundamental rights Those rights, whether or not explicitly stated in the Constitution, deemed to be basic and essential to a person's liberty and dignity.

gag order An order by a judge prohibiting certain parties from speaking publicly or privately about a particular case.

gambling Operating or playing a game for money in the expectation of gaining more than the amount played.

gay rights Summary term referring to the idea that persons should be permitted to engage in private homosexual conduct and be free from discrimination based on their sexual orientation.

gender-based classifications Laws that discriminate on the basis of gender.

gender-based peremptory challenges   A challenge to a prospective juror's competency to serve based solely on the prospective juror's gender.

gender equity   The idea that women should receive equal benefits conferred by government.

gender-neutral   Term for a law or practice that applies equally to males and females—that is, one that is nondiscriminatory. For example, rape laws traditionally proscribed acts by a male against a female, whereas newer sexual battery laws proscribe acts by or against a person of either gender and thus are gender-neutral.

general court-martial   A court-martial composed of three or more military members and a military judge or a military judge alone with jurisdiction to try the most serious offenses under the Uniform Code of Military Justice.

general objection   An objection raised against a witness's testimony or introduction of evidence when the objecting party does not recite a specific ground for the objection.

general warrant   A search or arrest warrant that is not particular as to the person to be arrested or the property to be seized.

gerrymander   To intentionally manipulate legislative district boundaries for political purposes.

good-faith exception   An exception to the exclusionary rule. Whereas the exclusionary rule bars the use of evidence obtained by a search warrant later found to be defective, the exception allows use of such evidence if the police acted in good faith that the warrant was valid.

good-time credit   Credit toward early release from prison based on good behavior during confinement (often referred to as "gain time").

grandfather clause   (1) In its modern, general sense, any legal provision protecting someone from losing a right or benefit as a result of a change in policy. (2) In its historic sense, a legal provision limiting the right to vote to persons whose ancestors held the right to vote prior to passage of the Fifteenth Amendment in 1870.

grand jury   A group of twelve to twenty-three citizens convened to hear evidence in criminal cases to determine whether indictment is warranted.

group rights   Rights that people have by virtue of membership in a group, as distinct from purely individual rights.

habeas corpus   "You have the body." *See:* habeas corpus, writ of.

habeas corpus, **writ of**   A judicial order issued to an official holding someone in custody, requiring the official to bring the prisoner to court for the purpose of allowing the court to determine whether that person is being held legally. *See also:* habeas corpus.

habitual offender   One who has been repeatedly convicted of crimes.

habitual offender statute   A law that imposes an additional punishment on a criminal who has previously been convicted of crimes.

handwriting exemplar   A sample of a suspect's handwriting.

hard-core pornography   Pornography that is extremely graphic in its depiction of sexual conduct.

harmless error   A procedural or substantive error that does not affect the outcome of a judicial proceeding.

harmless error analysis   Judicial determination as to whether a particular procedural error requires reversal of a lower court's judgment.

harmless error doctrine   The doctrine by which minor or harmless errors during a trial do not require reversal of the lower court's judgment by an appellate court. To be considered harmless, an error of constitutional magnitude must be found by the appellate court to be "harmless beyond any reasonable doubt."

hate crimes   Crimes in which the victim is selected on the basis of race, religion, or ethnicity.

hate speech   Offensive speech directed at members of racial, religious, or ethnic minorities.

hearing   A public proceeding in a court of law, legislature, or administrative body for the purpose of ascertaining facts and deciding matters of law or policy.

hearsay evidence   Statements made by someone other than a witness offered in evidence at a trial or hearing to prove the truth of the matter asserted.

heightened scrutiny   The requirement that government justify a challenged policy by showing that it is substantially necessary to the achievement of an important objective.

high crimes and misdemeanors   Offenses for which an official of the federal government may be impeached and removed from office by Congress.

holding   The legal principle drawn from a judicial decision.

homicide   The killing of a human being.

hot pursuit   (1) The right of police to cross jurisdictional lines to apprehend a suspect or criminal. (2) The Fourth Amendment doctrine allowing warrantless searches and arrests where police pursue a fleeing suspect into a protected area.

house arrest   A sentencing alternative to incarceration where the offender is allowed to leave home only for employment and approved community service activities.

human rights statutes   State laws protecting people from discrimination in a variety of forms.

hung jury   A trial jury unable to reach a verdict.

Hyde amendment   A federal law that prohibits the use of federal welfare funds to pay for nontherapeutic abortions.

hypothetical question   A question based on an assumed set of facts. Hypothetical questions may be asked of expert witnesses in criminal trials.

illegitimacy   The condition of being born out of wedlock.

imminent lawless action   Unlawful conduct that is about to take place and which is inevitable unless there is intervention by the authorities.

imminently dangerous or outrageous conduct   The type of action that, when resulting in someone's death, usually characterizes second-degree murder.

immunity   Exemption from civil suit or prosecution. *See also:* transactional immunity; use immunity.

impeachment   (1) A legislative act bringing a charge against a public official that, if proven in a legislative trial, will cause his or her removal from public office. (2) Impugning the credibility of a witness by introducing contradictory evidence or proving his or her bad character.

implied consent   An agreement or acquiescence manifested by a person's actions or inaction.

implied consent statute   A law providing that by accepting a license a driver arrested for a traffic offense consents to urine, blood, and breath tests to determine blood alcohol content.

implied powers   Governmental powers not stated in but implied by the Constitution.

implied powers, doctrine of   A basic doctrine of American constitutional law derived from the Necessary and Proper Clause of Article I, Section 8. Under this doctrine, Congress is not limited to exercising those powers specifically enumerated in Article I but rather may exercise powers reasonably related to the fulfillment of its broad constitutional powers and responsibilities.

Imports-Exports Clause   Article I, Section 10, Clause 2 of the Constitution, restricting state power to tax imports and exports.

impoundment   (1) Action by a president in refusing to allow expenditures approved by Congress. (2) In criminal law, the seizure and holding of a vehicle or other property by the police.

in camera   "In a chamber." In private; term referring to a judicial proceeding or conference from which the public is excluded.

incapacitation   The process of making it impossible for someone to do something.

incapacity   An inability, legal or actual, to act.

incarceration   Imprisonment.

incest   Sexual intercourse with a close blood relative or, in some cases, a person related by affinity.

inchoate offenses   Offenses preparatory to committing other crimes. Inchoate offenses include attempt, conspiracy, and solicitation.

incite   To provoke or set in motion.

inciting a riot   The crime of instigating or provoking a riot.

incorporation   The process by which most provisions of the Bill of Rights have been extended to limit state action by way of the Due Process Clause of the Fourteenth Amendment. Specific protections of the Bill of Rights are said to be incorporated within the Fourteenth Amendment's broad restrictions on the states.

inculpatory   That which tends to incriminate.

indefinite sentence   Form of criminal sentencing whereby a judge imposes a term of incarceration within statutory parameters, and corrections officials determine actual time served through parole or other means.

independent agencies   Federal agencies located outside the major cabinet-level departments.

independent counsel   A special prosecutor appointed to investigate and, if warranted, prosecute official misconduct.

independent source doctrine   The doctrine that permits evidence to be admitted at trial as long as it was obtained independently from illegally obtained evidence.

independent state grounds   The doctrine that an individual's claim to a right or benefit not supported by federal law will nevertheless be recognized by a federal court if a state court has found that the claimed right or benefit rests on a valid provision of state law.

indeterminate sentence   A prison sentence for an indefinite time, but within stipulated parameters, that allows correction officials to determine the prisoner's release date.

indictment   A formal document handed down by a grand jury accusing one or more persons of the commission of a crime or crimes.

indigency   Poverty; inability to afford legal representation.

indigent defendants   Defendants who cannot afford to retain private legal counsel and are therefore entitled to be represented by a public defender or a court-appointed lawyer.

indirect contempt   An act committed outside the presence of the court that insults the court or obstructs a judicial proceeding.

individual rights   In the traditional constitutional law sense, the legal protections for individuals against government actions that threaten life, liberty, or property.

ineffective representation   Representation by an attorney who is incompetent or less than reasonably effective.

inevitable discovery exception   An exception to the *Miranda* requirements and the fruit of the poisonous tree doctrine; allows the admission of evidence that was derived from inadmissible evidence if it inevitably would have been discovered independently by lawful means.

inflammatory remarks   Remarks by counsel during a trial designed to excite the passions of the jury.

in forma pauperis   "In the manner of a pauper." Waiver of filing costs and other fees associated with judicial proceedings to allow an indigent person to proceed.

information   A document filed by a prosecutor charging one or more persons with commission of crime.

inherent executive power   The powers of the president that flow from the nature of the office rather than from specific provisions of Article II.

inherently suspect   A law, policy, or classification that is, from a constitutional standpoint, questionable on its face.

inherent power   The power existing in an agency, institution, or individual by definition of the office.

initial appearance   After arrest, the first appearance of the accused before a judge or magistrate.

injunction   A judicial order requiring a person to do, or to refrain from doing, a designated thing.

in loco parentis   "In the place of the parent(s)."

inmate   One who is confined in a jail or prison.

in personam   Term referring to legal actions brought against a person, as distinct from actions against property. *See also: in rem.*

in propria persona   "In one's proper person." Term referring to the proper person to bring a legal action or make a motion before a court of law.

in re   "In the matter of."

in rem   Term referring to legal actions brought against things rather than persons. *See also: in personam.*

insanity   A degree of mental illness that negates the legal capacity or responsibility of the affected person.

insanity defense   A defense that seeks to exonerate the accused by showing that he or she was insane at the time of the crime and thus not legally responsible.

insufficient evidence Evidence that falls short of establishing that required by law; usually referring to evidence that does not legally establish an offense or a defense.

intelligible principle standard The doctrine whereby, in delegating power to the executive branch, Congress must provide a clear statement of policy to guide executive discretion.

intent A state of mind in which a person seeks to accomplish a given result through a course of action.

inter alia "Among other things."

intergovernmental tax immunity The doctrine that federal and state governments may not levy taxes on one another.

intermediate appellate courts Appellate courts positioned below the supreme or highest appellate court, whose primary function is to decide routine appeals not deserving review by the Supreme Court.

intermediate scrutiny *See*: heightened scrutiny.

interposition The archaic doctrine holding that when the federal government attempts to act unlawfully on an object within the domain of the state governments, a state may interpose itself between the federal government and the object of the federal government's action.

interpretation The process of assigning meaning to a text.

interpretivism The theory of constitutional interpretation holding that judges should confine themselves to the plain meaning of the text, the intentions of the Framers, and/or the historical meaning of the document.

interrogation Questioning of a suspect by police or questioning of a witness by counsel.

interrogatories Written questions put to a witness.

interstate agreements Formal agreements or compacts between or among states.

interstate commerce Commercial activity potentially extending beyond the boundaries of a state.

Interstate Commerce Act of 1887 Landmark act of Congress establishing the Interstate Commerce Commission.

interstate compacts Agreements between or among state governments, somewhat analogous to treaties.

intoxication A state of drunkenness resulting from the use of alcoholic beverages or drugs.

invalidate Annul, negate, set aside.

invasion of privacy A tort involving the unreasonable or unwarranted intrusion on the privacy of an individual.

inventory search An exception to the warrant requirement that allows police who legally impound a vehicle to conduct a routine inventory of the contents of the vehicle.

investigatory detention Brief detention of suspects by a police officer who has reasonable suspicion that criminal activity is afoot. *See also*: stop and frisk.

invidious Arousing animosity, envy, or resentment.

ipse dixit "He himself said it." An assertion resting on the authority of an individual.

ipso facto "By the mere fact"; by the fact itself.

irreparable injury An injury for which the award of money may not be adequate compensation and that may require the issuance of an injunction to fulfill the requirements of justice.

irresistible impulse A desire that cannot be resisted due to impairment of the will by mental disease.

Jim Crow laws Laws originating in the nineteenth century requiring various forms of racial segregation.

joinder The coupling of two or more criminal prosecutions.

joinder and severance of parties The uniting or severing of two or more parties charged with a crime or crimes.

joinder of offenses The uniting for trial in one case of different charges or counts alleged in an information or indictment.

joint resolution An act expressing the will of both houses of Congress in attempting to impose duties or limitations on parties outside the Congress; must be presented to the president for signature or veto.

judgment A judicial determination as to the claims made by parties to a lawsuit. In a criminal case, the court's formal declaration to the accused regarding the legal consequences of a determination of guilt.

judgment of acquittal (1) In a nonjury trial, a judge's order exonerating a defendant based on a finding that the defendant is not guilty. (2) In a case heard by a jury that finds a defendant guilty, a judge's order exonerating the defendant on the ground that the evidence was not legally sufficient to support the jury's finding of guilt.

judicial activism Approach to jurisprudence whose underlying philosophy is that judges should exercise power vigorously, as opposed to exercising judicial restraint.

judicial behavior The way judges make decisions; the academic study thereof.

judicial conference A meeting of judges to deliberate on the disposition of a case.

judicial federalism The constitutional relationship between federal and state courts of law.

judicial notice The act of a court recognizing, without proof, the existence of certain facts that are commonly known. Such facts are often brought to the court's attention through the use of a calendar or almanac.

judicial restraint Approach to jurisprudence whose underlying philosophy is that judges should exercise power cautiously and show deference to precedent and to the decisions of other branches of government, as opposed to exercising judicial activism.

judicial review Generally, the review of any issue by a court of law. In American constitutional law, the authority of a court to invalidate acts of government on constitutional grounds.

Judiciary Act of 1789 Landmark statute establishing the federal courts system.

jurisdiction "To speak the law." The geographical area within which, the subject matter with respect to which, and the persons over whom a court can properly exercise its power.

juris privati "The private law," including such areas as torts, contracts, and property.

jurist A person who is skilled or well versed in the law; often applied to lawyers and judges.

jury A group of citizens convened for the purpose of deciding factual questions relevant to a civil or criminal case.

jury instructions A judge's explanation of the law applicable to a case being heard by a jury.

jury nullification The act of a jury disregarding the court's instructions and rendering a verdict based on the consciences of the jurors.

jury pardon An action taken by a jury, despite the quality of the evidence, acquitting a defendant or convicting the defendant of a lesser crime than charged.

jury selection The process of selecting prospective jurors at random from lists of persons representative of the community.

jury trial A judicial proceeding to determine a defendant's guilt or innocence, conducted before a body of persons sworn to render a verdict based on the law and the evidence presented.

just compensation The constitutional requirement that a party whose property is taken by government under the power of eminent domain be justly compensated for the loss.

Just Compensation Clause Clause found in the Fifth Amendment requiring the federal government to provide owners reasonable and fair compensation when taking their property for a public use.

justiciability Appropriateness for judicial decision. A justiciable dispute is one that can be effectively decided by a court of law.

justifiable homicide Killing another in self-defense or defense of others when there is serious danger of death or great bodily harm to self or others, or when authorized by law.

justifiable use of force The necessary and reasonable use of force by a person in self-defense, defense of another, or defense of property.

justification A valid reason for one's actions.

juvenile A person who has not yet attained the age of legal majority.

juvenile court A judicial tribunal having jurisdiction over minors defined as juveniles who are alleged to be status offenders or to have committed acts of delinquency.

juvenile delinquency Actions of a juvenile in violation of the criminal law.

juvenile delinquency hearing Hearing in which a juvenile court determines whether a juvenile should be found to be delinquent. Analogous to a criminal trial in the adult justice system.

knock and announce The provision under federal and most state laws that requires a law enforcement officer to first knock and announce his or her presence and purpose before entering a person's home to serve a search warrant.

knowing and intelligent waiver A waiver of rights that is made with an awareness of the consequences.

laissez-faire capitalism The theory holding that a capitalist economy functions best when government refrains from interfering with the marketplace.

law clerk A judge's staff attorney.

lawmaking function One of the principal functions of an appellate court, often referred to as the law development function.

leading question A question that suggests an answer; permitted at a criminal trial on cross-examination of witnesses and in other limited instances.

least restrictive means test A judicial inquiry as to whether a particular policy that is being challenged as an infringement of some fundamental right is the least burdensome means of achieving the government's objective.

legislation Law enacted by a lawmaking body.

legislative veto A statutory provision under which a legislative body is permitted to overrule a decision of an executive agency.

legislature An elected lawmaking body such as the Congress of the United States or a state assembly.

Lemon test Three-part test set forth in *Lemon v. Kurtzman* (1971). To pass muster under the Establishment Clause, a law must have a secular purpose, must not have the principal effect of advancing or inhibiting religion, and must avoid excessive entanglement between government and religious institutions.

lex non scripta "The unwritten law" or common law.

liability A broad legal term connoting debt, responsibility, or obligation; the condition of being bound to pay a debt, obligation, or judgment. This responsibility can be either civil or criminal.

libel The tort of defamation through published material. *See:* defamation.

libertarianism A philosophy that stresses individual freedom as the highest good.

liberty The absence of restraint.

liberty of contract The freedom to enter into contracts without undue interference from government.

limited government An idea central to republican constitutionalism in which the power of government is limited by constitutional provisions specifically defining the nature and scope of governmental powers and prohibiting government from acting in detriment to individual rights and liberties.

limiting doctrines Doctrines by which courts may refuse to render a decision on the merits in a case. *See:* abstention; exhaustion of remedies; political questions doctrine; mootness; standing.

line-item veto Executive act nullifying certain portions of a bill.

lineup A police identification procedure in which a suspect is included in a lineup with other persons who are exhibited to a victim or witness.

literacy test A test of reading and/or writing skills, often given as a prerequisite to employment. At one time, literacy tests were required by many states as preconditions for voting in elections.

litigant A party to, or participant in, a legal action.

local aspects of interstate commerce Regulations of interstate commerce imposed by local governments in response to unique local conditions such as the shape of a harbor.

loitering Standing around idly; "hanging around."

loss of civil rights Forfeiture of certain rights, such as voting, as a result of a criminal conviction.

lottery A drawing in which prizes are distributed to winners selected by lot from among those who have participated by paying a consideration.

magistrate A judge with minor or limited authority.

Magna Carta The "Great Charter" signed by King John in 1215 guaranteeing the legal rights of English subjects. Generally considered the foundation of Anglo-American constitutionalism.

majority opinion An appellate court opinion joined in by a majority of the judges who heard the appeal.

mala in se "Evil in itself." Term referring to crimes like murder that are universally condemned.

malapportionment A condition that exists when legislative districts in a state or subdivisions of a county or municipality contain substantially unequal numbers of voters; may result naturally as a function of population shifts or through deliberate gerrymandering.

mala prohibita "Prohibited evil." Term referring to crimes that are wrong primarily because the law declares them to be wrong.

malfeasance Misconduct that adversely affects the performance of official duties.

malice aforethought The mental predetermination to commit an illegal act.

mandamus, **writ of** "We command." A judicial order commanding a public official or an organization to perform a specified duty.

mandate A command or order.

manifest necessity That is which clearly or obviously necessary or essential.

market participant exception The doctrine whereby states may impose regulations to inhibit competition by out-of-state competitors where the state is itself a participant in the market.

material Important, relevant, necessary.

memorandum decision A judicial decision rendered without a supporting Opinion of the Court.

mens rea "Guilty mind"; criminal intent.

militia Historically, a military force composed of all able-bodied citizens, in service only during time of war, rebellion, or emergency.

minimal scrutiny The most lenient form of judicial review of policies challenged as violations of civil rights and liberties.

Miranda **warning** The warning given by police to individuals who are taken into custody before they are interrogated. Based on the Supreme Court's decision in *Miranda v. Arizona* (1966), the warning informs persons in custody that they have the right to remain silent and to have a lawyer present during questioning, and that anything they say can and will be used against them in a court of law.

misappropriation Wrongful taking or diversion of funds or other property.

miscarriage of justice Decision of a court that is inconsistent with the substantial rights of a party to the case.

misdemeanor A minor crime usually punishable by a fine or confinement for less than one year.

misrepresentation An untrue statement of fact made to deceive or mislead.

mistake of fact Unconscious ignorance of a fact or belief in the existence of something that does not exist.

mistake of law An erroneous opinion of legal principles applied to a set of facts.

mistrial A trial that is terminated due to misconduct, procedural error, or a hung jury (one that is unable to reach a verdict).

mitigating circumstances Circumstances or factors that tend to lessen culpability.

mitigating factors *See:* mitigating circumstances.

mitigation Reduction or alleviation, usually of punishment.

mockery of justice test Judicial test for determining whether a defendant was provided adequate representation. The question is whether performance by counsel constituted a mockery of justice.

modern administrative state Term for the highly bureaucratized federal government that emerged in the twentieth century.

moment of silence Policy under which public school students are required to observe a minute of silence at the beginning of the school day.

monetary fines Sums of money offenders are required to pay as punishment for the commission of crimes.

monogamy The practice of having only one spouse, as distinct from bigamy or polygamy.

moot A point that no longer has any practical significance; academic.

mootness Term referring to a question that does not involve rights currently at issue in, or pertinent to, the outcome of a case.

moral individualism The doctrine that individuals, not society or government, should make moral choices.

motion An application to a court to obtain a particular ruling or order.

motion for a new trial A formal request made to a trial court to hold a new trial in a particular case that has already been adjudicated.

motion for rehearing A formal request made to a court of law to convene another hearing in a case in which the court has already ruled.

motion to dismiss A formal request to a trial court to dismiss the criminal charges against the defendant.

motive A person's conscious reason for acting.

myth of legality The belief that judicial decisions are a function of legal rules, procedures, and principles rather than the ideological leanings or policy preferences of judges.

narrowly tailored Term used to describe a policy that is carefully designed to achieve its intended goal with a minimal negative impact on civil liberties.

narrowness doctrine The doctrine that judicial decisions should be framed in the narrowest possible terms or based on the narrowest possible grounds.

national supremacy The doctrine that holds that when state and federal authority collide, the federal authority must prevail.

natural law Principles of human conduct believed to be ordained by God or nature, existing prior to and superseding human law.

natural rights   Rights believed to be inherent in human beings, the existence of which is not dependent on their recognition by government. In classical liberalism, natural rights are "life, liberty, and property." As recognized by the Declaration of Independence, they are "life, liberty, and the pursuit of happiness."

negligence   The failure to exercise ordinary care or caution.

neutral and detached officer   A judge or magistrate who is without an interest in the outcome of a case.

New Equal Protection   A modern interpretation of the Equal Protection Clause of the Fourteenth Amendment under which policies that impinge on fundamental rights or discriminate on the basis of suspect classifications are presumed invalid by the courts.

new federalism   Term for the variety of efforts in recent decades aimed at revitalizing the role of the states in the federal system or returning power to them.

New Jersey Plan   A plan introduced by the New Jersey delegation at the Constitutional Convention of 1787. It called for a unicameral legislature in which all states would be equally represented.

new property   Term referring to a person's interest in government benefits or entitlements.

Nineteenth Amendment   Amendment to the Constitution, adopted in 1920, which prohibits the denial of voting rights on account of gender.

Ninth Amendment   Amendment contained within the Bill of Rights that recognizes rights retained by the people even though they are not specifically enumerated in the Constitution.

no contest plea   A plea to a criminal charge that, although it is not an admission of guilt, generally has the same effect as a plea of guilty. *See also: nolo contendere.*

nolo contendere   "I will not contest it." Alternate term for a plea of no contest in a criminal case.

nondeadly force   Force that does not result in death.

nondelegation doctrine   The doctrine that Congress may not delegate its legislative authority to the executive branch.

noninterpretivism   A term referring to a variety of theories of constitutional interpretation, the common element of which is the rejection of interpretivism. *See also*: interpretivism.

nonunanimous verdicts   Jury verdicts rendered by a less-than-unanimous vote of the jurors.

notary public   A person empowered by law to administer oaths, to certify things as true, and to perform various minor official acts.

notice of appeal   Document filed with an appellate court notifying the court of an appeal from a judgment of a lower court.

nuisance   An unlawful or unreasonable use of a person's property that results in an injury to another or to the public.

nullification   The act of rendering something invalid; the process by which something may be invalidated. Historically, a doctrine under which states claimed the right to nullify actions of the national government.

obiter dicta   "Something said in passing." Incidental statements in a judicial opinion that are not binding and are unnecessary to support the decision.

objective test   A legal test based on external circumstances rather than the perceptions or intentions of an individual actor.

obscenity   Explicit sexual material that is patently offensive, appeals to a prurient or unnatural interest in sex, and lacks serious scientific, artistic, or literary content.

obstruction of justice   The crime of impeding or preventing law enforcement or the administration of justice.

open fields exception   An exception to the Fourth Amendment search warrant requirement, holding that Fourth Amendment protection does not apply to the open fields around a home, even if these open fields are private property.

opening statement   A prosecutor's or defense lawyer's initial statement to the judge or jury in a trial.

open public trial   A trial that is held in public and is open to spectators.

opinion   A written statement accompanying a judicial decision, authored by one or more judges, supporting or dissenting from that decision.

opinion concurring in the judgment   A judicial opinion in which the author agrees with the decision of the court, but for reasons other than those stated in the court's principal opinion.

opinion evidence   Testimony in which the witness expresses an opinion, as distinct from knowledge of specific facts.

Opinion of the Court   An opinion announcing both the decision of the court and its supporting rationale. The opinion can either be a majority opinion or a unanimous opinion.

oral argument   A hearing before an appellate court in which counsel for the parties appear for the purpose of making statements and answering questions from the bench.

ordinance   An enactment of a local governing body such as a city council or commission.

organized crime   Syndicates involved in racketeering and other criminal activities.

original intent, doctrine of   The doctrine holding that the Constitution should be interpreted and applied according to the intentions of the Framers, insofar as those intentions can be determined.

originalism   The doctrine that courts must preserve the original meaning of the Constitution.

original jurisdiction   The authority of a court of law to hear a case in the first instance.

original package doctrine   Archaic doctrine under which states were prohibited from imposing taxes on imported goods that, although no longer in the stream of commerce, remained in their original packages.

overbreadth doctrine   First Amendment doctrine that holds that a law is invalid if it can be applied to punish people for engaging in constitutionally protected expression.

overrule   To reverse or annul by subsequent action.

oversight   The responsibility of a legislative body to monitor the activities of government agencies it created.

oversight hearings   Formal hearings conducted for the purpose of monitoring actions by government agencies.

panel A set of jurors or judges assigned to hear a case.

pardon An executive action that mitigates or sets aside punishment for a crime.

parens patriae "The parent of the country." Term referring to the role of the state as guardian of minors or other legally disabled persons.

parliamentary system A democratic system of government in which there is no formal separation of the legislative and executive offices. The leader of the majority party in the parliament is the prime minister, or chief executive.

parochial legislation Legislation that favors narrow, localized interests.

parole The conditional early release from prison.

parole revocation hearing An administrative hearing held for the purpose of determining whether an offender's parole should be revoked.

partisan gerrymandering The intentional manipulation of legislative district lines in order to provide one political party a competitive advantage over another.

party (1) A person taking part in a legal transaction; includes plaintiffs and defendants in lawsuits but also has a far broader legal connotation. (2) In politics, an organization established for the principal purpose of recruiting and nominating candidates for public office.

pat-down search A manual search of the exterior of a suspect's outer garments.

patently offensive Plainly or obviously offensive; disgusting.

penal Of or pertaining to punishment.

pendency of the appeal The period after an appeal is filed but before the appeal is adjudicated.

penitentiary A prison.

penology The study or practice of prison management.

penumbra An implied right or power emanating from an enumerated right or power.

per curiam "By the court." Term referring to an opinion attributed to a court collectively, usually not identified with the name of any particular member of the court.

peremptory challenge An objection to the selection of a prospective juror in which the attorney making the challenge is not required to state the reason for the objection.

per se "By itself; in itself."

petition A written request, usually addressed to a court, asking for a specified action. Sometimes the term indicates written requests in an *ex parte* proceeding, where there is no adverse party. In some jurisdictions, the term refers to the first pleading in a lawsuit.

petitioner A person who brings a petition before a court of law.

petit jury A trial jury, usually composed of either six or twelve persons.

petty (petit) offenses Minor crimes for which fines or short jail terms are the only prescribed modes of punishment.

picketing Carrying signs of protest in the public forum.

places of public accommodation Businesses that open their doors to the general public.

plaintiff The party initiating legal action; the complaining party.

plain view Readily visible to the naked eye. *See also*: plain view doctrine.

plain view doctrine The Fourth Amendment doctrine under which a police officer may seize evidence of crime that is readily visible to the officer's naked eye as long as the officer is legally in the place where the evidence becomes visible.

plea bargain An agreement between a defendant and a prosecutor whereby the defendant agrees to plead guilty in exchange for some concession (for example, a reduction in the severity or number of charges brought).

plea of guilty A formal answer to a criminal charge in which the accused acknowledges guilt and waives the right to trial.

plea of not guilty A formal answer to a criminal charge in which the accused denies guilt and thus exercises the right to a trial.

plenary Full, complete; often used with reference to the nature and extent of governmental powers enumerated in the federal Constitution.

plenary review Full, complete review by an appellate court.

pluralism A social or political system in which diverse groups compete for status or power; the theory that the role of government is to serve as broker among competing interest groups.

plurality opinion An opinion that states the judgment of the Court but that does not have the endorsement of a majority of justices.

pocket veto The power of a chief executive to effectively veto legislation by not acting on a bill passed within ten days prior to adjournment of a legislative session.

police deception Intentional deception by police in order to elicit incriminating statements from a suspect.

police interrogation Questioning by the police of a suspect in custody.

police power The power of government to legislate to protect public health, safety, welfare, and morality.

police powers of the states The powers of state governments to enact laws to further the public health, safety, welfare, and morality.

political dissent Organized or public opposition to the government.

political question A question that a court believes to be appropriate for decision by the legislative or the executive branch of government and thus improper for judicial decision making.

political questions doctrine The doctrine that holds that courts should avoid ruling on political questions.

poll tax A tax that must be paid before a person is permitted to vote in an election.

polling the jury Practice in which trial judge asks each member of the jury to affirm that he or she supports the jury's verdict.

polygamy Plural marriage; having more than one spouse.

polygraph evidence Results of lie detector tests (generally inadmissible into evidence).

popular sovereignty The idea that political authority is vested ultimately not in the rulers but in the people they rule.

pornography Material that appeals to the sexual impulse or appetite.

postconviction relief Term applied to various mechanisms a defendant may use to challenge a conviction after other routes of appeal have been exhausted.

power of contempt The authority of a court of law to punish someone who insults the court or flouts its authority.

power to investigate The power of a legislative body to conduct hearings and subpoena witnesses in order to investigate an issue or area over which it has legislative authority.

power to regulate interstate commerce The power of Congress, and to a lesser extent the powers of state and local governments, to enact laws and regulations affecting commerce involving more than one state.

precedent A judicial decision cited as authority controlling or influencing the outcome of a similar case.

preemption In constitutional law, the doctrine under which a field of public policy, previously open to action by the states, is brought by the U.S. Congress within the primary or exclusive control of the national government.

preferred freedoms Certain freedoms, in particular the First Amendment freedom of speech, that are accorded greater protection than other activities. When a legislative measure that restricts preferred freedoms is challenged, the ordinary presumption that the restriction is constitutional is reversed in favor of the presumptive protection of free expression.

prejudicial error An error at trial that substantially affects the interests of the accused.

preliminary hearing A hearing held to determine whether there is sufficient evidence to hold an accused for trial.

preliminary injunction An injunction issued pending a trial on the merits of the case.

preparatory conduct Actions taken in order to prepare to commit a crime.

preponderance of evidence Evidence that has greater weight than countervailing evidence.

presentment A synonym for indictment.

presentment requirement As outlined in the Presentment Clause (Article I, Section 7) of the Constitution, the requirement that a bill that has passed both houses of Congress be "presented" to the president for signature or veto.

presidential immunity The barrier against bringing a civil suit against the president for any of his official actions.

presidential pardon Action by the president pardoning one or more persons for the commission of a crime.

presidential power to make foreign policy The president's broad authority to set policy as it relates to international relations and foreign affairs.

presidential war powers Term referring to the president's authority as commander in chief.

presumption (1) An inference drawn by reasoning. (2) A rule of law subject to rebuttal.

presumption of constitutionality The doctrine of constitutional law holding that laws are presumed to be constitutional with the

burden of proof resting on the plaintiff to demonstrate otherwise.

presumption of innocence The notion that the accused in a criminal trial is presumed innocent until proven guilty.

presumption of validity *See*: presumption of constitutionality.

preterm conference The Supreme Court's conference held prior to the beginning of its annual term in which the Court disposes of numerous petitions for certiorari.

pretextual stop An incident in which police stop a suspicious vehicle on the pretext of a motor vehicle infraction.

pretrial detention The holding of a defendant in custody prior to trial.

pretrial discovery The process by which the defense and prosecution interrogate witnesses for the opposing party and gain access to the evidence possessed by the opposing party prior to trial.

pretrial diversion program A program in which a first-time offender is afforded the opportunity to avoid a criminal conviction by participating in some specified treatment, counseling, or community service.

pretrial motion Any of a variety of motions made by counsel prior to the inception of a trial.

pretrial publicity Media coverage of a case that has the potential to deprive a defendant of the right to a fair trial by an impartial jury.

pretrial release The release of a defendant pending trial.

preventive detention Holding a suspect in custody before trial to prevent escape or other wrongdoing.

prima facie "On the face of it"; at first glance. Term referring to a point that will be considered true unless contested or refuted.

principals Persons whose conduct involves direct participation in a crime.

prior restraint An official act preventing publication of a particular work.

prisoners' rights The set of rights that prisoners retain or attempt to assert through litigation.

private property Property held by individuals or corporations, not by the public generally.

privilege In general, an activity in which a person may engage without interference. The term is often used interchangeably with "right" in American constitutional law, with reference to the Privileges and Immunities Clauses of Article IV and the Fourteenth Amendment of the Constitution.

privileges Rights extended to persons by virtue of law.

Privileges and Immunities Clause (1) Article IV, Section 2, Clause 1, of the Constitution, providing that "Citizens of each State shall be entitled to all Privileges and Immunities of Citizens in the several States." (2) Similar provision contained in Section 1 of the Fourteenth Amendment.

probable cause Knowledge of specific facts providing reasonable grounds for believing that criminal activity is afoot.

probable cause hearing A hearing held in a court to make a formal determination on an issue of probable cause.

probation Conditional release of a convicted criminal in lieu of incarceration.

probative   Tending to prove the truth or falsehood of a proposition.

pro bono   "For the good." Performing service without compensation.

procedural criminal law   The branch of the criminal law that deals with the processes by which crimes are investigated, prosecuted, and punished.

procedural due process   Set of procedures designed to ensure fairness in a judicial or administrative proceeding.

procedural law   The law regulating governmental procedure (for example, rules of criminal procedure).

profanity   Vulgar, coarse, or filthy language; irreverence toward sacred things.

pro forma   Merely for the sake of form.

prohibition, writ of   An appellate court order preventing a lower court from exercising its jurisdiction in a particular case.

promissory estoppel   The doctrine of contract law under which a promise that induces action on the part of the promissee may be legally enforceable.

pronouncement of sentence   Formal announcement of a criminal punishment by a trial judge.

proof beyond a reasonable doubt   The standard of proof in a criminal trial or a juvenile delinquency hearing.

proper forum   The correct court or other institution in which to press a particular claim.

property rights   The bundle of rights that exist relative to private ownership and control of property.

proportionality   The degree to which a particular punishment matches the seriousness of a crime or matches the penalty other offenders have received for the same crime.

proportional representation   An electoral system in which the percentage of votes received by a given political party entitles that party to the same percentage of seats in the legislature.

proportionate representation   The idea that certain groups should be represented by ensuring that the legislature is composed according to the proportion of such groups in society.

proscribe   To forbid; prohibit.

pro se   "On one's own behalf." *See also*: pro se defense.

prosecution   Initiation and conduct of a criminal case.

prosecutor   A public official empowered to initiate criminal charges and conduct prosecutions.

prosecutorial discretion   The leeway afforded prosecutors in deciding whether or not to bring charges and to engage in plea bargaining.

prosecutorial immunity   A prosecutor's legal shield against civil suits stemming from his or her official actions.

pro se **defense**   Representing oneself in a criminal case.

protective tariffs   Taxes on products imported from other nations, which increase their cost and thus make domestic products more appealing to consumers. Opposed by supporters of free trade.

provocation   An action or behavior that prompts another person to react through criminal conduct.

proximate cause   The cause that is nearest a given effect in a causal relationship.

prurient interest   An excessive or unnatural interest in sex.

public accommodations statute   A law prohibiting various forms of discrimination by businesses that open their doors to the general public.

public defender   An attorney responsible for defending indigent persons charged with crimes.

public drunkenness   The offense of appearing in public while intoxicated.

public figures   Public officials or persons who are in the public eye.

public forum   A public space generally acknowledged as appropriate for public assemblies or expressions of views.

public law   General classification of law consisting of constitutional law, administrative law, international law, and criminal law.

public safety exception   Exception to the *Miranda* requirement that police officers promptly inform suspects taken into custody of their rights to remain silent and have an attorney present during questioning. Under the public safety exception, police may ask suspects questions motivated by a desire to protect public safety without jeopardizing the admissibility of suspects' answers to those questions or subsequent statements.

punitive damages   A sum of money awarded to the plaintiff in a civil case as a means of punishing the defendant for wrongful conduct.

punitive isolation   Solitary confinement of a person who is incarcerated.

pure speech   Communication that is purely spoken.

putting witnesses under the rule   Placing witnesses under the rule that requires them to remain outside the courtroom except when testifying.

qua   As; in the character or capacity of.

quash   To vacate or annul.

quasi-judicial authority   The authority of certain regulatory or administrative agencies to make determinations with respect to the rights of private parties under their jurisdiction.

race-conscious remedies   Remedies to racial injustices that specifically take race into account.

racial gerrymandering   The intentional manipulation of legislative district boundaries in order to diminish or enlarge the political influence of African-American or other minority voters.

racially motivated peremptory challenges   Peremptory challenges to prospective jurors, based solely on racial animus or racial stereotypes.

rational basis test   The test of the validity of a statute inquiring whether it is rationally related to a legitimate government objective.

real property   Land and buildings permanently attached thereto.

reapportionment   The redrawing of legislative district lines so as to remedy malapportionment.

reasonable doubt standard   The standard of proof in a criminal trial under which a defendant must not be convicted of a crime if after hearing all the evidence, a reasonable person would have doubt as to the defendant's guilt. Sometimes the term "reasonable doubt" is equated to lack of moral certainty.

reasonable expectation of privacy A person's reasonable expectation that his or her activities in a certain place are private; society's expectations with regard to whether activities in certain places are private.

reasonable force The maximum degree of force that is necessary to accomplish a lawful purpose.

reasonable suspicion A reasonable person's suspicion that criminal activity is afoot.

reasoning The logic of a legal argument or judicial opinion.

rebuttal witnesses Witnesses called to dispute the testimony of the opposing party's witnesses.

reciprocal immunity *See*: intergovernmental tax immunity.

recognizance An obligation to appear in a court of law at a given time.

recusal A decision of a judge to withdraw from a case, usually due to bias or personal interest in the outcome.

recuse To disqualify oneself from participating in a court case.

redeeming social importance Value to society that redeems an otherwise worthless instance of expression.

referendum An election in which voters decide a question of public policy.

regulation A legally binding rule or order prescribed by a controlling authority; generally used with respect to the rules promulgated by administrative and regulatory agencies.

rehabilitation The process of restoring someone or something to its former status; a justification for punishment emphasizing reform rather than retribution.

released time programs Public school programs in which students are permitted to leave school grounds to attend religious exercises.

release on personal recognizance Pretrial release of a defendant based solely on the defendant's promise to appear for future court dates.

relevant evidence Evidence tending to prove or disprove an alleged fact.

Religion Clauses of the First Amendment The Establishment Clause and Free Exercise Clause of the First Amendment.

Religious Freedom Restoration Act (RFRA) Act of Congress designed to enhance religious freedom vis-à-vis government; declared unconstitutional by the Supreme Court in 1997.

religious speech Expression of a religious nature.

religious tests Tests to determine whether individuals hold "appropriate" religious convictions.

remand To send back, as from a higher court to a lower court, for the latter to take specified action in a case or to follow proceedings designated by the higher court.

remedy The means by which a right is enforced or a wrong is redressed.

removal power The power of the president to remove officials in executive departments and agencies.

rendition The act of one state in surrendering a fugitive to another state.

Rendition Clause Clause of Article IV, Section 2 of the Constitution, requiring states to surrender fugitives to other states upon proper request.

repeal A legislative act removing a law from the statute books.

reply brief A brief submitted in response to an appellee's answer brief.

reporters Books containing judicial decisions and accompanying opinions. *See*: case reporters.

representative democracy A form of government in which policy decisions are made by representatives chosen in periodic competitive elections. *See*: representative government.

representative government Form of government in which officials responsible for making policy are elected by the people in periodic free elections. *See*: representative democracy.

reprimands Minor punitive actions taken by military commanders for various infractions committed by military servicepersons.

resentencing A new sentencing hearing ordered by an appellate court.

reserved powers Powers reserved to the states or the people under the Tenth Amendment.

res judicata "A thing decided." A matter decided by a judgment, connoting the firmness and finality of the judgment as it affects the parties to the lawsuit; has the general effect of bringing litigation on a contested point to an end.

res nova "New thing." A new issue or case.

resolution A legislative act expressing the will of one or both houses of the legislature. Unlike a statute, a resolution has no enforcement clause. *See also*: concurrent resolution; joint resolution.

respondent A person asked to respond to a lawsuit or writ.

restitution The act of compensating someone for losses suffered.

restrictive covenant An agreement among property holders restricting the use of property or prohibiting the rental or sale of it to certain parties.

retribution Something demanded in payment for a debt; in criminal law, the demand that a criminal pay his or her debt to society.

retroactive Changing the legal status or character of past events or transactions.

reverse To set aside a decision on appeal.

review An examination by an appellate court of a lower court's decision.

revocation The withdrawal of some right or power (for example, the revocation of parole).

RICO Act The Racketeer Influenced and Corrupt Organizations Act, passed in 1970, which essentially prohibits infiltration of organized crime into organizations or enterprises engaged in interstate commerce.

rider A small provision attached to a contract, document, or bill.

right Anything to which a person has a just and valid claim.

right of confrontation The right to cross-examine witnesses for the opposing party in a criminal case.

right of cross-examination *See*: right of confrontation.

right of privacy   Constitutional right to engage in intimate personal conduct or make fundamental life decisions without interference by the state.

right to appeal   Statutory right to appeal decisions of lower courts in certain circumstances.

right to a speedy trial   Constitutional right to have an open public trial conducted without unreasonable delay.

right to be let alone   Another term for the right of privacy.

right to counsel   (1) The right to retain an attorney to represent oneself in court. (2) The right of an indigent person to have an attorney provided at public expense.

right to die   Controversial "right" to terminate one's own life under certain circumstances.

right to keep and bear arms   Right to possess certain weapons, protected against federal infringement by the Second Amendment to the Constitution.

right to refuse medical treatment   The right of a patient or patient's surrogate in some instances to refuse to allow doctors to perform medical treatment.

right to vote   The right of an individual to cast a vote in an election.

riot   A public disturbance involving acts of violence, usually by three or more persons.

ripeness   Readiness for review by a court of law. An issue is "ripe for review" in the Supreme Court when a case presents adverse parties who have exhausted all other avenues of appeal.

ripeness doctrine   The doctrine under which courts consider only those questions that are deemed to be "ripe for review."

roadblocks   Barriers set up by police to stop motorists.

robbery   The crime of taking money or property from a person against that person's will by means of force.

rule making   The power of a court or agency to promulgate rules; the process through which rules are promulgated.

rule of four   U.S. Supreme Court rule whereby the Court grants certiorari only on the agreement of at least four justices.

rule of law   The idea that law, not the discretion of officials, should govern public affairs.

rules of procedure   Rules promulgated by courts governing civil, criminal, and appellate procedure.

sanction   Penalty or other mechanism of enforcement.

saving construction, doctrine of   The doctrine that, given two plausible interpretations of a statute, a court will adopt the interpretation that prevents the statute from being declared unconstitutional.

scarcity theory   Theory holding that government can and should regulate access to the public airwaves, as these are scarce commodities.

school prayer   Various activities of a religious nature in the public schools.

school prayer decisions   Collective term for the Supreme Court's decisions of the 1960s prohibiting various activities of a religious nature in the public schools.

scientific evidence   Evidence obtained through scientific and technological innovations.

Scopes trial   Sensational criminal trial held in 1925 in Dayton, Tennessee, in which John Scopes, a high school biology teacher, was convicted under a state law (now defunct) prohibiting the teaching of evolution.

search and seizure   Term referring to the police search for and/or seizure of contraband or other evidence of crime.

search based on consent   A search of person or property conducted after a person voluntarily permits police to do so.

search incident to a lawful arrest   Search of a person placed under arrest and the area within the arrestee's grasp and control.

search warrant   A court order authorizing a search of a specified area for a specified purpose.

secession   Action by a state formally withdrawing from the Union.

Second Amendment   Amendment contained within the Bill of Rights guaranteeing the "right to keep and bear arms."

Section 1983 action   A federal lawsuit brought under 42 U.S. Code Section 1983 to redress violations of civil and/or constitutional rights.

secular government   Government that is not affiliated with or controlled by religious authorities.

secular humanism   The philosophy that man, not God, is the source of standards of right and wrong.

sedition   The crime of inciting insurrection or attempting to overthrow the government.

seditious speech   Expression aimed at inciting insurrection or overthrow of the government.

seduction   The common law crime of inducing a woman of previously chaste character to have sexual intercourse outside of wedlock on the promise of marriage.

seizure   Action of police in taking possession or control of property or persons.

selective incorporation   Doctrine under which selected provisions comprising most of the Bill of Rights are deemed applicable to the states by way of the Fourteenth Amendment.

selective prosecution   Singling out defendants for prosecution on the basis of race, religion, or other impermissible classifications.

self-representation   *See*: pro se defense.

sentence   The official pronouncement of punishment in a criminal case.

sentencing guidelines   Legislative guidelines mandating that sentencing conform to guidelines absent a compelling reason for departing from them.

sentencing hearing   A hearing held by a trial court prior to the pronouncement of sentence.

separate but equal doctrine   A now defunct doctrine that permitted racial segregation as long as equal facilities or accommodations were provided.

separation of church and state   First Amendment doctrine that holds that there must be a "wall of separation" between religion and government.

separation of powers Constitutional assignment of legislative, executive, and judicial powers to different branches of government.

sequestration Holding jurors incommunicado during trial.

seriatim Serially, individually.

set-aside Term for the affirmative action policies that reserve a certain proportion of government contracts for minority businesses.

Seventh Amendment Amendment contained within the Bill of Rights guaranteeing the right to a jury trial in federal civil suits.

severability The doctrine under which courts will declare invalid only the offending provision of a statute and allow the other provisions to remain in effect.

severability clause A clause found in a statute indicating that if any particular provision of the law is invalidated, the other provisions remain in effect.

sexual harassment Offensive interaction of a sexual nature in the workplace.

Shays's rebellion A 1786 uprising of farmers in Massachusetts led by Daniel Shays, a former Revolutionary Army captain. The rebellion was spawned by economic conditions that the rebels believed to be grossly unfair to farmers and working people. It was put down in January 1787. Shays and thirteen other leaders of the rebellion were tried for treason and sentenced to death. Two were executed. Shays and the other leaders were eventually pardoned by Massachusetts governor John Hancock.

Sherman Antitrust Act of 1890 A federal statute prohibiting any contract, combination, or conspiracy in restraint of trade. The act is designed to protect and preserve a system of free and open competition. Its scope is broad and reaches individuals and entities in profit and nonprofit activities as well as local governments and educational institutions.

show cause A court order requiring a party to appear and present a legal justification for a particular act.

showup An event in which a crime victim is taken to see a suspect to make an identification.

silver platter doctrine Doctrine under which federal and state authorities could share illegally obtained evidence before the exclusionary rule was made applicable to all jurisdictions.

similar fact evidence Evidence of facts similar to the facts in the crime charged. The test of admissibility is whether such evidence is relevant and has a probative value in establishing a material issue. Under some limited circumstances, evidence of other crimes or conduct similar to that charged against the defendant may be admitted in evidence in a criminal prosecution.

sine qua non "Without which not." A necessary or indispensable condition or prerequisite.

Sixth Amendment Amendment contained within the Bill of Rights guaranteeing the right to counsel and the right to trial by jury in criminal cases.

slander The tort of defaming someone's character through verbal statements.

small claims Minor civil suits.

sobriety checkpoints Roadblocks set up for the purpose of administering field sobriety tests to motorists who appear to be intoxicated.

social contract The theory that government is the product of agreement among rational individuals who subordinate themselves to collective authority in exchange for security of life, liberty, and property.

social Darwinism The theory that society improves through unrestricted competition and the "survival of the fittest."

sodomy Oral or anal sex between persons, or sex between a person and an animal (the latter is often referred to as bestiality).

solicitation (1) The crime of offering someone money or other thing of value in order to persuade that person to commit a crime. (2) An active effort on the part of an attorney or other professional to obtain business.

sovereign immunity A common law doctrine under which the sovereign may be sued only with its consent.

special prosecutor A prosecutor appointed specifically to investigate a particular episode and, if criminal activity is found, to prosecute those involved. Also referred to as an independent counsel.

specific performance A court-imposed requirement that a party perform obligations incurred under a contract.

Speech or Debate Clause Provision of Article I, Section 6, protecting members of Congress from arrest or interference with their official duties.

speedy and public trial An open and public criminal trial held without unreasonable delay; guaranteed by the Sixth Amendment to the Constitution.

spending power The power of the legislature to spend public money for public purposes.

standby counsel An attorney appointed to assist an indigent defendant who elects to represent himself or herself at trial.

standing The right to initiate a legal action or challenge based on the fact that one has suffered or is likely to suffer a real and substantial injury.

stare decisis "To stand by decided matters." The principle that past decisions should stand as precedents for future decisions. This principle, which supports the proposition that precedents are binding on later decisions, is said to be followed less rigorously in constitutional law than in other branches of the law.

state action doctrine The doctrine that limits constitutional prohibitions to official government or government-sponsored action, as opposed to action that is merely private in character.

state power to regulate interstate commerce The limited power of a state government to make and enforce rules affecting commerce that transcends the state.

state's attorney A state prosecutor.

states' rights The constitutional rights and powers reserved to state governments under the Tenth Amendment. Historically, the philosophy that states should be accorded broad latitude within the American federal system.

status offenses Noncriminal conduct on the part of juveniles that may subject them to the jurisdiction of the court.

statute A generally applicable law enacted by a legislature.

statute of limitations A law proscribing prosecutions for specific crimes after specified periods of time.

statutory construction The official interpretation of a statute rendered by a court of law.

statutory rape The strict-liability offense of having sexual intercourse with a minor.

stay To postpone, hold off, or stop the execution of a judgment.

stay of execution An order suspending the enforcement of a judgment of a court.

stewardship theory The theory that the president, being steward of the country, may exercise any and all powers he deems necessary to that end, unless they are specifically prohibited by the Constitution.

stop and frisk An encounter between a police officer and a suspect during which the latter is temporarily detained and subjected to a pat-down search for weapons.

stream of commerce doctrine The doctrine, first articulated by Justice Holmes in 1905, permitting federal regulation of commerce that is no longer of an interstate nature.

strict judicial scrutiny Judicial review of government action or policy in which the ordinary presumption of constitutionality is reversed.

strict liability offenses Offenses that do not require proof of the defendant's intent.

strict necessity, doctrine of The doctrine that a court should consider a constitutional question only when strictly necessary to resolve the case at bar.

strict neutrality The doctrine that government must be strictly neutral on matters of religion.

strict scrutiny The most demanding level of judicial review in cases involving alleged infringements of civil rights or liberties.

strip searches Searches of suspects' or prisoners' private parts.

sua sponte "Of its own will." Voluntarily, without coercion or suggestion.

subjective test A legal test based on the perceptions or intentions of an individual actor, rather than external circumstances.

subpoena "Under penalty." A judicial order requiring a person to appear in court in connection with a designated proceeding.

subpoena duces tecum "Under penalty you shall bring with you." A judicial order requiring a party to bring certain described records, papers, books, or documents to court.

substantial federal question A significant legal question pertaining to the U.S. Constitution, a federal statute, treaty, regulation, or judicial interpretation of any of the foregoing.

substantial step A significant step toward completion of an intended result.

substantive criminal law That branch of the criminal law that defines criminal offenses and defenses and specifies criminal punishments.

substantive due process Doctrine that the Due Process Clauses of the Fifth and Fourteenth Amendments require legislation to be fair and reasonable in content as well as application.

substantive law That part of the law that creates rights and proscribes wrongs.

sui juris "Under law"; having full legal rights.

summary decisions Decisions made by appellate courts without the submission of briefs or oral arguments.

summary judgment A decision rendered without extended argument where no material legal question is presented in a case.

summary justice Trial held by court of limited jurisdiction without benefit of a jury.

summary trial A bench trial of a minor misdemeanor.

summons A court order requiring a person to appear in court to answer a criminal charge.

Sunday closing laws Laws, now largely defunct, prohibiting business from opening on Sundays.

supervisory power The power of the Supreme Court to supervise the lower federal courts.

suppression doctrine *See*: exclusionary rule.

supra "Above."

Supremacy Clause Provision of Article VI of the Constitution making that document, and all federal legislation consistent with it, the "supreme Law of the Land."

suspect classification doctrine The doctrine that laws classifying people according to race, ethnicity, and religion are inherently suspect and should be subjected to strict judicial scrutiny.

suspended sentence A trial court's decision to place a defendant on probation or under community control instead of imposing an announced sentence, on the condition that the original sentence may be imposed if the defendant violates the conditions of the suspended sentence.

sustain To uphold.

symbolic speech An activity that expresses a point of view or message symbolically, rather than through pure speech.

taking Government action taking private property or depriving the owner the use and control thereof.

tax exemptions Rules under which certain organizations or individuals are not required to pay certain taxes.

taxing power The power of government to levy taxes.

taxpayer suits Suits brought by taxpayers to challenge certain government actions. Taxpayer suits as such are prohibited in the federal courts in that one does not acquire standing merely by virtue of paying taxes to support policies of which one does not approve.

Tenth Amendment Amendment to the Constitution reserving to the states powers not delegated to the federal government.

Terry **stop** *See*: stop-and-frisk.

Third Amendment Amendment found in the Bill of Rights prohibiting the military from quartering soldiers in citizens' homes without their consent.

third party A person not directly connected with a legal proceeding but potentially affected by its outcome.

third-party consent Consent, usually to a search, given by a person on behalf of another. For example, a college roommate who allows the police to search his or her roommate's effects.

Thirteenth Amendment Amendment to the Constitution, ratified in 1865, formally abolishing slavery.

time, place, and manner doctrine First Amendment doctrine holding that government may impose reasonable limitations on the time, place, and manner of expressive activities.

time, place, and manner regulations Reasonable government regulations as to the time, place, and manner of expressive activities protected by the Constitution.

tolling Ceasing. For example, someone who conceals himself or herself from the authorities generally causes a tolling of the statutes of limitation on prosecution of a crime.

tort A wrong or injury other than a breach of contract for which the remedy is a civil suit for damages.

totality of circumstances The entire collection of relevant facts in a particular case.

transactional immunity A grant of immunity applying to offenses to which a witness's testimony relates.

transcript A written record of a trial or hearing.

treason The crime of attempting by overt acts to overthrow the government, or of betraying the government to a foreign power.

treaty A legally binding agreement between one or more countries. In the United States, treaties are negotiated by the president but must be ratified by the Senate.

trespass An unlawful interference with one's person or property.

trial A judicial proceeding held for the purpose of making factual and legal determinations.

trial by jury A trial in which the verdict is determined not by the court but by a jury of the defendant's peers.

trial courts Courts whose primary function is the conduct of civil and/or criminal trials.

trial *de novo* "A new trial." Refers to trial court review of convictions for minor offenses by courts of limited jurisdiction by conducting a new trial instead of merely reviewing the record of the initial trial.

trial jury A fixed number of citizens, usually six or twelve, selected according to law and sworn to hear the evidence presented at a trial and to render a verdict based on the law and the evidence.

tribunal A court of law.

trimester framework The framework established in *Roe v. Wade* (1973) governing the validity of laws regulating abortion in the three stages of pregnancy.

true bill An indictment handed down by a grand jury.

trustee A person entrusted to handle the affairs of another.

trusty A prisoner entrusted with authority to supervise other prisoners in exchange for certain privileges and status.

tuition tax credits Vouchers that taxpayers may "spend" at schools of their choice, be they public or private.

Twenty-fifth Amendment Amendment ratified in 1967 dealing with issues of presidential disability and removal.

Twenty-first Amendment Amendment ratified in 1933 repealing the unpopular Eighteenth Amendment (1919) that had established Prohibition.

Twenty-second Amendment Amendment ratified in 1951 limiting presidents to two terms in office.

Twenty-sixth Amendment Amendment ratified in 1971 lowering the voting age in federal and state elections to 18.

two-party system A political system, such as that of the United States, organized around two major competing political parties.

two-witness rule A requirement that to prove a defendant guilty of perjury the prosecution must prove the falsity of the defendant's statements either by two witnesses or by one witness and corroborating documents or circumstances.

tyranny of the majority A political system in which the rights of the individual or minority group are not protected against the will of the majority.

ultra vires "Beyond the power"; beyond the scope of a prescribed authority.

umpire of the federal system Term that describes the Supreme Court's role in refereeing disputes between the national government and the states.

unalienable rights Rights that are vested in individuals by birth, not granted by government.

unanimity rule A decision rule requiring a unanimous vote.

unconstitutional as applied Declaration by a court of law that a statute is invalid insofar as it is enforced in some particular context.

unconstitutional per se A statute that is unconstitutional under any given circumstances.

unconventional religious practices Practices outside the religious mainstream.

unicameral legislature A one-house legislative body.

Uniform Code of Military Justice (UCMJ) A code of laws enacted by Congress that govern military servicepersons and define the procedural and evidentiary requirements in military law and the substantive criminal offenses and punishments.

unitary system A political system in which all power is vested in one central government.

universal suffrage The requirement that all citizens (at least all competent adults not guilty of serious crimes) be eligible to vote in elections.

unlawful assembly A group of individuals, usually five or more, assembled to commit an unlawful act or to commit a lawful act in an unlawful manner.

unreasonable searches and seizures Searches that violate the Fourth Amendment to the Constitution.

U.S. attorneys Attorneys appointed by the president with consent of the U.S. Senate to prosecute federal crimes in a specific geographical area of the United States.

U.S. Court of Appeals for the Armed Forces *See*: Court of Appeals for the Armed Forces.

U.S. Courts of Appeals The intermediate appellate courts of appeals in the federal system that sit in geographical areas of the United States and in which panels of appellate judges hear appeals in civil and criminal cases primarily from the U.S. District Courts.

U.S. District Courts The principal trial courts in the federal system that sit in ninety-four districts where usually one judge hears proceedings and trials in both civil and criminal cases.

use immunity A grant of immunity that forbids prosecutors from using immunized testimony as evidence in criminal prosecutions.

U.S. Sentencing Commission A federal body that proposes guideline sentences for defendants convicted of federal crimes.

U.S. Supreme Court The highest court in the United States, consisting of nine justices, with jurisdiction to review, by appeal or writ of certiorari, the decisions of lower federal courts and many decisions of the highest courts of each state.

vacate To annul, set aside, or rescind.

vagrancy The crime of going about without visible means of support (virtually archaic).

vagueness doctrine Doctrine of constitutional law holding unconstitutional (as a violation of due process) legislation that fails to clearly inform the person what is required or proscribed.

venire The set of persons summoned for jury duty. The actual jury is selected from the venire. *See:* voir dire.

venue The location of a trial or hearing.

verdict The formal decision rendered by a jury in a civil or criminal trial.

vested rights Rights acquired by the passage of time.

veto The power of a chief executive to block adoption of a law by refusing to sign the legislation.

viability That point in pregnancy where the fetus is able to survive outside the womb.

victim impact statements Statements during the sentencing phase of a criminal trial in which evidence is introduced relating to the physical, economic, and psychological impact that the crime had on the victim or victim's family.

victimless crimes Crimes in which no particular person appears or claims to be injured, such as prostitution or gambling.

Virginia Plan A plan introduced by James Madison, a member of the Virginia delegation to the Constitutional Convention of 1787. It called for a bicameral Congress, in which members of the House of Representatives would be elected by the people and members of the Senate would be elected by the state legislatures. State representation in both bodies would be based on population.

voice exemplar A sample of a person's voice; usually taken by police for the purpose of identifying a suspect.

void-for-vagueness doctrine *See:* vagueness doctrine.

voir dire "To speak the truth." The process by which prospective jurors are questioned by counsel and/or the court before being selected to serve on a jury.

voluntariness of confessions The quality of a confession having been freely given.

vote dilution The reduction or diminution of the voting power of individuals or minorities as a result of malapportionment, gerrymandering, or some other discriminatory practice.

voting blocs Groups of individuals who usually vote together.

Voting Rights Act of 1965 Landmark federal legislation protecting voters from racial discrimination.

waiver The intentional and voluntary relinquishment of a right, or conduct from which such relinquishment may be inferred.

waiver of juvenile court jurisdiction A relinquishment by a juvenile court to allow prosecution of a juvenile in an adult court.

waiver of *Miranda* rights A known relinquishment of the right against self-incrimination provided by the Fifth Amendment to the Constitution.

War Powers Resolution The 1973 act of Congress purporting to limit a president's authority to commit troops to a combat situation abroad.

warrant A court order authorizing a search, seizure, or arrest.

warrantless arrest An arrest made by police who do not possess an arrest warrant.

warrantless search A search made by police who do not possess a search warrant.

warrant requirement The Fourth Amendment's "preference" that searches be based on warrants issued by judges or magistrates.

weight of the evidence The balance or preponderance of the evidence. Weight of the evidence is to be distinguished from "legal sufficiency of the evidence," which is the concern of an appellate court.

well-regulated militia Body of citizens organized for military service but subject to government regulation.

white primary Historically, a primary election in which participation was limited to whites.

wiretap order A court order permitting electronic surveillance for a limited period.

wiretapping The use of highly sensitive electronic devices designed to intercept electronic communications.

writ An order issued by a court of law requiring the performance of some specific act.

writ of *certiorari* *See:* certiorari, writ of.

writ of error *See:* error, writ of.

writ of *habeas corpus* *See:* habeas corpus, writ of.

writ of *mandamus* *See:* mandamus, writ of.

writ of prohibition *See:* prohibition, writ of.

writs of assistance Ancient writs issuing from the Court of Exchequer in England granting sheriffs broad powers of search and seizure for the purpose of assisting in the collection of debts owed to the Crown.

yellow dog contracts Contracts, generally illegal, making the right to work conditioned upon the employee's agreement not to join a labor union.

zoning Laws regulating the use of land.

APPENDIX E
Internet Resources

NAME OF RESOURCES	DESCRIPTION	URL
American Civil Liberties Union	The premier civil rights/civil liberties interest group	http://www.aclu.org/
American Civil Rights Union	A conservative counterpart to the ACLU	http://www.civilrightsunion.org/
American Enterprise Institute	Conservative policy research organization that emphasizes economic issues	http://www.aei.org/
American Land Rights Association	An organization dedicated to protecting private property rights, especially in rural areas	http://www.landrights.org/
Americans United for Separation of Church and State	A site maintained by one of the best known antiestablishmentarian organizations	http://www.au.org/
Ballot Access News	A nonpartisan online newsletter reporting on the problems associated with ballot access for independent and third-party candidates	http://www.ballot-access.org/
Bureau of Justice Statistics	Agency with the U.S. Department of Justice responsible for collecting and disseminating data dealing with crime and the justice system	http://www.ojp.usdoj.gov/bjs/
Catholic League for Religious and Civil Rights	Site promoting the nation's largest Catholic civil rights organization	http://www.catholicleague.org/
Cato Institute	A leading libertarian think tank	http://www.cato.org/
Center for Voting and Democracy	Organization interested in the impact of different voting systems on voter turnout, representation, accountability, and the influence of money on elections	http://www.fairvote.org/
Center for the Study of the Presidency	An educational institution devoted to the study of the presidency and other aspects of American government and politics	http://www.cspresidency.org/
Christian Coalition	A political organization dedicated to public policies informed by conservative Christian ideas	http://www.cc.org/
Civil Rights Division, U.S. Department of Justice	Division of the Justice Department responsible for enforcing civil rights laws	http://www.usdoj.gov/crt/
Compassion and Choices	An organization supporting the "right to die"	http://www.compassionandchoices.org/
Congressional Quarterly	Congressional news, general background information on Members of Congress, information about bills sponsored, speeches made, roll call votes, etc.	http://www.cq.com/
C-SPAN Online	Gavel-to-gavel coverage of the U.S. House and other public affairs programming	http://www3.capwiz.com/c-span/
Eagle Forum	Phyllis Shlafly's organization—a conservative alternative to feminism	http://www.eagleforum.org/
Exploring Constitutional Law	Explores some of the great issues and controversies that surround our Nation's founding document	http://www.law.umkc.edu/faculty/projects/FTrials/conlaw/home.html
Federal Bureau of Investigation	The premier federal law enforcement agency	http://www.fbi.gov/
Federal Bureau of Prisons	Federal agency responsible for running the federal government's prison system	http://www.bop.gov/
Federal Courts Home Page (Administrative Office of the U.S. Courts)	A clearinghouse for information from and about the federal courts	http://www.uscourts.gov
Federal Judicial Center	The federal courts' agency for research and continuing education	http://www.fjc.gov
Federal Register Online	Federal Register searchable database	http://www.gpoaccess.gov/fr/index.html

NAME OF RESOURCES	DESCRIPTION	URL
Federalism Project (American Enterprise Institute)	Provides a conservative perspective	http://www.federalismproject.org/
FedWorld Information Network	National Technical Information Service, U.S. Department of Commerce	http://www.fedworld.gov/
Findlaw	A comprehensive legal Web site including a database of Supreme Court decisions and various constitutional law materials	http://findlaw.com
Freedom Forum	A nonpartisan foundation dedicated to freedoms of speech and press	http://www.freedomforum.org/
Hudson Institute	A nonpartisan policy research organization that promotes global security	http://www.hudson.org/
Institute for Justice	A libertarian alternative to the ACLU	http://www.ij.org/
Jurist	An excellent legal website	http://jurist.law.pitt.edu
Lambda Legal Defense and Education Fund	An interest group promoting the cause of gay rights	http://www.lambdalegal.org/
Legal Information Institute (Cornell University)	A searchable database of Supreme Court opinions	http://supct.law.cornell.edu/supct
Library of Congress	Links to various agencies within the Executive Branch	http://www.loc.gov/index.html
NAACP	The oldest and best known organization devoted to promoting civil rights for African Americans	http://www.naacp.org/
National Abortion Rights Action League	An interest group dedicated to maintaining legalized abortion	http://www.naral.org/
National Gay and Lesbian Task Force (NGLTF)	A leading gay rights organization	http://www.ngltf.org/
National Organization for Women	The leading interest group in the movement for women's rights	http://www.now.org/
National Rifle Association	The leading organization dedicated to promoting the right to keep and bear arms	http://www.nra.org/
Not Dead Yet	A national organization of people with disabilities who oppose the legalization of physician-assisted suicide	http://acils.com/notdeadyet/
Operation Rescue	An antiabortion interest group	http://www.operationsaveamerica.org
Oyez	A multimedia database about the U.S. Supreme Court	http://www.oyez.org/
Public Citizen	A pro-consumer, pro-democracy group founded by Ralph Nader	http://www.citizen.org/
Publius: The Journal of Federalism	A scholarly journal devoted to issues of federalism	http://publius.oxfordjournals.org
SCOTUSblog	An excellent blog on the Supreme Court, updated frequently	http://www.scotusblog.com/
Secular Web	A website devoted to promoting secular humanism	http://www.secular.org/
Southern Poverty Law Center	A prominent civil rights organization with a particular emphasis on combating "hate groups" and "hate crimes"	http://www.splcenter.org/
Supreme Court Database	Site providing access to the most comprehensive database on Supreme Court decision-making	http://supremecourtdatabase.org/index.php
Supreme Court of the United States	The Court's official website.	http://www.supremecourt.gov/
The White House	Information on the President and Vice President, events and tours at the White House, press releases, e-mail addresses, etc. Also includes links to offices within the Executive Office of the President	http://www.whitehouse.gov
Thomas Jefferson Center for the Protection of Free Expression	A nonprofit organization located in Charlottesville, Virginia devoted to the defense of free expression in all its forms	http://www.tjcenter.org/
U.S. Code	The United States Code in a searchable database	http://uscode.house.gov/search/criteria.shtml
U.S. Government Printing Office—Congress Page	Various Congressional informational resources	http://www.gpoaccess.gov/congress/index.html
U.S. Sentencing Commission	The federal agency responsible for promulgating federal sentencing guidelines	http://www.ussc.gov/
United States Supreme Court Home Page	The Supreme Court's own Web site	http://www.supremecourtus.gov

Table of Cases

Principal cases are in bold type. Non-principal cases are in roman type.

Index